Plymouth Argyle
The Modern Era
– A Complete Record –

PLYMOUTH ARGYLE

The Modern Era

— A Complete Record —

Series Editor: Clive Leatherdale
Series Consultant: Leigh Edwards

Andy Riddle

DESERT ISLAND BOOKS

Second edition published in 2008
First edition published in 2002

DESERT ISLAND BOOKS LIMITED
7 Clarence Road, Southend-on-Sea, Essex SS1 1AN
United Kingdom
www.desertislandbooks.com

British Library Cataloguing-in-Publication Data
A catalogue record for this book is available from the British Library

ISBN   978-1-874287-62-9

Printed in Great Britain
by Biddles Ltd, Kings Lynn

Photographs in this book are reproduced
by kind permission of Dave Rowntree

Contents

Preface

For most professional footballers, life is a roller coaster: elation one week, despair the next. Few players are fortunate enough to play at a top club, the Liverpools or Manchester Uniteds. Whenever I reflect on my twenty-year playing career, my mind blocks out negative periods and floods with memories of successful times, special matches and treasured goals.

Many of my happiest memories occurred during my two and a bit seasons with Argyle. During my first full season I scored my first League hat-trick, against Tranmere. I also came up against a former club, Blackpool, in the FA Cup and scored twice in a 2-0 victory at Home Park. My parents watched proudly from the Main Stand after the long trek from Scotland.

Playing in a promotion-winning team was another first for me. Tony Waiters had assembled talented players, but also a team of characters, prepared to work their socks off for one another. The dressing room camaraderie is something I miss since I finished playing. The togetherness of Argyle's players in 1974-75 was special and that bond remains today and will always be there.

During the following season – although it wasn't one of my best – I vividly remember my first League goal, at home to Sunderland, in front of a big crowd. After receiving the ball, wide on the halfway line, I beat four defenders before slotting it past Jim Montgomery in the visitors' goal. Probably the best goal of my entire career!

My other personal highlight of 1975-76 was my one and only game against the late great Bobby Moore – then with Fulham – around Boxing Day. We won 4-1 with two goals from yours truly.

My one regret about my time at Plymouth is that I didn't stay longer. Following promotion the team was broken up too hastily, and after two years of hard work, my deadly partnership with my good friend Paul Mariner was dismantled. Paul was the perfect foil for me. Although we were similar in many ways, I never felt as comfortable on a football pitch with any other striker. We both took pleasure in creating chances for one another through hard running, aerial challenges, subtle flicks, and we developed a knack of creating space for each other. A stream of crosses also assisted us from our wingers Hugh McAuley and Brian Johnson. Perhaps the club were under pressure financially. I don't know. We had the nucleus of a very good team, and who knows what we might have achieved had we stayed together.

I hold fond memories of Argyle fans and the people of Plymouth, who made my wife, Elaine, and I feel so at home. We still have friends in Plymouth and love to visit old haunts, although now that I am settled in Carlisle, my visits are too infrequent for my liking.

This was the first club where the fans gave me my own chant. I recently attended an ex-Argyle players' reunion and visited Home Park with former team-mates. The Main Stand is the only part of the ground to remain from my days. We sat in our old dressing room and swapped stories from bygone days, then took a nostalgic wander down the tunnel onto the pitch. Our discussion turned to matches and incidents from that promotion season, then I wandered off alone to the penalty area, reliving the past. Perhaps I had had too many from the night before, but when I stared up at the empty terraces it was an eerie feeling to hear thousands of the Argyle faithful singing 'Oh, Billy Billy'.

BILLY RAFFERTY

Author's Note

I saw my first match at Home Park (v Coventry) in August 1966 but it is now a distant memory. For the next eight years my Saturday afternoon trips to Plymouth from my home in deepest Cornwall were dependent on the reliability of my grandfather's Mini and my selection or otherwise for the local junior football team.

By 1974 I had some tactical inkling of how the game of football should be played and my abiding memory of all my years following the Pilgrims is the pleasure of watching that season's promotion side. To my mind, that was how football should be played. A rock-solid defence, with the likes of Furnell, Green, Saxton and Burrows, a creative but combative midfield pair like Randell and Delve, and a forward line containing two marauding wingers in Johnson and McAuley, who laid on chance after chance for two of the most prolific strikers ever to have worn the green shirt – Mariner and Rafferty. Everything came together under the charge of a charismatic, tactically brilliant manager in Tony Waiters.

When, therefore, I was commissioned by Desert Island Books to compile this book, I had no doubt when the 'modern era' began. Since then, Argyle have provided a roller coaster of emotions and many outstanding memories.

I am grateful to Paul Truscott, who generously allowed me to delve into his collection of press cuttings, thus saving me many extra hours of toil in the local library, also to Paul Hart and Tom Finnie, and Dave Rowntree for providing a selection of photographs from his vast archive.

Thank you to my publisher and editor, Clive Leatherdale, for your encouragement and guidance. It has been hard work but always enjoyable.

Finally to my wife, Joy-Anne, and children Sophie and Benjamin, thank you once again for you patience. Maybe next year I will decorate that bedroom!

ANDY RIDDLE
August 2008

Publishers' Note:
This book contains full details – line-ups for both sides, goalscorers, goal-times, referees, attendances, League positions after each game, cumulative points totals, plus a 50-word summary of key moments – of every first-team competitive match Argyle have played in the League, FA Cup and League Cup, beginning with 1974-75. Minor cup competitions have been excluded for reasons of space.

Introduction

The progress of Plymouth Argyle as a football club moved at a rapid pace during its early days. The definitive details of the formation of the club, to this day, have never been determined, with two theories abounding. The suggestion that the club was born in 1886 by a group of ex-college and public school pupils who took the name from the Argyll and Sutherland Highlanders – who at that time were stationed nearby – seems less credible than the theory that an Argyle Athletic Club was formed two years later at a meeting held at Argyle Terrace.

Whichever is correct, the fact remains that within the space of fifteen or so years, the city supported a professional football team. Some of the leading clubs in the country, such as Aston Villa and Notts County, were invited to play exhibition matches in the city. Crowds of 15,000-plus were attracted to the games, whereupon it was agreed to transform the club into a professional concern.

Directors were appointed and the first team-manager – Frank Brettell – was engaged. Irishman Brettell had an impressive track record, being a highly respected administrator within the game who had taken both Portsmouth and Tottenham into the professional ranks. He used his considerable contacts to build a side capable of holding its own in the competitive Southern and Western league competitions. The club's first ever professional match, a Western League fixture at West Ham on 1 September 1903, ended in a 1-0 victory.

The club more than held its own and by 1906 Brettell had retired, his job done. Robert Jack, a Scotsman, who was Brettell's first professional signing, returned to the club to commence a long association with it. Progress under Jack was steady. Argyle won the Southern League title in 1912-13. When the Football League expanded in 1920 by creating Division Three (North and South), Argyle were elected. Jack scoured the country for players and made regular incursions into Scotland to bring players down south. Distance mattered little in those days. Jack's endearing personality, the ideal of living in a mild South West climate and the opportunity to swap the life of a miner or factory worker for that of a footballer, was enough persuasion. Wages were of little consideration. In an oppressed economy, any form of employment was welcome.

Argyle soon became a leading light in the new division, finishing runners-up for six successive seasons from 1921-22, at a time when only the champions were promoted. This period brought together some of the legendary players in Argyle history, such as Sammy Black and Jack Leslie. The Division Three (South) championship was finally achieved in 1929-30, by which time future Arsenal and England star Ray Bowden had broken through into the first team. Two seasons later the aforementioned trio contributed 55 goals between them as the Pilgrims finished the Division Two campaign in fourth place.

Prior to the outbreak of war in 1939, Argyle were rarely out of the top half of Division Two. Crowds in excess of 20,000 at home matches became the norm. Jack remained in situ until the end of the 1937-38 season.

World War II saw the city become one of Hitler's prime targets. The club contested three league games before war was declared and the competition abandoned. A South West Regional League was created which Argyle won, but raising a team was a haphazard occupation. Thirty different players were used in 28 matches and crowds plummeted to the 2,000 mark. Only 896 watched Argyle hammer Bristol City 10-3 in February 1940, the only 'league' game played in the country on that day.

With peace on the horizon, the directors turned their thoughts to restoring the club to normality. There was much to do. Not only did the team have to be rebuilt, with many players having retired after losing six years from their careers, but Home Park itself had suffered. A Luftwaffe bomb had destroyed the grandstand and the stadium had fallen into neglect with the pitch weed-infested.

An interim Football League (South) was formed for the first post-war season, combining clubs from the First and Second Divisions. Guest players were permitted and no fewer than 72 players pulled on the green shirt that season. Argyle won only three matches, to finish bottom, but few cared. Huge crowds, deprived of so much for so long, flocked to Home Park, attracted by the visits of Arsenal, Wolves and Chelsea amongst others and the chance to see such star names as Tommy Lawton, Billy Wright and Cliff Bastin.

In fact, the war years and the National Service that followed brought to the city many servicemen who ended up on Argyle's books to stay. Bill Shortt, Ernie Edds and Gordon Astall, for example, all came to the club via this route.

Jack Tresarden, who had succeeded Jack as manager in 1938, resumed the post. The side struggled to nineteenth in the first proper league campaign and fared little better at the start of the following season. In modern parlance, the board considered that Tresarden had somewhat 'lost the plot', for his signings had included 42-year-old John Oakes. Whether Tresarden jumped or was pushed, his departure was the first of numerous manager-director conflicts to darken Argyle's history. In his place came assistant Jimmy Rae, another Scotsman who had served the club well as a pre-war full-back.

Reservations about Rae's appointment seemed justified at first and results failed to improve. Despite signings such as Neil Dougall and George Dews, the side failed to gel, with youngsters like Alex Govan and Len Boyd tossed into the deep end.

Despite the arrival of Jack 'Jumbo' Chisholm, Argyle were relegated in 1949-50. With hindsight, the drop down a division was not a bad thing, allowing, as it did, a number of players to find a level at which to acclimatise. Chisholm's influence as a leader of men both on and off the field was soon felt and the side finished the following season in fourth place as well as attracting a gate of 40,000 for an FA Cup visit from the mighty Wolves.

The 1951-52 season saw silverware arrive at Home Park as the side swept to the Division Three (South) title, losing only eight games. Rae was able to name the same eleven, week in, week out. Back in Division Two, the new-found confidence was confirmed by a fourth-place finish and hopes, the following season, of an even stronger promotion push to Division One.

Sadly, they did not materialise. Govan and Astall were sold to Birmingham, centre-forward Maurice Tadman's supply-line dried up, and Chisholm's injuries began to take their toll. Three seasons of struggle ensued, culminating in a return to Division Three. By this time Rae had gone, replaced by former Manchester United and England star, Jack Rowley.

Rowley set about rebuilding a team, and was rewarded with the inaugural Division Three title in 1958-59, thanks largely to the goals of Wilf Carter and Jimmy Gauld.

Rowley became the next manager to be driven out by boardroom disputes. Popular player Neil Dougall took charge without success. Apart from a brief revival under Ellis Stuttard, Argyle became perennial strugglers in Division Two, a succession of managers, including Malcolm Allison unable to give the side that extra push.

Following several flirts with relegation, the inevitable happened. With Derek Ufton at the helm the side won only three of the first 25 games of the 1967-68 season. In desperation, fading stars such as Alan Sealey, Mike Harrison and England international Alan Peacock were brought in, but spent most of the time on the treatment table.

Ufton was sacked and Northern Ireland boss Billy Bingham was recruited on the understanding that he would manage Argyle and Northern Ireland simultaneously. In any case, he arrived too late to make any difference.

The one bright spot during these dark years was the emergence of local talent such as Mike Bickle and Norman Piper but Bingham's inevitable club versus country conflicts came to the crunch. The Irishman left and Stuttard returned for a second spell in the manager's chair.

The club seemed marooned in the Third Division but Stuttard can be credited with important signings, such as those of Jim Furnell and Bobby Saxton, around whom future success was built. The affable Stuttard was made chief scout in October 1972, as the directors again plumped for new leadership. In came former England goalkeeper Tony Waiters, a man establishing a reputation as an excellent coach but who was untried at league level.

Waiters arrived with a vision for the club that extended beyond immediate first-team success. Having worked with the England Youth side, he realised the importance of developing youngsters for the future. He established an extensive scouting system and oversaw the improvement of facilities at the club, including the new training facility at Harper's Park.

Initial results were encouraging, as Waiters dragged the side away from the lower reaches of Division Three. The following season saw Argyle make national headlines as several giant-killing feats propelled them to the semi-finals of the League Cup. League results remained poor, however, and some cynics still questioned Waiters' ability to hack it in the rough and tumble of lower league football. But then came season 1974-75 ...

Chapter One

Shattered Dreams
1974-1977

LEAGUE DIVISION 3	**1974-75**
Division 3	2nd (promoted)
League Cup	1st round
FA Cup	4th round

During the summer of 1974 opinions were split regarding Argyle's likely fortunes. Optimists confidently predicted that the team would capitalise on their run to the previous season's League Cup semi-final, which had also provided a timely boost to the club's finances. Surely a side which could produce high class football against the likes of QPR and Burnley were near-certainties for promotion. Exciting youngsters such as Paul Mariner, Brian Johnson and Alan Rogers would complement the more experienced players.

Some older sages who had seen it all before were less sanguine. Turning it on in front of big crowds was fine, but doing the same on a bitterly cold Saturday at Halifax in front of 2,000 diehards on the terracing would really test the players' mettle. Promising youngsters had come and gone by the barrel-load over the years. Too often they looked world-beaters when they burst into the side, but faded into oblivion after the first-season euphoria had worn off.

Pre-season friendlies offered little support to the optimists as Argyle sides, considered near to full strength, succumbed to the 'might' of Stafford Rangers and Burscough. The bookies were also unimpressed. Crystal Palace were installed as title favourites at 14-1 with Argyle quoted at 25-1.

As the Pilgrims emerged for the opening match at Deepdale, most of the hype focused on Bobby Charlton's first appearance as Preston's player-manager. The travelling Pilgrimites had other things on their mind. Waiters had certainly been busy during the summer. Four new faces trotted out in the green and black stripes and a fifth, Ian Pearson, was on the bench. Brighton had forked out £30,000 to take unsettled midfield maestro Ernie Machin as their new captain, Under-23 cap Colin Sullivan had moved on to greater things with Norwich (Argyle receiving a record £70,000), and the reliable Neil Hague had followed local boy Derek Rickard to Bournemouth in a deal worth £15,000 to the Pilgrims. In their places came Phil Burrows (£16,000), a journeyman full-back from York,

Clive Griffiths on loan from Manchester United, John Delve (£30,000) a fringe player at QPR, and Mike Green (£19,000) who had skippered Bristol Rovers to promotion in the season just past. As for the result, Preston beat Argyle by a single goal.

As fans filed in for the first home game they noticed an immediate change. The standard match programme had been replaced by a newspaper-style publication costing eight pence. The new format was informative, but for those who liked to peruse their programme to while away a few minutes, anything more than a mild breeze would whip the pages away. Rain during the match caused sleepless nights for the club's apprentices faced with scraping soggy copies from the terraces on Monday morning.

Some things, of course, didn't change. Argyle's best-known fan, Umbrella Vi, stood in her usual place by the halfway line on the Lyndhurst side. Vi's green umbrella caricatured the emotions of the home fans. She would celebrate an Argyle goal with unrestrained twirling, without regard for fellow supporters nearby. When things weren't going so well, the umbrella would droop despairingly over the advertising hoardings and woe betide a suspect decision by a linesman, for Vi's umbrella would suddenly be thrust sword-like in his direction.

The sword thrusts outnumbered the twirls in the early weeks of the season. Four further away defeats were interspersed by a 4-1 home win over Tranmere, inspired by a Billy Rafferty hat-trick. By the end of September, ten league games had yielded just seven points and hopes of another money-spinning run in the League Cup were dashed in the first round by Green's former side, Bristol Rovers. Wonder-boy Mariner had found the net just three times. Johnson and Rogers hadn't even made the side. Pessimists 1 Optmists 0.

Changes were inevitable. The popular Steve Davey was dropped and eventually departed for Hereford, while Griffiths was recalled to Old Trafford to cover for the injured Jim Holton. A fit again Colin Randell was restored to midfield and Bobby Saxton brought back to bolster the defence. Johnson came in, too, and winger Hugh McAuley, well known to Waiters from his time at Liverpool, signed from the Anfield club for £12,000 to replace his ageing counterpart, Harry Burrows. Tough-tackling midfielder Peter Hardcastle joined from Blackpool to bolster the squad.

Fortunes changed dramatically as Waiters' revised line-up clicked into gear. In goal, the silver-haired Furnell continued to prove that appearances can be deceptive. The loyal John Hore came in at full-back for the suspended Peter Darke – who was then unable to regain his place – whilst his opposite number, Burrows, was consistency personified. Saxton and captain Green completed a solid back four. Delve buzzed here and there in midfield to complement the silky Randell. From mid-October the side embarked on a four-month unbeaten league run that extended to 15 February, when Argyle suffered a devastating 2-5 loss at promotion rivals Blackburn. In the meantime, crowds flocked back to Home Park. The modest 5,700 who had grudgingly paid £1 to sit or 50 pence to stand and witness the win over Tranmere had swelled to almost 29,000 by the time Blackburn paid a visit in early February.

League form also carried over into the FA Cup. A 3-2 win at a gloomy Dartford ground was followed by a dramatic 2-1 win over Crystal Palace, thanks to a penalty save by Jim Furnell. Two goals by Billy Rafferty against one of his former sides, Blackpool, earned Argyle a home tie against the Division One leaders, Everton.

Home Park was full to the rafters for the occasion. The Devonport End, host to the main chorus, was naturally packed. The structural strength of the Grandstand was put to the test, and below on the Mayflower Terrace young boys wriggled their way towards the railings at the front. The 'popular side' was more popular than ever and even Vi failed by a few yards to seize her customary position on halfway. Many others had little option but to risk exposure to the elements at the uncovered Barn Park End. Thirty-eight thousand were crammed in, leaving older supporters to reminisce on the 'good old days' and younger supporters to wonder how an extra 5,000 had squeezed in back in 1936 to create the club's all-time attendance record. Despite the massive home support, Vi's umbrella whirled just once: the Toffees showed too much class in front of the Match of the Day cameras.

Back in the league, the twin-strike partnership of Mariner and Rafferty grabbed the headlines. It was rare for one or both of their names not to appear on the scoresheet. Mariner had come from non-league Chorley the previous season. His raw talent was maturing quickly and scouts from top sides were soon keeping a close eye on his development. Rafferty had joined from Blackpool for £25,000 in March 1974 but cartilage problems had restricted him to just five games prior to this season. Surgery in the summer solved the problem and gave the well-built Scot a new lease of life.

Although the strikers grabbed the glory, they relied heavily on Waiters' policy of playing two wingers. To the delight of traditionalists, wide men were back in fashion, giving the elbow to Alf Ramsey's 'wingless wonders'. Players such as Eddie Gray (at Leeds), Willie Morgan (Manchester United), and Steve Heighway (Liverpool) were exciting crowds up and down the country. Argyle had Johnson on the right, McAuley on the left, but their differing styles were equally effective on their day. McAuley was the archetypal flankman – small, quick and tricky. Johnson was less speedy, but difficult to stop. Thirteen goals between them was an added bonus to the side.

That 2-5 defeat at Ewood Park terminated a run of sixteen unbeaten matches. A minor blip followed. Malcolm Allison returned to Home Park with Crystal Palace, vowing and getting revenge for their cup exit with a one-goal victory. A strike by Mariner earned two hard-fought-for points from the visit of Southend and things seemed back to normal with a 5-1 crushing of Hereford at Edgar Street. TV cameras returned to Plymouth for the match with mid-table Wrexham. On paper the Welsh side posed little threat but they had become something of a bogey side in recent times. An unexpected 3-0 win saw the visitors singing all the way back to north Wales.

Waiters soon got his side back on track. Another mini-run was put together and, with three games still remaining, promotion was clinched with a single-goal home triumph over Colchester in front of 23,551 fans. The only question remaining was whether Argyle could clinch the title. The final home game saw old rivals Port Vale applaud the Argyle players onto the pitch. Their admiration was short-lived as the boys from Burslem scooped a 1-1 draw. This dropped point was to prove crucial in the final reckoning, as Argyle were running neck and neck with Blackburn. The Lancashire side had a game in hand but their 0-2 defeat at Colchester increased the pressure on them.

Argyle's last game was a tricky visit to Peterborough, who had been on the promotion fringes for much of the season. A win would give the Pilgrims the title irrespective of Blackburn's result, thanks to superior goal-difference. Despite a mass exodus of fans to the Fens, it was not a good day. A 0-1 defeat was exacerbated by crowd trouble, with a number of 'fans' disgracing the club's name. News also came through that Rovers had cruised past Port Vale 4-1, a result that would leave everyone sweating on the result of Rovers' final game at Wrexham the following Monday. Sadly for Argyle, the Welsh side had shown no form since their emphatic triumph at Home Park and a goalless draw saw Gordon Lee's Blackburn lift the trophy.

Despite the disappointment of missing out on the title, a wave of excitement swept across the city. Long-awaited success had been mixed with an invigorating style of play not seen for many a year. The youth development system was beginning to unearth some real talent and the crowds were back. The optimists had won the argument. Roll on next season.

DID YOU KNOW?

**In May 1945 Argyle played Bristol City at Ashton Gate.
The competition? – the Welsh Cup!**

Match of the Season 1974-75
Bournemouth 3   Argyle 7

Division 3, 11 January 1975

Argyle rolled into Dean Court in their brand new team coach to find the home club in crisis. Heavy spending on new signings, including Derek Rickard and Neil Hague from Argyle, seemed justified when the Cherries touched the top four, but three points from a possible twenty had sent them plunging. Three players – Trevor Howard, Howard Goddard and the veteran John O'Rourke – 'top scored' with just three apiece. The board had sacked boss Trevor Hartley and installed Tony Nelson on a caretaker basis.

Waiters ensured against complacency. A Billy Rafferty goal had separated the sides a month earlier at Home Park. Bournemouth didn't score many, but their defence were a mean bunch.

Back at Home Park an abnormally large crowd of 2,375 watched the Combination League side share eight goals with their Fulham counterparts. The mystified Cottagers quickly learned they were not the main attraction. Attendees were able to purchase tickets for the forthcoming FA Cup-tie with Everton. The score from Dean Court was updated regularly and soon had the crowd rubbing their eyes and checking that 1 April had not arrived sooner than expected.

The match epitomised Waiters' preferred style of play. Constant raids down the flanks caused havoc and the midfield sprayed the ball around. Mariner and Rafferty both struck within the first thirteen minutes. Wingers Johnson and McAuley scored before half-time and Delve added another just after the break. Suddenly the Cherries found their feet. John Wingate, a former Pilgrim for one match, found the net. Green scored an unfortunate own-goal and Howard's effort made him leading scorer with four! Mariner and Randell added two more to the Argyle tally in the last three minutes to leave the Home Park scoreboard operator frantically searching for a seven in his box of numbers.

The statisticians were left rubbing their hands. No other league side had scored seven that season. More impressively, it was the first time any Argyle side had netted seven away from home.

The Cherries' next twelve matches yielded only four goals, and five more wins could not keep them up. Nelson didn't last long.

LEAGUE DIVISION 2   **1975-76**
Division 2   16th
League Cup   2nd round
FA Cup   3rd round

Transfer activity was less frenetic during the summer of 1975. This suggested that Waiters felt confident his squad could consolidate its place in Division Two. The flame-haired Mick Horswill, an FA Cup winner with Sunderland in 1973, arrived from Manchester City for £30,000, and Neil Rioch, brother of Scottish international, Bruce, came on a free transfer from Aston Villa. Defender Geoff Banton travelled south from Bolton. The latter two lacked experience and were unlikely to be more than squad players.

Argyle's green and black stripes, often bemoaned by players and fans alike for being unrecognisable on grey days, were discarded in favour of a predominantly all-white kit. A green and black stripe down each sleeve failed to appease traditionalists – who demanded that green be the dominant colour – and did little to suggest that the designers had added substantial overtime for their 'creativity'.

One thing that did not change was the matchday 'newspaper'. Despite a 25 percent hike in price to ten pence, the content had diminished, enlivened only by an occasional amusing player 'personal profile'. John Delve, for example, revealed that his favourite TV show was 'Jackanory' and he had considered being a pedalo owner in Spain as an alternative career.

One of the busiest members of the Argyle staff was groundsman Harry Elsworth. His attempts to present the Home Park pitch in pristine condition were regularly undermined by invading foxes, attracted no doubt by the wildlife in the adjoining zoo. A shotgun became an integral part of Harry's equipment.

The side selected for Argyle's opener at Nottingham Forest was one of the youngest put out by an Argyle manager in many a year. Veteran keeper Jim Furnell was demoted to the reserves and the promising Milija Aleksic was given his chance. The only other 30-something in the squad, Bobby Saxton, had to be content with a substitute berth to allow new boy Horswill a slot in the back four. Aged 21, Delve became one of the club's youngest ever captains.

Horswill made a quick impression, albeit mostly for the wrong reasons. An own-goal on his debut was followed by another against Oldham in late September. In the same match he compensated by scoring at the right end from 35 yards. His style could certainly be described as combative. Too much so for most referees, who regularly asked for his name. His first suspension was meted out by Christmas. He also suffered a broken nose, which required surgery, and was detained overnight in a Bournemouth hospital after being concussed in a first round League Cup win against the Cherries.

Argyle's early season form set the tone for the season. At home they were a force to be reckoned with. Until early December only one team, Bolton, left with both points. The story away from home was very different. Admittedly, the fixture list had been unwittingly unkind to the Pilgrims. The majority of trips seemed to pit the Greens against in-form sides. Nevertheless the concept of winning away from home seemed alien.

There were occasional glimmers of hope. Without the injured Rafferty and Johnson, Argyle faced a daunting trip to Southampton, hot tips for promotion. The Saints boasted an impressive line-up, including internationals Mick Channon and Jim McCalliog. They even had the luxury of another former England star, Peter Osgood, on the bench. Channon hit the only goal but the Saints' real hero was keeper Steve Middleton, who denied Argyle time and again.

A quick return to the City Ground brought an end to the League Cup campaign as Brian Clough's Forest turned around their indifferent league form to score a solitary goal.

There was much activity off the field as well. Bobby Howe, a former West Ham player and highly rated coach, was added to the backroom staff from Bournemouth who, in contrast to Argyle, were scrapping their youth system as part of a cost-cutting exercise. In November, Argyle announced that they had purchased Elm Cottage, a spacious property adjoining the Central Park area. Purchase and conversion costs were quoted at £30,000. This was the next phase in Waiters' plan, with the property intended to house the club's apprentices.

By this time, supporters had said goodbye to an old favourite. Stalwart defender Bobby Saxton had moved to local rivals Exeter for £4,000. Having lost his first-team place, the 32-year-old saw it as an opportunity to prolong his league career.

December saw a break from league action with a visit from the mighty Manchester United for a testimonial for Peter Middleton, whose career was tragically ended when he was knocked down by a car 48 hours after scoring a stunning goal on his Pilgrims debut in September 1972.

By mid-season Waiters was facing a dilemma. The bigger matches saw Argyle turn on the style, such as in the 4-0 Christmas win over Fulham, Bobby Moore *et al*. Well-earned draws in front of 20,000-plus crowds at Chelsea and Bristol City – not to mention taking the lead at leaders Sunderland – were interspersed with dismal defeats, such as that at Hull (0-4). By and large, the manager stayed true to the same hard core of thirteen or fourteen players.

The fringe players were too inexperienced, and to throw them in would have been risky with the side teetering on a relegation battle.

Interest in the FA Cup didn't last long. With automatic inclusion in the third round, the annual hope of a home tie against a glamour side was soon dispelled when the radio announced 'Hull City will play Plymouth Argyle'. It was difficult to envisage a worse draw, but come match-day the players knuckled down and forced the Tigers into a replay, which started disastrously. Alf Wood's goal after 25 seconds, followed by Sutton's slice into his own net, knocked the stuffing out of Argyle.

Lack of success on their travels made home results even more vital. A 1-3 home reverse to Notts County on 7 February prompted Waiters – but not the directors – to suggest that his job was on the line. Personnel changes were also afoot. Long-serving Johnny Hore was allowed to follow Saxton up the A38 to Exeter, initially on loan. The homesick Barrie Vassallo was released. Before the curtain came down Rioch had also gone and the club announced that Horswill was available for transfer after failing to temper his disciplinary problems.

That Notts County defeat prompted Waiters to recall 38-year-old Furnell. The manager stressed that no blame was attached to Aleksic but felt, given the side's predicament, that experience was needed in goal. Indeed, Aleksic's contributions had already attracted the interest of other clubs.

Furnell's comeback match was not one to savour, a 0-2 defeat at relegation-haunted Portsmouth, who played more than half the game with ten men. Successive 3-0 home wins over Bristol Rovers and Luton prompted a mini-revival, blunted by a three-goal beating by Chelsea's teenagers.

Relegation clouds still hovered. York and Pompey looked doomed but any one of seven clubs could be dragged down to join them. Waiters set a target of 38 points, which he considered to be sufficient to stay up. This helped to focus the players and they came away from Burnden Park having dented second-place Bolton's promotion hopes with a goalless draw.

A home win over Oldham saw the points target creep closer, though it was followed by a grim performance at doomed York. Goals by Peter Darke were rare, but the full-back's first strike for two years provided an unexpected Easter win over Southampton. A draw at Fulham saw Waiters' target attained and safety guaranteed. Waiters paid a glowing tribute to Furnell, going so far as to attribute Argyle's survival to him. Such praise failed to persuade Furnell to defer his retirement. With Oxford losing their final three games, the safety margin was more comfortable than at first imagined.

> **DID YOU KNOW?**
>
> Former Pilgrim, Eric Burgess, has a famous sister – Anthea Redfern – hostess of TV's The Generation Game and one-time wife of Bruce Forsyth.

Despite setting an unwanted record of becoming the first Argyle side ever to go through a season without an away win, several positive points emerged. Attendances averaged nearly 15,000 and many of the squad adapted well enough to the demands of Second Division football. Youngsters such as Dave Sutton and George Foster integrated easily into the side when called upon, and the Mariner-Rafferty partnership continued to earn rave reviews despite a reduced goal output.

For many supporters, the season ended on a note of regret. It was long anticipated that that prolific partnership would end sooner rather than later. England manager Don Revie had twice watched Mariner in action, and calls for his inclusion in the Under-23 side grew louder by the week. It was not a question of whether Argyle could hold on to their young star but for how long. Few then expected that it would be Rafferty's departure that came first.

The Scot was omitted from the final game at Carlisle and by a bizarre turn of events he eventually signed for them. The departure of such a favourite was hard to stomach, but the fee of just £20,000 seemed insulting. It was not one of Waiters' better decisions.

Match of the Season 1975-76
Sunderland 2   Argyle 1

Division 2, 17 January 1976

Argyle travelled to Roker Park with justifiable trepidation. Since their famous FA Cup final triumph over Leeds in 1973, Sunderland had retained an affection in the hearts of most neutrals. Despite producing one of the greatest cup shocks of all time, they had failed to storm out of the Second Division as many had predicted. The venerable Bob Stokoe was still in place as manager but the patience of many Wearsiders was wearing thin.

This finally seemed to be the season when their return to the First Division seemed inevitable. Since mid-September, they had set a storming pace at the top of the table. At Roker Park they were near invincible. Only Bristol Rovers had come away with so much as a point.

Their line-up showed some familiar names from the Wembley triumph, and Stokoe had added much-needed experience. Bobby

Moncur, a hero at rivals Newcastle, strengthened the defence, whilst perennial ace goalscorer 'Pop' Robson was as dangerous as ever, despite approaching the veteran stage.

Pilgrim fortunes had seen a recent upturn. A spell of three wins and a draw around Christmas was marred only by humiliation at home to Hull in the FA Cup. Waiters had a full squad at his disposal. The only question was whether or not to retain Dave Sutton in the back four or recall former Sunderland cup hero, Horswill, who was available after suspension. Sutton got the nod.

Argyle were back in their black and green stripes, their all-white kit clashing with the red and white stripes of their opponents. As the teams lined up for the kick-off a familiar face greeted full-back Peter Darke. Bearded winger Roy Greenwood was making his Roker debut, having recently signed from Hull for £150,000, and was about to lock horns with Darke for the *fourth* time this season.

Argyle started brightly and were well worth their half-time lead, thanks to Mariner's close-range header which evaded Joe Bolton's desperate attempts at a goal-line clearance. But within two minutes of the turnaround, Greenwood showed Darke a clean pair of heels to lay on Mel Holden's equaliser. Sunderland's ruthless streak now came to the fore. Mariner and Rafferty were the chief victims of bone-numbing tackles and Mariner limped off after 63 minutes. Substitute Horswill's return to Roker provoked jeers rather that cheers.

The Pilgrims barely had time to readjust when the diminutive Bobby Kerr headed past Aleksic. Horswill, his hackles already rising, entered the ref's notebook within eight minutes of coming on for a late lunge on Moncur, for which Dennis Longhorne soon exacted revenge.

Argyle continued to pressure their hosts. With five minutes still remaining, 29,000 whistling Rokerites were demanding the final whistle, but Sunderland held on to win.

Eventual runners-up, Bristol City became the only the second side to take a point from Roker as Stokoe's men clinched the title.

LEAGUE DIVISION 2	**1976-77**
Division 2	21st (relegated)
League Cup	1st round
FA Cup	3rd round

The close call of the previous season had made it obvious that team-strengthening was a priority. Despite healthy attendances and a profit in transfer dealings, funds were limited, despite a successful commercial section overseen by the enterprising Bill Pearce. His efforts over the previous season had swelled the Argyle coffers by £100,000.

Notwithstanding the club being heavily indebted to its bankers, the directors showed their commitment by loaning it £60,000. The question was, would the fans stick by the side? A poor start to the season would send the marginal supporters back to their armchairs.

Waiters' first task was to find a goalkeeper. Furnell had retired as expected and was taken on by the club's commercial department. In came Paul Barron – a promising young keeper who had been earning bright reviews with non-league Slough – and the more experienced Neil Ramsbottom.

The acquisition of midfielder Doug Collins added yet more experience. Collins had notched up almost 300 games for Grimsby and Burnley, many at Turf Moor in the top Division. If bringing Collins to Plymouth was a minor coup, the next signing was the stuff of headlines. Rumours abounded that Brian Hall – a regular in Liverpool's great team – was on Argyle's shopping list. Naturally the Pilgrims were not alone in their attempts to sign a player of such pedigree. The required transfer fee of £50,000 was seen as a stumbling block. No doubt Hall's wages were as well.

Although Hall and his wife appeared keen on the South West, the deal seemed doomed. Yet the fans weren't giving up hope. A '(H)all for Argyle' fund was created and various fund-raising events were organised throughout Devon, Cornwall and beyond. The scheme worked, raising £35,000. Hall arrived.

The backroom staff were also boosted by the arrival of another former goalkeeper of renown, Mike Kelly, who was to take charge of the reserve team.

As the new boys ran out for the first fixture, two familiar faces accompanied them. Mick Horswill had been given a reprieve after promising to behave himself, and the No 9 shirt was still filled by Paul Mariner. The summer months had been rife with transfer speculation over the young starlet, with virtually every First Division club mentioned as a possible buyer at one time or another. But for now, he remained a Pilgrim.

DID YOU KNOW?

Argyle twice entered the Anglo-Scottish Cup during the 1970s, but their longest
journey turned out to be a trip to Fulham.

One old friend was missing. Despite appearing in the pre-season
team photos, full-back Phil Burrows had moved to Hereford,
tempted by a higher wage. Hugh McAuley was also holding out for
a better deal, but remained on the books.

The unpopular white kit was still in place as the season commenced with a two-legged League Cup-tie with Devon rivals Exeter.
The pre-season build-up had given Waiters few clues as to his best
eleven. He obviously hadn't found it, as Fourth Division City
moved into the next round with ease.

Burrows' eve-of-season departure had added to Waiters' selection headaches, for he now found himself without a left-back.
Horswill, although not left-footed, was handed the No 3 shirt. Hall
and Collins were naturally given midfield berths but the young
Chris Harrison was preferred to John Delve. The experimental front
pairing of Mariner and Brian Johnson weighed in with a goal apiece
to get the season off to a bright start with a draw at Oldham, followed by a crushing 4-0 win over old rivals Blackburn.

A home defeat by Notts County presented the manager with a
fresh challenge. Right-back Peter Darke was suffering a crisis of
confidence and was on the receiving end of noisy barracking from
his own supporters, which prompted Waiters to pull him off. Darke
played in the next match at Orient but took a knock which inflicted
blurred vision. It was an opportune moment to replace him with
Colin Randell.

The passions generated by Brian Hall's arrival cooled somewhat
after the first few games. The club's record signing had failed to
ignite the side. The same could not be said of Mariner. Rather than
skulking over having to languish in the Second Division, he knuckled down to the job he was paid for, scoring goals. Only once in the
first seven games did he fail to find the net. Each new goal had
Argyle's bank manager rubbing his hands with glee.

A new Argyle 'Player of the Month' award had been introduced
by a local company. Unsurprisingly, Mariner was the first recipient.
Such was the desperation to keep him at Home Park that one suspects he would have won it without even playing.

By early October even the most optimistic fans accepted that
Mariner's Argyle days were numbered. A £125,000 bid from West
Brom was rejected. West Ham now seemed his likely destination, as
manager Ron Greenwood watched him at home to Luton.

In what proved to be his Argyle swansong, Mariner scored a typically brave goal against Cardiff. Greenwood was present again, but so too was Ipswich boss Bobby Robson. Talks with Robson began after the game and within a couple of days a deal was done. Mariner's value was set at £220,000, with Argyle receiving £175,000 in cash, plus two Ipswich fringe players – centre-forward Terry Austin and defender John Peddelty.

By October, the fruits of the youth policy were rewarded with selection for England Youth trials for four apprentices – Kevin Smart, John Uzzell, Gary Megson and Mike Trusson. But Mariner's departure seemed to knock the stuffing out of the first team. He had been a focal point on the pitch and was popular off it. It was not until the first day of 1977 that another win came Argyle's way.

By that time, another striker had joined the fold. Bruce Bannister had been one half of the 'Smash and Grab' partnership with Alan Warboys at Bristol Rovers that even out-scored Mariner and Rafferty. No one was quite sure if Bannister was Smash or Grab, or cared. Austin was proving a competent target-man but could not be expected to be another Mariner. Bannister seemed good value at £15,000, a forward capable of getting the goals desperately needed to halt Argyle's alarming slide towards the foot of the table. Argyle offloaded Jim Hamilton to Rovers as part of the deal.

A goal in Bannister's second game earned a draw with Southampton, but he too suffered from an inadequate supply line. That ammunition might have been provided by McAuley, but the winger had remained out of favour and transfer-listed since the early part of the season, since when he had been stagnating in the reserves. New Year's Day saw him restored to a first-team fixture at Home Park, this time debuting for his new club Charlton. A week later, Argyle were dumped unceremoniously out of the FA Cup by Oldham. Aleksic had also gone to Luton, initially on loan. The transfer was soon made permanent, the fee of £20,000 proving a bargain for the Hatters.

Another new face appeared on the scene. John Craven a no-nonsense utility player, arrived from Coventry for £20,000. After just two minutes of his debut against Oldham he made his first impact. Sadly it was on the Devonport End roof as he bludgeoned a chance over the bar. There were times when Craven made Horswill look like a choirboy. His first seven games yielded four bookings and, with Delve and Horswill also in the side, the inevitable suspensions mounted.

By the end of February, it seemed as if a new crisis was rearing its head almost daily. For one thing, the side was incapable of winning. Waiters fiddled around with his selections. Peddelty was employed in an unfamiliar midfield role, and Alan Rogers recalled after a long absence. Brian Hall's tepid performances had brought murmurings from the terraces. The pressure on the side was even beginning to tell on the usually mild-mannered Mike Green, who was sent off at Hereford after retaliating against the veteran Terry Paine.

Horswill demanded a transfer, claiming to be unsettled. Rumours abounded that Collins felt the same way. Waiters, inevitably, was feeling the heat. Aggrieved by what he perceived to be a lack of support from the directors when they vetoed the appointment of a youth-team coach and refused to improve the contract of assistant manager Keith Blunt, he launched a public attack on the board. From that point, the writing was on the wall. At Luton in mid-March, Hall was dropped. He promptly took issue with Waiters, as a result of which the player put his house up for sale. Two weeks later Waiters took the unprecedented step of circulating other clubs about his own availability, together with that of four of his backroom staff, including Kelly. Waiters confirmed that he had taken these steps without the knowledge or approval of the board. 'It is nothing to do with them,' he insisted.

Events off the field could hardly hide the fact that relegation was ever more probable. Argyle simply weren't scoring enough goals. A terrible 1-2 defeat at home to Hull in front of the season's lowest gate saw the crowd finally vent its spleen against the manager. The time had come, and Chairman Robert Daniel announced the sacking of Waiters. Assistant Keith Blunt resigned. Kelly was given the task of saving Argyle.

Kelly's first match in charge saw former Argyle favourite Billy Rafferty score the first of the northerners' three goals. It was a cathartic moment. The release of Rafferty had, with hindsight, been the first step in the demise of Waiters.

Kelly had a thankless task. Argyle drew with Wolves but defeat in the last two matches cemented a return to the Third Division wilderness. How things had changed in two years.

Match of the Season 1976-77

Sheffield United 1   Argyle 0

Division 2, 7 May 1977

Argyle's predicament was clear. Nothing less than a win at Bramall Lane would do, and even then there was no guarantee of avoiding the drop. Hereford, on 27 points, looked doomed. Cardiff had 31 points, Orient 32 and Carlisle 33, but all had games in hand.

Mike Kelly took charge for only his fourth game. His team selection was important but the more crucial question was, could he fire up his players? The off-field events of the last few weeks had obviously taken their toll on morale. Several players, notably Brian Hall, had little doubt that their futures lay away from Home Park. Only one change was made from the previous match, a 0-1 home defeat by Forest. Hall was relegated to the bench, with winger Alan Rogers drafted in.

If there was such a thing as ideal opponents, then perhaps the Blades were just that. Under Jimmy Sirrel, they had been marooned in mid-table for much of the season and had little to play for.

Prior to kick-off, Kelly was presented with three bottles of champagne by the Argyle Travel Club as a good-luck gesture. The home fans witnessed a presentation of their own. The choice of Keith Edwards as their player of the year was hardly controversial. Since Christmas nineteen-year-old Edwards had been unable to stop scoring, and had averaged a goal a game over the last thirteen matches.

The match itself was hardly a classic. No one expected it would be, what with the tension involved. Argyle had more than their fair share of possession but found difficulty in penetrating a determined United defence. Peddelty was dominating at the back, but a minute before half-time that man, or rather boy, Edwards struck again.

His goal blasted the Blades into action. Ramsbottom, as on numerous occasions during the season, was again Argyle's saviour. Hall's introduction made little difference. Austin missed two good chances and the match drifted to its inevitable conclusion.

Relegation was confirmed a few days later when all the other struggling teams picked up points from their games in hand. Kelly had failed in his unenviable task.

That final game had been a microcosm of Argyle's entire season. An even share of possession had produced no goals. Horswill had been booked yet again, saddling the club with one of the worst disciplinary records in the league. Brian Hall had been left on the bench. Ramsbottom, abused by certain sections of fans at the start of the season, had won them over with a series of defiant displays. Whatever the reasons, a difficult summer lay ahead.

How many players' autographs can you pick out from the 1974-75 promotion team?

Mike Green's shot against Sunderland beats the keeper but is blocked on the line

Lethal strike duo Paul Mariner (left) and Billy Rafferty

This copy to be Forwarded to Visiting Club

THE FOOTBALL LEAGUE, SEASON 1975-76

Percentage of Nett Takings (Ground and Stands) in accordance with Regulation 34

Receipts	£	p.	Payments	£	p.	
Date of Match :			Printing, Postage and Advertising ...	148	50	
11th October 1975						
v.Bolton Wanderers	8021	10	Gatemen	167	25	
Gross Takings—Ground, Stands, Enclosures, &c.			Police	344	19	
			Floodlighting ...	–	–	
			V.A.T. ...	594	02	
			St. John Ambulance	8	76	4% £ 270 – 33
			BALANCE ...	6758	38	
TOTAL	8021	10	TOTAL	8021	10	

herewith enclose Cheque value £ 270 – 33

" Percentage Cheques MUST be in the hands of the League Secretary WITHIN SIX DAYS of the game being played."

AMOUNT PAYABLE TO VISITING CLUB
Regulation 35

ACTUAL ATTENDANCE	VISITORS' ENTITLEMENT
PAID ADMISSIONS :	**PAID ADMISSIONS :**
ADULTS 9211	ADULTS 9211 at 13p £1197 – 43
SCHOOL CHILDREN 2860	SCHOOL CHILDREN 2860 at 7p £ 200 – 20
*SEASON TICKETS 2279	**SEASON TICKETS :**
	ACTUALLY SOLD, ADULTS 2578 at 13p £ 335 – 14
	ACTUALLY SOLD, S. CHILDREN 66 at 7p £ 4 – 62
COMPLIMENTARY TICKETS :	**COMPLIMENTARY TICKETS ISSUED :**
	SEASON TICKETS
SEASON *USED	DAY TICKETS .
DAY USED 245	LESS 250 ALLOWED at 13p £
ATTENDANCE 14,595	£1737 – 39
	Travelling Expenses in respect of postponed or abandoned matches under Regulation 22 (*if any*) £
	£

*Where the number " used " cannot be computed, insert number " issued."

NOTE.—The visiting Club is entitled to a minimum of £400.

Secretary G. A. Little

Date 15th October, 1975.

Club Plymouth Argyle

UPS41490 8.75

A fascinating insight into Argyle's accounts – against Bolton in October 1975

Chapter Two

The Road to Nowhere
1977-1983

LEAGUE DIVISION 3	**1977-78**
Division 3	19th
League Cup	1st round
FA Cup	3rd round

Despite relegation, the directors stood by Mike Kelly as manager. In came Lennie Lawrence to look after the reserves. It was a busy summer for transfers, sadly all of them in an outward direction. The traumatic last months of the previous season had led to speculation of a mass exodus. There were enough outgoings to give Kelly some sleepless nights, wondering what his first-choice side would be. As expected, Doug Collins and Bruce Bannister had moved on – to Sunderland and Hull respectively. Peter Darke tried pastures new at Torquay and player of the year Neil Ramsbottom went to Blackburn. Replacing them was, well, no one.

It might have been worse. Two players who seemed certainties to depart, Brian Hall and Mick Horswill, remained, although Hall was still officially transfer-listed.

There were mixed views as to Argyle's destiny for the coming season. The side had considerably less experience, but this was offset by the likelihood of youth players emerging, to boost morale and drive. The main concern was the lack of a proven goalscorer.

A long-standing feature was also missing as fans filed through the turnstiles for the first match. The 47-year-old roof of the Devonport End had been deemed unsafe and, without funds to replace it, had been demolished. The residence of Argyle's main choir suddenly seemed less hospitable. Many took refuge in the Lyndhurst Stand but the ground suddenly seemed to lack atmosphere.

The pre-season build up had a more competitive edge, for the club had entered the Anglo-Scottish Cup. The preliminary group saw them pitched against Birmingham and both Bristol clubs. Three points from three matches was not enough to progress, but the performances of certain youngsters, notably John Uzzell and Mike Trusson, gave cause for optimism.

The unpopular newspaper-style programme had been replaced by a more conventional issue. Strangely, the early editions carried cover pictures of the long departed Paul Mariner and Jim Furnell.

DID YOU KNOW?

Two Argyle goalkeepers from the 1970s – Milija Aleksic and Peta Bala'c
– both had Yugoslavian fathers.

The season proper started as it had twelve months earlier with a League Cup-tie against Exeter. Young Trusson struck twice to cancel out two Grecian penalties. With no away-goals rule, a goalless draw at Home Park took the tie into a replay. Argyle won the toss to stage it, but a single goal took promoted Exeter through.

The first two league games failed to yield a goal and the sceptics who asked where Argyle's goals would come from seemed to have a point. Struggling Hereford provided the first win, but Kelly took more heart from a 3-3 home draw with Walsall. It at least proved that his side could score, and Austin found the net twice.

Another favourite departed from Home Park at this time when Colin Randell added to the growing list of ex-Pilgrims at Exeter. Brian Bason, a sturdy utility player, came on loan from Chelsea but the end of the road for John Peddelty arrived in sad circumstances. A head injury proved serious enough to force him to bow to medical opinion and quit the game. The defender-cum-midfielder had played just 30 matches since arriving as part of the Paul Mariner deal.

News leaked out that Argyle were in negotiations to sign Fred Binney, Plymouth born, but who had somehow slipped through the net early in his career. That had proved to be a big mistake, for Binney had scored prolifically wherever he went. Many considered him unfortunate not to ply his trade at a higher level. Although he was now approaching the twilight of his career, he was still capable of bagging twenty goals a season.

At one point the deal seemed destined to fall through, with Binney unimpressed by Argyle's offer. Though he eventually signed, he was short of match fitness and initially kept in the reserves to get him up to speed.

The fans received a bonus in October when Home Park was chosen to host Manchester United's European Cup-Winners' Cup-tie against the crack French side, Saint-Etienne. United had been ordered to play their 'home' leg well away from Old Trafford as punishment for crowd disturbances. Over 31,000 crammed in to see Tommy Docherty's side defeat Saint-Etienne 2-0 to progress 3-1 on aggregate.

Back in Division Three, Argyle continued to slide, although Paul Barron attracted the attention of a number of clubs and John Craven revelled in the responsibility of skippering a struggling side. In the light of his frequent misdemeanours of the previous campaign, it says much that he contrived to stay out of the referees' notebook until mid-November.

After claiming just one point from three home matches in October, it was clear that measures had to be taken to strengthen the team. The fans were beginning to vote with their feet. The regular 15,000 from two years earlier had diminished to a paltry 4,600 for a midweek visit from Shrewsbury, Argyle's lowest crowd since the war. The directors again dug deep into their pockets to find £15,000 to bring Brian Taylor from Walsall. Taylor had looked a class act when facing the Pilgrims a few weeks earlier but – such was Argyle's wretched form – that could be said of most opponents!

Further changes to the side were made. In came another product of the youth system, Gary Megson. Hall's departure seemed imminent, ironically just as he was showing some of the form expected of him. Sure enough, he left for Burnley, which provided him with the move back north that he sought. Sadly, his career was cut short by injury after only 40-odd games for the Clarets.

Any hopes that the New Year would bring a change in fortunes evaporated, first, when Craven requested a transfer and, second, with defeat in the FA Cup at Mansfield. Bason, having had his earlier loan spell cut short when Chelsea recalled him, returned, this time permanently, for £35,000.

The new signings failed to appease the remaining supporters, particularly as Binney had remained largely out of favour since his arrival. When Jim Hamilton, a player who had virtually been ignored during his time as a Pilgrim, gave Carlisle a single goal victory at Home Park it was too much to take. The fans vented their anger at both Kelly and chairman Robert Daniel. The side had slumped to next to bottom and looked in grave danger of dropping to the Fourth Division for the first time.

The next home game saw an even lower crowd, 4,639. A 0-3 defeat at leaders Cambridge proved to be Kelly's last match in charge. Daniel was not going to make the same mistake twice and ring the changes too late to make any difference. Whether Kelly was sacked or asked to resign is open to speculation, though plainly he was unhappy with the situation. In front of local TV cameras, Kelly stormed out of Home Park, vociferously refusing interviews. Despite his reputation as a coach, few supporters were sorry to see him go.

Lennie Lawrence was given temporary command. His first game in charge saw one of the most bizarre matches ever staged at Home Park. A crowd of just 2,843 braved sub-zero temperatures to watch the Pilgrims take on Bradford City. City took a 25th-minute lead through David McNiven, who two minutes later was the victim of an astonishing assault by Horswill, who pursued his victim around the pitch. Referee Ron Crabb, who earlier in the season had been suspended by the Football League for failing to send off Leeds' Norman Hunter, needed little encouragement to despatch Horswill. Such was the ferocity of his attack that Horswill was even jeered by his own fans. Once play resumed, conditions worsened. In driving sleet and hail one of Mr Crabb's watches failed to function. More seriously, Mr Crabb was rapidly approaching the same condition. After 61 minutes he called a halt to the farce, before seeking medical treatment. The Argyle players returned to the changing room to be a greeted by a chastened but warm Horswill.

Lawrence's appointment coincided with the approach of transfer deadline day. The caretaker boss was soon wheeling and dealing. In came Keith Fear, Tyrone James and Steve Perrin, with Terry Austin moving to Walsall and Tony Waiters clinching the signing of Craven for his new club, Vancouver Whitecaps. Dave Sutton also went, on loan, to Huddersfield. With so many new faces the team was unlikely to gel overnight, but time was not on their side.

One win in six games did little to enhance Lawrence's CV. Just as most fans were beginning to lose hope, Daniel sprung a surprise by announcing the return of Malcolm Allison, the charismatic coach who had abruptly left Argyle thirteen years before. For some reason, Allison was given the title of 'consultant manager' with Lawrence remaining in his post.

Allison's impact was almost immediate. After witnessing a draw at home to Oxford, he called the players in for Sunday training to prepare them for a midweek match at Portsmouth. Pompey were almost as bitter rivals to Argyle as Exeter are today, so an astonishing 5-1 win – irrespective of their opponents' poor form – was all the more gratifying.

Allison was soon brought back down to earth. The next five games yielded just three points and Argyle were grateful to relegation rivals, who kept losing, and to Fred Binney, who suddenly started scoring, and scoring.

The crucial game was at home against Port Vale. The Potteries side had lost three on the trot and for them it was the final game of the season. They remained a point ahead of the Pilgrims, who occupied the last relegation spot. In a match of nerve-racking tension it was that man Binney again who struck twice in a 3-2 win. Allison had done the job asked of him. Survival was assured and a celebratory 6-0 thrashing of relegated Bradford City followed in the final game. Allison's future at Argyle was uncertain, but there was no doubt that the fans wanted him to stay.

Match of the Season 1977-78

Argyle 3   Port Vale 2

Division 3, 29 April 1978

Whatever financial inducements were made to Malcolm Allison to secure his return to Home Park, it was now time to earn his corn. The situation was stark. Vale were playing their final game of the season and stood one place outside the relegation zone with 36 points. Argyle were one point and one place behind them, but with a game in hand. A win would secure survival. Allison, seeking every possible advantage, urged the supporters to turn out in force. They obeyed. A crowd of 9,474 was the highest at Home Park for some time.

Tension filled the air as the two teams ran out. Vale were in the throes of an awful run, but were one of the division's draw specialists. They needed a win now, something they had not achieved for nine games. Despite their poor form there was a nagging memory that they had been a jinx side to Argyle in recent years. Encounters between the two teams were invariably physical. With this in mind, Allison relegated wafer-thin Alan Rogers to the bench. John Uzzell missed his first game of the season through injury. Brian Bason was restored to the side and Horswill asked to fill in at left-back.

With fans still filing in, Vale took the lead through top scorer Ken Beamish, who lashed in a left-foot volley. This only served to increase the crowd volume. Brian Johnson capitalised on a mistake by Graham Hawkins to send the sides in level at half-time.

Argyle started the second period on the offensive. Binney scored a typical goal, tapping in Johnson's corner, but a mistake by the inexperienced Hodge let Vale in again. Cometh the hour, cometh the man. Binney applied what was to prove the crucial goal. Minutes seemed like hours. Allison, ignoring his lifetime touchline ban, made regular sorties from the directors' box to the dugout, where Lennie Lawrence was directing operations.

The final whistle provoked scenes of jubilation to match that of any promotion celebration. Young boys leapt over the barriers. Fathers followed. Even the older generation made it onto the pitch, courtesy of helping hands. Within seconds the playing area was a carpet of green and white. From within, eleven white-shirted Pilgrims were eventually hoisted shoulder high.

The crowd refused to disperse until Allison and Lawrence took a bow. Eventually they appeared at the front of the grandstand with the customary bottles of champagne. The frustrations of the previous eight months were forgotten.

LEAGUE DIVISION 3	1978-79
Division 3	15th
League Cup	2nd round
FA Cup	1st round

Despite having a contract in his pocket, there were still question marks over Malcolm Allison's future at Argyle, as speculation at the end of the previous season had linked him with any number of high-profile positions. He remained at Home Park, however, and his summer transfer dealings gave a clue to the motivation behind his loyalty.

Big Mal was a well-known figure in the world of football. Brash, arrogant, a showman – these were just some of the labels attached to him. What was not in dispute was that as a coach he had numerous admirers. He was happiest when working with the players. With a number of promising youngsters coming through the ranks, and the raw talent of the likes of Gary Megson available to him, Allison saw a challenge that excited him. He saw no future for some players already on the books. Paul Barron went to Arsenal, Mick Horswill to Hull, Geoff Banton to Fulham, and Kevin Smart to Wigan. Tony Burns, an experienced keeper, was recruited from Crystal Palace, together with team-mate, Steve Brennan. It was clear that Allison relished the opportunity to mould a team from the up and coming talent now available to him.

Nor did he always agree on a player's best position. A pre-season friendly against Stoke illustrated the point, for the entire back four – Bason, Foster, Trusson and Rogers – had previously been midfielders or forwards.

Whilst Allison's line up raised a few eyebrows, there could be no complaints from traditionalists about Argyle's revamped shirts. Apart from a splash of white, green was back in favour. With regard to the stadium, there was no sign yet of a new roof for the Devonport End.

The season began well with two victories in the League and progression to the second round of the League Cup. Most players had settled quickly into the new roles they had been asked to play. The exception was Tony Burns. His experience had been preferred to the youthful promise of Martin Hodge, but Burns was proving erratic. A sharp save would invariably be followed by a schoolboy error. After a calamitous 1-4 home defeat by Mansfield, Hodge was restored.

The good news was that Fred Binney was producing the goods. By the end of September he had already notched eleven League and cup goals and was displaying the goal-poaching instincts on which he had built his reputation. The defence, however, was looking porous. The experiment of fielding Trusson as a central defender was soon abandoned and Colin Clarke, a man with over 400 games under his belt, was signed from Oxford – who had by then knocked Argyle out of the League Cup.

There were further comings and goings. Out went Brian Taylor after a relatively short spell as a Pilgrim. A fee of £35,000 took him to Preston. In his place, on loan, came another midfielder, Barry Silkman, a player well known it seems to Allison. After formalities were complete the newcomer was told that his new boss wanted a word with him. 'Good,' came Silkman's retort, 'I want to see him too, he owes me a fiver.'

Silkman quickly endeared himself to the home crowd. On his day he was one of the most skilful players around, looking more suited to the First Division stage. With socks down at his ankles he was capable of enough flashes of brilliance to have his loan period turned into a permanent contract, although the size of the fee was kept under wraps. Paradoxically, Silkman's arrival coincided with a run of results which sent Argyle spiralling down the table. At the end of September they had stood fourth. By the New Year they had slipped to twelfth.

The nadir of the season and, some would argue, of Argyle's entire history, came in the FA Cup. A 0-2 defeat at Worcester City marked the first occasion a Pilgrims side had lost to non-league opposition in the FA Cup. The result was hard to stomach, but not so hard as the ineptitude of Argyle's performance.

Inevitably, changes had to be made. Allison acknowledged that for all Rogers' qualities, he was no full-back. In came Brian McNeill from Bristol City for £15,000 and Allison also added Clevere Forde, a young non-league talent, and a promising 19-year-old, Lee Chapman, who was taken on loan from Stoke.

Argyle's dismal form and cup demise was too much for Big Mal. In mid-January, despite having two years left on his contract, he took little persuading to return to Manchester City, the club where he had forged his reputation in tandem with Joe Mercer. This time he would link up with City's general manager, Tony Book, whom Allison had brought to Home Park as a player during his first spell at the club. Argyle received £35,000 compensation for the loss of Allison and wasted little time in announcing former favourite, Bobby Saxton, as his successor.

Saxton's move to St James' Park had worked out well. He had kept a regular place in the side and when another former Argyle favourite, Johnny Newman, vacated the managerial seat in December 1976, Saxton occupied it as player-manager. Newman had guided City to the top of the Fourth Division and Saxton continued the good work. The Grecians finished the season as runners-up.

Taking over at Home Park was, in fact, a step down for Saxton as, at the time of his switch, City were riding high in sixth place in Division Three. His move to Argyle left Exeter with a few head-aches, not least because he also brought assistant Jack Edwards, physio Tony Long, and chief scout Jim Furnell with him.

Saxton's management style could not have been more different to Allison's. Saxton was a no-nonsense character, a pie and chips man, as opposed to champagne and cigars. The flashiness of Silk-man did not fit with his way of thinking. Despite having played just fourteen matches for the club, Argyle looked set to profit hand-somely from selling him. Allison was willing to pay £100,000 to take him to Maine Road until the deal initially fell through on medical grounds. Silkman went to Luton on loan until the move to City was finally concluded.

Keith Fear was another player who wanted to leave. Unable to secure a regular first-team spot, the former Bristol City man was 'unsettled', as they say. Saxton soon received a further blow. In a home game against Oxford, skipper George Foster suffered a broken leg that put him out for the season.

Despite these early setbacks, results started to improve. Saxton relied on the existing squad and it was Binney's goals that generally kept the team afloat. Progress was, however, blighted by inconsis-tency. A satisfying 4-2 home win over Exeter was followed two weeks later by a 0-5 reverse at Mansfield.

At least the fans had the consolation that their side did not have a relegation battle on its hands. With a mid-table finish on the cards, Saxton wasted no time in planning for the following season. In early April he announced that eight players, including Clarke, Fear and Brennan, as well as several youngsters, were available for transfer.

With safety guaranteed, Saxton chopped and changed his line-ups enabling him to run the rule over a number of youngsters, such as Kevin Hodges and Mark Graves. Deprived of the tension pro-vided by a relegation or promotion battle, crowds drifted away, the season being to all intents dead.

It was a foregone conclusion that Binney would be voted Ar-gyle's Player of the Year. His 28 goals made him the second top scorer in the country, behind Watford's Ross Jenkins. Binney was presented with his trophy at the final game and immediately ran over to plant a kiss on Umbrella Vi, because, he said, 'she keeps sending me nice messages'. At least everyone was smiling at the end of the season.

DID YOU KNOW?

Barry Silkman quickly ended his playing spell in Israel when he received call-up
papers for the Israeli Army.

Match of the Season 1978-79

Sheffield Wednesday 2   Argyle 3

Division 3, 23 September 1978

After a reasonable start to the season, confidence was running high
in the Argyle camp. Four wins from the first six League games had
restored some of the confidence in the players. The Owls were
languishing in mid-table on account of a miserable away record, but
at home they were a different proposition, having not lost at Hillsborough for the last fifteen League matches.

Under the management of the combative Jack Charlton, Wednesday were in much the same boat as Argyle. The once great club
had been stranded in the Third Division for too long but had put
their faith in a young squad. The one star name in the side was Ian
Porterfield, scorer of Sunderland's FA Cup winning goal in 1973.
Wearing the Owls' No 9 shirt was a young Tommy Tynan. Marking
him would be Colin Clarke, who was making his Argyle debut after
signing from Oxford.

Strangely, Argyle attracted Wednesday's largest home crowd of
the season so far, a shade over 12,000. By half-time most of them
were mystified by the fact that Wednesday were somehow a goal
up. Argyle's abrasive style of recent seasons had disappeared. The
cloggers had moved on to be replaced by ball-players such as Megson, Taylor and Perrin. For the first 45 minutes the Pilgrims sprayed
the ball around, producing flowing moves out of defence. Fred
Binney, who had scored in each of his last three games, somehow
missed two sitters and had two other chances that on another day
would have been put away. The real test would be how Argyle
would respond to Roger Wylde's header, just before the break.

The second period followed the pattern of the first. In the 69th
minute Binney finally buried a chance which had been beautifully
created by Megson. Five minutes later Binney was at it again, after
Perrin's powerful run had induced panic in the Wednesday defence.
It was the 150th goal of Binney's career.

Wednesday pulled back to 2-2 when substitute Ian Nimmo, who
had replaced Tynan, scrambled the ball home after Hodge had
fumbled a cross. To a man, Argyle's defenders insisted their keeper
had been impeded.

Two minutes later, all hell broke loose. Perrin again sent Binney bearing down on goal. He collided with his marker, Jeff Johnson, who went sprawling, but Binney recovered his poise to shoot past keeper Bob Bolder. The Owls howled. Irate players besieged the referee, claiming Johnson had been deliberately tripped. One fan raced on to confront the official and two others staged a mini protest on the far side of the pitch. Binney later claimed that the collision was accidental. As ever, the referee did not change his decision. Binney's goal counted. It was the first hat-trick by an Argyle player for 200 matches.

Charlton was generous in defeat, praising the quality of Argyle's football. He also had the last word. Binney's attempts to retrieve the match ball as a memento were laughed off. The Owls boss said: 'We can't afford to give away match balls in the Third Division.'

LEAGUE DIVISION 3   **1979-80**
Division 3   15th
League Cup   3rd round
FA Cup   1st round

As the players returned for pre-season training, there was a gaping hole in Saxton's team. The goalkeeping position was proving to be a headache. The unfortunate Tony Burns had moved on and Argyle had also swelled their coffers by accepting £135,000 from Everton for Martin Hodge. This left 17-year-old apprentice Neil Hards as Saxton's only option between the posts.

At least Saxton had skipper George Foster available again after his broken leg, while Colin Randell had returned from Exeter for a second spell at Home Park. Another new face belonged to the regally named Forbes Phillipson-Masters, a £35,000 signing from Southampton. It was fortunate that the defender played in the days before names appeared on the back of shirts.

Aside from the goalkeeping issue, the side looked solid enough. As long as Binney kept on scoring, there was every hope that Argyle might be up among the front runners. Saxton tried to solve his goalkeeping problem by offering £60,000 for Newcastle's Steve Hardwick. After deliberation, Hardwick decided to stay put.

For the second time, Argyle took part in the pre-season Anglo-Scottish Cup and, for the second time, they failed to survive their preliminary group ties, this time against Fulham, Birmingham and Bristol City. Hards played admirably early on, but was faced with some competition, temporarily at least, when Saxton signed David Brown on a month's loan from Middlesbrough.

Indifferent pre-season form had already encouraged mutterings from the terraces, particularly when it was belatedly announced that admission prices were to increase substantially. Even the privilege of standing would cost £1.30. At least Argyle made progress in the League Cup – just. A first-leg defeat at Fourth Division Newport saw Saxton lambast his defence. Hards was the hero in the return, saving Howard Goddard's last-minute penalty. Goddard followed up to net the loose ball but referee Lester Shapter ruled that the match had ended as soon as the ball struck Hards.

The League campaign started with a home win over Bury. Binney was soon on the goal trail, but in the next match he took an injury which – unbeknown to him at the time – would signal the end of his all too brief liaison with his home-town club.

With Binney out, the responsibility of scoring goals was heaped on the young shoulders of Mark Graves and Mike Trusson. Both had potential but needed a wiser head alongside them.

DID YOU KNOW?

**Argyle played just two matches in the short-lived Simod Cup in the 1980s.
They lost both of them 2-6.**

A shock aggregate League Cup victory over Chelsea provided only temporary respite for the beleaguered fans. A single-goal defeat at Grimsby followed, a result which left the Pilgrims just one place off the bottom. 'Here we go again,' bewailed the fans as the prospect of another relegation battle loomed large.

Saxton acted quickly. The directors were persuaded to part with much of the money received for the sale of Hodge, £75,000 of which went to Carlisle in exchange for David Kemp, a striker who terror- ised defences in the lower divisions, averaging a goal every two and a half games.

Kemp burst onto the scene, scoring twice on his debut in Ar- gyle's first ever match against Wimbledon. His lethal shooting saw him hailed as the new Messiah of Home Park, leaving the fans drooling in anticipation of a Kemp-Binney strike partnership.

That match saw an unusual plea from the players – please cut the grass. It was felt that the deep spongy turf hindered Argyle's passing game, not to mention sapping the energy of the team.

The Pilgrims and Dons did not have to wait long to meet again, having been paired in the League Cup. Wimbledon breathed a sigh of relief when they discovered that Kemp was cup-tied. A scoreless draw at Home Park took the tie back to Plough Lane where the Dons snatched victory in extra-time.

The uncertainty shrouding the occupancy of the No 1 jersey was finally settled with the £40,000 signing of Geoff Crudgington from Swansea, although initially he might have doubted the wisdom of his move. A visit to Chester produced an inept performance before 3,000 spectators. Binney wasted a penalty and Megson miskicked with the goal at his mercy.

With the restored Binney now partnering Kemp in the attack, it seemed only a matter of time before the goals started to flow. Sadly they did not. The partnership showed no immediate signs of 'click- ing' and was given little time to do so. Binney soon found himself back with the 'stiffs', who had interpreted the word a mite literally when including 42-year-old Jim Furnell in a recent reserve match.

A home defeat by Brentford consigned the Pilgrims to the bot- tom, following which the board demanded an explanation from Saxton. The manager denied the meeting was to discuss his future but inevitably, speculation began to mount. Player power, it seems, was also having an influence. The perpetrators were not named but

Megson, now rated in the £250,000 bracket, was summarily dropped and transfer listed. In came John Sims, a player Saxton had signed at Exeter.

Two home wins on the trot seemed to signal an upturn in fortunes, but a 2-5 thumping at Colchester was exacerbated by Kemp limping off with an injury that would keep him out for weeks. Binney seemed the obvious replacement, but by now he was so marginalised that, far from being recalled, he was offloaded in January to Hereford.

Argyle and Colchester were soon re-acquainted, this time in the FA Cup. An improved performance at Layer Road earned a replay — but an extra-time goal by Ian Allinson saw Argyle blow their chance of a home tie against Fourth Division Bournemouth, and with it a likely passport to a third-round clash against one of the big boys.

Some silverware did, in a manner of speaking, find its way to Home Park. When Nottingham Forest arrived for Ellis Stuttard's testimonial, manager Brian Clough brought along the European Cup and League Cup — for display purposes only.

Despite Kemp's absence, a few younger players were coming into their own. Kevin Hodges was maturing quickly and Leigh Cooper, who was also drafted in, took to league football like a duck to water.

To boost his attacking options, Saxton brought Jeff Cook on loan from Stoke. After initially keeping the bench warm, he soon showed what he was capable of. Two strikes against Hull on his full debut were followed by a goal in each of the next three games. The fans clamoured for him to sign permanently, but his form merely alerted Stoke to the fact that perhaps they had a talented striker on their hands. He was hastily recalled to the Potteries once his loan period had elapsed.

In February, Gary Megson's future was finally settled. Several clubs made enquiries about him, but he eventually followed Hodge to Goodison Park with Everton manager Gordon Lee paying Argyle £250,000.

Kemp's return to the starting line-up coincided with a defeat against lowly Wimbledon, who were rapidly proving themselves to be Argyle's new bogey side. It was the Pilgrims' first loss in ten games, a run which had freed them from relegation pressures. The apparent comfort of their mid-table position induced ill-judged complacency. The points gap separating Argyle from those below them was narrow and three successive away defeats suddenly had everyone looking over their shoulders again. Fortunately Kemp found a goalscoring ally in Mike Trusson, and six points from the final four games saw Argyle finish five points clear of the trap door.

As the curtain came down on another season, it was time to reflect on the plusses and minuses. The side had finished in fifteenth position with 44 points, an identical record to the previous campaign. Figures don't lie, which meant that despite the pre-season hopes there had been no progress. Saxton was a popular figure but results had been generally disappointing and none of the cash generated from the sale of Megson had been used for team strengthening. There was much to consider during the close season.

Match of the Season 1979-80
Chelsea 1   Argyle 2

League Cup, 2nd round, 2nd leg, 4 September 1979

Despite a creditable 2-2 draw in the first leg at Home Park a week earlier, even the most ardent fan gave Argyle little chance in the return. A dismal start to the season had been compounded by injuries. Striker Fred Binney was already out and Argyle had just come off the back of a 1-3 home defeat by Sheffield Wednesday, which had led Saxton to remark: 'many more performances like that and I won't be around.' The Owls' muscular approach had also put John Uzzell and Brian Bason in hospital, thereby denying the latter a nostalgic return to Stamford Bridge. On-loan goalkeeper David Brown was handed his Argyle debut.

The Blues were led by two footballing legends, Danny Blanchflower (manager) and Geoff Hurst (coach). Chelsea had taken the departure of star youngsters such as 'Butch' Wilkins in their stride and had begun their Second Division campaign well. Their youthful side was complemented by older heads such as Ron 'Chopper' Harris who, to the relief of Argyle's forwards, was left on the bench for this particular match. Chelsea even had the novelty of a foreigner in their ranks, Yugoslav goalkeeper Petar Borota.

The crowd of 14,112 was handsome by Argyle standards but not Chelsea's, for it proved to be their lowest of the season. Those who did bother to attend expected to see a comfortable home victory.

Argyle settled quickly. John Sparrow cleared a Trusson header off the line and Graves' effort was deflected into the side netting. On twelve minutes Chris Harrison, playing as a sweeper, ventured upfield to unleash a 25-yard shot which Borota could only help on its way. To their credit, the Pilgrims did not rest on their lead. Trusson hit the crossbar and Johnson went close with an overhead kick. Megson added noughts to his escalating transfer value with every touch, Brown grew in confidence, and the back four had the Chelsea front line in their pockets.

Whatever the normally mild-mannered Blanchflower said to his troops at half-time certainly stirred them up, for they came out with all guns blazing. Then, in the 68th minute, Chelsea were hit with a sucker punch. Hodges' shot was blocked, but Johnson followed up to fire into an empty net.

Three minutes later, man-mountain Micky Droy headed in a left-wing cross to halve the deficit, but the Pilgrims retained their composure to the final whistle.

Hopes that this would prove a turning point in Argyle's season soon foundered as they returned to losing ways in their next match, against Grimsby. But defeat also knocked the stuffing out of Chelsea, who lost their next two games and plummeted to eighteenth in the table before recovering. How much the defeat by Argyle played a part in Blanchflower's decision to resign shortly afterwards, only he will know, but Hurst took his place, leading Chelsea briefly to the top of the table before they slipped back to finish fourth.

LEAGUE DIVISION 3   **1980-81**
Division 3   7th
League Cup   1st round
FA Cup   3rd round

Home and away defeats by Portsmouth saw Argyle dumped from the League Cup before the Division Three campaign had even got underway. This soured the mood of supporters, as did the crowd violence that marred the home leg. No doubt a combination of booze and a summer heat-wave played its part in the trouble, which saw a corner flag flung into the crowd. The mayhem made national headlines and did nothing to help football's image or entice back a few of the missing thousands. Poor crowds, of course, were not exclusive to Home Park. They pervaded the game as a whole and had been testing soccer's administrators for some time. Ideas for making the game more attractive, such as awarding three points for a win, were bandied about, and some clubs had experimented by staging Sunday matches for the first time.

It was a case of 'as you were' at Home Park, with Saxton and his backroom staff remaining at the helm, overseeing pretty much the same squad of players who had struggled for most of the previous season. Mike Trusson, who had looked better than most, had gone to Sheffield United, with winger Donal Murphy arriving from Torquay for £65,000. The only other newcomer was John Peachey, a free transfer from Darlington.

Saxton sprang a surprise in the opening league game, preferring Mark Graves to Sims as attacking partner to Kemp. The campaign started unspectacularly, with three draws and a win in the first four matches. The new-style match programme attracted admiring comments. Priced at 30 pence, it was a great improvement on the previous season's token effort and was boosted by the inclusion of an insert, 'On Target', which was included in most clubs' publications and was reminiscent of the popular Football League Review of a few years earlier.

A thumping 4-1 win over Carlisle, with David Kemp getting a hat-trick against his former club, was like a bolt from the blue. Two away draws were followed by another 4-1 win, at home to Gillingham. This time Kemp only managed two but they were enough to make him the leading scorer in the country and to take Argyle to the top of the table. Handicapped by a meagre squad, Saxton had nevertheless found a forward combination that seemed to be working in tandem and the whole team was also working for each other. Team spirit, conspicuously lacking in recent times, was evident for all to see. Crudgington was consistency personified between the posts. The defence and midfield were functioning well as a unit, while Murphy had quickly settled and was also getting some useful goals. Although Sims – soon back in favour – was not a prolific scorer himself, he proved to be the ideal foil for Kemp.

Two further victories consolidated Argyle's pole position and clinched the September manager of the month award for Saxton. That particular honour was seen across football as something of a jinx, often signalling a downturn in its recipients' fortunes. Surely it couldn't happen this time. Argyle were playing too well.

The unbeaten run extended into October. It had to end some-time, of course. A home match with Blackpool demonstrated the fickle nature of the Pilgrims' fan base. Fewer than 5,000 had turned out for the first home league game of the season. Two months later, that figure had more than doubled. Nearly 11,000 – including the unemployed Malcolm Allison – saw Saxton receive his bottle of Bell's whisky on the pitch before the game, and then witnessed the jinx rear its ugly head again. Alan Ball's inspired Tangerines trav-elled back up the motorway with both points.

Two tough away matches followed. A 0-2 setback at Hudders-field set off a few alarm bells, but Kemp again showed his liking for settling old scores against former clubs by scoring twice in a fighting 3-1 midweek win at Pompey to get things back on track and con-tinue the joust with Chesterfield at the top of the table.

Form can be as fickle as an Argyle fan and, for no apparent reason, things started to go awry. The Kemp goal machine was by now receiving close attention from opposition defences and had stopped working to full capacity. Saxton continued to reiterate his belief that the team was playing well, but the simple truth was that Argyle could not win a match and were rapidly losing touch with the promotion pack.

Three successive home defeats soon sent Mr and Mrs Fickle back to their living room, as only 5,000 saw Kemp find his scoring boots to clinch a win over Walsall's walking wounded. That result left Argyle in eighth place, from where a good run of results could still lift them back into contention.

Unfortunately, that winning run did not materialise. Christmas arrived with only one more victory to Argyle's name. The saving grace was the FA Cup, which seemed to inspire the players. The draw was relatively kind, throwing up home ties against Division Three bedfellows Newport and Oxford, both of whom were both channelling their energies into avoiding relegation, not dreaming of Wembley.

The festive season saw a distinct lack of cheer or goodwill. Fierce rivals Exeter had the temerity not just to take both points away from

Home Park, but in the process overtake the Pilgrims in the table. A 0-3 tanking at Swindon the following day all but put paid to the promotion dream, and was so dispiriting that the team were locked in the dressing room for an hour after the game. The expression on Saxton's face when he eventually emerged made it clear they had not spent the time exchanging gifts. Little wonder, then, that there was minimal take up of the offer of half-price season tickets. Few were prepared to fork out £27.50 for a grandstand seat for the remainder of this lame-duck season.

The third round FA Cup draw threw up another home tie, this time against Charlton Athletic, who had stormed from nowhere to the top of Division Three on the back of thirteen wins and a draw in fourteen matches. On the day, the south London side were largely second best, but they scraped through thanks to a late Derek Hales goal.

January finally brought some transfer news. Saxton had been tracking Hull's former England Under-23 defender, Gordon Nisbet, since the previous May, but various offers had been rebuffed. The Yorkshire club's financial position had worsened in recent months, however, and they were suddenly keen to offload players. £30,000 exchanged hands as Hull's former captain signed for Argyle, in preference to a move to Carlisle or Swindon.

Nisbet's arrival signalled an upturn in fortunes as this topsy-turvy season contrived another twist. The clenched fist salute that invariably followed a Kemp goal was again seen on a regular basis. Apart from the inclusion of Nisbet, the one major change to the line up was the recall of Brian Johnson after a prolonged spell in the Combination League side. Johnson replaced Brian Bason, whose versatility would be missed, but the enticement of Crystal Palace's £80,000 cheque to lighten Argyle's ever darkening financial gloom was difficult to resist. The arrival of Nisbet also signalled the end for fellow full-back McNeill. Full-back was a position in which the club were well covered, and McNeill opted to ply his trade north of the border with Hearts.

Those keeping an eye on the reserves also had reasons to cheer. Jim Furnell's second strings had climbed into the top three of the Combination League, despite competing against the second elevens of Arsenal, Tottenham and other big clubs, whilst apprentice David Phillips had been selected for the Welsh youth team.

Transfer deadline day came and went without anyone noticing. That was not just common to Argyle. The game was not cash rich. Attendances in general had fallen but players' wages and transfer fees had gone the other way. There was general outrage when it was revealed that a Leeds player was reputed to be earning £600 a week. Saxton, in one of his programme notes, stated his belief that 25 percent of Football League players could be looking for other clubs at the end of the season.

Argyle's performances over the closing weeks could barely be faulted, although draws against bottom sides Blackpool and Hull needed to have been wins to generate the extra momentum needed to go all out for promotion – however remote that objective might have been. In the end, seventh place was a considerable improvement on recent seasons. Saxton had benefited from a settled side and had called upon only nineteen players, five of whom were used as stopgaps. The defence was sound enough, conceding less than a goal a game, but the 'goals for' column relied too heavily on Kemp. His 28 goals accounted for 44 percent of the side's total and left him as second top scorer in the division behind Exeter's goal-machine, Tony Kellow. The dismal results of the middle third of the season had done too much damage to be rectified.

Match of the Season 1980-81
Argyle 4   Carlisle 1

Division 3, 6 September 1980

These two sides went into the match having had contrasting starts to the new season. Argyle were unbeaten, albeit having drawn three of their four games. The Cumbrians, under the command of Martin Harvey, on the other hand, had managed only a solitary point at Huddersfield and had lost both home games, 0-3 and 1-4.

Saxton was in bullish mood after a pleasing performance in the previous week's 0-0 draw at Oxford. 'Last Saturday's standards are what we have to aim for every week,' he wrote in his programme notes.

The Carlisle squad contained a couple of faces familiar to Argyle fans – Jim Hamilton, who, unlike his spell at Home Park, had established himself as a first-team regular at Brunton Park, and Hugh McAuley, who was out of the favour and therefore did not play. Carlisle's forward line contained two players who, in time, would become well known to Pilgrim followers – Gordon Staniforth and a young, fresh faced Peter Beardsley.

Argyle's players clearly hadn't read Saxton's programme notes. They started untidily, until Harrison strode upfield to test Trevor Swinburne with a 25-yard shot. The ball carried too much power to be safely gathered, but only Kemp seemed to anticipate the probability of the keeper spilling it, and snapped up the rebound to give the Pilgrims an undeserved lead.

DID YOU KNOW?

A home match against Oxford in October 1975 saw the opposition's Roger Hynds
clear the ball into touch and knock off a policeman's helmet.

Six minutes later, Carlisle's Staniforth was left unmarked and
made no mistake. The visitors then received another boost, or so
they thought. Forbes Phillipson-Masters – never likely to be the
subject of that favourite chant 'There's only one ...' – was booked
for knocking the ball away to delay a free-kick. Within a minute he
was off. Beardsley showed too much speed for FPM and hared in
on goal, to which FPM responded by committing a professional foul
and dragging him back. Referee Tom Bune immediately flashed a
red card. The official was predictably harangued but everyone knew
that he had little option.

United thought their luck had changed. How wrong they were.
Saxton reshuffled his remaining ten players, but kept both Bason
and Murphy in wide positions. FPM's dismissal served only to
inspire the men in green. On the stroke of half-time, Murphy, a
teasing figure on the left, 'nutmegged' a defender and sent a low
cross into the area. Kemp swept a first-time shot into the net, his
100th league and cup goal. The crowd were still on their feet as the
half-time whistle went.

Five minutes into the second half, the same combination doubled
the punishment. Kemp's downward header from the winger's cross
had Swinburne sprawling along his goal-line in a desperate attempt
to claw the ball back. Mr Bune looked to his linesman, who hesitat-
ingly signalled the ball had crossed the line. Kemp was overjoyed at
bagging only the second hat-trick of his career. With the ball stuffed
up his shirt he performed a previously unseen version of the Irish
jig all the way back to the halfway line.

Murphy finished the rout with a header. Sadly only 4,854 were
there to see the win, not that it mattered to Kemp, who proudly left
the ground clutching the match ball.

Carlisle manager Martin Harvey paid for the defeat with his job.

DIVISION 3   **1981-82**
Division 3   10th
League Cup   2nd round
FA Cup   1st round

There was an unexpected turn of events during the summer of 1981. With Howard Kendall taking charge at Everton, Bobby Saxton was the man selected to fill the vacant managerial chair at Blackburn. Few could blame Saxton for jumping at the chance to move up another rung on the managerial ladder, but the choice surprised many given his lack of success at Home Park.

The directors took a month to mull over the potential candidates. Ian Greaves, who had spent a brief time at Home Park under Tony Waiters, seemed a likely successor, but they eventually plumped for Bobby Moncur. Having captained Newcastle to a Fairs Cup triumph in 1969 and earned sixteen Scottish caps, his playing pedigree was not in doubt. More importantly, as a manager he had in 1980 taken Hearts into the Scottish Premier League, although his subsequent achievements as Carlisle boss were less impressive. Nonetheless, the consensus over his selection was favourable. Saxton had been followed to Ewood Park by Jim Furnell, prompting a reshuffle at Home Park. Jack Edwards remained, but he was chosen to lead the reserves, whilst Moncur brought in Martin Harvey, an ex-Northern Ireland international, recently sacked by Carlisle, as his assistant.

On the playing side, the nucleus of the previous season's squad remained intact. It was hoped that more promising youngsters would break through in the manner of Kevin Hodges and John Uzzell. George Foster seemed a likely departure until proposed moves to Brighton or Middlesbrough fell through.

The first competitive games gave ample proof that pre-season friendlies are of little value in predicting league form. Argyle started their warm-ups confidently, narrowly losing 0-1 to a Southampton side containing Kevin Keegan, Alan Ball and Mick Channon. A few days later, another First Division side, Everton, struggled to a 1-1 draw in a match held up midway through the second half by flood-light failure. Immediately following the Southampton match, nego-tiations began with the aim of signing their full-back Mike McCartney, who had once been under Moncur's wing at Carlisle. The deal was agreed, with Argyle paying the Saints £50,000. But with the finances at Home Park becoming more parlous by the week, he would be the club's only pre-season signing.

A short-lived Football League Group Cup was introduced this season, with Argyle pitched into the same group as Bournemouth, Torquay and Newport. Two draws and a defeat clinched the wooden spoon and gave the first indications that tough times lay ahead.

The Football League had bitten the bullet and introduced three points for a win, in the hope of encouraging more attacking football. Clearly the Pilgrims had failed to grasp the concept, for they slumped to defeat against Oxford in front of the lowest ever opening day crowd at Home Park. 'The worst we've played,' was Bobby Moncur's verdict, a damning one considering the Group Cup performances.

The first round League Cup-tie at Chester came to a premature end when home keeper Grenville Millington collided with a goalpost, which snapped near the base. Desperate repairs failed to make one post out of two, whereupon the referee abandoned the game with twelve minutes remaining.

The depths of Argyle's financial plight came to light when the club published its annual accounts. The year to 31 May showed an operating loss of £129,273, blamed largely on the attendance levels which had fallen well short of the directors' break-even figure of 7,500. The continuing importance of the highly successful Argyle lottery was highlighted by the fact that the scheme had contributed more to income than gate receipts. Expenses were also appreciably higher, due partly to an increase in players' bonuses following what in Argyle terms had been a reasonable successful season.

These revelations prompted a stormy shareholders meeting in late September. Rather than the usual 'all in favour, let's go to the bar,' affair, the directors faced hostile questioning on a number of issues. The main complaint was the 25 percent hike in admission charges, which they had invoked at the start of the season in an attempt to increase revenue. The majority of those present felt that, given the dismal level of attendances, the scheme had backfired. A father and son would have to pay £3.30 to watch Argyle, and it seemed many fathers had voted with their feet and stayed at home.

Back on the field, the players were doing their best to help the financial situation by ensuring that win bonuses were a thing of the past. A second home defeat saw the attendance fall below the 4,000 mark for the first time since World War II.

That figure dropped to 2,300 when Argyle posted their first win of the season, as the protracted League Cup-tie with Chester was finally settled, but the club was clearly on the brink. Following a five-hour board meeting, the directors sanctioned urgent steps to rectify the situation, as well as ironically concluding a four-year contract with Moncur. The manager, away scouting, missed Argyle's first league point of the season, as a draw at Brentford took on triumphant proportions.

DID YOU KNOW?

Prior to a match in January 1976, Dave Sutton was knocked over in the Home Park car park by Paul Mariner's car. Sutton still played in the match.

That goalless draw provided only the briefest respite. New boy McCartney was injured and Kemp had forgotten where the net was. In front of more sparsely populated terraces, Nisbet's own-goal triggered a third successive home league defeat, this time against ten-man Chesterfield. Yet another sub-3,000 crowd witnessed Argyle's first home point, and goal, of the season as leaders Reading were held to a draw. Andy Rogers, a loan signing from Southampton, made his debut.

A trip to First Division Middlesbrough in the next round of the League Cup was the last thing Argyle needed, but they performed creditably to go into the home leg trailing only 1-2. Any hopes that this would trigger some league improvement were dashed by another home defeat, this time by Gillingham, with Foster sent off for good measure. The 1-2 defeat prompted respected local journalist Harley Lawer to pen an article entitled 'The Argyle crisis', in which he commented that the team's performances were among the worst he could ever recall.

The defeat by the Gills proved to be Kemp's last game for the club. Sadly out of touch, his commitment to the cause was questioned in some quarters. He was eventually loaned out to Gillingham and Brentford before joining the exodus to the United States.

There was no happy return for Moncur and Harvey to Carlisle, where a Gordon Staniforth hat-trick piled on the agony. Foster – for a second successive match – and McCartney were both sent off.

The demise of Kemp was lightened by the return of Jeff Cook, this time on a permanent basis for a fee of £25,000. A lot would depend on how he reacted to the weight of expectation now strung around his shoulders.

The misery on the pitch continued. An injury-time defeat at next-to-bottom Wimbledon left Argyle six points adrift, still winless. Two draws and six goals were all Argyle had to show from eleven league games, which must have left Moncur perusing his contract to double check that it was measured in 'years' not 'months'.

Another old favourite was set to end his time at Home Park. Foster paid dearly for his suspension. Unable to regain his place, he was loaned to Exeter before pursuing his career elsewhere.

A win would surely come sooner or later. It did, against the familiar foes of Chester, although no one quite expected it to be so emphatic. Cook's two goals confirmed his standing as the club's latest saviour. A scoreless draw against Middlesbrough was not enough to stay alive in the League Cup, but at least the perform-ance helped confidence.

Confidence was something decidedly absent in the boardroom. Argyle's financial dilemma was placing a strain on working relation-ships. Andy Rogers had shown up well whilst on loan. A fee of £50,000 was agreed with Southampton to make the transfer perma-nent but the more cautious directors baulked at the idea of paying out such a sum. Claim and counter claim followed over the financial commitment of some of the directors. Within days, a number of wealthy local businessmen were knocking at chairman Robert Daniel's door. He was happy to take them on board, so to speak, and eventually a deal was done whereby a substantial cash injection gave the club some short-term financial stability. Daniel remained chairman but the rest of the original board resigned. In a statement, Daniel revealed that he had paid twice the nominal value of the ex-directors' shares to enable the new directors to take their place. He confirmed that had the deal not been concluded 'there would have been no Plymouth Argyle'. To add to the fans' relief, admission prices were also cut.

How much these behind the scenes wranglings distracted the players is open to conjecture, but their happy conclusion coincided with a dramatic turnaround in results. Three successive wins lifted Argyle off the bottom, and from there they never looked back. Moncur was able to select a largely settled side week in, week out, although John Uzzell's consistency meant no place for McCartney. Cook lived up to expectations and Sims readily took on the mantle of goalscorer.

FA Cup progress was halted at the first hurdle by Gillingham, which meant a barren spell of fixtures before Christmas. Tottenham were tempted to Devon for a friendly, but even then only 6,000 turned out to see them, even though Argentinian stars Ossie Ardiles and Ricky Villa were in the Spurs side.

Fortunately, all the drama had been confined to the first months of the season. Moncur knuckled down to the job in hand and the players responded. In the end, finishing tenth was a minor miracle.

Match of the Season 1981-82
Argyle 5   Chester 1

Division 3, 24 October 1981

A paltry 2,646 were scattered around the vastness of Home Park awaiting the arrival of the two teams. These were the true fans, who would turn out through thick and thin. Unfortunately, thick was but a distant memory. Of course, they had seen it before this season, with crowds hovering around the 3,000 mark. Jokes about lack of deodorant and arriving early to get a place had worn thin. Even these (fool)hardy souls must have considered the weekly shopping trip as a real alternative.

Argyle were rooted to the foot of the table after their worst ever start to a season. Chester were hardly going great guns themselves, but they were already nine points ahead of the Pilgrims. The only encouraging sign was that they were also the one team Argyle had beaten so far, thanks to a penalty in a League Cup-tie.

Desperate times call for desperate measures. In the hope of motivating the players to greater efforts, the manager of Plymouth Gin promised a bottle of his finest for every player if Argyle scored more than three. Pigs and aviation sprung to mind.

Despite their dreadful league start, Moncur had kept faith with his players. He made only one change to his line-up, an enforced one, with Foster suspended after his recent 'double' sending off. Chris Harrison came in to replace him and goalkeeper Crudgington was appointed captain for the day.

Fate again seemed set to conspire against Argyle. Grenville Millington pulled off a wonder save from Hodges, and Rogers had an effort disallowed for offside. The match then turned. Chester were forced to reorganise after Gary Simpson was stretchered off with ligament damage. Within a minute Jeff Cook put Argyle ahead. Bryn Jones immediately responded with a shot that flew in off a post, but Randell restored Argyle's advantage before the interval. Such a lead was heralded a triumph, and the loyal few gave their heroes a standing ovation as they trudged off for their half-time pep talk.

Upon the resumption, a third goal from Sims was just the tonic Argyle needed to go with their gin. Chester were now theirs for the taking. Cook, who had warned beforehand 'don't expect miracles' slid through the mud for a fourth. Randell completed the rout with the final kick. It was all too much for Chester's John Cottam, who was booked as he trooped off the pitch after the final whistle.

The result proved to be a catalyst for both sides. With a league win finally under their belts, Argyle went from strength to strength. Chester, however, fell apart. They earned just five more wins that season and were knocked out of the FA Cup by non-league Penrith. Gaining just two points from their final seventeen matches sealed relegation early. Little wonder manager Cliff Sear lost his job.

LEAGUE DIVISION 3	1982-83
Division 3	8th
Milk Cup	1st round
FA Cup	3rd round

The transformation during the previous season at least proved that Moncur was not a quitter. Although he had not won over all the fans, he had silenced his critics and was ready for the challenge of a new campaign.

The pre-season build up included a friendly against Everton to raise money for the South Atlantic Dependents' Fund, following the Falklands conflict. The pre-match entertainment included a free-fall parachute drop by four Royal Marines. One of the quartet unfortunately missed Home Park altogether. Those present hoped it was not a prophetic message for the Argyle forwards.

Apart from the arrival of Ray Gooding from Coventry and Mike Carter from Bolton, there was little other transfer paperwork in secretary Graham Little's in-tray. The new board had kept a tight hold on the purse strings. Despite the injection of funds, the club would continue to lose money while attendances were so low.

From a fan's point of view, a retrograde step was taken in the fashion stakes. The hated all-white kit was back, but if it made it easier to pass to a team-mate – something unheard of at the start of the previous season – then so be it.

Other significant changes occurred within the structure of the club. On cost grounds, the reserve team was withdrawn from the Combination League, a decision that would have grave long-term implications. The reserves would instead compete in the Western League. This had the benefit of more local matches, at the expense of lower-grade football. The step up to league soccer from this level was huge, perhaps unbridgable. Later requests to be readmitted into the Combination set-up fell on deaf ears. The additional decision to pull Argyle's third team from the South Western League was perplexing, for it meant that the cream of the area's youngsters now found themselves pitted against an assortment of overweight has been's and never were's in Division Five of the Plymouth and District League. A win by 20 (twenty!) goals to nil in the opening fixture suggested they were playing slightly below the level their abilities deserved.

Everyone breathed a sigh of relief when Argyle won their opening league match. Southend were hardly a team to set the world alight, but over the years had proved to be something of a bogey side for the Pilgrims. A 2-0 first-leg League Cup win over Bournemouth followed, before the early-season jitters set in again.

DID YOU KNOW?

A dreary 0-0 draw against Bristol City at Home Park in January 1976 was brought to life by the away fans chanting 'We built the Concorde'.

Some of the Football League's new directives – introduced to get the game to clean up its act – soon came to the fore. Chris Harrison was shown the red card for a 'professional foul' on Reading's Kerry Dixon, and in the following game Newport keeper Mark Kendall was penalised for breaching the new rule on quick release of ball. Kevin Hodges scored from the resultant free-kick.

Although clear favourites to progress in the League Cup, Argyle threw away their two-goal advantage at Bournemouth and conceded a third, killer, goal in extra-time.

After six league games, Argyle were handily placed in seventh. Four games later they were twentieth. No goals and no points in four games gave Moncur a sense of *déjà vu*. Doubts were again raised as to his long-term future. The defence in particular was all over the place. Various permutations had been tried in the middle of the back four. Now, in came Lindsay Smith, a loan signing from Cambridge. His arrival signalled the end of Phillipson-Masters' Home Park career. By November he had moved to Bristol City.

Smith's arrival and the conversion of McCartney into a mid-fielder lent the side greater stability. Argyle embarked on a nine-match unbeaten run which propelled them back up the table again. The sequence delighted statisticians, for Argyle scored two goals – no more, no less – in each of those nine games. The improved form also carried over into the FA Cup, with wins over Exeter and Bristol Rovers being rewarded with a trip to Watford, who were challenging for the English championship. It was the sort of money-spinning tie Argyle's accountants had hoped for.

October saw more changes in the boardroom. Chairman Robert Daniel, who had not been in the best of health, announced that he would terminate his twenty-year association with Argyle in the summer, when he would quit as a director and sever his financial links with the club. This would allow the remaining directors time to bring in other businessmen to take over Daniel's shares and bank guarantee.

Argyle were grateful for Hodges' and McCartney's goals from midfield, and Sims was leading the attack with aplomb. The main concern was the lack of a regular scorer to complement him. New-boy Carter had not looked the part and was eventually released after less than a season at the club. Cook had been unable to sustain the standards he had set on his arrival. Smith had been a pillar of

strength in defence and a fee of £20,000 to make his move permanent looked a sound investment.

One of the busiest men around Home Park was groundsman
George Robertson, an Argyle stalwart. He had been a regular in the
first team for many years and had since served the club in various
capacities. The autumn of 1982 was proving particularly wet, and
Robertson and his staff did a sterling job in keeping the pitch
drained and playable.

The end of Argyle's unbeaten run after Christmas was particularly galling, for it came at the hands of local rivals Exeter, who
avenged their FA Cup defeat. But a win the following day over
fourth-placed Cardiff lifted Argyle back to seventh spot and seemingly handily placed for a promotion push. Three successive defeats
then sent them back to mid-table obscurity and prompted action
from Moncur to pep up his goal-shy attack.

To that end, in came all-action forward Kevin Bremner on a
month's loan from Colchester. Bremner scared the living daylights
out of defences and there was no doubting his commitment. His
debut against Orient ended with a booking and ripped shorts, but
several opponents – not least keeper Mervyn Day – were left nursing bumps and bruises. Bremner earned instant popularity with the
Home Park crowd, but many clubs saw him as ideally suited to
lower league football. One of them was Millwall, for whom he
signed after his loan period expired.

Moncur then seemingly stumbled across the answer to his attacking problems. The promising Dave Phillips, by now a Welsh Under-
21 international, had already been employed in midfield and at full-
back but the experiment of playing him up front in place of the
injured Cook showed that he also had an eye for goal. Phillips
possessed a ballistic shot and began finding the net regularly, relishing the opportunity of an extended run in the first team. His reputation spread far beyond the South West, and several clubs made a
note of him as one to watch for the future.

Argyle's topsy-turvy form continued. Four straight wins, for
example, were immediately followed by three successive defeats.
Aficionados of the Football Pools avoided Argyle's 'number' on the
coupon like the plague. Blowing hot and cold did little to attract
spectators back through the turnstiles. Gates continued to hover
around the 4,000 mark, far below the break-even figure which the
directors had budgeted for.

The team's attacking options were further enhanced by the
signing of Gordon Staniforth from Carlisle. Staniforth was known to
Moncur and Argyle fans alike as a forward who relished facing the
Pilgrims. He had an impressive scoring record for the Cumbrians

and if he could maintain it as a Pilgrim, then Argyle might still have a say in the promotion race.

Unfortunately, Staniforth took time to settle and the lack of goals in the end proved costly. The promotion push never materialised and the side failed to rise above eighth place. The curtain came down in regrettable circumstances. Portsmouth brought their legion of fans to Home Park to celebrate their championship success but the game was frequently interrupted by crowd invasions and violence. At one point the referee threatened to take the players off the pitch but was persuaded to desist by both managers.

Match of the Season 1982-83

Watford 2   Argyle 0

FA Cup, 3rd round, 8 January 1983

This was a Cup-tie that Argyle fans had drooled over since the names were pulled out of the hat. They had endured a dismal time in recent years in the FA Cup, and it seemed an age since Argyle had had the chance to pit themselves against a top club. That time had now come. Under the stewardship of up and coming Graham Taylor and the high-profile chairmanship of Elton John, Watford were going places. At the moment they were second behind Liverpool in the old First Division.

Although many Argyle fans bemoaned the fact that the tie was away, their disappointment was tempered by the anticipated boost to the club's coffers. Many supporters were determined to make the trip. Tickets were put on sale at the home league match with Cardiff and long queues soon formed. The Argyle Travel Club booked a 700-seat 'special' train, which would pick up at various stations throughout the South West. The return fare was £9.75. By half-time against Cardiff over 300 seats had already been sold.

Moncur's thoughts focused on the need to curb the attacking threat posed by his opponents, in particular the England forward Luther Blissett, and the wingers, Nigel Callaghan and John Barnes. Watford relied heavily on the long-ball game to exploit the trio's pace. Argyle experimented with various tactics in training but the players persuaded their manager to stick to their normal game.

The teams entered Vicarage Road to a maelstrom of noise from the 17,630 crowd. Argyle seemed undaunted and started confidently. Close marking and no-nonsense defending curbed Watford's forward momentum. Occasional counter-attacks were frustrated by poor passing but as half-time approached it seemed the teams would go in level.

But five minutes before the break Uzzell's mistimed tackle on Barnes earned the Argyle full-back a booking. From the resultant free-kick, Wilf Rostron found himself confronted with an open goal. He couldn't miss and Crudgington's half-hearted appeal for offside convinced nobody.

There was still time for Cook – who had become a proud father on the eve of the match – to equalise, but he shot meekly at Steve Sherwood.

On an ever-worsening surface, Argyle began the second period in a positive mood. Rogers shot against Sherwood's legs, Hodges blasted just wide, and Smith failed to connect with a header as Sherwood flapped at thin air. Oh, for a Binney or a Kemp.

With Argyle pushing forward in ever increasing numbers, it was perhaps inevitable that Watford would exploit the extra space. Callaghan broke clear on the left and crossed for Blissett to add to his already considerable goal-tally for the season. To their credit, Argyle kept Sherwood busy until the end, but to no avail. The generous applause afforded them by the home supporters was no less than they deserved.

Watford's Cup run ended in the fifth round but they maintained their second place in the league, albeit some distance behind champions Liverpool. No one, however, could have predicted the circumstances in which Argyle and Watford would meet again, fifteen months later.

Anxious faces at Home Park watch Paul Mariner challenge a Carlisle defender

Bobby Moore leads out Fulham at Home Park, December 1975

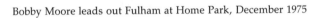

Physio Tommy Eggleston, Micky Horswill, coach Alan Brown, and Gary Megson

Brian Johnson celebrates scoring another goal at Home Park

Chairman Robert Daniel puffs on his cigar with manager Tony Waiters on his right

Colin Randell is challenged by Fulham's George Best, November 1976

A mud-splattered John Craven celebrates his goal against Oldham, January 1977

Bruce Bannister is dispossessed v Hereford, watched by Steve Davey, April 1977

## Chapter Three

Tommy Rolls into Town
1983-86

LEAGUE DIVISION 3	**1983-84**
Canon Division 3	19th
Milk Cup	2nd round
FA Cup	Semi-finals

After two successive top-ten finishes, many believed that Moncur had now unearthed the final piece of the jigsaw needed for a successful assault on promotion. In came Tommy Tynan, a £55,000 buy from cash-starved Newport. Tynan was one of the most prolific scorers in the lower leagues, as his tally of 33 the previous season illustrated. He had formed a lethal partnership with John Aldridge which had helped County to the quarter-finals of the European Cup-Winners' Cup. Such was Tynan's reputation that Moncur did not initially pursue the player, believing he would be out of Argyle's price range.

Moncur pinned his faith on the Tynan-Staniforth partnership to come up with the goods, and allowed the popular John Sims to move to Torquay. Jeff Cook, whose form had faltered, was also allowed to go, transferring to Halifax. A number of the club's youngsters had also been released, leaving the reserve side severely weakened.

The era of football sponsorship had well and truly arrived. Both the League and League Cup had new sponsors, offering considerable prize money for successful teams. Argyle's new silky green shirts were emblazoned with the name of local company Beacon Electrical. Little did the owners realise how much exposure their name would get in the coming months.

At boardroom level, Stuart Dawe had taken over as chairman, although Robert Daniel had been persuaded to remain as a director. It soon became clear that Moncur did not enjoy such a fruitful relationship with the new chairman. The idea of signing Tynan, in fact, originated with the directors. Moncur had set his mind on bringing Billy Rafferty back to Home Park, but the board were not willing to sanction his purchase. It proved to be the start of Moncur's downfall.

Tynan's initial form was unimpressive, mirroring the rest of the team. Yet again, Argyle seemed determined to give everyone else an early advantage. A mere two points from the first five games left them languishing in the bottom three. The only consolation was licking Swindon in the Milk Cup.

Argyle's new green strip caused some confusion. Swindon's keeper, Jimmy Allan caused the first-leg kick-off to be delayed by six minutes when he too donned his usual green jersey. Efforts to find an alternative failed and Allan was forced to play the match in an off-grey tracksuit top.

The elusive first league win came against Preston, courtesy of Andy Rogers, who had become a father for the first time the day before the game. Tynan missed a hatful and was awarded just one star for his performance by the local Sunday newspaper. It was not what Argyle fans had hoped for.

More signs of discord between the manager and board surfaced. The directors were keen to renew the Tynan-Aldridge partnership. Moncur, for some reason, was not. In view of the sheer scale of Aldridge's later triumphs, this was a grave mistake. Rumours were rife that Moncur's days were numbered, particularly as the board convened a number of times after the manager went public by stating that he had no intention of bidding for Aldridge.

A 4-0 midweek win over Scunthorpe gave notice that the side was beginning to gel but post-match events overshadowed all else. At 10.30pm, Chairman Dawe issued a statement confirming that Moncur and the club had parted company because of 'differences of opinion regarding club policy'. Compensation had been agreed and Martin Harvey was given temporary charge of team affairs.

The announcement coincided with the publication of Argyle's latest financial accounts. The club announced a loss of £34,378, a considerable improvement on the previous year when, under the old board, a crippling loss of £353,145 had everyone fearing the worst. The cynics suggested that Moncur would have gone earlier had the club been able to afford it.

Harvey seemed a likely candidate for the job, particularly after guiding the Pilgrims to a splendid home draw with mighty Arsenal in the second round of the Milk Cup. Gordon Nisbet scored a memorable goal past Pat Jennings. Instead the board plumped for a familiar face to take charge. John Hore, a loyal servant as a player, had guided non-league Bideford to two Western League titles. Many were surprised at his appointment, believing a more experienced man would be preferred. Hore, strangely, was not given any form of contract and was required to prove he was up to the job.

He made a promising start. Argyle won two and drew one of his first three games, before losing 0-1 at Highbury in the return leg of the Milk Cup.

DID YOU KNOW?

From his hotel room in Plymouth in April 1977 referee Alan Robinson spotted a French sailor vandalising his car and gave chase in his pyjamas.

Hore wasted no time before splashing out £7,000 on Tony Kellow, a player whose goalscoring record put even Tynan's to shame. Age was not on Kellow's side but, on paper at least, a Tynan-Kellow partnership could prove to be a lethal one.

Another arrival was Dave Lean, a friend of Hore's and an Argyle player in Billy Bingham's era. Lean, a successful manager at South Western League level, would run the reserve side.

Thoughts also turned to the late, lamented Devonport End roof. £30,000 was the quote to rebuild it. Two thirds of the funds would be available via the Football League Ground Improvement Trust. The rest would have to be found from public donations. No one was holding their breath.

League form soon settled down to its usual indifferent self. There seemed little to become excited about over the FA Cup either. A dour draw at Southend was a reasonable result considering Argyle's miserable record at Roots Hall. The replay was won in extra-time and a home draw with Barking seemed likely to ensure passage to the third round.

But the dream attacking partnership of Kellow and Tynan had failed to click, goals were in short supply, and full-back Nisbet was threatening to be top dog in the scoring charts. It took a late winner to overcome the part-timers of Barking, but hopes of a glamour tie in round three were dashed when Newport came out of the hat. Tynan may have relished the prospect, but no one else did. In fact, there were doubts as to whether the ex-County man would face his old side. The two teams met on league business over Christmas, but Tynan found himself dropped and demanded a transfer. One can only surmise the directors' feelings as they watched Aldridge sink Argyle with two goals to take his season's tally to nineteen.

In fact, Tynan was restored by the time the cup-tie came around, and scored from the spot in injury-time to earn a replay at Somerton Park. There, although few gave Argyle a chance, a late Andy Rogers goal put Argyle into round four. Surely this time they would catch a big fish. Out came ... Darlington! At least the tie was at home, which meant that the fifth round was within reach. Only once before, in 1953, had an Argyle side progressed that far.

Tynan's season, meanwhile, was going from bad to worse. After just three minutes of a match against another of his former clubs, Lincoln, he found himself sent off.

Hore urged his players not to get preoccupied with the Cup. Argyle had shown little improvement in the league and still hovered in the lower third of the table. The Cup-tie duly arrived but, despite languishing near the bottom of Division Four, Darlington also had pound signs flashing before their eyes, and raised their game accordingly. They took the lead and it needed a late Staniforth goal to finally overcome their plucky efforts.

Next came an away tie, against West Brom, a top division side. Tynan had come off the transfer list and had begun to find the net, and it was he who struck the only goal. The Baggies fans jeered their team and Argyle's dream continued.

Torquay were despatched 5-1 in the new Associate Members Cup, whereupon the club announced ticketing arrangements for the FA Cup quarter-final at home to second division strugglers Derby. Grandstand seat prices were increased from the normal £3.50 to £6, and fans would need to attend the next home game against Hull to obtain a voucher guaranteeing them a ticket. Needless to say, the Hull match brought all sorts of long-lost 'fans' out of the woodwork. The official attendance was 10,023 but there was evidence of some fans entering the ground twice or three times to obtain extra vouchers.

Whilst cup fever was spreading across the West Country, Hore was left scratching his head over Argyle's worrying league form. Although the team were eight points clear of the drop zone, he was only too aware of the distractions caused by the cup run, and that a losing sequence in the league could spell disaster.

Come the big day, over 34,000 jostled their way through the overworked Home Park turnstiles. Argyle outplayed a Derby side containing several internationals. Crudgington was a virtual spectator but luck deserted Argyle when Staniforth struck the woodwork with a shot that ricocheted along the goal-line before hitting the other upright. The Rams hung on grimly for a draw, which tipped the scales hugely in Derby's favour.

The replay mirrored the first game, but this time the luck was with Argyle, as Rogers' fluke goal propelled them into the semi-finals to face Watford.

Away from the spotlight, in the bread-and-butter league, Argyle were a shadow of their cup selves. In fact, their league position was becoming a huge worry. Confronted by a small squad and a backlog of fixtures, Hore was forced to draft in Neville Chamberlain on loan from Stoke, and Bradley Swiggs and Mark Smith from local clubs. A flu epidemic at the club was hardly opportune either.

Argyle were also marching onwards in the Associate Members Cup but a win over Brentford only added to the fixture congestion.

Preparations for the semi-final were less than ideal, with a mid-week fixture against Wimbledon having been re-arranged after a previous postponement. That brought another defeat, but at least everyone escaped without injury. The build-up then started in earnest. The national media descended on Home Park. Hore found himself with a microphone under his nose and a camera in his face wherever he went, but handled it all with calm assurance.

All points west of Taunton became ghost towns as hordes converged on Villa Park for the biggest match in Argyle history. To this day, those present can relive the agony of George Reilly's header that proved to be the match-winner, and the moment when Kevin Hodges' goal-bound shot was diverted wide by a divot. Argyle had won many friends but Watford had the ultimate prize.

The players had just 48 hours to drown their sorrows before the business of league survival resumed. Following an inept 1-2 defeat at Bolton, Hore barricaded his players in the dressing room for 50 minutes. Whatever he said failed to register. One point from the next four matches saw the team slip to twentieth. Other strugglers, bar the already doomed Exeter, were picking up points. A drastic upturn in form was required, and achieved. Ten points from the last four games saw Argyle finish five points above the trap-door.

The season had not yet run its course. Exeter were dumped from the Associate Members Cup before Millwall triumphed in the southern section semi-final. Argyle's small squad had played 64 competitive matches during the season. A three-day break in Jersey, courtesy of the club, was richly deserved.

Match of the Season 1983-84

Derby 0   Argyle 1

FA Cup, quarter-final replay, 14 March 1984

Not for the first time, Argyle were firm underdogs going into the match. Derby were not exactly setting the Second Division alight, but surely they could not play as badly as in the first match the previous Saturday, particularly in front of their own fans.

Argyle's followers had only four days to plan their exodus to the Baseball Ground. Phantom sick-notes and mythical family bereavements abounded as 5,000 fans made the trip.

The team's preparations included a training session at a Derby school on the afternoon of the tie. The session ended with winger Andy Rogers attempting to take a few accurate corner-kicks. Taking corners was a regular activity for him, though you would not have thought so. After three scuffed attempts, Hore called it a day.

Argyle were unchanged from the previous match. Hore's selection was not difficult, given the small squad he had inherited. Leigh Cooper, at 21, one of the club's youngest captain's – 'because no one else wanted to do it' – led out the side. Derby included three Scottish internationals – Archie Gemmill, Kenny Burns and John Robertson. It was Robertson who Argyle most feared, for he was living proof that appearances can be deceptive. Round-shouldered, podgy, he had an almost unique knack for making any football kit look scruffy. Yet he could win a game with one burst along the touchline.

Derby started brightly but in the eighteenth minute Rams' fullback John Barton slashed wildly at a clearance and presented Argyle with their first corner. Rogers, trying to put his afternoon's school experience out of his mind, strode over to take the flag-kick. His right-foot corner took the term 'inswinger' to new levels. The ball eluded both keeper Steve Cherry and the hapless Barton on the near post, and ended up nestling among a year's supply of toilet rolls in the far corner.

Any thoughts of sitting back on this surprise lead were put on the back burner. Argyle continued to press and Smith twice hit the woodwork. Derby became desperate. Robertson alternated between left and right flanks but had little joy with either Nisbet or Uzzell. Hodges shackled Gemmill in midfield and Cooper was everywhere. Rams boss Peter Taylor brought off top scorer Bobby Davison and replaced him with England veteran Dave Watson, a centre-half, a substitution that provoked jeers from home fans.

The final whistle uncorked ecstatic scenes from the Argyle contingent packed at one end. Taylor stormed out of the ground without speaking to his players or the press, who were too busy seeking out Rogers anyway. 'A pure fluke,' was the winger's succinct summary. No one cared.

Derby, by the way, ended up relegated.

LEAGUE DIVISION 3   **1984-85**
Canon Division 3   15th
Milk Cup   2nd round
FA Cup   2nd round

The most reliable method of predicting Argyle's finishing position this season was with a pin and a blindfold. There was still a buzz around the club after the FA Cup exploits of the previous season, but the form shown against the likes of West Brom and Derby now needed to be repeated against the Doncaster's and Wigan's of this world.

Another factor was the loss of two of the mainstays of the side. The Cup-run had not persuaded Lindsay Smith to stay, and he had moved to Millwall. Less of a surprise was the departure of Dave Phillips. Having graduated to the full Welsh squad there was little doubt that he would progress to greater things. Both deals had been administered by the newly introduced Transfer Tribunal. In both cases they had done Argyle few favours. Smith's fee was finalised at £17,500, whilst Phillips was initially valued at an insulting £65,000, with more to come, depending on appearances. To add insult to injury, Manchester City were only obliged to pay half the fee up front. Argyle had valued him at £200,000.

Hore bolstered the defence with the signings of Adrian Burrows, who had hovered around the lower league scene for a number of years, and Clive Goodyear from Luton. Phillips' midfield replacement was Russell Coughlin, yet another signing from Carlisle.

Another welcome newcomer to Home Park was the Devonport End roof. Work had proceeded throughout the summer to ensure the new structure was in place in time for the opening game. Kit-wise, there was little change, although the shirts were now adorned by new sponsors – Ivor Jones Insurance. Jones was a keen Argyle fan who in future years would find a place on the board.

A draw in a potentially difficult opening fixture at Burnley was followed by a narrow home win over Torquay in a first leg, Milk Cup-tie. Compared to recent seasons, this constituted a decent start, and with the new signings settling in quickly there seemed some cause for optimism. The nature of a home defeat by Reading put paid to that, and left Hore admitting the side needed further strengthening. Torquay were beaten again, at Plainmoor, but Hore missed the league draw at Lincoln, scouting on other players.

Hore's quest for new blood took him to a Friday night match at Doncaster, where his target was Rovers' striker Alan Brown. A deal looked likely, but Brown broke a leg in front of Hore's eyes, which meant the player was going nowhere.

DID YOU KNOW?

Brian Johnson once blasted a penalty so high over the Barn Park end that the ball was later recovered from the hippopotamus pen in the adjoining zoo.

Four points from the opening five matches had again left the side trying to play catch-up. A bizarre match at Bolton then started a remarkable sequence which left fans wondering whether to take along a pocket calculator as well as the obligatory flask and scarf as part of their match-day equipment.

The normally reliable Crudgington started the rot at Burnden Park by inexplicably fly-hacking at a shot on goal, kicking air, and leaving the ball to roll unhindered across the line. Further errors by Hodges and Burrows were also punished. With Burrows erring yet again and Nisbet handling on the line, Argyle found themselves 1-5 down when Crudgington took a blow to the hand. Nisbet took over between the posts but conceded two more. The final score, 2-7, constituted Argyle's biggest defeat since November 1972.

With reserve keeper Dave Philp deputising for the injured Crudgington, a 1-4 defeat at Birmingham in the Milk Cup left Hore under pressure. A first league win – 6-4 against nine-man Preston – did little to hide the concerns over the avalanche of goals conceded. A 3-3 draw at Gillingham followed. Argyle's last four matches had yielded 30 goals (eighteen of them into their own net). Such excitement suddenly attracted an additional 1,500 spectators for a home match with Hull. Perhaps inevitably, the match saw just one goal, with new on-loan keeper Les Sealey unable to prevent the visitors scoring.

Defeat by Birmingham in the home leg at least netted the club £2,500 in 'Milk money'. But it was the league trip to Derby, scene of one of Hore's greatest triumphs, that ironically sealed his downfall. A 1-3 defeat saw Argyle plunge to next to bottom. It was all too much for the directors who decided immediately on a change at the helm, motivated by the hope of making an early – rather than late – escape from yet another relegation battle. When the axe fell on Hore, reserve-team manager Dave Lean resigned.

Speculation over the identity of Hore's successor started immediately. Likely candidates included Don Megson, Gordon Lee and Ian Greaves, all vastly experienced. In the interim, Martin Harvey was again handed the caretaker role, but the team looked no less frail in defence. On the up side, Argyle embarked on another FA Cup run with a comfortable win over non-league Barnet.

Former Argyle favourite Johnny Newman divulged that he had been offered the managerial job but had decided to remain at Hereford. The directors interviewed five hopefuls, but plumped for Dave Smith, a canny Scot who had a fine record as a manager in the lower divisions.

Smith was initially happy to keep faith the playing staff he had inherited. His arrival certainly sparked a change in fortunes. Argyle notched up three straight league wins, although their cup dreams were shattered, ironically by Newman's Hereford. A 0-2 replay defeat denied Argyle a home tie against Arsenal, which would have undoubtedly produced a capacity crowd to see the return of former hero Paul Mariner.

Fortunately for the morale of Argyle's leaky defenders, Tommy Tynan was banging them in at the other end with ever increasing regularity. A Boxing Day hat-trick against Bristol City was spoilt only by one thing – the defence let in four!

Dave Smith's first signing was Kevin Summerfield, a free transfer from Cardiff, and the new boy debuted in a home win over Millwall. The press were exposed to the manager's quirky nature after the game. Waiting for his usual verbal summary of the match, the hacks were directed by Smith to a blackboard, where he had inscribed his comments. The new boss soon endeared himself to the fans. He dubbed himself the self-proclaimed 'Cider Man' and his programme notes were a cut above the bland 'we were unlucky, things will improve,' nonsense spouted by club managers up and down the country.

That defeat by Bristol City convinced Smith that his defence needed reinforcing. He signed Bolton's Northern Ireland international Gerry McElhinney for a fee of £32,000, but with the country in the midst of an icy grip, the newcomer had to wait for three weeks to make his Pilgrims debut.

The Irishman finally made his debut in a Freight Rover Trophy victory over Bournemouth, although the Cherries progressed after an aggregate win. Smith continued to shuffle his side, partly due to injuries, but he was unable to mastermind a string of wins, and the threat of relegation hovered over the club, despite a gap opening up over the bottom four. McElhinney soon won the hearts of supporters. Even those at the rear of the grandstand winced at the ferocity of the tackles flying in from the former boxer and Gaelic footballer. Sadly, there was little support for Tynan in the goalscoring stakes. Staniforth remained popular with the fans but did not score enough for some people's liking.

Winger Tony Obi was drafted in on loan from Aston Villa to add numbers as the injury crisis began to mount, but he made little impression. Tynan carried on scoring at a prolific rate, and the first of his brace against Lincoln in mid-April was his 28th of the season

– thus breaking Maurice Tadman's Argyle post-war scoring record which had stood since 1952.

That win over Lincoln was the second of three successive victories which at least guaranteed safety for another season. The main interest now lay in whether Tynan could break the all-time Argyle League scoring record over a season, currently held by Jack Cock who had scored 32 in 1926-27. A penalty against relegated Cambridge took Tynan's league tally to 31, but frustratingly he failed to find the net in the final two games. Nevertheless, no one had done more to rescue Argyle's season almost single-handedly. Tynan was the obvious winner of the Player of the Year, but strangely polled only 60 percent of the votes. One wondered whether the remaining 40 percent had actually watched a match.

The final home fixture saw Dave Smith presented with a watch by League sponsors Canon to mark his 35 years of involvement in the game as player, coach and manager.

A finishing position of fifteenth hardly represented progress but there were signs towards the end of the season that Smith was beginning to forge a useful side. If Tynan could continue his rich scoring vein, anything was possible. There was, however, bad news on the horizon.

Match of the Season 1984-85

Argyle 6　Preston 4

Division 3, 29 September 1984

In recent years, the Argyle faithful had become used to long waits to celebrate their first league victory of the season. A 2-7 collapse at Bolton on 22 September, followed by a 1-4 loss at Birmingham in a midweek Milk Cup-tie, suggested that the wait this season could be longer than usual.

Preston had conceded six goals themselves in both their last two games. Their manager, Alan Kelly, did not have fond memories of Home Park. He had been the Preston goalkeeper when Argyle put seven past them in 1963.

Injuries forced Hore into making changes but he probably would have done so anyway. Geoff Crudgington's pride had been injured at Bolton, but so had his hand, and part-timer Dave Philp took over between the posts for his League debut. Striker Tommy English had come to Home Park on trial after failing to find a club, but had to be content with the No 12 shirt.

A close-range header by Tynan gave Argyle a deserved lead, but then it all started to go wrong again. Jonathan Clark fired in from 30 yards after a linesman had spotted an infringement by Goodyear. Six minutes later the Argyle defence waved John Kelly through to shoot past Philp and send the visitors in at half-time 2-1 up.

The first half had given little hint of what was to follow in the second. Four minutes after the restart Clark struck again and the writing was on the wall. Hore responded by handing English his debut, replacing Mark Rowe. 'Nothing against Rowe,' Hore said later, 'but we needed more bodies in the box.'

Within two minutes, Kevin Hodges had reduced the arrears. Ninety seconds later, Clark concluded his participation when referee Ron Groves took exception to some choice language and sent off the Preston midfielder. Argyle immediately took advantage and Coughlin scored from 25 yards. Three goals each, with Preston a man short.

A slight lull allowed everyone to catch their breath before the goals started flowing again. Willie Naughton found himself clean through but Philp took his legs. Kelly scored from the spot to make it 3-4. Two minutes later, English made his mark by dribbling into the box. Down he went, and Groves pointed to the spot yet again. Protests from Preston players obliged the referee to seek refuge amidst the photographers behind the goal, but that did not save Tommy Booth from being booked for dissent. Staniforth made no mistake with the penalty. 4-4.

Seven minutes still remained, plenty of time for more goals. Preston player-coach Booth found himself in trouble again, this time for blocking Nisbet's surge down the right wing. The visitors were now down to nine. From the resultant free-kick, Hodges netted to put Argyle's noses ahead for the first time. English rounded things off with a sixth goal just before the final whistle. This was enough to see him hailed as the new hero. Hundreds of fans swarmed onto the pitch to carry him off shoulder high.

The wave of emotion was short-lived. Within a fortnight Hore had been sacked. English disappeared from view. After four substitute appearances and one full game in the Milk Cup, he eventually moved on to Colchester, where better times awaited.

The result precipitated a disastrous run for Preston. Relegation to the soccer basement awaited after they gathered just ten points from their next twenty matches. They were thrashed 1-6 by Norwich in the Milk Cup and 1-4 by non-league Telford in the FA Cup. Booth eventually took over from the beleaguered Kelly, who vowed never again to set foot in Home Park.

LEAGUE DIVISION 3   **1985-86**
Canon Division 3   2nd (promoted)
Milk Cup   1st round
FA Cup   3rd round

The usual optimism that precedes any new season was in short supply around Home Park during the summer of 1985. Day after day, or so it must have seemed to Dave Smith, came a knock on his office door or a phone call from yet another player wanting to move away from Home Park. Andy Rogers and Leigh Cooper fancied a change of scenery, Gordon Staniforth dug his heels in over signing a new contract, and Chris Harrison was set to move on after a well-deserved testimonial. Even physio Jimmy Goodfellow had quit. Worst of all, despite his personal success the previous season, Tommy Tynan was hankering for a move back north.

Cooper, having looked likely to move to Orient in exchange for John Cornwell, was eventually persuaded to stay. The rest of the malcontents were not. Rogers went to Reading, Harrison to Swansea, and Tynan – despite receiving sackloads of pleading fan-letters every day – signed for Norman Hunter's Rotherham for a paltry £25,000. Staniforth also left, although at least Argyle received a player in exchange.

Smith soon set about replacing the 'lost boys'. Garry Nelson, a winger discovered by Smith at Southend, was signed as Rogers' direct replacement. John Matthews, an experienced ex-Arsenal man who knew his way around the lower leagues, joined from Chesterfield and, after much haggling, Steve Cooper, a player Smith had admired for some time, joined from Newport, with Staniforth and £15,000 going in the opposite direction.

Changes were also afoot behind the scenes. On the eve of the season, Chairman Stuart Dawe stepped down, though he remained on the board. Peter Bloom was the man to take over, pledging himself not to become involved in team affairs.

For the fans, there was at least the consolation of watching the cream of the country's players parading their skills in pre-season. The Heysel tragedy had produced a ban on English sides playing even friendlies in Europe. This meant that Tottenham, Aston Villa, Luton, Southampton and Chelsea all warmed up for the season sampling the delights of Devon and Cornwall.

Argyle started in customary fashion, with defeats at York and home to Reading, interspersed with a 2-1 win over Exeter in the Milk Cup. Further bad news took the form of Kevin Summerfield fracturing a cheekbone in a training accident: he would miss several weeks. A new striker was clearly a priority. Smith had made it clear from the outset that Cooper was not seen as a direct replacement for Tynan. Ironically, the manager missed the first victory of the season, a 2-0 win at Swansea. He was away watching the marksman he had targeted. Who better to replace Tynan than a man who had matched his 31 league goals last season, not to mention adding another five in cup matches – Tranmere forward John Clayton. The sanity of those sitting on the League's valuation panel was again called into question, but on this occasion they did Argyle a favour. Their figure of £24,000 was surely a steal for a player who had been voted as one of Rothmans players of the season.

By early September, Exeter had triumphed on aggregate in the Milk Cup and a league draw at Brentford saw Argyle slump to twentieth in the table. The situation might have been worse but for the benevolence of referees who had conspired to award Argyle no fewer than five penalties. McElhinney had converted three out of four to lay an early unlikely claim for a Golden Boot.

Clayton had settled in and was proving to be a skilful acquisition but his goal output was hardly Tynanesque. Nevertheless, behind the scenes, Smith and his trusty sidekick, Martin Harvey, were moulding the team and tactics. A 3-0 win over Gillingham on the first day of October signalled the start of a run that would see their plans come to fruition.

The defence had suddenly taken on a steely quality. Crudgington was, well, Crudgington, reliable as ever. Nisbet was happily raiding down the flank, as only Nisbet could, and McElhinney, having relinquished penalty duties, was reminding older supporters of the great 'Jumbo' Chisholm with his whole-hearted performances. Matthews, stroking the ball around and strolling through games with ease, was proving the perfect midfield foil to the hustle and bustle of Coughlin, and Hodges and Nelson were rolling back the years with some good old-fashioned wing play. Steve Cooper was raw, but no one could recall another player jumping so high, even if his headers were rarely on target.

Following that Gillingham win, it was not until shortly before Christmas that the next defeat was tasted, when a three-goal lead was overturned by runaway leaders Reading. The winning run had included FA Cup victories over Aldershot and an uncompromising Maidstone. A study of the league tables showed Argyle in second place, prompting several extra fans to dust off their street maps and delve deep into their wardrobes for a green scarf. It was hardly fanatical support, but crowds of six or seven thousand were at least healthier than they had been for a while.

The 'glamour' of the FA Cup third round saw Argyle handed a trip to Hull. The preparation was hardly ideal. The first day of 1986 saw a crazy 4-4 draw at home to Cardiff. Both sides gave the impression that they had over-indulged the night before, but the Pilgrims pulled back from 2-4 down, despite losing Crudgington with an injury, forcing Nisbet to don the No 1 jersey.

A respectable draw at Hull counted for nothing when the Second Division side scored an early winner in the replay. A minor crisis ensued, and a slump to eighth place suggested that promotion was again off the agenda. The Freight Rover Trophy failed, unsurprisingly, to ignite renewed passion in either the players or fans, as only one point was gained from group matches against Bristol City and Walsall.

Arctic conditions saw no fewer than five matches postponed as Argyle completed just two league fixtures in February. This hardly helped restore cohesion. Smith, having relied on the same squad for most of the season, felt fresh blood was needed to pep things up. Striker Kevin Godfrey arrived on a month's loan from Orient. By the time he departed, he had participated in one draw and six wins. His final match, an evening fixture at Cardiff, saw Argyle collect yet another three points. It was perhaps the moment Smith sensed that something special was happening. Upon the final whistle he tossed his flat cap to the travelling fans. The loss of such a close friend dawned on him after the euphoria had died down. An appeal through the press saw the cap eventually returned to its follicly challenged home.

Smith then pulled off a master-stroke. Tynan had fallen out with Rotherham manager Norman Hunter after a training ground bust-up with a team-mate. Smith was in like a shot, and a loan deal was agreed to bring Tynan back to Home Park for the final nine games of the season. It was the morale booster both the team and the fans needed to sustain the winning momentum. No one, however, could have forecast the impact Tynan would make. His return to Home Park enticed a crowd of 13,000. The opponents, as fate would have it, were Rotherham, and Tynan scored twice in a 4-0 win. Hunter fumed that Smith had broken a 'gentleman's agreement' not to play Tynan in the fixture. Smith denied all knowledge. Two more Tynan goals followed in the next match as Bury were despatched. It was Argyle's ninth win on the trot. The sequence ended with a draw at Lincoln. No prizes for guessing the Argyle scorer.

Five thousand fans travelled to Wigan full of expectation but an off day had Smith apologising for the team's performance against their promotion rivals.

Things soon got back on track. A 4-1 win over Bolton earned three precious points and also improved the goal difference. Blackpool gave Argyle a scare, taking the lead before succumbing 1-3. A win against Bristol City would clinch promotion. With the Home Park capacity officially set at 20,000, Argyle announced a full house. In truth there were at least another 5,000 crammed in to whatever nooks and crannies they could find. Tynan grabbed an early goal to dispel the nerves and a stunning team performance ensured that the club finally waved goodbye to Division Three. Smith's cap was jettisoned again, this time for good.

Even members of the valuation panel would have voted for Dave Smith as April manager of the month. Tynan scored again in the final match to take his tally to ten in nine matches. Whilst his stunning return played a major part in sealing promotion, it overshadowed other equally significant contributions. Four other players made it to double figures in the goal stakes, and the devastating flank partnership of Hodges and Nelson became feared throughout the division. Fortunately, sense prevailed when it came to voting for Player of the Year, with Hodges rightly chosen.

Whilst Smith spent the summer plotting his next campaign, the fans had just one thought, 'Tommy must stay.'

Match of the Season 1985-86
Reading 4   Argyle 3

Division 3, 21 December 1985

It was billed not only as the Third Division's match of the day, but of the season. Argyle were on a roll after a run of fourteen unbeaten matches had seen them surge up the table into second place. Promotion was their only priority, not the championship, and for very good reasons. Ian Branfoot had assembled a Reading side that had taken the division apart. By mid-October their league record read: played 13, won 13. It was the best start to a season ever made by any club in any division. With less than half the campaign completed, Reading were fifteen points clear of Argyle.

Over 8,500, the Royals' biggest crowd of the season to date, packed into the ageing Elm Park stadium. When the home team was announced, every name was cheered to the rafters. Some of Reading's players were familiar to Argyle supporters. Tricky winger Andy Rogers had been a big favourite at Home Park until his summer move. There was also Kevin Bremner. 'Mad Max,' as he had been dubbed during his brief loan spell as a Pilgrim, was playing in Reading's midfield rather than up front, doubtless to the relief of Argyle's central defenders, who were fully aware of his physical approach. Reading's danger-man was ace goalscorer Trevor Senior, who had scouts flocking to his every match.

DID YOU KNOW?

Tommy Tynan played 19 games for Dallas Tornado during the 1976 North American Soccer League, scoring twice and being credited with four 'assists'.

Argyle's players were undaunted by the prospect of visiting the champions elect. Within ten minutes, Kevin Hodges had shot them into the lead. Two more goals either side of half-time put the Pilgrims three up. The previous cauldron of noise was now confined to the end where the Green Army had assembled. Reading had the name of their sponsors, 'Courage', emblazoned on their shirts. Their fans were beginning to wonder if too many free beer samples had been imbibed by the players before the game.

A simple tactical change by Ian Branfoot transformed the match. Bremner was pushed forward into attack. Within minutes, he was obstructed by Clive Goodyear, leaving Dean Horrix to convert the penalty. Worse was to follow. With Bremner in full cry, he set up Senior not once, but twice within a minute, to even things up at three goals apiece. Argyle were now hanging on, but three minutes after drawing level Reading were in front when Bremner himself tapped in. Both sets of fans were shell-shocked, one at the capitulation and the other at the comeback. The name on the Reading shirts had suddenly taken on a new meaning.

With the final seconds ticking by, Rogers raised the temperature by playing keep-ball at a corner flag. Nisbet took out his frustration on his former team-mate, for which he was sent down the tunnel a few seconds before the rest of his colleagues.

The morale-sapping defeat stopped Argyle in their tracks, and it took them several matches to regain some form. For Reading, it was just another step on the way to the championship. They led the table from start to finish.

Home Park stages this European tie after hooligans closed Old Trafford

Exeter's Alan Beer (left) tries to restrain an irate John Delve

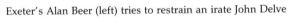

Manager Mike Kelly looks so bored he is reduced to practising origami

Chairman Robert Daniel looks more worried than manager Malcolm Allison

Allison celebrates after the 3-2 win over Port Vale confirms Argyle's survival

Bobby Moncur's Argyle squad for the 1982-83 season

Action v Derby in the FA Cup quarter-final. Note the absent Devonport End roof

Misery awaits Argyle, who lose 0-1 in their first ever FA Cup semi-final

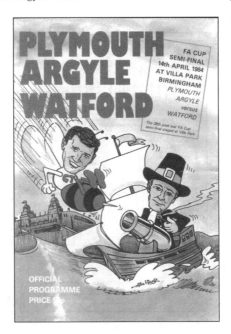

## Chapter Four

Middle of the Road 1986-1991

LEAGUE DIVISION 2	**1986-87**
Today Division 2	7th
Littlewoods Cup	1st round
FA Cup	4th round

After nine seasons among the also-rans of the Third Division, it was now a case of 'into the unknown'. If he felt any trepidation at the prospect of facing the likes of Leeds, Ipswich and Sunderland, Dave Smith kept it quiet. The lack of transfer activity underlined his faith in the players who had just done him proud. Two youngsters had been brought in, Harvey Lim, a goalkeeper on loan from Norwich, and Eddie McElhinney, younger brother of 'Rambo', who had arrived from Northern Ireland club Coleraine for £15,000.

The only newcomer of note was former Scottish international Stewart Houston, who arrived as trainer-coach in place of Martin Harvey, who had decided to move on.

Argyle fans were again treated to an entertaining pre-season, with the visits of Charlton and Chelsea. All except the Home Park team announcer also enjoyed the visit of Soviet side Torpedo Moscow, who provided some rich entertainment.

At least the club entered the new season with some financial stability. The latest accounts actually showed a profit of £107,000, although the lottery and commercial activities had again proved invaluable, as expenses exceeded gate receipts by £5,000 a week. The club also revealed new shirt sponsors in the form of the National and Provincial Building Society.

Of course, the possible return of Tommy Tynan had occupied minds over the summer, fuelled by the player's admission that he would be willing to come back. Tynan had returned to his club, Rotherham, where he seemed to be back in favour. His manager, Norman Hunter, had selected him for pre-season games and any hope of him again becoming a Pilgrim seemed pie in the sky.

So, the eleven who trotted out for the first game at Bradford City (drawn 2-2) were familiar faces. Three days later, there seemed little need for Tynan as Argyle raced into a 4-1 half-time lead at Cardiff in the Littlewoods Cup, only to allow the Fourth Division side to end up winning 5-4. It was one of Argyle's greatest ever collapses.

DID YOU KNOW?

**Entertainer Lionel Blair once spent a day training with Argyle
whilst appearing in a show in the city.**

The first home league game brought a 1-0 victory over last season's rivals, Reading. Forecasts of a 15,000 gate were wide of the
mark, but almost 10,000 was pretty healthy. The fact that the match
programme sold out half an hour before kick-off suggested that the
club had been caught by surprise at the size of the crowd.

A second leg home defeat by Cardiff had the moaners moaning
and the rest of the crowd singing 'There's only one Tommy Tynan'.
Whispers suggested he could be on his way back. Smith re-iterated
his 'no transfer policy' but on Saturday afternoon at Hull a familiar
shape filled the No 9 shirt. 'TT' had returned, with Argyle repaying
the original fee of £25,000 to Rotherham. It seemed likely that Tynan
would also have a new attacking partner. News leaked that Pompey
were ready to sell last-season's top scorer Nicky Morgan, who had
been displaced at Fratton Park by the arrival of Paul Mariner. In the
event, Morgan went to Stoke.

Argyle's dislike of the various supplementary cup competitions
concocted over recent years continued with a 2-3 defeat at Ipswich
in the Full Members' Cup.

Kevin Summerfield was the main, albeit unlikely, source of goals
during the early weeks, so long as he wasn't playing at Home Park.
He managed to score in each of the first six away matches, including that defeat at Ipswich, to send the 'statto's' rifling through their
record books.

Tynan's return again lifted spirits, as did the return of Kevin
Hodges from injury sooner than expected. It took Tynan seven
games to get off the mark, but his first goal earned a victory over
Sheffield United that saw the Pilgrims enter the top four. Five-figure
crowds were becoming the norm and suddenly everyone was paying tribute to the canny know-how of Dave Smith.

Sunderland became the first side to defeat Argyle in the league,
by which time Garry Nelson had been laid low by the effects of a
mystery virus which had also caused him to miss games last season.
The defeat was only a blip, for Argyle lost only once more before
the end of November. Renewed interest in the club brought a bonus
for Smith, who published his *Promotion Diary* – a quirky analysis of
the previous season's promotion campaign.

Argyle's winning ways saw Smith add to his whisky reserves, as
he was awarded another manager of the month prize. The curse
which seemed to traditionally follow such an award then struck in a

big way. December yielded just two points from five games, both in draws against sides chasing promotion.

With keeper Lim's three-month loan coming to an end, Steve Cherry – who, when with Derby, had inadvertently helped Argyle in that famous FA Cup quarter-final – arrived on a month's loan to provide some competition for Geoff Crudgington.

Cherry first saw action in the second half of Argyle's best win of the season, a 6-1 thrashing of Brian Clough's Nottingham Forest. Unfortunately, it did not earn three points as the match was a testimonial for John Uzzell. Over 6,000 fans braved a miserable evening to pay tribute to the popular defender.

Cherry's league bow came after Crudgington was dropped following a 3-2 win over leaders Oldham. Supporters could have been forgiven for thinking that Cherry was a bad omen. Despite some fine personal performances, he did not play in a winning side and Crudgington was recalled after Christmas.

The New Year brought an FA Cup third round tie at Bristol City. Five thousand Pilgrimites descended on Ashton Gate, causing the kick-off to be delayed by sixteen minutes. A draw saw the sides replay at Home Park, where Argyle triumphed in injury-time to set up a money-spinning tie at First Division leaders Arsenal.

The tie at Highbury generated phenomenal interest, as was to be expected. The 5,000 grandstand tickets on offer to Argyle fans were quickly snapped up, and an estimated 12,000 made the journey to north London on the day. Expectations were obviously high. Smith took flak for dropping Crudgington yet again, but it was doubtful whether his inclusion would have altered the score-line. Arsenal were simply on a different planet, and the 6-1 thrashing emphasised the gulf in class between the top of the First and Second Divisions. The defeat temporarily derailed Argyle's league form too, but despite taking only one point from the next three games, they still loitered around the all-important fifth place, which would seal a place in the newly introduced play-offs.

Poor Cherry had still not experienced the winning feeling and became the target for abuse from the Home Park crowd, angry at Crudgington's continued omission. The hiccup in form prompted Smith to contemplate new signings, and several players, including Liverpool's Gary Ablett, were rumoured to be on their way to Home Park.

Curiously, Argyle regained their form while Smith was away scouting, leaving Stewart Houston in charge. Houston jokingly nominated himself as manager of the month for his efforts. Cherry finally experienced the joy of victory and regained enough confidence to hold on to his place for the remainder of the season.

Smith's jaunts around the country were finally rewarded with the capture of Nicky Law from Blackpool for £35,000 – Law added to his growing entourage of central defenders – and striker Stewart Evans, a £50,000 buy from West Brom.

These additions were timely, for injuries were beginning to mount. Smith held things together and a riveting win at second placed Portsmouth seemed to put a play-off place beyond doubt. Two points dropped at home to relegation-threatened Huddersfield undid all the good work. Despite a week of preparation, Argyle came unstuck on Oldham's plastic pitch. With the final game at champions Derby unlikely to yield any reward, three points from the penultimate fixture, at home to Stoke, were essential. From the moment the referee unwittingly obstructed two Argyle defenders, allowing the visitors to take the lead, the writing was on the wall. Ipswich's draw at Sheffield United made Argyle's task virtually impossible. Three points and a hatful of goals were needed at the Baseball Ground, but Derby were in no mood to let Argyle spoil their party.

Despite the disappointment of the last three games, it had been an eventful season. Few would have predicted that Argyle would have made such an impact. The crowds, and Tynan, had returned and the feel-good factor was back in earnest at Home Park.

Match of the Season 1986-87
Argyle 2   Portsmouth 3

Division 2, 26 December 1986

Shorn of local derbies against Exeter or Torquay, Pompey had – in the eyes of Argyle fans – become public enemy number one. This was in the main due to the crowd trouble that had soured matches between the two sides. The self-styled 'Battle of the Ports' had unfortunately taken on a literal meaning in recent years.

A mouth-watering match was in prospect for various reasons. Pompey were the league leaders and their side contained a certain Paul Mariner, former God of Home Park. The visitors had also earned themselves a bad-boy reputation, although it was the players rather than their supporters who had saddled the club with that unwanted tag. A recent match at Sheffield United had seen three players – Billy Gilbert, Kevin Dillon and Mick Tait – sent off in the first half. To exacerbate matters, Mariner had put through his own net to inflict on Portsmouth only their third defeat of the season.

Unfortunately for Argyle, the three offenders' suspensions had not yet taken effect. What with the likes of hard-men Noel Blake and Mick Kennedy, it seemed that Argyle physio Malcolm Musgrove was set for a busy time. Of course, Pompey could play a bit as well. The skilful Vince Hilaire and Kevin O'Callaghan would pose a threat down the flanks. The main source of goals came not from Mariner – who was winding down his career and had scored just once this season – but Micky Quinn, who already had thirteen goals to his name.

Dave Smith had other worries too. Steve Cooper and Kevin Summerfield were injured and Clive Goodyear and Adrian Burrows found themselves omitted after a 0-3 capitulation at Ipswich in the previous match. Steve Cherry was still preferred to Geoff Crudgington, and Garry Nelson played despite a sleepless night when his wife presented him with a baby seven hours before kick-off.

Over 21,000 shrugged off the festive excesses to cram into Home Park for an 11.30 start. Any instructions Smith issued to keep a close eye on Quinn were forgotten as he was allowed to head the first goal. Seven minutes later Dillon made it 0-2. Argyle fought back in controversial manner. Tynan beat the offside trap but was brought down by Paul Hardyman. Referee Keith Burge, in his first league season, awarded a free-kick before his attention was attracted by Cornish linesman David James's vigorous flag-waving. After consultation, Burge pointed to the penalty spot and Coughlin converted. Post-match TV inquests showed the linesman to have got it wrong. It ought to have been a free-kick. Pompey's Hilaire, surprisingly omitted from the starting eleven, replaced the injured Hardyman, and it was the winger who restored Pompey's two-goal advantage with a header after Cherry failed to cut out a cross.

From that moment it was Argyle who did most of the attacking, as one would expect. Various parts of goalkeeper Alan Knight's anatomy were used to defy Tynan, and illegal use of Mick Tait's hand went unnoticed.

With thirteen minutes remaining, Hodges stabbed home at the second attempt to set up a frenzied finish, but Knight remained defiant. The matched turned ugly just before the final whistle when a tackle from O'Callaghan – normally the good boy in Pompey's class of rogues – left John Uzzell with a badly gashed shin. Uzzell and his manager were incensed. Uzzell claimed that his shinpad had saved him from a broken leg. Smith ordered the club photographer to take pictures of the injury and demanded that the authorities study the video of the match. Quinn added fuel to the fire by claiming that Uzzell had spat at him. These events overshadowed an otherwise enthralling game which saw Alan Ball's side continue on their march to eventual promotion.

LEAGUE DIVISION 2   **1987-88**
Barclays Division 2   16th
Littlewoods Cup   2nd round
FA Cup   5th round

The relative success of 1986-87 was helped by healthy attendances that helped to boost the club's finances, which showed a profit of almost £200,000. With funds available, Smith was determined to strengthen his squad, particularly in defence, where various combinations had failed to produce a unit that looked completely at ease. Uncharacteristically for a manager so adept at picking up a bargain, Smith splashed out a club record £170,000 for his namesake Mark, a central defender from Sheffield Wednesday. Clive Goodyear was the man to make way, £50,000 taking him to Wimbledon, with whom in May he would win the FA Cup.

Smith also made the tough decision to release Gordon Nisbet. Many thought he had another season left in him, including Exeter, who snapped him up on a free transfer. Garry Nelson was another departee. The popular winger yearned for a move back to the South East and Brighton paid out £72,500 for him. Determined to retain the formation that had served him well, Smith had to find a winger to replace Nelson. Doug Anderson came from Tranmere for £15,000 and another flank-man, Keith Furphy, came on trial after spending his career in the USA.

Several youngsters, such as Andy Morrison and the Rowbotham brothers, were also knocking on the door of first-team selection but much would depend on whether Tynan could find a partner to share some of his goalscoring responsibilities.

One other familiar face returned. Martin Harvey came back as number two, replacing Stewart Houston who had received an offer he couldn't resist to coach the Arsenal reserve side.

There was certainly optimism amongst the supporters. Season tickets (£110 for the grandstand and £65 for standing) were snapped up in the belief that this could be 'the year'.

Work also started on sprucing up the ageing Home Park. Five new flagpoles were erected at the Devonport End, and new terracing and a refreshment kiosk were planned for the corner known as the Spion Kop. A team of long-term unemployed were engaged to smarten up derelict areas outside the ground.

Amongst the early visitors were West Ham who came down for Kevin Hodges' testimonial. In the League, two substitutes were now allowed and the fixture list had some blank Saturdays. The composition of the divisions had been restructured. Division Two now contained 23 clubs, an odd number in more ways than one.

DID YOU KNOW?

Argyle's League Cup-tie at Chester in August 1981 had to be replayed after Chester keeper Grenville Millington snapped a goal-post, which could not be repaired.

The Argyle shop increased its range of products to cater for the demands of an ever-widening fan base. Replica shirts hit the shelves for the first time. A 'Sunday Independent' sponsored green top could be purchased for £12.50, or £16.50 for those of a larger waist-line. The shop's official price list also carried a warning that 'pirate' vendors were on the increase.

The first league match was one of the hardest. Manchester City, along with Aston Villa, had been surprisingly relegated, and gave the Second Division a formidable look. The Pilgrims, now skippered by Tommy Tynan, seemed undaunted by playing in front of 20,000 at Maine Road, and Nicky Law gave them the lead. One of the shocks of the opening day seemed on the cards until City scored twice in the last ten minutes.

The visit of Ipswich (0-0) for the first home league match drew a decent midweek crowd of 12,000. The 3,000 who stayed away from the next match missed a treat as six goals were put past Hudders-field. At the time, Argyle thought scoring six made them pretty special. In retrospect, that result lost some of its gloss, for the Terri-ers finished well adrift at the bottom. Among their numerous other defeats was a 1-10 mauling at Maine Road.

Two more Argyle victories followed, whereupon the club found itself above the clouds in top spot. There was a drawback. Smith must have cringed when named manager of the month. Sure enough, the curse struck again. The whole of September failed to bring a win. With several clubs tightly packed below Argyle, they were soon down in mid-table. Nor did the Littlewoods Cup herald a change in fortune. Exempt from the first round due to last season's high finish, a trip to Fourth Division Peterborough in the second should have held few fears. But rampant Posh scored four.

The supporters were becoming increasingly impatient with the situation. Mark Smith had looked a class defender, but his pairing with Nicky Law was not 'clicking', and goals were being shipped at an alarming rate. Some other new faces were struggling, in particu-lar Anderson and Stewart Evans, who had become targets for some crowd invective. Coughlin was still out with injury and Hodges was looking less of a threat than usual. As a possible sign of despera-tion, a visit to Stoke saw Tynan strangely employed in midfield.

A new signing seemed likely, with Smith embarking on various scouting missions. He was absent for the visit of Leeds but predicted an entertaining game. The Yorkshire side's glory days were well behind them – they languished below Argyle in the table – but they had conceded just ten goals so far. But now came one of those days. Everything Argyle touched seemed to fly past Mervyn Day and for the second time in a few weeks Argyle scored six.

The result again flattered to deceive and was followed by a home defeat by Millwall. A win over third-placed Hull lifted spirits, but only temporarily as the defensive failings were again horribly exposed. A youthful Ian Wright undid Argyle with a hat-trick as Crystal Palace scored five. It was the final proof that the defensive situation needed to be rectified. In a surprise move, Smith signed the promising Nicky Marker from Exeter. Marker could play in a number of positions but Smith was clearly intent on using him in the back four. A fee of £95,000 changed hands and Darren Rowbotham was included as part of the deal.

Marker's debut was hardly a success. Argyle again visited Maine Road, this time in the Simod Cup. City, fresh from their demolition of Huddersfield, racked up another six with striker Tony Adcock scoring his second hat-trick in four days. Argyle replied twice.

The plan to use Marker to shore up the defence was soon abandoned. He was pushed into midfield instead, with Gerry McElhinney – who had been languishing in the reserves for much of the season – recalled. The Irishman lasted just two games before Adrian Burrows was brought in. Burrows' days at Home Park had seemed numbered. Southend were keen to sign him after his loan spell at Roots Hall, but he resolved to fight for his place at Argyle.

Smith continued to chop and change, but Argyle even lost at Huddersfield, of all places. Coughlin, hampered by a persistent hamstring injury, moved to Blackpool for £75,000 and several other players were rumoured to be anxious to leave, among them Nicky Law, who handed in a transfer request.

Christmas at least brought some cheer. Faced with the customary mass shopping expeditions on the Saturday, Argyle put back the game with Bradford City to Sunday. The switch worked, and 11,000 saw Argyle's victory. Two more wins followed, but counted for little when lowly Reading inflicted a New Year's Day defeat.

With little to play for in the league, the fans craved some excitement in the FA Cup. After the debacle against Peterborough earlier in the season, few underestimated their Fourth Division rivals Colchester, but the U's were comfortably despatched. Revenge was gained over Manchester City in the league and Evans silenced the boo-boys by scoring the only goal against Shrewsbury, which sent Argyle through to the last sixteen of the FA Cup. On this occasion the draw was not so kind, sending Argyle back to Maine Road.

By this time, the condition of the Home Park pitch was causing concern. Despite outlaying £20,000 the previous season on re-surfacing, the pitch had not stood up well to recent heavy rainfall. Groundsman Mark Lewis had to put in long hours to keep it playable. As for the 60-odd fans enjoying a 'quiet' drink in the Far Post social club, gallons of rainwater had accumulated on the ageing roof which collapsed under the weight. Fortunately, no one was injured.

In the Cup, Argyle put up a brave fight at Maine Road before losing 1-3, but a bumper crowd produced net receipts of around £40,000 to provide some consolation.

The season was effectively dead. Relegation, barring a disastrous losing run, was unlikely. Tynan found reason to cheer when he notched the 200th goal of his career but there was little else to retain the interest of the fans. By the season's end, crowds had slumped back to the 6,000 mark. Only one point from six games near the end of the campaign meant a few nervous glances over the shoulder but the relegation candidates were well adrift.

The anticlimactic campaign left much for Smith to ponder, not least the future of eleven of the squad, whose contracts were up.

Match of the Season 1987-88

Reading 0   Argyle 1

Division 2, 29 August 1987

The Pilgrims travelled to Elm Park, handily positioned in fifth place. They headed a clutch of teams on four points thanks to the previous week's 6-1 hammering of Huddersfield. For the Royals, still under the stewardship of Ian Branfoot, the season had barely started. They had only one league game under their belt.

Reading no longer posed the same threat as two seasons earlier, when they had crushed Third Division opponents. Their squad had been weakened by the summer sale of Trevor Senior to Watford and Kevin Bremner to Brighton. Ex-Argyle winger Andy Rogers had earlier moved to Southend. The sale of Senior and Bremner had reaped a handy £390,000, some of which had been invested in new signings Francis Joseph, Colin Gordon and Mick Tait, but Senior's goalscoring had made him a Reading legend, and it was hard to see how they could be replaced.

Not surprisingly, Dave Smith kept faith with the same eleven who had disposed of Huddersfield. Urged on by their usual vocal away support, Argyle dominated the early exchanges. John Matthews and Kevin Summerfield quickly took control of the midfield and Keith Furphy's speed was inducing panic in Reading's defence.

Furphy had an early chance, but the ball took an unkind bobble off the firm surface.

Argyle continued to dominate as half-time approached. With a minute to go before the interval, Smith vacated his seat in the stand to undertake his usual practice of going to the dressing room to review his notes and pour the half-time cuppas. As he navigated the inner sanctum of Elm Park he heard, as he put it, 'a bit of noise'. Unbeknown to Smith, that 'noise' was the sound of Argyle supporters celebrating. Darren Rowbotham's cross had been headed on harmlessly by Stewart Evans. Intending to clear, Reading's Gary Peters nodded a looping header over his own goalkeeper, and was still shaking his head in disbelief as the half-time whistle blew.

Smith delivered his prepared half-time pep talk. Reading looked more determined and forced four corners in succession. On each occasion Steve Cherry confidently came out to claim the ball. The Green Army were soon chanting his name, a far cry from his early days with the club when he was more used to jeers than cheers.

Argyle soon regained their earlier dominance. Furphy missed several chances and Evans' shot scraped the crossbar. Reading attacks were becoming scarcer, but when they did press forward Nicky Law and Mark Smith tidied things up.

At the final whistle, the Argyle players trooped off, well satisfied with their afternoon's work. In the dressing room, Smith and coach Martin Harvey discussed the game. 'We must be well up with the leaders now,' commented Harvey. Smith questioned his assistant's judgment. 'Not with five points,' came the reply. Harvey quickly pointed out that Argyle's points tally was seven. It was the moment of realisation. Not only had Smith missed seeing the goal, he hadn't even realised it had been scored. For once he was speechless. With a towel over his head to hide his embarrassment, he slumped in the corner.

The win sent Argyle to the top of the Second Division for the first time since August 1962. For Reading, the result told a different story. Their fears over the loss of Senior proved well-founded. With Gordon emerging as top scorer with just ten, they averaged just a goal a game. It was not enough to stave off relegation.

LEAGUE DIVISION 2   **1988-89**
Barclays Division 2   18th
Littlewoods Cup   2nd round
FA Cup   4th round

The anticipated mass exodus of players seeking better contracts did not materialise. Those who did depart were not unexpected and, on recent form, would not be greatly missed. John Clayton, who had only fleetingly exhibited his undoubted skill, pursued a career in Dutch football with Fortuna Sittard for £60,000 The want-away Nicky Law had his wish granted and transferred to Notts County for £70,000, whilst Geoff Crudgington, as expected, called it a day. Steve Cooper also left, netting the club another £75,000 after his transfer to Barnsley, and the fans bade a fond farewell to Gerry McElhinney on his move to Peterborough.

There was, however, another departure that few anticipated. Scottish Premier League Dundee needed a new manager and Dave Smith was their choice. The chance to return to his home-town club and rub shoulders with Rangers and Celtic instead of Walsall and Shrewsbury proved irresistible. Argyle fans had mixed feelings. Smith was undoubtedly a shrewd and capable manager. But his recent reluctance to sign new players had lost some of their good-will, and there were signs that the board shared the supporters' frustrations.

But who would succeed him? Trevor Francis was the foremost name touted by the media. The Plymouth-born England international would have been a popular choice and, although now in his mid-30s, he would have still proved a useful asset as a player. However, it soon became clear that his name had been conjured up from nowhere. Though Tommy Tynan was listed among the hopefuls, the directors plumped for Ken Brown, a choice that brought almost universal nods of approval. Brown, like Smith before him, had been in the game for many years. His track record showed that he had twice led Norwich to promotion, not to mention winning the League Cup.

The delay in naming a new manager also meant a delay in signing new players. Brown needed to act quickly. He presumably faced few difficulties in landing his first catch, his son Kenny, who arrived from Norwich on a free transfer. Forward Sean McCarthy became the only other pre-season signing, joining from Swansea for £50,000. Discounting the youngsters on the fringes of selection, the squad had only fifteen players with serious league experience.

Yet another testimonial featured among the pre-season friendlies with Coventry providing the opposition for Leigh Cooper's benefit.

DID YOU KNOW?

**Former goalkeeper Rhys Wilmot took goal-kicks with his left foot
and drop-kicks with his right.**

The marketing men hadn't yet hit upon the idea of changing the kit for each new season, and Argyle turned out in a virtually identical strip to that of the previous campaign.

The season started promisingly enough with the long-ball game favoured by Smith soon abandoned. Tynan, reappointed captain, was quickly back on the goal trail, confirming that there was still plenty of life in him, despite approaching 33. Others soon found the net as well, as Hereford were emphatically despatched from the Littlewoods Cup, 6-2 on aggregate.

After coming a cropper (0-3) at leaders Watford, Tynan scored a thrilling hat-trick to demolish Stoke, but the away-day blues, so prevalent in the past, seemed to have returned to stay. The Littlewoods Cup yet again paired Argyle with Manchester City and a 0-1 defeat at Maine Road left the tie nicely poised for the second leg. Home crowds had been disappointing but nearly 9,000 turned out for a goal feast that saw City run out 6-3 winners. By coincidence, the sides met again at Home Park three days later in the league. The attendance reached five figures for the first time this season, but the match was an anticlimax, settled by one City goal.

Further misery lay in store. A five-goal hiding at Chelsea preceded Argyle's failure to beat ten-man Shrewsbury. Defeat at Barnsley left the side again hovering perilously above the relegation zone.

It was clear fresh faces were needed and Brown acted quickly to sign winger Mark Stuart from Charlton for £150,000. Stuart's debut, against Blackburn, saw two wingers in action, with Calvin Plummer – an earlier signing – operating on the right. With regular crosses to thrive upon, Tynan notched all four goals that sank Rovers.

The Simod Cup had often been unkind to the Pilgrims. This time young keeper Gary Penhaligon was given his chance, but could not have enjoyed Argyle's 2-6 defeat by Chelsea.

The next match saw Leigh Cooper's leg broken in a tackle by Portsmouth's remorseful Barry Horne. That game also marked the debut of Greg Campbell, a forward who had bought out his contract with Dutch side Sparta Rotterdam. His arrival put added pressure on McCarthy, whose goal output had been disappointing.

Brown's plans were thrown into further disarray by the revelation that Steve Cherry had failed to settle in the South West and had asked for a move. Brown again wasted little time in seeking a replacement. To replace Cherry, Alan Miller, a keeper with considerable potential, was signed on loan from Arsenal. Miller had already won England Under-21 honours, despite never having appeared in a first-team game for the Gunners.

With the teams above Argyle closely bunched, a run of five unbeaten matches – courtesy of Tynan's goals and Miller's saves – pitched the side back up to eighth. Christmas brought its usual doom and gloom, with three straight defeats before a welcome win over high-riding Watford.

Victory over Cambridge in the FA Cup earned a dream home tie against Everton in the fourth round. Much of the build-up focused on the threat posed by Tynan, who was still in prime form, but it was McCarthy – with his first goal since October – who put Argyle ahead. An unintentional handball by Adrian Burrows gave Everton a lifeline and Argyle an extra pay-day. The Goodison replay added to the record receipts of £100,000 which the home tie generated.

Everton made no mistake, but the match was marred by Graeme Sharp breaking Kevin Summerfield's leg. Ken Brown was irate, particularly as the 'tackle' went unpunished.

Perhaps unsurprisingly, Argyle were thrown out of their stride in subsequent matches, but the reliance on Tynan's goals was never more apparent. Six games brought just one goal as Tynan suffered a temporary drought. Miller, meanwhile, his loan spell expired, returned to Highbury. In a short space of time the young keeper had achieved hero status. The fans would have loved him to stay, but the Gunners realised his worth and were not prepared to release him. In an unprecedented move, the directors presented Miller with a watch to show their appreciation of his efforts. Despite being loaned to Chesterfield, Cherry was still on the books. Brown did not think he was the answer, so in came another of Arsenal's conveyor belt of exceptional young keepers, Rhys Wilmot.

With Argyle down to eighteenth, Brown also signed Millwall's David Byrne, a primarily right-sided player whose arrival meant the end was in sight for Plummer. Initially arriving on loan, Plummer had looked a world beater during his first games, but had then gone off the boil. A series of invisible displays soon had the crowd on his back and shattered his fragile confidence. Byrne looked lively and unveiled an awesome long throw which added to Argyle's armoury. Cherry, meanwhile, was transferred to Notts County.

Despite indifferent results and performances, the crowds held up fairly well, due in many cases mainly to the attractiveness of the opposition. Late-season matches against Barnsley and Oxford encouraged only the 5,000 diehards to turn out.

A 4-1 Easter Monday win over Swindon put relegation fears to bed, although Tynan blotted his copybook by throwing his captain's armband angrily to the ground after being substituted. The match also saw McCarthy find his scoring boots. Five goals in as many games from the big Welshman did much to ensure safety.

The Hillsborough tragedy cast a pall over football and drained what little there was left to enthuse over. Brown used the meaningless final matches to blood some youngsters, but was left to reflect on a hugely disappointing season which had also seen him lose two of his most reliable players to serious injuries. 'It has been a rubbish year,' was his succinct but accurate summary of his first year in charge. Argyle were once again indebted to Tynan's goals.

As a bonus for Argyle fans, Home Park was selected to stage an England Under-21 international against Poland. In preparation for the prestigious match, the pitch was given a once-over, and just days before the big game it resembled a ploughed field. A true playing surface was restored in time and a 10,000-plus crowd saw a 2-1 win for the home country, whose team was graced by Steve Bull, Paul Merson and Michael Thomas.

Match of the Season 1988-89

Argyle 1   Everton 1

FA Cup, 4th round, 28 January 1989

Victory over a stubborn Cambridge side in the third round handed Argyle a dream tie against the million pound men of Everton. Colin Harvey's side contained household names – Neville Southall, Tony Cottee, Kevin Ratcliffe, to name but a few. The opportunity to view such talent was a rare event and naturally there was the usual clamour for tickets that such matches bring.

As ever on these occasions, expectations were high that an upset was on the cards. The Toffees had been early leaders of the First Division and had proved difficult to beat, but their recent form was giving Harvey cause for concern. They had needed two games to overcome West Brom in the third round and had recently suffered three successive league defeats. Argyle, languishing in fifteenth place, were hardly in prime shape themselves, but the media's – and probably Harvey's – focus was on Tommy Tynan, who topped the Second Division scoring charts with 22 to his name.

The BBC, sensing an upset, despatched Match of the Day cameras to Home Park. Manager Ken Brown's team selection was predictable, although keeping faith with Sean McCarthy – goalless since 11 October – must have required much thought. McCarthy, aware of the need to rediscover his cutting edge, requested to wear Kevin Hodges' usual No 8 shirt instead of No 10. The only logic to such a request – which was granted – was that it was the number McCarthy wore at his previous club, Swansea.

It had been some time since Home Park embraced such a crowd. Over 27,000 stood and sat shoulder to shoulder to greet the two sides. To many of these fair-weather supporters, the visitors' faces seemed more familiar than those of the home side.

Spurred on by the vociferous support, Argyle started at a frantic pace and the blue shirts of Everton were soon in reverse gear. Everton's Stuart McCall pulled a shot wide in the sixth minute but for much of the first half Argyle were the more purposeful side. Brown's tactics soon became obvious – get the ball wide to Hodges and Stuart on the flanks. With more time on the ball than usual, Nicky Marker and Kevin Summerfield in midfield were able to find the wingers more frequently than they could have hoped.

The second half started in much the same way. Adrian Burrows and Mark Smith looked comfortable against the dangerous Everton front pairing of Cottee and Graeme Sharp, and it was little surprise when Argyle took the lead. Hodges' cross was pawed away by Southall to McCarthy, who fired in. The No 8 shirt had worked its magic. Home Park reverberated. Surely it was the goal that would set the Pilgrims on their way.

The Toffees were stung into action and Miller produced a stunning one-handed save from McCall. With a little over ten minutes remaining, Ian Snodin's cross was handled. The crowd were unsure of the identity of the culprit, but referee Danny Vickers was sure – and pointed to the spot. The official had been so close to the action all afternoon that he had been hit by the ball on three separate occasions. Burrows was deemed to be the offender, later verified by the TV cameras. Kevin Sheedy's left foot proved as reliable as usual, and for the first time the Everton fans packed behind Miller's goal had something to shout about.

The remaining minutes passed without incident, leaving Everton to breathe a sigh of relief and Argyle to anticipate another bumper pay-day from the replay.

Everton's class told in the return match four days later, and they fired four goals without reply. They marched all the way to Wembley, where they lost to Merseyside neighbours Liverpool.

LEAGUE DIVISION 2　　　　**1989-90**
Barclays Division 2　　　　16th
Littlewoods Cup　　　　2nd round
FA Cup　　　　3rd round

Much of the summer talk in the world of football centred around the ongoing repercussions of the Hillsborough tragedy. Clearly, drastic measures would have to be taken on ground improvements, which would involve considerable expenditure. This proved to be the focus of Chairman Peter Bloom's statement which accompanied Argyle's annual accounts. The club were still very much on an even keel financially and work had already been carried out at Home Park, including a new family stand and additional facilities behind the scenes.

The close-season comings and goings brought mixed reactions. Fortunately, Arsenal believed that Rhys Wilmot was more expendable than Alan Miller and the fans and Ken Brown were delighted to seal a permanent transfer for £100,000, after Wilmot's highly successful loan spell. Another player with top-flight experience, Andy Thomas, was signed from Bradford City for £70,000. There was a sad farewell to the loyal John Uzzell and the cultured if ageing John Matthews. Both were snapped up by Dave Smith, back in the South West after his brief sojourn at Dundee, and now managing Torquay. The ineffective Calvin Plummer had been sold to Chesterfield for £20,000.

Another likely departure was Mark Smith. Argyle's record signing had joined the unsettled brigade and yearned for a move back north. It was a blow to Brown's plans, as he had seen the classy defender as pivotal to his plans.

A comprehensive pre-season build-up was organised. Argyle took part in a soccer festival at Penzance. Other teams included a Liverpool youth side that contained Steve McManaman and Steve Staunton, both stars of the future. A near full-strength Argyle demolished Cornish side Porthleven 13-0. Keeper Wilmot was given a brief run out at centre-forward and gave Tommy Tynan a few sleepless nights by scoring an eleven minute hat-trick! The Brazilian champions, Botafogo, also brought their Latin American skills to Home Park in an entertaining encounter.

The league season saw Argyle in free-scoring mood. A 3-0 win at Portsmouth saw them up in third place. They were also through to the second round of the Littlewoods Cup, despite doing their best to toss away a three-goal first-leg lead against bottom of the league Cardiff. New boy Thomas had settled in well and, as a bonus, Mark Smith remained a Pilgrim, having yet to finalise a move elsewhere.

DID YOU KNOW?

Against Bury in April 1986 a dog wandered onto the Home Park pitch, prompting the
crowd to burst into a chorus of 'There's only one Jack Russell'.

The second round of the Littlewoods Cup again paired Argyle
with Arsenal. The two sides had clashed twice previously in recent
times, not that anyone at Home Park was complaining, as they
anticipated another night to remember and a boost to the bank
balance. A 2-0 win for Arsenal at Highbury in the first leg was not
as decisive as the score-line suggested. The Pilgrims gave a good
account of themselves, with only John Brimacombe's late own-goal
giving the Gunners some breathing space.

Another own-goal, this time at Home Park by David Byrne, gave
Arsenal an early lead and allowed the Gunners to relax and turn on
the style. Tynan's equaliser on the night proved but a token gesture, as the First Division giants romped to a 6-1 win.

The defeat only served to harden the Pilgrims' resolve. Three
straight wins carried them back up to third place. No one at that
time would have put money on Brown being dismissed within three
months, but he was. Defensively, the loss of Smith through injury
began to tell. Sean McCarthy and Brimacombe also missed matches
through injury, and age was beginning to catch up with Tynan,
although he was still knocking them in. A 0-3 defeat at Ipswich in
mid-October sparked a dismal run. Apart from a shock win at
Watford, it was to be March before the fans could celebrate another
victory. A 2-5 defeat at West Ham in the Zenith Data Systems Cup
was followed, more crushingly, by a third round FA Cup home
defeat by Oxford. It was at this match that the supporters' wrath
was directed at the board. But it was Ken Brown who would pay
the ultimate price.

The inevitable departure of Mark Smith had come in November,
with Argyle recouping much of their record fee when he signed for
Barnsley for £145,000.

The side's poor form saw the predictable arrival of several loan
signings in a desperate attempt to stem the tide. Jim Beglin, a one-
time Liverpool regular and Republic of Ireland international, arrived
from Leeds but was still recovering from a broken leg. His performances did not impress and seemed to serve only as a means to
regain match fitness. Julian Broddle signed for £70,000 from Barnsley to fill the problem left-back position, and Leigh Cooper and
Kevin Summerfield made welcome but brief returns to the side after
recovering from broken legs. Sadly, neither was the player they had
been pre-injury.

Geoff Crudgington's testimonial against Tottenham brought some welcome relief. The on-field antics of Paul Gascoigne, playing with a plaster cast on his arm, briefly lifted the gloom surrounding Home Park.

Brown's comments after yet another defeat, this time by Wolves, subconsciously detailed his own shortcomings. 'The players lacked commitment, pride and passion,' he said. But it was Brown's job to instil those qualities and he had failed. Many put it down to his lack of a hardline assistant. Brown was a decent chap. Probably too nice to be a football manager. The players liked him personally, but did they respect him? He had surprised many by retaining the existing backroom staff when he joined Argyle, rather than name his own assistant. Within days of the Wolves defeat, Brown was summoned to a board meeting and advised of his dismissal. Assistant manager Martin Harvey soon followed, although in his case amicably, with his contract being settled.

John Gregory, recently dismissed as Portsmouth manager, was immediately put in temporary charge with the usual promise of a permanent job if results went accordingly. They did not. Two more defeats saw the board move for a new man. The jungle telegraph suggested Dave Smith was ripe to return but the directors plumped instead for a former Argyle favourite, David Kemp.

Kemp's task was merely to keep Argyle in the Second Division. He had some coaching experience with Wimbledon and in Sweden, following his playing career, but it was still a gamble to take him on. The fans merely hoped that he was as good a manager as he had been a player. John Gregory remained for the moment as a player, appearing in his first match for two years. It helped earn a welcome three points at the expense of Sunderland, in what was Kemp's first game in charge. Gregory didn't last long, opting to move to Bolton.

Kemp wasted little time in bringing in fresh blood. Mark Fiore and Dean Blackwell (loan) arrived from the Dons. Striker Paul Robinson came from Scarborough and the highly experienced Danis Salman signed from Millwall. The Wimbledon connection continued with their former number two, Alan Gillett, brought in to take up a similar position. Despite this influx, there was little to shout about in terms of improved results. By the end of March the side had dropped into the bottom three and the visit of Ipswich enticed the season's lowest crowd of 6,793. At last they enjoyed a rare victory. Two more defeats followed. A study of the remaining fixtures did not make pretty reading. Leeds, Newcastle and Oldham were flying high and crucial matches against fellow strugglers Bournemouth and Bradford City also loomed.

A battling draw against leaders Leeds instilled some confidence. Kemp's mettle would now be tested but he came through with flying colours, thanks mainly to an unexpected source of goals – Sean McCarthy. The big Welshman had struggled to grab the number of goals expected of him since arriving at Home Park and had lived largely in the shadow of Tynan. But the game at West Brom marked the highlight of his career so far when he scored a hat-trick. Two days later he struck twice more to seal victory over Oldham. Argyle weren't out of the woods yet but their prospects were certainly brighter. Stoke were already doomed and Bradford City looked sure to join them, leaving only one relegation spot left. A draw at home to Newcastle left Argyle four points clear of the drop zone. Another against Watford in the penultimate match meant safety was assured, but that match was tinged with sadness, for it saw Tommy Tynan walk off the Home Park pitch for the last time. The club had already announced that he would be released, but the man who had gained legendary status as an Argyle hero would be granted a testimonial.

After yet another season of struggle it was apparent that changes were needed on the playing front if the club were to move upwards. David Kemp, showing little room for sentiment, announced the release of Leigh Cooper and Greg Campbell, and transfer-listed Summerfield, Stuart and Broddle. His job had just begun.

Match of the Season 1989-90
Argyle 1   Leeds 1

Division 2, 10 April 1990

In a season of poor performances, contenders for the title of 'match of the season' were few and far between, but the home fixture against leaders Leeds United provided the catalyst for a run which eventually steered Argyle away from the relegation zone.

Under Howard Wilkinson, Leeds were looking to recapture past glories. His side contained a mix of promising youngsters and experienced pros who had known the big time. Gordon Strachan was proving an inspirational skipper and was also their leading scorer. A return to Home Park lay in store for former Argyle loanees Lee Chapman and Jim Beglin. Beglin would be assured of some stick from the crowd after his uninspired performances in a green shirt earlier in the season.

The match was David Kemp's tenth in charge of Argyle and he had tasted victory just twice so far. After two successive defeats he had rung the changes. Skipper Nicky Marker was available again after suspension and returned to central defence. Kenny Brown was dropped for the first time and loan signing Dean Blackwell given the No 2 shirt. Tynan played in midfield, allowing Andy Thomas to push forward. Danis Salman returned from injury to displace Julian Broddle on the left-hand side of the defence.

Despite an evening kick-off, Argyle officials hoped to attract the biggest crowd of the season, but Leeds surprisingly sold only 1,800 of their allocation of 3,400 tickets.

Kemp's tactics focused on nullifying the threat of Strachan and his 'oppo' on the other flank, Gary Speed, which task Blackwell and Salman performed effectively. There was little to chose between the sides and chances were few and far between. Chapman broke the deadlock in the 28th minute, firing home from close range after good work by Beglin and John Hendrie, but Argyle were soon back on terms. Within two minutes McCarthy burst into the penalty area and was tripped by Peter Haddock. There was little dispute as ever-cheerful referee Roger Milford pointed to the spot. Tynan strode up to take the kick but was delayed whilst Beglin tried to tip keeper Mervyn Day on which way to go. His 'advice' was to no avail.

Kemp handed recent recruit Adam King his first taste of league soccer four minutes from the end, and after the game the Argyle manager expressed his satisfaction with the result.

For Leeds it proved another step on the way to the title, which they would claim on goal-difference over Sheffield United.

LEAGUE DIVISION 2   **1990-91**
Barclays Division 2   18th
Rumbelows Cup   3rd round
FA Cup   3rd round

Argyle's escape from relegation had come at a price. Kemp's recruits had cost over £100,000 and had done the job asked of them, but the prospect of another season of struggle necessitated further outlay. Mark Stuart and Sean McCarthy were sold to Bradford City for a combined £330,000. Much of that income went on recruiting nomadic striker Robbie Turner from Bristol City for £150,000 and defender-cum-midfielder Steve Morgan from Blackpool for £115,000. Dave Walter was also brought in from Exeter for £10,000 to provide goalkeeping cover for Rhys Wilmot.

Of course, some familiar faces would be missing. Tommy Tynan had linked up with Dave Smith at Torquay as player-coach. Youngster Peter Whiston had also moved to the Gulls. Leigh Cooper soon found a home at Aldershot, while Greg Campbell, seemingly with little prospect of first-team football at Home Park, went to Northampton. Julian Broddle was another who did not figure in Kemp's plans. He joined the exodus to Bradford City, initially on loan.

Another player was missing from the pre-season build up – John Brimacombe. The local lad had failed to recover from the ankle injury suffered the previous season and medical opinion had forced him to call it a day.

Kemp had turned his attentions to the youth set-up at Home Park. The club's centre of excellence, which had been established for seven years, underwent a major shake-up. Kemp was not convinced that the centre had unearthed enough potential first-team players, and asked his assistant Alan Gillett to oversee operations. Another former favourite, Gordon Nisbet, returned as youth-team manager.

Kemp's former connections played a major part in pre-season preparations. For the first time since the late 1960s, the squad ventured abroad for warm-up matches, with Sweden the destination. Wimbledon also paid a visit to Home Park in a friendly, during which Brimacombe was presented with an inscribed gold watch by his team-mates.

Ribero took over as the club's new kit suppliers, and promptly turned the clock back by producing a green and white striped design. Some supporters loved it, others hated it.

The stripes had to wait for their first league airing as the Pilgrims visited Newcastle for the first match bedecked in yellow shirts and green shorts.

DID YOU KNOW?

A sign of things to come. Gordon Nisbet and John Uzzell once 'arrested' an invading fan on the Home Park pitch. Nisbet went on to join the police after his playing days.

Young Owen Pickard, a prolific scorer in the reserves, was given the nod to lead the attack alongside Turner in the early matches. Many fans wondered how Tynan's goals would be replaced, and much expectation was heaped on the youngster, but the early goals came from an unlikely source – Andy Thomas – who found the net on eight occasions in the first ten league and cup matches. Two of those goals helped secure a surprise aggregate win over First Division Wimbledon in the Rumbelows Cup, much to the delight of Kemp and Gillett, but just one win in the first eight league games left Argyle seventeenth, facing another season of struggle.

The club was also labouring financially. Only 4,500 turned out to watch the Wimbledon game, leaving Kemp perplexed as to the poor response. He ventured to suggest that his Wimbledon long-ball background was working against him. The directors were more than perplexed; they were also concerned. Gate revenues were way below what was required. No home match had yet come near to attracting 8,000 spectators, which the club needed to break even. The annual accounts had for the first time in five years revealed a loss – £325,000 – partly due to Kemp's late-season spending spree. If the club hoped to attract sympathy with these figures, they shot themselves in the foot by admitting that one unnamed player had earned £65,000 for the year, and four others were in the £30,000 plus bracket.

Walter was drafted in for his debut in place of Wilmot, suspended after being sent off against the Dons. Argyle cruised to a comfortable victory over struggling Hull, thanks to two unlikely goals from Danis Salman, but the victory was tarnished by the loss of Andy Thomas with a back injury. As he trudged off the pitch, no one realised at the time that it would the last game of his career. The injury never healed and yet another Pilgrim was consigned to soccer's scrap-heap.

The next round of the Rumbelows Cup saw Argyle entertain the holders, Nottingham Forest, and the tie attracted a decent crowd in excess of 17,000. The Pilgrims raised their game, but Forest escaped a late penalty appeal to progress 2-1.

The squad was taking on an ever more depleted look. Turner's physical style was approved of by the Argyle fans but not by referees. He now faced suspension, as did Kevin Hodges, who was sent off for the first time in his long career in a thrashing at Port Vale.

Marker gashed a knee and Wilmot broke his nose. A familiar scenario was beginning to build. With no funds available to buy, a number of loan signings were employed, generally with little effect, and ever greater reliance was placed on youngsters such as Martin Barlow, the irony of which was not lost on some, given Kemp's pre-season thoughts on the centre of excellence.

Even Keith Edwards, once the scourge of Argyle, but now in the veteran stage, was given a try. He scored at leaders Oldham, but failed to have any impact.

For the fifth time, Argyle attempted to win a Zenith Data Systems Cup match. For the fifth time they failed, but they came close, losing a penalty shoot-out to Brighton. The New Year arrived with just five league wins under their belts and relegation staring Kemp in the face. The FA Cup also brought a familiar tale. A creditable draw at Middlesbrough – achieved despite Turner's expulsion – was the prelude to Argyle blowing the replay at home. The chance of another much-needed pay-day had gone. A week later, Argyle visited Ayresome Park again, this time in the league. It was Hodges' 471st full league game, breaking Sammy Black's all-time Argyle appearance record that had stood since the 1930s.

The word 'crisis' again reared its head. Even the most diehard fans were beginning to lose faith in manager, players and board alike, and with some justification. The style of play, akin to Wimbledon's 'famed' long-ball – whether Kemp denied it or not – was both unpopular and unsuccessful. Equally clearly, some players were not Second Division material. Strangely, the directors, having said no money existed for new signings, were now talking of up-grading the floodlights. The pressure was mounting on Kemp. Once a hero of the Home Park terraces as a player, he was now losing the fans' confidence. The local evening paper lambasted the style of play. Kemp reacted by declining all interviews.

These distractions obviously did nothing to improve form on the pitch. A one-man demolition by Teddy Sheringham saw the future England star score all four of Millwall's goals to push Argyle into the bottom three.

To add to the turmoil, a posse of local businessmen formed a consortium to take over the club, pledging to redevelop the area around Home Park. Their proposals included a new supermarket and a purpose-built athletics track, as well as a redesigned 20,000 all-seated football stadium, and the promise of £1.5 million to be available for team strengthening. The City Council dismissed the plans as 'too ambitious'. Meanwhile, the existing directors were negotiating to renew the lease of Home Park, with the existing one having just nineteen years to run. A proposed new 125-year lease would at least give the club some bargaining power with the banks, should additional funds be needed.

The humiliation at Millwall at least appeared to shake the players into action. Successive wins over Brighton and Port Vale were followed by a shock draw at leaders West Ham. Five more points were gained from the next three matches and this mini-revival was to prove crucial at the final count.

But the jitters returned and Kemp was forced to continually juggle the side in an attempt to find the winning formula. Another youngster, Ryan Cross, was drafted in for the final few games, and did himself justice, whilst Darren Tallon created an Argyle post-war record on his one and only Pilgrims' appearance by becoming the 33rd player to be used by the club in a season.

A 4-1 win over fellow strugglers Blackburn eased the pressure, but a four-goal defeat at Notts County – who were indebted to a hat-trick by future Pilgrim Dave Regis – meant relegation loomed large once more. A visit to doomed Hull in the penultimate game seemed to offer a lifeline, but the Pilgrims conjured up their worst performance of the season. Hull had fielded a number of untried youngsters who relished the opportunity given to them. Fortunately, other results went Argyle's way, but mathematically they still needed points from the final match.

Charlton were the visitors to Home Park. Thankfully from the Pilgrims' point of view, Athletic had little to look forward to but their summer holidays. A comfortable 2-0 win confirmed safety. At least the fans had Second Division soccer to look forward to, and a number of youngsters had shown promise. But in many respects that club had taken a backward step. Was Kemp the right man for the job? Questions still remained.

Match of the Season 1990-91

West Ham 2   Argyle 2

Division 2, 5 March 1991

The contrast between these two clubs could not have been more stark. The Hammers were flying, topping the table, having lost just two league games all season. Argyle were labouring in the bottom six. Twenty thousand-plus crowds were the norm at Upton Park. Money was no problem to the London side, and in Frank McAvennie they boasted a £1 million player. Argyle were losing money by the bucketload week after week. Both sides were managed by former playing favourites, but Billy Bonds had retained his popularity, Kemp was losing his.

The Hammers had carried their league form into the FA Cup, and once the Argyle fixture was out of the way were headed for a quarter-final tie with Everton. Pilgrim followers clung to the vain hope that this would prove a distraction.

Argyle's previous away match had also been in the capital, but a 1-4 defeat by Millwall had left the players' ears burning after a subsequent tongue-lashing by Kemp. Since then, two home wins had brought a welcome six points, but few expected points from Upton Park.

The team-sheet showed that Bonds had little intention of shielding his stars from pre-quarter-final injury. Central defender Tony Gale was laid low by a tummy bug, but his replacement, the lofty Colin Foster, seemed ready-made to cope with the aerial threat of Robbie Turner. Top scorer Trevor Morley was also out, but was replaced by Northern Ireland international Jimmy Quinn.

The wet surface soon intervened. In the nineteenth minute, Tim Breacker fired a low cross into the Argyle penalty area. The ball struck Marker and flew past Rhys Wilmot. Would conceding such a goal lead to Argyle capsizing?

To their credit, the answer was no. Inspired by the tireless running of Kevin Hodges, making his 500th league appearance, the Pilgrims fought back. Robbie Turner, capable of outjumping most defenders, did so twice to give Argyle a shock lead. The Hammers were facing their first home loss in thirteen months when Breacker sprinted forward again. This time his angled shot found the far corner of Wilmot's net.

A furious onslaught followed as Bonds' side went for the kill. With three minutes remaining, Stuart Slater was felled by Andy Clement, who had otherwise deputised effectively at left-back. A penalty was the outcome, and Argyle shoulders slumped. Perhaps they did not know the Hammers' wretched record with spot-kicks. Morley, Quinn and Julian Dicks had all missed in previous games, and with some trepidation George Parris stepped forward. The penalty was straight and true, but too straight. Wilmot's half-dive was enough to parry the ball to safety.

Both managers expressed their satisfaction at the result. West Ham went on to win their quarter-final before succumbing to Nottingham Forest in the semi-final. Promotion was theirs, though they relinquished top spot to Oldham.

Manager Dave Smith enjoys a moment with supporter 'Noddy' in the Far Post club

Kevin Summerfield (left) and Geoff Crudgington pose with snooker star Steve Davis

Tommy Tynan (left) celebrates Summerfield's goal against Leeds, October 1987

Assistant manager Martin Harvey bites someone's head off from the sidelines

Kevin Hodges marks his record number of Argyle appearances

Manager Peter Shilton goes over the head of assistant John McGovern

The League trophy in the Home Park dressing room during Arsenal's visit, July 1991

Arsenal's Tony Adams in action during Graham Little's testimonial, July 1991

Swindon player-manager Glenn Hoddle on his backside at Home Park, October 1991

Four of Shilton's big signings – Paul Dalton, Gary Poole, Warren Joyce, Steve Castle

Chapter Five

Off the field Shenanigans 1991-1995

LEAGUE DIVISION 2	**1991-92**
Barclays Division 2	22nd (relegated)
Rumbelows Cup	1st round
FA Cup	3rd round

Predictably, Argyle were amongst the favourites for relegation. Player of the year Kenny Brown had not renewed his contract and had gone to one of his father's former clubs, West Ham. With financial constraints the main consideration, Kemp was forced to add to his squad on the cheap. The quality of the new arrivals hardly inspired confidence. Striker Morrys Scott and midfielder Mark Quamina had played only a handful of league games between them, while goalkeeper Steve Morris had been an understudy at Swansea. The exception was ex-Norwich and Leicester defender Tony Spearing, who was signed to fill the problematic left-back position, which had never been adequately covered since the departure of John Uzzell.

The pre-season saw not one but two testimonials at Home Park. Long-serving club secretary Graham Little had retired, and was justifiably rewarded with a match against Arsenal. The club also fulfilled its promise of a benefit game for Tommy Tynan. Aston Villa provided the opposition. Little's job was renamed 'Chief Executive' and for the first time in the club's history was filled by a female, Liz Baker.

Another pre-season capture was that of Dwight Marshall. The striker had impressed during various friendlies and was signed from Grays Athletic for £35,000. Marshall took little time in adjusting to league soccer. Within nineteen minutes of his debut in the curtain raiser at home to Barnsley he scored to put Argyle ahead. The Pilgrims won 2-1. It was early days, but perhaps Kemp had unearthed a marksman who could fill Tommy Tynan's boots.

Shrewsbury provided the opposition in the Rumbelows Cup, which allowed Kevin Summerfield to snub his nose at Kemp for letting him go. Now captain of the Shrews, Summerfield scored in both legs as the Third Division side progressed on away goals.

Back in the league, two wins in the first three matches were followed by a backs-to-the-wall draw at Newcastle, but the rot soon set in. Marshall apart, the new signings were largely anonymous. Six defeats in seven matches saw the side plunge to the bottom, and the goals-against column took a battering. The pressure on Kemp intensified by the day. To curb the flow of goals he employed Robbie Turner in defence and achieved a scoreless draw at fellow strugglers Bristol Rovers. Turner was then suspended, and former Welsh international Jeff Hopkins was brought in on loan. Wilmot found himself less busy but so, usually, did his opposite number. Marshall apart, Argyle rarely threatened to score.

The crowds began to drift away in droves. The crisis was deepening. Another takeover approach saw local businessman Steve Tiller announce a £2 million rescue package. The effect of this was merely to cause division between the present directors, some of whom backed Tiller's consortium. Then, out of the blue, it was announced that millionaire Dan McCauley had seized power of the club, pledging to save it from its current demise. McCauley had previously had a financial interest in Devon's two other league sides, but for the moment the Argyle faithful cared little. Outgoing chairman Peter Bloom remained on the board, together with two other directors. The McCauley regime would be turbulent, but it would ultimately save the club.

McCauley was away on business for the first match under his reign. Had he been present he may have had second thoughts about his investment, as only 4,000 turned out to watch Argyle slump to another home defeat, this time against ten-man Watford. McCauley wasted little time in reaching for the cheque-book. A club record £200,000 was splashed out for Notts County's Dave Regis, who had punished Argyle the previous season with a hat-trick. The transformation of Turner into a defender proved to be one of Kemp's better decisions, and suddenly the side began to scrape a few wins. The problem was that playing Turner in defence meant he was absent in attack, where he was needed.

Another big-money signing, David Smith, arrived from Bristol City for £185,000, but the new man spent more time on the treatment table than on the pitch.

Argyle quickly waved goodbye to the FA Cup. Four goals by Carl Saunders inspired Bristol Rovers to a 5-0 win and a tie against Liverpool. 'Some of our players have got no brains,' was Kemp's succinct summary of the match. Strangely, the defeat came in the midst of one of Argyle's better spells. Dwight Marshall's three goals helped earn three points at Barnsley in mid-January that lifted the Pilgrims to the heady heights of eighteenth.

Another cup run ran into the buffers. Argyle had somehow won not one but two Zenith Data Systems Cup-ties. Victories over Millwall and Portsmouth had set up a southern area semi-final against Southampton. The Saints, including future stars Alan Shearer and Matthew Le Tissier, scraped through by a single goal.

Dutchman Erik van Rossum was signed on a short-term contract from Twente Enschede. He debuted in a home match against Cambridge, but another home defeat – this time against fellow long-ball exponents – spelled the end for Kemp. A board meeting the following Thursday confirmed his dismissal. McCauley knew the parting of the ways was inevitable but still had regrets. He confirmed that he had allowed Kemp more time, when other directors had insisted on his dismissal following the FA Cup debacle. The chairman paid tribute to Kemp's hard work and dedication, but at the end of the day Argyle were still a losing team.

Kemp's assistant, Alan Gillett, remained and was given temporary charge of team affairs, along with youth-team manager Gordon Nisbet. McCauley had publicly named the man he wanted to take over – former Argentinian World Cup star, Ossie Ardiles. But Ardiles politely refused. Ray Wilkins was also mentioned, but he was keen to continue his playing career in the top flight.

Gillett and Nisbet took charge for the first time at home to Brighton. The long-ball game was immediately consigned to memory, but a draw against the bottom club was a calamity. A week later, during a 0-2 defeat at Ipswich, Turner collided with Wilmot and suffered a double fracture of the leg. His season was over, and perhaps Argyle's was too.

McCauley seemed intent on bringing in a high-profile manager. On the Monday following the Ipswich game he held a press conference to unveil Peter Shilton. The goalkeeper who held the all-time England appearance record was still turning out for Derby at the age of 42 and insisted he was coming to Home Park as a player-manager, not manager. His appointment certainly excited the fans and generated huge publicity, but lurking in the background was the fear that Shilton was untried in management at any level.

Shilton wasted no time announcing his assistant, former Nottingham Forest team-mate, John McGovern. The duo received a rapturous welcome as they appeared for their first game in charge, ironically against Derby.

Their short-term task was obvious. Save Argyle from the drop. Their arrival seemed to inspire some players. Transfer-seeking Steve Morgan produced a scintillating performance against the Rams. With the threat of Shilton hovering over his first-team place, Rhys Wilmot was also on the transfer list, but for the time being was playing out of his skin in the attempt to keep Shilton at bay. For his part, the new manager appeared in no rush to grab the No 1 jersey.

DID YOU KNOW?

**Adam King came on as a substitute against Ipswich in October 1990
wearing a No 8 shirt.**

Despite the euphoria attending Shilton's arrival, results were no
better. Transfer deadline day brought the usual flurry of activity.
Striker Kevin Nugent had already arrived in a £200,000 deal from
Leyton Orient and was now joined by David Lee, on loan from
Chelsea, and the experienced Steve McCall, who had played top
flight and European football for Ipswich and Sheffield Wednesday.

But still the defeats piled up. Shilton finally selected himself for
his Pilgrims debut at Charlton. He kept a clean sheet in a creditable
draw against the promotion chasers, but he was soon crashing back
to earth. A home defeat by Southend dumped Argyle back to the
bottom. With just four points separating the last seven teams, there
was still time to string together a good run of results.

A first ever win at Roker Park against fellow strugglers Sunderland flattered to deceive. The Pilgrims simply lacked enough firepower. Marshall had excelled during his first season but Regis had
let everyone down, himself included. The final Saturday saw the
Pilgrims host Blackburn, needing all three points to give themselves
a chance of staying up. Sadly, a David Speedie hat-trick silenced the
17,000 Home Park crowd.

Shilton conceded that the task of trying to avoid relegation had
been harder than he had imagined. Whilst the fans were naturally
crestfallen, the standard of football under his leadership had improved immeasurably. With funds available, and Shilton's high
profile likely to attract better players, the mood was not as despondent as might have been imagined. Surely relegation would be just
a short-term setback.

Match of the Season 1991-92

Argyle 0   Cambridge 1

Division 2, 11 February 1992

In a season of under-achievement, candidates for Match of the
Season were in short supply, but the visit of Cambridge encom-
passed in miniature the shape of the whole campaign.

Argyle's much-maligned long-ball game had been woefully
misguided, given that the side were 21st before kick-off, yet Kemp –
stubbornly refusing to admit to such labels – had stayed true to that
approach. The visitors, under John Beck, employed a similar game,

but Beck was the acknowledged 'expert' in the art of hoofing the ball upfield at every opportunity, proof of which was that Cambridge were headed for the play-offs. Besides, Cambridge had a Dion Dublin in their ranks. Argyle didn't.

Despite Argyle's lowly position they were unbeaten in eight at home, but two successive away defeats had forced Kemp to ring the changes. Dutch Under-21 international Erik van Rossum came into the back four for his Pilgrims debut, releasing Robbie Turner back to his favoured forward position, and relegating record signing Dave Regis to the bench. Expensive buy David Smith was passed fit and able, and he too made his home debut, some six weeks after signing.

Beck's tactics were more subtle than critics gave him credit for. Above all, he had the players to carry them out, notably the towering dual strike-force of Dion Dublin and John Taylor. It is fair to say that at that time Cambridge could, and did, put the willies up everyone. Their squad happened to contain no fewer than five past or future Argyle players. Tony Dennis was previously a Pilgrim, whilst keeper Jon Sheffield, Chris Leadbitter, Mick Heathcote and Neil Heaney would all appear in Argyle green later in their careers.

The only goal came in the fourteenth minute. Naturally, Dublin was involved, flicking on a corner for Michael Cheetham to apply the finishing touch. It wasn't Argyle's evening. Nicky Marker and Smith banged the woodwork either side of the interval, and several other chances were created and squandered. Frustration set in, culminating in the expulsion of Kemp from the dug-out with twelve minutes remaining for firing a verbal volley at a linesman. It would be a sad end for a man who, as a player, was once a hero of the Home Park terraces. Kemp's sacking was confirmed a few days later. The irony that his downfall was brought about by Beck's long-ball tactics was not lost on some.

Beck, meanwhile, was gushing in his praise of Argyle. 'I can't believe we have won. I thought Plymouth were absolutely magnificent,' he enthused. It was an opinion shared by few. United maintained their form to the end of the season before falling at the play-off hurdle.

LEAGUE DIVISION 2   **1992-93**
Barclays Division 2 (new style)   14th
Coca-Cola Cup   3rd round
FA Cup   3rd round

During the summer every club was promoted. The advent of the Premier League meant each division was elevated upwards. Argyle found themselves back in Division Two, though relatively speaking things were just as they were.

Peter Shilton paved the way for major personnel changes. With 30 players on Argyle's books, it was obvious that the squad had to be trimmed. Seven professionals, most of them Kemp's recruits, were released, and another seven were transfer-listed. The re-building began with the early-summer acquisition of Preston skipper Warren Joyce for £160,000. Joyce voiced his pleasure at not having to play any longer on Deepdale's plastic pitch.

Changes within the structure of Home Park also made headlines that summer. Chief Executive Liz Baker needed all her diplomatic skills when grandstand season-ticket holders were advised that, following the implementation of safety changes, they could not be guaranteed their usual seat. Home Park's official capacity was cut from 19,930 to 18,000, due partly to the number of broken seats in the Lyndhurst Stand, which were deemed unusable and dangerous. In the end, a decision was made to completely replace the seating at a cost of £60,000, with green seats interspersed with white ones to spell out PAFC.

The gap between the standard of the first and the reserve team was also a worry. Shilton rightly perceived that the step up from Western League football was too great. In an attempt to be readmitted to the Football Combination League – Reading having dropped out – the club circulated other clubs with the offer of a £500 'sweetener' to every side visiting Home Park. The ploy worked to a certain degree, with a place secured in the second division of the league. The club also remained in the Western League.

Despite relegation, season-ticket sales were healthy and sponsorship deals gave cause for encouragement. Belief in Shilton's ability was evident. There was no disputing Chairman Dan McCauley's commitment either, as his cheque-book took a regular airing. Suddenly, six-figure transfers were becoming the norm. Steve Castle arrived from Orient for £195,000, winger Paul Dalton came from Hartlepool in a deal valued at an Argyle record £250,000 – with young defender Ryan Cross going the other way – and Gary Poole was signed from Barnet. Goalkeeper Ray Newland arrived as cover for Shilton, as Wilmot's departure seemed only a matter of time.

Striker Paul Boardman, son of comedian Stan, joined from Knowsley United to provide goals and a few new gags.

Pre-season friendlies included Luton coming down for a second testimonial for long-serving Kevin Hodges. That aside, Argyle's preparations were decidedly low key, with warm-ups restricted in the main to local non-league sides. Shilton had vowed to improve Argyle's woeful disciplinary record and was soon practising what he preached. He hauled Tony Spearing off the pitch after the player was involved in a fracas during a friendly at Bodmin.

McCauley's company, Rotolok, were revealed as the new shirt sponsors. Argyle were now kitted out in shirts designed by Admiral, still sporting green and white stripes, but with a broader stripe.

The early matches saw Dalton and Castle missing through injury. Argyle were quickly into cup action, with Shilton rolling back the years to restrict West Brom to a one-goal first-leg lead in the Coca-Cola Cup.

Another new face joined the scene. Winger Craig Skinner arrived on loan from Blackburn and impressed in the first home league game, as the Pilgrims produced a thrilling brand of attacking soccer to destroy Bradford City. West Brom were despatched in the second leg of the Coca-Cola Cup but, at Hull, Shilton was sent off for the first time in his long career.

Part of McCauley's financial outlay was recouped by the sale of club captain Nicky Marker to Blackburn. The fee, £500,000, smashed Argyle's transfer record receipts. As part of the deal, Skinner's loan was made permanent and defender Keith Hill joined him from Ewood Park. Marker's departure was, of course, a blow to supporters, even if it was inevitable. He had developed considerably over the years and was now an asset to any club.

Marker's loss was not felt so badly, in part because of sterling performances by certain players. Steve McCall's experience was invaluable, making his £25,000 fee look a bargain. Andy Morrison played above his years, and Marc Edworthy looked as though he had been born into league football. Another bonus was the sparkling form of Dave Regis. Few had expected Regis to be around Home Park for another season, but a loan spell at Bournemouth seemed, temporarily at least, to rejuvenate him. Regis was suddenly doing what a striker should do, and his goals against Luton in particular helped the Pilgrims progress to the third round of the Coca-Cola Cup.

Joyce enjoyed his return to Preston, helping Argyle to their first away win since April. While Home Park was acquiring a reputation as a fortress, too many points were being squandered on grounds up and down the country. The fans hoped for improvement once

Dalton and Castle were fit. Neither had yet appeared in a league game, added to which, Marshall was also on the treatment table.

All three regained fitness around the same time, which meant that Regis, despite his recent improved form, had to make way. Half of his original £200,000 fee was recouped as Stoke took him off Argyle's hands.

Robbie Turner also returned to fitness earlier than expected. His broken leg had not been expected to mend until Christmas, but by early November he was back, albeit briefly. After just two games, he was on his travels again, this time to Exeter.

All told, injuries proved a major disruption. Joyce, Spearing, Evans, Morrison and Shilton himself all had spells on the sidelines. Boardman, looking useful in the reserves, was given his first-team chance and made a scoring debut, but the injury jinx soon struck him down. Kevin Hodges was another name absent from the team sheet, but in his case for a different reason. The appearance record holder had finally bade a fond farewell to Home Park and moved to Torquay.

By Christmas the side were stranded in mid-table and out of the Coca-Cola Cup, following defeat by Third Division Scarborough. The first questions were starting to be asked about Shilton's managerial ability, particularly after a Boxing Day defeat at Exeter. Any loss to the Grecians was hard to stomach at the best of times, but the manner of Argyle's 0-2 capitulation saw the players booed off the field by 1,000 travelling fans. They had seen little evidence of passion in the heat of battle.

For the moment, the FA Cup kept the season alive. Wins over Dorking and Peterborough saw Argyle drawn at Premier League Ipswich, but the East Anglian side proved too strong. There was also an early chance to gain revenge over Exeter in the Autoglass Trophy. With the early ties being contested on a round-robin basis, both sides gained a point in a 1-1 draw at Home Park.

Another away defeat, this time at Bolton, left Shilton admitting to being perplexed by the wretched away form. But home form was beginning to suffer as well. The strikers lacked confidence and more goals were needed. A 0-0 home draw with Hull saw the crowd dip below 5,000 and the side was jeered and slow-handclapped. There were signs of friction between Shilton and Dan McCauley. The chairman's patience was wearing thin. He had expected some return from the funds he had poured into the club, but at the moment there was none in sight. Shilton's honeymoon period was well and truly over.

Kevin Nugent was one player who suffered more than his fair share of abuse. No one doubted his effort or commitment, but his lack of goals could not be concealed. A hat-trick against Mansfield momentarily silenced his critics but he needed more of the same to keep them quiet for long.

Much was made of Shilton's impending 1,000th league appearance, but when he took another injury everything had to be put on hold. Ray Newland was drafted in, having played a few matches earlier in the season, but his confidence was even lower than that of the strikers. Great saves were interspersed with howlers, and it was a pity Newland was in goal when Burnley ended Argyle's eighteen-match unbeaten home run.

The injury crisis became so severe that the reserves were forced to field former Argyle favourites Gordon Nisbet and Steve Davey, who had a combined age of 86! The situation was exacerbated by continued disciplinary problems. Hill and Morrison both suffered sendings off and subsequent suspensions.

Marshall was allowed to go on loan to Middlesbrough, but the arrival of 19-year-old Lee Hodges on loan from Tottenham sparked the side briefly into life. It did not last. The final quarter of the season passed without so much as a whimper. Dalton and Castle performed manfully, with Castle netting a hat-trick at West Brom, but displays at Home Park were nothing short of miserable.

A humiliating 0-3 home defeat by Exeter brought the feud between chairman and manager into the open. McCauley had endured a self-imposed period of silence but this defeat was too much to take. He already harboured misgivings about Shilton's transfer dealings, and had recently blocked the proposed signing of Torquay defender Wes Saunders. Now, Shilton's post-defeat comments, to the effect that he was not receiving the full backing of the board, stung McCauley into action. His response was tantamount to a vote of no confidence in the management team. He also suggested that the players' wages should be withheld after such an abject display. The feud between manager and chairman was just warming up.

Four points from their final six home games saw Argyle finish in the bottom half. No one was happy with that.

Match of the Season 1992-93
Argyle 0   Exeter 3

Division 2, 10 April 1993

A blood-curdling defeat at the hands of Argyle's deadly rivals may seem a strange choice as Match of the Season, but its significance cannot be overlooked as, with hindsight, it was a significant milestone in the reign and eventual demise of Peter Shilton.

DID YOU KNOW?

Former manager Neil Warnock has many strings to his bow.
One of them is being a qualified chiropodist.

Argyle had produced a toothless display when losing 0-2 at Exeter on Boxing Day. The fans and, presumably the players, were looking for revenge. Surely the team would be fired up for this one.

Before the game, City manager Alan Ball shared his thoughts on local derbies: 'Derby matches are all about optimism in the opposition penalty area and pessimism in your own,' he spouted. How true his comments were to prove.

The teams ran out to be greeted by a crowd of 9,391, double the recent Home Park attendances. City sported their garish away strip, purple shirts illuminated by white splashes. Yellow shorts hardly complemented the design. The fashion police were out in force.

With injuries playing a major part in team selection, Shilton – sidelined himself – retained the jittery Ray Newland in goal. 'Jock' Morrison was available after suspension and fit-again striker Paul Boardman was given another chance, following his scoring debut.

The Grecians, like Argyle, hadn't climbed out of second gear all season, and had toiled around the lower third of the table. Their team had few stars, although Kevin Bond was an experienced defender and striker Ronnie Jepson would need to be watched.

City started confidently. Argyle threatened on rare occasions but Bond was always there to tidy up. With the home defence having little confidence in Newland and *vice versa* a disaster was waiting to happen. The hapless keeper threatened to deal with a through ball, Keith Hill threatened to help out, and in the end neither player did anything. The lurking Jepson was left facing an empty net

Shilton juggled his formation at half-time but to no avail. Morrison, an old head on young shoulders, tried his best to induce some passion into his team-mates, also to no avail. Michael Evans looked lively after replacing the redundant Boardman, but Steve Morgan presented former Argyle trialist John Hodge with another goal, and three minutes from time the winger ran through a static defence. The Grecians celebrated in front of their ecstatic supporters long after the Pilgrims had been booed off.

Shilton's post-match comments reiterated his frustration at not – in his opinion – being permitted to strengthen his defence. This sideswipe at the board reopened some festering wounds. Chairman Dan McCauley's response left no one in any doubt where he stood on the matter. The marriage made in heaven was under strain and was never to recover. A bitter divorce was on the horizon.

LEAGUE DIVISION 2   1993-94
Endsleigh Division 2   3rd (play-offs)
Coca-Cola Cup   1st round
FA Cup   4th round

The pressure on Shilton, as he prepared for the new season, was intense. He, like everyone else, knew that a poor start would mean goodbye. After making noises about strengthening the squad at the end of the previous season, he finally got his way. He embarked on another spending spree, funded by selling Gary Poole to Southend for £350,000 and Andy Morrison to Blackburn for £400,000. Both deals yielded substantial profits. Poole had arrived on a free transfer only twelve months previously, while Morrison had come up through the youth ranks. Warren Joyce and Steve Morgan were the other significant departures, boosting the coffers by a further £300,000.

Shilton, confident in the knowledge of which areas of the team needed strengthening, set about a recruitment campaign. Wayne Burnett arrived from Blackburn as part of the Morrison deal, and central defender Andy Comyn was signed from Derby for £165,000. The defence was further boosted by the signings of Mark Patterson, a direct replacement for Poole and Dominic Naylor.

The goalkeeping position was causing concern. While Shilton could not go on for ever, Newland was not up to the task. Nineteen-year-old Alan Nicholls was brought in from non-league Cheltenham for an initial fee of £5,000.

A less publicised departure was that of youth-team manager Gordon Nisbet. Having been instrumental in setting up the newly formed South West Youth League, he had finally decided to quit football to pursue a career in the police force.

Long-serving Adrian Burrows was rewarded with a testimonial as part of the pre-season build-up. Sheffield Wednesday, boasting the likes of Trevor Francis, Des Walker and Chris Waddle, turned on the style as Argyle's opponents, running out 5-0 victors.

Argyle soon had some silverware to show in the trophy cabinet. The Devon Professional Bowl was re-introduced after a six-year absence, and wins over Exeter and Torquay clinched the trophy.

The league campaign did not start as planned. Argyle's new-look defence conceded five goals in the first two league matches, and another three in the Coca-Cola first leg at Birmingham. To add to the club's woes, Keith Hill was sent off at Hull. Fortunately, scoring goals did not seem to be a problem. Steve Castle was banging them in at will from midfield, and by mid-September he had already notched up seven, helping Argyle to fourth place.

DID YOU KNOW?

Against West Brom in March 1991, the referee failed to spot that both
Argyle substitutes were wearing No 14 shirts.

Nisbet's youth-team vacancy was finally filled – by chance. Ian
Bowyer, a former team-mate of Shilton and McGovern at Nottingham Forest, had noticed on Teletext that there were some personnel
changes afoot at Home Park. A phone call to McGovern set the ball
rolling.

Back on the field, few could complain about a lack of entertainment. Goals were flying in at both ends. Argyle's No 1 jersey continued to be swapped around like a hot potato. Newland was no
more convincing. Nicholls was also given an early chance, but
suspension, followed by a broken toe, gave Shilton the chance to
move closer to the magic 1,000-game mark.

Argyle's dislike of supplementary cup competitions was again in
evidence with a lacklustre defeat by Swansea in the Autoglass
Trophy. Another defeat at home to Exeter confirmed Argyle's non-
participation in later rounds.

Castle was proving to be a revelation in midfield. Always in the
thick of the action, his goals were providing something of a lifeline,
given the paucity of scoring efforts from the regular forwards. It was
no coincidence that when Castle suffered a barren patch in late
October and early November, the side picked up only three points
from four games. This prompted Shilton to seek another striker,
with Bristol City's Wayne Allison his main target. The purse strings
were tightening, however. Despite a healthy profit from transfer
dealings, the club was still seriously in the red. The wage bill was
soaring and gates were far too low to cover it. Dan McCauley had
ploughed almost £2 million into the club, and the directors were
unwilling to throw good money after bad. The message to Shilton
was 'offload some players before we can buy again'.

The first round draw of the FA Cup handed Argyle a first ever
visit to Marlow. Two goals from Paul Dalton dismissed thoughts of
an upset.

Shilton's search for a goalscorer at least had the effect of stirring
Dwight Marshall into action. The lively forward had been blighted
with injuries since his promising first season, but suddenly came
good with a hat-trick at Bradford City. The Valley Parade success
sparked a run of seven wins on the trot and earned Shilton his first
Manager of the Month award. Shortly after Marshall's threesome,
Castle repeated the feat at Stockport, scoring three times in six
minutes to register the fastest hat-trick in Argyle history.

The winning run included an FA Cup success against Gillingham, and by the turn of the year Argyle were lying in second place. Word was getting out that the side was playing some quality football and the stay-aways were beginning to return. Four successive 10,000-plus crowds went away amply entertained.

Thanks in part to a kindly draw, the cup run continued. Third Division Chester were overcome to set up a fourth round tie with First Division strugglers Barnsley. With home advantage, Argyle started as favourites, but they were taken to a replay and lost by a single goal at Oakwell.

The transformation in Argyle's fortunes had the effect of turning the spotlight on Shilton in a different way. The chairman seemed so satisfied with the way of things – what with the team winning and the turnstiles clicking – that there was talk of Shilton and McGovern being head-hunted by a bigger club.

Shilton, himself, had to contend with watching from the sidelines. Despite remaining just five matches short of his 1,000th league game, there was no chance of ousting the in-form Nicholls, who in March completed a remarkable transition from non-league soccer by being called up for the England Under-21 squad. Unfortunately, a clash of fixtures forced the club to withdraw him. Nicholls' first cap was only delayed, however. He was awarded it at the end of the season, against France.

In February, further plans regarding the refurbishment of Home Park were revealed. The intention was to install seating into the Devonport End and to replace the roof and seats in the main grandstand, as well as extend the structure. The total cost was estimated at £1.5 million, clearly out of the club's depth, but the hope was that the Ground Improvement Trust would provide two thirds of the outlay.

The chase for promotion got serious as winter turned to spring. Reading had been runaway leaders for some time, and although they were flagging they still looked assured of promotion. Argyle found themselves heading the chasing pack, but seven clubs were still in contention. The Pilgrims' scoring record could yet play a significant part.

The bandwagon continued to roll with just the occasional bump along the way. A win at Exeter for the first time in 66 years exorcised the humiliation of the previous season's debacle, and the visit of leaders Reading brought out another big crowd. The Royals were defeated 3-1 and suddenly, within the space of three weeks, their lead had been cut from fourteen points to two.

Another away win, this time at Rotherham, lifted Argyle above Reading at the top, and also installed the Pilgrims as the leading scorers in the country. Promotion, if not the championship, seemed theirs for the taking, but for some inexplicable reason the players then froze. A home defeat by lowly Cardiff was followed by two away losses. Those nine dropped points were to prove the difference between success and failure.

It appeared that Argyle were back on schedule. Two more goals from Castle helped defeat Bradford City in the penultimate game of the season, leaving them in second place. But crucially, both Port Vale and Stockport had a game in hand, and neither slipped up. A combination of favourable results could still see Argyle promoted, but all three sides won on the final day to leave the Pilgrims facing the nail-biting adventures of the play-offs.

Burnley were the semi-final opponents. Despite the harsh dismissal of Adrian Burrows – the first of his career in what proved to be his final game – a scoreless draw at Turf Moor left Argyle the favourites. More than 17,500 packed into Home Park for the second leg, but a nervy performance let the Clarets through. Despite finishing twelve points behind Argyle, they went on to clinch promotion to (the new) Division One.

In spite of that crushing disappointment, there was greater cause for optimism at Home Park than for many a year. The youth team won the first ever South West Youth League, and a member of that side, Chris Twiddy, won Welsh youth honours. The style of play of the first team was more attractive than anything seen since the era of Tony Waiters. With exciting talent such as Castle, Dalton and Nicholls on the books, there was much to look forward to.

Match of the Season 1993-94

Hartlepool 1   Argyle 8

Division 2, 7 May 1994

Argyle went into the last game of the season knowing that they had to win and rely on Port Vale losing to stand any chance of promotion. Stockport were also in the frame. Level on points with Argyle, they had a superior goal-difference. So Argyle not only had to win, but win handsomely.

If Shilton could have chosen his final day opponents, he would undoubtedly have picked Hartlepool. The word crisis had oft been associated with the Pilgrims over the years, but the current plight at the Victoria Ground had put Argyle's previous ups and downs into perspective. Already relegated by a wide distance, the Hartlepool players were engaged in a training strike over delayed wage payments, and were only meeting up on match-days.

The prospect of turning out to see Argyle's free-scoring side in action failed to excite the residents of Hartlepool. Of the 2,300 inside the ground, an estimated 1,500 were travelling Pilgrim supporters, many in fancy dress or green wigs.

With Kevin Nugent injured, Richard Landon, a recent £15,000 recruit from Bedworth, retained his place up front. Hartlepool, who presumably didn't know who was playing until they turned up, had chopped and changed their side all season. Only one player in their current line-up, Nick Peverell, had played in their first match, back in August. Despite having won just nine games all season, Hartlepool had reserved their best displays for high-flying opposition, as a recent 4-1 win over Burnley illustrated.

Argyle dominated from the start. Dalton, on his return to his former club, was in ebullient mood on the left and tormented the Pool defenders. The only surprise was that it took half an hour to break the deadlock, when Marshall scored after Dalton had again induced confusion in the home penalty area.

Within ten minutes, Argyle player of the year Steve McCall was on hand to fire in only his second of the season. This opened the floodgates. Within four minutes it was 4-0, Landon and the inevitable Dalton scoring.

'More of the same,' was Shilton's simple half-time message. And that's what he got. Landon stuck out a leg to bag his second goal, and Castle's remarkable tally for a midfield player was raised to 21 for the season. Nicholls, presumably surprised at being called into action, fumbled and presented Peverell with a consolation goal for the home side.

Landon must have wondered what all the fuss was about. League football seemed easy, and he completed his hat-trick when hapless keeper Steve Jones dived over his scuffed shot. By now the Argyle fans were cruelly chanting 'You're worse than San Marino'. Sadly for the few Hartlepool fans present, it was probably true. But Argyle hadn't finished yet. Dalton thumped a last-minute shot into the roof of the net, causing even the home fans to applaud the contribution of their former favourite.

The 8-1 win was the biggest away victory in Argyle's history. Even the hard to please Dan McCauley paid tribute to the players and, in particular, Landon, whose signing he had criticised only a few weeks earlier. Too bad the result could not secure promotion.

LEAGUE DIVISION 2   **1994-95**
Endsleigh Division 2   21st (relegated)
Coca-Cola Cup   1st round
FA Cup   3rd round

A season of high expectation lay in store. Much would hinge on how the players reacted to last season's play-off nightmare. What, in fact, transpired was one of the most traumatic seasons in the club's history.

In the belief that success breeds success, Shilton retained virtually all of the previous season's squad. Of the departures, Adrian Burrows and Ray Newland's had been expected. Dwight Marshall had joined Luton.

The season's first blow was administered even before a ball had been kicked. The club's prize asset, Steve Castle, requested a transfer. Although the goalscoring midfielder would attract a healthy fee, Shilton hoped to dissuade him from moving if he could.

Only one signing of note was made. Peter Swan, an experienced defender, was captured for a club record outlay of £300,000 from Port Vale, and was immediately installed as club captain in place of the unsettled Castle.

The proposed structural changes to the stadium were still on hold, but at least Home Park saw the benefits of a 'spring clean' in preparation for the new campaign. Colin Wheatcroft, under his title of 'Park Superintendent', had made some startling discoveries. For example, the corner flags had to be replaced as the old ones were not regulation size. The 20-year-old wooden goalposts and crossbars were now replaced with metal ones. This was just as well. The crossbars were found not to be true, and could not have withstood many more burly goalkeepers using them as monkey-bars. With new-style goal nets and a fresh lick of paint here and there, the ground was at last taking on a more aesthetically pleasing look.

The playing strip had also changed. Green and black stripes, not dissimilar to the design worn by the 1974-75 promotion side, were back. Perhaps it was a good omen. Perhaps not.

The pre-season friendlies did little more than crock key players. Castle and goalkeeper Alan Nicholls suffered knocks and missed games. With Shilton still unfit, several guest custodians, including Jonathan Gould, Ian Andrews and Ken Veysey, were called upon, before YTS lad James Dungey was plunged into action. Shilton had to find a regular No 1 and tried to bring back former Argyle favourite Martin Hodge. The board initially vetoed the idea, but at the eleventh hour 35-year-old Hodge did sign, and was drafted in for the first league game of the season, against Brentford.

DID YOU KNOW?

A remote-controlled jeep was sent careering around the penalty area at half-time during a dull goalless draw at home to Bristol Rovers in February 1992.

That first match started well. Despite Shilton having to omit five injured regulars, Swan scored within eighteen minutes of his debut. Then it all went horribly wrong. The Bees scored five, inflicting on Argyle their worst ever opening day home defeat.

The team had an early chance to make amends in the Coca-Cola Cup, but a first visit to Walsall's new Bescot stadium saw two Pilgrims sent off and four more goals conceded. The almost meaningless return leg attracted fewer than 3,000 to Home Park but at least Argyle won on the night. Any notions that the worst was over were quickly dispelled. The events of the next few weeks were to reach almost farcical proportions.

A second successive 1-5 home league defeat (this time to Bradford City) left everyone incredulous. Chairman McCauley publicly blasted the team's performance. The one player able to hold his head up high was new goalkeeper Martin Hodge!

The fans' patience ran out. A proposed Travel Club trip to the next game, at Hull, was cancelled through lack of interest. For those who might otherwise have travelled, it proved a wise decision. Following Argyle's 0-2 defeat Shilton took a sideswipe at the board, demanding support 'from everyone within the club'. Argyle then lost 2-4 at Birmingham. Mark Patterson was carted off to hospital with a head injury, and former flop, Dave Regis, scored twice for the opposition.

Home Park's next game saw Huddersfield rub salt into the wounds. Two goals in the first nine minutes led to Hodge being substituted at half-time. Nicholls replaced him but was then sent off, leaving Castle to don the keeper's jersey. Peter Swan's unimpressive start to his Argyle career was already incurring the wrath of the supporters.

Swan was omitted from the next match, but not on account of his form – his wife had just given birth. Without him, Argyle put up the shutters against Cambridge. Afterwards, Shilton's sidekick, John McGovern, announced his resignation for 'personal reasons'. Speculation was rife that McGovern would team up with another former Forest colleague, Archie Gemmill, recently appointed manager at Rotherham.

Three successive wins – without the loss of a goal – lifted some of the gloom but relations between manager and chairman deteriorated. Ian Bowyer had stood in for McGovern as Shilton's number two, but McCauley decided things were so bad that Shilton did not need an assistant. He also aired his reservations regarding further loan signings.

An Auto Windscreens Shield defeat by Exeter in front of an eerily empty Home Park was the least of Shilton's worries. The injury crisis was worsening with every game. Down to fourteen fit professionals, the dismissal of Nicholls at Stockport exacerbated the problem. The local newspaper, the *Evening Herald*, ridiculed the goings on at Home Park in the strongest possible terms, prompting McCauley to ban the paper's football correspondent from the press box. He was forced to file his match report from the comfort of the Lyndhurst Stand.

For the time being, the war of words between McCauley and Shilton cooled down. The chairman agreed to a verbal ceasefire in what he described as a 'zero relationship' with his manager. As predicted, McGovern joined Rotherham and took pleasure in seeing his new charges send Argyle home pointless.

Fresh faces appeared on the scene. Despite McCauley's dislike of loan signings, it was clear that there was no other option. Youngsters such as Dungey, Danny O'Hagan and Marcus Crocker had been thrown into the first team before they were ready. Micky Quinn, renowned for his girth as much as for his goalscoring feats, duly arrived on loan. Quinn, often subjected to terrace taunts on the subject of pies and eating, quickly won over the sceptics, even though he failed to score. After three games his one-month loan period was up and he departed.

History was made with Argyle's first round FA Cup-tie at Kettering, transmitted live by Sky TV, who were hoping for an upset. The Pilgrims scraped through.

The crisis between manager and chairman now came to a head. Shilton suffered personal humiliation when McCauley went public about the former England star's private financial plight. Shilton's position seemed untenable, for he had lost the confidence of just about everyone. Had results improved, he might have clung on, but – the FA Cup apart – they did not. One bad result followed another, one feeble loan signing followed another, and indiscipline among the players led to several dismissals and suspensions that cast the club in a bad light. Although Shilton had to go, technically he was not sacked, but merely suspended. Whatever, no one expected to see him back.

The popular Steve McCall was given the title of 'acting player-manager'. His first match was a demanding FA Cup-tie at Premiership Nottingham Forest. The outcome was predictable but, tellingly, the players at least showed some effort.

March saw a brief respite from the gloom. Home Park was chosen to stage an England Under-15 international against Belgium. Despite a bitterly cold evening, more than 6,000 turned out to watch the home side win 7-0 with a young Michael Owen scoring a hat-trick.

McCall's priority was to drag his side away from the bottom of the league. Sadly, he inherited a squad low on confidence, desire, and numbers. Results were no better and no worse, prompting McCauley to propose that an experienced hand might be drafted in to assist McCall. It was not a suggestion to which McCall took a liking. A man of principle, he resigned his post after just sixteen games in charge, but remained on the staff as a player to help the battle against the drop.

Former boss Dave Smith was approached regarding a return to the Home Park hot seat, but after giving the matter much thought he turned the offer down, believing the job should go to a younger man. He recommended giving it to another former Home Park favourite, George Foster.

In fact, the man in the right (or wrong!) place at the right time was another former England international, Russell Osman. Sacked earlier in the season as manager of Bristol City, he had been training with Argyle and was now given the unenviable task of staving off relegation. His desire could not be faulted, as he agreed to work on an expenses only basis. Five points from his first three games in charge initially gave hope, but a home defeat by Birmingham before Home Park's biggest gate of the season left Argyle with one foot over the precipice.

A shock victory at Wycombe in the penultimate match gave a flicker of hope, but matters were now in others' hands. Argyle needed Shrewsbury to beat Bournemouth in midweek, but it didn't happen. The final match saw Argyle run out knowing that next season they would be playing basement league football for the first time in the club's history. It was a sad state of affairs but, frankly, was nothing more than they deserved.

Match of the Season 1994-95
Brentford 7   Argyle 0

Division 2, 17 December 1994

Chairman Dan McCauley – not usually given to understatement – did precisely that when he summarised Argyle's season as an 'under-achievement'. Victories were so few and far between that it seems unfair to pick out a winning match as the pick of the bunch.

Instead, the collapse at Brentford proved to be a microcosm of the entire season.

Peter Shilton came into the match a shadow of the figure who twelve months earlier had Argyle producing some of the most flowing and entertaining football seen at Home Park for many a year. The week preceding the visit to Brentford had again seen him berated by his chairman for various off-field matters. It was a wonder that he found time to choose his squad, a task in itself given the lack of available players.

Somehow, Shilton cobbled together a team. Having eliminated the injured and suspended, he came up with a list of ten fit and able players. To make up the numbers, YTS lad Simon Dawe was drafted in, with the manager's 16-year-old son, Sam, named as a substitute. To accommodate everyone in reasonably familiar positions, striker Kevin Nugent was asked to play in midfield, and right-back Mark Patterson was switched to the left to allow Dawe to remain on his favoured right-hand side.

Brentford, having come away from Home Park on the opening day with a 5-1 win, had not sustained that early tempo and seemed by December to be destined for a mid-table finish. But within eight minutes, the Bees were two up. Argyle regrouped, and contained their hosts until the interval, but an error by Peter Swan shortly after the break resulted in a third goal. A fourth soon followed. By this time, Brentford manager David Webb was urging his team to throttle back, but none of his players wanted to miss the party. They were all keen to get in on the act, sensing that the hapless Pilgrims were there for the taking. The Greens' defence had looked at sixes and sevens from the off, and their uncertainty quickly spread throughout the side.

More goals followed, but even at six down the loyal band of travelling Argyle supporters could be heard urging their team on. A seventh goal on the stroke of full-time, however, proved to be the straw that broke the camel's back. Brentford had condemned Argyle to their biggest defeat in 34 years, and the third worst in their history. A prophetic chorus of 'Bye bye Shilton' broke out.

The result re-ignited Brentford's season. They lost just three more games. Missing out on automatic promotion, they succumbed to Huddersfield in the play-off semi-finals in a penalty shoot-out.

Shilton's 1992-93 squad. The squiggles all over the photo are players' autographs

Argyle have just lost the play-off semi-final to Burnley. Steve Castle looks dejected

A proud Neil Warnock surveys Wembley prior to the 1996 play-off final v Darlington

Scorer Ronnie Mauge celebrates after the defeat of Darlington at Wembley, May 1996

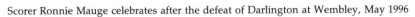

Dressing room joy after Argyle beat Colchester in the play-off semi-final, May 1996

A much-prized possession. The programme from the Division 3 play-off final, 1996

Four players in this picture were sent off, making a total of five, against Chesterfield

Argyle beat the Gambian national team 2-1 during this end of season African trip

Chapter Six

The Yo-Yo Years
1995-2002

LEAGUE DIVISION 3   **1995-96**
Endsleigh Division 3   4th (promoted via play-offs)
Coca-Cola Cup   1st round
FA Cup   3rd round

After the disasters of the previous season, Chairman Dan McCauley pledged to restore the club's fortunes. Clearly, it needed a complete overhaul. Not only was a new manager needed, but there would undoubtedly be plenty of comings and goings on the playing front, particularly as eleven of the twelve players offered new contracts had said no thanks.

One player who would not be around under the new manager was Player of the Year Marc Edworthy. The cultured youngster had been the one bright light in a black season, and by the end of May he had transferred to Crystal Palace for £350,000.

The first task was to select the new boss. Russell Osman had done well enough during his brief spell in charge. Twelve points from eight games could not avert the drop but he had done enough for McCauley to admit that Osman was a leading candidate.

Amongst the other names banded about, that of Neil Warnock kept surfacing. A friend of McCauley when he was briefly manager at Torquay, Warnock was trying to guide Huddersfield out of the Second Division via the play-offs. But all was not sweetness and light between Warnock and the Terriers' chairman, and eight days after Huddersfield's Wembley victory Warnock quit, gathered his passport, and set off for the Maldives for a well-earned break. McCauley tracked down his hotel, whereupon a sequence of phone calls and faxes resulted in Warnock signing a three-year deal.

On returning to England, Warnock wasted little time in rebuilding the side. With the full financial backing of McCauley, he quickly identified his likely targets. Several players who had previously worked with him jumped at the chance of doing so again. At the same time, Warnock swept through the deadwood at Home Park. Some of those shown the door were players whom the fans were sorry to see leave.

Mick Jones, a trusty sidekick of Warnock at previous clubs, was named as his assistant. Nobody could dispute that in new physiotherapist Norman Medhurst – who had worked with the England squad for twenty years – the club had secured one of the best in the business.

Along with a new team came new shirts. The green and black stripes had, not surprisingly, been discarded, and were replaced by a 'modern' gaudy design which prompted one fan to pen a letter suggesting that the strip 'disturbs the mind'.

Warnock used the pre-season to examine various options. In eight friendlies he called upon no fewer than 42 players, and it was therefore no surprise that the eleven who ran out for the first league match of the season contained seven who were making their Argyle debuts.

The supporters had high hopes of a rapid escape from football's basement, a view shared by bookmakers who, having noted Argyle's spending spree, installed them as championship favourites. It should, however, have surprised no one that with such a turnover in personnel the team were performing like perfect strangers – which is what they were. By August Bank Holiday the Pilgrims propped up the entire Football League with four defeats from four matches. They had also been eliminated from the Coca-Cola Cup by Birmingham. Starts don't come any worse than that. The more superstitious fans attributed the dreadful start partly to a change in Argyle's theme tune. The long-standing *Semper Fidelis* had been replaced by *Simply The Best*. A more inappropriate tune at that time it was difficult to imagine.

Realistically, the poor start was partly down to goalkeeper Nicky Hammond. The experienced keeper had performed like a novice and crucial errors sapped the confidence of the defence. In normal circumstances Alan Nicholls would have stepped into the breach, but his career was now on a downward spiral. Injuries had played a part, but not as much as the indiscipline he had displayed both on and off the field. A drink-driving charge proved to be the final straw and the club sacked him.

A visit to Gigg Lane to face Bury was hardly likely to stir the soul, but it proved to be the turning point in Argyle's season. Warnock pulled off a masterstroke by making one of his new recruits, Ronnie Mauge, captain for the day against his former club. The midfielder had a blinder and, spurred on by his example, Argyle swept to a 5-0 win.

A new-found confidence suddenly swept through the side. The defence tightened up, and in attack Adrian Littlejohn's speed and ability were more than a match for most Third Division defenders. Warnock was still on the look-out for players and wisely decided to forego the pleasure of watching another Auto Windscreens Shield defeat – this time by Peterborough – to run the rule over Bristol City's Ian Baird. He liked what he saw and Baird, so often the scourge of Argyle defenders over the years, was soon on his way to Home Park. Kevin Nugent went in the opposite direction and was valued at £75,000 more than Baird – which meant that handy sum swelled Argyle's piggy-bank.

By the time of Argyle's first Devon derby, against Torquay, they had climbed to fourth place, but behind the scenes things were not going so smoothly. McCauley was in dispute with another director, Dennis Angilley. Shortly afterwards, another board member, Ivor Jones, resigned, having taken exception to McCauley's alleged claim that the club was subsidising its directors.

The McCauley-Angilley dispute reared its ugly head again at the AGM, where there was talk of Angilley launching a hostile takeover bid. Warnock threatened to walk out if that came about, and the whole sorry affair threatened to undermine Argyle's valiant efforts to secure promotion.

The FA Cup had taken supporters to pastures new. The first round draw saw a trip to Slough and the second round tie at Kingstonian was chosen for live coverage on Sky TV. The match was hardly likely to break audience records but the £60,000 fee was welcome, for it coincided with the release of Argyle's latest financial report. The relegation season had seen the club haemorrhage £500,000, with liabilities now standing at almost £2.5 million.

The Cup-tie at Kingstonian gave Argyle fans their first chance to pay tribute to Alan Nicholls, who had lost his life in a motorcycle accident days earlier. For all his shortcomings, he was well-liked by all who met him and his loss shrouded the club in gloom.

In the league the side continued to hover in the top six. Club funds received a further boost when a near full-house was recorded for the FA Cup third round tie with Coventry. Despite taking an early lead and the Sky Blues being reduced to ten men, the Premiership side triumphed in the end, 3-1.

Warnock began preparations for the final run in. His attentions were centred mainly on the goalkeeping position. He had recouped the £40,000 he had paid for Hammond by selling him to Reading, but this left only Kevin Blackwell and young James Dungey. Blackwell had done sterling work for most of the season, considering he was brought to the club mainly to run the youth team. Australian-born Andy Petterson arrived on loan from Charlton and endeared himself to the fans by saving a penalty on his debut. After Petterson's loan spell had expired, Steve Cherry returned to Home Park for his second stint as a Pilgrim, a move that surprised almost everyone, considering his urge to leave during his first spell.

DID YOU KNOW?

Despite being on loan from Argyle, George Foster was voted
Exeter City's Player of the Year for 1981-82.

Despite the odd hiccup, Warnock maintained the momentum.
One-nil victories were becoming a speciality. Transfer deadline day
saw Canadian international Carlo Corazzin added to the squad for
£150,000 to intensify competition for places among the strikers. A
bad defeat at Fulham (0-4) threatened to de-rail the promotion train,
but Corazzin made his mark on his home debut, against Mansfield,
coming off the bench with minutes left and slotting home a penalty
to break the deadlock.

The ongoing saga of the future of Home Park took another twist
when the City Council announced plans for a new £25 million
'Tradium'. The idea looked exciting in prospect, but no one was
holding their breath.

Back in the real world, it was still nip and tuck at the top of the
table but, having put a home defeat by Darlington behind them,
Argyle were now on a roll. It was not quite the fairytale finish of
1985-86, but five wins from the last six games was enough to secure
a play-off place. It might have been better, but Bury's last-day win
secured the final automatic promotion spot.

Colchester were Argyle's play-off opponents. On paper it ought
to have been an uneven contest. Warnock had spent £1 million on
new players. U's boss Steve Wignall's sole purchase was future
Pilgrim Paul Gibbs, on whom he had spent the princely sum of
£2,000. But football matches are not won on paper.

The first leg was to be played in Essex. Demand for tickets was
great, but the bad news was that Argyle were allowed only 1,200.
As a partial peace offering, a giant screen was erected at Home Park
and the match relayed live. Argyle conspired to give one of their
worst performances for many a month. They were grateful to escape lightly, having been punished by nothing more than a wonder
goal from Mark Kinsella. Three nights later, they turned the tables
with a 3-1 win. Wembley here we come.

The Saturday of the May Bank Holiday weekend normally sees
traffic streaming into Devon and Cornwall, but this year it was
different. It seemed everyone was leaving. From nowhere, an extra
20,000 Argyle fans sprung up. An Argyle appearance at Wembley
was, after all, a less than once in a lifetime experience.

With an estimated 30,000 Argyle following at the national stadium, green and white dominated the Wembley terraces. Stories
emerged of exiled fans jetting in from various parts of the world.

The match itself hardly lived up to the occasion, but tension was high and Argyle's opponents, Darlington, were doughty fighters. One moment of inspiration from Ronnie Mauge settled the outcome and skipper Mick Heathcote, the backbone of the side, climbed the steps to take the trophy. Thousands of tears filled thousands of eyes. The disasters of twelve months earlier were long since forgotten. There was a sad note to the day, however, as news emerged that a supporter had died following a fight outside the ground.

The traditional open top bus tour and civic reception followed. Thousands more greeted their heroes. Perhaps Argyle were, after all, simply the best.

Match of the Season 1995-96

Argyle 3   Colchester 1
> Division 3, play-off semi-final, 2nd leg, 15 May 1996

With Colchester holding a single-goal advantage from the first leg, the wily Warnock tried to gain a psychological advantage over his opponents by dismissing the U's as a small town club and complained that his players had been subjected to missile throwing at Layer Road. In reality, of course, he knew as much as anyone that Steve Wignall's side were formidable foes. They had taken four league points from Argyle, and in Mark Kinsella possessed a player who could turn a game single-handedly.

Wignall selected the same eleven but had the insurance of top scorer Tony Adcock on the bench. Warnock brought in Mauge for Chris Billy, a player who for some reason had not been taken by Argyle fans to their hearts.

Five hundred U's supporters had made the arduous midweek trip but they were silenced after only three minutes when Michael Evans brought the tie level. Ironically, considering all Warnock's preparations, the move started from a mis-kick by Cherry. The crowd cared little. They were up for the battle and the goal only increased the volume.

Shortly before half-time Argyle were awarded a fortuitous free-kick. Chris Leadbitter, possessor of the sweetest left foot at Home Park curled a free-kick of Brazilian proportions past the despairing Carl Emberson to put the Pilgrims 2-1 ahead on aggregate.

Wignall gambled on introducing his top scorer for the second half, but Argyle continued to press. On the hour, Leadbitter's left foot was in action again, sending the fleet-footed Littlejohn clear. U's despairing defender Tony McCarthy had only one option and took it, clipping Littlejohn's heel. The referee reached for his pocket but, to the amazement of most and relief of some, he brandished only a yellow card. Warnock was livid. His rant at the nearby linesman was sufficiently florid for the referee to be summoned and Warnock to be 'sent off'. Never one to conform, he refused to take the traditional route for such offenders to the directors' box, but vaulted the perimeter fencing to conduct operations from the Mayflower Terrace.

Within minutes the dangerous Kinsella repeated his first-leg feat by firing a shot past Cherry from 25 yards. The advantage, courtesy of the away goals rule, was now back with Colchester.

Extra-time loomed, but there was still time for another right-wing dribble from the elusive Barlow. His cross eluded Emberson and was met by the diving figure of full-back Paul Williams, whose excursions into opposition penalty areas were as frequent as total eclipses of the sun. 'Charlie' launched his 5ft 6in frame into mid-air and made perfect contact, heading the ball into the roof of the net.

Minutes later the referee's whistle sparked a mass pitch invasion. Warnock and his players were engulfed. At long last, Argyle were 'going to Wem-ber-ley'.

LEAGUE DIVISION 2   **1996-97**
Nationwide Division 2   19th
Coca-Cola Cup   1st round
FA Cup   3rd round

In contrast to the previous close season when the majority of players were jumping ship, most of Neil Warnock's expensively assembled squad were keen to capitalise on the promotion success and were only too eager to play for a manager who obviously commanded respect. The nomadic Ian Baird had moved on to Brighton and Steve McCall had teamed up with two former Pilgrims, Kevin Hodges and Garry Nelson, to form the new managerial team at Torquay but, by and large, the rest of the squad were fit and raring to go.

The mood quickly soured. Before the season had even started, Warnock faced challenges both on and of the field. He had hoped to sign several players, namely Dean Kiely, Mark Kinsella and Barry Hayles – all, as it turned out, future Premiership stars – but Chairman McCauley was having none of it, baulking at the prospect of paying out combined fees of £400,000. Moreover, the existing players were unhappy over bonus payments and the denial of a close-season break, which they had been given to understand was part of their reward for winning promotion. These problems took their toll on the relationship between McCauley and Warnock, and the ongoing saga of former director Dennis Angilley's attempts to buy out McCauley fanned the flames. McCauley, as it happened, had changed his mind and was apparently no longer happy to sell.

There were also problems over the Wembley play-off shirts. McCauley had demanded the return of the shirts worn at Wembley, but the players naturally wished to keep them as souvenirs. A situation that could and should have been amicably resolved suddenly got out of hand, and there was even talk of McCauley issuing threats of legal action.

As if the club did not have enough to worry about, Warnock faced a pre-season injury crisis. Once again the goalkeeping position was causing headaches. Steve Cherry had departed for a second time, leaving only the inexperienced James Dungey and youth-team coach Kevin Blackwell to contest the No 1 jersey. Dungey then suffered a serious knee injury in training. The visit of Ruud Gullit's Chelsea for a friendly should have been an occasion to savour, but in the second half 'Mr Reliable' Mark Patterson suffered a broken leg in a clash with goalkeeper Kevin Hitchcock, which looked likely to keep him out for most of the season. Gullit added fuel to the fire by criticising Argyle's physical approach to the game.

> **DID YOU KNOW?**
>
> Lee Phillips became the youngest ever Pilgrim at 16 years, 43 days when he came on
> as a last-minute sub against Gillingham in October 1996. He never touched the ball.

Warnock acted quickly to solve his goalkeeping crisis. In a move that shocked everyone, ex-Liverpool and Southampton star Bruce Grobbelaar signed on the eve of the season. This constituted a huge gamble, in more ways than one. Grobbelaar might add a few hundred to the gate, but for one thing he was 38, for another he was facing a Crown Court hearing into allegations of match-fixing.

Tony James had also been signed from Hereford to bolster the defence as the league campaign kicked off in 90 degree temperatures. Brentford administered Argyle's traditional first round exit from the Coca-Cola Cup but things started well in the league. A Friday night victory over Preston in front of Sky TV cameras established the Pilgrims as the early leaders. Yet by the time of the Coca-Cola second leg Warnock's future was again in doubt, following well-aired differences of opinion with his chairman. A threatened anti-McCauley protest by the crowd did not materialise, but within weeks of the Wembley triumph everything was going pear-shaped.

These events had an adverse effect on results. One of four successive defeats was a farcical trip to Stockport. Warnock's choice of hotel was vetoed by the board on cost grounds. As a form of protest, he ordered the players to drive the 300 miles on the morning of the match. If nothing else, it was symptomatic of the manager's disillusionment.

Argyle's cause was not helped by losing Grobbelaar and Carlo Corazzin to international call-ups, added to which, striker Adrian Littlejohn had forgotten where the net was.

There was little doubt where the allegiance of fans lay in the Warnock v McCauley feud. Warnock's style of play was not always pretty to watch but the supporters always found him approachable and forthright in his views. During the home match against Bristol City some fans demanded the chairman's dismissal by brandishing red cards at him. Unperturbed, McCauley responded with a smile and a thumbs up.

Meanwhile, the City Council reiterated their plans for stadium development. McCauley had expressed reservations over the proposals but was assured that the club would get a new stadium – 'without having to pay a pound. The tradium will go ahead, the funding is there and the commitment is there.'

Back on the pitch, matters degenerated to a level appropriate to a Sunday League outfit. The players arrived at Burnley with only 30 minutes to spare, after traffic delays. Then, just days after trouncing Fulham in the first round of the FA Cup, the lowest home crowd of the season were subjected to such a dire performance against Chesterfield that even Warnock left the ground before the final whistle, leaving assistant Mick Jones to face the press and skipper Mick Heathcote grovelling to the fans in apology.

Those expecting Argyle's annual accounts to bring some much-needed cheer were in for a fall. Despite the revenue generated by the Wembley success, the club made a profit of only £142,544, due mainly to a surplus on transfer fees. Naturally, McCauley had his say, criticising the size of the wage bill and questioning the performance of the commercial department. McCauley's comments again incurred the wrath of Warnock who took the unprecedented step of issuing a statement to the press. It amounted to a damning indictment of his relationship with the chairman. Clearly, resignation was on his mind if matters were not resolved.

Could it get any worse? Well, yes, actually. Midfielder Ronnie Mauge, described by Warnock as 'a likeable rogue' on signing him, lived up to his reputation and found himself remanded in Exeter Prison on charges which, shall we say, were of a serious nature. He was released on bail on the understanding that he only entered Plymouth for training and matches. Warnock took him under his wing, inviting him to live in his Cornish home. In the circumstances it was surprising that he should pick Mauge for the local derby FA Cup-tie with Exeter. Again the match featured live on Sky TV and at last, Argyle came up trumps, winning 4-1.

A rare Auto Windscreens Shield win over Bournemouth was marred by a broken leg for Lee Phillips, who had earlier become the youngest ever player to appear in the Argyle first team.

Having kissed goodbye to hopes of the FA Cup with a home defeat by Peterborough, league results took centre stage. The club could not pull away from the relegation zone. Grobbelaar was now in the midst of his trial, the sordid details of which were headline news. To his credit, he remained faithful to Argyle during this difficult time. On the field it was the Grobbelaar of old, alternating between brilliance, flamboyance and downright eccentricity.

After a disappointing goalless draw with struggling Wycombe, Warnock set a survival target of 50 points. But he would not be around to see if it was achieved. On the Monday he was travelling to watch a non-league match when his mobile phone rang. On the other end was Chief Executive Roger Matthews, who informed him that his services were no longer required. McCauley had deemed him to be in breach of contract by continually criticising the running of the club in the media.

Assistant Mick Jones was handed the task of saving the Pilgrims, with the promise of the job on a permanent basis if he impressed. There was no doubt that the fans would back him, but such was the sense of frustration over the sacking of Warnock that McCauley began receiving death threats.

At least the youth set-up seemed to be heading in the right direction. The club officially opened the Argyle Hotel, which was to be used as a base for the club's youngsters, and announced the development of various soccer academies throughout Devon and Cornwall.

Dreams of another Wembley appearance vanished when Northampton knocked Argyle out of the Auto Windscreens Shield, but it was a nondescript league match at Chesterfield which grabbed the national headlines, as five players were sent off.

Hopes of avoiding relegation took a nosedive with the departure of striker Michael Evans to Southampton, but the temptation of a record incoming fee of £500,000 proved too great. That income was used to reduce Argyle's debts, rather than invest in new players. The transfer deadline saw just one new signing, Simon Collins from Huddersfield for £40,000, whilst local student Steve Perkins was also given a chance.

With the departure of Evans, and Littlejohn still struggling to shoot straight, goals began to dry up. Fortunately, despite the odd Grobbelaar howler, the defence closed ranks and eked out several important draws. Patterson returned from injury, but he had hardly been missed. His deputy, Chris Billy, had won over the fans with some gutsy displays which would see him voted Player of the Year. In the end, the odd point here and there proved important. A win at home to Walsall clinched safety. Jones had done his job.

Despite avoiding relegation, the fans were in no mood to rejoice. The final home game was followed by a small on-pitch demonstration, led by the recently formed 'McCauley Out Action Group'.

The beleaguered squad were treated to an end of season trip to the Gambia, where they secured a 2-1 win over the national team.

Match of the Season 1996-97

Chesterfield 1   Argyle 2

Division 2, 22 February 1997

The infamous happenings which took place during this game made it easy to overlook the importance of the result, but the battling qualities which the side displayed for new manager Mick Jones augured well for the team during the relegation battle ahead.

Jones, in only his third league in charge, chose to recall Bruce Grobbelaar in goal, despite the Zimbabwean international being in the midst of his match-fixing trial.

The Spireites, for their part, were capturing headlines for their FA Cup giant-killing. Having recently defeated Nottingham Forest, they were now through to the last eight and would go on to controversially lose to Middlesbrough in a semi-final replay.

The game was tetchy from the start, and took a turn for the worse from Argyle's point of view when combative Ronnie Mauge was sent off in the 35th minute for a two-footed lunge at Chris Beaumont.

Mauge's dismissal only served to steel Argyle's resolve. After 63 minutes, the impressive Mickey Evans, who was being watched by a Southampton scout, scored with a shot which deflected in off Jamie Hewitt. A few minutes later Mark Saunders made it 2-0 as Hewitt again diverted a shot past Billy Mercer.

Argyle continued to battle for every ball, yet with five minutes remaining Jon Howard pulled one back. Chesterfield poured forward, sensing they could square the game, but with two minutes left on the clock the contest erupted. As Grobbelaar leapt to collect a cross he was felled by an elbow from Darren Carr. With the keeper prostrate, mayhem ensued around him. Tony James remonstrated and, suddenly, seventeen players were sucked into a mass brawl in the goalmouth. Punches, kicks and assorted bear-hugs and strangleholds were exchanged. Referee Richard Poulain eventually restored some order, or so he thought. Richard Logan and Kevin Davies decided to take their own personal skirmish into a second round. By the letter of the law, everyone involved could have been dismissed, but Mr Poulain eventually chose to brandish 'only' four more red cards – to Carr for committing the original challenge, to James for seeking retribution, and to Logan and Davies for their prolonged bout of fisticuffs. It was the first time five players had been dismissed in a Football League game.

Grobbelaar groggily got to his feet, but was concussed. Wisely Mr Poulain blew for full-time 90 seconds later. Argyle's eight remaining men left the pitch with smiles from ear to ear, knowing they had secured a vital three points.

The result helped to eventually secure Jones the manager's job on a permanent basis, but the furore surrounding what became known as the 'Battle of Saltergate' saw both the police and the Football League launch their own investigations. Eventually both clubs escaped with a fine for their collective misdemeanours.

LEAGUE DIVISION 2   **1997-98**
Nationwide Division 2   22nd (relegated)
Coca-Cola Cup   1st round
FA Cup   1st round

Few were under any illusions that the forthcoming campaign would be anything but a struggle. The squad available to Mick Jones looked weaker than the previous season's crew. With a limited budget available, Jones's new recruits – Graham Anthony, non-league striker Padi Wilson, and St Lucian international Earl Jean – were hardly out of the top drawer. Jones also pursued Nottingham Forest striker Steve Guinan, who impressed during a friendly against Sheffield Wednesday, but to no avail.

Jones decided at an early stage that Bruce Grobbelaar carried too much baggage. His Crown Court proceedings had still not been resolved and had gone to a re-trial.

Problems mounted for Jones almost from day one. The club was forced to call off their first friendly at St Blazey after the Football League pointed out that the match was due to be played before the official opening of the season. Teenager Lee Phillips broke his leg for a second time in eight months. Defender Mark Patterson refused to sign a new contract for 'personal reasons', Mark Saunders and Ronnie Mauge were holding out for better deals, and Tony James and Jason Rowbotham were long-term injury victims. Simon Collins also suffered injury in a friendly at Falmouth. Chris Curran was allowed to leave, joining Exeter for £20,000.

Jones was also busy making backroom changes. Kevin Blackwell was promoted from the youth team to be his assistant and, in turn, his place was taken up by a former Pilgrim favourite, Kevin Summerfield. The directors also found a few pennies to finance the position of reserve-team coach, which was given to Gary Clayton. Clayton had made only one appearance the previous season, due to a career-threatening knee injury, and had been among those players released.

The other significant arrival on the playing front was goalkeeper Jon Sheffield, who was signed from Peterborough for an initial fee of £45,000. Sheffield soon found himself overworked. It would be late September before he tasted victory in an Argyle shirt, by which time the Pilgrims had also been emphatically despatched from the Coca-Cola Cup by Oxford.

Of course, there were also the customary off-the-field shenanigans to cope with. By early September, Dan McCauley was apparently threatening not just to sell the club but close it. He brandished plans to build a supermarket on the Home Park site if the City

Council did not renew the lease on the ground, which had only thirteen years to run. If there were any buyers for the club out there, the asking price was a cool £3 million. Former Argyle hero Tommy Tynan emerged as a potential buyer. He threw his hat into the ring by forming a potential consortium under a 'Pilgrims for the People' banner.

Not for the first time, the local *Evening Herald* newspaper expressed its opinion of Mr McCauley's actions. This time he responded by banning the paper not just from the press box, but from the ground completely. The paper's editor, showing great initiative, hired a 50ft crane to hoist its reporter and photographer above the pitch.

By the end of October, Argyle had mustered just a solitary win, leaving themselves next to bottom. Patterson had moved to Gillingham and, in a bid to cut costs, four players – Graham Anthony, James Dungey, Steve Perkins and Chris Leadbitter – were released and four office staff made redundant. Attendances had fallen below 4,000. Several of the remaining faithful were indignant when Devon County Council suddenly issued prohibition notices, forcing the closure of the Lyndhurst and Mayflower stands on safety grounds and insisting on improvements to the Lyndhurst roof and public address system.

This latest farce at least exacted an apology for the inconvenience from McCauley via his programme notes. By now he had chosen to stay clear of Home Park, as he and his wife had been subject to verbal abuse by a section of supporters.

Three successive wins in early November lightened the atmosphere. Individually, several players were performing well. Sheffield was more than an adequate replacement for Grobbelaar, Corazzin – despite frequent trans-Atlantic trips to represent Canada – regularly demonstrated his somersault celebration after scoring, Mark Saunders, like Mauge, had put his contract dispute well and truly behind him, and Martin Barlow was showing some of the best form of his career. It just needed the side to gel as a unit.

The visit of Oldham brought the return of Neil Warnock, who had quickly found employment as the Latics' manager. The former Argyle boss was afforded a tremendous reception and had the last laugh as he led his side to victory. The match saw spectators being asked to sign a 'Save Argyle' petition, which was to be presented to the Football League.

By this time, Argyle's interest in cup competitions had ended for another season. A disappointing replay defeat by lowly Third Division Cambridge had killed the FA Cup dream, and a penalty shoot-out at Northampton had ended Auto Windscreeens hopes.

The end of year shareholders' meeting witnessed a mellower McCauley. Having been re-elected as chairman with 29 votes for, none against, and 30 abstentions, he announced a potential major sponsorship deal for the club with a multinational company. He also announced that his Rotolok company would continue to finance the club until the end of the season. He even lifted the Home Park ban on the local press. He was, however, keen to stress that the club was still on the market and that he intended writing to the Football League to give provisional notice of Argyle's resignation.

The takeover saga soon reached soap opera proportions. The Tynan consortium looked doomed to failure after insufficient finance was raised. Other local businessmen cobbled plans together but there were a lot of words and little action.

Back on the field, victories were so rare that relegation looked a real threat. With only Corazzin to carry the burden of scoring, Argyle were unable to string a run of results together. Draws were now not enough, but wins were all too infrequent. Jones had been frustrated in his attempts to bolster his attack. After enquiring about various players – including Marco Gabbiadini, Leo Fortune-West and Kevin Francis – he attempted to set up a loan deal with Chelsea for their striker Mark Stein, only to be told that the Blues would sell him but not loan him. Weeks later the same player went on loan to Bournemouth in time for him to make his debut against the Pilgrims. Some new faces did eventually find their way to Home Park, but none with the potency of Stein. Phil Starbuck had been in the game for a while, but the remainder – Barry Conlon, Stephen Woods and particularly Darren Currie – while they had potential, could not compensate for the wise old heads that were desperately needed.

Unexpected home wins over high flyers Bristol City and Wrexham brought renewed hopes of safety, but Argyle were undone at Oldham by one Adrian Littlejohn, former star of the Home Park parish. Littlejohn had lost his way with Argyle to such an extent that he was considered dispensable and exchanged for Starbuck.

A home win against Blackpool, achieved despite the expulsion of Jason Rowbotham on the stroke of half-time, again lifted the side out of the bottom four, but the position was incredibly congested at the bottom. With four games remaining, Argyle were only five points behind Oldham, who were in the top half.

A draw at Millwall followed, but luck deserted the Pilgrims in their next home game. They struck the woodwork on three occasions, but Northampton striker Chris Freestone's aim was truer. His hat-trick would mean much biting of nails at Home Park over the closing two weeks of the season.

DID YOU KNOW?

After Tommy Tynan's hat-trick against Stoke in September 1988, the match ball became trapped on the Lyndhurst Stand roof. It was retrieved the following Monday.

On the financial front, there was still no sign of the much-vaunted new sponsor. With the end of the season nigh, McCauley suggested that he might be prepared to sacrifice some of his monopoly shareholding – if a wealthy entrepreneur was prepared to invest – and that he had no intention of abandoning the club.

Argyle's final home game brought a visit from Gillingham, who still harboured play-off ambitions. The match seemed to be heading for a draw when a last-minute Gills goal stunned the Home Park crowd into silence. All now rested on the final game at Burnley, where a 1-2 defeat confirmed the ignominy of relegation.

For Mick Jones, there was a sting in the tail. In the midst of his summer holiday he was advised that the board had decided to terminate his contract. His loyalty to the club, his knowledge of the game, and the respect he had gained from the players, had not been enough. He had paid the ultimate price for relegation.

Match of the Season 1997-98
Burnley 2   Argyle 1

Division 2, 2 May 1998

Argyle's sickening last-gasp defeat against Gillingham had left them filling the final relegation spot. With Burnley drawing their game in hand in midweek, both sides went into this relegation decider on 49 points, but Burnley had the better goal-difference. Brentford had 50 points. There were no other teams in the equation. Southend and Carlisle were already down and the other teams couldn't be caught. In short, Argyle had to win and hope that Brentford would draw at best. With Brentford facing a tough game at play-off seeking Bristol Rovers, Burnley and Argyle would both be going for a win.

Under the charge of former England star Chris Waddle, Burnley had struggled all season. Their early form had made Argyle's start look reasonably impressive, and it was mid-October before they registered their first win. Only the goals of striker Andy Cooke had given them a lifeline. For Argyle, Chris Billy was injured, so Mick Jones shuffled his line-up, recalling the experienced Phil Starbuck.

The do-or-die game attracted the second largest Second Division attendance of the season, with the sizeable Argyle contingent determined not to finish second in the volume stakes.

Despite the obvious tension, the football was pretty good. The Clarets took an early lead, with Cooke heading his nineteenth goal of the season. It did not last long. The tricky Darren Currie wriggled his way down the left and crossed for Mark Saunders to head past the flat-footed Chris Woods and leave several Burnley defenders staring accusingly at each other. The home side launched a ferocious response, hitting the woodwork twice before Cooke was at it again, sneaking in front of Mick Heathcote to guide another header past Sheffield.

As the game moved into the second half, Jones initiated a tactical change as the Pilgrims went all out to save the game and their season. Ronnie Mauge replaced the ineffective Starbuck. Defender Paul Williams and midfielder Martin Barlow were sacrificed for more attacking options.

With the match nearing its conclusion, Burnley were happy to fall back and soak up pressure. That was a dangerous ploy. Substitute Earl Jean sent a twenty-yard shot narrowly over, having been convinced it was on its way in, and then missed another glorious chance when he shot straight at Woods. If only the chance had fallen to the in-form Carlo Corazzin.

The final whistle ended the agony. News filtered through of Brentford's defeat. Burnley were safe. The Pilgrims would have been had they won. Some Argyle players went over to pay tribute to the fans, who had been magnificent throughout. Young defender Paul Wotton, Plymouth through and through, was in tears. He was not the only one.

Despite pleas not to do so, hundreds of jubilant Burnleyites swarmed onto the pitch. Among them were a mindless few who threw missiles at the Green Army. The majority of both sets of supporters good-naturedly exchanged handshakes and scarves.

It was assistant manager Kevin Blackwell, who had never before experienced relegation in his long career, who expressed the feeling of many fans by making a veiled attack on the board, claiming Argyle had been a 'rudderless ship'. Relegation was hardly likely to help team-building. Ten players would be out of contract on 1 July. Many were expected to leave, but it would not be Jones's problem.

LEAGUE DIVISION 3	**1998-99**
Nationwide Division 3	13th
Worthington Cup	1st round
FA Cup	3rd round

Whenever in the past Argyle had invited back former star players – David Kemp and Johnny Hore – to manage the club, the outcome had been tears all round. Paying no heed, the man chosen to succeed Mick Jones was Argyle's all-time record appearance holder, Kevin Hodges. Hodges had transformed the fortunes of Torquay during his spell there, taking them from perennial strugglers to a Wembley play-off, where they had lost to Colchester. Naturally, the Gulls were unhappy at losing both Hodges and Steve McCall, who followed Hodges to Home Park as his assistant following the departure of Kevin Blackwell.

The fact that McCall was still playing – despite his advancing years – was a bonus to Hodges, whose first task was to rebuild the squad after the exodus of out-of-contract players. The main area of concern was the forward line. With Corazzin moving to Northampton and the late-season loan signings not retained, the attack consisted of the diminutive Earl Jean and the inexperienced Lee Phillips, who had again recovered from a broken leg.

Valuable experience had also been lost with the departures of Chris Billy, Paul Williams, Mark Saunders and Richard Logan. Sadly, under the Bosman ruling, that accumulated talent failed to earn a penny for the club. Tony James, who had become the forgotten man of Home Park – having been injured for sixteen months and facing another knee operation – was also allowed to leave. He went to train with Neil Warnock's Bury.

The pre-season friendlies saw a number of players brought in on trial. Some were quickly despatched from whence they came, but a few showed promise. In the end, Hodges mustered a reasonable squad, augmented by the additions of experienced pros such as Lee Power, Paul Gibbs and Chris Hargreaves, together with the untried potential of Richard Flash. A friendly at Saltash brought another setback for Jason Rowbotham, whose injury would keep him out for the season.

Some stability was restored at board level. Dan McCauley was still in the chair, but had recruited three more businessmen with expertise in various fields to boost the number of directors to six.

There was an unusual problem on the agenda during one of the early board meetings. Argyle had changed kit suppliers. The new manufacturers had not only failed to deliver replicas of the new *Evening Herald*-sponsored green and black shirts for the fans to purchase, but had also been unable to supply the 'official' shorts to the first team because 'they were not ready'. The solution was to go to a local sports shop, where 40 pairs of plain black shorts were purchased at £4.50 a pair. The errant kit eventually arrived after Argyle had been forced to wear their bargains in the first two league games.

With another former old boy, Sean McCarthy, signing a three-year contract on the eve of the season, the league campaign began with 37-year-old McCall orchestrating a win over Rochdale. Unable to play because of blistered feet, he was missed as Portsmouth sank the Pilgrims in the first leg of the Worthington Cup.

It wasn't long before three successive wins saw Argyle storm up to third place. Strangely, it was the form away from home that gave most encouragement. Wins at Rotherham, Peterborough and Brighton were countered by failure to beat either Scarborough or bottom of the table Hull at Home Park, despite both sides having men sent off.

October saw the return of a familiar face, when Dwight Marshall came back for his second spell as a Pilgrim. Was he the answer to Argyle's goalscoring problems? None of the other strikers had yet shown an aptitude for bulging the net, with Power being particularly disappointing.

The home match against Brentford saw the late introduction of 16-year-old YTS player Darren Bastow as a substitute. Who? asked most of the fans, as his name was announced, but they did not have to wait long to see that the youngster could play a bit. With one of his first touches, his twenty-yard shot took a deflection and looped over the keeper to seal a 3-0 win. At one point it had looked as though the game might not go ahead. A dispute over stewards' pay was only settled at the last minute and the fans were locked out of the ground until 7pm.

Suddenly, Argyle hit a poor patch. Five straight league losses sent them plummeting towards mid-table. They were also fortunate to scrape through to the second round of the FA Cup, after two goalless draws against non-league Kidderminster resulted in a penalty shoot-out which Argyle won.

Injuries were playing a major part in Hodges' team selection, to the extent that he was forced to name himself among the substitutes for the second round FA Cup-tie at Wycombe. Without surplus funds to buy, he was soon utilising a number of loan signings, with variable success. Craig Taylor, Guy Branston and Howard Forinton were the pick of the bunch, with Forinton soon achieving hero status by scoring in both games against Exeter. The injuries provided openings to other youngsters, such as Jon Beswetherick and

Jon Ashton, whilst Bastow soon proved to be a precocious talent. Eager to protect the youngster, Hodges banned him from talking to the press, but word was soon getting around that Argyle had a real talent on their hands. His development was a tribute to the work done by Kevin Summerfield with the youth squad. Several of his young charges had impressed and looked to be knocking on the door of first-team selection. Some were given their opportunity in an Auto Windscreens Shield tie at Brentford. Hodges' team selection suggested that he was not overly concerned with progressing in the competition, and a 0-2 defeat was unlikely to leave him suffering a sleepless night.

Interest in the FA Cup was maintained with a thrilling home replay victory over Wycombe, as another teenager, Terry Sweeney, scored his first goal for the club on his home debut, sweeping the ball in from 30 yards to set up a money-spinning home tie with Derby County.

By contrast, the league season was threatening to fizzle out. The Plymouth public certainly thought so, as crowds slumped to around 4,000, although the Derby Cup-tie rekindled some interest. Almost 17,000 turned out, hoping for one of the Cup upsets of the day, but it wasn't to be. Jim Smith's men hardly had to extend themselves as they cruised to a 3-0 win.

Hodges remained up-beat, knowing that a good league run would put his side back in the play-off frame. Three straight wins in mid-February proved his point as Argyle moved up to fifth. Hoping to add impetus, he recruited another former favourite, Nicky Marker, on loan. Marker was out of favour at Sheffield United but, having sampled Premiership and European football with Blackburn, he was not short of experience. Regrettably, injuries and age had taken their toll. Marker was largely anonymous and in his four games Argyle failed to win or even score.

Transfer deadline day saw the arrival of two more loan signings. Mark Sale, all 6ft 3in of him, and Steve Guinan were Hodges' final bets to boost Argyle's play-off ambitions, but their debut match at Chester put another dent in those hopes as a 2-3 defeat was compounded by a serious injury to keeper Jon Sheffield. As if things couldn't get worse, Marshall was inadvertently injured by a fan who ran on to celebrate Argyle's opening goal.

Argyle's forwards had struggled to find the net for most of the season, but Guinan ran riot against Scunthorpe, scoring a hat-trick as the Pilgrims rattled up five. The arrival of the new, albeit temporary strike-force, convinced Earl Jean that his future lay elsewhere. He had not helped his cause after storming out of the ground after being substituted against Hartlepool a few weeks earlier.

DID YOU KNOW?

The need for replacement seating in the Lyndhurst Stand was highlighted when a
seat collapsed under the not inconsiderable weight of a policeman.

With seven games remaining, Argyle were on the fringe of the
play-off zone but toothless home defeats by Brighton and particularly Southend left their ambitions in tatters and some fans questioning Hodges' motivational abilities.

Two more goals by Guinan in a win at Swansea had the fans
crying out for him to sign permanent terms. They certainly needed
something to cheer them up after another season of anticlimax. The
mood was not helped by happenings at the final home game. A
faulty fire alarm led to fans being locked out of the ground and the
kick-off delayed by half an hour. Once the match had started, a
stink bomb was tossed into the directors' box. The final whistle saw
the popular Ronnie Mauge engage in a solo lap of honour, seemingly confirming the rumours that he would not be in a green shirt
come August.

Argyle's season drifted to a close. Defeats against the bottom
two clubs in the final matches saw them finish in the lowest position in the club's history.

And what of the new stadium project? It seemed that in this case
no news was bad news.

Match of the Season 1998-99
Carlisle 2   Argyle 1

Division 3, 8 May 1999

The importance of this game for the two sides could not have been
more contrasting. For Argyle it was a meaningless match. Stranded
in mid-table they had little to play for except their pride and, in a
few cases, a new contract. Things were very different for Carlisle.
They were the 92nd club in the league and staring Conference
football in the face. Their cause had hardly been helped by Argyle
going down without a whimper at Scarborough in midweek. That
result had given the Yorkshire side a one-point advantage over the
Cumbrians.

Kevin Hodges fielded a relatively young and inexperienced side,
mainly through necessity, with injuries still ravaging his squad. His
counterpart, Nigel Pearson, had similar problems, borne more out
of financial constraints than injuries. Three weeks earlier, when he
was facing life without a goalkeeper, the Football League had

granted special dispensation to allow Carlisle to borrow Jimmy Glass from Swindon, *after* the transfer deadline had passed.

More than 7,500 crammed into Brunton Park for what was the most important game in Carlisle's history. Argyle may have been on to a hiding to nothing, but they were determined to hold firm.

There was a sickening blow just before half-time. Argyle's peroxide Paul Gibbs, recently named in the PFA's hypothetical divisional team of the year, was left writhing after a crunching collision with Tony Hopper. The crack could be heard around the ground. The unfortunate defender was taken to hospital where a double fracture of the leg was diagnosed.

The Pilgrims seemed undaunted by this setback. Shortly after half-time, Lee Phillips – having his best game in an Argyle shirt – finally broke his scoring duck after a trademark slide-rule pass from home-town 'boy' Steve McCall.

Scarborough were drawing, so Carlisle needed to conjure up two goals from somewhere. Their skipper, David Brightwell, brought the home crowd to life with a 30-yard pile-driver that speared past Dungey.

As the game entered injury-time it was confirmed that Scarborough had gained a point. Many Carlisle fans were already in tears, others couldn't bear to watch the final death-throes. A draw was no good.

Five minutes of injury-time passed. Hearts thumped each time referee Fraser Stretton put his whistle to his lips, but there was one final hope as he awarded Carlisle a corner. Ten blue shirts and the red one of keeper Glass piled forward. Graham Anthony, briefly a Pilgrim, swung the ball over. It was met powerfully by Scott Dobie's head. Dungey did well to parry the effort, but the ball fell at the feet of Glass six yards out. Instinctively, he swung at the ball and sent it into the bottom corner. Pandemonium. Hundreds invaded the pitch. Many more couldn't believe what they had just witnessed.

Eventually the playing area was cleared. Mr Stretton primed the players for a quick dash. Dungey was already on the halfway line as the final whistle sparked another mass invasion.

Carlisle's heroes emerged in the directors' box after a few minutes, hurling boots, shinpads, socks and even shorts to the masses below. The Argyle fans who had made the long trip stayed to witness the remarkable scenes. Their team might have lost, but no one would have missed the occasion.

Glass, the hero, was still being interviewed by the press an hour after the game. He never played for the club again.

LEAGUE DIVISION 3   **1999-2000**
Nationwide Division 3   12th
Worthington Cup   1st round
FA Cup   4th round

Having used no fewer than 35 players the previous season, Hodges was craving for stability in his side, which might encourage the consistency needed to mount a realistic promotion challenge.

A few of the younger players had the benefit of some experience behind them and would play an important role during the coming season. Jon Beswetherick would be needed to replace Paul Gibbs, who faced most of the season on the sidelines after his broken leg at Carlisle. Jon Ashton had shown promise and, of course, great things were expected of Darren Bastow, provided Argyle could hold on to him.

Several familiar faces were missing as the players reported for pre-season training. Ronnie Mauge had left as expected and moved to Bristol Rovers, Dwight Marshall and Simon Collins were also gone, and there was no Richard Flash, who had been advised to quit the game following his injury the previous season.

New faces had taken their place. Paul McGregor, who had briefly hit the highlights with Nottingham Forest when scoring in a UEFA Cup-tie against Lyon in 1995, promised to make his mark, both on the field and in the flamboyant fashion stakes. Wayne O'Sullivan, experienced keeper Kenny Veysey and the regal sounding Barrington Belgrave also arrived on free transfers. Chris Leadbitter returned for a second spell from Torquay and young Ian Stonebridge, formerly on Tottenham's books, was given a chance to resurrect his career. But there was no Steve Guinan. The striker who made such an impression at the back end of the last campaign had chosen to fight for his place at Forest.

The highlight of pre-season was a testimonial for long-serving Martin Barlow. Fulham provided the opposition, but Barlow himself was only able to take the kick-off before being substituted. A groin injury had recently required surgery, which was likely to keep him out for several weeks.

The league season began with defeat at Southend and an uncharacteristic dismissal for skipper Mick Heathcote. Poor home form saw a slide towards the nether reaches of the table, and there were mixed fortunes for the strikers. Paul McGregor displayed plenty of skill but desperately needed a goal to boost his confidence. Martin Gritton, having been given a second chance following his university studies, showed flashes of style, and Stonebridge, unknown at the start of the season, earned rave reviews and scored a few goals.

With just six league games under his belt, he was selected for the England Under-18 squad, with whom he went on to win four caps, scoring twice.

Twin 1-4 defeats by Walsall ensured that Argyle failed to progress beyond the first round of the League Cup, under its different guises, for the seventh successive season. Those defeats prompted Hodges to strengthen his defence with the signing of Craig Taylor from Swindon for £30,000. Taylor had impressed during a short loan spell the previous season.

A 5-0 trouncing of Orient sparked a run of results which saw a steady rise through the table. Bastow, disappointing in early games with the weight of expectation on his shoulders, rediscovered some form after spending a week with Derby, and McGregor was beginning to turn on the style, having finally got a goal under his belt. Two goals from McGregor sealed an FA Cup replay win over Brentford, and he then turned on the style for the visit of table-toppers Barnet. The Sunday match saw Argyle in dazzling mood, with Beswetherick rampant on the overlap, and McGregor scoring a stunning hat-trick.

McGregor's contribution was badly missed as Argyle paid their first ever visit to league newcomers Cheltenham. The home side's officials were taken aback at the size of the Argyle following and delayed the kick-off by fifteen minutes, but the outcome was a 0-2 defeat on what would become a new Argyle bogey ground.

The FA Cup provided the main source of excitement. The second round brought another visit from Brighton. The earlier league match between the two sides had been an X-rated but thrilling affair, with the Seagulls' prolific striker, Darren Freeman, throwing his shirt angrily into the crowd after being substituted. The Cup-tie didn't produce any goals, but the tackles were soon flying in thick and fast, and Freeman and team-mate Danny Cullip were both red-carded.

The replay saw Argyle installed as underdogs, but a 25-yard rocket from Chris Hargreaves carried Argyle through to a third round tie at Reading. Argyle were again in new surroundings, with a first visit to the impressive Madejski Stadium. Hargreaves produced another thumping goal to take the Second Division strugglers back to Home Park, where Mick Heathcote's long legs came in handy as he poked home the winner two minutes from time.

Home Park attendances had again been generally disappointing, but the Boxing Day league fixture against Torquay drew a surprisingly healthy crowd of almost 15,000. The Gulls were enjoying their best season for some time and were currently top dogs in Devon. A battling draw ensured Argyle remained beneath them in the table but Torquay would return in January to knock Argyle out of the Auto Windscreens Shield.

Perhaps it was symbolic that the final match of the 1990s, at Swansea, ended in defeat. It had been one of the most turbulent decades in the club's history, with a few high spots but too many low ones, with internal wranglings, poor performances and supporter unrest dominating the headlines.

For some months the club had not been plagued by off-field problems. That changed when young starlet Bastow was axed from the side for disciplinary reasons. Details were kept under wraps but the club confirmed that as a result on his misdemeanours he might not play for some time.

The fourth round FA Cup draw paired Argyle with Preston. Only two years previously the sides had been rivals in Division Two, but their paths had subsequently taken different directions. Under David Moyes, Preston were now on the verge of Premiership football. Two own-goals and a penalty hardly helped Argyle's cause as North End cruised through. They were by far the most impressive side to visit Home Park that season.

With Argyle once again treading water in mid-table, the fans grew restive at the lack of investment in new players. Craig Middleton arrived on loan from Cardiff and scored a couple of useful goals, but the purse strings were being tightly held and there was a feeling that this would be another season of obscurity. With McCall and Leadbitter regular visitors to the treatment room, and Barlow's injury taking longer than expected to heal, the midfield positions caused Hodges a few headaches. Defender Paul Wotton was drafted into the middle of the park and did well enough, but the side was lacking a creative spark.

Reading, having been impressed with Beswetherick during the Cup encounters, tabled a bid of £150,000 for the defender. As much as it must have been tempting, Argyle resisted it.

A personal highlight for veteran Sean McCarthy arrived during the match against York. Since returning to Home Park he had been bedevilled by various injuries and had waited a long time to notch the 200th goal of his career. But at last he reached that milestone.

Barlow finally returned to action in early March but his comeback lasted just 23 minutes as another injury ended a disastrous season for him.

For no obvious reason, Argyle were a different proposition when they played away. At Home Park, they were unbeaten, although too many points had been dropped through a glut of draws, but their away results were as bad as any in the division. At Torquay, however, McGregor was at his imperious best, illuminating Argyle's

4-0 win. By this time, Steve Guinan – the player most fans had hoped to see in a Pilgrims shirt at the beginning of the season – was back, after being sacked by Cambridge.

A rare but majestic goal from Jason Rowbotham clinched a home win over Northampton but that four-goal win at Plainmoor proved to be a flash in the pan. Heavy defeats at Macclesfield and Orient dashed any lingering hopes of making the play-offs, and the final home game mirrored that of twelve months earlier, with an evident lack of commitment on display. This time, Hull came to Home Park and finally ended Argyle's unbeaten home run.

The final match, at Mansfield, saw Guinan finally get off the mark. Twelfth place represented only a marginal improvement on the previous season. The fans' patience was wearing thin and time was running out for Hodges.

Match of the Season 1999-2000
Torquay 0   Argyle 4

Division 3, 25 March 2000

This was a vital match for both sides. Argyle were keen to turn around their woeful away form to maintain a push for the play-offs. Torquay, under Wes Saunders, had been having one of their best seasons for many a while, and still harboured play-off ambitions themselves.

No one was more desperate for success than Pilgrims boss Kevin Hodges, for he also used to manage Torquay. As usual, he chopped and changed his line-up, giving loan signing Craig Etherington his Argyle debut and including the returning Steve Guinan. Jason Rowbotham also returned to the side, as sweeper.

The Plainmoor terraces were dominated by green but the majority of Argyle fans massed at one end soon received a good soaking, for the kick-off was greeted by a hailstorm. The deluge did little to help the already saturated playing surface either, and disrupted the early exchanges.

The home side received an early blow when leading scorer Tony Bedeau was stretchered off with ankle ligament damage after falling awkwardly. Two minutes later Argyle took the lead. Stand-in skipper Craig Taylor found himself unmarked to head in a Beswetherick cross.

'Bezzie' was causing problems with his rampaging runs down the left flank, and it was he who also set up the second goal when United keeper Stuart Jones crucially hesitated over a cross and the fleet-footed Paul McGregor nipped in to make it 2-0.

DID YOU KNOW?

Former Argyle boss Mick Jones was sacked as manager of Peterborough United
after just 12 days of the 1989-90 season.

The Gulls enjoyed a dominant ten-minute spell in the second half, but this was a day when each Pilgrim seemed on top of his game. Taylor and Barrett were solid at the back, Hargreaves was having one of his best matches for the club, and the new front combination of McGregor and Guinan were displaying an understanding born from their days at Nottingham Forest.

A sweeping move led to number three, as McGregor was presented with an open goal. Eight minutes later, he completed his second hat-trick of the season, cheekily 'nutmegging' Jones.

A minute later, both McGregor and Guinan were substituted, allowing them to take the plaudits from the Green Army. Even some of the home fans joined in the applause, and the match sponsors broke with tradition by awarding McGregor the man of the match award rather than a home player.

Perhaps taken aback by the novelty of an Argyle win away from home, the authorities selected three Pilgrims – Barrett, Jon Sheffield and Sean McCarthy – for random drug tests after the match. McGregor left clutching the match ball and exclaiming his delight at moving closer to taking £100 off his manager. Hodges had wagered that, as he had failed to score before mid-October, he would not reach fifteen for the season. McGregor won his bet, grabbing sixteen in league and League Cup.

Unlike Argyle, Torquay did not fade. It required a last-day home defeat by Northampton to stop them from reaching the play-offs. For the first time in many years, they finished 'top dogs' in Devon.

LEAGUE DIVISION 3   **2000-01**
Nationwide Division 3   12th
Worthington Cup   1st round
FA Cup   1st round

With no fewer than seventeen players out of contract, Kevin Hodges knew he was in for a busy summer of negotiation. He also knew that another mediocre start would signal the end of his tenure. Two mid-table seasons were not what the supporters wanted or expected, but the mega-budgets of the Shilton and Warnock eras were gone and Hodges had been forced to work within strict financial constraints.

Yet again, under freedom of contract rules, Argyle had waved goodbye to players without recouping any fees. Jason Rowbotham, Jon Ashton and Barrington Belgrave had all been released. Chris Hargreaves had gone to Northampton and Paul Gibbs to Brentford. The career of Darren Bastow also seemed to have been cut short. He had gone AWOL since his problems of last season and appeared uninterested in pursuing a career that might have carried him a long way.

The new players signed by Hodges seemed of good pedigree. Terry Fleming had recently captained Lincoln, and Jason Peake brought with him bags of experience. Reserve keeper John Hodges was recruited from Leicester to put pressure on Jon Sheffield.

Hodges set a tough test for his charges pre-season. After Argyle had disposed of Charlton, fellow Premiership sides West Ham and Everton both visited Home Park. The rare opportunity to watch such star names as Paolo di Canio and Paul Gascoigne attracted five figure crowds to both matches, giving an early and much needed boost to the Argyle coffers.

The Everton match saw the first appearance of another new face. Martin Phillips was predicted by his then Exeter manager, Alan Ball, to become 'Britain's first £10 million player'. Things hadn't quite gone according to plan, allowing Argyle to sign the winger from Portsmouth for £25,000. Phillips was, nevertheless, a tricky customer, likely to cause problems for Third Division defenders.

Home Park had become something of a fortress during the previous campaign but any hopes of another long unbeaten home run ended on the opening day, when Orient defeated an Argyle side bereft of the injured Heathcote, Gritton and Leadbitter, and the suspended Taylor and McGregor.

After an encouraging draw at promotion favourites Hull, the traditional exit from the Worthington Cup followed, administered on this occasion by Bristol Rovers.

By mid-September, Britain was in the grip of a sudden fuel crisis, but Argyle were having a crisis of their own. A 1-4 defeat at Shrewsbury left them in the bottom three and without three central defenders. With Heathcote still injured, Taylor was stretchered off and Barrett dismissed. Hodges, still denied transfer funds, brought in former Welsh international Paul Mardon, who hadn't played a first-team game for seventeen months, on loan.

By now, the pressure was mounting on Hodges. Two of his new signings, Peake and Fleming, had shown no form at all, and the overall standard of football was inexcusable. Attendances were some of the lowest in the club's history. The fans and, perhaps more importantly, the chairman, were losing patience.

A 2-5 humiliation at Cheltenham left Hodges on the brink. What he needed most was a convincing victory over Barnet in the next home game, but the jeers and boos which rang out around Home Park as the final whistle blew told its own story. Another home defeat, the fourth in competitive matches this season, blew the final whistle on Hodges.

It was difficult not to feel sorry for the man. Hodges had been a popular and loyal servant as a player but management was a different ball game. He had worked under difficult circumstances but in the end he had to go. Perhaps, as many had said, he was too nice a figure to succeed in such a cut-throat game. He accepted his dismissal with grace and wished the club good luck.

With assistant Steve McCall, also leaving, youth team manager Kevin Summerfield was temporarily handed the reins. He had a burgeoning reputation as a coach and would be considered a front runner for the job if results improved.

His first match in charge could not have been more onerous – a trip to runaway leaders Chesterfield, who had won eight of their first ten games. Summerfield dropped Peake and Fleming and welcomed back the fit-again Heathcote. Argyle lost 1-2 but earned praise for their performance.

Two successive wins followed, doing Summerfield's cause no harm. There was also a noticeable upturn in the form of Paul McGregor, who until recently had been a shadow of himself.

Despite Summerfield's claim to the manager's job, McCauley let it be known that he favoured an experienced hand on the tiller, with Carlisle boss Ian Atkins his personal choice. Another unlikely name was mentioned – former Scottish international Paul Sturrock, who had previously managed St Johnstone and Dundee United, where he had made his name. His availability was brought to the board's attention by former Argyle player David Byrne, who had known Sturrock from his own time in Scottish football.

DID YOU KNOW?

In August 1987, having missed Argyle score at Reading on the stroke of half-time, manager Dave Smith remained unaware of the fact until after the final whistle.

Six candidates, including Paul Sturrock, were interviewed at McCauley's Rotolok factory. On the last day of October, after much discussion by the board, Sturrock was revealed as the new man at the helm.

Summerfield took charge for the final time in the local derby at Torquay, with Sturrock watching from the directors' box. A draw left Argyle in twentieth position and Sturrock under no illusions over the size of the task in hand. One of his first engagements was to address the shareholders' AGM. He promised to leave fans with a 'nice taste for next season' but also warned of 'dark and grumpy days to come'.

One thing he could not control was the weather. A particularly wet autumn caused various postponements and it would be eighteen days before he would take charge of the side. A late Peake goal saved Argyle from embarrassment at non-league Chester in the FA Cup. More rain led to more postponements and did little to help the saturated Home Park pitch. A problem with the drainage was identified, and despite many hours of work by the ground-staff the playing surface was the worst for many a year.

Sturrock's first game in charge at Home Park was not one to remember. Chester returned in the FA Cup replay and stunned the Pilgrims with an extra-time winner. It was only the second occasion that a non-league side had beaten the Pilgrims, and the first at Home Park. It was, in theory, the worst defeat ever for the club.

Sturrock soon showed that he was his own man. He seemingly had the backing of the board, something Hodges had not enjoyed. At Exeter, Sturrock unveiled new signings David Worrell, Brian McGlinchey and Frenchman David Friio, with another Frenchman, goalkeeper Romain Larrieu, watching from the stands. Out went Kevin Nancekivell, who had been given a taste at league football at the age of 29, youngster Jamie Morrison-Hill, and the popular Adam Barrett, who signed for Mansfield.

Larrieu was handed his debut in an LDV Vans Trophy match with Bristol City at Home Park. 'Typical foreign goalkeeper,' was muttered more than once by the spartan band of spectators, as Larrieu did his best to make a hash of every cross that came his way. But he kept a clean sheet in a 3-0 win and pulled off a couple of late saves which suggested that he had played in goal before, after all.

A second abortive trip to Rochdale followed. 'What a waste of life,' was Paul McGregor's reaction as the coach pulled into Home Park after yet another trip to Lancashire had revealed the Spotland ground in a worst condition than Home Park.

Sturrock's rebuilding gathered momentum. More players arrived on loan or short-term contracts, whilst former favourite Mickey Evans re-signed from Bristol Rovers in a £30,000 deal. But there was heartache for a few. The under-performing Peake and Fleming were allowed to leave, and Martin Barlow was told that he had no future at Home Park. Sturrock's strategy became clear. He was building for the future, a point made by the board when he was appointed. The cull continued. Lee Phillips, Sheffield and the seemingly uninterested Paul McGregor were all told they could leave.

The position of assistant manager also needed resolving. For a while it seemed that Sturrock's former sidekick, John Blackley, would also venture south. In the end it didn't happen and Sturrock was more than happy to appoint Summerfield, with whom he had quickly built a good working relationship. Another new signing was Sean Evers from Reading. Two years earlier he had been valued at £500,000. Sturrock singled him out as the man he would build his midfield around.

Another problem which Sturrock needed to address was that of player discipline, or rather indiscipline. Several sendings off had given the club one of the worst records in the league.

As the end of the season approached, a few of the more optimistic supporters still clung to the hope of a play-off position. Sturrock later admitted that he was happy that the team failed on that score. He needed time to fully assess his players and take stock.

Not that his plans all went according to the book. Craig Taylor broke an ankle against Southend towards the end of the season, and Player of the Year Wayne O'Sullivan announced that he was starting afresh in Australia. Both players had figured in Sturrock's thoughts for the following season.

In the final analysis, Argyle finished in twelfth position, identical to the previous year. Had Sturrock made the impression expected of him? Only time would tell.

Match of the Season 2000-01

Argyle 3   Chesterfield 0

Division 3, 10 March 2001

The visit of league leaders Chesterfield had been eagerly awaited. It would be a measure of the progress Argyle had made under Paul

Sturrock. The Spireites had been the runaway leaders of the division, having lost only twice in the league. Save for one week after a defeat by Barnet, they had not relinquished top spot since day one. Whether they would be promoted or not was another question. News of serious financial irregularities had filtered out of Saltergate. The Football League were investigating and if found guilty severe punishment could be meted out. Docking of points, denial of promotion, and even expulsion from the league had been mentioned.

Spice to the occasion was added by the fact that the visitors were managed by Argyle old boy Nicky Law. The former curly haired central defender, now completely shorn, was afforded the usual hostile reception reserved for returning ex-Pilgrims.

Despite their league dominance, the Spireites had no real stars in their team, but they had been rumoured to have been splashing out mega-bucks in wages to attract the right players. In Mike Pollitt, they possessed one of the best keepers in the lower divisions, and striker Luke Beckett would need close watching.

The turnover of players at Home Park showed no signs of slackening, with Stuart Elliott making his debut at full-back in place of David Worrell, victim of a broken ankle. Elliott had the air of a naughty schoolboy, and had lived up to that earlier in the season when he was sent off against the Pilgrims whilst still a Darlington player. On the bench was another new boy, Sean Evers, recipient of a big build up by Sturrock, who claimed Evers would be an integral part of Argyle's future.

A crowd of less than 5,500 was disappointing, but those who turned up saw a promising opening by Argyle, crowned by a David Friio header in the twentieth minute. The Frenchman was on a short-term contract but had quickly become the darling of the Home Park faithful. With his Gallic colleague, Romain Larrieu, in the Argyle goal also improving with every game, everyone was hoping that the pair would be quickly tied on longer deals.

A superb double save from Larrieu proved the turning point of the game. Chesterfield had looked threatening but, when Martin Phillips scored his first Argyle goal, their challenge subsided. Old warhorse Sean McCarthy, preferred to Ian Stonebridge in attack, justified his inclusion with the third goal, turning in a cross from substitute Michael Meaker from close range.

The victory gave credence to Sturrock's claim that on their day Argyle could match any side in the division. Faced with other distractions, Chesterfield crumbled, winning only two more games. The 'punishment' for their financial misdemeanours was the docking of nine points, but they still had sufficient to gain promotion.

LEAGUE DIVISION 3   **2001-02**
Nationwide Division 3   1st (champions)
Worthington Cup   1st round
FA Cup   2nd round

Paul Sturrock's homework was finished. It was exam time. Certainly the players were left in no doubt of his determination as they departed for their summer holidays with the promise of the hardest pre-season they had ever experienced.

The final 'victim' of Sturrock's new broom was Sean McCarthy. Ever more prone to injury and disciplinary problems, he did not figure in the manager's plans and found a new home up the road at Exeter. Two more players were added to the squad. Graham Coughlan had captained Livingston to two successive Scottish divisional titles but was strangely not considered good enough to mix it in the Scottish Premier League. Sturrock knew of his qualities. His free transfer would turn out to be the bargain of the season. Lee Hodges also arrived. Argyle fans with good memories will have remembered him as a fresh-faced youngster who arrived on loan from Tottenham in February 1993. Since then Hodges had drifted around the lower leagues and was now out on a limb.

Since the end of the previous season, there was the promise that work on the new stadium would start in earnest. Barr Construction had successfully tendered and were waiting for the nod. The word was that work would start as soon as the season was over, but summer drifted on without a bulldozer chugging into life. The deal hinged on the granting of a new lease on Home Park by the City Council, who were also heavily involved in funding the project. New stadium plans had been in the pipeline for years but nothing had come this close. Dan McCauley took a huge gamble, shelling out £500,000 to get the work started. Once that happened the consequences of the deal not being completed didn't bear thinking about. Fortunately, within days, contracts were signed and a new 125-year lease granted.

Phase one commenced, involving the demolition and rebuilding of three sides of the ground. Phase two, to be started at later date, would see the Grandstand side and offices rebuilt.

McCauley's gamble would be the last significant move of his turbulent and controversial reign as club chairman. On the eve of the season, news broke that he was prepared to sell his shares to a new five-man consortium, headed by director Paul Stapleton, who would become the new chairman. Also appointed to the board was 88-year-old Michael Foot, former leader of the Labour Party and a lifelong Argyle fan. McCauley would remain on the board with an equal shareholding until the liabilities to the bank and his company, Rotolok were repaid. Many supporters rejoiced at his reduced power base. There was no doubt that some of his actions had divided opinion, but in the cold light of day the fact remains that without him there may not have been a Plymouth Argyle Football club to support, and for that he deserves praise, not censure. Certainly, McCauley had been the catalyst for the new stadium.

The new stadium would accompany a season to remember. One player who would not figure in Sturrock's plans was Steve Guinan. The striker had been cast into the wilderness and was forced to train with the youth team. The pre-season build up included a trip back to Sturrock's homeland, where the Greens played four friendlies. Another pre-season fixture involved a testimonial for Mick Heathcote against Premiership Sunderland, one of his former clubs. Heathcote had been a stalwart of the Argyle defence for several seasons and no one begrudged him such an accolade, but the match prompted the first controversy of the new season. The game proved to be Heathcote's last in a green shirt. Having missed much of the previous campaign through injury, Sturrock had given him the pre-season to prove his fitness. Heathcote had come through several games and was subsequently offered a twelve-month deal. But 'Hector' felt he deserved an extra year and when Shrewsbury manager Kevin Ratcliffe came on the phone offering what he wanted, he was off for his second spell as a Shrew.

Ironically, Argyle's first league game was at home to Shrewsbury. Heathcote received a mixed reception. A minority believed he had taken the money and ran. Most, however, appreciated his contribution to Argyle and his need to give himself and his young family a regular wage for another year.

It was Heathcote who had the last laugh. Ratcliffe's side, one of the favourites for relegation, left with all three points despite playing more than half the match a man short. Further defeats followed, and Argyle soon found themselves in the bottom three and, yet again, dumped from the Worthington Cup at the first hurdle, despite an impressive showing at First Division Watford. It was not the start anyone had envisaged.

The lack of atmosphere at Home Park was mooted as a possible cause for the poor early form. The appearance of the stadium was changing by the day, and even on non-match days fans were arriving to pay their last respects to their favourite viewing spot. Spectators were restricted to one side of the ground and the capacity cut, temporarily to 7,500. The Devonport End, Lyndhurst Road side, and Barn Park End were populated only by a few orange-helmeted construction workers cum ball-boys. Two of the floodlight pylons had also been demolished and temporary lighting installed. With the tree-lined Central Park in the background, it was easy to imagine how the ground must have looked 80 years earlier.

Arguably, the turning point of Argyle's season came on virgin territory at Rushden and Diamonds. A splendid fight-back from two down lifted morale. From then on there was no looking back.

In the space of ten days, Argyle won two Devon derbies away from home, the win at Exeter made even more pleasurable by Ian Stonebridge's last-gasp winner. The result proved to be the end of the road for Grecians boss Noel Blake, just as it had a week earlier for Swansea manager John Hollins, following defeat at Home Park. Argyle's inspired form was proving an execution ground for opposing managers.

There was more good news. After protracted negotiations, a work permit was granted for dreadlocked Canadian international Jason Bent, a player Sturrock had admired for some time.

With Luton's Joe Kinnear adding spice to the race for the title with some inflammatory pre-match remarks, a deeply satisfying win over the Hatters' saw fourth place gained to complete an unbeaten September. There was little to mull over for the manager of the month panel. At the same time, Sturrock junior – Blair – moved south to try his luck. The decision over his future would rest with the coaching staff, not his father, who vowed to treat him like any other player.

A second successive manager of the month award followed as Argyle refused to be beaten. Mediocre teams that previous Argyle sides would have struggled to overcome were now despatched without mercy. A club record run of nineteen unbeaten matches included a first round FA Cup victory over a brave Whitby Town. Argyle had chosen to make the long journey north by plane and were back home in time to witness the second round draw – and the debut of another Scottish import, Marino Keith – on Match of the Day. After cruising to a 3-0 lead in the replay, despite the first-half dismissal of Mickey Evans, Argyle's defence went to sleep and allowed Whitby not one but two moments of glory.

The long unbeaten run was finally ended in a second round FA Cup replay at Bristol Rovers, who had belied their lowly league position with a gutsy display at Home Park in the first encounter.

Argyle continued to head the table week in, week out. In normal circumstances such form would have seen them romp away with the championship by a country mile, but Kinnear's Hatters refused to get off their backs.

Neil Heaney, a player who had briefly tasted the good life with Arsenal and Southampton, was brought in from Dundee United but lacked match fitness. Meanwhile, Sturrock junior was trying his best to keep dad happy by regularly coming off the bench to set up vital goals.

The Boxing Day match against Torquay saw the opening of the two ends of the revamped Home Park, which filled rapidly with a crowd of over 13,000. The occasion motivated the lowly Gulls as much as Argyle, and the match ended 2-2.

The home game with Scunthorpe saw Argyle suffer their one major injury blow of the season when Brian McGlinchey hobbled off with what transpired to be a broken ankle. The doughty Irishman had personified Argyle's resolute defence, but would now miss the rest of the season. Happily, Jon Beswetherick returned, his confidence restored after he had taken a first-half mauling at Exeter.

The following home game against Oxford saw the opening of the Lyndhurst side, thus raising the capacity to over 20,000. Although only 8,000 people were in the ground, it looked an impressive sight. Chairman Paul Stapleton came on the pitch before the start to pay tribute to the contribution of his predecessor, Dan McCauley. For once, the often vilified McCauley was roundly applauded.

The Pilgrims continued on their merry way. Sturrock, with another manager of the month award to his name, refused to talk about the 'p' word, but promotion was as good as certain. It was finally clinched with yet another away win, this time at Rochdale. The aim now was the title.

Luton, however were still breathing down Argyle's necks, and a defeat at Hartlepool and a home draw with Southend saw the Pilgrims relinquish top spot for the first time since October. On the same day, Luton won their twelfth match in a row and were banging in goals left, right and centre.

The key was Argyle's game in hand, but they faced two tough matches in the north in the space of three days. A win at Carlisle was followed by the news that Luton had amazingly only drawn at home to Macclesfield. The initiative was back with the Greens. A Monday night at Darlington was not the most salubrious surroundings in which to clinch a championship, but who cared. Argyle had won a title for the first time since 1959.

The final home game saw young and old turn out for party time. The new Home Park was near capacity. The visitors, Cheltenham, needed a win themselves to clinch promotion but Sturrock demanded the professionalism that his side had displayed all season. A 2-0 win prompted wild celebrations as the trophy was presented to captain Paul Wotton.

Every player was cheered to the rafters as they lifted the trophy in turn. Keeper Larrieu had grown in stature with every game and had proudly kept an improbable 27 clean sheets during the season. Now he was talked about as a £1 million player. The defence had been the key to the success. Only 28 goals had been conceded all season. The central defenders, Coughlan and Wotton, had been outstanding and Coughlan had also finished as top scorer to boot, clinching every player of the year award going. Another significant factor was that both players had avoided suspension. Bent, once fit, had shown flashes of why Sturrock rated him so highly. Marino Keith had seized his chance with some stunning goals during the run in. Lee Hodges had been an unsung hero but a vital cog in the Argyle machine. David Friio had dominated midfield battles and, along with Larrieu, Coughlan and Wotton, were chosen by their fellow professionals for the hypothetical PFA Select side. But the biggest cheer was reserved for the management team of Kevin Summerfield and Paul Sturrock. Was Sturrock the best manager Argyle had ever had? At that moment he was. Earlier in the season the directors had revealed their five-year plan for the club with the objective of First Division football. That might have seemed mere words to some, but the board and the manager evidently believed them.

The following day saw the traditional open top bus ride and civic reception. Thousands lined the streets. Long-suffering fans suddenly had new hope to go with their new ground.

Match of the Season 2001-02

Argyle 2   Luton 1

Division 3, 29 September 2001

Luton manager Joe Kinnear had been in more than ebullient mood during the build up to the game. After all, a man who had been in charge of Wimbledon's infamous 'Crazy Gang' was hardly likely to be the shy and retiring type, but his comments were to inadvertently provide the catalyst for Argyle's drive for the Third Division championship.

The Hatters came to Home Park as leaders. According to Kinnear, it was not just the Home Park stadium that would be one-sided. His players shared his confidence. 'I don't think there will be too many problems in us beating Plymouth,' predicted striker Steve Howard.

Sturrock made a tactical change for the occasion, bringing in Jason Bent for his full debut, partly to curb the left-sided menace of Frenchman Jean-Louis Valois, supposedly one of the best players in the Third Division.

DID YOU KNOW?

When a team loses its first two home games, it is likely they will get relegated. This happened to Argyle in 2001-02 but they were subsequently crowned champions.

Kinnear's chest puffed a little larger as Dean Crowe gave his side a fourteenth-minute lead. It was perhaps inevitable that the diminutive striker would score. He had, very briefly, been a Pilgrim and had come on as a substitute in Argyle's opening game when on loan from Stoke, but within days had returned north, citing 'family problems'.

Within seven minutes, Martin Phillips had levelled. With referee Andy Hall seeing things that 5,700 others hadn't, the game threatened to boil over. According to Mr Hall, Mickey Evans elbowed Chris Coyne and was accordingly sent off. Evans protested his innocence to no avail, although he would later have the decision rescinded on appeal. With the referee also giving an airing to his yellow card on six occasions in the first half alone, it seemed inevitable that its red counterpart would get at least one more dose of daylight before the afternoon was out.

With Evans out of the equation, Argyle regrouped, leaving Stonebridge as the lone striker, a formation regularly used in away matches. In first-half stoppage time, Friio stooped to head in Wotton's corner to put the ten men ahead.

The second half typified the resolute defence which would guide Argyle through the season. Valois fired a free-kick against the crossbar but was otherwise anonymous, and was substituted near the end. The Hatters ran out of ideas and Mr Hall's cards remained in his pocket. The loss of three points saw Luton also lose top spot and drop to third, with Argyle one place below.

The defeat did nothing to quieten Kinnear. At his post-match press conference, further derogatory remarks about his opponents inflamed the situation. One such comment described Argyle defender Graham Coughlan as a 'Joe Soap centre-half'. A few months later, when Coughlan clutched an armful of awards, the player could no longer resist a dig at Kinnear's expense. 'Not bad for a Joe Soap,' he pointedly remarked.

Paul Sturrock later revealed that Kinnear's comments had done his team-talk for him that day. Kinnear's pre-match comments, pinned to the Argyle dressing-room wall, provided the perfect motivation, not only for that one game, but the whole season.

The same could certainly be said for the Green Army. Of all the Home Park terrace chants over the season, 'Are you watching Joe Kinnear?' had more airplay than most.

Carlo Corazzin (centre) sees red at Bristol Rovers, in the first game of 1997-98

Paul McGregor with the match-ball after his hat-trick at Torquay, March 2000

The Lyndhurst Side under water as a result of drainage problems during 2000-01

Inside the Rochdale dressing room as Argyle clinch promotion with a 3-1 win

Cheltenham have been beaten and Argyle celebrate the Division Three trophy

Skipper Paul Wotton holds aloft the Division Three championship trophy, April 2002

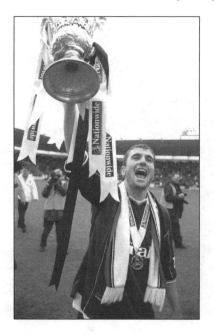

Demolition of the Devonport End as Argyle implement plans to rebuild Home Park

Four Argyle managers – Neil Dougall, Bobby Saxton, Paul Sturrock, Johnny Hore

The author, Andy Riddle, gets his hands on the Division Three trophy

Argyle mascot Pilgrim Pete with Sophie Riddle, the author's daughter

Chapter Seven

Chasing the Dream
2002-2008

LEAGUE DIVISION 2	**2002-03**
Nationwide Division 2	8th
Carling Cup	1st round
FA Cup	3rd round

On the back of such a dominant season, Paul Sturrock was understandably content to rely on many of the same squad for the forthcoming campaign, adding just three foot-soldiers – winger David Beresford, striker Nathan Lowndes, and centre-half Stuart Malcolm. The latter pair were a gamble, both having hogged the treatment room for long periods at their previous clubs. Jon Beswetherick had joined Sheffield Wednesday, and there seemed no future for striker Martin Gritton, who was interesting Torquay, or the much-vaunted Sean Evers who, given Sturrock's public admiration for his ability, will probably rank as the Scotsman's worst acquisition. Success was also a big factor in ensuring that some of the more influential and talented players, such as Friio and Larrieu – who had been attracting attention from bigger clubs – did not see their futures elsewhere. Home Park was a good place to be.

It was not unreasonable to hope that the momentum of the previous campaign could continue. Argyle were tipped as dark horses for another tilt at the title, the bookies making them third favourites behind Wigan and Cardiff. Sturrock was, as ever, cautious in his optimism, suggesting that many other sides had steamrollered their way through one division only to find life on the next rung a little wobblier.

Pre-season revolved around another trip to Scotland. With Lowndes looking impressive, three wins from four games provided the necessary confidence boost, although reality quickly hit home when an attractive fixture against Premiership Charlton resulted in a 5-1 win for Alan Curbishley's men.

Some pride was restored with a 2-2 draw at home to Nottingham Forest but Mickey Evans suffered a suspected fractured cheekbone, necessitating an operation, although the wonders of modern medicine would see him fit for the opening league encounter.

There was action off the field as well. The new 'Pilgrims Way' wall was unveiled, comprising over 1,600 bricks, each containing messages which supporters had paid for. The club had the use of a new team coach and had also been successful in gaining admission to the Avon Insurance Combination League, meaning some more competitive fixtures for the reserve side, and hopefully bridging the ever widening gap between the standard of first and second-team football. Chairman Paul Stapleton celebrated his first year at the helm by announcing that completion of the stadium rebuild was a priority.

Sturrock missed the opening league encounter, at fellow-promoted Mansfield, due to a virus. Perhaps it was just as well. The normally watertight defence conceded four goals against a Stags side missing six first-choice players. The performance led to an early reading of the riot act in a 45-minute players meeting on the Monday.

Coughlan's injured hamstring saw him miss the first home game, giving Malcolm an unexpected early opportunity. Sturrock, still not fighting fit, was forced to retire to the dressing room during the second half after feeling faint, thereby missing the late action that saw McGlinchey's red card and Wotton's last-minute free-kick secure a fortunate three points.

The victory sparked an unbeaten run, save of course, for the customary first round Carling Cup exit. By the end of August second place had been attained. Amid this early excitement there was a slight concern that the forwards were sharing a mutual goal-drought. The goals were coming from elsewhere.

This early success had also led opposing teams to sit up and take notice. Sturrock knew the run could not last forever, and further bolstered his squad with defender Hasney Aljofree and Frenchman Osvaldo Lopes, who had been the most impressive of a number of pre-season trialists.

The promising start soon became a distant memory. The lack of a regular goalscorer began to take its toll, and a run of eight games without a win suddenly turned Argyle into possible relegation candidates. Sturrock brought in David Norris on loan from Bolton and the busy midfielder soon made his mark with a debut goal to give the Pilgrims an unlikely win at high-flying Crewe. Seven days later a heavy home defeat by Blackpool epitomised the inconsistency that had infiltrated the side. To make matters worse, Larrieu had suffered a finger injury and replacement McCormick had a really bad game at Tranmere. Bad enough to persuade Sturrock to seek a temporary replacement in Australian Danny Milosevic, a Leeds second string. The Aussie's debut didn't last 90 minutes. He was subjected to roughhouse tactics from Oldham in a bruising encounter.

DID YOU KNOW?

As a boy, having been told he would be too small for a goalkeeper, Peter Shilton is said to have spent hours hanging by his arms from the stairs in an attempt to grow.

A point from the Oldham match spurred for an eight-game unbeaten run which all but dispensed with any relegation worries and brought a sense of belief that the play-offs were a possibility. Further experience was added in the form of loan-signing Tony Barras, a no-nonsense central defender, and ex-Scottish international Paul Bernard, another player whose career had been blighted by injury. Norris continued to impress, and £25,000 made his move to Home Park permanent.

The inconsistency remained, leaving the Greens rooted just outside the play-off zone, although the gap with the teams above was ever widening. The frustrating results were perfectly illustrated by a 6-1 thrashing of Peterborough, which was followed by an away defeat at lowly Chesterfield, who had not won in their previous ten games. In addition, there was an FA Cup defeat by non-league Dagenham to contend with. The defence had again looked solid, but the lack of a regular goalscorer was taking its toll.

By early April, Sturrock decided that getting new players took priority. He missed a couple of games to go scouting. With the play-offs looking unlikely, the planning for next season had begun early.

In the end, eighth place was a respectable enough finish, although there was a sixteen-point gap to the play-off zone. The nucleus of the team had readily adapted to the demands of a higher division and with stability at both boardroom and management level, a few tweaks here and there on the playing side would surely lead to a competitive new campaign.

Match of the Season 2002-03

Wigan 0   Argyle 1

Division 2, 29 March 2003

If there is such a thing as a home banker this looked like it. Argyle travelled to the JJB Stadium stranded in mid-table, as they had been for much of the season. Inconsistency had cost them dear, dropping points in games they were expected to win. It had proved a frustrating season in many ways. Expectations were high after the previous campaign, when the title had been clinched with some aplomb. Nevertheless, the players had little to play for except professional pride and, in a few cases, a new contract, hopefully.

Wigan, on the other hand, had done what Argyle had achieved a year earlier, winning almost at will. They had practically superglued themselves to the top spot and were currently a whole fourteen points above their nearest rivals, Crewe. They needed just ten more points from their remaining seven games to assure themselves of promotion. In reality it was less. That statistic relied on third-placed Cardiff winning every remaining match.

The Latics had lost only four times the whole season and just once at home, back in August. Chairman Dave Whelan had poured some of his wealth into the new stadium and player-salaries. Despite a posh new arena, success on the field had eluded them, so Whelan, together with manager Paul Jewell, invested on experienced players such as keeper John Filan and defender Matt Jackson. The danger-man, though, was Nathan Ellington, who had cost £1.2 million and was described by Graham Coughlan as one of his most feared opponents, for his lightning pace if nothing else.

Despite Wigan's winning habit, they regularly failed to even half fill the JJB. Situated in the soccer hot-bed of the North West, football fans were spoilt for choice. Hence a crowd of just 7,203 shuffled through the turnstiles. After two minutes, on-loan Grant Smith's volley was tipped over by Filan. Smith was again at the centre of the action when the Latics conceded two successive free-kicks. The first led to Ian Stonebridge heading over, and the second resulted in a spectacular overhead-kick from Hasney Aljofree that went wide.

By the midway point of the first half, Romain Larrieu in the Argyle goal must have been ruing his decision not to bring a good book to read. Any threat from Ellington was soon snuffed out and Wigan lacked any creativity. Their main source of danger came from the long throws of muscular Canadian defender Jason DeVos.

On 35 minutes the Pilgrims got their just reward. Stonebridge expertly controlled a long ball on his chest and laid it off to Marino Keith. The Scottish striker broke through a tackle and, never one to be afraid of having a shot, hit a stinging drive that the overworked Filan could only parry onto a post and then over the line.

No doubt Jewell's Scouse tones went into overdrive during the interval. Whatever was said, though, failed to inspire his men. It was comfortable for Argyle and the home side almost had to rely on the benevolence of Larrieu when the Frenchman scuffed a goal-kick to Andy Liddell, who shot high, wide, and handsome.

Paul Sturrock's men remained in control to the end. DeVos was thrown forward to add height to the attack, but to little effect, with Coughlan winning most of his aerial battles.

The defeat proved a mere blip on Wigan's season. They did not lose again and racked up a century of points.

NATIONWIDE DIVISION 2   **2003-04**
Nationwide Division 2   1st (champions)
Carling Cup   1st round
FA Cup   1st round

Gone were a number of fringe players and loanees, to be replaced by two Birmingham City imports – Tony Capaldi, who had impressed during the final game of the previous season, and Peter Gilbert, who arrived on an initial three-month loan. Both were distinctly left-sided players. The squad had been trimmed to just 21 players, threadbare by modern standards.

Pre-season involved a trip to the beautiful Austrian resort of Obertraun. Against German side SV Wacker Burghausen, young defender Paul Connolly was sent off.

An opening-day draw against Grimsby in 90 degree temperatures was followed by the traditional Carling Cup exit. An unkind pairing had sent the Pilgrims on a midweek trip to Colchester. A solitary win in the opening five league games was not the start anyone had wanted. Victory at Brentford was welcome, but it came at a cost. Larrieu had suffered a serious knee injury. It would end his season and, with no replacement forthcoming, Luke McCormick was again entrusted with the keeper's jersey.

Some pundits suggested that, given Argyle's indifferent form, it was not only another goalkeeper who was needed. The perma-smiling Congolese international Eugene Kangualungu arrived on a three-month deal, to the consternation of those in the club shop responsible for printing shirts.

Any doubts about McCormick's ability to take on Larrieu's mantle were soon dispelled. Another impressive string of results saw a home defeat by Bristol City as the only blot on the landscape. City's winner came from a mistake by Gilbert, which prompted abuse from a minority of 'supporters' who were rightly vilified by Sturrock the day after.

October proved to be the springboard. Friio returned after a four-match absence through injury to face managerless Tranmere. Suddenly it was the old Friio, orchestrating the midfield and playing a crucial role in the six-goal demolition of the woeful Merseysiders. Bristol City made a quick return visit as LDV Van Trophy holders, but it was Argyle who were in the driving seat with Gilbert among the scorers in a 4-0 win.

A visit to third-placed Port Vale looked to be more of a test. It was not. Friio was again inspired as a 5-1 win pushed Argyle into second place. The day was spoilt by the late arrival of a number of Argyle fans after delays on the M6 and the fact that Jason Bent was racially abused by Andreas Lipa – on Vale's anti-racism day! Lipa later sent a letter of apology to Bent, who took the matter no further. Two more goals from Friio spurred the Greens to another win, at Sheffield Wednesday, earning top spot.

These awe-inspiring results grabbed national headlines. Suddenly it was a damage limitation exercise for opposition managers. Next up were Blackpool. Manager Steve McMahon had obviously been reading the Joe Kinnear manual of mind games as he claimed, pre-match, that his side were better man-for-man. When the team sheets appeared, however, they did not reinforce his boasts, with top scorer Scott Taylor left on the bench. It was shut-up-shop time, but a single strike from Marino Keith sent Argyle three points clear at the top.

This outstanding month brought a blizzard of awards. Sturrock had no contenders for 'Manager of the Month', Friio was Second Division player of the month, and the LDV victory was named as performance of round one by the sponsors.

Friio was again at the centre of the action, being one of three players sent off in a feisty affair with a fired up Oldham.

The question of goalkeeping cover came up again. McCormick had done little wrong and whoever came in would be classed as a back-up. Finnish international Jani Viander was the first of a few who would be given an opportunity. Meanwhile, David Beresford had joined Tranmere. The fleet-footed winger had shown speed but little else, even in reserve games, to impress Sturrock.

Casting league form aside, Argyle conspired to exit two cup competitions, losing on penalties at home to Wycombe in the LDV and at Third Division Northampton in the FA Cup.

A new striker was rumoured to be on the shopping list with Reading's Nathan Tyson and Torquay's David Graham mentioned in despatches. Sturrock had made no secret of his admiration for The Gulls' forward but, scarily, his wage demands were too much for Argyle's strict salary cap.

Back in the league, a Friioless Argyle produced their worst performance in a 0-3 defeat at promotion rivals QPR. It prompted Sturrock to shuffle his pack; even captain Wotton was left out.

Results soon got back on track, although the club parted company with chief executive, John McNulty. He had played a pivotal role in the new stadium development but had been absent through illness recently. The manner of his dismissal later saw him successfully contend that he had been unfairly dismissed.

Another string of wins saw the Pilgrims go into Christmas as leaders. A press conference announced an 'exciting new signing', whereupon a number of names, including Paul Gascoigne, were bandied about. It transpired that Paul Sturrock had signed a new contract until 2008. Argyle had secured the services of one of their most popular managers ever, or so we thought.

The year ended with Wotton scoring Argyle's 5,000th league goal in a win at Bournemouth, another manager of the month award for Sturrock, as well as the Tissot Managers Performance League, which rewarded the most successful manager over a three-year period. The prize was presented by the previous holder, Claudio Ranieri at Chelsea's salubrious Stamford Bridge.

The New Year started with a seven-goal demolition of Chesterfield. It was time to say goodbye to the still-smiling Kangualungu and Brian McGlinchey, who had signed full-time for Torquay.

There was a treat for the fans attending the home game against Rushden when legendary Argyle forwards Paul Mariner and Billy Rafferty were reunited for the first time in several years. The familiar old chants came back which brought a tingle to the spine of the older supporters and prompted the younger to ask 'how good were they?'

A 2-0 win at Stockport set a club record of seven consecutive clean sheets. With nearest rivals QPR beaten at Bournemouth, the Pilgrims now had a five-point cushion at the top.

If that seemed comfortable, it wasn't. One point from the next three games saw top spot snatched by the form team of the division, Bristol City, who had won ten on the trot. Normal order was resumed with three straight wins and, with the Bristolians finally losing, top spot was regained.

All seemed rosy, but suddenly news emerged that Sturrock had been given permission to talk to Southampton, football-speak for 'I'm off'. Sure enough, a day later he was pictured at St Mary's stadium brandishing a red and white scarf, with a contract in his back pocket which Argyle could never have matched.

As usual, money had talked. No one could blame Sturrock for taking the opportunity to manage a Premiership team, something which his new contract had allowed, but the main feeling among the Argyle faithful was one of panic. Would the season fall apart?

Sturrock's sidekicks, Kevin Summerfield and John Blackley, were put in temporary charge. It was expected that the duo would follow Sturrock, but it was later confirmed that that would wait until after the season had ended. Players and fans alike rallied to the cause for their first game in charge, with McCormick's penalty save securing a goalless draw at Notts County.

The two automatic promotion spots were now being contested by just three teams, Argyle, QPR and Bristol City, but form began to desert Argyle again. Draws at Luton and at home to Wrexham, when over 80 former players were paraded at Home Park as part of the club's centenary celebrations, was followed by defeat at Barnsley, when Summerfield's lone-striker tactics received criticism.

Further defeats at Bristol City and Oldham only made the need for a new manager more urgent. The usual suspects, Peter Reid, Trevor Francis and John Gregory had been mentioned, but news leaked that another Scot, Bobby Williamson, was to be the man. Williamson's appointment was announced in time for the match at home to QPR. Argyle's rivals had also looked tense in recent weeks and had dropped unexpected points. A win for Argyle would clinch promotion. A tense match saw the deadlock broken by Evans' bullet header. Friio added another and promotion and the title were sealed in front of a full house.

For the second time in three years the final match was a celebration party. Evans deservedly won the player of the year award. A fit 'Trigger' had been a revelation, when many expected him to play only a supporting role. McCormick, Connolly and Gilbert had come of age, Friio and Norris had been crucial, and the rest of the team had shown great spirit, particularly after the loss of the manager. Credit should also go to Summerfield and Blackley who held things together. As for new manager Williamson, he had three wins from three games and a title. Easy, this management business.

Match of the Season 2003-04
Argyle 7 Chesterfield 0

Division 2, 3 January 2004

Paul Sturrock's side went into the New Year in pole position and another routine victory was predicted. Routine victories had become, well, routine, and The Spireites' form hardly gave confidence to their 160 travelling fans who had made the long journey, although their team had picked up a first away win for a year, at Barnsley, the previous weekend. A long second half of the season looked in prospect for Roy McFarland's men.

There was only one blot on the Argyle landscape. The day before, Sturrock had been named 'Manager of the Month', an award that mythically meant the onset of a poor run of results. To add credence to this notion, the man himself pointed out that the last time such an honour had been bestowed upon him, his team failed to win their next four games.

Sturrock chose the same eleven who had beaten Brentford in the previous game. That meant Paul Wotton and David Norris had to settle for the bench, both having served a one-match suspension.

Perfection. In all walks of life we seek it, no more so than in sport. Yet it rarely happens. In football it has never been achieved and never will. The reason? Well there are eleven people out there trying to spoil everything you do. Yet, during the first thirteen minutes of this match everyone present at Home Park witnessed the nearest to perfection that they are likely to see.

Four minutes after referee Hill's first blast of his whistle, 'Buster' Phillips received a pass from Friio, cut inside full-back Alan O'Hare and curled in a cross. Distracted perhaps by the sight of the un-shaven Evans bearing down on him, Carl Muggleton dropped the ball, leaving Lee Hodges with the simple task of scoring. 1-0.

Standard fare ensued for the next seven minutes. Okay, perhaps that part wasn't perfect, but then Aljofree floated a free-kick to-wards Evans. Panic ensued again amongst the Chesterfield defend-ers and Capaldi prodded home the loose ball. 2-0.

Within a minute, Argyle had forced a corner. Coughlan's usual reliable head failed to make proper contact and all but Lowndes believed the ball to be going out of play. The flame-haired striker retrieved the ball and fired it past the hapless Muggleton. 3-0.

Another four minutes, another corner. Capaldi's inswinger was met by an unmarked Friio. 4-0.

Most home fans were still on their feet applauding when Argyle surged forward once more. Evans was again a central figure, receiv-ing the ball from the left and teeing up Lowndes to stroke home – 5-0 – although there was already some debate amongst the stunned fan-base as to the exact score.

Surely this couldn't continue. It didn't, not for another nineteen minutes. Then a Connolly cross found the head of Evans, whose nod down was met by Friio to smash home another. 6-0.

In between, Chesterfield had gained some possession and actu-ally created a couple of chances. Mark Allott's shot and Glynn Hurst's header were both high, and on a normal day would have been greeted by a few discontented ooh's and aah's from the home fans. Instead they were greeted with derision. Would anyone have cared too much if they had gone in?

One can only hazard a guess at the content of McFarland's half-time team talk. Jibes among the crowd became more ridiculous by the minute. Sneak on a couple of extra players and see if anyone notices, was one. Perhaps the former England centre-half would bring himself on to shore up his defence, was another. Perhaps not so ridiculous after all, on reflection.

Admirably, McFarland switched to a 4-3-3 formation, which if nothing else had the effect of disrupting Argyle's play. On the basis of the first half, it was not unreasonable to expect a double-figure score, but the half-time break slowed the momentum and an element of normality prevailed. How inconsiderate that we had to wait until the 89th minute for another goal. Friio again rushed towards a Stonebridge corner and nodded in, although later he conceded that he had mistimed his header and that his hat-trick had indeed been completed courtesy of his Gallic mouth.

A quick scour of the records revealed it to be the biggest Home Park victory since 1936. Even Sturrock himself was shocked at the manner of the victory. 'Scary' was his description of those glorious thirteen minutes.

CHAMPIONSHIP   **2004-05**
Championship   17th
Carling Cup   1st round
FA Cup   3rd round

The step up to the Championship was huge. Argyle were suddenly small fish in a big pond, competing against sides such as Sunderland, West Ham and Leeds, with massive financial resources and able to attract top quality international players. Very few of the squad had experience at this level. Neither, of course, did manager Williamson, who still had to prove himself and come out of Sturrock's shadow.

As his predecessor had done on a number of occasions, Williamson recruited heavily from Scotland, bringing in Lee Makel, Steven Milne, Keith Lasley and most impressively, Stevie Crawford, a Scottish international. They were hardly household names but all experienced players, and the fact that they were prepared to come to Plymouth perhaps said something about the respect Williamson enjoyed. Also joining was French defender Mathias Doumbe, who had also been plying his trade in Scotland with Hibs.

Jason Bent and Martin Phillips had been told at the end of the previous season that they would be released. Ian Stonebridge had moved to Wycombe for a 'nominal' fee having never really fulfilled his early promise.

On the return from another pre-season tour of Austria, Argyle hosted Portsmouth and were taken apart 1-5 as the crowd marvelled at the skill and speed of Yakubu and Lua-Lua. Sturrock also brought his Southampton team for a friendly but a much-improved Argyle performance resulted in a 3-1 win.

Off the field, Ginsters extended their shirt sponsorship deal for another three years. On the stadium development front there were no developments. Chairman Stapleton revealed that the remaining side would not be redeveloped until 2006, but that there was scope to increase the capacity to 30,000 should circumstances warrant it.

With Hasney Aljofree absent after knee surgery, Argyle entered the Championship with a 0-0 draw against Millwall, who had lost the FA Cup final only three months earlier.

After two away wins, the Greens found themselves temporarily topping the table. It was a far better start than anyone had imagined but surely the visit of Sunderland would prove a test. After a dream start when Wotton blasted a free-kick past Thomas Myrhe from near the touchline, Crawford underlined his class with a superb finish. Although the Black Cats pulled one back they returned to Wearside with their tails between their legs.

DID YOU KNOW?

Whilst a Barnet player, Lee Hodges slipped on a bar of soap in the shower, giving himself a groin injury.

After such an encouraging start surely Argyle could make rare progress in the Carling Cup, which brought a local derby of sorts at Yeovil. But no. In a match that went into extra-time, Lee Johnson, son of the manager, grabbed a hat-trick, although it was a bizarre incident that grabbed the headlines. After the ball was kicked out to allow Coughlan to receive treatment, Johnson played the ball back to McCormick. Unfortunately, it soared over the keeper into goal. To their credit, from the restart, Argyle allowed Crawford to dribble unopposed into their net to restore the *status quo ante*.

Meanwhile, Sturrock's short love affair with Southampton had come to a bitter end, prompting speculation that he would return to Home Park, rumours quickly dispelled by Stapleton.

Four successive defeats saw a slump to mid-table. Tony Capaldi had, however, established himself in the Northern Ireland team and the Republic of Ireland manager, Brian Kerr, had been checking on Coughlan. And not before time!

Sturrock was not unemployed for long, being snapped up by Sheffield Wednesday. He was quick to move for Aljofree, which would also assist his rehabilitation from his knee surgery. His stay was short-lived though, cut short by a shoulder injury.

Capaldi was also in the wars, collecting a broken fibula which would keep him out for six weeks.

Argyle continued to beat the teams they were expected to beat, such as Rotherham and Gillingham, and with the odd point gained here and there, a mid-table position was stabilised. Another bonus was the form of Doumbe, whose impressive performances had dislodged Wotton from the central defensive role.

More personnel changes followed. Defensive coach John Blackley had rejoined Sturrock at Hillsborough, to be replaced by another Scot, Jocky Scott, who had been directing the reserves at Sunderland. McCormick, displaced by Larrieu, had joined Boston on loan.

November began encouragingly. Argyle led 2-0 at half-time against Reading, and went off to a standing ovation, only to be pulled back to all-square. Four days later they ended the last unbeaten record in the English leagues with a 2-0 win at Wigan.

Nathan Lowndes joined Port Vale for £25,000, never having cemented a regular place at Home Park.

With Argyle ever more in the public eye, some players found themselves attracting attention. Rumour had it that Everton were interested in Doumbe, whilst Gilbert was being watched by Wales manager John Toshack after some impressive performances in the Under-21 side.

The Toffees would get a closer look at Doumbe when the FA Cup third round draw sent Everton to Home Park. The BBC announced this as their choice for live Match of the Day coverage, no doubt sniffing a possible Cup upset. The event would also boost the Argyle coffers by another £150,000.

Results wise, Argyle were beginning to look shaky. Defeats by Crewe and Derby left them seventeenth, and the mood was not helped by the news that Crawford and Makel had not settled in the West Country and wanted to return 'home'. With Blair Sturrock also moving on, to Kidderminster, Williamson brought in Icelandic midfielder Bjarni Gudjonsson on a free from Coventry, and striker Scott Taylor from Blackpool for £100,000 – Argyle's most expensive signing for seven years.

The club's annual accounts also showed a rarity – a profit! £629,097, thanks in the main to larger crowds, increased merchandise, and other commercial activities.

January brought the much-anticipated clash with Everton. Argyle did not disgrace themselves in losing 1-3, and Gudjonsson scored a lovely goal. But three successive league defeats saw Argyle slip to twentieth, and scoring goals was becoming a problem.

Four trialists played in a friendly at Torquay. One, Hungarian Akos Buzsaky, was taken on loan from Porto. He was not the only arrival. Young Southampton striker Dexter Blackstock quickly impressed. The board also splashed £250,000 on Everton striker Nick Chadwick, who had notched the Toffees' third goal in the FA Cup-tie. The biggest shock was the departure of Friio. A two and half year contract took the Frenchman to Nottingham Forest for £100,000, a fee which many supporters felt was hardly value for money for such a natural match-winner.

With the new signings taking time to settle, a five-goal thrashing by West Ham only enhanced the relegation fears and provoked mumblings over the future of Williamson. The pressure was eased by two 3-0 wins against Sheffield United and Crewe, opening up a seven-point gap to the relegation zone.

Results continued to be topsy-turvy. A 5-1 win over Brighton was followed four days later by the reverse score at Sunderland. Meanwhile, Sturrock was still sniffing around his former players. A £50,000 bid for Evans was turned down, but the same fee saw Steve Adams rejoin his old boss. Marino Keith also departed on a free to Colchester. Transfer deadline day saw Jason Dodd arrive on loan, again from Southampton, but he was recalled after four matches with the Saints in the midst of both an injury crisis and a relegation battle. The same fate befell Blackstock.

Whilst the away form had been dismal, Argyle continued to rely on their home performances. A crucial win against strugglers Watford came courtesy of Buzaky's first goal for the club. The Hungarian playmaker was quickly becoming a firm favourite with the Home Park faithful, and went a long way to softening the blow of Friio's departure. By the end of the season there was a 'sign him on' campaign. His stock was rising all the time as, presumably, was his transfer fee.

Relegation was avoided by three points. It was a close call but at least the fans could relax and enjoy the final game that saw Wotton overwhelmingly voted 'player of the year'. David Worrell bid farewell after being told he was to be released.

Match of the Season 2004-05

Argyle 3 Sheffield United 0

Championship, 22 February 2005

Three days earlier, Argyle had taken a five-goal thrashing at West Ham, while the Blades had held mighty Arsenal to a draw in the FA Cup – at Highbury! United's Cup exploits had damaged their league form, however, and three successive defeats had seen them lose ground in the promotion chase. Manager Neil Warnock would have them fired up for this one.

Bobby Williamson had rung the changes after the Upton Park capitulation, making six changes, with only Buzsaky surviving a cull of the midfield quartet. Within three minutes a sweet strike on the turn from Coughlan gave home fans a rare glimpse of the ability that had made the Irishman a prolific striker in his youth.

The goal carried a double whammy. In a vain attempt to save, goalkeeper Paddy Kenny had injured his hip. As the half wore on, his limp became more pronounced and kicking more difficult. After 28 minutes he had no choice but to go off, giving Warnock another problem as he had no substitute goalkeeper.

Skipper Phil Jagielka donned the keeper's jersey, something he had done earlier in the season when Kenny had been sent off. This provided another spur to Argyle, as Jagielka was probably the Blades most influential player.

United's defence protected their keeper until the interval, but soon after the change-around Wotton hit a bullet that would have beaten most keepers. Even Warnock had an air of resignation as a late diving header from substitute Dexter Blackstock made it three.

CHAMPIONSHIP

CHAMPIONSHIP	**2005-06**
Championship	14th
Carling Cup	2nd round
FA Cup	3rd round

In many ways there was now even more pressure on Williamson, now that expectations were higher. Many fans had been unhappy with his style of play although, in fairness, few sides scrap to avoid relegation with panache. Doumbe and Buzsaky aside, Williamson's signings had been disappointing, and some thought that, tactically at least, he was not in the same league as Sturrock.

There had been the usual summer departures, notably Graham Coughlan, who had rejoined Sturrock at Sheffield Wednesday. As for the intake, they didn't lack experience. Full-backs Anthony Barness and Rufus Brevett had played in the Premiership. The arrival of veteran Nigerian World Cup star Taribo West prompted disbelief, excitement, and a blaze of publicity. Winger Bojan Djordjic had persuaded Manchester United to pay £1 million for him as a 16-year-old, but he had failed to deliver at Old Trafford or Ibrox. If he could not produce on these stages, could he do it at Home Park? There was relief all round when the board bowed to popular demand to make Buzsaky's signing permanent.

Fans had their first glimpse of West in home friendlies against FC Bruges and OFK Belgrade. Both games were goalless. It then emerged that West had visa and passport problems. He returned to Italy to sort matters out and would miss the first few games.

On the opening day, a last-minute Chadwick goal beat promotion favourites Reading at the Madjeski. Four consecutive defeats, interspersed by a rare Carling Cup win (over Peterborough) saw the side plummet to 21st. West had reappeared, but his – and the team's – woeful performance against Brighton was the final straw. Williamson was sacked, having never endeared himself to the fans or emerged from the shadow of Sturrock.

Jocky Scott was put in temporary charge but a home draw with Crewe left the Greens next to bottom. Following a Carling Cup defeat at Barnet, the new manager was announced as former Stoke boss Tony Pulis, who had been in the crowd for the Brighton debacle. He had been dismissed from the Potteries club for 'failing to exploit foreign markets', a new entry in the 'Football Chairman's Book of Excuses to Sack Your Manager'.

Pulis's remit was simple. Avoid relegation. Whilst his was not a universally popular choice (Sturrock, of course, having been hotly tipped to return), he was the type of manager who would at least restore discipline and the work ethic.

DID YOU KNOW?

Taribo West holds an Olympic gold medal, having been part of
the winning Nigeria squad at the 1996 Atlanta Games.

Pulis quickly showed West the door. The Nigerian's age was a
secret. Guesses ranged from 33 (unlikely) to 44 (nearer the mark,
judging by performances) but whatever, he was well past his sell-by
date. Other Williamson recruits, Brevett, Djordjic, Gudjonsson and
Mendes, were also frozen out.

Despite his best efforts, Pulis could not extricate Argyle from the
relegation zone. He masterminded a satisfying 2-0 win over Stoke,
but otherwise Argyle were either losing or drawing. A Guy Fawkes-
night defeat at Ipswich saw the Greens in 23rd spot.

Stifled by the unpopular transfer window and a meagre budget,
Pulis began to dip into the loan market. In came towering West
Ham defender Elliott Ward and midfielder Jason Jarrett. Both players gave their all and Ward, in particular, quickly endeared himself
to Argyle fans.

In the run up to Christmas, confidence was restored and results
improved. At home to Crystal Palace, Chadwick scored after twelve
seconds, the fastest goal in Argyle history.

2006 started with a heavy home defeat by Leeds. Five days later
FA Cup dreams ended for another year with defeat at Wolves, only
eight days after Argyle had drawn at Molineux in the league. The
only bright spot was the return the versatile Lee Hodges after a
long-term back injury. The end of Jarrett's loan spell saw him em-
bark on a nomadic trip around the Championship. He was quickly
back at Home Park, this time in a Norwich shirt, and would later be
seen again in the colours of Preston. In place of Jarrett came long-
haired Frenchman Lilian Nalis. Going through the out-door was
Mendes.

The arrival of Nalis coincided with a run of one defeat in eleven
games, during which time there were more comings and goings. In
came former Juventus striker Vincent Pericard, on loan from Portsmouth. He quickly got the fans on his side by bagging a hat-trick on
his home debut, against Coventry, a match which saw the farewell
appearance of the much-missed Ward. He returned to West Ham's
first team and a £1 million move to Coventry in the summer showed
why Ward did not become a permanent Pilgrim.

By early April another season of Championship football had
been secured and Pulis had done his job. The football hadn't been
pretty, but that was out of necessity. Pulis later revealed how much
work he felt was needed when he arrived. There had been an air of

despondency around Home Park and he was also concerned about the player's fitness levels.

Near the end of the season Mickey Evans announced his departure. A local boy, he had never been a prolific goalscorer, but no defender ever had an easy game against him. It was fitting, then, that his final match saw him head a memorable goal. His farewell lap of honour was met with many a tear. Nice one Trigger!

Match of the Season 2005-06
Reading 1 Argyle 2

Championship, 6 August 2005

Opening-day matches are hard to predict. The previous campaign had seen Reading narrowly miss out on the play-offs, losing just three home games. Manager Steve Coppell would field probably the most settled side in the league. Nine of his players today had started at Home Park nine months previously. The exceptions were the new strike-force of Leroy Lita – a £1 million signing from Bristol City – and the much cheaper Kevin Doyle, an import from Cork.

Bobby Williamson also had a few choices to make, opting for Larrieu in goal instead of McCormick, and fielding new full-backs in Barness and Brevett. A visit to the Madjeski is always a favourite for Argyle supporters, being an easy hop up the motorway. The Green Army comprised almost a quarter of the 16,000 attendance.

On the lush surface, the deadlock was broken in the 21st minute. Brevett crossed to the near post. Evans anticipated this but the Reading defenders did not, and the Argyle striker turned the ball in. Buzsaky, celebrating his call up to the Hungarian squad, almost doubled Argyle's lead after half-time, but his left-foot shot was saved by the shaven-headed Marcus Hahnemann.

The Royals' main threat came from Glen Little, 6ft-plus and pedestrian in pace. He was hardly the archetypal winger, yet he was tricky and dangerous. In the 54th minute Little's teasing cross found the head of Lita, who scored past an exposed Larrieu.

It was now a question of Argyle hanging on. With referee Paul Taylor studying his watch, Wotton fired in a last desperate shot. The ball deflected off a defender into the path of Chadwick, who swung a leg, made feeble contact, then watched as the ball wrong-footed Hahnemann and dribbled in.

As the season wore on, the magnitude of that victory became ever more apparent. Reading never lost at home again and, indeed, lost only once away. They dominated the division to secure their place in the Premiership. So this was the shock result of the season.

CHAMPIONSHIP   2006-07
Championship   11th
Carling Cup   1st round
FA Cup   Quarter-finals

After two seasons of Championship football, Argyle seemed to have a solid platform on which to build. But, with pre-season imminent, that platform was shaken.

At Stoke City, it was all-change again. The Icelandic consortium that had rid itself of Pulis before, had been ousted by Peter Coates, a friend of his. Manager Johan Boskamp had also departed and Coates wanted Pulis back. The Argyle board finally relented, admitting it would be churlish to stand in Pulis's way. Nevertheless, the manner of the departure, and its timing left a bad taste.

A day before the players were due back for training, Argyle's latest manager was announced as Ian Holloway, who had been on 'gardening leave' following an acrimonious departure from QPR, who had told him to speak to Leicester about their managerial vacancy, only to then sack him for doing so!

Holloway was well liked in the game. His Bristolian burr, witticisms, and eccentricity endeared himself to most, and did not mask a deep knowledge of the game. Chairman Stapleton believed he had found a long-term manager who would guide the Pilgrims to the promised land. Holloway himself made all the right noises, and local journalists rubbed their hands at the prospect of some rich copy.

The pre-season trip to Austria was 'interesting'. Argyle had chosen a different base to their usual one, but Real Madrid boss Fabio Capello wanted his team to use the same hotel. An inducement was offered to persuade Argyle to decamp to another hotel. As well as financial compensation, Capello offered to play Argyle in a friendly, which settled the matter. Madrid were missing some of their more famous names but still fielded a star-studded team. Coach trips from Plymouth were hastily arranged and Argyle put up a creditable display in losing 0-1.

Less creditable was the incident over an evening meal when young striker Chris Zebroski for some reason smashed a glass water-jug over the head of skipper Paul Wotton, who required over 100 stitches. Zebroski would have his contract terminated.

Holloway pulled off a coup by paying an initial £200,000 for Manchester United forward Sylvan Ebanks-Blake, who was unlikely to see much first-team action at Old Trafford. Also joining was 34-year-old Millwall striker Barry Hayles for what appeared to be a rather high £100,000. Holloway had known Hayles for many years.

DID YOU KNOW?

In 2003, director Michael Foot became the oldest registered player in English football history when he was included in the official Argyle squad as a 90th birthday present.

Remarkably, Wotton was fit for the opening day, with Hayles grabbing a debut goal. Wins at Colchester and Sunderland lifted the Greens to third, which was another encouraging start. But then Sturrock brought his Sheffield Wednesday team to Home Park and stole the points. Despite fielding a strong side, Argyle fell to Walsall in the Carling Cup.

Hayles was justifying his transfer fee with some barnstorming performances and the team played more stylish football than under the previous two managers. The spirit was also there, typified by a fight-back from three goals down at home to Cardiff to snatch a point.

Holloway also stamped his authority. He lost patience with Djordjic, who was exiled to the South Western League team with the Under-18s. Djordjic scored five goals in one such match, if only to illustrate the gulf in class.

The squad, still relatively small, now had a solid look to it. The defence looked secure with Dutch centre-half Marcel Seip quickly impressing. Nalis and Wotton provided a solid midfield duo, with Norris and Buzsaky providing the flair, and the attacking combination of Hayles and Ebanks-Blake developing a good understanding with each other.

By late October Argyle lay fifth. Birmingham came to Home Park and ended Plymouth's unbeaten seven-match run, despite being under the cosh for much of the game.

A number of youth-team players were emerging. Gary Sawyer, Luke Summerfield, Reuben Reid and 16-year-old Dan Gosling had all come into first-team contention, testimony to the work of club staff over a number of seasons. Gosling, in particular, took the eye. He had played against Real Madrid and when given a first-team opportunity rarely looked out of place.

A 1-0 win over Hull was marred by a serious injury to Wotton, who suffered cruciate ligament damage after landing awkwardly. It ended Wotton's season, and it was ironic that such a combative player, who had remained injury free for much of his career, should be incapacitated in such a manner.

Coincidence possibly, but without their talisman Argyle's campaign began to lose momentum. Having fought his way back into the team, Djordjic was showing the best form of his Argyle career when he suffered a fractured cheekbone against West Brom.

During the January transfer window Holloway signed Kevin Gallen on loan from QPR, where he had given Holloway excellent service. England Under-18 international Scott Sinclair brought a raw talent. The squad was also enhanced by Hungarians Peter Halmosi (a winger from Debrecen) and central defender Krisztian Timar (Ferencvaros). Argyle also spent £300,000 on New Zealand striker Rory Fallon, equalling the club's outgoing transfer record. It showed that the board was serious about a promotion push.

There were groans when the 'glamour' of the FA Cup third round sent the Pilgrims to Peterborough. The Greens scraped through after a replay, only to be sent to Barnet. With a concerted push for the play-offs in the offing, the Cup was seen as a distraction, but the League Two opponents were brushed aside thanks to a super goal from Sinclair. The wonder-kid collected the ball outside his own area and weaved past several Bees before slotting the ball home. It was voted the goal of the round.

Round five brought Championship leaders Derby to Home Park, but there was still the matter of league points to be gained. Injuries to Chadwick and Buzsaky had tightened Holloway's options. Vital points were being dropped as Argyle struggled to break back into the top ten.

Over 18,000 paid to see Derby but the Rams did not look up for the fight. Gallen was a constant thorn in their side, scoring one penalty and missing another. Cup fever began to grip Plymouth.

The eight quarter-finalists comprised Argyle and seven Premiership sides, including Manchester United and Chelsea. A home draw was forthcoming, but opponents Watford meant mixed emotions. The Hornets were next to bottom of the Premiership and beatable. There was also the opportunity to avenge the FA Cup semi-final defeat by them 23 years earlier, but it would have been nice to get one of the 'big two' to Home Park.

With minds possibly elsewhere, further league points were dropped. Argyle seemed marooned in mid-table with the gap to the play-offs widening by the week.

The big day finally arrived. Live BBC coverage dictated an early evening kick-off, which displeased the Watford fans who would have to make their way home late on a Sunday night. Argyle dominated the game but could not find their way past keeper Ben Foster, on loan from Manchester United. A Bouazza left-foot strike which McCormick barely saw ended Cup dreams once again.

It wasn't long before the 'the week from hell' arrived, as Holloway put it. The Cup run had disrupted the fixture list. A game at Burnley needed to be rearranged and was squeezed between other away trips to Ipswich and Leeds. It was all too much. Three away games in eight days took its toll on players and fans alike. Three defeats, and comprehensive ones at that, effectively ended any fading hopes of a play-off spot.

Holloway took responsibility but rallied his troops again. The season ended with five straight wins, and finishing eleventh was the Pilgrims' best for twenty years.

It had been an 'if only' season in many ways, but there were many positive signs. Sinclair had returned to Chelsea, his perform-ances adding to his transfer value and putting him out of Argyle's reach, but Seip, Timar and Halmosi had shown rapid improvement. Ebanks-Blake was another to adapt quickly to the demands of Championship football, whilst Hayles had given his all to silence his critics. The veteran Nalis clinched the player of the year award, having held the side together after the enforced absence of Wotton, whilst Gosling looked a star in the making. The traumatic events of the previous summer seemed a long way off.

Match of the Season 2006-07
Argyle 0 Watford 1

FA Cup, 3rd round, 11 March 2007

Home Park was packed in anticipation of Argyle reaching the semi-finals. The day reunited the managers from that previous encounter with Watford 23 years earlier. Graham Taylor was part of the BBC punditry team, and John Hore the special guest of Argyle.

The outcome was too close to call. Argyle still had half an eye on the play-offs. For their part, Adie Boothroyd's men had surprised everyone by reaching the Premiership, albeit via the play offs, but they were set for an immediate return, being ten points adrift of safety. Watford had only won three Premiership games all season. Their 'up and at 'em' style had proved fruitless in their new cul-tured environment.

Ian Holloway had endured an unwanted midweek fixture at Sheffield Wednesday, where he rested certain players. His main problem was who to choose up front. Hayles had missed six games with a broken toe and was now sick, whilst record signing Rory Fallon was Cup-tied, having played in an earlier round for Swansea. Warhorse Kevin Gallen was given the nod.

Boothroyd had been boosted by the return of England goal-keeper Ben Foster after a two-match absence and opted for a tradi-tional 4-4-2 formation.

From the off, Watford started to punt long balls forward but they proved meat and drink for the formidable Krisztian Timar. The

Hornets' style of play, however, compressed Argyle's midfield and generally unsettled the home side.

In the 21st minute Watford produced a clever set-piece between Steve Kabba and Tommy Smith. The ball found its way to the left foot of Frenchman Hameur Bouazza on the edge of the area. He has probably not hit a sweeter shot in his career. 0-1.

Inevitably, from then on Watford allowed Argyle to come at them, which merely allowed Foster the opportunity to show why he was an England keeper.

The second half began with Hayles thrown into the fray, replacing the inexperienced Gosling. Watford were battered but emerged with a semi-final spot. Boothroyd admitted his side were fortunate.

CHAMPIONSHIP   **2007-08**
Championship   10th
Carling Cup   3rd round
FA Cup   4th round

Little did we know what a traumatic season lay in store. After all, everything seemed rosy in the Home Park garden. There was continued stability, both financially and at boardroom level, with the club finally owning the freehold of Home Park. The manager was seemingly set for the long term. It was the quietest summer, transfer wise, for many a year, with only French midfielder Nadjim 'Jimmy' Abdou signing after a pre-season trial. Holloway had lost Kevin Gallen to MK Dons, and the expected departure of Tony Capaldi finally materialised. Now an established international, he had largely been frozen out since he made his disenchantment clear, back in January. Many Argyle fans felt a sense of betrayal, given that the club had given him his first chance of league football. Cardiff eventually came up with a wage deal to meet his demands. To rub salt in the wounds Argyle received not a penny, thanks to Monsieur Bosman.

The Greens began their league campaign where they had ended the previous one – at Hull. Young Gosling missed the opening games with good reason. He was part of the England squad taking part in the Under-17 World Cup in South Korea.

Early arrivals at the home opener against Ipswich would have been greeted by a ghostly white Holloway being lifted into an ambulance. It was a worrying moment but news emerged that a kidney stone was to blame and the boss was soon back at work.

Early season performances were encouraging but the results were not. One win in the first five games left the side down in eighteenth, following a home draw with Cardiff. Of course, Capaldi was not roundly applauded. If he had collected all the £10 notes being waved in his direction, he may have been persuaded to stay!

In the midst of this, Argyle had reached the relatively uncharted waters of the third round of the Carling Cup, thanks to home wins over Wycombe and Doncaster. Their reward for this remarkable achievement was a trip to Premiership West Ham. The Greens gave the Hammers a fright or two, but with extra-time looking a certainty, Dean Ashton grabbed a late winner.

The Upton Park performance boosted confidence and with the teams tightly packed a run of ten points from a possible twelve, culminating in a fine win at Charlton, saw the team rise to fourth, mainly on the back of a rock-solid defence in which Timar was outstanding.

The first loanee of the season arrived in the shape of winger Lee Martin, another talent off the Manchester United production line. It was the second time Holloway had tried to sign the youngster, previously losing out to Stoke.

As one wide man arrived, another left. Bojan Djordjic was one of the most talented players to pull on an Argyle shirt. Sadly, few fans ever saw that talent. You do not get signed by Sir Alex Ferguson for £1 million as a 16-year-old without having some ability. Yet there was something about the Djordjic psyche that had left a succession of managers frustrated. He was also one of the most affable characters around Home Park, always willing to have a chat with the fans. He eventually returned to Swedish football.

Another departure was Akos Buzsaky. A crowd favourite, he was capable of turning a match single handed. He was also capable of making little contribution. He left for moneybags QPR, initially on loan.

Striker Jermaine Easter arrived from Wycombe on loan, only to see his new team suffer a temporary dip in form. An easy win over a woeful Norwich seemed to get the season back on track but then a bombshell dropped.

Leicester were looking for yet another manager and the word on the street was that Holloway was their number one choice. Speculation began to mount, prompting Holloway to declare his undying love of all things Argyle and dismissing the rumours as 'poppycock'.

Even Leicester chairman Milan Mandaric denied outright any interest in 'Ollie' but the tune soon changed. The prospect of doubling his salary and a move to a 'bigger' club was quickly draining the love from Holloway's veins. It quickly became apparent that he wanted to go, but things threatened to get messy. The board, understandably upset, refused him permission to talk to the Foxes. This led to Holloway's resignation but Argyle refused to budge saying that he was still under contract.

In the end, Argyle relented, being in a no-win situation. It was obvious Holloway had no intention of managing Argyle again and on the day he was due in the Argyle club shop to sign copies of his newly released autobiography he was pictured at the Walkers Stadium, brandishing a blue and white scarf above his head and being unveiled as Leicester's *fifth* manager of 2007.

The vitriol from supporters was unprecedented. Sadly, this led to Holloway's wife being verbally abused whilst shopping in a local supermarket, a shameful incident.

Holloway's sidekicks, Tim Breacker and Des Bulpin, were expected to follow him but took charge for a potentially difficult match at Sheffield United. The players seemed less affected. Of course, many had seen managers come and go, and they rallied superbly to snatch an unexpected win to move into fourth place.

Despite the rush of candidates for the managerial vacancy, there was only one real contender. Cue a certain Paul Sturrock. The Scot was now in charge at Swindon, having pulled them up from League Two. He had, however, remained friends with Argyle chairman Paul Stapleton. A compensation deal was quickly brokered and for the second time Paul Sturrock was unveiled as Plymouth's manager.

There was no fairytale start, with a talented West Brom leaving Home Park with the points. For Sturrock, it was a case of consolidating Argyle's position until the January transfer window. What he did not envisage was the amount of recruitment he would need to do. Argyle ended 2007 in sixth place, but when the transfer window opened all hell broke loose.

Thirty-one days later, the Argyle squad had a very different look. Lee Martin's loan spell had ended. Clearly a real talent, a troublesome hamstring had curtailed his recent involvement and he opted to go to Sheffield United. Predictably, Hayles followed Holloway. Argyle made a £50,000 profit on a player who had scored just twice in the current campaign.

The top clubs had quickly been alerted to the talents of Gosling and the 17-year-old gained a dream move to Everton for an initial fee of £1 million.

The next departee was more unexpected. Sylvan Ebanks-Blake had proved to be one of Holloway's best acquisitions and was top scorer. There was outrage when he opened talks with Wolves, and when the striker left for £1.5 million it prompted questions as to the exact nature of the club's long-term ambitions. Again it emerged that the club's hands were tied. The player's contract allowed him to talk to any club prepared to pay the said amount, and highlighted both the complexity of modern-day contracts and the gulf in financial clout between Argyle and most of their Championship rivals.

If that was not enough, the last day of January saw Norris sign for Ipswich, who had long admired a player who had been Argyle's most consistent performer for several seasons. Argyle were reluctant sellers, as half the fee would go to his former club, Bolton.

Ipswich twisted some Wanderers arms to reduce their percentage, and with Norris, clearly unsettled, wanting to go, the player described by Sturrock as his best signing left for pastures new for £2 million.

Over the space of a couple of months, many of the team's mainstays had left and needed to be replaced. To make matters worse, the impressive Peter Halmosi was generating much interest.

Sturrock had to earn his corn, and quickly, if he was to keep the season on track. There was comfort in the knowledge that he had done it before at Argyle, bringing in unknowns such as Friio, Coughlan and Larrieu.

Easter's move was made permanent, Jim Paterson and Chris Clark arrived from north of the border, Jamie Mackie, who had been catching the eye at Exeter, moved down the A38, Frenchman Yoan Folly, a player Sturrock had signed twice previously with former clubs came in, and a new club record £500,000 secured the services of Scottish striker Steve MacLean, another player well known to the manager.

In fairness to the new boys, they settled quickly. FA Cup interest ended at the fourth round stage after a brave defeat at Portsmouth. The south coast rivals went on to lift the trophy and Clark's goal was the only one they conceded on their way. League form was also maintained until some disappointing results in March left the side playing catch up.

Scottish internationals Russell Anderson and Gary Teale came in on loan, both with Premiership experience. Another bonus was the return of Wotton after his long-term knee injury. The skipper had worked hard in his recovery and his comeback was akin to getting another new player.

Argyle's season effectively ended with a home defeat by Charlton who, in the previous few weeks would have had trouble winning a raffle. The afternoon had started dramatically with Seip walking out after refusing to be a substitute. The Addicks also had keeper Nicky Weaver sent off early on, but still managed to nick the three points. Seip was fined and transfer listed. Sadly it looked like the talented defender had played his last game in a green shirt.

There were more twists and turns. Prior to the final home game, Sturrock announced that five other players would be leaving. The least surprising name was Nick Chadwick, whose injuries meant he was never able to achieve a prolonged run in the side. Paul Connolly had decided his future lay elsewhere. Again, Argyle would receive no fee for a player they had nurtured over the years. As for Lee Hodges, he had been a loyal servant to Argyle. A Mr Dependable, he had appeared in every position for the club.

The other two departures shocked the most. Lilian Nalis had reached the veteran stage but many felt he had another season in him. The final name on the list was one Paul Wotton. The man was Argyle through and through. Earlier in the season he had declined a loan move, stating that he only wanted to play for one club in his career. He was not the most talented, but certainly one of the most committed, as his fight-back from injury showed. His turbo-charged free-kicks would be long remembered. It was a devastating blow for the player and Sturrock described the decision as the toughest he had ever made.

After such a drain it was testimony to everyone that the club maintained their season-by-season improvement, finishing in tenth place. And Holloway? He was relieved of his duties after his Leicester team were relegated.

Sadly, this soap opera season had a devastating end. On 8 June goalkeeper Luke McCormick was arrested after being involved in an early morning accident on the M6 motorway in which two young boys were tragically killed and their father seriously injured. The club subsequently cancelled his contract 'by mutual consent' with the matter to follow the due legal process.

Match of the Season 2007-08

Bristol City 1 Argyle 2

Championship, 15 March 2008

In footballing terms, Paul Sturrock was suffering the week from hell. Firstly, the Pilgrims had lost a rain-swept midweek fixture at doomed Scunthorpe. Secondly, during the course of that 0-1 defeat they had lost keeper Luke McCormick, sent off for handling outside the area. An automatic one-match ban rendered 'Super Luke' unavailable for Ashton Gate. With Larrieu still sidelined through illness, Sturrock somehow had to find an experienced custodian.

By Friday morning it looked likely that youth-team keeper Lloyd Saxton would be entering the cauldron, but at the last minute Leicester boss Ian Holloway offered the services of Scottish international Rab Douglas. Douglas was signed on an emergency one-game loan, and was introduced to his new team-mates on the morning of the game.

As well as being forced to replace his goalkeeper, Sturrock made six other changes from the eleven that had started at Scunthorpe. Paul Wotton started a game for the first time in fifteen months, reclaiming the captain's armband to boot. There was a kit change too. Argyle's normal away kit comprised yellow shirts and green shorts. The shorts were dropped, if you will pardon the expression, to be replaced by yellow versions which did not match the hue of the shirts.

The Robins topped the table. After gaining promotion from League One they had proved to be the surprise package of the Championship. They were a team similar to Argyle – without any real stars –although they numbered £1 million striker Lee Trundle among the subs. They had gained a reputation in recent years of blowing their chances at the death, but manager Gary Johnson, once a contender for the Argyle job, was determined not to let it happen this time.

For the opening minutes Argyle were virtually entrenched in their own half. The Greens gradually edged their way back. With the fourth official signalling one minute of first-half stoppage time, Gary Teale sent in a low right-wing cross. Fallon was first to react, diverting a low left-foot shot past flamboyant Brazilian keeper Adriano Basso.

In teeming rain the 2,000-strong Green Army did not have to wait too long for more rejoicing. On the hour a Teale corner found Connolly at the far post. The full-back nodded the ball back and Kiwi Fallon bundled the ball in.

City, having started the match full of neat football, now resorted to high balls aimed at big man Dele Adebola and substitute Tamas Vasko. The tactic almost worked, with Wotton clearing off the line. Trundle, a major disappointment since his big-money move, was introduced into the fray and it was he who pulled a goal back from the spot after Jermaine Easter had charged down a free-kick using his hand.

City continued to press, with referee Bates mysteriously accumulating six minutes of stoppage time. Argyle, however, held out to regain a place in the top six. It was the start of City's downfall. They lost form and an automatic promotion place and eventually lost in the play-off final at Wembley.

And Rab Douglas was gone as quickly as he arrived.

The Beast – Hungarian centre-half Krizstian Timar

An Argyle dream-team strike partnership – Tommy Tynan and Mickey Evans

Local boy Mark Damerell

Mike Green, Mark Graves and Darren Tallon at an Argyle golf day

GUIDE TO SEASONAL SUMMARIES

Col 1:   Match number (for league fixtures); Round (for cup-ties).
        e.g.2:1 means 'Second round; first leg.'
        e.g.4R means 'Fourth round replay.'

Col 2:   Date of the fixture and whether Home (H), Away (A), or Neutral (N).

Col 3:   Opposition.

Col 4:   Attendances. Home gates appear in roman; Away gates in *italics*.
Figures in **bold** indicate the largest and smallest gates, at home and away.
Average home and away attendances appear after the final league match.
N.B. Home attendances are those registered with the Football League
and should be taken as accurate.

Col 5:   Respective league positions of Argyle and their opponents after the match.
Argyle's position appears on the top line in roman.
Their opponents' position appears on the second line in *italics*.
For cup-ties, the division and position of opponents is provided.
        e.g.2:12 means the opposition are twelfth in Division 2.

Col 6:   The top line shows the result: W(in), D(raw), or L(ose).
The second line shows Argyle's cumulative points total.

Col 7:   The match score, Argyle's given first.
Scores in **bold** indicate Argyle's biggest league win and heaviest defeat.

Col 8:   The half-time score, Argyle's given first.

Col 9:   The top line shows Argyle's scorers and times of goals in roman.
The second line shows opponents' scorers and times of goals in *italics*.
A 'p' after the time of a goal denotes a penalty; 'og' an own-goal.
The third line gives the name of the match referee.

Team line-ups: Argyle line-ups appear on the top line, irrespective of whether
they are home or away. Opposition teams appear on the second line in *italics*.
Players of either side who are sent off are marked !
Argyle players making their league debuts are displayed in **bold**.
In the era of squad numbers, players' names are positioned as far as
possible as if they were still wearing shirts 1 to 11.

Substitutes: Names of substitutes appear only if they actually took the field.
A player substituted is marked *
A second player substituted is marked ˆ
A third player substituted is marked "
These marks indicate the sequence of substitutions.

N.B.   For clarity, all information appearing in *italics* relates to opposing teams.

LEAGUE DIVISION 3 — SEASON 1974-75

Manager: Tony Waiters

Results

No	Date	V	Opponent	Att	Pos	Pt	F-A	H-T	Scorers, Times	Ref
1	17/8	A	PRESTON	11,663		0	L 0-1	0-0	Morley 60	P Richardson
2	24/8	H	GRIMSBY	8,531	12/22	2	W 2-1	1-0	Mariner 23, Rafferty 73; Lewis 87	T Bune
3	30/8	A	SOUTHEND	8,063	20/1	2	L 1-2	1-1	Rafferty 11; Cunningham 14, Worthington 51	A Hamil
4	4/9	A	ALDERSHOT	3,756	/2	2	L 3-4	3-1	Burrows H 31, Rafferty 40, Green 44; Dean 27, Brodie 50, Brown 62, Walton 83	J Homewood
5	7/9	H	TRANMERE	5,752	11/21	4	W 4-1	2-0	Mariner 28, Rafferty 40, 63, 76p; Allen 54	C Lawthon
6	14/9	A	SWINDON	5,445	17/10	4	L 0-2	0-0	Hubbard 54, Eastoe 64	A Porter
7	17/9	A	COLCHESTER	5,389	18/4	4	L 0-1	0-0	Packer 90	T Spencer
8	21/9	H	GILLINGHAM	5,556	17/18	5	D 1-1	0-1	Randell 58; Lindsey 44p	T Glasson
9	24/9	H	HEREFORD	5,519	15/17	7	W 1-0	1-0	Mariner 12	K Salmon
10	28/9	A	WREXHAM	3,814	18/14	7	L 1-5	0-0	Green 65; Thomas 47, 59, 88, Smallman 49, 90	D Richardson
11	1/10	H	HUDDERSFIELD	5,324	/9	9	W 2-0	1-0	Randell 11, Mariner 65	D Nippard

Line-ups (1–11 and 12 sub used)

No	Side	1	2	3	4	5	6	7	8	9	10	11	12
1	Argyle	Furnell	Darke	Burrows P	Hore	Griffiths	Green	Delve	Davey	Rafferty	Mariner*	Burrows H	Pearson
1	Preston	Brown	McMahon	Spark	Charlton	Bird	Sadler	Lamb	Morley	Elwiss	Coleman*	Burns	Smith
2	Argyle	Furnell	Darke	Burrows P	Hore	Griffiths	Green	Delve	Davey	Mariner*	Rafferty	Burrows H	Pearson
2	Grimsby	Wainman	Beardsley	Booth	Hubbard	Wigginton	Gray	Barton	Fletcher	Hickman	Lewis	Boylen	
3	Argyle	Furnell	Darke	Burrows P	Hore	Griffiths	Green	Delve	Davey	Rafferty	Mariner	Burrows H	
3	Southend	Cawston	Dyer	Worthington	Elliott	Townsend	Moody	Coulson	Brace	Guthrie	Taylor	Cunningham	
4	Argyle	Furnell	Darke	Burrows P	Hore*	Griffiths	Green	Delve	Davey	Rafferty	Hardcastle	Burrows H	Mariner
4	Aldershot	Johnson	Walden	Jopling	Sainty*	Dean	Richardson	Walton	Brown	Howarth	Joslyn	Brodie	Harley
5	Argyle	Furnell	Darke	Burrows P	Delve*	Griffiths	Green	Mariner	Davey	Rafferty	Hardcastle	Burrows H	Hore
5	Tranmere	Johnson	Mathias	Flood	Veitch	Moore	Pafios	Coppell	Allen	Mitchell	Crossley	Young*	Webb
6	Argyle	Furnell	Darke	Burrows P	Green	Griffiths	Delve	Mariner	Davey	Rafferty	Hardcastle	Randell	
6	Swindon	Barron	McLaughlin	Trollope	Hubbard	Potter	Prophett	Moss	Syrett	Eastoe	Butler	Jenkins	
7	Argyle	Furnell	Darke I	Burrows P	Hardcastle	Griffiths	Green	Hore	Mariner	Rafferty*	Saxton	Randell	Davey
7	Colchester	Walker	Smith A	Smith L	Leslie	Packer	Morgan	Thomas	Svarc	Froggatt	Lindsay	Cook	
8	Argyle	Furnell	Darke	Provan	Griffiths	Saxton	Green	Hore	Hardcastle*	Mariner	Rafferty	Randell	Davey
8	Gillingham	Hillyard	Lindsey	Ley	Jacques	Galvin	Hill	Chadwick	Jacks	Richardson	Wilks	Yeo	
9	Argyle	Furnell	Darke	Provan	Griffiths	Saxton	Delve	Hore	Mariner	Rafferty*	Hardcastle	Burrows H	Tyler
9	Hereford	Hughes	Emery	Byrne	Morgan	Rylands	Rudge	Kemp	Fear*	Redrobe	McNeil	Layton	
10	Argyle	Furnell	Darke	Provan	Green	Griffiths	Saxton	Randell	Mariner	Davey	Hardcastle	Burrows H*	Hardcastle
10	Wrexham	Lloyd	Jones	Fagg	Evans	May	Thomas	Tinnion	Whittle	Davies	Smallman	Griffiths	
11	Argyle	Furnell	Darke	Provan	Delve	Saxton	Green	Randell	Hardcastle	Mariner	Rafferty	Burrows H	McGinley
11	Huddersfield	Poole	Hutt	Garner	Pugh	Saunders	Dolan	Hoy*	Smith	Gowling	Summerill	Chapman	

Match notes

1 — Preston (A): Preston boss Bobby Charlton makes his playing comeback and admits his side were fortunate. Hore hits a post and Delve's shot (35) hits the crossbar and appears to cross the line. Morley climbs first to head the only goal. Pearson makes his league debut, replacing the injured Mariner.

2 — Grimsby (H): A third successive defeat for Tommy Casey's side. Mariner prods in Burrows' (H) corner and Rafferty scores from 25 yards for his first Argyle goal. Davey and Rafferty hit posts. Lewis gives the Mariners' late hope but misses a last minute chance. Barton is booked for a foul on Delve.

3 — Southend (A): Three wins out of 3 for Southend but Arthur Rowley is unhappy with his side's showing. Argyle's lead is cancelled out by a free kick taken as they arrange their defensive 'wall'. Worthington admits his ambitious 25 yard winner was 'lucky'. Darke is booked for deliberate handball.

4 — Aldershot (A): Argyle open with a string of corners but Dean's header is deemed over the line after Hore clears from under the crossbar. Burrows' response is a 30 yard screamer. Tom McAnearney's half time pep talk does the trick as the Shots dominate the second half, aided by defensive lapses.

5 — Tranmere (H): Jake King's young side have no answer to the on-song Rafferty. Young is stretchered off (19). Mariner's header precedes the onset of heavy rain. Rafferty completes his hat-trick from the spot after Davey is pulled back by Eddie Flood. Delve picks up his third booking of the season.

6 — Swindon (A): Swindon are smarting from a 6-2 hammering at Crystal Palace a week earlier. Argyle are without Harry Burrows with a broken hand but have new chief coach, Alan Brown on the bench. Hubbard beats Furnell with a low drive and Syrett brilliantly sets up Eastoe for an easy second.

7 — Colchester (A): Darke is booked (21) for kicking the ball away and dismissed 20 minutes later for obstructing Cook. Davey is cautioned within 30 seconds of coming on. Ten man Argyle hold United until injury time, when Mick Packer's first goal for the club finds the top corner from 30 yards.

8 — Gillingham (H): The referee dominates, booking Galvin (foul on Mariner) and Saxton (handball) within the first twelve minutes, and later, Rafferty. Lindsey handles (34) but Ron Hillyard saves Rafferty's penalty. Lindsey is more successful after Darke handles. Randell scores directly from a corner.

9 — Hereford (H): Burrows returns from injury to set up Mariner's winner. Refereeing decisions again make the headlines as Darke and Layton are booked for innocuous challenges, prompting Tony Waiters to report Mr Salmon to the Football League. Darke appeals his sending off at Colchester.

10 — Wrexham (A): Mickey Thomas makes light of the treacherous conditions to score his first hat-trick but Smallman's last minute shot from 20 yards is the pick of the bunch. Arfon Griffiths is the midfield architect. Green is thrown in attack in desperation and scores after two goal-line clearances.

11 — Huddersfield (H): Furnell is a virtual spectator as Argyle dominate. Saxton and Green effectively nullify the dangerous Gowling. Mariner's sixth-minute effort is ruled offside but Randell's volley soon makes amends. Poole is kept busy but is deceived by Mariner's speculative effort from the right wing.

Match-by-match league log (Plymouth Argyle). Team line-up column headers (top row):

Furnell · Darke · Delve · Provan · Burrows P · Saxton · Green · Delve · Randell · Mariner · Rafferty · Hardcastle · Burrows H

---

12 H WALSALL · 5/10 · 2-1 · W · 11 · 5,765 · 7 · 11
Rafferty 36, Delve 84
Andrews 40
Opponents: Kearns | Harrison | Fry | Robinson | Saunders | Atthey | Sloan | Andrews | Wright | Buckley | Caswell
Ref: C Thomas

Walsall are fresh from a 6-0 thrashing of Brighton. Rafferty ends his minor drought by scoring from six yards. George Andrews, once close to becoming a Pilgrim, equalises. Former Argyle loanee, Kearns, keeps the Pilgrims at bay until Delve, from 30 yards, hits his first Greens goal

---

13 A PORT VALE · 12/10 · 0-2 · L · 11 · 3,634 · 13 · 11
Horton 25, Woodward 84
Opponents: Connaughton | Brodie | Dulson | Chadwick | Summerscales | Horton | Lacey | McLaren | Williams* | Bailey | Sharp | Woodward
Ref: R Kirkpatrick

Seven away defeats on the trot for Argyle as Roy Sproson's Vale maintain their unbeaten home record. Persistent foul play from both sides disrupts the game. Horton's first-time shot flies in and Woodward shoots into an empty net. Williams is stretchered off (58) with concussion.

---

14 H ALDERSHOT · 15/10 · 1-0 · W · 13 · 5,517
Rafferty 44
Opponents: Johnson | Walden | Jopling* | Dean | Walker | Brown | Howarth | Bell | Brodie | Sainty | Johnson | Richardson
(Joslyn)
Ref: E Read

Argyle's seventh lowest crowd since the war see Mariner and Rafferty combine for the only goal. The Pilgrims announce they have agreed the £12k transfer of winger Hugh McAuley from Liverpool. Darke suffers a bruised foot and skipper Green has stitches inserted in an eye wound.

---

15 H PETERBOROUGH · 19/10 · 2-0 · W · 11 · 6,843 · 2
Green 36, Rafferty 77
Opponents: Steele | Bradley* | Lee | Walker | Turner | Carmichael | Murray | Nixon | Galley | Hill | Robson | Gregory
Ref: H Powell

Posh top the table after a midweek win but new boy McAuley sets up both goals. Saxton's woeful back-pass gives Galley an early chance but he fails to capitalise. Driving rain fails to silence the vociferous visiting fans, who have travelled through the night. Turner is booked for a foul.

---

16 A BURY · 26/10 · 1-0 · W · 17 · 4,697 · 15 · 17
Forrest 9(og)
Opponents: Forrest | Hoolickin | Kennedy | Williams | Hulme | Holt | Spence | Rowland | Buchan* | Tinsley | Hamstead | Duffey
Ref: D Turner

Waiters issues instructions to capitalise on keeper John Forrest's lack of height (5' 9"). Johnson obliges by chipping from 25 yards. The ball strikes the crossbar, hits Forrest on the back and goes in. Duffey makes his debut after signing from Crewe but Argyle's defence remain sound.

---

17 A CHARLTON · 2/11 · 2-0 · W · 19 · 8,495 · 6
Johnson 52, McAuley 76
Opponents: Franklin | Curtis | Tumbridge* | Bowman | Young | Horsfield | Powell | Cripps | Hunt | Flanagan | Peacock | Dunphy
Ref: R Clay

Argyle win at the Valley for the first time since 1931. Former Pilgrim, Andy Nelson, recalls long-term injury victim, Mike Flanagan. Rafferty finds the net (50) but is ruled offside. Johnson's long ball floats over everyone for the first goal and McAuley seals the win with a rare header.

---

18 H WATFORD · 9/11 · 1-1 · D · 20 · 8,063 · 14
Johnson 35
Markham 88
Opponents: Rankin | Walsh | Williams | Keen | Goodeve | Lees | Morrissey | Bond | Jenkins | Craker* | McCettigan | Markham
Ref: T Reynolds

Days of rain tests Home Park's new drainage system. Argyle's newspaper style programme has a new editor and a new printer. Watford player-manager Mike Keen recalls himself. Johnson's shot finds it way through crowd of players. Furnell fails to cut out a cross, to gift the equaliser.

---

19 A CRYSTAL PALACE · 16/11 · 3-3 · D · 21 · 19,308 · 6
Rafferty 23, Johnson 31, Mariner 66
Whittle 2, Sw'hurst 51, Hinshelw'd 72
Opponents: Hammond | Jump | Cannon | Jeffries | Evans | Venables | Whittle | Hinshelwood | Taylor* | Swindlehurst | Lindsay
Ref: A Grey

This thriller sees Palace lead after 70 seconds. Rafferty levels from 25 yards and Johnson's scoring run continues whilst Taylor is off the pitch injured. Crowd trouble at half-time and five Argyle fans run the length of the pitch. Swindlehurst nets from 30 yards after a retaken free-kick.

---

20 A CHESTERFIELD · 30/11 · 2-1 · W · 23 · 4,663 · 18
Rafferty 22, Mariner 83
Shanahan 47p
Opponents: Tingay | O'Neil | Burton | Barlow | Winstanley | Kowalski | Darling | Moss | Shanahan | McKewan | Wilson | Vassallo
Ref: C White

Darke is suspended after his appeal fails. Rafferty is injured whilst heading the first but resumes after treatment. Argyle protest that Burrows' collision with Darling was accidental but Shanahan sends Furnell the wrong way. Delve is booked for dissent (56). Mariner's low shot seals it.

---

21 H BOURNEMOUTH · 7/12 · 1-0 · W · 25 · 9,897
Rafferty 65
Opponents: Charlton | Payne | Miller | Delaney | Hague | Howard | O'Rourke | Goddard | Greenhalgh | Parodi
Ref: H New

Griffiths has returned to Man Utd after his loan spell. Cherries have former Home Park favourites Hague and Welsh in the side and Rickard on the bench. Rafferty outpaces everyone for the only goal. Payne is booked for no apparent reason and Delve's name is taken again for dissent.

---

22 A BRIGHTON · 21/12 · 2-2 · D · 26 · 9,913 · 21
Rafferty 9, 11
Binney 77, Towner 80
Opponents: Grummitt | Tiler | Wilson | Mason | Rollings | Winstanley | Towner | Binney | Mellor | O'Sullivan | Walker
Ref: H Robinson

Even home fans applaud Argyle's flowing football. Rafferty increases his season's tally to 16 with two well-taken goals. Plymouth-born Fred Binney leads the comeback as he heads Brighton's first and makes the second. Ex-Pilgrim skipper, Ernie Machin, is kept on the subs' bench.

---

23 H SWINDON · 26/12 · 4-3 · W · 28 · 18,027 · 5
Randell 42, Delve 47, Mar' 65, Raf' 77p
Moss 22, 31, McLaughlin 49
Opponents: Barron | Dixon | Hubbard | Prophet | Burrows | Trollope | Moss | McLaughlin | Eastoe | Jenkins | Anderson | Rogers
Ref: A Robinson

Swindon have slipped from second after two successive defeats, but boast in Peter Eastoe the division's top scorer. Swindon's early dominance is rewarded, but the Pilgrims' fight-back is completed when McAuley, yet to finish on a losing Argyle side is brought down in the penalty area.

LEAGUE DIVISION 3 — SEASON 1974-75

Manager: Tony Waiters

Results

No	Pos	Date	Att	Opp Pos	Pt	Res	F-A	H-T
24	3	A HALIFAX 28/12	2,063	18	29	D	1-1	1-1
25	2	A BOURNEMOUTH 11/1	7,362	20	31	W	7-3	4-0
26	2	H CHESTERFIELD 18/1	13,005	24	33	W	3-0	1-0
27	2	A WATFORD 1/2	8,563	14	35	W	3-1	1-0
28	1	H BLACKBURN 4/2	28,744	2	37	W	2-1	0-0
29	1	H CHARLTON 8/2	22,946	3	38	D	1-1	0-0
30	2	A BLACKBURN 15/2	17,734	1	38	L	2-5	2-1
31	4	H CRYSTAL PALACE 22/2	21,002	5	38	L	0-1	0-1
32	3	H SOUTHEND 28/2	16,321	13	40	W	1-0	0-0
33	2	A HEREFORD 8/3	9,296	11	42	W	5-1	1-0
34	3	H WREXHAM 15/3	14,855	11	42	L	0-3	0-1

Line-ups, Scorers, Times and Referees

24 — HALIFAX
Argyle: 1 Furnell, 2 Hore, 3 Burrows P, 4 Delve, 5 Green, 6 Saxton, 7 Johnson, 8 Mariner, 9 Rafferty, 10 Hardcastle, 11 McAuley
Halifax: 1 Smith, 2 Luckett, 3 Collins, 4 McHale, 5 Rhodes, 6 Phalan, 7 Jones, 8 Blair, 9 Downes, 10 Gwyther, 11 Quinn
Scorers: McAuley 39 / Blair 1 — Ref: G Trevett
Argyle don a new all-white strip for this gate-lashed game. Blair heads in Gwyther's cross after 30 seconds. Rafferty misses an open goal but McAuley dives in to head the equaliser. Hardcastle, replacing tendon-injury victim Randell, is booked, as is Saxton who now faces suspension.

25 — BOURNEMOUTH
Argyle: 1 Furnell, 2 Hore, 3 Burrows P, 4 Sutton, 5 Green, 6 Delve, 7 Randell, 8 Johnson, 9 Mariner, 10 Rafferty, 11 McAuley
Bournemouth: 1 Charlton, 2 Payne, 3 Parodi, 4 Howard, 5 Merrick, 6 Hague, 7 Miller*, 8 Goddard, 9 Wingate, 10 O'Rourke, 11 Buttle, 12 Greenhalgh
Scorers: Rr7, M'13,88, J'39, McA'45, D'49, Rn'90 / Wingate 61, Green 75(og), Howard 77 — Ref: W Gow
Argyle travel to Dean Court in their new £25k state-of-the-art team coach. Neil Hague heads the managerless Cherries' only first-half chance wide. Wingate and Green's own-goal after a scramble gives home fans hope. Randell finishes the job with a goal two minutes into injury-time.

26 — CHESTERFIELD
Argyle: 1 Furnell, 2 Hore, 3 Burrows P, 4 Sutton, 5 Green, 6 Delve*, 7 Randell, 8 Mariner, 9 Rafferty, 10 Johnson, 11 McAuley, 12 Vassallo
Chesterfield: 1 Tingay, 2 Holmes, 3 Burton, 4 O'Neil, 5 Winstanley, 6 Barlow, 7 Darling, 8 Moss, 9 Kowalski, 10 Bellamy, 11 Phillips
Scorers: Delve 28, Mariner 80, Vassallo 84 — Ref: D Nippard
Joe Shaw's Spireites have plunged to the foot of the table after losing seven of the last nine matches. Rafferty looks poised to score but slips in the mud. Vassallo, replacing the injured Delve, completes the scoring with his first league goal. Steve Davey is named available for transfer.

27 — WATFORD
Argyle: 1 Furnell, 2 Hore, 3 Burrows P, 4 Saxton, 5 Green, 6 Delve, 7 Randell, 8 Johnson, 9 Mariner, 10 Rafferty, 11 McAuley
Watford: 1 Rankin, 2 How, 3 Williams, 4 Joslyn, 5 Goodeve, 6 Markham, 7 Scullion, 8 Bond, 9 Mercer, 10 Mayes*, 11 Keen
Scorers: Markham 41(og), Johnson 63, Mariner 81 / Goodeve 90 — Ref: J Hough
Over 1,000 Argyle fans make the journey to Vicarage Road. Mariner, having missed the Everton cup-tie, returns from injury and his shot hits the post, strikes Markham on the rebound, and flies in for the opener. Five players are booked, including Markham and the inevitable Delve.

28 — BLACKBURN
Argyle: 1 Furnell, 2 Hore, 3 Burrows P, 4 Saxton, 5 Green, 6 Delve, 7 Randell, 8 Johnson, 9 Mariner, 10 Rafferty, 11 McAuley
Blackburn: 1 Jones, 2 Burgin, 3 Wood, 4 Metcalfe, 5 Hawkins, 6 Fazackerley, 7 Beamish, 8 Oates, 9 Martin, 10 Parkes, 11 Heaton*, 12 Hickman
Scorers: Rafferty 61, Johnson 86 / Beamish 90 — Ref: J Bent
The biggest league gate at Home Park since 1960 see Argyle take over from their opponents at the top. Rovers are without broken-leg victim, Jimmy Mullen. Hawkins helps Rafferty's shot over the line and Johnson scores on a counter-attack. Blackburn's goal comes in injury-time.

29 — CHARLTON
Argyle: 1 Furnell, 2 Hore, 3 Burrows P, 4 Saxton, 5 Green, 6 Delve, 7 Randell, 8 Johnson, 9 Mariner, 10 Rafferty, 11 McAuley
Charlton: 1 Tutt, 2 Curtis, 3 Warman, 4 Bowman, 5 Goldthorpe, 6 Young, 7 Powell, 8 Hales, 9 Horsfield, 10 Hunt, 11 Peacock
Scorers: Rafferty 67 / Warman 80 — Ref: M Taylor
Another top of the table clash. Charlton fulfil Andy Nelson's pledge that they are looking for a win, and attack with gusto. Rafferty outjumps the defence to head home. Warman converts Powell's overhead kick. Rafferty's last-minute penalty strikes an upright after Hunt had handled.

30 — BLACKBURN
Argyle: 1 Furnell, 2 Hore, 3 Burrows P, 4 Saxton, 5 Green, 6 Delve, 7 Randell, 8 Johnson, 9 Mariner, 10 Rafferty, 11 McAuley
Blackburn: 1 Jones, 2 Heaton, 3 Burgin, 4 Metcalfe, 5 Hawkins, 6 Fazackerley, 7 Beamish, 8 Oates, 9 Martin, 10 Parkes, 11 Hickman
Scorers: McAuley 16, Jones 19(og) / Beam 39, Martin 53, 87, Hickm'n 56, 85 — Ref: K McNally
England boss, Don Revie, attends the match to watch Mariner and sees the Pilgrims lose their 16-match unbeaten league record. Argyle's early lead is aided by Jones punching into his own net. A penalty sparks crowd trouble but Furnell saves from Martin (23) before Rovers run riot.

31 — CRYSTAL PALACE
Argyle: 1 Furnell, 2 Hore, 3 Burrows P, 4 Delve, 5 Green, 6 Saxton, 7 Randell, 8 Johnson*, 9 Mariner, 10 Rafferty, 11 McAuley, 12 Vassallo
Crystal Palace: 1 Burns, 2 Mulligan, 3 Wall, 4 Johnson, 5 Jeffries, 6 Evans, 7 Whittle, 8 Holder, 9 Hill, 10 Swindlehurst, 11 Taylor
Scorers: Swindlehurst 31 — Ref: A Hamil
Argyle announce an annual profit of £2,678. Malcolm Allison's prediction that his side would end the Pilgrims' unbeaten home run comes true. The only goal comes after a well-rehearsed free-kick. The ref lectures Evans, goes to his pocket but pulls out his handkerchief to blow his nose.

32 — SOUTHEND
Argyle: 1 Furnell, 2 Hore, 3 Burrows P, 4 Delve, 5 Green, 6 Hardcastle, 7 Randell, 8 Vassallo*, 9 Mariner, 10 Rafferty, 11 McAuley, 12 Darke
Southend: 1 Webster, 2 Worthington, 3 Taylor, 4 Elliott*, 5 Townsend, 6 Dyer, 7 Little, 8 Brace, 9 Guthrie, 10 Silvester, 11 Ford, 12 Love
Scorers: Mariner 67p — Ref: D Lloyd
Mariner's penalty, after Rafferty had been felled by Dave Worthington, seals a dour victory. Vassallo's full debut is not a happy one as he is booked and then goes off with cramp. The crowd vent their feelings about the continued omission of Davey. U's win only two more matches.

33 — HEREFORD
Argyle: 1 Blyth, 2 Hore, 3 Burrows P, 4 Hardcastle*, 5 Green, 6 Saxton, 7 Randell, 8 Johnson, 9 Mariner, 10 Rafferty, 11 McAuley, 12 Vassallo
Hereford: 2 Emery, 3 Byrne, 4 Roberts, 5 Tucker, 6 McLaughlin, 7 Gregory, 8 Deacy*, 9 Galley, 10 McNeil, 11 Tyler, 12 Silkman
Scorers: Hardcastle 21, Mariner 51, Rafferty 81, 88, [Vassallo 90] / McNeil 70 — Ref: P Reeves
Hardcastle, in for the suspended Delve, nets his first league goal to inspire the Greens. On-loan goalkeeper Jim Blyth is blameless as Argyle's wingers create havoc. A happier day for Vassallo as he blasts in the best goal of the match. Dixie McNeil finishes the season with 32 goals.

34 — WREXHAM
Argyle: 1 Furnell, 2 Hore, 3 Burrows P, 4 Delve, 5 Green, 6 Saxton, 7 Randell, 8 Johnson, 9 Mariner, 10 Rafferty, 11 McAuley
Wrexham: 1 Lloyd, 2 Jones, 3 Fogg, 4 Evans, 5 May, 6 Thomas, 7 Tinnion, 8 Sutton, 9 Davies, 10 Whittle, 11 Griffiths
Scorers: Griffiths 19, Davies 77, Whittle 78 — Ref: B Daniels
In front of the 'Match of the Day' cameras, Wrexham score their fourth successive victory over the Pilgrims. The Welsh side are missing Dave Smallman, transferred to Everton for £75k, but Griffiths scores with a solo effort and two defensive blunders gift the points to the Robins.

#	Date	Opponent	Venue	Att	Res	Score	Pos	Pts	Scorers	Referee
	18/3			22,068			7	44	Charlton 85	Ref: P Walters
36	21/3	TRANMERE	A	3,040	W	3-1	24	46	Green 3, Johnson 8, Rafferty 34 / Crossley 78	Ref: P Partridge
37	28/3	HALIFAX	H	19,580	W	2-0		48	Collins 74 (og), McAuley 80	Ref: M Sinclair
38	29/3	BRIGHTON	H	19,396	D	2-2	19	49	Green 21, Mariner 53 / Fell 1, Burrows 32(og)	Ref: D Civil
39	31/3	GILLINGHAM	A	11,200	D	2-2	10	50	Green 69, Rafferty 88 / Shipperley 2, Yeo 40	Ref: R Clay
40	5/4	BURY	H	14,940	W	2-1	15	52	Rafferty 24, Johnson 73 / Spence 13	Ref: A Hart
41	8/4	HUDDERSFIELD	A	2,947	W	2-0	23	54	Mariner 23, 69	Ref: J Hunting
42	12/4	WALSALL	A	7,404	D	0-0	8	55		Ref: J Goggins
43	15/4	COLCHESTER	H	23,551	W	1-0	13	57	Mariner 50	Ref: A Lees
44	19/4	PORT VALE	H	22,447	D	1-1	4	58	Delve 67 / Brownhill 47	Ref: A Turvey
45	22/4	GRIMSBY	A	9,052	D	1-1	14	59	Mariner 70 / Boylen 82	Ref: P Willis
46	26/4	PETERBOROUGH	A	11,176	L	0-1	5	59	Robson 42	Ref: J Williams

Home Average 14,060
Away 7,813

Line-ups and match reports

18/3 — Tunks, McMahon, Burns, Stiles, Bird, Spark, Barter*, Coleman, Elwiss, Holden, Charlton, Smith.
Rafferty and Phil Burrows are chosen for the PFA's Third Division All-Star side. A good crowd turns out to see Preston's ageing stars. Hore, on the overlap, sets up Mariner for the first. Charlton looks to have clinched a point with a powerful shot but Mariner's late header steals it.

36 TRANMERE — Furnell, Hore, Burrows P, Saxton, Green, Delve, Vassallo, Randell, Johnson, Mariner, Rafferty, McAuley; Johnson, Webb, Mathias, Moore, Philpotts, Palios*, Crossley, Kenny, Allen, McBurney, Young, Woodin.
McAuley's family attend the match and see him inspire another win on a mudbath. Green heads in a free-kick. Johnson punishes a defensive error and Rafferty combines with Mariner for the third. Hore heads onto the roof of his own net. Paul Crossley scores directly from a free-kick.

37 HALIFAX — Furnell, Hore, Burrows P, Saxton, Green, Delve, Vassallo, Randell, Johnson, Mariner, Rafferty, McAuley; Smith, Smith, Collins, McHale, Rhodes, Phelan, Jones, Ford, Downes!, Campbell, Blair.
Town frustrate Argyle but then self destruct. Steve Downes, angered by a tackle, runs 20 yards to head-butt Green and is sent off (50) although Green later confirms there was no contact. John Collins deflects Mariner's shot and McAuley evades four tackles to score a brilliant solo goal.

38 BRIGHTON — Furnell, Hore, Burrows P, Saxton, Green, Delve, Vassallo, Randell, Johnson, Mariner, Rafferty, McAuley; Grummitt, Tiler, Wilson, Mason, Piper, Winstanley, Towner, Machin, Marlowe, Fell, O'Sullivan.
Brighton's players watch the previous day's match from the stands as Waiters calls the crowded fixtures 'a farce'. Fell scores after 29 seconds. After Green's reply, Fell's shot hits Furnell, Burrows' knee and the back of the net. Machin runs the show. Mariner nods in to rescue a point.

39 GILLINGHAM — Furnell, Hore, Burrows P, Saxton, Green, Delve, Vassallo, Randell, Johnson, Mariner, Rafferty, McAuley; Hillyard, Wiltshire, Ley, Galvin, Shipperley*, Tydeman, Jacks, Richardson, Gauden, Chadwick, Yeo, O'Donnell.
Alan Brown's fitness regime pays off as Argyle claw a two-goal deficit in the Priestfield mud. Yeo initially claims the first but is credited only with the second. Green scores against one of his former clubs and after Dave Shipperley goes off injured, Rafferty clinically shoots home.

40 BURY — Furnell, Hore, Burrows P, Saxton, Green, Delve, Vassallo, Randell, Johnson, Mariner, Rafferty, McAuley; Forrest, Hoolickin, Kennedy, Nicholson, Hulme, Darcy, Buchan*, Riley, Spence, Rowland, Williams, Rudd.
The Easter exertions continue to prove too much for Randell's tendon. Michael Foot MP sees the Pilgrims win yet again. Spence silences the crowd's 'Oggie Oggie' chant. Rafferty is unmarked and Forrest only parries Johnson's shot. Rudd and Delve are unpunished after fisticuffs.

41 HUDDERSFIELD — Furnell, Hore, Burrows P, Saxton, Green, Delve, Vassallo, Randell, Johnson, Mariner, Rafferty, McAuley; Taylor, Sweeney, Garner, Dolan, Saunders, Hart, Maitland, Smith, Dungworth*, Gowling, Gray, Garwood.
In a blizzard, Mariner reinforces his claims for England Under-23 honours. Defeat virtually seals Huddersfield's three-year slide through the divisions. Disillusioned Terriers boss, Bobby Collins, says his players 'must be disgusted with themselves'. Furnell's fingertips deny Dolan.

42 WALSALL — Furnell, Hore, Burrows P, Saxton, Green, Delve, Vassallo, Randell, Johnson, Mariner, Rafferty, McAuley; Kearns, Brown, Harrison, Robinson, Saunders, Atthey, Caswell, Andrews, Wright, Buckley, Birch.
Both sides spurn chances. Kearns fumbles Mariner's first-minute shot but no one follows up. Burrows clears Wright's bullet header off the line. Mariner clutches his shoulder for most of the second half after receiving a kick. Two more points will confirm the Pilgrims' promotion.

43 COLCHESTER — Furnell, Hore, Burrows P, Saxton, Green, Delve, Vassallo, Randell, Johnson, Mariner, Rafferty, McAuley; Walker, Dominey*, Cook, Packer, Harford, Smith L, Leslie, Svarc, Froggatt, Foley, Lindsay, Bunkell.
Police watch helplessly as spectators surge onto the pitch at the final whistle as the Greens' return to Division Two, after a seven-year absence, is confirmed. Walker pulls off a string of fine saves but drop-kicks the ball against Rafferty's back and the ball drops invitingly for Mariner.

44 PORT VALE — Furnell, Hore, Burrows P, Saxton, Green, Delve, Vassallo, Randell!, Johnson, Mariner, Rafferty, McAuley; Connaughton, Lacey, Dulson, Ridley, Harris, Horton, Woodward*, Brownhill, Williams, Bailey, McLaren, Sharp.
Vale players applaud Argyle onto the pitch but then try to spoil the party. Brownhill heads in unmarked and Randell, never before booked in his career, is sent off (64) for a foul on McLaren. Delve's back-header goes in off a post. Mr Turvey's decisions continue to baffle everyone.

45 GRIMSBY — Furnell, Hore, Burrows P, Saxton, Green, Delve, Vassallo, Randell, Johnson, Mariner, Rafferty, McAuley; Wainman, Marley, Govier, Hubbard, Barton, Gray, Lewis, Partridge, Lumby*, Boylen, Booth, Brown.
Tony Waiters is linked with Newcastle. Grimsby's best crowd of the season see their side continue a nine-match unbeaten run which has taken them clear of relegation. Rafferty's overhead kick hits the bar and Mariner nets the rebound. The unmarked Boylen dents Argyle's title hopes.

46 PETERBOROUGH — Furnell, Hore, Burrows P, Saxton, Green, Delve, Vassallo, Randell*, Johnson, Mariner, Rafferty, McAuley; Steele, Bradley, Winfield, Murray, Turner, Hobson, Nixon, Gregory, Hall, Hill, Robson, Vassallo.
Five thousand Pilgrim followers invade East Anglia but crowd-trouble mars the day. Rafferty is voted Third Division Player of the Year by the Daily Express. In an uncompromising match, Robson scores after Argyle fail to clear. Blackburn win on the following Monday to take the title.

LEAGUE DIVISION 3 (CUP-TIES)

Manager: Tony Waiters

SEASON 1974-75

League Cup

#		Opponent	Date	Res	Pos	Att		F-A	H-T	Scorers, Times, and Referees	1	2	3	4	5	6	7	8	9	10	11	12 sub used
1	A	BRISTOL ROV	20/8	D		8,974	2:	0-0	0-0	Ref: B Newsome	Furnell	Darke	Burrows P	Hore	Griffiths	Green	Delve	Davey	Rafferty	Mariner	Burrows H	
											Eadie	*Jacobs*	*Parsons*	*Aitken*	*Taylor*	*Stanton*	*Jones*	*Staniforth*	*Warboys*	*Bannister*	*Rudge**	*Fearnley*
1R	H	BRISTOL ROV	27/8	L	12	11,213	2:12	0-1	0-0	Warboys 86 Ref: B Newsome	Furnell	Darke	Burrows P	Hore	Griffiths	Green	Delve	Davey	Rafferty*	Mariner	Burrows H	Pearson
											Eadie	*Jacobs*	*Parsons*	*Aitken*	*Taylor*	*Prince*	*Jones*	*Stanton*	*Warboys*	*Bannister*	*Fearnley*	

Match 1: In an unexciting game, new skipper Green stars against his former club, curbing the threat of 'Smash and Grab' Bruce Bannister and Alan Warboys. Mr Newsome upsets both managers by booking five players, including Davey Green and Delve, all for dissent, in a 14-minute spell.

Match 1R: No repeat of Argyle's semi-final exploits last season as Warboys' late 25-yard drive puts Don Megson's Rovers through. Green wastes a late chance by handling to control the ball. Rafferty injures tendons and Delve and Prince have a running battle, with both ending in the notebook.

FA Cup

#		Opponent	Date	Res	Pos	Att		F-A	H-T	Scorers, Times, and Referees	1	2	3	4	5	6	7	8	9	10	11	12 sub used
1	A	DARTFORD	23/11	W	10	4,384	SL:18	3-2	1-1	Randell 38, 88, Mariner 89 Henderson 40, 86 Ref: R Glasson	Furnell	Hore	Burrows P	Saxton	Green	Delve	Randell	Johnson*	Mariner	Rafferty	McAuley	Rogers
											Keen	*Payne*	*Shovelar*	*Carr*	*Burns*	*Mitchell*	*Light*	*Henderson*	*Moy*	*Robinson*	*Halliday*	
2	H	CRYSTAL PALACE	14/12	W	6	17,473	3	2-1	0-1	Green 71, Rafferty 76 Swindlehurst 22 Ref: E Read	Furnell	Hore	Burrows P	Saxton	Green	Delve	Randell	Johnson*	Mariner	Rafferty	McAuley	Rogers
											Burns	*Mulligan*	*Cannon*	*Venables*	*Jeffries*	*Evans*	*Chatterton*	*Whittle*	*Swindlehurst*	*Hinshelw'd**	*Taylor*	*Lindsay*
3	H	BLACKPOOL	4/1	W	3	23,143	2:8	2-0	1-0	Rafferty 33, 60 Ref: A Hamil	Furnell	Hore	Burrows P	Saxton	Green	Delve	Hardcastle*	Johnson	Mariner	Rafferty	McAuley	Rogers
											Burridge	*Curtis*	*Bentley*	*Hatton*	*Hart*	*Alcock*	*Moore**	*Ainscow*	*Walsh*	*Davies*	*Evanson*	*Tong*
4	H	EVERTON	25/1	L	2	38,000	1:1	1-3	0-2	Vassallo 59 Pearson 7, Lyons 37, 76 Ref: W Gow	Furnell	Hore	Burrows P	Saxton	Green	Delve	Randell	Johnson	Vassallo	Rafferty	McAuley	
											Davies	*Scott*	*Seargeant*	*Clements*	*Kenyon*	*McNaught*	*Marshall**	*Dobson*	*Pearson*	*Lyons*	*Telfer*	*Bernard*

Match 1 (Dartford): Watling Street reverberates with Henderson's second for the Southern League champions. In the gloomy conditions, substitute Rogers' ginger hair stands out and he sets up Mariner's leveller. Randell's second saves Argyle's blushes, leaving Dartford boss, Ernie Morgan, distraught.

Match 2 (Crystal Palace): Hero Furnell is mobbed by fans at the final whistle as he saves Venables' injury-time spot-kick after Green had fouled Whittle. Green's chip cancels out Swindlehurst's opener. Rafferty volleys the winner. A policeman's hat finds its way onto the pitch, so Ian Evans decides to wear it.

Match 3 (Blackpool): In front of his parents, who have travelled from Scotland, the in-form Rafferty climbs to the top of the national scoring charts with two strikes against his former team. Hardcastle is stretchered off (75) after a clash with Pool skipper, Hatton, who is booed for the remainder of the game.

Match 4 (Everton): Home Park is stunned into silence when the team is announced. Mariner is out injured. The Toffees are without star striker, Bob Latchford. In front of a full house, and TV cameras, Everton's class tells. Vassallo ensures he will never forget his full debut by converting Randell's pass.

Final League Table

#	Team	P	Home					Away					Pts
			W	D	L	F	A	W	D	L	F	A	
1	Blackburn	46	15	7	1	40	16	7	9	7	28	29	60
2	PLYMOUTH	46	16	5	2	38	19	8	6	9	41	39	59
3	Charlton	46	15	5	3	51	29	7	6	10	25	32	55
4	Swindon	46	18	3	2	43	17	3	8	12	21	41	53
5	Crystal Pal	46	14	8	1	48	22	4	7	12	18	35	51
6	Port Vale	46	15	6	2	37	19	3	9	11	24	35	51
7	Peterborough	46	10	9	4	24	17	9	3	11	23	36	50
8	Walsall	46	15	5	3	46	13	3	8	12	21	39	49
9	Preston	46	16	5	2	42	19	3	6	14	21	37	49
10	Gillingham	46	14	6	3	43	23	3	8	12	22	37	48
11	Colchester	46	13	7	3	45	22	4	6	13	25	41	47
12	Hereford	46	14	6	3	42	21	2	8	13	22	45	46
13	Wrexham	46	10	8	5	41	23	5	7	11	24	32	45
14	Bury	46	13	6	4	38	17	3	6	14	15	33	44
15	Chesterfield	46	11	7	5	37	25	5	5	13	25	41	44
16	Grimsby	46	12	8	3	35	19	3	5	15	20	45	43
17	Halifax	46	11	10	2	33	20	2	7	14	16	45	43
18	Southend	46	11	9	3	32	17	2	7	14	14	34	42
19	Brighton	46	14	7	2	38	21	2	3	18	18	43	42
20	Aldershot*	46	13	5	5	40	21	1	6	16	13	42	38
21	Bournemouth	46	9	6	8	27	25	4	6	13	17	33	38
22	Tranmere	46	12	4	7	39	21	2	5	16	16	36	37
23	Watford	46	9	7	7	30	31	1	10	12	22	44	37
24	Huddersfield	46	9	6	8	32	29	2	4	17	15	47	32
		1104	309	155	88	921	506	88	155	309	506	921	1103

* deducted 1 pt

Notes

Double wins: (6) Bournemouth, Bury, Chesterfield, Hereford, Huddersfield, Tranmere.

Double defeats: (1) Wrexham.

Won from behind: (2) Bury, Swindon.

Lost from in front: (3) Aldershot, Blackburn, Southend.

High spots: Sixteen-match unbeaten run mid season.
The Mariner-Rafferty partnership.
Capacity attendance against league leaders Everton in FA Cup.
Two appearances on 'Match of the Day'.
Promotion after six seasons in Division 3.

Low spots: Two points from final three games cost the championship.
Five defeats in first seven matches.
Departure of ever popular Steve Davey to Hereford.

Player of the Year: Paul Mariner.

Ever presents: (3) Jim Furnell, Mike Green, Bill Rafferty.

Hat-tricks: (1) Bill Rafferty.

Leading scorer: Bill Rafferty (26).

Appearances and Goals

Name	Lge	Sub	LC	Sub	FAC	Sub	Lge	LC	FAC	Tot
Burrows, Harry	10		2							1
Burrows, Phil	39		2		4					
Darke, Peter	19		2		2					
Davey, Steve	6	2	2				5			5
Delve, John	42		2		4					
Furnell, Jim	46		2		4					
Green, Mike	46		2		4		6		1	7
Griffiths, Clive	10	1			1					
Hardcastle, Peter	12	1			1		1			1
Hore, John	33		2		4					
Johnson, Brian	32				4		8			8
Mariner, Paul	45		2		3		20		1	21
McAuley, Hugh	32		2		4		5			5
Pearson, Ian		2		1						
Provan, David	7									
Rafferty, Bill	46		2		4		23		3	26
Randell, Colin	36		2		3		4		2	6
Rogers, Alan		1				3				
Saxton, Bobby	38				4					
Sutton, Dave	2									
Vassallo, Barrie	5	5					2		1	3
(own-goals)							4			4
21 players used	506	16	22	1	44	3	79		8	87

LEAGUE DIVISION 2 — Manager: Tony Waiters — SEASON 1975-76

Argyle players listed in roman, opponents in *italics*. Asterisk (*) = player substituted.

No	Date	1	2	3	4	5	6	7	8	9	10	11	12 sub used
1	A NOTT'M FOREST 16/8	Aleksic	Hore	Burrows	Horswill	Green	Delve	Randell*	Johnson	Rafferty	Pearson	McAuley	Saxton
		Middleton	*Anderson*	*Clark*	*Chapman*	*O'Kane*	*McGovern*	*Lyall*	*Richardson*	*O'Hare*	*Robertson*	*Bowyer*	
2	H CHARLTON 23/8	Aleksic	Hore	Burrows	Randell	Green	Delve	Horswill	Mariner	Rafferty	Pearson	McAuley*	Pearson
		Tutt	*Penfold*	*Warman*	*Bowman*	*Giles*	*Young*	*Powell*	*Hales*	*Hunt*	*Flanagan*	*Peacock*	
3	A SOUTHAMPTON 29/8	Aleksic	Hore	Burrows	Randell	Green	Delve	Horswill	Mariner	Pearson*	Foster	McAuley	Saxton
		Middleton	*Rodrigues*	*Steele*	*Holmes*	*Bennett*	*Blyth*	*O'Brien**	*Channon*	*Stokes*	*McCalling*	*Peach*	*Osgood*
4	H SUNDERLAND 6/9	Aleksic	Hore	Burrows	Randell	Green	Delve	Horswill	Johnson*	Mariner	Rafferty	McAuley	Vassallo
		Montgomery	*Malone !*	*Bolton*	*Gibb*	*Clarke*	*Moncur*	*Kerr*	*Halom*	*Holden**	*Robson*	*Towers*	*Porterfield*
5	A ORIENT 13/9	Aleksic	Hore	Burrows	Delve	Green	Saxton	Horswill	Johnson	Mariner	Rafferty	McAuley	
		Jackson	*Fisher*	*Roffey*	*Bennett*	*Hoadley*	*Walley*	*Roeder*	*Grealish*	*Queen**	*Mooney*	*Allder*	*Cotton*
6	H YORK 20/9	Aleksic	Hore	Burrows	Horswill	Green	Vassallo	Randell	Johnson	Foster	Rafferty	McAuley	
		Crawford	*Stone*	*Downing*	*Pollard*	*Swallow*	*Topping*	*McMordie*	*Woodward*	*Seal*	*Jones*	*Wann*	
7	A LUTON 24/9	Aleksic	Hore	Burrows	Horswill	Green	Delve	Randell	Johnson	Mariner	Rafferty	McAuley	Foster
		Barber	*Ryan John*	*Buckley*	*Anderson*	*Faulkner*	*Futcher P*	*King*	*Husband*	*Futcher R*	*Ryan Jim*	*Seasman*	
8	A OLDHAM 27/9	Aleksic	Hore	Burrows	Horswill	Green	Delve*	Randell	Johnson	Mariner	Rafferty	McAuley	Foster
		Ogden	*Branagan*	*Whittle*	*Bell*	*Hicks*	*Holt*	*Blair*	*Chapman*	*Husband*	*Robins*	*Groves*	
9	H CARLISLE 4/10	Aleksic	Hore	Burrows	Horswill	Green	Delve	Randell	Johnson	Mariner	Rafferty	McAuley	
		Burleigh	*Spearritt*	*Gorman*	*O'Neill*	*Green*	*Parker*	*Martin*	*Barry**	*Prudham*	*Clarke*	*Laidlaw*	*Owen*
10	H BOLTON 11/10	Aleksic	Hore	Burrows	Horswill*	Green	Delve	Randell	Johnson	Mariner	Rafferty	McAuley	Pearson
		Siddall	*Nicholson*	*Dunne*	*Greaves*	*Jones P*	*Allardyce*	*Byron*	*Jones G**	*Whatmore*	*Reid*	*Thompson*	*Walsh*

No	Att	Pos	Pt	F-A	H-T	Scorers, Times, and Referees
1	13,083	–	L 0	0-2	0-1	Horswill 32(og), O'Hare 82. Ref: J Bent
2	14,201	17 (22)	W 2	1-0	1-0	Johnson 37. Ref: E Read
3	18,000	18 (1)	L 2	0-1	0-1	Channon 32. Ref: P Walters
4	18,304	15 (4)	W 4	1-0	0-0	Rafferty 47. Ref: M Sinclair
5	5,010	18 (16)	L 4	0-1	0-0	Grealish 48. Ref: K Baker
6	12,818	17 (20)	D 5	1-1	0-1	Rafferty 82, Seal 45. Ref: B Daniels
7	9,226	–	D 6	1-1	0-1	Johnson 60, Husband 20. Ref: C Thomas
8	8,227	18 (7)	L 6	2-3	1-1	Mariner 33, Horswill 74, Jones 2, Horswill 88(og), Robins 89. Ref: W Johnson
9	12,875	14 (20)	W 8	2-1	1-0	McAuley 34, Burrows 75, Clarke 76. Ref: C White
10	14,595	14 (4)	L 8	2-3	1-0	Johnson 30p, 90, Whatmore 81, 82, Reid 90. Ref: R Challis

Match notes

1. Mariner is suspended and Delve is appointed captain. After numerous outbreaks of crowd trouble, Forest boss Brian Clough confronts the hooligans and order is restored. Debutant Horswill deflects Lyall's shot with his head and O'Hare pounces after some poor defensive work.

2. The Addicks feel robbed as Derek Hales has two efforts disallowed, both for offside. Horswill's fierce shot deflects off Mariner and Johnson runs in to head home. Six fans, identified as troublemakers at the Forest match, are refused entry. Another spate of bookings angers the crowd.

3. England striker Mick Channon wants to leave the Saints but still gives his all to plunder the only goal. Steve Middleton produces several great saves to deny an injury-weakened Argyle. Osgood comes on to near hysteria. Saints boss, Lawrie McMenemy, praises Aleksic's performance.

4. Argyle apply early pressure and Delve and Rafferty have shots cleared off the line. Dick Malone has an eventful match. Lectured after fouling McAuley, he almost scores and is then dismissed (33) for kicking Mariner. Rafferty weaves his way from halfway for a superb solo effort. Rafferty hits the upright in injury-time.

5. Saxton is called up as a late replacement after Randell is taken ill on the way to London. Grealish scores on the turn from six yards. Rafferty chases after the referee after a penalty appeal is turned down. Mariner twice goes off for treatment. Rafferty hits the upright in injury-time.

6. Fans are invited to suggest a name for Argyle's new training ground. Jimmy Seal promises manager Wilf McGuiness he will score, and keeps to his word to notch his sixth goal in nine matches against the Pilgrims. Rafferty is accused of diving by the ref but makes amends to equalise.

7. Barber is unemployed during the first half as Aleksic defies Luton. Husband darts in to net Jim Ryan's parried free-kick. Faulkner's poor pass goes straight to Johnson who slots home left-footed. Mariner's header hits the side netting. Bobby Howe joins the Home Park coaching staff.

8. Latics' 100% home record remains intact. Aleksic fails to hold Whittle's shot for the opener. Horswill's 35-yard rocket is his first for Argyle. Aleksic appears to be obstructed as Horswill turns the ball into his own net. Waiters is to be reported to the FA for remarks made to the referee.

9. Bobby Saxton has joined Exeter for £4,000. McAuley scores with his second attempt after his first shot hits Johnson. Rafferty hits the bar from 25 yards before Burrows scores his first league goal for the club. Clarke's header brings an immediate response but Argyle hang on to the win.

10. Bolton are unbeaten in nine matches. New penalty-taker Johnson slots home after Paul Jones's foul on Mariner. Johnson still has time to reply. Whatmore nets twice before Reid's goals in injury-time seals Argyle's first home defeat since March. Horswill suffers a badly broken nose.

18/10 — A WEST BROM
Osborne, Mulligan, Wilson, Cantello, Wile, Robertson, Martin, Brown, Hurst, Giles, Johnston
Brown 41; Ref: P Partridge
11,149 — 15 — 8
Horswill's nose has recovered sufficiently. Mariner's header hits the bar (19) and minutes later, Osborne blocks Johnson's header with his leg. Green subdues 1966 World Cup hero, Geoff Hurst, but his strike-partner heads in Mulligan's cross. Willie Johnston torments Argyle's defence.

12 — H BLACKBURN — 21/10 — D 2-2 — 14,371 — 9
Aleksic, Hore, Burrows, Horswill, Green, Delve, Randell, Johnson, Mariner, Rafferty, McAuley
Jones, Wilkinson, Hutt, Metcalfe, Waddington, Fazackerley, Beamish, Oates, Hindson, Svarc, Parkes
Delve 50, Rafferty 72; Beamish 31, Hutt 78; Ref: B Stevens
Form continues to elude Argyle as they struggle against a Rovers side fielding a makeshift back four. Delve's first of the season responds to Beamish's solo effort. Rafferty looks to have clinched two points but Hutt, on loan from Huddersfield, scores off the post from outside the box.

13 — H OXFORD — 25/10 — W 2-1 — 12,491 — 11
Aleksic, Burton, Burrows, Horswill, Green, Delve*, Randell, Johnson, Mariner, Rafferty, McAuley
Taylor, Shuker, Hynd, Clarke C, Jeffrey*, Houseman, Tait, Clarke D, Foley, Aylott, McGrogan
Mariner 65, 77; Tait 62; Ref: M Taylor
Horswill plays despite needing an operation on his nose. Hore is dropped. Hynd's clearance knocks a policeman's helmet off. Referee Taylor lectures the Oxford bench for dissent. Tait heads home a corner but Mariner's second, a classic diving header, gives an improved Argyle a win.

14 — A CHELSEA — 1/11 — D 2-2 — 20,096 — 12
Aleksic, Darke, Burrows, Rioch, Green, Delve, Randell, Johnson, Mariner, Rafferty, McAuley
Bonetti, Locke, Harris, Stanley, Dempsey, Droy, Britton, Wilkins, Maybank, Hutchinson, Garner
Mariner 70, 75; Britton 4, Wilkins 57; Ref: D Civil
Under a constant dark sky, Rioch makes his debut after a 'free' from Villa. Chelsea are missing David Hay, due to a family bereavement. An error from Darke gifts Britton the first. Ray Wilkins scores with a rare header. On-song Mariner proves a handful and he silences the crowd.

15 — A NOTTS CO — 4/11 — L 0-1 — 9,234 — 12
Aleksic, Darke, Burrows, Delve, Rioch, Green, Randell, Johnson, Mariner, Rafferty, McAuley*
McManus, Richards, O'Brien, Needham, Probert, Stubbs*, Carter, Mann, Scanlon, Bolton
Scanlon 57; Ref: C Seel
Ron Fenton's County are the surprise package of the division so far. McManus needs two attempts to stop Rioch's pile-driver. Scanlon heads home Richards' free-kick. Argyle announce the purchase of Elm Cottage for £20000, which will be used to house their young professionals.

16 — H PORTSMOUTH — 8/11 — W 3-1 — 13,885 — 14
Aleksic, Lloyd, Burrows, Delve, Rioch, Green, Foster, Johnson, Mariner, Rafferty, Pearson
Lawler, Wilson, Piper, Went, Hand, Marinello, Roberts, Graham, Kamara*, Mellows, Cahill
Johnson 51, Rafferty 84, 90; Piper 82; Ref: W Gow
The final ten minutes livens up a tedious 'Battle of the Ports'. Randell fails a late fitness test. Pompey are on a run of nine successive defeats. Norman Piper scores on his return to Home Park. New loan signing, Jim Hamilton, from Sunderland, scores a debut hat-trick for the reserves.

17 — A BRISTOL ROV — 15/11 — D 0-0 — 14,121 — 15
Aleksic, Eadie, Burrows, Darke, Green, Delve, Randell, Johnson*, Mariner, Rafferty, Rioch
Williams, Parsons, Day, Taylor, Prince, Stephens, Smith, Warboys, Bannister, Fearnley
Ref: A Porter
A blood and thunder match on a greasy surface produces only one booking. Horswill, for a foul on Bannister. Darke leaves the pitch for twelve minutes to receive two stitches in an eye wound. David Williams clears Johnson's shot off the line. Highlights are shown on The Big Match.

18 — H WEST BROM — 22/11 — W 2-1 — 17,380 — 17
Aleksic, Osborne, Burrows, Horswill, Green, Delve, Randell, Johnson, Mariner, Rafferty, McAuley
Mulligan, Wilson, Trewick*, Wile, Robertson, Martin, Brown T, Brown A, Mayo, Giles, Edwards
Wile 11(og), Mariner 78; Giles 90; Ref: D Reeves
Albion's eleven-match unbeaten run is ended. Unchallenged, Wile heads past Osborne. Rafferty plays on after a clash of heads despite blurred vision. Each of Albion's back four are booked, all for fouls. Darke clears Brown's shot off the line. Player-boss, Giles, scores in stoppage time.

19 — A HULL — 29/11 — L 0-2 — 5,098 — 13
Aleksic, Darke*, Burrows, Horswill, Green, Delve, Randell, Johnson, Mariner, Rafferty, Rioch
Wealands, Daniel, Devries, Galvin, Croft, Roberts, Gibson*, Grimes, Fletcher, Wood, Greenwood, Hawley
Greenw'd 37, 57, Wood 40, Grimes 47; Ref: I Smith
Five coachloads of supporters make the long journey north to witness the Pilgrims' worst display of the season and it could have been worse. Fletcher puts the ball in the net (5) but Wood is adjudged to have fouled Aleksic. Argyle reshuffle their defence but it makes little difference.

20 — H BLACKPOOL — 6/12 — L 1-2 — 12,422 — 18
Aleksic, Wood, Burrows, Horswill, Green, Delve, Randell*, Johnson, Mariner, Rafferty, McAuley
Hatton, Alcock, Bentley, Suddaby, Hart, Tong, Weston, Walsh, Ainscow*, Betts, Vassallo, Evanson
Mariner 79; Walsh 21, 82; Ref: A Lees
Argyle are unchanged despite the previous week's abysmal showing. Top scorer Walsh gives Pool the lead. Hatton is booked for time-wasting after only 25 minutes. Mariner cuts in from the left to level with a fine solo goal but Horswill's poor back-pass lets Walsh in for his second.

21 — A CHARLTON — 12/12 — L 0-2 — 7,095 — 17
Aleksic, Tutt, Burrows, Horswill, Green, Sutton, Randell, Johnson*, Mariner, Rafferty, McAuley
Curtis, Warman, Bowman, Giles, Goldthorpe, Powell, Hales, Flanagan, Hunt, Peacock, Foster
Flanagan 11, Darke 19(og); Ref: G Kew
The Addicks find form after four successive defeats. Flanagan shoots in from an acute angle and Darke deflects Powell's shot. Johnson hits the bar from 30 yards. Mariner misses from the spot (75) as Graham Tutt makes his first ever penalty save. Horswill's booking means suspension.

LEAGUE DIVISION 2 — Manager: Tony Waiters — SEASON 1975-76

No		Opponent	Date	Att	Pos	Opp Pos	Pt	F-A	H-T	Scorers, Times, and Referees
22	H	NOTT'M FOREST	20/12	10,545	17	13	19	W 1-0	0-0	Mariner 57 / Ref: A Robinson
23	A	BRISTOL CITY	26/12	21,471	18	3	20	D 2-2	1-1	Mariner 27, 48 / Merrick 34, Collier 58 / Ref: D Wallace
24	H	FULHAM	27/12	24,054	16	9	22	W 4-0	4-0	Randall 17, Rafferty 22, 38, [Johnson 40] / Ref: L Burden
25	H	ORIENT	10/1	11,934	12	14	24	W 3-0	2-0	Randall 1, Rafferty 8, Mariner 74 / Ref: E Read
26	A	SUNDERLAND	17/1	29,737	14	1	24	L 1-2	1-0	Mariner 40 / Holden 47, Kerr 67 / Ref: A Morrissey
27	H	BRISTOL CITY	24/1	17,887	11	2	25	D 0-0	0-0	Ref: T Bosi
28	A	BLACKBURN	31/1	8,525	13	18	25	L 1-3	1-2	Foster 41 / Svarc 30, 59, Hird 31 / Ref: P Reeves
29	H	NOTTS CO	7/2	11,576	15	4	25	L 1-3	0-2	Rafferty 89 / Probert 28, Scanlon 44, Vinter 87 / Ref: D Lloyd
30	A	PORTSMOUTH	14/2	9,509	17	21	25	L 0-2	0-1	Busby 12, Macken 67 / Ref: B Newsome
31	H	BRISTOL ROV	21/2	11,183	14	10	27	W 3-0	1-0	Johnson 45, Rafferty 49, Mariner 59 / Ref: J Homewood

Line-ups (Argyle, then *opponent* in italics)

No	1	2	3	4	5	6	7	8	9	10	11	12 sub used
22	Aleksic	Darke	Burrows	Horswill	Sutton	Delve	Randall	Johnson	Mariner	Rafferty	McAuley	Robertson
22	*Wells*	*Anderson*	*Clark*	*McGovern*	*Chapman*	*Richardson*	*Curran**	*O'Neill*	*O'Hare*	*Butlin*	*Bowyer*	
23	Aleksic	Darke	Burrows	Sutton	Green	Delve	Randall	Johnson	Mariner	Rafferty	McAuley	Whitehead
23	*Cashley*	*Sweeney*	*Drysdale*	*Gow*	*Collier*	*Merrick*	*Tainton*	*Ritchie*	*Mann*	*Cheesley**	*Fear*	
24	Aleksic	Darke	Burrows	Sutton	Green	Delve	Randall	Johnson	Mariner	Rafferty	McAuley	Howe
24	*Mellor*	*Curbush*	*Strong*	*Mullery*	*Lacy*	*Moore**	*Conway*	*Mitchell*	*Busby*	*Slough*	*Barrett*	
25	Aleksic	Darke	Burrows	Sutton	Green	Delve	Randall	Johnson	Mariner	Rafferty	McAuley	
25	*Jackson*	*Fisher*	*Payne*	*Bennett*	*Everett*	*Walley*	*Cunningham*	*Roeder*	*Bullock*	*Queen*	*Heppolette*	
26	Aleksic	Darke	Burrows	Sutton	Green	Delve	Randall	Johnson	Mariner	Rafferty	McAuley	Henderson
26	*Montgomery*	*Malone*	*Bolton*	*Longhorn*	*Clarke*	*Moncur*	*Kerr**	*Holden*	*Halom*	*Robson*	*Greenwood*	
27	Aleksic	Darke	Burrows	Sutton	Green	Delve	Randall*	Horswill	Mariner	Rafferty	McAuley	Johnson
27	*Cashley*	*Sweeney*	*Drysdale*	*Gow*	*Collier*	*Merrick*	*Tainton*	*Ritchie*	*Mann*	*Fear*	*Brolly*	
28	Aleksic	Darke	Burrows	Sutton	Green	Delve	Horswill	Johnson	Mariner	Foster	McAuley	
28	*Jones*	*Wilkinson*	*Wood*	*Metcalfe*	*Hawkins*	*Fazackerley*	*Hird*	*Oates*	*Svarc*	*Parkes*	*Wagstaffe*	
29	Aleksic	Darke	Burrows	Sutton	Green	Delve*	Randall	Johnson	Mariner	Foster	McAuley	Vinter
29	*McManus*	*Richards*	*O'Brien*	*Probert*	*Needham*	*Stubbs*	*King*	*Sims*	*Bradd*	*Mann**	*Scanlon*	
30	Furnell	Horswill	Burrows	Sutton	Green	Delve	Randall	Foster	Mariner	Rafferty	McAuley	Eames
30	*Lloyd*	*Lawler*	*Wilson*	*Roberts**	*Mellows*	*Cahill*	*Busby*	*Piper*	*Graham*	*Macken*	*Kamara*	
31	Furnell	Horswill	Burrows	Sutton	Green	Delve*	Randall	Johnson	Mariner	Rafferty	McAuley	Staniforth
31	*Eadie*	*Jacobs*	*Bater*	*Day*	*Taylor*	*Prince**	*Stephens*	*Smith*	*Warboys*	*Bannister*	*Dobson*	

Match notes

22 — Hore looks set to move to Exeter after failing to regain his place. Nineteen-year-old keeper Peter Wells pulls off some stunning save but is unable to stop Mariner's soaring header. Mariner also somehow scoops over from point-blank range but the two points are most welcome.

23 — Green returns to replace the suspended Horswill. City lose top scorer Cheesley with a pulled hamstring (19). The defence is static as Merrick's diving header cancels out Mariner's opener. Mariner is denied a hat-trick when Sweeney clears off the line. Delve now also faces suspension.

24 — Randall gets his first of the season and Rafferty ends his lean spell as Argyle dominate the first half to the extent that Bobby Moore is taken off at half-time. Substitute Howe sees two goals scored as he warms up ready to come on. Fulham attack in the second half but chase a lost cause.

25 — Sutton plays despite being knocked over by Mariner's car in the car park before the game! Argyle complete the signing of Jim Hamilton for £10k. David Payne plays his first match for the O's for two years after a broken leg but cannot prevent two early goals which kill the game.

26 — Sunderland are unbeaten at home but are given a shock as Mariner's header gives Argyle an interval advantage. Darke marks new signing Roy Greenwood for the fourth time this season. Holden equalises and Kerr, the smallest player on the pitch, heads in to keep the unbeaten record.

27 — The fixture is brought forward as both sides are out of the FA Cup. An ill-tempered affair produces the first goalless draw at Home Park for almost two years. Horswill is booked for the second time in as many games since his suspension. City fans chant 'We built the Concorde'.

28 — The frosty pitch passes a 9.30 inspection. Svarc scores the first and makes the second before Foster, surprisingly selected ahead of Rafferty, scores his first league goal after Hird's mistake. Metcalfe's long-range shot is turned onto the bar by Aleksic but Svarc is first to the rebound.

29 — Waiters claims his job is on the line following this latest defeat. County defend solidly and score two breakaway goals. McManus pulls off a string of saves, prompting his manager to call for his selection for Ireland. Mick Vinter scores for the fourth time in recent games as a sub.

30 — Furnell is recalled at the age of 38 and is soon in action. Busby, on loan from QPR, scores from close range. Kamara is sent off (42) for retaliation on Horswill. Six players are also booked. Another loanee, Macken, from Derby, hammers the second after a drop-ball is not cleared.

31 — Argyle announce they are prepared to release the homesick Vassallo. A rain-sodden pitch passes a 1 o'clock inspection after the referee helps the groundstaff. A well-rehearsed free-kick sets up a comfortable win to take Argyle closer to safety. Delve suffers stud marks on his neck.

32. 24/2 — Att 13,927 — pos 29
FT 1-0 (HT ...)
Ref: P Walters
Opponents (Luton): *Barber, Ryan John, Buckley, Chambers, Faulkner*, Futcher P, Husband, King, Fuccillo, West, Aston (Pollock)*
The match is played at a furious pace. Randell takes the first with style. Rafferty scores twice in a minute before going off with cramp. Keith Barber prevents a larger victory as the Hatters plunge to their biggest defeat of the season. Faulkner is booked after only two minutes for a foul.

---

33. A OXFORD 28/2 — Att 5,778 — 13 D 20 30 — FT 2-2 (HT 1-0)
Mariner 24, McAuley 58 / *Tait 59, 82*
Ref: G Trevitt
Argyle: Furnell, Darke, Burrows, Sutton, Green, Foster, Horswill, Johnson, Mariner, Clarke D*, McAuley
Oxford: *Burton, Taylor, Shuker, Lowe, Clarke C, Houseman, Jeffrey, Foley, Tait, Duncan (Gibbins)*
Randell and Delve are suspended. Shuker, Houseman and Tait are back for Oxford after missing the midweek match. All three had been sent off the previous week. With a two-goal lead, the Greens look to have clinched their first away win, but Tait scores twice to deny the victory.

---

34. H CHELSEA 6/3 — Att 20,638 — 17 L 9 30 — FT 0-3 (HT 0-1)
Stanley 24, Britton 47, Swain 56
Ref: A Hamil
Argyle: Furnell, Darke, Burrows, Sutton, Green, Foster, Horswill, Johnson, Mariner, Rafferty*, McAuley (Hardcastle)
Chelsea: *Bonnetti, Locke, Harris, Stanley, Wicks, Hay, Britton, Wilkins, Finnieston, Swain, Lewington*
Mariner has pleurisy. Hore joins Exeter on loan. Chelsea field one of the youngest sides in their history. Charlie Cooke is out with a broken arm. Furnell punches straight to Stanley for the first and Ray Wilkins' superb dummy sets up Britton. Swain's goal comes direct from a corner.

---

35. A BOLTON 13/3 — Att 21,147 — 15 D 2 31 — FT 0-0 (HT 0-0)
Ref: J Yates
Argyle: Furnell, Darke, Burrows, Sutton, Green, Foster, Horswill, Johnson, Randell, Rafferty*, McAuley (Foster)
Bolton: *Siddall, Walsh, Dunne, Greaves, Jones P, Allardyce, Byrom, Whatmore*, Jones G, Reid, Thompson (Morgan)*
Argyle dent Wanderers' promotion hopes with a solid defensive display. Darke effectively shackles former England winger Peter Thompson. Gary Jones's 'goal' is disallowed for offside (38). New signing, Scottish international Willie Morgan, is brought on to rapturous applause.

---

36. H HULL 20/3 — Att 10,631 — 17 D 14 32 — FT 1-1 (HT 1-1)
Johnson 30p / *McIntosh 26*
Ref: T Bune
Argyle: Furnell, Darke, Burrows, Sutton, Green, Foster, Horswill, Johnson, Mariner, Rafferty*, McAuley (Pearson)
Hull: *Wealands, Daniel, Devries, Galvin, Croft, Roberts, Lyall, Grimes, Sunley, Fletcher*, McIntosh (Hemmerman)*
Mr Bune whistles twice in the first five seconds for infringements, and sets the tone for the afternoon. McIntosh is hero and villain as he puts Hull ahead after a one-two between Lyall and Sunley, but then fouls McAuley. Johnson tucks away the penalty. Mariner hits a post late on.

---

37. A BLACKPOOL 27/3 — Att 5,497 — 17 D 15 33 — FT 0-0 (HT 0-0)
Ref: B Martin
Argyle: Furnell, Darke, Burrows, Delve, Green, Foster, Horswill, Johnson, Mariner, Rafferty*, McAuley* (Pearson)
Blackpool: *Wood, Hatton, McEwan, Suddaby, Alcock / Ainscow, Suddick, Walsh, Bentley, Evanson, ...*
Argyle announce that Horswill can leave after failing to curb his disciplinary problems. Blackpool hit the woodwork twice in the second half before Ainscow is sent off. An away victory still eludes the Pilgrims.

---

38. H OLDHAM 3/4 — Att 9,782 — 13 W 15 35 — FT 2-1 (HT 1-0)
Randell 10, Burrows 83 / *Whittle 70*
Ref: R Lewis
Argyle: Furnell, Darke, Burrows, Sutton, Green, Delve, Horswill, Johnson, Randell, Rafferty*, McAuley (Groves)
Oldham: *Platt, Wood, Whittle, Hicks, Edwards, Holt, Robins, Bell, Shaw, Chapman, Groves*
Rioch is the latest player allowed to leave after only three appearances. Furnell is penalised (59) for handling and Oldham score from the free-kick. Burrows rare goal gives Argyle vital points.

---

39. A YORK 10/4 — Att 3,646 — 16 L 21 35 — FT 1-3 (HT 0-1)
Mariner 58 / *Pollard 12, Holmes 52, Cave 71*
Ref: R Chadwick
Argyle: Furnell, Darke, Burrows, Sutton, Green, Delve, Horswill, Johnson, Mariner, Rafferty*, McAuley (Seal)
York: *Crawford, Scott, Downing, Holmes*, James, Topping, Cave, Pollard, Hinch, Woodward, McMordie (Seal)*
England manager Don Revie again watches Mariner, who obliges with a lovely header. York are almost relegated. Burrows has an unhappy return to his old club and is at fault for York's first two goals. Mariner has another disallowed for handball before Micky Cave nets a rebound.

---

40. H SOUTHAMPTON 16/4 — Att 25,305 — 13 W 5 37 — FT 1-0 (HT 0-0)
Darke 83
Ref: R Challis
Argyle: Furnell, Darke, Burrows, Sutton, Green, Delve, Horswill, Johnson, Mariner, Rafferty*, McAuley (Stokes)
Southampton: *Turner, Rodrigues, Peach, Holmes, Blyth, Steele, Channon, Gilchrist, Osgood, McCalling, Stokes*
A large Easter crowd give Furnell a half-time standing ovation after a superb display. Argyle dominate against the high-flying Saints. Darke's cross from way out on the right flies over Ian Turner to virtually save the Greens from relegation. It is the full-back's first goal for two years.

---

41. A FULHAM 19/4 — Att 6,913 — 14 D 12 38 — FT 0-0 (HT 0-0)
Ref: R Toseland
Argyle: Furnell, Darke, Burrows, Sutton, Green, Mellor, Horswill, Johnson, Mariner, Rafferty*, McAuley (Johnson)
Fulham: *Mellor, James, Fraser, Lloyd, Lacy, Howe, Mitchell, Conway*, Slough, Camp, Dowie (Barrett)*
Argyle reach Waiters' 38-point safety target at a sunny Craven Cottage with an organised display. Furnell is outstanding, prompting Waiters to claim that he has saved Argyle from relegation. The match is Rafferty's final Argyle appearance. Burrows clears off the line from Lacy.

---

42. A CARLISLE 24/4 — Att 7,038 — 16 L 19 38 — FT 0-2 (HT 0-1)
Clarke 6, McVitie 86
Ref: D Richardson
Argyle: Furnell, Harrison, Burrows, Sutton, Green, Delve, Horswill, Randell, Mariner, Foster, McAuley
Carlisle: *Ross, Carr, Gorman, Barry, Green, Bonnyman, McVitie, O'Neill, Clarke, Owen, Martin (Johnson)*
Two points save the U's from relegation. Argyle's luxury coach breaks down and they arrive at the ground at the last minute. Harrison makes a competent debut. Green, returning to his home town, is twice denied by Ross from long range. Transfer-listed Horswill impresses as sweeper.

Home Average 14,800
Away 11,497

LEAGUE DIVISION 2 (CUP-TIES)　　　Manager: Tony Waiters　　　SEASON 1975-76

League Cup

League Cup	Att	F-A	H-T	Scorers, Times, and Referees	1	2	3	4	5	6	7	8	9	10	11	12 sub used
1:1 H BOURNEMOUTH 19/8	W 10,849 4:	2-0	1-0	Rafferty 6, Hague 84(og) Ref: K Salmon	Aleksic *Baker*	Hore *Payne*	Burrows *Russo*	Randell *Benson*	Green *Morgan*	Delve *Hague*	Horswill *Nightingale*	Foster *Howard*	Pearson *Goddard*	Rafferty *Rickard*	McAuley *Cunningham*	
1:2 A BOURNEMOUTH 26/9	W 3,203 4:17	2-1	1-1	Burrows 30, Mariner 83 Rickard 20 Ref: K Salmon (Argyle win 4-1 on aggregate)	Aleksic *Baker*	Hore *Payne*	Burrows *Miller*	Randell *Benson**	Green *Morgan*	Delve *Hague*	Horswill* *Redknapp*	Mariner *Rickard*	Pearson *Goddard*	Rafferty *Nightingale*	McAuley *Buttle*	Saxton *Reeves*
2 A NOTT'M FOREST 9/9	L 8,978 12	0-1	0-0	Bowyer 84 Ref: R Perkin	Aleksic *Middleton*	Hore *Anderson*	Burrows *Gunn*	Horswill *Clark*	Green *Chapman*	Delve *Richardson*	Randell *O'Neill*	Johnson* *McGovern*	Mariner *O'Hare*	Rafferty *Bowyer*	McAuley *Robertson*	Vassallo

Match notes:

1:1 — Foster discovers he is playing only 45 minutes before kick off after Johnson suffers back spasms. After Rafferty's goal, the visitors miss good chances. Green fouls Nightingale but Aleksic holds Howard's penalty (38). Hague deflects Rafferty's shot. A fussy referee books six players.

1:2 — Neil Hague flicks on Buttle's corner for Rickard to score the first. After a retaken free-kick, Burrows crashes in his first goal for the Pilgrims. Horswill spends the night in hospital after being carried off with concussion (60). Mariner's long-range effort sends Cherries' fans home early.

2 — Promotion favourites, Forest's early season form has been far from impressive. Aleksic pulls off a string of outstanding saves but is powerless to stop Bowyer's late header from O'Neill's cross. Both left wingers, McAuley and Robertson, are dangerous but both sides waste chances.

FA Cup

FA Cup	Att	F-A	H-T	Scorers, Times, and Referees	1	2	3	4	5	6	7	8	9	10	11	12 sub used
3 A HULL 3/1	D 6,515 18	1-1	0-1	Rafferty 68 Grimes 17 Ref: K McNally	Aleksic *Wealands*	Darke *Banks*	Burrows *McGill*	Sutton *Galvin*	Green *Croft*	Delve *Roberts*	Randell *Grimes*	Johnson *Lyall*	Mariner *Hawley*	Rafferty *Wood*	McAuley *Greenwood*	
3R H HULL 6/1	L 20,208 18	1-4	0-2	Green 61 Wood 1, 74, Sutton 31(og), Hawley 86 Ref: K McNally	Aleksic *Wealands*	Darke *Daniel*	Burrows *Banks*	Sutton *Hawley*	Green *Croft*	Delve *Roberts*	Randell *Grimes*	Johnson *Lyall*	Mariner *Wood*	Rafferty *Galvin*	McAuley *Greenwood*	

Match notes:

3 — Controversial referee Mr McNally has one of his quieter days and only books three players. Aleksic fails to hold a cross and Grimes pounces. Mariner hits the woodwork before Rafferty's first-time shot clinches a replay. Croft's back-pass eludes Wealands who chases back to recover.

3R — Fans are still arriving as Wood heads in after 25 seconds. A minute later Croft clears off the line from Johnson. Sutton slices into his own net from a corner. Green's shot provides hope but another Wood header kills the game. Hawley's late goal seals a fourth-round tie at Roker Park.

League Table — Home and Away

Pos	Team	P	W	D	L	F	A	W	D	L	F	A	Pts
1	Sunderland	42	19	2	0	48	10	5	6	10	19	26	56
2	Bristol City	42	11	7	3	34	14	8	8	5	26	21	53
3	West Brom	42	10	9	2	29	12	10	4	7	21	21	53
4	Bolton	42	12	5	4	36	14	8	7	6	28	24	52
5	Notts Co	42	11	6	4	33	13	6	5	8	27	28	49
6	Southampton	42	18	2	1	49	16	3	5	13	17	34	49
7	Luton	42	13	6	2	38	15	6	4	11	23	36	48
8	Nott'm For	42	13	1	7	34	18	4	11	6	21	22	46
9	Charlton	42	11	5	5	40	34	4	7	10	21	38	42
10	Blackpool	42	9	9	3	26	23	4	7	10	14	27	42
11	Chelsea	42	7	9	5	25	20	5	7	9	28	34	40
12	Fulham	42	9	8	4	26	14	4	6	11	18	33	40
13	Orient	42	10	6	5	21	12	3	8	10	16	27	40
14	Hull	42	9	5	7	29	23	5	6	10	16	26	39
15	Blackburn	42	8	6	7	27	22	4	8	9	18	28	38
16	PLYMOUTH	42	13	4	4	36	20	0	8	13	12	34	38
17	Oldham	42	11	8	2	37	24	2	4	15	20	44	38
18	Bristol Rov	42	7	9	5	20	15	4	7	10	18	35	38
19	Carlisle	42	9	8	4	29	22	3	5	13	16	37	37
20	Oxford	42	7	7	7	23	25	4	4	13	16	34	33
21	York	42	8	3	10	28	34	2	5	14	11	37	28
22	Portsmouth	42	4	6	11	16	23	5	1	15	17	38	25
		924	229	131	102	684	423	102	131	229	423	684	924

Double wins: (0).
Double defeats: (1) Notts Co.

Won from behind: (1): Oxford.
Lost from in front (3) Bolton, Oldham, Sunderland.

High spots: Big increase in home support.
Continued attacking 4-2-4 formation.
Taking half-time lead at leaders Sunderland.
Mariner-Rafferty partnership continued to earn rave reviews.

Low spots: Failure to win a single away match in league.
End of season departure of Bill Rafferty to Carlisle.
Retirement of Jim Furnell.

Player of the Year: Paul Mariner.
Ever presents: (1) Phil Burrows.
Hat-tricks: (0).
Leading scorer: Paul Mariner (16).

Appearances and Goals

Player	Lge	Sub	LC	Sub	FAC	Sub	Lge	LC	FAC	Tot
Aleksic, Milija	29		3		2					
Burrows, Phil	42		3		2	2	2	1		3
Darke, Peter	26		2		2	2	1			1
Delve, John	38		3		2		1			1
Foster, George	9	7	1				1			1
Furnell, Jim	13									
Green, Mike	40		3		2		1			1
Hardcastle, Peter		1								
Harrison, Chris	1									
Hore, John	12	1	3							
Horswill, Mick	32		3		1		1			1
Johnson, Brian	35	2	1		2		8			8
Mariner, Paul	38		2		2		15	1		16
McAuley, Hugh	40		3		2		2			2
Pearson, Ian	6	4	2							
Rafferty, Bill	38	1	3		2	2	12	1	1	14
Randell, Colin	36		3		2	2	4			4
Rioch, Neil	3	2			1					
Saxton, Bobby	1	2			1					
Sutton, Dave	22		2		2					
Vassallo, Barrie	1	2		1						
(own-goals)								1	1	2
21 players used	462	22	33	2	22		48	4	2	54

LEAGUE DIVISION 2 — Manager: Tony Waiters > Mike Kelly — SEASON 1976-77

Match details

No	Match	Date	Att	Pos	Pt	F-A	H-T	Scorers, Times, and Referees
1	A OLDHAM	21/8	7,378		D 1	2-2	1-1	Mariner 20, Johnson 77 / Chapman 36, Irving 61 / Ref: P Partridge
2	H BLACKBURN	24/8	13,553		W 3	4-0	2-0	Collins 7, Johnson 45, Hall 73, [Mariner 77] / Ref: E Read
3	H NOTTS CO	28/8	14,539	9 / 12	L 3	1-2	1-1	Mariner 45 / Sims 41, Vinter 74 / Ref: E Hughes
4	A ORIENT	4/9	4,808	10 / 22	D 4	2-2	2-2	Green 36, Mariner 43 / Hoadley 23, 24 / Ref: R Glasson
5	H CHELSEA	11/9	18,356	16 / 5	L 4	2-3	0-0	Hall 79, Mariner 82 / Britton 57p, Swain 78, Finnieston 85 / Ref: D Lloyd
6	A MILLWALL	18/9	9,883	18 / 6	L 4	0-3	0-2	Lee 5, 73, Salvage 31p / Ref: R Lewis
7	H BOLTON	25/9	12,564	18 / 3	D 5	1-1	1-1	Mariner 24 / Mariner 36(og) / Ref: K Salmon
8	H LUTON	2/10	12,187	15 / 16	W 7	1-0	0-0	Johnson 48p / Ref: D Nippard
9	A BLACKPOOL	9/10	12,647	10 / 5	W 9	2-0	2-0	Collins 8, Horswill 39 / Ref: K McNally
10	H CARDIFF	16/10	14,198	10 / 20	D 10	2-2	1-1	Mariner 6, Hall 49p / Evans 10, Dwyer 53 / Ref: R Crabb

Line-ups

No	Team	1	2	3	4	5	6	7	8	9	10	11	12 sub used
1	Argyle	Ramsbott'm	Darke	Horswill	Harrison	Sutton	Green	Hall	Johnson	Mariner	Collins	McAuley	
1	Oldham	*Platt*	*Branagan*	*Whittle*	*Bell**	*Hicks*	*Hurst*	*Chapman*	*Shaw*	*Halom*	*Irving*	*Groves*	*Robins*
2	Argyle	Ramsbottom	Darke*	Horswill	Harrison	Sutton	Green	Johnson	Hall	Mariner	Collins	McAuley	Delve
2	Blackburn	*Bradshaw*	*Wilkinson**	*Bailey*	*Metcalfe*	*Wood*	*Fazackerley*	*Hawkins*	*Svarc*	*Beamish*	*Parkes*	*Wagstaffe*	*Mitchell*
3	Argyle	Ramsbottom	Darke*	Horswill	Harrison	Sutton	Green	Hall	Johnson	Mariner	Collins	McAuley	Rogers
3	Notts Co	*McManus*	*Richards*	*O'Brien*	*Probert*	*Needham*	*Stubbs*	*McVay**	*Vinter*	*Sims*	*Smith*	*Mann*	*Benjamin*
4	Argyle	Ramsbottom	Darke*	Horswill	Harrison	Green	Sutton	Hall	Johnson	Mariner	Collins	McAuley	Delve
4	Orient	*Jackson*	*Roffey*	*Fisher*	*Allen*	*Hoadley*	*Roeder*	*Cunningham*	*Heppolette*	*Clarke*	*Possee*	*Grealish*	
5	Argyle	Ramsbottom	Randell	Horswill	Harrison*	Sutton	Green	Delve	Johnson	Mariner	Hall	Rogers	Hamilton
5	Chelsea	*Bonetti*	*Locke*	*Wilkins G*	*Stanley*	*Wicks*	*Hay*	*Britton*	*Wilkins R*	*Finnieston*	*Lewington*	*Swain*	
6	Argyle	Ramsbottom	Randell	Horswill	Harrison*	Sutton	Green	Delve	Johnson	Mariner	Hall	Rogers	Foster
6	Millwall	*Goddard*	*Evans*	*Donaldson*	*Brisley*	*Kitchener*	*Hazell*	*Lee*	*Seasman*	*Shanahan*	*Walker*	*Salvage*	
7	Argyle	Ramsbottom	Randell	Horswill	Delve	Sutton	Green	Hall	Harrison	Mariner	Johnson*	Collins	Rogers
7	Bolton	*Siddall*	*Ritson*	*Dunne*	*Greaves*	*Jones*	*Allardyce*	*Morgan*	*Whatmore*	*Taylor*	*Reid*	*Thompson*	
8	Argyle	Ramsbottom	Randell	Horswill	Delve	Sutton	Green	Hall	Harrison	Mariner	Collins	McAuley	
8	Luton	*Barber*	*Price*	*Buckley*	*West*	*Faulkner*	*Futcher P*	*Ryan*	*Husband*	*Deans**	*Futcher R*	*Fuccillo*	*Hill*
9	Argyle	Ramsbottom	Randell	Horswill	Delve	Sutton	Green	Hall	Johnson	Mariner*	Collins	Harrison	Hamilton
9	Blackpool	*Wood*	*Gardner*	*Bentley*	*Ronson*	*Hart*	*Suddaby*	*Ainscow*	*Suddick*	*Walsh*	*Hatton*	*Farley*	
10	Argyle	Barron	Randell	Horswill	Delve	Sutton	Green	Hall	Harrison	Mariner	Collins	Hamilton	
10	Cardiff	*Irwin*	*Dwyer*	*Charles**	*Buchanan*	*Went*	*Larmour*	*Sayer*	*Livermore*	*Evans*	*Alston*	*Anderson*	*Pethard*

Match notes

1. With Hall, Argyle's new £50k signing from Liverpool, prompting in midfield, the Pilgrims soon threaten a much-awaited away win. The back-in-favour Horswill is soon hobbling after an injury. Latics get on top after Mariner's well-taken goal. Johnson nets from six yards to level matters.

2. New boys Collins and Hall open their accounts as Argyle find early form. The inexperienced Harrison impresses in midfield, as does the new strike partnership of Mariner and Johnson. Jim Smith's Rovers are well beaten. Mariner misses a re-taken spot-kick (90), by blazing wide.

3. County boss, Ron Fenton says 'We love playing here.' as his side gain their fifth successive win over Argyle. Sims hits the crossbar but makes amends minutes later. Mariner scrambles an equaliser but Vinter gives County their just rewards. Waiters slams the minority who jeer Darke.

4. Hoadley scores Orient's first league goals of the season. His second is scooped back from the line but the referee adjudges it to be over. The outstanding Ramsbottom is furious and throws the ball at Mr Glasson, but escapes with a lecture. Darke is replaced, suffering blurred vision.

5. The game bursts into life after Randell upends Lewington, and Britton scores from the spot. Swain fires home a great individual effort. Mariner maintains his prolific scoring run. Five are booked including Chelsea trainer, Norman Medhurst, who comes onto the pitch without permission.

6. Not a happy day for Green as the ball rebounds from him for the first and he then brings down Seasman to conceded a penalty. Play is halted after someone in the crowd uses a whistle. Delve, Mariner and Hall are all booked within the space of a minute. Hall's late effort is disallowed.

7. Mariner, now linked with a number of clubs, outjumps three defenders to score with a header but then beats Ramsbottom after his lunge diverts Neil Whatmore's shot. Ex-England winger Peter Thompson torments Argyle. Visiting manager Ian Greaves praises Argyle's performance.

8. Mariner's days at Home Park are numbered as he is watched by West Ham and Ipswich. West Brom have already had a bid turned down. In a dreary affair, Hall is brought down by West for a penalty which Hatters boss, Harry Haslam describes as 'worse than the Great Train Robbery.'

9. A strange choice for BBC's 'Match of the Day'. Motorway delays mean Argyle arrive only 30 minutes before kick-off. Another 'phantom' whistler delays the match. Collins' lovely free-kick and a rare Horswill goal give the Greens their first away win in 28 attempts.

10. Mariner says farewell with a goal as his move to Ipswich nears completion. Barron, on his league debut, has barely touched the ball before Cardiff equalise. Hall is fouled but recovers to convert the spot-kick. Horswill chases a spectator around the pitch and into the arms of the law.

11 · A · 23/10 — 10,258 (12, 11)
Eddie Day, Williams, Aitken, Taylor, Prince, Stephens, Fearnley, Warboys, Bannister, Powell
Prince 11
Ref: T Reynolds
Seventeen-year-old apprentice Trusson has the unenviable task of replacing Mariner, who travels to Ipswich the next day to finalise his move. Torrential rain before the game creates a greasy surface. Prince hammers in a partial clearance before Hall's late deflected shot steals a point.

12 · H · BURNLEY · 30/10 — 0-1 — 14,704 (14 L, 17, 11)
Ramsbottom, Randell, Stevenson, Newton, Delve, Noble, Sutton, Thompson, Ingham, Rodaway, Hall; Harrison, Smith, Peddelty, Austin, Collins, Hamilton*, Johnson, Flynn, Summerbee
Smith 58
Ref: A Lees
Austin and Peddelty, part of the Mariner deal, make their debuts. Skipper Green is dropped. Collins is made captain against his former club. Malcolm Smith, on loan from Middlesbrough, gets the only goal. Mike Summerbee provides the entertainment by making fun of the referee.

13 · A · CHARLTON · 5/11 — 1-3 — 13,617 (17 L, 3, 11)
Wood, Hammond, Berry, Hunt, Delve, Slough, Sutton, Giles, Powell, Curtis, Hall; Hamilton, Hales, Flanagan
Hall 81p
Hales 6, 80, Flanagan 57
Ref: R Toseland
Charlton notch their fifth successive home win at a stroll. The Pilgrims have no answer to the power of Derek Hales, talked of as an England possible, who makes it sixteen for the season. Hall's penalty after Giles pushes Collins is scant consolation.

14 · H · FULHAM · 13/11 — 2-2 — 25,335 (14 D, 15, 12)
Barron, Mellor, James, Strong, Collins, Slough, Sutton, Howe, Moore, Best, Peddelty; Hamilton, Evanson, Mitchell, Marsh, Johnson, Bullivant*, Greenaway
Austin 33, Johnson 59
Mitchell 30, Howe 90
Ref: L Burden
The crowds flock to see Bobby Campbell's stars. George Best and Rodney Marsh turn on the magic to give Argyle problems and Marsh sets up the opener. Horswill grabs Best around the neck. Austin's first goal for the club sparks a revival. Howe's goal completes the entertainment.

15 · A · HULL · 20/11 — 1-3 — 8,161 (18 L, 11, 12)
Barron, Wealands, Daniel, De Vries, Johnson, Bremner, Sutton, Croft, Haigh, Nisbet, Peddelty; Hamilton*, Lord, Hawley, Hemmerman, Galvin*, Collins, Delve, Staniforth
Harrison 88
Staniforth 65, Hawley 76, [Hemmerman 80]
Ref: K Hackett
Waiters brands his team 'a soft touch' as Argyle rarely threaten the Tigers' unbeaten home record. Sub Gordon Staniforth scores with his first touch. Poor defensive work gifts John Kaye's Hull the points. Harrison slides in for his first ever league goal at a good pass from Collins.

16 · H · CARLISLE · 27/11 — 1-0 — 10,204 (18 L, 20, 12)
Ramsbottom, Burleigh, Hoolickin, Carr, Johnson, Bonnyman, Sutton, MacDonald, Moncur, Peddelty*; Harrison, Barry, Lathan, Foster, Clarke, McAuley
Clarke 78
Ref: J Bent
Rafferty returns to run the home defence ragged and make a mockery of his £20k transfer fee. Player-manager Bobby Moncur commands the defence. McAuley, out of favour and transfer-listed, comes on the biggest cheer of the afternoon. Clarke's header finishes off a flowing move.

17 · A · WOLVES · 4/12 — 0-4 — 16,370 (20 L, 4, 12)
Pierce, Palmer, Parkin, Daley, Delve, Munro, Green, McAlle, Hibbitt, Richards, Hall; Harrison, Richards, Sunderland, Foster, Patching, Gould
Richards 29, 85, Sunderland 43, [Hibbitt 69]
Ref: M Sinclair
Green is recalled to replace the concussed Peddelty. Only Ramsbottom prevents a rout as Sammy Chung's free-scoring Wolves run riot on a frosty pitch. Sunderland's left-foot volley from 18 yards is the pick of the goals. Richards' second is Wolves 41st league goal of the season.

18 · H · SHEFFIELD UTD · 11/12 — 0-0 — 8,827 (20 D, 6, 13)
Brown, Franks, Garner, Longhorn, Colquhoun, Kenworthy, Green, Woodward, Dornan, Hamson, Hall; Peddelty, Austin, Guthrie, Collins, Trusson, Hamilton
Ref: A Robinson
Despite the lack of goals there is plenty of goalmouth action. Ramsbottom's legs deny Woodward breaking United's post-war scoring record. Blades' debutant Dornan cracks a shot against the crossbar. Peddelty impresses in a new midfield role. Delve wastes two good late chances.

19 · A · NOTT'M FOREST · 18/12 — 1-1 — 15,180 (20 D, 3, 14)
Middleton, Anderson, Clark, Barrett, Delve, Lloyd, Green, Bowyer, O'Neill, O'Hare, Hall; Peddelty, O'Neill, Bowery, Chapman, Collins, Woodcock
Austin 12
Barrett 88
Ref: J Reynolds
A dramatic start as Woodcock is brought down by Peddelty in the area (4) but Ramsbottom blocks Colin Barrett's spot-kick. Bannister, a £15k signing from Bristol Rovers sets up Austin's goal. Argyle look set to dent Forest's promotion hopes but Barrett atones for his earlier error.

20 · H · SOUTHAMPTON · 27/12 — 1-1 — 24,787 (20 D, 15, 15)
Wells, Andrusz'ski, Peach, Holmes, Peddelty, Blyth, Green, Ball, Channon, Steele, Hall; Osgood, Austin, Bannister, McCalliog, MacDougall, Collins
Bannister 59
MacDougall 44
Ref: T Spencer
The referee initially allows Delve's 'goal' after just 30 seconds and then changes his mind. On an icy pitch, Bannister, playing in gym-shoes in the second half, scores after Peddelty's header hits the post. Ted MacDougall is a constant threat but Alan Ball has a quiet debut for the Saints.

21 · H · CHARLTON · 1/1 — 1-0 — 13,445 (19 W, 11, 17)
Wood, Hammond, Warman, Tydeman, Peddelty, Berry, Green, Curtis, Burman, Powell, Hall; Delve, Flanagan, Austin, Bannister, Peacock, McAuley, Collins
Austin 33
Ref: C Thomas
Hugh McAuley moves to Charlton and ironically makes his debut at Home Park. Andy Nelson slams his defenders as 'dreamers' as a clever Bannister free-kick sets up Austin. A strong wind spoils the game. McAuley misses a sitter. Argyle gain their first victory in twelve matches.

LEAGUE DIVISION 2

Manager: Tony Waiters > Mike Kelly — SEASON 1976-77

No	Date	Opponent	Att	Pos	Pt	F-A	H-T	Scorers, Times, and Referees
22	A 3/1	BURNLEY	10,399	18 / 20	W 19	2-0	1-0	Green 44, Austin 84 — Ref: P Willis
23	H 22/1	OLDHAM	9,200	16 / 8	D 20	2-2	0-1	Austin 47, Craven 65 / Hicks 11, Whittle 66 — Ref: B James
24	A 5/2	NOTTS CO	9,079	18 / 10	L 20	0-2	0-1	Needham 13, Mann 58 — Ref: R Matthewson
25	A 9/2	HEREFORD	5,002	17 / 22	D 21	1-1	1-1	Hall 41 / Layton 15 — Ref: K Baker
26	H 12/2	ORIENT	9,551	17 / 21	L 21	1-2	1-1	Rogers 38 / Possee 32, Cunningham 50 — Ref: D Biddle
27	A 19/2	CHELSEA	22,154	17 / 1	D 22	2-2	0-1	Austin 52, Bannister 67p / Swain 2, Britton 61p — Ref: J Sewell
28	H 26/2	MILLWALL	10,437	17 / 6	D 23	2-2	1-1	Hall 45, 73 / Shanahan 6, Summerill 78 — Ref: E Hughes
29	A 2/3	BLACKBURN	7,755	—	L 23	0-2	0-1	Waddington 43p, Svarc 85 — Ref: T Bosi
30	A 5/3	BOLTON	18,496	17 / 2	L 23	0-3	0-2	Whatmore 2, 88 Jones P 29p — Ref: K Ridden
31	A 12/3	LUTON	12,793	17 / 4	D 24	1-1	1-0	Foster 12 / Aston 46 — Ref: R Robinson

Line-ups (Argyle row plain, opponents in italic)

No	1	2	3	4	5	6	7	8	9	10	11	12 sub used
22	Ramsbottom	Randell	Horswill	Delve	Sutton	Green	Hall	Harrison	Austin	Bannister	Collins	
22	*Stevenson*	*Scott*	*Brennan*	*Noble*	*Thomson*	*Rodaway*	*Cochrane*	*Smith*	*Morley*	*Flynn*	*Ingham*	
23	Ramsbottom	Randell	Horswill	Craven	Peddelty	Green	Hall	Harrison	Austin	Bannister	Rogers	
23	*Platt*	*Wood*	*Whittle*	*Bell*	*Hicks*	*Hurst*	*Robins*	*Irving*	*Halom*	*Chapman*	*Valentine*	
24	Ramsbottom	Randell	Horswill	Craven	Peddelty	Green	Hall	Harrison	Austin	Bannister	Rogers	
24	*McManus*	*Richards*	*O'Brien*	*Bushy*	*Needham*	*Stubbs*	*Carter*	*Vinter*	*Bradd*	*Mann*	*Smith*	
25	Ramsbottom	Randell	Horswill	Craven	Peddelty	Green !	Hall	Delve	Austin	Bannister	Rogers	
25	*Hughes*	*Byrne*	*Ritchie*	*Layton*	*Jefferson*	*Lindsay*	*Paine*	*Preece*	*Galley*	*Peters*	*Davey*	
26	Ramsbottom	Randell	Horswill	Delve	Craven	Peddelty	Hall	Collins*	Austin	Bannister	Rogers	Banton
26	*Jackson*	*Fisher*	*Roffey*	*Grealish*	*Hoadley*	*Roeder*	*Cunningham*	*Allen*	*Possee*	*Queen*	*Whittle*	
27	Ramsbottom	Randell	Horswill	Delve	Green	Peddelty	Hall	Craven	Austin	Bannister	Rogers	
27	*Phillips*	*Locke*	*Wilkins G*	*Stanley*	*Wicks*	*Hay*	*Britton*	*Wilkins R*	*Mayhank*	*Lewington*	*Swain*	
28	Ramsbottom	Randell	Darke	Craven	Sutton	Peddelty	Hall	Delve	Austin	Bannister	Rogers	
28	*Goddard*	*Evans*	*Moore*	*Brisley*	*Kitchener*	*Hazell*	*Lee**	*Shanahan*	*Summerill*	*Walker*	*Donaldson*	*Salvage*
29	Ramsbottom	Randell	Darke	Sutton	Peddelty	Delve	Craven	Harrison	Austin	Bannister	Rogers*	Collins
29	*Bradshaw*	*Fazackerley*	*Wood*	*Waddington**	*Keeley*	*Hawkins*	*Hird*	*Taylor*	*Svarc*	*Parkes*	*Wagstaffe*	*Mitchell*
30	Ramsbottom	Peddelty	Darke	Delve	Sutton	Green	Hall	Harrison*	Austin	Bannister	Collins	
30	*McDonagh*	*Nicholson*	*Dunne**	*Greaves*	*Jones P*	*Allardyce*	*Morgan*	*Whatmore*	*Jones G*	*Reid*	*Waldron*	
31	Ramsbottom	Smart	Darke	Peddelty	Sutton	Horswill	Randell	Foster	Austin	Bannister	Rogers	
31	*Aleksic*	*Price*	*Buckley*	*Chambers*	*Faulkner*	*Futcher P*	*Husband*	*West*	*Geddis*	*Fuccillo*	*Aston*	

22 — Burnley: Collins masterminds a victory against his old club in a vital relegation battle. Bannister is again inspirational and contributes to both goals. Harry Potts' side are in crisis and in the midst of a run of 14 games without a win. A number of their fans stage a protest after the final whistle.

23 — Oldham: The match goes ahead despite pools of water on the surface. Debutant Craven, a £20k signing from Coventry, misses a sitter (2), ballooning the ball over the Devonport End roof. He later makes amends but Whittle's deflected free-kick is allowed after the referee consults his linesman.

24 — Notts Co: County gain their first home win since the end of October. David Needham rises above everyone to head home Mann's corner and later (73) hits the bar with another headed effort. Mann finishes a fine solo run for the second. Horswill is booed throughout following a foul on Carter.

25 — Hereford: Layton heads home a corner to give the division's bottom side an early lead. Argyle's plight worsens when Green is sent off for retaliation (18) after a foul by veteran Terry Paine. Hall equalises with a diving header. Waiters writes to the Football League to complain about the referee.

26 — Orient: Argyle concede a goal from a corner for the fourth consecutive match when Possee forces home Grealish's flag-kick. Laurie Cunningham, described by his manager, George Petchey, as the most skilful player he has ever seen, scores a cheeky winner between Ramsbottom's legs.

27 — Chelsea: Again Argyle concede from a corner when Swain gives the Blues an early lead. After Austin's leveller, Green fouls Mayhank and Ian Britton converts the penalty. Bannister scores after Randell's shot hits Britton on the arm. Delve chips in from 25 yards (85) but it is then disallowed.

28 — Millwall: Hall finally finds form and answers his critics with two fine goals. Argyle's disciplinary problems mount. Green and Horswill are suspended and Craven and Delve now face a similar fate. Waiters denies rumours that Collins wants a transfer. Darke is recalled after a long absence.

29 — Blackburn: Argyle's season goes from bad to worse. Waiters and the directors are in conflict. Horswill requests a transfer and wants to return north. Rovers are awarded a penalty when Svarc appears to slip. Craven is booked for the fourth time in seven games. Ramsbottom fumbles for the second.

30 — Bolton: The Greens never recover from Whatmore's early strike after a defensive mix-up. Waiters is appalled by the penalty, claiming Garry Jones had been practising in swimming baths. Whatmore's second is a goal to remember as he flicks the ball over Green, beats two defenders and scores.

31 — Luton: A much-changed Argyle upset the form-book to end the Hatters run of nine successive wins. Hall is unhappy at being dropped and wants talks with Waiters. New boy Smart handles the experienced John Aston well. Both sides blame the bright sun for mistakes which lead to both goals.

Column headings (Argyle line-up): Ramsbottom · Smart · Darke · Horswill · Sutton · Peddelty · Randell · Foster · Austin · Bannister · Rogers

---

32 — 19/3
Foster 4, Bannister 78
8,893 | 5 | 26
Ref: D Smith
Argyle: Ramsbottom · Smart · Darke · Horswill · Summerbee* · Hart · Suddaby · Weston · Spence · Walsh · Hatton · Bentley
Opp (italic): Wood · Gardner · Harrison · ... · McEwan · Rogers
Waiters carries out a pre-match inspection of the swamp-like conditions in his bare feet. Randell revels in the mud, setting up Foster for the first. Rogers is upended by Suddaby for a penalty. Ramsbottom needs four stitches in a shin wound and is fortunate not to be sent off for a foul.

---

33 A CARDIFF 26/3
Austin 87
9,587 | 19 | 28 | W | 1-0
Ref: D Reeves
Ramsbottom · Smart · Darke · Horswill · Sutton · Peddelty · Randell · Foster · Austin · Bannister · Rogers
Healey · Dwyer · Attley · Campbell · Went · Larmour · Grapes · Livermore · Evans · Friday · Buchanan
Austin pounces on Healey's error to ease Argyle's relegation fears. The headlines are made away from the pitch. The disillusioned Waiters and Hall have both put their houses up for sale. The manager also circulates his availability to other clubs, together with four of his backroom staff.

---

34 H BRISTOL ROV 2/4
Peddelty 23, Williams 67
10,307 | 17 | 29 | D | 1-1
Ref: A Robinson
Ramsbottom · Smart · Darke · Horswill · Sutton · Peddelty · Randell · Foster · Austin · Bannister · Rogers
Eadie · Williams · Parsons · Day · Taylor · Prince · Stephens · Fearnley · Stanforth · Aitken · Britten · Hamilton*
Peddelty scores on his 22nd birthday from Horswill's long throw. Williams equalises after Darke's poor clearance. Mr Robinson is not in the best of form after having a disturbed night when, clad in his pyjamas, he chased a French sailor who had vandalised his car outside his hotel.

---

35 A SOUTHAMPTON 8/4
Bannister 21, Peach 38, MacDougall 51, 80, [Channon 82]
20,914 | 29 | L | 1-4
Ref: W Gow
Ramsbottom · Smart · Darke · Craven! · Sutton · Peddelty · Foster · Randell · Austin · Bannister · Delve* · Rogers
Wells · Rodrigues · Peach · Holmes · Blyth · Waldron · Ball · Channon · Osgood · Williams · MacDougall · Hebberd*
Without tonsillitis victim Horswill, Argyle employ Craven as a sweeper to curb the threat of Saints' lethal forward line. The plan backfires. Peach scores from 30 yards. Ted MacDougall makes it 20 for the season and Mick Channon beats four players to notch a brilliant solo effort.

---

36 H HEREFORD 9/4
Bannister 2, 69, Davey 22
9,787 | 22 | 31 | W | 2-1
Ref: A Lees
Ramsbottom · Randell · Darke · Craven · Sutton · Peddelty · Hall · Foster · Trusson* · Bannister · Rogers · Delve
Charlton · Emery · Ritchie · Jefferson · Marshall · Sheedy · Coughlin · Spiring · Davey · McNeil · Briley · Carter*
Bannister puts Argyle ahead after 90 seconds. Steve Davey scores against his old side but is replaced, suffering from a fractured cheekbone (50) following an elbow in the face. McNeil's feeble penalty (81) goes straight at Ramsbottom. Craven is sent off (89) for persistent misconduct.

---

37 A FULHAM 11/4
Mitchell 54, Maybank 77
11,710 | 15 | 31 | L | 0-2
Ref: K Burns
Ramsbottom · Darke · Horswill · Craven · Sutton · Peddelty · Hall · Foster · Austin · Bannister · Delve
Peyton · Evans · Strong · Storey · Lacy · Moore · Best · Maybank · Warboys · Mitchell · Slough
Argyle start the brighter and Delve's drive strikes an upright. Ramsbottom appears to be impeded for Mitchell's opener but the referee ignores vigorous protests. A piece of vintage George Best dribbling sets up Maybank for an easy second as they leap-frog the Pilgrims in the table.

---

38 H HULL 16/4
Hall 89
Dobson 54, 83
8,694 | 12 | 31 | L | 1-2
Ref: E Read
Ramsbottom · Darke · Horswill · Craven* · Sutton · Peddelty · Hall · Foster · Trusson · Bannister · Delve · Johnson
Wealands · Daniel · Nisbet · Bremner · Croft · Haigh · Gibson · Lord · Sunley · Dobson · Stewart
Argyle's season hits a new low as Hull, with four 18-year-olds in the side gain their first away win of the season. Ian Dobson scores his first ever league goals. Waiters is booed, the crowd slow-handclap and the terraces are sparsely populated by the time Hall scores his late goal.

---

39 A CARLISLE 23/4
Hall 90
Rafferty 8, McCartney 31p, Tait 84
7,751 | 21 | 31 | L | 1-3
Ref: K McNally
Ramsbottom · Smart · Horswill · Craven · Sutton* · Peddelty · Hall · Foster · Austin · Bannister · Delve · Randell
Ross · Hoolickin · McCartney · Martin · MacDonald · Parker · McVitie · Bonnyman · Tait · Rafferty · O'Neill
Chairman Robert Daniel sacks Waiters after last week's dismal showing. Mike Kelly takes charge of the side. Billy Rafferty comes back to haunt Argyle as he scores the first and is then brought down by Peddelty for a penalty. Tait side-foots home the third as relegation looms large.

---

40 H WOLVES 30/4
16,795 | 1 | 32 | D | 0-0
Ref: B Daniels
Ramsbottom · Horswill · Delve · Sutton · Peddelty · Hall · Foster · Austin · Bannister · Randell
Pearce · Palmer · Parkin · Daley · Munro · McAlle · Hibbitt · Richards · Sunderland · Patching · Carr · Todd*
Hundreds of Wolves fans travel west to see their side gain the point needed to clinch promotion. Argyle come close to spoiling the party when Delve's overhead flick deceives Pearce but the ball is scrambled off the line. Wolves' boss Sammy Chung compliments Argyle's performance.

---

41 H NOTT'M FOREST 2/5
Bannister 19
Woodcock 29, Withe 52
13,542 | 3 | 32 | L | 1-2
Ref: B Stevens
Ramsbottom · Smart · Horswill · Delve · Craven · Peddelty · Randell · Foster · Austin · Bannister · Delve
Middleton · Anderson · Clark · Chapman · Lloyd · Bowyer · McGovern · O'Neill · Withe · Woodcock · Robertson
Brian Clough describes his side as magnificent as Forest keep their promotion hopes alive. Argyle seem doomed as other clubs have games in hand. Bannister nets an astute header. Woodcock and Withe take their joint tally to 33. Ramsbottom's saves justify his Player of the Year tag.

---

42 A SHEFFIELD UTD 7/5
Edwards 44
12,227 | 11 | 32 | L | 0-1
Ref: D Richardson
Ramsbottom · Smart · Horswill · Craven* · Delve · Peddelty · Foster · Delve · Austin · Bannister · Rogers · Hall
Brown · Cutbush · Garner · Franks · Colquhoun · Kenworthy · Woodward · Stainrod · Edwards · Longhorn · McKee · Calvert*
Surprise away wins by Bristol Rovers and Cardiff condemn Argyle to the drop. Keith Edwards scores the only goal, his 14th in as many games. Argyle are prepared to release the unsettled Bannister and Randell. Several other players are queuing to see the manager about their futures.

Home 13,329 · Away 11,746 · Average

LEAGUE DIVISION 2 (CUP-TIES)

Manager: Tony Waiters > Mike Kelly

SEASON 1976-77

League Cup

		Att	F-A	H-T	1	2	3	4	5	6	7	8	9	10	11	12 sub used	Scorers, Times, and Referees
1:1 H EXETER	14/8	8,688 4:	0-1 L	0-1	Barron	Darke*	Horswill	Randell	Sutton	Green	Hall	Harrison	Mariner	Collins	McAuley	Johnson	Kellow 21
					Key	*Templeman*	*Hooker*	*Hore*	*Saxton*	*Hatch*	*Hodge*	*Kellow*	*Morrin*	*Beer*	*Jordan*		Ref: W Gow

Argyle's unimpressive pre-season form is carried into their first competitive match of the season. On a baking hot day, City keeper Richard Key indulges in little more than sunbathing as the Grecians dominate. Collins' speculative effort from 45 yards is the best Argyle can muster.

		Att	F-A	H-T	1	2	3	4	5	6	7	8	9	10	11	Scorers, Times, and Referees
1:2 A EXETER	18/8	8,859 4:	0-1 L	0-1	Ramsbottom	Darke	Horswill	Randell	Sutton	Green	Hall	Johnson	Mariner	Collins	McAuley	Jordan 38
					Key	*Templeman*	*Hooker*	*Hore*	*Saxton*	*Hatch*	*Hodge*	*Kellow*	*Clapham*	*Beer*	*Jordan*	Ref: D Biddle

(Argyle lost 0-2 on aggregate)

Key is busier in this second leg but defies the Pilgrims by pulling fine saves from Mariner, Hall and Johnson. Mike Jordan fires home from 20 yards after a neat interchange with Tony Kellow. Grecians' boss John Newman is delighted with his side's aggregate win over his former club.

FA Cup

		Att	F-A	H-T	1	2	3	4	5	6	7	8	9	10	11	Scorers, Times, and Referees
3 A OLDHAM	8/1	9,889 7	18 0-3 L	0-2	Ramsbottom	Delve	Horswill	Peddelty	Sutton	Green	Hall	Harrison	Austin	Bannister	Johnson	Whittle 36, Halom 38, Robins 70
					Platt	*Wood*	*Whittle*	*Bell*	*Hicks*	*Hurst*	*Chapman*	*Robins*	*Halom*	*Irving*	*Valentine*	Ref: E Read

Jimmy Frizzell's Oldham cruise through to the next round. Maurice Whittle enhances his dead-ball reputation with a goal direct from a free-kick. Halom stabs into an empty net and Robins finishes it off with a well-placed shot. Ramsbottom has x-rays after the game on a rib injury.

League Table

Pos & Team	P	Home					Away					Pts
		W	D	L	F	A	W	D	L	F	A	
1 Wolves	42	15	3	3	48	21	7	10	4	36	24	57
2 Chelsea	42	15	6	0	51	22	6	7	8	22	31	55
3 Nott'm For	42	14	3	4	53	22	5	11	5	24	21	52
4 Bolton	42	15	2	4	46	21	5	9	7	29	33	51
5 Blackpool	42	11	7	3	29	17	8	6	7	29	25	51
6 Luton	42	13	5	3	39	17	8	1	12	28	31	48
7 Charlton	42	14	5	2	52	27	2	11	8	19	31	48
8 Notts Co	42	11	5	5	29	20	8	5	8	36	40	48
9 Southampton	42	12	6	3	40	24	5	4	12	32	43	44
10 Millwall	42	9	6	6	31	22	6	7	8	26	31	43
11 Sheffield Utd	42	9	8	4	32	25	5	4	12	22	38	40
12 Blackburn	42	12	4	5	31	18	3	5	13	11	36	39
13 Oldham	42	11	6	4	37	23	3	4	14	15	41	38
14 Hull	42	9	8	4	31	17	4	3	14	14	36	37
15 Bristol Rov	42	8	9	4	32	27	4	4	13	21	41	37
16 Burnley	42	8	9	4	27	20	3	5	13	19	44	36
17 Fulham	42	9	7	5	39	25	2	6	13	15	36	35
18 Cardiff	42	7	6	8	30	30	2	10	9	26	37	34
19 Orient	42	4	8	9	18	23	5	8	8	19	32	34
20 Carlisle	42	7	7	7	31	33	4	5	12	18	42	34
21 PLYMOUTH	42	5	9	7	27	25	3	7	11	19	40	32
22 Hereford	42	6	9	6	28	30	2	6	13	29	48	31
	924	224	138	100	781	509	100	138	224	509	781	924

Appearances & Goals

Name	Lge	Sub	LC	Sub	FAC	Sub	Lge	LC	FAC	Tot
Austin, Terry	29						7			7
Bannister, Bruce	24					1	7			7
Banton, Geoff				1						
Barron, Paul	3		1							
Collins, Doug	22	1	2				2			2
Craven, John	15		1				1			1
Darke, Peter	15		2							
Delve, John	28	4			1					
Foster, George	14	1								
Green, Mike	22		2			1	2			2
Hall, Brian	36	1	2			1	10			10
Hamilton, Jim	6	2								
Harrison, Chris	21		1				1			1
Horswill, Mick	37		2			1	1			1
Johnson, Brian	12	3	1	1			4			4
Mariner, Paul	10		2				7			7
McAuley, Hugh	4	1	2							
Peddelty, John	29									
Ramsbottom, Neil	39		1		1					
Randell, Colin	34	1	2							
Rogers, Alan	15	4								
Smart, Kevin	9									
Sutton, Dave	34		2		1		1			1
Trusson, Mike	4									
24 players used	462	19	22	1	11		46			46

Odds & ends

Double wins: (1) Blackpool.

Double defeats: (3) Carlisle, Hull, Notts Co.

Won from behind: (0).

Lost from in front: (2) Nott'm For , Southampton .

High spots: Surprise draw at Chelsea. Holding free-scoring Wolves to a goalless draw at home. Neil Ramsbottom winning over the fans to be elected 'Player of the Year'.

Low spots: Sacking of Tony Waiters with only four matches of the season remaining, following season-long murmurings of discontent between the manager and the board. Inevitable sale of Paul Mariner. Poor disciplinary record. Two League Cup defeats against Exeter.

Player of the Year: Neil Ramsbottom.

Ever presents: (0).

Hat-tricks: (0).

Leading scorer: Brian Hall (10).

LEAGUE DIVISION 3   Manager: Mike Kelly > Malcolm Allison   SEASON 1977-78

No	Date	Att	Pos	Pt	F-A	H-T	Scorers, Times, and Referees	1	2	3	4	5	6	7	8	9	10	11	12 sub used
1	H PRESTON 20/8	7,154		D 1	0-0	0-0	Ref: S Bates	Barron	Smart	Uzzell	Horswill	Foster	Craven	Johnson	Delve	Austin	Trusson	Rogers	
								Tunks	_McMahon_	_Wilson_	_Doyle*_	_Baxter_	_Cross_	_Coleman_	_Brown_	_Thomson_	_Elwiss_	_Bruce_	_Burns_
2	A CARLISLE 27/8	4,853	18	D 2	0-0	0-0	Ref: N Midgley	Barron	Smart	Uzzell	Horswill	Foster	Craven	Delve	Johnson	Trusson	Hall	Rogers	
								Swinburne	_Carr_	_McCartney_	_Tait_	_MacDonald_	_Parker_	_McIlfie_	_Ludlam_	_Lathan_	_Rafferty_	_Martin_	
3	H HEREFORD 3/9	5,732	24	W 4	2-0	0-0	Trusson 57, Rogers 78; Ref: A Lees	Barron	Smart	Uzzell	Horswill	Foster	Craven	Delve	Johnson	Austin*	Trusson	Rogers	Hall
								Hughes	_Emery_	_Ritchie_	_Layton_	_Jefferson_	_Sheedy_	_Briley_	_Holmes_	_Sinclair_	_McNeil_	_Spring_	
4	A COLCHESTER 9/9	5,719	1	L 4	1-3	0-0	Hall 58; _Williams 48, Gough 73, Dowman 83_; Ref: C Downey	Barron	Smart	Uzzell	Horswill	Foster	Craven	Johnson*	Delve	Austin	Trusson	Hall	Peddelty
								Walker	_Cook_	_Williams_	_Leslie*_	_Packer_	_Dowman_	_Garwood_	_Gough_	_Froggatt_	_Bunkell_	_Allison_	_Dyer_
5	H WALSALL 13/9	5,958	13	D 5	3-3	1-1	Hall 23, Austin 57, 82; _Buckley 34, Craven 70(og), Caswell 77_; Ref: R Crabb	Barron	Smart	Uzzell	Horswill	Foster	Craven	Hall	Delve	Austin	Trusson	Rogers	
								Kearns	_Taylor_	_Caswell_	_Hynd_	_Serella_	_Newton_	_Robertson_	_Bates_	_Denerley_	_Buckley_	_Birch*_	_Evans_
6	H CAMBRIDGE 17/9	6,022	14	L 5	0-1	0-1	_Uzzell 45(og)_; Ref: A Robinson	Barron	Smart	Uzzell	Horswill	Foster	Craven	Hall	Delve	Austin	Trusson*	Rogers	Peddelty
								Webster	_Batson_	_Murray_	_Stringer_	_Fallon_	_Howard_	_Watson_	_Streete_	_Morgan_	_Finney_	_Biley_	
7	A BRADFORD C 24/9	4,031	23	W 7	1-0	1-0	Hall 45; Ref: G Courtney	Barron	Smart	Uzzell	Craven*	Foster	Delve	Harrison	Austin	Johnson	Rogers	Hall	
								Downsboro'	_Hardcastle_	_Spark_	_Middleton_	_Nicholls_	_Fretwell*_	_Watson_	_Dolan_	_Cooke_	_Wright_	_Martinez_	_Podd_
8	A SHEFFIELD WED 27/9	8,515	8	D 8	1-1	0-1	Austin 89; _Wylde 42_; Ref: P Richardson	Barron	Smart	Uzzell	Bason	Foster	Peddelty*	Hall	Delve	Austin	Horswill	Rogers	
								Turner	_Walden_	_Rushbury_	_Mullen_	_Cusack_	_Leman_	_Wylde_	_Johnson_	_Prendergast_	_Porterfield_	_Bradshaw_	_Trusson_
9	H GILLINGHAM 1/10	12,399	7	L 8	1-3	0-1	Hall 55; _Richardson 45p, 56, Price 87_; Ref: T Reynolds	Barron	Smart	Uzzell	Bason	Foster	Craven	Hall	Delve	Austin	Trusson	Rogers	
								Hillyard	_Williams_	_Armstrong*_	_Knight_	_Shipperley_	_Crabbe_	_Nichol_	_Hunt_	_Price_	_Westwood_	_Richardson_	_Weatherly_
10	H SHREWSBURY 4/10	4,661	5	D 9	2-2	2-1	Hall 35, Austin 40; _Nixon 28, Atkins 73p_; Ref: T Spencer	Barron	Smart	Uzzell	Bason	Foster	Craven	Hall	Delve	Austin	Binney	Rogers*	
								Mulhearn	_King_	_Leonard_	_Durban_	_Griffin_	_Atkins_	_Irvine_	_Hornsby_	_Lindsay_	_Bates_	_Nixon_	_Horswill_
11	A CHESTER 8/10	3,367	16	D 10	1-1	0-0	Rogers 72; _Hall 81(og)_; Ref: M Scott	Barron	Smart	Uzzell	Delve	Foster	Craven	Hall	Bason*	Austin	Trusson	Rogers	
								Lloyd	_Raynor_	_Walker_	_Storton_	_Delgado_	_Oakes_	_Crossley_	_Jeffries_	_Kearney_	_Edwards_	_Phillips_	_Johnson_

Match notes:

1. Argyle continue their unwanted record of not winning an opening day league match since 1962. Trusson's second-minute effort is disallowed. Austin hits the post twice. Foster continues to shine as a central defender. Nobby Stiles' side rarely threaten but seem content with a point.
2. Argyle fail to score for the fourth successive match but concentrate on keeping Billy Rafferty quiet. Carlisle's smallest crowd for years see a mistake littered game. Barron is the busier keeper. New skipper Craven has an impressive match. Uzzell is booked for deliberate handball.
3. The Greens end their goal drought and send Hereford to their third successive defeat. Argyle hit the woodwork on five occasions. Trusson swings a boot at Johnson's cross to open the scoring and Hughes admits to a cameraman that he did not see Rogers' first-time shot fly past him.
4. Williams scores only his third goal in over 400 appearances for the U's. After Hall's equaliser Argyle get on top and manager Bobby Roberts admits he would have settled for a point. Two more make it four wins out of five for United as they maintain their top of the table position.
5. Hall finally displays the form expected of him and scores a lovely left-foot goal. Alan Buckley responds with his 99th league goal for Walsall. Denmelly's shot wickedly deflects off Craven. Dave Mackay's Saddlers are now unbeaten in twelve league and cup matches away from home.
6. Cambridge rarely threaten but in first-half stoppage time, Barron comes to collect a cross. Uzzell gets their first and his back-header trickles into an empty goal. Argyle have plenty of possession but use it to little effect. Foster is thrown into the attack in vain as the slide continues.
7. Brian Bason joins Argyle on a month's loan from Chelsea and talks commence to bring Fred Binney to Home Park. Hall ghosts in to head home Johnson's corner in an uninspiring match. Craven is taken off with a groin strain. Barron continues to improve with every game he plays.
8. Bason has an impressive debut but Binney's transfer is in doubt. Foster, two days short of his 21st birthday, is appointed skipper for the absent Craven. Dennis Leman creates both goals with one good pass and one bad one. Peddelty suffers a head injury which eventually ends his career.
9. The Gills go top after their first win at Home Park in 31 attempts. Mr Reynolds, whose decisions caused a riot during a midweek World Cup match in Austria, is at it again when he penalises Craven for a harmless challenge. Kelly believes his side are fearful of playing at home.
10. The lowest crowd since the war watch Argyle fight back from a goal down. Hornsby wrong-foots everyone to set up Nixon. Hall and Austin convert headers but Barron, trying to gather a loose ball, rashly challenges Bates and Atkins converts. Binney signs but lacks match practice.
11. A blood-splattered Craven is inspirational. Argyle are frustrated by Chester's offside trap. Rogers finishes off a sweeping move but Hall lunges at an Edwards cross to divert past Barron. The keeper pulls off a great save from Kearney and Craven clears off the line in the dying minutes.

Plymouth Argyle — Match Record (matches 12–23)

Home team line‑up shown in roman, opponents in italic. Substitutes marked *.

---

12 — A ROTHERHAM — 11/10 — W 2:1 (HT 2:1) — Pos 12 — Att 6,286
Scorers: Hall 28p, Binney 39 / *Phillips 5*
Ref: R Chadwick

Argyle: Barron, Smart, Uzzell, Bason, Craven, Hall, Delve, Foster, Austin, Binney, Rogers*, Harrison
Rotherham: *McAllister, Forrest, Breckin, Rhodes*, Green, Finney, Phillips, Stancliffe, Gwther, Goodfellow, Crawford, Womble*

A great start for Rotherham when Phillips runs unchallenged from halfway to score after a poor Delve pass. Breckin handles Binney's cross and Hall slams in the penalty. Binney gets his first goal for his home‑town club as Argyle continue to prefer playing away from Home Park.

---

13 — H TRANMERE — 15/10 — D 0:0 (HT 0:0) — Pos 14 (opp 1) — Att 6,156
Scorers: *Moore 51*
Ref: R Glasson

Argyle: Barron, Smart, Uzzell, Bason, Craven, Hall, Delve, Foster, Austin, Binney, Rogers
Tranmere: *Johnson, Mathias, Flood, Parry, Evans, Peplow, Palios, Philpotts, Moore, Tynan, Allen*

The Argyle players spend Friday night in a local hotel to prepare for the game. Remarkably, Tranmere field the same eleven that have started every match this season. Ronnie Moore heads home Peplow's cross as Johnny King's Rovers play a simple long‑ball game to great effect.

---

14 — A OXFORD — 22/10 — L 1:2 (HT 1:1) — Pos 18 (opp 5) — Att 5,727
Scorers: Austin 35 / *Curran 43, Bodel 62*
Ref: A Cox

Argyle: Barron, Smart, Uzzell, Bason, Craven, Hall, Taylor, Foster, Austin, Binney, Rogers*
Oxford: *Burton, Kingston, Fogg, Bodel, Jeffrey, McBrogan, Foley, Clarke, Curran, Duncan, Harrison*

New 15k signing from Walsall, Brian Taylor is included but Bason is set to return to Chelsea to cover injuries. Austin's well‑directed header gives Argyle hope. Hugh Curran's equaliser sparks crowd trouble. Bodel gets the winner whilst Taylor is off the pitch receiving treatment.

---

15 — H PORTSMOUTH — 29/10 — W 3:1 (HT 2:0) — Pos 15 (opp 23) — Att 6,594
Scorers: Austin 10, Taylor 42, Johnson 47 / *Kemp 88*
Ref: E Read

Argyle: Barron, Smart, Uzzell, Megson, Craven, Hall, Taylor, Foster, Austin, Harrison, Johnson
Portsmouth: *Middleton, Roberts, Viney, Ellis, Cahill, Denyer, Kemp, Foster, Piper N, Mellows, Barnard*

Gary Megson has a league debut to remember as he has a hand in Argyle's first two goals. Taylor scores a beauty on his home debut. Recalled Johnson puts the game beyond Pompey just after the break. David Kemp scores a late consolation to take his season's personal tally to eleven.

---

16 — A WREXHAM — 5/11 — L 0:2 (HT 0:2) — Pos 16 (opp 1) — Att 8,548
Scorers: *Roberts 44, Shinton 45*
Ref: K Baker

Argyle: Barron, Smart, Uzzell, Craven, Foster, Megson, Taylor, Austin, Johnson, Harrison
Wrexham: *Davies, Hill, Dwyer, Davis, Roberts, Shinton, Sutton, McNeil, Whittle*, Cartwright, Lyons*

Argyle are without Hall who is expected to sign for Burnley. Wrexham manager Arfon Griffiths declares the Pilgrims as the best footballing side he has seen this season. Roberts digs the ball out of the mud for the first and, seconds later, Shinton chips over Barron from ten yards.

---

17 — H CHESTERFIELD — 12/11 — W 2:0 (HT 0:0) — Pos 15 (opp 18) — Att 5,572
Scorers: Austin 75, Johnson 84
Ref: D Hutchinson

Argyle: Barron, Smart, Uzzell, Horswill, Megson, Craven, Foster, Taylor, Austin, Johnson, Harrison, Rogers
Chesterfield: *Tingay, Badger*, Burton, Kowalski, Cottam, O'Neill, Harris, Tartt, Simpson, Cammack, Hepplolette, Dearden*

Hall has departed as expected. Rogers torments Len Badger all afternoon and the full‑back is replaced late in the game. It is Rogers who sets up Austin's opener. Johnson seals the victory when scoring a defence‑splitting move. Tartt is booked (29) for kicking the ball away.

---

18 — A PETERBOROUGH — 19/11 — L 0:1 (HT 0:1) — Pos 18 (opp 3) — Att 6,528
Scorers: *Robson 23*
Ref: H Robinson

Argyle: Barron, Smart, Uzzell, Taylor, Megson, Johnson, Foster, Craven, Austin, Harrison, Rogers
Peterborough: *Barron, Hindley, Lee, Doyle, Ross, Slough, Turner, Sargent, Earle, McEwan, Robson*

Boro's two veterans make telling contributions. Tommy Robson scores the only goal in his 350th match for Posh and keeper Jim Barron makes several fine saves. Craven tarnishes his unblemished disciplinary record this season by being booked for tripping debutant Billy McEwan.

---

19 — H BURY — 3/12 — L 0:1 (HT 0:1) — Pos 19 (opp 16) — Att 4,766
Scorers: *Stanton 27*
Ref: K Cooper

Argyle: Barron, Smart, Uzzell, Taylor, Megson, Craven, Foster, Austin, Graves*, Harrison, Rogers
Bury: *Forrest, Keenan, Kennedy, Hatton, Stanton, Bailey, Tucker, Rowland, McIlwraith, Suddick, Robins*

With three strikers injured, 16‑year‑old Mark Graves is told he is playing only 30 minutes before kick‑off. New Bury boss Bob Stokoe is delighted with his side's performance. Spurs and Coventry send scouts to watch Megson, and Arsenal are reported to be interested in Barron.

---

20 — A PORT VALE — 9/12 — D 3:3 (HT 1:2) — Pos 18 (opp 21) — Att 3,650
Scorers: Austin 38, 87, Horswill 63 / *Beamish 7, Smart 29(og), Lamb 50*
Ref: J Bray

Argyle: Barron, Smart, Uzzell, Harrison, Johnson, Craven, Foster, Megson, Austin, Horswill, Rogers
Port Vale: *Connaughton, McGifford, Griffiths, Ridley, Dulson, Harris, Ford, Lamb, Brownbill, Beamish, Bailey*

With a strong wind behind them, Vale, looking for their first win in twelve matches, take an early lead. Smart then helps Dave Harris's header in. Argyle stage a great fight‑back from 1‑3 down. The outstanding Horswill gets a deserved goal and then sets up Austin for a late equaliser.

---

21 — H EXETER — 26/12 — D 2:2 (HT 1:1) — Pos 18 (opp 17) — Att 12,349
Scorers: Johnson 44, Craven 87 / *Roberts 35, Kellow 84*
Ref: E Hughes

Argyle: Barron, Smart, Uzzell, Megson, Harrison*, Craven, Foster, Johnson, Austin, Rogers, Holman
Exeter: *Key, Templeman, Hore, Bowker, Jennings*, Hatch, Saxton, Kellow, Randall, Roberts, Taylor, Heale*

Four minutes after City take the lead, Nicky Jennings is taken off having been struck in the face by the ball. Johnson hits both uprights in the second half before Kellow appears to give Exeter the points. Craven scores for the first time since his debut. Taylor goes to hospital for checks.

---

22 — A SWINDON — 27/12 — L 1:3 (HT 1:1) — Pos 19 (opp 9) — Att 9,732
Scorers: Binney 22 / *Moss 12, Guthrie 82, Kamara 85*
Ref: L Shapter

Argyle: Barron, Smart, Uzzell, Megson, Harrison, Craven, Foster, Johnson, Austin, Binney, Rogers
Swindon: *Allan, McLaughlin, Trollope, Kamara, Ford, Prophett, Thomas, Moss, Guthrie, Stroud, Cunningham*

Taylor has blood poisoning and Austin knee‑ligament damage. Argyle recall Binney for the first time in two months. Kelly says he needs reinforcements. Late goals again prove costly as Guthrie and Kamara take advantage of Argyle pushing forward to score a flattering victory.

---

23 — H WREXHAM — 31/12 — L 0:1 (HT 0:1) — Pos 20 (opp 1) — Att 7,415
Scorers: *Shinton 33*
Ref: B Stevens

Argyle: Barron, Smart*, Uzzell, Horswill, Foster, Megson, Johnson, Binney, Harrison, Rogers, Delve
Wrexham: *Davies, Hill, Dwyer, Davis, Roberts, Thomas, Sutton, Shinton, Whittle, McNeil, Cartwright*, Lyons*

The Robins, containing a number of Welsh internationals, regain their top spot with their third successive win at Home Park. Dixie McNeil's pass gets the Greens defence in a dither and Bobby Shinton scores. Dai Davies pulls off some fine saves. Uzzell's late strike goes just wide.

LEAGUE DIVISION 3

Manager: Mike Kelly > Malcolm Allison — SEASON 1977-78

Column headings: No · Date · Att · Pos · Pt · F-A · H-T · Scorers, Times, and Referees · 1 · 2 · 3 · 4 · 5 · 6 · 7 · 8 · 9 · 10 · 11 · 12 sub used

---

24 · A LINCOLN · 2/1
Att 6,262 · Pos 20 · Pt 19 · **D 2-2** (H-T 2-2)
Scorers: Austin 1, Neale 44(og) | Austin 9(og), Neale 26 — Ref: D Clarke

1	2	3	4	5	6	7	8	9	10	11	12
Barron	Harrison	Uzzell	Delve	Foster	Craven	Johnson	Megson	Austin	Horswill	Binney	Cockerill
Grotier	*Guest*	*Neale*	*Leigh*	*Wigginton*	*Cooper*	*Fleming*	*Graham**	*Harford*	*Hubbard*	*Jones*	

To add to Argyle's woes, Craven requests a transfer. Austin and cricket playing Phil Neale set their own quiz question by sharing out the goals. Austin scores after 52 seconds but then heads into his own net. Neale scores from 20 yards and then slices an Argyle free-kick past Grotier.

---

25 · A PRESTON · 14/1
Att 6,500 · Pos 5 · Pt 19 · **L 2-5** (H-T 1-3)
Scorers: Foster 7, Johnson 67p (Elwiss 82) | Bax'13, C'man 22, T'mson 28, B'ce 79 — Ref: A Jenkins

1	2	3	4	5	6	7	8	9	10	11	12
Barron	Harrison	Uzzell	Bason	Foster	Craven	Delve	Megson	Austin	Rogers	Johnson	Doyle
Tunks	*McMahon*	*Cameron*	*Burns*	*Barter*	*Cross**	*Coleman*	*Haselgrave*	*Thomson*	*Elwiss*	*Bruce*	

Bason returns on a £35k transfer. Foster celebrates his 50th league appearance a goal but Preston strike three times in 15 minutes. New Argyle physio Dennis Loze is kept busy. Johnson scores from the spot after he was fouled by Doyle. Nobby Stiles' men continue their promotion push.

---

26 · H CARLISLE · 21/1
Att 4,744 · Pos 13 · Pt 19 · **L 0-1** (H-T 0-1)
Scorers: — | Hamilton 16 — Ref: T Spencer

1	2	3	4	5	6	7	8	9	10	11	12
Barron	Harrison	Uzzell	Bason	Foster	Banton	Delve	Megson	Austin	Craven	Rogers*	Sutton
Swinburne	*Carr*	*McCartney*	*MacDonald*	*Lathan*	*Parker*	*McVitie*	*Bonnyman*	*Tait*	*Rafferty*	*Hamilton*	

Injuries force a re-shuffle but the fans vent their anger at Kelly and Chairman Robert Daniel as Argyle slump to another home defeat. Jim Hamilton shows that the Pilgrims were hasty in jetting him go by powering home from 20 yards after Rafferty's shot rebounds off Barron.

---

27 · A HEREFORD · 28/1
Att 4,737 · Pos 22 · Pt 21 · **W 3-1** (H-T 2-1)
Scorers: Austin 7, Craven 40, Megson 75 | Davey 9 — Ref: G Owen

1	2	3	4	5	6	7	8	9	10	11	12
Barron	Harrison	Uzzell	Banton	Delve	Foster	Bason	Taylor	Austin	Craven	Megson	Redrobe
Mellor	*Jefferson**	*Ritchie*	*Layton*	*Marshall*	*Sheedy*	*Briley*	*Stephens*	*Barton*	*Davey*	*Spring*	

The Greens grab two vital points in this bottom of the table clash. Taylor is back after a lengthy illness and Craven is used as a striker. Austin gets a faint touch on Bason's corner but Steve Davey soon responds. Craven slams in through a crowd of players. Megson scores his first goal.

---

28 · H COLCHESTER · 4/2
Att 4,639 · Pos 6 · Pt 22 · **D 1-1** (H-T 1-1)
Scorers: Taylor 5 | Rowles 28 — Ref: W Gow

1	2	3	4	5	6	7	8	9	10	11	12
Barron	Harrison	Uzzell	Bason*	Foster	Banton	Delve	Megson	Austin	Craven	Taylor	Horswill
Walker	*Cook*	*Wignall*	*Leslie*	*Packer*	*Dowman*	*Foley*	*Gough*	*Rowles*	*Allison*	*Dyer*	

The attendance is a new post-war low. Taylor cracks in a beauty from 30 yards. Recent signing Eddie Rowles equalises. Bason limps through most of the first-half after being injured in the build up to Argyle's goal. Craven is close with a header from 25 yards from Walker's mis-kick.

---

29 · A CAMBRIDGE · 11/2
Att 4,745 · Pos 1 · Pt 22 · **L 0-3** (H-T 0-3)
Scorers: — | Cozens 8, Fallon 38, Morgan 45 — Ref: D Reeves

1	2	3	4	5	6	7	8	9	10	11	12
Barron	Harrison	Uzzell	Bason	Foster	Megson	Banton	Taylor	Austin	Craven	Delve	
Webster	*Howard*	*Smith*	*Stringer*	*Watson*	*Fallon*	*Cozens*	*Spriggs*	*Morgan*	*Finney*	*Biley*	

Surprise leaders Cambridge score a convincing victory. Cozens scores from a half-cleared corner. Fallon heads home Watson's free-kick and Biley sets up Morgan on the stroke of half-time. Argyle recover their poise in the second period but a Craven overhead kick is their best effort.

---

30 · A GILLINGHAM · 25/2
Att 9,120 · Pos 1 · Pt 23 · **D 1-1** (H-T 1-1)
Scorers: Megson 34 | Crabbe 6 — Ref: C White

1	2	3	4	5	6	7	8	9	10	11	12
Barron	Harrison	Uzzell	Craven	Foster	Banton	Bason	Fear	Austin	Taylor	Megson	
Hillyard	*Williams*	*Armstrong*	*Overton*	*Knight*	*Crabbe*	*Nicholl*	*Hunt**	*Price*	*Westwood*	*Richardson*	*Hughes*

Reserve team boss Lennie Lawrence takes charge of the side following Kelly's resignation. Argyle face a side leading the league for the sixth time this season. Barron saves Richardson's penalty (70) to secure an unlikely point. Fear debuts after his £20,000 transfer from Bristol City.

---

31 · H CHESTER · 4/3
Att 5,322 · Pos 11 · Pt 24 · **D 2-2** (H-T 1-1)
Scorers: Fear 25, Uzzell 57 | Oakes 44, Mellor 84 — Ref: D Biddle

1	2	3	4	5	6	7	8	9	10	11	12
Barron	Harrison	Uzzell	Bason	Foster	Banton	Craven	Taylor	Austin	Megson	Fear	
Lloyd	*Raynor*	*Walker*	*Storton*	*Delgado*	*Oakes*	*Jones*	*Jeffries*	*Mellor*	*Crossley*	*Phillips*	

Fear scores on his home debut. Player-manager Alan Oakes equalises with a deflected shot. Debutant Ian Uzzell scores his first senior goal. Mellor equalises again but it leaves Chester still looking for their first away win of the season. Barron is rumoured to be on his way to Arsenal.

---

32 · A WALSALL · 7/3
Att 6,722 · Pt 24 · **L 0-1** (H-T 0-1)
Scorers: — | Buckley 2 — Ref: P Richardson

1	2	3	4	5	6	7	8	9	10	11	12
Barron	Harrison	Uzzell	Taylor	Foster	Craven	Banton	Megson	Austin	Horswill	Fear	
Kearns	*Macken*	*Caswell*	*Harrison*	*Serella*	*Evans*	*Dennehy*	*Bates*	*Wood*	*Buckley*	*King*	

Alan Buckley's 25th of the season is enough to give Walsall the points and extend their unbeaten run to eleven matches. Rumours abound on the eve of transfer deadline day. Sutton and Austin look set to leave and two unnamed players expected to replace them. Barron stays though.

---

33 · H TRANMERE · 10/3
Att 3,712 · Pos 5 · Pt 25 · **D 1-1** (H-T 0-0)
Scorers: Perrin 63 | Allen 77 — Ref: R Chadwick

1	2	3	4	5	6	7	8	9	10	11	12
Barron	Harrison	Uzzell	Bason	Foster	James	Fear	Taylor	Perrin	Horswill	Megson	
West	*Mathias*	*Flood*	*Parry*	*Philpotts*	*Evans*	*Peplow*	*Palios*	*Moore*	*Tynan*	*Allen*	

Craven has also gone but new boys Perrin and James settle in well. It is Perrin a 30k signing from Crystal Palace who gives Argyle the lead with a well-taken goal. Russ Allen heads the equaliser but then sees his penalty saved by Barron (72) after Megson's foul on Ronnie Moore.

---

34 · H LINCOLN · 13/3
Att 5,208 · Pt 25 · **L 1-2** (H-T 1-1)
Scorers: Perrin 3 | Wigginton 36, Harding 65 — Ref: S Bates

1	2	3	4	5	6	7	8	9	10	11	12
Barron	Harrison	Uzzell	Bason*	Foster	James	Taylor	Megson	Perrin	Horswill	Fear	
Grotier	*Guest*	*Leigh*	*Neale*	*Wigginton*	*James*	*Cooper*	*Graham*	*Harford*	*Hubbard*	*Harding*	*Johnson*

Argyle's dismal home form continues. On a wet evening, Perrin scores again but, Megson excepted, every Pilgrim has an off-night. Lincoln have remained in the Westcountry after a drubbing at Exeter and are unfortunate not to win by a hatful as several good chances go begging.

Plymouth Argyle — Season match record (games 35–46)

#	Venue	Opponent	Date	HT	FT	Result	Pts	Pos	Att	Scorers (Argyle)	Scorers (Opponents)	Referee
35	H	OXFORD	18/3	1-1	2-1	W	27	21	5,726 (17)	Fear 33, Johnson 86	Bodel 41	M Sinclair
36	A	PORTSMOUTH	21/3	2-0	5-1	W	29	19	11,010 (24)	Trusson 29, Binney 38, 90, Taylor 65, [Fear 69]	Piper S 73	J Taylor
37	H	SWINDON	25/3	0-1	0-2	L	29	21	9,174 (8)	—	Cunningham 10, Guthrie 74	D Nippard
38	A	EXETER	28/3	0-0	0-0	D	30	21	8,334	—	—	J Homewood
39	H	SHEFFIELD WED	4/4	1-1	1-1	D	31	20	7,694 (16)	Fear 41p	Wylde 15	E Read
40	A	CHESTERFIELD	8/4	1-2	1-4	L	31	22	3,996 (11)	Binney 7	Fern 15, 52, Cammack 33, Simpson 86	A Hamil
41	H	ROTHERHAM	11/4	1-1	1-1	D	32	21	5,018 (20)	Foster 24	Gwyther 34	A Lees
42	H	PETERBOROUGH	15/4	1-0	1-0	W	34	21	5,678 (4)	Binney 40	—	L Shapter
43	A	BURY	22/4	0-1	1-1	D	35	21	3,177 (13)	Binney 90	Rowland 8	B Martin
44	A	SHREWSBURY	25/4	0-3	1-3	L	35	21	2,308	Fear 61p	Biggins 12, Atkins 20p, Irvine 28	M Peck
45	H	PORT VALE	29/4	1-1	3-2	W	37	20	9,474 (21)	Johnson 28, Binney 52, 68	Beamish 2, Froggatt 59	L Burden
46	H	BRADFORD C	1/5	4-0	6-0	W	39	19	7,862 (22)	Harrison 13, Taylor 25, 30, Perrin 39, [Foster 84, Fear 89]	—	R Crabb

Home Average 6,887 — Away 6,046

Line-ups and match reports

35 — Oxford (H)
Argyle: Barron, Harrison, Uzzell, Bason, Foster, James, Johnson, Taylor, Perrin, Fear*, Megson, Trusson
Oxford: Burton, Kingston, Fogg, Briggs, Bodel, Jeffrey, Seacole, Taylor, Foley, Curran, Duncan
Malcolm Allison returns to Home Park as consultant manager and witnesses a much-improved performance. An early mix up sees Harrison kick Foster in the head. Johnson's header goes in off a post. Despite the two welcome points, Allison calls the players in for Sunday training.

36 — Portsmouth (A)
Argyle: Barron, James, Uzzell, Bason, Foster, Fear, Johnson, Taylor, Binney, Perrin*, Megson, Trusson
Portsmouth: Middleton, Roberts*, Taylor, Ellis, Cahill, Pullar, Denyer, Lathan, Garwood, Mellows, McCaffrey, Piper
Allison's revised tactics pay dividends. Megson is used as a sweeper and Binney recalled after three months. Perrin limps off (21) but Trusson soon makes his mark. Binney intercepts Cahill's throw back to Middleton for number two. Taylor scores the goal of the night from 20 yards.

37 — Swindon (H)
Argyle: Barron, James, Uzzell, Megson, Foster, Johnson, Taylor, Binney, Fear, Trusson, Rogers
Swindon: Allan, McLaughlin, Ford, Kanara, Carter, Prophett, Moss, Cunningham*, Guthrie, McHale, Trollope, Bates
'Umbrellas Vi' forsakes her usual spot for a seat in the directors box. Argyle are unable to maintain their recent improved form. Cunningham gives Swindon a good start. Allison defies his lifelong touchline ban to make a brief sojourn to the dugout. Guthrie heads in Moss's cross.

38 — Exeter (A)
Argyle: Barron, Horswill, Uzzell, Bason, Foster, James, Megson, Taylor*, Binney, Fear, Trusson, Rogers
Exeter: Key, Templeman, Hore, Delve, Giles, Hodge, Kellow, Randell, Bowker, Holman, Hatch
Both sides struggle on a heavy pitch. Twice Foster ventures upfield to test Key. Bobby Saxton's side have little to play for but ex-Pilgrims Hore and Delve relish the challenge and have outstanding games. City have a late penalty appeal turned down when Uzzell upends Hodge.

39 — Sheffield Wed (H)
Argyle: Barron, Horswill, Uzzell, Bason*, Foster, James, Rogers, Taylor, Binney, Fear, Trusson, James
Sheffield Wed: Bolder, Walden, Grant, Rushbury, Dowd, Mullen, Wylde, Porterfield, Tynan, Johnson, Hornsby
Wednesday continue their climb to safety with their ninth point from five games. Tommy Tynan is prominent up front for the Owls and sets up the first goal for Roger Wylde. Fear equalises from the spot after Mullen fouls Binney. Wylde hits the post and Binney's late effort is offside.

40 — Chesterfield (A)
Argyle: Barron, Harrison, Uzzell, Foster, James, Rogers, Taylor, Binney, Fear, Perrin, Simpson
Chesterfield: Letheran, Tartt, Burton, Pollard, Cottam, O'Neill, Cammack, Fern, Simpson, Walker, Kowalski
Allison attends the match despite a car crash on the M1 the previous evening. Binney's early strike is no avail, as defensive blunders gift the points to Arthur Cox's Spireites. Fern eludes seven defenders for his first. Foster's awful back-pass to Cammack sums up Argyle's afternoon.

41 — Rotherham (H)
Argyle: Barron, Taylor, Uzzell, James, Foster, Harrison, Fear, Perrin, Binney, Rogers
Rotherham: McAllister, Forrest, Breckin, Rhodes, Stancliffe, Green, Finney, Phillips, Gwyther, Goodfellow, Nix
United leave Home Park the happier side as Argyle drop another vital home point. Foster powers in a header from 18 yards but Rotherham respond through David Gwyther's close range effort. Horswill hits the post. Rotherham are happy to defend but look dangerous on the break.

42 — Peterborough (H)
Argyle: Hodge, Taylor, Uzzell, James, Foster, Harrison, Binney, Perrin, Rogers
Peterborough: Waugh, Hindley, Hughes, Doyle, Turner, Ross, Slough, McEwan, Butlin, Anderson, Robson
Barron misses his first game of the season through illness. Nineteen-year-old debutant, Martin Hodge is largely untroubled by the Posh attack. Binney is in inspirational form and deserves his goal, heading in Harrison's cross. Despite some worrying moments Argyle get a valuable win.

43 — Bury (A)
Argyle: Hodge, Forrest, Uzzell, Harrison, Foster, Fear, Johnson, Binney, Perrin, Trusson, Robson
Bury: Forrest, Keenan, Kennedy, Hatton, Tucker, Wilson, Stanton, Farrell, Rowland, Whitehead, Robins
Binney does it again. His header is the last touch of the match. Hodge is unsighted as Rowland scores. Farrell and Rowland hit the woodwork as Argyle, with Fear as sweeper and Uzzell at centre-half, take time to settle. Other results are favourable and surviving the drop is still possible.

44 — Shrewsbury (A)
Argyle: Hodge, Uzzell*, James, Taylor, Foster, Horswill, Rogers, Harrison, Binney, Perrin, Fear, Bason
Shrewsbury: Mulhearn, Leonard, King, Keay, Hayes, Lindsay*, Irvine, Maguire, Biggins, Atkins, Turner, Griffin
The match is effectively over after half an hour. Part-timer Steve Biggins scores with a header, his seventh goal in eight games. Ian Atkins converts a penalty after Sammy Irvine is obstructed. Irvine gets a fine third. Fear pulls one back after Foster's header is handled on the line.

45 — Port Vale (H)
Argyle: Hodge, Bason, James, Taylor, Johnson, Horswill, Harrison, Binney, Perrin, Fear, Beamish*
Port Vale: Connaughton, Bentley, Dulson, Ridley, Harris, Hawkins, Bramage, Moore, Froggatt, Beamish*, Bailey, Satcliffe
The players are carried high as two points secure Argyle's place in Division Three. Vale, without a win in nine games, stun the crowd with Ken Beamish's 16th of the season. Johnson seizes on an error and the on-song Binney strikes twice more with typical opportunism.

46 — Bradford C (H)
Argyle: Hodge, Harrison, Bason, James, Foster, Johnson, Horswill, Taylor, Binney, Perrin, Fear
Bradford C: Downsbro', Podd, Wood, Johnson*, Baines, Middleton, Gallagher, Dolan, Cooke, McNiven, Hutchins, Wright
Argyle totally demoralise already relegated Bradford. Ex-Plymouth coach Bryan Edwards is in charge for the first time as City's new general manager. Taylor's goals are the pick. Foster celebrates his Player of the Year award with a goal. It is referee Ron Crabb's final game.

LEAGUE DIVISION 3 (CUP-TIES) Manager: Mike Kelly > Malcolm Allison SEASON 1977-78

League Cup

	Att		F-A	H-T	Scorers, Times, and Referees
1:1 A EXETER 13/8	6,712	D	2-2	2-1	Trusson 38, 42 / Robertson 8p, 55p / Ref: L Burden

1	2	3	4	5	6	7	8	9	10	11	12 sub used
Barron	Smart	Uzzell	Horswill	Foster	Craven	Delve	Johnson*	Austin	Trusson	Rogers	Sutton
Baugh	*Templeman*	*Hore*	*Weeks*	*Saxton*	*Hatch*	*Hodge*	*Kellow*	*Robertson*	*Beer*	*Jennings*	*Holman*

A game of four penalties. Craven fouls Lammie Robertson who converts the re-taken spot-kick. After Trusson's first goals in senior football, Barron fouls Kellow and Robertson converts again. Craven pushes Beer (76) but Barron's save prevents Robertson completing his hat-trick.

1:2 H EXETER 16/8	7,639	D	0-0	0-0	Ref: D Nippard (Argyle draw 2-2 on aggregate)

1	2	3	4	5	6	7	8	9	10	11
Barron	Smart	Uzzell	Horswill*	Foster	Craven	Johnson	Delve	Austin	Trusson	Rogers
Baugh	*Templeman*	*Hore*	*Weeks**	*Saxton*	*Hatch*	*Hodge*	*Kellow*	*Bowter*	*Beer*	*Jennings*

Little excitement to match the first-leg thriller. Both sides miss chances. Youngsters Uzzell and Trusson continue to impress. Argyle introduce a player of the match award won by Horswill. With away goals ignored Argyle win the toss of a coin to decide the venue for a third match.

1R H EXETER 23/8	8,776	L	0-1	0-0	Beer 83 / Ref: B Stevens

1	2	3	4	5	6	7	8	9	10	11	12 sub used
Barron	Smart	Uzzell	Horswill	Foster	Craven	Johnson	Delve	Austin*	Trusson	Rogers	Hall
Baugh	*Templeman*	*Hore*	*Weeks**	*Saxton*	*Hatch*	*Hodge*	*Kellow*	*Bowter*	*Beer*	*Jennings*	*Robertson*

Tony Waiters returns from Canada to watch Argyle. With extra-time looming, Alan Beer latches on to Hodges' pass. Beer and Delve hit the woodwork. Transfer-listed Hall is brought on to replace hamstring victim, Austin. Newly promoted City now meet cup-holders Aston Villa.

FA Cup

1 A BATH CITY 26/11	7,866	18	D	SL:1	F-A 0-0	H-T 0-0	Ref: L Burden

1	2	3	4	5	6	7	8	9	10	11	12 sub used
Barron	Smart	Uzzell	Taylor	Foster	Craven	Megson	Harrison	Austin	Johnson*	Rogers	Horswill
Allen	*Ryan*	*Rogers M*	*Burns*	*Bourne*	*Gover*	*Griffin*	*Gibbs*	*Provan*	*Rogers P*	*Higgins*	

Bath manager, Brian Godfrey admits his side were too keyed up as the tackles flew in thick and fast. Johnson requires two stitches in a shin wound. Megson has a late effort disallowed for offside (88). City, without both their skipper and leading scorer, live to fight another day.

1R H BATH CITY 29/11	5,455	18	W	SL:1	2-0	2-0	Taylor 9, 14 / Ref: L Burden

1	2	3	4	5	6	7	8	9	10	11	12 sub used
Barron	Smart	Uzzell	Taylor	Foster	Craven	Trusson*	Megson	Austin	Harrison	Rogers	Horswill
Allen	*Ryan*	*Rogers M*	*Burns*	*Bourne*	*Gover*	*Tavener*	*Gibbs*	*Provan*	*Rogers P*	*Higgins*	

Taylor robs Tavener on the halfway line and shoots past Allen from 30 yards. A header five minutes later ensures there is no giant-killing act. Allen rugby tackles Trusson in the area but goes unpunished. Argyle play their best football of the season in the first half but fade later on.

2 H CAMBRIDGE 17/12	5,850	18	W	4	1-0	1-0	Johnson 31p / Ref: D Nippard

1	2	3	4	5	6	7	8	9	10	11	12 sub used
Barron	Smart	Uzzell	Horswill	Foster	Craven	Johnson	Megson	Austin	Harrison	Rogers	
Webster	*Batson*	*Smith L*	*Stringer*	*Fallon*	*Howard*	*Watson**	*Spriggs*	*Morgan*	*Finney*	*Biley*	*Cozens*

United boss, Ron Atkinson, fumes at the decision to award a penalty against Malcolm Webster for jumping with his foot extended. Even Kelly admits his surprise. Johnson finds the right corner of the net with the spot-kick. Drifting fog descends over the pitch during the second half.

3 A MANSFIELD 7/1	7,402	19	L	2:20	0-1	0-1	Miller 21 / Ref: E Read

1	2	3	4	5	6	7	8	9	10	11	12 sub used
Barron	Harrison	Uzzell	Horswill	Foster	Craven	Johnson	Megson	Austin	Binney*	Delve	Rogers
Arnold	*Pate*	*Foster B*	*Sharkey**	*Foster C*	*Wood*	*Miller*	*Goodwin*	*Syrett*	*Hodgson*	*Aston*	*Phillips*

Hopes of a money-spinning cup run are dashed at Field Mill. Stags skipper Sandy Pate returns after a ten month injury absence. Johnny Miller's 25 yard drive after a run from halfway is the decisive moment. Dave Syrett, a pre-season target for the Pilgrims, is the main threat.

League Table

Pos	Team	P	Home					Away					Pts
			W	D	L	F	A	W	D	L	F	A	
1	Wrexham	46	14	8	1	48	19	9	7	7	30	26	61
2	Cambridge	46	19	3	1	49	11	4	9	10	23	40	58
3	Preston	46	16	5	2	48	19	4	11	8	15	19	56
4	Peterborough	46	15	7	1	32	11	5	9	9	15	22	56
5	Chester	46	14	8	1	41	24	2	14	7	18	32	54
6	Walsall	46	12	8	3	35	17	6	9	8	26	33	53
7	Gillingham	46	11	10	2	36	21	4	10	9	31	39	50
8	Colchester	46	10	11	2	36	16	5	7	11	19	28	48
9	Chesterfield	46	14	6	3	40	16	3	8	12	18	33	48
10	Swindon	46	12	7	4	40	22	4	9	10	27	38	48
11	Shrewsbury	46	11	7	5	42	23	5	8	10	21	34	47
12	Tranmere	46	13	7	3	39	19	3	8	12	18	33	47
13	Carlisle	46	10	9	4	32	26	4	10	9	27	33	47
14	Sheffield Wed	46	13	7	3	28	14	2	6	12	22	38	46
15	Bury	46	7	13	3	34	22	6	6	11	22	34	45
16	Lincoln	46	10	8	5	35	26	5	7	11	18	35	45
17	Exeter	46	11	8	4	30	18	4	6	13	19	41	44
18	Oxford	46	11	10	2	38	21	2	4	17	26	46	40
19	PLYMOUTH	46	7	8	8	33	28	4	8	10	28	40	39
20	Rotherham	46	11	5	7	26	19	2	8	13	25	49	39
21	Port Vale	46	7	11	5	28	23	1	9	13	18	44	36
22	Bradford C	46	11	6	6	40	29	1	4	18	16	57	34
23	Hereford	46	9	9	5	28	22	0	5	18	6	38	32
24	Portsmouth	46	4	11	8	31	38	3	6	14	10	37	31
		1104	272	192	88	869	504	88	192	272	504	869	1104

Odds & ends

Double wins: (3) Bradford C, Hereford, Portsmouth.

Double defeats: (3) Cambridge, Swindon, Wrexham.

Won from behind: (2) Port Vale, Rotherham.

Lost from in front (4) Chesterfield, Lincoln, Oxford, Preston.

High spots: Magnificent win at Portsmouth.

Exciting victory over Port Vale (h) to avoid relegation.

Introduction of youth-team products, Uzzell, Megson and Trusson.

Transformation of George Foster into central defender.

Low spots: Career-ending injury to John Peddelty.

Departure of unsettled Brian Hall.

Season-long battle to avoid relegation.

Acrimonious departure of Mike Kelly in front of local TV cameras.

Player of the Year: George Foster.

Ever presents: (1) George Foster.

Hat-tricks: (0).

Leading scorer: Terry Austin (11).

Appearances and Goals

Player	Appearances						Goals			
	Lge	Sub	LC	Sub	FAC	Sub	Lge	LC	FAC	Tot
Austin, Terry	29		3		4		11			11
Banton, Geoff	6									
Barron, Paul	41		3		4					
Bason, Brian	22	1								
Binney, Fred	18				1		9			9
Craven, John	30		3		4		2			2
Delve, John	19	1	3		1					
Fear, Keith	17									
Foster, George	46		3		4		6			6
Graves, Mark	1						3			3
Hall, Brian	13	1					6			6
Harrison, Chris	29	2			4		1			1
Hodge, Martin	5	3								
Horswill, Mick	29	3	3		2	2	1			1
James, Tyrone	12	1								
Johnson, Brian	20	2	3		3		6		1	7
Megson, Gary	24				4		2			2
Peddelty, John	1	3								
Perrin, Steve	11									
Rogers, Alan	28	1	3		3		3			3
Smart, Kevin	23	1	3		3		2			2
Sutton, Dave						1				
Taylor, Brian	26	1			2		5	2		7
Trusson, Mike	12		3		1		2		2	4
Uzzell, John	44		3		4		1			1
(own-goals)							1			1
25 players used	506	20	33	2	44	3	61	2	3	66

LEAGUE DIVISION 3 — Manager: Malcom Allison > Bobby Saxton — SEASON 1978-79

In each line-up cell the top name is Plymouth Argyle; the italic name is the opponent.

No	Date		Att	Pos	Pt		F-A	H-T	1	2	3	4	5	6	7	8	9	10	11	12 sub used	Scorers, Times, and Referees
1	19/8	A CHESTERFIELD	3,895		2	W	3-1	0-1	Burns _Letheran_	Bason _Tartt_	Rogers _Salmons*_	Trusson _O'Neill_	Foster _Cottam_	Perrin _Hunter_	Fear _Cammack_	Megson _Fern_	Binney _Simpson_	Taylor _Flavell_	Johnson _Kowalski_	Johnson _Dearden_	Fear 48, Binney 56, Megson 70 / Cottam 24 / Ref: N Glover After a half-time roasting from Allison, Argyle look a different side. Bason has a hand in all three Pilgrims goals. Cottam scores from 25 yards. Fear levels from close range and then Binney scores with a spectacular overhead kick after practising the trick in training. Megson seals it.
2	26/8	H LINCOLN	7,806	5	4	W	2-1	1-1	Burns _Grotier_	Bason _Wright_	Rogers _Leigh_	Trusson _Fleming_	Foster _Wigginton_	Perrin _Cooper_	Fear _Hobson_	Megson _Ward*_	Binney _Harland_	Taylor* _Hughes_	Johnson _Harding_	Levy _Sunley_	Megson 43, Perrin 78 / Harding 32 / Ref: W Bombroff In baking heat, Lincoln's busy style unsettles the Greens early on. Taylor goes off suffering a deep gash on his foot (25) and new boy Levy finds the going tough. Harding shows great skill to open the scoring but headers from Megson and Perrin continue Argyle's promising start.
3	1/9	A SOUTHEND	5,936	8	4	L	1-2	1-1	Burns _Cawston_	Bason _Dudley_	Rogers _Yates_	Trusson _Laverick_	Foster _Walker_	Perrin _Hadley_	Fear _Morris_	Graves* _Pountney_	Brennan _Parker_	Megson _Polycarpou_	Johnson _Fell_	Harrison	Megson 10 / Pountney 21, Parker 90 / Ref: C Downey Megson continues his rich scoring vein to give Argyle an early lead in this Friday night encounter. Ron Pountney heads home Colin Morris's corner and Morris also sets up the winner for Derrick Parker in injury-time. Cawston denies Graves with a spectacular full-length diving save.
4	9/9	H MANSFIELD	6,052	15	4	L	1-4	1-2	Burns _Arnold_	Bason _Curtis_	Rogers _Foster B*_	Brennan* _Goodwin_	Foster _Saxby_	Perrin _McClelland_	Megson _Miller_	Fear _Martin_	Binney _Syrett_	Trusson _Hodgson_	Johnson _Bird_	Graves _Foster C_	Binney 38 / Syrett 14, Martin 21, Saxby 53, Miller 87 / Ref: B Stevens Argyle launch their club lottery scheme but their on-the-field enterprise is non-existent. After an error-prone performance the fans lose patience with Allison's new-look defence and heckle the manager. Burns is twice at fault as the previously winless Stags are made to look world-class.
5	12/9	A BURY	3,361		6	W	2-1	1-1	Burns _Forrest_	Hodges _Keenan*_	Rogers _Kennedy_	Brennan _Lugg_	Foster _Tucker_	Perrin _Bailey_	Megson _Wilson_	Taylor _Farrell_	Binney _Rowland_	Trusson _Robins_	Johnson _Taylor_	Fear _Hatton_	Perrin 42, Binney 84 / Robins 1 / Ref: P Richardson The error-prone Burns is dropped and Hodge recalled. Kevin Hodges makes his debut for the injured Bason. Bury have yet to win this season and fall to another Binney goal with the match evenly poised. Robins scores after only 27 seconds to claim the fastest goal of the season so far.
6	16/9	H SWINDON	6,099	8	8	W	2-0	1-0	Hodge _Ogden_	Bason _McLaughlin_	Rogers _Ford_	Brennan* _McHale_	Foster _Aizlewood_	Perrin _Stroud_	Trusson _Miller*_	Taylor _Carter_	Binney _Guthrie_	Megson _Kamara_	Johnson _Bates_	Fear _Gilchrist_	Bason 40, Binney 80 / Ref: D Biddle Bason, Argyle's outstanding player so far this season, scores a spectacular goal after a powerful surge from inside his own half. Ogden denies him a second when he saves a well-struck volley. Binney's header from six inches somehow hits the bar but he makes amends minutes later.
7	23/9	A SHEFFIELD WED	12,088	6	10	W	3-2	0-1	Hodge _Bolder_	Bason _Blackhall_	Rogers _Grant_	Brennan _Rushbury_	Foster _Smith_	Clarke _Mullen_	Megson _Wylde_	Fear _Porterfield_	Binney _Tynan*_	Perrin _Johnson_	Johnson _Hornsby_	Uzzell _Nimmo_	Binney 69, 74, 81, Wylde 42, Nimmo 79 / Ref: D Clarke Jack Charlton's Owls are unbeaten in 15 home matches. Binney is at the heart of the action. He again misses from inches before Wylde's header puts the home side ahead. Binney levels and his second is his 150th in league soccer. He completes his hat-trick from a difficult angle.
8	25/9	A TRANMERE	1,907		10	L	1-2	0-0	Hodge _Johnson_	Bason _Mathias*_	Rogers _Flood_	Taylor _Parry_	Foster _Bramhall_	Clarke _Palios_	Megson _Craven_	Fear _O'Neil_	Binney _Moore_	Evans _Evans_	Johnson _McAuley_	Johnson _Postlewhite_	Johnson 90 / Evans 51, Moore 60 / Ref: K Walmsley Argyle remain in the north over the weekend but the euphoria of Hillsborough is short-lived. Hodge saves brilliantly from Ronnie Moore but the ball goes to Evans who scores from an acute angle. Moore scores on the turn. Argyle stage a late rally but Johnson's goal comes too late.
9	30/9	H ROTHERHAM	6,705	4	12	W	2-0	2-0	Hodge _McAlister_	Bason* _Pugh_	Rogers _Breckin_	Taylor _Finney_	Foster _Green_	Clarke _Forrest_	Megson _Dawson_	Fear _Phillips_	Binney _Gwyther_	Perrin _Crawford_	Johnson _Smith_	Trusson	Binney 18, 21 / Ref: E Read The Millers never look likely to end their run of 25 away matches without a win. After two early goals, Binney misses an easier chance for another hat-trick when he puts Taylor's clever back-heel wide. Clarke has an impeccable game but the defence looks more solid of late.
10	7/10	A CARLISLE	5,731	5	13	D	1-1	0-0	Hodge _Swinburne_	Bason _Hoolickin_	Rogers* _McCartney_	Taylor _MacDonald_	Foster _Ludham_	Clarke _Parker_	Megson _McVitie_	Fear _Bonnyman_	Binney _Kemp_	Perrin _Tait_	Johnson _Hamilton_	Graves _Maguire_	Perrin 62 / Bonnyman 48 / Ref: T Farley Argyle become only the second side to score at Brunton Park this season. Jim Hamilton rattles the crossbar before Phil Bonnyman finishes a move he started. Swinburne is yards off his line as Perrin's header floats over him. Graves comes on and almost turns the game Argyle's way.
11	14/10	H SHREWSBURY	9,901	4	14	D	1-1	0-1	Hodge _Wardle_	Bason ! _King_	Rogers _Leonard_	Megson _Turner_	Foster _Griffin_	Clarke _Hayes_	Silkman _Chapman_	Fear _Lindsay_	Binney _Atkins_	Perrin _Biggins_	Johnson _Maguire_	Johnson	Bason 55 / Atkins 27 / Ref: A Glasson Shrewsbury's well-worked corners finally bring a reward when Ian Atkins converts Graham Turner's flick-on. New boy Silkman shows some nice touches. Bason scores with a screamer but then incurs the wrath of Allison by being sent off for dissent (89), having already been booked.

12 A CHESTER 18/10 — 5 D 15 — 3,921 6 — 0-0 0-0

Hodge	Trusson	Rogers	Silkman	Foster	Clarke	Brennan	Fear	Binney	Perrin	Johnson
Millington	Nickeas	Walker	Storton	Delgado	Oakes	Jones	Livermore	Edwards	Mellor	Phillips

Chester recover well after being on the wrong end of a 2-6 drubbing at Tranmere the previous week. Hodge keeps Argyle in the game with a number of stunning saves. Mellor's shot finally beats him but crashes off the crossbar. Player-manager Alan Oakes recalls himself after injury.

Ref: T Morris

13 A WALSALL 21/10 — 7 L 15 — 5,552 16 — 1-2 1-1
Binney 39 / Buckley 32, Stragia 73

Hodge	Kearns	Rogers	Foster	Clarke	Brennan	Silkman	Fear	Binney	Perrin	Johnson
Macken	Harrison	Stragia	Serella	King	Birch	Waddington	Austin	Buckley	McDonough	

The only surprise is that the game produces just three goals as numerous attempts are made from both sides. Buckley lashes in from 25 yards. Silkman, socks rolled down, stuns the crowd with his speed and ability. Terry Austin hits the bar off his knee. Stragia beats Hodge's dive.

Ref: S Bates

14 H BLACKPOOL 28/10 — 8 D 16 — 8,886 10 — 0-0 0-0

Hodge	Foster	Rogers	Megson*	Trusson	Clarke	Silkman	Fear	Binney	Perrin	Johnson	Harrison
Ward	Gardner	Pashley	Thompson	Suddaby	McEwan	Weston	Ronson	Spence*	Chandler	Wagstaffe	Sermanni

Silkman again stars after pleading with Allison to play, claiming his pulled muscle only hurts when he walks. Megson angrily storms off (25) after suffering an early injury. McEwan hits the bar (10). In the closing minutes, Ward parries Fear's shot straight to Trusson who miskicks.

Ref: T Spencer

15 A COLCHESTER 3/11 — 13 L 16 — 4,564 10 — 1-2 1-0
Binney 45 / Bunkell 75, Gough 90

Hodge	Hodges	Rogers	Silkman	Foster	Clarke	Fear*	Megson	Binney	Perrin	Trusson
Walker	Cook	Packer*	Hodge	Wignall	Dowman	Foley	Gough	Bunkell	Lee	Allinson	Dyer

Allison is looking to strengthen the side and has a £175k bid for Alan Buckley turned down. Fear splits the defence to set up Binney on the stroke of half-time. Bunkell equalises with Argyle appealing for offside. In injury-time, Gough scrambles the ball in from Allinson's corner.

Ref: J Martin

16 H SOUTHEND 11/11 — 13 D 17 — 6,890 7 — 1-1 1-1
Silkman 44 / Fell 16

Hodge	Bason	Rogers	Megson	Foster	Clarke	Silkman	Fear	Binney	Perrin*	Johnson
Cawston	Dudley	Stead	Laverick	Cusack	Moody	Fell	Pountney	Parker	Polycarpou	Morris

Silkman is the new Home Park hero as he gives another man-of-the-match performance. He thunders home a 30-yard effort, hits the woodwork and leaves the field covering his face with his shirt in mock embarrassment. Fell gives U's the lead when he heads in from under the crossbar.

Ref: W Bombroff

17 H PETERBOROUGH 14/11 — W 19 — 7,398 — 3-2 2-0
Binney 40, Rogers 42, Green 76(og) / Bason 57(og), Cunningham 85

Hodge	Bason	Rogers	Silkman	Foster	Clarke	Megson	Fear	Binney	Graves	Upton
Waugh	Hindley	Styles	Doyle	Green	Ross	Robertson	McEwan	Butlin	Sargent*	Cunningham	Robson

Colin Upton marks his debut by nodding on for Binney to get the opener. Rogers spears in a 30-yarder from Fear's free-kick. Bason's back-pass is out of Hodge's reach. Green steers Rogers' centre past his own keeper before Dave Cunningham's header gives Argyle a late scare.

Ref: E Hughes

18 A LINCOLN 18/11 — 8 D 20 — 3,670 24 — 3-3 1-2
Fear 6, Binney 81p, Clarke 90 / Fleming 21p, 26p, Hobson 56

Hodge	Bason	Rogers	Silkman	Foster	Clarke	Megson	Fear*	Binney	Perrin	Johnson
Turner	Guest	Leigh	Fleming	Smith	Cooper	Hobson	Ward	Tynan	Watson	Harding

Fear side-foots in from 20 yards before controversy strikes. Clarke pushes Ward and Fleming scores from the spot as Burns clears debris from behind the goal. The kick is eventually re-taken. Foster fouls Watson in the area. Binney's penalty follows a handball. Clarke steals a point.

Ref: D Hutchinson

19 H WATFORD 9/12 — 9 D 21 — 11,907 1 — 1-1 0-1
Silkman 57 / Jenkins 43

Hodge	Bason	McNeill	Silkman	Foster	Clarke	Megson	Chapman	Forde	Perrin	Fear
Sherwood	Stirk	Harrison	Train	Bolton	Garner	Downes	Blissett	Jenkins	Joslyn	Mercer

Argyle's three new boys all have impressive debuts. The tall Ross Jenkins heads in his 22nd goal of the campaign from Ian Bolton's free-kick. Silkman finishes a brilliant solo run by beating Steve Sherwood from 25 yards. The draw is enough to put Watford top on goal difference.

Ref: L Burden

20 H CHESTERFIELD 16/12 — 8 D 22 — 6,740 11 — 1-1 0-1
Megson 78 / Kowalski 13

Hodge	Burns	McNeill	Silkman	Foster	Clarke	Megson	Fear	Binney	Perrin*	Chapman
Letheran	Hunter	Burton	Flavell	Cottam	Prophett	Tartt	Kowalski	Fern*	Salmons	Cammack	Walker

Steve Cammack misses an easy chance only two minutes after Andy Kowalski's early strike. Gian Letheran keeps them in the game with some fine saves. The industrious Megson gets a deserved equaliser. The Spireites appeal vociferously for a late penalty after Fern is brought down.

Ref: D Lloyd

21 A BRENTFORD 26/12 — 10 L 22 — 7,360 20 — 1-2 0-0
Smith 71, 74

Hodge	Burns	McNeill	Silkman	Foster	Clarke	Fear	Megson	Binney	Chapman	Forde
Bond	Salman	Tucker	McNichol	Kruse	Graham J	Graham W*	Glover	Smith	Allder	Phillips	Fraser

Binney intercepts Barry Tucker's back pass to score but is denied a hat-trick by having an effort disallowed and a penalty appeal turned down after being pulled back by Pat Kruse. Dean Smith scores twice for the Bees who concede their first goal at Griffin Park for 434 minutes.

Ref: A Grey

22 A GILLINGHAM 30/12 — 12 L 22 — 5,951 4 — 0-2 0-1
Nicholl 30, Westwood 70

Hodge	Burns	McNeill	Hodges	Foster	Clarke	Fear	Megson	Binney	Graves	Chapman
Hillyard	Sharpe	Armstrong	Overton	Weatherley	Crabbe	Nicholl	Hughes	Jolley	Westwood	Richardson

Gills boss Gerry Summers gambles on playing youngster Terry Jolley instead of the fit again seasoned campaigner, Ken Price. The move pays off as Jolley has a hand in both goals, with Nicholl's shot going in off a post and Westwood getting to the ball ahead of Burns and McNeill.

Ref: B Daniels

23 A SWINDON 20/1 — 8 W 24 — 7,780 5 — 3-1 0-1
Binney 60, 71 Trusson 62 / Carter 16

Hodge	Uzzell	McNeill	Bason	Foster	Clarke	Bason	Megson	Binney	Trusson	Rogers
Ogden	Hamilton	Ford	McHale	Aizlewood	Lewis*	Miller	Carter	Gilchrist	Bates	Kamara	Williams

Argyle give Saxton a winning start which had looked unlikely following Roy Carter's header. Binney equalises with a cheeky back-heel from Bason's cross. Trusson has time to pick his spot and Binney is unmarked to slot home the third. Uzzell has a header ruled out for offside (51).

Ref: R Robinson

LEAGUE DIVISION 3

Manager: Malcom Allison > Bobby Saxton — SEASON 1978-79

No	Date	V	Opponent	Att	Pos	Pt	Res	F-A	H-T	Scorers, Times, and Referees
24	27/1	H	SHEFFIELD WED	8,596	*18*	26	W	2-0	1-0	Binney 33p, 84. Ref: A Robinson
25	3/2	H	TRANMERE	7,418	8 / *23*	27	D	2-2	2-1	Trusson 10, 38 / *Moore 4p, Parry 87*. Ref: C Thomas
26	10/2	A	ROTHERHAM	5,237	8 / *8*	27	L	0-1	0-0	*Gwyther 76*. Ref: B Martin
27	17/2	H	CARLISLE	6,294	8 / *7*	29	W	2-0	2-0	Binney 11, 38. Ref: M Sinclair
28	20/2	H	OXFORD	7,098	8	29	L	0-1	0-0	*Berry 57*. Ref: B Stevens
29	24/2	A	SHREWSBURY	6,087	9 / *2*	29	L	0-2	0-1	*Maguire 20, Chapman 63*. Ref: G Nolan
30	27/2	H	EXETER	12,637		31	W	4-2	3-1	Binney 12p, Bason 13, J'nson 29, Fear 82 / *Delve 20, Sims 52*. Ref: E Read
31	3/3	H	WALSALL	6,487	7 / *18*	33	W	1-0	0-0	Megson 90. Ref: T Bune
32	10/3	A	BLACKPOOL	4,879	7 / *12*	34	D	0-0	0-0	Ref: P Partridge
33	12/3	A	MANSFIELD	4,325		34	L	0-5	0-1	*Syrett 45, 52, Carter 72, 89, Hamilton 83* / New. Ref: A McDonald
34	17/3	H	COLCHESTER	5,342	8 / *14*	35	D	1-1	0-1	Binney 82 / *Dyer 2*. Ref: E Hughes

Line-ups (Argyle in roman, opponents in *italic*)

No	1	2	3	4	5	6	7	8	9	10	11	12 sub used
24	Hodge	Uzzell	McNeill	Bason	Foster	Clarke	Silkman	Megson	Binney	Trusson	Rogers	Grant
	Turner	*Blackhall*	*Rushbury*	*Mullen*	*Pickering*	*Johnson*	*Wylde*	*Lowey*	*Taylor*	*Porterfield**	*Hornsby*	*McAuley*
25	Hodge	Uzzell	McNeill	Bason	Foster	Clarke	Harrison	Trusson	Binney	Fear	Rogers	Rogers
	Johnson	*Mathias*	*Flood*	*Bramhall*	*Postlewhite*	*Parry*	*Peplow**	*Craven*	*Moore*	*Evans*	*Palios*	*McAuley*
26	Hodge	Uzzell	McNeill	Bason	Foster	Clarke	Megson	Harrison	Binney	Trusson	Rogers	
	McAlister	*Forrest*	*Brackin*	*Stancliffe*	*Green*	*Flynn*	*Dawson*	*Phillips*	*Gwyther*	*Crawford*	*Smith*	
27	Hodge	Uzzell	McNeill	Clarke	Foster	Bason	Harrison	Megson	Binney	Trusson*	Rogers	Graves
	Swinburne	*Hoolickin*	*Collins*	*MacDonald*	*Tait*	*Parker*	*McVitie*	*Bonnyman*	*Ludham*	*Kemp*	*Hamilton*	
28	Hodge	Uzzell	McNeill	Clarke	Foster*	Bason	Megson	Harrison	Binney	Perrin	Rogers	Graves
	Burton	*McIntosh*	*Fogg*	*Briggs*	*Bodel*	*Duncan*	*Jeffrey*	*Berry*	*Berry*	*Seacole*	*Hodgson*	
29	Hodge	Uzzell	McNeill	Harrison	Clarke	James	Graves*	Bason	Perrin	Johnson	Rogers	Hodges
	Wardle	*King*	*Leonard*	*Turner*	*Griffin*	*Keay*	*Chapman*	*Atkins*	*Tong*	*Biggins*	*Maguire*	*Maguire*
30	Hodge (Fear 82)	Uzzell	McNeill	Harrison	Clarke	James	Bason	Megson	Binney*	Johnson	Rogers	Hodges
	O'Keefe	*Templeman*	*Hore*	*Randall*	*Giles*	*Roberts*	*Neville*	*Pearson*	*Sims*	*Sims*	*Rogers*	*Hatch*
31	Hodge	Harrison	McNeill	James	James	Clarke	Fear	Waddington	Johnson	McDonough	Rogers	Fear
	Turner	*Harrison*	*Caswell*	*Jones*	*Serella*	*Stragia*	*King*	*Austin*	*McDonough*	*McDonough*	*Macken*	
32	Hodge	Clarke	McNeill	Harrison	James	Johnson	Johnson	Megson	Binney	Trusson	Rogers	Macken
	Hesford	*Malone*	*Pashley*	*Thompson*	*Suddaby*	*McEwan*	*Kerr*	*Jones*	*Spence*	*Davidson*	*Weston*	
33	Hodge	Harrison	McNeill	Clarke	James	Bason!	Johnson	Megson	Binney	Trusson	Rogers	Weston
	New	*Dawkins*	*Foster*	*Curtis*	*Saxby*	*Bird*	*Hamilton*	*Carter*	*Syrett!*	*Martin*	*Miller*	
34	Walker	McNeill	Uzzell	James	Clarke	Johnson	Megson	Harrison*	Binney	Trusson	Rogers	Fear
	Cook	*Wright*	*Hodge*	*Wignall*	*Gough*	*Packer*	*Foley*	*Dyer*	*Lee*	*Lee*	*Allison*	*Allen*

24. Maurice Setters takes charge of the Owls with Jack Charlton away scouting. Binney misses three sitters before Mick Pickering upends Trusson in the area. Rogers' corner is headed in at the near post and only Chris Turner's finger-tips deny Binney a second hat-trick against Wednesday.

25. A dramatic start with Foster deemed to have fouled Moore. His weak penalty hits Hodge's knee and goes in via a post. Trusson hits back twice but Clarke chests the ball to Parry to equalise. Foster, already booked, kneels in front of Mr Thomas to receive a severe lecture after a foul.

26. Conditions are difficult with one end of the pitch frozen. The first half is a dull stalemate but United dominate the second half with Argyle defending the frozen end. Hodge clears the ball out of the ground as he gets to Foster's weak back-pass first. Gwyther scores after Smith's run.

27. Bason plays like a man possessed after getting married the previous day. Binney's first is a well-struck left foot volley and the second a header. Again he is denied a hat-trick when the ref strangely disallows a header for an infringement on Swinburne when no Argyle player is near him.

28. A disastrous evening as Foster, in his 99th league appearance breaks his leg after a tackle on Plymouth-born Colin Duncan. Binney has an effort disallowed for handball and Bodel clears Perrin's shot off the line. Paul Berry's goal is a sloppy one as Hodge advances but fails to collect.

29. Graham Turner's side are on a real roll. Unbeaten in 14 matches they are also in the midst of an FA Cup run which sees them reach the last eight. Foster's replacement, James, gives them a helping hand with a woeful back-pass. Veteran Sammy Chapman shoots home from 18 yards.

30. In a lively contest, Binney scores from the spot after Giles fouls Megson. Bason, having been up all night with toothache, and an afternoon at the dentist, defies the pain to score. Johnson, back after a loan spell at Torquay, drills home from 25 yards after O'Keefe's poor goal-kick.

31. Both sides get bogged down in the mud as Argyle struggle, with Walsall resorting to a nine-man defence at times. Saddlers boss Frank Sibley fumes after Megson's header trickles in off a post after a linesman had signalled full-time to Mr Bune. Hodge's leg saves Waddington's shot.

32. Blackpool's main threat, Derek Spence, is shackled by James and the N Irish international fails to score for the first time in six matches. Megson adds to his growing reputation with a classy display and almost scores with an overhead kick. Johnson heads Rogers' goal-bound shot too high.

33. It all goes wrong for Argyle at Field Mill as they suffer their biggest defeat since late 1972. After being penalised for an innocuous foul, Bason is sent off for swearing at the ref (32). Dave Syrett, originally dropped by Billy Bingham, starts the rout and on loan Mike Carter nets twice.

34. U's squad arrives in Plymouth at 1am on Saturday morning after their coach was stranded for six hours at Heston services. Saxton lays into his players and apologises to fans for the performance. Dyer scores after 66 seconds. Binney's goal is the eleventh of his career against Colchester.

Plymouth Argyle — season results (matches 35–46)

Column players (Argyle line-up / opponents in italics)

---

35 · A PETERBOROUGH · 24/3 — 10 · L · 1-2 · 1-1 · att 4,039 · 21 · 35
Argyle: Hodge, Uzzell, McNeill, James, Clarke, Bason, Johnson, Megson, Binney, Binney, Harrison, Rogers
Opp.: *Waugh, Hindley, Styles, Doyle, Smith, Ross, Guy, Sharkey*, Cooke, McEwan, Cliss, Robson*
Johnson 25 | Cooke 45, Smith 90
Ref: C Downey
With an away point seemingly in the bag, Megson needlessly obstructs Guy. From Doyle's free-kick, Tony Smith heads in with seconds left on the clock. With a strong wind at their backs, Argyle took the lead through Johnson's left-foot shot. Joe Cooke scores from Posh's first corner.

36 · A SWANSEA · 31/3 — 10 · L · 1-2 · 0-0 · att 11,412 · 2 · 35
Argyle: Hodge, McNeill, Harrison, Uzzell*, Bartley, James, Johnson, Fear, Binney, Megson, Harrison, Trusson
Opp.: *Crudgington, Smith, Phillips, Stevenson, Charles*, Attley, James, Curtis, Waddle, Callaghan, Boersma*
Stevenson 62, Waddle 69 | Megson 74
Ref: D Civil
Stevenson's controversial opener is allowed despite Hodge being pinned to the ground by Waddle at the time. Hodge is booked for his protests. Waddle appears to steer the ball in with a hand for the second. Rogers leaves ex-Liverpool hard-man Tommy Smith stranded to set up Megson.

37 · H BURY · 3/4 — W · 3-0 · 1-0 · att 4,728 · 37
Argyle: Hodge, Uzzell, ...
Opp.: *Forrest, Constantine, Stanton, Ritson, Tucker*, Whitehead, Lugg, Wilson, Beamish, Gregory, Taylor, Madden*
Tucker 21(og), Harrison 52, Clarke 72
Ref: T Spencer
Clarke lays claim to the first goal but the records credit it as an own-goal against Billy Tucker who is injured in the incident and goes off five minutes later. Forrest makes a great point-blank save but Harrison nets the rebound. No doubt about the third as Clarke thunders a shot home.

38 · H HULL · 7/4 — 10 · L · 3-4 · 1-2 · att 5,816 · 11 · 37
Argyle: Hodge, Uzzell*, Nisbet, Skipper, Haigh, Roberts, Horswill, Edwards, Bannister, Galvin*, Hood
Opp.: *Blackburn, Hawker, Croft*
Trusson 38, Binney 71p, Clarke 88 | Edwards 12, 14, Skipper 47, Bannister 74
Ref: K Salmon
A comedy of errors at both ends. Horswill, on his return to Home Park, is booked after only seven seconds for fouling Megson. Argyle's static defence gift Hull the first three. Binney's penalty comes after Trusson appears to trip over his own feet. Hodge drops a cross for Hull's fourth.

39 · A OXFORD · 11/4 — L · 2-3 · 1-1 · att 3,299 · 37
Argyle: Hodge, Burton, Taylor, Fogg, Briggs, Bodel, Duncan, Graydon, Jeffrey, Berry, Trusson, Seacole, Hodgson
Opp.: italics
Johnson 10, 85 | Graydon 39, 79p, Berry 57
Ref: J Taylor
Johnson shoots home from the edge of the box. Ray Graydon's corners cause problems all evening and he eventually scores directly from one. Harrison fouls Jason Seacole. Graydon's spot-kick is saved but is ordered to be re-taken after Hodge is adjudged to have moved too early.

40 · H BRENTFORD · 14/4 — 11 · W · 2-1 · 1-0 · att 6,344 · 15 · 39
Argyle: Hodge, McNeill*, Tucker, Salman, Kruse, McNichol, Carlton, Fraser, Aller, Graham J, Phillips, Smith
Opp.: *Bond, Shrubb**
Binney 38p, Johnson 61 | Carlton 84
Ref: A Robinson
Saxton gambles by leaving out both central defenders, James and Clarke. Uzzell and McNeil are drafted in as central defenders. Megson scores but Carlton makes Argyle sweat. his legs swept from underneath by Jim McNichol. Binney sends Len Bond the wrong way. Johnson scores the only goal.

41 · A EXETER · 17/4 — L · 0-1 · 0-0 · att 8,022 · 39
Argyle: Hodge, Uzzell, Hore, Bason, Randell, Giles, Roberts, Neville, Rogers, Upton*, Binney, Sims, Johnson, Perrin, Trusson, Delve, Fear, Hatch
Opp.: *Main, Templeman*
Rogers 78
Ref: J Homewood
Argyle start the livelier and Johnson and Trusson go close. Binney almost breaks clear in the 70th minute but Ian Main beats him to the ball. Pete Rogers, recently signed from Bath City, scores the only goal when the ball runs loose following John Sims' aerial challenge on Hodge.

42 · H GILLINGHAM · 21/4 — 11 · W · 2-1 · 1-1 · att 5,868 · 4 · 41
Argyle: Hodge, McNeill, Sharpe, Barker, Overton, Weatherley, Hughes, Nichol, White, Price, Westwood, Funnell
Opp.: *Hillyard*
Johnson 45, 52 | Funnell 4p
Ref: W Bombroff
The game is halted after ten minutes when a spectator's yellow anorak is deemed to be clashing with Gillingham's shirts. Shortly after, Funnell finishes off a brilliantly executed free-kick. Johnson scores with his thigh and his head. McNeill receives stitches in a head wound at half-time.

43 · H CHESTER · 24/4 — D · 2-2 · 1-2 · att 4,686 · 42
Argyle: Hodge, McNeill, Nickeas, Burns, Clarke, Starton, Raynor, Uzzell, Oakes, Jones, Livermore, Edwards, Phillips, Harrison, Rogers, Henderson
Opp.: *Lloyd*
Johnson 41, Megson 88 | Raynor 4p, Edwards 29
Ref: J Martin
Rayner hammers home a penalty after handball is awarded. Welsh international Ian Edwards evades several tackles to notch his 23rd of the season. A shot from 18 yards gives Johnson his sixth in five games and, late on, Megson dives into a crowded goalmouth to head the equaliser.

44 · A WATFORD · 28/4 — 13 · D · 2-2 · 0-1 · att 14,816 · 2 · 43
Argyle: Hodge, McNeill, Harrison, James, Hodges, Uzzell, Bolton, Graves*, Downes, Blissett, Trusson, Forde, Harrison, Binney
Opp.: *Stirk, Sherwood, Strik, Joslyn, Garner, Jenkins, Mercer, Train*
Trusson 63, Megson 74 | Joslyn 34, Mercer 52
Ref: B Hill
With an average age of just 20, Argyle bounce back to put the brakes on Watford's promotion drive. Already two down, Hodge blocks Ian Bolton's spot-kick (60) after Megson collides with Mercer. Trusson climbs higher than two defenders to head in and Megson coolly finishes.

45 · A HULL · 1/5 — L · 1-2 · 0-0 · att 3,646 · 43
Argyle: Hodge, McNeill, Nisbet, Skipper, Hawker*, Hood, McDonald, Trusson, Roberts, Horswill, Edwards, Megson, Binney, Harrison, Forde
Opp.: *Wealands*
Binney 68 | Horswill 50, Edwards 88
Ref: G Flint
After a dull first half, Argyle old boy Mick Horswill crashes in Gordon Nisbet's cross. Binney scores with a curling 25 yarder. Keith Edwards shot goes under Hodge's body for his 22nd of the season. Hull keeper Jeff Wealands is penalised on three occasions for taking too many steps.

46 · H SWANSEA · 5/5 — 15 · D · 2-2 · 1-0 · att 13,406 · 2 · 44
Argyle: Hodge, McNeill, James, Hodges, Bason, Uzzell, Stevenson, Attley*, Megson, Harrison, Binney, Trusson, Johnson
Opp.: *Crudgington, Evans, Bartley, Phillips, Toshack, Curtis, Waddle, Callaghan, Charles*
Binney 30, Bason 55 | Curtis 54, Toshack 78
Ref: R Lewis
In front of Match of the Day cameras a large Welsh contingent boost the crowd, with John Toshack's Swans hoping for promotion. Binney opens the scoring with a header from a tight angle having earlier celebrated his Player of the Year award by planting a kiss on Umbrella Vi.

Average · Home 7,526 · Away 6,023

LEAGUE DIVISION 3 (CUP-TIES) Manager: Malcom Allison > Bobby Saxton SEASON 1978-79

League Cup

			Att	F-A	H-T	1	2	3	4	5	6	7	8	9	10	11	12 sub used	Scorers, Times, and Referees
1:1	H	TORQUAY	7,725	1-1 D	0-0	Hodge	Bason	Rogers	Trusson	Foster	Megson	Johnson	Taylor	Binney	Perrin	Fear		Parsons 81(og)
		12/8	4			*Turner*	*Parsons*	*Payne*	*Darke*	*Green*	*Dunne*	*Coffill*	*Cooper**	*Murphy*	*Wilson*	*Raper*	*Lawrence*	Lawrence 76
																	Lawrence	Ref: C White

Local rivals frighten Argyle with some fine play. Allison complains about the treatment meted out to Megson. Les Lawrence scores within 20 seconds of coming on, nodding in player-manager Mike Green's free-kick from halfway. Parsons heads past Turner with Binney pressurising.

			Att	F-A	H-T	1	2	3	4	5	6	7	8	9	10	11	12 sub used	Scorers, Times, and Referees
1:2	A	TORQUAY	6,999	2-1 W	0-0	**Burns**	Bason	Rogers	Trusson	Foster	Perrin	Fear	Megson	Binney	Taylor	Johnson		Binney 63, 90
		15/8	4			*Turner*	*Parsons*	*Payne*	*Wilson*	*Green*	*Dunne**	*Coffill*	*Darke*	*Cooper*	*Murphy*	*Raper*	*Lawrence*	Murphy 56
																	Lawrence	(Argyle win 3-2 on aggregate) Ref: L Burden

Donal Murphy finally breaks the stalemate after Raper's shot is only parried by on-loan Tony Burns. Binney heads in after Johnson's fine wing-play. Dunne goes off with a gashed head (70). Binney takes advantage of the five minutes of injury-time to pounce on Megson's pass.

			Att	F-A	H-T	1	2	3	4	5	6	7	8	9	10	11	12 sub used	Scorers, Times, and Referees
2	A	OXFORD	4,255	1-1 D	0-1	Burns	Bason	Rogers	**Brennan**	Foster	Perrin	Megson	Fear	Harrison	Trusson	Johnson		Fear 60
		30/8	24			*Burton*	*Kingston*	*Fogg*	*Briggs*	*Stott*	*Jeffrey*	*McGrogan*	*Taylor*	*Foley*	*Seacole*	*Duncan*		Seacole 10
																		Ref: R Challis

Argyle re-shuffle without the injured Binney. Brennan plays at sweeper and Harrison plays in an unfamiliar forward role. Trusson's error sets up Seacole who heads in after his shot rebounds off Burns. Fear replies with a header as Argyle come from behind for the fifth match in a row.

			Att	F-A	H-T	1	2	3	4	5	6	7	8	9	10	11	12 sub used	Scorers, Times, and Referees
2R	H	OXFORD	8,524	1-2 L	1-0	Burns	Bason	Rogers	Graves	Foster	Perrin	Megson	Fear	Binney	Trusson	Johnson		Fear 22p
		5/9	24	aet		*Burton*	*Taylor*	*Fogg*	*Briggs*	*Bodel*	*Jeffrey*	*McGrogan*	*Sweetzer*	*Foley**	*Seacole*	*Duncan*	*White*	Sweetzer 78, Seacole 113
																		Ref: S Bates

Fear is the hero and villain. He scores from the spot after Megson is brought down by Bodel. Sweetzer, playing his first full game, equalises and Seacole gives the U's the lead in extra-time. With 30 seconds left, Binney is fouled by Les Taylor but Roy Burton saves Fear's penalty.

FA Cup

			Att	F-A	H-T	1	2	3	4	5	6	7	8	9	10	11	12 sub used	Scorers, Times, and Referees
1	A	WORCESTER	8,253	0-2 L	0-1	Hodge	Bason	Rogers	Silkman	Foster	Clarke	Megson	Fear	Binney	Perrin	Brennan*	Trusson	Phelps 13, Williams J 88
		25/11	SL:1			*Cumbes*	*Barton*	*Punsheon*	*Tudor*	*Phelps*	*Deehan*	*Williams J*	*Stevens*	*Williams B*	*Lawrence*	*Allner**	*Martin*	Ref: B Stevens

Argyle slump to their first ever defeat to a non-league side with an inept display. City boss Nobby Clark claims he could have played in goal himself given Jim Cumbes' lack of action. Malcolm Phelps scores with a powerful header and Jim Williams compounds the embarrassment.

League Table

	Team	P	Home W	D	L	F	A	Away W	D	L	F	A	Pts
1	Shrewsbury	46	14	9	0	36	11	7	10	6	25	30	61
2	Watford	46	15	5	3	47	22	7	7	9	36	30	60
3	Swansea	46	16	6	1	57	32	8	6	9	26	29	60
4	Gillingham	46	15	7	1	39	15	6	10	7	26	27	59
5	Swindon	46	17	2	4	44	14	8	5	10	30	38	57
6	Carlisle	46	11	10	2	31	13	4	12	7	22	29	52
7	Colchester	46	13	9	1	35	19	4	8	11	25	36	51
8	Hull	46	12	9	2	36	14	7	2	14	30	47	49
9	Exeter	46	14	6	3	38	18	3	9	11	23	38	49
10	Brentford	46	14	4	5	35	19	5	5	13	18	30	47
11	Oxford	46	10	8	5	27	20	4	10	9	17	30	46
12	Blackpool	46	12	5	6	38	19	6	4	13	23	40	45
13	Southend	46	11	6	6	30	17	4	9	10	21	32	45
14	Sheffield Wed	46	9	8	6	30	22	4	11	8	23	31	45
15	PLYMOUTH	46	11	9	3	40	27	4	5	14	27	41	44
16	Chester	46	11	9	3	42	21	3	7	13	15	40	44
17	Rotherham	46	13	3	7	30	23	4	7	12	19	32	44
18	Mansfield	46	11	7	5	30	24	5	8	10	21	28	43
19	Bury	46	6	11	6	35	32	5	9	9	24	33	42
20	Chesterfield	46	10	5	8	35	34	3	9	11	16	31	40
21	Peterborough	46	8	7	8	26	24	3	7	13	18	39	36
22	Walsall	46	7	6	10	34	32	3	6	14	22	39	32
23	Tranmere	46	4	12	7	26	31	2	4	17	19	47	28
24	Lincoln	46	5	7	11	26	38	2	4	17	15	50	25
		1104	265	174	113	847	541	113	174	265	541	847	1104

Odds & ends

Double wins: (3) Bury, Sheffield Wed, Swindon.
Double defeats (3) Hull, Mansfield, Oxford.

Won from behind: (6) Bury, Chesterfield, Gillingham, Lincoln, Sheffield Wed, Swindon.
Lost from in front: (5) Brentford, Colchester, Oxford, Peterborough, Southend.

High spots: Goalscoring form of Fred Binney.
Five wins in first seven games suggesting promotion candidates.
Performances of Gary Megson, attracting attention of bigger clubs.
Impressive form of young goalkeeper, Martin Hodge.
Five wins in first seven matches suggesting promotion candidates.

Low spots: Abysmal FA Cup performance at non-league Worcester.
Inspirational defender, George Foster suffering broken leg v Oxford.
Three wins from final 15 matches saw a slump to mis-table.

Player of the Year: Fred Binney.
Ever presents: (0).
Hat-tricks: (1) Fred Binney.
Leading scorer: Fred Binney (28).

Appearances and Goals

Player	Lge	Sub	LC	Sub	FAC	Sub	Goals Lge	LC	FAC	Tot
Bason, Brian	36		4		1					4
Binney, Fred	42	1	3	1	1	1	26	2		28
Brennan, Steve	6									
Burns, Tony	8		3							
Chapman, Paul	3	1								
Clarke, Colin	35						3			3
Fear, Keith	23	5	4	1			3		2	5
Forde, Clevere	4	1								
Foster, George	28		4							
Graves, Mark	6	5	1							
Harrison, Chris	21	2	1				1			1
Hodge, Martin	38				1					
Hodges, Kevin	11	1	1			1				
James, Tyrone	15									
Johnson, Brian	33		4				9			9
Levy, Tony		1								
McNeill, Brian	27									
Megson, Gary	42		4		1		8			8
Perrin, Steve	22		4		1		3			3
Rogers, Alan	38		4		1	1	1			1
Silkman, Barry	14						2			2
Taylor, Brian	8		2							
Trusson, Mike	24	3	4	1			5			5
Upton, Colin	2	1								
Uzzell, John	20	1								
(own-goals)							2		1	3
25 players used	506	22	44		11	1	67	5		72

LEAGUE DIVISION 3

Manager: Bobby Saxton — SEASON 1979-80

No		Date		Att	Pos	Pt	F-A	H-T	Scorers, Times, and Referees
1	H	18/8	BURY	5,547		W 2	2-0	2-0	Binney 16, 18p / Ref: B Stevens
2	A	21/8	MILLWALL	5,153		L 2	1-2	0-1	Hodges 64 / O'Callaghan 25, Lyons 60 / Ref: J Bray
3	A	25/8	CHESTERFIELD	5,510	17	L 2	1-3	0-1	Graves 65 / Birch 42, 53, Moss 50 / Ref: N Glover
4	H	1/9	SHEFFIELD WED	6,208	20	L 2	1-3	0-1	Hodges 90 / McCulloch 2, Porterfield 75, Curran 84 / Ref: A Glasson
5	A	8/9	GRIMSBY	7,326	23	L 2	0-1	0-1	Cumming 33 / Ref: D Webb
6	H	15/9	WIMBLEDON	5,744	19	W 4	3-0	1-0	Kemp 44, 47, Trusson 75 / Ref: T Spencer
7	H	18/9	OXFORD	5,635		D 5	1-1	0-0	Kemp 89 / Berry 58 / Ref: W Bombroff
8	A	21/9	SOUTHEND	4,699	23	L 5	1-4	1-3	Kemp 8 / Pountney 7, Tuohy 16, Morris 27, [Gray 51] / Ref: D Letts
9	H	29/9	BLACKPOOL	5,693	21	D 6	2-2	2-1	Binney 30, 33 / Kellow 26, Jones 74 / Ref: E Read
10	A	6/10	CHESTER	2,818	23	L 6	0-1	0-1	Henderson 38 / Ref: A Hamil
11	H	9/10	MILLWALL	5,353		D 7	1-1	1-0	Kemp 33 / Lyons 47 / Ref: A Robinson

Line-ups (Argyle player / opponent)

No	1	2	3	4	5	6	7	8	9	10	11	12 sub used
1	Hards / Forrest	James / Constantine	Harrison / Kennedy	Randell / Waldron	Phill'-Mastrs / Howard	Foster / Lugg !	Bason / McIlwraith	Megson / Wilson*	Binney / Beamish	Hodges / Gregory	Johnson* / Taylor	Perrin / Madden
2	Hards / Jackson	Harrison / Donaldson	Harrison / Roberts	Phill'-Mastrs / Chatterton	Foster / Blyth	Hodges /	Megson / Seasman	Graves / Lyons*	Binney / Mehmet	Randell / O'Callaghan	Johnson / Kinsella	
3	Hards / Letheran	Harrison / O'Neill	Bason / Kowalski	Hodges / Tartt	Phill'-Mastrs / Green	Foster / Hunter	Randell / Birch	Megson / Moss	Graves / Walker	Trusson / Salmons	Johnson / Ridley	
4	Cox / Blackhall	Harrison / Grant	Hodges / Smith	Uzzell* / Mullen	Phill'-Mastrs / Hornsby	Bason / Curran	Megson / Porterfield	Graves / Ford	Trusson / Fleming	Randell / McCulloch	Johnson / King	Ball
5	Brown / Batch	Harrison / Moore D	Hodges / Moore K	Uzzell* / Waters	Phill'-Mastrs / Wigginton	Foster / Stone	Megson / Brolly	Graves* / Ford	Trusson / Liddell*	Randell / Mitchell	Johnson / Cumming	Bason / Lester
6	Brown / Goddard	Harrison / Jones	Hodges / Galliers	Uzzell* / Perkins	Phill'-Mastrs / Bowgett	Bason / Haverson	Megson / Leslie*	Kemp / Parsons	Trusson / Denny	Randell / Cork	Johnson / Knowles	Downes
7	Brown / Burton	Harrison / Taylor	Hodges / Fogg	Phill'-Mastrs / Briggs	Foster / Stott	Bason / Jeffrey	Megson / Graydon	Kemp / Duncan	Trusson / Berry	Randell / Cooke*	Johnson / Hodgson	Binney / McGrogan
8	Brown / Cawston	Harrison / Dudley	McNeill / Moody*	Phill'-Mastrs / Cusack	Foster / Yates	Bason* / Stead	Megson / Otulakowski	Kemp / Morris	Trusson / Pountney	Hodges / Tuohy	Johnson / Gray	Binney / Walker
9	Brown / McAlister	Harrison / Pashley	McNeill / Doyle	Bason / Suddaby !	James / McEwan	Foster / Oakes	Randell / Malone	Kemp / Kellow	Kellow / Smith	Harrison / Jones	Johnson / Weston*	Binney / Kerr
10	Crudgington / Millington	Harrison / Raynor	McNeill / Storton	James / Cottam	Foster / Burns	Bason / Oakes	Megson / Jones	Kemp / Ruggiero	Kellow / Edwards	Randell / Henderson	Johnson / Walker	Binney
11	Crudgington / Jackson	Harrison / Chatterton	McNeill / Gregory	James / Kinsella	Foster / Tagg	Bason / Blyth	Megson / Towner	Kemp / Mehmet	Kellow / Mitchell	Binney / Lyons	Fear / Seasman	Harrison

Match 1 (Bury): Binney scores his first from an impossible angle and gets his second from the spot after Megson is challenged by Waldron. Ray Lugg, already booked, is sent off (90) for attempting to wrestle the ball from Binney who is carrying the ball. Danny Wilson is taken off in a wheelchair.

Match 2 (Millwall): In a fast flowing game, highly rated 17-year-old Kevin O'Callaghan puts the Lions ahead. Hodges gets his first league goal after a one-two with Graves. John Lyons a £60k summer signing from Wrexham put Millwall back in front. John Jackson thwarts Plymouth in the latter stages.

Match 3 (Chesterfield): Two errors by Phillipson-Masters gift the Spireites an unassailable lead. Argyle's defence cannot cope with Ernie Moss who rounds off a fine performance by chipping over Hards. Graves, leading the attack for the injured Binney, bundles in his first league goal from Johnson's pass.

Match 4 (Sheffield Wed): Wednesday's physical approach dominates the game. Uzzell and Bason end up in hospital and the ref asks skipper Ian Porterfield to lecture his team. Manager Jack Charlton blames the length of the grass for slowing the ball up. The speed of debutant Gary Ball is Argyle's main threat.

Match 5 (Grimsby): Brown and Liddell clash leaving Liddell needing four stitches and Brown receiving treatment behind the goal. Trusson takes over the keeper's jersey for six minutes but does not make a save. Cumming finishes off a four man move for the only goal. Randell hits a post from 25 yards.

Match 6 (Wimbledon): David Kemp demonstrates why Saxton paid £75k for his services. He ignores flying boots to nod in his first and then hits a first time shot past Goddard. The in-form Johnson sets up Trusson. Saxton also complains about the length of the grass and will ask the groundsman to cut it.

Match 7 (Oxford): After Berry heads home Hodgson's corner, the ref bewilders everyone by allowing Megson's shot (72) to count after a linesman signals the ball is over the line. He is then called back by the Oxford players for a second look and disallows it. Kemp saves Argyle's blushes late on.

Match 8 (Southend): 'I will buy because we are not good enough,' growls Saxton after a humiliating defeat. The Shrimpers score at will after Kemp's beautifully taken equaliser. McNeil has an unhappy return to first-team action by getting himself booked and having his hand trodden on in a skirmish.

Match 9 (Blackpool): Kellow scores with a diving header. Binney scores twice, both from half chances as he links well with Kemp. Pool are reduced to ten men when Suddaby is sent off for a second booking. New manager Stan Ternent is also booked for protesting. Garry Jones gets a soft equaliser.

Match 10 (Chester): A defensive mistake again costs dearly when James misses a cross and Edwards holds off Crudgington and Foster to give Henderson an easy task. Millington had earlier saved Binney's penalty (30) after a handball was spotted. Megson misses a sitter from Kemp's clever back-heel.

Match 11 (Millwall): Fear is recalled to replace flu victim Randell. Kemp drills home a free-kick from the edge of the box to produce an interval lead. Lyons scores with a diving header from Mitchell's cross. The speedy Tony Towner causes some problems but the Lions are happy to return with one point.

Plymouth Argyle match records (continued)

No.	V	Opponent	Date	Result	Score	Scorers	Att.	Pos.	Ref.
12	A	BLACKBURN	13/10	L	0-1	Brotherston 85	6,026	17 · 7	A Saunders
13	H	ROTHERHAM	20/10	W	1-0	Kemp 63	4,850	23 · 7 · 9	R Lewis
14	A	SWINDON	23/10	L	1-2	Kemp 77 / Mayes 7, Rowland 25	6,514	9	D Vickers
15	H	BRENTFORD	27/10	L	0-1	Graham 62	5,206	24 · 5 · 9	D Hedges
16	A	OXFORD	31/10	D	1-1	Trusson 80 / Foley 74	3,824	10	J Warner
17	A	BURY	3/11	L	1-2	Trusson 77 / Johnson 23, Madden 25p	2,641	23 · 22 · 10	B Newsome
18	H	SWINDON	6/11	W	2-0	Trusson 18, Sims 88	4,157	12	C Thomas
19	H	CARLISLE	10/11	W	4-2	Johnson 27p, Randall 56, Kemp 59 / Ludlam 18, Bannon 64 (MacD'ald 76 og)	5,216	21 · 19 · 14	L Burden
20	A	COLCHESTER	16/11	L	2-5	Kemp 42, Cook 69 (og) / Lee 5, Packer 7, 58, Hodge 23, Gough 55	3,520	21 · 3 · 14	A Grey
21	A	SHEFFIELD UTD	1/12	L	2-3	Hodges 38, Randall 69 / Speight 33, Sabella 41, Bourne 90p	14,101	23 · 1 · 14	T Farley
22	H	BARNSLEY	8/12	W	2-1	Sims 59, Hodges 77 / Graham 16	5,311	22 · 15 · 16	D Lloyd
23	A	MANSFIELD	21/12	D	0-0	—	3,000	17	M Baker

12 — BLACKBURN (A), 13/10
Opponents (italic): Arnold, Round*, Morley, Coughlin, Keeley, Fazackerley, Brotherston, Parkes, Crawford, Kendall, Stonehouse.
Argyle hit rock bottom as Blackburn gain their first home victory of the season. Noel Brotherston runs onto McNeill's weak back-pass and toe-pokes the ball through Crudgington's legs. Binney is booked (69) for standing on the ball whilst organising a defensive wall at a free-kick.

13 — ROTHERHAM (H), 20/10
Opponents (italic): Mountford, Forrest, Tiler, Rhodes, Stancliffe, Breckin, Gooding, McEwan, Fern, Finney.
Hards is added to the squad with Crudgington doubtful, forcing 42-year-old Jim Furnell to appear for the reserves. Despite the presence of three Rotherham defenders on the line, Kemp's sizzling volley flies in to break the deadlock. Trusson and Breckin are booked for kicking each other.

14 — SWINDON (A), 23/10
Opponents (italic): Allan, Templeman, Lewis, McHale, Tucker, Stroud, Miller, Carter, Rowland, Mayes, Williams. (subs Johnson*, Binney)
Yet again Argyle give themselves an uphill task. Alan Mayes notches his 13th of the season and the unmarked Andy Rowland heads in. Kemp knocks in a rebound after Allan fails to hold Hodges' shot.

15 — BRENTFORD (H), 27/10
Opponents (italic): Bond, Salman, Tucker, McNichol, Kruse, Fraser, Carlton, Graham, Smith, Phillips, Holmes.
The directors meet Saxton after this latest crisis but Saxton denies it was to discuss his future. After Bond brilliantly saves Kemp's penalty (10) the confidence drains away from Argyle. After a series of attacks, Jackie Graham gets the all-important goal. Slow-handclapping ensues.

16 — OXFORD (A), 31/10
Opponents (italic): Burton, Fogg, Briggs, Foster, Stott, Jeffrey, Graydon, Duncan, Cooke, Berry, Foley, Hodgson*.
Amid rumours of dressing-room unrest, Saxton omits Megson and includes John Sims a £22k purchase from Exeter. The performance is much improved. Foley outpaces James to score within two minutes of coming on. Trusson levels with his first touch of the game from 25 yards out.

17 — BURY (A), 3/11
Opponents (italic): Forrest, Ritson, Halford, Howard, Waldron, Whitehead, Mullen, Madden, Johnson, Wilson, Hilton.
Reserve striker Steve Johnson hurtles in to head a great goal. Phillipson-Masters suffers concussion in the clash. Hodges' tackle on Waldron looks outside the area but Madden scores from the spot. Trusson again scores immediately after coming off the bench. Kemp hits the post.

18 — SWINDON (H), 6/11
Opponents (italic): Allan, Templeman, Lewis, Tucker, Stroud, Bates, Carter, Rowland, Mayes*, Johnson, Williams, Miller.
World Cup referee Clive Thomas is on top form booking seven players including five from Swindon. Trusson, back in the starting line-up after his recent scoring exploits, does it again, expertly tucking the ball past Allan. Sims celebrates his home debut by wrapping up the points.

19 — CARLISLE (H), 10/11
Opponents (italic): Swinburne, Hoolickin, Winstanley, MacDonald, Ludlam, Parker, McVitie*, Bonnyman, Hamilton, Bannon, Staniforth, Beardsley.
A thrill a minute game. United take the lead whilst Bason is off the field receiving treatment. Johnson levels after Kemp is challenged by Parker. Kemp scores with a header from a kneeling position and MacDonald bizarrely knocks the ball into an empty net instead of out of play.

20 — COLCHESTER (A), 16/11
Opponents (italic): Walker, Cook, Packer, Leslie, Wignall, Downan, Hodge, Gough, Foley, Lee, Rowles.
U's hit five in a match for the first time in five years. Colchester fully exploit Argyle's defensive frailties. Kemp inevitably scores but then limps off injured. Sims shot brushes Cook on the way in but by then it is too late. The two sides are due meet again next week in the FA Cup.

21 — SHEFFIELD UTD (A), 1/12
Opponents (italic): Conroy, Cutbush, Tibbatt, Kenworthy, McPhail, Ludlam, Garner, Bourne, Matthews, Speight, Sabella.
Argyle give the leaders a fright. Hodges' fine goal equalises Speight's header. Alex Sabella shows off some of his South American genius with a stunning goal. Randall pulls back another before Bason chases 20 yards and inexplicably lunges thigh high at Bourne in the penalty area.

22 — BARNSLEY (H), 8/12
Opponents (italic): Springett, Flavell, Collins, Glavin, Riley, McCarthy, Banks, Graham, Aylott, Lester, Pugh.
Allan Clarke is without recognising Norman Hunter. Graham heads in Ronnie Glavin's cross to give the visitors an interval lead. Despite being up all night with a virus, Sims has a hand in both goals as veteran Peter Springett is powerless to stop Sims header and Hodges shot.

23 — MANSFIELD (A), 21/12
Opponents (italic): Arnold, Thompson, Wood, Curtis, Bird, McClelland, Thomson, Taylor, Austin, Lathan*, Mann, Allen. (sub Cook)
An icy pitch is deemed playable. Argyle pick up a useful point, surviving severe pressure during the second period The unlucky Cooper strikes the woodwork for the third successive match. Terry Austin is the main threat with his aerial power and has a 'goal' disallowed for offside.

No	Date	Team	Result	F-A	H-T	Att	Pos	Pt	Scorers, Times, and Referees
24	H 26/12	READING	W	2-0	2-0	6,484	19		Randell 22, Kearney 39(og) — Ref: W Bombroff
25	H 29/12	CHESTERFIELD	W	1-0	0-0	6,425	18	21	Ridley 54(og) — Ref: E Read
26	A 1/1	EXETER	D	2-2	0-1	10,489	22		Randell 60, 79 / Hatch 4, Rogers P 48 — Ref: T Spencer
27	H 5/1	HULL	W	5-1	2-0	6,341	14	24	Cook 17, 63, Sims 35, 78, Harrison 47 / Norrie 60 — Ref: D Letts
28	A 12/1	SHEFFIELD WED	W	1-0	1-0	13,287	13	26	Cook 38 — Ref: A Dobson
29	H 19/1	GRIMSBY	D	1-1	1-1	6,310	13	27	Cook 13 / Cumming 20 — Ref: M Bidmead
30	H 26/1	GILLINGHAM	D	2-2	0-1	6,413	13	28	Bason 58, Cook 74 / Hughes 13, Price 64 — Ref: B Stevens
31	A 16/2	BLACKPOOL	W	3-1	0-1	3,302	12	30	Hodges 47, Graves 73, Kemp 85 / Fletcher 32 — Ref: G Courtney
32	A 19/2	WIMBLEDON	L	1-3	0-2	3,488	12	30	Kemp 84p / Leslie 14, Parsons 15, Cork 48 — Ref: D Hodges
33	H 23/2	BLACKBURN	L	0-1	0-0	6,918	14	30	Garner 46 — Ref: T Bune
34	A 1/3	ROTHERHAM	L	1-3	0-1	3,840	14	30	Kemp 50 / Gooding 28, Henson 70, 80 — Ref: R Banks

Line-ups (1 – 11, 12 sub used)

No	1	2	3	4	5	6	7	8	9	10	11	12 sub used
24 Argyle	Crudgington	James	Harrison	Randell	Foster	Phill'Masters	Hodges	Cooper	Sims	Bason	Graves*	Cook
24 Reading	Death	Joslyn	White	Bowman	Kearney	Moreline	Earles	Kearns	Heale	Sanchez*	Lewis	Williams
25 Argyle	Crudgington	James	Harrison	Randell	Foster	Phill'Masters	Hodges	Cooper	Sims	Bason	Graves	Cook
25 Chesterfield	Kendall	Tartt	O'Neill	Ridley	Green	Kowalski	Birch	Moss	Walker	Salmons	Crawford	
26 Argyle	Crudgington	James	Harrison	Randell	Foster	Phill'Masters	Hodges	Cooper	Sims	Bason	Graves*	Cook
26 Exeter	Main	Mitchell*	Hatch	Hare	Giles	Roberts P	Neville	Rogers P	Bowker	Delve	Pullar	Roberts L
27 Argyle	Crudgington	James	Harrison	Randell	Foster	Phill'Masters	Hodges	Cooper	Sims	Cook	Bason	Farley
27 Hull	Blackburn	Nisbet	Skipper	Croft	Dobson	Devries	Roberts	Moss*	Edwards	Haigh	Norrie	
28 Argyle	Crudgington	James	Harrison	Randell	Foster	Phill'Masters	Hodges	Cooper	Sims	Cook	Bason	Leman
28 Sheffield Wed	Bolder	Blackhall	Williamson	Smith	Pickering	Hornsby	King*	Johnson	Mellor	McCulloch	Curran	
29 Argyle	Crudgington	James	Harrison	Randell	Foster	Phill'Masters	Hodges	Cooper	Sims	Bason	Cook	Kilmore
29 Grimsby	Batch	Stone	Moore K	Waters	Wigginton	Crombie	Brolly	Ford	Drinkell	Mitchell	Cumming*	
30 Argyle	Crudgington	James	Harrison	Trusson	Foster	Phill'Masters	Hodges	Cooper	Sims	Bason	Cook	Walker
30 Gillingham	Hillyard	Ford*	Barker	Overton	Weatherly	Crabbe	Nicholl	Hughes	Price	Bruce	Richardson	
31 Argyle	Crudgington	James	Harrison	Trusson	Foster	Phill'Masters	Hodges	Cooper	Sims	Bason	Graves*	Fletcher
31 Blackpool	Hesford	Gardner	Pashley	Brocklebank	Malone	Doyle	Noble	Kellow*	MacDougall	Weston	Harrison	
32 Argyle	Crudgington	James	Harrison	Randell	Foster	Phill'Masters	Hodges	Cooper	Sims	Bason	Kemp	
32 Wimbledon	Beasant	Briley	Jones	Galliers	Smith	Cunningham	Ketteridge	Parsons	Leslie	Cork	Lewington	
33 Argyle	Crudgington	James	Harrison	Randell	Foster	Phill'Masters	Hodges	Cooper	Sims	Bason	Kemp	
33 Blackburn	Arnold	Rathbone	Branagan	Kendall	Keeley	Fazackerley	Brotherston	Crawford	Garner	McKenzie	Parkes	
34 Argyle	Crudgington	Hodges	McNeill*	Randell	Foster	Phill'Masters	Harrison	Bason	Sims	Kemp	Cooper	Johnson
34 Rotherham	Brown	Forrest	Breckin	Tiler	Stancliffe	Green	Gooding	Halom	Fern	Henson	Rhodes	

Match reports

24. Bason and Hodges cause chaos down the right side as Argyle continue their improved form. Randell, back to his creative best, scores with a diving header and Death looks to have Bason's shot covered before Kearney's touch sends it out if his reach. Cook almost adds a third late on.

25. On loan goalkeeper, Mark Kendall shows why he is highly rated by Tottenham with a series of fine saves. It takes a pacy, well-placed shot to beat him which sadly comes from his own defender John Ridley who is attempting to stop Randell. Crudgington makes a vital save from Moss.

26. Peter Hatch notches the first league goal of the 1980's to give City an early lead. Delve and Neville miss good chances before Rogers pounces on a back-pass. Randell on his return to St James Park, strikes after Delve slips. The Welshman's second finds the top corner from 25 yards.

27. On-loan Jeff Cook endears himself to the home crowd with two goals, the second coming from an overhead kick whilst lying on his back. Sims' first comes from a header after he outjumps Gordon Nisbet. Newly appointed Hull boss Mike Smith claims Randell could play for Wales.

28. A tale of two goalkeepers. Crudgington's handling and dominance of his area is superb. Bob Bolder makes a hash of Cooper's corner and punches it towards his own goal to allow Cook to pounce. The error does little to appease Jack Charlton who fumes at another home defeat.

29. In pouring rain, both goals come from headers. On three occasions Argyle shots leave muddy ball-marks on the woodwork as Cook, Sims and Hodges all go close. Both managers praise the performance of referee Mr Bidmead. David Kemp is given the all-clear to resume playing.

30. Cook's golden run continues as he scores a valuable equaliser. Hughes nods past Crudgington. Bason scores with a sizzling drive after good interplay with Hodges. Price squeezes in Richardson's cross. Steve Bruce is booked for a challenge which sends Foster onto the running track.

31. After three weeks without a match, Argyle struggle to find their rhythm. New £30k signing Paul Fletcher opens the scoring. Hodges' clinical finish sets the Greens on their way. Pool's smallest crowd of the season call for manager Stan Ternent's head. Alan Ball looks set to take over.

32. Argyle's ten match unbeaten run comes to an end at Plough Lane. Two goals in 30 seconds set the Dons on their way to a third straight win. Kemp scores from the spot after being brought down himself. Dave Beasant, replacing the suspended Ray Goddard, is largely unemployed.

33. A dull affair with only player-manager Howard Kendall trying to inspire his side. Duncan McKenzie is kept on a tight rein. Perhaps inevitably it is an error which creates the only goal when Cooper's attempted clearance from Brotherston's free-kick is sliced straight to Simon Garner.

34. Saxton vows to make changes after an inept display. The first goal is a catastrophe. McNeill is not expecting Crudgington's throw and Mick Gooding nips in to put the ball into an empty net. Henson scores twice in his second game for the Millers. Brown and Halom are debutants.

Football match-by-match records and reports (Plymouth Argyle). Top team name listed is Argyle; italic names are the opposing team.

No	Venue / Date	Opponent	Score (FT / HT)	Result	Pos / Pts	Attendance	Scorers	Ref
35	A 8/3	BRENTFORD	0-0 / 0-0	—	15 / 31	6,460	—	M Heath
36	H 15/3	CHESTER	1-0 / 1-0	W	14 11 / 33	4,095	Bason 33	P Jackson
37	A 22/3	CARLISLE	1-2 / 0-1	L	16 11 / 33	3,611	Trusson 89	D Richardson
38	H 29/3	COLCHESTER	2-0 / 2-0	W	16 5 / 35	4,330	Trusson 2, 35	M Robinson
39	H 1/4	MANSFIELD	0-0 / 0-0	D	16 / 36	4,669	—	A Glasson
40	A 5/4	READING	0-1 / 0-1	L	36	7,466	—	A Gunn
41	H 7/4	EXETER	2-0 / 1-0	W	38	10,214	Sims 25p, Kemp 60	M Baker
42	A 12/4	HULL	0-1 / 0-1	L	18 19 / 38	5,369	—	M Scott
43	H 19/4	SHEFFIELD UTD	4-1 / 1-0	W	16 9 / 40	6,322	Trusson 32, Sims 61, Kemp 70, 78, Casey 90	S Bates
44	H 22/4	SOUTHEND	0-0 / 0-0	D	41	5,392	—	A Seville
45	A 26/4	BARNSLEY	0-0 / 0-0	D	15 14 / 42	10,231	—	M Baker
46	A 3/5	GILLINGHAM	1-0 / 1-0	W	15 16 / 44	4,020	Sims 5	H Robinson

Home Average 5,776 — Away Average 5,960

Match reports

35 (Brentford): Saxton, as promised, makes a number of changes and sees his side gain a well-earned point. Bees boss Bill Dodgin concedes that Argyle were the better team. Trusson revels in his midfield role. Danis Salman clears a Sims shot off the line but there is little else to excite the crowd.

36 (Chester): Intended referee John Martin arrives at the ground with 25 minutes remaining, having been informed that the match kicked off at 7.30. Former ref Ron Crabbe is drafted in to run the line in a natty track-suit and borrowed boots. Bason gets the only goal when he nets Johnson's cross.

37 (Carlisle): Argyle endure snow and ice on their long trip north. Graves, again preferred to Kemp, goes off (30) with a gashed knee. Peter Beardsley puts Carlisle ahead rounding two defenders. Paul Bannon seems to have put the game beyond doubt but Trusson gives the home side a late scare.

38 (Colchester): United's recent slump continues as Trusson dominates the game. As well as two goals, he hits the bar and forces Mick Walker into a brilliant save. Packer pulls down Sims (75) but Walker again saves to deny the hat-trick. U's boss Bobby Roberts and five of his players are booked.

39 (Mansfield): Although Argyle dominate they create few clear-cut chances. Rod Arnold saves well from Bason's long-range effort and twice Arthur Mann clears off the line from Kemp. Eighteen goal Terry Austin is subdued. The Stags continue to frustrate and Mick Jones is the happier manager.

40 (Reading): Ollie Kearns scores unchallenged from Reading's first corner with Crudgington rooted to his line. Argyle are undaunted by the Royals' fine home record but again fail to find the net with Kemp still looking to find his pre-injury form. Jerry Williams has a tenth-minute effort ruled out.

41 (Exeter): Hodges cross causes confusion in the goalmouth and results in the referee pointing to the spot for a reason that was obvious to no one. Sims, without a goal in three months, scores against his former club. City look out of touch and it is little surprise when Kemp nods in a second.

42 (Hull): It's the same old story with Argyle having the better of the game but failing to capitalise. With other sides near the bottom winning, relegation remains a real possibility. In windy conditions, good football proves difficult on a bumpy pitch. Craig Norrie scores his first home league goal.

43 (Sheffield Utd): It could have been so much different. Crudgington gets the better of a one on one with Flood (18) and saves Kenworthy's penalty (39) after Hodges had nudged Garner. Trusson scores direct from a free-kick and Sims superbly flicks the ball over his head before despatching a shot.

44 (Southend): Southend, desperately needing points, show the greater determination but the match lacks any real excitement. Argyle do not win their first corner until the 53rd minute. Mervyn Cawston makes fine saves from Kemp and Trusson. Derek Spence causes a few anxious moments.

45 (Barnsley): A point is enough to stave off relegation worries. Playing a stubborn possession game, Argyle fail to win a single corner for the whole match but still produce enough chances to win the game. Johnson and Randell hit posts and Crudgington pushes Glyn Riley's shot onto an upright.

46 (Gillingham): Saxton misses the match through illness as Jack Edwards and Jim Furnell take charge. Sims early strike comes after Hillyard fails to hold Johnson's 20 yard shot. Phillipson-Masters shines in defence despite playing with three stitches in a head wound. Kemp misses a sitter.

Line-ups (best reading)

- 36 Chester — Argyle: Crudgington, James, Harrison, Randell, Foster, Phill'-Masters, Trusson, Graves*, Sims, Bason, Johnson, Hodges. Chester: Millington, Raynor, Walker, Storton, Cottam, Jeffries, Phillips T, Jones*, Rush, Phillips R, Henderson, Sutcliffe.
- 37 Carlisle — Argyle: Crudgington, James, Harrison, Randell, Foster, Phill'-Masters, Trusson, Graves*, Sims, Bason, Johnson, Hodges. Carlisle: Swinburne, Hoolickin, McCartney, MacDonald, Ludlam, Winstanley, McIlvie, Houghton, Bannon 88, Hamilton*, Beardsley 38, Collins.
- 38 Colchester — Argyle: Crudgington, James, Harrison, Randell, Foster, Phill'-Masters, Trusson, Kemp, Sims, Bason*, Johnson, Hodges. Colchester: Walker, Cook, Packer, Leslie, Wignall, Dowman, Hodge, Rowles, Wright, Lee, Allinson.
- 39 Mansfield — Argyle: Crudgington, James, Harrison, Randell, Foster, Phill'-Masters, Trusson, Kemp, Sims, Bason, Johnson. Mansfield: Arnold, Dawkins, Mann, Curtis, McClelland, Burrows, Lathan, Pollard, Austin, Bird, Allen.
- 40 Reading — Argyle: Crudgington, James, Harrison, Randell, Foster, Phill'-Masters, Trusson, Bason, Sims, Kemp, Johnson*, Hodges. Reading: Death, Joslyn, White, Bowman, Hetzke, Moreline, Kearney, Williams, Kearns 2, Sanchez, Wanklyn*, Earles.
- 41 Exeter — Argyle: Crudgington, James, Harrison, Randell, Foster, Phill'-Masters, Trusson, Kemp, Sims, Bason, Hodges. Exeter: Main, Rogers M, Hatch, Hore, Giles, Roberts P, Neville*, Rogers P, Delve, Pullar, Roberts L.
- 42 Hull — Argyle: Crudgington, James, Harrison, Randell, Foster, Phill'-Masters, Trusson, Kemp, Sims, Bason, Hodges. Hull: Norman, Nisbet, Devries*, Croft, Roberts D, Moss, Edwards, Tait, Deacy, Norrie 6, Marwood.
- 43 Sheffield Utd — Argyle: Crudgington, James, Harrison, Randell, Foster, Phill'-Masters, Trusson, Kemp, Sims, Hodges, Johnson. Sheffield Utd: Poole, Cutbush, Renwick, Kenworthy, McPhail, Jones, Casey 90, Speight, Flood, Sabella, Garner*, Verde.
- 44 Southend — Argyle: Crudgington, James, Harrison, Randell, Foster, Phill'-Masters, Trusson, Kemp, Sims, Hodges, Johnson. Southend: Cawston, Dudley, Yates, Stead, Moody, Cusack, Gray, Pountney, Spence, Mercer, Otulakowski.
- 45 Barnsley — Argyle: Crudgington, James, Harrison, Randell, Foster, Phill'-Masters, Trusson, Kemp, Sims, Hodges, Johnson. Barnsley: Pierce, Cooper, Chambers, Banks, Evans, McCarthy, Hunter, Lester, Riley, Parker, Downes.
- 46 Gillingham — Argyle: Crudgington, James, Harrison, Randell, Foster, Phill'-Masters, Trusson, Kemp, Sims 5, Hodges, Johnson. Gillingham: Hillyard, Sharpe, Overton, Bruce, Crabbe, Weatherly, White, Duncan*, Richardson, Price, Adams, Walker.

LEAGUE DIVISION 3 (CUP-TIES) Manager: Bobby Saxton SEASON 1979-80

League Cup

1:1 A NEWPORT 11/8 — Att 4,574 (4:) — F-A 0-1 L — H-T 0-0
Scorers: Tynan 80. Ref: A Seville

Pos	1	2	3	4	5	6	7	8	9	10	11	12 sub used
Argyle	Hards	James	Harrison	Bason	Phill'-Masters	Foster	Randell	Megson	Binney	Trusson*	Johnson	Hodges
Newport	*Plumley*	*Walden*	*Relish*	*Davies*	*Oakes*	*Bruton**	*Vaughan*	*Lowndes*	*Goddard*	*Tynan*	*Moore*	*Thompson*

Seventeen-year-old Neil Hards is thrust into the side to solve Argyle's goalkeeping crisis and is the only player to emerge with credit. Saxton is furious at his side's display. Tommy Tynan nets the only goal, seizing upon Hards' only error. Several outbreaks of crowd trouble mar the day.

1:2 H NEWPORT 14/8 — Att 4,505 (4:) — F-A 2-0 W — H-T 1-0
Scorers: Binney 40, Bason 85. Ref: L Shapter — (Argyle won 2-1 on aggregate)

Pos	1	2	3	4	5	6	7	8	9	10	11	12 sub used
Argyle	Hards	James	Harrison	Phill'-Masters	Foster	Bason	Megson	Hodges	Binney	Randell	Johnson	Johnson
Newport	*Plumley*	*Walden*	*Relish*	*Davies*	*Oakes*	*Bruton**	*Vaughan*	*Lowndes*	*Goddard*	*Tynan*	*Moore*	*Thompson*

After a typical piece of Binney opportunism, the game ends dramatically. Bason puts Argyle ahead on aggregate. County are awarded a penalty when Foster fouls Howard Goddard (90). Hards saves and Goddard nets the rebound but Mr Shapter has blown for time before the ball goes in.

2:1 H CHELSEA 28/8 — Att 10,802 (2:4) — F-A 2-2 D — H-T 2-2
Scorers: Trusson 4, 11 / Fillery 2, 37. Ref: J Martin

Pos	1	2	3	4	5	6	7	8	9	10	11	12 sub used
Argyle	Hards	Hodges	Harrison	Phill'-Masters	Foster	Bason	Megson	Graves	Trusson	Randell	Johnson	
Chelsea	*Borota*	*Locke*	*Stride*	*Wilkins*	*Droy*	*Harris*	*Britton*	*Bannon*	*Langley*	*Aylott**	*Fillery*	*Bumstead*

A much improved performance sees Argyle rattle their more illustrious opponents. Fans are still arriving as the first two go in. Trusson, only playing due to the continuing absence of Binney, scores a superb solo goal. After Fillery's second, the Blues are happy to settle for a draw.

2:2 A CHELSEA 4/9 — Att 14,112 (2:6) — F-A 2-1 W — H-T 1-0
Scorers: Harrison 12, Johnson 68 / Droy 71. Ref: A Gunn — (Argyle won 4-3 on aggregate)

Pos	1	2	3	4	5	6	7	8	9	10	11	12 sub used
Argyle	Brown	James	Harrison	Foster	Phill'-Masters	Hodges	Megson	Graves	Trusson	Randell	Johnson	Johnson
Chelsea	*Borota*	*Chivers*	*Sparrow*	*Bumstead*	*Droy*	*Sitton*	*Britton**	*Bannon*	*Langley*	*Aylott*	*Walker*	*Harris*

Argyle put indifferent league form behind them to record a shock win. David Brown, on loan from Middlesbrough, plays a blinder. Harrison moves up from his sweeper's role to shoot home from 25 yards. Johnson scores into an empty net. Droy's header fails to inspire a fightback.

3 H WIMBLEDON 25/9 — Att 6,090 (24) — F-A 0-0 D — H-T 0-0
Ref: S Bates

Pos	1	2	3	4	5	6	7	8	9	10	11	12 sub used
Argyle	Brown	Hodges	McNeill	James	Foster	Bason	Megson	Trusson	Binney	Randell	Harrison	Harrison
Wimbledon	*Goddard*	*Perkins*	*Downes*	*Galliers*	*Bowgett*	*Cunningham*	*Richards*	*Parsons*	*Leslie*	*Cork*	*Knowles*	

Fresh from a recent 3-0 league win over the Dons, Argyle start as clear favourites. Lacking the cup-tied Kemp, the attack looks weak with little support for the recalled Binney. No one looks capable of scoring and Dario Gradi's Wimbledon are content to take the tie back to Plough Lane.

3R A WIMBLEDON 2/10 — Att 5,042 (19) — F-A 0-1 L aet — H-T 0-0
Scorers: Leslie 112. Ref: D Johnson

Pos	1	2	3	4	5	6	7	8	9	10	11	12 sub used
Argyle	Brown	Hodges	McNeill	James	Foster	Bason	Harrison	Trusson	Binney	Randell	Johnson*	Forde
Wimbledon	*Goddard*	*Perkins*	*Jones*	*Galliers**	*Bowgett*	*Cunningham*	*Ketteridge*	*Parsons*	*Leslie*	*Cork*	*Lewington*	*Diadulewicz*

The Dons progress to a fourth round meeting with Swindon although boss Gradi admits he would rather concentrate on getting his side away from the bottom of the league. Once again the value of Kemp is highlighted by his absence. John Leslie gets the only goal, scoring on the turn.

FA Cup

1 A COLCHESTER 24/11 — Att 4,064 (3) — F-A 1-1 D — H-T 0-1
Scorers: Hodges 85 / Rowles 28. Ref: M Baker

Pos	1	2	3	4	5	6	7	8	9	10	11	12 sub used
Argyle	Crudgington	James	McNeill	Randell	Foster	Phill'-Masters	Hodges	Cooper*	Sims	Bason	Graves	Allinson
Colchester	*Walker*	*Cook*	*Packer*	*Leslie*	*Wright*	*Downman*	*Hodge*	*Gough*	*Foley*	*Lee*	*Rowles**	*Harrison*

Argyle are not relishing a return to Layer Road only eight days after a 2-5 thrashing in the league but put up a much-improved performance. Leigh Cooper is brought in for his first senior appearance. Man of the match Hodges scores a deserved equaliser after Rowles' first-half strike.

1R H COLCHESTER 27/11 — Att 6,926 (3) — F-A 0-1 L aet — H-T 0-0
Scorers: Allinson 100. Ref: M Baker

Pos	1	2	3	4	5	6	7	8	9	10	11	12 sub used
Argyle	Crudgington	James	McNeill	Randell	Foster	Phill'-Masters	Hodges	Cooper*	Sims	Bason	Graves	Allinson
Colchester	*Walker*	*Cook*	*Packer*	*Leslie*	*Wright*	*Downman*	*Hodge*	*Gough*	*Foley*	*Lee*	*Allinson*	*Harrison*

Both sides defend well until Phillipson-Masters fails to clear Lee's cross and Ian Allinson, back in the side after a family illness, scores in extra-time. Argyle have three penalty appeals turned down but none of them are too convincing. A visit from Bournemouth awaits the winners.

Pos	Team	P	Home						Away						Pts
			W	D	L	F	A		W	D	L	F	A		
1	Grimsby	46	18	2	3	46	16		8	8	7	27	26		62
2	Blackburn	46	13	5	5	34	17		4	12	7	24	19		59
3	Sheffield Wed	46	12	6	5	44	20		9	10	4	37	27		58
4	Chesterfield	46	16	5	2	46	16		7	6	10	25	30		57
5	Colchester	46	10	10	3	39	20		10	2	11	25	36		52
6	Carlisle	46	13	6	4	45	26		6	6	12	21	30		48
7	Reading	46	14	5	4	43	19		2	10	11	23	46		48
8	Exeter	46	14	5	3	38	22		3	7	13	22	46		48
9	Chester	46	14	6	3	29	18		3	7	13	20	39		47
10	Swindon	46	15	4	4	50	20		4	4	15	21	43		46
11	Barnsley	46	10	7	6	29	20		6	7	10	24	36		46
12	Sheffield Utd	46	13	5	5	35	21		5	5	13	20	45		46
13	Rotherham	46	13	4	6	38	24		6	6	12	20	42		46
14	Millwall	46	14	6	3	49	23		2	7	14	16	36		45
15	PLYMOUTH	46	13	7	3	39	17		3	5	15	20	38		44
16	Gillingham	46	8	9	6	26	18		6	5	12	23	33		42
17	Oxford	46	10	4	9	34	24		4	9	10	23	38		41
18	Blackpool	46	10	7	6	39	34		5	4	14	23	40		41
19	Brentford	46	10	6	7	33	26		5	5	13	26	47		41
20	Hull	46	11	7	5	29	21		1	9	13	22	48		40
21	Bury	46	10	4	9	30	23		6	3	14	15	36		39
22	Southend	46	11	6	6	33	23		3	4	16	14	35		38
23	Mansfield	46	9	9	5	31	24		1	7	15	16	34		36
24	Wimbledon	46	6	8	9	34	38		4	6	13	18	43		34
		1104	287	144	121	893	530		121	144	287	530	893		1104

Appearances and Goals

Player	App Lge	Sub	LC	Sub	FAC	Sub	Goals Lge	LC	FAC	Tot
Ball, Gary		1								
Bason, Brian	41	1	5		2		2	1		3
Binney, Fred	7	3	4				4	1		5
Brown, David	5		3				5			5
Cook, Jeff	4	3								
Cooper, Leigh	14				2					
Crudgington, Geoff	37				2					
Fear, Keith	1									
Forde, Clevere						1				
Foster, George	46		6		2		2			2
Graves, Mark	14		2		2					
Hards, Neil	4		3	1						
Harrison, Chris	41		6				1	1		2
Hodges, Kevin	41	3	5	1	2		5		1	6
James, Tyrone	35	2	5		2					
Johnson, Brian	25	1	5				1	1		2
Kemp, David	27	2					15			15
McNeill, Brian	15		2		2					
Megson, Gary	12		5							
Perrin, Steve		1								
Phil'-Masters, Forbes	38		4		2		5			5
Randell, Colin	42		6		2		7			7
Sims, John	31									
Trusson, Mike	25	2	5		2		8	2		10
Uzzell, John	1									
(own-goals)							4			4
25 players used	506	19	66	2	22	1	59	6	1	66

Double wins: (0).
Double defeats: (1) Blackburn.

Won from behind: (3) Barnsley, Blackpool, Carlisle.
Lost from in front: (0)

High spots: Ten-match unbeaten run mid-season to climb away from relegation zone.
Superb win v Chelsea (a) in League Cup replay.
Impact of new signings, David Kemp, John Sims and Geoff Crudgington.

Low spots: Two wins in first twelve matches, leaving Argyle bottom of the table at end of October.
Mid-season injury to David Kemp.
Failure to retain popular loan signing, Jeff Cook.

Player of the Year: George Foster.
Ever presents: (1) George Foster.
Hat-tricks: (0).
Leading scorer: David Kemp (15).

LEAGUE DIVISION 3   Manager: Bobby Saxton   SEASON 1980-81

No	Date		Att	Pos	F-A	Pt	H-T	Scorers, Times, and Referees	1	2	3	4	5	6	7	8	9	10	11	12 sub used
1	A 16/8	COLCHESTER	2,061		2-2	D 1	1-0	Kemp 18, Murphy 46, Hodge 53, Gough 90, Ref: D Letts	Crudgington / Walker	Harrison / Cook	Uzzell / Cotton	Cooper / Gough	Foster / Wignall	Phill'-Masters / Packer	Hodges / Hodge	Kemp* / Rowles*	Graves / Foley	Bason / Lee	**Murphy** / Allinson	**Peachey** / Leslie
								All four goals have a special quality. Kemp heads in with U's defenders appealing for offside. Graves smashes a first-time shot against the crossbar and Murphy follows up. Hodge and, with the last kick, Gough both smash in powerful shots to conclude a highly entertaining match.												
2	H 19/8	CHESTER	4,823		2-0	W 3	0-0	Kemp 55, Bason 71, Ref: B Stevens	Crudgington / Millington	Harrison / Jeffries	Uzzell / Walker	Cooper / Storton	Foster / Cottam*	Phill'-Masters / Oakes	Hodges / Burns	Kemp / Kearney	Graves / Birch	Bason / Jones	Murphy / Ludlam	Phillips
								Cooper's effort (42) is initially allowed but the referee changes his mind after linesman, Graham Butland, a former Plymouth city councillor spots an infringement. Kemp scores a typical opportunist goal from close range. Bason powers a free-kick through the 'wall' from 25 yards.												
3	H 23/8	CHARLTON	6,023		1-1	D 4	1-1	Murphy 45, Berry 13, Ref: A Glasson	Crudgington / Wood	Harrison / Gritt	Uzzell / Warman	Cooper / Shaw	Foster / Berry	Phill'-Masters / Tydeman	Hodges / Powell	Kemp* / Walsh	Graves* / Ostergaard*	Bason / Smith	Murphy / Robinson	Sims / Walker
								The Addicks take a controversial lead when Mr Glasson overrules a linesman to award a corner. Les Berry powers Powell's flag-kick against the bar and then nets the rebound. Murphy powers in an unstoppable header. After two wins, Mike Bailey's side drop their first point of the season.												
4	A 30/8	OXFORD	3,398	18	0-0	D 5	0-0	Ref: A Gunn	Crudgington / Burton	Harrison / Fogg	Uzzell / Smithers	Randall / Jeffrey	Foster / Briggs	Phill'-Masters / Shotton	Hodges / Brock	Kemp / Taylor	Sims / Cooke	Bason / Foley*	Murphy / Lythgoe	Murphy / Seacole
								Veteran Roy Burton stands firm against a barrage of shots. Argyle's domination looks in vain when a penalty is awarded following Harrison's mild challenge on Foley. Justice is done when Shotton blasts the spot-kick a yard wide. U's boss Bill Asprey comes under fire from the fans.												
5	H 6/9	CARLISLE	4,854	23	4-1	W 7	2-1	Kemp 17, 45, 81, Murphy 50, Staniforth 23, Ref: T Bune	Crudgington / Swinburne	Harrison / Hooljckin	Uzzell / Collins	Randall / MacDonald	Foster / Houghton	Phill'-M'ters ! / Parker	Hodges / McVitie	Kemp / Metcalfe	Sims* / Beardsley*	Bason / Hamilton	Murphy / Staniforth	Graves / Coady
								Argyle ignore the early dismissal of Phillipson-Masters (25). The centre half is sent off for tripping Peter Beardsley only a minute after being booked. Kemp scores a glorious hat-trick and celebrates his third goal by dancing back to the centre circle with the ball stuffed up his shirt.												
6	A 13/9	CHESTERFIELD	5,561	8	2-2	D 8	1-1	Graves 18, Kemp 76, Hunter 39, Walker 48, Ref: G Owen	Crudgington / Turner	Harrison / Stirk	Uzzell / O'Neill	Randall / Wilson*	Foster / Green	James / Hunter	Hodges / Birch	Kemp / Bonnyman	Graves* / Walwyn	Bason / Ridley	Murphy / Walker	Peachey / Moss
								Kemp's flick eludes Bill Green and Graves gives the Pilgrims the lead. Hunter's looping header goes out of everyone's reach and in off a post. Phil Walker scores from Wilson's throw before Hunter fails to spot Kemp lurking behind him. The Argyle striker nips in to steal a back-pass.												
7	A 17/9	READING	5,859	6	1-1	D 9	0-1	Murphy 89, Sanchez 20, Ref: R Challis	Crudgington / Death	Harrison / Joslyn	Uzzell / Henderson	Randall / Bowman	Foster / Hicks	Phill'-Masters / Hetzke	Hodges / Earles	Kemp / Wanklyn	Sims* / Dixon	Bason / Sanchez	Murphy / Beavon	Graves
								Argyle maintain their unbeaten start but only just. With 30 seconds remaining, Kemp dummies Bason's cross to leave Murphy clear. Steve Death saves but Murphy knocks in the rebound. Sanchez gives Reading the lead when his swerving 20-yard shot takes an uneven bounce.												
8	H 20/9	GILLINGHAM	6,719	17	4-1	W 11	2-1	Kemp 7, 69, Hodges 30, Bason 46, Price 37, Ref: V Callow	Crudgington / Hillyard	Harrison / Walker	Uzzell / Ford	Randall / Overton	Foster / Weatherly	Phill'-Masters / Hughes	Hodges / Bruce	Kemp / Duncan	Sims / Price	Bason / Westwood	Murphy / Dunn*	Bottiglieri
								Two more from Kemp make him the country's leading scorer and take Argyle to the top of the table. Saxton sympathises with his opposite number Gerry Summers as the Gills play their part. Hodges' goal catches the eye as he weaves past two defenders and blasts in from 20 yards.												
9	A 27/9	NEWPORT	6,878	24	2-0	W 13	0-0	Sims 49, Kemp 53, Ref: D Vickers	Crudgington / Dowler	Harrison / Walden	Uzzell / Relish*	Randall / Bruton	Foster / Oakes	Phill'-Masters / Tynan	Hodges / Vaughan	Kemp / Lowndes	Sims / Gwyther	Bason / Aldridge	Murphy / Moore	Elsey
								Argyle establish their longest opening unbeaten run since the war. After a quiet first half, Murphy is the inspiration as he creates havoc. Sims gets the first and Kemp delights the big Argyle following with a header. The blood-splattered Foster epitomises the Pilgrims' new-found spirit.												
10	H 30/9	READING	11,480		2-1	W 15	1-1	Bason 26, Kemp 60, Beavon 9, Ref: C Thomas	Crudgington / Death	Harrison / Joslyn	Uzzell / Henderson	Randall / Bowman	Foster / Hicks	Phill'-Masters / Hetzke	Hodges / Lewis	Kemp / Webb	Sims / Dixon	Bason / Sanchez !	Murphy / Beavon	
								Murphy's stray pass goes to Beavon who shoots home from 25 yards. Bason completes a three-man move to equalise. Kemp heads the winner. Future Cup final hero Lawrie Sanchez causes controversy. Having already been booked, he is sent off (63) for comments made to Uzzell.												
11	A 4/10	SHEFFIELD UTD	12,401	11	0-0	D 16	0-0	Ref: D Allison	Crudgington / Richardson	Harrison / Ryan	Uzzell / Houston	Randall / Kenworthy	Foster / McPhail	Phill'-Masters / Matthews	Hodges / Tibbott	Kemp / Trusson	Sims / Wiggan	Bason / Hatton	Murphy / Peters	
								Saxton is named as Third Division Manager of the Month. Despite their domination, Argyle are unable to defeat a woeful Blades' side who are booed off the pitch. Coach Martin Peters makes three tactical changes to no avail. Trusson apologises to the fans for the team's performance.												

No	Venue	Opponent	Date	Result	Score	Pos	Attendance	Scorers	Referee
12	(H)	FULHAM	7/10	—	—	18	11,547	Bason	Ref: E Read
13	H	BLACKPOOL	11/10	L	0-2	18	10,698	Morris 36, 77	Ref: J Martin
14	A	HUDDERSFIELD	18/10	L	0-2	18	11,655	Robins 65, Kennedy 90	Ref: A Dobson
15	A	PORTSMOUTH	21/10	W	3-1	20	15,635	Kemp 5, 52, Sims 82 / Garner 6	Ref: R Lewis
16	H	BARNSLEY	25/10	L	1-3	20	8,911	Sims 37 / Lester 71, Riley 73, Glavin 89	Ref: A Seville
17	H	BRENTFORD	28/10	L	0-1	20	7,249	Smith 63	Ref: H King
18	A	HULL	1/11	L	0-1	20	3,367	Deacy 42	Ref: J Worrall
19	A	FULHAM	4/11	D	0-0	21	3,507	—	Ref: J Hunting
20	H	WALSALL	8/11	W	2-0	23	5,022	Kemp 78, 88	Ref: A Robinson
21	A	CHESTER	12/11	L	0-1	23	2,247	Ludlam 62	Ref: D Richardson
22	H	COLCHESTER	15/11	D	1-1	24	4,905	Kemp 78 / Bremner 38	Ref: D Hutchinson
23	A	MILLWALL	29/11	D	1-1	25	3,385	Hodges 17 / Mehmet 90	Ref: R Toseland

Match reports

12. Fulham (7/10) — Fulham: Peyton, Clement, Strong, Beck, Brown, Hatter, Gale, O'Driscoll, Davies, Lock*, Goodlass, Greenaway; sub Johnson.
Argyle are now one of only two unbeaten sides in the league. On a rain swept evening, Murphy is kept quiet by ex-England defender, Dave Clement. Bason scores the winner direct from a free-kick with Fulham believing it was indirect. Four Cottagers are booked for protesting.

13. H Blackpool (11/10) — Argyle: Crudgington, Harrison, Uzzell*, Randell, Foster, Hodges, Cooper, Kemp, Sims, Bason, Murphy. Blackpool (italic): Hesford, Simmonite, Williams, Ball, McEwan, Morgan, Hockaday, Morris, Ashurst, Deary.
The Manager of the Month jinx strikes. Saxton receives his award on the pitch before the game and Argyle go on to lose their unbeaten record. Two strikes from Colin Morris see him overtake Kemp in the scoring charts. Player-manager, Alan Ball orchestrates the victory from midfield.

14. A Huddersfield (18/10) — Huddersfield (italic): Rankin, Brown, Robinson, Stanton, Topping, Harvey, Kindon, Robins, Laverick, Cowling, James.
Argyle are distinctly second best in this top of the table clash. Ian Robins gets the breakthrough after a dazzling run down the wing by Brian Stanton. With most of the Argyle side up for a corner, Crudgington is totally exposed after a quick counter attack as Kennedy slots past him.

15. A Portsmouth (21/10) — Portsmouth (italic): Mellor, Viney, Brisley*, McLaughlin, Aizlewood, Garner, Gregory, Tait, Showers, Bryant, Rogers, Barnard.
Argyle bounce back with Kemp and Bason back to their best. Mellor barely sees Kemp's shot for his first but Garner equalises seconds later after Gregory hits the post. A demoralising second half is hardly the best preparation for Frank Burrows' side who face a Cup tie at Anfield.

16. H Barnsley (25/10) — Barnsley (italic): New, Joyce, Glavin, Chambers, Banks, McCarthy, Evans, Parker*, Aylott, Lester, Downes, Riley.
Argyle look world-beaters in the first half but have only a Sims' goal to show for their efforts. Norman Hunter admits his side were 'useless' in the first period but the introduction of Glyn Riley at half-time inspires the visitors. Lester and Riley get two in two minutes and Glavin taps in.

17. H Brentford (28/10) — Brentford (italic): McKellar, Shrubb, Hill, Salman, Kruse, Smith, Hurlock, Harris, Booker, Walker, Crown, Graves.
For the first time in nine years, Argyle fall to a third successive home defeat. Dean Smith gets to David Crown's pass before Foster to score the only goal. Harrison comes close for the Greens when his hopeful, high looping cross lands on the roof of the net. Bason hits the post. (43).

18. A Hull (1/11) — Hull (italic): Norman, Nisbet, Haigh, Swann, Roberts D, Marwood, Moss, Edwards, Whitehurst, Deacy.
The slide continues. Argyle's defenders stand transfixed believing Nick Deacy to be offside as he scores bottom of the table Hull's first goal in almost nine hours of football. A mixture of desperate defending and inspired heroics by goalkeeper Tony Norman keep Kemp and Co at bay.

19. A Fulham (4/11) — Fulham (italic): Peyton, Clement*, Strong, Beck, Brown, Gale, O'Driscoll, Davies, Peters, Wilson, Goodlass, Greenaway.
A familiar tale as Argyle dominate but have nothing to show for their efforts against the managerless Cottagers. Dave Clement is replaced after only seven minutes with hamstring trouble. Bason is stretchered off but returns. The match is watched by Fulham's lowest crowd of the season.

20. H Walsall (8/11) — Walsall (italic): Turner, Macken, Caswell*, Serella, Hart, Waddington S, O'Kelly, Smith, Buckley, Paul, Harrison.
The fans have to endure a freezing cold day and a dire match. The turning point comes when the referee fails to spot Sims control with his hand before setting up Kemp's opener. Walsall lose Caswell with injury and finish with three others limping including player-boss Alan Buckley.

21. A Chester (12/11) — Chester (italic): Millington, Raynor, Jeffries, Burns, Cottam, Ludlam, Sutcliffe, Phillips, Birch, Jones, Gendall.
Bearing little resemblance to the team that led the division only a few weeks before, Saxton describes this latest performance as a shambles. Steve Ludlam sidesteps two tackles to score. The introduction of Hodges spurs Argyle to their best period of the match in the last 15 minutes.

22. H Colchester (15/11) — Colchester (italic): Walker, Cook, Rowles, Leslie, Wignall, Packer, Hodge, Foley, Bremner, Lee, Allinson.
Kevin Bremner scores his first league goal after Cook's 40 yard free-kick is only parried. After Kemp's leveller, U's are convinced Bremner's last-minute header is over the line but BBC cameras prove otherwise. Three U's fans attempt to get in for free but do so via the police hut roof.

23. A Millwall (29/11) — Millwall (italic): Jackson, Roberts, Robinson, Blyth, Kitchener, Sitton, Kinsella, Mehmet, Martin*, Dibble, Bartley, McKenna.
Despite Hodges well-struck goal, Argyle fail to beat the struggling Lions who are without a manager and field a mix of teenagers and veterans. Dave Mehmet's last-minute equaliser goes a little way to appease the disenchanted home fans who chant for the resignation of their chairman.

Manager: Bobby Saxton   SEASON 1980-81

Match results

No	Date	Venue / Opponent	Att	Pos	Pt	F-A	H-T	Scorers, Times, and Referees
24	6/12	H ROTHERHAM	6,155	8 / 6	W 27	3-1	1-0	Murphy 42p, 87, Kemp 55 / Fern 50 / Ref: L Burden
25	20/12	A BURNLEY	5,678	9 / 3	L 27	1-2	0-1	Murphy 67p / Taylor 12, 48 / Ref: T Mills
26	26/12	H EXETER	14,792		L 27	0-2	0-2	Kellow 25p, Pullar 31 / Ref: D Letts
27	27/12	A SWINDON	9,710	11 / 18	L 27	0-3	0-0	Carter 57, Greenwood 68, Rowland 70 / Ref: A Ward
28	10/1	A BARNSLEY	12,355	13 / 2	L 27	1-2	0-1	Kemp 90 / Lester 11, Aylott 71 / Ref: T Farley
29	17/1	H MILLWALL	4,847	10 / 16	W 29	2-0	2-0	Murphy 34, Cooper 37 / Ref: D Civil
30	24/1	H OXFORD	5,121		W 31	3-0	2-0	Cooper 9, 59, Kemp 41 / Ref: T Spencer
31	31/1	A CHARLTON	8,127	8 / 1	D 32	1-1	0-1	Kemp 76 / Walsh 33 / Ref: B Hill
32	7/2	H CHESTERFIELD	6,305	8 / 7	W 34	1-0	0-0	Johnson 54 / Ref: A Glasson
33	14/2	A CARLISLE	3,924	8 / 20	L 34	0-2	0-0	Staniforth 75, Beardsley 79 / Ref: R Chadwick
34	21/2	H NEWPORT	4,315	9 / 18	W 36	3-2	0-1	Johnson 52p, Hodges 67, Sims 77 / Gwyther 9, Tynan 50 / Ref: D Lloyd

Line-ups (Argyle top row; opponents in italics; 12 = sub used)

No	1	2	3	4	5	6	7	8	9	10	11	12 sub used
24	Crudgington	McNeill	Uzzell	Hodges	Foster	Phill*-Masters	Cooper	Kemp	Sims	Bason	Murphy	
24	*Mountford*	*Forrest*	*Breckin*	*Rhodes*	*Stancliffe*	*Mullen*	*Fern*	*Gooding*	*Moore**	*Carr*	*Hensan*	*Winn*
25	Crudgington	McNeill	Harrison	Hodges	Phill*-Masters	Foster	Cooper	Kemp	Sims	Bason	Murphy	
25	*Stevenson*	*Laws*	*Holt*	*Scott*	*Overson*	*Dobson*	*Cassidy*	*Potts*	*Hamilton*	*Taylor*	*Cavener*	
26	Crudgington	McNeill*	Harrison	Hodges	Foster	Phill*-Masters	Cooper	Kemp	Sims	Bason	Murphy	
26	*Bond*	*Rogers M*	*Hatch*	*Forbes*	*Roberts L*	*Roberts P*	*Pearson*	*Rogers P*	*Kellow*	*Delve*	*Pullar*	*Johnson*
27	Crudgington	James	Harrison*	Randell	Lewis	Phill*-Masters	Cooper	Kemp	Sims	Bason	Murphy	
27	*McAllister*	*Henry*	*Peach*	*Kamara*	*Stroud*	*Miller*	*Carter*	*Rowland*	*Greenwood*	*Hughes**	*Johnson*	*Rideout*
28	Crudgington	Nisbet	Harrison	Hodges	Foster	Phill*-Masters	Cooper	Kemp	Sims	Bason	Murphy	
28	*Pierce*	*Joyce*	*Chambers*	*Glavin*	*Banks*	*McCarthy*	*Evans*	*Parker*	*Aylott*	*Lester*	*Downes*	
29	Crudgington	Nisbet	Harrison	Hodges	Foster	Phill*-Masters	Cooper	Kemp	Sims	Johnson	Murphy	
29	*Jackson*	*Martin*	*Roberts*	*Chatterton*	*Tagg*	*Blyth*	*Kinsella*	*Mehmet*	*Mitchell*	*Bartley**	*Massey*	*Dibble*
30	Crudgington	Nisbet	Harrison	Hodges	Foster	Phill*-Masters	Cooper	Kemp	Sims	Johnson	Murphy*	
30	*Burton*	*Doyle*	*Fogg*	*Jeffrey*	*Cooke*	*Briggs*	*Jones*	*Berry*	*Thomas**	*Foley*	*Smithers*	*Lythgoe*
31	Crudgington	Nisbet	Harrison	Hodges	Foster	Phill*-Masters	Cooper	Kemp	Sims	Collins*	Johnson	
31	*Johns*	*Gritt*	*Madden*	*Shaw*	*Berry*	*Tydeman*	*Powell*	*Naylor*	*Walsh*	*Walker*	*Robinson*	*Murphy*
32	Crudgington	Nisbet	Harrison	Hodges	Foster	Phill*-Masters	Cooper	Kemp	Sims	Johnson	Murphy	
32	*Turner*	*Tartt*	*O'Neill*	*Wilson*	*Green*	*Hunter*	*Birch*	*Moss*	*Kowalski*	*Salmons**	*Walker*	*Ridley*
33	Crudgington	Nisbet	Harrison	Hodges	Foster	Phill*-Masters	Cooper	Kemp	Sims	Johnson	Murphy	
33	*Swinburne*	*Haigh*	*Coady*	*Hamilton*	*Houghton*	*Parker*	*Coughlin*	*Campbell*	*Brown*	*Beardsley*	*Staniforth*	
34	Crudgington	Nisbet	Harrison	Hodges	Foster	Phill*-Masters	Cooper	Kemp	Sims	Randell	Johnson	
34	*Plumley*	*Walden*	*Relish**	*Davies*	*Oakes*	*Tynan*	*Vaughan*	*Lowndes*	*Gwyther*	*Elsey*	*Moore*	*Warriner*

Match reports

24 — Murphy scores from the spot after Carr has two attempts at upending Hodges. Fern equalises with a diving header before Kemp's rising shot finishes off a precision four man move down the left. Kemp's bicycle kick hits the woodwork. Murphy intercepts Breckin's back-pass to score.

25 — Steve Taylor gives the Clarets the lead with an easy header and gets his second after the defence is caught square. Murphy's penalty prowess comes to the fore again after Kemp's slow-motion dive. Crudgington raises the biggest cheer when he has to change his shorts on the pitch.

26 — City overtake Argyle in the table after winning this local derby. Tony Kellow notches his 20th of the season after Cooper handles in the area. Dave Pullar extends the lead from Kellow's pass. Argyle look set to sign experienced England Under-23 defender Gordon Nisbet from Hull.

27 — A third defeat in a week puts the pressure on Saxton. Town are now unbeaten in six games since John Trollope has taken charge. All three goals stem from the wing where Miller gives James a torrid time. Argyle do not force a save from debut boy McAlister until the 88th minute.

28 — Barnsley manage only three shots in the game but score twice to extend their unbeaten run to 18 matches. Lester score after good work by Banks and Glavin. Aylott pounces on loose ball. Kemp gets the final touch to Foster's effort. Nisbet is booked on his debut for a flying tackle.

29 — Crudgington almost opens the scoring when his gale assisted drop-kick bounces fractionally over the bar. Johnson centres for Murphy to head in. Cooper claims his first goal when his free-kick scatters the wall. Millwall boss Peter Anderson suffers his first defeat since taking over.

30 — Argyle easily repeat their cup win over Oxford. For the second time in a week Cooper scores from a free-kick. Kemp heads goal number 22 for the season and Cooper then strikes again with a 30 yard rocket. Saxton praises the much maligned Sims who plays a part in all three goals.

31 — After just two minutes, Jeremy Collins almost scores with his first kick in league football. The leaders go ahead through Paul Walsh. Mr Hill awards a penalty when the ball hits Collins on the arm but Crudgington smothers Walsh's spot-kick. Kemp beats two defenders to head home.

32 — Dejected Chesterfield manager, Frank Barlow bemoans his side's luck as Argyle rarely threaten. Johnson's 35 yard free-kick takes a wicked deflection off Les Hunter and soars over keeper John Turner's head. Crudgington pulls off a wonder save from the highly rated Phil Walker.

33 — Peter Beardsley shows why he is interesting bigger clubs by inspiring lowly Carlisle to a much-needed victory. He skips past Harrison for the first and leaves two defenders flat-footed to score the second. He is then fouled by Foster (81) but Crudgington saves Staniforth's penalty.

34 — County, with one eye on their forthcoming Cup Winners Cup quarter final, let a two goal lead slip. In incessant rain, Johnson's penalty starts the comeback after Kemp tangles with Grant Davies. Hodges' cross flies over Gary Plumley and Sims notches his first goal in ten matches.

Football results grid (read in reading order; each match lists Argyle lineup, opponents' lineup in italics, scorers, referee and match report).

28/2 — opponents: *Sutton · Walker · Ford · Bruce · Weatherly · White · Nicholl* · Duncan · Price · Lee · Adams · Richardson*
4,396 20 38
Ref: A Grey
Full back Andy Ford commits a schoolboy error when he plays the ball across his own area and Sims nips in to score. Argyle are happy to defend in the second half. Price looks set to score but a last-ditch tackle by Nisbet saves the day as the home fans scream for a penalty.

---

36 A BLACKPOOL 8 L 0-0 0-1 38   3,933 23 38
Crudgington · Nisbet · Harrison* · Hodges · Foster · Phill'Masters · Cooper · Kemp · Press · Randell · Murphy
Hesford · Gardner · Pashley · McEwan · Stragia · Ashurst · Morgan · Conn · Thompson* · Morris · Noble · Bamber
Morris 54
Ref: M Heath
Johnson's second minute booking sets the tone as the referee never lets the match flow. Colin Morris, so often the scourge of Argyle gets the winner. Foster has an 89th minute effort disallowed as Mr Heath adjudges that he had used Phillipson-Masters' shoulders to gain extra height.

---

37 H HUDDERSFIELD 8 D 0-0 0-0 39   5,433 2
Crudgington · Nisbet · Harrison · Hodges · Foster · Phill'Masters · Cooper · Kemp · Sims · Randell · Murphy
Freeman · Brown · Robinson · Stanton · Sutton · Hanvey · Lillis · Kennedy · Austin · Robins · Johnson · Cowling
Ref: M Bidmead
Saxton admits he is now planning for next season after another lacklustre performance. Sims hits a post and Johnson forces a good save from Neil Freeman but there is little else to entertain. Former Pilgrim Dave Sutton performs solidly as the Terriers maintain their promotion push.

---

38 H PORTSMOUTH 8 W 1-0 1-0 41   6,042 6
Crudgington · Nisbet · Harrison · Hodges · Foster · Phill'Masters · Cooper* · Kemp · Sims · Peachey · Murphy
Mellor · McLaughlin · Viney · Doyle · Aizlewood · Ellis · Gregory · Tait · Rafferty · Barnard · Rogers* · Graves · Perrin
Murphy 7
Ref: E Read
In appalling conditions, Murphy deflects Cooper's corner and Peter Mellor allows the ball to squirm under his body. At half-time, Cooper is rushed to hospital after a hard tackle but no bones are broken. A wind-assisted Crudgington clearance narrowly misses after eluding Mellor.

---

39 A BRENTFORD 7 W 1-0 1-0 43   5,870 12
Crudgington · Nisbet · Harrison · Hodges · Foster · Phill'Masters · Collins · Kemp · Sims · Randell · Murphy
McKellar · Tucker · Hill · Salman · Kruse · Hurlock · Funnell · Roberts · Johnson · Walker · Crown* · Booker
Kemp 38
Ref: K Baker
Bees boss, Fred Callaghan, watching from his preferred position in the press box, is not amused by his side's showing and orders them in for Sunday training. Kemp ends his minor drought by side-footing in Hodges cross. After Danis Salman stumbles Sims misses an easy chance.

---

40 H HULL 7 D 0-0 0-0 44   4,668 24
Crudgington · Nisbet · Harrison · Hodges · Foster · Phill'Masters · Collins · Kemp · Sims · Randell · Murphy
Norman · Hoolickin · Booth · Ferguson · Eccleston · Richards · Marwood · Swann · Whitehurst · Mutrie · Deacy
Ref: D Hedges
Argyle fail to break down an already doomed Hull side. Yet again, keeper Tony Norman is their saviour. Randell almost scores after 15 seconds and later chips over Norman only to see his shot rebound off the crossbar. The Tigers finally win their first corner in the 86th minute.

---

41 A WALSALL 8 W 3-1 1-0 46   3,556
Crudgington · Nisbet · Harrison · Hodges · Foster · Phill'Masters · Johnson · Kemp · Sims · Randell · Murphy
Green · Macken · Harrison · Mower · Serella · Hart · Rees · Caswell* · O'Kelly · Penn · Waddington · P Buckley
Hodges 5, Kemp 54, 70 — Penn 60
Ref: M Dimblebee
There are no excuses for either side as the match is played on a near-perfect surface. Kemp converts crosses by Sims and Murphy with his head. His first goal is his 100th in league football. Don Penn pegs one back. Crudgington makes vital saves from Penn and Brian Caswell.

---

42 H SHEFFIELD UTD 7 W 1-0 0-0 48   4,897
Crudgington · Nisbet · Harrison · Hodges · Foster · Phill'Masters · Johnson · Kemp · Sims · Randell · Murphy
Conroy · Casey · Garner · Houston · Trusson · Wiggan · Givens · Charles · Hatton · Ryan
Hodges 79
Ref: S Bates
Both sides miss chances. Stewart Houston clears a Johnson shot off the line. A bad clearance from Crudgington goes straight to ex-Green Mike Trusson who shoots tamely wide. Johnson and Nisbet are involved in some clever exchange of passes down the right to set up Hodges' winner.

---

43 H SWINDON 8 D 0-0 0-0 49   6,369
Crudgington · Nisbet · Harrison · Hodges · Foster · Phill'Masters · Johnson · Kemp · Sims · Randell · Murphy
Allan · Henry · Peach · Kamara · Lewis · Stroud · Miller · Carter · Rowland · Rideout · Williams
Ref: A Hamil
Swindon boss John Trollope apologises to fans for his side's negative play which does little to contribute to a boring afternoon. It's the Robins' fourth consecutive scoreless draw away from home. Johnson comes closest when he hits the crossbar and Allan superbly saves from Murphy.

---

44 A EXETER 7 D 1-1 0-0 50   8,491 10
Crudgington · Nisbet · Harrison · Hodges · Foster · Phill'Masters · Johnson · Kemp · Sims · Randell · Murphy
Main · Rogers M · Sparrow · Forbes · Roberts L · Roberts P · Prince · Rogers P · Kellow · Delve* · Pratt · Hatch
Sims 81 — Kellow 54
Ref: M Baker
Brian Godfrey's City have the best of the early exchanges and take the lead when the prolific Tony Kellow heads his 31st of the season. On his return to St James Park, Sims heads in Johnson's free-kick. Phillipson-Masters, already facing suspension, is booked for deliberate handball.

---

45 H BURNLEY 5 W 2-1 1-0 52   4,331 8
Crudgington · Nisbet · Harrison · Hodges · Foster · Phill'Masters · Uzzell · Kemp · Sims · Randell · Murphy
Stevenson · Wood · Laws · Phelan* · Overson · Dobson · Young · Robertson · Hamilton · Cassidy · Potts
Kemp 26, 71 — Cavener 89
Ref: J Martin
Kemp celebrates his Player of the Year award with two more goals. The first is a gift following a defensive mix-up between former England internationals Alan Stevenson and Martin Dobson. Uzzell, playing superbly at centre-half, takes a battering from Irishman Billy Hamilton.

---

46 A ROTHERHAM 7 L 1-2 1-1 52   11,497 1
Crudgington · Nisbet · Harrison · Hodges · Foster · Phill'Masters · Johnson · Kemp · Sims · Randell · Murphy
Mountford · Forrest · Breckin · Gooding · Stancliffe · Mullen · Towner · Seasman · Moore · Fern · Henson
Sims 35 — Moore 15, Fern 80
Ref: P Tyldesley
Rotherham fans flood the pitch after their side gain the point necessary to clinch the title. In front of an unguarded goal, Ronnie Moore fails to connect with a header but soon makes amends after Sims loses possession on the edge of the area. Veteran Rodney Fern clinches the match.

Home 6,766
Away 6,673
Average 6,766

LEAGUE DIVISION 3 (CUP-TIES) Manager: Bobby Saxton SEASON 1980-81

League Cup

	Att		F-A	H-T	Scorers, Times, and Referees	1	2	3	4	5	6	7	8	9	10	11	12 sub used
1:1 H PORTSMOUTH 8/8	7,036	L	0-1	0-1	Laidlaw 42 / Ref: S Bates	Crudgington *Mellor*	James *McLaughlin*	McNeill *Viney*	Randell *Barnard*	Foster *Aizlewood*	Phill'-Masters *Garner*	Hodges *Gregory*	Kemp *Laidlaw*	Sims *Tait*	Bason *Brisley*	Johnson* *Rogers*	Graves
1:2 A PORTSMOUTH 12/8	11,997	L	1-2	1-1	Kemp 6 / Gregory 20, Rogers 82 / Ref: C Downey / (Argyle lost 1-3 on aggregate)	Crudgington *Mellor*	James *McLaughlin*	Harrison *Viney*	Randell *Brisley*	Foster *Aizlewood*	Phill'-Masters *Garner*	Hodges *Gregory*	Kemp *Laidlaw*	Sims *Tait*	Bason* *Barnard*	Murphy *Rogers*	Graves

1:1 Sadly, numerous outbreaks of terrace violence provide the main memory of the afternoon. With little change in personnel from last season, Argyle again look toothless. Up front, Kemp and Sims barely get a touch. Joe Laidlaw curls the ball around a defensive wall for the only goal.

1:2 Murphy, a new £65k signing from Torquay, provides Kemp with a perfect pass to allow the striker to score. Ex-Argyle winger Alan Rogers sends over a harmless-looking cross but Foster slips on the rain-soaked surface and Dave Gregory takes advantage. Rogers' corner flies in.

FA Cup

			Att		F-A	H-T	Scorers, Times, and Referees	1	2	3	4	5	6	7	8	9	10	11	12 sub used
1 H NEWPORT 22/11	8	W	6,719	18	2-0	0-0	Kemp 65, Murphy 75 / Ref: A Glasson	Crudgington *Kendall*	McNeill *Walden*	Harrison *Relish**	Hodges *Davies*	Foster *Oakes*	Phill'-Masters *Tynan*	Cooper *Bailey*	Kemp *Lowndes*	Sims *Gwyther*	Bason *Elsey*	Murphy *Moore*	Aldridge
2 H OXFORD 13/12	8	W	7,264	20	3-0	0-0	Sims 47, Kemp 69, Murphy 78p / Ref: A Robinson	Crudgington *Burton*	McNeill *Briggs*	Harrison *Smithers*	Hodges *Jeffrey*	Phill'-Masters *Wright*	Foster *Shotton*	Cooper *Brock*	Kemp *Cassells*	Sims *Cooke*	Bason *Graydon*	Murphy *Lythgoe*	
3 H CHARLTON 3/1	11	L	9,499	1	1-2	1-0	Kemp 11 / Powell 48, Hales 85 / Ref: E Read	Crudgington *Johns*	McNeill *Gritt*	Harrison *Madden*	Hodges *Shaw*	Foster *Berry*	Phill'-Masters *Tydeman**	Cooper *Powell*	Kemp *Walker*	Sims *Hales*	Bason *Walsh*	Murphy *Naylor*	Robinson

1 The deadlock is broken by one of the goals of the season. Bason starts the move with a 40-yard run before Murphy and Sims combine to set up a waist high volley for Kemp. It is Mr Glasson's ninth time in charge at Home Park and the first time Argyle win at home under his control.

2 Beleaguered Oxford boss Bill Asprey loses three new players from his depleted squad with a stomach bug hours before kick-off. His eight-man defence holds out until Sims strikes and then sets up Kemp. Murphy finishes the job from the spot after Kemp turns too quickly for Shotton.

3 After a miskick by Steve Gritt lets Kemp in, only the brilliance of Nicky Johns denied the Argyle striker a hat-trick. Colin Powell scores direct from a corner and Derek Hales' late strike stuns the home crowd. Charlton boss Mike Bailey admits he would have been happy with a draw.

Odds & ends

Double wins: (4) Gillingham, Newport, Portsmouth, Walsall.
Double defeats: (2) Barnsley, Blackpool.

Won from behind: (2) Newport, Reading.
Lost from in front: (1) Barnsley.

High spots: Twelve-match unbeaten run at start of season.
Scoring prowess of David Kemp.
Good defensive record.

Low spots: Four successive league defeats around Christmas thwarted promotion hopes.
Summer departure of manager Bobby Saxton to Blackburn.
Collecting only one point from possible eight against bottom two sides, Blackpool and Hull.

Player of the Year: David Kemp.
Ever presents: (3) Geoff Crudgington, George Foster, David Kemp.
Hat-tricks: (1) David Kemp.
Leading scorer: David Kemp (28).

Appearances & Goals

Player	Lge	Sub	LC	Sub	FAC	Sub	Lge	LC	FAC	Tot
Bason, Brian	28	1	2		3		4			4
Collins, Jeremy	3									
Cooper, Leigh	28				3		3			3
Crudgington, Geoff	46		2		3					
Foster, George	46		2		3					
Graves, Mark	4	4		2						
Harrison, Chris	45		1				1			1
Hodges, Kevin	39	2	2		3		5			5
James, Tyrone	9	1	2							
Johnson, Brian	15	3	1				2			2
Kemp, David	46		2		3		24	1	3	28
McNeill, Brian	5		1		3					
Murphy, Donal	40	2	1		3		9		2	11
Nisbet, Gordon	19									
Peachey, John	1	2								
Phil' Masters, Forbes	44		2		3					
Randell, Colin	30		2		3					
Sims, John	42	1	2		3		8		1	9
Uzzell, John	16									
(own-goals)										
19 players used	**506**	*16*	22	*2*	33		56	1	6	63

League Table

	P	Home					Away					Pts
		W	D	L	F	A	W	D	L	F	A	
1 Rotherham	46	17	6	0	43	8	7	7	9	19	24	61
2 Barnsley	46	15	5	3	46	19	6	12	5	26	26	59
3 Charlton	46	14	6	3	36	17	11	3	9	27	27	59
4 Huddersfield	46	14	6	3	40	11	7	8	8	31	29	56
5 Chesterfield	46	17	4	2	42	16	6	6	11	30	32	56
6 Portsmouth	46	14	5	4	35	19	8	4	11	20	28	53
7 PLYMOUTH	46	14	5	4	35	18	5	9	9	21	26	52
8 Burnley	46	13	5	5	37	21	5	9	9	23	27	50
9 Brentford	46	7	9	7	30	25	7	10	6	22	24	47
10 Reading	46	13	5	5	39	22	5	5	13	23	40	46
11 Exeter	46	9	9	5	36	30	7	4	12	26	36	45
12 Newport	46	11	6	6	38	22	4	7	12	26	39	43
13 Fulham	46	8	7	8	28	29	6	10	7	29	35	43
14 Oxford	46	7	8	8	20	24	6	9	8	19	23	43
15 Gillingham	46	9	8	6	23	19	3	10	10	25	39	42
16 Millwall	46	10	9	4	30	21	4	5	14	13	39	42
17 Swindon	46	10	6	7	35	27	3	9	11	16	29	41
18 Chester	46	11	5	7	25	17	4	6	13	13	31	41
19 Carlisle	46	8	9	6	32	29	6	4	13	24	41	41
20 Walsall	46	8	9	6	43	43	5	6	12	16	31	41
21 Sheffield Utd	46	12	6	5	38	20	2	6	15	27	43	40
22 Colchester	46	12	7	4	35	22	2	4	17	10	43	39
23 Blackpool	46	5	9	9	19	28	4	5	14	26	47	32
24 Hull	46	7	8	8	23	22	1	8	14	17	49	32
	1104	265	162	125	808	529	125	162	265	529	808	1104

LEAGUE DIVISION 3 — Manager: Bobby Moncur — SEASON 1981-82

Line-ups

No	Date	1	2	3	4	5	6	7	8	9	10	11	12 sub used
1	H OXFORD 29/8	Crudgington	Nisbet	McCartney	Harrison	Phill'Masters	Cooper	Hodges	Kemp	Sims	Randell	Collins*	Phillips
		Burton	*Doyle*	*Fogg*	*Jeffrey*	*Briggs*	*Shatton*	*Jones*	*Foley*	*Cassells*	*Page*	*Smithers*	
2	A BURNLEY 5/9	Crudgington	Nisbet	McCartney	Harrison*	Foster	Cooper	Hodges	Kemp	Sims	Randell	Murphy	Phillips
		Stevenson	*Laws*	*Holt*	*Young*	*Overson*	*Dobson*	*Cavener*	*Taylor*	*Hamilton*	*Cassidy*	*Potts*	
3	H LINCOLN 12/9	Crudgington	Nisbet	McCartney	Harrison	Foster	Cooper	Hodges	Kemp	Sims	Randell	Murphy*	Dennis
		Felgate	*Thompson T*	*McVay*	*Gilbert**	*Turner P*	*Carr*	*Shipley*	*Cockerill*	*Hobson*	*Cunningham*	*Cammack*	*Neale*
4	A BRENTFORD 19/9	Crudgington	Nisbet	Uzzell	Harrison	Foster	Rowe	Hodges	Kemp	Sims	Randell	Dennis	
		McKellar	*Tucker*	*Hill*	*Salman*	*Whitehead*	*Hurlock*	*Shrubb*	*Roberts*	*Booker*	*Harris*	*Walker*	*Musker*
5	A BRISTOL CITY 22/9	Crudgington	Nisbet	Uzzell	Harrison	Foster	Cooper	Hodges	Kemp	Sims	Randell	Dennis*	Murphy
		Moller	*Stevens*	*Sweeney*	*Aitken*	*Rodgers**	*Nicholls*	*Tainton*	*Mann*	*Mabbutt*	*Harford*	*Hay*	*Musker*
6	H CHESTERFIELD 26/9	Crudgington	Nisbet	Uzzell	Harrison	Foster	Cooper*	Hodges	Kemp	Sims	Randell	Dennis	Murphy
		Turner	*Bellamy*	*O'Neill*	*Tartt*	*Green !*	*Ridley*	*Windridge*	*Henderson*	*Bonnyman*	*Kowalski*	*Crawford*	
7	H READING 29/9	Crudgington	Nisbet	Uzzell	Harrison	Foster	Murphy	Hodges	Kemp	Sims	Randell	Rogers	
		Fearon	*Williams*	*Cullen*	*Wood*	*Hicks*	*Hetzke*	*Earles*	*Kearney*	*Heale*	*Beavon*	*Sanchez*	
8	A SOUTHEND 3/10	Crudgington	Nisbet	Uzzell	Harrison	Foster	Cooper*	Murphy	Kemp	Sims	Randell	Rogers	
		Cawston	*Hadley*	*Yates*	*Pennyfather*	*Moody*	*Cusack*	*Gray**	*Otulakowski*	*Spence*	*Mercer*	*Nelson*	*Greaves*
9	H GILLINGHAM 10/10	Crudgington	Nisbet	Uzzell	Harrison	Foster!	Cooper	Murphy	Kemp	Sims	Phillips	Rogers	
		Hillyard	*Sitton*	*Ford*	*Bruce*	*Weatherly*	*Bowman*	*White*	*Duncan*	*Adams*	*Lee*	*Price*	
10	A CARLISLE 17/10	Crudgington	Nisbet	McCartney	Phill'Masters	Foster!	Cooper	Hodges	Cook	Sims	Randell	Rogers	
		Swinburne	*Parker*	*Rushbury*	*Haigh*	*Ashurst*	*Larkin*	*Coughlin*	*Beardsley*	*Lee*	*Robson*	*Staniforth*	
11	A WIMBLEDON 20/10	Crudgington	Nisbet	McCartney	Phill'Masters	Foster	Cooper	Hodges	Cook	Sims	Randell	Rogers	
		Beasant	*Brown*	*Jones**	*Galliers*	*Smith*	*Suddaby*	*Boyle*	*Leslie*	*Lazarus*	*Downes*	*Hodges*	*Joseph*

Match details

No	Scorers, Times, and Referees	Att	Pos	Pt	F-A	H-T	Res
1	Cassells 20 — Ref: L Burden	4,089	—	0	0-1	0-1	L
2	Dobson 79p — Ref: D Owen	4,022	23 / 11	0	0-1	0-1	L
3	Gilbert 36, Cockerill 55 — Ref: V Callow	3,323	24 / 6	0	0-2	0-1	L
4	Ref: B Hill	4,890	23 / 9	1	0-0	0-0	D
5	Sims 15, Hodges 32 / Harford 2, Nicholls 61, Mann 72 — Ref: H Taylor	7,471	—	1	2-3	2-1	L
6	Nisbet 47(og), Henderson 84 — Ref: R Milford	3,451	23 / 2	1	0-2	0-0	L
7	Hodges 70 / Heale 42 — Ref: B Stevens	2,745	—	2	1-1	0-1	D
8	Nelson 11, Mercer 29, Greaves 80 — Ref: M Bodenham	3,470	23 / 16	2	0-3	0-2	L
9	Phillips 84 / Lee 11, Bowman 51 — Ref: E Read	3,094	23 / 7	2	1-2	0-1	L
10	Cook 50 / Staniforth 22, 53p, 57 — Ref: R Chadwick	3,630	—	2	1-3	0-1	L
11	Randell 85 / Joseph 80, Boyle 90 — Ref: D Axcell	2,114	24 / 23	2	1-2	0-0	L

Match reports

1 — H OXFORD (29/8): A disappointing start for new manager Moncur. In front of Argyle's lowest ever opening day attendance, the Pilgrims never compete and are unable to cope with the lively Keith Cassells and Peter Foley. It is Cassells who gets the all-important goal, easily converting a Smithers pass.

2 — A BURNLEY (5/9): Randell is forced to switch to centre half when Harrison requires five stitches in head wound after an off the ball clash with Billy Hamilton. The ref ignores a penalty appeal when McCartney appears to handle but awards a spot-kick three minutes later when Randell pushes Taylor.

3 — H LINCOLN (12/9): The attendance slumps to under £4k for the first time since the war. At half-time it is announced that Mr Callow is unwell and an appeal goes out for a replacement, leading to a ten-minute delay in starting the second half. David Gilbert scores his first league goal with a fine solo effort.

4 — A BRENTFORD (19/9): With Moncur absent on a scouting mission, Argyle grab their first point of the season in a drab affair. The Bees remain unbeaten but by the end their fans jeer their efforts. Crudgington saves the Greens on several occasions and is booked for bringing down Bob Booker outside the area.

5 — A BRISTOL CITY (22/9): An error from Crudgington gifts City an early lead. Sims finally gets Argyle's first league goal of the season and Hodges gives them a surprise lead. Plymouth born Alan Nicholls levels and Mann scores from 35 yards. Foster is off the field for 22 minutes to have five stitches inserted.

6 — H CHESTERFIELD (26/9): Another disastrous afternoon. Henderson's miscued shot is going well wide until Nisbet toe-pokes it past his own keeper. Sims accidentally breaks Bill Green's nose but the big defender retaliates and is sent off (74). Henderson heads in the second. Dennis is Argyle's main threat.

7 — H READING (29/9): Another new post-war low attendance. Andy Rogers starts his month's loan from Southampton with a lively display. The first half is played in thick fog. Gary Heale gets his sixth of the season from 20 yards. Hodges equalises to give the Pilgrims their first home point of the season.

8 — A SOUTHEND (3/10): Moncur describes this latest defeat as an humiliation. Only Crudgington keeps the score down. Garry Nelson slots home a partially cleared corner. Keith Mercer caps a fine display with a goal and Danny Greaves, son of Jimmy, scores within five minutes of coming on as substitute.

9 — H GILLINGHAM (10/10): Can it get any worse? Randell drops out in the morning with tonsillitis, yet another home defeat and Foster is sent off (89) for aiming a punch at Trevor Lee. Phillips celebrates his first full game with a goal but Rogers aside, the players produce a dismal display as the crisis deepens.

10 — A CARLISLE (17/10): With Peter Beardsley everywhere, Gordon Staniforth, a Moncur signing when Carlisle boss, scores a glorious hat-trick. His second comes from the spot after Beardsley is tripped. McCartney, against his old side, and Foster, for the second successive match, are dismissed for bad fouls.

11 — A WIMBLEDON (20/10): Fellow strugglers Wimbledon gain their second win in four days to leave Argyle six points adrift at the bottom. Sub Francis Joseph gives Dave Bassett's Dons the lead but Randell hits back with a 25-yard special. On-loan Terry Boyle scores with the last kick to add to Argyle's woes.

(Plymouth Argyle season match-by-match record — rotated table, page 257)

12 (partial, top of page)
- Cook 37, 65, Randell 41, 90, Sims 70 | Jones 39
- Att: 2,646 | 20 | 5 | 3-1
- Opposition: Millington, Needham, Raynor, Starton, Cottam, Oakes, Jones, Simpson*, Ludam, Phillips, Burns, Howat
- Ref: S Bates
- Moncur finds the secret of success as each player is promised a bottle of gin by a local benefactor if the team scores three. The returning Jeff Cook provides the inspiration. Chester are forced to reorganise after Simpson is carried off (36). Randell scores with the last kick of the game.

---

13 · A WALSALL · 31/10 — 24 · W · 5 · 8 · 1-0 · Sims 22 · Att 4,549
- Opposition (Walsall): Green, Macken, Caswell, Beech, Seralla, Hart, Smith*, Loveridge, Penn, Rogers, Waddington, S O'Kelly
- Ref: G Flint
- Despite being without the suspended Foster and McCartney, Argyle's transformation continues against Alan Buckley's high-flying Saddlers. Sims throws himself at Rogers' cross to head the ball home. The defence looks rock solid Cook and Rogers non-stop running causes havoc.

---

14 · H FULHAM · 3/11 — 24 · W · 11 · 3-1 · Cook 27, 58p, Sims 76 | Davies 81 · Att 4,915
- Opposition (Fulham): Peyton, Hopkins, Strong, O'Driscoll*, Brown, Gale, Davies, Wilson, Coney, O'Sullivan, Lewington, Peters
- Ref: C Thomas
- Cook repays another instalment on his £25k fee. He converts Sims' knock-down to give Argyle the lead. Fulham skipper Les Strong is given a torrid time by Rogers and brings him down in the area. Cook sends Peyton the wrong way. Sims and Gordon Davies both score with headers.

---

15 · H PORTSMOUTH · 7/11 — 23 · D · 12 · 0-0 · Att 6,275
- Opposition (Portsmouth): Knight, Ellis, Viney, Doyle, Aizlewood, Rollings, Hemmerman, Gregory, Rafferty, Tait, Crown
- Ref: D Hutchison
- Mr Hutchison becomes the third referee at Home Park this season to retire at half-time after he is struck in the back by a clearance. Argyle force a total of 21 corners but are unable to pass the defiant Alan Knight, who adds to his reputation as one of most promising keepers around.

---

16 · A NEWPORT · 14/11 — 21 · W · 18 · 15 · 1-0 · Sims 54 · Att 4,427
- Opposition (Newport): Kendall, Walden*, Relish, Davies, Oakes, Bailey, Vaughan, Lowndes, Waddle, Aldridge, Elsey, Tynan
- Ref: D Reeves
- The arguments over the legitimacy of Sims' goal rage long after the match has finished. A linesman indicates offside against Cook and then lowers his flag again as Sims pounces. Crudgington again produces some excellent saves as the Pilgrims' slow climb up the table continues.

---

17 · H DONCASTER · 28/11 — 21 · W · 9 · 18 · 4-2 · Sims 39, 60, Hodges 45, Cook 63 | Nimmo 7, Snodin I 42 · Att 4,341
- Opposition (Doncaster): Boyd, Russell, Cooper, Snodin I, Lister, Dowd, Pugh, Nimmo, Douglas, Snodin G, Little
- Ref: D Letts
- Billy Bremner's side, the early leaders in the division, suffer their fourth successive defeat. Snodin's goal is the pick as he finishes a 40 yard run. Sims' second comes off his back as he inadvertently deflects Nisbet's 30-yard piledriver.

---

18 · A HUDDERSFIELD · 5/12 — 21 · D · 15 · 19 · 0-0 · Att 6,949
- Opposition (Huddersfield): Taylor, Brown, Burke, Lillis, Sutton, Wilson, Stanton, Kennedy, Austin*, Robins, Cowling, Fletcher
- Ref: J Lovatt
- Both sides miss good chances. Cook swerves around the advancing Dick Taylor but then loses his balance and screws his shot wide. Dave Cowling hits a post (46). Sims looks set to score but his legs get in a tangle when trying to force the ball in. Terriers fans jeer Terry Austin.

---

19 · H SWINDON · 26/12 — · W · 22 · 2-1 · Hodges 3, Cook 41 | Rowland 89 · Att 8,185
- Opposition (Swindon): Allan, Baddeley, Williams, Hughes, Lewis, Graham, Emmanuel, Carter R, Rowland, Rideout, Pritchard
- Ref: A Seville
- The Swindon defence is still sorting itself out and allows Hodges too much freedom to give Argyle the perfect start. Rogers is at his best and sends over a series of dangerous crosses. After sustained pressure, Cook fires in. Andy Rowland's effort comes too late to make a difference.

---

20 · A EXETER · 28/12 — · D · 23 · 1-1 · Harrison 85p | Kellow 70 · Att 9,144
- Opposition (Exeter): Main, Mitchell, Rogers M, Prince, Foster, Cooke, Roberts L, Kellow, Delve, Pullar, Dennis
- Ref: C Downey
- Foster makes his debut for City on loan after failing to regain his place at Home Park. Tony Kellow gets his inevitable goal. Phillipson-Masters somehow shoots wide with the goal at his mercy. Harrison defies the incessant rain to score from the spot after Martyn Rogers pushes Hodges.

---

21 · H BRISTOL ROV · 2/1 — 15 · W · 8 · 26 · 4-0 · Cooper 51, 67, Cook 69p, 75 · Att 7,058
- Opposition (Bristol Rovers): Thomas, Gillies, McCaffrey*, Parkin, Mabbutt, Williams D, Stephens, Penny, Williams B, Barrett
- Ref: J Martin
- With various boardroom disputes now resolved things take a turn for the better. Bobby Gould is so disgusted with his side's display that he gives them only five minutes to board the team bus. Cook and Cooper share the goals including a penalty when Brian Williams upends Rogers.

---

22 · H BURNLEY · 9/1 — 14 · D · 19 · 27 · 1-1 · Hodges 74 | Young 47 · Att 5,065
- Opposition (Burnley): Stevenson, Laws, Wharton, Dixon, Overson, Dobson, Steven, Cassidy, Hamilton, Taylor, Young
- Ref: R Milford
- Sub zero temperatures and failing snow give further strength to the argument for summer soccer. A rare Nisbet error hands Kevin Young the opener. Hodges' persistence is finally rewarded. As the weather closes in Burnley abandon attempts to travel home and remain in Plymouth.

---

23 · A PRESTON · 16/1 — 16 · L · 23 · 27 · 0-1 · Bruce 41 · Att 4,936
- Opposition (Preston): Hodge, Taylor, McAteer, Bell, Booth, O'Riordan, Anderson, Doyle, Elliott, Naughton, Bruce
- Ref: G Owen
- Gordon Lee takes charge of his first home game for Preston and includes ex-Pilgrim Martin Hodge on loan from Everton. Alex Bruce scores with a splendid half-volley from the corner of the penalty area. Argyle rarely threaten as they suffer their first defeat for almost three months.

LEAGUE DIVISION 3　　　Manager: Bobby Moncur　　　SEASON 1981-82

No	Date	Att Pos	Pt	F-A	H-T	Scorers, Times, and Referees	1	2	3	4	5	6	7	8	9	10	11	12 sub used
24	A READING 23/1	2,789/ 7 15	D 28	2-2	0-2	Cooper 58, Hodges 69 / Beavon 21, Dixon 43 / Ref: M Dimblebee	Crudgington / Fearon	Nisbet / Williams*	Uzzell / Lewis	Harrison / Webb	Phill'·Mast's* / Hicks	Cooper / Barnes	Hodges / Beavon	Cook / Earles	Sims / Dixon	Phillips / Sanchez	Rogers / Donnellan	Rowe / Cullen
25	H BRENTFORD 30/1	5,008 10	W 31	1-0	1-0	Hodges 29 / Ref: K Barratt	Crudgington / McKellar	Nisbet / Salman	Uzzell / Tucker	Harrison / McNichol	James / Whitehead	Cooper / Hurlock	Hodges / Kamara	Cook / Booker	Sims / Sweetzer	Randell / Bowles	Rogers / Roberts*	Bowen
26	A LINCOLN 6/2	2,970 14	L 31	0-2	0-1	Thompson 24, Cockerill 81 / Ref: A Challinor	Crudgington / Felgate	Nisbet / Carr	Uzzell / Neale	Harrison / Cockerill	James / Peake	Cooper / Thompson	Hodges / Shipley	Cook / Turner	Sims / Cammack	Randell / Cunningham	Rogers / Gilbert	
27	H BRISTOL CITY 9/2	5,260 11	W 34	2-1	1-0	Cook 38, Hodges 64 / Chandler 71 / Ref: G Napthine	Crudgington / Moller	Nisbet / Stevens	Uzzell / Hay	Harrison / Newman	James / Williams	Cooper / Nicholls	Hodges / Musker	Cook / Bray	Sims / Chandler	Randell / Harford	Rogers / Economou	
28	H SOUTHEND 13/2	5,058 12	D 35	0-0	0-0	Ref: A Glasson	Crudgington / Keeley	Nisbet / Stead	Uzzell / Yates	Harrison / Hadley	James / Moody	Cooper / Cusack	Hodges / Nelson	Cook / Gray	Sims / Dudley	Randell / Mercer	Rogers / Otulakowski	
29	A CHESTERFIELD 20/2	4,381 13	D 36	2-2	1-1	Sims 37, Cook 60 / Ridley 30, Crawford 46 / Ref: D Civil	Crudgington / Turner	Nisbet / Stirk	Uzzell / O'Neill	Harrison / Wilson	James / Green	Cooper / Ridley	Hodges / Carroll*	Cook / Henderson	Sims / Bonnyman	Randell / Kowalski	Rogers / Crawford	Windridge
30	A GILLINGHAM 27/2	4,835 14	L 36	2-3	2-1	Sims 23, 40 / Bruce 2, Cascarino 47, Kemp 62 / Ref: D Hedges	Crudgington / Hillyard	Nisbet / Sharpe	Uzzell / Adams	Harrison / Bruce	James / Shaw	Cooper / Duncan	Hodges / Powell	Cook / Tydeman	Sims / Miller*	Randell / Kemp	Rogers / Price	Cascarino
31	H CARLISLE 6/3	3,272 13	W 39	1-0	0-0	Sims 64 / Ref: C White	Crudgington / Swinburne	Nisbet / Parker	Uzzell / Rushbury	Harrison / Houghton	Phill'·Masters / Ashurst	Cooper / Crabbe*	Hodges / Coughlin	Cook / Robson	Sims / Bannon	Randell / Lee	Rogers / Staniforth	Larkin
32	A CHESTER 13/3	1,988 13	W 42	3-0	1-0	Uzzell 38, Hodges 56, Sims 86 / Ref: B Martin	Crudgington / Harrington	Nisbet / Cottam	Uzzell / Raynor	Harrison / Storton	Phill'·Masters / Zelem	Cooper / Oakes	Hodges / Cooke*	Cook / Jones	Sims / Simpson	Randell / Needham	Rogers / Henderson	Phillips
33	A FULHAM 16/3	5,105 10	W 45	3-1	2-1	Sims 3, Cooper 40, Cook 53 / Tempest 27 / Ref: I Borrett	Crudgington / Peyton	Nisbet / Lock	Uzzell / Strong	Harrison / O'Driscoll*	Phill'·Masters / Brown	Cooper / Hopkins	Hodges / Davies	Cook / Wilson	Sims / Tempest	Randell / O'Sullivan	Rogers / Parker	Beck
34	H WALSALL 20/3	5,134 8	W 48	4-1	3-0	Cook 12, 18, Nisbet 40, Rogers 49 / Penn 47 / Ref: B Stevens	Crudgington / Green	Nisbet / Horne	Uzzell / Sinnott	Harrison / Beech*	Phill'·Masters / Serella	Cooper / Hart	Hodges / Rees !	Cook / Caswell !	Sims / Penn	Randell / O'Kelly	Rogers / Waddington S Loveridge	Beck

Match reports

24 — Defeat looks inevitable until Cooper smashes a 30-yard volley against his home town side. Hodges' low drive completes the comeback after Beavon streaks clear to score and Kerry Dixon eludes Uzzell to make it two. Fears that Phillipson-Masters has broken his leg prove unfounded.

25 — After a series of narrow misses, Hodges latches onto a loose ball to despatch it past David McKellar. James plays immaculately in his first senior game for a year to keep Stan Bowles anonymous. Five players are booked for varied reasons despite the almost total lack of foul play.

26 — Argyle's worst performance for several weeks. Glenn Cockerill's long throw causes confusion in the defence and Steve Thompson knocks in Tony Cunningham's flick. David Felgate produces a wonder save to deny Hodges. Cockerill clinches the three points with an easy chance.

27 — Donal Murphy leaves to team up again with Bobby Saxton at Blackburn. City slip nearer to relegation despite the efforts of giant Swede, Jan Moller. Nisbet sets up the first goal for Cook and Hodges maintains his recent scoring run. Ricky Chandler notches his maiden league goal.

28 — A bumpy pitch and strong wind makes for very poor entertainment. As visiting manager, Dave Smith leaves his seat in the directors box after 20 minutes, one wag suggest that he is going home. Southend, missing six key players, show great discipline and Argyle are bereft of ideas.

29 — Headers from Ridley and Sims cancel each other out before Alan Crawford scores one of the goals of the season. From the kick off, he dribbles from halfway and chips over Crudgington to put the Spireites ahead within nine seconds of the restart. No Argyle player had touched the ball.

30 — Despite 22 attempts on goal, Argyle come away pointless. Steve Bruce scores after 75 seconds but Argyle dominate the first half as Sims gives them an interval lead. On-loan David Kemp scores for the first time in eight matches as the Gills beat Argyle for the third time this season.

31 — Bob Stokoe's Carlisle are denied top spot as Sims silences his critics with an amazingly agile header that seems beyond him. Moncur's pre-match statement that United's defence is the best in the third division is well founded as they defend resolutely in driving rain and thick mud.

32 — Home fans are left wondering quite how their side put five past third placed Chesterfield in midweek. By the end they chant for the sacking of manager Alan Oakes as Argyle cruise to victory. Uzzell scores only his second ever goal and Hodges and a header from Sims complete the job.

33 — Despite a midfield quagmire, Randell orchestrates a superb victory over Malcolm MacDonald's leaders. Sims scores yet again, Cooper chips over Peyton and Cook seizes on an error. Dale Tempest scores his first league goal as the Cottagers miss Tony Gale on England Under-21 duty.

34 — Walsall, angered by Harrison's tackle on Ken Beech which results in him being stretchered off, lose their discipline. Five are booked and skipper Caswell (48) for abusive language and Rees (77) for two bookings are dismissed. Rogers finally gets his first goal after 31 matches.

Lineup column headers (also the line-up for the match of 27/3):

Knight	McLaughlin	Sullivan	Doyle	Aizlewood	Ellis	Berry	Rafferty	Senior	Tait	Crown*	Wimbleton
Crudgington	Kendall	Walden	Vaughan	Uzzell	Phill'-Masters	Cooper	Oakes	Thomas	Hodges	Cook	Rogers
Crudgington	Bond	Rogers M	Mitchell	Uzzell	Harrison	Cooper	Foster	Giles	Hodges	Cook	Rogers
Crudgington	Allan	Henry	Baddeley	Uzzell	Harrison	Cooper	Lewis	Stroud	Hodges	Carter R	Rogers
Crudgington	Beasant	Thoams	Smith	Uzzell	Harrison	Cooper	Morris	Belfield	Hodges	Elliott	Rogers
Crudgington	Cox	Brown	Burke	Uzzell	Harrison	Cooper	Valentine	Hanley	Hodges	Hatte*	Rowe
Crudgington	Sansome	Stevens	Chatterton	McCartney	Harrison	Cooper	Madden	Shinton	Hodges	Anderson	Rogers
Crudgington	Humphries S	Russell	Lister	McCartney	Harrison	Cooper	Crawford	Wigginton	Hodges	Liddell*	Rogers
Crudgington	Burton	Fogg	Smithers	McCartney	Harrison	Cooper	Briggs	Shotton	Hodges	Foley	Rogers
Crudgington	Hodge	Anderson	Naughton	McCartney	Harrison	Cooper	Westwell	O'Riordan	Hodges	Kelly	Rogers
Crudgington	Thomas	Jones	Slatter	Uzzell	Harrison	Cooper	Parkin	McCaffrey	Hodges	Barrett*	Rogers
Crudgington	Gleasure	Martin	Robinson	Uzzell	Phillips	Cooper	Kitchener	Roberts	Dennis	Hayes*	Rogers

Substitutes / additional names (in order across the row):
- Newport: Bishop, Elsey, Johnson, Tynan, Aldridge, Moore
- Exeter: Pratt*, Rogers P, Kellow, Delve, Robertson, Hatch
- Swindon: Abbley, Quinn, Carter M, Graham, Emmanuel
- Wimbledon: Armstrong, Hughes*, Leslie, Evans, Joseph, Gage, Rowe
- Huddersfield: Stanton, Lillis, Wilson, Cowling, Purdie, Kennedy
- Millwall: Allardyce, Roberts*, Martin, West, Neal, Horrix
- Doncaster: Ham*, Pugh, Douglas, Snodin G, Dawson, Bennett, Uzzell
- Oxford: Train, Lawrence, Hebberd*, Brock, Thomas, Kearns
- Preston: McAteer, Doyle, Elliott, Bell, Bruce, Neal
- Bristol Rov: Stephens, Curle, Williams D, Williams B, Randall
- Millwall: Chatterton, Massey, West, Dibble, Harrix

27/3 — Pos 15, Pts 48, Att 9,551
Scorer (against): Rafferty 85. Ref: A Gunn

Two ex-Pilgrims play a major part in Argyle's downfall. Colin Sullivan subdues Rogers and Bill Rafferty scores the only goal when he controls Trevor Senior's lob and cracks home from twelve yards. Steve Berry's header is goal-bound until Hodges chests it away off the line.

36 — H NEWPORT 2/4 — HT 0-0, L 1-2, Pos 13 (opp 20), Pts 48, Att 5,148
Hodges 56; Elsey 58, Bishop 82. Ref: L Burden

The club experiment with Friday night soccer. Newport gain their first ever win at Home Park thanks to two rare errors from Crudgington. Argyle's lead through Hodges is short-lived as the keeper fails to cut out Moore's cross and later spills Tommy Tynan's mis-hit shot to Bishop.

37 — H EXETER 9/4 — HT 1-0, W 2-1, Pts 51, Att 9,458
Nisbet 43, Sims 50; Kellow 58p. Ref: S Bates

Sims revels in the local derby atmosphere and creates a goal from nothing by beating two players and lobbing Len Bond. Paul Giles is upended by Nisbet for a penalty. The defender had already thrashed in a 25-yard special to pocket a £5 bet from his manager for unexpectedly scoring.

38 — A SWINDON 10/4 — HT 0-0, W 2-0, Pos 9 (opp 21), Pts 54, Att 4,056
Rogers 75, 80. Ref: A Hamil

Having conceded ten goals in their previous two matches, Swindon recall Kevin Baddeley to counter the threat of Rogers. After a quiet first period, the winger switches wings to great effect and scores both goals. Uzzell sets up the first and Nisbet's over-ambitious shot is steered in.

39 — H WIMBLEDON 14/4 — HT 0-0, W 2-0, Pos 6 (opp 23), Pts 57, Att 4,748
Nisbet 68, Sims 84. Ref: T Spencer

The struggling Dons have three players booked to take their season's tally-caution to 67. The introduction of Rowe proved the turning point as he has a hand in the move which sees Nisbet execute a smartly taken goal. Uzzell and Joseph both hit the woodwork before Sims settles it.

40 — H HUDDERSFIELD 17/4 — HT 1-0, D 1-1, Pos 7 (opp 12), Pts 58, Att 5,434
Sims 3; Kennedy 80p. Ref: T Bune

Missing six regulars, the Terriers rely on the offside law to thwart Argyle. Sims scores with a lovely header. Uzzell's desperate lunge on Mark Lillis results in a penalty which Mark Kennedy smashes in. The biggest cheer is reserved for the eccentric Mr Bune who falls flat on his face.

41 — A MILLWALL 20/4 — HT 1-2, L 1-2, Pos 9 (opp 13), Pts 58, Att 2,562
Cook 42; Horrix 15, Allardyce 38. Ref: J Hunting

Any outside chance of promotion is ended as player-manager Peter Anderson inspires his side from midfield. Dean Horrix's swirling shot is deflected off Nisbet. Big Sam Allardyce heads the second before Cook ends his recent barren spell with a header that loops over Paul Sansome.

42 — A DONCASTER 24/4 — HT 0-2, D 2-2, Pos 9 (opp 19), Pts 59, Att 3,894
Sims 62, Cook 81; Dawson 14, Douglas 27. Ref: K Walmsley

Mike Ham's debut lasts only 35 minutes as he is carried off with an ankle injury. Rovers have only two shots in the first half and score from both. Sims reduces the deficit after Cook's shot rebounds off a post and Cook himself deprives Billy Bremner's men of vital relegation points.

43 — A OXFORD 28/4 — HT 0-0, L 0-1, Pos 9 (opp 2), Pts 59, Att 6,957
Kearns 84. Ref: M Baker

Substitute Ollie Kearns keeps the U's in the promotion hunt by scoring only six minutes after replacing the out of sorts Trevor Hebberd. Despite having little to play for, Argyle produce a battling performance. Oxford take only one point from their remaining games to miss out.

44 — H PRESTON 1/5 — HT 0-1, L 0-3, Pos 10 (opp 14), Pts 59, Att 3,319
Kelly 32, Bell 66, Elliott 84. Ref: D Lloyd

John Kelly's precision shot through a crowded area gives Preston the lead. Cook is sent off (43) for lashing out at Doyle after a penalty claim is turned down. Two more clinical finishes complete a dismal afternoon which ends with the crowd calling for the resignation of the chairman.

45 — A BRISTOL ROV 8/5 — HT 1-2, W 3-2, Pos 11 (opp 16), Pts 62, Att 4,025
Uzzell 24, Sims 63, Rogers 78; Williams B 10p, Williams D 27. Ref: M James

Uzzell's rare right-foot shot makes amends for his early misdemeanour when he sends Keith Curle sprawling in the box. The game continues to see-saw as Argyle fight back. Rogers rounds Martin Thomas for the winner minutes after spurning an easier chance when he lofts the ball over.

46 — H MILLWALL 15/5 — HT 2-0, W 2-1, Pos 10 (opp 9), Pts 65, Att 3,193
Hodges 29, Cooper 42; Horrix 68. Ref: C Thomas

Moncur switches a number of players to different positions in this meaningless match. Dennis, in for the suspended Cook, looks lively and Phillips adapts well to his unfamiliar full-back role. Millwall never give up and deserve their goal when Dean Horrix ghosts in unnoticed.

Home 4,792
Away 4,727
Average 4,792

LEAGUE DIVISION 3 (CUP-TIES)　　　Manager: Bobby Moncur

League Cup		Att	F-A	H-T	Scorers, Times, and Referees	1	2	3	4	5	6	7	8	9	10	11	12 sub used
1:1 A CHESTER 8/9	23 D	1,690 14	1-1	1-1	Storton 36(og) / Jones 26 / Ref: N Glover	Crudgington	Nisbet	McCartney	Harrison	Foster	Cooper	Hodges	Kemp	Sims	Randell	Murphy	
					Millington	*Needham*	*Raynor*	*Storton*	*Cottam*	*Oakes*	*Jones*	*Simpson*	*Ludlam*	*Howat*	*Sutcliffe*	

Argyle make a second trip to Sealand Road when the previous week's tie is abandoned after 78 minutes due to a collapsed goalpost. Two stunning saves by Crudgington keep Argyle in the match. Bryn Jones shoots low into the net. Hodges' harmless cross hits Storton and goes in.

League Cup		Att	F-A	H-T	Scorers, Times, and Referees	1	2	3	4	5	6	7	8	9	10	11	12 sub used
1:2 H CHESTER 15/9	24 W	2,348 8	1-0	1-0	Dennis 41p / 8 / Ref: H King / (Argyle won 2-1 on aggregate)	Crudgington	Nisbet	Uzzell	Harrison	Foster	Rowe	Hodges	Kemp	Sims	Randell	Dennis	Cooke
					Millington	*Needham*	*Raynor*	*Storton*	*Cottam*	*Oakes*	*Jones*	*Simpson*	*Ludlam*	*Howat**	*Sutcliffe*	

For the second successive match the referee is replaced at half-time after feeling unwell. Seventeen-year-old apprentice Tony Dennis in his first full match coolly slots home the penalty after Storton fouls Kemp. Another teenager, Mark Rowe also impresses with his ball distribution.

League Cup		Att	F-A	H-T	Scorers, Times, and Referees	1	2	3	4	5	6	7	8	9	10	11	12 sub used
2:1 A MIDDLESBRO 6/10	23 L	8,201 1:20	1-2	1-0	Kemp 13 / Ashcroft 72, Thomson 73 / Ref: J Worrall	Crudgington	Nisbet	McCartney	Uzzell	Foster	Cooper	Hodges	Kemp	Sims	Randell	Rogers	
					Platt	*Craggs*	*Bolton*	*Angus*	*Baxter*	*McAndrew*	*Cochrane*	*Otto*	*Ashcroft*	*Shearer*	*Thomson*	

The Pilgrims produce a vastly improved performance against the First Division strugglers. Kemp gives them a shock lead but two goals in the space of 80 seconds in the second half spare Boro's blushes. Foster plays soundly against the side who almost bought him during the summer.

League Cup		Att	F-A	H-T	Scorers, Times, and Referees	1	2	3	4	5	6	7	8	9	10	11	12 sub used
2:2 H MIDDLESBRO 27/10	24 D	6,402 1:21	0-0	0-0	Ref: T Spencer / (Argyle lost 1-2 on aggregate)	Crudgington	Nisbet	McCartney	Harrison	Phill'-Masters	Cooper*	Hodges	Cook	Sims	Randell	Rogers	Murphy
					Platt	*Nattrass*	*Bolton*	*Angus*	*Baxter*	*McAndrew*	*Cochrane*	*Otto*	*Woof**	*Hodgson*	*Thomson !*	*Shearer*

Boro go on the defensive after being reduced to ten men on 29 minutes when Bobby Thomson is dismissed for his second bookable offence, when he upends Hodges. Platt keeps Argyle at bay with some fine saves to set up a money-spinning fourth round tie with Liverpool at Anfield.

FA Cup

FA Cup		Att	F-A	H-T	Scorers, Times, and Referees	1	2	3	4	5	6	7	8	9	10	11	12 sub used
1 H GILLINGHAM 21/11	21 D	5,471 1	0-0	0-0	Ref: E Read	Crudgington	Nisbet	McCartney	Harrison	Phill'-Masters	Cooper	Hodges	Cook	Sims	Randell*	Rogers	Phillips
					Hillyard	*Sharpe*	*Ford*	*Bruce*	*Weatherly*	*Bowman*	*Powell*	*Duncan*	*White*	*Ovard*	*Price*	

Gills boss Keith Peacock, without a number of key players, is the happier of the two managers as Argyle face an unwanted midweek trip to Kent for a replay. Hodges comes closest to breaking the deadlock when his crisp shot hits the post and rebounds along the face of the goal.

FA Cup		Att	F-A	H-T	Scorers, Times, and Referees	1	2	3	4	5	6	7	8	9	10	11	12 sub used
1R A GILLINGHAM 24/11	21 L	7,370 1	0-1	0-0	Bowman 51 / Ref: E Read	Crudgington	Nisbet	McCartney!	Harrison	Phill'-Masters	Cooper	Hodges	Cook*	Sims	Phillips	Rogers	Dennis
					Hillyard	*Sharpe*	*Ford*	*Bruce*	*Weatherly*	*Bowman*	*Powell*	*Tydeman*	*White*	*Lee**	*Price*	*Duncan*

McCartney becomes the second Argyle player to be dismissed twice this season when he is sent off in the last minute for retaliation. Ritchie Bowman's goal dashes Argyle's hopes of a lucrative cup run and with it the hope of some much needed cash to fund some new signings.

	P	W	D	L	F	A	W	D	L	F	A	Pts
1 Burnley	46	13	7	3	37	20	8	10	5	29	25	80
2 Carlisle	46	17	4	2	44	21	6	7	10	21	29	80
3 Fulham	46	12	9	2	44	22	9	6	8	33	29	78
4 Lincoln	46	13	7	3	40	16	8	7	8	26	24	77
5 Oxford	46	10	8	5	28	18	9	6	8	35	31	71
6 Gillingham	46	14	5	4	44	26	6	6	11	20	30	71
7 Southend	46	11	7	5	35	23	7	8	8	28	28	69
8 Brentford	46	8	6	9	28	22	11	5	7	28	25	68
9 Millwall	46	12	4	7	36	28	6	9	8	26	34	67
10 PLYMOUTH	46	12	5	6	37	24	6	6	11	27	32	65
11 Chesterfield	46	12	4	7	33	27	6	6	11	24	31	64
12 Reading	46	11	6	6	43	35	6	5	12	24	40	62
13 Portsmouth	46	11	10	2	33	14	3	9	11	23	37	61
14 Preston	46	10	7	6	25	22	6	6	11	25	34	61
15 Bristol Rov*	46	12	4	7	35	28	6	5	12	23	37	61
16 Newport	46	9	10	4	28	21	5	7	11	26	33	58
17 Huddersfield	46	10	5	8	38	25	5	7	11	26	34	57
18 Exeter	46	14	4	5	46	33	2	5	16	25	51	57
19 Doncaster	46	9	9	5	31	24	4	8	11	24	44	56
20 Walsall	46	10	7	6	32	23	3	7	13	19	32	53
21 Wimbledon	46	10	6	7	33	27	4	5	14	28	48	53
22 Swindon	46	9	5	9	37	36	4	8	11	18	35	52
23 Bristol City	46	7	6	10	24	29	4	7	12	16	36	46
24 Chester	46	2	10	11	16	30	5	1	17	20	48	32
* 2 pts deducted	1104	258	155	139	827	594	139	155	258	594	827	1499

	Lge	Sub	LC	Sub	FAC	Sub	Lge	LC	FAC	Tot
Collins, Jeremy	1									
Cook, Jeff	35		1		2		16			16
Cooper, Leigh	43		3		2		5			5
Crudgington, Geoff	46		4		2					
Dennis, Tony	4	2	1			1				1
Foster, George	10		3							
Ham, Mike	1									
Harrison, Chris	43		3		2		1			1
Hodges, Kevin	46		4		2		11			11
James, Tyrone	6									
Kemp, David	9		3				1			1
McCartney, Mike	16	2	1		2					
Murphy, Donal	4	2	1	1						
Nisbet, Gordon	45		4		2		3			3
Phillips, David	6	2			1	1	1			1
Phil'-Masters, Forbes	31		1		2					
Randell, Colin	38		4		1		3			3
Rogers, Andy	40		2		2		4			4
Rowe, Mark	2	2	2		1					
Sims, John	46		4		2		18			18
Uzzell, John	34	1	2				2			2
(own-goals)									3	3
21 players used	506	9	44	1	22	2	64		3	67

Double wins: (5) Bristol Rov, Chester, Fulham, Swindon, Walsall.

Double defeats: (4) Gillingham, Lincoln, Oxford, Preston.

Won from behind: (2) Bristol Rov, Doncaster.

Lost from in front: (3) Bristol City, Gillingham, Newport.

High spots: Only eight defeats in 35 matches after disastrous start. Immediate success of Jeff Cook-John Sims partnership. Consistency in second half of season with relatively unchanged side.

Low spots: Two points from first eleven matches leaving the side at bottom of the table. Disappointing level of attendances. Loss of form and departure of David Kemp.

Player of the Year: John Sims.

Ever presents: (3) Geoff Crudgington, Kevin Hodges, John Sims.

Hat-tricks: (0).

Leading scorer: John Sims (18).

LEAGUE DIVISION 3 — Manager: Bobby Moncur — SEASON 1982-83

No	Date	Att	Pos	Pt	F-A	H-T	Scorers, Times, and Referees	1	2	3	4	5	6	7	8	9	10	11	12 sub used
1	H SOUTHEND 28/8	3,850		W 3	1-0	1-0	Harrison 4	Crudgington	Nisbet	Uzzell	Harrison	Phill'-Masters	Cooper	Hodges	Phillips	Sims	Gooding	Rogers	Carter
							Ref: A Glasson	Cawston	Stead	Pountney	Clark	Moody	Cusack	Otulakowski	Phillips	Mercer*	Pennyfather	Nelson	Greaves
2	A READING 4/9	2,102	12 / 9	L 3	2-3	0-2	Cook 59p, Uzzell 68, Earles 1, Dixon 44, 81	Crudgington	Nisbet	Uzzell	Harrison !	Phill'-Mast's*	Cooper	Hodges	Cook*	Sims	Gooding	Rogers	Carter
							Ref: B Daniels	Judge	Williams*	Richardson	Beavon	Hicks	Wood	Baston	Earles	Dixon	Sanchez	Donnellan	White
3	A NEWPORT 7/9	3,741		D 4	2-2	0-1	Cook 58, Hodges 78, Tynan 2, Gwyther 66	Crudgington	Nisbet	Uzzell	Harrison	McCartney	Cooper	Hodges	Gooding	Cook	Sims	Rogers	
							Ref: K Salmon	Kendall	Jones	Vaughan	Relish	Stroud	Lowndes	Bailey	Elsey	Gwyther	Tynan	Moore	
4	H ORIENT 11/9	3,649	6 / 9	W 7	2-0	1-0	Hodges 33, 64	Crudgington	Nisbet	Uzzell	Harrison	McCartney	Cooper	Hodges	Cook*	Sims	Gooding	Rogers	Carter
							Ref: E Read	Day	Osgood	Peach*	Foster	Gray	Vincent	Godfrey	Donn	Blackhall	Smith	Taylor	Cornwell
5	A SHEFFIELD UTD 18/9	13,604	11 / 5	L 7	1-3	0-0	Sims 84, Kenworthy 59, Young 81, 85	Phillips	Nisbet	Uzzell	Nisbet	McCartney	Cooper	Hodges	Cook*	Sims	Gooding	Rogers	Carter
							Ref: R Chadwick	Conroy	Henderson	Houston	McHale	McPhail	Kenworthy	Curran	Trusson	Edwards	Young	Charles	
6	H WREXHAM 25/9	3,628	7 / 16	W 10	2-0	1-0	Gooding 22, Rogers 88	Crudgington	Nisbet	Phillips	Phill'-Masters	McCartney	Cooper	Hodges	Cook	Sims	Gooding	Rogers	Carter
							Ref: J Martin	Niedzwiecki	Hill	Davis	Hunt	Dowman	Keay	Bater	Gregory	Fox	McNeil*	Burton	Baker
7	H BRISTOL ROV 28/9	3,542		L 10	0-4	0-0	Randall 59, 89, Kelly 75, Williams D 76 Kite	Crudgington	Nisbet	Harrison	Phill'-Masters	McCartney	Cooper	Hodges	Cook*	Sims	Gooding	Rogers	Carter
							Ref: A Robinson	Slatter	Williams B 76	Williams G	Parkin	McCaffrey	Holloway	Williams D	Kelly*	Randall	Barratt		Sherwood
8	A WIGAN 2/10	5,011	15 / 11	L 10	0-3	0-2	Bradd 31, 44, O'Keefe 63	Crudgington	Nisbet	Harrison	Phill'-Masters	Uzzell	Cooper	Hodges	McCartney	Rogers*	Carter	Rowe	
							Ref: A Saunders	Tunks	McMahon	Lloyd*	Methven	Weston	Langley	Cribley	Gemmill	O'Keefe	Bradd	Houghton	Glenn
9	A BRADFORD C 9/10	4,690	19 / 2	L 10	0-4	0-1	Campbell 32, 48, Gallagher 51p, Gray 54 McManus	Crudgington	Nisbet	Uzzell	Harrison	Phill'-Masters	Cooper	Hodges	Carter*	Sims	McCartney	Rogers	Dennis
							Ref: A Shaw	Leigh	Podd	Chapman	Lester	Cooke	McFarland	Gray	Gallagher	Campbell	Ellis	Mellor	
10	H LINCOLN 16/10	2,921	20 / 1	L 10	0-2	0-1	Bell 29, Hobson 90	Crudgington	Nisbet	Uzzell	Harrison	Smith	Cooper	Hodges	Carter*	Sims	McCartney	Rogers	Phillips
							Ref: D Hedges	Felgate	Carr	Neale	Cockerill	Peake	Thompson	Burke	Turner	Hobson	Bell	Shipley	
11	H BOURNEMOUTH 19/10	2,525	/ 2	W 13	2-0	1-0	Hodges 17, Sims 77	Crudgington	Nisbet	Uzzell	Harrison	Smith	Cooper	Hodges	Cook	Sims	McCartney	Rogers	Carter
							Ref: V Callow	Leigh	Heffernan	Sulley	Spackman	Brignull	Compton	Williams	Morgan	Funnell	Graham*	Dawtry	

Match reports

1. Hodges break finally beats the offside trap. Appeals for a penalty go unheeded as he is tackled by Pennyfather. Stead makes a second tackle and this time Mr Glasson awards the spot-kick. Harrison's attempt is blocked by Mervyn Cawston but he follows up to turn the rebound in.

2. Some of Reading's third lowest crowd since the war are still arriving as Earles opens the scoring. Harrison becomes an early victim of the new professional foul rule when he is dismissed for tripping Dixon (30). A similar offence by Wood on Hodges brings a penalty but no dismissal.

3. Tommy Tynan heads in a cross from Kevin Moore. Cook pounces after County fail to clear a corner. David Gwyther is allowed time and space to send in an unstoppable shot. Mark Kendall falls foul of the FA directive on releasing the ball. The resultant free-kick leads to Hodges' goal.

4. Both sides are unusually captained by their goalkeepers. Cooper and Hodges combine for the latter to score. David Peach is stretchered off (42) with a leg injury. Mervyn Day is penalised for taking too many paces and Gooding tees up the free-kick for Hodges to blast in his second.

5. Both sides struggle on Sheffield's hottest day for 21 years. After a monotonous first period, the game bursts into life. Kenworthy rises above everyone to meet Charles' corner. Alan Young gets a second before Sims finishes a four-man move. Young picks his spot with time to spare.

6. Wrexham's under-strength side is further weakened when the dangerous Dixie McNeil is forced off after just eleven minutes to have stitches inserted in a leg wound. Gooding scores his first Pilgrims goal since his free transfer from Coventry and Rogers scores with a rare header.

7. Moncur describes his side's performance as the worst he has seen. Rovers win at Home Park for the first time in 26 years. Argyle survive for almost an hour until the Pirates cut loose. Player-manager David Williams scores from 25 yards and Randall takes his season's tally to seven.

8. Wigan are full of confidence after scoring six at Doncaster in midweek. Archie Gemmill makes his home debut. Veteran Les Bradd scores twice and ex-Argyle man Eamon O'Keefe gets a third as the Pilgrims come away from their first ever visit to Springfield Park empty-handed.

9. The pressure is on Moncur as Argyle's season threatens to fall apart. The defence have no answer to Irish international Bobby Campbell who is denied a hat-trick when Phillipson-Masters upends him in the area. Gallagher sends Crudgington the wrong way and Gray lobs in the fourth.

10. Loan signing Lindsay Smith from Cambridge meets his new team-mates only two hours before kick-off. Even the pre-match marching band have difficulty standing in the gale-force wind. Despite the conditions, Lincoln show why they top the table as Bell and Hobson score easily.

11. Only the true diehards turn out on a rainswept evening to see their side regain some form. Hodges' shot takes a deflection to leave Ian Leigh stranded and Sims ignores Tom Heffernan's flying boot to bravely head the second. Nisbet suffers a gashed shin and Smith is booked again.

No	Venue	Opponent	Date	Att	Pos	W/D/L	FT	HT
12		(23/10)		3,149	16	16		
13	H	BRENTFORD	30/10	4,036	14	9	W	2-0
14	A	MILLWALL	2/11	3,097	13	18	D	2-2	2-1
15	A	DONCASTER	8/11	2,942		21	D	2-2	0-0
16	H	OXFORD	13/11	3,908	11	10	W	2-1	1-0
17	A	PRESTON	27/11	3,633	11	22	D	2-2	0-2
18	H	HUDDERSFIELD	4/12	4,227	10	4	W	2-1	2-0
19	H	GILLINGHAM	18/12	4,179	8	12	W	2-0	1-0
20	A	EXETER	27/12	9,168	9	13	L	0-1	0-0
21	H	CARDIFF	28/12	8,631	7	4	W	3-2	1-2
22	A	PORTSMOUTH	1/1	15,856	8	2	L	1-2	0-2
23	A	SOUTHEND	14/1	3,082	10	9	L	1-3	0-2

12 — 23/10
Argyle: Crudgington, Nisbet, Uzzell, Harrison, Smith, Cooper, Hodges, Cook, Sims, McCartney, Rogers
Opp: Turner, Bellamy, Wilson, Green, Henson, Strik, Henderson, Walker, Kowalski, Windridge, Dawson
Hodges 72, Nisbet ??
Walker 76
Ref: B Guy
An injury to John Stirk proves crucial. He goes off for seven minutes to have a head wound stitched and during that time Argyle score twice. Hodges, with his back to goal, volleys in Rogers' cross and Nisbet's swerving shot confuses John Turner. Robert Daniel is to quit as chairman.

13 — BRENTFORD (H) 30/10
Argyle: Crudgington, Nisbet, Uzzell, Harrison, Smith, Cooper, Hodges, Cook, Sims, McCartney, Rogers
Brentford: Roche, Rowe, Harris*, McNichol, Whitehead, Hurlock, Kamara, Booker, Mahoney, Bowles, Roberts, Bowen
Cook 67, Sims 77
Ref: R Milford
The Bees come to Home Park as the highest scorers in the Football League but it is Paddy Roche who is the busier keeper. Cook's shot takes a wicked deflection off Alan Whitehead with Roche going the other way. Sims smashes an unstoppable 20-yard screamer into the top corner.

14 — MILLWALL (A) 2/11
Argyle: Crudgington, Nisbet, Uzzell, Harrison, Smith, Cooper, Hodges, Cook, Sims, McCartney, Rogers
Millwall: Sansome, Stevens, Madden, Massey, Allardyce*, Carr, Neal, Horrix, Martin, Chatterton, Hayes
Cooper 26, Madden 44(og)
Chatterton 45p, Massey 49
Ref: D Axcell
Cooper opens the scoring from a well-rehearsed free-kick. Lawrie Madden turns a Nisbet cross into his own net. Smith is astonished when Mr Axcell awards a penalty for a foul and Nicky Chatterton pulls one back from the spot. Andy Massey levels from a free-kick to share the points.

15 — DONCASTER (A) 8/11
Argyle: Crudgington, Nisbet, Uzzell, Harrison, Smith, Cooper, Hodges, Cook, Sims, McCartney, Rogers
Doncaster: Peacock, Russell, Watson, Snodin I*, Wigginton, Cawthorne, Douglas, Owen, Austin, Snodin G, Lister, Humphries
McCartney 52, Hodges 90
Russell 80, Austin 87
Ref: J Hough
After a mediocre first half the game reaches a pulsating climax. McCartney gets his first Argyle goal. A 30-yard strike by Billy Russell is followed by Terry Austin slotting home to seemingly clinch the match. Hodges has other ideas and nets a last-gasp equaliser from eight yards.

16 — OXFORD (H) 13/11
Argyle: Crudgington, Nisbet, Uzzell, Harrison, Smith, Cooper, Hodges, Cook, Sims, McCartney, Rogers
Oxford: Butcher, Linney, Grant, Fogg, Shotton, Brock, Jones, Vinter, Whatmore, Thomas*, Foley
McCartney 34, Sims 64
Fogg 78p
Ref: C Thomas
There's no stopping McCartney as he gets his second goal in a week. Sims' diving header looks to have put the game beyond Jim Smith's men. Uzzell goes sprawling in an effort to stop Foley and handles. Although Crudgington gets a hand to Fogg's penalty it carries too much power.

17 — PRESTON (A) 27/11
Argyle: Crudgington, Nisbet, Uzzell, Harrison, Smith, Cooper, Hodges, Cook, Sims, McCartney, Rogers
Preston: Litchfield, Westwell, McAteer, O'Riordan, Coleman, Gowling, Walsh, Sayer, Elliott, Naughton, Houston
Cooper 83, Hodges 85
McAteer 18, Elliott 32
Ref: T Mills
Argyle, looking for their first win at Deepdale since 1964, suffer an early blow when Andy McAteer scores from a free-kick after Crudgington had taken too many steps. Goal-machine Steve Elliott notches his 15th of the season before Cooper and Hodges complete a fine comeback.

18 — HUDDERSFIELD (H) 4/12
Argyle: Crudgington, Nisbet, Uzzell, Harrison, Smith, Cooper, Hodges, Cook, Sims, McCartney, Rogers
Huddersfield: Cox, Brown, Burke, Stanton, Sutton, Valentine*, Lillis, Doyle, Sayer, Wilson, Cowling, Pugh
Cook 13p, Hodges 40
Wilson 66
Ref: D Letts
Mick Buxton's side have risen rapidly from the bottom of the table following seven successive wins. Cook sends Brian Cox the wrong way after Hodges ankles had been clipped by Doyle. Hodges' shot soars in the wind over Cox and Phil Wilson hits a swerving 20-yard consolation.

19 — GILLINGHAM (H) 18/12
Argyle: Crudgington, Nisbet, Uzzell, Harrison, Smith, Cooper, Hodges, Cook, Sims, McCartney, Rogers
Gillingham: Hillyard, Sitton, Adams, Shaw, Weatherly, Tydeman, Powell*, Johnson, Cascarino, White, Price, Miller
Sims 35, Rogers 64
Ref: D Lloyd
The Gills are going through a rough patch and have won only one of their last nine matches. The returning Ron Hillyard still looks far from fit. Cook has a hand in both goals. His shot hits the post and Sims follows up. His through pass then sets up Rogers to score with an angled shot.

20 — EXETER (A) 27/12
Argyle: Hards, Nisbet, Uzzell, Harrison, Smith, Cooper, Hodges, Cook*, Sims, McCartney, Rogers
Exeter: Bond, Rogers M, Viney, Harle, Marker, McEwan, Neville, Rogers P, Kellow, Delve, Carter
Neville 65
Ref: D Civil
Hards replaces the injured Crudgington for this local derby. Danger-man Tony Kellow for once shakes off the attentions of Smith to set up the only goal. Dave Harle has a chance to put the game beyond doubt. With Argyle appealing for offside he races through but puts his shot wide.

21 — CARDIFF (H) 28/12
Argyle: Hards, Nisbet, Uzzell, Harrison, Smith, Cooper, Hodges, Carter, Sims, McCartney, Rogers
Cardiff: Dibble, Jones, Mullen*, Tong, Dwyer, Bennett G, Bennett D, Gibbins, Hatton, Giles, Lewis, Maddy
Sims 12, 78, Carter 59
Hatton 13, Bennett G 43
Ref: T Spencer
The opportunity to buy tickets for next week's cup clash at Watford draws a healthier than usual attendance. Both teams respond with a highly entertaining game. Sims and Bob Hatton trade goals within a minute of each other. Carter opens his Argyle account and Sims clinches it.

22 — PORTSMOUTH (A) 1/1
Argyle: Crudgington, Nisbet, Uzzell, Harrison, Smith, Cooper, Hodges, Carter*, Sims, McCartney, Rogers
Portsmouth: Knight, McLaughlin, Sullivan, Doyle, Howe, Aizlewood*, Webb, Tait, Rafferty, Biley, Ellis
McLaughlin 73(og)
Webb 34, Smith 35(og)
Ref: A Ward
Future England man Neil Webb opens the scoring before two own-goals dominate proceedings. Smith, with time to spare, rolls the ball back to Crudgington but fails to notice the keeper coming out to collect the ball himself. McLaughlin sends Cooper's corner spinning past Knight.

23 — SOUTHEND (A) 14/1
Argyle: Crudgington, Nisbet, Uzzell, Phillips, Smith, Cooper, Hodges, Cook, Sims, McCartney, Rogers
Southend: Cawston, Stead, Yates, Clark, Hadley, Cusack, Pountney, Phillips, Mercer, Otulakowski*, Nelson, Pennyfather
Phillips 85
Mercer 16, Yates 26, Phillips 86
Ref: M Dimblebee
The Pilgrims never look likely to break their Roots Hall jinx which has seen them lose on eight of their last nine visits to Essex. Phillips' 25-yard screamer is the only bright spot as defensive errors gift three points to the Shrimpers. Moncur makes noises about needing a new striker.

LEAGUE DIVISION 3 — SEASON 1982-83

Manager: Bobby Moncur

No 24 — H 22/1 NEWPORT — Lost 2-4 (H-T 1-2) — Att 4,287 · Pos 12 · Pt 34
Scorers: Vaughan 19 (og), Cook 64 / Tynan 13, 20, Elsey 82, Lowndes 90 — Ref: J Bray

	1	2	3	4	5	6	7	8	9	10	11	12 sub used
Argyle	Crudgington	Nisbet	Phillips	Harrison	Smith	Cooper	Hodges	Cook	Sims	McCartney	Rogers	Pulis
Newport (7)	*Kendall*	*Boyle*	*Relish**	*Bailey*	*Oakes*	*Stroud*	*Lowndes*	*Aldridge*	*Tynan*	*Vaughan*	*Elsey*	*Smith*

Argyle are torn apart by the renowned Tommy Tynan-John Aldridge combination. Vaughan back-heads a clearance over his own keeper. Sims somehow blasts over from five yards. Harrison, back from suspension, has a nightmare match as defensive errors once again prove expensive.

No 25 — A 29/1 ORIENT — Won 2-0 (H-T 2-0) — Att 2,699 · Pos 10 · Pt 37
Scorers: McCartney 18p, Hodges 34 — Ref: I Borrett

	1	2	3	4	5	6	7	8	9	10	11	12 sub used
Argyle	Crudgington	Nisbet	Uzzell	Harrison	Smith !	Cooper	Hodges	Bremner	Sims	McCartney	Rogers	
Orient (14)	*Day*	*Roffey*	*Peach*	*Foster*	*Cunningham*	*Cornwell*	*Osgood*	*Godfrey*	*Houchen*	*Blackhall**	*Sussex*	*Smith*

Kevin Bremner, on loan from Colchester, finishes with a booking and ripped shorts but ensures the Orient defenders know they have been in a game. Day's fingertips cannot keep out McCartney's spot-kick after Peach fells Rogers. Smith is dismissed (87) for elbowing Keith Houchen.

No 26 — H 1/2 READING — Won 3-0 (H-T 2-0) — Att 3,504 · Pt 40
Scorers: Williams 19 (og), Bremner 39, [McCartney 55pl] — Ref: S Bates

	1	2	3	4	5	6	7	8	9	10	11	12 sub used
Argyle	Crudgington	Nisbet	Uzzell	Harrison	Smith	Cooper	Hodges	Bremner	Sims	McCartney	Rogers	
Reading	*Judge*	*Tutty*	*Richardson*	*Beavon*	*Williams*	*White*	*Matthews**	*Stant*	*Price*	*Bason*	*Doherty*	*McMahon*

A makeshift Reading side contains three part-timers. Jerry Williams heads over Judge. Bremner gets the second and is brought down by Steve Richardson for McCartney's penalty. The Royals' plight is highlighted when sales rep Des MacMahon replaces bricklayer Mark Matthews.

No 27 — A 5/2 BRISTOL ROV — Lost 0-2 (H-T 0-0) — Att 6,556 · Pos 8 · Pt 40
Scorers: Platnauer 66, Ball 88 — Ref: E Scales

	1	2	3	4	5	6	7	8	9	10	11	12 sub used
Argyle	Crudgington	Nisbet	Uzzell	Harrison	Smith	Cooper	Hodges	Bremner	Sims*	McCartney	Rogers	Phillips
Bristol Rov (3)	*Kite*	*Slatter*	*Williams B*	*Holloway*	*Parkin*	*McCaffrey*	*Ball*	*Williams D*	*Platnauer*	*Randall*	*Barratt*	

Argyle's second visit to Eastville this season ends in disappointment. Bobby Gould's side take the lead when Nicky Platnauer scores after his initial shot is blocked. Alan Ball makes victory safe with his first Rovers goal. Argyle put summer signing Mike Carter on the transfer list.

No 28 — H 8/2 WALSALL — Drew 0-0 (H-T 0-0) — Att 3,148 · Pos 8 · Pt 41
Ref: J Martin

	1	2	3	4	5	6	7	8	9	10	11	12 sub used
Argyle	Crudgington	Nisbet	Uzzell	Harrison	Smith	Cooper	Hodges	Bremner	Sims	McCartney	Rogers	
Walsall (21)	*Green*	*Caswell*	*Mower*	*Beech*	*Sinnott*	*Hart*	*Shakespeare*	*Preece*	*Kearns*	*Buckley**	*O'Kelly*	*Round*

The Saddlers get what they came for as they grab another point towards their climb away from the relegation zone. Peter Hart and Lee Sinnott keep Sims and Bremner quiet. Ron Green pulls off a fine save from Rogers but there is little else to excite the fans on a bitterly cold evening.

No 29 — H 19/2 BRADFORD C — Won 3-1 (H-T 1-0) — Att 3,644 · Pos 8 · Pt 44
Scorers: Cooper 37, McCartney 81p / Cooke 50 — Ref: T Bune

	1	2	3	4	5	6	7	8	9	10	11	12 sub used
Argyle	Crudgington	Nisbet	Uzzell	Harrison	Ham	Cooper	Hodges	Bremner	Sims	McCartney	Rogers	
Bradford C (11)	*Ramsbottom*	*Abbot*	*Chapman*	*Lester*	*Jackson*	*Cherry*	*McCall*	*Cooke**	*Campbell*	*Black*	*Ellis*	*Gray*

The drama occurs at lunchtime. Crudgington suffers burns to his back when he throws a burning pan of fat out of his house. Nisbet prepares to play in goal and Moncur to name himself as sub but Crudgington defies the pain. Player-manager Trevor Cherry fouls Sims for the penalty.

No 30 — A 26/2 LINCOLN — Won 2-1 (H-T 0-1) — Att 3,915 · Pos 8 · Pt 47
Scorers: Hodges 63, Phillips 81 / Bell 22p — Ref: D Vickers

	1	2	3	4	5	6	7	8	9	10	11	12 sub used
Argyle	Crudgington	Nisbet	Uzzell	Harrison	Ham	Cooper	Hodges	Cook*	Sims	McCartney	Rogers	Phillips
Lincoln (3)	*Felgate*	*Simmonite*	*Neale*	*Cockerill*	*Peake*	*Thompson*	*Burke**	*Turner*	*Hobson*	*Bell*	*Shipley*	*Kelly*

The result only inflames the discontent at Sincil Bank as fans invade the pitch at the end to call for the head of chairman Gilbert Blades. Mr Vickers awards a penalty against Harrison when the ball strikes his hand. The Argyle players return to the team bus through a police cordon.

No 31 — H 1/3 MILLWALL — Won 3-1 (H-T 0-1) — Att 4,114 · Pt 50
Scorers: Sims 84, Phillips 87, 89 / Neal 10 — Ref: A Hamil

	1	2	3	4	5	6	7	8	9	10	11	12 sub used
Argyle	Crudgington	Nisbet	Uzzell	Harrison	Smith	Rowe	Hodges	Phillips	Sims	McCartney	Rogers	
Millwall	*Wells*	*Martin*	*Stride*	*Lovell*	*Madden*	*Roberts !*	*Bremner*	*Neal**	*Aylott*	*Massey*	*Chatterton*	*Robinson*

A quick return to Home Park for Kevin Bremner as he signs for the Lions. Millwall look set to hang on to Dean Neal's early goal until Paul Roberts is sent off (72) for remarks made to a linesman. Phillips repays Moncur's faith in playing him up front with two fine strikes late on.

No 32 — H 5/3 CHESTERFIELD — Won 2-0 (H-T 0-0) — Att 4,466 · Pos 8 · Pt 53
Scorers: Phillips 70, Rogers 83 — Ref: B Stevens

	1	2	3	4	5	6	7	8	9	10	11	12 sub used
Argyle	Crudgington	Nisbet	Uzzell	Harrison	Smith	Cooper*	Hodges	Phillips	Sims	McCartney	Rogers	Carter
Chesterfield (21)	*Turner*	*Stirk*	*Partridge*	*Thrower**	*Bellamy*	*O'Neill*	*Windridge*	*Plummer*	*Henderson*	*Kowalski*	*Kendall*	*Atherzych*

Phillips is at it again as he gives the Pilgrims the lead. Opposition manager Frank Barlow is fuming, claiming that Phillips was offside. Argyle take route one for their second as Rogers latches on to a flick from Crudgington's goal-kick to steer past Turner and make it four wins in a row.

No 33 — A 11/3 BRENTFORD — Lost 0-2 (H-T 0-0) — Att 4,967 · Pos 8 · Pt 53
Scorers: Joseph 57, Kamara 82 — Ref: D Brazier

	1	2	3	4	5	6	7	8	9	10	11	12 sub used
Argyle	Crudgington	Nisbet	Uzzell	Harrison	Smith	Cooper	Hodges	Phillips	Sims	McCartney	Rogers	Roberts
Brentford (14)	*Roche*	*Rowe*	*Wilkins*	*McNichol*	*Whitehead*	*Hurlock*	*Kamara*	*Joseph*	*Cassells*	*Bowles*	*Roberts*	

Brentford dent Argyle's outside promotion hopes although Moncur is far from despondent over his team's performance. Francis Joseph lobs Crudgington from the edge of the penalty area after Smith fails to clear. Chris Kamara drives home the second. Roche saves well from Phillips.

No 34 — A 15/3 BOURNEMOUTH — Lost 0-1 (H-T 0-1) — Att 4,258 · Pt 53
Scorers: Nightingale 44 — Ref: M Robinson

	1	2	3	4	5	6	7	8	9	10	11	12 sub used
Argyle	Crudgington	Nisbet	Uzzell	Harrison	Smith	Cooper	Hodges	Phillips	Sims	McCartney	Rogers	
Bournemouth	*Leigh*	*Heffernan*	*Sulley*	*Spackman*	*Brignull*	*Impey*	*Carter**	*Beck*	*Morgan*	*Lee*	*Nightingale*	*Graham*

Neither side deserve to lose but the Cherries create more clear-cut chances. Trevor Lee challenges Crudgington and the ball ricochets to Mark Nightingale to pick his spot. Argyle route most of their attacks through Rogers but, a Sims shot apart, never seriously threaten Ian Leigh's goal.

#	H/A	Date	Opponent	Att	Pos	Res	—	Score	Pts
35	A	19/3	(Doncaster)	3,406	22			1-2	53
36	A	26/3	OXFORD	4,786	9	D	7	1-1	54
37	H	1/4	EXETER	8,856		W		1-0	57
38	A	2/4	CARDIFF	7,226	8	D	3	0-0	58
39	A	9/4	HUDDERSFIELD	9,277	9	L	2	0-2	58
40	H	16/4	SHEFFIELD UTD	3,665	8	W	10	3-1	61
41	H	19/4	WIGAN	3,097		L		0-2	61
42	A	23/4	GILLINGHAM	3,356	9	L	15	1-2	61
43	H	30/4	PRESTON	2,912	8	D	19	1-1	62
44	A	2/5	WALSALL	3,473	9	L	11	0-2	62
45	A	7/5	WREXHAM	2,250	8	W	19	3-2	65
46	H	14/5	PORTSMOUTH	14,173	8	L	1	0-1	65

35 (19/3) — Phillips 23 / Walker 19, 66. Ref: J Deakin
Argyle: Crudgington, Nisbet, Uzzell, Harrison, Smith, Cooper, McCartney, Hodges, Rogers, Austin*, Sims, Phillips
Opp: Boyd, Russell, Johnson, Snodin G, Humphries, Lister, Walker, Mell, Mann, Robertson, Douglas
The headline writers rub their hands in glee as former dustman Colin Walker scores twice to secure a shock victory for lowly Rovers. Uzzell is left standing by Stewart Mell to set up the first. Billy Russell's long throw causes confusion for number two.

36 OXFORD (A) — Cooper 23 / Hebberd 3p. Ref: M Heath
Argyle: Crudgington, Nisbet, Uzzell, Harrison, Smith, Cooper, Hodges, Phillips, Rogers, Staniforth, Sims
Oxford: Hardwick, Attley, Smithers, Lawrence*, Briggs, Shotton, Jones, Whatmore, Vinter, Brock, Biggins
Moncur finally gets his man with the capture of Gordon Staniforth from Carlisle. Cooper concedes an early penalty when he handballs when attempting to clear. He soon makes amends with a fine 20 yard effort. United press in the second half and retain their unbeaten home record.

37 EXETER (H) — Sims 47. Ref: A Seville
Argyle: Crudgington, Nisbet, Uzzell, Harrison, Smith, Cooper, Hodges, Phillips, Rogers, Staniforth, Sims
Exeter: Bond, Rogers M, Viney, Harle, Marker, Phillips, Neville, Rogers P, Crown, Delve*, Pratt
City surprisingly leave out the menacing Tony Kellow. Sims continues his fine scoring record against his former club when he applies the finishing touch after Hodges header hits the crossbar. Len Bond prevents a bigger victory. Uzzell is booked on his 150th Argyle appearance.

38 CARDIFF (A) — 0-0. Ref: T Holbrook
Argyle: Crudgington, Nisbet, Uzzell, Harrison, Smith, Cooper, Hodges, Phillips, Rogers, Staniforth, Sims
Cardiff: Steele, Jones, Mullen, Tong, Dwyer, Bennett G, Bennett D, Gibbins, Hatton*, Hemmerman, Micallef, Bodin
Len Ashurst admits his promotion-chasing side have lost their sparkle after they leave the pitch to cries of 'what a load of rubbish'. Both sides have justifiable penalty claims turned down. Rogers has a late chance to clinch the points but after a 40-yard run he shoots weakly at Steele.

39 HUDDERSFIELD (A) — Hanvey 60, Brown 72p. Ref: N Glover
Argyle: Crudgington, Nisbet, Uzzell, Harrison, Smith, Cooper, Hodges, Phillips, Rogers, Staniforth, Sims
Huddersfield: Cox, Brown, Burke, Stanton, Sutton*, Ham, Hanvey, Lillis, Russell, Doyle, Wilson, Cowling, Pugh
Keith Hanvey finally breaks the deadlock, heading in Pugh's corner. The ref penalises Harrison when Mark Lillis falls in the area. Moncur describes it as the worst decision he has ever seen but Malcolm Brown converts the spot-kick. Terriers skipper Dave Sutton injures a knee.

40 SHEFFIELD UTD (H) — Phillips 46, Nisbet 67, Staniforth 89 / Morris 28. Ref: A Robinson
Argyle: Crudgington, Nisbet, Uzzell, Harrison, Smith, Cooper, Hodges, Phillips, Rogers, Staniforth, Sims
Sheff Utd: Waugh, Smith, Henderson, Richardson, West, Houston, Towner, Trusson, Morris, Brazil*, Charles, Edwards
An uncharacteristic slip by Nisbet gives the Blades an interval lead. Tony Towner propels a massive clearance towards his own goal and Phillips pounces. Nisbet atones for his earlier error with a thundering header from Uzzell's cross. Staniforth scores from an unlikely angle.

41 WIGAN (H) — O'Keefe 70, Butler 72. Ref: C Thomas
Argyle: Crudgington, Nisbet, Uzzell, Harrison, Smith, Cooper, Hodges, Phillips, Rogers, Dennis, Sims*
Wigan: Tunks, Langley, Weston, Barrow, Walsh, Methven, Sheldon, Cribley, Lowe, O'Keefe, Butler
With Dennis replacing the unwell Sims, Argyle lack any forward height to pose a threat to the Wigan defence. O'Keefe makes Argyle pay for releasing him on a free transfer, ten years earlier, with a 20-yard shot. The Latics take three points from their first ever visit to Home Park.

42 GILLINGHAM (A) — Phillips 80 / Cascarino 6, 16. Ref: D Letts
Argyle: Crudgington, Nisbet, Uzzell, Harrison, Smith, Cooper, Hodges, Phillips, Rogers, Dennis*, Sims
Gillingham: Hillyard, Sharpe, Adams, Sitton, Shaw, Tydeman, Johnson, Bowman, Mehmet*, Weatherly, Cascarino, Horrix
A jittery defence is punished by Tony Cascarino. Micky Adams' long throw is met first by the tall striker who heads over Crudgington. Smith then commits defensive suicide with a misjudged back-pass which the future Irish international intercepts. Phillips' response comes too late.

43 PRESTON (H) — Smith 89 / Booth 34. Ref: A Glasson
Argyle: Crudgington, Nisbet, Uzzell*, Harrison, Smith, Cooper, Hodges, Phillips, Rowe, Staniforth, Sims
Preston: Hodge, Hinnigan, McAteer, O'Riordan, Booth, Lodge, Sayer, Gowling*, Elliott, Naughton, Bell, Kelly
Martin Harvey takes charge with Moncur away scouting. Joe Hinnigan's header hits the bar and Tommy Booth reacts quickest to nod in the rebound. Preston boss Gordon Lee is upset when his side concede Smith's late equaliser. Rowe impresses at left-back after Uzzell is injured.

44 WALSALL (A) — Buckley 61, Penn 68. Ref: D Richardson
Argyle: Crudgington, Nisbet, Rowe, Harrison, Smith, Cooper, Hodges, Phillips, Rogers, Staniforth, Sims
Walsall: Kearns M, Caswell, Mower, Shakespeare, Simnott, Hart, Penn, Preece, Summerfield, Buckley, O'Kelly*, Kearns O
Argyle win lots of friends with their attractive play but yet again come away without the points. Kevin Summerfield creates both Saddlers goals. Player-manager Alan Buckley notches his 200th for the club and Don Penn celebrates a return from a four-month injury absence.

45 WREXHAM (A) — Sims 13, Rogers 56, 86 / Gregory 5, Muldoon 34. Ref: J Hough
Argyle: Crudgington, Nisbet, Rowe, Ham, Smith, Cooper, Hodges, Phillips, Rogers, Staniforth, Sims
Wrexham: Niedzwiecki, King, Bater, Savage, Dowman, Keay, Jones, Burton*, Hunt, Muldoon, Gregory, Cunningham
The Welshmen's plight deepens as Argyle come from behind twice. Dowman scores from close range but two from Rogers sinks Wrexham and does struggling rivals Exeter a favour too. Muldoon scores from ten yards to give Gregory an easy chance. Sims volleys from ten yards to level.

46 PORTSMOUTH (H) — Biley 59. Ref: K Cooper
Argyle: Crudgington, Nisbet, Uzzell, Harrison, Smith, Cooper, Hodges, Phillips, Rogers, Staniforth, Sims
Portsmouth: Knight, Ellis, Sullivan, Doyle, Tait, Aizlewood, Webb, Dillon, Rafferty, Biley, Rogers
A massive influx of fans from the South coast celebrate Pompey's championship success. Sadly the match is marred by a crowd invasion four minutes from time which forces Mr Cooper to take the players off the pitch. The match resumes but similar scenes again greet the final whistle.

Home 14,173
Away 5,341
Average 4,532

LEAGUE DIVISION 3 (CUP-TIES)   Manager: Bobby Moncur   SEASON 1982-83

Milk Cup

		Att	F-A	H-T	Scorers, Times, and Referees	1	2	3	4	5	6	7	8	9	10	11	12 sub used
1:1 H BOURNEMOUTH 31/8	W	3,103	2-0	0-0	Sims 84, 87 Ref: T Stevens	Crudgington	Nisbet	Uzzell	Harrison	Phill'/Masters	Cooper	Hodges	Cook	Sims	Gooding	Rogers	
						Allen	*Heffernan*	*Sulley*	*Spackman*	*Brignull*	*Imray*	*Carter*	*Williams*	*Morgan*	*Crawford*	*Dawtrey*	

Sims continues last season's form with two late goals when a draw looks inevitable. He cleverly chips over Kenny Allen for his first and then sees his speculative shot from wide on the left fly just inside the post to give Argyle a clear advantage to take to the second leg at Dean Court.

		Att	F-A	H-T	Scorers, Times, and Referees	1	2	3	4	5	6	7	8	9	10	11	12 sub used
1:2 A BOURNEMOUTH 14/9	L	3,353 16	0-3 aet	0-1	Funnell 17, Brignull 84, Morgan 111 Ref: C Downey (Argyle lost 2-3 on aggregate)	Crudgington	Nisbet	Uzzell	Harrison	McCartney	Cooper*	Hodges	Cook	Sims	Gooding	Rogers	Carter
						Allen	*Sulley*	*O'Donnell*	*Brignull*	*Compton*	*Carter*	*Williams*	*Morgan*	*Funnell*	*Crawford*	*Mundee**	*Dawkins*

Tony Funnell puts the Cherries ahead when Sulley's through ball hits McCartney on the back. Argyle look to be heading for the second round until Brignull heads in from close range. Cook hits the upright in extra-time before Trevor Morgan stabs home after a goalmouth scramble.

FA Cup

		Att	F-A	H-T	Scorers, Times, and Referees	1	2	3	4	5	6	7	8	9	10	11	12 sub used
1 H EXETER 20/11	W	10,202 16	2-0	0-0	Hodges 60, Sims 81 Ref: E Read	Crudgington	Nisbet	Rowe	Harrison	Smith	Cooper	Hodges	Cook	Sims	McCartney	Rogers	
						Bond	*Rogers M*	*Viney*	*Harle*	*Marker*	*McEwan*	*Neville*	*Rogers P*	*Kellow*	*Delve*	*Pullar*	

Peter Rogers misses a glorious chance when he rounds Crudgington but misses an open goal. Cook hits the woodwork (55). Seventeen-year-old Nicky Marker does a good job in marking Sims but cannot prevent the wily striker setting up Hodges' goal and scoring the second himself.

		Att	F-A	H-T	Scorers, Times, and Referees	1	2	3	4	5	6	7	8	9	10	11	12 sub used
2 A BRISTOL ROV 11/12	D	9,018 2	2-2	1-1	Rogers 33, Sims 59 Williams D 45, 47 Ref: L Burden	Crudgington	Nisbet	Uzzell	Harrison	Smith	Cooper	Hodges	Cook	Sims	McCartney	Rogers	
						Kite	*Slatter*	*Williams B*	*Williams G*	*Parkin*	*McCaffrey*	*Holloway*	*Williams D*	*Stephens**	*Randall*	*Barrett*	*Withey*

Rogers again shows his liking for the Eastville stadium by scoring from 20 yards. David Williams equalises in first-half injury-time and gets another immediately after the re-start from 35 yards. Sims levels on his return from injury to send the 1,000 travelling Argyle fans home happy.

		Att	F-A	H-T	Scorers, Times, and Referees	1	2	3	4	5	6	7	8	9	10	11	12 sub used
2R H BRISTOL ROV 20/12	W	9,130 2	1-0	0-0	McCartney 54 Ref: L Burden	Crudgington	Nisbet	Uzzell	Harrison !	Smith	Cooper	Hodges	Cook	Sims	McCartney	Rogers	
						Kite	*Slatter*	*Williams B*	*Williams G*	*Parkin*	*McCaffrey*	*Channon*	*Williams D**	*Stephens*	*Withey*	*Barrett*	*Platnauer*

A heavy downpour before kick-off threatens the match. Both sides battle in the mud. Neil Slatter fails to clear Rogers' cross and McCartney slams the ball home. Harrison is dismissed (65) for elbowing Stephens in retaliation. Rovers are unable to convert their late pressure into goals.

		Att	F-A	H-T	Scorers, Times, and Referees	1	2	3	4	5	6	7	8	9	10	11	12 sub used
3 A WATFORD 8/1	L	17,630 1:2	0-2	0-1	Rostron 40, Blissett 73 Ref: R Lewis	Crudgington	Nisbet	Uzzell	Phillips	Smith	Cooper	Hodges	Cook	Sims	McCartney	Rogers	
						Sherwood	*Rice*	*Rostron*	*Taylor*	*Sims*	*Bolton*	*Callaghan*	*Blissett*	*Gilligan*	*Jackett*	*Barnes*	

Argyle put up a brave show against their high-flying illustrious opponents. Cook, who became a father during the night, almost celebrates with a goal as his shot flashes past a post. Wilf Rostron scores from a John Barnes free-kick. England's Luther Blissett ends the giant-killing dream.

	P	W	D	L	F	A	W	D	L	F	A	Pts
		Home					**Away**					
1 Portsmouth	46	16	4	3	43	19	11	6	6	31	22	91
2 Cardiff	46	17	5	1	45	14	11	6	6	31	36	86
3 Huddersfield	46	15	8	0	56	18	8	5	10	28	31	82
4 Newport	46	13	7	3	40	20	10	2	11	36	34	78
5 Oxford	46	12	9	2	41	23	3	10	10	30	30	78
6 Lincoln	46	17	1	5	55	22	6	6	11	22	29	76
7 Bristol Rov	46	16	4	3	55	21	6	5	12	29	37	75
8 PLYMOUTH	46	15	2	6	37	23	4	6	13	24	43	65
9 Brentford	46	14	4	5	50	28	6	6	13	38	49	64
10 Walsall	46	14	5	4	38	19	3	8	12	26	44	64
11 Sheffield Utd	46	16	3	4	44	20	3	4	16	18	44	64
12 Bradford C	46	11	7	5	41	27	6	6	12	27	42	61
13 Gillingham	46	12	4	7	37	29	4	9	10	21	30	61
14 Bournemouth	46	11	7	5	35	20	5	6	12	24	48	61
15 Southend	46	10	8	5	41	28	5	6	12	25	37	59
16 Preston	46	11	10	2	35	17	4	3	16	25	52	58
17 Millwall	46	12	7	4	41	24	2	6	15	23	53	55
18 Wigan	46	10	4	9	35	33	5	5	13	25	39	54
19 Exeter	46	12	4	7	49	43	2	8	13	32	61	54
20 Orient	46	10	6	7	44	38	3	5	15	20	50	54
21 Reading	46	10	8	5	37	28	2	9	12	27	51	53
22 Wrexham	46	11	6	6	40	26	1	9	13	16	50	51
23 Doncaster	46	6	8	9	38	44	3	3	17	19	53	38
24 Chesterfield	46	6	6	11	28	28	2	7	14	15	40	37
	1104	297	137	118	1005	612	118	137	297	612	1005	1519

Odds & ends

Double wins: (3) Chesterfield, Orient, Wrexham.
Double defeats: (3) Bristol Rov, Portsmouth, Wigan.
Won from behind: (5) Cardiff, Lincoln, Millwall, Sheff Utd, Wrexham.
Lost from in front: (0).
High spots: Emergence of David Phillips as goalscoring midfield player.
Penetrative right-sided combination of Kevin Hodges and Gordon Nisbet.
Excellent scoreless draw at promoted Cardiff.
Nine-match unbeaten run in mid-season to pull away from relegation zone.
Low spots: Inconsistency cost possible promotion place.
Losing in League Cup first round after leading 2-0 from first leg.
Further decrease in home attendances.
Four-match losing run from end of September, scoring nil and conceding 13 goals.
Player of the Year: Gordon Nisbet.
Ever presents: (2) Kevin Hodges, Gordon Nisbet.
Hat-tricks: (0).
Leading scorer: John Sims (14).

Appearances & Goals

Player	Lge	Sub	LC	Sub	FAC	Sub	Goals Lge	LC	FAC	Tot
Bremner, Kevin	5						1			1
Carter, Mike	6	6				1	1			1
Cook, Jeff	19	1	2		4		5			5
Cooper, Leigh	45		2		4		4			4
Crudgington, Geoff	44		2		4					
Dennis, Tony	3									
Gooding, Ray	7	2	2				1			1
Ham, Mike	4									
Hards, Neil	2									
Harrison, Chris	41		2		3		1			1
Hodges, Kevin	46		2		4		11		1	12
McCartney, Mike	33		1		4		5		1	6
Nisbet, Gordon	46		2		4		2			2
Phillips, David	20	3			1		8			8
Phill-Masters, Forbes	6				1					
Rogers, Andy	44		2		4		5		1	6
Rowe, Mark	6	2		1		4				
Sims, John	42	1	2		4		10	2	2	14
Smith, Lindsay	34				4		1			1
Staniforth, Gordon	11						1			1
Uzzell, John	42		2		3		1			1
(own-goals)							4			4
21 players used	**506**	**13**	**22**	**2**	**44**	**3**	**61**	**2**	**5**	**68**

CANON DIVISION 3

Manager: Bobby Moncur > John Hore

SEASON 1983-84

---

1. H WIGAN — 27/8 — Att 3,730 — D — Pt 1 — F-A 0-0 — H-T 0-0

1	2	3	4	5	6	7	8	9	10	11	12 sub used
Crudgington	Nisbet	Uzzell	Harrison	Smith L	Forbes	Hodges	Phillips	Tynan	Staniforth	Rogers	
Tunks	*Cribley*	*Comstive*	*Butler*	*Walsh*	*Methven*	*Bruce*	*Barrow*	*Lowe*	*Taylor*	*Houghton*	

Ref: L Burden

Argyle parade their new signings, Tommy Tynan (£55k from Newport) and part-timer Dick Forbes, who impresses. Despite totally dominating the match, the Pilgrims' finishing is woeful and this, combined with desperate defence, see the Latics take an unlikely point back to Lancashire.

---

2. A MILLWALL — 3/9 — Att 4,611 — L — Pos 18/9 — Pt 1 — F-A 0-1 — H-T 0-0

1	2	3	4	5	6	7	8	9	10	11	12 sub used
Crudgington	Nisbet	Uzzell	Harrison	Smith L	Forbes	Hodges	Phillips	Tynan	Staniforth	Rogers	
Sansome	*Lovell*	*Stride*	*Robinson*	*Nutton*	*Cusack*	*Bremner*	*Lowndes*	*Martin**	*Otulakowski*	*Chatterton*	*Neal*

Lovell 86 — Ref: B Hill

Only skipper Crudgington earns his wages as he defies Millwall. With an undeserved point beckoning, he is powerless to stop Steve Lovell's volley. Once again the Pilgrims attack looks toothless and the fans are still waiting to see how Tynan managed to score 33 times last season.

---

3. A ROTHERHAM — 6/9 — Att 4,488 — L — Pos 9 — Pt 1 — F-A 0-2 — H-T 0-1

1	2	3	4	5	6	7	8	9	10	11	12 sub used
Crudgington	Nisbet	Uzzell	Harrison!	Smith L	Cooper	Hodges	Phillips	Tynan	Staniforth	Rogers	
Stevenson	*Forrest*	*Crosby*	*O'Dell**	*Johnson*	*McEwan*	*Rhodes*	*Kilmore*	*Moore*	*Mitchell*	*McBride*	*Walker*

Kilmore 31, McBride 81p — Ref: J Bray

Yet again Argyle fire blanks. Free-transfer Kevin Kilmore nicks his third goal in three games to give George Kerr's side the lead. Harrison is booked for a mistimed tackle and four minutes later is sent off for obstructing Forrest. Smith is convinced Moore dived but McBride converts.

---

4. H GILLINGHAM — 10/9 — Att 3,192 — D — Pos 20/17 — Pt 2 — F-A 1-1 — H-T 0-0

1	2	3	4	5	6	7	8	9	10	11	12 sub used
Crudgington	Nisbet	Uzzell	Harrison	Smith L	Cooper	Hodges	Phillips*	Tynan	Staniforth	Rogers	
Hillyard	*Sage*	*Garner*	*Sitton*	*Shaw*	*Handford*	*Daniel**	*Johnson*	*Leslie*	*Mehmet*	*Weatherly*	*Cascarino*

Nisbet 79, Sitton 53 — Ref: E Read

At last! Full-back Nisbet finally breaks Argyle's scoring duck after seven hours of football. Even a draw looks unlikely after Tony Cascarino flicks on Dave Mehmet's corner for John Sitton to score easily. Rowe's corner is partially cleared and Nisbet's trusty right boot does the rest.

---

5. A LINCOLN — 17/9 — Att 3,103 — L — Pos 22/14 — Pt 2 — F-A 1-3 — H-T 1-1

1	2	3	4	5	6	7	8	9	10	11	12 sub used
Crudgington	Phillips	Uzzell	Harrison	Smith L	Cooper	Hodges	Rowe	Tynan	Staniforth	Rogers	
Felgate	*Simmonite*	*Neale*	*Cockerill*	*Thompson*	*Houghton*	*Thomas**	*Turner*	*Hobson*	*Jack*	*Shipley*	*Stradder*

Tynan 36 — Hobson 30, 88, Jack 70 — Ref: J Lovatt

Tynan's impressive scoring record against the club where he endured a miserable time continues. His lob over David Felgate answers Gordon Hobson's opener. Argyle's back four have difficulty with the pace of Hobson and he gets his second after Ross Jack headed the Imps in front.

---

6. H PRESTON — 24/9 — Att 3,674 — W — Pos 20/10 — Pt 5 — F-A 1-0 — H-T 0-0

1	2	3	4	5	6	7	8	9	10	11	12 sub used
Crudgington	Nisbet	Uzzell	Ham	Smith L	Cooper*	Hodges	Rowe	Tynan	Staniforth	Rogers	
Litchfield	*Clark*	*McAteer*	*Jones**	*Booth*	*Lodge*	*Walsh*	*Sayer*	*Elliott*	*Naughton*	*Houston*	*Himnigan*

Rogers 61 — Ref: R Milford

Rogers celebrates becoming a father by scoring the only goal when he runs on to Staniforth's pass. Argyle miss a hatful of chances with Tynan the main culprit as he squanders three good opportunities. Cooper suffers a nasty knee injury which may necessitate a cartilage operation.

---

7. H SCUNTHORPE — 27/9 — Att 3,821 — W — Pt 8 — F-A 4-0 — H-T 2-0

1	2	3	4	5	6	7	8	9	10	11	12 sub used
Crudgington	Nisbet	Uzzell	Harrison	Smith L	Cooper	Hodges	Rowe	Tynan	Staniforth	Rogers	
Neenan	*Longden*	*Pointon*	*Brolly*	*Green*	*Hunter*	*Boxall**	*Holden*	*Cowling*	*Lester*	*Dey*	*O'Berg*

Staniforth 5, 33, Rowe 70, Rogers 76 — Ref: C Thomas

Events after the match overshadow Argyle's biggest win of the season. At 10.30 it is announced that Moncur has resigned due to differences of opinion over club policy. Coach Martin Harvey is put in temporary command. On the field the Iron are crushed with Staniforth at his best.

---

8. A BURNLEY — 1/10 — Att 6,766 — L — Pos 18/8 — Pt 8 — F-A 1-2 — H-T 1-0

1	2	3	4	5	6	7	8	9	10	11	12 sub used
Crudgington	Nisbet	Uzzell	Harrison	Smith L	Cooper	Hodges	Rowe	Tynan	Staniforth	Rogers	
Hansbury	*Scott*	*Wharton*	*Phelan*	*Overson*	*Flynn*	*Dobson*	*Gow*	*Hamilton*	*Waldron**	*Hutchison*	*Phillips* *Reeves*

Flynn 21(og) — Hamilton 66, Scott 88 — Ref: D Shaw

John Bond concedes that his team of fading stars were fortunate. Hansbury juggles with Flynn's back-header before knocking it into the roof of the net to give Argyle a farcical lead. Hamilton's shot squirms under Crudgington and Derek Scott is left totally unmarked to head the winner.

---

9. A BOURNEMOUTH — 8/10 — Att 3,759 — L — Pos 19/22 — Pt 8 — F-A 1-2 — H-T 1-2

1	2	3	4	5	6	7	8	9	10	11	12 sub used
Crudgington	Nisbet	Uzzell	Harrison	Smith L	Cooper	Hodges	Rowe	Tynan	Pearson	Phillips	
Leigh	*La Ronde*	*Sulley*	*Beck*	*Brignall*	*Nightingale*	*Schiavi*	*Williams*	*Morgan*	*Graham*	*Thompson*	

Pearson 14 — Morgan 28, Thompson 34 — Ref: R Lewis

The euphoria of a midweek draw with Arsenal is soon forgotten at a bleak Dean Court. Pearson, in his first Argyle start for seven years, gets an early strike. Two defensive errors by Crudgington and Smith gift the Cherries their goals and give new boss Don Megson only his second win.

---

10. H OXFORD — 15/10 — Att 2,990 — W — Pos 16/7 — Pt 11 — F-A 2-1 — H-T 0-1

1	2	3	4	5	6	7	8	9	10	11	12 sub used
Crudgington	Nisbet	Uzzell	Harrison	Smith L	Cooper	Hodges	Rowe	Tynan	Pearson	Phillips	
Hardwick	*Hinshelwood*	*McDonald*	*Thomas*	*Briggs*	*Shotton*	*Lawrence*	*Barnett*	*Biggins*	*Hebberd*	*Brock*	

Nisbet 59, Phillips 79 — Lawrence 24 — Ref: J Deakin

Incessant rain and gale-force winds greet new manager Johnny Hore. With the wind at their backs, U's force ten first half corners and George Lawrence converts one of them. Nisbet becomes Argyle's top scorer with another 25-yard screamer. Phillips bends one around Hardwick.

---

11. H BRISTOL ROV — 18/10 — Att 4,896 — D — Pos 12 — F-A 1-1 — H-T 0-0

1	2	3	4	5	6	7	8	9	10	11	12 sub used
Crudgington	Nisbet	Uzzell	Harrison	Smith L	Cooper	Hodges	Rowe	Tynan	Pearson*	Phillips	
Kite	*Slatter*	*Williams B*	*Bater**	*Parkin*	*Holloway*	*McCaffrey*	*Pulis*	*Stephens*	*Randall*	*Williams G*	*White*

Phillips 59 — Williams G 53 — Ref: A Seville

Tynan receives an award from Rothmans before the match for his previous season's scoring exploits. Two Welsh Under-21 internationals score. Geraint Williams volleys in after good work by Ian Holloway and Neil Slatter and Phillips responds with a well-struck shot from Rowe's cross.

12 A 22/10 HULL — 8,807 — 16 — W — 2-1 — 3 — 15 — 0-1
Smith L 53, Tynan 78 / McClaren 28
Ref: P Tyldesley

| Crudgington | Nisbet | Uzzell | Harrison | Smith L | Cooper | Hodges | Rowe | Tynan | Staniforth | Phillips |
| Norman | McNeil | Hollifield | Roberts D | Skipper | Askew | Marwood | McClaren | Whitehurst | Mattie | Swann* | Flounders |

Crudgington's penalty save helps Argyle to become the first side to defeat the Tigers this season. Uzzell is punished for a handball (66) but Brian Marwood's spot-kick is saved at the second attempt. Smith's shot and Tynan's close-range header turn the form book upside down.

13 H 29/10 SHEFFIELD UTD — 5,458 — 16 — L — 0-1 — 4 — 15 — 0-0
Phillistkirk 80
Ref: D Letts

| Crudgington | Nisbet | Uzzell | Harrison | Smith L | Cooper | Hodges | Rowe | Tynan* | Staniforth | Phillips |
| Waugh | Heffernan | Bolton | Arnott | Stancliffe | Kenworthy | Morris | Phillistkirk | Edwards | McHale | Brazil | Pearson |

Argyle fail to transfer their Milk Cup form to the league as another three points are thrown away. Tynan's sloppy pass goes to Kevin Arnott who crosses to the waiting Tony Phillistkirk, who scores his first league goal. Hodges holds his head in shame after slicing a chance well wide.

14 A 31/10 PORT VALE — 3,466 — 14 — W — 1-0 — 24 — 18 — 1-0
Phillips 10
Ref: D Owen

| Crudgington | Nisbet | Uzzell | Harrison | Smith L | Cooper | Hodges | Rowe | Tynan | Staniforth | Phillips |
| Pearce | Tartt | Shankland | Hunter | Ridley | Cegielski | Earle | Oakes | Bright | O'Keefe | Fox |

Vale's injury crisis forces 42 year old coach Alan Oakes into action. Phillips exchanges passes with Tynan and shoots in from near the penalty spot. The goal seals Argyle's first ever win at Vale Park in 18 attempts.

15 A 5/11 BRENTFORD — 4,183 — 15 — D — 2-2 — 19 — 19 — 1-1
Tynan 42, Hodges 69 / Mahoney 2, Cassells 71
Ref: M Taylor

| Crudgington | Nisbet | Uzzell | Harrison | Smith L | Cooper | Hodges | Rowe | Tynan* | Staniforth* | Phillips |
| Swinburne | Rowe | Roberts P | Salman | Whitehead | Booker | Mahoney | Joseph | Cassells | Bullivant | Roberts G | Pearson |

Crudgington's first touch is to pick the ball out of the net as Tony Mahoney rises unchallenged to head in a free-kick. Tynan's brilliant scissors kick levels. Hodges' first of the season puts the Greens ahead but Cassells scrambles home after Paul Roberts' massive throw causes confusion.

16 H 12/11 BOLTON — 4,624 — 9 — W — 2-0 — 8 — 22 — 1-0
Kellow 3, Phillips 66
Ref: B Stevens

| Crudgington | Nisbet | Uzzell | Harrison | Smith L | Forbes | Hodges | Rowe | Tynan | Kellow | Phillips |
| Farnworth | Borrows | Deakin | Joyce | McElhinney | Valentine | Thompson | Chandler | Foster* | Caldwell | Redfearn | Berry |

Ace striker Tony Kellow makes a sensational start to his debut as he meets Nisbet's cross and powers in an unstoppable header. Phillips rifles in a poor clearance. Bolton, who thumped Walsall 8-1 a few weeks earlier, fight back and Crudgington is forced to make three crucial saves.

17 A 3/12 BRADFORD C — 2,955 — 14 — L — 0-2 — 22 — 22 — 0-0
Hawley 53p, Haire 62
Ref: N Ashley

| Crudgington | Nisbet | Uzzell | Harrison | Smith L | Cooper* | Hodges | Rowe | Tynan | Kellow | Phillips |
| McManus | Padd | Withe | Mccall | Pickering | Cherry | Haire | Hawley | Campbell | Yarath | Ellis* | Gray |

City gain their first home win of the season. Hawley converts from the spot after Harrison is penalised for handball. Garry Haire capitalises on some hesitancy to snatch a second. Another penalty is awarded when Uzzell fouls Campbell but Crudgington guesses correctly this time.

18 A 17/12 ORIENT — 2,684 — 14 — L — 2-3 — 5 — 22 — 2-1
Nisbet 14, 28 / McNeil 25, Cornwell 55, 84
Ref: H Taylor

| Crudgington | Nisbet | Uzzell | Harrison | Smith L | Cooper | Hodges | Rowe* | Tynan | Kellow | Phillips |
| Key | Cornwell | Corbett | Roffey | Sussex | Hales | Godfrey | Brooks | Houchen | Kitchen | McNeil |

Orient's opener is highly controversial. From a corner, the ball goes a yard out of play. Houchen plays it back in, with the defence assuming he was returning it for a goal-kick. Play continues and McNeil scores. Nisbet carries on scoring but John Cornwell's aerial power proves decisive.

19 H 26/12 EXETER — 10,387 — 14 — D — 2-2 — 20 — 23 — 1-0
Staniforth 41, Kellow 72 / Neville 77, Pratt 82
Ref: T Bune

| Crudgington | Nisbet | Uzzell | Harrison | Smith L | Cooper | Hodges | Rowe | Kellow | Staniforth | Rogers |
| Bond | Kirkup | Viney | O'Connor | Webster | McEwan | Neville | Rogers P | Pratt | Francis* | Marker | Ling |

After Staniforth's goal, Argyle threaten to run riot as Smith hits the bar and Ling clears off the line. Grecians' legend Kellow scores against his former side. Neville is City's hero as he scores and is then brought down by Smith. Crudgington saves McEwan's penalty but Pratt follows up.

20 A 27/12 NEWPORT — 5,154 — 17 — L — 0-2 — 9 — 23 — 0-1
Aldridge 14, 65
Ref: M Robinson

| Crudgington | Nisbet | Uzzell | Harrison | Smith L | Cooper* | Hodges | Rowe | Kellow* | Staniforth | Rogers |
| Kendall | Jones L | Matthewshon | Reid | Oakes | Boyle | Micallef | Aldridge | Chamberlain* | Carter | Lewis | Relish |

The dropped Tynan watches from the stand as his former goalscoring partner, John Aldridge, heads two more goals to take his season's tally to 19. Crudgington, making his 500th league appearance, acrobatically denies Aldridge a hat-trick. The ineffective Kellow is replaced by Phillips.

21 H 31/12 SOUTHEND — 3,978 — 14 — W — 4-0 — 16 — 26 — 1-0
Hodges 13, Clark 46(og), Tynan 57p, [Rogers 86]
Ref: V Callow

| Crudgington | Nisbet | Uzzell | Harrison | Smith L | Cooper | Hodges | Phillips | Tynan | Staniforth | Rogers |
| Cawston | Stead | Collins | Ferguson | Clark | Moody | Pountney | Kellock | McDonough | Fuccillo* | Shepherd |

The match bears no resemblance to the earlier dour FA Cup-ties between the two sides. Paul Clark scores the goal of the match, inexplicably smashing a shot past his own keeper. Transfer-seeking Tynan scores his first penalty for the club after Steve Collins bowled over Rogers.

22 A 2/1 WALSALL — 4,856 — 15 — L — 2-3 — 5 — 26 — 1-2
Smith L 36, Tynan 73 / Hart 6, Summerfield 18, Buckley 79
Ref: A Buksh

| Crudgington | Nisbet | Uzzell | Harrison | Smith L | Cooper | Hodges | Phillips | Tynan | Staniforth* | Rogers* |
| Green | Caswell | Mower | Shakespeare | Brazier | Hart | Rees* | Brown | O'Kelly | Summerfield | Childs | Buckley | Kellow |

Walsall are brimming with confidence after reaching the Milk Cup quarter-finals. Argyle are again caught out by a set-piece when Peter Hart heads in Kenny Mower's free-kick. Manager Alan Buckley scores within 75 seconds of coming on to thwart the Pilgrims spirited fightback.

23 H 21/1 LINCOLN — 3,804 — 15 — D — 2-2 — 12 — 27 — 1-0
Cooper 23, 52 / Thomas 57, Cockerill 73
Ref: J Martin

| Crudgington | Phillips | Uzzell | Nisbet | Smith L | Cooper | Hodges | Pearson | Tynan! | Staniforth | Rogers |
| Felgate | Simmonite | Neale | Cockerill | Walker | Saxby | Houghton | Thomas | Strodder* | Jack | Shipley | Burke |

Tynan sets a new but unwanted league record when he is red-carded after just three minutes for allegedly spitting at Alan Walker. David Felgate is penalised for handling outside his area and Cooper scores. The skipper then smashes in from 30 yards before Argyle's ten men tire.

CANON DIVISION 3   Manager: Bobby Moncur > John Hore   SEASON 1983-84

No	Date	1	2	3	4	5	6	7	8	9	10	11	12 sub used	Att	Pos	Pt	F-A	H-T	Scorers, Times, and Referees
24	H BURNLEY 4/2	Crudgington	Nisbet	Uzzell	Harrison	Smith L	Cooper	Hodges	Phillips	Pearson*	Staniforth	Rogers	Kellow	5,104	15 / 8	28	D 1-1	0-0	Staniforth 63 / Tueart 57 / Ref: C Downey
		Hansbury	*Scott*	*Donachie*	*Phelan*	*Overson*	*Flynn*	*Tueart*	*Dobson*	*Hamilton*	*Daley*	*Hutchison*							
25	A PRESTON 11/2	Crudgington	Nisbet	Uzzell	Harrison	Smith L	Cooper	Hodges	Phillips	Kellow*	Staniforth	Rogers	Rowe	4,370	17 / 16	28	L 1-2	0-2	Staniforth 87 / Twentyman 17, Naughton 22 / Ref: A Challinor
		Litchfield	*Clark*	*Himigan*	*Jones*	*Twentyman*	*Farrelly*	*Kelly*	*Walsh*	*Elliott*	*Naughton*	*Houghton**	*McAteer*						
26	H PORT VALE 14/2	Crudgington	Nisbet	Uzzell	Harrison	Smith L	Cooper	Hodges	Phillips	Tynan	Staniforth	Rogers		3,552	15 / 24	31	W 3-0	0-0	Staniforth 54, Tynan 76, 84 / Ref: L Burden
		Siddall	*Sproson*	*Shankland*	*Hunter*	*Ridley*	*Cegielski*	*Gore*	*Young*	*Henderson**	*O'Keefe*	*Fox*	*Bright*						
27	H HULL 25/2	Crudgington	Nisbet	Uzzell	Harrison	Smith L	Cooper	Hodges	Phillips	Tynan	Staniforth	Rogers		10,023	15 / 5	34	W 2-0	1-0	Tynan 35p, Phillips 68 / Ref: E Read
		Norman	*McNeil*	*Hollifield*	*Swann*	*Skipper*	*Booth*	*Marwood*	*McClaren*	*Whitehurst*	*Taylor*	*Roberts G*							
28	A SHEFFIELD UTD 28/2	Crudgington	Nisbet	Uzzell	Harrison	Ham	Cooper	Hodges*	Phillips	Tynan	Staniforth	Rogers		9,541		34	L 0-2	0-1	Charles 37, Morris 67 / Ref: R Bridges
		Tomlinson	*Heffernan*	*Bolton*	*Arnott*	*Stancliffe*	*Charles*	*Morris*	*Atkins*	*Edwards*	*McHale*	*Garner*	*Rowe*						
29	A BRISTOL ROV 3/3	Crudgington	Nisbet	Uzzell	Harrison	Ham	Cooper	Hodges	Phillips	Tynan	Kellow	Rogers		5,619	17 / 5	34	L 0-2	0-1	Bannon 19, White 69 / Ref: H King
		Cashley	*Slatter*	*Williams B*	*Pulis*	*Parkin*	*McCaffrey*	*Holloway*	*Bater*	*White*	*Bannon**	*Williams D*	*Randall*						
30	H BRENTFORD 6/3	Crudgington	Nisbet	Uzzell	Harrison	Ham	Cooper	Hodges	Phillips	Tynan	Cassidy	Rogers		4,332		35	D 1-1	0-0	Phillips 59 / Hurlock 76 / Ref: T Spencer
		Roche	*Wilkins*	*Price*	*Fisher*	*Roberts P*	*Gray*	*Kamara*	*Finney*	*Joseph*	*Cassells**	*Roberts G*	*Mahoney*						
31	H BOURNEMOUTH 17/3	Crudgington	Nisbet	Uzzell	Harrison	Smith L	Cooper	Hodges	Phillips	Tynan	Staniforth	Rogers		7,235	17 / 18	38	W 1-0	1-0	Staniforth 12 / Ref: R Milford
		Leigh	*Nightingale*	*Sulley*	*Beck*	*Brown*	*Brignull*	*O'Driscoll*	*Savage*	*Rafferty*	*Williams*	*Graham*							
32	H MILLWALL 20/3	Crudgington	Nisbet	Uzzell	Harrison	Smith L	Cooper	Hodges	Phillips	Tynan	Rowe	Rogers		4,507		38	L 0-1	0-0	Nutton 66 / Ref: J Bray
		Sansome	*Stevens*	*Stride*	*Lovell*	*Nutton*	*Cusack*	*McLeary*	*Neal*	*White*	*Otulakowski*	*Bremner*							
33	A OXFORD 24/3	Crudgington	Nisbet	Hardwick	Harrison	Smith L*	Cooper	Rowe	Phillips	Tynan	Chamberlain	Rogers	Ham	7,777	17 / 1	38	L 0-5	0-2	McDonald 11p, 64p, Biggins 33, 50, 55 / Ref: A Ward
		Hinshelwood	*McDonald*	*Brock**	*Todd*	*Shotton*	*Jones*	*Biggins*	*Vinter*	*Hebberd*	*Rhodes-Brown*	*Phillips*							
34	H ROTHERHAM 30/3	Crudgington	Nisbet	Smith M	Harrison	Smith L	Cooper	Hodges	Phillips	Tynan	Staniforth	Rogers		4,736	17 / 23	39	D 1-1	0-0	Tynan 65 / Simmons 90 / Ref: D Hedges
		Mimms	*Forrest*	*Crosby*	*Trusson*	*Johnson*	*Pickering*	*Eley*	*Birch*	*Simmons*	*Mitchell*	*Kilmore*							

24 — H BURNLEY. A highly entertaining match with Burnley's experienced side producing some flowing football. Smith miskicks on the edge of the box and Hamilton swings a shot against the crossbar. Former England man Dennis Tueart reacts quickest. Staniforth shows great opportunism to level.

25 — A PRESTON. Preston ignore their dire financial plight to leap-frog above Argyle in the league. Only a council grant has saved them from closure and the second half is delayed by four minutes to allow Tom Finney to launch an appeal. Poor defensive work again proves to be Argyle's downfall.

26 — H PORT VALE. The match proves a useful boost ahead of the forthcoming FA Cup fifth-round match. Vale show why they are at the bottom. Tynan looks refreshed after a two-match suspension and demonstrates his finishing ability. Crudgington spends a quiet 32nd birthday in the Argyle goal.

27 — H HULL. The attendance is inflated as many people pay twice in order to obtain vouchers for FA Cup quarter-final tickets. A revitalised Tynan finds the net from the spot after he was impeded by Swann. After Phillips goal, Tynan is brought down by Norman (86) but his second penalty is weak.

28 — A SHEFFIELD UTD. Watching Derby manager Peter Taylor must be pleased with what he saw as his cup opponents show little to fear. Twenty-seven goal striker Keith Edwards is kept quiet but the equally dangerous Colin Morris puts the game beyond Argyle after Charles heads his first of the season.

29 — A BRISTOL ROV. Martin Harvey is left in charge with Hore away watching Derby. Argyle's cup form continues to elude them in the league. Ham, in for the injured Smith, makes a hash of a clearance to let in Paul Bannon. Crudgington punches a cross back to Holloway who sets up Steve White.

30 — H BRENTFORD. Watford loanees, Neil Price and Francis Cassidy, make their only Argyle appearances. Three regulars are missing to protect them from injury before the big cup game but two more home points are dropped to leave the Pilgrims looking over their shoulder towards the relegation zone.

31 — H BOURNEMOUTH. Back to the important issue of gaining league points. Staniforth scores with a piercing shot. Billy Rafferty brings the best out of Crudgington on two occasions and also sends a header against the bar. Even in mid-March fans are buying season tickets to guarantee a semi-final ticket.

32 — H MILLWALL. A flu virus sweeps Home Park affecting five of the sixteen players available. Lions' boss George Graham is not impressed with his side's display, despite them gaining their first away win of the campaign. Mike Nutton scores the only goal after being sent clear by Kevin Bremner.

33 — A OXFORD. With the flu epidemic spreading, the Greens field an even weaker side. Part-timer Mark Smith endures a nightmare debut and concedes one of the penalties. Lindsay Smith concedes the other. Steve Biggins scores a 22-minute hat-trick which includes Oxford's 100th goal of the season.

34 — H ROTHERHAM. Tynan scores after collecting a pass from Staniforth and is unfortunate not to complete a hat-trick when the woodwork denies him twice. He at least avoids a booking which would have seen him miss the semi-final. Staniforth needs stitches after an ugly challenge by Mike Trusson.

35 A WIGAN 3/4 — 1-1 — 40 — 2,756

| Crudgington | Nisbet | Smith M | Harrison | Smith L | Cooper | Smith L | Hodges | Phillips | Tynan | Staniforth | Rogers | Rowe |
| Tunks | Cribley | Aspinall | Kelly | Walsh | Methven | Langley | Johnson | Phillips | Barrow | Lowe | Butler |

Tynan 86 / Johnson 11 — Ref: J Lovatt

Argyle gain their first away point for five months. Despite his lean start to the season, Tynan looks like reaching the 20 goal mark again. Lowe is fouled by Crudgington two yards outside the area but a penalty is given (88). Justice is done when Johnson crashes the kick against the bar.

---

36 A SCUNTHORPE 7/4 — 0-1 — 17 L 21 — 40 — 2,780

| Crudgington | Nisbet | Uzzell | Harrison | Smith L | Cooper | Hodges | Phillips | Staniforth* | Tynan | Rogers | Chamberlain |
| Neenan | Longden | Pointon | Matthews | Green | Pratley | Brolly | Cammack | Bell | Whitehead | Graham |

Bell 29, Brolly 79, Cammack 89 — Ref: L Dilkes

Fellow strugglers Scunthorpe drag Argyle further into relegation danger with an emphatic victory. Uzzell's weak challenge is punished by Derek Bell. Dead-ball specialist Mike Brolly somehow shoots through an eight-man wall and Steve Cammack heads in from under the bar.

---

37 H WIMBLEDON 10/4 — 1-2 — 18 L 2 — 40 — 6,471

| Crudgington | Nisbet | Rowe | Harrison | Smith L | Cooper | Hodges | Phillips | Staniforth* | Tynan | Rogers | Chamberlain |
| Beasant | Peters | Winterburn | Galliers | Morris | Hatter | Evans | Ketteridge | Cork | Gage* | Hodges | Fishenden |

Tynan 43p / Hatter 67p, Cork 81 — Ref: K Cooper

Half-price admission tempts a few more 'fans' from their armchairs. With one eye on Saturday's semi-final, Argyle are no match for Dave Bassett's high-flyers. Steve Hatter concedes a penalty and scores one after Smith clatters Alan Cork. Nisbet turns Cork's shot into his own net.

---

38 A BOLTON 16/4 — 1-2 — 40 — 3,266

| Crudgington | Nisbet | Uzzell | Harrison | Smith L | Cooper | Hodges | Phillips | Staniforth* | Tynan | Rogers | Chamberlain |
| Farnworth | Borrows | Deakin | Joyce | McElhinney | Valentine | Thompson | Chandler | Caldwell | Whatmore | Bell |

Tynan 59p / Chandler 39p, Bell 68 — Ref: K Redfern

The Bolton public are clearly not impressed with the visit of the FA Cup semi-finalists, which attracts Wanderers' lowest crowd for 51 years. Hore holds a 50 minute inquest after the match into another inept display. Graham Bell sweeps the winner after a penalty for each side.

---

39 H NEWPORT 20/4 — 0-1 — 19 L 10 — 40 — 7,654

| Crudgington | Nisbet | Uzzell | Harrison | Smith L | Cooper | Hodges | Phillips | Tynan | Staniforth | Rogers |
| Kendall | Jones V | Relish | Reid | Oakes | Boyle | Lilygreen* | Matthewson | Carter | Randall | Williams | Green |

Green 85 — Ref: T Holbrook

A shirt-sleeved crowd see County gain the three point with a classic smash and grab act. On the defensive for most of the game, substitute Phil Green lobs Crudgington after an error gives the ball away. Mark Kendall is booked three times from time for kicking the ball into the crowd.

---

40 A EXETER 21/4 — 1-1 — 19 D 24 — 41 — 6,870

| Crudgington | Nisbet | Uzzell | Harrison | Smith L | Cooper | Hodges | Phillips | Tynan* | Staniforth | Rogers | Chamberlain |
| Crabtree | Kirkup | Viney | O'Connor | Webster | Marker | Ling* | Pratt | Harrower | McDonough | Howarth |

Staniforth 62 / Pratt 9 — Ref: G Napthine

Dan MacAuley hires a plane to 'buzz' the ground before the match to support his takeover bid for City. A point each does little for either side. Staniforth is the first Argyle player other than Tynan to score a league goal for nine matches. City have now gone 17 games without winning.

---

41 A WIMBLEDON 28/4 — 0-1 — 20 L 2 — 41 — 3,706

| Crudgington | Nisbet | Uzzell | Harrison | Smith L | Cooper | Rowe | Phillips | Chamberlain | Staniforth | Rogers* | Hodges |
| Beasant | Peters | Winterburn | Galliers | Morris | Hatter | Evans | Ketteridge | Cork | Gage | Thomas |

Winterburn 3 — Ref: A Gunn

A good evening for Nigel Winterburn as he wins the Dons' player of the year award and scores his first goal for the club. Argyle come back after this early setback to force eight corners in the opening twelve minutes. Staniforth's shot cannons off an unwitting Dave Beasant's legs.

---

42 A GILLINGHAM 1/5 — 1-2 — 19 L — 41 — 3,103

| Crudgington | Nisbet | Uzzell | Harrison | Rowe | Cooper | Hodges | Phillips | Swiggs | Chamberlain | Staniforth | Rogers* |
| Fry | Sage | Sitton | Bruce | Handford | Shaw | Cochrane | Musker | Leslie | Mehmet | Cascarino* | Weatherly |

Chamberlain 56 / Leslie 15, Shaw 78 — Ref: K Salmon

Phillips is absent, winning his first Welsh cap against England. Local boy Bradley Swiggs is drafted in. John Leslie gives the Gills the lead, knocking on Steve Bruce's long throw. Chamberlain claims his first Pilgrims goal. Irish international Terry Cochrane sets up Shaw's winner.

---

43 H WALSALL 5/5 — 3-1 — 20 W 6 — 44 — 5,144

| Crudgington | Nisbet | Uzzell | Harrison | Smith L | Cooper | Rowe | Phillips | Chamberlain | Staniforth* | Rogers | Hodges |
| Godden | Hart | Mower | Shakespeare | Brazier | Hawker | Rees ! | Bamber* | Kelly | Preece | O'Kelly | Summerfield |

Rogers 59, Staniforth 82, 90p / Kelly 56 — Ref: J Martin

Mr Martin, who sent Tynan off after three minutes earlier in the season, is at it again, dismissing Mark Rees for two yellows (17). Crudgington is the hero, saving O'Kelly's penalty (45) after Harrison brings down Dave Bamber. Argyle make the extra man count in the second period.

---

44 A SOUTHEND 7/5 — 1-1 — 20 D 22 — 45 — 3,540

| Crudgington | Nisbet | Uzzell | Harrison | Smith L | Cooper | Rowe | Phillips | Chamberlain | Staniforth | Rogers | Hodges |
| Pritchard | Stead* | Collins | Phillips | May | Whymark | Clark | Kellock | Shepherd | Fuccillo | Rogers | Gymer |

Chamberlain 8 / May 86 — Ref: J Ashworth

Cooper celebrates his 23rd birthday by sending over the corner to supply Chamberlain with Argyle's opener. Bobby Moore's side are even more desperate for points than Argyle. Warren May's goal from Alan Rogers' cross is probably not enough to save them from the drop.

---

45 H BRADFORD C 9/5 — 3-0 — 19 W 7 — 48 — 5,744

| Crudgington | Nisbet | Uzzell | Harrison | Smith L | Cooper | Rowe* | Phillips | Chamberlain | Staniforth | Rogers | Hodges |
| McManus | Abbott | Withe | McCall | Clegg | Jackson | Haire | Hawley* | Campbell | Yorath | Ellis | Gray |

Smith L 12, Staniforth 62, Hodges 66 — Ref: R Lewis

The Greens find form when it matters to virtually secure their Division Three future. Smith finds himself all alone to shoot home from Nisbet's free-kick. Eric McManus is in top form but can do little to stop Staniforth adding to the lead and Hodges from crashing home from 20 yards.

---

46 H ORIENT 12/5 — 2-1 — 19 W 11 — 51 — 7,664

| Crudgington | Nisbet | Uzzell | Harrison | Smith L | Cooper | Hodges | Phillips | Chamberlain | Staniforth* | Rogers | Swiggs |
| Shoemake | Hales | Wilkins | Corbett | Cunningham | Banfield | Silkman* | Brooks | Sussex | Godfrey | McNeil | Harvey |

Chamberlain 29, Smith L 31, Hodges 55 / Sussex 25 — Ref: A Seville

Scenes more reminiscent of promotion greet the final whistle as the drop is avoided. Andy Sussex gives Orient the lead with their only chance of the match. Two quick responses follow and Hodges second half goal seals a crucial victory. The players are mobbed as they leave the pitch.

Home Average 5,336
Away Average 4,703

CANON DIVISION 3 (CUP-TIES)   Manager: Bobby Moncur > John Hore   SEASON 1983-84

Milk Cup

Milk Cup	Att		F-A	H-T	Scorers, Times, and Referees	1	2	3	4	5	6	7	8	9	10	11	12 sub used
1:1 A SWINDON 30/8	3,343	4:	L 0-1	0-0	Hockaday 55 Ref: D Vickers	Crudgington	Nisbet	Uzzell	Harrison	Smith L	Forbes	Hodges	Phillips	Tynan	Staniforth	Rogers	
						Allan	*Henry*	*Bailie*	*Emmanuel*	*Gray*	*Graham*	*Hockaday*	*Richardson*	*Rowland*	*Mayes*	*Nelson*	

The start of the match is delayed by six minutes as Jimmy Allan's jersey clashes with Argyle's new all-green shirts. Andy Rowland twice goes close and Phillips grazes the bar just before half-time. Summer signing Dave Hockaday nets the winner, heading in Garry Nelson's free-kick.

Milk Cup	Att		F-A	H-T	Scorers, Times, and Referees	1	2	3	4	5	6	7	8	9	10	11	12 sub used
1:2 H SWINDON 12/9	20	4:20	W 4-1	1-0	Smith L 16, Staniforth 56, Tynan 69, Nelson 78 [Nisbet 77] Ref: T Holbrook (Argyle won 4-2 on aggregate)	Crudgington	Nisbet	Uzzell	Harrison	Smith L	Forbes	Hodges	Rowe	Tynan	Staniforth	Rogers	
						Allan	*Bailie*	*Baddeley*	*Emmanuel*	*Henry*	*Graham*	*Batty***	*Rowland*	*Quinn*	*Nelson*	*Barnard*	

Argyle emphatically progress to the next round as they finally find their shooting boots. Smith gives them the lead when Staniforth is off the pitch receiving treatment. Tynan gets his first goal for the club with a nice header. Garry Nelson drives home from 20 yards but it is all too late.

Milk Cup	Att		F-A	H-T	Scorers, Times, and Referees	1	2	3	4	5	6	7	8	9	10	11	12 sub used
2:1 H ARSENAL 4/10	18	1:12	D 1-1	1-0	Nisbet 22, Rix 59 Ref: T Spencer	Crudgington	Nisbet	Uzzell	Harrison	Smith L	Cooper	Hodges	Rowe	Tynan	Staniforth	Rogers*	Phillips
						Jennings	*Robson*	*Sansom*	*Whyte*	*O'Leary*	*Hill*	*Sunderland*	*Davis*	*Woodcock***	*Nicholas*	*Rix*	*Talbot*

Terry Neill's collection of internationals are matched all the way. Cooper's corner finds Nisbet who hits a stinging 25-yarder past Pat Jennings. Rogers goes to hospital for x-rays on an ankle injury. Graham Rix saves the Gunners' blushes when he combines well with Charlie Nicholas.

Milk Cup	Att		F-A	H-T	Scorers, Times, and Referees	1	2	3	4	5	6	7	8	9	10	11	12 sub used
2:2 A ARSENAL 25/10	16	1:12	L 0-1	0-1	Sunderland 43 Ref: A Robinson (Argyle lost 1-2 on aggregate)	Crudgington	Nisbet	Uzzell	Harrison	Smith L	Cooper	Hodges	Rowe	Tynan	Staniforth	Phillips*	Pearson
						Jennings	*Robson*	*Sansom*	*Whyte*	*O'Leary*	*Hill*	*Sunderland*	*Davis*	*Woodcock*	*Nicholas*	*Rix*	

Terry Neill lavishes praise on Argyle after another fighting display. Alan Sunderland makes the breakthrough when he seizes on Rix's blocked shot. Substitute Pearson is so nearly the hero when his near-post flick is turned away for a corner by the outstretched leg of Pat Jennings.

FA Cup

FA Cup	Att		F-A	H-T	Scorers, Times, and Referees	1	2	3	4	5	6	7	8	9	10	11	12 sub used
1 A SOUTHEND 19/11	9	17	D 0-0	0-0	Ref: M Bodenham	Crudgington	Nisbet	Uzzell	Harrison	Smith L	Cooper	Hodges	Rowe	Tynan	Kellow	Phillips	
						Keeley	*Stead*	*Collins*	*Pennyfather*	*Turner*	*Moody*	*Ferguson*	*Kellock***	*McDonough*	*Shepherd*	*Phillips*	*Pountney*

A disallowed penalty appeal provides the main talking point. Hodges beats the offside trap but, with only John Keeley to beat, Chris Turner tackles him from behind. The play is scrappy but Argyle are happy to take a draw from Roots Hall which has not been a happy hunting ground.

FA Cup	Att		F-A	H-T	Scorers, Times, and Referees	1	2	3	4	5	6	7	8	9	10	11	12 sub used
1R H SOUTHEND 22/11	9	17	W 2-0 aet	0-0	Stead 93(og), Tynan 117 Ref: M Bodenham	Crudgington	Nisbet	Uzzell	Harrison	Smith L	Cooper	Hodges	Rowe	Tynan	Kellow	Phillips	
						Keeley	*Stead*	*Collins*	*Pennyfather***	*Turner*	*Moody*	*Ferguson*	*Pountney*	*McDonough*	*Shepherd*	*Phillips*	*Clark*

These two well-matched sides battle out another stalemate for the first 90 minutes. Disaster then strikes the U's as Micky Stead, under no pressure, miscues a clearance which finds the corner of his own net. Tynan gets to Phillips free-kick first to send the Pilgrims into round two.

FA Cup	Att		F-A	H-T	Scorers, Times, and Referees	1	2	3	4	5	6	7	8	9	10	11	12 sub used
2 H BARKING 10/12	19	L:17	W 2-1	1-0	Rowe 30, Smith L 86, Groom 74 Ref: T Spencer	Crudgington	Nisbet	Uzzell	Ham	Smith L	Phillips	Hodges	Rowe	Tynan*	Kellow	Rogers	Staniforth
						Root	*Wright*	*Watts*	*Cooper*	*Groom*	*Reeves*	*Shirt*	*Kean*	*Armstrong***	*Tappin*	*Crown*	*Ralph*

Argyle find it difficult to raise their game against the part-timers, who have won only four games this season. Rowe's sweetly struck 25-yard shot fails to ignite the home side. Electrician Andy Groom equalises from the edge of the box. Smith's winner goes in via a Barking shoulder.

FA Cup	Att		F-A	H-T	Scorers, Times, and Referees	1	2	3	4	5	6	7	8	9	10	11	12 sub used
3 H NEWPORT 7/1	15	10	D 2-2	0-1	Hodges 61, Tynan 90p, Aldridge 11, 84 Ref: D Reeves	Crudgington	Nisbet	Uzzell	Harrison	Smith L	Cooper	Hodges	Phillips	Tynan	Staniforth	Rogers	
						Kendall	*Jones*	*Relish*	*Reid*	*Boyle!*	*Matthewson*	*Micallef*	*Aldridge*	*Chamberlain*	*Carter*	*Lewis*	

Argyle try their best to gift Newport the tie with some defensive howlers. Rogers is robbed in his own area for the opener and Uzzell's back-pass lets Aldridge in again. Hodges is fouled by Carter in injury-time and Tynan slots home the penalty. Terry Boyle is sent off in the tunnel.

FA Cup	Att		F-A	H-T	Scorers, Times, and Referees	1	2	3	4	5	6	7	8	9	10	11	12 sub used
3R A NEWPORT 10/1	15	10	W 1-0	0-0	Rogers 84 Ref: D Reeves	Crudgington	Phillips	Uzzell	Harrison	Smith L	Cooper	Hodges	Forbes*	Tynan	Staniforth	Rogers	Pearson
						Kendal	*Jones*	*Relish*	*Reid*	*Boyle*	*Matthewson***	*Micallef*	*Aldridge*	*Chamberlain*	*Carter*	*Lewis*	*Woodruff*

A piece of quick thinking by Staniforth sees the Pilgrims through to the fourth round. On a rain-soaked pitch the home side have more of the play but Argyle defend resolutely. With extra-time approaching, Staniforth dummies Phillips' cross and Rogers appears in the middle to score.

FA Cup	Att		F-A	H-T	Scorers, Times, and Referees	1	2	3	4	5	6	7	8	9	10	11	12 sub used
4 H DARLINGTON 28/1	15	4:19	W 2-1	1-1	Uzzell 40, Staniforth 81, Todd 28 Ref: R Milford	Crudgington	Nisbet	Uzzell	Harrison	Smith L	Phillips	Hodges	Phillips	Tynan	Staniforth	Rogers	
						Barber	*Craggs*	*Johnson*	*Honour***	*Smith*	*Barton*	*Cartwright*	*Todd*	*Gilbert*	*Walsh*	*McLean*	*Davies*

Attempts by goal-shy Staniforth to change his luck by wearing new boots pay off as he rescues Argyle from another replay and leaves Darlo boss Cyril Knowles in despair. A rare Uzzell goal cancels out Todd's opener. The Pilgrims move into round five for the first time since 1953.

Match results

Rnd	H/A	Opponent	Date	Pos	Res	Score	HT	Scorers	Att	Ref
	A	WEST BROM	18/2		W		0-0	Tynan 38	23,795	Ref: P Willis
QF	H	DERBY	10/3	17	D	0-0	0-0		34,365	Ref: B Stevens
QF	A	DERBY	14/3	17	W	1-0	1-0	Rogers 18	26,906	Ref: B Stevens
SF	N	WATFORD	14/4	20	L	0-1	0-1	Reilly 13	43,858 (at Villa Park)	Ref: J Worrall

Line-ups

v West Brom — Crudgington, Nisbet, Uzzell, Harrison, Smith L, Cooper, Hodges, Phillips, Tynan, Staniforth, Rogers
Opponents: Barron, Whitehead, Statham, Zondervan, McNaught, Bennett, Jol, Thompson, Perry*, MacKenzie, Morley / Luke

v Derby (10/3) — Crudgington, Nisbet, Uzzell, Harrison, Smith L, Cooper, Hodges, Phillips, Tynan, Staniforth, Rogers
Opponents: Cherry, Barton, Buckley, Gemmill, Burns, Powell, Futcher, Davison, Wilson, Hooks*, Robertson / Watson

v Derby (14/3) — Crudgington, Nisbet, Uzzell, Harrison, Smith L, Cooper, Hodges, Phillips, Tynan, Staniforth, Rogers
Opponents: Cherry, Barton, Buckley, Gemmill, Burns, Powell, Futcher, Davison*, Wilson, Plummer, Robertson / Watson

v Watford (14/4) — Crudgington, Nisbet, Uzzell, Harrison, Smith L, Cooper, Hodges, Phillips, Tynan, Staniforth, Rogers
Opponents: Sherwood, Bardsley, Price, Taylor, Terry*, Sinnott, Callaghan, Johnston, Reilly, Rostron, Barnes / Jobson

Match notes

Tynan comes off the transfer list to send 6,000 travelling Pilgrim fans home ecstatic. A former Pilgrim, Paul Barron, has no chance as Tynan volleys past a crowd of defenders. The victory is particularly sweet for Nisbet who was previously released by Baggies' manager Johnny Giles.

The shots on target count tells its own story. Argyle 12, Derby 2. Staniforth comes agonisingly close when Cherry finger-tips a save onto a post. The ball rebounds along the line and hits the other upright. Surely Derby cannot play as badly at the Baseball Ground in the replay.

Rogers scores one of the most famous goals in the club's history when he floats in a corner which eludes Steve Cherry's grasp. The ball strikes the underside of the bar and goes in. A small dog delays play for two minutes. Peter Taylor storms out without talking to his players or press.

Devon and Cornwall are deserted as 24,000 fans travel to Villa Park. Lanky George Reilly shatters the Wembley dream when he heads home John Barnes' wicked cross. Hodges' shot in the dying seconds looks destined for the corner net until a divot diverts the ball agonisingly wide.

Final League Table

Pos	Team	P	Home W	D	L	F	A	Away W	D	L	F	A	Pts
1	Oxford	46	17	5	1	58	22	11	6	6	33	28	95
2	Wimbledon	46	15	5	3	58	35	11	4	8	39	41	87
3	Sheffield Utd	46	14	7	2	56	18	10	4	9	30	35	83
4	Hull	46	16	5	2	42	11	7	9	7	29	27	83
5	Bristol Rov	46	16	4	3	47	21	4	9	10	21	33	79
6	Walsall	46	14	4	5	44	22	8	5	10	24	39	75
7	Bradford C	46	11	9	3	46	30	9	2	12	27	35	71
8	Gillingham	46	13	4	6	50	29	7	6	10	24	40	70
9	Millwall	46	16	4	3	42	18	2	9	12	29	47	67
10	Bolton	46	13	6	4	36	17	5	6	12	20	43	64
11	Orient	46	13	5	5	40	27	5	4	14	31	54	63
12	Burnley	46	12	5	6	52	25	4	9	10	24	36	62
13	Newport	46	11	9	3	35	27	5	5	13	23	48	62
14	Lincoln	46	11	4	8	42	29	6	11	7	17	33	61
15	Wigan	46	11	5	7	26	18	5	8	10	20	38	61
16	Preston	46	12	5	6	42	27	3	6	14	24	39	56
17	Bournemouth	46	11	5	7	38	27	5	2	16	25	46	55
18	Rotherham	46	10	5	8	29	17	5	5	14	28	47	54
19	PLYMOUTH	46	11	8	4	41	30	3	7	13	28	49	51
20	Brentford	46	8	9	6	41	38	3	7	13	28	49	49
21	Scunthorpe	46	9	9	5	40	31	0	10	13	14	42	46
22	Southend	46	8	9	6	34	24	2	5	16	21	52	44
23	Port Vale	46	10	4	9	33	29	1	6	16	18	54	43
24	Exeter	46	4	8	11	27	39	2	7	14	23	45	33
		1104	286	142	124	996	590	124	142	286	590	996	1514

Appearances & Goals

Player	Lge	Sub	LC	Sub	FAC	Sub	Goals Lge	LC	FAC	Tot
Cassidy, Francis	1									
Chamberlain, Neville	7	4					3			3
Cooper, Leigh	43		3		9		3			3
Crudgington, Geoff	46		4		10					
Forbes, Dick	3		1		1					
Ham, Mike	5	1			1					
Harrison, Chris	44		4		9					
Hodges, Kevin	41	2	4		10		4		1	5
Kellow, Tony	8	2			3		2			2
Nisbet, Gordon	44		4		9		4		2	6
Pearson, Ian	5	3			1	1	1			1
Phillips, David	39	3	2	1	10		6			6
Price, Neil	1									
Rogers, Andy	36	1	3		8		4		2	6
Rowe, Mark	24	4	3		3		1		1	2
Smith, Lindsay	42		4		10		4	1	1	6
Smith, Mark	3									
Staniforth, Gordon	36	3	4		7	1	11	1	1	13
Swiggs, Bradley	1	1								
Tynan, Tommy	35		4		10		12	1	3	16
Uzzell, John	42		4		10		1			1
(own-goals)							2		1	3
21 players used	506	24	44	2	110	2	56	5	11	72

Odds & ends

Double wins: (2) Hull, Port Vale.

Double defeats: (4) Millwall, Newport, Sheffield Utd, Wimbledon.

Won from behind: (4) Hull, Orient, Oxford, Walsall.

Lost from in front: (4) Bournemouth, Burnley, Orient, Wimbledon.

High spots: Reaching semi-finals of the FA Cup for the first time in the club's history.

Holding Arsenal to a draw in the Milk Cup first leg.

The signing of Tommy Tynan from Newport.

Winning three of the final four league matches to avoid relegation.

Low spots: Poor league form despite cup success.

Departure of Bobby Moncur as manager over differences of opinion in club policy.

Dismal run of only one win in 15 matches in late season.

Player of the Year: Gordon Staniforth.

Ever presents: (1) Geoff Crudgington.

Hat-tricks: (0).

Leading scorer: Tommy Tynan (16).

CANON DIVISION 3

Manager: John Hore > Dave Smith — SEASON 1984-85

No		Date	Att / Pos	Pt	H-T	F-A	Scorers, Times, and Referees	1	2	3	4	5	6	7	8	9	10	11	12 sub used
1	A	25/8	6,613 / —	D 1	1-0	1-1	BURNLEY. Hodges 33 / Taylor 83 / Ref: K Redfern	Crudgington / Hansbury	Nisbet / Scott	Uzzell / Hampton	Harrison / Phelan	Goodyear / Overson	Burrows / Hird	Hodges / Grewcock	Cooper / Powell	Tynan / Taylor	Staniforth / Biggins	Coughlin / Hutchison	Rogers
2	H	1/9	5,509 / 19	L 2	1-0	1-2	READING. Staniforth 40 / Horrix 51, Senior 87 / Ref: K Cooper	Crudgington / Judge	Nisbet / Richardson	Uzzell / White	Harrison / Beavon	Goodyear / Hicks	Burrows / Wood	Hodges / Duncan	Cooper / Horrix	Tynan / Senior	Staniforth / Sanchez	Coughlin* / Crown	Rogers
3	A	8/9	2,171 / 18	D 2	0-2	2-2	LINCOLN. Hodges 67, Tynan 81 / Hobson 15, Turner 43 / Ref: P Vanes	Crudgington / Felgate	Nisbet / Redfearn	Uzzell / McCarrick	Harrison / Walker	Goodyear / Strodder	Burrows / Thompson	Hodges / Shipley	Cooper / Turner	Tynan / Hobson	Staniforth / Thomas	Coughlin / Mair	
4	H	15/9	4,933 / 17	D 3	0-0	0-0	BOURNEMOUTH. / Ref: H King	Crudgington / Leigh	Nisbet / Nightingale	Uzzell / Sulley	Harrison / Beck	Goodyear / Brown	Burrows / Savage	Hodges / O'Driscoll	Cooper* / Morrell	Tynan / Rafferty	Staniforth / Thompson	Coughlin / Schiavi	Rowe
5	H	18/9	4,537 / 17	D 4	0-1	1-1	YORK. Staniforth 55p / Houchen 30 / Ref: B Stevens	Crudgington / Jones	Nisbet / Evans	Uzzell / Hay	Harrison / Stragia	Goodyear / MacPhail	Burrows / Haslegrave	Hodges / Ford	Cooper* / Houchen	Tynan / Walwyn	Staniforth / Byrne	Coughlin / Nicholson*	Rogers / Hood
6	A	22/9	3,876 / 21	L 4	1-3	2-7	BOLTON. Coughlin 31, Tynan 69 [Oghani 45] / Joyce 7, Cald'l 16, 57, 87, Ch'ler 62p, 88, Farnworth / Ref: A Saunders	Crudgington / Farnworth	Nisbet / Borrows	Uzzell / Phillips	Harrison* / Joyce	Goodyear / McElhinney	Burrows / Valentine	Hodges / Thompson	Cooper / Chandler	Tynan / Oghani	Staniforth / Caldwell	Coughlin / Bell	Rogers
7	H	29/9	4,258 / 16	W 7	1-2	6-4	PRESTON. Tyn'16, Hod'59,86, Cough'63, Star'84p, Clark 37, 49, Kelly 43, 82p [English 89] / Ref: R Groves	Philip / Litchfield	Nisbet / Jones	Rowe* / Rudge	Harrison* / Twentyman	Goodyear / Booth !	Burrows / Clark !	Hodges / Kelly	Cooper / Farrelly	Tynan / Houghton	Staniforth / Naughton	Coughlin / Houston	English
8	A	2/10	4,442 / 18	D 8	2-0	3-3	GILLINGHAM. Tynan 8, Nisbet 12, Rogers 48 / Oakes 53, Cascarino 82, Hinnigan 84 / Ref: K Miller	Philip / Hillyard	Nisbet / Hinnigan	Rowe / Sage	Harrison / Oakes	Goodyear / Weatherly*	Burrows / Shaw	Hodges* / Musker	Rogers / Johnson	Tynan / Leslie	Staniforth / Mehmet	Coughlin / Cascarino	English / Shiners
9	H	6/10	5,705 / 22	L 8	0-1	0-1	HULL. / Flounders 38 / Ref: T Spencer	Sealey* / Norman	Nisbet / Roberts D	Rowe* / Pearson	Harrison / McClaren	Goodyear / Skipper	Burrows / McEwan	Hodges / Flounders	Rogers / Horton	Tynan / Whitehurst	Staniforth / Askew	Coughlin / Roberts G	English
10	A	13/10	11,316 / 23	L 8	1-0	1-3	DERBY. Tynan 38 / Buckley 58p, Davison 60, 81 / Ref: N Midgley	Sealey / Burridge	Nisbet / Palmer	Rowe / Buckley	Cooper / Powell	Goodyear / Streete	Burrows / Burns	Hodges / Taylor	Rogers* / Wilson	Tynan / Davison	Staniforth / Hooks	Coughlin / Robertson	English
11	H	20/10	4,067 / 18	W 11	0-0	1-0	ROTHERHAM. Rogers 66 / Ref: D Letts	Sealey / Mimms	Nisbet / Forrest	Uzzell / Mitchell	Harrison / Trusson	Rowe / Crosby	Burrows / Pickering	Hodges / Birch	Rogers / Gooding	Tynan / Dungworth*	Staniforth / Simmons	Coughlin / Kilmore	English / Rhodes

Match reports

1. BURNLEY — A baking hot day plays an important part in Argyle's fortunes. Hodges rounds Hansbury and his shot eludes two defenders on the line. Overson hoists a hopeful high ball into the area. Crudgington is blinded by the sun and former West Ham FA Cup hero, Alan Taylor takes advantage.

2. READING — Hore admits his side needs strengthening after another poor display. Steve Wood's trailing leg upends Hodges and although Alan Judge blocks Staniforth's spot-kick he follows up to net the rebound. Dean Horrix and the prolific Trevor Senior make it two wins out of two for the Royals.

3. LINCOLN — The ref ignores a linesman's flag to allow Hobson to open the scoring. Tynan fluffs a penalty which he hits weakly straight at Felgate. Hodges is not told that his house had been broken into on Friday evening until after the match. Hore is elsewhere spying on potential new signings.

4. BOURNEMOUTH — The match is dire without one single incident worthy of comment. Hore's quest for new players takes him to a Friday night match at Doncaster to tie up a deal with striker Alan Brown. The Argyle boss cannot believe his luck when his intended target suffers a broken leg against Lincoln.

5. YORK — York old boy Staniforth causes the most problems. He is brought down with a 'professional foul' by Jones who avoids being red-carded. Keith Houchen opens the scoring although Keith Walwyn claims he has the final touch. Staniforth's spot-kick levels after Hodges is brought down.

6. BOLTON — A comedy of errors. Crudgington fly-kicks at Joyce's shot and misses. Hodges' back-pass sets up Caldwell. Nisbet handles for Chandler's penalty. At 5-2 Crudgington injures a hand and is replaced by Nisbet, who sinks to his knees to stop Chandler's shot and completely misses it.

7. PRESTON — On loan Tom English comes off the bench to alter the course of the match. Two-goal Jonathan Clark is sent off for foul language and player-coach Tommy Booth follows him for persistent misconduct. At 4-4, English is brought down for a penalty and then scores another himself.

8. GILLINGHAM — Another thriller means Argyle's last four matches have yielded 30 goals. At 3-0 the Pilgrims appear to be cruising. All three came from the edge of the 18-yard box. Keith Oakes sets off a remarkable recovery. Philip drops a cross to Cascarino. Joe Hinnigan heads in from 15 yards.

9. HULL — Much-travelled Les Sealey arrives on a month's loan from Luton. An extra 1,500 fans turn out hoping for another scoring extravaganza but only see Andy Flounders given the freedom of the penalty area to head in. Player-manager Brian Horton makes his 650th league and cup appearance.

10. DERBY — No repeat of last season's cup heroics on the same pitch. The tide turns with the departure of Rogers who is left in agony by Charlie Palmer's tackle. Sealey's dash at Kevin Wilson ends in a penalty decision. The keeper barely sees Bobby Davison's bullet header or his powerful shot.

11. ROTHERHAM — Martin Harvey finds himself in charge as Hore is sacked despite the cup run of last season. Coughlin wonders what he has to do to score as he hits the bar and forces Bobby Mimms into two spectacular saves all in a ten-minute spell. Rogers' deep cross floats on the wind over Mimms.

League Matches 12–23

12. ORIENT (A) — 23/10 — Lost 0-2 (positions 22 / 20; Att 2,310; 11)
Scorers: Godfrey 9, 37, Brooks 62
Ref: A Robinson
- Argyle: Sealey, Nisbet, Uzzell*, Harrison, Rowe, Burrows, Hodges, Rogers, Tynan, Staniforth, Coughlin, Cooper
- Orient: Wilmot, Hales, Stride, Corbett, Cunningham, Foster, Silkman, Brooks, Jones, Cornwell, Godfrey
- Report: Barry Silkman demonstrates that he has lost none of the skill seen during his brief spell as a Pilgrim. Kevin Godfrey's first takes a cruel deflection off Uzzell. Rhys Wilmot looks safe and secure in the Orient goal. Cooper is stretchered off in the last minute with ligament damage.

13. DONCASTER (A) — 26/10 — Lost 3-4 (positions 23 / 5; Att 4,688; 11)
Scorers: Tynan 24, 28, Hodges 82; Bar'w'th 54, 58, Douglas 57, Philliben 63
Ref: D Shaw
- Argyle: Sealey, Nisbet, Goodyear, Harrison, Rowe, Burrows, Hodges, Rogers, Tynan, Staniforth, Coughlin, Cooper
- Doncaster: Peacock, Russell, Yates, Snodin I, Philliben, Lister, Buckley, Butterworth, Douglas, Harle, Snodin G*, Kowalski
- Report: Questions are again asked of the defence as Argyle once more throw away a seemingly emphatic lead. Rovers score four times in a nine-minute spell. The crossbar denies Tynan a hat-trick. John Philliben scores his first ever league goal. Coughlin is booked for the fifth time this season.

14. BRISTOL ROV (H) — 3/11 — Won 3-2 (positions 20 / 2; Att 5,818; 14)
Scorers: Nisbet 58, Tynan 62, Harrison 82; Slatter 6, Randall 48
Ref: D Letts
- Argyle: Sealey, Nisbet, Uzzell, Harrison, Rowe, Burrows, Hodges, Rogers, Tynan, Staniforth, Coughlin
- Bristol Rov: Cashley, Slatter, Williams B, Williams G, Parkin, McCaffrey, Holloway, Williams D, Stephens, Randall, O'Connor
- Report: Speculation links former Argyle skipper Johnny Newman with the managerial vacancy. The home fans are grateful that Paul Randall converts only one of his many chances. Nisbet's long-range shooting sets up a tremendous comeback. A rare Harrison header seals an unlikely victory.

15. BRADFORD C (H) — 6/11 — Drew 0-0 (positions 21 / 3; Att 4,578; 15)
Ref: L Burden
- Argyle: Philip, Nisbet, Uzzell, Harrison, Rowe, Burrows, Hodges, Rogers, Tynan, Staniforth, Coughlin*, Goodyear
- Bradford C: McManus, Cherry, Withe, McCall, Jackson, Evans, Hendrie, Goodman*, Campbell, Abbott, Ellis, Fletcher
- Report: Paul Bannon arrives on loan from Bristol Rovers. Sealey has returned to Luton. Defences dominate, with player-manager Trevor Cherry marshalling his side. Philip produces a good save from Bobby Campbell. Peter Jackson's lob lands on the roof of the net in the closing minutes.

16. WIGAN (A) — 10/11 — Lost 0-1 (positions 21 / 14; Att 3,121; 15)
Scorers: Newell 1
Ref: T Holbrook
- Argyle: Philip, Nisbet, Uzzell, Harrison, Rowe*, Burrows, Hodges, Rogers, Tynan, Staniforth, Goodyear, Bannon
- Wigan: Tunks, Cribley, Knowles, Kelly, Walsh, Methven, Butler, Barrow, Johnson, Newell, Langley
- Report: Both sides are looking for new managers. The defence is nowhere to be seen as Mike Newell gallops clear from halfway to slot past Philp. Steve Johnson is pulled down in the area by Philip (58). Johnson's spot-kick thuds against the bar. Newell's follow up is disallowed for offside.

17. WALSALL (H) — 24/11 — Lost 1-3 (positions 21 / 10; Att 4,907; 15)
Scorers: Tynan 50; Handysides 66, Shakesp're 69, Childs 90
Ref: T Bune
- Argyle: Crudgington, Nisbet, Uzzell, Harrison, Rowe, Burrows, Goodyear, Rogers, Tynan, Staniforth*, Coughlin, Bannon
- Walsall: Cherry, Caswell, Mower, Shakespeare, Brazier, Hart, Handysides, Kelly, Preece, Buckley*, Jones, Childs
- Report: Manager Alan Buckley's decision to substitute himself after Tynan's goal transforms his side's fortunes. After taking an hour just to force a corner, the Saddlers score twice in four minutes. Buckley's replacement, Gary Childs, adds another in injury-time to rub salt in the wounds.

18. SWANSEA (A) — 1/12 — Won 2-0 (positions 21 / 23; Att 3,124; 18)
Scorers: Tynan 22, Staniforth 79
Ref: K Barratt
- Argyle: Crudgington, Nisbet, Uzzell, Harrison, Rowe*, Burrows, Rogers, Hodges, Tynan, Staniforth, Coughlin
- Swansea: Rimmer, Marustik*, Evans, Lewis, Stevenson, Richardson, Saunders, Richards, Cole, Mardenboro'h, Pascoe, Loveridge
- Report: Tynan and Staniforth make light of the mud and rain to run the Swans defence ragged and set up Argyle's first away league win for 13 months. Tynan's agile leap powers the ball in from Rogers' centre. Staniforth spots Jimmy Rimmer off his line and coolly chips the ball over him.

19. CAMBRIDGE (H) — 15/12 — Won 2-0 (positions 20 / 24; Att 3,675; 21)
Scorers: Hodges 72, Tynan 82
Ref: J Martin
- Argyle: Crudgington, Nisbet, Rowe, Harrison, Cooper*, Burrows, Rogers, Hodges, Tynan, Staniforth, Coughlin, Rowbotham
- Cambridge: Branagan, Clark*, Bennett, Beattie, Moyes, Sinton, Spriggs, Cooke, Pyle, Finney, Rayment
- Report: Argyle finally grind down a side who are in freefall through the divisions and have won only once in 17 games. Seventeen-year-old Darren Rowbotham comes on as Smith's only remaining fit player. A small boy runs the length of the pitch at half-time to score into an empty net.

20. MILLWALL (H) — 22/12 — Won 3-1 (positions 16 / 5; Att 4,557; 24)
Scorers: Tynan 2, Coughlin 47, Staniforth 56; Lovell 41p
Ref: J Deakin
- Argyle: Crudgington, Nisbet, Rowe, Harrison, Summerfield, Burrows, Rogers, Hodges, Tynan, Staniforth, Coughlin
- Millwall: Sansome, Stevens, Roffey, McLeary, Smith, Lowndes, Cusack, Fashanu*, Neal, Lovell, Otulakowski, Bremner
- Report: It takes Tynan only 66 seconds to notch up another goal to keep up his record of having scored in every match under Smith's charge. Rowe's clumsy challenge on Otulakowski sees Lovell level from the spot. Summerfield has a constructive debut. Bremner breaks his collar-bone.

21. BRISTOL CITY (A) — 26/12 — Lost 3-4 (positions 17 / 8; Att 10,339; 24)
Scorers: Tynan 24, 42, 53; Hutchinson 20, 33, Walsh 27, 87p
Ref: M Robinson
- Argyle: Crudgington, Nisbet, Goodyear !, Harrison, Rowe, Ham, Rogers, Hodges, Tynan, Staniforth, Cooper, Summerfield
- Bristol City: Waugh, Llewellyn, Rogers, Phil'-Masters Curle, Pritchard, Hutchinson, Stroud, Walsh, Riley, Neville
- Report: Smith threatens to report the ref as Walsh seals the game with a late penalty after Pritchard fell in the area. Hat-trick hero Tynan blots his copybook with an awful pass to Goodyear which leaves Riley clear. The already cautioned Argyle defender pulls him back and is dismissed.

22. NEWPORT (A) — 29/12 — Lost 0-1 (positions 17 / 16; Att 3,003; 24)
Scorers: Chamberlain 62
Ref: J Moules
- Argyle: Crudgington, Nisbet, Goodyear, Harrison, Summerfield, Burrows, Rogers, Hodges, Tynan !, Staniforth, Cooper*, Harrison
- Newport: Kendall, Jones, Matthewson, Pulis, Boyle, Carter, Giles, Reid, Cooper, Chamberlain, Lewis
- Report: The players attend a 'clear the air' meeting on Sunday after a frustrating defeat. Ex-Argyle loan striker Neville Chamberlain gets his fifth goal in three matches after Crudgington fails to collect a corner. Tynan is red-carded (84) against his old club after throwing a punch at Roy Carter.

23. BRENTFORD (H) — 1/1 — Drew 1-1 (positions 18 / 15; Att 6,946; 25)
Scorers: Tynan 25; Cassells 65
Ref: E Read
- Argyle: Crudgington, Nisbet, Goodyear, Harrison, Summerfield*, Burrows, Rogers, Hodges, Tynan, Staniforth, Coughlin, Rowbotham
- Brentford: Phillips, Roberts P, Murray, Booker, Salman, Wignall, Cooke, Kamara, Cassells, Torrance, Roberts G*, Alexander
- Report: New defender Gerry McElhinney is introduced to the crowd before the start. Smith is unhappy with his current defence and brings only the back four and Coughlin in for extra training. Brentford's goal stands despite two players in offside positions. Tynan gets his 16th of the season.

CANON DIVISION 3 — Manager: John Hore > Dave Smith — SEASON 1984-85

No	Date	1	2	3	4	5	6	7	8	9	10	11	12 sub used	Att	Pos	Pt	F-A	H-T	Scorers, Times, and Referees
24	A BOURNEMOUTH 26/1	Crudgington	Nisbet	Uzzell	Ham*	McElhinney	Cooper	Rogers	Hodges	Summerfield	Staniforth	Coughlin	Harrison	3,695	19	25	0-1	0-0	Thompson 58 — Ref: E Scales
		Smeulders	*Nightingale*	*Sulley*	*Savage*	*Brown*	*Howlett*	*O'Driscoll*	*Russell*	*Rafferty*	*Thompson*	*Morrell*							League action resumes after a three week lay-off due to the weather. Argyle miss the suspended Tynan and never threaten. The evergreen Billy Rafferty has a hand in the goal, setting up Mark Nightingale who crossed to the unmarked Ian Thompson. Ham goes off with a calf strain.
25	A PRESTON 2/2	Crudgington	Nisbet	Uzzell	Ham	McElhinney	Cooper	Rogers	Hodges	Tynan	Staniforth	Summerfield*	Goodyear	3,248	19 W	28	2-1	0-1	Goodyear 60, Hodges 69 — Kelly 11 — Ref: K Hackett
		Campbell	*Farrelly*	*McAteer*	*Twentyman*	*Gibson*	*Clark*	*Kelly*	*Rudge*	*Naughton**	*Houghton*								Preston, without a win since November, get an early boost when John Kelly shoots home. Geoff Twentyman's back-pass falls yards short of Campbell. Then Goodyear, on for the injured Summerfield, pounds in to lob the keeper. Hodges weaves past a defender to clinch three points.
26	H BOLTON 9/2	Crudgington	Nisbet	Uzzell	Burrows	McElhinney	Cooper	Rogers	Hodges	Tynan	Staniforth*	Goodyear	Harrison	4,978	19 W	31	2-0	1-0	Tynan 16, Goodyear 58 — Ref: C Downey
		Farnworth	*Borrows*	*Deakin*	*Joyce*	*Came*	*Valentine*	*Thompson*	*Chandler*	*Foster*	*Caldwell**	*Bell*	*Rudge*						Bolton boss Charlie Wright storms out of Home Park claiming that his star striker, Tony Caldwell, had been kicked out of the match by some over-vigorous defending. Tynan drills a shot between two defenders on the line. Goodyear, revelling in his new midfield role, gets another.
27	A YORK 12/2	Crudgington	Nisbet	Uzzell	Burrows	McElhinney	Cooper	Rogers	Hodges	Tynan	Summerfield	Harrison		4,820	19 D	32	0-0	0-0	Ref: D Richardson
		Astbury	*Hay*	*Senior*	*Stragia*	*MacPhail*	*Haselgrave*	*Ford*	*Banton*	*Butler*	*Atkinson*	*Pearce*							York are on a roll, having beaten Arsenal in the FA Cup and not conceded a goal for eight matches. On a frozen pitch Tynan misses a chance to dent that record but Mike Astbury saves his penalty (33) after Hodges, playing his 250th league game, is brought down by Ricky Sbragia.
28	A BRISTOL ROV 23/2	Philip	Nisbet	Uzzell	Burrows	McElhinney	Rowe	Rogers	Hodges	Tynan	Summerfield*	Obi*	Rowbotham	5,953	19 L	32	0-1	0-1	Williams B 45 — Ref: R Lewis
		Cashley	*Slatter*	*Williams B*	*Bater*	*Parkin*	*Jones*	*Holloway*	*Williams D*	*Stephens*	*Randall*	*O'Connor**	*Bannon*						Injury-stricken Argyle include Tony Obi, on loan from Villa. The midfield are often left chasing shadows but hold out until seconds before half-time. Brian Williams' 20-yard shot seems covered by Philip until McElhinney's deflection leaves the keeper stranded. Tynan scrapes the bar.
29	H DONCASTER 2/3	Philip	Nisbet	Uzzell*	Burrows	McElhinney	Goodyear	Rogers	Hodges	Tynan	Summerfield	Obi*	Coughlin	5,019	18 W	35	2-1	1-0	Summerfield 2, Tynan 51 — Snodin I 88 — Ref: D Hedges
		Peacock	*Russell*	*Snodin G*	*Snodin I*	*Philliben*	*Lister*	*Buckley*	*Butterworth*	*Douglas*	*Harle !*	*Kowalski*							Summerfield opens his Argyle account from the first attack. Ian Snodin, back from midweek England Under-21 duty in Israel, enhances his growing reputation with a fine performance. Harle is sent off (82) for an ugly foul on Uzzell leaving blood seeping through the defender's sock.
30	H ORIENT 5/3	Philip	Nisbet	Uzzell	Coughlin	McElhinney	Goodyear	Rogers	Hodges	Tynan	Summerfield	Obi		4,770	16 D	36	1-1	1-0	Uzzell 18 — Sussex 66 — Ref: L Burden
		Wilmot	*Cunningham*	*Castle*	*Corbett*	*Foster*	*Silkman*	*Godfrey*	*Juryeff*	*Jones*	*Cornwell**	*Sussex*	*Mountford*						Uzzell's header, his first goal for 14 months, opens the scoring. Tommy Cunningham is dominant at the back for the O's. Barry Silkman displays typical panache by back-heeling a free-kick for Andy Sussex to smash the equaliser. Orient do not win a corner until the 84th minute.
31	A ROTHERHAM 9/3	Crudgington	Nisbet	Uzzell	Coughlin*	McElhinney	Goodyear	Rogers	Hodges	Tynan	Summerfield	Obi*	Burrows	4,111	14 W	39	2-0	1-0	Summerfield 2, Tynan 49 — Ref: R Guy
		Mimms	*Forrest*	*Mitchell*	*Trusson*	*Pickering*	*Crosby*	*Birch*	*Gooding*	*Richardson*	*Simmons*	*Kilmore**	*Dungworth*						Yet another early strike from Summerfield sets Argyle on their way to a shock win. Tynan misses a sitter before making amends by shooting past Bobby Mimms despite stumbling. Uzzell concedes a penalty (73) by fouling Richardson but Mick Gooding hits his shot against a post.
32	H DERBY 16/3	Crudgington	Nisbet	Uzzell	Coughlin	McElhinney	Goodyear	Rogers	Hodges	Tynan	Summerfield	Obi*	Staniforth	6,117	15 L	39	0-1	0-0	Davison 62 — Ref: T Spencer
		Sutton	*Palmer*	*Buckley*	*Lewis*	*Hindmarch*	*Blades*	*Micklewhite*	*Christie*	*Davison*	*Devine*	*Robertson**	*Powell*						Storm-force winds wreck any chance of flowing football. Tynan comes closest. His cross-field pass is caught by the wind. Steve Sutton furiously back-pedals as the ball is almost blown into the net. Davison scores with a brave header. Robertson has a running feud with Nisbet.
33	H GILLINGHAM 19/3	Crudgington	Nisbet	Uzzell	Coughlin	Burrows	Goodyear	Rogers	Hodges	Tynan	Summerfield	Staniforth		4,852	16 D	40	1-1	0-1	Tynan 77p — Mehmet 38p — Ref: R Milford
		McDonagh	*Sage*	*Hinnigan*	*Oates*	*Musker*	*Shaw*	*Cochrane*	*Shearer*	*Robinson*	*Mehmet*	*Cascarino*							Keith Peacock's Gills are happy to boost their promotion challenge with a point but cannot snatch all three. Crudgington races off his line and brings down Terry Cochrane. Skipper Dave Mehmet scores from the spot. Tynan reciprocates after Russell Musker fouls Hodges in the area.
34	A HULL 23/3	Crudgington	Nisbet	Uzzell	Coughlin	Burrows	Goodyear	Rogers	Hodges	Tynan	Summerfield*	Staniforth	Harrison	6,947	17 D	41	2-2	1-2	Tynan 2, 50 — Roberts G 21 Flounders 36 — Ref: T Simpson
		Norman	*Swann*	*Hollifield*	*Williams**	*Skipper*	*McEwan*	*Flounders*	*McClaren*	*Whitehurst*	*Askew*	*Roberts G*	*Massey*						Hull twice take advantage of fouls by Burrows on Billy Whitehurst by scoring from the resultant free-kicks. Tynan takes his season's tally to 23 with another two goals. Crudgington gives his side a late scare when he rushes out but heads the ball straight to Massey who delays his shot.

#	Venue	Opponent	Date	Score (HT)	Pos	—	Pts	Att.	Argyle scorers	Opposition scorers	Referee
35	H	BURNLEY	26/3	2-2 (2-1) D	17	21	42	4,383	Tynan 10p, 21	Biggins 24, Hird 78	K Cooper
36	A	BRADFORD C	30/3	0-1 (0-0) L	18	1	42	6,552	—	McCall 68	G Courtney
37	H	BRISTOL CITY	5/4	1-0 (0-0) W	16	5	45	9,959	Staniforth 79	—	M Robinson
38	A	BRENTFORD	8/4	1-3 (1-1) L	17	15	45	4,043	Tynan 40p	Cassells 33, 56p, Roberts 85	D Brazier
39	H	WIGAN	13/4	1-0 (1-0) W	16	18	48	4,159	Tynan 31	—	D Letts
40	H	LINCOLN	16/4	2-0 (0-0) W	14	18	51	4,228	Tynan 79, 88	—	R Gifford
41	A	WALSALL	20/4	3-0 (1-0) W	14	8	54	2,775	Tynan 36, Hodges 69, 73	—	M Scott
42	A	READING	24/4	1-1 (0-1) D	14	8	55	2,296	Staniforth 61	Hicks 17	A Ward
43	H	SWANSEA	27/4	1-2 (0-1) L	15	20	55	4,994	Tynan 64	Parlane 19, Marustik 52	J Martin
44	A	CAMBRIDGE	4/5	1-1 (0-1) D	16	24	56	1,435	Tynan 50p	McDonough 2p	A Buksh
45	H	NEWPORT	6/5	1-0 (1-0) W	16	17	59	5,079	Hodges 39	—	A Robinson
46	A	MILLWALL	11/5	0-2 (0-1) L	15	2	59	13,460	—	Cusack 30p, Lowndes 73	D Axcell

Home 5,133 Away 4,971 Average 5,133

Line-ups (Argyle in roman, opponents in italics)

35 Burnley — Crudgington, Nisbet, Uzzell, Coughlin, Rogers, Goodyear, Burrows, McElhinney, Hodges, Tynan, Summerfield*, Staniforth / *Hansbury, Palmer, Hampton, Phelan, Grewcock*, Hird, Overson, Jackson, Scott, Devine, Biggins, Hutchison, Lawrence*

36 Bradford C — Crudgington, Nisbet, Uzzell, Coughlin, Rogers, Goodyear, Burrows, McElhinney, Hodges, Tynan, Staniforth, Ellis / *McManus, Abbott, Withe, McCall, Evans, Hendrie, Jackson, Walsh, Singleton, Campbell, Hawley*

37 Bristol City — Crudgington, Nisbet, Uzzell, Coughlin, Rogers, Goodyear, Burrows, McElhinney, Hodges, Tynan, Staniforth / *Shaw, Stevens, Newman, Curle, Riley*, Hughes, Neville, Pritchard, Walsh, Hutchinson, Johnson*

38 Brentford — Crudgington, Nisbet, Uzzell, Coughlin, Rogers, Goodyear, Burrows, McElhinney, Hodges, Tynan, Staniforth / *Phillips, Salman, Murray, Millen, Kamara, Hurlock, Fisher, Cooke, Cassells, Booker, Roberts, Goodyear*, Rowbotham*

39 Wigan — Crudgington, Nisbet, Rowbotham, Coughlin, Rogers, Goodyear, Burrows, McElhinney, Hodges, Tynan, Staniforth / *Tunks, Butler, Mitchell, Kelly, Barrow, Methven, Walsh, Lowe, Newell*, Jewell, Langley, Aspinall*

40 Lincoln — Crudgington, Nisbet, Rowbotham*, Coughlin, Rogers, Goodyear, Burrows, McElhinney, Hodges, Tynan, Staniforth / *Naylor, Strodder, Neale, Redfearn, Collins!, Thompson, Walker, McGinley, Shipley, Jack, McCarrick, Harrison, Thomas*

41 Walsall — Crudgington, Nisbet, Harrison, Coughlin, Rogers, Goodyear, Burrows, McElhinney, Hodges, Tynan, Staniforth / *Cherry, Kelly, Mower, Shakespeare, Hart, Brazier, Handysides, O'Kelly, Elliott, Naughton, Childs*, Jones*

42 Reading — Crudgington, Nisbet, Harrison, Coughlin*, Rogers, Goodyear, Burrows, McElhinney, Hodges, Tynan, Staniforth / *Westwood, Peters, Richardson, Beavon, Burvill, Hicks, Wood, White, Crown, Harrix, Christie*, Cooper, Roberts*

43 Swansea — Crudgington, Nisbet, Harrison, Coughlin, Rogers, Goodyear, Burrows, McElhinney, Hodges, Tynan, Staniforth* / *Rimmer, Lewis, Sullivan, Price, Parlane, Stevenson, Marustik!, Turner, Waddle, Cooper, Pascoe*

44 Cambridge — Crudgington, Nisbet, Goodyear, Coughlin, Rogers, Goodyear, Burrows, McElhinney, Hodges, Tynan, Staniforth / *Key, Osgood, Bennett, Rayment, Sinton, Moyes, Beattie, Finney, Cooper, Spriggs, McDonough*, Massey*

45 Newport — Crudgington, Nisbet, Harrison, Coughlin, Rogers, Goodyear, Burrows, McElhinney, Hodges, Tynan, Staniforth* / *Kendall, Jones, Relish, Reid, Matthewson, Boyle, Kent, Emmanuel, Cooper, Giles, Chamberlain, Summerfield*

46 Millwall — Crudgington, Nisbet, Uzzell, Uzzell, Rowbotham, Goodyear, Burrows, McElhinney, Hodges, Tynan, Rowbotham, Staniforth, Cooper, Summerfield / *Sansome, Hinshelwood, Stevens, Briley, Lowndes, Cusack, Smith, Fashanu, Chatterton, Brenner, Otulakowski*

Match reports

35. Struggling Burnley are the Jekyll and Hyde team of the division, having actually won by 7-0 and 9-0 margins. Hodges is too quick for 37-year-old Tommy Hutchison, who gifts Argyle a penalty. Uzzell does likewise on Mike Phelan and Kevin Hird notches his 21st goal of the season.

36. The leaders are pushed all the way by Argyle. It takes a scrambled goal by Stuart McCall to settle it, with both sides claiming a handball in the build-up to the goal. Northern Ireland team-mates McElhinney and Bobby Campbell show little sympathy for each other in a bruising duel.

37. On four minutes, another early goal looks on the cards until Tynan slips at the crucial second. The otherwise impressive John Shaw makes a hash of Rogers' high cross and palms the ball to Staniforth, who makes no mistake from close range. The goal inspires a rousing finale.

38. Keith Cassells finally strikes with his third clear-cut chance of the first half. Phillips' challenge on Hodges is deemed illegal and Tynan grabs another penalty. Cassells gets his second from the spot after Hurlock is the meat in a Hodges-Nisbet sandwich. Roberts blasts a fine third goal.

39. Tynan overtakes Trevor Senior at the top of the third division scoring charts with his 27th of the season. For once his goal comes from outside the area. Visiting boss Bryan Hamilton is impressed. Wigan's two apprentices, Warren Aspinall and Jim Mitchell, are both yellow-carded.

40. Two more goals from Tynan sets a new Argyle post-war scoring record for one season, breaking Maurice Tadman's previous best. Lincoln do their homework and employ two wingers to stop Nisbet and Rowbotham attacking. Stuart Naylor lets the second goal slip through his hands.

41. The Argyle fans are quick to remind Steve Cherry of last season's FA Cup quarter-final when Andy Rogers' corner eluded him. Who else but Tynan opens the scoring but Hodges upstages him with two splendid strikes. He misses a hat-trick by shooting across the face of an open goal.

42. Smith maintains his impressive record of never being beaten at Reading as a manager. Argyle are caught off-guard from Derek Christie's long throw and Royals' skipper Martin Hicks scores his first of the season. For once Tynan doesn't score but fellow striker Staniforth equalises.

43. The struggling Swans gain three vital points. Tempers boil over, due mainly to some strange refereeing decisions. The frustrated Marustik is given his marching orders for throwing the ball at a ball-boy. Coughlin and Alan Waddle end up lying on the ground exchanging punches.

44. Beleaguered United have won only four points since Boxing Day. Two hundred Argyle fans swell the sparse crowd in anticipation of a rout. Within 90 seconds Burrows handles and Roy McDonough converts. Frustration sets in until the ball strikes Keith Osgood's elbow in the area.

45. Smith receives a watch from league sponsors Canon before the match to mark his 35 years in the game. Argyle are without Goodyear, who has had a toenail removed. Staniforth goes off with double vision (30). Hodges reaches double figures for the season firing in an angled volley.

46. A mass invasion at the final whistle prevents Millwall players from doing a lap of honour to celebrate promotion. The elusive Otulakowski is sent flying by McElhinney and Dave Cusack's penalty sends Crudgington the wrong way. Lowndes' second sends the crowd into raptures.

Milk Cup

	Att		F-A	H-T	Scorers, Times, and Referees	1	2	3	4	5	6	7	8	9	10	11	12 sub used
1:1 H TORQUAY 27/8	5,689 *4:*	W	1-0	0-0	Goodyear 60	Crudgington	Nisbet	Uzzell	Harrison	Goodyear	Burrows	Hodges	Cooper	Tynan	Staniforth	Coughlin	
					Ref: A. Seville	*Allen*	*Dawkins*	*Anderson*	*Impey*	*Compton*	*Whitehouse*	*Carter*	*Laryea*	*Mooney*	*Barnes*	*Hall*	
1:2 A TORQUAY 4/9	3,003 *4:19*	W	1-0	1-0	Staniforth 20	Crudgington	Nisbet	Uzzell	Harrison	Goodyear	Burrows	Hodges	Cooper	Tynan	Staniforth	Coughlin	
					Ref: E Read (Argyle won 2-0 on aggregate)	*Allen*	*Dawkins*	*Anderson*	*Whitehouse*	*Compton*	*Impey*	*Wakefield*	*Laryea*	*Mooney*	*Barnes*	*Hall*	
2:1 A BIRMINGHAM 25/9	7,964 *2:2*	L	1-4	1-1	Staniforth 38 *[Rees 86]* Clarke 40, Hopkins 61, Harford 65, Ref: J Hough	Philip	Nisbet	Rowe	Harrison	Goodyear*	Burrows	Hodges	Rogers	Tynan	Staniforth	Coughlin	Uzzell
						Prudhoe	*Roberts*	*Hagan*	*Wright*	*Armstrong*	*Daly**	*Kuhl*	*Clarke*	*Harford*	*Halsall*	*Hopkins*	*Rees*
2:2 H BIRMINGHAM 9/10	4,650 *2:5*	L	0-1	0-1	Clarke 26 Ref: R Milford (Argyle lost 1-5 on aggregate)	Philip	Nisbet	Rowe	English	Goodyear	Burrows	Hodges	Rogers	Tynan	Staniforth	Coughlin	
						Prudhoe	*Roberts*	*Hagan*	*Wright*	*Armstrong*	*Halsall !*	*Kuhl*	*Clarke*	*Harford*	*Bremner*	*Storer**	*Jones*

1:1 — Argyle take a slender lead to Plainmoor thanks to new £40k signing from Luton, Clive Goodyear. After Tynan misses two good chances, the new boy shoots through a crowded penalty area past the unsighted Kenny Allen. Cooper's diving header hits a post and rolls along the line.

1:2 — Torquay, still without a goal this season, optimistically make the match all-ticket but sell only half of them. Staniforth scores with an angled shot from Coughlin's corner. Mr Read is as busy as usual, booking six players, including Coughlin for the third time in as many matches.

2:1 — From Rogers' left-wing cross, Staniforth nips in to give Argyle a surprise lead. Gerry Daly sets up two of the goals from free-kicks. Wayne Clarke scores with a superb volley from the edge of the 18-yard box. Sub Tony Rees gives Brum a comfortable cushion for the second leg.

2:2 — Wayne Clarke's seventh goal of the season from Coughlin's misplaced pass kills the tie. Transfer-seeking Mick Halsall is sent off (31) for a late tackle on acting skipper Nisbet. Clarke almost follows for disputing the decision. Argyle receive 'Milk' money of £2,500 as losers.

FA Cup

	Att		F-A	H-T	Scorers, Times, and Referees	1	2	3	4	5	6	7	8	9	10	11	12 sub used
1 H BARNET 17/11	5,568 *GL:14*	W	3-0	1-0	Goodyear 25, Tynan 69, Staniforth 86 Ref: H King	Crudgington	Nisbet	Uzzell	Harrison	Goodyear	Burrows	Rogers	Rowe	Tynan	Staniforth	Coughlin	
						Phillips	*Brown*	*Pittaway**	*Millett*	*Baldrey*	*Evans*	*Stein !*	*Ferguson*	*Margerrison*	*Atkins*	*Mahoney*	*Ragan*
2 H HEREFORD 8/12	7,882 *4:4*	D	0-0	0-0	Ref: R Milford	Crudgington	Nisbet	Uzzell	Harrison	Cooper	Burrows	Rogers	Hodges	Tynan	Staniforth	Coughlin	
						Rose	*Price*	*Bray*	*Hicks*	*Pejic*	*Emery*	*Harvey*	*Delve*	*Phillips*	*Kearns*	*Dalziel*	
2R A HEREFORD 12/12	6,956 *4:4*	L	0-2	0-1	Kearns 5, Phillips 58 Ref: R Milford	Crudgington	Nisbet	Uzzell	Harrison	Cooper	Burrows	Rogers	Hodges	Tynan	Staniforth	Coughlin	
						Rose	*Price*	*Bray*	*Hicks*	*Pejic*	*Emery*	*Harvey*	*Delve*	*Phillips*	*Kearns*	*Dalziel*	

1 — Dave Smith takes charge for the first time against Barry Fry's non-leaguers. Crudgington returns after an eight-week lay-off. Staniforth, the victim of a number of tough tackles, slots home a penalty for handball which only the linesman sees. Stein protests too much and is red-carded.

2 — Johnny Newman's side are typically well organised and give the Pilgrims a few scary moments. Ollie Kearns and Stewart Phillips have shots cleared off the line and Phillips misses an easy tap-in. Coughlin, Argyle's best player, has three long-range shots but all go narrowly wide.

2R — A home tie against Arsenal and the return of Paul Mariner to Home Park is not enough to inspire the Pilgrims. John Delve creates the first goal for Ollie Kearns. Tynan's header beats Rose but hits Keith Hicks' knee on the line. Phillips shoots into an empty net after Price breaks clear.

League Table

	P	W	D	L	F	A	W	D	L	F	A	Pts
		Home					Away					
1 Bradford C	46	15	6	2	44	23	13	4	6	33	22	94
2 Millwall	46	18	5	0	44	12	8	7	8	29	30	90
3 Hull	46	16	4	3	46	20	9	8	6	32	29	87
4 Gillingham	46	15	5	3	54	29	10	3	10	26	33	83
5 Bristol City	46	17	2	4	46	19	7	7	9	28	28	81
6 Bristol Rov	46	15	6	2	37	13	6	6	11	29	35	75
7 Derby	46	14	7	2	40	20	5	6	12	25	34	70
8 York	46	13	5	5	42	22	7	4	12	28	35	69
9 Reading	46	8	7	8	31	29	11	5	7	37	33	69
10 Bournemouth	46	16	3	4	42	16	3	8	12	15	30	68
11 Walsall	46	9	7	7	33	22	6	6	8	25	30	67
12 Rotherham	46	11	6	6	36	24	7	5	11	19	31	65
13 Brentford	46	13	5	5	42	27	3	9	11	20	37	62
14 Doncaster	46	11	5	7	42	33	6	3	14	30	41	59
15 PLYMOUTH	46	11	7	5	33	23	4	7	12	29	42	59
16 Wigan	46	12	6	5	36	22	3	8	12	24	42	59
17 Bolton	46	12	5	6	38	22	4	1	18	31	53	54
18 Newport	46	9	6	8	30	30	4	7	12	25	37	52
19 Lincoln	46	8	11	4	32	20	3	7	13	18	31	51
20 Swansea	46	7	5	11	31	39	5	6	12	22	41	47
21 Burnley	46	6	8	9	30	24	5	5	13	30	49	46
22 Orient	46	7	7	9	30	36	4	6	13	21	40	46
23 Preston	46	9	5	9	33	41	4	2	17	18	59	46
24 Cambridge	46	2	3	18	17	48	2	6	15	20	47	21
	1104	274	136	142	889	614	142	136	274	614	889	1520

Odds & ends

Double wins: (2) Preston, Rotherham.
Double defeats: (1) Derby.

Won from behind: (1) Bristol Rov Preston (h & a).
Lost from in front: (4) Derby, Doncaster, Reading, Walsall.

High spots: Goalscoring exploits of Tommy Tynan, earning 'Golden Boot' award.
Amazing comeback against Preston (h)
Four-match spell in September-October saw a total of 30 goals scored for and against.

Low spots: Comedy of errors against Bolton (a).
FA Cup defeat against 4th Division Hereford.
Disappointing away form.
End of season departure of Tommy Tynan to Rotherham.

Player of the Year: Tommy Tynan.
Ever presents: (1) Gordon Nisbet.
Hat-tricks: (1) Tommy Tynan.
Leading scorer: Tommy Tynan (32).

Appearances / Goals

	Lge	Sub	LC	Sub	FAC	Sub	Lge	LC	FAC	Tot
	Appearances						Goals			
Bannon, Paul			2							
Burrows, Adrian	38	1	4		3					
Cooper, Leigh	19	2	2		2					
Coughlin, Russell	37	1	4		3		3			3
Crudgington, Geoff	33		2		3					
English, Tom	4	1					1			1
Goodyear, Clive	31	2	4		1		2	1	1	4
Ham, Mike	6									
Harrison, Chris	28	5	3		3		1			1
Hodges, Kevin	45		4		2		10			10
McElhinney, Gerry	20	1								
Nisbet, Gordon	46		4		3		2			2
Obi, Tony	5									
Philp, Dave	7	2								
Rogers, Andy	39	3	2		3		2			2
Rowbotham, Darren	3	4			1					
Rowe, Mark	14	1	2		1					
Sealey, Les	6									
Staniforth, Gordon	40	1	4		3		7	2	1	10
Summerfield, Kevin	15	2	2				2			2
Tynan, Tommy	45		4		3		31		1	32
Uzzell, John	29	2	1	1	3		1			1
22 players used	506	29	44	1	33		62	3	3	68

CANON DIVISION 3

Manager: Dave Smith

SEASON 1985-86

No	Date	Att	Pos	Pt	F-A	H-T	Scorers, Times, and Referees	1	2	3	4	5	6	7	8	9	10	11	12 sub used
1	A 17/8 York	4,246		L 0	1-3	0-2	McElhinney 55p / Canham 11, Walwyn 44, Gabbiadini 57 Astbury — Ref: J Worrall	Crudgington	Nisbet	Goodyear	Uzzell	McElhinney	Matthews	Hodges	Coughlin	Cooper S	Rowbotham	Nelson	Mills
							(opp)	*Westwood*	*Hood*	*Evans*	*McAughtrie*	*MacPhail*	*Haselgrave*	*Ford*	*Gabbiadini**	*Walwyn*	*Houchen*	*Canham*	*Mills*
2	H 24/8 Reading	4,261	22, 5	L 0	0-1	0-1	Senior 23 — Ref: R Milford	Crudgington	Nisbet	Uzzell	Goodyear	McElhinney	Matthews	Hodges	Coughlin	Cooper S	Cooper L	Nelson	
							(opp)	*Westwood*	*Bailie*	*Richardson*	*Beavon*	*Hicks*	*Wood*	*Williams*	*White*	*Senior*	*Horrix*	*Burvill*	
3	A 26/8 Swansea	3,906		W 3	2-0	0-0	McElhinney 55p, Cooper S 81 — Ref: B Stevens	Crudgington	Nisbet	Uzzell	Goodyear	McElhinney	Matthews	Hodges	Coughlin	Cooper S	Cooper L	Nelson	
							(opp)	*Rimmer*	*Lewis*	*Sullivan*	*Price*	*Stevenson*	*Marustik*	*Hutchison*	*Turner*	*Waddle*	*Andrews*	*Pascoe*	
4	H 31/8 Notts Co	5,105	19, 11	L 3	0-1	0-1	Harkouk 13 — Ref: R Groves	Crudgington	Nisbet	Cooper L	Burrows	McElhinney	Matthews	Hodges	Coughlin	Cooper S	Clayton	Nelson	
							(opp)	*Leonard*	*Richards*	*Clarke*	*Benjamin*	*Sims*	*Yates*	*McParland*	*Goodwin*	*Young*	*Harkouk*	*Hunt*	
5	A 7/9 Brentford	3,927	20, 3	D 4	1-1	0-1	Cooper S 89p / Lynch 25 — Ref: K Baker	Crudgington	Nisbet	Goodyear	Burrows	McElhinney	Rowbotham	Hodges	Coughlin	Cooper S	Clayton	Nelson	
							(opp)	*Phillips*	*Salman*	*Murray*	*Millen*	*Wignall*	*Hurlock*	*Lynch*	*Cooke*	*Booker*	*Alexander*	*Cooper**	*Torrance*
6	H 14/9 Newport	3,686	15, 7	W 7	2-0	1-0	Burrows 31, Nelson 79 — Ref: A Robinson	Crudgington	Nisbet	Goodyear	Burrows	McElhinney	Matthews	Hodges	Coughlin	Cooper S	Clayton	Nelson	
							(opp)	*Kendall*	*Pulis*	*Relish*	*Reck*	*Dowman*	*Boyle*	*Carter*	*James*	*McManus**	*Staniforth*	*Lewis*	*Peacock*
7	A 17/9 Doncaster	2,904		L 7	0-1	0-1	Woods 37 — Ref: A Banks	Crudgington	Nisbet	Goodyear*	Burrows	McElhinney	Matthews	Hodges	Coughlin	Cooper S	Clayton	Nelson	Rowbotham
							(opp)	*Peacock*	*Caswell*	*Rushbury*	*Humphries*	*Brown*	*Cusack*	*Buckley*	*Dobbin*	*Douglas*	*Woods**	*Butterworth*	*Harle*
8	H 21/9 Wolverhampton	5,241	14, 24	W 10	3-1	1-0	Cooper S 44p, Nelson 50, 62 / Edwards 49 — Ref: K Cooper	Crudgington	Nisbet	Goodyear	Burrows	McElhinney	Matthews	Hodges	Coughlin*	Cooper S	Clayton	Nelson	Rowbotham
							(opp)	*Flowers*	*Wright*	*Barnes*	*Stoutt*	*Clarke*	*Cartwright*	*Dougherty**	*Ainscow*	*Edwards*	*King*	*Crainie*	*Morrisey*
9	A 28/9 Bolton	4,270	18, 13	L 10	1-3	0-3	Clayton 65 / Joyce 13, Caldwell 39, Rudge 44 — Ref: G Aplin	Crudgington	Nisbet	Goodyear	Burrows	McElhinney	Matthews	Hodges	Coughlin	Cooper S	Clayton	Nelson	
							(opp)	*Farnworth*	*Fitzpatrick*	*Scott*	*Thompson*	*Came*	*Allardyce*	*Joyce*	*Caldwell*	*Rudge*	*Hartford*	*Walker*	
10	H 1/10 Gillingham	4,135	13, 9	W 13	3-0	1-0	Hodges 44, Nelson 53, Cooper S 83p — Ref: A Seville	Crudgington	Nisbet	Goodyear	Cooper L	McElhinney	Matthews	Hodges	Coughlin	Cooper S	Clayton	Nelson	
							(opp)	*Hillyard*	*Hinnigan*	*Macowat*	*Oakes*	*Collins*	*Shaw*	*Cochrane*	*Sage*	*Elsey**	*Mehmet*	*Cascarino*	*Hales*
11	H 5/10 Bristol Rov	5,662	11, 20	W 16	4-2	3-0	Clayton 13, Coughlin 19, Hodges 36, Morgan 78, 81 [Parkin 72(og)] — Ref: L Robinson	Crudgington	Nisbet	Cooper L	Goodyear	McElhinney	Matthews	Hodges	Coughlin	Cooper S	Clayton	Nelson	
							(opp)	*Green*	*Davies*	*Bater*	*Stevenson*	*Parkin*	*England*	*Badock**	*Spring*	*Morgan*	*Randall*	*O'Connor*	*White*

Match notes

1. The unsettled Tynan has gone to Rotherham. Despite an extensive pre-season programme with matches against five First Division sides, Argyle struggle to find cohesion. Burly striker Keith Walwyn proves a handful as York show why they are one of the favourites for promotion.
2. A pre-match cloudburst creates conditions more akin to mid-February. Trevor Senior, the striker Smith tried to sign during the close season, does the damage knocking in Horrix's shot which rebounds off the crossbar. Westwood saves McElhinney's spot-kick after Nelson is fouled.
3. For the fourth successive match Argyle are awarded a penalty when Nelson is brought down by Welsh international Paul Price. McElhinney makes no mistake, to lead the goalscoring charts. Cooper, Tynan's replacement, demonstrates his aerial power by heading in Coughlin's corner.
4. Smith complains afterwards that one time Argyle target, Rachid Harkouk, is at least a yard offside when he scores the vital goal. Argyle rely on the aerial route to Cooper with little success. Despite the lack of points Smith is reasonably happy and predicts that 'someone will cop it soon.'
5. Mr Baker needs a police escort from the pitch after he awarded a late penalty. He is a long way from the action as Nelson stumbles as he and Danis Salman give chase. Bees' boss Frank McLintock, already booked for coaching, is livid. McElhinney breaks his nose for the eighth time.
6. Burrows heads in a pin-point cross from Coughlin. Precision passing also makes the second with Nelson applying the finishing touch to Clayton's pass. Argyle are grateful that former Welsh international winger Leighton James shows little appetite for becoming involved.
7. Clayton is permitted to play wearing a plaster cast after breaking a finger against Newport. Neil Woods collects a through ball and coolly rounds Crudgington to score into an empty net. Smith's desperation to rescue a point sees him use a substitute for the first time this season.
8. Bill McGarry's squad is ravaged with injuries and he is forced to field a very inexperienced side. Nelson then takes advantage of naïve defending to easily score twice more.
9. Memories of last season's 2-7 fiasco on the same ground come flooding back when Nisbet's poor pass allows Warren Joyce to give Wanderers an early lead. As Asa Hartford pulls the strings in midfield, Bolton cruise to a three-goal lead. Clayton's first for Argyle is scant consolation.
10. Gills' keeper Ron Hillyard usually performs miracles at Home Park but this time he is powerless to stop a convincing victory. Hodges starts things off with an angled drive and Nelson finishes a move he started. Peter Shaw handles to give Argyle their seventh penalty this season.
11. Rovers have only twelve fit players available. A three-goal half-time lead seems scant reward for such first-half domination. Wide-men Hodges and Nelson tear Rovers apart. Cooper and Clayton finally click. Parkin turns Nisbet's cross past Green. Two late defensive errors prove costly.

The followed club is Plymouth Argyle. Each match lists Argyle's line-up (roman) paired with the opponents' line-up (italic). The two figures after the attendance are the opponents' league position and Argyle's cumulative points.

No	V	Opponent	Date	Att	Opp pos	Pts	Res	Score	Scorers (Argyle / Opponent)	Referee
12	A	WALSALL	12/10	4,253	2	17	D	2-2	Nelson 50, 90 / Rees 44, 68	I Hemley
13	A	ROTHERHAM	19/10	2,942	18	18	D	1-1	Hodges 49 / Tynan 86	J Hendrick
14	H	LINCOLN	22/10	6,552	15	21	W	2-1	Hodges 47, Nelson 89 / Ward 65	R Hamer
15	A	DERBY	26/10	11,433	4	24	W	2-1	Hodges 7, Goodyear 30 / Davison 45	K Breen
16	H	CHESTERFIELD	2/11	7,522	13	25	D	0-0	—	R Lewis
17	H	BOURNEMOUTH	5/11	6,186	16	28	W	2-1	Hodges 42, Cooper S 56 / Newson 30	P Vanes
18	A	BURY	9/11	2,975	13	31	W	1-0	Clayton 38 / —	D Phillips
19	H	WIGAN	23/11	6,714	10	34	W	2-1	Summerfield 68, Coughlin 85p / Methven 70	D Hedges
20	A	BLACKPOOL	30/11	6,184	6	35	D	1-1	Nelson 83 / Stonehouse 28p	J Key
21	H	DARLINGTON	14/12	6,036	20	38	W	4-2	Hodges 37, 64, Cooper S 45, S'field 58 / MacDonald 76, Airey 88	R Gifford
22	A	READING	21/12	8,512	1	38	L	3-4	Hodges 10, Cooper S 44p, Clayton 48 / Horrix 69p, Senior 79, 80, Bremner 83	D Axcell
23	A	BRISTOL CITY	26/12	8,298	12	38	L	0-2	— / Walsh 7p, Neville 36	D Vickers

12 — WALSALL (A)
Walsall: Cherry, Jones, Mower*, Shakespeare, Hawker, Matthews, Rees, Cross, O'Kelly, Elliott, Naughton, Kelly
Two goals from Mark Rees seem certain to preserve Walsall's 100% home record. His second comes after running unchallenged from halfway. Nisbet and Clayton combine to set up Nelson. With two minutes of injury-time played, Nelson slots the ball home from the dead-ball line.

13 — ROTHERHAM (A)
Argyle: Crudgington, Nisbet, Cooper L, Matthews!, McElhinney, Hodges, Coughlin, Cooper S, Clayton, Nelson, Goodyear; sub Emerson
Rotherham: O'Hanlon, Forrest, Dungworth, Smith, Trusson, Pickering, Birch, Gooding*, Tynan, Simmons, Pugh
Ten-man Argyle come so close to holding on to their slender lead. Hodges finds the corner of the net with a low drive. Matthews, already booked and spoken to on more than one occasion, is red-carded after a late tackle on Simmons (58). Predictably, Tommy Tynan grabs a goal.

14 — LINCOLN (H)
Argyle: Crudgington, Nisbet, Cooper L, Matthews, McElhinney, Hodges, Coughlin, Cooper S, Clayton, Nelson, Goodyear
Lincoln: Greygoose, Meacham, McCarrick, Redfearn, West, Strodder, Toman, Turner, Latchford, Ward, McGinley
The Imps come closest to scoring in the first half when Matthews' back-pass goes straight to Bob Latchford. Hodges scores his 50th league goal with a volley before Warren Ward equalises. Nelson scores his seventh of the season after he rounds Dean Greygoose to put into an empty net.

15 — DERBY (A)
Argyle: Crudgington, Nisbet, Cooper L, Matthews, McElhinney, Hodges, Coughlin, Cooper S, Clayton, Nelson*, Goodyear
Derby: Wallington, Palmer, Buckley, Williams, Hindmarch, MacLaren, Micklewhite, Christie, Davison, McLaren*, Chandler, Garner
Smith does an impromptu war dance on the pitch at the end of another victory at the Baseball Ground. Mark Wallington fails to hold Clayton's stinging drive and Hodges pounces. County's keeper then totally misses Coughlin's corner and Goodyear heads in. Davison pulls one back.

16 — CHESTERFIELD (H)
Argyle: Crudgington, Nisbet, Cooper L, Summerfield, McElhinney, Hodges, Coughlin, Cooper S, Clayton, Nelson*, Goodyear; sub Rowbotham
Chesterfield: Marples, Scrimgeour, O'Neill, Williamson, Baines, Hunter, Reid, Moss, Walker, Henderson, Spooner*, Hewitt
Argyle miss the guile of the suspended Matthews as they are unable to break down a resolute defence. Chris Marples shows why he is also Derbyshire's wicket-keeper with some competent handling. Veteran Ernie Moss almost snatches the points with the Spireites' first shot (70).

17 — BOURNEMOUTH (H)
Argyle: Crudgington, Nisbet, Cooper L, Matthews, McElhinney, Hodges, Coughlin, Cooper S, Clayton, Nelson, Summerfield
Bournemouth: Smeulders, Heffernan, Sulley, Newson, Brown, Beck, O'Driscoll, Russell, Clarke, Howlett, Lewis*, Morrell
Smith pays tribute to a good size crowd who turn out despite poor weather and other counter attractions. Argyle suddenly find themselves in the promotion race after another three points. Hodges continues his good run of scoring and Cooper gets his first Pilgrims goal from open play.

18 — BURY (A)
Argyle: Crudgington, Nisbet, Cooper L, Matthews*, McElhinney*, Hodges, Coughlin, Cooper S, Clayton, Nelson, Summerfield
Bury: Hughes, Dixon, Bramhall, Dobson, Valentine, Hill, White, Madden*, Bedford, Jakub, Young, Kerr
The Shakers are still re-grouping to leave Clayton unmarked on the edge of the box from Coughlin's quickly taken free-kick. The striker makes no mistake. Argyle are forced to re-shuffle their line up at half-time when McElhinney remains in the dressing room after a bang on the head.

19 — WIGAN (H)
Argyle: Crudgington, Nisbet, Cooper L, Matthews, McElhinney, Hodges, Coughlin, Cooper S*, Clayton, Nelson, Summerfield
Wigan: Tunks, Butler, Knowles, Kelly, Cribley, Lowe, Methven, Barrow, Newell, Langley, Cook, Matthews
The whistle dominates as Mr Hedges awards 58 free-kicks. Wigan soon recover from Summerfield's goal with Colin Methven smashing an unstoppable shot past Crudgington. From 20 yards away, the ref decides that Alex Cribley's foul on Clayton takes place in the penalty area.

20 — BLACKPOOL (A)
Argyle: Crudgington, Nisbet, Cooper L, Matthews, McElhinney, Hodges, Coughlin, Cooper S, Clayton, Nelson, Summerfield
Blackpool: O'Rourke, Moore, Law, Stonehouse, Hetzke, Davies, Greenall, Britton, Stewart, Windridge, Dyer
Pool are awarded a harsh penalty after McElhinney cannot evade Paul Stewart's fierce cross and the ball strikes him on the arm. Nelson saves a point when he completes a fine move involving Hodges and Coughlin. Some late pressure fails to end the Tangerines' unbeaten home record.

21 — DARLINGTON (H)
Argyle: Crudgington, Nisbet, Cooper L*, Matthews, McElhinney, Hodges, Coughlin, Cooper S, Clayton, Nelson, Summerfield
Darlington: Barber, Evans, Morgan, Tupling*, Green, Lloyd, Roberts, Ward, Airey, Paskett, McLean, MacDonald
Cyril Knowles' side play their part in a highly entertaining game. Cooper's effort is the pick of the six goals. He smashes in from 25 yards to cheer himself up after failing his driving test for the second time. Play is delayed when sub Rowbotham appears wearing a number eleven shirt.

22 — READING (A)
Argyle: Crudgington, Nisbet!, Cooper L, Goodyear, McElhinney, Hodges, Coughlin, Cooper S, Clayton, Nelson, Summerfield
Reading: Westwood, Peters, Bailie, Wood, Hicks, Rogers, Horrix, Senior, Bremner, Gilkes*, Burvill
At 3-0 up Argyle look set to close the 15-point gap on runaway leaders Reading but then collapse dramatically. Goodyear chops down Kevin Bremner and Horrix's spot-kick provides the catalyst for a dramatic comeback. Nisbet is dismissed (90) for kicking ex-Pilgrim Andy Rogers.

23 — BRISTOL CITY (A)
Argyle: Crudgington, Nisbet, Cooper L, Goodyear, McElhinney, Hodges, Coughlin, Cooper S, Clayton, Nelson, Summerfield
Bristol City: Waugh, Llewellyn, Newman, Curle, Moyes, Riley, Pritchard, Hutchinson, Walsh, Tong, Neville
The normally prolific Nelson wastes four good scoring opportunities. Summerfield sends Howard Pritchard sprawling and Alan Walsh gives City the lead. Steve Neville sneaks in at the far post to head a second. Referee Vickers is replaced at half-time after suffering a back injury.

CANON DIVISION 3 — Manager: Dave Smith — SEASON 1985-86

No		Date	Att	Pos	Pt	F-A	H-T	Scorers, Times, and Referees	1	2	3	4	5	6	7	8	9	10	11	12 sub used
24	H	SWANSEA 28/12	8,622	3	23	2-0	1-0	Clayton 21, 50 — Ref: C Downey	Crudgington	Nisbet	Sullivan	Goodyear	McElhinney	Summerfield	Hodges	Coughlin	Cooper S	Clayton	Nelson	Matthews
									Hughes	*Hough*	*Sullivan*	*Price*	*Harrison*	*Emmanuel*	*McHale*	*Gibbins*	*McCarthy*	*Hutchison*	*Davis*	
25	H	CARDIFF 1/1	8,920	3	21	4-4	2-2	Nel' 33, Sum' 41, Clayt' 83, Hodges 88; Turner 35, Ford 40, Vaugh' 53, Mul' 59p — Ref: R Hamer	Crudgington*	Nisbet	Cooper L	Goodyear	McElhinney	Summerfield	Hodges	Coughlin	Cooper S	Clayton	Nelson	Matthews
									Smelt	*Curtis*	*Giles*	*Ford*	*Stevenson*	*Mullen*	*Christie*	*Vaughan*	*Turner*	*Farrington*	*Micallef*	
26	A	NOTTS CO 11/1	4,953	6	42	0-2	0-1	Hunt 26, McParland 73 — Ref: L Dilkes	Crudgington	Nisbet	Cooper L	Goodyear	McElhinney	Matthews	Hodges	Coughlin	Cooper S*	Clayton	Nelson	Coughlin
									Leonard	*Fairclough*	*Clarke*	*Benjamin*	*Sims**	*Davis*	*McParland*	*Goodwin*	*Waitt*	*Edge*	*Hunt*	*Robinson*
27	H	YORK 18/1	5,942	7	43	2-2	1-1	Brimacombe 6, Coughlin 68p; Walwyn 31, 48 — Ref: R Milford	Crudgington	Nisbet	Uzzell*	Brimacombe	McElhinney	Matthews	Hodges	Coughlin	Cooper S*	Clayton	Nelson	Cooper L
									Leaning	*Senior*	*Hood*	*McAughtrie*	*MacPhail*	*Mills*	*Ford*	*Banton*	*Walwyn*	*Houchen*	*Canham*	
28	A	NEWPORT 25/1	3,007	8	43	1-3	1-2	Clayton 7; Staniforth 30, Berry 38, Hodges 50(og) — Ref: M Reed	Crudgington	Nisbet	Cooper L	Goodyear	McElhinney	Matthews	Hodges	Coughlin	Cooper S	Clayton	Nelson	Mardenboro'
									Kendall	*Jones L*	*Jones P*	*Berry*	*Carter*	*Boyle*	*Gill*	*Relish*	*Latchford*	*Staniforth**	*Lewis*	
29	H	BRENTFORD 1/2	4,873	7	46	2-0	1-0	Nelson 30, 55 — Ref: R Groves	Crudgington	Nisbet	Cooper L	Goodyear	McElhinney	Matthews	Hodges	Coughlin	Cooper S	Clayton	Nelson	Alexander
									Phillips	*Joseph*	*Murray**	*Salman*	*Evans*	*Hurlock*	*Lynch*	*Sinton*	*Millen*	*Cooke*	*Booker*	
30	H	DONCASTER 15/2	4,827	8	46	0-1	0-0	Douglas 81 — Ref: I Hemley	Crudgington	Nisbet	Cooper L	Goodyear	McElhinney	Matthews	Hodges	Coughlin	Cooper S	Clayton	Nelson	Brown
									Rhodes	*Stead*	*Rushbury*	*Humphries*	*Flynn*	*Cusack*	*Buckley*	*Douglas*	*Dobbin*	*Philliben*	*Brown*	
31	A	GILLINGHAM 4/3	3,490	8	47	1-1	0-0	Summerfield 86; Cascarino 59 — Ref: M Bodenham	Crudgington	Nisbet	Cooper L	Goodyear	McElhinney	Summerfield	Hodges	Coughlin	Godfrey	Clayton	Nelson	
									Hillyard	*Sage*	*Elsey*	*Oakes*	*Weatherly*	*Hinnigan*	*Cochrane*	*Hales*	*Robinson*	*Shearer*	*Cascarino*	
32	A	BRISTOL ROV 8/3	4,667	8	50	2-1	1-0	Coughlin 16p, Godfrey 80; Morgan 74 — Ref: M Scott	Crudgington	Nisbet	Cooper L	Goodyear	McElhinney	Summerfield	Hodges	Coughlin*	Godfrey	Clayton	Nelson	Rowbotham
									Green	*Scales*	*Tanner*	*Stevenson*	*Parkin*	*Jones*	*Francis*	*Penrice*	*Morgan*	*White*	*O'Connor*	
33	A	WOLVERHAMPTON 11/3	2,367	6	53	3-0	2-0	Coughlin 22p, Summer'd 24, Clayton 82 — Ref: D Hutchinson	Crudgington	Nisbet	Cooper L	Goodyear	McElhinney	Summerfield	Hodges	Coughlin	Godfrey	Clayton	Nelson*	Rowbotham
									Barrett	*Palmer*	*Barnes*	*Streete*	*Zelem*	*Purdie*	*Eli*	*Holmes*	*Mutch*	*Edwards*	*Chapman*	
34	H	WALSALL 15/3	6,079	5	56	2-0	1-0	Cooper L 34, Coughlin 59 — Ref: R Hamer	Crudgington	Nisbet	Cooper L	Goodyear	McElhinney	Summerfield	Hodges	Coughlin	Godfrey	Clayton	Rowbotham	Rees
									Prudhoe	*Taylor*	*Mower*	*Jones*	*Hawker*	*Hart*	*Childs*	*Cross*	*Daley*	*Elliott*	*Naughton**	

24. The Swans are struggling to survive. Only the High Court has recently saved them from going out of business. Clayton has a chance for a hat-trick when Hough pushed Hodges to concede a penalty Cooper stands down to give Clayton the honours but Mike Hughes pulls off a fine save.

25. Both Smith and Alan Durban bemoan their side's defending. At 2-4 down, Argyle suffer another blow as Nisbet is forced to don the keeper's jersey when Crudgington suffers a nasty facial injury. Hodges scoops the ball off the line with his hand but makes amends with a late equaliser.

26. Unpredictable goalkeeper Mick Leonard does his best to give Argyle a head start. He rushes out to the touchline to meet Nelson, who easily evades him and passes to Clayton who hesitates in front of an open goal. That sets the tone for an off day as County easily cruise to victory.

27. Ex-Dockyard worker John Brimacombe has a dream debut, hooking in Nelson's corner. Keith Walwyn shows why he has scored 21 times this season by banging in the only two chances to fall his way. McAughtrie fouls Clayton. Coughlin becomes Argyle fourth different penalty taker.

28. After Clayton's early goal it all goes to pieces. Staniforth shows some of his old magic. Goodyear swings at a clearance and misses, leaving Berry to score. Hodges passes back to Crudgington who is practically standing next to him. Cooper hits a penalty too close to Kendall (60).

29. Smith has been away scouting for most of the week and jokes that he should stay away more often after seeing his side regain form. Visiting England manager Bobby Robson is impressed with two-goal Nelson who looks back to his best. Phillips saves Clayton's point-blank header.

30. Some woeful finishing reminds the Argyle faithful just how much the team misses Tynan. Dave Cusack's under-rated side have surprised a lot of teams this season and fully deserve to win by more than one. Crudgington fails to hold Stead's shot and Colin Douglas grabs the rebound.

31. The Greens finally get back to league action. Smith includes his new loan signing, Kevin Godfrey from Orient, who looks lively. The ever dangerous Tony Cascarino powers home his 19th of the season. Summerfield, in for the suspended Matthews, scores after Clayton hits the bar.

32. Rovers protest strongly against the decision to award handball against Vaughan Jones. Coughlin coolly slots in the penalty to end Ron Green's run of five consecutive clean sheets. Trevor Morgan for once escapes McElhinney's clutches to score. Godfrey gets a well-deserved winner.

33. The once mighty Wolves looked doomed for the drop. Peter Zelem is penalised for handling and Coughlin makes no mistake with his spot-kick. Godfrey again plays his part by laying on the goals for Summerfield and Clayton as thoughts of a promotion push are revived again.

34. Both sets of fans and manager Alan Buckley leave Home Park wondering how Walsall are so far up in the table. The Saddlers fail to get one shot on target as Crudgington has one of the easiest afternoons of his long career. Both goals come courtesy of powerful long-range shots.

18/3 — 2-1 — att. 1,828
Marples, Hewitt, O'Neill, Williamson*, Baines, Bellamy, Brown, Scrimgeour, Henderson, Moss, Godfrey, Clayton, Rowbotham, Batty, Cooper S, Walker
Henderson 2
Ref: G Napthine
The Greens suffer a setback when Henderson scores after just 80 seconds from Williamson's corner with question marks against the marking. Summerfield equalises when he calmly steers the ball past Marples. Cooper comes on and looks rejuvenated after a spell in the reserves.

36 DERBY 22/3 H 4 W 59 62 — 0-1 4-1 — att. 11,769 (pos. 3)
Crudgington, Nisbet, Cooper L, Buckley, Uzzell, Williams, Summerfield, Pratley, McEhinney, MacLaren, Micklewhite, Coughlin*, Hodges, Christie, Godfrey, Davison, Clayton, Gregory, Rowbotham, Chandler, Cooper S
Clayton 47, 56, Rowbot'm 79, Hodges 83
Christie 12
Ref: G Ashby
County have lost only four league matches all season but Argyle sweep them aside. Three defenders all leave the ball to each other to gift Christie the opener. Clayton demonstrates a knack for scoring which he failed to show as a Derby player. Rowbotham kicks off his goal record.

37 CARDIFF 28/3 A W 65 — 2-0 2-1 — att. 3,834
Smelt, Marustik, Giles, Ford, Brignull, Mullen, McLaughlin, Vaughan, Nardiello, Micallef, Foley, Crudgington, Nisbet, Uzzell, Hodges, Coughlin, Matthews, Godfrey*, Clayton, Rowbotham, Cooper S
Hodges 10, Matthews 29
Nardiello 49
Ref: M Dimblebee
Two thousand travelling Argyle fans account for more than half the attendance. A penalty is given when Lee Smelt dives at the feet of Hodges. Smelt requires four minutes of treatment to a head injury. This disconcerts Rowbotham, whose spot-kick is parried but Hodges follows up.

38 BOURNEMOUTH 5/4 A W 68 — 2-0 3-1 — att. 5,351 (pos. 14)
Smeulders, O'Hanlon, Sulley, Newson, Morrell, Beck, O'Driscoll*, Williams, Clarke, Thompson, O'Connor, Nightingale, Crudgington, Nisbet, Uzzell, Heffernan, Coughlin, Hodges, Matthews, Tynan, Cooper S, Nelson*
Cooper S 12, Coughlin 44p, Hodges 84
Beck 72
Ref: J Moules
Smith surprises everyone by bringing Tynan back on loan until the end of the season. Cooper, playing his best game of the season, triggers another victory with a superb header. Coughlin scores from the spot after Cooper is bowled over and Hodges beats Smeulders' despairing dive.

39 ROTHERHAM 8/4 H W 71 — 4-0 — att. 13,034
Hughes, Dixon, Hill, Robinson, Gooding, Pickering, Birch, Pepper, Trusson, Horner, Crudgington, Nisbet, Cooper L, Crosby, Coughlin, Hodges, Matthews, Tynan, Cooper S, Nelson*, Summerfield, Simmons
Pickering 17(og), Tynan 33, 59,
[Summerfield 89]
Ref: K Cooper
Tommy is back! The crowd are thrilled by their hero's homecoming. Millers' manager Norman Hunter is not, claiming Argyle have broken a gentleman's agreement in playing the striker against the team he belongs to. Smith denies such an agreement as his side carry on winning.

40 BURY 12/4 H W 74 — 2-0 3-0 — att. 13,626 (pos. 19)
Hughes, Dixon, Hill, Robinson, Valentine, White, Bramhall*, Pashley, Cross, Jakub, Crudgington, Nisbet, Cooper L, Coughlin, Hodges, Matthews, Tynan, Cooper S, Nelson, Harris, Young
Hodges 12, Tynan 30, 59
Ref: R Gifford
No Argyle side has won nine on the trot since 1930. Tynan poaches two more trademark goals from inside the six-yard box. Hodges nicks the ball away from a fumbling Hughes to open the scoring. A dog wanders aimlessly on the pitch to a chorus of 'There's only one Jack Russell'.

41 LINCOLN 16/4 A D 75 — 0-1 1-1 — att. 2,297
Swinburne, Hodson, Redfearn, Daniel, West, Stradder, McInnes, Turner, White, Kilmore, Mair, Crudgington, Nisbet, Cooper L, Coughlin, Hodges, Matthews*, Tynan, Cooper S, Nelson*
Tynan 54
West 3
Ref: P Tyldesley
At a rain-swept Sincil Bank, Argyle find themselves under pressure for the first time in weeks. Gary West's early goal gives hope to the Imps who are battling for every point to fight against relegation. Tynan, inevitably, gets the equaliser against one of his former clubs.

42 WIGAN 19/4 A L 75 — 0-3 — att. 9,485 (pos. 3)
Stewart, Cribley, Knowles, Walsh, Beesley, Methven, Lowe, Jewell, Aspinall*, Langley, Griffiths, Crudgington, Nisbet, Cooper L, Goodyear, Coughlin, Hodges, Matthews*, Tynan, Cooper S, Nelson, Barrow
Jewell 30, 67, Lowe 55
Ref: G Aplin
Smith apologises to the 5,000 travelling fans for his side's uncharacteristic display. Griffiths' vicious swerving cross takes Crudgington by surprise and Paul Jewell nips in. David Lowe punishes Goodyear's mistake. Jewell's superb control gives him time to smash in number three.

43 BOLTON 22/4 H W 78 — 4-1 — att. 12,183
Felgate, Scott, Phillips, Came, Thompson, Neal, Sutton, Burrows, Crudgington, Nisbet, Cooper L, Goodyear, Coughlin, Hodges, Summerfield, Tynan, Clayton, Oghani, Caldwell*, Hartford, Gavin, Bell, Nelson
Hodges 72, Coughlin 85p, Tynan 86,
Sutton 17 [Burrows 90]
Ref: A Robinson
There is much biting of nails as Bolton look to have put another obstacle in the way of Argyle's promotion push. Former defender Dave Sutton gives the visitors the lead. Hodges equalises and Scott handles. Tynan and Burrows finish off to crucially improve the Greens' goal-difference.

44 BLACKPOOL 26/4 H W 81 — 3-1 — att. 14,975 (pos. 12)
O'Rourke, Moore, Walsh, Conroy, Law, Greenall, Deary, Stewart, Thompson, Sendall, Crudgington, Nisbet, Cooper L, Goodyear, Coughlin, Hodges, Matthews*, Tynan, Clayton, Nelson
Nelson 50, Coughlin 78p, Tynan 88
Stewart 30
Ref: J Martin
Another nerve-racking game follows much the same pattern as the previous one. Pool cling on to a lead until Nelson slams in a first-time shot. Mr Martin finally relents after a number of penalty appeals are turned down. Coughlin coolly slots home. Tynan nicks Clayton's header.

45 BRISTOL CITY 29/4 H W 84 — 4-0 — att. 19,900
Waugh, Llewellyn, Williams, Curle, Moyes, Riley, Pritchard, Newman, Harle, Walsh, Neville, Crudgington, Nisbet, Cooper L, Goodyear, Coughlin, Hodges, Matthews, Tynan, Summerfield, Nelson
Tynan 22, 64, Nelson 54, Coughlin 60
Ref: J Deakin
The Greens are going up. A stunning performance clinches promotion. City have no answer to the rampaging Pilgrims. Coughlin scores direct from a corner. Tynan's second starts a party amongst the capacity crowd. Smith's trademark flat cap is last seen spiralling into the night air.

46 DARLINGTON 3/5 A W 87 — 0-0 2-0 — att. 3,306 (pos. 15)
Asbury, Evans, Morgan, Tupling, Douglas, Lloyd, Roberts, Ward, Airey, Woodcock, Robinson, Crudgington, Nisbet, Cooper L, Goodyear, Coughlin, Hodges, Matthews*, Tynan, Summerfield, Nelson, Cooper S
Hodges 65, Tynan 84
Ref: J McAuley
Not surprisingly, Smith is named as April manager of the month. One thousand fans make the long journey north to see their heroes finish the season in style. Hodges cuts through two players to score a superb goal and Tynan incredibly notches his tenth goal in less than a month.

Home 8,297
Away 4,715
Average

CANON DIVISION 3 (CUP-TIES)

Manager: Dave Smith

SEASON 1985-86

Milk Cup

	Att	F-A	H-T	Scorers, Times, and Referees	1	2	3	4	5	6	7	8	9	10	11	12 sub used
1:1 H EXETER 20/8	4,754 4:	W 2-1	1-0	Summerfield 15, McElhinney 63p / Pratt 71p / Ref: J Deakin	Crudgington *Shaw*	Nisbet *Kirkup**	Cooper L *King**	Goodyear *McNichol*	McElhinney *McCaffrey*	Matthews *Marker*	Hodges *Ling*	Coughlin *Kellow*	Cooper S *Morgan*	Summerfield *Pratt*	Nelson *Crawford*	*Viney*

A mixed evening for Summerfield. After heading the opening goal he is later fouled by Aiden McCaffrey leading to McElhinney's penalty. After the match it is revealed that he has suffered a fractured cheekbone. Cooper brings down Martin Ling and Ray Pratt scores from the spot.

	Att	F-A	H-T	Scorers, Times, and Referees	1	2	3	4	5	6	7	8	9	10	11	12 sub used
1:2 A EXETER 4/9	3,362 4:21	L 0-2	0-2	Kimble G 20, Marker 44 / Ref: J Martin / (Argyle lost 2-3 on aggregate)	Crudgington *Shaw*	Nisbet *Kirkup*	Cooper L* *Viney*	Burrows *McNichol*	McElhinney *Impey*	Matthews *Marker*	Hodges *Ling*	Coughlin *Kimble A*	Cooper S *Morgan*	Clayton *Kimble G*	Nelson *Crawford*	*Goodyear*

Injury-hit City call up the 19-year-old Kimble twins. The Grecians have fared no better in the league than Argyle but show more cohesion to progress to the next round. The tricky Martin Ling sets up Garry Kimble to level on aggregate and Nicky Marker's header puts City through.

FA Cup

	Att	F-A	H-T	Scorers, Times, and Referees	1	2	3	4	5	6	7	8	9	10	11	12 sub used
1 H ALDERSHOT 16/11	7,209 4:17	W 1-0	1-0	Coughlin 20 / Ref: B Stevens	Crudgington *Coles*	Nisbet *Blankley*	Cooper L *Gillard**	Goodyear *Fern*	McElhinney *Smith*	Summerfield *Morris*	Hodges* *Staff*	Coughlin *Johnson*	Cooper S *Duncan*	Clayton *Foyle*	Nelson *McDonald*	Rowbotham *Fielder*

In front of the second largest cup attendance of the day, the Shots produce slick football which belies their fourth division status. Out-of-sorts striker Martin Foyle misses several chances. Coughlin beats two defenders to score a memorable goal. Veteran Ian Gillard is stretchered off.

	Att	F-A	H-T	Scorers, Times, and Referees	1	2	3	4	5	6	7	8	9	10	11	12 sub used
2 H MAIDSTONE 7/12	7,597 GL:17	W 3-0	2-0	Cooper L 12, Nelson 29, Summerfield 84 / Ref: R Milford	Crudgington *Richardson*	Nisbet *Thompson*	Cooper L *Borg*	Goodyear *Pittaway*	McElhinney *Glover*	Summerfield *Fergusson*	Hodges *Hill*	Coughlin *Reynolds*	Cooper S *Cugley*	Clayton *Barnes*	Nelson *Tiltman**	*Joyce*

For the second year running Barry Fry brings a non-league side to Home Park. Despite some uncompromising tackling, Maidstone put up little resistance as Argyle play some slick football. Their one chance comes from the spot after McElhinney handled but Barnes' shot is smothered.

	Att	F-A	H-T	Scorers, Times, and Referees	1	2	3	4	5	6	7	8	9	10	11	12 sub used
3 A HULL 4/1	6,776 2:8	D 2-2	2-1	Clayton 29, Cooper S 33 / Flounders 20, 56 / Ref: J Worrall	Philip *Norman*	Burrows *Jobson*	Cooper L *Swann*	Goodyear *Doyle*	McElhinney *Skipper*	Summerfield *McEwan*	Hodges *Ring*	Matthews *Bunn*	Cooper S *Flounders*	Clayton *Askew*	Nelson *Roberts*	

A trip to Boothferry Park is hardly the glamour tie Argyle had hoped for. Philip admits blame for Hull's first when he mistimes a punch. Argyle fight back on a pitch that is getting harder by the minute in freezing conditions. Andy Flounders gets his second to take the tie to a replay.

	Att	F-A	H-T	Scorers, Times, and Referees	1	2	3	4	5	6	7	8	9	10	11	12 sub used
3R H HULL 7/1	13,940 2:8	L 0-1	0-1	Roberts 6 / Ref: J Deakin	Philip *Norman*	Burrows *Jobson*	Cooper L *Swann*	Goodyear *Doyle*	McElhinney *Skipper*	Matthews *McEwan*	Hodges *Horton*	Summerfield* *Bunn*	Cooper S *Flounders*	Clayton *Askew*	Nelson *Roberts*	Uzzell

Gareth Roberts gets the vital early breakthrough and the Tigers are then happy to soak up pressure. Manager Brian Horton recalls himself and controls the midfield. Summerfield unsuccessfully claims that his shot is over the line before Norman scoops it back. Hull now face Brighton.

Final League Table

Pos	Team	P	W	D	L	F	A	W	D	L	F	A	Pts
1	Reading	46	16	3	4	39	22	13	4	6	28	29	94
2	PLYMOUTH	46	17	3	3	56	20	9	6	8	32	33	87
3	Derby	46	13	7	3	45	20	10	8	5	35	21	84
4	Wigan	46	17	4	2	54	17	6	10	7	28	31	83
5	Gillingham	46	14	5	4	48	17	8	8	7	33	37	79
6	Walsall	46	15	7	1	59	23	7	2	14	31	41	75
7	York	46	16	4	3	49	17	4	7	12	28	41	71
8	Notts Co	46	12	6	5	42	26	7	8	8	29	34	71
9	Bristol City	46	14	5	4	43	19	4	9	10	26	41	68
10	Brentford	46	8	8	7	29	29	10	4	9	29	32	66
11	Doncaster	46	7	10	6	20	21	9	6	8	25	31	64
12	Blackpool	46	11	6	6	38	19	5	6	11	28	36	63
13	Darlington	46	10	7	6	33	33	5	6	12	22	45	58
14	Rotherham	46	13	5	5	44	18	2	7	14	17	41	57
15	Bournemouth	46	9	6	8	41	31	6	3	14	24	41	54
16	Bristol Rov	46	9	8	6	27	21	5	5	14	24	54	54
17	Chesterfield	46	10	6	7	41	30	3	8	12	20	34	53
18	Bolton	46	10	4	9	35	30	5	4	14	19	38	53
19	Newport	46	7	8	8	35	33	4	10	9	17	32	51
20	Bury	46	11	7	5	46	26	1	6	16	17	41	49
21	Lincoln	46	7	9	7	33	34	3	7	13	22	43	46
22	Cardiff	46	7	5	11	22	29	5	4	14	31	54	45
23	Wolves	46	6	6	11	29	47	5	4	14	28	51	43
24	Swansea	46	9	6	8	27	27	2	4	17	16	60	43
		1104	268	145	139	941	609	139	145	268	609	941	1511

Appearances and Goals

	Lge	Sub	LC	Sub	FAC	Sub	Lge	LC	FAC	Tot
Brimacombe, John	1						1			1
Burrows, Adrian	7		1		2		2			2
Clayton, John	36				4		11	1		12
Cooper, Leigh	39	1	2		4		1		1	2
Cooper, Steve	34	4	2		4		8	1		9
Coughlin, Russell	44	1	2		2		10	1		11
Crudgington, Geoff	46		2		2					
Godfrey, Kevin	7						1			1
Goodyear, Clive	41		1	1	4		2			2
Hodges, Kevin	46		2		4		16			16
Matthews, John	29	2	2		2		1			1
McElhinney, Gerry	44		2		4		2		1	3
Nelson, Garry	41	1	2		4		13		1	14
Nisbet, Gordon	46		2		2					
Philp, Dave						2				
Rowbotham, Darren	7	7					1			1
Summerfield, Kevin	21	5	1		4		7		2	9
Tynan, Tommy	9						10			10
Uzzell, John	8					1				
(own-goals)							2			2
19 players used	506	21	22	1	44	2	88	2	6	96

Double wins: (7) Bournemouth, Bristol Rov, Bury, Darlington, Derby, Swansea, Wolves.

Double defeats: (3) Doncaster, Notts Co, Reading.

Won from behind: (5) Blackpool, Bolton, Bournemouth, Chesterfield, Derby.

Lost from in front: (2) Newport, Reading.

High spots: Winning 13 of final 15 games to gain promotion.

Exciting style of play utilising two wide men, Hodges and Nelson.

Triumphant return of Tommy Tynan on loan.

Full house for match v Bristol City (h).

Low spots: Losing at leaders Reading after being 3-0 ahead.

Being knocked out of Milk Cup by local rivals Exeter.

Player of the Year: Kevin Hodges.

Ever presents: (1). Kevin Hodges.

Hat-tricks: (0).

Leading scorer: Kevin Hodges (16).

TODAY DIVISION 2

Manager: Dave Smith

SEASON 1986-87

No	Date	V	Team	Att	Pos	Pt	Res	F-A	H-T	Scorers, Times, and Referees
1	23/8	A	BRADFORD C	5,104		1	D	2-2	1-1	Coughlin 24, Summerfield 84 / Ormondroyd 17, Matthews 82(og) / Ref: I Hendrick
2	30/8	H	READING	9,659	9	4	W	1-0	0-0	Hodges 53 / Ref: B Stevens
3	6/9	A	HULL	6,451	8	7	W	3-0	3-0	Cooper S 13, 34, Summerfield 45 / Ref: C Trussell
4	13/9	H	BRIGHTON	9,423	8	8	D	2-2	0-0	Nelson 67, Matthews 80 / Connor 77, Penney 88 / Ref: R Gifford
5	20/9	A	BARNSLEY	4,163	8	9	D	1-1	1-1	Summerfield 14 / May 41 / Ref: J Bray
6	30/9	A	BLACKBURN	5,300	5	12	W	2-1	0-1	Summerfield 66, Rowbotham 73 / Fazackerley 17p / Ref: J McAuley
7	4/10	H	LEEDS	11,923	6	13	D	1-1	0-0	Cooper S 60 / Baird 46 / Ref: P Vanes
8	11/10	A	GRIMSBY	4,155	6	14	D	1-1	1-0	Cooper S 22 / Moore 50 / Ref: T Mills
9	14/10	H	SHEFFIELD UTD	11,003	4	17	W	1-0	0-0	Tynan 63 / Ref: K Cooper
10	18/10	H	SUNDERLAND	13,482	6	17	L	2-4	0-2	Hodges 51, Tynan 59 / Buchanan 7, 15, Armstrong 79, [Lemon 87] / Ref: R Milford

Line-ups (1–12, 12 = sub used)

1 — v Bradford C

	1	2	3	4	5	6	7	8	9	10	11	12
Argyle	Crudgington	Nisbet	Cooper L	Uzzell*	McElhinney	Matthews	Hodges	Coughlin	Summerfield	Clayton	Nelson	Goodyear
Bradford	*Litchfield*	*Oliver*	*Withe*	*McCall**	*Jackson*	*Evans*	*Hendrie*	*Ormondroyd*	*Campbell*	*Abbott*	*Graham*	*Singleton*

2 — v Reading

	1	2	3	4	5	6	7	8	9	10	11	12
Argyle	Crudgington	Nisbet	Cooper L	Goodyear	Uzzell	Matthews	Hodges	Coughlin	Summerfield	Clayton	Nelson	
Reading	*Westwood*	*Bailie*	*Richardson*	*Beavon*	*Hicks*	*Peters*	*Rogers**	*Hurlock*	*Senior*	*Bremner*	*Canoville*	*White*

3 — v Hull

	1	2	3	4	5	6	7	8	9	10	11	12
Argyle	Crudgington	Nisbet	Cooper L	Goodyear	Uzzell	Matthews	Summerfield	Coughlin	Tynan	Cooper S	Nelson	
Hull	*Norman*	*Jobson*	*Swann*	*Heard*	*Skipper*	*Williams*	*Parker*	*Bunn*	*Flounders*	*Askew**	*Roberts*	*Saville*

4 — v Brighton

	1	2	3	4	5	6	7	8	9	10	11	12
Argyle	Crudgington	Nisbet	Cooper L	Goodyear	Uzzell	Matthews	Summerfield	Coughlin	Tynan	Cooper S*	Nelson	Rowbotham
Brighton	*Digweed*	*Berry*	*Hutchings*	*Wilson*	*Gatting*	*O'Reilly**	*Penney*	*Saunders*	*Rowell*	*Connor*	*Jasper*	*O'Regan*

5 — v Barnsley

	1	2	3	4	5	6	7	8	9	10	11	12
Argyle	Crudgington	Nisbet	Cooper L	Goodyear	McElhinney	Matthews	Summerfield	Coughlin	Tynan	Clayton	Nelson*	Uzzell
Barnsley	*Baker*	*Joyce*	*Gray*	*Thomas*	*May*	*Futcher*	*Lowndes*	*Foreman*	*Chandler**	*Dobbin*	*Agnew*	*Beresford*

6 — v Blackburn

	1	2	3	4	5	6	7	8	9	10	11	12
Argyle	Crudgington	Nisbet	Cooper L	Goodyear	McElhinney	Matthews	Summerfield	Coughlin	Tynan	Clayton*	Nelson	Rowbotham
Blackburn	*O'Keefe*	*Price*	*Branagan*	*Barker*	*Fazackerley*	*Mail*	*Brotherston*	*Sellars*	*Diamond*	*Garner*	*Patterson*	

7 — v Leeds

	1	2	3	4	5	6	7	8	9	10	11	12
Argyle	Crudgington	Nisbet	Cooper L	Goodyear	McElhinney	Matthews	Summerfield	Coughlin	Tynan	Rowbotham	Nelson*	Cooper S
Leeds	*Day*	*Aspin*	*Haddock*	*Ormsby*	*Ashurst*	*Rennie*	*Stiles*	*Sheridan*	*Baird*	*Edwards*	*Ritchie*	

8 — v Grimsby

	1	2	3	4	5	6	7	8	9	10	11	12
Argyle	Crudgington	Nisbet	Cooper L	Goodyear	Uzzell	Matthews	Brimac'be*	Coughlin	Tynan	Cooper S	Nelson*	Summerfield
Grimsby	*Batch*	*Burgess*	*Cumming*	*Bonnyman*	*Lyons**	*Moore*	*Henshaw*	*Walsh*	*Hobson*	*O'Riordan*	*Turner*	*Rawcliffe*

9 — v Sheffield Utd

	1	2	3	4	5	6	7	8	9	10	11	12
Argyle	Crudgington	Nisbet	Cooper L	Goodyear	Uzzell	Matthews	Hodges	Coughlin	Tynan	Cooper S	Nelson	Summerfield
Sheffield Utd	*Burridge*	*Barnsley*	*Pike*	*Dempsey*	*Smith*	*Eckhardt*	*Morris*	*Frain*	*Withe*	*Foley*	*Beagrie*	

10 — v Sunderland

	1	2	3	4	5	6	7	8	9	10	11	12
Argyle	Crudgington	Nisbet	Cooper L	Goodyear	Uzzell	Matthews	Hodges	Coughlin	Tynan	Cooper S	Nelson	Summerfield
Sunderland	*Hesford*	*Burley*	*Kennedy*	*Armstrong*	*Hetzke*	*Bennett*	*Lemon*	*Doyle*	*Swindlehurst*	*Gray*	*Buchanan*	

Match notes

1. The lanky Ian Ormondroyd gives Bradford the lead at a sparsely populated Odsal Stadium. Coughlin equalises after good work by Hodges. Uzzell goes off with a cut eye. Matthews' slight touch puts the Bantams back in front. Summerfield's angled shot gains a well-earned point.

2. Summerfield misses a good chance after only 15 seconds. Mr Stevens takes an age to decide that Bailie's challenge on Clayton (9) is illegal. Coughlin's spot-kick is saved. Hodges thumps in a left-foot drive. The Royals are denied a last-minute penalty when Senior appears to be held.

3. Tynan is back, which seems to inspire fellow striker Cooper. He smashes home a 20-yard volley and then rises above everyone to head home. Summerfield glides in to head a third. Crudgington is fortunate to escape a red card after bringing down Frankie Bunn on the edge of the box.

4. In driving wind and rain, only the brilliance of Perry Digweed combats Argyle's first-half dominance. Nelson finally beats the keeper with a header. Connor outpaces Uzzell for the equaliser. Matthews finds the corner from 30 yards. Penney dashes from halfway to pinch a point.

5. Crudgington defies his 34 years to produce a series of elastic saves. Summerfield scores yet another goal away from Home Park, finishing off a flowing move involving Tynan and Clayton. May lashes home from 18 yards for Barnsley's first goal since the opening day of the season.

6. Chris Price is fouled by Nelson and Derek Fazackerley sends Crudgington the wrong way. Rowbotham's introduction inspires the Greens. Summerfield maintains his record of scoring in every away match by pouncing on a back-pass. The substitute scores with a 20-yard drive.

7. Things look bleak when Nelson is replaced after 30 minutes and then McElhinney hobbles to the dressing room at half-time. The Irishman limps through the second period as Ian Baird puts Leeds ahead within 30 seconds of the restart. S Cooper blasts home a poor clearance.

8. S Cooper's shot balloons off a defender past a startled Batch. Player-manager Mick Lyons replaces himself at half-time. Kevin Moore scores the Mariners' first home goal of the season. Summerfield misses a last-minute chance as he hits the crossbar when it looks easier to score.

9. Argyle continue to be the surprise team of the division. Hodges makes a shock comeback after six weeks, having received treatment for a knee injury at Lilleshall. Tynan finally breaks his duck when he intercepts Brian Smith's suicidal back-pass and steers the ball past John Burridge.

10. Dave Buchanan soon shows why he was plucked from non-league obscurity with two goals. His 25-yard shot is deflected in and Goodyear can only help the second into the net. Hodges scores from an impossible angle. Crudgington spills a pass to Armstrong and Lemon is unmarked.

Season match-by-match record (away = A, home = H)

No.	H/A	Opponent	Date	Seq	Res	Pos	Pts	FT	HT	Att
11	H	(Ipswich)	21/10			8	20	2-0		12,569
12	A	MILLWALL	25/10	4	L	13	20	1-3	0-1	3,558
13	H	CRYSTAL PALACE	1/11	4	W	10	23	3-1	1-1	11,708
14	A	SHREWSBURY	8/11	4	D	20	24	1-1	1-0	3,821
15	H	WEST BROM	15/11	3	W	7	27	1-0	0-0	14,697
16	A	HUDDERSFIELD	22/11	3	W	20	30	2-1	1-1	4,874
17	H	OLDHAM	29/11	3	W	1	33	3-2	2-1	17,265
18	A	STOKE	6/12	3	L	12	33	0-1	0-0	10,043
19	H	DERBY	13/12	3	D	4	34	1-1	0-1	15,812
20	A	IPSWICH	19/12	5	L	3	34	0-3	0-1	11,538
21	H	PORTSMOUTH	26/12	5	L	1	34	2-3	1-2	21,249

---

11 — H (Ipswich) 21/10
Opponents (Ipswich): Cooper, Yallop, Zondervan, Atkins, Cranson, Gleghorn, Brennan, D'Avray*, Deehan, Wilson, Stockwell.
Ref: R Hamer
…deserve their wages. Steve Cherry joins Argyle on a month's loan from Walsall. Ipswich manager Bobby Ferguson fumes at his players, saying only three of them deserve their wages. Coughlin scores from a twice-taken penalty after Cranson fouls Tynan. The on-song Summerfield scores a fine solo goal.

12 — A MILLWALL 25/10 (1-3)
Scorers: Walker 71(og); Sheringham 31, Stevens 79, Salman 81.
Argyle: Crudgington, Nisbet, Cooper L, Goodyear*, Matthews, McElhinney, Hodges, Coughlin, Tynan, Cooper S, Summerfield, Burrows.
Millwall: Sansome, Coleman N, Stevens, Byrne, McLeary, Walker, Briley, Morgan, Sheringham, Marks, Salman.
Ref: B Hill
The linesmen are busiest as both sides continually employ successful offside traps. David Byrne sets up Keith Stevens' goal and Danis Salman scampers away from everyone to score. Alan Walker scores an own-goal from 25 yards. Teddy Sheringham turns sharply to open the scoring.

13 — H CRYSTAL PALACE 1/11 (3-1)
Scorers: Tynan 9, 78, Summerfield 59; Taylor 40.
Argyle: Crudgington, Nisbet, Cooper L, Goodyear, Matthews, McElhinney, Hodges, Coughlin, Tynan, Cooper S, Summerfield.
Palace: Wood, Stebbing, Sparrow, Taylor, Cannon, Irvine, Higginbottom, Gray*, Droy, Wright, Otulakowski, Finnigan.
Ref: G Ashby
Palace show why they have conceded ten goals in three games with some poor defending. Jim Cannon inexplicably passes to Tynan for the first. Kevin Taylor sneaks in to level. Droy nods the ball away from Wood to gift Summerfield an easy goal. Tynan scores with a fine header.

14 — A SHREWSBURY 8/11 (1-1)
Scorers: Matthews 44; McNally 64p.
Argyle: Crudgington, Nisbet, Cooper L, Goodyear, Matthews, Burrows, Hodges, Coughlin, Tynan, Clayton, Cooper S.
Shrewsbury: Perks, Williams, Johnson, Leonard, McNally, Franklin, Pearson, Hackett*, Brown, Robinson, Daly, Tester.
Ref: R Guy
Matthews scores with a left-foot pile-driver from 22 yards. A through ball leaves Crudgington exposed and he brings down Gary Leonard in the box. Bernard McNally's penalty squeezes in between fingertips and post. Argyle have chances but wayward finishing lets them down.

15 — H WEST BROM 15/11 (1-0)
Scorer: Nisbet 61.
Argyle: Crudgington, Nisbet, Cooper L, Goodyear, Matthews, Burrows, Hodges, Coughlin, Tynan, Clayton, Summerfield.
West Brom: Naylor, Whitehead, Cowdrill, Palmer, Dickinson, Hopkins, Anderson, MacKenzie, Williamson, Crooks, Dyson.
Ref: J Martin
The Pilgrims reach the heady heights of third place thanks to Nisbet's first goal for two years. Tynan lays off Cooper's free-kick for the full back to thunder in and find the target from 25 yards. Ron Saunders' side rarely threaten and do not force their first corner until the 87th minute.

16 — A HUDDERSFIELD 22/11 (2-1)
Scorers: Clayton 38, Tynan 73; Webster 12.
Argyle: Crudgington, Nisbet, Cooper L, Goodyear, Matthews*, Burrows, Hodges, Coughlin, Tynan, Clayton, Summerfield.
Huddersfield: Cox, Brown, Burke, Banks, Webster, Winter, McDermott, Raynor*, Shearer, Wilson, Cork, Cowling.
Ref: D Hedges
Poor marking leaves Simon Webster free to head home from a corner. Mr Hedges ignores a linesman's flag to allow Clayton to pounce after a goalmouth scramble. Terriers boss Mick Buxton confronts the referee at half-time. Matthews rescues a lost cause for Tynan to head in.

17 — H OLDHAM 29/11 (3-2)
Scorers: Clayton 10, Burrows 18, Tynan 71; Milligan 35, Futcher 84.
Argyle: Crudgington, Nisbet, Cooper L, Goodyear, Matthews, Burrows, Hodges, Coughlin*, Tynan, Clayton, Rowbotham.
Oldham: Goram, Irwin, Donachie*, Hoolickin, Williams, Palmer, Henry, Wright, Milligan, Futcher, Callaghan.
Ref: R Groves
Argyle stun Joe Royle's leaders with two early goals. Burrows gives a faultless display. Tynan rounds off a flowing move with a diving header. Ron Futcher punishes a mix-up between Nisbet and Crudgington. Bell's Manager of the Month Smith dances on the pitch at the end.

18 — A STOKE 6/12 (0-1)
Scorer: Berry 64p.
Argyle: Cherry, Nisbet, Cooper L*, Goodyear, Burrows, Hodges, Rowbotham, Coughlin, Tynan, Clayton, Summerfield.
Stoke: Fox, Dixon, Parkin, Talbot, Berry, Ford, Morgan, Kelly, Saunders, Heath, Bould.
Ref: R Wiseman
Argyle's first visit to the Victoria Ground for 22 years ends in defeat. The ref is replaced by linesman Mr Hoare at half-time after suffering bruised ribs. Cherry has an outstanding debut but is penalised for shoving his arms around an opponent. George Berry crashes home the penalty.

19 — H DERBY 13/12 (1-1)
Scorers: Tynan 90; Micklewhite 37.
Argyle: Cherry, Nisbet, Cooper L, Goodyear, Matthews, Burrows, Hodges, Coughlin, Tynan, Clayton, Summerfield.
Derby: Wallington, Sage, Forsyth, Williams, MacLaren, Gee*, Davison, Gregory, Harbey, Lillis, Micklewhite.
Ref: T Holbrook
Cherry keeps Argyle in the game with a string of fine saves against his former club but is unable to prevent Gary Micklewhite planting the ball out of his reach after Cooper misses a cross. In injury-time, Hodges is fouled and Matthews' quick free-kick finds Tynan who cannot miss.

20 — A IPSWICH 19/12 (0-3)
Scorers: Wilson 11, Brennan 47, 76.
Argyle: Cherry, Nisbet, Cooper L, Goodyear, Matthews*, Burrows, Hodges, Coughlin, Tynan, Clayton, Nelson; sub Summerfield.
Ipswich: Cooper, Yallop, Zondervan, Atkins, Dozzell, Humes, Cole, Brennan, Deehan, Wilson, Stockwell.
Ref: R Lewis
Argyle are outclassed by an impressive Ipswich side. Kevin Wilson shoots them into the lead after hesitation in the defence. Paul Cooper tips Coughlin's 30-yard drive onto the bar. Mark Brennan scores twice after good build-ups. Nelson returns after two months and goes close.

21 — H PORTSMOUTH 26/12 (2-3)
Scorers: Coughlin 31p, Hodges 77; Quinn 13, Dillon 20, Hilaire 53.
Argyle: Cherry, Nisbet, Cooper L*, Goodyear, Matthews*, Burrows, Hodges, Coughlin, Tynan, Clayton, Nelson; sub Rowbotham.
Portsmouth: Knight, Swain, Dillon, Hardyman*, Blake, Gilbert, O'Callaghan, Kennedy, Mariner, Quinn, Hilaire, Tait.
Ref: K Burge
Pompey's bad boy reputation is not helped by O'Callaghan's shocking tackle on Uzzell. A free-kick is awarded when Hardyman brings down Tynan outside the area but the linesman indicates a penalty. Micky Quinn scores his 18th of the season. Coughlin sends Knight the wrong way.

TODAY DIVISION 2   Manager: Dave Smith   SEASON 1986-87

No	Date	V	Team	Att	Pos	Res	—	Pt	F-A	H-T	Scorers, Times, and Referees	1	2	3	4	5	6	7	8	9	10	11	12 sub used
22	27/12	A	WEST BROM	12,678	8	D	7	35	0-0	0-0	Ref: P Don	Crudgington	Nisbet	Goodyear	Burrows	McElhinney	Matthews	Hodges	Coughlin	Tynan	Clayton	Nelson	
												Naylor	*Whitehead*	*Cowdrill*	*Singleton*	*Dyson*	*Dickinson*	*Hopkins*	*Anderson*	*MacKenzie*	*Williamson*	*Crooks*	
											Crudgington is recalled and produces several good saves. He rushes 15 yards outside the penalty area to rob Bobby Williamson. Albion fans are unhappy with their team's display, which is largely down to Argyle's effective defending. By the end, two games in two days takes its toll.												
23	1/1	A	BIRMINGHAM	8,696	6	L	11	35	2-3	0-1	Goodyear 69, Tynan 86 / Kuhl 13, Clarke 58, Mortimer 83 / Ref: T Holbrook	Crudgington	Nisbet	Goodyear	Burrows	McElhinney	Matthews	Hodges	Coughlin	Tynan	Cooper L	Nelson	Kennedy
												Hansbury	*Ranson*	*Roberts*	*Williams*	*Hart**	*Mortimer*	*Bremner*	*Clarke*	*Rees*	*Kuhl*	*Handysides*	
											Kuhl nips in to head home after Rees's shot is pushed onto a post. Wayne Clarke gets his 19th goal of the season. Goodyear's goal sparks a mini revival. Blues suffer a setback (38) when Tom Williams' attempted tackle on Nelson catches debutant team-mate Paul Hart, breaking his leg.												
24	3/1	H	HULL	11,697	5	W	17	38	4-0	2-0	Tynan 30, 70, Hodges 35, Nels' 60 / Ref: B Stevens	Crudgington	Nisbet	Cooper L	Goodyear	Burrows	Matthews*	Hodges	Coughlin	Tynan	Nelson	Rowbotham	Brimacombe
												Norman	*Williams*	*Heard*	*Parker*	*Skipper*	*Buckley*	*Horton**	*Bunn*	*Flounders*	*Jobson*	*Roberts*	*Saville*
											Captain McElhinney is dropped. Tynan is appointed stand-in skipper and responds with two goals. He surprises Norman with a header and then sets up Hodges who scores from 25 yards with a weak shot. Nelson pounces on a loose ball and Tynan loops another header over Norman.												
25	24/1	H	BRADFORD C	11,582	5	W	20	41	3-2	1-0	Tynan 23, Summ'field 46, Hodges 90 / McCall 77, 89 / Ref: A Ward	Crudgington	Nisbet	Goodyear	Summerfield	Burrows	Matthews	Hodges	Coughlin	Tynan	Nelson	Rowboth'm*	Brimacombe
												Litchfield	*Abbott*	*Goddard*	*McCall*	*Oliver*	*Evans*	*Hendrie*	*Clegg*	*Ormondroyd*	*Palin**	*Ellis*	*Leonard*
											Smith has only twelve fully fit players available. The Bantams, under caretaker boss Terry Dolan, look anything but a bottom of the table side. Tynan scores again with his head. Stuart McCall's late goal looks to have clinched a point but Hodges fires home a loose ball in stoppage time.												
26	7/2	A	READING	6,853	6	L	16	41	0-2	0-1	Senior 39, 55 / Ref: A Buksh	Cherry	Nisbet	Cooper L	Burrows	McElhinney	Matthews	Rowbotham	Coughlin*	Tynan	Nelson	Goodyear	Hodges
												Westwood	*Bailie*	*Richardson*	*Beavon*	*Hicks*	*Wood*	*Williams*	*Taylor*	*Senior*	*Bremner*	*Hurlock*	
											A 35-minute dressing room inquest follows a dismal display. Trevor Senior gets the better of a tussle with McElhinney to fire home the first although there is more than a suspicion of handball. The prolific scorer then heads home from close range following Terry Hurlock's cross.												
27	14/2	H	BLACKBURN	9,884	4	D	17	42	1-1	1-0	Summerfield 29 / Ainscow 87 / Ref: K Cooper	Cherry	Nisbet	Cooper L	Burrows	McElhinney	Matthews	Rowboth'm*	Coughlin	Tynan	Summerfield	Nelson	Hodges
												Mimms	*Price*	*Rathbone*	*Barker*	*Keeley*	*Mail*	*Miller*	*Sellars*	*Diamond*	*Garner*	*Branagan**	*Ainscow*
											Nelson misses a glorious chance to add to Summerfield's header when he rounds Mimms but somehow fails to hit the target. McElhinney is penalised for pushing Keeley. Cherry silences his barrackers by saving Barker's penalty with his leg. Ainscow punishes some poor defending.												
28	21/2	A	SHEFFIELD UTD	6,982	5	L	12	42	1-2	0-1	Coughlin 68p / Foley 32, Frain 55 / Ref: N Ashley	Cherry	Nisbet	Cooper L*	Burrows	McElhinney	Matthews	Hodges	Coughlin	Tynan	Summerfield	Goodyear	Goodyear
												Burridge	*Wilder*	*Pike*	*Arnott*	*Stancliffe*	*Barnsley*	*Frain*	*Foley*	*Withe*	*Dempsey*	*Beagrie**	*Phillskirk*
											Argyle are linked with Liverpool's Gary Ablett. Steve Foley converts Peter Beagrie's cross. David Frain's blistering shot puts the Blades two up. Coughlin scores from the spot after Pike needlessly handles. Argyle never look like gaining their first win at Bramall Lane since the war.												
29	28/2	H	BARNSLEY	9,588	4	W	19	45	2-0	1-0	Nelson 9, 88 / Ref: R Gifford	Cherry	Nisbet	Uzzell	Goodyear	McElhinney	Matthews*	Hodges	Coughlin	Tynan	Cooper S	Nelson	Brimacombe
												Baker	*Joyce*	*Cross*	*Ogley*	*Gray*	*Futcher*	*Hedworth*	*Agnew*	*Dobbin*	*MacDonald*	*Clarke**	*Beresford*
											Two corners in the first minute set the tone as Argyle dominate. Defenders stand rooted to the spot as Nelson sneaks in to net Coughlin's cross. Matthews goes off (27) with a gashed leg. Allan Clarke's side play the final 25 minutes with ten men through injury. Nelson heads in a second.												
30	7/3	H	MILLWALL	9,525	4	W	11	48	1-0	0-0	Tynan 80 / Ref: R Groves	Cherry	Nisbet	Uzzell	Goodyear	McElhinney	Brimacombe	Hodges	Coughlin	Tynan	Cooper S*	Nelson	Clayton
												Horne	*Morgan*	*Coleman N*	*Hurlock*	*Coleman P*	*McLeary*	*Sheringham*	*Mehmet*	*Armstrong*	*Booker*		
											The Pilgrims are grateful that Gerry Armstrong has an off day as the Irish striker misses two sitters. All three officials fail to see McElhinney's handball in the area, which leaves Lions' boss John Docherty fuming. Tynan nets from close range with the referee about to award a penalty.												
31	14/3	A	SUNDERLAND	10,062	5	L	15	48	1-2	1-1	Tynan 38 / Buchanan 45, Lemon 52 / Ref: J Worrall	Cherry	Nisbet	Uzzell	Law	McElhinney	Brima'be*	Hodges	Coughlin	Tynan	Clayton	Nelson	Goodyear
												Hesford	*Burley*	*Gray*	*Armstrong*	*Hetzke*	*Bennett*	*Lemon*	*Doyle*	*Swindlehurst*	*Proctor*	*Buchanan*	
											Tynan gives Argyle a deserved lead when he twists and turns Hetzke before drilling home a well-placed shot. Despite Buchanan's equaliser, the Wearsiders are booed off at half-time. Cherry is deceived by Mark Lemon's swerving shot which bounces off the keeper's chest and in.												

32	H	GRIMSBY		5	W	5-0	2-0	Nisbet 11, 57, Tynan 45, 75,	Cherry	Nisbet	Cooper L	Law	McElhinney	Matthews	Hodges	Coughlin	Tynan	Clayton	Nelson	
	21/3		9,671	*12*	51			[Clayton 78]	*Batch*	*McDermott*	*Agnew*	*Turner*	*Crombie*	*Halsall*	*Robinson*	*Henshaw*	*Walsh**	*O'Riordan*	*Cumming*	*Burgess*
								Ref: J Deakin	A 25-yard strike from Nisbet, a goal from Tynan on the stroke of half-time, and some strange decisions by referee Deakin is all to much for Mariners' boss Mick Lyons, who remonstrates with the officials at the interval. Nisbet improves on his earlier effort with a shot from 30 yards.											
33	A	LEEDS		5	L	**0-4**	0-2		Cherry	Nisbet	Cooper L	Law	McElhinney*	Matthews	Hodges	Coughlin	Tynan	**Evans**	Nelson	Rowbotham
	28/3		*18,618*	*7*	51			*Sheridan 6p, Baird 41, 64, 78*	*Day*	*Aspin*	*MacDonald*	*Aizlewood*	*Ashurst*	*Ormsby*	*Ritchie*	*Sheridan**	*Pearson*	*Baird*	*Adams*	*Edwards*
								Ref: J Lloyd	Ian Baird is tormentor-in-chief for the FA Cup semi-finalists as he is brought down by McElhinney in the box and then goes on to complete a hat-trick. By the end Argyle are reduced to ten men through injury and two more, including new £50k signing Stewart Evans, are hobbling.											
34	H	SHREWSBURY		5	W	3-2	1-2	Tynan 7, 66, Nelson 73	Cherry	Burrows	Cooper L	Law	McElhinney	Matthews	Hodges	Brimacombe	Tynan	Clayton*	Nelson	Rowbotham
	4/4		**8,905**	*18*	54			*Brown 2, Robinson 17*	*Perks*	*Williams*	*Green*	*Leonard**	*Pearson*	*Linighan*	*McNally*	*Hackett*	*Brown*	*Robinson*	*Tester*	*Steele*
								Ref: G Ashby	After heavy rain, spectators are only admitted at 2.15 following a third pitch inspection. The Shrews score with their first attack. Tynan soon equalises but Robinson puts the visitors back in front. Tynan bravely gets his head to a Matthews thunderbolt. Nelson wrong-foots Steve Perks.											
35	A	BRIGHTON		5	D	1-1	1-1	Tynan 35	Cherry	Brimacombe	Cooper L	Law	Uzzell	Matthews	Hodges	Coughlin*	Tynan	Clayton	Nelson	Rowbotham
	7/4		*6,483*	*22*	55			*Armstrong 19*	*Digweed*	*Brown*	*Hutchings*	*Wilson*	*Isaac*	*Young*	*Crumplin**	*Gatting*	*Armstrong*	*Connor*	*Hughes*	*Jasper*
								Ref: D Vickers	Argyle's re-shuffled defence have difficulty in coping with the speed of Terry Connor and Darren Hughes and the latter sets up the unmarked Gerry Armstrong to head the opening goal. Tynan springs the offside trap to equalise. Coughlin limps off to add to Smith's injury worries.											
36	A	CRYSTAL PALACE		5	D	0-0	0-0		Cherry	Brimacombe	Cooper L	Law	Uzzell	Matthews	Hodges	Coughlin	Tynan	Clayton	Nelson	
	11/4		*10,589*	*6*	56				*Wood*	*Finnigan*	*O'Doherty*	*Taylor*	*O'Reilly*	*Cannon*	*Irvine*	*Gray*	*Bright*	*Wright*	*Barber*	
								Ref: K Miller	The two play-off contenders are locked in a stalemate, with George Wood's soaring kicks providing most of the danger. Mark Bright almost scores from a long clearance, leaving the confused Cherry and Law exchanging angry words. Brimacombe continues to impress at right-back.											
37	H	BIRMINGHAM		6	D	0-0	0-0		Cherry	Brimacombe	Cooper L	Law	Uzzell	Matthews	Hodges	Coughlin	Tynan	Clayton	Nelson*	Goodyear
	18/4		13,372	*12*	57				*Tomlinson*	*Ashley*	*Dicks*	*Williams*	*Overson*	*Bird*	*Frain*	*Handysides*	*Whitton*	*Rees*	*Wigley*	
								Ref: R Hamer	Birmingham boss John Bond is forced to field three 17 year olds to bolster his injury ravaged side and operates the sweeper system to great effect. Goalkeeper Paul Tomlinson, playing his last game on loan for the Blues, copes admirably with everything Argyle can throw at him.											
38	A	PORTSMOUTH		4	W	1-0	0-0	Summerfield 74	Cherry	Brimacombe	Cooper L	Law	Uzzell	Matthews	Hodges	Coughlin	Tynan	Clayton*	Nelson	Summerfield
	20/4		*17,171*	*2*	60				*Knight*	*Swain*	*Hardyman*	*Dillon*	*Blake*	*Ball*	*O'Callaghan*	*Kennedy*	*Russell**	*Quinn*	*Hilaire*	*Tait*
								Ref: T Holbrook	Argyle's first away win for five months means out-of-touch Pompey lose their unbeaten home record and the league leadership. Just two minutes after coming on as a substitute, Summerfield ghosts in to intercept a bad back-pass by Noel Blake and give Alan Knight no chance.											
39	H	HUDDERSFIELD		5	D	1-1	0-0	Law 77	Cherry	Goodyear*	Cooper L	Law	Uzzell	Matthews	Hodges	Coughlin	Tynan	Summerfield	Nelson	Evans
	25/4		13,342	*21*	61			*Cork 50*	*Cox*	*Trevitt*	*Burke*	*Banks*	*Webster*	*Jones*	*Ward**	*Cork*	*Shearer*	*Wilson*	*Mitchell*	*Cooper*
								Ref: V Callow	Duncan Shearer gives the home defence an early warning when he goes close in the first minute. Banks threads a pass through to David Cork, who gives the Terriers the lead. Brian Cox dislocates a finger and minutes later misses a Matthews corner to gift Law his first Pilgrims goal.											
40	A	OLDHAM		6	L	1-2	0-2	Law 60	Cherry	Goodyear	Cooper L	Law	Uzzell	Matthews	Summerf'ld*	Coughlin	Tynan	Evans	Nelson	Hodges
	2/5		*6,542*	*3*	61			*Williams 2, Palmer 43*	*Goram*	*Irwin*	*Barlow*	*Henry*	*Linighan*	*Moore*	*Palmer*	*Ormondroyd*	*Cecere*	*Milligan*	*Williams*	
								Ref: D Shaw	Despite a week's preparation, Argyle fail to adapt to Oldham's synthetic pitch. They get the worst possible start when Cherry is caught in two minds and the ball drifts goalwards. Gary Williams scores but Goodyear slips when poised to clear. Palmer increases the lead. Law prods in.											
41	H	STOKE		6	L	1-3	0-2	Coughlin 55p	Cherry	Nisbet	Uzzell	Law	McElhinney	Matthews*	Hodges	Coughlin	Tynan	Evans	Nelson	Summerfield
	4/5		13,774	*8*	61			*Saunders 35, 38, Talbot 46*	*Fox*	*Dixon*	*Mills*	*Talbot*	*Hemming*	*Berry*	*Ford*	*Parkin**	*Morgan*	*Saunders*	*Gayle*	*Kelly*
								Ref: J Deakin	Referee Deakin inadvertently sets up the first goal. The ball rebounds off him and then he obstructs two defenders allowing Saunders time to shoot. Talbot's header leaves the Pilgrims play-off dreams on a knife-edge. Peter Fox saves Coughlin's first penalty but moves too early.											
42	A	DERBY		7	L	2-4	1-0	Nelson 9, 85 *[Gregory 90]*	Cherry	Nisbet	Uzzell	Law	Burrows	Matthews	Hodges*	Coughlin	Tynan	Evans	Nelson	Summerfield
	9/5		**20,798**	*1*	61			*Davison 70, Callaghan 80, Mickle' 81,*	*Steele*	*Blades*	*Forsyth*	*Williams*	*Hindmarch*	*MacLaren*	*Micklewhite*	*Gee**	*Davison*	*Gregory*	*Callaghan*	*Lillis*
	Home		Away					Ref: T Mills	Derby have already clinched the championship but deny Argyle a surprise victory with a late flurry. Nelson races clear to open the scoring. Hindmarch clears an Evans header off the line which the striker claims was in. John Gregory scores in the fourth minute of injury-time.											
Average	12,387		8,785																	

TODAY DIVISION 2 (CUP-TIES)

Manager: Dave Smith

SEASON 1986-87

Littlewoods Cup

Littlewoods Cup	Att		H-T	F-A	Scorers, Times, and Referees	1	2	3	4	5	6	7	8	9	10	11	12 sub used
1:1 A CARDIFF	2,503	4:	4-1	4-5 L	Nisbet 4, Coughlin 22, 38, Summ' 41 / Vau' 31,57, Turn' 55, Boyle 70, Wh' 83 Moseley / Ref: G Ashby	Crudgington	Nisbet	Cooper L	Uzzell	McElhinney*	Matthews	Hodges	Coughlin	Summer'ld^	Clayton	Nelson	Good'/Coop'S
					Moseley		*Kerr*	*Sherlock*	*Wimbleton*	*Brignull*	*Boyle*	*Giles**	*Turner*	*Wheeler*	*Vaughan*	*Rogers*	*Curtis*
1:2 H CARDIFF	5,829	4:14	0-0	0-1 L	Giles 63 / Ref: J Martin / (Argyle lost 4-6 on aggregate)	Crudgington	Nisbet	Cooper L	Uzzell	McElhinney*	Matthews	Hodges*	Coughlin	Summerfield	Clayton^	Nelson	Burr'/Coop'S
					Moseley		*Kerr*	*Sherlock*	*Wimbleton*	*Brignull*	*Boyle*	*Giles*	*Turner*	*Wheeler*	*Curtis*	*Rogers*	

FA Cup

FA Cup	Att		H-T	F-A	Scorers, Times, and Referees	1	2	3	4	5	6	7	8	9	10	11	12 sub used
3 A BRISTOL CITY	16,943	3:7	0-0	1-1 D	Summerfield 49 / Riley 56 / Ref: J Martin	Crudgington	Nisbet	Cooper L	Goodyear	McElhinney*	Matthews	Hodges	Coughlin	Tynan	Summerfield	Nelson	Brimacombe
					Waugh		*Newman*	*Williams*	*Moyes*	*MacPhail*	*Marshall*	*Riley*	*Llewellyn*	*Fitzpatrick*	*Walsh*	*Neville*	
3R H BRISTOL CITY	14,142	3:7	0-0	3-1 W aet	Summerf'd 95, Nelson 110, Tynan 118 / Marshall 109 / Ref: J Martin	Crudgington	Nisbet	Uzzell	Goodyear	McElhinney*	Matthews^	Hodges	Coughlin	Tynan	Summerfield	Nelson	Burr'/Rowb'm
					Waugh		*Newman*	*Williams*	*Moyes*	*MacPhail*	*Tanner**	*Riley*	*Llewellyn*	*Fitzpatrick*	*Walsh*	*Neville*	*Marshall*
4 A ARSENAL	39,029	1:1	0-3	1-6 L	Rowbotham 68 [Davis 77, Rocastle 79/ / Nic'las 23, Quinn 36, Anders'n 42, 75, / Ref: J Bray	Cherry	Nisbet	Cooper L	Summerfield	Burrows	Matthews*	Hodges	Coughlin	Tynan	Clayton^	Nelson	Uzz'l/Rowb'm
					Lukic		*Anderson*	*Sansom*	*O'Leary*	*Williams*	*Adams*	*Rocastle*	*Davis*	*Quinn*	*Nicholas*	*Hayes**	*Grov^/Caes'*

1:1 CARDIFF — The crowd go home happy after a nine-goal spectacular but Smith does not, after seeing Argyle surrender a three-goal lead to new relegated Cardiff. Nisbet scores from 35 yards and Coughlin from 40. Vaughan adds to the long-range efforts. Robbie Turner's goal sparks the comeback.

1:2 CARDIFF — Rumours abound of the return of Tynan. On this form the Argyle attack needs him after a number of chances go begging. David Giles admits his goal was a fluke as he hit a hopeful cross into the area that floats over Crudgington. Frank Burrows is delighted with his side's efforts.

3 BRISTOL CITY — The kick-off is delayed by 16 minutes as 2,000 fans are still trying to get in at 3 o'clock. David Moyes is slow to react and Summerfield takes advantage to slot past Keith Waugh. The Argyle defence is also at fault when no one closes down Neville and he slips a pass to Glyn Riley.

3R BRISTOL CITY — Four goals in extra-time makes up for the lack of excitement in the first 90 minutes. Smith's double substitution pays dividends. Summerfield slides in to open the scoring. Marshall responds but Nelson shows he has recovered from his long running virus by firing in. Tynan finishes it.

4 ARSENAL — Cherry replaces the axed Crudgington but probably wishes he didn't. The Gunners give Argyle a football lesson in front of 12,000 travelling fans. Rocastle gives a supreme performance in midfield. Rowbotham's goal briefly raises hopes. Substitute Groves is injured after ten minutes.

League Table

	P	W	D	L	F	A	W	D	L	F	A	Pts
1 Derby	42	14	6	1	42	18	11	3	7	22	20	84
2 Portsmouth	42	17	2	2	37	11	6	7	8	16	17	78
3 Oldham	42	13	6	2	36	16	9	3	9	29	28	75
4 Leeds	42	15	4	2	43	16	4	7	10	15	28	68
5 Ipswich	42	12	6	3	29	10	5	7	9	30	33	64
6 Crystal Pal	42	12	4	5	35	20	7	1	13	16	33	62
7 PLYMOUTH	42	12	6	3	40	23	4	7	10	22	34	61
8 Stoke	42	11	5	5	40	21	5	5	11	23	32	58
9 Sheffield Utd	42	10	8	3	31	19	5	5	11	19	30	58
10 Bradford C	42	10	5	6	36	27	5	5	11	26	35	55
11 Barnsley	42	8	7	6	26	23	6	6	9	23	29	55
12 Blackburn	42	11	4	6	30	22	4	6	11	15	33	55
13 Reading	42	11	4	6	33	23	3	7	11	19	36	53
14 Hull	42	10	6	5	25	22	3	8	10	16	33	53
15 West Brom	42	8	6	7	29	22	5	6	10	22	27	51
16 Millwall	42	10	5	6	27	16	4	4	13	12	29	51
17 Huddersfield	42	9	6	6	38	30	4	6	11	16	31	51
18 Shrewsbury	42	11	3	7	24	14	4	3	14	17	39	51
19 Birmingham	42	8	9	4	27	21	3	8	10	20	38	50
20 Sunderland*	42	8	6	7	25	23	4	6	11	24	36	48
21 Grimsby	42	5	8	8	18	21	5	6	10	21	38	44
22 Brighton	42	7	6	8	22	20	2	6	13	15	34	39
	924	232	122	108	693	438	108	122	232	438	693	1264

* play-offs-down

Notes

Double wins: (1) Hull.

Double defeats: (2) Stoke, Sunderland.

Won from behind: (3) Blackburn, Huddersfield, Shrewsbury.

Lost from in front: (2) Derby, Sunderland.

High spots: Highest league finish since 1961-62.

Permanent return of Tommy Tynan.

Average home gate increased by over 4,000.

Low spots: Only one point from final four matches cost play-off place.

Double defeat by 4th Division Cardiff in Littlewoods Cup.

Totally outclassed by Arsenal in FA Cup.

Player of the Year: Tommy Tynan.

Ever presents: (0).

Hat-tricks: (0).

Leading scorer: Tommy Tynan (19).

Appearances and Goals

Player	Appearances						Goals			
	Lge	Sub	LC	Sub	FAC	Sub	Lge	LC	FAC	Tot
Brimacombe, John	8	3					1			1
Burrows, Adrian	16	1	1		1					
Cherry, Steve	21									
Clayton, John	20	1	2	1			3			3
Cooper, Leigh	35		2		2					
Cooper, Steve	10	2	2	2			4			4
Coughlin, Russell	40		2		3		5	2		7
Crudgington, Geoff	21		2		2					
Evans, Stewart	4	1								
Goodyear, Clive	27	5	1	1	2		1			1
Hodges, Kevin	33	2	2		3		5			5
Law, Nicky	12						2			2
Matthews, John	39		2		3		2			2
McElhinney, Gerry	20	1	1		2					
Nelson, Garry	30	2	2		3		7		1	8
Nisbet, Gordon	35		2		3		3	1		4
Rowbotham, Darren	7	9				2	1		1	2
Summerfield, Kevin	24	4	2		3		9	1	2	12
Tynan, Tommy	40		2		3		18		1	19
Uzzell, John	20	1	2		1	1	1			1
(own-goals)										
20 players used	462	31	22	4	33	5	62	4	5	71

BARCLAYS DIVISION 2 — SEASON 1987-88

Manager: Dave Smith

No	Date		Att	Pos	Pt	F-A	H-T	Scorers, Times, and Referees	1	2	3	4	5	6	7	8	9	10	11	subs used
1	A 15/8	MANCHESTER C	20,046		L 0	1:2	0:1	Law 36 / Stewart 81, Varadi 90 / Ref: A Seville	Cherry	Brimacombe	Cooper L	Coughlin*	Law	Smith	Matthews	Summerfield	Tynan	Evans	Furphy^	Cooper S/Uzzell
								(opp)	*Nixon*	*Gidman*	*Hinchcliffe*	*Clements*	*Brightwell†*	*Redmond*	*White*	*Stewart*	*Varadi*	*Scott**	*McNab*	*Adcock/Simpson*
2	H 18/8	IPSWICH	11,901		D 1	0:0	0:0	Ref: R Gifford	Cherry	Brimacombe	Cooper L	Law	Smith	Matthews	Cooper S*	Summerfield	Tynan	Evans	Furphy^	Rowboth'm D/Clayton
								(opp)	*Hallworth*	*Stockwell*	*Harbey*	*Yallop*	*Dozzell*	*Cranson*	*Lowe*	*Brennan*	*Woods*	*Zondervan*	*Gleghorn*	
3	H 22/8	HUDDERSFIELD	8,881	5 / 21	W 4	6:1	2:0	Evans 15, Furphy 28, Tynan 48, 67, Ward 85 [Law 60, Summerfield 89] Ref: K Burge	Cherry	Brimacombe	Cooper L	Rowboth'm D	Law	Smith	Matthews	Summerfield	Tynan	Evans	Furphy*	Coughlin/Uzzell
								(opp)	*Cox*	*Trevitt*	*Burke*	*Banks*	*Webster*	*Tucker*	*Mitchell^*	*May*	*Shearer*	*Cowling^*	*Cork*	*Bray/Ward*
4	A 29/8	READING	6,658	1 / 21	W 7	1:0	1:0	Peters 44(og) Ref: A Gunn	Cherry	Brimacombe	Cooper L	Rowboth' D*	Law	Smith	Matthews	Summerfield	Tynan	Evans	Furphy	Cooper S
								(opp)	*Francis*	*Jones*	*Richardson*	*Beavon**	*Hicks*	*Peters*	*Tait*	*Gordon**	*Horrix*		*Smillie*	*Joseph/White*
5	H 31/8	SHEFFIELD UTD	14,504	1 / 17	W 10	1:0	1:0	Evans 37 Ref: R Milford	Cherry	Brimacombe	Cooper L	Rowboth' D*	Law	Smith	Matthews	Summerfield	Tynan	Evans	Furphy	Hodges
								(opp)	*Leaning*	*Barnsley*	*Pike*	*Kuhl*	*Stancliffe*	*Eckhardt*	*Marsden^*	*Withe**	*Cadette*	*Dempsey*	*Beagrie*	*Philliskirk/Wilder*
6	A 5/9	BARNSLEY	6,976	2 / 1	L 10	1:2	0:0	Tynan 85 / Wylde 60, 70p Ref: R Nixon	Cherry	Brimacombe	Cooper L	Hodges	Law^	Smith	Matthews	Summerfield	Tynan	Evans	Furphy*	Coughlin/Uzzell
								(opp)	*Baker*	*Joyce*	*Cross*	*Thomas*	*Gray*	*Futcher*	*Wylde*	*Agnew*	*Lowndes*	*MacDonald*	*Clarke*	
7	H 12/9	WEST BROM	10,578	5 / 20	D 11	3:3	0:1	Tynan 69, 83, Clayton 72, Gray 12, 84, Palmer 90 Ref: D Hutchinson	Cherry	Brimacombe	Cooper L	Matthews	Law	Smith	Anderson*	Summerfield	Tynan	Evans	Clayton^	Rowboth'/D/Cooper S
								(opp)	*Naylor*	*Palmer*	*Cowdrill*	*Bennett**	*Reilly*	*Bradley*	*Hopkins*	*Goodman**	*Gray*	*Singleton*	*Morley*	*Williamson/Dickinson*
8	A 16/9	BRADFORD C	11,009	7 / 1	L 11	1:3	0:1	Matthews 52, Abbott 20p, 70p, 78 Ref: K Breen	Cherry	Brimacombe	Cooper L	Anderson	Law	Smith^	Matthews	Summerf'ld*	Tynan!	Evans	Clayton	Cooper S/Uzzell
								(opp)	*Tomlinson*	*Mitchell*	*Goddard^*	*McCall*	*Oliver*	*Evans*	*Hendrie*	*Sinnott*	*Futcher*	*Abbott*	*Ellis**	*Thorpe/Ormondroyd*
9	A 19/9	LEICESTER	8,872	12 / 17	L 11	0:4	0:3	Wilson 27, Ford 31, Newell 43, [Rantanen 59] Ref: A Buksh	Cherry	Brimacombe	Cooper L	Matthews^	Law	McElhinney*	Anderson	Rowboth' D*		Evans	Clayton*	Hodges/Uzzell
								(opp)	*Cooper*	*Morgan*	*James*	*Osman*	*Walsh*	*Ramsey*	*Ford*	*Newell*	*Rantanen^*	*Mauchlen*	*Wilson^*	*McAllister/Moran*
10	H 26/9	BIRMINGHAM	8,912	14 / 8	D 12	1:1	1:1	Tynan 11, McElhinney 43(og) Ref: K Cooper	Crudgington	Brimacombe	Cooper L	Matthews	Law	Smith	Hodges	Summerfield	Tynan	Evans	Anderson^	Clayton/Matthews
								(opp)	*Hansbury*	*Ranson*	*Dicks*	*Williams*	*Overson*	*Trewick*	*Bremner*	*Handysides*	*Whitton**	*Rees*	*Wigley*	*Kennedy*
11	A 29/9	BOURNEMOUTH	6,491	13	D 13	2:2	1:1	Hodges 16, Clayton 65, Aylott 12, Brooks 86 Ref: J Martin	Crudgington	Brimacombe	Cooper L	Matthews	Law	Smith	Hodges	Summerfield	Tynan	Evans	Cooper S*	Clayton
								(opp)	*Peyton*	*Newson*	*Morrell*	*Brooks*	*Williams*	*Whitlock*	*O'Driscoll*	*Heffernan*	*Aylott*	*Cooke*	*O'Connor**	*Keane*

Match commentaries:

1. Relegated City get a shock as Argyle take the lead after forcing six corners in succession. Law nods in from Matthews' flag-kick. New record £170k signing Smith marshals the defence superbly. Paul Stewart equalises and Cherry's weak goal-kick leads to Imre Varadi's late winner.

2. A combination of the crossbar and fine goalkeeping by Jon Hallworth combine to deny Summerfield a hat-trick. Ipswich also have chances to win the game. Cherry saves at the second attempt from Woods and David Lowe inexplicably passes to Gleghorn with the goal at his mercy.

3. Evans goes down on one knee to score his first goal for almost a year. Furphy loops a header over Cox although Tynan claims he gets a touch. Tynan then scores a rare goal from outside the area as he fires in from 25 yards. Law blots his copybook with a feeble back-pass to let Ward in.

4. The laugh is on manager Smith as he remains blissfully unaware of the result until after the final whistle. Having left his seat early he misses Gary Peters' looping header over his own keeper. Assuming he saw the goal, no one tells Smith until he mentions his satisfaction with a point.

5. Argyle remain the surprise leaders of the division after a hard-fought win. Matthews' well-directed free-kick finds the head of Evans who gives Andy Leaning no chance. Argyle hang on grimly in the second period. Brimacombe does well to contain the tricky wing-play of Peter Beagrie.

6. Smith is voted manager of the month. The Tykes put Argyle under constant pressure in a bruising battle. The only surprise is that it takes them an hour to score when Roger Wylde stabs home. The ball strikes Law's arm and Wylde scores from the spot. Tynan gets a late consolation.

7. Andy Gray celebrates his Albion debut with an early goal. Clayton marks his debut while Martin Harvey is holding up his number to be subbed. When Cherry saves Reilly's twice-taken penalty it looks all over but Ron Atkinson's side fight back. Carlton Palmer clinches a point in injury-time.

8. Little goes right for Argyle as City go top. Smith concedes the first penalty when he fouls Hendrie and later goes off with concussion. Tynan is dismissed (44). Matthews levels from 30 yards. Cooper up-ends Ron Futcher for another spot-kick. Greg Abbott then seals his hat-trick.

9. The Foxes parade their new £400k strike force of Newell and Rantanen who both scored on their midweek debuts. City dominate to the extent that Smith predicts they will be champions. It could have been worse but the ref rules that McElhinney's handball in the area was accidental.

10. Argyle's rapid slide down the table continues despite taking an early lead. Smith's header is blocked on the line but Tynan nets the rebound. McElhinney knocks Rees's cross past his own keeper. Crudgington pulls off a miraculous last-minute save from the unmarked Andy Kennedy.

11. Steve Cooper receives an ankle injury in the first minute and is soon replaced. Aylott lets fly from 20 yards for the first. Hodges lobs over Peyton. Clayton volleys in from an acute angle but the Cherries gain a deserved point when the influential Brooks finds the corner of the net.

Football results table — Plymouth Argyle match log.

(continued)

Spink	Gage	Gallacher	Lillis	Sims	Keown	Birch	Aspinall	McInally*	Hunt	Walters	Evans

3/10 — 10,515 — 8 — 13

Walters 2, 39, Lillis 9
Ref: H King

Villa cruise to their fifth successive away victory. Alan McInally's shot hits the post and rebounds invitingly to Mark Walters who makes no mistake. Lillis and Smith both score with headers. Matthews' pass goes straight to Walters who scores with ease. Evans hits the bar late on.

---

13 A STOKE 10/10 — 8,275 — 9 — 13 — 0-1 — L

| Crudgington | Brimacombe | Cooper L | Tynan | Smith | Law | Hodges | Summerfield | Clayton | McInally* | Evans | Rowbotham J |
| Fox | Dixon | Carr | Parkin | Berry | Bould | Daly* | Saunders^ | Shaw | Anderson* | Heath | Allinson/Hemming |

Heath 11
Ref: N Midgley

Tynan uncharacteristically misses several good chances as Stoke win a match that will not remain in the memory for long. Phil Heath outjumps everyone to provide a rare piece of quality. Stoke's fans are frustrated by Argyle's unadventurous play and heavy reliance on the offside law.

---

14 H LEEDS 17/10 — 9,358 — 16 — 16 — 6-3 — W

| Crudgington | Rowboth'm J* | Cooper L | Tynan | Smith | Williams | Hodges | Summerfield | Clayton | Brimacombe | Tynan | Rowbotham D |
| Day | Aspin | Adams* | Haddock | Ashurst | Williams | De Mange | Sheridan | Taylor | Pearson^ | Snodin | Stiles/Swan |

Clayton 9, 84, Sum'f'd 11, 49, Smith 72, [Tynan 90]
Taylor 12, Snodin 18, 87
Ref: R Groves

Argyle confound everyone including their absent manager to rip apart a Leeds defence that had previously conceded only ten goals all season. United gradually lose their composure and discipline as Clayton and Summerfield in particular take advantage of some Kamikaze defending.

---

15 H MILLWALL 20/10 — 8,958 — 8 — 16 — 1-2 — L

| Crudgington | Rowboth'm J | Cooper L | Tynan | Smith | Law | Hodges | Summerf'ld^ | Clayton | Brimacombe | Tynan | Rowbotham D/Evans |
| Horne | Salman | Coleman | Hurlock | McLeary | Walker | Lawrence | Briley | Cascarino | Sheringham | Cascarino | Anthrobus |

Evans 35
Cascarino 24, Sheringham 76
Ref: J Deakin

The Lions bring Argyle down to earth as danger men Cascarino and Sheringham are allowed too much freedom. Argyle lose Summerfield and Matthews with injury before half-time. Cascarino scores with a 20-yard volley. Evans soon replies but Sheringham taps in Les Briley's cross.

---

16 A BLACKBURN 24/10 — 6,014 — 15 — 17 — 1-1 — D

| Cherry | Rowboth'm J | Cooper L | Matthews | Smith | Law | Hodges | Evans | Clayton | Cooper S | | |
| Gennoe | Price | Sulley | Ainscow | Mail | Hendry | Miller | Reid | Patterson* | Garner | Sellars | Curry |

Evans 55
Sellars 90p
Ref: G Tyson

Cherry returns from injury to give a man of the match display. Matthews is booked for time-wasting whilst waiting for Law to take a throw-in. Evans heads in from virtually on the goal-line. In the closing seconds the ref spots Law handling and Sellars makes no mistake from the spot.

---

17 H HULL 31/10 — 8,550 — 3 — 20 — 3-1 — W

| Cherry | Brimacombe | Cooper L | Matthews* | Smith | Law | Hodges | Coughlin | Tynan | Clayton | Evans | |
| Norman | Palmer | Heard | Jobson | Parker | Skipper | Roberts | Thompson* | Saville ! | Askew | Williams | Bunn |

Smith 5, Clayton 18, Tynan 21p
Saville 34
Ref: D Elleray

Hull are on a great run having lost only once in 15 games but are stunned by Smith's early header. Clayton makes it two and Pat Heard sends Hodges tumbling. Tynan slots home Argyle's first penalty of the season. Tigers scorer Andy Saville is sent off for foul and abusive language.

---

18 A CRYSTAL PALACE 3/11 — 7,424 — 20 — 1-5 — L

| Cherry | Brimacombe | Cooper L | Matthews | Smith | Law | Hodges | Coughlin | Tynan | Clayton* | Evans | |
| Wood | O'Doherty | Burke | Gray | Cannon | Nebbeling | Redfearn | Thomas | Bright | Wright | Salako* | Barber/Stebbing |

Brimacombe 89
Wright 19, 65, 88, Gray 50, Neb'ling 82
Ref: M Bodenham

Ian Wright gives a preview of the form that will take him on to England honours. Argyle's defence are unable to cope with his speed as he scores a superb hat-trick. Andy Gray also shows great pace to score and Nebbeling is left unmarked. Brimacombe scores with a late header.

---

19 A SWINDON 14/11 — 9,616 — 12 — 21 — 1-1 — D

| Cherry | Brimacombe | Cooper L | McElhinney | Marker | Smith | Law | Hodges | Coughlin | Tynan | Anderson | Cooper S |
| Flowers | Hockaday | King | Kamara | Parkin | Calderwood | Bamber | Barnard | Quinn^ | Foley* | Barnes | O'Regan/White |

Evans 11
Barnes 45
Ref: T Mills

Tim Flowers, who arrived on loan from Southampton only 24 hours before the match, denies Argyle on several occasions but is powerless to stop Evans heading in from Anderson's cross. With the Argyle defence anticipating an offside flag, Bobby Barnes runs through to equalise.

---

20 H MIDDLESBROUGH 21/11 — 9,728 — 2 — 21 — 0-1 — L

| Cherry | Brin'combe^ | Cooper L | McElhinney | Marker | Smith | Law | Hodges | Coughlin | Tynan | Evans* | Anderson | Cooper S/Summerf'd |
| Pears | Glover | Cooper | Mowbray | Parkinson ! | Pallister | Slaven | Kernaghan | Hamilton | Kerr | Ripley | |

Hamilton 39
Ref: R Gifford

Boro's rock solid defence have conceded just 14 goals in 20 matches and are uncompromising in thwarting any Argyle attack. Marker ends up with stud marks on his hip. Gary Parkinson is sent off for two illegal challenges on Anderson, who is the Pilgrims most effective attacker.

---

21 A OLDHAM 28/11 — 4,516 — 15 — 24 — 1-0 — W

| Cherry | Brimacombe | Cooper L | Burrows | Smith | Marker | Hodges | Coughlin | Tynan | Cooper S | Anderson | |
| Gorton | Irwin | Barrett | Flynn | Kelly | Linghan | Palmer | Henry | Ritchie | Wright | Williams* | Cecere |

Tynan 52
Ref: P Danson

Unlike last season's visit, Argyle cope well with the Boundary Park plastic. Transfer-listed Burrows is recalled and plays an outstanding game at the back. Hodges outsprints Earl Barrett and crosses to Tynan who, despite having his back to goal, manages to stab the ball past Gorton.

---

22 H SHREWSBURY 5/12 — 7,603 — 14 — 27 — 2-0 — W

| Cherry | Brimacombe | Cooper L | Burrows | Smith | Law | Hodges | Coughlin* | Tynan | Cooper S | Anderson | Summerfield |
| Parks | Green | Williams | Leonard | Moyes | Linighan | Priest | McNally | Brown | Robinson | Narbett* | Tester |

Hodges 67, Cooper S 81
Ref: K Burge

The Shrews come looking for a point after losing nine of their last ten matches. They manage to frustrate Argyle until Summerfield lays on a chance for Hodges. S Cooper scores after the ball bounces off Moyes. Five bookings include Linighan for an off the ball scuffle with Tynan.

---

23 A HUDDERSFIELD 12/12 — 5,747 — 21 — 27 — 1-2 — L

| Cherry | Brimacombe | Law | Burrows | Smith | Marker | Hodges* | Summerfield | Tynan | Cooper S | Anderson | Clayton |
| Martin | Trevitt | Bray | Banks | Mitchell | Walford | Barham* | Hutchings | Cooper | May | Cork | Ward |

Cooper S 82
Cork 37, 74
Ref: J Rushton

The Terriers recently suffered a 1-10 thrashing at Man City but look a different proposition under new boss Malcolm MacDonald. Dave Cork finds the net from Graham Cooper's cross. He scores again after a run by Ian Banks. Cooper replies after Mitchell allows a pass to elude him.

BARCLAYS DIVISION 2

SEASON 1987-88

Manager: Dave Smith

No	Date		Att Pos	F-A	Pt	H-T	Scorers, Times, and Referees
24	20/12	H BRADFORD C	11,350 / 14	W 2-1	30	2-0	Cooper S 29, Smith 41 / McCall 75 / Ref: R Milford
25	26/12	A BIRMINGHAM	9,166 / 15	W 1-0	33	0-0	Tynan 65p / Ref: J Ireland
26	28/12	H LEICESTER	15,581 / 19	W 4-0	36	0-0	Ramsey 46(og), Smith 47, Tynan 63, [Anderson 76] / Ref: P Durkin
27	1/1	H READING	13,298 / 22	L 1-3	36	0-0	Tynan 73p / Gilkes 74p, Jones 77, Moran 82 / Ref: M Bodenham
28	2/1	A WEST BROM	8,445 / 19	L 0-1	36	0-1	Goodman 32 / Ref: T Mills
29	16/1	H MANCHESTER C	13,291 / 10	W 3-2	39	0-2	Tynan 64, Smith 65, Evans 85 / Stewart 13, McNab 30 / Ref: K Cooper
30	13/2	A IPSWICH	10,476 / 9	W 2-1	42	1-1	Law 41, Summerfield 64 / Deehan 25 / Ref: R Lewis
31	27/2	A ASTON VILLA	16,142 / 1	L 2-5	42	1-3	Tynan 7, Hodges 83 [Thompson 75] / Gray S 20p, Platt 23, Birch 27, 77 / Ref: J Kirkby
32	5/3	A LEEDS	18,115 / 7	L 0-1	42	0-0	Baird 75 / Ref: J Ashworth
33	12/3	H STOKE	8,749 / 10	W 3-0	45	2-0	Tynan 32, 34, Uzzell 85 / Ref: J Carter
34	19/3	A HULL	5,172 / 11	D 1-1	46	1-0	Evans 13 / Parker 64 / Ref: R Bridges

Line-ups (columns 1–11 and subs used)

No	1	2	3	4	5	6	7	8	9	10	11	subs used
24	Crudgington	Brimacombe	Law	Burrows	Marker	Smith	Hodges	Summerfield	Tynan	Cooper S	Anderson*	Evans
	Tomlinson	Mitchell*	Staunton*	McCall	Oliver	Evans	Hendrie	Sinnott	Futcher	Palin	Leonard	Abbott/Ormondroyd
25	Cherry	Brimacombe	Law	Burrows	Marker	Smith	Hodges	Summerfield*	Tynan	Cooper S	Anderson	Cooper L
	Godden	Ranson	Dicks	Roberts	Overson	Trewick	Bremner	Childs	Kennedy*	Rees	Wigley	Whitton
26	Cherry	Brimacombe	Law	Burrows	Marker	Smith	Hodges	Summerfield	Tynan	Cooper S	Anderson	Anderson
	Andrews	Ramsey	Venus	Morgan	Brien	MacDonald*	Ford^	Mauchlen	Newell	McAllister	Osvold	James/Cusack
27	Cherry	Brimacombe	Law*	Burrows	Marker	Smith	Hodges	Matthews	Tynan	Cooper S^	Anderson	Cooper L/Evans
	Francis	Bailie	Gilkes	Beavon	Hicks	Curle	Jones	Madden	Tait	Moran	Williams	Williams
28	Cherry	Brimacombe	Cooper L	Burrows	Marker	Smith	Hodges	Matthews	Tynan	Evans	Anderson*	Cooper S
	Powell	Dickinson	Cowdrill	Palmer	North	Kelly	Hopkins	Goodman	Gray	Robson*	Morley^	Lynex/Williamson
29	Cherry	Brimacombe	Cooper L	Burrows	Marker	Smith	Hodges	Matthews	Tynan	Cooper S^	Anderson*	Summerfield/Evans
	Nixon	Gidman	Hinchcliffe	Clements	Brightwell^	Redmond	White	Stewart	Adcock*	McNab	Lake	Varadi/Simpson
30	Cherry	Law	Cooper L	Burrows	Marker	McElhinney	Hodges	Matthews	Tynan	Evans	Summerfield	Summerfield
	Hallworth	Yallop	Harbey	Atkins	Humes*	Dozzell	Lowe	Stockwell	Deehan	Wark	Gleghorn	Brennan/Woods
31	Cherry	Brimacombe	Cooper L	Burrows	Marker	McElhinney^	Hodges	Matthews	Tynan	Cooper S	Summerfield	Morrison
	Spink	Gage	Gallacher	Gray A	Evans	Keown	Birch	Daley	Thompson	Gray S	Platt	
32	Cherry	Brimacombe	Cooper L	Burrows	Marker	Smith	Hodges*	Matthews	Tynan	Cooper S	Summerfield	Evans
	Day	Williams*	Adams	Aizlewood	Ashurst	Swan	Batty	Sheridan	Baird	Pearson	Snodin	Rennie
33	Cherry	Brimacombe	Uzzell	Burrows	Marker	Smith	Hodges^	Matthews	Tynan	Evans*	Summerfield	Clayton/Anderson
	Barrett	Beeston	Carr	Parkin	Bould	Berry	Ford	Henry	Morgan*	Shaw	Hackett^	Heath/Hemming
34	Cherry	Brimacombe	Uzzell	Burrows	Marker	Smith	Hodges^	Matthews	Tynan	Evans*	Summerfield	Clayton/Cooper L
	Norman	Williams	Heard	Jobson	Skipper	Parker	Roberts	Saville	Dyer^	De Mange	Barnes	Payton

Match notes

24 — Coughlin joins Blackpool in a shock move. Sunday soccer comes to Home Park and is deemed a success. With Cherry injured, Crudgington plays his second match in 24 hours. Cooper scores for the third match running and Smith scores from close range. McCall nets from 30 yards.

25 — Argyle taste victory at St Andrews for the first time ever. Anderson has his best game yet for the Greens as he torments the City defence. Not for the first time, Brian Roberts chops him down but this time it is in the area. Tynan makes no mistake. Steve Wigley heads against the bar.

26 — City are failing to live up to Smith's early season prediction of league champions. They are without Steve Walsh who is serving a nine-match suspension. After a frustrating first half, Ramsey's slice past his own keeper opens the floodgates. Anderson scores his first goal for the club.

27 — The struggling Royals complete an unlikely away double having won at Crystal Palace a few days earlier. Hicks handles Evans header and Tynan scores another penalty. Law trips Linden Jones a minute later for Gilkes to reply. Jones puts the visitors ahead and Steve Moran seals it.

28 — Former Throstle Evans has a golden chance to silence the Hawthorns crowd. After Steve Cooper beats two players Evans shot is scrambled back to him by Hopkins. The lanky striker then blasts the second shot wildly over. Goodman beats two defenders to Dickinson's free-kick.

29 — There seems no way back after Paul Stewart grabs his 21st of the season and Neil McNab completes a flowing move. A double substitution works wonders. Tynan scores with an overhead kick. Smith notches another header and Evans caps a remarkable comeback with a low shot.

30 — Deehan rises above a static defence to head in. Town boss John Duncan labels Law's equaliser a fluke but the transfer-listed defender insists his curling shot over Hallworth was intentional. Summerfield embarks on a mazy run from halfway and beats three defenders before scoring.

31 — Flying winger Tony Daley has a hand in all of Villa's goals, and Tynan's opener as his misplaced pass finds the Argyle striker. Cherry trips Daley after a mix-up with Brimacombe. Stuart Gray makes no mistake from the spot. New £200k signing David Platt scores on his debut.

32 — Ian Baird returns from a brief spell at Portsmouth to score his customary goal against Argyle. The Pilgrims miss three good chances in the first 20 minutes. Gary Williams scoops Tynan's flick off the line. In the dying seconds Evans is a toenail away from connecting in front of goal.

33 — Tynan grabs the headlines as he scores the 200th league goal of his career, but the real hero is Uzzell, returning from a long spell of injury. The defender sets up the first two with a long-throw and a cross and then completes a memorable display by heading his first goal for three years.

34 — The Tigers have slumped from promotion candidates to mid-table in a few weeks. Summerfield's first-time cross results in Evans and the ball ending up in the back of the net. Peter Barnes misses an open goal after Cherry fails to bring him down. Gary Parker hammers in a free-kick.

No	Venue	Date	Pos	Result	Score	HT	Attendance
35	H	26/3	13	W	3-0	1-0	12,359
36	H	4/4	14	W	1-0	1-0	13,299
37	A	9/4	14	L	2-3	2-3	11,052
38	H	15/4		D	0-0	0-0	8,059
39	A	19/4	15	L	0-1	0-1	9,052
40	H	23/4	15	L	1-3	0-1	8,370
41	H	26/4	15	L	1-2	0-0	6,310
42	A	30/4	15	L	1-3	0-1	16,615
43	H	2/5	14	W	1-0	0-0	6,084
44	A	7/5	16	L	1-2	0-1	4,510

35. BLACKBURN (H, 26/3) — W 3-0 (1-0)
Evans 40, Burrows 81, Hodges 90
Argyle: Cherry, Brimacombe, Uzzell, Burrows, Marker, Smith, Hodges, Matthews, Tynan, Evans, Summerfield Cooper L
Blackburn: Gennoe, Price, Sulley, Barker, Hendry, Mail^, Reid, Archibald, Ardiles*, Garner, Sellars Ainscow/Miller
Ref: D Elleray
Rovers boss Don Mackay is not a happy man. His side are outplayed and he complains that the water is too hot in the showers. The much-feted debut of Argentinian star Ossie Ardiles comes to a premature end after a strong tackle by Marker. Uzzell needs eight stitches in a toe wound.

36. SWINDON (H, 4/4) — W 1-0 (1-0)
Evans 12
Argyle: Cherry, Brimacombe, Cooper L, Burrows, Marker, Smith, Hodges, Matthews, Tynan, Evans*, Summerfield Clayton
Swindon: Digby, Hockaday, King, Gittens, Parkin, Wegerle*, Bamber, Foley, O'Regan, Quinn, Barnes White
Ref: M Bodenham
Evans scores for the third successive match after Summerfield takes advantage of a slip by Jon Gittens. Northern Ireland striker Jimmy Quinn misses three chances as Smith clears off the line, he hits the crossbar and then puts an easy header wide. Cherry saves well from Dave Bamber.

37. MILLWALL (A, 9/4) — L 2-3 (2-3)
Hodges 2, Summerfield 30
O'Callagh^ 7p, Cascarino 9, Sher'm 12
Argyle: Cherry, Brimacombe, Cooper L, Burrows, Marker, Smith, Hodges, Matthews, Tynan, Evans, Summerfield
Millwall: Horne, Stevens, Coleman, Hurlock, Wood, McLeary, Carter, Briley, Sheringham, Cascarino, O'Callaghan* Horrix
Ref: M Bailey
Hodges' hopeful 25-yard shot sails in to spark a frantic first 15 minutes. O'Callaghan levels from the spot after Smith grabs Cascarino, who then executes a stunning overhead kick. Sheringham powers in a header. Summerfield volleys in but a later effort is strangely ruled out for offside.

38. BARNSLEY (H, 15/4) — D 0-0 (0-0)
Argyle: Cherry, Brimacombe, Cooper L, Burrows, Marker, Smith, Hodges, Matthews, Tynan, Evans, Summerfield
Barnsley: Baker, Joyce, Cross, Thomas, McGugan, Jeffels, Currie, Blair, Lowndes, Beresford, Rees* Coatsworth
Ref: K Miller
A thick fog envelopes the ground as Argyle drop their first home points since New Year's Day. A fine save from Clive Baker denies Marker his first goal for the club. David Currie provides the main threat as Tykes manager Allan Clarke declares himself satisfied with one point.

39. SHEFFIELD UTD (A, 19/4) — L 0-1 (0-1)
Morris 84
Argyle: Cherry, Brimacombe, Cooper L, Burrows, Marker, Smith, Hodges, Matthews, Tynan, Evans, Summerfield
Sheffield Utd: Benstead, Carr, Powell, Barnsley, Stancliffe, Smith, Philliskirk*, Agana, Cadette, Beagrie, Hetherston Morris
Ref: L Dilkes
The Blades well rehearsed offside trap holds them in good stead for the full 90 minutes. Tynan's desperation for a goal leads him to hurriedly stab at a chance from six yards. Peter Beagrie, for once, gets the better of Brimacombe and crosses for Colin Morris to grab a late winner.

40. CRYSTAL PALACE (H, 23/4) — L 1-3 (0-1)
Evans 85
Barber 43, Bright 47, 81
Argyle: Cherry, Brimacombe, Cooper L*, Burrows, Marker, Smith, Hodges, Matthews, Tynan, Evans, Summerfield Cooper S
Palace: Suckling, Finnigan, Burke, Pennyfather, Nebbeling, Cannon, Redfearn*, Thomas, Bright, Barber, Salako Pemberton
Ref: R Hamer
Eccentric refereeing upsets players and supporters alike. Phil Barber heads the opener. Smith shepherds the ball over the line for a goal-kick but Mr Hamer mysteriously awards a free-kick from which Mark Bright scores. He scores his 22nd of the season late on before Evans replies.

41. BOURNEMOUTH (H, 26/4) — L 1-2 (0-0)
Hodges 52
Pulis 68, Brooks 72
Argyle: Cherry, Brimacombe, Cooper L*, Burrows, Marker, Smith, Hodges, Matthews, Tynan, Evans, Summerfield Law
Bournemouth: Peyton, Pulis, Morrell, Brooks, Williams, Whitlock, O'Driscoll, Aylott, Newson, Cooke*, Close* Richards/Langan
Ref: R Groves
Hodges celebrates the birth of his daughter by scoring against the club who released him as a youngster. Peyton shows why he has been called into the Eire squad with some excellent saves. Pulis equalises after Aylott's shot is blocked and then sets up Brooks to score from 20 yards.

42. MIDDLESBROUGH (A, 30/4) — L 1-3 (0-1)
Clayton 75
Ripley 34, Kernaghan 64, Hamilton 66
Argyle: Cherry, Brimacombe, Uzzell, Clayton, Marker, Smith, Hodges, Matthews, Tynan, Evans, Summerfield
Middlesbrough: Pears, Parkinson, Cooper, Mowbray, Hamilton, Pallister, Slaven, Ripley, Kernaghan, Kerr, Burke* Glover
Ref: S Lodge
Bruce Rioch's side, needing a win, start nervously. Smith gives them an unexpected boost when he lobs over Cherry and Stuart Ripley rolls into an unguarded net. New England cap Gary Pallister goes close. Alan Kernaghan and Gary Hamilton maintain Boro's promotion hopes.

43. OLDHAM (H, 2/5) — W 1-0 (0-0)
Marker 69
Argyle: Cherry, Brimacombe, Uzzell, Burrows, Marker, Smith, Hodges, Matthews, Tynan^, Evans^, Summerfield Cooper S/Clayton
Oldham: Rhodes, Irwin, Barrett, Flynn, Marshall, Milligan, Palmer, Donachie^, Barlow^, Wright, Ritchie Cecere/Edmonds
Ref: H King
Free scoring Oldham fail to score for the first time in 24 matches. Cooper launches himself into a spectacular overhead kick but Marker gets there first to head his first goal for the Pilgrims. Argyle receive a late scare when Cherry is forced to punch the ball away from outside the area.

44. SHREWSBURY (A, 7/5) — L 1-2 (0-1)
Clayton 82
Geddis 37, 72
Argyle: Cherry, Brimacombe, Uzzell, Burrows, Marker, Smith, Hodges, Matthews^, Cooper S*, Clayton, Law Tynan/Evans
Shrewsbury: Perks, Green, Williams, Priest^, Pratley, Linighan, Kasule, McNally, Geddis, Brown^, Bell Melrose/Narbett
Ref: J Worrall
Argyle have little to play for and it shows. Tynan is left on the bench but replaces Cooper (52) who is suffering from blistered feet. McNally impresses watching Northern Ireland manager Billy Bingham. David Geddis scores two with his head. Clayton wastes a last-minute chance.

Home 10,280 Average Away 9,574

BARCLAYS DIVISION 2 (CUP-TIES)

Manager: Dave Smith

SEASON 1987-88

Littlewoods Cup

	Att	F-A	H-T	Scorers, Times, and Referees	1	2	3	4	5	6	7	8	9	10	11	subs used
2:1 A PETERBOROUGH 23/9 · 12 L	3,843 4:15	1-4	0-3	[Riley 75] Tynan 69 / Lawrence 19, Gooding 27, Halsall 41 / Ref: P Don	Crudgington / *Shoemake*	Brimacombe / *Paris*	Cooper L / *Gunn*	McElhinney / *Gooding*	Law / *Pollard*	Smith / *Price*	Hodges / *Lawrence*	Matthews* / *Collins*	Tynan / *Riley*	Evans / *Halsall*	Anderson^ / *Luke*	Cooper S/Clayton
2:2 H PETERBOROUGH 6/10 · 17 D	5,524 4:14	1-1	0-0	Clayton 86 / Gooding 81 / Ref: R Hamer (Argyle lost 2-5 on aggregate)	Crudgington / *Neenan*	Brimacombe / *Paris*	Cooper L / *Gunn*	Law / *Gooding*	Smith / *Pollard*	Matthews* / *Price*	Hodges / *Luke*	Clayton / *Halsall*	Tynan / *Lawrence*	Evans / *Riley*	Rowboth'm D / *Collins*	Rowbotham J

Fourth division Posh expose Argyle's brittle confidence. Crudgington replaces the injured Cherry but is regularly left exposed. Gooding cracks in a shot from the edge of the box. Tynan drops into midfield and he scores from 20 yards. Riley looks offside as he sweeps in the fourth.

Noel Cantwell's side come determined to defend their first-leg lead. Without the suspended Tynan, Argyle lack the cutting edge needed to break through. Mick Gooding rubs salt in the wounds when he latches onto David Riley's pass. Clayton's late 25-yard strike is academic.

FA Cup

	Att	F-A	H-T	Scorers, Times, and Referees	1	2	3	4	5	6	7	8	9	10	11	subs used
3 H COLCHESTER 11/1 · 13 W	10,351 4:3	2-0	2-0	Cooper S 41, Matthews 44 / Ref: I Hemley	Cherry / *Walton*	Brimacombe / *Hinshelwood*	Cooper L / *Hedman*	Burrows / *Chatterton**	Marker / *Hill*	Smith / *Keane*	Hodges / *White*	Matthews / *Wilkins*	Tynan / *Tempest*	Cooper S / *English*	Anderson / *Grenfell*	Walsh
4 H SHREWSBURY 30/1 · 13 W	12,749 19	1-0	1-0	Evans 14 / Ref: D Hutchinson	Cherry / *Perks*	Cooper L / *Green*	Law / *Williams B*	Burrows / *Priest**	Marker / *Moyes*	Smith / *Linighan*	Hodges / *Williams W*	Matthews / *McNally*	Tynan / *Brown^*	Evans / *Geddis*	Summerf'ld* / *Bell*	Clayton · *Kasule/Tester*
5 A MANCHESTER C 20/2 · 13 L	29,206 10	1-3	0-1	Tynan 77 / Scott 7, Simpson 77, Moulden 89 / Ref: K Redfern	Cherry / *Nixon*	Cooper L / *Gidman*	Law* / *Hinchcliffe*	Burrows / *Seagraves*	Marker / *McNab*	McElhinney / *Redmond*	Hodges / *White*	Matthews / *Stewart*	Tynan / *Varadi**	Evans / *Scott*	Clayton^ / *Moulden*	Summerfield/Cooper S · *Simpson*

U's boss Roger Brown locks his side in the dressing room for 45 minutes after the game accusing his players of lack of effort. S Cooper almost makes a hash of his goal when he makes poor contact. The same cannot be said for the second, as Matthews drills home from 10 yards.

The match survives a 12.30 pitch inspection but is played in driving rain and sleet. Evans' header proves vital. A clash between Evans and Linighan results in a broken nose for the defender and a penalty for Argyle which Tynan misses. Cooper clears off the line in the final minute.

City are fortunate to retain eleven men when Stewart is only booked for elbowing McElhinney. Scott's opener is hotly disputed as Argyle appeal for offside. Simpson's speed leads to City's second. Tynan immediately responds from close range. Moulden accepts a simple chance.

League table

	Team	P	Home					Away					Pts
			W	D	L	F	A	W	D	L	F	A	
1	Millwall	44	15	3	4	45	23	10	4	8	27	29	82
2	Aston Villa	44	9	7	6	31	21	13	5	4	37	20	78
3	Middlesbro*	44	15	4	3	44	16	7	8	7	19	20	78
4	Bradford C	44	14	3	5	49	26	8	8	6	25	28	77
5	Blackburn	44	12	8	2	38	22	9	6	7	30	30	77
6	Crystal Pal	44	16	3	3	50	21	6	6	10	36	38	75
7	Leeds	44	14	4	4	37	18	5	8	9	24	33	69
8	Ipswich	44	14	3	5	38	17	5	6	11	23	35	66
9	Manchester C	44	11	4	7	50	28	8	4	10	30	32	65
10	Oldham	44	13	4	5	43	27	5	7	10	29	37	65
11	Stoke	44	12	6	4	34	22	5	5	12	16	35	62
12	Swindon	44	10	7	5	43	25	6	4	12	30	35	59
13	Leicester	44	12	5	5	35	20	4	6	12	27	41	59
14	Barnsley	44	11	4	7	42	32	4	7	11	19	30	57
15	Hull	44	10	8	4	32	22	4	7	11	22	38	57
16	PLYMOUTH	44	12	4	6	44	26	4	4	14	21	41	56
17	Bournemouth	44	7	7	8	36	30	6	3	13	20	38	49
18	Shrewsbury	44	7	8	7	23	22	4	8	10	19	32	49
19	Birmingham	44	7	9	6	20	24	4	6	12	21	42	48
20	West Brom	44	8	7	7	29	26	4	4	14	21	43	47
21	Sheffield U**	44	8	6	8	27	28	5	1	16	18	46	46
22	Reading	44	5	7	10	20	25	5	5	12	24	45	42
23	Huddersfield	44	4	6	12	20	38	2	4	16	21	62	28
		1012	246	127	133	830	559	133	127	246	559	830	1391

* play-offs-up
** play-offs-down

Appearances and Goals

Player	Appearances						Goals			
	Lge	Sub	LC	Sub	FAC	Sub	Lge	LC	FAC	Tot
Anderson, Doug	17	2	1		1		1			1
Brimacombe, John	42		2	1	1	1	1			1
Burrows, Adrian	23			3			1			1
Cherry, Steve	37			3		3				
Clayton, John	12	8	1	1	1	1	7	1		8
Cooper, Leigh	33	4	2		1					
Cooper, Steve	14	9	1		1	1	3		1	4
Coughlin, Russell	7	1								
Crudgington, Geoff	7		2							
Evans, Stewart	31	6	2		1		10		1	11
Furphy, Keith	6						1			1
Hodges, Kevin	35	2	2		3		6			6
Law, Nicky	25	1	2		2		3			3
Marker, Nicky	26				3		1			1
Matthews, John	34	1	2		3		1		1	2
McElhinney, Gerry	6		1		1					
Morrison, Andy		1								
Rowbotham, Darren	5	4	1		1					
Rowbotham, Jason	3	1		1						
Smith, Mark	41		2		2		6			6
Summerfield, Kevin	32	5	1		2		5			5
Tynan, Tommy	42	1	1		3		16	1	1	18
Uzzell, John	6	4					1			1
(own-goals)							2			2
23 players used	484	50	22	3	33	3	65	2	4	71

Odds & ends

Double wins: (1) Oldham.

Double defeats: (4) Aston Villa, Crystal Pal, Middlesbrough, Millwall.

Won from behind: (2) Ipswich, Man City (h).

Lost from in front: (5) Aston Villa, Bournemouth, Man City (a), Millwall, Reading.

High spots: Division leaders at end of August.

Capture of highly rated Nicky Marker from Exeter.

Nine goal thriller against Leeds.

Low spots: Failure to maintain early season form.

Disappointing drop in home attendances.

End of season departure of Dave Smith.

Littlewoods Cup defeat against 4th Division Peterborough.

Player of the Year: Steve Cherry.

Ever presents: (0).

Hat-tricks: (0).

Leading scorer: Tommy Tynan (18).

BARCLAYS DIVISION 2   Manager: Ken Brown   SEASON 1988-89

No	Date	1	2	3	4	5	6	7	8	9	10	11	subs used	Scorers, Times, and Referees	Att	Pos	Pt	F-A	H-T
1	A WALSALL 27/8	Cherry	Brimacombe	Cooper L	Burrows	Marker	Smith	Hodges	Matthews	Tynan*	McCarthy	Summerfield	Evans	Tynan 37, Marker 45 / Taylor A 64, 77 / Ref: T Fitzharris	6,178		D 1	2-2	2-0
		Barber	Doman	Taylor M	Shakesp'e*	Forbes	Hart	Pritchard	Goodwin	Taylor A	Christie	Naughton	Hawker	New manager Ken Brown looks to have the perfect start when Marker's powerful shot adds to Tynan's opener. Newly promoted Walsall fight back with two goals from new £90k signing Alex Taylor. His second comes from a free-kick after Cherry was penalised for too many steps.					
2	H HULL 3/9	Cherry	Brimacombe	Cooper L	Burrows	Marker	Smith	Evans	Matthews	Tynan	McCarthy*	Summerfield	Uzzell	Tynan 54, Skipper 60(og) / Ref: J Deakin	8,202	7 13	W 4	2-0	0-0
		Norman	Jobson	Jacobs	Warren	Skipper	Terry	Dyer	Roberts	Moore	Saville	Edwards*	Payton	A superb passing display gives the Argyle faithful heart for the new season. Norman appears to have Burrows' header covered but Tynan nips in to divert the ball into the net. Marker's cross clips Peter Skipper's heel to leave Norman stranded, although Tynan claims the final touch.					
3	A WATFORD 10/9	Cherry	Brimacombe	Cooper L	Burrows	Marker	Smith	Plummer	Matthews	Tynan	McCarthy	Summerfield		Wilkinson 13, Bamber 77, Porter 89p / Ref: A Seville	12,040	11 1	L 4	0-3	0-1
		Coton	Gibbs	Falconer	Jackett	Holdsworth	McClelland	Hodges*	Wilkinson	Bamber	Porter	Holden	Thomas	Watford maintain their 100% record with a convincing win. Holden escapes his marker and his low cross is touched in by Paul Wilkinson. McCarthy is fortunate to stay on after lashing out at Gibbs. Cherry looks to have fouled Wilkinson outside the box but a penalty is awarded.					
4	H STOKE 17/9	Cherry	Brown	Cooper L	Burrows	Marker	Smith	Plummer	Matthews	Tynan	McCarthy	Brimacombe		Tynan 35, 44, 64, Marker 54 / Ref: K Burge	7,823	9 23	W 7	4-0	2-0
		Fox	Gidman^	Carr	Kamara	Beeston	Henry	Hackett	Ford	Stainrod*	Saunders	Beagrie	Shaw/Morgan	Tynan grabs the headlines with a hat-trick but the hero is loan signing Plummer who torments the Stoke defence for 90 minutes. Marker scores the goal of the match after running from halfway and beating three defenders. Tynan's match ball is recovered from the stand roof on Monday.					
5	A LEICESTER 21/9	Cherry	Brown	Cooper L	Burrows*	Marker	Smith	Plummer	Matthews	Tynan	McCarthy	Brimacombe	Summerfield	Newell 58 / Ref: D Elleray	9,117	7	L 7	0-1	0-0
		Cooper	Mauchlen	Spearing	Ramsey	Walsh	Brown	Weir	Cross	Newell	McAllister	Quinn	Morgan	Referee Mr Elleray turns a blind eye to valid penalty appeals for both sides. Scottish international winger Peter Weir proves to be the thorn in Argyle's side and it is he who lays on the winner for Mike Newell. Marker almost deceives Paul Cooper who grabs the ball from under the bar.					
6	H WEST BROM 24/9	Cherry	Brown	Cooper L	Burrows	Marker	Smith	Plummer	Matthews	Tynan	McCarthy	Brimacombe		Tynan 53 / Phillips 85 / Ref: P Durkin	8,539	13 9	D 8	1-1	0-0
		Naylor	Alliston	Burrows	Talbot	Whyte	North	Hopkins	Goodman !	Phillips	Palmer*	Anderson	Cork	Cherry is accused of feigning injury after Goodman is sent off (11) for violent conduct. The lump on the keeper's face suggests otherwise. The game degenerates into a midfield stalemate. Tynan's header looks enough for three points but Stewart Phillips punishes defensive indecision.					
7	A CRYSTAL PALACE 1/10	Cherry	Brown	Cooper L	Burrows	Marker	Smith	Plummer	Matthews*	Tynan*	McCarthy	Brimacombe	Summerfield/Evans	Brimacombe 45 / Wright 33, Thomas 38, Bright 43, [Pardew 79] / Ref: I Hemley	8,047	19 18	L 8	1-4	1-3
		Parkin	Pemberton	Burke	Pardew	Hopkins	O'Reilly	Redfearn	Thomas	Bright	Wright	Barber		The writing is on the wall when Wright and Pemberton hit the woodwork in the first 15 minutes. Palace look a potent attacking force and yet this is their first league win of the season. The Wright-Bright partnership again causes problems. Alan Pardew scores with a superb volley.					
8	A BIRMINGHAM 4/10	Penhaligon	Brown	Cooper L	Burrows	Marker	Smith	Plummer	Matthews	Tynan	McCarthy	Brimacombe		Tynan 75 / Ref: E Parker	4,921	6	W 11	1-0	0-0
		Thomas	Ranson	Roberts	Atkins	Overson	Bird*	Bremner	Langley^	Whitton	Robinson	Wigley	Childs/Morris	Both keepers make their debuts but Martin Thomas is the busier. Penhaligon, deputising for the flu-stricken Cherry, shows some confident handling. Tynan's goal after Marker retrieves a ball that seems destined to go out of play condemns Brum to their eighth loss in nine games.					
9	H BRADFORD C 8/10	Cherry	Brown	Cooper L	Burrows	Marker	Smith	Plummer	Matthews	Tynan	McCarthy	Brimacombe		Tynan 20, 36, McCarthy 25 / Jewell 51 / Ref: K Cooper	6,855	8 6	W 14	3-1	3-0
		Tomlinson	Mitchell	Goddard	Banks	Oliver	Jackson	Thomas*	Sinnott	Ormondroyd	Kennedy	Jewell	Abbott	Tynan, looking sharper than ever after shedding half a stone in a summer fitness regime, plunders two more goals. McCarthy also finds the net after Brimacombe's shot was blocked. The Bantams employ Peter Jackson as a sweeper but are unable to contain the lively Plymouth attack.					
10	H MANCHESTER C 15/10	Cherry	Brown	Cooper L	Burrows	Marker	Uzzell	Plummer	Matthews*	Tynan	McCarthy	Brimacombe	Summerfield	Gayle 49 / Ref: K Cooper	10,158	14 4	L 14	0-1	0-0
		Dibble	Gleghorn	Hinchcliffe	Gayle	Biggins	Redmond	White	Moulden	Morley	McNab	Hughes^	Beckford	What an anti-climax after the nine-goal League Cup thriller between the two sides only three days earlier. Over-fussy refereeing and blatant time-wasting only add to Argyle's and the fans' frustrations. Brian Gayle is unchallenged as he heads Hinchcliffe's corner in at the far post.					
11	A CHELSEA 22/10	Cherry	Brown	Cooper L	Burrows	Marker	Smith	Plummer*	Matthews*	Nicholas	McCarthy	Brimacombe	Uzzell/Hodges	Dixon 18, Durie 25, 42, Roberts 34p, [Dorigo 88] / Ref: D Hutchinson	12,658	16 5	L 14	0-5	0-4
		Freestone	Clarke	Dorigo	Roberts	McLaughlin	Wood	McAllister^	Nicholas	Dixon	Durie	Wilson K	Wilson C	A shambolic display from Argyle gets the result it deserves. Cherry can barely kick after pulling a muscle. Burrows misdirects a back-pass to gift Chelsea their first and unnecessarily handles to concede the penalty. Freestone does not have a shot to save. Brown orders Sunday training.					

12 — H SHREWSBURY — 25/10

Argyle: Cherry, Brown, Cooper L, Williams !, Burrows, Marker, Smith, Hodges, Summerfield, Tynan, McCarthy, Brimacombe

Shrewsbury: Green Run, Green Rich, Bell^, Moyes, Finley, Brown, Priest*, Melrose, Irvine, Thomas, Rougvie/Griffiths

Another morale-sapping performance against a Shrewsbury side that played half the match with ten men after skipper Brian Williams was red-carded (43) for aiming a blow at Tynan. The injured Cherry is still unable to kick. Seventeen-year-old substitute Carl Griffiths twice goes close.

D 0-0 (0-0) — 6,298 — 19 15

Ref: P Vanes

---

13 — A BARNSLEY — 29/10

Argyle: Cherry, Brown, Cooper L, Burrows, Marker !, Smith, Hodges, Summerfield, Tynan, McCarthy, Brimacombe* Uzzell

Barnsley: Baker, Joyce, Beresford, Thomas, Shotton, Futcher, Rees, Dobbin, Cooper, MacDonald, Broddle

Steve Cooper gives his former team-mates a torrid afternoon as Argyle fail to cope with his physical style. Allan Clarke's £100k signing scores the first and makes the second. Mr Danson books six players for various offences and takes a firm line with Marker after he flattened Broddle.

L 1-3 (0-1) — 5,485 — 7 15

Marker 49 / Cooper 19, Thomas 57, Dobbin 70

Ref: P Danson

---

14 — H BLACKBURN — 5/11

Argyle: Cherry, Brown, Cooper L, Marker !, Uzzell, Plummer, Summerfield, Tynan, McCarthy !, Stuart

Blackburn: Gennoe, Atkins, Millar*, Dawson, Hill, Mail, Gayle, Reid, Curry^, Ainscow/Kennedy, Sellars

Who said Tynan was past his best? The prolific striker gives a master class in finishing with the aid of a plentiful supply of chances from new boy Stuart and Plummer. McCarthy, already booked for dissent, sees red after consigning Keith Hill to the Home Park turf with an elbow.

W 4-3 (3-0) — 7,823 — 4 18

Tynan 6, 39, 40, 73 / Reid 52, Garner 61, Kennedy 84

Ref: G Ashby

---

15 — A PORTSMOUTH — 12/11

Argyle: Cherry, Brown, Cooper L*, Burrows, Uzzell, Brimacombe, Smith, Hodges, Summerfield, Tynan, McCarthy^, Matthews/Campbell G

Portsmouth: Knight, Neill, Sandford*, Kuhl, Hogg, Ball, Chamberlain, Horne, Aspinall, Quinn, Hardyman, Kelly

Another defeat is overshadowed by the loss of Cooper with a broken leg (51) after a tackle by Barry Horne. Play is delayed by six minutes to administer treatment on the pitch. Argyle are already two down after Chamberlain outpaces the defence and Quinn outwits the offside trap.

L 0-2 (0-2) — 11,572 — 3 18

Chamberlain 27, Quinn 45

Ref: P Don

---

16 — A OXFORD — 19/11

Argyle: Cherry, Brown, Uzzell, Burrows, Marker !, Smith, Hodges, Matthews, Tynan, Plummer, Stuart

Oxford: Judge, Bardsley, Phillips, Mustoe, Briggs, Greenall, Reck^, Foyle, Simpson, Lewis, Purdie*, Heath/Hill

Injuries and suspensions forces Brown to re-shuffle the side. Tynan scores the only goal after Plummer chests down Uzzell's towering cross to give Argyle their first ever win at the Manor Ground. Stuart continues his impressive form on the wing since his £150k arrival from Charlton.

W 1-0 (1-0) — 5,429 — 18 21

Tynan 30

Ref: G Pooley

---

17 — H OLDHAM — 26/11

Argyle: Miller, Brown, Uzzell, Burrows, Brimacombe, Summerfield, Plummer, Hodges, Tynan, Campbell G, Stuart

Oldham: Rhodes, Irwin, Barrett, Skipper, Flynn^, Milligan, Palmer, Kelly, Barlow*, Ritchie, Wright, Phillskirk/Warhurst

The new boys make their mark. Campbell, in his first full game, scores with a beautiful chip over the advancing Rhodes. Miller, on loan from Arsenal, makes a world-class save from Andy Ritchie which even has Latics boss Joe Royle applauding. Hodges ends his recent goal drought.

W 3-0 (2-0) — 7,829 — 17 24

Tynan 8, Campbell G 35, Hodges 88

Ref: R Gifford

---

18 — A IPSWICH — 3/12

Argyle: Miller, Brown, Uzzell, Burrows, Brimacombe, Summerfield, Plummer*, Hodges, Tynan, Campbell G, Stuart

Ipswich: Forrest, Yallop, Hill, Zondervan, Redford*, Lingham, Lowe, Dozzell, Wark, Atkinson, Stockwell, D'Avray

Young Canadian international Craig Forrest makes a hash of Brown's free-kick and the ball comes off Campbell's back and rolls in. Burrows slips to allow David Lowe the equaliser. Stuart scores directly from a free-kick. Substitute Mitch D'Avray is allowed to head in unchallenged.

D 2-2 (2-1) — 9,929 — 7 25

Campbell G 3, Stuart 45 / Lowe 19, D'Avray 76

Ref: J Ashworth

---

19 — H BRIGHTON — 6/12

Argyle: Miller, Brown, Uzzell, Brimacombe, Summerfield, Plummer, Hodges, Tynan, Campbell G, Stuart

Brighton: Keeley, Chivers, Dublin, Wilkins, May, Gatting, Nelson, Curbishley, Bremner, Owers^, Crumplin*, Wood/Codner

Tynan finishes off a one-two with Campbell. John Crumplin has an unhappy evening. With the goal at his mercy he allows Miller to scramble back. He then appears to head off the line but a penalty is given. Manager Barry Lloyd later claims the referee had apologised for his decision.

W 3-0 (1-0) — 8,133 — 28

Tynan 39, 51p, Plummer 53

Ref: H King

---

20 — H BOURNEMOUTH — 10/12

Argyle: Miller, Brown, Uzzell, Brimacombe, Summerfield, Plummer, Hodges, Tynan, Campbell G*, Stuart

Bournemouth: Peyton, O'Driscoll, Morrell, Bond, Williams, Brooks, O'Connor, Clarke, Aylott, Bishop, Blissett, McCarthy

Former England international, Luther Blissett continues his lethal form by scoring his seventh goal for the Cherries in only his fourth game. Summerfield quickly responds with a lethal strike which goes in via the crossbar. Harry Redknapp's men look the likelier winners by the end.

D 1-1 (0-0) — 10,619 — 11 29

Summerfield 57 / Blissett 53

Ref: A Ward

---

21 — H SUNDERLAND — 18/12

Argyle: Carter, Brown, Uzzell, Brimacombe, Marker, Summerfield, Plummer, Hodges, Tynan, Campbell G, Stuart

Sunderland: Carter, Bennett, Gray, Ord, MacPhail, Doyle, Owers, Armstrong, Gates, Gabbiadini, Pascoe

Argyle bow to the attraction of Christmas shopping and switch to a Sunday kick-off. Defensive errors prove expensive. Brown's mistake gifts the second to Pascoe. Tynan sends Tim Carter the wrong way after Hodges was fouled. Marker's back-pass is intercepted by Marco Gabbiadini.

L 1-4 (0-2) — 13,498 — 13 29

Tynan 56p / Armstrong 27, Pascoe 43, Gab'dini 64, [Gates 85]

Ref: K Burge

---

22 — A SWINDON — 26/12

Argyle: Miller, Brown, Uzzell, Marker, Summerfield, Smith, Hodges, Tynan, McCarthy, Stuart

Swindon: Digby, Hockaday, King, Jones, Parkin, Gittens, Foley, Shearer, Henry, MacLaren, Geddis

A misunderstanding between Burrows and Miller proves costly as Duncan Shearer nips in to score. Hodges' surging runs from midfield cause consternation in the home defence. Miller makes two fine saves from Tommy Jones but Argyle fail to benefit from a strong wind behind them.

L 0-1 (0-1) — 7,883 — 12 29

Shearer 6

Ref: A Buksh

---

23 — A LEEDS — 31/12

Argyle: Miller, Brown, Uzzell, Burrows, Marker, Smith, Hodges, Tynan, McCarthy, Stuart

Leeds: Day, Aspin, Snodin, Aizlewood, Blake, Rennie, Whitlow, Baird, Sheridan, Davison*, Hilaire, Pearson

Argyle defend stoutly until Ian Baird anticipates Marker's return to Miller and scores easily. The game degenerates into a midfield battle with a number of x-rated tackles going unpunished. Glyn Snodin gets a brilliant second after a burst from halfway. Day's trailing foot denies Tynan.

L 0-2 (0-0) — 24,043 — 11 29

Baird 55, Snodin 77

Ref: P Wright

BARCLAYS DIVISION 2

SEASON 1988-89

Manager: Ken Brown

No	Date		Att	Pos	Pt	F-A	H-T	Scorers, Times, and Referees	1	2	3	4	5	6	7	8	9	10	11	subs used
24	H 2/1	WATFORD	12,142	16 *4*	32	1-0	0-0	Summerfield 89 Ref: P Durkin	Miller *Coton*	Brown *Gibbs*	Uzzell *Rostron*	Burrows *Sherwood**	Marker *Miller*	Smith *McClelland*	Summerfield *Redfearn*	Hodges *Wilkinson*	Tynan *Thompson*	McCarthy *Falconer*	Stuart *Holden^*	Holdsworth/Porter *Holdsworth/Porter*
25	A 14/1	BRIGHTON	8,504	16 *20*	33	2-2	1-1	Tynan 40, Stuart 54 Bremner 33, May 88 Ref: I Hemley	Miller *Keeley*	Rowbotham *Chivers*	Uzzell *Dublin*	Burrows *Wilkins*	Marker *May*	Smith *Gatting*	Summerfield *Nelson*	Hodges *Curbishley*	Tynan *Bremner*	McCarthy* *Owers**	Stuart *Wood^*	Campbell G *Cooper/Crumplin*
26	H 21/1	WALSALL	11,505	15 *24*	36	2-0	0-0	Tynan 62, Marker 77 Ref: K Cooper	Miller *Barber*	Rowbotham *Dornan*	Uzzell *Mower*	Burrows *Shakespeare Forbes*	Marker *Hart*	Smith *Rees*	Summerfield *Goodwin^*	Hodges *Banton**	Tynan *Bertschin*	McCarthy* *Hawker*	Stuart *Christie/Jones*	Campbell G *Christie/Jones*
27	H 4/2	BIRMINGHAM	7,721	14 *23*	36	0-1	0-1	Robinson 13 Ref: K Cooper	Miller *Thomas*	Brown *Ashley*	Uzzell *Trewick*	Burrows *Atkins*	Marker *Overson*	Smith *Langley*	Matthews *Roberts*	McCarthy *Tait*	Tynan *Frain*	Hodges* *Robinson*	Stuart *Wigley*	Campbell G
28	A 11/2	BRADFORD C	8,693	16 *19*	37	1-1	1-0	McCarthy 36 Costello 89 Ref: J Watson	Miller *Evans M*	Brown *Mitchell*	Uzzell *Oliver**	Burrows *Abbott*	Marker *Jackson*	Smith *Evans D*	Matthews^ *Thomas*	McCarthy *Sinnott*	Tynan* *Leonard*	Hodges *Goddard^*	Stuart *Jewell*	Campbell G/Plummer *Costello/Banks*
29	H 18/2	CHELSEA	13,180	16 *1*	37	0-1	0-1	Dixon 18 Ref: R Hamer	Miller *Beasant*	Brown *Clarke*	Uzzell *Dorigo*	Burrows *Roberts*	Marker *McLaughlin*	Smith *Bumstead*	Matthews^ *Nicholas*	McCarthy *Mitchell*	Tynan *Dixon*	Hodges *Durie^*	Stuart *Hazard**	Plummer *Wilson K/Lee*
30	A 25/2	MANCHESTER C	22,451	17 *1*	37	0-2	0-1	McNab 12p, Biggins 54 Ref: H Taylor	Wilmot *Dibble*	Brown *Lake*	Uzzell *Taggart**	Burrows *Gayle*	Marker *Megson*	Smith *Redmond*	Matthews *White*	McCarthy* *Morley*	Tynan *Gleghorn*	Hodges *McNab*	Stuart *Biggins^*	Plummer *Hinchcliffe/Moulden*
31	A 28/2	SHREWSBURY	2,978	16 *1*	37	0-2	0-1	Kelly 27, McGinlay 72 Ref: J Worrall	Wilmot *Perks*	Brown *Green*	Uzzell *Williams*	Burrows *Bell*	Marker *Pratley*	Smith *Finley*	Matthews* *Brown*	McCarthy *Kelly*	Tynan *McGinlay**	Hodges *Griffiths*	Stuart *Thomas*	Plummer *Osbourne*
32	H 4/3	PORTSMOUTH	8,131	18 *14*	37	0-1	0-0	Quinn 81 Ref: D Hutchinson	Wilmot *Gosney*	Brown *Neill*	Rowbotham *Whitehead*	Burrows *Dillon*	Marker *Hogg*	Smith *Maguire*	Matthews^ *Chamberlain*	McCarthy* *Horne*	Tynan *Quinn*	Hodges *Connor**	Stuart *Kelly*	Plummer/Pickard *Aspinall*
33	A 11/3	BLACKBURN	7,462	16 *3*	40	2-1	1-0	Stuart 29, Tynan 83 Hildersley 73 Ref: A Dawson	Wilmot *Gennoe*	Brown *Atkins*	Uzzell *Sulley*	Burrows *Reid*	Marker *Hendry*	Smith *Hill^*	Matthews *Gayle*	McCarthy *Hildersley*	Tynan *Byrne*	**Campbell D** *Diamond**	Stuart *Sellars*	Garner/Finnigan
34	H 18/3	LEICESTER	6,703	18 *15*	41	1-1	1-0	Stuart 14 Cross 52 Ref: G Ashby	Wilmot *Hodge*	Rowbotham *Mauchlen*	Uzzell *Spearing*	Burrows *Kennedy*	Marker *Walsh*	Smith *Paris*	Matthews* *Reid*	**Byrne** *Cross*	Tynan *Newell*	Pickard *McAllister*	Stuart *Mills*	Hodges

24 — WATFORD: The game looks to be heading for the scoreless draw it deserves when an element of good fortune gives Argyle all three points. With only 50 seconds left, McCarthy's mis-hit shot turns into a perfect pass to Summerfield who scores past his former Birmingham team-mate Tony Coton.

25 — BRIGHTON: Kevin Bremner opens the scoring with a header. Tynan plays the 500th full league game of his career and marks the occasion with a goal. He also crosses for Stuart to execute a simple tap-in. Calls for the board to resign from disgruntled Albion fans are silenced by May's equaliser.

26 — WALSALL: Even at this early stage of the season, Walsall, under new manager John Barnwell, look doomed for the drop as Argyle consign them to their 14th consecutive defeat. Tynan is again at the centre of the action scoring the first with a header and then setting up Marker with a 40-yard pass.

27 — BIRMINGHAM: A case of after the Lord Mayor's show as Argyle produce an uninspiring performance after the thrills of last week's FA Cup-tie. Steve Wigley runs clear and crosses for the unmarked Colin Robinson. Kevin Langley comes closest to scoring for the Greens when he heads over his own bar.

28 — BRADFORD C: Terry Yorath takes charge of City for the first time and finds himself having to play his fourth-choice keeper. Uzzell takes Paul Jewell's legs (11) but Miller palms away Abbott's spot-kick. McCarthy heads in from a tight angle. Peter Costello leaps high to head home the equaliser.

29 — CHELSEA: Former England striker Kerry Dixon looks two yards offside as he scores the only goal. Some rugged tackles from both sides go unpunished. The need for repairs to a net causes a five-minute delay. Dave Beasant is twice punished for taking a step too far out of his area for drop-kicks.

30 — MANCHESTER C: Manager Brown spends 30 minutes with the ref to question the legitimacy of both City goals. Marker brings down Morley. Neil McNab sends Wilmot the wrong way. The keeper redeems himself when he saves a second penalty from the same player after he felled Wayne Biggins (20).

31 — SHREWSBURY: The goal drought continues as the Shrews gain a comfortable victory. Sweeper Tony Kelly, on loan from West Brom, lets fly from 25 yards. John McGinlay, making his home debut, scores from close range after Wilmot slipped to give Shrewsbury their first home win for four months.

32 — PORTSMOUTH: Argyle's afternoon is summed up as early as the 13th minute when McCarthy's goal-bound shot flattens Tynan. The Pilgrims are totally bereft of ideas and only Wilmot saves them from a heavier defeat. Debutant Pickard's error leads to Mickey Quinn's cross.

33 — BLACKBURN: David Campbell arrives on loan from Charlton to pep up Argyle's flailing attack. Tynan robs Colin Hendry to set up Stuart. Ronnie Hildersley equalises. Tynan's farcical winner comes after a soaring clearance lands in mud and the lack of bounce deceives Gennoe who is 30 yards out.

34 — LEICESTER: Despite pouring rain and an already sodden pitch, Argyle produce a six-man passing move which results in Stuart and the ball in the back of the net. Nicky Cross levels with an angled drive. New boy Byrne and Stuart cause problems on both wings. Tynan fluffs a good late chance.

35 — A HULL, 25/3

0-3 (HT 0-2) — Pos 20, 19, 41 — Att 5,851

Scorers: Edwards 4, 69, Jobson 33
Ref: L Dikes

Argyle: Wilmot, Howbotham, Uzzell, Burrows, Matthews, McCarthy, Tynan, Byrne, Stuart
Hull: Hesford, Murray^, Jacobs, Swan, Terry, McParland, Roberts*, Whitehurst, Edwards, Bell, Payton/Jenkinson

After seven successive defeats, Hull parade £350k of new signings in Peter Swan and Ian McParland. Richard Jobson's first goal of the season from 30 yards sandwiches two fortunate strikes from Keith Edwards. Smith's clearance is deemed in and a free-kick deflects off Byrne's arm.

36 — H SWINDON, 27/3

4-1 (HT 3-0) — Pos 18, 9, 44 — Att 8,487

Scorers: Marker 13, Tynan 16p, McCarthy 34, 51. Jones 67
Ref: J Moules

Argyle: Wilmot, Brown, Uzzell, Burrows, Smith, Matthews, McCarthy, Tynan*, Byrne, Stuart, Campbell G
Swindon: Digby, Hockaday, Bodin, Gittens, Calderwood, Foley, McLoughlin, Shearer, MacLaren, White

Swindon keeper Fraser Digby has a nightmare. He drops Byrne's long throw at Marker's feet. He then pulls down Marker. Tynan scores from the spot. McCarthy taps in after Stuart's shot is fumbled. Calderwood loses possession on halfway and McCarthy runs clear to make it four.

37 — A STOKE, 1/4

2-2 (HT 0-2) — Pos 17, 11, 45 — Att 8,363

Scorers: Tynan 51p, McCarthy 78. Bamber 25, Henry 42
Ref: R Pawley

Argyle: Wilmot, Brown, Uzzell, Burrows, Marker, Smith, Matthews, McCarthy, Tynan, Byrne, Stuart, Hodges
Stoke: Barrett, Butler, Carr, Kamara, Higgins^, Berry, Hackett, Bamber*, Saunders, Henry, Morgan/Shaw

Arsenal turn down a £100k bid for Wilmot who gifts the first when he parries the ball and Dave Bamber accepts an easy chance. Burrows' error leads to the second. Tynan scores from the spot after Stuart is fouled but misses a second penalty when Scott Barrett guesses correctly.

38 — A SUNDERLAND, 4/4

1-2 (HT 0-2) — Pos 45 — Att 8,003

Scorers: Tynan 63. Armstrong 6, 17
Ref: S Lodge

Argyle: Wilmot, Brown, Uzzell, Burrows, Marker, Smith, Matthews, McCarthy, Tynan, Byrne, Stuart
Sunderland: Carter, Bennett, Gray, Lemon, MacPhail, Ord, Owers, Armstrong, Gates, Gabbiadini, Atkinson*, Williams

Defensive errors deny Argyle the chance to bring anything back from their longest trip of the season. The defence is slow to react after Wilmot saves well from Gabbiadini and Armstrong pounces. He then strikes again after Brown and Matthews dally. Tynan grabs his 26th of the season.

39 — H LEEDS, 9/4

1-0 (HT 0-0) — Pos 18, 48 — Att 9,365

Scorer: McCarthy 86
Ref: R Groves

Argyle: Wilmot, Brown, Uzzell, Burrows, Smith, Byrne, McCarthy, Tynan, Matthews, Stuart, Hodges
Leeds: Day, Aspin, Snodin^, Williams, Blake, Fairclough, Strachan, Baird, Shutt*, Whitlow, Pearson/Rennie

Despite spending a million pounds, Leeds slump to a second successive defeat to end their play-off dreams. Uzzell marshals Gordon Strachan superbly. McCarthy gives Mervyn Day no chance from close range. Stuart, booked only once before this season, receives an eighth yellow.

40 — A WEST BROM, 15/4

2-2 (HT 0-1) — Pos 19, 49 — Att 11,358

Scorers: Brown 68, McCarthy 90. Brown 25(og), West 52
Ref: P Don

Argyle: Wilmot, Brown, Uzzell, Burrows, Marker, Smith, Matthews, McCarthy, Tynan, Byrne, Hodges
West Brom: Naylor, Bradley*, Albiston, Talbot, Whyte, North, Ford, Goodman, West, Robson, Anderson, Bartlett

Colin West heads against the bar and Brown heads back to where Wilmot had been to gift the opener. West scores the second on the turn. Argyle fail to capitulate and Brown makes amends by side-footing home. McCarthy equalises with two minutes of injury-time already played.

41 — H CRYSTAL PALACE, 22/4

0-2 (HT 0-1) — Pos 19, 49 — Att 8,492

Scorers: Bright 12, 54
Ref: K Burge

Argyle: Wilmot, Brown, Uzzell, Burrows, Marker, Smith, Byrne, McCarthy, Tynan, Matthews, Stuart, Hodges
Crystal Palace: Suckling, Pemberton!, Burke, Madden, Hopkins, O'Reilly, Salako, Pardew, Bright, Barber, Shaw

There is an element of good fortune about both Palace goals. Mark Bright mis-hits the first and admits his second was an intended cross. John Pemberton, booked for a foul on Stuart, is red-carded for swearing. Referee Burge lectures Palace manager Steve Coppell after the dismissal.

42 — H BARNSLEY, 25/4

1-2 (HT 1-1) — Pos 19, 49 — Att 5,468

Scorers: Byrne 21. Currie 2, Shotton 86
Ref: J Deakin

Argyle: Wilmot, Brown, Uzzell, Burrows, Smith, Byrne, McCarthy, Tynan, Matthews, Stuart, Hodges
Barnsley: Baker, Joyce, Broddle, Dobbin, Shotton, Futcher, Robinson, Agnew, Lowndes, Currie, MacDonald

Argyle again pay the penalty for slack defending. Wilmot fails to cut out John MacDonald's cross and David Currie scores within 90 seconds of the start. Byrne opens his Pilgrims' account with a header at good work by Tynan. Malcolm Shotton heads home MacDonald's corner.

43 — A OLDHAM, 29/4

2-2 (HT 1-2) — Pos 18, 50 — Att 4,614

Scorers: Marker 26, Campbell G 80. Irwin 24, Wright 31
Ref: T West

Argyle: Wilmot, Brown, Uzzell^, Burrows, Marker, Smith, Byrne, Brimacombe, Tynan, Matthews*, Stuart, Hodges/Campbell G
Oldham: Hallworth, Irwin, Barrett, Henry, Marshall, Holden, Palmer, Kelly, Bunn*, Milligan, Wright, Hartford

Denis Irwin's free-kick penetrates Argyle's wall to put Latics in front. Marker's header provokes severe Oldham pressure. Palmer misses an open goal and Smith clears off the line. Jon Hallworth's clanger, when he takes his eye off Ian Marshall's back-pass, allows Campbell to level.

44 — H IPSWICH, 1/5

0-1 (HT 0-1) — Pos 20, 50 — Att 6,484

Scorer: Humes 40
Ref: K Cooper

Argyle: Wilmot, Brown, Uzzell, Burrows, Marker, Smith, Byrne, Brimacombe, Tynan, McCarthy, Hodges, Stuart
Ipswich: Forrest, Baltacha, Harbey, Zondervan*, D'Avray, Linighan, Lowe, Redford, Wark, Stockwell, Humes, Yallop

Ipswich boss John Duncan can thank his keeper, Craig Forrest, for keeping his side in the game after the Canadian international pulls off a string of great saves. Tony Humes fires home the only goal from the edge of the penalty area as Argyle's poor end of season run continues.

45 — H OXFORD, 6/5

3-1 (HT 0-0) — Pos 18, 15, 53 — Att 4,989

Scorers: Burrows 75, McCarthy 77, Stuart 88. Ford 86
Ref: R Milford

Argyle: Wilmot, Brown, Uzzell, Burrows, Marker, Morrison, Byrne*, McCarthy, Tynan, Garner^, Stuart, Barlow/Whiston
Oxford: Hucker, Slatter*, Phillips, Shelton, Lewis, Evans, Bardsley, Mustoe^, Nogan, Durnin, Hill, Heath/Ford

With little at stake, Brown bloods some youngsters. A dismal first half produces little excitement. Burrows goal from two yards finally wakes everyone up. McCarthy scores with a first time-effort. Mike Ford lashes home Lee Nogan's cut-back. Stuart's drive deflects off Micky Lewis.

46 — A BOURNEMOUTH, 13/5

0-0 (HT 0-0) — Pos 18, 12, 54 — Att 7,230

Ref: A Buksh

Argyle: Wilmot, Brown, Brimacombe, Burrows, Campbell G, Morrison, Byrne^, Tynan, Whiston*, Stuart, Hodges/Plummer
Bournemouth: Smeulders, Newson, Morrell, Teale, Shearer, O'Driscoll, Holmes, Brooks, Mundee, Bishop, Blissett

The Cherries are looking to finish in their highest ever league position but 21-goal striker Luther Blissett is the chief culprit as a number of chances go begging. Jan Smeulders' fine save denies Whiston a goal on his full debut. Burrows clears off the line from Peter Shearer's header.

Home 8,628 Away 9,253 Average 9,253

BARCLAYS DIVISION 2 (CUP-TIES)   Manager: Ken Brown   SEASON 1988-89

Littlewoods Cup

Littlewoods Cup	Att		F-A	H-T	Scorers, Times, and Referees	1	2	3	4	5	6	7	8	9	10	11	subs used
1:1 A HEREFORD 29/8	2,353 4:	W	3-0	2-0	Summerf'd 6, Marker 26, McCarthy 85 Ref: R Milford	Cherry	Brimacombe	Cooper	Burrows	Marker	Smith	Hodges	Matthews	Tynan	McCarthy	Summerfield	
						Rose	*Jones*	*Crane*	*Stevens*	*Devine*	*Bowyer*	*Mardenboro'*	*Maddy*	*Stant*	*Benbow**	*McLoughlin*	*Williams*
1:2 H HEREFORD 6/9	4,772 4:12	W	7-3	2-1	McCarthy 3, 66, Marker 27, Stant 1, Tester 50 Ref: R Groves (Argyle won 6-2 on aggregate)	Cherry	Brimacombe	Cooper	Burrows	Marker	Smith	Uzzell	Matthews	Tynan	McCarthy	Summerfield	
						Rose	*Williams*	*Crane*	*Stevens*	*Devine*	*Maddy*	*Mardenboro'*	*Benbow*	*Stant*	*Tester*	*McLoughlin*	
2:1 A MANCHESTER C 28/9	9,454 8	L	0-1	0-1	White 12 Ref: K Breen	Cherry	Brown	Cooper	Burrows	Marker	Smith	Plummer	Matthews	Tynan	McCarthy	Brimacombe	
						Dibble	*Biggins**	*Hinchcliffe*	*Gayle*	*Brightwell*	*Redmond*	*White*	*Moulden^*	*Morley*	*McNab*	*Lake*	*Simpson/Beckford*
2:2 H MANCHESTER C 12/10	8,794 4	L	3-6	2-2	Smith 27, McC' 33, Ty'n 48 (Lake 89) Big's 5, Gleg'16,90, M'den 74, McN' 80 Ref: R Hamer (Argyle lost 3-7 on aggregate)	Cherry	Brown	Cooper	Burrows	Marker	Smith	Plummer*	Matthews^	Tynan	McCarthy	Brimacombe	
						Dibble	*Glephorn*	*Hinchcliffe*	*Gayle*	*Biggins**	*Redmond*	*White*	*Moulden*	*Morley*	*McNab*	*Lake*	*Beckford*

Argyle virtually assure themselves a place in round two with an accomplished display. Kevin Rose, making his 300th consecutive appearance, is powerless to stop Summerfield's left-foot volley. Marker coolly finishes and McCarthy scores his first goal for the club from a Tynan cross.

Any thoughts of an easy passage are soon put aside when Phil Stant scores after 45 seconds. McCarthy soon heads a reply. Marker continues his scoring run. Tester levels after Smith's error. McCarthy crashes home another and is denied a hat-trick by a linesman's flag for offside.

Argyle give themselves a fighting chance after a spirited display against Mel Machin's men. They are far from dispirited after David White scores from Andy Hinchcliffe's corner. Both goalkeepers have good games with Andy Dibble making a particularly fine save from Marker.

Brown's instructions not to concede an early goal are ignored as Biggins scores from close range. Nigel Gleghorn gives Argyle a mountain to climb. Dibble saves Tynan's penalty (23) after David White handles. McNab does not make the same mistake after Matthews fouls Beckford.

FA Cup

FA Cup	Att		F-A	H-T	Scorers, Times, and Referees	1	2	3	4	5	6	7	8	9	10	11	subs used
3 H CAMBRIDGE 7/1	8,648 4:11	W	2-0	0-0	Tynan 52, Summerfield 59 Ref: D Elleray	Cherry	Brown	Uzzell	Burrows	Marker	Smith	Summerfield	Hodges	Tynan	McCarthy	Stuart	
						Vaughan	*Bailie*	*Kimble*	*Daish*	*Chapple*	*Turner*	*Clayton*	*Ryan*	*Dublin**	*Taylor*	*Croft^*	*Reilly/Leadbitter*
4 H EVERTON 28/1	27,566 1:9	D	1-1	0-0	McCarthy 62, Sheedy 79 Ref: D Vickers	Miller	Brown	Uzzell	Burrows	Marker	Smith	Summerfield	McCarthy	Tynan	Hodges	Stuart	
						Southall	*Snodin*	*vd Hauwe*	*Ratcliffe*	*Watson*	*Bracewell*	*Steven*	*McCall*	*Sharp*	*Cottee*	*Sheedy*	
4R A EVERTON 31/1	28,542 1:9	L	0-4	0-2	Sharp 23, 48, Nevin 36, Sheedy 84 Ref: D Vickers	Miller	Brown	Uzzell	Burrows	Marker	Smith	Summerf'ld*	McCarthy	Tynan	Hodges^	Stuart	
						Southall	*Snodin**	*vd Hauwe*	*Ratcliffe*	*Watson*	*Steven*	*Nevin^*	*McCall*	*Sharp*	*Cottee*	*Sheedy*	*Matthews/Campbell G Wilson/Clarke*

Cambridge put up stubborn resistance. Tynan finally breaks the deadlock when he side-foots in a Stuart shot that looked to be going wide. A deft flick from Summerfield settles the tie. U's regret not starting with George Reilly as the big striker proves a handful when he comes on.

McCarthy's request to swap shirt numbers with Hodges pays off as the Welsh striker scores his first goal since October. Most of the crowd are mystified when a penalty is awarded but Match of the Day cameras later reveal the ball hitting Burrows' hand. Sheedy makes no mistake.

Argyle's big night out is marred by the broken leg suffered by Summerfield after a tackle by Graeme Sharp. The Scottish international puts the Toffees ahead. Pat Nevin pounces on Miller's parry. Sharp converts his second header of the evening and Sheedy atones for an earlier miss.

Home / Away league table

	Team	P	W	D	L	F	A	W	D	L	F	A	Pts
1	Chelsea	46	15	6	2	50	25	14	6	3	46	25	99
2	Manchester C	46	12	8	3	48	28	10	8	5	29	25	82
3	Crystal Pal*	46	15	6	2	42	17	8	6	9	29	32	81
4	Watford	46	14	5	4	41	18	8	7	8	33	30	78
5	Blackburn	46	16	4	3	50	22	6	7	10	24	37	77
6	Swindon	46	13	8	2	35	15	7	8	8	33	38	76
7	Barnsley	46	12	8	3	37	21	8	6	9	29	37	74
8	Ipswich	46	13	3	7	42	23	9	4	10	29	38	73
9	West Brom	46	13	7	3	43	18	5	11	7	22	23	72
10	Leeds	46	12	6	5	34	20	5	10	8	25	30	67
11	Sunderland	46	12	8	3	40	23	4	7	12	20	37	63
12	Bournemouth	46	13	3	7	32	20	5	5	13	21	42	62
13	Stoke	46	10	9	4	33	25	5	5	13	24	47	59
14	Bradford C	46	8	11	4	29	22	6	3	14	23	37	56
15	Leicester	46	11	6	6	31	20	2	10	11	25	43	55
16	Oldham	46	9	10	4	49	32	2	11	10	26	40	54
17	Oxford	46	11	6	6	40	34	3	6	14	22	36	54
18	PLYMOUTH	46	11	4	8	35	22	3	8	12	22	44	54
19	Brighton	46	11	5	7	36	24	3	4	16	21	42	51
20	Portsmouth	46	10	6	7	33	21	3	6	14	20	41	51
21	Hull	46	7	9	7	31	25	4	5	14	21	43	47
22	Shrewsbury	46	4	11	8	25	31	4	7	12	15	36	42
23	Birmingham	46	6	4	13	21	33	2	7	14	10	43	35
24	Walsall	46	3	10	10	27	42	2	6	15	14	38	31
		1104	261	163	128	884	581	128	163	261	581	884	1493

* promoted after play-offs

Appearances / Goals

Player	Lge	Sub	LC	Sub	FAC	Sub	Lge	LC	FAC	Tot
Barlow, Martin	24	1	4				1			1
Brimacombe, John	39		2		3		1			1
Brown, Kenny	43		4		3		1			1
Burrows, Adrian	13									
Byrne, David	1									
Campbell, David										
Campbell, Greg	6	7				1	3			3
Cherry, Steve	15		4		1					
Cooper, Leigh	15		4							
Evans, Stewart	1	2								
Garner, Darren	1									
Hodges, Kevin	23	8	1	1	3		1			1
Marker, Nicky	42	1	4		3		6	2		8
Matthews, John	29	1	4	1						
McCarthy, Sean	37	1	4		3		8	4	1	13
Miller, Alan	13		4		2					
Morrison, Andy	2									
Penhaligon, Gary	1									
Pickard, Owen	1	1								
Plummer, Calvin	17	6	2				1			1
Rowbotham, Jason	5									
Smith, Mark	35		4		3			1		1
Stuart, Mark	32				3		5			5
Summerfield, Kevin	17	3	2	1	3		2	1	1	4
Tynan, Tommy	46		4		3		24	1	1	26
Uzzell, John	30	3	4		3					
Whiston, Peter	1	1	1							
Wilmot, Rhys	17									
(own-goals)							1			1
28 players used	506	35	44	2	33	2	55	9	3	67

Odds & ends

Double wins: (2) Blackburn, Oxford.
Double defeats: (6) Barnsley, Chelsea, Crystal Pal, Manchester C, Portsmouth, Sunderland.
Won from behind: (0).
Lost from in front: (0).
High spots: Virtuoso performance from Tommy Tynan v Blackburn (h). Nine-goal thriller v Man City (h) in Littlewoods Cup. Superb performances of on-loan goalkeepers, Miller and Wilmot. Holding First Division Everton (h) to a draw in the FA Cup.
Low spots: Broken legs suffered by both Leigh Cooper and Kevin Summerfield. End-of-season release of long-serving John Uzzell. Poor away record.

Player of the Year: Tommy Tynan.
Ever presents: (1) Tommy Tynan.
Hat tricks: (2) Tommy Tynan (2).
Leading scorer: Tommy Tynan (26).

BARCLAYS DIVISION 2

Manager: Brown > Gregory > Kemp — SEASON 1989-90

No	Date	H/A	Opponent	Att	Pos	Opp	Pt	Res	F-A	H-T	Scorers, Times	Referee
1	19/8	H	OXFORD	8,509	—	—	3	W	2-0	0-0	Stuart 48, 64	Ref: K Burge
2	26/8	A	WEST HAM	20,231	11	1	3	L	2-3	0-1	Stuart 54, 77 / Kelly 21, Allen 51, Keen 76	Ref: T Holbrook
3	2/9	H	BARNSLEY	7,708	8	16	6	W	2-1	0-0	Campbell 75, McCarthy 90 / MacDonald 86	Ref: R Groves
4	9/9	A	OLDHAM	4,940	11	15	6	L	2-3	0-1	McCarthy 50, Thomas 71 / Palmer 28, Holden 54, Ritchie 69	Ref: A Wilkie
5	12/9	A	PORTSMOUTH	6,865	3	22	9	W	3-0	1-0	Tynan 22, 76p, Thomas 89	Ref: M James
6	16/9	H	SHEFFIELD UTD	10,884	5	1	10	D	0-0	0-0		Ref: B Stevens
7	23/9	A	WOLVERHAMPTON	13,762	11	17	10	L	0-1	0-0	Paskin 90	Ref: A Ward
8	26/9	A	SWINDON	6,862	12	16	10	L	0-3	0-1	Jones 37, King 77, Bodin 86	Ref: D Vickers
9	30/9	H	BRIGHTON	7,610	11	6	13	W	2-1	1-0	Hodges 42, Tynan 74 / Wood 51	Ref: G Ashby
10	7/10	H	STOKE	6,940	7	21	16	W	3-0	1-0	Hodges 44, Tynan 52p, Thomas 74	Ref: R Lewis
11	14/10	A	MIDDLESBROUGH	15,003	4	20	19	W	2-0	0-0	Stuart 66, Thomas 84	Ref: M Peck

Line-ups (positions 1–11) and subs used

1. H OXFORD
Argyle: Wilmot, Brown, Brimacombe, Marker, Burrows, Smith, Byrne, McCarthy, Tynan, Thomas, Stuart
Oxford: Hucker, Bardsley, Phillips J, Phillips L, Foster, Greenall, Penney^, Mustoe*, Foyle, Durnin, Simpson. Subs: Ford/Smart
> Argyle gain an opening-day win for the first time in seven seasons. Stuart capitalises on a mistake by ex-England defender Steve Foster to drill the ball past Peter Hucker. He then cleverly chips over the defence and scores via the crossbar. Want-away Smith plays soundly at the back.

2. A WEST HAM
Argyle: Wilmot, Brown, Brimacombe, Marker, Burrows, Smith, Byrne, McCarthy, Tynan, Thomas, Stuart
West Ham: Parkes, Potts, Dicks, Gale, Martin, Keen, Ward, Kelly, Allen, Brady, Paris
> Both sides play their part in an entertaining game. Despite attempts by Brown to clear off the line, David Kelly's header goes in. Martin Allen gets a debut goal. Stuart scores from 25 yards. Kevin Keen pounces on a loose ball. Stuart jinks his way through to shoot past Phil Parkes.

3. H BARNSLEY
Argyle: Wilmot, Brown, Brimacombe, Marker, Burrows, Smith, Byrne^, McCarthy, Tynan^, Thomas, Stuart. Subs: Hodges/Campbell
Barnsley: Baker, Shotton, Broddle, Dobbin, Banks, Futcher, Lowndes, Agnew, MacDonald*, Currie, Robinson. Sub: Cooper
> Barnsley dominate for long periods and only the brilliance of Wilmot defies them. Campbell scores immediately after replacing Tynan. Steve Cooper robs Smith and crosses for John MacDonald's equaliser. McCarthy takes advantage of three minutes of injury-time to secure the win.

4. A OLDHAM
Argyle: Wilmot, Brown, Brimacombe, Marker, Burrows, Smith, Hodges, McCarthy, Tynan, Thomas, Stuart
Oldham: Rhodes, Irwin, Barlow, Henry, Barrett, Warhurst, Palmer, Ritchie, Bunn, Milligan, Holden
> Argyle once again succumb to the Boundary Park plastic. Roger Palmer scores after Mike Milligan crashes a shot against the bar. McCarthy's goal threatens a revival but defensive errors by Marker and Brown allow the Latics to restore their lead. Thomas scores his first for Argyle.

5. A PORTSMOUTH
Argyle: Wilmot, Brown, Brimacombe, Marker, Burrows, Smith, Hodges, McCarthy, Tynan, Thomas, Stuart
Portsmouth: Knight, Hogg, Maguire, Fillery, Sandford, Ball, Wigley, Kuhl, Chamberlain, Connor, Black*. Sub: Whittingham
> Wilmot denies Pompey twice with fine saves before Tynan opens the scoring with a header. The ever-improving McCarthy celebrates his 24th birthday with a fine run which ends in Maguire conceding a penalty for handball. With the home side pushing forward Thomas drills in a shot.

6. H SHEFFIELD UTD
Argyle: Wilmot, Brown, Brimacombe, Marker, Burrows, Smith, Hodges, McCarthy, Tynan, Thomas*, Stuart. Sub: Byrne
Sheffield Utd: Tracey, Hill, Pike, Booker, Stancliffe, Morris, Whitehouse, Gannon, Deane, Francis*, Bryson. Sub: Bradshaw
> A dour scoreless draw confounds the experts who predict a highly entertaining match between two free-scoring sides. Both managers blame the strong wind for spoiling the game. Thomas wastes the best chance when he ignores the unmarked McCarthy and tries a speculative shot.

7. A WOLVERHAMPTON
Argyle: Wilmot, Brown, Brimacombe, Marker, Burrows, Byrne, McCarthy, Tynan, Thomas, Stuart
Wolverhampton: Kendall, Bellamy, Venus, Streete, Clarke, Vaughan, Bennett, Gooding, Bull, Mutch^, Dennison*. Subs: Downing/Paskin
> A number of curious decisions, mostly in Argyle's favour, enrages the Molineux crowd. Marker and Burrows nullify the threat of Steve Bull and Andy Mutch. McCarthy misses a hat-trick of chances. Substitute John Paskin supplies the killer blow in the second minute of injury-time.

8. A SWINDON
Argyle: Wilmot, Brown, Brimacombe, Marker, Burrows, Byrne!, Hodges, McCarthy, Tynan, Thomas, Stuart. Sub: Thomas
Swindon: Digby, Hockaday, King, McLoughlin, Calderwood, Gittens, Jones*, Shearer^, Close!, Simpson!, MacLaren. Subs: Bodin/Galvin
> Tom Jones heads in to score Swindon's first goal for 344 minutes. Byrne and Shaun Close are dismissed after a clash (50) which is spotted by a linesman. Simpson follows (57) after a fracas with Brown. Phil King lobs over Wilmot from 25 yards. Bodin scores from the edge of the area.

9. H BRIGHTON
Argyle: Wilmot, Brown, Brimacombe, Marker, Burrows, Morrison, Byrne, Campbell, Tynan, Thomas, Stuart. Sub: Thomas
Brighton: Keeley, Chivers, Dublin, Curbishley, Bissett, Gatting, Nelson, Wood, Bremner, Codner, Wilkins*. Sub: Crumplin
> Hodges ends Argyle's minor drought with his first goal for ten months. Paul Wood equalises from Kevin Bremner's cross. Garry Nelson causes a few flutters in the home defence. Byrne's long throw creates confusion from which Tynan strikes for his first home goal of the season.

10. H STOKE
Argyle: Wilmot, Brown, Brimacombe, Marker, Burrows, Morrison, Byrne, Hodges*, Tynan, Campbell, Stuart. Sub: Thomas
Stoke: Barrett, Butler, Statham, Kamara, Cranson, Beeston, Hackett^, Palin, Beagrie, Biggins, Saunders. Subs: Bamber
> It is not one of Stoke manager Mick Mills' better days. Pre-match injury worries and the need to borrow Argyle's black shorts are compounded by calls for his head by the travelling fans. Tynan's penalty after Statham trips Campbell is sandwiched by two well-placed shots past Barrett.

11. A MIDDLESBROUGH
Argyle: Wilmot, Brown, Brimacombe, Marker, Burrows, Morrison, Hodges, Thomas, Tynan, Campbell, Stuart. Sub: Campbell
Middlesbrough: Poole, Coleman, Mohan, Mowbray, Kernaghan, Putney, Slaven, Proctor, Davenport*, Gill^, Comfort. Subs: Ripley/Cooper
> The Pilgrims' roller-coaster season continues with a fine win at struggling Boro. Bruce Rioch's big-money signings fail to make any impact. Stuart fires a low shot into the corner. Thomas celebrates his recall with a fine all-round performance which is capped by a well-taken goal.

Plymouth Argyle — Season results and line-ups (matches 12–23)

Left-hand figures per match: Argyle league position · Opponents' league position · Argyle points.

No.	V	Opponent	Date	Att.	Arg Pos	Opp Pos	Pts	Res	Score	Scorers	Referee
12		(Leicester City)	17/10	10,037	—	24	22			Reid 84	Ref: J Carter
13	A	IPSWICH	21/10	10,362	5	14	22	L	0-3	Kiwomya 20, 68, Milton 29	Ref: P Don
14	H	BLACKBURN	28/10	6,876	6	9	23	D	2-2	McCarthy 13, 45 / Gayle 16, Sellars 52	Ref: R Gifford
15	A	LEEDS	1/11	26,791	6	2	23	L	1-2	Thomas 38 / Strachan 36p, Davison 62	Ref: J Lloyd
16	H	BRADFORD C	4/11	7,152	10	18	24	D	1-1	Tynan 65 / Campbell 62	Ref: R Milford
17	A	WATFORD	11/11	9,401	8	18	27	W	2-1	Tynan 56, Thomas 83 / Redfearn 84	Ref: K Barratt
18	A	SUNDERLAND	18/11	15,033	10	4	27	L	1-3	Campbell 37 / Gabbiadini 2, Owers 27, Ord 50	Ref: S Lodge
19	H	PORT VALE	25/11	7,034	10	14	27	L	1-2	Tynan 5 / Cross 15, 24	Ref: P Jones
20	A	OXFORD	2/12	4,403	11	15	27	L	2-3	Thomas 37, Tynan 78p / Evans 14, Simpson 61, Phillips J 85	Ref: I Hemley
21	H	PORTSMOUTH	10/12	9,988	12	21	27	L	0-2	Chamberlain 41, Whittingham 52	Ref: D Hedges
22	H	WEST BROM	26/12	9,782	13	19	28	D	2-2	Thomas 74, Summerfield 85 / Goodman 11, 29	Ref: R Hamer
23	H	HULL	29/12	8,588	14	23	28	L	1-2	Campbell 67 / Swan 40, Terry 87	Ref: K Burge

Line-ups (Argyle above, opponents below)

17/10 (Leicester City) — Leicester: Hodge, Mauchlen, Johnson*, Ramsey, James^, Reid, Clarke, Kitson, McAllister, Paris; subs Oakes/Morgan.
Hodge breaks the Argyle appearance record and scores in his 492nd game with a tame shot that sneaks under Martin Hodge. Thomas finishes from close range and his shot deflects off Allan Evans. City respond to David Pleat's half-time talk and Paul Reid fires home from 25 yards.

13 IPSWICH — Argyle: Wilmot, Brimacombe, Marker, Burrows, Morrison^, Hodges, Thomas, Tynan*, Campbell, Stuart, Thomas; sub McCarthy/Whiston. Ipswich: Forrest, Stockwell, Thompson, Zondervan, Yallop, Linighan, Lowe, Dazzell, D'Array, Kiwomya, Milton.
Despite injuries to key players, Ipswich stroll to victory over a lethargic Argyle. Chris Kiwomya puts Town ahead from close range. Simon McCarthy gets another after good work by Lowe. Milton returns from injury to net a second.

14 BLACKBURN — Argyle: Wilmot, Brimacombe, Marker, Burrows, Morrison^, Hodges, Thomas, McCarthy*, Campbell, Stuart, Thomas; sub Campbell/Byrne. Blackburn: Collier, Atkins, Sulley, Reid, Hendry, Gayle, Irvine, Stapleton, Garner*, Sellars, Finnigan.
McCarthy makes an impression on his return to the starting line-up with both goals. Howard Gayle. The strong wind plays a part as Sellars' corner curls over Wilmot. Scott Sellars takes advantage of Brown's mistake to set up close.

15 LEEDS — Argyle: Wilmot, Brimacombe, Marker, Burrows, Hodges, Byrne, McCarthy*, Thomas, Campbell, Stuart, Thomas; sub Speed. Leeds: Day, Sterland, Whitlow, Jones*, Fairclough, Haddock, Strachan, Batty, Davison, Williams, Speed.
Leeds early pressure pays off when Wilmot's despairing dive fells Davison and Gordon Strachan scores with the spot-kick. Thomas finishes off a good move down the right with a header. The midfielder turns from hero to villain when his long back-pass is intercepted by Davison.

16 BRADFORD C — Argyle: Wilmot, Brimacombe, Marker, Burrows, Hodges, Byrne, McCarthy*, Thomas, Campbell, Stuart, Thomas; sub Campbell. Bradford: Evans M, Timmin, Mitchell, Aizlewood, Sinnott, Jackson, Campbell, Evans D, Adcock, Quinn, Jewell.
In driving rain, City surprise everyone with some fast-flowing football. The new electronic scoreboard scores from a narrow angle. The new electronic scoreboard flashes into life to proclaim Tynan's headed equaliser from Byrne's corner.

17 WATFORD — Argyle: Wilmot, Coton, Marker, Burrows, Hodges, Byrne, Campbell, Tynan, Thompson, Porter, Hodges; sub Stuart. Watford: Coton, Gibbs, Drysdale, Falconer, Holdsworth, Roeder, Redfearn, Wilkinson, Thompson, Porter, Hodges.
The game threatens to boil over at times. Brown is booked for throwing the ball at Glyn Hodges in retaliation. Campbell and Tony Coton are involved in a flare-up after the final whistle. A vintage Tynan goal and a 25-yard strike from Thomas prove enough. Neil Redfearn responds.

18 SUNDERLAND — Argyle: Wilmot, Carter, Marker, Burrows, Hodges, Byrne, Campbell, Gates, Gabbiadini, Pascoe, Thomas; sub Brady. Sunderland: Carter, Agboola, Hardyman*, Bennett, Ord, Owers, Atkinson, Armstrong, Gates, Gabbiadini, Pascoe.
Brown's pre-match instruction to be wary of Gabbiadini's speed is soon forgotten as the striker races onto a long ball within two minutes. Only a desperate foul from behind by Burrows prevents a repeat (11). Wilmot is booked for booting the ball upfield before the free-kick is taken.

19 PORT VALE — Argyle: Wilmot, Grew, Marker, Burrows, Hodges, Morrison, Campbell, Tynan, Cross, Beckford, Thomas; sub Jeffers. Port Vale: Grew, Mills, Hughes, Walker, Aspin, Glover, Porter, Earle, Cross, Beckford, Jeffers.
Despite an early header from Tynan, Argyle sorely miss the injured Brimacombe and Byrne. Robbie Earle's powerful run creates the equaliser. Nicky Cross scores his second as the defence are caught flat-footed by Simon Mills' through ball. The game fizzles out after this early flurry.

20 OXFORD — Argyle: Wilmot, Kee, Marker, Burrows, Hodges, Morrison, Campbell, Tynan, Stein, Beauchamp^, Thomas; subs Durnin/Simpson. Oxford: Kee, Phillips J, Lewis, Foster, Evans, Mustoe*, McClaren, Penney, Stein, Beauchamp^, Phillips J 85.
Irish international Jim Beglin is brought in on loan to cover for the injured Brimacombe. Sloppy defending proves costly as Argyle lose a game they dominate. A point looks safe when Tynan scores from the spot after Paul Kee brings down Byrne. Jimmy Phillips pops up for the winner.

21 PORTSMOUTH — Argyle: Wilmot, Knight, Marker, Burrows, Hodges, Campbell*, Tynan, Whittingham, Gilligan, Black, Thomas; sub Pickard/Damerell. Portsmouth: Knight, Chamberlain, Beresford*, Maguire, Ball, Wigley, Kuhl, Whittingham, Gilligan, Black.
Brown slams the performance as pathetic. Mark Chamberlain produces a goal worthy of a greater occasion as he rides the tackle before angling a low shot past Wilmot. Guy Whittingham increases Pompey's lead. Local boy Mark Damerell is given his first taste of league soccer.

22 WEST BROM — Argyle: Wilmot, Naylor, Marker, Burrows, Hodges, Campbell, Tynan*, Goodman, West, McNally, Thomas; sub Robson / Anderson^ / Cartwright/Bartlett. West Brom: Naylor, Dobbins, Harbey, Robson*, North, Whyte, Ford, Goodman, West, McNally, Summerfield 85.
Don Goodman puts Brian Talbot's side in the driving seat with two first-half goals. Tynan is upset at being replaced. Thomas continues his scoring form with a header. Summerfield returns after eleven months on the sidelines to score after good work by the on-loan Mark Robson.

23 HULL — Argyle: Wilmot, Hesford, Marker, Burrows, Hodges, Campbell, Tynan, Swan, Terry 87, Thomas; sub Robson / Roberts* / Doyle / Jenkinson. Hull: Hesford, Brown, Jacobs, Jobson, Terry, Shaw, Askew, Payton, Swan, Roberts*.
The quest for fresh blood becomes more urgent after Brown witnesses another inept display. Peter Swan puts the Tigers ahead after Wilmot parries Nicky Brown's shot. Campbell restores hope. Steve Terry scores from Askew's free-kick after Marker is harshly penalised for a foul.

Match summary (positions in *italics* shown as Argyle / opponent):

No	V	Date	Opponents	Att	Pos (Argyle / opp)	Pt	Res	F-A	H-T	Scorers, Times	Ref
24	A	1/1	BOURNEMOUTH	6,939	17 / 15	29	D	2-2	0-1	Tynan 77p, Thomas 83 / Holmes 20, Williams 66	P Durkin
25	H	13/1	WEST HAM	11,671	16 / 10	30	D	1-1	1-0	Tynan 2 / Quinn 56	M Reed
26	A	20/1	BARNSLEY	7,224	16 / 23	31	D	1-1	0-0	Thomas 73 / Smith 80	J Ashworth
27	H	3/2	WOLVERHAMPTON	10,873	18 / 6	31	L	0-1	0-1	Mutch 21	R Gifford
28	A	10/2	SHEFFIELD UTD	13,530	19 / 2	31	L	0-1	0-1	Deane 43	J Martin
29	A	24/2	PORT VALE	7,254	20 / 9	31	L	0-3	0-0	Hughes 51, Beckford 74, Mills 83	K Hackett
30	H	3/3	SUNDERLAND	7,299	19 / 7	34	W	3-0	2-0	Tynan 31, 73, McCarthy 39	A Gunn
31	A	7/3	BRIGHTON	7,418	20 /	34	L	1-2	0-1	Stuart 81 / Morrison 50og, Gotsmanov 54	M Bailey
32	H	10/3	SWINDON	8,364	21 / 2	34	L	0-3	0-2	White 31, 57, Shearer 32	J Deakin
33	A	17/3	STOKE	9,452	20 / 24	35	D	0-0	0-0	—	V Callow
34	H	20/3	MIDDLESBROUGH	7,185	21 / 20	35	L	1-2	0-1	Byrne 72 / Baird 37, Brennan 51	H King

Line-ups (each cell = Argyle player / *opponent player*):

No	1	2	3	4	5	6	7	8	9	10	11	subs used
24	Wilmot / Peyton	Beglin / Bond	Brown / Morrell	Marker / Teale	Williams / Williams	Hodges / Peacock	Robson / Lawrence	Campbell* / Shearer	Tynan / Holmes	Thomas / Brooks*	Summerfield / Blissett	Garner / Newson
25	Wilmot / Suckling	Brown / Potts	Broddle / Dicks	Marker / Gale	Williams / Martin	Hodges / Devonshire*	Summerfield / Allen	McCarthy* / Bishop	Tynan / Keen^	Thomas / Morley	Robson / Quinn	Campbell / Brady/Paris
26	Wilmot / Baker	Brown / Dobbin	Broddle* / Taggart	Marker / Futcher	Burrows / Shotton	Hodges / Smith	Summerfield / Lowndes	McCarthy / Agnew*	Tynan / Glover	Thomas / Gray	Robson / Archdeacon^	Whiston / Cross/Robinson
27	Wilmot / Kendall	Brown / Bennett	Broddle / Venus	Marker / Westley	Burrows / Downing*	Hodges / Streete	Summerfield / Jones	McCarthy* / Cook	Tynan* / Bull	Thomas / Mutch	Robson / Dennison	Whiston/Stuart / Thompson
28	Wilmot / Tracey	Brown / Hill	Broddle / Barnes	Marker / Webster	Burrows / Stancliffe	Hodges / Morris	Summerfield / Bradshaw	Campbell* / Gannon^	Tynan / Agana^	Thomas / Deane	Robson / Bryson	Stuart / Booker/Wood
29	Grew / Mills	Brown / Hughes	Cooper* / Walker	Marker / Aspin	Burrows / Glover	Hodges / Porter	Summerfield / Earle	Stuart / Cross	Tynan / Beckford	Broddle / Jeffers	—	Campbell
30	Wilmot / Norman	Brown / Kay	Broddle / Hardyman^	Marker / Bennett	Burrows / MacPhail	Hodges^ / Atkinson	Morrison / Bracewell	McCarthy* / Armstrong	McCarthy^ / Hauser^	Gregory / Gabbiadini	Stuart / Owers	Sum'field/Brimac'mbe / Agboola/Hawke
31	Wilmot / Digweed	Brown / Chivers	Broddle / Chapman	Marker / Curbishley	Burrows / Gatting	Hodges / Dublin	Morrison / Gotsmanov	McCarthy! / Barham	Tynan / Bremner	Gregory* / Crumplin	Stuart / Wilkins	Brimacombe
32	Wilmot / Digby	Brown / Kerslake	Broddle / Bodin	Summerf'ld* / McLoughlin	Burrows / Calderwood	Hodges / Gittens	Morrison / Jones	McCarthy / White	McCarthy^ / Shearer	Gregory / MacLaren	Gregory^ / Simpson	Whiston/Byrne
33	Wilmot / Fox	Brown / Butler	Cooper / Carr	Blackwell / Beeston	Burrows / Blake	Hodges / Sandford	Morrison / Smith	McCarthy* / Ellis*	McCarthy / Kevan	Byrne / Biggins	Fiore / Brooke	Morgan
34	Wilmot / Pears	Brown / Parkinson	Salman / Phillips	Marker / Kernaghan	Burrows / Coleman	Hodges / McGee	Morrison^ / Slaven^	McCarthy^ / Proctor	McCarthy^ / Baird	Blackwell / Brennan	Fiore / Davenport	Campbell/Byrne / Ripley

Match reports:

24 — Bournemouth: Against the run of play, Matty Holmes chips over Wilmot from 25 yards. John Williams marks his recall by slotting home a penalty after Shaun Teale fouls Thomas, who goes on to score his 13th of the season after good play by the impressive Robson.

25 — West Ham: A dramatic start as the referee fails to play advantage as Marker bursts through on goal. Justice is done when Tynan touches in the resultant free-kick. Tynan's goal is disallowed (68) for pushing, although keeper Suckling later admits he lost the ball. Jimmy Quinn heads the equaliser.

26 — Barnsley: Barnsley, with three players making their home debuts, employ a seven-man defence in a bid to improve the worst goals-against record in the division. Thomas breaks down the barrier when he feeds off Tynan's pass. Mark Smith scores against his former side with a far-post header.

27 — Wolverhampton: A poor performance and another home defeat signals the end for Brown, who is dismissed two days later. Only Wilmot emerges with any credit. Argyle are grateful that Steve Bull and Andy Mutch uncharacteristically miss a number of chances, although the two combine for the winner.

28 — Sheffield Utd: Despite the victory, courtesy of Brian Deane's header, Blades boss Dave Bassett lambasts his players. John Gregory takes charge of Argyle with the promise of a permanent job if results improve. He sees a much-improved performance from recent weeks with Stuart going close.

29 — Port Vale: Vale Park continues to be an unhappy hunting ground for Argyle. Cooper makes his comeback after 15 months. A downpour just prior to kick-off makes the already sodden surface virtually unplayable. Mistakes lead to the first two goals. Simon Mills scores with a cross-cum-shot.

30 — Sunderland: David Kemp takes charge for the first time. Gregory plays his first league game for almost two years. Hardyman is stretchered off to hospital after just eight minutes with concussion. Tynan finds his scoring boots again. McCarthy sweeps in a shot after a mistake by Reuben Agboola.

31 — Brighton: Argyle have not won at Brighton since 1952. Morrison slices Ian Chapman's cross into his own net. Wilmot fails to hold Barham's shot to present Gotsmanov with an easy chance. McCarthy, already booked for dissent, is sent off (87) when his head collides with Digweed's elbow!

32 — Swindon: The gap between top and bottom is all too obvious as Ossie Ardiles' men gain another three points in their quest for promotion. The concept of passing to a team-mate seems alien to most Pilgrims. Two goals in 90 seconds kills the game. White's second finishes a fine run by Simpson.

33 — Stoke: Gregory's short spell at Home Park ends as he departs for Bolton. The performances of the two new boys help to produce a much improved performance. Only some wayward finishing by McCarthy prevents an easy Argyle victory. Cooper successfully comes through 90 minutes.

34 — Middlesbrough: A home defeat by fellow strugglers Boro plunges Argyle further into relegation trouble. Ian Baird scores yet another goal against the Pilgrims when he nips in to intercept Morrison's back-pass. Mark Brennan lets fly from the left wing. Byrne scores with a header from Brown's cross.

35 — A LEICESTER 24/3

Pos 22 · 9,395 · 14 · 36 · D 1-1 (0-1)

Marker 58 / McAllister 28p · Ref: A Bennett

Argyle: Wilmot, Brown, Salman, Marker!, Burrows, Morrison, Byrne*, Hodges, Tynan*, Campbell, Fiore*, Blackwell
Leicester: Hodge, Mauchlen, Paris, Mills, Walsh, James, Ramsey*, Oldfield^, Kelly, McAllister, Reid, Wright/North

Early chances are squandered. Salman fouls Paul Reid and Gary McAllister sends Wilmot the wrong way from the spot. The ex-Argyle keeper presents his former team with the equaliser when he fumbles Marker's shot. Marker is dismissed (88) for a second yellow after a foul on Kelly.

36 — H IPSWICH 31/3

Pos 21 · 6,793 · 9 · 39 · W 1-0 (0-0)

Morrison 68 · Ref: B Stevens

Argyle: Wilmot, Brown, Salman, Marker, Burrows, Morrison, Byrne, McCarthy, Tynan*, Hodges, Fiore, Pickard
Ipswich: Forrest, Stockwell, Thompson, Baltacha*, Gayle, Linighan, Lowe, Redford*, Wark, Dozzell, Milton, Palmer/Meade

Argyle produce a shambolic first-half performance with Ipswich only marginally better. The second period produces an improved showing from both sides with Tynan twice going close with headers and Lowe missing a glorious chance. Morrison's powerful header proves enough.

37 — A NEWCASTLE 3/4

Pos 21 · 16,558 · 39 · L 1-3 (1-1)

Hodges 3 / Quinn 41, McGhee 53p, 54 · Ref: K Breen

Argyle: Wilmot, Brown, Salman^, Marker, Burrows, Morrison, Byrne, McCarthy, Dillon, Quinn, Fiore, Pickard/Blackwell
Newcastle: Burridge, Scott, Sweeney, Aitken, Anderson^, Ranson, Brock*, Dillon, Quinn, McGhee, Askew, Gallacher/Kristensen

Hodges gives Argyle a dream start as he sprints away from the defence. Mick Quinn scores the 200th goal of his career. Within a minute McGhee strikes again as he heads in Kevin Brock's cross.

38 — A BLACKBURN 7/4

Pos 21 · 7,492 · 6 · 39 · L 0-2 (0-0)

Sellars 56, 78 · Ref: A Seville

Argyle: Broddle, Blackwell, Marker, Burrows, Morrison, Byrne, McCarthy, Miller, Garner, Fiore*, Campbell
Blackburn: Gennoe, Atkins, Dawson, Reid, Moran, Gayle*, Millar, Stapleton, Garner, Sellars, Irvine

Simon Garner misses an easy first-half chance when he weakly strokes the ball towards an empty net, but Broddle clears off the line. Scott Sellars opens the scoring with defenders appealing for offside. Sellars gets his second after his first shot was cleared off the line by McCarthy.

39 — H LEEDS 10/4

Pos 22 · 11,382 · 1 · 40 · D 1-1 (1-1)

Tynan 30p / Chapman 28 · Ref: R Milford

Argyle: Wilmot, Blackwell, Salman, Marker, Burrows, Morrison*, Byrne, McCarthy, Batty, Chapman, Hendrie^, Speed, Thomas, King, Davison
Leeds: Day, Sterland, Beglin, Jones, Fairclough, Haddock, Strachan, Batty, Chapman, Hendrie^, Speed, Davison

Argyle drop into the relegation zone despite a battling performance against Howard Wilkinson's leaders. Lee Chapman gives United the lead after good work by Beglin. McCarthy is brought down by Haddock. Beglin's advice to Day regarding Tynan's penalty technique is to no avail.

40 — H BOURNEMOUTH 14/4

Pos 21 · 7,520 · 20 · 43 · W 1-0 (0-0)

Tynan 60p · Ref: G Ashby

Argyle: Wilmot, Blackwell, Salman, Marker, Burrows, Hodges, Byrne*, McCarthy, Aylott, Holmes, Blissett, Thomas, Pickard, Cadette
Bournemouth: Peyton, Mundee*, Coleman, Shearer, Miller, Peacock, O'Driscoll, Brooks, Aylott, Holmes, Blissett, Cadette

Harry Redknapp is without his entire first-choice defence through injury. Gavin Peacock's shot smashes against a post. Argyle recover and immediately net a penalty when Paul Miller trips Hodges. Tynan keeps his cool to send Gerry Peyton the wrong way and secure a vital win.

41 — A WEST BROM 16/4

Pos 19 · 9,728 · 16 · 46 · W 3-0 (1-0)

McCarthy 23, 59, 72 · Ref: D Hedges

Argyle: Wilmot, Naylor, Burgess*, Shakespeare, North, Whyte, Ford, Goodman, Bannister^, King, McNally, Bradley, Fiore, Hackett/Foster
West Brom: Naylor, Burgess*, Harbey, Shakespeare, North, Whyte, Ford, Goodman, Bannister^, King, Bradley, Hackett/Foster

McCarthy, so often the culprit of missed chances this season, scores the first hat-trick of his career to give the Pilgrims an unlikely victory at the Hawthorns. He gives Stacey North a torrid time and it is the defender's slip that allows the Welshman to run clear to score his third goal.

42 — H OLDHAM 18/4

Pos 17 · 8,146 · 9 · 49 · W 2-0 (2-0)

McCarthy 18, 45 · Ref: R Wiseman

Argyle: Wilmot, Brown, Fiore, Marker, Burrows, Hodges, Byrne, McCarthy, Bunn, Holden, Milligan, Thomas, King, Adams
Oldham: Hallworth, Irwin, Barlow, Henry, Barrett, Warhurst*, Redfearn, Ritchie, Bunn, Holden, Milligan, Adams

Joe Royle's side seem to have their minds on their forthcoming Littlewoods Cup final. McCarthy completes a memorable week with another two goals. He races clear of Paul Warhurst to slot in the first via Jon Hallworth's legs and heads in King's corner on the stroke of half-time.

43 — H NEWCASTLE 21/4

Pos 18 · 11,702 · 3 · 50 · D 1-1 (1-1)

Tynan 12 / McGhee 25 · Ref: A Ward

Argyle: Wilmot, Brown, Fiore, Marker, Burrows, Hodges, Byrne, McCarthy, Quinn, McGhee, Kristensen, Thomas*, King, Salman
Newcastle: Burridge, Scott, Stimson, Aitken, Anderson, Bradshaw, Brock*, Dillon, Quinn, McGhee, Kristensen, Salman

The Magpies are looking for their seventh straight win. Argyle fail to take advantage of Tynan's header and allow United back in the game. McGhee makes it 25 for the season. Mr Ward's notebook fills rapidly. Three visitors are booked for dissent within three minutes of each other.

44 — A HULL 24/4

Pos 17 · 5,256 · 16 · 51 · D 3-3 (3-3)

Fiore 46, Burrows 49, Thomas 77 / Swan 10, Shotton 83, Hunter 85 · Ref: R Hart

Argyle: Wilmot, Brown*, Salman, Marker, Burrows, Hodges, Byrne, McCarthy, Swan, Payton, Swan, King*, Thomas, Hunter/Atkinson
Hull: Hesford, Brown^, Jacobs, Jobson, Shotton, Doyle, Roberts, Payton, Swan, Palin*, Hunter/Atkinson

Kemp is furious with his players after they let a two-goal lead slip. Payton heads against the bar and Peter Swan is the first to react. Fiore scores his first league goal. Burrows and Thomas seem to have secured the points but Hull rally and score twice from dead-ball situations.

45 — H WATFORD 28/4

Pos 18 · 8,564 · 15 · 52 · D 0-0 (0-0)

Ref: K Cooper

Argyle: Wilmot, Brown, Salman, Marker, Burrows, Hodges, Byrne, McCarthy, Penrice, Falconer, Thomas^, King/Morrison
Watford: Coton, Gibbs, Williams, Richardson, Holdsworth, Roeder, Ashby, Wilkinson, Penrice, Falconer, Drysdale

Home fans bid farewell to Tynan who plays his last game. A point ensures Argyle's safety but there is little else to remember the afternoon by. The main entertainment is provided by the officials. The referee is struck in the midriff by a clearance and a linesman trips over his own feet.

46 — A BRADFORD C 5/5

Pos 16 · 4,903 · 23 · 55 · W 1-0 (1-0)

McCarthy 22 · Ref: D Axcell

Argyle: Wilmot, Brown, Salman, Marker, Burrows, Hodges, Byrne, McCarthy, Pickard, Morrison, Aizlewood, Jewell, Woods*, Fiore, King/Tinnion, Costello
Bradford C: Tomlinson, Mitchell, Graham, Duxbury, Oliver, Simnott, Adcock, Woods*, Aizlewood, Jewell, Tinnion, Costello

Argyle's spirited finish to the season continues against already relegated City. After McCarthy's diving header from Byrne's free-kick, neither side show too much enthusiasm on a sweltering afternoon. Brown appears to handle inside the area but Mr Axcell awards a free-kick instead.

Home 8,749 · Away 10,383 · Average 8,749

BARCLAYS DIVISION 2 (CUP-TIES) — Manager: Brown > Gregory > Kemp — SEASON 1989-90

Littlewoods Cup

1:1 A CARDIFF — 22/8 — W 3-0 (0-0) — Att 2,620
Scorers: Tynan 57, 70p, McCarthy 62. Ref: P Vanes

1	2	3	4	5	6	7	8	9	10	11	subs used
Wilmot	Brown	Marker	Burrows	Brimacombe	Smith	Byrne	McCarthy	Tynan	Thomas	Stuart	
Wood	*Rodgerson*	*Gibbins*	*Abraham*	*Perry*	*Lynex*	*Curtis*	*Morgan*	*Kelly*	*Gilligan*	*Pike**	*Fry*

Bluebirds manager Frank Burrows pays tribute to Tynan, saying that it was an education for his defenders to play against him. The prolific striker heads the Pilgrims in front. Brimacombe's shot flies off McCarthy's knee. Tynan scores from the spot after Gibbins fouled McCarthy.

1:2 H CARDIFF — 29/8 — 11 — L 0-2 (0-1) — Att 5,728 — 4:24
Scorers: Pike 29, Morgan 76. Ref: P Durkin. (Argyle won 3-2 on aggregate)

1	2	3	4	5	6	7	8	9	10	11	subs used
Wilmot	Brown	Brimacombe	Marker	Burrows	Smith	Byrne*	McCarthy	Tynan	Thomas	Stuart	Hodges
Wood	*Rodgerson*	*Daniel*	*Lynex*	*Abraham*	*Perry*	*Curtis**	*Morgan*	*Gilligan*	*Kelly*	*Pike^*	*Gummer/Fry*

Argyle get a scare against the league's bottom club who are now without a manager. Veteran George Wood pulls off some fine saves as the Greens create a hatful of chances. Chris Pike heads in Alan Curtis's free-kick. Curtis also has a hand in the second as he sets up Jon Morgan.

2:1 A ARSENAL — 19/9 — 5 — L 0-2 (0-1) — Att 26,865 — 1:6
Scorers: Smith 7, Brimacombe 87(og). Ref: P Alcock.

1	2	3	4	5	6	7	8	9	10	11	subs used
Wilmot	Brown	Brimacombe	Marker	Burrows	Smith	Hodges	McCarthy	Tynan	Thomas	Stuart	
Lukic	*Dixon*	*Winterburn*	*Thomas*	*O'Leary*	*Adams*	*Rocastle*	*Richardson*	*Smith*	*Merson**	*Marwood*	*Groves*

Argyle leave Highbury with a sense of injustice. Thomas tests Lukic after only 11 seconds. The travelling Argyle fans fear the worse when Alan Smith heads in. McCarthy has a header disallowed for offside (64). David Rocastle's harmless-looking cross is turned in by Brimacombe.

2:2 H ARSENAL — 3/10 — 11 — L 1-6 (1-1) — Att 17,360 — 1:3
Scorers: Tynan 32 (Groves 68, Smith 70) Byrne 13(og), Thomas 50, 75, 86, Ref: M Bodenham. (Argyle lost 1-8 on aggregate)

1	2	3	4	5	6	7	8	9	10	11	subs used
Wilmot	Brown	Brimacombe	Marker	Burrows	Morrison	Hodges*	Byrne	Tynan^	Campbell	Stuart	Thomas/Pickard
Lukic	*Dixon**	*Winterburn*	*Thomas*	*Adams*	*O'Leary*	*Rocastle*	*Richardson*	*Smith*	*Groves^*	*Hayes*	*Caesar/Merson*

Rocastle's shot takes a huge deflection off Byrne to put the Gunners ahead. Tynan restores hope after Campbell hit the bar. Arsenal are ruthless in the second half. Michael Thomas's first goal looks offside. With a comfortable aggregate lead, a lesson in one-touch soccer follows.

FA Cup

3 H OXFORD — 6/1 — 17 — L 0-1 (0-0) — Att 7,384 — 12
Scorers: Simpson 77. Ref: R Gifford.

1	2	3	4	5	6	7	8	9	10	11	subs used
Wilmot	Brown	Whiston	Marker	Burrows	Hodges	Byrne	Morrison	Tynan	Thomas	Summerfield	
Kee	*Smart*	*Phillips*	*Lewis*	*Foster*	*Evans*	*Heath*	*McClaren*	*Durnin*	*Stein*	*Simpson*	

Argyle carry their poor league form into the cup. A seventh home match without a win leaves supporters chanting for the Board's resignation. Brown's cause is not helped by having only 14 fit players to choose from. Paul Simpson sends U's through after Wilmot fails to gather a cross.

	P	W	D	L	F	A	W	D	L	F	A	Pts
		Home					**Away**					
1 Leeds	46	16	6	1	46	18	8	7	8	33	34	85
2 Sheffield Utd	46	14	5	4	43	27	10	8	5	35	31	85
3 Newcastle	46	17	4	2	51	26	5	10	8	29	29	80
4 Swindon	46	12	6	5	49	29	8	8	7	30	30	74
5 Blackburn	46	10	9	4	43	30	9	8	6	31	29	74
6 Sunderland*	46	10	8	5	41	32	8	6	9	29	32	74
7 West Ham	46	14	5	4	50	22	6	7	10	30	35	72
8 Oldham	46	15	7	1	50	23	4	7	12	20	34	71
9 Ipswich	46	13	7	3	38	22	6	5	12	29	44	69
10 Wolves	46	12	5	6	37	20	6	8	9	30	40	67
11 Port Vale	46	11	9	3	37	20	4	7	12	25	37	61
12 Portsmouth	46	9	8	6	40	34	6	8	9	22	31	61
13 Leicester	46	10	8	5	34	29	5	6	12	33	50	59
14 Hull	46	7	8	8	27	31	7	8	8	31	34	58
15 Watford	46	11	6	6	41	28	3	9	11	17	32	57
16 PLYMOUTH	46	9	8	6	30	23	5	5	13	28	40	55
17 Oxford	46	8	7	8	35	31	7	2	14	22	35	54
18 Brighton	46	10	6	7	28	27	5	3	15	28	45	54
19 Barnsley	46	7	9	7	22	23	6	6	11	27	48	54
20 West Brom	46	6	8	9	35	37	7	7	10	32	34	51
21 Middlesbro	46	10	3	10	33	29	3	8	12	19	34	50
22 Bournemouth	46	8	6	9	30	31	4	6	13	27	45	48
23 Bradford C	46	9	6	8	26	24	0	8	15	18	44	41
24 Stoke	46	4	11	8	20	24	2	8	13	15	39	37
	1104	252	165	135	886	640	135	165	252	640	886	1491

* promoted
after play-offs

Odds & ends

Double wins: (0).

Double defeats: (3) Port Vale, Swindon, Wolves.

Won from behind: (0).

Lost from in front: (2) Newcastle, Port Vale.

High spots: Eight-match unbeaten run at end of season to pull away from relegation zone.

Quality midfield play from new signing Andy Thomas.

Consistency of defence.

Low spots: Early season departure of unsettled record signing, Mark Smith.

Six-goal thrashing at home to Arsenal in Littlewoods Cup.

Failure of any new or loan signings (except Thomas) to make any impact.

End of season departure of Tommy Tynan to Torquay.

Player of the Year: Nicky Marker.
Ever presents: (2) Adrian Burrows, Rhys Wilmot.
Hat-tricks: (1) Sean McCarthy.
Leading scorer: Tommy Tynan (18).

Appearances / Goals

Player	Lge	Sub	LC	Sub	FAC	Sub	Lge	LC	FAC	Tot
	Appearances						**Goals**			
Barlow, Martin	5	1								
Beglin, Jim	5									
Blackwell, Dean	5	2								
Brimacombe, John	18	2	4							
Broddle, Julian	9									
Brown, Kenny	44		4		4					
Burrows, Adrian	46		4		1		1			1
Byrne, David	28	4	3		1		1			1
Campbell, Greg	15	7	1				3			3
Cooper, Leigh	2									
Damerell, Mark		1								
Fiore, Mark	11	1	1				1			1
Garner, Darren		1								
Gregory, John	3									
Hodges, Kevin	43	1	2	1		1	4			4
King, Adam	5	3								
Marker, Nicky	43		4		1		1			1
McCarthy, Sean	30	2	3				11	1		12
Morrison, Andy	18	1	1		1		1			1
Pickard, Owen	1	4				1				
Robson, Mark	7									
Salman, Danis	10	1								
Smith, Mark	6		3							
Stuart, Mark	23	2	4				6			6
Summerfield, Kevin	8	2			1		1			1
Thomas, Andy	33	3	3		1		12			12
Tynan, Tommy	44		4		1		15	3		18
Whiston, Peter	3	5								
Wilmot, Rhys	46		4		1					
(own-goals)							1			1
29 players used	506	43	44	3	11		58	4		62

BARCLAYS DIVISION 2 — Manager: David Kemp — SEASON 1990-91

No	V	Date	Opponent	Att	Pos	Pt	F-A	H-T	Scorers, Times, and Referees
1	A	25/8	NEWCASTLE	23,984		0	L 0-2	0-1	Kristensen 3, Quinn 66. Ref: D Allison
2	H	28/8	WATFORD	7,734		1	D 1-1	1-0	Thomas 40; McLaughlin 84. Ref: J Deakin
3	H	1/9	MIDDLESBROUGH	6,266	19/17	2	D 1-1	0-1	Thomas 60; Slaven 45. Ref: P Durkin
4	A	8/9	BRISTOL CITY	14,283	17/5	3	D 1-1	0-1	Thomas 68; Morgan 17. Ref: P Jones
5	H	15/9	LEICESTER	6,336	14/20	6	W 2-0	1-0	Hodges 35, Pickard 75. Ref: H King
6	H	18/9	OXFORD	5,859	14/19	7	D 2-2	0-0	Burrows 53, Thomas 77; Foyle 62, Stein 86. Ref: J Martin
7	A	22/9	WOLVERHAMPTON	15,137	16/13	7	L 1-3	1-3	Turner 26; Bull 36, 42, Mutch 44. Ref: A Bennett
8	A	29/9	PORTSMOUTH	8,636	17/16	7	L 1-3	1-0	Thomas 19; Clarke 49, 89, Kuhl 54. Ref: G Pooley
9	H	2/10	WEST BROM	5,617	15/17	10	W 2-0	1-0	Thomas 38, Fiore 47. Ref: K Cooper
10	H	6/10	IPSWICH	5,935	15/13	11	D 0-0	0-0	Ref: R Lewis
11	A	13/10	SHEFFIELD WED	23,489	16/1	11	L 0-3	0-2	Wilson 4, Sheridan 43, 63. Ref: A Wilkie

Line-ups (Argyle player / opponent, italic = opponent)

No	1	2	3	4	5	6	7	8	9	10	11	subs used
1	Wilmot / Burridge	Brown / Scott	Morgan / Sweeney	Marker / Aitken	Burrows / Kristensen	Hodges / Ranson	Byrne / Dillon	Morrison / Anderson	Turner / Quinn	Thomas / Howey	Fiore* / O'Brien	Pickard
2	Wilmot / James	Brown / Williams*	Morgan / Dublin	Marker / Roeder	Burrows / Holdsworth	Hodges / McLaughlin	Byrne* / Thomas	Morrison / Wilkinson	Turner / Kennedy	Thomas / Falconer	Pickard / Porter	King / Bazeley
3	Wilmot / Pears	Brown / Cooper	Morgan / Phillips	Marker / Mowbray	Burrows / Kernaghan	Hodges / Wark	Byrne / Slaven	Morrison* / Mustoe	Turner / Ripley	Thomas / Russell	Pickard / Hendrie	Robinson
4	Wilmot / Sinclair	Brown / Llewellyn	Morgan / Aizlewood	Marker / May	Burrows / Shelton	Hodges / Rennie	Byrne / Bent	Fiore / Newman	Turner / Taylor*	Thomas / Morgan	Pickard / Smith	Pickard / Allison
5	Wilmot / Hodge	Brown / Mills	Morgan^ / Spearing	Marker / Hill	Burrows / Walsh	Hodges / James	Byrne / Wright	Fiore / Oldfield	Turner / Reid*	Thomas / Davies*	Pickard* / Kelly	King, Morrison / North, Ramsey
6	Wilmot / Kee	Brown / Robinson	Morgan* / Ford	Marker / Phillips	Burrows / Foster*	Hodges / Melville	Byrne / Penney	Fiore / Lewis	Turner / Foyle	Thomas / Stein	Adcock / Simpson	King / Smart
7	Wilmot / Stowell	Brown / Ashley	Summerfield / Steele	Marker / Bellamy	Burrows / Hindmarch	Hodges / Downing	Byrne / Thompson	Fiore / Cook	Turner / Bull	Thomas / Mutch	Adcock* / Dennison*	Robinson / Paskin
8	Wilmot / Gosney	Brown / Neill	Morgan / Beresford	Marker / Kuhl	Burrows / Butters*	Hodges / Black	Byrne / Wigley	Fiore* / Stevens	Turner / Clarke	Thomas / Aspinall	Salman / Murray^	Robinson / Powell, Maguire
9	Wilmot / Naylor	Brown / Hodson	Morgan / Harbey	Marker / Robson	Burrows / Bradley	Hodges / Strodder	Byrne / Ford	Fiore / West	Turner / Bannister	Thomas / McInally	Salman / Shakesp're*	Hackett
10	Wilmot / Forrest	Brown / Yallop	Morgan / Zondervan	Marker / Stockwell	Burrows / Gayle	Hodges / Linghan	Byrne* / Gregory	Fiore / Redford	Turner / Hill	Thomas / Kiwomya	Salman / Milton	King
11	Wilmot / Pressman	Brown / Nilsson	Morgan / King	Marker / Palmer	Burrows / Shirtliff	Hodges / Pearson	Byrne / Wilson	Fiore / Sheridan	Turner / Francis*	Thomas* / Williams	Salman^ / Worthingt'n^	Pickard, Morrison / Whitton, McCall

Match notes

1. After a promising pre-season, the Pilgrims quickly come back down to earth against the championship favourites. From their first attack, Bjorn Kristensen fires in from the edge of the box. There is more than a suspicion of offside for Mick Quinn's goal. Turner has a promising debut.

2. Kemp is delighted with his side's performance as they dominate the game. Fortune favours Argyle when Thomas appears to aim a pass to the offside Turner but mis-hits past a stranded David James. A defensive lapse allows the unmarked Joe McLaughlin to head in Gary Porter's cross.

3. After a confident start, slack defending by Morgan allows Bernie Slaven to open his account for the season. Thomas smashes a shot in from 20 yards from Byrne's free-kick. Slaven misses a chance from virtually on the goal-line and later manages to hook the ball over an open goal.

4. A dramatic start sees a penalty awarded when Rob Newman flattens Turner (2). Thomas's spot-kick lacks power and Ronnie Sinclair saves. Nicky Morgan gives City the lead after Marker is slow to clear. Thomas swivels to score the equaliser. Five Argyle players receive cautions.

5. A combination of Wilmot's brilliance and a hapless Leicester attack allow the Greens to gain their first win of the season. Hodges fires a shot between Tony James's legs to leave Martin Hodge unsighted. Pickard gets his first senior goal when he gets a faint touch to Fiore's corner.

6. Individual errors prove expensive. After an uninspiring first half, Burrows heads in via the crossbar. From Simpson's free-kick everyone but King moves out for offside leaving Foyle free to head in. Thomas volleys in. Burrows needlessly concedes a corner from which Stein levels.

7. A well worked set-piece leads to Turner's first goal for Argyle. Defensive failings then come to the fore again as England striker Steve Bull makes his presence felt. His powerful running creates pandemonium as he scores twice and also lays on a third for strike partner Andy Mutch.

8. Another promising start goes to waste. Turner gives Pompey's new £325k signing, Guy Butters, such a torrid time that he is replaced at half-time. Kuhl's shot takes a cruel deflection. Argyle have a strong case for a penalty ignored when Gosney appears to pin Marker to the ground.

9. Turner again proves to be the danger-man as the Throstles' defenders have difficulty in coping with his physical style. He lays on Thomas's seventh of the season. Darren Bradley underhits a pass to Naylor and Fiore nips in. The Baggies reliance on a long-ball game has little effect.

10. Wilmot is the hero as he pulls off a string of fine saves. Turner misses a great opportunity when he shoots straight at Forrest. Play is delayed when substitute King takes to the field wearing a number eight shirt. He then changes to number 14 despite being programmed to wear twelve.

11. Plymouth-born veteran Trevor Francis shows that even at the age of 36 he oozes class. He goes off near the end to a standing ovation. Danny Wilson heads the Owls into an early lead. John Sheridan scores twice and the only surprise is that Wednesday do not win by a greater margin.

No	Venue	Opponent	Date	Result	Score	Att	Ref
			20/10			6,267	Ref: J Key
13	H	NOTTS CO	23/10	D	0-0	6,651	Ref: J Carter
14	H	HULL	27/10	W	4-1	5,039	Ref: A Seville
15	A	CHARLTON	3/11	W	1-0	5,239	Ref: A Smith
16	A	BRIGHTON	10/11	L	2-3	7,305	Ref: R Pawley
17	H	MILLWALL	17/11	W	3-2	6,542	Ref: R Groves
18	H	WEST HAM	24/11	L	0-1	11,490	Ref: R Hamer
19	A	PORT VALE	1/12	L	1-5	6,717	Ref: T Lunt
20	A	WATFORD	8/12	L	0-2	6,361	Ref: V Callow
21	H	NEWCASTLE	16/12	L	0-1	7,845	Ref: T Holbrook
22	A	OLDHAM	21/12	L	3-5	11,296	Ref: D Phillips
23	H	BARNSLEY	26/12	D	1-1	5,668	Ref: C Wilkes

Scorers

- NOTTS CO (0-0)
- HULL (4-1): Morrison 39, Salman 48, 82, Turner 70
- CHARLTON (1-0): Turner 9
- BRIGHTON (2-3): Turner 13, Barlow 89 — Barham 24, Small 64, Codner 78
- MILLWALL (3-2): Robinson 27, 27, Marker 70p — Sheringham 47, Rae 85
- WEST HAM (0-1): McAvennie 62
- PORT VALE (1-5): Ampadu 2 — Jeffers 23, Ford 37, Beckford 67, 86, [Walker 78]
- WATFORD (0-2): Wilkinson 56, 74
- NEWCASTLE (0-1): Peacock 86
- OLDHAM (3-5): Edwards 6, Brown 25, 67 [Barrett 49] — Redfearn 2, 61, Palmer 44, 85
- BARNSLEY (1-1): Morgan 54 — Rammell 84

Match notes

20/10 — Barlow has a lively first full league game. Morgan's challenge on Alan Irvine (54) is more clumsy than malicious but deemed worthy of a penalty. Wilmot dives to save John Millar's spot-kick. Argyle are awarded a penalty for handball but a linesman changes Mr Key's decision.

NOTTS CO — Lack of goals is not the only concern as the club announce they are losing £8,000 per week with no money available for new players and attendances 2,000 below break-even. Craig Short handles Barlow's cross but Thomas misses his second penalty of the season as Cherry blocks.

HULL — Sheep farmer Walter replaces the suspended Wilmot. Salman, with only twelve goals in 15 years as a pro, scores twice from outside the box. Turner goes one better with a wind-assisted sizzler from 30 yards. Thomas goes off with a back injury that will eventually end his career.

CHARLTON — A fine display by Walter gives Kemp a selection headache with Wilmot available next week. Ampadu, on loan from Arsenal, has a promising debut, setting up Turner's goal and having a shot kicked off the line by Mark Reid. Turner faces a ban after picking up his sixth yellow card.

BRIGHTON — A dreadful back-pass by Gary Chivers allows Turner to give Argyle the lead. Mark Barham heads the equaliser. Eire international John Byrne gives the Pilgrims defence a hard time and he sets up the next two goals. Barlow rounds off a good display with a curling shot past Digweed.

MILLWALL — With Turner suspended, Robinson has a dream full debut by scoring twice in 37 seconds. His second comes after Ampadu regains possession from the kick-off and the new striker scores from 30 yards. Ian Dawes is penalised for handball and Marker takes over the penalty-taking role.

WEST HAM — Argyle impress Hammers boss Billy Bonds but West Ham show why they are still unbeaten this season. A million pound striker takes his only chance of the game. There is some amusement when the referee singles out George Parris for a booking when the true offender is Breacker.

PORT VALE — Ampadu scores from Argyle's first attack but it then all goes badly wrong. Marker is carried off with a gashed knee (22). After an earlier booking Hodges is dismissed (30). Vale score at regular intervals thereafter. YTS lad Evans is given a 20-minute debut.

WATFORD — The absence of a number of key players through injury begins to take its toll. McAllister arrives on loan from Wimbledon. The introduction of the creative Gary Penrice for the second half turns the game. Two goals from Paul Wilkinson give Watford their first home win of the season.

NEWCASTLE — The inability to score continues to concern Kemp as Argyle United to gain their first away win for three months. The decision to switch to a Sunday kick-off does little to attract a bigger crowd. Gavin Peacock scores the all-important goal at the far post from a Kevin Brock cross.

OLDHAM — An explosive start with Neil Redfearn scoring after 77 seconds. On-loan Edwards provides a slight touch to Hodges' corner to level. Brown pushes forward at every opportunity and fires home two well-struck efforts. Despite conceding five by the end, Argyle are far from disgraced.

BARNSLEY — Kemp's injury worries mount as Brown goes off with a hamstring injury and Wilmot suffers a broken nose after connecting with Andy Rammell's boot. Carl Tiler hits the bar and then clears off his line from Edwards. Mark Smith provides the opening for Rammell to equalise.

BARCLAYS DIVISION 2 — Manager: David Kemp — SEASON 1990-91

Results

No	Date		Opponent	Att	Pos	Opp Pos	Res	Pt	F-A	H-T	Scorers, Times, and Referees
24	29/12	H	BRISTOL ROV	8,469	20	10	D	24	2-2	2-2	Jones 9(og), Turner 33 / Saunders 9, 43; Ref: A Ward
25	1/1	A	SWINDON	9,736	22	13	D	25	1-1	0-0	Turner 51 / Foley 90; Ref: R Nixon
26	12/1	A	MIDDLESBROUGH	14,198	21	5	D	26	0-0	0-0	Ref: R Shepherd
27	19/1	H	BRISTOL CITY	8,074	17	12	W	29	1-0	0-0	Robinson 74; Ref: R Gifford
28	2/2	H	LEICESTER	8,172	21	19	L	29	1-3	1-2	Marker 42 / Wright 33, Kelly 40, James 57; Ref: K Lupton
29	16/2	A	MILLWALL	8,388	22	6	L	29	1-4	1-1	Garner 36 / Sheringham 1, 51, 61, 67; Ref: K Burge
30	23/2	H	BRIGHTON	5,384	21	6	W	32	2-0	2-0	Morgan 17, Burrows 37; Ref: M Reed
31	2/3	H	PORT VALE	5,145	19	16	W	35	2-0	0-0	Turner 48, 75; Ref: B Stevens
32	5/3	A	WEST HAM	18,933	18	1	D	36	2-2	0-1	Turner 50, 75 / Marker 19(og), Breacker 78; Ref: A Gunn
33	13/3	A	WEST BROM	8,673	18	20	W	39	2-1	1-1	Hodges 41, Turner 80 / Palmer 6; Ref: R Wiseman
34	16/3	H	PORTSMOUTH	6,586	18	19	D	40	1-1	1-0	Brown 41p / Kuhl 81; Ref: R Hamer

Line-ups (Argyle / opponent in italics)

No	Team	1	2	3	4	5	6	7	8	9	10	11	subs used
24	Argyle	Walter	Clement	Morgan	McAllister	Burrows	Salman	Barlow	Hodges	Turner	Edwards*	Morrison*	Adcock*
24	Bristol Rov	*Parkin*	*Bloomer*	*Twentyman*	*Yates*	*Mehew**	*Jones*	*Holloway*	*Reece*	*White*	*Saunders**	*Pounder*	*Nixon*
25	Argyle	Walter	Clement	Morgan	McAllister	Burrows	Salman	Barlow	Hodges	Turner	Adcock	Morrison	
25	Swindon	*Digby*	*Kerslake*	*Bodin*	*Hazard*	*Lorenzo*	*Gittens*	*Jones*	*Shearer*	*White**	*MacLean*	*Foley*	*Summerbee*
26	Argyle	Walter	Morgan	Phillips…	Marker	Brown	Salman	Barlow	Hodges	Turner	Adcock	Morrison	Ripley
26	Middlesbrough	*Pears*	*Cooper^*	*Phillips*	*Mowbray*	*Coleman*	*Putney*	*Slaven*	*Mustoe**	*Baird*	*Kerr*	*Hendry*	*McGee*
27	Argyle	Walter	Brown	Morgan	Marker	Burrows	Salman	Barlow	Hodges	Robinson	Adcock	Morrison	
27	Bristol City	*Leaning*	*Llewellyn*	*Scott*	*May*	*Bryant*	*Aizlewood*	*Rennie**	*Newman*	*Allison*	*Morgan*	*Smith*	*Donowa*
28	Argyle	Walter	Brown	Morgan	Marker	Burrows	Salman	Barlow*	Hodges	Robinson	Adcock^	Morrison	McAllister, Clement
28	Leicester	*Muggleton*	*Mauchlen*	*Gibson*	*North*	*Madden*	*James*	*Wright*	*Reid*	*Oldfield*	*Mills**	*Kelly*	*Peake*
29	Argyle	Walter	Brown	Morgan	Marker	Burrows	Salman	Barlow*	Hodges	Robinson	Robinson	Garner	Meade
29	Millwall	*Branagan*	*Cunningham*	*Dawes*	*Waddock*	*Thompson*	*McLeary*	*Stephenson*	*Goddard*	*Sheringham*	*Rae*	*McGlashan*	
30	Argyle	Wilmot	Brown	Morgan	Marker	Burrows	Salman	Barlow	Hodges*	Turner	Morrison	Fiore	Clement
30	Brighton	*Digweed*	*Crumplin*	*Gatting*	*Wilkins*	*Stemp*	*Chapman*	*Barham**	*Byrne*	*Wade**	*Codner*	*Walker*	*Robinson, McGrath*
31	Argyle	Wilmot	Clement	Morgan	Marker	Burrows	Salman	Barlow	Hodges	Turner	McAllister	Fiore	Van der Laan, Ford
31	Port Vale	*Grew*	*Mills*	*Platnauer*	*Walker*	*Aspin*	*Glover*	*Porter^*	*Earle*	*Millar**	*Beckford*	*Jeffers*	
32	Argyle	Wilmot	Brown	Morgan	Marker	Burrows	Salman	Barlow	Hodges	Turner	Clement	Fiore*	
32	West Ham	*Miklosko*	*Breacker*	*Parris*	*Foster*	*Bishop*	*Hughton**	*Keen*	*McAvennie*	*Slater*	*Potts*	*Quinn*	*Allen*
33	Argyle	Wilmot	Brown	Morgan	Marker	Burrows	Salman	Barlow*	Hodges	Turner	Clement*	Fiore	Damerell, Morrison
33	West Brom	*Rees*	*Hodson*	*Robson*	*Roberts*	*Burgess*	*Dobbins^*	*Ford*	*Parkin*	*Bannister !*	*Palmer^*	*Anderson*	*Raven, Shakespeare*
34	Argyle	Wilmot	Brown	Morgan	Marker	Burrows	Salman	Barlow	Hodges	Turner	Morrison	Fiore^	Clement
34	Portsmouth	*Gosney*	*Stevens**	*Daniel*	*Aspinall*	*Hogg*	*Russell*	*Wigley*	*Kuhl*	*Whittingham*	*Murray*	*Anderton*	*Awford*

Match reports

24 — Bristol Rov: Errors are inevitable on a pitch covered in pools of water. Rovers skipper, Vaughan Jones, attempts to head Morgan's cross over the bar but only succeeds in beating Parkin. The impressive Carl Saunders strikes twice. Turner makes a welcome return by sliding in for Argyle's second.

25 — Swindon: Argyle look set to end their dismal run when Turner scores with a close-range header. The Swindon supporters turn against their side who look bereft of attacking ideas. Steve Foley's injury-time equaliser is barely deserved and does little to pacify unhappy Robins boss Ossie Ardiles.

26 — Middlesbrough: Argyle return to Ayresome Park for the second successive Saturday and produce the same result. Boro test the strength of the woodwork and Ian Baird's shot is cleared off the line. Marker is outstanding in defence. Paul Kerr and Stuart Ripley test the strength of the woodwork and Ian Baird's shot is cleared off the line.

27 — Bristol City: City manager Jimmy Lumsden is determined not to see his side repeat last week's humiliating 0-4 home defeat by Swindon and employs a five man defence. The ploy seems to have worked until Robinson rises to head Brown's free-kick. Morrison's header had earlier hit the woodwork.

28 — Leicester: Troubled City have just parted company with manager David Pleat. Their plight could have been worse as Argyle miss three good chances including a missed penalty by Marker (12) after Madden fouled Robinson. Kelly looks offside as he sets up an easy opener for Tommy Wright.

29 — Millwall: Argyle succumb to a one-man show by future England star Teddy Sheringham. The striker becomes the country's leading scorer as he fully exploits Argyle's poor defending to take his season's tally to 25. Garner provides the one bright spot for the Greens as he scores from 20 yards.

30 — Brighton: Injuries force Hodges to play as a makeshift forward. Fortunately for Argyle, Albion put up little resistance. Fiore's presence disorientates Digweed and the ball runs invitingly to Morgan who scores into an unguarded net. Burrows gets ahead of the defence from Barlow's corner.

31 — Port Vale: Vale come closest to scoring in the first half when Salman over hits a back-pass which Wilmot tips over the bar. Turner and Neil Aspin enjoy a match-long physical battle. Turner comes out the winner with two headed goals while Aspin ends up with a blood-spattered shirt and shorts.

32 — West Ham: Tim Breacker's low cross deflects in off Marker. Argyle fight back and Turner puts them in front with two headers. Breacker levels. Disaster strikes as Clement fouls Stuart Slater (87) but George Parris becomes the fourth Hammer to miss a penalty this season as Wilmot saves.

33 — West Brom: Even Albion boss Bobby Gould is surprised that Palmer's header counts as the ball does not appear to cross the line. Hodges equalises after Turner's header hits the bar. Bannister is dismissed (54) for a second foul. Turner's head does it again. Both Argyle subs wear number 14.

34 — Portsmouth: Brown is given the penalty responsibilities and he coolly sends Andy Gosney the wrong way after Awford fouls Turner. Kemp vents his anger at the officials after Kuhl's goal is allowed to stand. Guy Whittingham is at least ten yards offside but deemed not to be interfering with play.

Plymouth Argyle — end-of-season fixture and results record

No	Date	V	Opponent	Pos	W/D/L	Pts	Att	HT	FT	Scorers	Ref
	19/3		(Sheffield Wednesday)	3		41	7,806			MacKenzie 87	P Vanes
36	22/3	A	IPSWICH	17	L	41	9,842	0-1	1-3	Fiore 71 / Morgan 20(og), Goddard 70, 85	J Carter
37	30/3	A	BARNSLEY	18	L	41	6,142	0-1	0-1	Agnew 27p	M Peck
38	1/4	H	OLDHAM	19	L	41	8,852	0-1	1-2	Fiore 62 / Ritchie 31, Adams 61	P Durkin
39	6/4	A	BRISTOL ROV	20	D	42	5,668	0-0	0-0		P Alcock
40	9/4	H	WOLVERHAMPTON	17	W	45	7,618	0-0	1-0	Hodges 64	J Deakin
41	13/4	H	SWINDON	18	D	46	6,712	2-1	3-3	Morrison 14, Salman 44, Viveash 81(og) / Hazard 30, Shearer 56, 64	A Seville
42	17/4	A	OXFORD	18	D	47	4,295	0-0	0-0		J Moules
43	20/4	H	BLACKBURN	17	W	50	5,122	4-0	4-1	Burrows 4, 38, Turner 10, 19 / Stapleton 87	M Pierce
44	27/4	A	NOTTS CO	20	L	50	7,370	0-1	0-4	Draper 31, Regis 73, 75, 88p	P Harrison
45	4/5	A	HULL	21	L	50	3,175	0-1	0-2	Thompson 24, Hunter 52	P Wright
46	11/5	H	CHARLTON	18	W	53	6,816	1-0	2-0	Pitcher 25(og), Turner 63	H King

Home Average 6,851 · Away Average 10,144

19/3 (Sheffield Wednesday) — Opponent line-up: Turner, Anderson, King, Palmer, Shirtliff, Pearson, Francis*, Sheridan, Hirst, Williams, McCalf^; sub Watson/MacKenzie^.
The Pilgrims look like putting a dent in the best away record in the division when Morgan strikes after Chris Turner fails to hold Brown's high ball. The recall of Trevor Francis fails to ignite Wednesday. For the eighth time this season, Argyle concede a goal in the last ten minutes.

36 IPSWICH (A) — Wilmot, Brown, Marker, Burrows, Salman, Morgan, Barlow*, Hodges^, Turner, Morrison, Fiore; sub Damerell/Clement. Ipswich: Forrest, Yallop, Thompson, Stockwell, Linighan, Gayle, Palmer, Goddard, Whitton, Dozzell, Kiwomya.
John Lyall's side are boosted when Morgan accidentally turns David Linighan's header past Wilmot. Paul Goddard finishes clinically. Within a minute Fiore rounds off a fine performance with a goal. As Argyle attack Goddard exploits defensive gaps to convert Dozzell's superb pass.

37 BARNSLEY (A) — Wilmot, Brown, Marker, Burrows, Clement, Barlow*, Hodges^, Turner, Morrison, Fiore; sub Damerell/Meade. Barnsley: Baker, Dobbin, Rimmer, Smith, Tiler, O'Connell, Rammell, Saville, Agnew, Archdeacon.
Burrows' feeble pass to Wilmot forces the keeper to trip Andy Rammell. Steve Agnew, who's balding pate seems to be everywhere converts. Turner incenses the home crowd when an off the ball clash with Mark Smith sees the ex-Argyle man return with his head swathed in bandages.

38 OLDHAM (H) — Wilmot, Brown, Marker, Burrows, Salman, Clement*, Hodges^, Turner, Morrison, Fiore; subs Barlow/Meade. Oldham: Hallworth, Halle*, Henry, Barrett, Jobson, Adams, Ritchie, Warhurst, Redfearn, Holden; sub Kane.
A classy display by Andy Ritchie has Kemp ranking the experienced forward as the best striker he has seen this season. Ritchie strikes a superb volley from a wide angle and also creates the second for Neil Adams. Fiore gives Halle a real run-around and scores a deserved goal.

39 BRISTOL ROV (A) — Wilmot, Brown, Marker, Burrows, Cross, Morgan, Hodges, Turner, Morrison, Fiore; sub Pounder/Boothroyd. Bristol Rovers: Parkin, Alexander, Twentyman, Sealy*, Jones, Clark, Holloway, Reece, White, Saunders; sub Bailey^.
The performance of debutant Ryan Cross is the one bright spot at a miserably wet and windy Twerton Park. Neither goalkeeper is really tested. Most of the action is confined to the final ten minutes as both sides create chances but over-eager attempts on goal sum up a frustrating match.

40 WOLVERHAMPTON (H) — Wilmot, Brown, Marker, Burrows, Meade*, Morgan*, Hodges, Turner, Morrison, Fiore; sub Clement. Wolves: Lange, Bennett, Thompson, Hindmarch, Roberts*, Birch, Todd, Bull, Mutch, Dennison; sub Burke.
Injury-hit Wolves have nothing to play for and it shows. Hodges knows little about his goal as Morgan's powerful shot strikes him to leave Tony Lange flat-footed. Marker keeps Steve Bull under wraps. Argyle suffer a late scare when Paul Birch hammers a free-kick against the bar.

41 SWINDON (H) — Wilmot, Brown, Marker, Burrows, Salman, Morgan^, Hodges, Turner, Morrison, Fiore; subs Clement/Cooper. Swindon: Digby, Kerslake, Viveash*, Hazard, Calderwood, Lorenzo, Shearer, MacLaren, Rideout, Foley; sub Simpson.
New Swindon boss Glenn Hoddle's game plan revolves around stopping Turner. Morrison blasts in a half-volley. Mike Hazard finishes off a five-man move. Salman scores with a 25-yard volley. Duncan Shearer is twice left unmarked. Digby is not where Adrian Viveash thinks he is.

42 OXFORD (A) — Wilmot, Brown, Cross, Burrows, Salman, Garner*, Hodges^, Turner, Morrison, Fiore; subs Clement/Cooper. Oxford: Veysey, Smart, Ford, Evans, Melville, Beauchamp, Nogan, Stein, Foyle, Simpson.
Ken Veysey passes a late fitness test to play a starring role as Brian Horton's side equal a club record of 13 unbeaten matches. The keeper is finally beaten by Marker's header but the ball strikes an upright. Two long-range efforts from Martin Foyle are the best Oxford can muster.

43 BLACKBURN (H) — Wilmot, Brown, Marker, Burrows, Salman, Cross, Hodges^, Turner, Morrison, Fiore; subs Barlow/Cooper. Blackburn: Mimms, Atkins, Reid I, Hill, Dobson, Irvine, Richardson, Livingstone, Stapleton, Sellars.
A disjointed Blackburn wonder what's hit them as Argyle fly into an early three-goal lead, all from set-pieces. Burrows slots home his second with the panache of a regular scorer. Paul Reid is red-carded (84) for violent conduct after kicking out at Turner who is lying on the ground.

44 NOTTS CO (A) — Walter, Brown, Cross, Burrows, Salman, Tallon*, Hodges^, Turner, Morrison, Fiore; subs Robinson/Barlow, Chapman/Bartlett. Notts Co: Cherry, Palmer, Paris, Yates, Short, Draper^, Thomas, King, Regis, Johnson^.
Kemp is forced to field four teenagers as his side is decimated by injury and suspension. Paul Reid is red-carded (84) for violent conduct after kicking out at Turner who is lying on the ground. Fiore brings down Gary Chapman to give Dave Regis the chance to complete his first league hat-trick.

45 HULL (A) — Walter, Brown, Cross, Burrows, Salman, Garner*, Adcock, Turner, Morrison, Fiore; subs Barlow, Smith. Hull: Wilson, Hockaday*, Thompson, Mail, Buckley, Warren, Ngata, Hunter, Jenkinson, Calvert.
The odds on an Argyle victory increase when Terry Dolan decides to blood number of youngsters which still leaves relegation a possibility. The 'Tigers' stroll to their first home win in nine matches.

46 CHARLTON (H) — Wilmot, Brown, Marker, Burrows, Salman, Barlow, Hodges, Turner, Morrison*, Fiore; subs Evans/Cross, Gritt/Gorman. Charlton: Bolder, Salako, Reid, Peake, Balmer, Lee*, Pitcher, Mortimer, Dyer^, Minto.
Argyle save themselves from the drop. The Addicks show little interest in making the match into a meaningful contest. Brown has an early chance to celebrate his player of the year award but blasts his spot-kick five yards wide (12). Darren Pitcher heads into his own unguarded net.

BARCLAYS DIVISION 2 (CUP-TIES) Manager: David Kemp SEASON 1990-91

Rumbelows Cup

			Att		H-T	F-A		Scorers, Times, and Referees	1	2	3	4	5	6	7	8	9	10	11	subs used
2:1	H	WIMBLEDON 25/9	17	1:15	0-0	1-0	W	Thomas 67 — Ref: K Cooper	Wilmot	Brown	Morgan	Marker	Burrows	Hodges	Byrne	Fiore*	Turner	Thomas	Salman	King
			4,506						*Segers*	*Joseph*	*Phelan*	*Barton*	*Scales*	*Curle*	*Fairweather Kruszynski*	*Kruszynski*	*Gayle**	*Sanchez*	*Cotterill*	*Cork*

The return of the experienced Salman helps to tighten the defence. The Dons miss the absent John Fashanu. Thomas, playing up front, scores from close range. Hans Segers is embarrassed when he is robbed by Byrne as he dribbles outside his area but John Scales scoops off the line.

			Att		H-T	F-A		Scorers, Times, and Referees	1	2	3	4	5	6	7	8	9	10	11	subs used
2:2	A	WIMBLEDON 10/10	15	1:10	1-0	2-0	W	Thomas 1, Fiore 63 — Ref: M Pierce (Argyle won 3-0 on aggregate)	Wilmot !	Brown	Morgan	Marker	Burrows	Hodges	Byrne*	Fiore	Turner	Thomas	Salman	Morrison
			3,473						*Segers*	*Joseph*	*Phelan*	*Barton*	*Blackwell*	*Curle*	*Gayle**	*Kruszynski Fashanu*	*Fashanu*	*Cork*	*Fairweather^*	*Newhouse/McGee*

Thomas shrugs off Dean Blackwell to give Argyle a useful cushion. Fiore scores with a header against his former club. With the tie safe, Wilmot is sent off (83) for a professional foul on Kruszynski. Marker takes over in goal but has little to do in the remaining seven minutes.

			Att		H-T	F-A		Scorers, Times, and Referees	1	2	3	4	5	6	7	8	9	10	11	subs used
3	H	NOTT'M FOREST 31/10	14	1:10	0-2	1-2	L	Salman 83 — Parker 13, Jemson 36 — Ref: A Gunn	Walter	Brown	Morgan	Marker	Burrows	Salman	Barlow	Fiore*	Turner	Adcock	Morrison	Byrne
			17,467						*Crossley*	*Laws*	*Pearce*	*Walker**	*Chettle*	*Keane*	*Crosby*	*Parker*	*Clough*	*Jemson^*	*Gaynor*	*Wassall/Starbuck*

Cup holders Forest progress to the last 16 but not before being given a fright or two. Garry Parker scores from 18 yards from a half-cleared corner. Nigel Jemson cleverly wrong-foots Marker before shooting past Walter. Salman's third goal in five days gives Argyle some late hope.

FA Cup

			Att		H-T	F-A		Scorers, Times, and Referees	1	2	3	4	5	6	7	8	9	10	11	subs used
3	A	MIDDLESBROUGH 5/1	22	5	0-0	0-0	D	Ref: P Tyldesley	Walter	Brown	Salman	Marker	Burrows	Morgan	Barlow	Hodges	Turner !	Adcock*	Morrison	Fiore
			13,042						*Pears*	*Cooper*	*Phillips**	*Mowbray*	*Coleman*	*Proctor^*	*Slaven*	*Mustoe*	*Baird*	*Kerr*	*Hendrie*	*McGee/Ripley*

Argyle welcome back Marker and Brown. Paul Kerr misses the best chance when he blazes over from six yards. The game ends on a sour note. Barlow requires treatment after a foul by John Hendrie. As soon as play resumes Turner exacts revenge on the Boro man and is sent off.

			Att		H-T	F-A		Scorers, Times, and Referees	1	2	3	4	5	6	7	8	9	10	11	subs used
3R	H	MIDDLESBROUGH 14/1	21	5	1-1	1-2	L	Marker 27p — Baird 10, Kerr 90 — Ref: P Tyldesley	Walter	Brown	Salman	Marker	Burrows	Salman	Barlow	Hodges	Turner	Adcock	Morrison	Fiore
			6,956						*Pears*	*Parkinson*	*Phillips*	*Mowbray*	*Coleman*	*Putney*	*Slaven**	*Wark*	*Baird*	*Kerr*	*Ripley*	*Hendrie*

The third meeting between these two sides in ten days finally produces some goals. Ian Baird strikes with his 13th goal of the season from Jimmy Phillips' corner. Marker scores from the spot after Adcock is brought down by Tony Mowbray. Kerr wins it for Boro in injury-time.

League Table

	P	W	D	L	F	A	W	D	L	F	A	Pts
1 Oldham	46	17	5	1	55	21	8	8	7	28	32	88
2 West Ham	46	15	6	2	41	18	9	9	5	19	16	87
3 Sheffield Wed	46	12	10	1	43	23	10	6	7	37	28	82
4 Notts Co*	46	14	4	5	45	28	9	7	7	31	27	80
5 Millwall	46	11	6	6	43	28	9	7	7	27	23	73
6 Brighton	46	12	4	7	37	31	9	3	11	26	38	70
7 Middlesbro	46	12	4	7	36	17	8	5	10	30	30	69
8 Barnsley	46	13	7	3	39	16	6	5	12	24	32	69
9 Bristol City	46	14	5	4	44	28	6	2	15	24	43	67
10 Oxford	46	10	9	4	41	29	4	10	9	28	37	61
11 Newcastle	46	8	10	5	24	22	6	7	10	25	34	59
12 Wolves	46	11	6	6	45	35	2	13	8	18	28	58
13 Bristol Rov	46	9	7	7	29	20	4	6	13	27	39	58
14 Ipswich	46	9	8	6	32	28	4	10	9	28	40	57
15 Port Vale	46	10	4	9	32	24	5	8	10	24	40	57
16 Charlton	46	8	7	8	27	25	5	10	8	30	36	56
17 Portsmouth	46	10	6	7	34	27	4	5	14	24	43	53
18 PLYMOUTH	46	10	10	3	36	20	2	7	14	18	48	53
19 Blackburn	46	8	6	9	26	27	6	4	13	25	39	52
20 Watford	46	5	8	10	24	32	7	7	9	21	27	51
21 Swindon	46	8	8	9	31	30	4	8	11	34	43	50
22 Leicester	46	12	4	7	41	33	2	4	17	19	50	50
23 West Brom	46	7	11	5	26	21	3	7	13	26	40	48
24 Hull	46	6	10	7	35	32	4	5	14	22	53	45
	1104	253	163	136	866	615	136	163	253	615	866	1493

* promoted
after play-offs

Double wins: (2) Charlton, West Brom.
Double defeats: (2) Newcastle, Oldham.

Won from behind: (2) Hull, West Brom.
Lost from in front: (5) Brighton, Oldham, Portsmouth, Port Vale, Wolves.

High spots: Solid home record, losing only 3 matches.
Surprise draw against West Ham (a).
Martin Barlow wins Barclays 'Young Eagle of the Month' award.

Low-spots: Enforced retirement of Andy Thomas with a back injury.
Heavy reliance on loan and poor quality signings.
Lack of goal scorer to support Robbie Turner.
Worst away scoring record in the Division.

Player of the Year: Kenny Brown.
Ever presents: (0).
Hat-tricks: (0).
Leading scorer: Robbie Turner (14).

Appearances / Goals

	Lge	Sub	LC	Sub	FAC	Sub	Lge	LC	FAC	Tot
Adcock, Paul	9	3	1	2			1			1
Ampadu, Kwame	6									
Barlow, Martin	25	5					1			1
Brown, Kenny	43		3		3		3			3
Burrows, Adrian	45		3		3		4			4
Byrne, David	11	3	2		1					
Clement, Andy	8	8								
Cooper, David		3								
Cross, Ryan	6	1								
Damerell, Mark		4								
Edwards, Keith	3		1				1			1
Evans, Michael	1	3								
Fiore, Mark	38		3			1	3		1	4
Garner, Darren	5						1			1
Hodges, Kevin	40	2	2	2	2		3			3
King, Adam	4	4				1				
Marker, Nicky	39		3		3		2	1		3
McAllister, Brian	7	1								
Meade, Raphael	2	3								
Morgan, Steve	40		3		3		3			3
Morrison, Andy	27	5	1	1	2		2			2
Pickard, Owen	4	3					1			1
Robinson, Paul	7	4					3			3
Salman, Danis	35		3		3	2	3	1		4
Summerfield, Kevin	1									
Tallon, Darren										
Thomas, Andy	14		2				6	2		8
Turner, Robbie	39		3		3		14			14
Walter, Dave	10		1		2					
Wilmot, Rhys	36		2		2					
(own-goals)							3			3
30 players used	506	52	33	3	22	1	54	4	1	59

BARCLAYS DIVISION 2 Manager: Kemp > Gillett & Nisbet > Shilton SEASON 1991-92

Each match lists the Argyle line-up (roman) above the opponents' line-up (italic).

No	Date		Att	Pos	Pt	F-A	H-T	Scorers, Times, and Referees	1	2	3	4	5	6	7	8	9	10	11	subs used
1	17/8	H BARNSLEY	6,352		W 3	2-1	1-0	Marshall 19, Turner 46	Wilmot	Salman	**Spearing**	Marker	Cross	Morgan	Barlow	**Marshall**	Turner	Morrison	Fiore*	Clement
								Pearson 74	*Whitehead*	*Bishop*	*Williams*	*Banks*	*Davis*	*Taggart*	*O'Connell*	*Rammel*	*Pearson*	*McCord**	*Graham*	*Fleming*
								Ref: G Ashby												
2	24/8	A LEICESTER	11,852	15 / 6	L 3	0-2	0-1		Wilmot	Salman	Spearing	Marker	Cross	Morgan	Quamina*	Marshall	Turner	Morrison	Clement^	Barlow/Fiore
								Gibson 15, Kitson 62	*Poole*	*Mills*	*Platnauer*	*Fitzpatrick*	*Walsh*	*James*	*Oldfield*	*Gibson*	*Wright**	*Kelly^*	*Kitson*	*Russell/Ward*
								Ref: D Gallagher												
3	31/8	H MILLWALL	5,369	7 / 19	W 6	3-2	2-1	Marshall 28, Burrows 41, Wood 90(og)	Wilmot	Clement	Spearing	Marker	Burrows	Morgan	Barlow	Marshall	Turner	Morrison^	Evans*	Scott/Edworthy
								Rae 45, Burrows 84(og)	*Davison*	*Dawes*	*Cooper*	*McGlashan*	*Thompson*	*McLeary**	*Kerr*	*Colquhoun*	*Falco*	*Rae*	*Barber*	*Wood*
								Ref: P Durkin												
4	4/9	A NEWCASTLE	19,543	11 / 17	D 7	2-2	1-0	Salman 41, Marshall 63	Wilmot*	Clement	Spearing	Marker	Burrows	Morgan	Barlow	Marshall	Turner	Morrison	Edworthy^	Salman
								Carr 82, Quinn 85	*Smicek*	*Neilson*	*Elliott*	*O'Brien*	*Scott*	*Bradshaw*	*Clark*	*Peacock^*	*Quinn*	*Carr*	*Roche**	*Makel/Hunt*
								Ref: M Peck												
5	7/9	H CHARLTON	5,602	17 / 12	L 7	0-2	0-0		Walter	Clement	Spearing*	Marker	Burrows	Morgan	Barlow	Marshall	Turner	Morrison	Evans^	Scott/Edworthy
								Pitcher 51p, Nelson 74	*Bolder*	*Pitcher*	*Minto*	*Peake*	*Webster*	*Gatting*	*Lee*	*Bacon^*	*Leaburn*	*Nelson**	*Walsh*	*Dyer/Gritt*
								Ref: R Groves												
6	14/9	A GRIMSBY	5,432	19 / 11	L 7	1-2	0-1	Burrows 68	Walter	Salman	Spearing	Marker	Burrows	Morgan	Barlow	Marshall	Scott^	Morrison	Edworthy*	Fiore/Clement
								Jobling 8, Jones 58	*Sherwood*	*McDermott*	*Jobling*	*Futcher*	*Lever*	*Dobbin*	*Watson^*	*Gilbert*	*Jones*	*Agnew*	*Woods**	*North/Smith*
								Ref: R Pawley												
7	17/9	A SOUTHEND	4,585	17	L 7	1-2	0-1	Marshall 71	Walter	Salman	Spearing	Marker	Burrows	Morgan	Barlow	Marshall	Evans	Morrison	Clement	
								Angell 31, Benjamin 79	*Sansome*	*Austin*	*Powell*	*Sussex*	*Scully*	*Prior*	*Ansah*	*Cornwell*	*Tilson*	*Benjamin*	*Angell*	
								Ref: M James												
8	21/9	H MIDDLESBROUGH	5,280	20 / 1	D 8	1-1	1-0	Burrows 35	Walter	Salman	Spearing	Marker	Burrows	Morgan	Barlow	Marshall	Scott	Morrison	Fiore*	Clement
								Wilkinson 68	*Pears*	*Parkinson^*	*Phillips*	*Mowbray*	*Kernaghan*	*Falconer*	*Slaven*	*Proctor**	*Wilkinson*	*Ripley*	*Hendrie*	*Mustoe/Fleming*
								Ref: J Martin												
9	28/9	A OXFORD	3,726	20 / 22	L 8	2-3	0-1	Fiore 63, Barlow 82	Walter	Clement	Spearing*	Marker	Burrows	Morgan	Barlow	Marshall	Scott	Quamina	Fiore	Clement
								Nogan 15, Simpson 85, Penney 86	*Veysey*	*Robinson*	*Smart*	*Phillips**	*Foster*	*Melville*	*Magilton*	*Penney*	*Aylott*	*Nogan*	*Simpson*	*Beauchamp*
								Ref: J Deakin												
10	5/10	H SWINDON	6,208	22 / 3	L 8	0-4	0-2		Wilmot	Salman	Spearing*	Marker	Burrows	Morgan	Barlow	Marshall	Turner	Quamina	Fiore	Damerell
								Shearer 8, 27, 62, 85	*Digby*	*Kerslake*	*Summerbee*	*Hoddle^*	*Calderwood*	*Taylor*	*Hazard*	*Shearer*	*Simpson*	*MacLaren*	*White*	*Jones*
								Ref: K Cooper												
11	12/10	A BLACKBURN	10,830	24 / 7	L 8	2-5	0-2	Marshall 54, Barlow 86	Wilmot	Salman	Clement	Marker	Burrows	Morgan	Barlow	Marshall	Turner !	Cross*	Fiore^	Quamina/Evans
								Moran 10, Garner 45, 62, Speedie 49, 56p	*Mimms*	*Duxbury*	*Atkins*	*Reid*	*Hill*	*May*	*Irvine**	*Moran*	*Speedie*	*Garner*	*Richardson*	*Livingstone/Sellars*
								Ref: T Holbrook												

Match commentaries:

1. New signing Marshall takes little time in making his mark as he spectacularly opens the new season with an overhead kick. Turner gives his side a two-goal cushion after scoring seconds after the interval. New £135k signing John Pearson gives Mel Machin's side hope with a header.

2. Colin Gibson springs the offside trap to evade the onrushing Wilmot and slot into an empty net. City's long-ball game continues to trouble the Argyle defence. Paul Kitson increases the lead when he scores after Steve Walsh nods on Tony James' long throw. Quamina has a quiet debut.

3. Bruce Rioch has spent heavily following the £2m sale of Sheringham but his side come off second best in an entertaining game. Burrows looks to have given Millwall a point when he turns the ball past Wilmot but Steve Wood suffers the same fate in the fourth minute of injury-time.

4. Argyle appear in unfamiliar sponsorless blue shirts. Wilmot is injured in a clash with Mick Quinn (33). Marker takes over between the posts. Sub Salman scores with his first touch. Turner is attacked by a fan after celebrating Marshall's goal and needs three stitches in a head wound.

5. Argyle old boy Garry Nelson proves to be a thorn in Argyle's side. He wins the penalty after having his heels clipped by Marker to allow Darren Pitcher to score. Nelson himself gets the second and later reveals that he was close to returning to Home Park during the summer.

6. Kemp bemoans his leaky defence and the lack of cash available to him. Kevin Jobling fires in a loose ball. Murray Jones has the freedom of the penalty area to stretch the lead. Burrows' header sparks an assault on the Grimsby goal. Barlow's late effort (87) is ruled out for handball.

7. Marker is deployed as a sweeper in an attempt to tighten up the defence. Walter pulls off a number of impressive saves but is powerless to stop Brett Angell's close-range shot. Marshall equalises from ten yards. Ian Benjamin nets the winner after Walter needlessly concedes a corner.

8. Argyle are without Morrison after a training injury. Falconer handles in the area. Barlow is the latest player to take on and fail with the penalty duties as Steve Pears saves (51).

9. Sixty seconds of defensive madness deny Argyle a rare away win. Barlow's goal from Turner's nod down seems enough. Walter, suffering from an earlier blow to the head, flaps at a cross and Simpson scores. Then he fumbles and David Penney swoops to lift Oxford off the bottom.

10. Wilmot is recalled after Walter's mishaps at Oxford but probably wishes he wasn't. Glenn Hoddle displays all his old magic. Duncan Shearer gives a perfect display of goalscoring opportunism. The announcer even credits him with a fifth, not realising it had been ruled out for offside.

11. Kenny Dalglish is announced as Rovers new boss 45 minutes before kick-off. Turner is red-carded (37) for an errant elbow on Kevin Moran. Garner's first appears offside. Kemp remonstrates with the ref at half-time. Speedie's spot-kick after Marker's foul only adds to Kemp's woes.

Plymouth Argyle — Season match-by-match record (matches 13–23)

#	Date	V	Opponent	Score	Res	Pos	Att	Referee
—	19/10	A	(Bristol Rovers)			23	5,049	G Pooley
13	26/10	H	WATFORD	0-1	L	24	4,090	A Smith
14	2/11	H	WOLVERHAMPTON	1-0	W	23	4,200	M Pierce
15	5/11	A	BRISTOL CITY	0-2	L		7,735	K Barratt
16	8/11	A	TRANMERE	0-1	L	12	7,490	D Phillips
17	16/11	H	PORT VALE	1-0	W	23	4,363	C Wilkes
18	23/11	H	SUNDERLAND	1-0	W	23	6,007	K Cooper
19	30/11	A	BRIGHTON	0-1	L	24	6,713	D Axcell
20	7/12	H	IPSWICH	1-0	W	23	4,986	M Bodenham
21	20/12	H	NEWCASTLE	2-0	W	24	5,048	K Burge
22	26/12	A	CAMBRIDGE	1-1	D	22	7,105	A Buksh
23	28/12	A	MILLWALL	1-2	L	22	6,980	G Willard

Scorers
- 13 Watford: Bazeley 21
- 14 Wolverhampton: Marshall 35
- 15 Bristol City: Morgan 15, Allison 28
- 16 Tranmere: Aldridge 73p
- 17 Port Vale: Marshall 84
- 18 Sunderland: Fiore 72
- 19 Brighton: O'Reilly 90
- 20 Ipswich: Fiore 26
- 21 Newcastle: Regis 23, Barlow 77
- 22 Cambridge: Turner 86p; Dublin 79
- 23 Millwall: Morgan 28; McCarthy 40, McGinlay 52

Opponent line-ups (as printed)
- 19/10: Parkin, Alexander, Twentyman, Yates, Marker, Cross, Skinner, Mehew, Reece, White*, Browning; Pounder, Purnell
- 13 Watford: James, Gibbs!, Drysdale, Dublin, McLaughlin, Putney, Bazeley*, Blissett*, Holdsworth, Porter; Nicholas, Butler
- 14 Wolverhampton: Stowell, Ashley, Venus, Bennett, Madden, Downing, Birch, Cook, Steele, Dennison*, Thompson; Taylor
- 15 Bristol City: Leaning, Llewellyn, Scott, May, Bryant, Aizlewood!, Shelton, Rennie, Allison, Morgan, Smith; Scott/Barlow
- 16 Tranmere: Nixon, Higgins, Brannan, Irons, Vickers, Morrissey, Malkin*, Martindale, Nolan, Aldridge, Cooper; Edworthy
- 17 Port Vale: Grew, Mills S, Hughes, Porter^, Aspin, Glover, Jalink, V der Laan*, Foyle, Jeffers; Mills B/Kent
- 18 Sunderland: Norman, Kay, Rogan, Bennett, Ball, Davenport, Bracewell, Rush, Armstrong, Byrne^, Pascoe*; Owers/Russell
- 19 Brighton: Beeney, Crumplin, Gallacher, Briley^, Chivers, O'Reilly, Robinson, Meade*, Gall, Codner, Walker; Farrington/Chapman
- 20 Ipswich: Forrest, Johnson, Thompson, Stockwell, Wark, Linighan, Milton, Palmer*, Whitton!, Dozzell, Kiwomya; Morrison, Yallop
- 21 Newcastle: Wright, Bradshaw*, Bodin, Roche, Scott, Appleby, Makel*, Peacock, Kelly, Hunt, Brock; Watson/Howey
- 22 Cambridge: Vaughan, Fensome, Kimble, Bailie*, Dennis, Chapple, O'Shea, Wilkins, Dublin, Taylor, Philpott; Rowett
- 23 Millwall: Branagan, Cunningham, Dawes, Thompson, McCarthy, McLeary, Stephenson, Verveer, Bogie, McGinlay, Kerr; Clement

Plymouth Argyle's goalkeeper throughout these matches was Wilmot; the full Argyle XI (Marker, Clement, Salman, Barlow, Morgan, Marshall, Hopkins, Fiore, Regis, Meaker, Spearing, Turner, Morrison, Edworthy, Cross, Evans, Scott and others) is printed in the second line of each fixture.

Match reports

19/10 — Turner is included as a central defender in a desperate attempt to stop leaking goals. Managerless Rovers soak up some early pressure and begin to look the more dangerous side. Morrison's return from injury lasts just 35 minutes as he is taken to hospital for x-rays on an ankle.

13 Watford — New chairman Dan McAuley is away on business and misses another abysmal performance. Wilmot gifts the only goal as he unwisely rushes to meet a free-kick and Bazeley finds himself confronted by an unguarded net. Nigel Gibbs is sent off (26) for a retaliatory kick on Fiore.

14 Wolverhampton — Wolves look toothless in attack as they miss the lethal Bull and Mutch partnership when both players fail late fitness tests. Marshall's header brings a welcome victory. Morgan gives a commanding performance in midfield. Evans misses a late chance when his shot hits Stowell's leg.

15 Bristol City — Yet again Argyle fail to gain anything from playing against ten men for much of the game. Nicky Morgan scores after Cross loses possession. Wayne Allison shrugs off four tackles to lob Wilmot from 20 yards. Mark Aizlewood gets a red card (31) for aiming a head-butt at Clement.

16 Tranmere — With new signing Regis looking lively, the Pilgrims give an improved performance. Ace marksman John Aldridge is kept quiet until he breaks clear and is brought down by Wilmot. The former Liverpool striker recovers to score from the spot after his characteristic shuffling run-up.

17 Port Vale — It isn't pretty to watch but Argyle fans are grateful for three points. It could have been so much different, but Robin van der Laan is guilty of a glaring miss. Turner returns from suspension and is again dominant in defence. Seventeen-year-old YTS lad Steve Jones gets a short run-out.

18 Sunderland — The pressure on Kemp eases with a second straight win. Meaker, on loan from QPR, marks his first full league game with a rasping drive that Tony Norman pushes onto the bar. Paul Bracewell attempts a 40-yard back-pass but Fiore is alert to his intentions and intercepts to score.

19 Brighton — With Regis struggling to justify his record £200k price tag, Argyle again rarely threaten to score. Barlow comes closest but his shot is cleared off the line by John Crumplin. A minute and a half into stoppage time, Gary O'Reilly rises to head home via post from Clive Walker's corner.

20 Ipswich — Turner continues to perform outstandingly in defence but is also badly missed up front. Fiore nips in to take advantage of Mick Stockwell's mis-control to slot home. Steve Whitton is booked for an off the ball incident with Spearing and then sees red after a clash with Turner (51).

21 Newcastle — Argyle ease themselves out of the bottom three. Regis's first goal for the club finally arrives when he gets the final touch with the ball bobbing around in the six-yard box. Barlow's drive from the edge of the area goes through the legs of Northern Ireland international Tommy Wright.

22 Cambridge — The match proceeds at a fast and furious pace without either side looking threatening. Dion Dublin's faint touch gives United the lead. Wilmot keeps Argyle in the game when he turns Wilkins' drive onto a post. Fensome needlessly handles Fiore's cross. Turner scores from the spot.

23 Millwall — Millwall recover from a 0-4 Boxing Day thrashing by Watford. The dangerous Paul Stephenson sets up both goals after Morgan's header puts the Pilgrims ahead. Morrison is fortunate to escape with only a booking after running ten yards to launch a two-footed lunge on Alan McLeary.

BARCLAYS DIVISION 2   Manager: Kemp > Gillett & Nisbet > Shilton   SEASON 1991-92

No	Date	V	Team	Att	Pos	OppPos	Res	F-A	H-T	Pt	Scorers, Times, and Referees
24	1/1	H	PORTSMOUTH	8,887	19	9	W	3-2	2:1	28	Turner 7, Morrison 11, Marshall 73 / Powell 13, Chamberlain 81 / Ref: G Singh
25	11/1	H	LEICESTER	5,846	21	7	D	2-2	2-0	29	Witter 2, Fiore 20 / Turner 51(og), Thompson 65 / Ref: K Cooper
26	18/1	A	BARNSLEY	5,322	18	21	W	3-1	3-0	32	Marshall 16, 19, 39 / Saville 60 / Ref: A Dawson
27	1/2	H	BRISTOL ROV	6,631	19	15	D	0-0	0-0	33	Ref: R Gifford
28	4/2	A	PORTSMOUTH	10,467	21	4	L	1-4	0-2	33	Regis 87 / P'ell 25, Wh'ham 42 74, Marker 67(og) / Ref: K Morton
29	8/2	A	WATFORD	7,260	21	16	L	0-1	0-0	33	Blissett 68 / Ref: I Borrett
30	11/2	H	CAMBRIDGE	4,290	21	4	L	0-1	0-1	33	Cheetham 14 / Ref: K Burge
31	22/2	H	BRIGHTON	5,259	20	24	D	1-1	1-0	34	Smith 33 / Gall 82 / Ref: H King
32	29/2	A	IPSWICH	12,852	22	2	L	0-2	0-0	34	Kiwomya 49, Whitton 82 / Ref: A Ward
33	7/3	H	DERBY	8,864	23	6	D	1-1	1-1	35	Morrison 25 / Simpson 17 / Ref: J Deakin
34	10/3	H	BRISTOL CITY	9,734	20	23	W	1-0	0-0	38	Marshall 49 / Ref: M Pierce

Line-ups (positions 1–11, subs used)

24 H PORTSMOUTH
Argyle: Wilmot, Spearing, Salman, Marker, Morrison, Morgan, Barlow, Marshall, Regis, Fiore*, Turner — sub: Edworthy
Portsmouth: Knight, Awford, Beresford, Burns^, Symons, Butters, Neill, Kuhl, Powell, Chamberlain, Anderton* — subs: Aspinall/Wigley
Turner and Morrison give Argyle the perfect start to the new year by cashing in on set-pieces. Darryl Powell quickly responds. Marshall ends his recent poor run with a curling shot. Darren Anderton goes close and Mark Chamberlain gives Pompey a late boost with a close-range shot.

25 H LEICESTER
Argyle: Wilmot, Spearing, Clement, Witter, Morrison, Morgan, Barlow, Marshall, Regis, Fiore*, Turner — sub: Salman
Leicester: Muggleton, Mills, Reid, Smith, Walsh, Gordon, Oldfield, Thompson, Wright, Willis, Kitson
Loan signing Tony Witter scores with his first touch in league football when he heads in Barlow's free-kick. Fiore sends a looping header just under the bar. Turner inadvertently heads Steve Thompson's corner past a startled Wilmot. Thompson needs no assistance to score the leveller.

26 A BARNSLEY
Argyle: Wilmot, Spearing, Clement, Marker, Morrison, Morgan, Witter, Marshall, Regis*, Salman, Turner — sub: Fiore
Barnsley: Butler, Fleming^, Bishop, Bullimore*, Davis, Taggart, Rammell, Redfearn, Saville, Currie, Archdeacon — subs: O'Connell/Graham
Turner is restored to the attack with great effect as the Barnsley defenders are unable to cope with his aerial power. Marshall takes advantage to score his first hat-trick. Andy Saville's token reply does little to pacify the home fans who stage a 'Mel Machin out' post-match demonstration.

27 H BRISTOL ROV
Argyle: Wilmot, Spearing!, Clement, Marker, Fiore*, Morgan, Barlow, Marshall, Regis, Fiore*, Turner — sub: Edworthy
Bristol Rov: Parkin, Alexander, Moore, Yates, Maddison, Skinner, Mehew, Reece, White, Saunders, Pounder
Argyle's determination not to suffer another drubbing from Rovers after the FA Cup debacle makes for poor entertainment. An away fan sends a remote controlled toy jeep racing around the penalty area during half-time. Spearing is sent off (83) for persistent misconduct after a caution.

28 A PORTSMOUTH
Argyle: Wilmot, Spearing, Clement*, Marker, Edworthy, Morgan, Witter, Marshall, Regis, Salman, Turner — sub: Garner
Portsmouth: Knight, Hendon, Beresford, Powell, Symons, Butters, Neill, Kuhl, Whittingham, Burns, Anderton
The pressure mounts on Kemp after another poor display. High-riding Pompey bounce back from two successive defeats but are never required to extend themselves. Late replacement Guy Whittingham scores two well-taken goals. Regis finally finds the net again but it is all too late.

29 A WATFORD
Argyle: Wilmot, Spearing, Smith, Marker, Edworthy, Morrison, Garner*, Marshall, Regis, Salman, Turner — sub: Fiore
Watford: James, Gibbs, Drysdale, Dublin, Holdsworth, McLaughlin, Hessenthaler, Nogan, Blissett, Porter*, Putney — sub: Butler
Despite three changes Argyle produce another drab display in the first half. Things improve slightly during the second period but David James shows why he is so highly rated with three fine saves. Watford are little better but Luther Blissett's goal puts another nail in Kemp's coffin.

30 H CAMBRIDGE
Argyle: Wilmot, Spearing, Salman, Marker, V Rossum, Morgan, Morrison, Marshall, Smith, Fiore*, Turner — sub: Regis
Cambridge: Sheffield, Fensome, Kimble, Dennis, Daish, O'Shea, Cheetham*, Leadbitter, Dublin, Wilkins*, Taylor — subs: Heaney/Heathcote
Record signing Regis is dropped. U's boss John Beck describes Argyle's performance as 'magnificent' but they cannot finds a way past second choice keeper Jon Sheffield. Kemp's dismissal to the stand (78) for remarks to a linesman proves to be his farewell. He is sacked on Thursday.

31 H BRIGHTON
Argyle: Wilmot, Salman, Fiore, Marker, Edworthy, Morrison, Barlow, Marshall, Regis, Smith, Marshall — sub: Turner
Brighton: Digweed, Munday, Gallacher, Wilkins, Burrows, McCarthy, Robinson, Meade, Gall, Cadner, Clarkson
Caretaker managers Nisbet and Gillett immediately abandon the unpopular long-ball game. Smith gets his first goal since his £185k arrival from Bristol City. Bottom of the table Albion are without six regulars but put up a spirited show and Mark Gall gives them a point via a post.

32 A IPSWICH
Argyle: Wilmot, Spearing, Morrison, Marker, Van Rossum, Morgan, Hodges, Garner*, Regis, Smith, Turner* — subs: Barlow/Clement
Ipswich: Forrest, Johnson*, Thompson, Stockwell, Wark, Linghan, Milton, Palmer, Whitton, Dozzell*, Kiwomya — subs: Goddard/Zondervan
Argyle battle hard in the first half. Disaster strikes when Kiwomya takes advantage of a collision between Wilmot and Turner. Celebrations are muted as it is obvious that Turner is seriously injured. After five minutes of treatment he is stretchered away with a double fracture of the leg.

33 H DERBY
Argyle: Wilmot, Salman, Spearing, Edworthy*, Morrison, Morgan, Van Rossum, Garner*, Regis, Marshall, Morgan — subs: Smith/Hodges
Derby: Taylor, Kavanagh, Round, Williams G, Coleman, Comyn, McMinn*, Ormondroyd, Gabbiadini, Williams P, Simpson — sub: Micklewhite
The new managerial team of Shilton and McGovern are greeted with rapturous applause. Paul Simpson threatens to spoil the occasion as he converts Ormondroyd's defence-splitting pass. Garner sets up Morrison for the equaliser. Morgan's powerful display impresses the new boss.

34 H BRISTOL CITY
Argyle: Wilmot, Salman, Spearing, Marker, Van Rossum, Morrison, Hodges, Edwards, Regis, Marshall, Morgan — sub: Bent
Bristol City: Welch, Llewellyn, Scott, May, Bryant, Osman, Mellan, Morgan*, Allison, Gavin, — sub: Gavin
City are plunged deeper into relegation trouble as Shilton gains his first win. Morgan's brilliant back-heel sets up Spearing, whose cross is dropped by Keith Welch and Marshall pounces. Transfer-seeking Wilmot is in top form. Allison claims that his late header goes over the line.

No	Venue	Opponent	Date	W/D/L	Score	Pos		Pts	Att
35	A	WOLVERHAMPTON	14/3		0-0	21	11	38	11,556
36	H	TRANMERE	21/3	W	1-0	21	13	41	7,447
37	A	DERBY	24/3	L	0-2			41	13,799
38	A	PORT VALE	28/3	L	0-1	22	24	41	5,310
39	H	GRIMSBY	31/3	L	1-2	23	17	41	6,274
40	A	CHARLTON	4/4	D	0-0	23	4	42	6,787
41	H	SOUTHEND	11/4	L	0-2	24	10	42	7,060
42	A	SUNDERLAND	16/4	W	1-0			45	28,813
43	A	MIDDLESBROUGH	18/4	L	1-2			45	15,086
44	H	OXFORD	20/4	W	3-1	20	21	48	9,735
45	A	SWINDON	25/4	L	0-1	21	8	48	10,463
46	H	BLACKBURN	2/5	L	1-3	22	6	48	17,459

35 — WOLVERHAMPTON (A)
Argyle: Wilmot, Salman, Van Rossum, Morrison, Marker, Hodges, Smith, Fiore, Marshall, Morgan — Garner/Burrows
Wolves: Stowell, Ashley, Venus, Bennett, Mountfield, Madden, Birch, Cook, Bull, Rankine, Thompson
Venus 71 — Ref: R Poulain
Only two sides of the Molineux ground holds supporters as the stadium is being re-developed. Steve Bull is denied the goal which would give him the all-time Wolves scoring record. The goal comes from an unlikely source as Mark Venus strikes from 25 yards to liven up a drab affair.

36 — TRANMERE (H)
Argyle: Wilmot, Hodges, Spearing, Morrison, Marker, Barlow, Regis, Smith, Marshall, Morgan
Tranmere: Nixon, Higgins, Nolan, Harvey, Vickers, Morrissey, Aldridge, Nevin, Muir, Thomas
Morgan 79 — Ref: K Cooper
Wilmot and Morgan, now both on the transfer list, are the heroes. The keeper is unfazed by John Aldridge's stuttering approach and saves his spot-kick (37) after Spearing fouled John Morrisey. Morgan shoots on the turn from the edge of the box. Shilton is away on a scouting mission.

37 — DERBY (A)
Argyle: Wilmot, Hodges, Spearing, Morrison, Marker, Barlow*, Regis, Fiore*, Marshall^, Morgan — Scutt/Nugent
Derby: Sutton, Kavanagh, Williams G, Coleman, Comyn, Johnson, Kitson, Gabbiadini, Williams P*, Simpson, McMinn
Johnson 17, McMinn 73 — Ref: A Flood
Argyle's goal-shy attack fail to test Steve Sutton on his Derby debut. Tommy Johnson avoids Marker's challenge to stab home from six yards. New £200k signing Kevin Nugent is introduced for the final half-hour. Ted McMinn's angled drive makes it an unhappy return for Shilton.

38 — PORT VALE (A)
Argyle: Wilmot, Hodges, Spearing, Lee, Marker, Barlow^, McCall, Nugent, Marshall*, Morgan — Smith/Regis
Port Vale: Grew, Aspin, Hughes, Walker, Swan, Lowe, Van der Laan, Cross*, Foyle, Kent, Allan
Walker 34p — Ref: M Reed
Despite the impressive debuts of Lee and McCall, Argyle slump to defeat against the bottom club. Wilmot, so often the hero, is now the culprit as he fouls David Lowe and Ray Walker's penalty sends him the wrong way. McCall shows why he has played at the top level for so long.

39 — GRIMSBY (H)
Argyle: Wilmot, Hodges, Morgan, Marker, Burrows, Lee, McCall, Nugent, Marshall, Smith
Grimsby: Sherwood, McDermott, Agnew, Lever, Rodger, Cunnington, Ford, Gilbert, Smith, Mendonca, Woods
McCall 61 / Mendonca 16, Woods 76 — Ref: R Hamer
Defensive errors again prove crucial. Smith's pass gets stuck in the mud and Clive Mendonca runs 50 yards to round Wilmot. Poor marking leads to Neil Woods second. McCall's curling shot eludes Sherwood. Nugent will miss the rest of the season with a broken bone in his foot.

40 — CHARLTON (A)
Argyle: Shilton, Hodges, Morgan, Morrison, Marker, Lee*, McCall*, Regis, Marshall, Fiore
Charlton: Bolder, Pitcher, Minto, Webster, Balmer, Lee*, Bumstead, Leaburn, Whyte, Walsh, Barness
Ref: A Smith
With Charlton homeless, the match is played at Upton Park. Shilton selects himself and inspires a fine defensive performance. The 42 year old pulls off two agile saves. McCall goes off injured and leaves Argyle bereft of attacking ideas. Marshall hits the bar but lack of goals is a worry.

41 — SOUTHEND (H)
Argyle: Shilton, Hodges*, Morgan, Morrison, Marker, Burrows, McCall, Regis, Marshall, Smith*
Southend: Sansome, Austin, Powell, Jones, Scully, Prior, Ansah, Cornwell, Tilson, Benjamin, Angell
Marker 17(og), Benjamin 75 — Ref: D Gallagher
Argyle hit rock bottom as they crash to defeat. Marker gets to Andy Ansah's fierce cross first but only succeeds in turning the ball past his own keeper. Burrows' acrobatic header hits the crossbar. Skipper Ian Benjamin's perfectly placed header stuns the crowd into silence.

42 — SUNDERLAND (A)
Argyle: Shilton, Cross, Morgan, Morrison, Marker, Burrows, McCall, Evans, Marshall, Smith
Sunderland: Norman, Kay, Rogan, Bennett, Hardyman^, Rush, Mooney, Goodman, Armstrong, Byrne*, Atkinson — Davenport/Owers
Marshall 67 — Ref: A Bennett
Shilton's decision to draft in Cross and Evans pays dividends as the Pilgrims score their first ever victory at Roker Park. Morgan crashes a shot against the crossbar. Twenty-one year old striker John Byrne is shackled by Morrison. Marshall scores the all-important goal from a pass by Evans.

43 — MIDDLESBROUGH (A)
Argyle: Shilton, Cross, Morgan, Morrison, Marker, Fiore, Lee, Hodges !, Evans, Marshall*, Smith
Middlesbrough: Pears, Fleming, Phillips, Mohan, Proctor, Hendrie*, Falconer, Wilkinson, Payton, Ripley* — Slaven/Parkinson
Marshall 27 / Ripley 28, Falconer 66 — Ref: N Midgeley
A Marshall goal gives Argyle hopes of a north-east double but Stuart Ripley equalises within a minute. Referee Midgeley is forced to retire at half-time with a calf injury. Hodges saves a goal-bound shot with his hand and is sent off (77). Shilton saves the resultant penalty from Payton.

44 — OXFORD (H)
Argyle: Shilton, Cross, Morgan, Morrison, Marker, Fiore, Lee, Evans, Marshall*, Smith — Pickard
Oxford: Veysey, Smart, Penney, Lewis, Evans, Melville, Magilton !, Beauchamp, Aylott, Bannister, Allen* — Durnin
Morrison 16, Marker 27, Lee 51 / Bannister 25 — Ref: A Ward
Argyle give themselves a lifeline and need one more win. Morrison's powerful header opens the scoring. Marker soon cancels out Bannister's response. Lee's first goal for the club clinches it. Magilton incenses manager Brian Horton by getting himself sent off for foul language (55).

45 — SWINDON (A)
Argyle: Shilton, Cross, Morgan^, Morrison, Marker, Garner*, Lee, Evans, Fiore, Smith
Swindon: Digby, Kerslake, Badin, Jones^, Calderwood, Taylor, Hazard, Gibson, Ling, Hoddle, Mitchell* — Close/Waddock
Taylor 26 — Ref: S Lodge
The hand of fate deals several blows to Shilton. Leading scorer Marshall is injured and Morgan pulls a hamstring to force playmaker McCall into the left-back slot. Plymouth born Shaun Taylor is voted Swindon's player of the year before the match and celebrates with a headed goal.

46 — BLACKBURN (H)
Argyle: Shilton, Cross, Morgan, Morrison, Marker, Garner, Lee, Evans^, Marshall*, Smith — Fiore/Nugent
Blackburn: Mimms, Brown, Wright, Cowans, Moran, Hendry, Wilcox^, Atkins, Speedie*, Newell, Sellars — Richardson/Price
Smith 12 / Speedie 41, 44, 67 — Ref: K Burge
Kick-off is delayed for 15 minutes to allow everyone in. Smith gives Argyle hope with an early goal but Kenny Dalglish's expensively assembled side keep their play-off hopes alive. David Speedie gives a demonstration of lethal finishing to condemn the Pilgrims to relegation.

Home 6,739
Away 9,772
Average 9,772

BARCLAYS DIVISION 2 (CUP-TIES)

Manager: Kemp > Gillett & Nisbet > Shilton   **SEASON 1991-92**

Rumbelows Cup

		Att		F-A	H-T	Scorers, Times, and Referees	1	2	3	4	5	6	7	8	9	10	11	subs used
1:1 A	SHREWSBURY 20/8	2,152 3:	D	1-1	0-1	Morrison 84	Wilmot	Salman	Spearing	Marker	Cross	Morgan	Barlow	Marshall	Turner	Morrison	Fiore*	Clement
						Summerfield 7	*Hughes*	*Gorman*	*Lynch*	*Henry*	*Heathcote*	*Blake*	*Smith*	*Summerfield*	*Spink*	*Hopkins*	*Lyne*	
						Ref: P Danson												

Argyle protest bitterly about Kevin Summerfield's opener. Mick Heathcote's header is saved by Wilmot but the former Argyle man, now the Shrews skipper, appears to knock the ball from the keeper's grasp. Morrison sends a rasping volley past Hughes from a half-cleared corner.

		Att		F-A	H-T	Scorers, Times, and Referees	1	2	3	4	5	6	7	8	9	10	11	subs used
1:2 H	SHREWSBURY 27/8	3,580 3:6	D	2-2 aet	1-0	Barlow 23, Turner 59,	Wilmot	Salman*	Spearing	Marker	Cross	Morgan	Barlow	Marshall	Turner I	Morrison	Fiore^	Clement/Scott
						Summerfield 57, Carr 85	*Hughes*	*Gorman*	*Lynch*	*Henry*	*Heathcote*	*Blake**	*Smith*	*Summerfield*	*Spink*	*Hopkins^*	*Lyne*	*Carr/Griffiths*
						Ref: D Frampton												
						(Argyle lost on away goals)												

Marker does his burgeoning reputation no harm by setting up Barlow with a superb run out of defence. Summerfield turns back time with a well-taken goal. Turner's header looks to have won it but Carr sends the match into overtime. Turner is dismissed (95) for elbowing Griffiths.

FA Cup

		Att		F-A	H-T	Scorers, Times, and Referees	1	2	3	4	5	6	7	8	9	10	11	subs used
3 A	BRISTOL ROV 5/1	6,767 21	L	0-5	0-2	*Alexander 36, Saunders 42, 51, 60, 70 Parkin*	Wilmot	Spearing	Salman*	Burrows	Morrison	Morgan	Barlow	Marshall	Regis	Fiore	Turner	Edworthy
						Ref: D Elleray	*Alexander*	*Alexander*	*Twent'man**	*Yates*	*Madison*	*Skinner*	*Cross*	*Reece*	*Browning*	*Saunders*	*Stewart*	*Pounder*

Kemp labels some of his players as 'brainless' after a disaster at Twerton Park. Ian Alexander heads through Wilmot's legs. Carl Saunders then slots home every chance he gets. The pain of the defeat is only exacerbated when the fourth round draw matches Rovers with Liverpool.

Plymouth Argyle — Season Statistics

Final League Table (Division Two)

Pos	Team	P	Home W	D	L	F	A	Away W	D	L	F	A	Pts
1	Ipswich	46	16	3	4	42	22	8	9	6	28	28	84
2	Middlesbro	46	15	6	2	37	13	8	5	10	21	28	80
3	Derby	46	11	4	8	35	24	12	5	6	34	27	78
4	Leicester	46	14	4	5	41	24	9	4	10	21	31	77
5	Cambridge	46	14	9	0	34	19	9	8	6	31	28	74
6	Blackburn*	46	14	5	4	41	21	7	6	10	29	32	74
7	Charlton	46	9	7	7	25	23	11	4	8	29	25	71
8	Swindon	46	15	3	5	38	22	3	12	8	31	33	69
9	Portsmouth	46	15	6	2	41	12	4	6	13	24	39	69
10	Watford	46	9	6	8	25	23	6	8	8	26	25	65
11	Wolves	46	11	6	6	36	24	7	4	12	25	30	64
12	Southend	46	11	5	7	37	26	6	11	6	26	37	62
13	Bristol Rov	46	11	9	3	43	29	5	5	13	17	34	62
14	Tranmere	46	9	9	5	37	32	9	5	10	19	24	61
15	Millwall	46	10	4	9	32	32	7	6	10	32	39	61
16	Barnsley	46	11	4	8	27	25	5	7	11	19	32	59
17	Bristol City	46	10	8	5	30	24	5	3	7	25	47	54
18	Sunderland	46	10	8	5	36	23	4	3	16	25	42	53
19	Grimsby	46	7	5	11	36	28	7	6	10	22	34	53
20	Newcastle	46	9	8	6	38	30	4	5	14	28	54	52
21	Oxford	46	10	6	7	39	30	3	5	15	27	43	50
22	PLYMOUTH	46	11	5	7	26	26	2	4	17	16	38	48
23	Brighton	46	7	7	9	36	37	5	4	14	20	40	47
24	Port Vale	46	7	8	8	23	25	3	7	13	19	34	45
		1104	262	144	144	824	594	146	144	262	594	824	1512

* promoted after play-offs

Appearances and Goals

Player	Lge	Sub	LC	Sub	FAC	Sub	Goals Lge	LC	FAC	Tot
Barlow, Martin	23	5	2		1		3		1	4
Burrows, Adrian	14	1	1		1		3			3
Clement, Andy	20	6			2					
Cross, Ryan	12		2							
Damerell, Mark		1				1				
Edworthy, Marc	7	8	1		1					
Evans, Michael	11	2								
Fiore, Mark	25	7	2		1		4			4
Garner, Darren	8	2								
Hodges, Kevin	11	3								
Hopkins, Jeff	8									
Jones, Steve		1								
Lee, David	9									
Marker, Nicky	44		2				1			1
Marshall, Dwight	44	2	2		1		14			14
McCall, Steve	9									
Meaker, Michael	4									
Morgan, Steve	45		2		1		2			2
Morrison, Andy	29	1	2		1		3		1	4
Nugent, Kevin	2	1								
Pickard, Owen	2	2								
Quamina, Mark	4	1								
Regis, Dave	21	3	1		1		2			2
Salman, Danis	26	2	2		2		1			1
Scott, Morrys	3	3				1				
Shilton, Peter	7									
Smith, David	14	4					2			2
Spearing, Tony	30		2		1					
Turner, Robbie	25		2		1		3		1	4
Van Rossum, Erik	9									
Walter, Dave	5									
Wilmot, Rhys	34		2		1					
Witter, Tony	3						1			1
(own-goals)							1			1
33 players used	506	54	22	3	11	1	42		3	45

Odds & ends

Double wins: (2) Barnsley, Sunderland.

Double defeats: (5) Blackburn, Grimsby, Southend, Swindon, Watford.

Won from behind: (0).

Lost from in front: (4) Blackburn, Middlesbrough, Millwall, Oxford.

High spots: Shock appointment of Peter Shilton as manager.
Tremendous support in vital final match of season.
Discovery of Dwight Marshall from non-league football.

Low spots: Losing final league match and failing to avoid relegation.
Worst away record in the division.
Averaging less than a goal a game.
Heavy FA Cup defeat at Bristol Rov.
Lack of impact from big-money signings, Regis and Smith.

Player of the Year: Dwight Marshall.
Ever presents: (0).
Hat-tricks: (1) Dwight Marshall.
Leading scorer: Dwight Marshall (14).

BARCLAYS DIVISION 2 (New style)

Manager: Peter Shilton

SEASON 1992-93

---

1. A MANSFIELD — 15/8 · Att 4,166 · D · Pt 1 · F-A 0-0 · H-T 0-0
Ref: T Holbrook

	1	2	3	4	5	6	7	8	9	10	11	subs used
Argyle	Shilton	Poole	McCall	Burrows	Marker	Morrison	Joyce	Garner^	Nugent	Marshall	Evans*	Hodges, K/Fiore
Mansfield	*Pearcey*	*Parkin*	*Charles*	*Spooner*	*Gray*	*Holland*	*Ford*	*Fairclough*	*Stant*	*Wilkinson**	*Withe*	*McLoughlin*

The inclusion of experienced new signings give the Argyle side a more solid look and Shilton feels aggrieved that the new campaign does not start with a win. Joyce has a good opportunity to mark his debut spectacularly but he delays his shot. Poole also has an impressive first match.

---

2. H BRADFORD C — 22/8 · Att 6,504 · Pos 13 · W · Pt 4 · F-A 3-0 · H-T 1-0
Scorers: Poole 14, Skinner 49, Marshall 75 · Ref: J Carter

	1	2	3	4	5	6	7	8	9	10	11	subs used
Argyle	Shilton	Poole	McCall	Morrison	Burrows	Marker	Joyce	Skinner	Nugent	Marshall	Evans	Partridge/Margerison
Bradford C	*Pearce*	*Duxbury M^*	*Richards*	*Duxbury L*	*Blake*	*Oliver*	*Jewell**	*McCarthy*	*Torney*	*Tinnion*	*Reid*	

Argyle play with a style that has not been seen at Home Park for a long time. Poole's shot from wide on the right is caught on the wind and catches out Chris Pearce. The on-loan Skinner caps a lively debut with an 18-yard shot. Marshall opens his account with an angled drive.

---

3. A HULL — 28/8 · Att 4,194 · L · Pt 4 · F-A 0-2 · H-T 0-0
Scorers: Hockaday 79, Lund 87 · Ref: P Harrison

	1	2	3	4	5	6	7	8	9	10	11	subs used
Argyle	Shilton !	Poole	Spearing	Morrison	Burrows	Marker	Skinner	Joyce	Nugent^	Marshall	McCall*	Garner/Evans, France/Allison
Hull	*Fettis*	*Hockaday*	*Heard*	*Mail*	*Hobson**	*Warren*	*Norton*	*Atkinson*	*Lund*	*Windass*	*Jenkinson^*	

Shilton is sent off (26) for the first time in his long career when he brings down Graeme Atkinson in the box when the striker through on goal. Marker takes over and immediately saves Leigh Jenkinson's penalty. The defence protect Marker admirably until two late goals seal the points.

---

4. H LEYTON ORIENT — 5/9 · Att 7,319 · Pos 6 · W · Pt 7 · F-A 2-0 · H-T 1-0
Scorers: Marker 16, Adcock 85 · Ref: K Cooper

	1	2	3	4	5	6	7	8	9	10	11	subs used
Argyle	Shilton	Poole	Morgan S	Morrison	Walker	Marker	Skinner	Joyce	Nugent	Marshall^	McCall	Adcock, Kitchen/Tomlinson
Leyton Orient	*Turner*	*Zoricich*	*Howard*	*Hales*	*Day**	*Whitbread*	*Achampong*	*Livett*	*Jones*	*Taylor*	*Ludden^*	

Alan Walker arrives on a monthly contract. Marker blasts a half-volley past Chris Turner. Adcock comes on to score his first senior goal. Orient manager Peter Eustace's enthusiasm lands him in trouble as he regularly breaches the new guideline that coaches must remain seated.

---

5. H STOKE — 12/9 · Att 8,208 · Pos 16 · D · Pt 8 · F-A 1-1 · H-T 0-1
Scorers: Walker 83; Stein 34 · Ref: K Cooper

	1	2	3	4	5	6	7	8	9	10	11	subs used
Argyle	Kite	Poole	Morgan S	Morrison	Walker	Marker	Skinner	McCall	Nugent*	Marshall	Evans^	Adcock
Stoke	*Sinclair*	*Butler*	*Harbey*	*Cranson*	*Overson*	*Foley*	*Ware*	*Stein*	*Biggins**	*Russell*	*Kelly*	

Phil Kite arrives on loan from Sheffield Utd to replace the suspended Shilton. The dangerous Mark Stein nips in to claim his sixth goal of the season. Argyle step up their attacking efforts and are rewarded with Walker's header. Lou Macari admits his side are happy with a point.

---

6. A HUDDERSFIELD — 15/9 · Att 4,411 · L · Pt 8 · F-A 1-2 · H-T 1-1
Scorers: Marker 30; Jackson 23, Roberts 52 · Ref: P Jones

	1	2	3	4	5	6	7	8	9	10	11	subs used
Argyle	Kite	Poole	Morgan S	Edworthy	Morrison	Marker	Skinner	Regis	Nugent*	Marshall	McCall	Adcock
Huddersfield	*Elliott*	*Parsley*	*Charlton*	*Donovan*	*Dyson*	*Jackson*	*Barnett*	*Robinson*	*Roberts*	*Lampkin*	*Onuora*	

Regis returns from a month's loan at Bournemouth but Walker has departed. The Terriers gain their first points of the season as Argyle again flatter to deceive away from Home Park. Peter Jackson scores from close range. Marker strikes from 20 yards. Iwan Roberts hits the winner.

---

7. A FULHAM — 19/9 · Att 5,439 · Pos 18 · L · Pt 8 · F-A 1-3 · H-T 0-0
Scorers: Adcock 83; Brazil 48, 75, Nebbeling 65 · Ref: G Poll

	1	2	3	4	5	6	7	8	9	10	11	subs used
Argyle	Shilton	Poole I	Morgan S	Edworthy	Marker	McCall	Skinner^	Adcock	Marshall	Regis*	Joyce	Marshall/Barlow
Fulham	*Stannard*	*Morgan*	*Pike*	*Ferney*	*Nebbeling*	*Thomas*	*Hails*	*Marshall*	*Farrell*	*Brazil*	*Kelly*	

Argyle's bright start to the season seems a distant memory as they suffer another away defeat and another red card. Poole is harshly dismissed for a second caution (35). Gary Brazil scores twice and Gavin Nebbeling finishes off some good work by Hails. Adcock justifies his inclusion.

---

8. H BOLTON — 26/9 · Att 6,829 · Pos 15 · W · Pt 11 · F-A 2-0 · H-T 2-0
Scorers: Regis 6, Nugent 18; Darby 88 · Ref: R Hamer

	1	2	3	4	5	6	7	8	9	10	11	subs used
Argyle	Shilton	Poole	Morgan S*	Hill	Morrison	Barlow	Skinner	Joyce	Nugent	Regis	McCall	Edworthy
Bolton	*Branagan*	*Brown*	*Burke*	*Kelly**	*Came**	*Winstanley*	*Green*	*Stubbs*	*Walker*	*Phillistirk*	*Patterson*	*Darby/Fisher*

Two goals is little reward for Argyle's stunning first-half performance. The revitalised Regis strikes again and Nugent opens his Pilgrims' account. Julian Darby gets a late consolation. John McGovern undertakes the press conference to talk about beating the club who sacked him.

---

9. A BURNLEY — 29/9 · Att 8,676 · D · Pt 12 · F-A 0-0 · H-T 0-0
Ref: J Kirkby

	1	2	3	4	5	6	7	8	9	10	11	subs used
Argyle	Shilton	Edworthy	Spearing	Hill	Morrison	Poole	Skinner	Joyce	Nugent	Regis	McCall	
Burnley	*Beresford*	*Measham*	*Jakub*	*Davis*	*Pender*	*Randall*	*Mooney*	*Farrell*	*Heath*	*Conroy*	*Harper*	

The goalless scoreline is a tribute to the ability of both goalkeepers. Forty-three year old Shilton shows he is still up there with the best and the promising young Marlon Beresford does his growing reputation no harm. Adrian Heath looks the most likely scorer and needs careful marking.

---

10. A PRESTON — 3/10 · Att 4,401 · Pos 10 · W · Pt 15 · F-A 2-1 · H-T 2-1
Scorers: Joyce 26, Regis 34; Davidson 36 · Ref: R Nixon

	1	2	3	4	5	6	7	8	9	10	11	subs used
Argyle	Shilton	Edworthy	Spearing	Hill	Morrison	Garner	Skinner	Joyce	Nugent	Regis	McCall	
Preston	*Farnworth*	*Davidson*	*Fowler L*	*Tinkler*	*Flynn*	*Callaghan*	*Ashcroft*	*Cartwright*	*Leonard*	*Ellis*	*James*	

Argyle finally gain an away win on the Deepdale plastic. Joyce, captain for the day in the absence of the suspended Poole, scores against his former club and then sets up Regis. Shilton's former Derby colleague, Jon Davidson, replies with the keeper unsighted but Argyle hang on.

---

11. H CHESTER — 10/10 · Att 7,182 · Pos 8 · W · Pt 18 · F-A 2-0 · H-T 1-0
Scorers: Poole 32p, 74p · Ref: R Groves

	1	2	3	4	5	6	7	8	9	10	11	subs used
Argyle	Shilton	Edworthy	Spearing	Hill	Morrison	Poole	Skinner	Joyce	Adcock	Regis*	Barlow^	Marshall/Dalton
Chester	*Stewart*	*Preece*	*Whelan*	*Butler*	*Abel*	*Garnett*	*Thompson*	*Barrow*	*Rimmer*	*Bishop*	*Kelly*	

The absence of McCall and Nugent ensures that no one will claim an ever-present record this season. Penalty king Poole scores twice from the spot. Garnett's trip on Joyce leads to the first award. Poole sends his second penalty into the opposite corner after Marshall is felled by Abel.

17/10 — 6,584 · 8 · 18 · Sandeman 14, Glover 37, Taylor 56 · Ref: T Fitzharris

Musselwhite | Sandeman | Sulley | Walker | Swan | Glover | Taylor | Aspin | Cross | Houchen | Kerr

Argyle's traditional nightmare at Vale Park strikes again. Dalton makes his long awaited first full appearance after a lengthy injury. Vale punish defensive lapses. Shilton has little chance with any of the goals, in particular, Ian Taylor's who lashes home a shot from close range.

---

13 · H · WIGAN · 24/10 — W 2-0 · HT 2-0 · 8 · 20 21 · 5,967 · Joyce 36, Castle 45 · Ref: P Durkin

Argyle: Shilton, Spearing, Edworthy, Castle, Poole, Morrison, Joyce, Nugent, Marshall, Dalton, Barlow — Worthington* Griffiths^, Pilling/Powell
Wigan (italic): Adkins, Makin, Parkinson, Robertson, Jones, Appleton, Langley, Daley

Regis moves to Stoke. Joyce opens the scoring after Nigel Adkins fails to hold Marshall's shot. Castle marks his delayed debut with a header on the stroke of half-time. Steve Appleton hits the post in the second half but Wigan look less of a threat after they replace Bryan Griffiths.

---

14 · A · READING · 31/10 — L 0-3 · HT 0-1 · 11 · 12 21 · 5,088 · Jones 34, Quinn 50, McPherson 66 · Ref: A Ward

Argyle: Shilton, Edworthy, Castle, Poole, Morrison, Joyce, Nugent, Marshall, Dalton
Reading (italic): Hislop, Gooding, Hopkins, McPherson, Richardson, Taylor, Quinn, Dillon, Jones, McGhee*, Lambert

Argyle's Jekyll and Hyde form continues. Shaka Hislop's legs save Reading after Marshall breaks free. Tom Jones finishes a superb four-man move with a 20-yard shot. Jimmy Quinn is given too much space. Gilkes misses an open goal. Shilton fails to hold Dillon's corner for the third.

---

15 · A · SWANSEA · 3/11 — D 0-0 · 22 · 5,430 · Ref: G Ashby

Argyle: Shilton, Poole, Edworthy, Castle, Hodges K, Morrison, Joyce, Nugent, Marshall, Turner
Swansea (italic): Freestone, Lyttle, Walker*, Ford, Harris, Coughlin, Cullen, West, Comforth, Legg, Jenkins

Shilton opts for experience by recalling Hodges and welcomes back Turner after an eight-month absence. Russell Coughlin shows that he has lost none of his passing ability and he comes closest to scoring from 35 yards. Hodges has an unconvincing appeal for a penalty turned down.

---

16 · H · ROTHERHAM · 7/11 — W 2-1 · HT 1-0 · 10 · 8 25 · 6,519 · Hutchings 44(og), Nugent 56 · Currie 51 · Ref: R Milford

Argyle: Shilton, Poole, Morrison, Castle, Hodges K*, Joyce, Nugent, Marshall, Turner — Skinner/Richardson
Rotherham (italic): Mercer, Pickering, Hutchings, Banks, Johnson, Law, Hazel, Todd*, Cunningham, Currie, Barrick

Phil Henson's side prove a tough nut to crack. Morgan's cross is chested down by Chris Hutchings but the ball trickles over the line. David Currie belts the ball away in frustration and is booked. Currie levels with a great left foot shot. Nugent wins it after good work by Skinner.

---

17 · A · STOCKPORT · 20/11 — L 0-3 · HT 0-0 · 12 · 4 25 · 5,377 · Francis 49, 57, Preece 84 · Ref: T West

Argyle: Newland, Poole, Dryden, Castle, Morgan S, Morrison*, Nugent, Marshall, Turner — Hodges K/Matthews
Stockport (italic): Redfern, Williams P* Frain, Todd, Barras, Williams B, Ward, Gannon, Francis, Beaumont, Preece

Dryden arrives from Exeter on loan with Turner making the opposite journey. The defence have no answer to giant striker Kevin Francis who takes his goal tally to 14. Morrison goes off with a cut eye. Dryden clears off the line. Andy Preece sweeps home the third after a Francis run.

---

18 · H · BOURNEMOUTH · 28/11 — W 2-1 · HT 1-0 · 9 · 18 28 · 6,408 · Boardman 21, Nugent 58 · Burrows 77(og) · Ref: J Martin

Argyle: Newland, Dryden, Poole, Castle, Morgan S, Garner, Nugent, Marshall, Boardman — Mundee/Murray
Bournemouth (italic): Bartram, Pennock, Morrell, Morris, Watson, McGorry, Wood, O'Driscoll, Lovell*, Morgan, Rowland^

Comedian Stan Boardman's son Paul is given his chance after scoring twelve times for the reserves this season and responds with a shot from three yards. Argyle look to be coasting after Nugent's goal but Burrows puts Tony Pulis's side back in it when he heads past his own keeper.

---

19 · H · HARTLEPOOL · 12/12 — D 2-2 · HT 2-1 · 11 · 7 29 · 5,996 · Nugent 12, Castle 20 · Johnrose 30, Saville 60 · Ref: M Pierce

Argyle: Newland, Hodge, Morgan S, Castle, Barlow, Garner, Nugent, Marshall, Dalton
Hartlepool (italic): Hodge, Cross R, Cross P, McGuckin, Emerson, MacPhail, Johnrose, Olson, Saville, Honour, Johnson

The visitors fly to Plymouth on the morning of the match but seem to have their heads in the clouds as Nugent pounces for the opener. Martin Hodge lets Castle's 35-yard drive slip through his grasp. Lenny Johnrose pulls one back. A one-two creates an easy chance for Andy Saville.

---

20 · A · BRIGHTON · 19/12 — L 1-2 · HT 0-1 · 12 · 7 29 · 5,872 · Nugent 62 · Nogan 31, Codner 51 · Ref: C Wilkes

Argyle: Newland, Dryden, Poole, Castle, Morgan S, Joyce, Garner^, Marshall, Dalton* — Morgan S/Barlow/Edwards
Brighton (italic): Beeney, Chivers, Chapman, Wilkins, McCarthy, Bissett, Crumplin, Kennedy*, Nogan, Codner, Walker

Slack marking allows Kurt Nogan to score his first league goal for Albion as Plymouth's away jinx strikes again. Robert Codner is left all alone to stroke home the second. Argyle are finally spurred into action and Nugent scores a splendid goal with a curling shot from 25 yards.

---

21 · A · EXETER · 26/12 — L 0-2 · HT 0-1 · 14 · 15 29 · 6,534 · Whiston 6, Daniels 74 · Ref: R Hamer

Argyle: Shilton, Miller, Hill, Morgan S, Burrows, Joyce, Barlow, Marshall, Castle — Garner*/Adcock
Exeter (italic): Miller, Cook, Tonge, Daniels, Whiston, Bailey, Kelly, Moran, Gallen, Hodge

A frenetic opening sees City lead through Peter Whiston's header and have three efforts disallowed in the first 17 minutes. An unimpressed Alan Ball confronts the referee at half-time. Scott Daniels' second ensures Argyle's 64-year wait for a league win at St James Park continues.

---

22 · H · WEST BROM · 28/12 — D 0-0 · 14 · 2 30 · 11,370 · Ref: K Burge

Argyle: Shilton, Naylor, Edworthy, Dryden, Morrison, Joyce, Skinner^, Castle, Marshall — Morgan S*/Dalton/Barlow, Hackett/Garner
West Brom (italic): Naylor, Reid*, Lilwall, Shakespeare Raven, Stroder, Donovan^, Hamilton, Taylor, McNally, Robson

Dalton drives back from Middlesbrough where he has been visiting his sick mother over Xmas. His appearance for the last 30 minutes almost swings the game. Nugent hits the woodwork with a spectacular volley. Gary Robson goes close for Albion with an ambitious overhead kick.

---

23 · A · BOLTON · 16/1 — L 1-3 · HT 1-3 · 16 · 6 30 · 8,256 · Dalton 26 · Walker 15, S'graves 17, Morrison 41(og) · Ref: J Winter

Argyle: Shilton, McCall, Morgan S, Hill, Joyce, Castle, Marshall, Nugent* — Evans/Barlow, Green*/McGinlay
Bolton (italic): Branagan, Brown, Burke, Lee, Seagraves, Winstanley, Green*, Kelly, Walker, Patterson, Stubbs

Wanderers are still on a high after a shock 2-0 FA Cup win at Anfield in midweek. Nineteen-goal Andy Walker gives them the lead and Mark Seagraves adds a second after McGinlay's shot rebounds from a post. Dalton scores a dazzling solo goal. Morrison deflects a shot past Shilton.

BARCLAYS DIVISION 2 (New style)   Manager: Peter Shilton   SEASON 1992-93

Positions key: 1–11 = team line-up (Argyle plain / opponent *italic*); symbols ^ and * denote substituted players, ! denotes dismissal/caution.

---

24. H FULHAM — 23/1
Att 5,703 · Pos 14 / 11 · D · 31 pts · F-A 1-1 · H-T 0-0
Scorers, Times and Referees: Castle 79p / *Morgan 88*. Ref: K Cooper

	1	2	3	4	5	6	7	8	9	10	11	subs used
Argyle	Shilton	McCall	Morgan S	Hill	Morrison	Garner	Marshall	Castle	Nugent	Evans	Dalton	
Fulham	*Stannard*	*Morgan*	*Pike*	*Newson*	*Nebbeling*	*Thomas**	*Hails*	*Marshall*	*Eckhardt*	*Brazil*	*Onwere^*	*Ferney / Farrell*

The Home Park groundstaff work overtime to make the pitch playable after heavy rain. Jim Stannard is the Cottagers' saviour on more than one occasion but is unable to stop Castle's powerfully struck penalty after Marshall was fouled by Nebbeling. Simon Morgan levels with a header.

---

25. H HULL — 26/1
Att 4,612 · D · 32 pts · F-A 0-0 · H-T 0-0
Ref: R Milford

	1	2	3	4	5	6	7	8	9	10	11	subs used
Argyle	Shilton	McCall	Morgan S	Hill	Morrison	Joyce	Marshall	Castle	Nugent*	Evans	Dalton	Adcock
Hull	*Wilson*	*Hockaday*	*Hobson*	*Mail*	*Wilcox*	*Abbott*	*Norton*	*Atkinson*	*Caruthers*	*Windass*	*Lund*	

The fans' discontent with Argyle's recent slide begins to surface as a grim display is met with jeers and slow handclapping by the end. Chances are few and far between with Dalton trying his luck with a 35-yard free-kick and Atkinson almost takes advantage of a poor Shilton clearance.

---

26. A BRADFORD C — 30/1
Att 5,528 · Pos 15 / 7 · D · 33 pts · F-A 0-0 · H-T 0-0
Ref: T Lunt

	1	2	3	4	5	6	7	8	9	10	11	subs used
Argyle	Shilton	McCall	Morgan S	Hill	Morrison	Burrows	Joyce	Castle	Nugent*	Marshall	Dalton	
Bradford C	*Whitehead*	*Jenkins*	*Heseltine*	*Duxbury L*	*Blake*	*Oliver*	*Jewell*	*Duxbury M*	*McHugh*	*Tinnion**	*Reid*	*Torpey*

The Bantams' third scoreless draw in a row means the Valley Parade faithful have yet to witness a goal in 1993. Twenty-one goal striker Sean McCarthy is missing through injury. Dalton twice goes close with Noel Blake clearing off the line and Phil Whitehead saving with his legs.

---

27. H MANSFIELD — 6/2
Att 4,630 · Pos 15 / 22 · W · 36 pts · F-A 3-2 · H-T 0-1
Scorers: Nugent 49, 55, 69 / *Wilkinson 4, 56*. Ref: P Scoble

	1	2	3	4	5	6	7	8	9	10	11	subs used
Argyle	Newland	Poole	Morgan S	Hill	Morrison	Joyce	Edworthy	Castle	Nugent	Marshall*	Dalton	Crocker
Mansfield	*Pearcey*	*Peer*	*Withe*	*Foster^*	*Walker**	*Fairclough*	*Stringfellow*	*Holland*	*Wilkinson*	*Castledine*	*Charles*	*Gray / Noteman*

The board give Shilton a vote of confidence. Newland replaces the injured manager and is immediately involved in a mix-up with Dalton to present Steve Wilkinson with an open goal. Nugent suddenly finds his scoring boots with a superb hat-trick with McCall the main creator.

---

28. A LEYTON ORIENT — 13/2
Att 5,804 · Pos 15 / 4 · L · 36 pts · F-A 0-2 · H-T 0-1
Scorers: *Achampong 9, Otto 82*. Ref: G Pooley

	1	2	3	4	5	6	7	8	9	10	11	subs used
Argyle	Newland	Poole	Morgan S	Hill	Morrison	Joyce	Edworthy	Castle*	Nugent	McCall	Dalton	Crocker
Leyton Orient	*Heald*	*Bellamy*	*Howard*	*Carter*	*Whitbread*	*Ludden*	*Warren**	*Achampong^*	*Ryan*	*Otto*	*Cooper*	*Hackett / Okai*

Another error by Newland gifts Orient the lead. He remains rooted to his line as Kenny Achampong stabs in from close range. He atones later with a penalty save as Adrian Whitbread misses O's third spot-kick in a row after McCall handles. Ricky Otto rounds Newland to clinch it.

---

29. H BURNLEY — 20/2
Att 5,905 · Pos 16 / 7 · L · 36 pts · F-A 1-2 · H-T 1-1
Scorers: Nugent 23 / *Pender 4, 84*. Ref: J Carter

	1	2	3	4	5	6	7	8	9	10	11	subs used
Argyle	Newland	Poole	Morgan S	Hill	Burrows	Morrison	Edworthy	Castle	Nugent	Crocker*	Dalton	Barlow
Burnley	*Beresford*	*Monington*	*Wilson*	*Davis*	*Pender*	*Deary*	*Harper*	*Farrell*	*Heath*	*Conroy*	*Slawson**	*Painter*

Argyle's 18-match unbeaten home run comes to an end. Slack marking allows John Pender to rise unchallenged and head home John Deary's corner. Nugent replies. Poole misses a penalty (64) as Marlon Beresford saves after bringing down Nugent. Pender connects with a half-volley.

---

30. A CHESTER — 27/2
Att 2,163 · Pos 15 / 23 · W · 39 pts · F-A 2-1 · H-T 0-0
Scorers: Butler 48(og), Hodges L 48 / *Rimmer 61*. Ref: B Coddington

	1	2	3	4	5	6	7	8	9	10	11	subs used
Argyle	Newland	Poole	Morgan S	Hill !	Morrison	Burrows	McCall	Castle	Nugent	Hodges L	Dalton	
Chester	*Stewart*	*Preece**	*Allbiston*	*Butler*	*Abel*	*Kelly*	*Thompson^*	*Wheeler*	*Rimmer*	*Bishop*	*Pugh*	*Comstive / Morton*

Argyle's first visit to the new Deva Stadium brings a rare away win. Stewart looks poised to gather Castle's header until the ball strikes Barry Butler. Just 39 seconds later, on-loan Lee Hodges celebrates his league debut with a goal. Hill, already booked, is sent off (88) for encroaching.

---

31. H PRESTON — 6/3
Att 5,201 · Pos 15 / 19 · W · 42 pts · F-A 4-0 · H-T 3-0
Scorers: Hodges L 14, Leonard 22(og), Castle 32, [Evans 87]. Ref: K Cooper

	1	2	3	4	5	6	7	8	9	10	11	subs used
Argyle	Newland	Poole	Morgan S	Hill	Morrison	McCall	Barlow	Castle	Nugent	Hodges L^	Dalton*	Joyce / Evans
Preston	*Johnstone*	*Ainsworth*	*Lucas*	*Fowler J*	*Flynn^*	*Greenall*	*Whalley*	*Cartwright**	*Norbury*	*Leonard*	*Ashcroft*	*Callaghan / James*

A spectacular overhead kick by Hodges sets Argyle up for a convincing win. Mark Leonard's attempted clearance loops over Glenn Johnstone. Castle's header prompts John Beck to use both his subs by the 40th minute. Evans joins the goal spree when he pounces on a loose clearance.

---

32. H BLACKPOOL — 9/3
Att 5,959 · Pos 11 / 21 · W · 45 pts · F-A 2-1 · H-T 1-0
Scorers: Poole 41p, Castle 69 / *Bamber 70*. Ref: D Frampton

	1	2	3	4	5	6	7	8	9	10	11	subs used
Argyle	Newland	Poole	Morgan S	Hill	Morrison !	McCall	Barlow	Castle	Nugent	Hodges L*	Dalton	Evans
Blackpool	*Dickins*	*Davies**	*Thornber*	*Horner*	*Briggs*	*Gore*	*Mitchell*	*Sinclair*	*Bamber*	*Gouck^*	*Eyres*	*Murphy / Bonner*

Argyle survive the early dismissal of Morrison (19) whose bad foul on Andy Gouck leaves the Pool player needing five stitches in a knee wound. Poole slots home his fourth penalty of the season when Steve Thornber trips Dalton. Castle and Dave Bamber both score with headers.

---

33. A ROTHERHAM — 13/3
Att 4,276 · Pos 13 / 9 · D · 46 pts · F-A 2-2 · H-T 1-1
Scorers: Dalton 9, Nugent 79 / *Morrison 4(og), Wilder 82p*. Ref: A Dawson

	1	2	3	4	5	6	7	8	9	10	11	subs used
Argyle	Newland	Poole	Morgan S	Hill	Morrison	Burrows	Barlow	Castle	Nugent	Hodges L	Dalton*	Evans
Rotherham	*Clarke*	*Pickering*	*Wilder*	*Banks**	*Law*	*Gridelet*	*Hazel*	*Buckley**	*Flounders*	*Varadi*	*Barrick*	*Richardson / Howard*

Morrison has a personal nightmare. His attempted clearance gives Rotherham the lead and he later concedes a penalty by barging Nicky Law to the ground. He is also cautioned to ensure another suspension. John Buckley is carried off unconscious after a clash of heads with Poole.

---

34. H SWANSEA — 20/3
Att 6,233 · Pos 13 / 10 · L · 46 pts · F-A 0-1 · H-T 0-1
Scorers: *Bowen 27*. Ref: S Dunn

	1	2	3	4	5	6	7	8	9	10	11	subs used
Argyle	Newland	Poole	Morgan S	Hill	Morrison	McCall	Barlow*	Castle	Nugent	Hodges L	Dalton	Evans
Swansea	*Freestone*	*Lyttle*	*Jenkins*	*Walker*	*McMahon*	*Ford*	*Bowen*	*Coughlin*	*Hayes**	*Comforth*	*Legg*	*Wimbleton*

A mistake by Newland proves costly. Steve Jenkins' cross appears to be going out of play but Newland needlessly palms the ball back across his goal leaving Jason Bowen to easily score his seventh goal in four matches. Freestone is booked late on for taking too long over a goal-kick.

Date		Result	Att	Pos	Pld
23/3			4,150	15	49

Bartram Mundee Masters Morrell Watson Pennock Wood Shearer Fletche* Ekoku Rowland Murray

Fletcher 60
Ref: P Taylor

Argyle reward their large following with a fine performance which Shilton ranks as the best since he took over. After going a goal down, the introduction of Evans turns the tide. Within three minutes Plymouth grab the lead through Castle's diving header and Dalton's angled drive.

---

36 27/3 H STOCKPORT 13 L 49 3-4 6,132 3 49

Newland Poole McCall Hill* Burrows Edworthy Barlow Castle Nugent Evans^ Dalton Garner/Hodges L
Kite Connelly Williams P Frain Miller Finley^ Gannon Ward Francis Beaumont Duffield* James/Flynn

Nugent 23, Dalton 37, 54
Williams P 34, Francis 41, 73, 81
Ref: R Hamer

Six foot seven inch Kevin Francis again proves a handful for the Argyle defenders as he takes his season's goal total to a remarkable 34. It all starts so well with Nugent notching his 13th of the season. Dalton seizes on an error by Alan Finley but the play-offs now look out of reach.

---

37 30/3 H HUDDERSFIELD L 49 1-3 4,986 49

Newland Clarke McCall Hill Burrows Morgan S^ Barlow Castle Nugent Evans* Dalton Joyce/Adcock
Parsley Charlton Robinson Cooper Jackson Barnett O'Regan Roberts Onuora Dunn

Dalton 8
Onuora 9, 67, Barnett 77
Ref: P Durkin

Argyle again let an early lead slip. Within a minute of Dalton's goal, Iffy Onuora's shot is dived on by Newland but a linesman rules the ball over the line. Onuora scores another and then Joyce's first touch after coming on sends a clearance straight to Gary Barnett who fires a shot in.

---

38 3/4 A BLACKPOOL 13 D 50 1-1 4,397 20 50

Newland Dickins McCall Hill Burrows Morgan S Joyce Castle Nugent Evans Dalton
Davies Burgess Horner Briggs Gore Leitch Sinclair Bamber Beech Eyres* Cook

Castle 74
Eyres 37
Ref: C Trussell

Morgan plays with a plaster cast on a broken hand. With strong wind and rain in their faces, Argyle go behind to a suspiciously offside David Eyres goal. Castle scores from close range after missing an earlier easy chance. Leitch heads wide in the last minute with the goal at his mercy.

---

39 5/4 A HARTLEPOOL 13 L 50 0-0 1,822 16 50

Newland Hodge McCall Hill Burrows Morgan S Joyce Castle Nugent Evans* Dalton Adcock
Cross R Nobbs Gilchrist MacPhail Emerson* Southall Olsson Gallacher Honour Tait Peverell

Honour 60
Ref: J Key

Hartlepool gain their first win in 21 matches at a bleak, rainswept Victoria Park. Poor finishing lets Argyle off the hook despite some uncertain defending. Brian Honour gets the winner after Morgan dithers over a clearance in his own penalty area. Dalton's late shot skims the crossbar.

---

40 10/4 H EXETER L 50 0-3 9,391 15 50

Newland Miller McCall Hill Morrison Morgan S Joyce^ Castle Nugent Boardman* Dalton Evans/Barlow
White Cook Bailey Daniels Brown Bond Minett Jepson Storer Hodge

Storer 37, Hodge 58, 87
Ref: M Bodenham

Defensive suicide leads to City's biggest ever league win at Home Park. Stuart Storer pounces on indecision between Newland and Hill. Morgan makes a hash of a clearance and John Hodge slides in a shot. Hodge has his boss Alan Ball dancing on the pitch after scoring again.

---

41 12/4 A WEST BROM 14 W 53 5-2 16,130 4 53

Newland Lange McCall Hill Morrison Morgan S Barlow Castle Nugent Evans Dalton
Lilwall Bradley Raven* Burgess Hunt Hamilton Taylor Mellon* Donovan Reid/Heggs

Castle 15, 42, 47, Dalton 71, Barlow 74
Taylor 10, Donovan 83
Ref: E Wolstenholme

Argyle respond superbly to the local derby drubbing. After the unmarked Bob Taylor puts Ossie Ardiles' side onto the lead, Castle takes matters into his own hands. He completes his hat-trick directly from a free-kick after Tony Lange is penalised for handling outside the area.

---

42 17/4 H BRIGHTON W 56 3-2 4,924 7 56

Newland Beeney McCall Hill Morgan S Edworthy Burrows Castle Nugent Evans Dalton
Myall Gallacher Wilkinson Foster Chivers Crumplin^ Byrne Codner Edwards* Farrington/Wilkins

Castle 20, Burrows 29, McCall 67
Nogan 12, 90
Ref: R Groves

Shilton, away in search of another defender, misses an eye-catching display from Edworthy. Kurt Nogan heads Albion the lead. Castle is soon on the goal-trail again. Burrows slams in his first goal for two years. McCall makes it three. Nogan makes it 20 for the season in stoppage time.

---

43 24/4 H PORT VALE 14 L 56 0-1 5,563 2 56

Shilton Musselwhite Aspin McCall Hill Morgan S Barlow Castle Nugent Evans Dalton Crocker
Porter Kent Swan Glover Slaven Van der Laan Cross* Kerr^ Taylor Foyle/Billing

Cross 9
Ref: H King

Linesman Kevin Pike is at the centre of the action. He ignores three offside Port Vale players to allow Nicky Cross to score. He then takes over in the middle after Mr King injured a hamstring. Vale manager John Rudge is highly satisfied with his side's 20th clean sheet of the campaign.

---

44 28/4 A STOKE 15 L 56 0-1 19,718 1 56

Shilton Fox McCall Hill Morgan S Barlow Morgan J Castle Evans Dalton
Butler Sandford Cranson Overson Gleghorn Stein Kevan Foley Shaw^ Ware^ Regis/Russell

Gleghorn 5
Ref: D Elleray

Sixteen-year-old Jamie Morgan makes his debut. Nigel Gleghorn's early strike is enough to give Lou Macari's men the title. Thirty-two goal danger-man Mark Stein is never a threat. The atmosphere becomes more intimidating near the end as Stoke fans gather around the perimeter.

---

45 1/5 A WIGAN 14 W 59 2-0 1,432 23 59

Shilton Adkins McCall Hill Morgan S Barlow Morgan J Joyce Evans Dalton
Doolan Tankard Johnson Piling Langley Skipper White Nugent Sharratt Griffiths

Dalton 45, Morgan S 84
Ref: J Brandwood

In contrast to the euphoria at Stoke, Argyle condemn Wigan to relegation in front of the smallest ever league crowd at Springfield Park. Dalton curls a superb free-kick around the wall on the stroke of half-time. An indirect free-kick inside the area is tapped to S Morgan to blast home.

---

46 8/5 H READING 14 D 60 2-2 5,137 8 60

Newland Francis McCall Hill Edworthy Burrows Barlow Morgan J Nugent Evans Dalton
Holzman Gooding McPherson Williams Parkinson Gilkes Dillon Quinn Lovell* Taylor Lambert

Poole 26p, Joyce 44
Lovell 45, Gilkes 55
Ref: M Pierce

The Royals are unhappy at the penalty decision when Nugent goes tumbling following a slight nudge by Adrian Williams. Joyce levels as Argyle's run of poor home form continues. Stuart Lovell responds within 40 seconds. Michael Gilkes levels as Argyle attempts at hooking the ball in.

Home 6,377
Away 6,080
Average 6,377

BARCLAYS DIVISION 2 (CUP-TIES) Manager: Peter Shilton SEASON 1992-93

Coca-Cola Cup

	Att	F-A	H-T	Scorers, Times, and Referees	1	2	3	4	5	6	7	8	9	10	11	subs used
1:1 A WEST BROM 19/8	8,264 1:	L 0-1	0-1	Taylor 27 / Ref: R Wiseman	Shilton *Naylor*	Poole *Hodson*	Spearing *Liwall*	Morrison *Bradley*	Burrows *Strodder*	Marker *Shakespeare*	Joyce *Garner*	McCall *Hamilton*	Nugent *Taylor**	Marshall *McNally*	Evans *Robson*	*Ampadu*
1:2 H WEST BROM 25/8	7,866 1:1	W 2-0	1-0	Marker 12, Poole 79p / Ref: D Frampton (Argyle won 2-1 on aggregate)	Shilton *Naylor*	Poole *Hodson**	Spearing *Liwall*	Morrison *Bradley*	Burrows *Strodder*	Marker *Shakespeare*	Joyce *Garner*	McCall *Hamilton*	Nugent *Taylor*	Marshall *Raven*	Evans *Robson*	*Coldicott*
2:1 A LUTON 23/9	3,702 1:21	D 2-2	0-1	Regis 50, 70 / Claridge 10, 75 / Ref: A Gunn	Shilton *Petterson*	Poole *Linton*	Morgan S *James*	Hill *Salton**	Morrison *Peake^*	Edworthy *Johnson*	Skinner *Claridge*	Joyce *Kamara*	Nugent *Gray*	Regis *Preece*	McCall *Oakes*	*Rees/Campbell*
2:2 H LUTON 6/10	8,946 1:22	W 3-2	1-0	Nugent 4, Poole 51, Regis 54 / Claridge 61, Preece 69 / Ref: M Bodenham (Argyle won 5-4 on aggregate)	Shilton *Petterson*	Edworthy *Linton*	Spearing *James**	Hill *Salton*	Morrison *Peake^*	Poole *Johnson*	Skinner* *Claridge*	Joyce *Kamara*	Nugent* *Gray*	Regis *Preece*	Garner *Rees*	Adcock *Oakes/Dreyer*
3 H SCARBOROUGH 27/10	8,619 3:5	D 3-3	0-1	Dalton 49, Joyce 80, Nugent 83 / Curran 24, Jules 51, Ashdjian 87 / Ref: R Gifford	Shilton *Evans*	Poole *Thompson*	Spearing *Mudd*	Edworthy *Lee*	Morrison *Hirst*	Castle *Curran*	Skinner* *Ashdjian*	Joyce *Himsworth*	Nugent *Mooney*	Marshall *Foreman*	Dalton *Jules**	Barlow *Wheeler*
3R A SCARBOROUGH 11/11	3,466 3:8	L 1-2	1-0	Dalton 9 / Mooney 55, Mockler 63 / Ref: D Allison	Shilton *Ford*	Poole *Thompson*	Morgan S *Mudd*	Hill *Lee*	Morrison *Hirst*	Joyce *Curran*	Evans* *McGee**	Castle *Himsworth*	Nugent *Mooney*	Marshall^ *Foreman*	Dalton *Wheeler*	Garner/Edworthy *Mockler*

1:1 — Shilton rolls back the years with a series of outstanding saves culminating in turning away Ian Hamilton's spot-kick (89) after a Burrows foul. Bob Taylor outjumps Burrows to head the only goal although only the width of a post denies him a second after good work by Gary Strodder.

1:2 — Argyle progress in style as they pepper Stuart Naylor's goal. Marker's strike from the edge of the box is hit with sufficient power to slip through Naylor's hands. Poole seems to have answered Argyle's perennial penalty taking problem by coolly slotting in after Strodder handles.

2:1 — Marker departs for Blackburn. Messy defending lets in Steve Claridge for an early goal. Regis finally justifies some of his £200k price tag with both Argyle goals. Marvin Johnson is stretchered off on the hour. Claridge heads his second to ensure a good crowd for the return fixture.

2:2 — The tie seems dead and buried as Argyle race into a three-goal lead. The introduction of the highly rated Scott Oakes turns the game and an error from Shilton, when he fails to hold the substitute's shot, gives the Hatters hope. David Preece narrows the deficit but the Greens hang on.

3 — Shilton has little to do except pick the ball out of the net on three occasions. Late goals from Joyce and Nugent look enough to send Argyle through but Paul Mudd's free-kick skids off the head of Morrison to the unmarked John Ashdjian to give the Pilgrims an unwanted trip north.

3R — Argyle's hopes of a fourth-round tie against Arsenal or Derby are dashed at the McCain Stadium. Shilton is unable to take goal-kicks because of a groin injury. Dalton latches on to Evans' through ball. Tommy Mooney levels. Sub Andy Mockler scores with his first touch of the game.

FA Cup

	Att	F-A	H-T	Scorers, Times, and Referees	1	2	3	4	5	6	7	8	9	10	11	subs used
1 A DORKING 15/11	3,200 D1:1	W 3-2	1-1	Dalton 32, 64, Marshall 47 / Grainger 21, Lumn 86 / Ref: D Gallagher	Newland *Orkney*	Poole *Bird*	Morgan S *Rains**	Hill *Welch*	Morrison *Mariner*	Joyce *Tutt*	Adcock *Robson*	Castle *Grainger*	Nugent *Lunn*	Marshall *Hanlan*	Dalton *Anderson*	*Thornton*
2 H PETERBOROUGH 9/12	6,057 1:12	W 3-2	2-0	Marshall 34, 37, Castle 75 / Philliskirk 74, Sterling 76 / Ref: P Durkin	Newland *Bennett*	Poole *Bradshaw*	Morgan S *Robinson*	Hill *Halsall*	Burrows *Luke*	Garner *Welsh*	Barlow *Sterling*	Castle *Iorfa**	Nugent *Adcock*	Marshall *Philliskirk*	Dalton *Ebdon*	*Barnes*
3 A IPSWICH 12/1	12,803 P:5	L 1-3	1-1	Castle 32 / Thompson 7, Dozzell 70, Whitton 86p / Ref: M Reed	Shilton *Baker*	McCall *Johnson*	Morgan S *Stockwell*	Hill *Wark**	Morrison *Whelan*	Joyce *Williams*	Skinner* *Guentchev*	Castle *Whitton*	Nugent *Dozzell*	Evans *Kiwomya*	Dalton *Youds*	Marshall *Youds*

1 — The match starts at 1pm as the Meadowbank ground floodlights are not up to league standard. John Rains' Chicks take the lead when 6ft 5in striker Carey Anderson sets up accountant Phil Grainger. Fitness begins to tell in the mud. Dalton and Marshall ensure there is no cup shock.

2 — Posh, fresh from a 9-1 win over Kingstonian in the previous round, barely know what's hit them as Marshall score two quickfire goals. Tony Philliskirk's header sparks a crazy two minutes which sees Castle score from the re-start and Worrell Sterling immediately repeat the feat.

3 — An early goal brings visions of a thrashing at the hands of the Premiership high-flyers. Neil Thompson's 30-yard drive swerves sufficiently to deceive Shilton. Castle scores direct from a free-kick. McCall completes an unhappy return to Portman Road by bringing down Kiwomya.

Home / Away

		P	W	D	L	F	A	W	D	L	F	A	Pts
1	Stoke	46	17	4	2	41	13	10	8	5	32	21	93
2	Bolton	46	18	2	3	48	14	9	7	7	32	27	90
3	Port Vale	46	14	7	2	44	17	12	4	7	35	27	89
4	West Brom*	46	17	3	3	56	22	8	8	7	32	32	85
5	Swansea	46	12	7	4	38	17	6	9	8	27	30	73
6	Stockport	46	11	11	1	47	18	8	4	11	34	39	72
7	Leyton Orient	46	16	4	3	49	20	5	5	13	20	33	72
8	Reading	46	14	4	5	44	20	4	11	8	22	31	69
9	Brighton	46	13	4	6	36	24	6	5	11	27	35	69
10	Bradford C	46	12	5	6	36	24	6	9	8	33	43	68
11	Rotherham	46	9	7	7	30	27	8	7	8	30	33	65
12	Fulham	46	9	9	5	28	22	7	8	8	29	33	65
13	Burnley	46	11	8	4	38	21	4	6	12	19	38	61
14	PLYMOUTH	46	11	6	6	38	28	5	6	12	21	36	60
15	Huddersfield	46	10	6	7	30	22	7	3	13	24	39	60
16	Hartlepool	46	8	6	9	19	23	6	6	11	23	37	54
17	Bournemouth	46	7	10	6	28	24	5	7	11	17	28	53
18	Blackpool	46	9	9	5	40	30	3	6	14	23	45	51
19	Exeter	46	5	8	10	26	30	6	9	8	28	39	50
20	Hull	46	9	5	9	28	26	4	6	13	18	43	50
21	Preston	46	8	5	10	41	47	5	3	15	24	47	47
22	Mansfield	46	7	8	8	34	34	4	3	16	18	46	44
23	Wigan	46	6	6	11	26	34	4	5	14	17	38	41
24	Chester	46	6	2	15	30	47	2	3	18	19	55	29
		1104	259	146	147	875	604	147	146	259	604	875	1510

* promoted after play-offs

Appearances / Goals

	Appearances						Goals			
	Lge	Sub	LC	Sub	FAC	Sub	Lge	LC	FAC	Tot
Adcock, Paul	2			1	1		2			2
Barlow, Martin	17			1	1		1			1
Boardman, Paul	2						1			1
Burrows, Adrian	20		2		3		1			1
Castle, Steve	31		2		3		11		2	13
Crocker, Marcus	1	3								
Dalton, Paul	30	2	2		3		9	2	2	13
Dryden, Richard	5									
Edworthy, Marc	14	1	3	1						
Evans, Michael	16	7	3		1		1			1
Fiore, Mark	1									
Garner, Darren	8	2	1	1	1					
Hill, Keith	36		3		3					
Hodges, Kevin	2	2								
Hodges, Lee	6	1								
Joyce, Warren	28	2	6		2		2	2		4
Kite, Phil	2									
Marker, Nicky	7		2				2	1		3
Marshall, Dwight	21	3	4		2	1	3	1		4
McCall, Steve	35		3		3	1	1			1
Morgan, Jamie	3									
Morgan, Steve	35	1	2		3		1			1
Morrison, Andy	29		6		2					
Newland, Ray	21				2					
Nugent, Kevin	45		6		3		11	2		13
Poole, Gary	39		6		2		5	2		7
Regis, Dave	7		2				2		3	5
Shilton, Peter	23		6		1					
Skinner, Craig	12	1	3		1		1			1
Spearing, Tony	5		4							
Turner, Robbie	2									
Walker, Alan	2									
(own-goals)							3			3
32 players used	506	40	66	4	33	1	59	11	7	77

Odds & ends

Double wins: (4) Bournemouth, Chester, Preston, Wigan.

Double defeats: (4) Exeter, Huddersfield, Port Vale, Stockport.

Won from behind: (4) Bournemouth, Brighton, Mansfield, West Brom.

Lost from in front: (2) Huddersfield, Stockport.

High spots: Outstanding midfield play of new signing, Steve Castle.

Emergence of several 'home-grown' youngsters into the side.

Superb 5-2 win at promotion candidates, West Brom.

Record incoming fee of £350,000 from Southend for Gary Poole.

Low spots: End of Kevin Hodges' long association with the club.

Inevitable departure of Nicky Marker and Andy Morrison to Premiership side, Blackburn.

0-3 home defeat by local rivals, Exeter.

Coca-Cola Cup run ended by Third Division Scarborough.

Player of the Year: Steve McCall.

Ever presents: (0).

Hat-tricks: (2) Steve Castle, Kevin Nugent.

Leading scorers: Steve Castle, Paul Dalton, Kevin Nugent (13).

ENDSLEIGH DIVISION 2

Manager: Peter Shilton

SEASON 1993-94

No	Date	Venue / Opponent	Att	Pos	Pt	F-A	H-T	Scorers, Times, and Referees
1	14/8	H STOCKPORT	6,863	—	L 0	2-3	0-1	Evans 86, Comyn 88 / Francis 36, 67, Preece 80 — Ref: R Groves
2	21/8	A HULL	3,580	17	D 1	2-2	1-1	Castle 44, 78 / Brown 42, Windass 71p — Ref: W Burns
3	28/8	H PORT VALE	6,072	11	W 4	2-0	0-0	Marshall 51, Castle 57 — Ref: K Cooper
4	31/8	A BLACKPOOL	3,865	—	L 4	1-2	0-0	Castle 82 / Griffiths 51p, Watson 73 — Ref: R Poulain
5	4/9	A SWANSEA	4,616	10	W 7	1-0	0-0	Dalton 50 — Ref: K Cooper
6	11/9	H LEYTON ORIENT	5,657	8	W 10	3-1	1-1	Castle 38, 64, Hill 57 / Barnett 20 — Ref: S Dunn
7	14/9	H ROTHERHAM	6,293	4	W 13	4-2	4-2	Nugent 24, Comyn 29, Castle 38, [Dalton 45] / Varadi 7, 23 — Ref: C Wilkes
8	18/9	A READING	6,209	5	L 13	2-3	0-1	Nugent 55, Castle 76p / Quinn 21 89, Gooding 67 — Ref: G Ashby
9	25/9	A CARDIFF	6,362	4	W 16	3-2	2-0	Nugent 35, 44, Comyn 50 / Stant 59, Millar 86 — Ref: J Brandwood
10	2/10	H HUDDERSFIELD	6,646	4	W 19	2-0	1-0	Castle 14, Trevitt 76(og) — Ref: M Bodenham
11	9/10	A BURNLEY	10,488	6	L 19	2-4	1-1	Castle 11, Dalton 69 / Eyres 8, Monington 58, Peel 65, 73 — Ref: K Hackett

Line-ups

No	Team	1	2	3	4	5	6	7	8	9	10	11	subs used
1	Argyle	Newland	Patterson	Naylor	Hill	Comyn	McCall	Burnett	Castle	Nugent*	Marshall	Dalton	Evans
1	Stockport	Edwards	Connelly	Wallace	Frain	Flynn	Finley	James	Ward	Francis	Ryan	Preece*	Beaumont
2	Argyle	Newland	Patterson	Naylor	Hill !	Comyn	Edworthy	Barlow	Castle	Nugent	Marshall	Evans*	McCall
2	Hull	Wilson	Mitchell	Hobson	Warren	Allison	Abbott	Norton	Moran^	Brown	Windass	Atkinson	Lee
3	Argyle	Nicholls	Patterson	Naylor	Hill	Comyn	McCall	Barlow	Castle	Nugent*	Marshall	Dalton	Evans
3	Port Vale	Musselwhite	Kent	Tankard	Aspin	Swan	Glover	Slaven	Van der Laan	Cross	Kerr*	Taylor	Billing
4	Argyle	Newland	Patterson	Naylor	Hill	Comyn	McCall*	Barlow	Castle	Evans^	Marshall	Dalton	Edworthy/Boardman
4	Blackpool	Martin	Davies	Cook	Beech	Briggs*	Gore	Watson	Bonner	Bamber	Sheedy	Griffiths^	Quinn/Mitchell
5	Argyle	Shilton	Patterson*	Naylor	Edworthy	Comyn	McCall*	Barlow	Castle	Evans	Marshall	Dalton	Burrows
5	Swansea	Freestone	Jenkins	Ford	Walker	Harris	Jones	Chapple^	Bowen	Torpey	Comforth^	Hayes	Hodge/Cook
6	Argyle	Shilton	Patterson	Naylor	Hill*	Comyn	McCall	Barlow	Castle	Evans^	Marshall	Dalton	Edworthy
6	Leyton Orient	Turner	Hendon	Howard^	Hackett	Kitchen	Bellamy	Carter	Barnett	Taylor*	West	Putney	Lakin/Benstock
7	Argyle	Nicholls	Patterson	Naylor	Hill*	Comyn	McCall*	Barlow	Castle	Nugent	Marshall	Dalton	Evans
7	Rotherham	Mercer	Pickering	Jacobs	Banks	Richardson	Law	Hazel	Goodwin	Helliwell	Varadi	Wilder	
8	Argyle	Nicholls	Patterson	Naylor	Hill	Comyn	McCall	Barlow	Castle	Nugent	Evans	Dalton	
8	Reading	Hislop	Hopkins	Kerr	McPherson	Williams	Parkinson	Gikes	Dillon	Quinn	Lovell*	Gooding	Gray
9	Argyle	Nicholls	Patterson	Naylor	Hill	Comyn	McCall	Barlow	Castle	Nugent	Skinner	Dalton	
9	Cardiff	Kite	James	Searle	Perry	Knill	Ratcliffe	Bird	Brazil	Stant	Thompson	Millar	
10	Argyle	Shilton	Patterson	Naylor	Hill*	Comyn	McCall	Barlow	Castle	Nugent	Marshall	Dalton	Edworthy
10	Huddersfield	Francis	Trevitt	Harkness	Starbuck	Dyson	Jackson	Dunn	Robinson	Booth*	Williams	Wells^	Roberts/Hicks
11	Argyle	Shilton	Patterson	Naylor	Burrows	Comyn	McCall	Barlow	Castle	Nugent	Marshall	Dalton	Skinner
11	Burnley	Beresford	Monington	Thompson	Davis	Pender	Randall	Francis*	Deary	Heath	Russell	Eyres	Peel

Match reports

1. Stockport — The giant Kevin Francis, who was best man at Argyle debutant Mark Patterson's wedding, does it again with two more goals against Argyle to add to the five he netted against them last season. The introduction of Evans breathes some life into the Argyle attack but they leave it too late.

2. Hull — Linton Brown is presented with an easy chance after a defensive tangle. Castle soon levels. A clumsy challenge by Comyn on Dean Windass is deemed worthy of a penalty. Windass himself scores. Castle gets his second. Hill, booked earlier, is red-carded (87) for upending Brown.

3. Port Vale — Nicholls has a fine league debut and makes a great save from Bernie Slaven's quickly taken free-kick. Marshall looks to be back to his best. He scores a cheeky goal by pushing the ball to one side of Paul Musselwhite and running around the other. He also sets up Castle's angled shot.

4. Blackpool — Newland, in for the suspended Nicholls, is at fault when his poor clearance goes to Mark Bonner who is fouled by Naylor. Griffiths scores from the spot. Marshall is sent off (68) for kicking and pushing the towering Dave Bamber. Castle's spot-kick is saved but he nets the rebound.

5. Swansea — Argyle grab all the points despite a corner count of 14-1 in the Swans' favour. Dalton scores a brilliant solo goal when he robs Shaun Chapple on the halfway line and beats two defenders. Shilton does his bit by pushing away John Ford's penalty (79) after the tumbling Evans handles.

6. Leyton Orient — Another all-action performance by Castle sets up a comfortable victory. Dalton's mazy run opens up the defence for the first. Hill scores his first Pilgrims goal after Chris Turner punched the ball straight to him. Castle is quickest to react after McCall's shot crashes against the bar.

7. Rotherham — Much travelled striker Imre Varadi heads over Nicholls and then pounces on Nicky Law's long throw. Nugent passes a late fitness test and scores his first goal for 16 matches. Comyn's header levels and Castle nets his seventh of the season to ensure a standing ovation at half-time.

8. Reading — Shilton is unable to celebrate his 44th birthday with three points. The lively Michael Gilkes sets up Jimmy Quinn's opener. Castle scores yet again, this time from the spot, after former Argyle loanee Jeff Hopkins fouled Dalton. Quinn makes it 10 for the side with a tremendous shot.

9. Cardiff — The ref refuses to allow Crocker to be a sub as he is wearing a protective cast on his arm. Comyn goes off for ten minutes to have four stitches in a facial wound. Phil Kite does well to hold Skinner's cheeky back-heel but fails to hang onto Dalton's header which leads to Comyn's goal.

10. Huddersfield — Nicholls' fractured toe means a 994th league appearance for Shilton. Neil Warnock's side provide uncompromising opposition in a match of seven bookings. Castle scores again. Simon Trevitt beats Dalton to a cross but is horrified when his attempted clearance sneaks inside a post.

11. Burnley — Shilton plays despite an overnight stomach upset. The Clarets have won every home match this season. Patterson fails to cut out a cross and allows Eyres to score. Castle quickly equalises. Dalton scores another solo goal. Sub Nathan Peel becomes an instant hero with two strikes.

Player columns (left to right): Nicholls · Patterson · Naylor · Burrows · Comyn · McCall · Barlow · Castle · Nugent · Burnett · Dalton · Marshall

12 — H YORK 16/10 — 2-1 (1-1) · 5,982 · 10 · 22
Scorers: Dalton 18, Comyn 63 / Barnes 44 · Ref: P Durkin
Team: Nicholls, Patterson, Naylor, Burrows, Comyn, McCall, Barlow, Castle, Nugent, Burnett*, Dalton, Marshall
Subs: Kiely, McMillan, Hall, Pepper, Tuttill, Atkin, McCarthy, Cooper*, Barnes, Swann, Barratt, Naylor
Burnett makes an impressive return after his opening-day injury. Former Argyle striker Steve Cooper limps off (28). Dalton finally repeats his away form at Home Park. Paul Barnes seizes on a rebound. Shots rain in on Kiely's head but only Comyn's header goes in.

13 — A BRISTOL ROV 23/10 — 0-0 (0-0) · 7,758 · 4 · 23
Ref: R Wiseman
Team: Nicholls, Patterson, Naylor, Burrows, Comyn, McCall, Barlow, Castle, Nugent, Skinner, Dalton, Marshall
Subs: Parkin, Channing, Madison, Browning, Wright^, McLean, Sterling, Taylor, Stewart, Waddock, Archer, Clark
Argyle fail to score in a league match for the first time this season against a side that have won their last six games. Castle clears a Clark shot off the line but then misses from the spot (71) when Brian Parkin saves.

14 — H WREXHAM 30/10 — 1-1 (0-0) · 6,977 · 18 · 24
Scorers: Barlow 89 / Bennett 77 · Ref: A Smith
Team: Nicholls, Patterson, Naylor, Burrows, Comyn, McCall, Barlow, Castle, Nugent, Skinner*, Dalton, Marshall
Subs: Marriott, Phillips, Hardy, Lake, Hunter, Pejic, Bennett, Owen, Connolly, Watkin, Cross !, Marshall
Wrexham arrive with the worst away record in the division. Jonathan Cross is booked (6) for a foul on Naylor and is red-carded (32) for an exact repeat. Castle misses his third penalty of the season (43) as Marriott saves. Barlow's late strike cancels out Bennett's 20th of the season.

15 — A CAMBRIDGE 2/11 — 0-2 (0-1) · 3,135 · 14 · 24
Scorers: Claridge 24, Rowett 85 · Ref: P Danson
Team: Nicholls, Patterson, Naylor, Burrows, Comyn, McCall, Barlow, Castle^, Nugent, Skinner*, Dalton, Marshall/Burnett
Subs: Filan, Jeffrey, Barrick, O'Shea^, Heathcote, Daish, Livett, Claridge, Fowler, Danzey, Flatts*, Rowett/Nyamah
The lack of goals from the forward line is again highlighted as Castle has one of his quieter games and no one else looks capable of scoring. Mick Heathcote, who had earlier hit a post, heads against the bar and Steve Claridge follows up. Gary Rowett cracks in a powerful drive.

16 — H BRENTFORD 6/11 — 1-1 (1-0) · 6,407 · 12 · 25
Scorers: Dalton 4, Allon 70 · Ref: R Milford
Team: Nicholls, Patterson, Naylor, Burrows, Comyn, McCall, Barlow, Castle, Nugent, Skinner*, Dalton, Marshall
Subs: Dearden, Grainger, Hutchings, Bates, Westley, Ratcliffe, Stephenson, Smith, Peters*, Allon, Gayle, Crocker/Bennett
With the club heavily in debt, the board tell Shilton he must offload one or two players before he can buy a new striker. Argyle dominate after Dalton's early goal but Dave Webb's side show gritty resilience and take advantage of slack defence when Joe Allon is unmarked to head in.

17 — A BRADFORD C 20/11 — 5-1 (3-0) · 5,204 · 9 · 28
Scorers: Comyn 3, Marshall 5, 76, 85, Nugent 15 / Nicholls 84(og) · Ref: N Barry
Team: Nicholls, Edwards, Naylor, Burrows, Comyn, McCall, Barlow, Castle, Nugent, Skinner*, Dalton, Marshall
Subs: Bowling, Stapleton, Lawford, Duxbury L, Blake, Richards, McHugh, Robson, McCarthy, Reid, Showler
Marshall responds to the club's quest for a new striker as Argyle romp to their biggest away win for 15 years. City manager Frank Stapleton plays in midfield in his injury-hit side. Second-choice keeper Ian Bowling has an unhappy time. Nicholls spills Showler's corner over the line.

18 — H HARTLEPOOL 27/11 — 2-0 (1-0) · 5,881 · 21 · 31
Scorers: Castle 40, Nugent 73 · Ref: D Frampton
Team: Nicholls, Patterson, Naylor, Burrows, Comyn, McCall, Barlow, Castle, Nugent, Marshall, Dalton, Skinner
Subs: Carter, Cross, Skedd*, Tait, MacPhail, Gilchrist, Southall, Johnrose, Houchen, Watten, West
Player-manager John MacPhail's newly appointed skipper, Brian Honour, comes close to giving Hartlepool the lead when he hits the upright from 25 yards. Nugent superbly volleys in from McCall's flighted free-kick.

19 — H HULL 11/12 — 2-1 (2-0) · 6,460 · 8 · 34
Scorers: Burnett 21, Castle 45 / Windass 82 · Ref: K Cooper
Team: Nicholls, Patterson, Naylor, Burrows, Comyn, McCall, Barlow, Castle, Nugent, Burnett, Dalton, Marshall
Subs: Wilson, Allison, Lee, Warren, Dewhurst, Abbott, Norton, Moran, Brown, Windass, Atkinson*, Skinner/Hargreaves
Burnett notches his first Argyle goal when his inswinging corner bounces once and flies in. Castle outjumps the defence to head in. Future Pilgrim Chris Hargreaves soon makes an impact He tests Nicholls with a 35-yard free-kick and his corner is finished off by Dean Windass.

20 — A STOCKPORT 17/12 — 3-2 (0-0) · 4,174 · 2 · 37
Scorers: Castle 50, 55, 56 / Preece 57, Frain 74 · Ref: J Rushton
Team: Nicholls, Patterson, Naylor, Burrows*, Comyn, McCall, Barlow, Castle, Nugent, Burnett, Dalton, Marshall
Subs: Edwards, Todd, Wallace, Frain, Flynn, Gannon^, Miller, Emerson*, Francis, Beaumont, Preece, Ward/Ryan
In front of Newcastle manager Kevin Keegan, Castle's close-range shot and two headers single-handedly destroys promotion rivals Stockport as he grabs the fastest hat-trick in Argyle history. County battle back gamely, but for once the defence subdues dangerman Kevin Francis.

21 — H FULHAM 28/12 — 3-1 (1-1) · 15,609 · 21 · 40
Scorers: Nugent 35, Dalton 79, Onwere 85(og) / Morgan 18 · Ref: M Bodenham
Team: Nicholls, Patterson, Naylor, Burrows, Comyn, McCall, Barlow, Castle, Nugent, Marshall, Dalton, Skinner
Subs: Stannard, Morgan, Herrera, Onwere, Jupp, Angus, Hails, Bedrossian^, Farrell, Brazil, Baah*, Tierling/Haworth
Cottagers boss Don Mackay bemoans the fact that his side play their second match in two days whilst Argyle have enjoyed an eleven-day break. Simon Morgan's gives the visitors a deserved lead. The game is still evenly poised when Onwere turns Marshall's cross past Stannard.

22 — A BOURNEMOUTH 1/1 — 1-0 (0-0) · 6,990 · 14 · 43
Scorer: Marshall 56 · Ref: P Alcock
Team: Nicholls, Patterson*, Naylor, Burrows, Comyn, McCall, Barlow, Castle, Nugent, Burnett, Dalton, Marshall
Subs: Bartram, Pennock, Mitchell, Chivers, Watson, Parkinson, O'Connor, McGorry*, Fletcher, Cotterill, Aspinall, Edworthy/Murray
Three thousand Pilgrim followers get a soaking but go home happy as Marshall's close-range header maintains the promotion challenge. The tackling becomes more physical and an uncharacteristic nasty challenge by McCall on Mark O'Connor causes a free-for-all near the touchline.

23 — H BRIGHTON 3/1 — 1-1 (0-1) · 15,334 · 21 · 44
Scorers: Castle 70 / Nogan 40 · Ref: K Cooper
Team: Nicholls, Edworthy, Naylor, Hill, Comyn, McCall, Burnett*, Castle, Nugent, Marshall, Dalton, Evans
Subs: Rust, Chapman, Simmonds, Pates, Foster, McCarthy, Flatts*, Case, Nogan, Funnell, Edwards, Geddes
The pitch passes an 11am inspection. With ex-England man Steve Foster a rock-like figure in defence and 39-year-old Jimmy Case running the midfield, Liam Brady's side threaten to spoil Argyle's fine home record. Castle's 20-yard effort cancels out Kurt Nogan's earlier strike.

ENDSLEIGH DIVISION 2

Manager: Peter Shilton

SEASON 1993-94

No	Date	Att	Pos	Pt	F-A	H-T	Scorers, Times, and Referees	1	2	3	4	5	6	7	8	9	10	11	subs used
24	A YORK 15/1	4,115	2 D 9 45		0-0	0-0	Ref: J Parker	Nicholls / *Kiely*	Edworthy / *McMillan*	Naylor / *Hall*	Hill / *Swann*	Comyn / *Tutill*	McCall / *Stancliffe*	Burnett / *McCarthy*	Castle / *Blackstone*	Nugent / *Barnes*	Marshall* / *Bushell*	Dalton / *Canham*	Barlow

With Nugent twice going close within the first five minutes, few would have predicted a no-score draw. Both defences gradually dominate with Shilton having a fine game. Ian Blackstone, replacing the suspended Steve Cooper, looks lively but is well marshalled by Comyn.

No	Date	Att	Pos	Pt	F-A	H-T	Scorers, Times, and Referees	1	2	3	4	5	6	7	8	9	10	11	subs used
25	H BURNLEY 22/1	10,595	2 W 6 48		3-2	2-0	Marshall 31, Nugent 32, 67, Heath 66, Philliskirk 82 — Ref: C Wilkes	Nicholls / *Beresford*	Edworthy / *Joyce**	Naylor / *Thompson*	Hill / *Davis*	Comyn / *Pender*	McCall / *Monington*	Burnett / *Philliskirk*	Castle / *Deary*	Nugent / *Heath*	Marshall / *Russell^*	Dalton / *Eyres*	Farrell/Francis

Shilton receives the December manager of the month award. Ex-Pilgrim Warren Joyce appears in the warm-up with 'Guess Who?' and 'Judas' emblazoned on his track suit. The match lives up to its billing as Burnley fight to the last. New signing Philliskirk causes a few late flutters.

No	Date	Att	Pos	Pt	F-A	H-T	Scorers, Times, and Referees	1	2	3	4	5	6	7	8	9	10	11	subs used
26	H BRISTOL ROV 5/2	13,318	4 D 3 49		3-3	2-3	Marshall 13, Dalton 29, Evans 76, Skinner 11, Archer 24, Sterling 33 — Ref: P Durkin	Nicholls / *Parkin*	Patterson / *Alexander^*	Naylor / *Maddison*	Hill / *Browning*	Comyn / *Clark*	McCall / *McLean*	Burnett / *Sterling*	Castle / *Taylor**	Evans / *Skinner*	Marshall / *Waddock*	Dalton / *Archer*	Hardyman/Stewart

Argyle fight back on three occasions against a team with the best away record in the division. Hill aside, the defence look unusually unsure and three times Comyn puts Nicholls under pressure with poor passes. Evans, deputising for the injured Nugent, caps a fine game with an equaliser.

No	Date	Att	Pos	Pt	F-A	H-T	Scorers, Times, and Referees	1	2	3	4	5	6	7	8	9	10	11	subs used
27	A BARNET 12/2	2,854	3 D 24 50		0-0	0-0	Ref: G Willard	Nicholls! / *Phillips*	Patterson / *Haylock*	Naylor / *Mitchell**	Hill / *Close!*	Comyn / *Walker*	McCall / *Barnett*	Burnett^ / *Wilson*	Castle / *Cooper*	Landon* / *Haag*	Marshall / *Gibson*	Dalton / *Scott*	Evans/Newland, Lynch

A dour affair is livened up by second-half shenanigans. With feelings running high over a declined penalty appeal by Barnet, Nicholls throws the ball at Shaun Close (75) who retaliates by head-butting the Argyle keeper. Referee Willard has little choice but to dismiss both players.

No	Date	Att	Pos	Pt	F-A	H-T	Scorers, Times, and Referees	1	2	3	4	5	6	7	8	9	10	11	subs used
28	A PORT VALE 19/2	9,093	4 L 6 50		1-2	1-1	Marshall 8, Taylor 29, Lowe 61 — Ref: B Coddington	Nicholls / *Musselwhite*	Patterson / *Aspin*	Naylor / *Stokes*	Hill / *Kent*	Comyn / *Swan*	McCall / *Glover*	Burnett / *Lowe*	Castle* / *Porter*	Evans / *Taylor*	Marshall^ / *Foyle*	Dalton / *Cross*	Evans/Barlow

Marshall gives the Pilgrims an ideal start when he shrugs off Peter Swan's challenge to drive a low shot home. Ian Taylor outjumps a static defence to equalise. On-loan David Lowe celebrates his Vale debut when the winner as Argyle once again come away from Vale Park pointless.

No	Date	Att	Pos	Pt	F-A	H-T	Scorers, Times, and Referees	1	2	3	4	5	6	7	8	9	10	11	subs used
29	H BLACKPOOL 22/2	7,102	3 W 53		2-1	0-0	Marshall 48, Nugent 81, Rodwell 58 — Ref: S Dunn	Nicholls / *Martin*	Patterson / *Bonner*	Naylor / *Cook*	Hill / *Horner*	Comyn / *Briggs*	McCall / *Gore*	Burnett* / *Rodwell*	Castle / *Watson*	Nugent / *Bamber*	Marshall* / *Gouck*	Barlow / *Beech*	Evans

Nugent returns after a four-match absence during which time Argyle have failed to win, and scores a crucial goal to clinch a hard-earned win. With football difficult on a rain-soaked pitch, both sides miss chances with Watson's effort (56) ruled out for offside and Castle hitting a post.

No	Date	Att	Pos	Pt	F-A	H-T	Scorers, Times, and Referees	1	2	3	4	5	6	7	8	9	10	11	subs used
30	H SWANSEA 26/2	8,930	3 W 17 56		2-1	1-1	Evans 16, McCall 52, Torpey 38 — Ref: R Milford	Newland / *Freestone*	Patterson / *Jenkins**	Naylor / *Cook*	Hill / *Walker*	Comyn / *Harris*	McCall / *Pascoe*	Burnett / *Hodge^*	Castle / *Rush*	Nugent / *Torpey*	Marshall* / *Cornforth*	Evans / *Ampadu*	Skinner, Chapple/McFarlane

The match goes ahead despite 24 hours of heavy rain. Marshall limps off after only two minutes with a hamstring injury. Evans cuts in from the left to score but Torpey levels when he is left unmarked in front of goal. McCall scores the winner with his first goal for almost a year.

No	Date	Att	Pos	Pt	F-A	H-T	Scorers, Times, and Referees	1	2	3	4	5	6	7	8	9	10	11	subs used
31	A EXETER 2/3	6,601	2 W 22 59		3-2	0-1	Gavin 48(og), Burnett 51, Evans 76, Cooper 28, Adekola 82 — Ref: M Pierce	Nicholls / *Fox*	Patterson / *Minett*	Naylor / *Robinson*	Hill* / *Cooper*	Comyn / *Daniels*	McCall / *Ross**	Burnett / *Storer*	Castle / *Coughlin*	Nugent / *Turner*	Evans / *Morgan^*	Skinner / *Gavin*	McCarthy, Brown/Adekola

Mark Cooper puts City in front from close range. Patterson's low cross is turned into his own net by Mark Gavin. Good work by Evans leads to Burnett's 20-yard shot. Evans scores a third. Adekola ensures a few anxious moments. Argyle win at Exeter for the first time in 66 years.

No	Date	Att	Pos	Pt	F-A	H-T	Scorers, Times, and Referees	1	2	3	4	5	6	7	8	9	10	11	subs used
32	A LEYTON ORIENT 5/3	5,334	2 L 9 59		1-2	0-2	Castle 55, Bogie 5, Carter 9 — Ref: M Bailey	Nicholls / *Newell*	Patterson / *Hendon**	Naylor / *Howard*	Burrows / *Austin*	Comyn / *West*	McCall / *Barnett*	Burnett* / *Carter*	Castle / *Putney^*	Nugent / *Benstock*	Evans / *Cooper*	Dalton / *Bogie*	Skinner, Taylor/Ludden

Argyle never recover from two early setbacks. Ian Bogie is inexplicably allowed to run unchallenged to shoot past Nicholls. Cooper's header is parried by Nicholls but the ball goes straight to the feet of Danny Carter. Castle scores against his former club.

No	Date	Att	Pos	Pt	F-A	H-T	Scorers, Times, and Referees	1	2	3	4	5	6	7	8	9	10	11	subs used
33	H BARNET 8/3	7,595	2 W 62		1-0	0-0	Evans 90 — Ref: R Groves	Nicholls / *Phillips*	Patterson / *Haylock*	Naylor / *Wilson*	Burrows / *Hoddle*	Comyn / *Walker*	McCall / *Newson*	Burnett^ / *Lynch^*	Castle / *Cooper*	Nugent / *Gibson*	Evans / *Dolby**	Dalton / *Scott*	Skinner, Haag/Marwood

Nicholls is pulled out of the England Under-21 squad. Bottom of the table Barnet come for a draw and almost get it. Evans notches the winner in the fifth of the eight minutes Mr Groves adds on to compensate for injuries and some extravagant time-wasting by Ray Clemence's side.

No	Date	Att	Pos	Pt	F-A	H-T	Scorers, Times, and Referees	1	2	3	4	5	6	7	8	9	10	11	subs used
34	H READING 12/3	14,953	2 W 1 65		3-1	1-1	Nugent 18, 72, Dalton 54, Kerr 27 — Ref: K Cooper	Nicholls / *Hislop*	Patterson / *Wallace*	Naylor / *Kerr*	Burrows / *Hopkins*	Comyn / *Williams*	McCall / *Gooding*	Burnett / *Taylor^*	Castle / *Gilkes*	Nugent / *Quinn*	Evans / *Lovell*	Dalton / *Jones*	Lambert

One time runaway leaders Reading have their lead cut to two points. Shaka Hislop hoofs Adrian Williams' back-pass straight at Nugent who makes no mistake. Dylan Kerr equalises. Nicholls makes a point-blank save from 32-goal Jimmy Quinn. Some crowd trouble mars the day.

No.	Venue	Opponent	Date	Att.	Pos	Pts	Result	HT	FT
35	A	ROTHERHAM	15/3	2,982	19	68	W	0-0	3-0
36	H	CARDIFF	19/3	9,587	21	68	L	1-2	1-2
37	A	HUDDERSFIELD	26/3	5,619	20	68	L	0-0	0-1
38	A	BRIGHTON	30/3	9,500		68	L	1-2	1-2
39	H	EXETER	2/4	12,986	22	71	W	0-0	1-0
40	A	FULHAM	4/4	5,819	20	72	D	0-1	1-1
41	H	BOURNEMOUTH	9/4	7,971	15	75	W	1-0	2-0
42	H	CAMBRIDGE	16/4	8,872	9	75	L	0-1	0-3
43	A	BRENTFORD	23/4	6,173	13	76	D	0-1	1-1
44	A	WREXHAM	26/4	2,518		79	W	2-0	3-0
45	H	BRADFORD C	30/4	10,985	10	82	W	1-1	3-1
46	A	HARTLEPOOL	7/5	2,382	23	85	W	4-0	8-1

Home Average 9,003 Away 5,451

---

35. ROTHERHAM (A) — Nugent 76, Evans 78, 88 — Ref: K Breen

Argyle: Nicholls, Patterson, Naylor, Comyn, Burrows, McCall*, Burnett, Castle, Nugent, Evans, Dalton, Skinner
Rotherham: Clarke, Wilder, Jacobs, Brien, Williams^, Barras, Banks, Goodwin, Helliwell, Goater*, Roberts, Varadi/Hazel

The Pilgrims top the table and become the country's leading scorers. Nicholls is the busier of the two keepers until Nugent's header. The much-improved Evans scores twice more. The only blot on the evening is an ankle injury to McCall that may keep him out for up to three weeks.

36. CARDIFF (H) — Evans 17 — Stant 25, 31 — Ref: M Bodenham

Argyle: Nicholls, Patterson, Naylor, Comyn, Burrows, Skinner*, Burnett, Castle, Nugent, Evans, Dalton, Barlow
Cardiff: Williams, Fereday, Searle, Wigg, Brock, Perry, Bird, Richardson, Stant, Dale, Griffith

Without six first-team regulars, the struggling Bluebirds pull off the shock result of the day. The in-form Evans notches his eighth of the season before one-time Argyle target, Phil Stant, punishes an error by Patterson. Stant scores again and comes close to a hat-trick in the final minute.

37. HUDDERSFIELD (A) — Booth 46 — Ref: K Lupton

Argyle: Nicholls, Patterson, Naylor, Comyn, Burrows, McCall, Burnett, Castle, Nugent, Evans, Dalton, Skinner
Huddersfield: Francis, Billy, Cowan, Starbuck, Scully, Mitchell, Clayton, Bullock, Booth, Jepson, Dunn

The Terriers have three players, Cowan, Scully and Baldry, making their debuts. Manager Neil Warnock praises Gary Clayton as the midfielder effectively stifles the threat of Castle. Andy Booth runs onto Phil Starbuck's pass with Comyn and Patterson waiting for an offside decision.

38. BRIGHTON (A) — Evans 76 — Nogan 61, Dickov 89 — Ref: A Smith

Argyle: Nicholls, Patterson, Naylor, Comyn, Burrows, McCall, Burnett, Castle !, Nugent, Evans, Dalton, Skinner
Brighton: Rust, Munday, Pates, Foster^, Wilkins, McCarthy, Crumplin*, Dickov, Nogan, Codner, Chapman, Kennedy/Fox

Argyle crash to a controversial third successive defeat. Kurt Nogan notches his 22nd of the season. Argyle look the likelier winners after Steve Foster goes off with a dead leg. Arsenal loanee Paul Dickov scores after a foul on Burrows. Castle is sent off for carrying his protests too far.

39. EXETER (H) — Dalton 47 — Ref: R Gifford

Argyle: Nicholls, Patterson, Naylor, Comyn, Burrows, McCall, Burnett, Castle, Nugent, Evans*, Dalton, Barlow
Exeter: McKnight, Llewellyn, Brown, Cooper, Daniels, Ross^, Storer, Bailey, Turner, Minett, Gavin, Mehew/Phillips

Argyle complete the double over their local rivals but are made to fight. Dalton turns smartly to shoot under the diving Alan McKnight. Hill is fortunate to escape with just a booking when he brings down Stuart Storer but City boss Terry Cooper sportingly agrees with the decision.

40. FULHAM (A) — Nugent 75 — Morgan 21 — Ref: P Foakes

Argyle: Nicholls, Patterson, Naylor, Comyn, Burrows, McCall*, Burnett, Castle, Nugent, Evans, Dalton, Barlow
Fulham: Stannard, Morgan, Pike, Jupp*, Thomas, Ferney, Brazil, Farrell, Herrera, Landon, Bedrossian

Evans may miss the rest of the season with a knee injury. With a gale-force wind blowing off the Thames, Argyle's promotion challenge looks to be off course when Simon Morgan heads in. Landon almost scores with his first touch. Nugent's header finally beats the superb Stannard.

41. BOURNEMOUTH (H) — Marshall 15, Castle 68 — Ref: R Gifford

Argyle: Nicholls, Patterson*, McCall, Comyn, Hill, Barlow, Burnett, Castle, Nugent, Marshall, Dalton, Edworthy
Bournemouth: Bartram, Chivers, Skinner, Watson, Morris, Burns, O'Connor, McElhatton, Murray*, Cotterill, Russell, Mean

Arsenal boss George Graham attends the game. Mr Gifford officiates at Home Park for a second successive Saturday after replacing the unwell Mr King. Chris Burns' headed clearance strikes Justin Skinner and the ball loops out of Bartram's reach. Castle gets his first for nine games.

42. CAMBRIDGE (H) — Joseph 19, Corazzin 72, 87 — Ref: K Cooper

Argyle: Nicholls, Edworthy, Naylor*, Comyn, Hill, McCall, Burnett, Barlow, Nugent, Marshall^, Dalton, Skinner/Landon
Cambridge: Filan, Joseph*, Barrick, Heathcote, Craddock, Granville, Jeffrey, Middleton, Butler, Hyde, Corazzin, Cheetham

Cambridge manage only three shots but score with all of them. Argyle dominate but look unlikely to breach a U's defence well marshalled by Mick Heathcote. Canadian international Carlo Corazzin demonstrates his finishing ability. He lobs Nicholls from 25 yards for his second goal.

43. BRENTFORD (A) — Landon 84 — Smith 24 — Ref: D Frampton

Argyle: Nicholls, Patterson, Naylor*, Hill, Comyn, McCall, Burnett*, Barlow, Nugent, Marshall, Dalton, Burrows/Landon
Brentford: Dearden, Statham, Grainger, Bates, Thompson, Ashby, Smith^, Hutchings, Annon, Manuel, Harvey, Ratcliffe

A dispirited Bees side are looking for their first win in 13 games. Makeshift striker David Thompson lays on Paul Smith's opener. Urged on by 1,500 fans, Argyle finally equalise when Richard Landon heads in his first league goal to leave the Pilgrims in second spot on goals scored.

44. WREXHAM (A) — Barlow 6, Marshall 19, Dalton 86 — Ref: E Wolstenholme

Argyle: Nicholls, Marriott, Williams, Comyn, Burrows, McCall, Barlow, Castle, Nugent, Marshall, Dalton, Cross
Wrexham: Jones, Williams, Brammer, Sertori, Pejic, Bennett, Owen, Connolly, Watkin, Taylor*

Just what the doctor ordered. Barlow beats Andy Marriott from ten yards and Marshall coolly slots in the second. Dalton is back to his best and rounds things off late on with a spectacular effort. Wrexham boss Brian Flynn praises Argyle as the best side his team have faced this season.

45. BRADFORD C (H) — Castle 11, 87, Landon 76 — Tomlinson G 9 — Ref: P Vanes

Argyle: Nicholls, Tomlinson P, Hill, Comyn, Burrows, McCall*, Burnett, Barlow, Landon, Marshall, Dalton, Burnett
Bradford C: Hoyle, Williams, Duxbury L, Sinnott, Richards, Duxbury M*, Robson, Tomlinson G, Stapleton*, Reid, Tolson/Power

Graeme Tomlinson shoots City into an early lead against the run of play. The inspirational Castle rediscovers his early season form and soon replies with a far-post header. Landon sends in a brave diving header and Castle curls a free-kick around the defensive wall for a superb third.

46. HARTLEPOOL (A) — Marshall 30, McCall 40, Landon 43,51,79, Peverell 71 [Dalton 44, 90, Castle 60] — Ref: B Hill

Argyle: Nicholls, Patterson*, Hill, Comyn, Burrows, McCall, Barlow, Castle, Nugent, Marshall, Dalton, Naylor
Hartlepool: Jones, Garrett, Ingram, Tait, Gilchrist, Skedd^, Peverell, Olsson, Houchen*, Halliday, Southall, West/Lynch

The notion that Pool play like strangers rings true as they are in the midst of a training strike over delayed wages and only meet up on match days. Argyle set a new club record with their biggest ever away win. Port Vale's win at Brighton means Argyle are destined for the play-offs.

ENDSLEIGH DIVISION 2 (CUP-TIES)

Manager: Peter Shilton

SEASON 1993-94

Play-offs

		Att	F-A	H-T	Scorers, Times, and Referees	1	2	3	4	5	6	7	8	9	10	11	subs used
SF 1 15/5	A BURNLEY	18,794	D 0-0	0-0	Ref: K Cooper	Nicholls	Patterson	Hill	Burrows !	Comyn	McCall	Barlow	Castle	Landon^	Marshall*	Dalton	Burnett/Nugent
		3		7		*Beresford*	*Parkinson*	*Thompson*	*Davis*	*Pender*	*Joyce*	*McMinn**	*Deary*	*Heath*	*Francis*	*Eyres*	*Lancashire*

Argyle still look on course for a Wembley appearance after a battling display at Turf Moor. In what proves to be his last Argyle appearance, Burrows is booked in the fourth minute and harshly receives a red card for the first time when the ball appears to strike his shoulder (50).

		Att	F-A	H-T	Scorers, Times, and Referees	1	2	3	4	5	6	7	8	9	10	11	subs used
SF 2 18/5	H BURNLEY	17,515	L 1-3	1-2	Marshall 15 / Francis 29, 31, Joyce 81 / Ref: T Holbrook / (Argyle lost 1-3 on aggregate)	Nicholls	Patterson	McCall	Hill	Comyn	Burnett*	Barlow	Castle	Landon^	Marshall	Dalton	Naylor/Nugent
		3		7		*Beresford*	*Parkinson*	*Thompson*	*Davis*	*Pender*	*Joyce^*	*McMinn*	*Deary*	*Heath*	*Francis^*	*Eyres*	*Farrell/Peel*

Marshall sends the home fans wild with delight as he grabs the lead with a 15-yard shot. The Argyle defence never look comfortable against lone striker John Francis who scores twice in quick succession. Warren Joyce pounces on a Nicholls fumble to end Argyle's Wembley dream.

Coca-Cola Cup

		Att	F-A	H-T	Scorers, Times, and Referees	1	2	3	4	5	6	7	8	9	10	11	subs used
1:1 17/8	A BIRMINGHAM	9,304	L 0-3	0-2	Parris 21, Frain 30, Peschisolido 58 / Ref: J Parker	Newland	Patterson	Naylor	Hill	Comyn	McCall	Garner	Castle	Evans	Marshall	Dalton*	Edworthy
		2:				*Miller*	*Hiley*	*Frain*	*Parris*	*Whyte*	*Dryden*	*Downing**	*McMinn^*	*Peschisolido*	*Saville*	*Smith*	*Mardon/Donowa*

Terry Cooper's side take a stranglehold on the tie with a convincing victory. The influential George Parris opens the scoring with a 30-yard blockbuster. John Frain brushes off several challenges to score and Canadian international Paul Peschisolido shoots home from 18 yards.

		Att	F-A	H-T	Scorers, Times, and Referees	1	2	3	4	5	6	7	8	9	10	11	subs used
1:2 24/8	H BIRMINGHAM	3,659	W 2-0	0-0	Barlow 66, Marshall 90 / Ref: R Milford / (Argyle lost 2-3 on aggregate)	Nicholls	Patterson	Naylor	Hill	Comyn	McCall	Barlow	Castle	Nugent	Marshall	Dalton	Donowa
		17 2:18				*Miller*	*Hiley*	*Frain*	*Dryden*	*Mardon*	*Whyte*	*Fenwick*	*Smith*	*Shutt*	*Saville*	*Moulden^*	*Donowa*

Argyle leave it too late to overcome the first-leg deficit but put up an encouraging show. Barlow cracks home a low shot. Everyone, except Mr Milford, is convinced that Chris Whyte handled in the area. Marshall scores a second in injury-time after Kevin Miller fumbles Dalton's shot.

FA Cup

		Att	F-A	H-T	Scorers, Times, and Referees	1	2	3	4	5	6	7	8	9	10	11	subs used
1 13/11	A MARLOW	2,700	W 2-0	0-0	Dalton 64, 89 / Ref: J Brandwood	Nicholls	Patterson	Naylor	Burrows	Comyn	McCall	Burnett	Castle	Nugent	Skinner*	Dalton	Marshall
		8 DL:3				*Mitchell K*	*Mitchell S*	*Holmes*	*Baron*	*Ferguson*	*Regan^*	*Lay*	*Chatlin^*	*Blackman*	*Buraglo*	*Watkins*	*Malins/Dell*

Argyle produce a professional performance at the compact Alfred Davis Memorial Ground to impart a first home defeat of the season on Dave Russell's side. Argyle's first comes direct from a free-kick. Dalton later admits he thought it was indirect and was aiming for Castle's head.

		Att	F-A	H-T	Scorers, Times, and Referees	1	2	3	4	5	6	7	8	9	10	11	subs used
2 4/12	H GILLINGHAM	6,051	W 2-0	1-0	Nugent 28, 59 / Ref: R Groves	Nicholls	Edworthy*	Naylor	Burrows	Comyn	McCall	Burnett	Castle	Nugent	Marshall	Dalton	Evans
		5 3:16				*Banks*	*Dunne*	*Palmer*	*Butler*	*Clark*	*Breen^*	*Reinelt*	*Forster*	*Baker*	*Smith*	*Micklewhite*	*Green*

Argyle comfortably reach the third round as Gills boss Mike Flanagan berates his side for lack of commitment. It could have been a different story but Richard Green blazes a penalty over the bar (74) after Comyn innocuously tackles Forster. Nugent maintains his good scoring run.

		Att	F-A	H-T	Scorers, Times, and Referees	1	2	3	4	5	6	7	8	9	10	11	subs used
3 8/1	H CHESTER	9,170	W 1-0	0-0	Nugent 84 / Ref: K Burge	Nicholls	McCall	Naylor	Hill	Comyn	McCall	Skinner	Castle	Nugent	Marshall*	Dalton	Bishop/Rimmer
		2 3:4				*Felgate*	*Preece*	*Jakub**	*Jenkins*	*Came*	*Greenall*	*Thompson*	*Lightfoot*	*Wheeler^*	*Leonard*	*Pugh*	*Bishop/Rimmer*

The recalled Skinner proves the main threat to Graham Barrow's side. Chester have plenty of possession but rarely threaten. With a replay looming, Nugent, now recovered from flu, scores his tenth of the season to ensure a safe passage and an eagerly awaited fourth-round draw.

		Att	F-A	H-T	Scorers, Times, and Referees	1	2	3	4	5	6	7	8	9	10	11	subs used
4 29/1	H BARNSLEY	12,760	D 2-2	0-1	Marshall 50, Dalton 59 / Payton 41, Taggart 71 / Ref: D Frampton	Nicholls	Edworthy	Naylor	Hill	Comyn	McCall	Burnett	Castle	Nugent*	Marshall	Dalton	Skinner
		2 1:23				*Butler*	*Eaden*	*Fleming*	*Wilson*	*Taggart*	*Bishop*	*O'Connell*	*Redfearn*	*Rammell*	*Payton*	*Archdeacon*	

Andy Payton catches Nicholls off his line to give the Tykes the lead before two high quality goals turn things around. Marshall curls a left-foot shot in from an almost impossible angle and Dalton beats three defenders before scoring. Gerry Taggart's header takes the tie back to Oakwell.

		Att	F-A	H-T	Scorers, Times, and Referees	1	2	3	4	5	6	7	8	9	10	11	subs used
4R 9/2	A BARNSLEY	10,913	L 0-1	0-0	O'Connell 65 / Ref: D Frampton	Nicholls	Patterson	Naylor	Hill	Comyn	McCall	Burnett*	Castle	Evans	Marshall^	Dalton	Skinner/Edworthy
		4 1:22				*Butler*	*Eaden*	*Fleming*	*Wilson*	*Taggart*	*Bishop*	*O'Connell*	*Redfearn*	*Rammell*	*Payton*	*Archdeacon*	

Barnsley move into the last 16 and an away tie at Oldham as Argyle's 15-match unbeaten run ends. Nicholls almost single-handedly defies Viv Anderson's side with a string of fine saves. He can do nothing about Brendan O'Connell's winner which has a look of offside about it.

Home / Away League Table

	P	W	D	L	F	A	W	D	L	F	A	F	A	Pts
			Home						Away					
1 Reading	46	15	6	2	40	16	11	5	7	41	28			89
2 Port Vale	46	16	6	1	46	18	10	4	9	33	28			88
3 PLYMOUTH	46	16	4	3	46	26	9	6	8	42	30			85
4 Stockport	46	15	3	5	50	22	9	10	4	24	22			85
5 York	46	12	7	4	33	13	9	5	9	31	27			75
6 Burnley*	46	17	4	2	55	18	4	6	13	24	40			73
7 Bradford C	46	13	5	5	34	20	6	9	8	27	33			70
8 Bristol Rov	46	10	8	5	33	26	10	2	11	27	33			70
9 Hull	46	9	9	5	33	20	9	5	9	29	34			68
10 Cambridge	46	11	5	7	38	29	8	4	11	41	44			66
11 Huddersfield	46	9	8	6	27	26	8	6	9	31	35			65
12 Wrexham	46	13	4	6	45	33	4	7	12	21	44			62
13 Swansea	46	12	7	4	37	20	4	5	14	19	38			60
14 Brighton	46	10	7	6	38	29	5	7	11	22	38			59
15 Rotherham	46	11	4	8	42	30	4	9	10	21	30			58
16 Brentford	46	7	10	6	30	28	6	9	8	27	27			58
17 Bournemouth	46	8	7	8	26	27	6	6	9	25	32			57
18 Leyton Orient	46	11	9	3	38	26	3	5	15	19	45			56
19 Cardiff	46	12	7	6	39	33	3	8	12	27	46			54
20 Blackpool	46	12	2	9	41	37	4	3	16	22	38			53
21 Fulham	46	7	6	10	20	23	7	4	12	30	40			52
22 Exeter	46	8	7	8	38	37	3	5	15	14	46			45
23 Hartlepool	46	8	3	12	28	40	1	6	16	13	47			36
24 Barnet	46	4	6	13	22	32	1	7	15	19	54			28
	1104	264	144	144	879	629	144	144	264	629	879			1512

* promoted after play-offs

Odds & ends

Double wins: (6) Bournemouth, Bradford City, Exeter, Hartlepool, Rotherham, Swansea.

Double defeats: (1) Cambridge.

Won from behind: (5) Bradford City, Exeter, Fulham, Orient, Rotherham.

Lost from in front: (2) Cardiff, Port Vale.

High spots: Scored more goals than any other side in the league.

Equalled club's biggest victory with an 8-1 win at Hartlepool.

Peter Shilton wins December 'Manager of the Month' award.

Exciting style of play to reach play-offs.

Alan Nicholls selected for England Under-21 side.

High tally of goals from midfielder Steve Castle

Low spots: Defeat in play-off semi-finals against Burnley.

Adrian Burrows controversially sent off in play-off first leg, for the only time in his career, in what was his final match.

Three successive defeats in March cost automatic promotion.

Player of the Year: Steve McCall.

Ever presents: (1) Andy Comyn.

Hat-tricks: (3) Steve Castle, Richard Landon, Dwight Marshall.

Leading scorer: Steve Castle (21).

Appearances and Goals

	Appearances						Goals			
	Lge	Sub	LC	Sub	FAC	Sub	Lge	LC	FAC	Tot
Barlow, Martin	22	4	1				2	1		3
Boardman, Paul						1				
Burnett, Wayne	30	2			5		2			2
Burrows, Adrian	20	2			2		2			2
Castle, Steve	44		2		5		21			21
Comyn, Andy	46		2		5		5			5
Crocker, Marcus		1								
Dalton, Paul	40		2		4	1	12		3	15
Edworthy, Marc	7	5		1	2	1				
Evans, Michael	16	6	1		1	1	9			9
Garner, Darren		2								
Hill, Keith	28	1	2		3		1			1
Landon, Richard	3	3					5			5
Marshall, Dwight	28	3	2		4	1	12	1	1	14
McCall, Steve	44	1	1		5		2			2
McCarthy, Alan	1	1								
Naylor, Dominic	42	1	2		5					
Newland, Ray	4	1	1							
Nicholls, Alan	38				5					
Nugent, Kevin	39	1	1		4		14		3	17
Patterson, Mark	41	2			3					
Shilton, Peter	4									
Skinner, Craig	9	7			2	2				
(own-goals)							3			3
23 players used	506	39	22	1	55	5	88	2	7	97

ENDSLEIGH DIVISION 2

Manager: Shilton > McCall > Osman — SEASON 1994-95

---

1 — H BRENTFORD — 13/8 | Att 7,976 | Pt 0 (L) | F-A 1-5 | H-T 1-3
Scorers: Swan 18 / Smith 26, Forster 37, 88, Stephenson 45, Fernandes 45 [Taylor 71] — Ref: S Dunn

	1	2	3	4	5	6	7	8	9	10	11	subs used
Argyle	Hodge	Patterson*	Hill	Comyn	**Swan**	**Payne**^	Barlow	Burnett	Nugent	Evans	Skinner	Edworthy/Landon
Brentford	Hurdle	Hutchings	Westley	Bates	**Smith**	Parris	Harvey	Taylor	Forster	Stephenson		

Argyle suffer their biggest ever opening-day loss at home. Despite the hammering, eleventh-hour signing Martin Hodge wins the man of the match award. £300k record signing Peter Swan marks his debut with a goal but the Bees' new arrival, Nicky Forster, tears the defence apart.

---

2 — A BRIGHTON — 20/8 | Att 8,309 | Pos 17/16 | Pt 1 (D) | F-A 1-1 | H-T 0-0
Scorers: Bradshaw 69 / Chamberlain 53 — Ref: P Foakes

	1	2	3	4	5	6	7	8	9	10	11	subs used
Argyle	Hodge	Edworthy*	Naylor	Comyn	Swan*	Hill	Barlow	**Bradshaw**	Nugent	Evans	Dalton	Burnett/Chamberlain
Brighton	Rust	Munday	Pates	Chapman*	Foster	McCarthy	Minton	McDougald	Nogan	Codner	Wilkins	

Darren Bradshaw arrives on loan from Peterborough to bolster Shilton's depleted squad and he equalises with a diving header. Swan goes off injured (32) after being kicked in the back. Former England winger Mark Chamberlain comes on at half-time for his Seagulls debut and scores.

---

3 — H BRADFORD C — 27/8 | Att 6,469 | Pos 20/1 | Pt 1 (L) | F-A 1-5 | H-T 0-4
Scorers: Dalton 83 / Jewell 23, 33, 39, Shutt 41, 48 — Ref: G Singh

	1	2	3	4	5	6	7	8	9	10	11	subs used
Argyle	Hodge	Edworthy*	Naylor	Comyn	Swan	Bradshaw	Barlow	Castle	Nugent	Shaw	**Dalton**	Twiddy
Bradford C	Tomlinson	Liburd	Jacobs	Duxbury	Sinnott	Richards	**Shutt**	Kamara	Taylor	**Jewell**	Murray	

Another shambolic home defeat brings pressure on Shilton. Paul Jewell is gifted a hat-trick by poor defending and Carl Shutt adds two more. City take their foot off the pedal in the second half. Dalton pounces on a mistake by Dean Richards. New boy Shaw has little chance to shine.

---

4 — A HULL — 30/8 | Att 3,384 | Pos 22 | Pt 1 (L) | F-A 0-2 | H-T 0-0
Scorers: Mann 53, Lee 62 — Ref: K Lynch

	1	2	3	4	5	6	7	8	9	10	11	subs used
Argyle	Hodge	Patterson	Naylor	Hill	Swan	Bradshaw	Burnett	Castle	Nugent	Shaw	Dalton*	Twiddy
Hull	Fettis	Lowthorpe	Graham	Hobson	Dewhurst	**Mann**	Atkinson	**Lee**	Brown	Windass	Lawford	

With five regulars missing, the Pilgrims slump to another defeat. Shaw wastes an opportunity when he shoots straight at Alan Fettis after being put through by Castle. Neil Mann scores his first ever league goal after a mix-up between Patterson and Hodge. Chris Lee heads in bravely.

---

5 — A BIRMINGHAM — 3/9 | Att 13,202 | Pos 22/8 | Pt 1 (L) | F-A 2-4 | H-T 0-2
Scorers: Castle 58, Nugent 80 / Regis 40, 89, Wallace 44, Tait 47 — Ref: J Parker

	1	2	3	4	5	6	7	8	9	10	11	subs used
Argyle	Bennett	Patterson*	Naylor	Comyn	Swan	Barlow	Burnett	**Castle**	**Nugent**	Shaw	Twiddy	Bradshaw
Birmingham	Bennett	Hiley*	Scott	Ward^	Whyte	Daish	Harding	Claridge	**Regis**	**Tait**	**Wallace**	Donowa/Dominguez

Shilton's game plan is again put into disarray when Patterson is taken to hospital with a head injury. Dave Regis demonstrates finishing ability that was rarely evident during his time at Home Park. Nugent claims Argyle's second although Liam Daish appears to get the final touch.

---

6 — H HUDDERSFIELD — 10/9 | Att 5,464 | Pos 22/4 | Pt 1 (L) | F-A 0-3 | H-T 0-2
Scorers: Booth 7, 9, 89 — Ref: J Holbrook

	1	2	3	4	5	6	7	8	9	10	11	subs used
Argyle	Hodge^	Bradshaw	Naylor	Comyn*	Swan	Burnett	Barlow	Castle	Nugent*	Shaw	Twiddy	Hill/Nicholls !
Huddersfield	Francis	Billy	Cowan	Logan	Scully	Mitchell	Baldry	Bullock*	**Booth**	Dunn^	Reid	Dyson/Jepson

Can it get any worse? Argyle use three different keepers during the match. Hodge goes off injured at half-time. Nicholls is sent off (77) for bringing down Andy Booth. Castle takes over. Booth, already interesting top clubs, grabs a hat-trick. Bullock escapes after elbowing Burnett.

---

7 — H CAMBRIDGE — 13/9 | Att 3,824 | Pos 22 | Pt 2 (D) | F-A 0-0 | H-T 0-0
Ref: M Pierce

	1	2	3	4	5	6	7	8	9	10	11	subs used
Argyle	Nicholls	Bradshaw	Naylor	Hill	Comyn*	Barlow	Burnett	Castle	Nugent	Shaw	Twiddy	
Cambridge	Filan	Hunter	Barrick	Craddock	O'Shea	Granville*	Fowler	Lillis^	Rush	Corazzin	Rattle	Hyde/Morah

Shilton's number two, John McGovern, quits for personal reasons. Swan is left out after his wife gives birth and ironically Argyle produce their best defensive performance of the season. Corazzin heads Shaw's shot over the bar and Burnett's well-struck drive goes straight at John Filan.

---

8 — A CARDIFF — 17/9 | Att 5,674 | Pos 22/21 | Pt 5 (W) | F-A 1-0 | H-T 0-0
Scorers: Castle 69 — Ref: J Rushton

	1	2	3	4	5	6	7	8	9	10	11	subs used
Argyle	Nicholls	Patterson	Naylor	Hill	Comyn	Barlow	Burnett	**Castle**	Nugent*	Shaw*	Twiddy	Swan/Landon
Cardiff	Williams	Brazil	Scott	Aizlewood	McLean	Perry	Oatway^	Richardson	Thompson	Dale	Griffith*	Bird/Baddeley

Swan is left on the bench. Nicholls saves Carl Dale's weak penalty (38) after the forward is tripped by Hill. Shaw's loan spell ends after he goes off with a serious-looking knee injury. Castle is back to his best and deservedly scores the only goal with a long-range shot from 25 yards.

---

9 — H CHESTER — 24/9 | Att 5,329 | Pos 21/24 | Pt 8 (W) | F-A 1-0 | H-T 1-0
Scorers: Twiddy 4 — Ref: P Rejer

	1	2	3	4	5	6	7	8	9	10	11	subs used
Argyle	Hodge	Patterson	Naylor	Hill*	Comyn	Barlow	Burnett	Morgan	Nugent	Landon^	**Twiddy**	Swan/Evans
Chester	Newland	Jenkins	Burnham	Alsford	Whelan*	Shelton	Page	Priest^	Lightfoot	Chambers	Anthrobus	Preece/Fitcroft

Mike Pejic's side arrive at Home Park with only one point to their name. Twiddy's early strike, his first senior goal, eases the pressure. Chester show little as an attacking force with Leroy Chambers fluffing their only good chance. Ray Newland receives a warm reception from the fans.

---

10 — A LEYTON ORIENT — 1/10 | Att 4,140 | Pos 19/21 | Pt 11 (W) | F-A 2-0 | H-T 2-0
Scorers: Landon 14, 38 — Ref: A Butler

	1	2	3	4	5	6	7	8	9	10	11	subs used
Argyle	Nicholls	Patterson	Naylor	Hill	Comyn	Barlow*	Burnett	Morgan	Skinner	**Landon**	Twiddy	Nugent/Edworthy
Leyton Orient	Heald	Howard	Austin	Purse	Hague	Carter^	Lakin	Cockerill	Gray	West	Dempsey*	Barnett/Bogie

Shilton's decision to drop Nugent for the first time and allow Landon to lead the attack pays dividends as the former Bedworth striker scores twice with two shots from 20 yards. Colin West blazes over after a free-kick near the penalty spot is given against Nicholls for time-wasting.

---

11 — A OXFORD — 8/10 | Att 6,550 | Pos 19/2 | Pt 11 (L) | F-A 0-1 | H-T 0-1
Scorers: Byrne 18 — Ref: P Wright

	1	2	3	4	5	6	7	8	9	10	11	subs used
Argyle	Nicholls	Patterson*	Naylor	Hill	Comyn	Barlow	Burnett	Morgan	Skinner	Landon*	Twiddy	Nugent/Edworthy
Oxford	Whitehead	Robinson	Ford M	Dyer	Elliott	Ragan	Massey	Smith	**Byrne**	Moody*	Allen^	Lewis/Rush

The working relationship between Shilton and chairman Dan McCauley continues to worsen. Argyle's mini-revival comes to an end against Denis Smith's charges. Chris Allen's corner is flicked on by Paul Moody and Eire international John Byrne applies the finishing touch for the winner.

Season results table (reading columns left-to-right: match no., venue, opponent, date; league position / number / points; result; HT score; attendance; team line-ups with Argyle above opponents; scorers; referee; match report).

12 — H WYCOMBE, 15/10
Pos 18 · 5 · 12 pts — **2–2** (HT 2–1) · Att 6,864
Argyle: Nicholls, Hill, Naylor, Swan, Comyn, Burnett, Barlow, Morgan, Skinner, Landon, Twiddy — sub O'Hagan
Wycombe: Hyde, Cousins, Brown, Crossley, Evans, Ryan, Carroll, Thompson*, Regis, Garner^, Stapleton — sub Hutchinson/Langford
Scorers: Skinner 2pp, Barlow 29 / Regis 28, 84
Ref: C Wilkes
Skinner converts Argyle's first penalty for almost a year after Matt Crossley handles. Even at 36, Cyrille Regis outpaces Comyn to level. Regis's second is controversial with Mr Wilkes, whose decisions baffle everyone for most of the game, ignoring claims of a foul on Nicholls.

13 — A STOCKPORT, 22/10
Pos 17 · 4 · 15 pts — **W 4–2** (HT 2–1) · Att 5,652
Argyle: Nicholls!, Patterson, Naylor, Hill*, Comyn, Burnett, Barlow, Edworthy, Skinner, Landon, Twiddy^ — sub O'Hagan/Dungey
Stockport: Ironside*, Connelly, Todd^, Eckhardt, Flynn, Dinning, Gannon, Ward, Francis, Armstrong, Chalk — sub Edwards/Beaumont
Scorers: Edworthy 24, O'Hagan 30, Landon 55, 87 / Chalk 1, Chalk 68
Ref: N Barry
Shilton picks his only fit 14 players. Martyn Chalk scores after just 31 seconds. Hill is stretchered off with a dislocated shoulder (22). Kevin Francis scores his customary goal. Nicholls is booked for time-wasting (72), throws the ball down in disgust, and is immediately sent off.

14 — H BLACKPOOL, 29/10
Pos 19 · 5 · 15 pts — **L 0–2** (HT 0–1) · Att 6,285
Argyle: Nicholls, Patterson, Naylor, Edworthy, Comyn, Burnett, Barlow, O'Hagan*, Skinner, Landon, Crocker
Blackpool: Martin, Brown, Burke, Bradshaw, Thompson, Homer, Mitchell, Beech, Watson*, Ellis, Quinn — sub Griffiths
Scorers: — / Watson 37, Ellis 63
Ref: R Harris
Argyle's home form lets them down again. Twiddy has a chance in the first minute but hesitates over his shot. Andy Watson opens the scoring with a clinical finish. Tony Ellis puts in a claim for goal of the season with a stupendous strike which flies in via the underside of the crossbar.

15 — H PETERBOROUGH, 1/11
Pos — · 15 pts — **L 0–1** (HT 0–1) · Att 4,145
Argyle: Nicholls, Patterson, Naylor, Edworthy, Comyn, Burnett, Barlow, Morgan, Crocker, Landon*, Twiddy — sub Nugent
Peterborough: Prudhoe, Ashley, Spearing, Ebdon, Breen, Clark, Farrell, McGorry, Williams, Charley, Henry
Scorers: — / Henry 6
Ref: J Holbrook
Yet again the Greens' young side fail to deliver the goods at Home Park. Nicholls is only able to palm away Sean Farrell's cross and Liburd Henry is on hand to score. Only Nicholls prevents a heavier loss. The fact that full-back Patterson is Argyle's most effective attacker says it all.

16 — A ROTHERHAM, 5/11
Pos 20 · 16 · 15 pts — **L 1–3** (HT 0–1) · Att 2,848
Argyle: Hodge, Patterson, Naylor, Edworthy, Comyn, Burnett^, Barlow, Morgan, Nugent, Crocker*, Skinner
Rotherham: Clarke, Wilder, James, Williams, Breckin, Brien, Hayward, Marginson*, Varadi, Goater, Roscoe — sub Hurst
Scorers: Skinner 75 / Goater 17, 80, Varadi 64
Ref: P Richards
Millers' joint manager John McGovern can afford a smile after seeing his new side despatch Argyle. Shaun Goater scores after Tony Brien's header is blocked. Patterson mysteriously throws in to Karl Marginson who sets up Imre Varadi. Skinner side-foots home. Goater scores again.

17 — H WREXHAM, 19/11
Pos 17 · 9 · 18 pts — **W 4–1** (HT 2–1) · Att 6,936
Argyle: Nicholls, Patterson, Naylor, Edworthy, Comyn, Burnett^, Barlow, Skinner, Nugent, Quinn, Morgan
Wrexham: Marriott, Jones, Hardy, Hughes, Hunter, Humes^, Bennett^, Owen, Watkin, Durkan, Phillips/Cross
Scorers: Hughes 6(og), Burnett 39, Phillips 75(og), Durkan 21 [Barlow 89]
Ref: K Cooper
The surprise arrival of the prolific Mick Quinn on loan raises spirits. Two bizarre own-goals help Argyle on their way. Bryan Hughes heads past his own keeper from fully 20 yards and Wayne Phillips swings wildly at a cross and sends the ball speeding past a helpless Andy Marriott.

18 — A YORK, 26/11
Pos 17 · 14 · 18 pts — **L 0–1** (HT 0–0) · Att 3,185
Argyle: Nicholls, Patterson, Naylor, Edworthy!, Comyn, Burnett, Barlow, Skinner, Nugent*, Quinn, Twiddy*
York: Kiely, McMillan, Wilson, Pepper, Atkin, Barras, McCarthy, Naylor*, Baker, Canham, Jordan
Scorers: — / McCarthy 78
Ref: G Cain
Twiddy suffers concussion after being hit in the face by the ball. Free-transfer signing, Micky Ross, comes on for his debut. Jon McCarthy is unmarked as he heads in Paul Wilson's cross. Edworthy uncharacteristically loses his cool and is dismissed (87) for aiming a kick at Wilson.

19 — H BRIGHTON, 10/12
Pos 19 · 17 · 18 pts — **L 0–3** (HT 0–0) · Att 6,091
Argyle: Nicholls, Patterson, Naylor, Swan, Comyn, Burnett, Barlow, Dawe*, Quinn, Ross, Twiddy*
Brighton: Rust, Smith, Chapman, Minton, Tuck, McCarthy, Myall, Akinbiyi, Nogan, Codner, Munday* — sub McGarrigle
Scorers: — / Codner 55, 68, Akinbiyi 70
Ref: S Dunn
Argyle slump to a sixth home defeat of the season against Liam Brady's side who had not won for twelve matches. Seventeen-year-old YTS debutant Simon Dawe keeps Robert Codner quiet. When Dawe is taken off, Codner immediately strikes by scoring from near the centre circle.

20 — A BRENTFORD, 17/12
Pos 19 · 9 · 18 pts — **L 0–7** (HT 0–2) · Att 4,492
Argyle: Hodge, Patterson, Naylor, Dawe, Comyn, Burnett*, Barlow, Nugent, Evans*, Ross*, Shilton
Brentford: Dearden, Hutchings, Grainger, Bates, Ashby, Smith*, Ratcliffe, Harvey, Taylor, Forster, Annon — sub Mundee
Scorers: — / Annon 3, Smith 8, Taylor 48, 56, [Forster 50, Mundee 74, Harvey 87]
Ref: R Harris
After a week of off-the-field troubles and speculation, another woeful performance rounds off a miserable week for Shilton. David Webb's side run riot against Argyle for the second time this season to condemn Argyle to their biggest defeat for 34 years. Five Pilgrims are also booked.

21 — A SWANSEA, 26/12
Pos 21 · 12 · 18 pts — **L 0–3** (HT 0–3) · Att 4,859
Argyle: Nicholls, Patterson, Hill, Swan, Comyn, Burnett*, Barlow, Dawe, Evans^, Ross, Barber
Swansea: Freestone, Barnhouse, Walker, Basham, Ford, Chapple, Hayes, Burns*, Torpey, Ampadu, Hodge^ — sub Penney/Perrett
Scorers: — / Hodge 4, Hayes 28, 43
Ref: P Vanes
The most generous defence in the Football League is again in benevolent mood. Martin Hayes' cross is not cleared and John Hodge scores with an overhead kick. Hayes then punishes more sloppy defensive work. Latest loan signing Phil Barber plays his first match of the season.

22 — H CREWE, 2/1
Pos 20 · 7 · 21 pts — **W 3–2** (HT 1–2) · Att 6,802
Argyle: Nicholls, Patterson, Naylor, Swan, Hill, Edworthy, Barlow, Nugent, Ross*, Crocker, Barber
Crewe: Smith M, Booty, Smith G, Wilson, Macauley, Gardiner*, Tierney, Collins, Clarkson^, Lennon, Murphy — sub Barr/Edwards
Scorers: Patterson 30, Evans 83, 89 / Murphy 13, Clarkson 40
Ref: M Pierce
Future England star, Danny Murphy, puts Crewe in front. Patterson crashes home his first for the club. Clarkson looks offside but is allowed to continue and slot past Nicholls. Evans, finally free of injury, earns a 'super-sub' tag by scoring twice after coming on for the injured Ross.

23 — A BOURNEMOUTH, 14/1
Pos 20 · 22 · 22 pts — **D 0–0** (HT 0–0) · Att 4,913
Argyle: Nicholls, Patterson, Naylor, Hill, Comyn, Burnett, Barlow, Nugent*, Evans, Landon/Dawe, Barber
Bournemouth: Andrews, Young, O'Connor^, Morris, Murray, Pennock, McElhatton*, Robinson, Mean, Fletcher, Brissett — sub Watson/Jones
Scorers: — / —
Ref: P Alcock
Bournemouth's biggest crowd of the season so far celebrate prematurely when Steve Jones heads in (86). With the players piling on top of him, referee Alcock decides that Jason Brissett was offside. Nugent adds his name to the injury list when he requires several stitches in a knee wound.

ENDSLEIGH DIVISION 2

Manager: Shilton > McCall > Osman

SEASON 1994-95

Match details

No	Date	V	Opponents	Res	Att	Pos	Pt	F-A	H-T	Scorers, Times, and Referees
24	21/1	H	ROTHERHAM	D	5,484	20 / 15	23	0-0	0-0	Ref: C Wilkes
25	28/1	A	BLACKPOOL	L	3,599	20 / 7	23	2-5	1-0	Patterson 30, Dalton 60; Watson 62, 90, Ellis 65, Mellon 68, 86. Ref: K Lupton
26	4/2	H	YORK	L	5,572	20 / 11	23	1-2	1-0	Skinner 44; Baker 70, Naylor 82. Ref: J Holbrook
27	7/2	A	SHREWSBURY	L	3,029	20 / 17	23	2-3	1-0	Nugent 21, Evans 86; Spink 49, 81, Withe 58. Ref: R Poulain
28	11/2	A	PETERBOROUGH	W	4,318	20 / 18	26	2-1	1-0	McCall 3, Nugent 85; Farrell 54. Ref: P Foakes
29	18/2	H	BOURNEMOUTH	L	5,435	20 / 21	26	0-1	0-1	McElhatton 45. Ref: K Cooper
30	21/2	A	WREXHAM	L	3,030	20 / —	26	1-3	1-0	Castle 32; Bennett 61, 90, Hughes 67. Ref: K Lynch
31	25/2	H	LEYTON ORIENT	W	5,173	20 / 23	29	1-0	0-0	Landon 71. Ref: G Singh
32	4/3	A	CHESTER	L	1,823	21 / 24	29	0-1	0-1	Rimmer 2. Ref: U Rennie
33	11/3	A	BRADFORD C	L	5,399	21 / 10	29	0-2	0-0	Power 73, 87p. Ref: E Wolstenholme
34	18/3	H	HULL	W	4,839	20 / 9	32	2-1	2-1	Nugent 10, Evans 19; Ormondroyd 13. Ref: P Rejer

Line-ups

No	Team	1	2	3	4	5	6	7	8	9	10	11	subs used
24	Argyle	Nicholls	Edworthy	Naylor	Hill	Comyn	Burnett	Skinner	Barlow	Landon	Evans	Barber*	Dalton
24	Rotherham	Clarke	Wilder	James	Richardson	Monington	Breckin	Hayward	McGlashan	Davison*	Goater	Roscoe	Varadi
25	Argyle	Nicholls	Patterson	Naylor	Hill	Comyn	Burnett	Skinner	Barlow	Gee	Landon^	McCall*	Burnett/Dalton
25	Blackpool	Martin	Rowett	Darton	Bradshaw	Morrison	Horner	Quinn	Mellon	Watson	Ellis	Gouck	
26	Argyle	Nicholls	Patterson	Naylor	Hill	Comyn	Burnett	Skinner*	Barlow	Gee	Nugent	Burnett	Evans/Dalton
26	York	Kiely	McMillan	Wilson	Pepper	Tutill^	Atkin	McCarthy	Murty*	Baker	Jordan	Hall	Canham/Naylor
27	Argyle	Nicholls	Patterson	Naylor	Hill	Comyn	Burnett	Wotton	Barlow	Gee*	Nugent!	Dalton	Evans/Castle
27	Shrewsbury	Edwards	Simkin	Withe	Taylor	Smith*	Lynch	Stevens	Evans	Spink	Walton	Currie	Seabury
28	Argyle	Nicholls	Patterson	Naylor	Hill	Swan	Burnett	Barlow	Wotton	Evans*	Nugent	Dalton	Skinner/Castle
28	Peterborough	Keeley	Ashley	Spearing	Etdon	Breen	Clark	Williams	Soloman	Farrell	Charlery	Moran*	Morrison
29	Argyle	Nicholls	Patterson	Naylor	Hill	Swan	Burnett	Barlow	Castle	Gee*	Nugent	Dalton	Evans/Wotton
29	Bournemouth	Andrews	McEhatton	Beardsmore	Morris	Murray	Pennock	Holland	Robinson	Jones	Fletcher	Brissett**	Mean
30	Argyle	Hodge	Patterson!	Naylor	Hill	Swan	Burnett	Castle	Castle	Landon	Gee	Dalton	Skinner
30	Wrexham	Marriott	Jones	Hardy	Hughes	Hunter	Pejic	Quigley	Connolly	Watkin	Cross		
31	Argyle	Hodge	Patterson	Naylor	Hill	Comyn	Barlow	Wotton^	Castle*	Landon	Gee	Dalton	Burnett/Skinner
31	Leyton Orient	Heald	Hendon	Austin	Bellamy	Purse	Bogie	Carter	Cockerill	Warren	West	Dempsey	
32	Argyle	Hodge	Patterson	Naylor	Hill	Comyn	Twiddy^	Barlow	Castle	Nugent*	Landon	Dalton	Evans/Wotton
32	Chester	Felgate	Jenkins	Ratcliffe	Preece	Whelan	Jackson	Priest^	Shelton	Page	Rimmer	Hackett^	Flitcroft/Gardiner
33	Argyle	Hodge	Edworthy	Huxford	Swan	Comyn	Burnett	Burnett	Castle	Nugent	Evans*	Dalton	Morgan/Ross
33	Bradford C	Tomlinson	Huxford	Jacobs	Robson	Mitchell*	Richards	Showler	Verveer	Taylor	Hamilton	Murray	Shutt/Power
34	Argyle	Hodge	Edworthy	Naylor	Swan	Comyn	Burnett	Evans	Castle	Nugent	Ross	Dalton	
34	Hull	Fettis	Lee	Graham^	Dakin	Dewhurst	Joyce	Allison	Mann*	Brown	Windass	Ormondroyd	Peacock/Lawford

Match reports

24 — ROTHERHAM. The match is one of only 16 in the whole league to survive torrential rain. Argyle's goal drought continues and their injury plight is highlighted by the inclusion of a far from fit Dalton as sub. Andy Hayward comes closest to breaking the deadlock when his angled shot strikes an upright.

25 — BLACKPOOL. Blackpool are jeered off the pitch at half-time as they trail to a 30-yard Patterson strike. Sam Allardyce switches his skipper, Andy Morrison, into midfield and his fierce determination combined with more defensive generosity and a malfunctioning offside trap transforms the match.

26 — YORK. York boss Alan Little gets an early 40th birthday present as City push the Pilgrims deeper into relegation trouble. Paul Baker scores from close range and Glenn Naylor beats the offside trap. Skinner's shot but the ball rebounds off Dean Kiely and goes in.

27 — SHREWSBURY. Mixed fortunes for Nugent. After putting Argyle ahead with his first goal since Easter last year, he was sent off (31) for a verbal outburst against a linesman. To make matters worse, he also receives a club fine for damaging a dressing room door. The defence is again in suicide mode.

28 — PETERBOROUGH. McCall is instrumental in the first win under his stewardship as he drives in a half-cleared corner. The Shrews fail to capitalise on a free-kick from six yards when Nicholls handles a back-pass. Ken Charlery outpaces Naylor to set up Andy Farrell's goal. Nugent heads a late winner.

29 — BOURNEMOUTH. Swan expresses a desire to leave Home Park. Castle makes a welcome start after a long absence with jaundice. McCall goes off (29) with blurred vision. Nicholls misses Brissett's corner and Michael McElhatton has the easy task of scoring to giving the struggling Cherries a boost.

30 — WREXHAM. Argyle take a 1-0 lead for the fourth successive away match but again throw it away. Bryan Hughes' shot trickles past three players and creeps in. Patterson sees the red card after bringing down Watkin (89) having been booked earlier. Bennett scores his 37th of the season in injury-time.

31 — LEYTON ORIENT. An inept Orient show why they have managed to gain only one point on their travels this season. Landon consolidates his place at the top of the Argyle scoring charts with only his fifth of the campaign. Argyle survive an early spell of pressure and Gary Bellamy tests the woodwork.

32 — CHESTER. Chester already looked doomed before the pre-match announcement of Derek Mann as their new manager inspires them to a rare win. Naylor carelessly hacks into touch and, from the resultant throw, Don Page lays on Stuart Rimmer's goal. Argyle are restricted to long-range efforts.

33 — BRADFORD C. After an evenly matched first hour, the introduction of Lee Power turns the game. He knows little of his first as Verveer's driving cross strikes him and goes in. There is no apparent contact by Comyn as John Taylor drops like a stone for a penalty. McCall brands the decision 'a joke'.

34 — HULL. A 'Kids for a Quid' scheme is introduced. Hull are strangely allowed to wear their green away shirts. Nugent fires in a 20-yard shot. The lanky Ian Ormondroyd levels. Evans nets a spectacular volley. Tigers boss Terry Dolan races onto the pitch after a clash between Ross and Graham.

Match summary

No	Date	Opponent	H/A	Att	Opp pos	Result	Pts	Score
	21/3	[cropped]		12,099			32	
36	25/3	CARDIFF	H	5,611	21 / 22	D	33	0-0
37	28/3	STOCKPORT	H	4,618		L	33	0-2
38	1/4	CAMBRIDGE	A	3,913	19	D	34	1-1
39	4/4	BRISTOL ROV	H	6,743		D	35	1-1
40	8/4	SHREWSBURY	A	5,089	18	W	38	1-0
41	15/4	BRISTOL ROV	A	7,068	4	L	38	0-2
42	17/4	SWANSEA	H	5,890	10	W	41	2-1
43	19/4	BIRMINGHAM	H	8,550		L	41	1-3
44	22/4	CREWE	A	3,786	7	D	42	2-2
45	29/4	WYCOMBE	A	6,850	6	W	45	2-1
46	6/5	OXFORD	H	4,953	7	D	46	1-1

Home Average 5,832 · Away 5,310 · Average 5,832

21/3 (Att 12,099 · pos 32)
Dyson 1, Booth 48 — Ref: G Cain
Opponents: Francis, Dyson, Williams, Bullock, Scully, Sinnott, Dunn*, Duxbury, Booth, Jepson, Reid; Baldry
Report: The Terriers move back to the top. Hodge is immediately tested by Iain Dunn's low cross. Swan heads Lee Duxbury's cross as far as Jon Dyson who lets fly from 25 yards. Andy Booth holds off Edworthy to notch his 26th goal of the season. Naylor almost scores from 30 yards.

36 · 25/3 · CARDIFF (H) — D 0-0 (pts 33)
Ref: P Vanes
Cardiff: Williams, Brazil, Searle, Griffith*, Young, Perry, Wigg, Nicholls, Pearson^, Richardson, Millar; Baddeley/Milsom
Report: More vital home points are dropped against fellow relegation candidates. Ross squanders the best chance but with only David Williams to beat hurries his shot. Nugent plays the second half with his head swathed in bandages. Patterson goes off with blood pouring from a head wound.

37 · 28/3 · STOCKPORT (H) — L 0-2 (pts 33)
Graham 2, Dinning 57 — Ref: C Wilkes
Stockport: Dickins, Connelly, Todd, Oliver, Flynn, Dinning, Gannon, Ward, Helliwell, Armstrong*, Graham; Beaumont
Report: Another home defeat prompts McCauley to suggest help for McCall. The manager rejects the idea and resigns two days later but remains as a player. Deniol Graham scores after just 89 seconds to leave Argyle with another mountain to climb. Tony Dinning scores from Ward's cross.

38 · 1/4 · CAMBRIDGE (A) — D 1-1 (pts 34)
Landon 62 / Butler 76p — Ref: D Orr
Cambridge: Sheffield, Joseph, Campbell, Thompson, Heathcote, Hayrettin, Hyde*, Danzey^, Butler, Corazzin, Pack; Hunter/Nyamah
Report: Linesman Richard Saunders takes over from the injured Mr Orr. Landon gives Argyle the rare luxury of a lead but Steve Butler scores from the spot after Corazzin goes tumbling. Castle is booked for protesting and is shown the red card for continuing his protests after the final whistle.

39 · 4/4 · BRISTOL ROV (H) — D 1-1 (pts 35)
Nugent 6 / Miller 60 — Ref: P Rejer
Bristol Rovers: Parkin, Pritchard, Maddison, Channing, Clark, Tillson, Sterling, Miller, Clarke; Browning, Archer
Report: New boss Osman's faith in the same starting line-up seems to be rewarded when Nugent strikes early with a deflected shot. The under-worked Nicholls blunders when he comes to collect a David Pritchard cross but gets in a tangle with Swan and allows Paul Miller an easy equaliser.

40 · 8/4 · SHREWSBURY (A) — W 1-0 (pts 38)
Patterson 25 — Ref: S Dunn
Shrewsbury: Clarke T, Seabury, Lynch*, Taylor, Williams, Scott, Spink, Walton, Smith; Castle/Ross, Withe/Stevens
Report: Winger Skinner is named as substitute goalkeeper. McCall returns and shows that he is still willing to give his all despite recent events. Patterson runs from halfway, beats two players and despatches a shot past Clarke. Nicholls makes a brilliant one-handed save near the end.

41 · 15/4 · BRISTOL ROV (A) — L 0-2 (pts 38)
Taylor 50, Wright 65 — Ref: J Rushton
Bristol Rovers: Parkin, Pritchard, Maddison, Channing, Clark, Wright, Evans, Stewart^, Skinner^, Taylor; Ross, Archer/Browning
Report: John Ward's promotion-chasing side pull off their expected win. Gareth Taylor heads in Worrell Sterling's cross. Nicholls is rooted to his line as Ian Wright is allowed a free header from Justin Channing's corner. Argyle maintain their record of never having scored at Twerton Park.

42 · 17/4 · SWANSEA (H) — W 2-1 (pts 41)
Swan 42, Nugent 60 / Hodge 40 — Ref: J Holbrook
Swansea: Freestone, Jenkins, Clode, Walker, Ford, Pascoe, Bowen*, Torpey, Ampadu^, Cornforth, Hodge; Hayes/Thomas
Report: Nicholls gifts the Swans the lead. He attempts to fly-hack the ball away but miskicks and John Hodge can scarcely believe his luck as he is confronted by an empty net. Swan, playing with pain-killing injections, levels with a header. Nugent's brave header clinches three vital points.

43 · 19/4 · BIRMINGHAM (H) — L 1-3 (pts 41)
Dalton 90 / Whyte 49, Claridge 74, 83 — Ref: R Harris
Birmingham: Bennett, Poole, Frain, Ward, Whyte, Daish, Hunt*, Claridge, Francis, Cooper^, Robinson; Dominguez/Otto
Report: Old adversary Kevin Francis returns with his new side and is in the thick of the action. He accidentally tramples on Nicholls and is the victim of two fouls in quick succession by Swan which sees the defender sent off (72). Claridge's solo effort, his 24th of the season, seals the victory.

44 · 22/4 · CREWE (A) — D 2-2 (pts 42)
Gardiner 45(og), Dalton 81p / Lennon 7, Adebola 82 — Ref: K Breen
Crewe: Gayle, Booty, Smith, Barr, MacAuley, Gardiner*, Tierney, Collins, Adebola, Lennon, Clarkson^; Murphy/Edwards
Report: Dungey plays after the League refuse to allow Argyle to sign another keeper. Neil Lennon lobs Dungey for the opener. Argyle can thank Mark Gardiner for their comeback as he helps Nugent's header into his own net and then handles to allow Dalton to blast home from the spot.

45 · 29/4 · WYCOMBE (A) — W 2-1 (pts 45)
Hill 4, Landon 65 / Bell 47 — Ref: J Lloyd
Wycombe: Hyde, Cousins, Howard, Crossley, Evans, Brown, Carroll, Bell, McGavin, Hemmings, Thompson*; Garner
Report: Argyle keep their hopes of avoiding the drop alive with a shock win against Martin O'Neill's promotion hopefuls. Hill opens the Pilgrims an ideal start by converting Dalton's pass. The excellent Dungey has no chance with Mickey Bell's equaliser. Landon coolly slots past Paul Hyde.

46 · 6/5 · OXFORD (H) — D 1-1 (pts 46)
Nugent 12 / Ford R 51 — Ref: C Wilkes
Oxford: Whitehead, Robinson, Collins, Lewis, Elliott, Gilchrist^, Ford R, Murphy, Massey*, Rush, Allen; Smith/Wanless
Report: Bournemouth's midweek win has already condemned Plymouth to the drop. Both sides toil in the heat with little to play for. Nugent gently guides a shot past Phil Whitehead. Bobby Ford scores from 20 yards The crowd invade the pitch at the end and stripping the players of their kit.

ENDSLEIGH DIVISION 2 (CUP-TIES)   Manager: Shilton > McCall > Osman   SEASON 1994-95

Coca-Cola Cup

1:1 A WALSALL 16/8 — Att 2,810 3: — L F-A 0-4 — H-T 0-0
Scorers, Times, and Referees: O'Connor 85; Wilson 53, 74, Lightbourne 76. Ref: G Pooley

	1	2	3	4	5	6	7	8	9	10	11	subs used
Argyle	Hodge	Payne	Edworthy	Comyn !	Swan	Hill	Barlow !	Burnett	Nugent	Evans	Skinner*	Morgan
Walsall	*Wood*	*Evans**	*Rogers*	*Watkiss*	*Marsh*	*Palmer*	*O'Connor*	*Ntamark*	*Wilson*	*Lightbourne*	*Mehew*	*Lillis*

A disastrous first visit to the new Bescot Stadium sees Skinner injured and Comyn (25 foul on Lightbourne) and Barlow (65 dissent) sent off. Northern Ireland forward Kevin Wilson proves a thorn in the side with two well-taken goals. Hodge again excels. Things can only get better.

1:2 H WALSALL 23/8 — Att 2,801 3:7 — W F-A 2-1 — H-T 1-0
Scorers, Times, and Referees: Swan 31, Castle 55, Wilson 75. Ref: C Wilkes. (Argyle lost 2-5 on aggregate)

	1	2	3	4	5	6	7	8	9	10	11	subs used
Argyle	Hodge	Bradshaw	Edworthy	Comyn	Swan	Hill	Barlow	Castle*	Nugent	Evans^	Dalton	Twiddy/Landon
Walsall	*Wood*	*Evans*	*Rogers*	*Watkiss*	*Marsh*	*Palmer*	*O'Connor*	*Ntamark*	*Lightbourne**	*Wilson*	*Mehew*	*Butler*

Argyle produce a much-improved performance despite having little chance of progression to the next round. Dalton's gem of a free-kick is disallowed for being taken too quickly. Castle's free-kick is allowed to follow up Swan's earlier thunderbolt. Kevin Wilson taps in a rebound.

FA Cup

1 A KETTERING 13/11 — Att 4,602 VC:5 — W F-A 1-0 — H-T 0-0
Scorers, Times, and Referees: Skinner 46. Ref: G Singh

	1	2	3	4	5	6	7	8	9	10	11	subs used
Argyle	Hodge	Patterson	Naylor	Edworthy	Comyn	Burnett	Barlow	Skinner	Nugent	Evans	Twiddy	Magee/Wright
Kettering	*Benstead*	*Smith*	*Ashby*	*Holden*	*Oxbrow*	*Taylor**	*Martin^*	*Stringfellow*	*Alford*	*Thomas*	*Brown*	

The match kicks off at four o'clock and is shown live on Sky TV. Despite a single goal victory, Argyle never look in danger of being on the wrong end of a cup upset and Hodge has a quiet afternoon. Skinner scores 42 seconds into the second half after Nugent's shot hits the upright.

2 H BOURNEMOUTH 3/12 — Att 6,739 24 — W F-A 2-1 — H-T 2-0
Scorers, Times, and Referees: Ross 3, 30, Jones 46. Ref: G Ashby

	1	2	3	4	5	6	7	8	9	10	11	subs used
Argyle	Nicholls	Patterson	Naylor	Edworthy	Swan	Burnett	Barlow	Patterson	Nugent*	Ross	Evans^	Landon/Shilton
Bournemouth	*Andrews*	*Young*	*Pennock**	*Watson*	*Robinson*	*Leadbitter*	*Beardsmore^*	*Mean*	*Morris*	*Jones*	*Russell*	*McElhatton/Murray*

Ross becomes an instant hero on his home debut. The manager's son becomes the youngest ever player to play first-team football for Argyle. Swan and Comyn both wear number five in the second half. Cherries boss Mel Machin keeps his side locked in for an hour after the match.

3 A NOTT'M FOREST 7/1 — Att 19,821 P:4 — L F-A 0-2 — H-T 0-2
Scorers, Times, and Referees: Collymore 6, Gemmill 16. Ref: D Elleray

	1	2	3	4	5	6	7	8	9	10	11	subs used
Argyle	Nicholls	Patterson	Naylor	Swan	Hill	Edworthy	Barlow	Skinner	Nugent*	Burnett	Barber*	Evans, Webb
Forest	*Crossley*	*Lyttle*	*Pearce*	*Haaland*	*Chettle*	*Stone*	*Phillips*	*Gemmill*	*Roy^*	*Collymore*	*Woan*	

McCall takes the hot seat from the sacked Shilton and faces Frank Clark's stars. The travelling Green Army fear the worst as Forest race into a two-goal lead through Stan Collymore and Scott Gemmill who latches onto an error by Burnett. A gutsy display ensures no further goals.

League table

Pos	Team	P	Home W	D	L	F	A	Away W	D	L	F	A	Pts
1	Birmingham	46	15	6	2	53	18	10	8	5	31	19	89
2	Brentford	46	14	4	5	44	15	11	6	6	37	24	85
3	Crewe	46	14	3	6	46	33	11	5	7	34	35	83
4	Bristol Rov	46	15	7	1	48	20	7	9	7	22	20	82
5	Huddersfield*	46	14	5	4	45	21	8	10	5	34	28	81
6	Wycombe	46	13	7	3	36	19	8	8	7	24	27	78
7	Oxford	46	13	6	4	30	18	8	6	9	36	34	75
8	Hull	46	13	6	4	40	18	8	5	10	30	39	74
9	York	46	13	4	6	37	21	8	5	10	30	30	72
10	Swansea	46	13	8	5	23	13	9	6	8	34	32	71
11	Stockport	46	12	3	8	40	29	12	3	8	23	31	65
12	Blackpool	46	11	4	8	40	36	9	5	9	24	34	64
13	Wrexham	46	10	7	6	38	27	6	8	9	27	37	63
14	Bradford	46	8	6	9	29	32	9	6	8	28	32	60
15	Peterborough	46	9	11	5	26	29	9	7	7	28	40	60
16	Brighton	46	9	10	4	25	15	9	7	11	29	38	59
17	Rotherham	46	12	6	5	36	26	2	8	13	21	35	56
18	Shrewsbury	46	9	9	5	34	27	4	5	14	20	35	53
19	Bournemouth	46	9	4	10	30	34	4	7	12	19	35	50
20	Cambridge	46	8	9	6	33	28	3	6	14	19	41	48
21	PLYMOUTH	46	7	6	10	22	36	5	4	14	23	47	46
22	Cardiff	46	5	6	12	25	31	6	5	14	21	43	38
23	Chester	46	5	6	12	23	42	1	5	17	14	42	29
24	Leyton Orient	46	6	6	11	21	29	0	2	21	9	46	26
		1104	252	149	151	824	617	151	149	252	617	824	1507

* promoted after play-offs

Appearances & Goals

Player	Lge	Sub	LC	Sub	FAC	Sub	Goals Lge	LC	FAC	Tot
Barber, Phil	4					1	2			2
Barlow, Martin	40	2	2		3		2			2
Bradshaw, Darren	5	1	1				1			1
Burnett, Wayne	25	7	1		3		1			1
Castle, Steve	23	3	1				3		1	4
Comyn, Andy	30		2		2					
Crocker, Marcus	3	2								
Dalton, Paul	23	3	1		1		4			4
Dawe, Simon	3	1								
Dungey, James	3									
Edworthy, Marc	24	3	2		3		1			1
Evans, Michael	12	11	2		2	1	4			4
Gee, Phil	6									
Hill, Keith	32	2	2		1		1			1
Hodge, Martin	17	2	2		1					
Landon, Richard	18	6	1		1	1	7			7
McCall, Steve	7									
Morgan, Jamie	6	2				1	1			1
Naylor, Dominic	42				3					
Nicholls, Alan	26	1			2					
Nugent, Kevin	34	3	2		3		7			7
O'Hagan, Danny	1	2								
Patterson, Mark	37	1	1		3		3			3
Payne, Ian	1		1							
Quinn, Mick	3									
Ross, Micky	11	6			1			2		2
Shaw, Graham	6									
Shilton, Sam	1	1				1				
Skinner, Craig	21	3	1		2		3	1		4
Swan, Peter	24	3	2		2		2		1	3
Twiddy, Chris	13	2	1		1	1	1			1
Wotton, Paul	5	2								
(own-goals)							3			3
32 players used	506	68	22	3	33	3	45	2	3	49

Odds & ends

Double wins: (1) Leyton Orient.

Double defeats: (6) Birmingham, Blackpool, Bradford City, Brentford, Huddersfield, York.

Won from behind: (3) Crewe, Stockport, Swansea.

Lost from in front: (5) Blackpool, Brentford, Shrewsbury, Wrexham, York.

High spots: Emergence of Marc Edworthy as classy defender. Number of promising youngsters given first-team opportunities. Fighting display at Premiership side Nottingham Forest in FA Cup.

Low spots: Well-publicised, acrimonious departure of Peter Shilton. Lack of regular goalscorer. Relegation to lowest division for first time in the club's history. Over-reliance on loan signings. Disastrous 0-7 defeat at Brentford. First two home league matches both resulted in 1-5 defeats. Poor disciplinary record.

Player of the Year: Marc Edworthy.

Ever presents: (0).

Hat-tricks: (0).

Leading scorers: Richard Landon, Kevin Nugent (7).

ENDSLEIGH DIVISION 3 — Manager: Neil Warnock — SEASON 1995-96

No	Date	Att	Pos	Pt	F-A	H-T	Scorers, Times, and Referees	1	2	3	4	5	6	7	8	9	10	11	subs used
1	A COLCHESTER 12/8	3,585	—	L 0	1-2	0-1	Littlejohn 54 / Betts 15, Locke 59 / Ref: A D'Urso	Hammond	Patterson*	Williams	Burnett	Heathcote	Hill*	Billy	Mauge	Littlejohn	Nugent	Leadbitter*	Hodgs'n/Tw'dy/Evans
							Emberson	*Locke*	*Betts*	*McCarthy*	*Caesar*	*Cawley*	*Kinsella*	*English !*	*Whitton*	*Adcock*	*Cheetham**	Dennis
2	H PRESTON 19/8	6,862	24 11	L 0	0-2	0-0	Hammond 64(og), Bryson 75 / Ref: P Rejer	Hammond	Patterson*	Williams	Burnett	Heathcote	Hill*	Billy	Mauge	Littlejohn	Nugent	Clayton^	L'dbit'r/Evans/Hodgs'n
							Vaughan	*Fensome**	*Sharp*	*Atkinson^*	*Kidd*	*Moyes*	*Fleming*	*Bryson*	*Wilkinson*	*Magee*	*Saville*	Ainsworth/Squires
3	A CHESTER 26/8	2,660	23 5	L 0	1-3	0-1	Williams 53 / Bishop 44, 62, Regis 82 / Ref: S Baines	Hammond	Twiddy^	Williams	Burnett*	Heathcote	Hill	Billy	Mauge	Littlejohn	Nugent*	Clayton	O'Hagan/Evans/L'dbit'r
							Stewart	*Flitcroft*	*Preedy*	*Jenkins*	*Jackson*	*Alsford*	*Fisher*	*Priest*	*Regis^*	*Milner**	*Bishop*	Rimmer/Murphy
4	H HEREFORD 29/8	5,608	—	L 0	0-1	0-1	White 32 / Ref: G Singh	Hammond	Saunders*	Williams	Clayton	Heathcote	Hodgson	Billy	Mauge	Littlejohn	Nugent*	Leadbitter*	Evans/O'Hag'n/Patrs'n
							MacKenzie	*Clarke*	*Preedy*	*Smith*	*Cross*	*Preece*	*Pounder*	*Wilkins*	*Lyne*	*White**	*Fishlock*	Pick
5	A BURY 2/9	3,040	24 14	W 3	5-0	3-0	Evans 28, 79, Clayton 40, Billy 45, [Littlejohn 89] / Ref: R Pearson	Blackwell	Patterson	Williams	Clayton	Heathcote	Hodgson	Billy	Mauge*	Littlejohn*	Evans	Leadbitter*	Saunders/O'Hagan
							Bracey	*Cross*	*Bimson*	*Reid*	*Lucketti*	*Hughes !*	*Daws**	*Carter*	*Stant*	*Rigby*	*Pugh*	Richardson
6	H LEYTON ORIENT 9/9	6,292	23 11	D 4	1-1	1-0	Evans 19 / Watson 81 / Ref: C Wilkes	Blackwell	Patterson*	Williams	Clayton*	Heathcote	Hodgson	Billy	Mauge	Littlejohn*	Evans	Leadbitter*	S'nders/O'Hag'n/Shilt'n
							Caldwell	*Hendon**	*Stanislaus*	*Chapman*	*Bellamy*	*McCarthy*	*Kelly*	*Cockerill*	*Inglethorpe**	*West*	*Brooks*	Austin/Watson
7	H DONCASTER 12/9	4,858	—	W 7	3-1	2-1	Evans 22, Billy 27, Littlejohn 84 / Hill 11(og) / Ref: K Leach	Blackwell	Patterson	Williams	Burnett	Heathcote	Hill	Billy	Mauge	Littlejohn	Evans	Leadbitter	Knight/Maxfield
							Sucking	*Kirby**	*Parrish*	*Moore*	*Wilcox*	*Carmichael**	*Schofield*	*Brabin*	*Jones*	*Brodie*	*Warren*	
8	A BARNET 16/9	2,557	13 24	W 10	2-1	0-0	Evans 67p, Littlejohn 88 / Cooper 74 / Ref: J Brandwood	Blackwell	Patterson	Williams	Burnett*	Heathcote	Hill	Billy^	Mauge	Littlejohn	Evans	Leadbitter	Saunders/Nugent
							Taylor	*Gale*	*McDonald*	*Pardew*	*Primus*	*Thomas*	*Dyer*	*Robbins*	*Wilson*	*Cooper*	*Scott*	
9	A WIGAN 23/9	2,631	10 12	W 13	1-0	0-0	Littlejohn 79 / Ref: J Lloyd	Blackwell	Patterson	Williams	Burnett*	Heathcote	Hill	Billy	Mauge	Littlejohn	Evans^	Leadbitter	Saunders/Nugent
							Farnworth	*Butler*	*Ogden*	*Greenall*	*Pender*	*Martinez*	*Kilford*	*Lightfoot*	*Mutch**	*Rimmer^*	*Diaz*	Lyons/Seba/Benjamin
10	H LINCOLN 30/9	6,643	5 24	W 16	3-0	3-0	Minett 4(og), Evans 6, Littlejohn 19 / Ref: R Gifford	Blackwell	Patterson	Williams	Barlow	Heathcote	Hill	Baird	Mauge*	Littlejohn	Evans	Leadbitter	Clayton/Magee
							Leaning	*Minett*	*Johnson A*	*Wanless*	*Carbon*	*Davis*	*Hulme**	*Onwere*	*Johnson D*	*Huckerby*	*Appleton*	Dixon
11	H FULHAM 7/10	6,681	4 12	W 19	3-0	2-0	Littlejohn 20, Baird 24, 77 / Ref: A Wiley	Blackwell	Patterson*	Williams	Barlow	Heathcote	Hill	Baird	Mauge*	Littlejohn	Evans	Leadbitter	Clayton
							Lange	*Jupp*	*Taylor**	*Mison*	*Angus*	*Blake**	*Thomas*	*Morgan*	*Brazil*	*Conroy*	*Moore*	Bolt/Cusack

Match notes

1. Seven debutants tells the story of how busy Warnock has been during the summer. Bettis scores from 20 yards, and four minutes later Tony English is dismissed for a second booking. Argyle look favourites but do not bargain for Locke's 35-yarder. Littlejohn equalises off a post.

2. Argyle look totally incapable of scoring, and then gift Preston two goals. Hammond is at fault for the first when he comes to collect Jamie Squires' corner and inexplicably pushes the ball into his own net. Ian Bryson is then left in acres of space to slide the ball under Hammond.

3. Warnock calls his side in for Sunday training as the pre-season bookies' favourites for promotion suffer their fifth successive league and cup defeat. Eddie Bishop scores twice with ease and the evergreen Cyrille Regis powers home a trademark header from David Flitcroft's corner.

4. Hammond's torrid start to his Argyle career continues as he fails to gather a long throw and veteran Steve White reacts the quickest. With the forward line again in lacklustre form, the crowd begin to vent their anger even at this early stage. Warnock praises his players' commitment.

5. Blackwell replaces the discarded Hammond. Argyle suddenly remember how to score as they run riot. Mauge, captain for the day against his former side, is inspirational. Hughes is sent off (68) for fouling the elusive Littlejohn. Clayton scores the pick of the goals from 25 yards.

6. Hopes of a revival in form are dashed as the O's make Argyle struggle. Evans has a simple task to score after Mauge's header hits the crossbar. Heathcote is penalised (68) for tripping Chapman but Blackwell saves Colin West's spot-kick. Mark Watson scores his first ever league goal.

7. Hill and Blackwell give Rovers a head start. The defender rolls the ball back to his keeper who completely miskicks. Evans levels. Billy scores from a sitting position after Perry Suckling misses Littlejohn's cross. Heathcote has a header cleared off the line. Littlejohn finishes Rovers off.

8. Evans breaks the deadlock from the spot after Billy is brought down by David MacDonald. Mark Cooper has the freedom of a very wet Underhill to equalise. Littlejohn outpaces Linvoy Primus to score a late winner and send the 1,000 soaked Argyle followers home happy.

9. The Latics feel robbed as two penalty appeals, both against Patterson, are turned down. Firstly, he handles but the referee deems it accidental. He then trips Spaniard Isidro Diaz but play goes on. Littlejohn again is in the right spot. Wigan sack manager Graham Barrow after this loss.

10. The experienced Baird is soon involved, pressurising Jason Minett to head firmly past his own keeper. Evans nets the 4,500th goal of Argyle's football league existence. Baird is involved again as he is the centre-piece of a clever passing move which Littlejohn finishes with aplomb.

11. Cottagers boss Ian Branfoot expresses envy at Argyle's spending power. His inexperienced side are outclassed as the Pilgrims' remarkable recovery continues with Baird again showing why he has played in the top flight. Behind the scenes, six fringe players look set to depart.

No		Venue	Date	Pos	Res	HT	FT	Scorers	Att	Opp Pos	Pts	Ref
12	A	MANSFIELD	14/10	4	D	1-1	1-1	Heathcote 9 / Ireland 30	3,164	15	20	K Lynch
13	H	TORQUAY	21/10	4	W	2-3	4-3	Littlejohn 7, 37, 85, Mauge 78 / Ndah 15, 22, Partridge 39	11,695	23	23	R Harris
14	A	DARLINGTON	28/10	6	L	0-0	0-2	Himsworth 53, Naylor 85	2,352	7	23	M Riley
15	A	SCARBOROUGH	31/10		D	1-0	2-2	Leadbitter 16, Littlejohn 47 / Charles 67, Trebble 90	1,876		24	N Barry
16	H	CARDIFF	4/11	6	D	0-0	0-0		7,434	21	25	S Mathieson
17	A	HARTLEPOOL	18/11	6	D	2-0	2-2	Evans 11p, Mauge 35 / Ingram 48, Howard 61	1,830	18	26	T Leake
18	H	ROCHDALE	25/11	5	W	0-0	2-0	Littlejohn 48, Evans 86	6,558	4	29	J Rushden
19	H	WIGAN	9/12	4	W	1-1	3-1	Barlow 8, Littlejohn 75, 88 / Farrell 12	5,931	11	32	M Pierce
20	A	LINCOLN	16/12	4	D	0-0	0-0		2,801	23	33	J Brandwood
21	H	CAMBRIDGE	23/12	4	W	0-0	1-0	Mauge 75	7,135	7	36	R Gifford
22	A	GILLINGHAM	26/12	4	L	0-0	0-1	Butler S 83p	9,651	1	36	G Pooley
23	H	EXETER	1/1	4	D	0-2	2-2	Baird 58, 79 / Came 2, Buckle 45	12,427	12	37	K Leach

12 – A MANSFIELD 14/10
Argyle: Blackwell, Patterson, Williams, Barlow*, Heathcote, Hill, Baird, Mauge, Littlejohn, Evans, Leadbitter — Clayton
Mansfield: Bowling, Boothroyd, Sedgemore, Doolan, Howarth, Peters, Ireland, Parkin, Harper, Hadley, Kerr

Barlow, one of the players who looks likely to leave, sets up Heathcote's header with a flighted free-kick. Simon Ireland heads in Kerr's high cross to give the Stags their eighth draw of the season. The Pilgrims are infuriated when Mr Lynch ignores Ian Bowling's bear-hug on Evans.

13 – H TORQUAY 21/10
Argyle: Blackwell, Patterson, Williams, Barlow*, Heathcote, Hill, Baird, Mauge, Littlejohn, Evans, Leadbitter* — Magee|Logan|Barlow
Torquay: Bayes, Curran, Kelly, O'Riordan^, Gore!, Barrow, Jack, Coughlin, Partridge, Ndah* — Hodges/Laight

Heathcote ignores a week of toothache to play his usual commanding game. Mr Harris books eight players, including manager Don O'Riordan for waving an imaginary flag at a linesman. Ian Gore is sent off for his second bookable offence. Littlejohn's lethal left foot strikes three times.

14 – A DARLINGTON 28/10
Argyle: Blackwell, Patterson, Williams, Clayton", Heathcote, Hill, Baird*, Mauge, Littlejohn, Evans, Leadbitter — Magee|Logan|Barlow
Darlington: Pollitt, Shaw, Barnard, Appleby, Crosby, Gregan, Himsworth, Olsson, Painter*, Naylor, Bannister — Gaughan

After a dull first half, Jim Platt's men go for broke as they push up in numbers. Mark Barnard's third attempt at a cross finds Gary Himsworth, who nets from 20 yards. Blackwell pulls off a fine save from Robbie Painter but the rebound fall to Glen Naylor who taps into an empty net.

15 – A SCARBOROUGH 31/10
Argyle: Blackwell, Patterson, Williams, Clayton, Barlow, Hill, Logan^, Mauge, Littlejohn, Evans^, Leadbitter — Wotton/Baird
Scarborough: Ironside, Knowles, Lucas, D'Auria, Hicks, Rockett, Charles, Todd, Page*, Trebble, Kinnaird — Ritchie

Argyle remain in the north as they take on Warnock's former side. Logan replaces the still dentally inconvenienced Heathcote. Boro refuse to throw in the towel. In stoppage time they have a shot cleared off the line and one disallowed before Neil Trebble's shot takes a deflection.

16 – H CARDIFF 4/11
Argyle: Blackwell, Patterson, Williams, Clayton, Barlow^, Hill, Logan, Mauge, Littlejohn, Evans^, Leadbitter^ — Billy/Magee
Cardiff: Williams, Brazil, Searle, Rodgerson, Jarman, Young, Fleming, Adams*, Howarth, Wigg, Gardner — Bird

A real bore-draw. Bluebirds boss Kenny Hibbitt designs a game plan which involves keeping eight men behind the ball and Littlejohn quiet. Sadly for the crowd, it works a treat. Warnock apologises to the fans labelling the match as the worst he has seen for two or three seasons.

17 – A HARTLEPOOL 18/11
Argyle: Blackwell, Patterson, Williams, Clayton, Barlow, Hill, Billy^, Mauge, Littlejohn, Evans, Leadbitter — Logan
Hartlepool: Horne, Ingram, McAuley, Billing, McGuckin, Henderson, Sloan^, Lowe*, Dixon, Halliday, Canham* — Howard/Houchen/Tait

Evans gives Argyle an early lead from the spot after Billy is brought down by Tony Canham. Pool protests fall on deaf ears. Mauge's header from 10 yards looks to have put the game beyond reach but Ingram's first ever goal sparks a spirited comeback. Steve Howard clinches a point.

18 – H ROCHDALE 25/11
Argyle: Blackwell, Patterson, Williams, Clayton^, Heathcote, Hill, Billy*, Mauge, Littlejohn, Evans, Leadbitter — Baird/Saunders
Rochdale: Gray, Thompstone, Formby, Martin, Bayliss, Butler, Thompson, Deary, Shaw, Whitehall, Peake* — Half^/Moulden

An unimaginative first half produces a number of hopeful long balls which both defences deal with easily. With his ears still ringing from a half-time rollicking from Warnock, Littlejohn fires home a superb goal after turning Butler in and out. Evans scores from the edge of the area.

19 – H WIGAN 9/12
Argyle: Blackwell, Patterson, Williams, Clayton, Barlow, Hill, Baird, Barlow, Littlejohn, Evans, Leadbitter
Wigan: Farnworth, Carragher, Butler^, Greenall, Pender, Farrell, Diaz*, Martinez, Sharp, Biggins, Leonard — Kilford/Black

Wigan are undefeated in eight matches under new boss John Deehan but meet their match in Littlejohn. His second comes after he races clear from halfway. The striker is made captain for the day by the superstitious Warnock, who thinks Argyle always lose when Heathcote is skipper.

20 – A LINCOLN 16/12
Argyle: Blackwell, Patterson, Williams, Clayton, Heathcote, Hill, Baird, Logan, Littlejohn, Evans, Leadbitter — Alcide
Lincoln: Richardson, Fleming, Whitney*, Barnett, Holmes, Brown G, Ainsworth, Onwere, Brown G, Carbon*, Brown S — Johnson A/Johnson D

Only six shots during the whole match tells its own story. John Beck's Imps field only two players who played in the earlier fixture only a few weeks earlier. Behind the scenes unrest make most of the headlines, with Warnock threatening to quit if Chairman Dan McAuley sells the club.

21 – H CAMBRIDGE 23/12
Argyle: Blackwell, Patterson, Williams, Clayton, Heathcote, Hill, Baird, Mauge*, Littlejohn, Evans, Leadbitter^ — Curran
Cambridge: Davies, Joseph Marc, Vowden^, Stock*, Craddock, Raynor, Joseph Matt, Middleton, Turner, Corazzin, Granville — Kydd/Robinson

Chris Curran surprisingly signs from Torquay. United's direct style sees them route most attacks through the returning Robbie Turner, but Heathcote deals with everything thrown at him. Mauge celebrates his return from injury with a vicious dipper from the edge of the box.

22 – A GILLINGHAM 26/12
Argyle: Blackwell, Patterson, Williams, Clayton!, Heathcote, Hill, Baird, Mauge*, Littlejohn, Evans, Leadbitter^ — Logan/Billy
Gillingham: Stannard, Micklewhite^, Naylor, Butler T, Harris, Green, Martin, Ratcliffe, Butler S, Bailey, Puttnam* — Fortune-West/Smith

Argyle fail to penetrate Gills' scrooge-like defence which has conceded just seven league goals. Leadbitter's first-minute booking sets the tone with little seasonal goodwill in evidence. Clayton is sent off for handling on the line. Debutant Steve Butler scores from the resultant spot-kick.

23 – H EXETER 1/1
Argyle: Blackwell, Patterson, Williams, Clayton^, Heathcote, Hill*, Baird, Mauge, Littlejohn, Evans, Leadbitter* — Curran/Logan/Billy
Exeter: Fox, Parsley, Hughes, Buckle, Blake, Cooper, Gavin, Hare^, Came, Bradbury, Bailey — Anderson

Mark Came easily lays claim to the first goal of the year as he scores after just 94 seconds in a morning kick-off. The Pilgrims' first-half display does little to improve the flu-stricken manager's state of health. Baird's header pulls one back and three substitutions have the desired effect.

ENDSLEIGH DIVISION 3

Manager: Neil Warnock

SEASON 1995-96

No	Date	Opponent	Att	Pos	Pt	F-A	H-T	Scorers, Times, and Referees
24	A 13/1	PRESTON	11,126	2	37	2-3 (L)	1-2	Heathcote 22, Saunders 89 / Bryson 37, Davey 42, Cartwright 50 / Ref: N Barry
25	H 20/1	COLCHESTER	5,800	5	38	1-1 (D)	1-0	Baird 30 / Greene 89 / Ref: D Orr
26	H 23/1	SCUNTHORPE	4,712	12	38	1-3 (L)	0-2	Logan 89 / Hope 20, Turnbull 32, McFarlane 81 / Ref: M Fletcher
27	A 30/1	NORTHAMPTON	3,911		38	0-1 (L)	0-1	Sampson 16 / Ref: A D'Urso
28	H 3/2	CHESTER	5,114	3	41	4-2 (W)	3-0	Barlow 12, Mauge 13, Partridge 32, Priest 70, Richardson 84 [Williams 72] / Ref: J Rushton
29	A 10/2	SCUNTHORPE	2,789	12	42	1-1 (D)	1-1	Evans 23 / McFarlane 4 / Ref: D Laws
30	A 17/2	DONCASTER	2,338	7	43	0-0 (D)	0-0	Ref: J Lloyd
31	H 20/2	BURY	4,536		46	1-0 (W)	0-0	Heathcote 79 / Ref: P Rejer
32	H 24/2	BARNET	6,426	11	47	1-1 (D)	1-0	Partridge 7 / Gale 72 / Ref: M Fletcher
33	A 27/2	LEYTON ORIENT	3,374		50	1-0 (W)	0-0	Logan 64 / Ref: G Pooley
34	H 2/3	GILLINGHAM	8,485	1	53	1-0 (W)	0-0	Barlow 70 / Ref: G Singh

Line-ups (Argyle player / opposition player):

No	1	2	3	4	5	6	7	8	9	10	11	subs used
24	Blackwell / Vaughan	Billy / Bishop	Williams / Barrick	Logan / Atkinson	Heathcote / Wilcox	Curran / Moyes	Saunders / Davey	Mauge / Bryson	Littlejohn ! / Saville	Evans / McDonald	Leadbitter* / Cartwright	Baird
25	Petterson / Emberson	Billy / Fry	Williams / McCarthy	Logan / Betts	Heathcote / Greene	Curran / Cawley	Baird / Kinsella	Mauge / Dennis	Littlejohn^ / Abrahams	Evans / Adcock	Leadbitter* / Gregory*	Saunders/Hill, Duguid
26	Petterson / Samways	Williams / Walsh	Saunders / Wilson	— / Ford	Heathcote / Hope	Curran / Bradley	Baird / Jones*	Mauge^ / D'Auria	Littlejohn* / McFarlane	Evans / Turnbull	Billy" / Nicholson	Logan/Barlow/P'tridg', Housham
27	Petterson* / Turley	Patterson* / Sampson	Williams / Maddison	Saunders / Hunter	Heathcote / Warburton	Clayton / O'Shea	Baird / Armstrong	Logan / Grayson	Partridge / Thompson^	Evans / White	Barlow / Burns^	Billy/Norton/Worboys
28	Petterson / Stewart	Patterson / Davidson	Williams / Burnham*	Mauge / Shelton*	Heathcote / Jackson	Clayton* / Whelan	Baird / Fisher	Logan / Priest	Partridge^ / Regis"	Evans / Rimmer	Barlow / Nateman	Billy/O'Hagan, Rogers/R'dson/Milner
29	Petterson / Butler	Patterson / Walsh	Williams / Wilson	Saunders / Clarkson	Heathcote / Knill	Clayton / Bradley	Baird / Jones	Logan / D'Auria	Partridge / McFarlane	Evans ! / Eyre^	Barlow / Patterson	Ford
30	Petterson / Suckling	Patterson* / Murphy	Williams / Parrish	Mauge / Moore	Heathcote / Colcombe	Clayton / Warren	Baird / Schofield	Logan / Brabin	Partridge^ / Jones	Evans / Kirby	Barlow / Smith	Evans, Billy
31	Cherry / Kelly	Patterson / West	Williams / Edwards^	Mauge / Daws	Heathcote / Lucketti	Clayton / Jackson	Baird / Rigby*	Logan / Matthews	Partridge^ / Carter	Evans^ / Johnrose	Barlow / Pugh	Littlejohn/Billy, Johnson/Paskin
32	Cherry / Taylor	Patterson / Gale	Williams / Dyer	Mauge / Pardew	Heathcote / Primus	Clayton / Howarth	Baird / Hodges*	Logan / Thompson^	Partridge / Simpson	Littlejohn / Devine	Barlow / Wilson	Cooper/Robbins
33	Cherry / Fearon	Patterson / Hendon	Williams / Austin	Mauge / Arnott	Heathcote / Bellamy	Clayton / McCarthy	Baird / Kelly	Logan / Cockerill	Littlejohn / Inglethorpe^	Evans / West	Barlow / Chapman^	Brooks/Baker
34	Cherry / Stannard	Patterson / Green*	Williams / Naylor	Mauge / Smith	Heathcote / Harris	Clayton / Butler	Baird / Martin	Logan / Castle	Littlejohn / Fortune-West	Evans / Freeman^	Barlow / Carpenter	Rattray/Bailey

24 — Heathcote gives Argyle the lead despite a robust challenge on Vaughan. Gary Peters' side then take charge. Blackwell errs for the second to reinforce Warnock's desire for another keeper. Littlejohn is dismissed for remarks to a linesman. Evans misses a penalty after a foul on Billy.

25 — On-loan Andy Petterson is soon in the action, bringing down Abrahams but then saving Betts' spot-kick (25). Baird's free-kick loops off the head of a defender to leave Emberson flat-footed. In desperation, U's throw centre-half David Greene forward and he side-foots an equaliser.

26 — The visitors are forced to use the Pilgrims' second-choice yellow kit after their own white shirts clash with Argyle's. It makes little difference. The Greens fail to cope with the visitors' long-throw tactic and Andy McFarlane's height. Scott Partridge arrives on loan from Bristol City.

27 — Littlejohn is missing after a hernia operation. Argyle dominate the game but succumb to Ian Sampson's shot which deflected off Heathcote's heel. Cobblers' keeper Billy Turley plays superbly on his home debut, saving twice from Evans when scoring looked a foregone conclusion.

28 — Barlow pulls the strings as Argyle overcome their promotion rivals with ease. Heathcote is given the captain's armband back and breaks the jinx but he somehow misses from a yard out. Logan fouls Andy Milner but Petterson makes his second successive Home Park penalty save.

29 — A mixed evening for Evans. He justifies the award of a new contract by scoring but, having been booked, is red-carded in the last minute by rookie ref Mr Laws for an innocuous challenge on Paul Wilson. Logan's clearance goes straight to Andy McFarlane who gratefully slots in.

30 — The two promotion chasing sides are well-matched. Petterson saves with his legs from Brabin and Mauge has an effort ruled out for offside. Sammy Chung's side have reached the heady heights of fourth place but are on the slide. Steve Cherry signs for Argyle for the second time.

31 — A freezing night and Argyle's recent form persuades only the die-hards to don overcoats. Gary Kelly is kept warm and busy by a dominant Argyle. The goal comes in unlikely fashion. Everyone misses Barlow's corner except Heathcote, who produces a spectacular overhead-kick.

32 — Partridge returns to Bristol and bids farewell with a goal. Littlejohn looks set to increase the lead when he is hauled down by Pardew. Cherry claims he was impeded by the keeper for the equaliser when Shaun Gale lobs the ball over him from 25 yards after the keeper had weakly punched clear.

33 — Orient prove to be little threat, even on their own turf. Logan and Heathcote are immovable at the back. Fearon pulls off a blinding save to stop Clayton's 30-yard volley. Mauge misses a sitter. The O's have two optimistic penalty claims turned down but manage only one shot on target.

34 — The mean Gills machine rolls into town boasting the best defensive record and worst disciplinary record in the league. Barlow's volley from a difficult angle beats Stannard. Tony Pulis claims it was Gills' best performance for some time, leaving fans wondering how bad the worst was.

No	V	Date	Opponent	Att	Fig.	Res	Pts	Score	HT
35	A	9/3	[CAMBROSE?]	2,785	23	W	56	3-2	
36	H	16/3	NORTHAMPTON	7,001	10 / 3	W	59	1-0	0-0
37	A	23/3	EXETER	6,185	12 / 3	D	60	1-1	1-1
38	A	30/3	FULHAM	5,667	17 / 5	L	60	0-4	0-1
39	H	2/4	MANSFIELD	6,375		W	63	1-0	0-0
40	H	6/4	DARLINGTON	8,990	7 / 5	L	63	0-1	0-1
41	A	8/4	TORQUAY	4,269	24 / 5	W	66	2-0	1-0
42	H	13/4	SCARBOROUGH	6,949	23 / 5	W	69	5-1	
43	A	16/4	HEREFORD	4,739		L	69	0-3	0-2
44	A	20/4	CARDIFF	3,374	22 / 4	W	72	1-0	0-0
45	A	27/4	ROCHDALE	2,355	15 / 5	W	75	1-0	0-0
46	H	4/5	HARTLEPOOL	11,526	20 / 4	W	78	3-0	1-0

Home 7,120 Away 3,872 Average

---

35 — A 9/3
Scorers: Billy 5, Logan 68, Baird 81 / Hyde 54, Cozazzin 74p — Ref: R Harris
Line-up: Cherry, Davies, Patterson, Wanless*, Williams, Granville, Logan, Vowden, Heathcote, Cradock, Clayton, Raynor, Billy, Joseph, Baird, Middleton, Littlejohn, Richards^, Evans, Corazzin, Barlow, Beall, Leadbitter, Hyde/Robinson
Report: Half-time sub Micah Hyde causes the Pilgrims' defence problems. The blood-splattered Heathcote plays a blinder. Clayton's miscued drive comes off Logan. Barlow fouls Tony Richards and Carlo Corazzin nets the penalty. Baird's wayward shot hits a defender's back and goes in.

36 — H 16/3 NORTHAMPTON
Scorer: Evans 82 — Ref: D Orr
Line-up: Cherry, Woodman, Patterson, Norton, Williams, Grayson^, Billy, Hunter, Heathcote, Sampson, Clayton, O'Shea, Baird, Williams, Littlejohn, Peer, Evans, Thompson", Barlow, White, Burns*, Gibb/Doherty/Warboys
Report: It takes a goal of farcical proportions to finally break down the Cobblers' stubborn defence. Barlow's cross runs off a defender's back, onto Heathcote's arm and into the six-yard box. Evans prepares to lash it in but misses completely. The ball hits his hip and spins gently goalwards.

37 — A 23/3 EXETER
Scorers: Clayton 9 / Logan 18(og) — Ref: S Mathieson
Line-up: Cherry, Fox, Patterson, Parsley, Williams, Foster*, Billy, Hughes, Heathcote, Blake, Clayton, Richardson, Baird, Gavin, Littlejohn, Cooper, Evans, Braithwaite, Barlow, Bailey, Came, Sharpe^/Anderson
Report: Clayton's swerving effort from 20 yards is due reward for Argyle's early dominance. The heavy surface does its best to disrupt play. Mark Cooper's shot appears to be going well wide until Logan sticks out a leg and deflects it over Cherry. The Greens win the shot count 21-4.

38 — A 30/3 FULHAM
Scorers: Scott 6, Morgan 51, Conroy 68, [Brooker 84] — Ref: K Leach
Line-up: Cherry, Lange, Patterson, Williams, Billy, Herrera, Heathcote, Angus^, Clayton, Blake, Baird*, Brooker, Littlejohn^, Cusack, Evans, Conroy, Corazzin, Scott, Barlow^, McAree^, Hamill/Simpson
Report: Illman and Corazzin sign on transfer deadline day. The squad and 400 fans travel to London by train. Warnock brands the display a disgrace as the Cottagers take Argyle apart to end the unbeaten run. Scott finishes a four-man move and Morgan scores the goal of the day from 25 yards.

39 — H 2/4 MANSFIELD
Scorer: Corazzin 89p — Ref: B Knight
Line-up: Cherry, Bowling, Patterson, Boothroyd, Williams, Hackett, Mauge, Doolan, Heathcote, Timons, Clayton, Wood, Billy*, Ireland, Littlejohn^, Harper, Evans, Hadley, Barlow, Slawson*, Corazzin, Robinson
Report: A scoreless draw looks likely as Ian Bowling pulls off a string of fine saves. Long-term absentee McCall comes on to great applause. Four minutes after coming on, Corazzin is fouled by Simon Wood. Patterson looks set to take the penalty but the Canadian takes responsibility.

40 — H 6/4 DARLINGTON
Scorer: Painter 22 — Ref: S Baines
Line-up: Cherry, Newell, Patterson, Bramwell, Williams", Barnard, Mauge, Appleby, Heathcote, Crosby, Hill^, Gregan, McCall, Carss, Littlejohn, Gaughan, Evans, Painter, Barlow^, Blake*, Corazzin, Carmichael, Lit'john/Billy/L'dbitter, Bannister
Report: Another blow in the race for promotion as a number of chances go begging. Robbie Painter is so surprised at being ruled onside that he scuffs his shot but still beats a surprised Cherry. McCall puts in a vintage performance in midfield but cannot unlock a well organised Darlo defence.

41 — A 8/4 TORQUAY
Scorers: Mauge 5, Littlejohn 76 — Ref: J Rushton
Line-up: Cherry, Bayes, Patterson, Winter, Williams, Stamps*, Mauge, Barrow, Heathcote, Watson, Clayton, Coughlin, Leadbitter", Ndah^, Littlejohn, Datway, Evans, Baker, Barlow, Williams, Hancox, Hall/Jack
Report: The Gulls are destined to finish bottom but escape demotion to Conference football when Stevenage's ground is deemed unsuitable for league soccer. Mauge heads in Barlow's corner. Cherry's clearance finds Littlejohn who sprints past everyone to score.

42 — H 13/4 SCARBOROUGH
Scorers: Mauge 26, Barlow 46, 77, Ritchie 90p [Littlejohn 71, 90] — Ref: G Barber
Line-up: Cherry, Ironside, Patterson, Knowles, Williams, Lucas, Mauge, Charles, Heathcote, Hicks, Clayton*, Rockett^, Leadbitter", Wells, Littlejohn, Fairclough, Evans^, Sansam*, Barlow, Magee, McCall/Corazzin/Billy, Sunderland/Page
Report: The goals-scored column gets an important boost against a poor Scarborough side. Only Ian Ironside, the woodwork and the refusal of the referee to award a penalty when Heathcote is fouled prevents a rout. Veteran Andy Ritchie is handed a consolation spot-kick after he is fouled.

43 — A 16/4 HEREFORD
Scorers: White 12, 39, 51p — Ref: S Bennett
Line-up: Cherry, De Bont, Patterson, Watkiss, Williams^, Lloyd, Mauge, Brough, Heathcote, Downing, McCall, James, Leadbitter, Stoker, Littlejohn, Watkins, Evans^, White*, Barlow*, Hargreaves^, Billy/Hill/Corazzin, Pitman, Lyne/Steele
Report: One time Argyle target Steve White defies his thirty-seven years to deal the Pilgrims a serious blow. He firstly finishes off a one-two with Watkins and then heads home from six yards. Mauge fouls Brough and his second hat-trick of the season is completed from the penalty spot.

44 — A 20/4 CARDIFF
Scorer: Evans 60 — Ref: I Hemley
Line-up: Cherry, Williams, Patterson, Rodgerson, Williams, Fleming, Mauge, Harding, Heathcote, Jarman, Clayton, Young, Leadbitter, Osman, Littlejohn, McGarry, Evans, Philiskirk*, Barlow, Dale, Curran, Gardner*, Flack/Vick
Report: The Bluebirds have not won for ten games and do little to suggest that sequence would be broken. Heathcote pushes Tony Philliskirk, leaving Cherry to face a penalty for the third successive match. Carl Dale's kick balloons off the keeper's leg. Evans runs clear to score off a post.

45 — A 27/4 ROCHDALE
Scorer: Evans 70 — Ref: F Stretton
Line-up: Cherry, Key, Patterson, Thackeray, Williams, Peake, Billy, Deary, Heathcote, Bayliss*, Clayton^, Butler, Leadbitter, Thompson, Littlejohn, Hall, Evans, Lancaster, Barlow, Whitehall, Curran, Stuart, Barlow, Thompstone
Report: Buckets and spades seem more appropriate given the amount of sand on the Spotland pitch. Evans is again at the centre of the action. He is booed throughout after a fifth-minute clash with Lance Key. The forward then side-foots home the winner. Clayton's season is ended by injury.

46 — H 4/5 HARTLEPOOL
Scorers: Billy 2, Heathcote 49, Logan 77 — Ref: R Gifford
Line-up: Cherry, Jones, Patterson, Ingram", Williams, McAuley, Billy, Henderson, Heathcote", McGuckin, Barlow, Lee, Leadbitter^, Gallagher*, Logan, Howard, Littlejohn, Halliday, Evans*, Allon, Corazzin, Canham, Corz'n/O'Haq'n/Mauge, Walton/Hutt
Report: A convincing win but Bury's victory means the play-offs beckon. Billy scores the fastest league goal of the day. Heathcote celebrates his player of the year award with a header. Logan atones for an early miss when he ends up in the net but not the ball, by heading in a corner.

ENDSLEIGH DIVISION 3 (CUP-TIES) Manager: Neil Warnock SEASON 1995-96

Play-offs

	Att	F-A	H-T	Scorers, Times, and Referees	1	2	3	4	5	6	7	8	9	10	11	subs used
SF A 12/5 COLCHESTER 4 L	6,511 / 7	0-1	0-1	Kinsella 44 — Ref: M Pierce	Cherry *Emberson*	Patterson *Fry*	Williams	Billy *McCarthy*	Heathcote	Barlow^ *Cawley*	Leadbitter *Kinsella*	Logan *Dennis*	Littlejohn	Evans* *McGleish*	Curran *Gibbs**	Corazzin/Mauge, Locke/Whitton

The match is beamed to Home Park on a giant TV screen. On a rutted surface, the U's overrun an off-colour Argyle but have only Kinsella's 30-yard effort to show for their dominance. Heathcote misses the ball from under the bar. Billy shoots wide with only Carl Emberson to beat.

	Att	F-A	H-T	Scorers, Times, and Referees	1	2	3	4	5	6	7	8	9	10	11	subs used
SF H 15/5 COLCHESTER 4 W	14,525 / 7	3-1	2-0	Evans 3, Leadbitter 41, Williams 85; Kinsella 66 — Ref: J Kirkby (Argyle won 3-2 on aggregate)	Cherry *Emberson*	Patterson *Fry*	Williams *Betts*	Billy *McCarthy*	Heathcote *Caesar"*	Barlow *Cawley*	Leadbitter *Kinsella*	Logan *Dennis*	Littlejohn	Evans *Reinelt**	Curran *Gibbs^*	Curran, Reinelt*, Adcock/Whitton/Locke

Evans' left-foot shot gives Argyle a dream start. Leadbitter's curling free-kick beats Emberson. Warnock is 'sent off' after McCarthy is only booked for fouling Littlejohn and watches the match from the terraces. With extra-time looming Williams sends the Greens to Wembley.

	Att	F-A	H-T	Scorers, Times, and Referees	1	2	3	4	5	6	7	8	9	10	11	subs used
F N 25/5 DARLINGTON 4 W (at Wembley)	43,431 / 5	1-0	0-0	Mauge 65 — Ref: W Burns	Cherry *Newell*	Patterson *Brumwell*	Williams *Barnard*	Mauge *Appleby*	Heathcote *Crosby*	Barlow *Gregan*	Leadbitter *Bannister*	Logan *Gaughan**	Littlejohn *Painter*	Evans *Blake*	Curran *Carss*	Curran, Carmichael

Thirty thousand fans form a mass exodus to watch Argyle at Wembley for the first time ever. The match is far from a classic, with tension running high. Mauge's twisting header from Patterson's cross seals promotion. Heathcote walks the thirty-nine steps to collect the trophy.

Coca-Cola Cup

	Att	F-A	H-T	Scorers, Times, and Referees	1	2	3	4	5	6	7	8	9	10	11	subs used
1:1 A 15/8 BIRMINGHAM 3 L	7,964 / 1	0-1	0-1	Cooper 44 — Ref: J Lloyd	Hammond *Bennett*	Patterson *Poole*	Williams *Cooper*	Burnett *Ward**	Heathcote *Edwards*	Hill *Whyte*	Billy *Donowa*	Mauge *Claridge"*	Littlejohn *Bowen*	Nugent *Otto*	Clayton *Tait^*	Hunt/Forsyth/Muir

Hammond is the busier keeper but Argyle have chances in the first half. Nugent looks set to score but needs too much time and Bennett robs him. Gary Cooper dribbles past three players before scoring. Mauge and Cooper are involved in a skirmish. Burnett impresses in defence.

	Att	F-A	H-T	Scorers, Times, and Referees	1	2	3	4	5	6	7	8	9	10	11	subs used
1:2 H 22/8 BIRMINGHAM 24 L	6,529 / 1:10	1-2	1-0	Heathcote 45; Edwards 51, Hunt 53 — Ref: C Wilkes (Argyle lost 1-3 on aggregate)	Hammond *Bennett*	Twiddy *Poole*	Williams *Cooper*	Burnett *Ward**	Heathcote *Edwards*	Hill *Whyte*	Billy *Hunt^*	Mauge *Claridge*	Littlejohn *Bowen*	Nugent* *Castle*	Clayton* *Hiley**	Saund/O'Hagan/Evans, Donowa/Forsyth/Dor'ty

Heathcote misses a header from just two yards but soon atones for his error by putting Argyle level on aggregate. Edwards equalises when Clayton fails to clear and Hammond somehow allows Hunt's corner-kick to creep in at the near post. Brum are then content to sit on their lead.

FA Cup

	Att	F-A	H-T	Scorers, Times, and Referees	1	2	3	4	5	6	7	8	9	10	11	subs used
1 A 11/11 SLOUGH 6 W	3,030 / VC12	2-0	0-0	Harvey 61(og), Heathcote 77 — Ref: P Durkin	Blackwell *Preddie*	Patterson *Honor*	Williams *Clement*	Clayton *Paris*	Heathcote *Baron*	Hill *Harvey*	Billy* *Catlin*	Mauge *Bushay"*	Littlejohn *West*	Evans *Pickett^*	Leadbitter *Fiore^*	Logan, Rake/Blackman/Lee

Match of the Day cameras are present, hoping to capture an upset. The non-leaguers match Argyle until Billy's vicious cross is touched in by Lee Harvey. Heathcote rises above everyone to put the tie beyond doubt. Ex-Pilgrim Andy Clement clears off the line from Mauge's header.

	Att	F-A	H-T	Scorers, Times, and Referees	1	2	3	4	5	6	7	8	9	10	11	subs used
2 A 3/12 KINGSTONIAN 5 W	2,961 / IC:8	2-1	1-1	Leadbitter 8, Littlejohn 84; Warden 44 — Ref: R Harris	Blackwell *Root*	Patterson *Brooker*	Williams *Riley*	Clayton* *Finch*	Heathcote *Nebbeling*	Hill *Fisher*	Billy^ *Warmington*	Mauge *Luckett**	Littlejohn *Warden*	Evans *Akuamoah*	Leadbitter* *Wingfield**	Baird/Magee/Logan, Bolton/Stevens

The Argyle fans pay tribute to former keeper Alan Nicholls who was tragically killed in a motor-cycle accident the previous week. A Sunday lunchtime kick-off accommodates Sky TV coverage. Littlejohn produces some magic to secure a third-round place amongst the big boys.

	Att	F-A	H-T	Scorers, Times, and Referees	1	2	3	4	5	6	7	8	9	10	11	subs used
3 H 6/1 COVENTRY 4 L	17,721 / P:17	1-3	1-0	Baird 19; Pickering 53, Salako 55, Telfer 58 — Ref: G Willard	Blackwell *Ogrizovic*	Billy *Pickering*	Williams *Hall*	Logan *Shaw*	Heathcote *Williams*	Hill *Busst !*	Baird* *Richardson*	Mauge^ *Telfer*	Littlejohn *Whelan*	Evans *Dublin*	Leadbitter *Salako*	Twiddy/Saunders

A giant-killing act looks likely when, already a goal down, David Busst is red carded for a professional foul on Evans. Ron Atkinson's pep talk does the trick. Pickering's intended cross loops over Blackwell and five minutes later it is all over as the impressive Salako takes charge.

Football League Division Three — Final Table

	Team	P	W	D	L	F	A	W	D	L	F	A	Pts
1	Preston	46	14	5	4	44	20	9	12	2	34	16	86
2	Gillingham	46	16	6	1	33	6	6	11	6	16	14	83
3	Bury	46	11	6	6	33	21	11	7	5	33	27	79
4	PLYMOUTH*	46	14	5	4	41	20	8	7	8	27	29	78
5	Darlington	46	10	6	7	30	21	10	12	1	30	21	78
6	Hereford	46	13	5	5	40	22	7	9	7	25	25	74
7	Colchester	46	13	7	3	37	22	5	11	7	24	29	72
8	Chester	46	11	9	3	45	19	7	7	9	27	31	70
9	Barnet	46	13	6	4	40	21	5	10	8	25	26	70
10	Wigan	46	15	3	5	36	22	5	7	11	26	35	70
11	Northampton	46	9	10	4	32	30	9	3	11	19	22	67
12	Scunthorpe	46	11	8	7	36	19	4	7	12	31	31	60
13	Doncaster	46	9	9	6	25	22	7	2	13	24	41	59
14	Exeter	46	9	9	5	25	26	4	9	10	21	31	57
15	Rochdale	46	7	8	8	32	33	7	5	11	25	28	55
16	Cambridge	46	8	8	7	34	30	6	4	13	27	41	54
17	Fulham	46	8	8	7	39	26	4	9	10	18	37	53
18	Lincoln	46	8	7	8	32	32	5	7	11	25	47	53
19	Mansfield	46	6	10	7	25	29	5	10	8	29	35	53
20	Hartlepool	46	8	9	6	30	24	4	4	15	17	43	49
21	Leyton Orient	46	11	8	3	29	22	1	7	15	15	41	47
22	Cardiff	46	8	6	9	24	28	3	6	14	17	42	45
23	Scarborough	46	5	11	7	22	28	3	5	15	17	41	40
24	Torquay	46	4	9	10	17	36	1	5	17	13	48	29
		1104	239	175	138	781	565	138	175	239	565	781	1481

* promoted after play-offs

Season Notes

Double wins: (5) Bury, Cambridge, Rochdale, Torquay, Wigan.

Double defeats: (3) Darlington, Hereford, Preston.

Won from behind: (2) Doncaster, Torquay.

Lost from in front: (1) Preston.

High spots: Club's first ever appearance at Wembley. Estimated 30,000 supporters attended play-off final. Play-off semi-final away leg beamed live to TV screen at Home Park. Climbed from bottom position to 4th place.

Low spots: Missed out on automatic promotion by one point. Disastrous start to season saw the club propping up the league for the first time in its history.

Behind the scenes dispute over retention of players' play-off shirts.

Tragic death of former keeper Alan Nicholls on 26 Nov, aged only 23.

Player of the Year: Mick Heathcote.

Ever presents: (1) Paul Williams.

Hat-tricks: (1) Adrian Littlejohn.

Leading scorer: Adrian Littlejohn (18).

Appearances and Goals

Player	Lge	Sub	LC	Sub	FAC	Sub	Lge	LC	FAC	Tot
Baird, Ian	24	3		1		1	5	1		6
Barlow, Martin	25	3					5			5
Billy, Chris	22	10		3		3	4			4
Blackwell, Kevin	20									
Burnett, Wayne	6	2		2						
Cherry, Steve	16									
Clayton, Gary	32	4	2		2	2	2			2
Corazzin, Carlo	1	5					1			1
Curran, Chris	6	2								
Evans, Michael	41	4		1		3	12			12
Hammond, Nicky	4		2		2					
Heathcote, Mick	44		2		3		4	1	1	6
Hill, Keith	21	3	2		2					
Hodgson, Doug	3	2								
Leadbitter, Chris	29	4		3		3	1		1	2
Littlejohn, Adrian	40	2	2		3		17	1		18
Logan, Richard	25	6	1			1	4			4
Magee, Kevin		4				1				
Mauge, Ronnie	36	1	2		3		7			7
McCall, Steve	2	2		2						
Nugent, Kevin	4	2	2							
O'Hagan, Danny		6				1				
Partridge, Scott	6	1					2			2
Patterson, Mark	42	1	1		2					
Patterson, Andy	6									
Saunders, Mark	4	6	1	1	1	1	1			1
Shilton, Sam		1								
Twiddy, Chris	1	1	1							
Williams, Paul	46		2		3		2			2
Wotton, Paul		1				1	1		1	
(own-goals)							1		1	4
30 players used	506	74	22	3	33	6	68	5	3	76

NATIONWIDE DIVISION 2

Manager: Neil Warnock > Mick Jones   **SEASON 1996-97**

No	Date	Att	Pos	Pt	F-A	H-T	Scorers, Times, and Referees	1	2	3	4	5	6	7	8	9	10	11	subs used
1	H 17/8 YORK	9,035		W / 3	2-1	0-0	Corazzin 61, Heathcote 65 / Pepper 79p / Ref: R Harris	Grobbelaar / Warrington	Billy / McMillan	Williams / Atkinson	Mauge / Randall	Heathcote / Atkin	Curran / Barras	Leadbitter / Hinsworth	Logan / Bushell*	Littlejohn / Bull	Evans / Tolson	Corazzin / Stephens'n^	Pepper / Murty
2	A 24/8 WREXHAM	3,920	2 / 15	D / 4	4-4	2-1	Evans 10, Littlejohn 25, 63, Logan 66 / Phillips 42, 73, Connolly 71, 87 / Ref: S Mathieson	Grobbelaar / Marriott	Billy / McGregor	Williams / Brace	Mauge / Phillips	Heathcote / Soloman	Curran / Carey	Leadbitter / Chalk	Logan / Russell*	Littlejohn / Connolly	Evans / Watkin^	Corazzin / Ward	Owen / Skinner
3	A 27/8 WATFORD	7,349	/	W / 7	2-0	1-0	Billy 32, Littlejohn 79 / Ref: A D'Urso	Grobbelaar / Miller	Billy / Page	Williams / Porter	Mauge / Palmer	Heathcote / Millen	James / Johnson	Leadbitter / Bazeley	Logan / Andrews*	Littlejohn / White	Evans / Johnson	Saunders / Mooney	Lowndes
4	H 30/8 PRESTON	9,209	1 / 14	W / 10	2-1	1-1	Evans 3, Logan 66 / Wilkinson 41 / Ref: P Rejer	Grobbelaar / Moilanen	Billy / Kay	Williams / Barrick	Mauge / Atkinson^	Heathcote / Wilcox	James / Moyes	Leadbitter / Davey	Logan / Bryson	Littlejohn / Saville	Evans / Wilkinson	Saunders* / Kilbane	Barlow / McDonald
5	H 7/9 NOTTS CO	8,109	3 / 17	D / 11	0-0	0-0	Ref: G Singh	Grobbelaar / Ward	Billy / Wilder	Williams / Baraclough	Mauge / Derry	Heathcote / Murphy	James / Hogg	Leadbitter / Kennedy	Logan / Robinson	Littlejohn / Wikes*	Evans / Jones	Barlow* / Agana	Corazzin / Martindale
6	A 10/9 BRENTFORD	5,377	6 / 1	L / 11	2-3	1-1	Mauge 44, Corazzin 83 / Smith 31, Asaba 71, Bent 84 / Ref: M Pierce	Grobbelaar / Dearden	Billy / Hurdle	Williams / Anderson	Mauge / Ashby	Curran ! / Bates	James / McGhee*	Leadbitter / Asaba	Logan / Smith	Littlejohn / Forster	Evans / Bent	Corazzin / Taylor	Barlow / Hutchings
7	A 14/9 STOCKPORT	5,087	9 / 22	L / 11	1-3	1-2	Evans 27p / Gannon 1, 10, Armstrong 51 / Ref: I Cruikshanks	Grobbelaar / Jones	Billy / Connelly	Williams / Todd	Mauge / Bennett	Curran / Flynn	James / Gannon	Leadbitter* / Durkan	Logan* / Marsden	Littlejohn / Angell	Evans / Armstrong	Corazzin^ / Jeffers	Heathcote / Barlow / Saunders
8	H 21/9 BRISTOL ROV	8,879	11 / 12	L / 11	0-1	0-0	Archer 78 / Ref: K Leach	Grobbelaar / Collett	Billy / Martin	Williams / Lockwood	Mauge / Browning	Heathcote / Clark	James / Power	Leadbitter / Holloway	Logan* / Gurney	Littlejohn / Cureton^	Evans / Archer	Barlow / Skinner	Corazzin / Beadle
9	A 28/9 CREWE	3,797	15 / 3	L / 11	0-3	0-1	Barr 14, Adebola 61, Murphy 85 / Ref: T Hellbron	Blackwell / Taylor	Billy / Unsworth	Williams / Smith	Saunders* / Westwood	Heathcote / Macauley	Corazzin^ / Whalley*	Leadbitter / Rivers*	Leadbitter* / Savage	Littlejohn / Adebola	Evans / Murphy	Barlow / Barr	Logan / Wotton / Little / Johnson
10	H 1/10 PETERBOROUGH	4,929	/	D / 12	1-1	1-1	James 13 / Regis 28 / Ref: B Knight	Grobbelaar / Tyler	Billy / Carter*	Williams / Clark	Curran / O'Connor	Heathcote / Heald	James / Welsh	Leadbitter* / Willis	Corazzin / Payne	Littlejohn / Farrell*	Evans / Regis	Barlow / Houghton^	Logan / Boothroyd / Ebdon / Rowe
11	H 5/10 MILLWALL	7,507	16 / 6	D / 13	0-0	0-0	Ref: J Brandwood	Blackwell / Carter	Billy / Doyle	Williams / Rogan^	Curran / Webber^	Heathcote / Harle	James / Savage	Corazzin / Bowry	Logan / Neil	Littlejohn / Hartley	Evans* / Dolby	Barlow / Dair^	Simpson / Newman / Hockton / Robertson

Match reports

1. Argyle are without Patterson, who breaks a leg in a pre-season friendly against Chelsea. The arrival of the flamboyant Grobbelaar adds a few hundred to the gate. Two headers give Argyle a comfortable lead. Nigel Pepper scores from the spot after Corazzin fouled Andy McMillan.

2. Argyle manage to squander a 4-1 lead as Brian Flynn's side pull level in a 16-minute spell. It could have been worse but Grobbelaar saves Karl Connolly's penalty (61) after a reckless challenge by Leadbitter on Wayne Phillips. Ex-Pilgrim Craig Skinner is instrumental in the comeback.

3. Debutant Tony James gives a man of the match performance despite travelling down from Manchester with Warnock during the day, after attending a transfer tribunal. Kenny Jackett's men have little answer to a confident Argyle who strike twice from close in after good build-ups.

4. The Friday evening kick-off accommodates live Sky TV coverage. Evans cannot fail to miss from five yards after good work by Billy. Steve Wilkinson continues his prolific start with his sixth goal in four matches. Logan caps a fine performance by shooting home from close range.

5. Unbeknown to Warnock, Corazzin takes on penalty-taking responsibilities and has a spot-kick saved (75) after Williams was fouled by Agana. Phil Robinson heads the ball out of Grobbelaar's hands and scores. The goal is allowed but Grobbelaar's protests change Mr Singh's mind.

6. Skipper Heathcote is concerned about his form and asks to be dropped. Paul Smith scores the goal of the match from 25 yards. Argyle repeat their Wembley goal routine with the same result. Curran is sent off (74) for a professional foul on Asaba. Mauge needs stitches in a cut chin.

7. Warnock's travel plans are blocked on financial grounds. Incredibly he instructs the players to drive 300 miles to the match on the Saturday morning. The shambles continues on the pitch as Argyle are well beaten by a County side that had scored just once in their previous six games.

8. Corazzin expresses his surprise at being left out after being told he was the best player at Stockport. With the goal yawning Barlow miscues his shot from five yards. Sub Peter Beadle makes an immediate impression by setting up Lee Archer for Rovers first away League goal this season.

9. Injuries and Grobbelaar's international duty leave Warnock with only 14 to choose from. Heathcote returns but is given a testing time by Dele Adebola, who creates Barr's opener and scores with a crisp shot. Danny Murphy is first to react after Blackwell beats away Colin Little's shot.

10. James is injured in the process of scoring but resumes after treatment. Dave Regis makes his Posh debut and inevitably scores to send manager Barry Fry on his familiar touchline sprint. Fry is unimpressed by his two wingers, Carter and Houghton, and replaces them both at half-time.

11. Goalkeepers dominate with both Blackwell and Tim Carter pulling off impressive saves. Blackwell also saves Dave Savage's penalty (21) after the same player was brought down by Logan. Debutant Simpson's shot is handled in the area but the referee rules the contact to be accidental.

12/10 — 3,720 / 20 / 16

| Wood | Ntamark | Marsh | Viveash | Thomas | Mountfield | Blake | Bradley^ | Lightbourne | Wilson | Ricketts* | Watson/Keates |

Corazzin begins a spell of international duty. Littlejohn ends his goal drought by chipping over the advancing Trevor Wood to score against his former club. Grobbelaar spends his spare moments conducting the crowd singing. Disgruntled home fans stage an after-match demonstration.

Ref: T Leake

---

13 — A BOURNEMOUTH — 15/10 — L 0-1 — 16 — 3,818 / 17

| Grobbelaar | Williams | Mauge | Heathcote | James* | Simpson^ | Curran | Corazzin^ | Evans | Barlow | Logan/Rowbotham/Illman |
| Marshall | Young | Beardsmore Coll | Cox^ | Gordon | Omoyinmi^ | Robinson | Fletcher | Watson^ | Dean | Murray/Howe/Rawlinson |

Fletcher 17

Ref: M Bailey

The unmarked Steve Fletcher heads in from what is a rare Bournemouth attack. Such is Argyle's domination that Grobbelaar spends much of the second half wandering up to the halfway line. The Pilgrims' misfortune is summed up when James is injured in a collision with Corazzin.

---

14 — H BRISTOL CITY — 19/10 — D 0-0 — 9,645 / 9 / 17

| Grobbelaar | Williams | Mauge | Heathcote | James | Simpson | Curran | Corazzin* | Evans | Barlow | Illman |
| Naylor | Owers | Edwards | Barnard | Taylor | Hewlett* | Goodridge^ | Carey | Agostino | Goater^ | McLeary/Kuhl/Seal |

Ref: P Richards

Fans brandish red cards at chairman McCauley in a call for him to resign. The Pilgrims' lack of firepower is never more evident as Joe Jordan's side keep their third successive clean sheet. Argyle claim that Illman's corner goes over the line but the referee merely blows for full-time.

---

15 — A BURNLEY — 26/10 — L 1-2 — 9,602 / 10 / 17

| Grobbelaar | Williams | Mauge | Heathcote* | James | Simpson | Curran | Illman | Evans | Barlow^ | Logan/Rowbotham |
| Beresford | Eyres | Harrison | Winstanley | Overson | Matthew | Smith | Nogan | Barnes | Gleghorn |

Evans 73
Nogan 28, Eyres 47p

Ref: R Poulain

Argyle do not have the best preparation as they arrive only half an hour before kick-off because of traffic problems. Warnock then complains that the dressing-room is too hot. David Eyres' penalty, after Billy was harshly penalised for fouling Paul Smith, adds to Kurt Nogan's opener.

---

16 — H GILLINGHAM — 29/10 — W 2-0 — 4,787 / 20

| Grobbelaar | Billy | Mauge | Heathcote | James | Simpson | Curran | Illman* | Evans | Barlow | Phillips |
| Gould | Green | Butters | Smith | Thomas* | Hessenthaler O'Connor^ | Ratcliffe | Onura | Bailey | Armstrong | Butler/Manuel |

Evans 59, Illman 66

Ref: P Rejer

Argyle dominate but need to be patient. Heathcote (twice) and Simpson hit the woodwork in the space of eight minutes. Illman's goal caps a fine performance. He is replaced with two minutes left by Phillips who becomes the youngest ever player to appear in Argyle's first team.

---

17 — H LUTON — 2/11 — D 3-3 — 7,134 / 8 / 21

| Grobbelaar | Billy^ | Mauge* | Heathcote | James | Simpson | Curran | Illman^ | Evans | Barlow | Leadbitter/Rowboth/Phillips |
| Feuer | James | Thomas I | Waddock | Davis | Johnson | Hughes | Alexander | Douglas^ | Thorpe | Showler* | Guentchev/Grant |

Mauge 32, Evans 71p, 74
Thorpe 10, 64, 86

Ref: A Wiley

Grobbelaar claims an assist when his clever pass to Evans leads to Mauge's opener. The two sides' in-form strikers then dominate with Tony Thorpe claiming the first hat-trick of his career. Mitchell Thomas is dismissed (71) for handling on the line and Evans slots in the spot-kick.

---

18 — A WYCOMBE — 9/11 — L 1-2 — 5,456 / 24 / 21

| Dungey | Billy | Mauge* | Heathcote | James | Simpson^ | Curran | Illman | Evans | Barlow | Leadbitter/Corazzin |
| Cheesewr't Kavanagh | Bell^ | McCarthy | Evans | Crossley | Carroll | Brown | Davis | McGavin | De Souza | Farrell |

Williams 39
Brown 23, McGavin 74

Ref: S Bennett

Wanderers go all out to impress new manager John Gregory. With Grobbelaar playing for Zimbabwe, Dungey is preferred to Blackwell but can do little about either goal. Steve Brown is left unmarked. Former Argyle trialist Miguel De Souza strongly challenges to set up the winner...

---

19 — H CHESTERFIELD — 19/11 — L 0-3 — 4,237 / 21

| Grobbelaar | Billy | Mauge* | Heathcote | James | Leadbitter | Curran^ | Illman* | Evans | Barlow | Littlejohn/Corazzin/Simpson |
| Mercer | Hewitt | Jules | Curtis | Williams | Davies* | Holland | Lormor | Gaughan^ | Perkins | Howard/Morris |

Lormor 7, Davies 57, Holland 79

Ref: G Pooley

Three days after thrashing Fulham in the cup, Argyle produce such a wretched showing that Warnock joins many fans in leaving the ground early. Skipper Heathcote apologises on behalf of the team. Warnock issues a statement regarding the off-the-pitch problems at Home Park.

---

20 — A BURY — 23/11 — L 0-1 — 3,582 / 3 / 21

| Grobbelaar | Billy | Mauge | Heathcote | James | Simpson | Curran | Leadbitter* | Littlejohn | Barlow | Corazzin |
| Kiely | West | Pugh | Daws | Lucketti | Jackson | Butler | Johnson^ | Carter | Johnrose | Matthews^ Armstrong/Rigby |

Carter 6

Ref: D Allinson

A mistake by Heathcote when he fails to clear Dean West's corner leads to the crucial goal by Mark Carter. Mauge, captain for the day, leads by example. Dean Kiely, who came close to signing for Argyle in the summer, has little to do to keep him warm in the freezing temperatures.

---

21 — H BURNLEY — 30/11 — D 0-0 — 6,289 / 8 / 22

| Grobbelaar | Billy | Mauge | Heathcote | James | Simpson^ | Leadbitter | Littlejohn | Evans* | Barlow | Corazzin/Saunders |
| Beresford | Parkinson | Eyres | Harrison | Swan | Weller | Smith | Nogan | Cooke | Gleghorn |

Ref: M Pierce

Warnock and opposing manager Adrian Heath are both warned by the referee for shouting at their players. Mauge is unavailable, having been remanded in custody after a court appearance. Paul Smith's inswinging corner flies straight in but the referee spotted a foul on Grobbelaar.

---

22 — A BLACKPOOL — 3/12 — D 2-2 — 2,690 / 23

| Grobbelaar | Billy | Wotton | Heathcote | James | Simpson^ | Leadbitter | Littlejohn | Evans* | Barlow^ | Corazzin/Saunders/Illman |
| Banks | Bryan | Barlow | Lydiate | Bradshaw | Banner | Onwere | Malkin | Ellis | Philpott* | Thorpe |

Wotton 10, Littlejohn 24
Philpott 40, Malkin 56

Ref: D Pugh

A bitterly cold and wet night gives credence to the argument for a mid-winter break. Wotton scores his first league goal with a strong header. Littlejohn looks sharp in scoring. Pool fight back after a half-time rollicking from Gary Megson. Malkin outjumps everyone to grab a point.

---

23 — H SHREWSBURY — 14/12 — D 2-2 — 5,075 / 14 / 24

| Grobbelaar | Billy | Mauge | Heathcote | James | Wotton* | Leadbitter* | Littlejohn | Evans | Barlow | Logan/Illman |
| Edwards | Seabury | Dempsey | Currie | Spink | Whiston | Brown | Cope | Anthrobus | Evans | Berkley |

Mauge 58, Evans 80
Spink 45, Evans 47

Ref: A D'Urso

Dean Spink scores in first-half injury-time for the weakened Shrews. With some harsh words from Warnock still ringing in their ears, Argyle immediately go out and concede another to Paul Evans. The lively Illman comes on for the second half and plays a part in both Argyle goals.

NATIONWIDE DIVISION 2

Manager: Neil Warnock > Mick Jones — SEASON 1996-97

No	Date	Opponent	Att	Pos (Arg/Opp)	Pt	Result F-A	H-T	Scorers, Times, and Referees	1	2	3	4	5	6	7	8	9	10	11	subs used
24	21/12	A ROTHERHAM	2,269	17/24	27	W 2-1	2-1	Illman 9, Evans 10 / Breckin 31 — Ref: T West	Grobbelaar	Billy	Williams	Mauge	Heathcote*	James	Wotton	Leadbitter*	Illman^	Barlow	Evans	Logan/Littlejohn
									Cherry	*Blades*	*Roscoe*	*Garner*	*Monington*	*Breckin*	*Hayward*	*McGlashan*	*McDougald*	*Druce**	*Glover*	*Bowyer/Glover*
25	26/12	H BRENTFORD	9,525	20/1	27	L 1-4	0-1	Illman 59 / Forster 7, 87, Asaba 71, Omigie 77 — Ref: F Stretton	Grobbelaar	Billy	Dearden	Mauge	Heathcote	James	Wotton*	Leadbitter*	Illman*	Evans	Barlow	Logan/Littlejohn/Corazzin
									Dearden	*Hurdle*	*Anderson*	*Ashby*	*Bates*	*McGhee*	*Asaba**	*Smith*	*Forster*	*Omigie*	*Bent*	*Statham*
26	11/1	H CREWE	4,767	15/9	30	W 1-0	0-0	Logan 90 — Ref: M Fletcher	Dungey	Billy	Williams	Curran	Heathcote	James	Corazzin^	Saunders*	Littlejohn	Barlow	Evans	Logan/Illman
									Kearton	*Barr*	*Billing**	*Westwood*	*Macauley*	*Whalley*	*Charnock*	*Savage*	*Moralee**	*Murphy*	*Adebola^*	*Smith/Little/Tierney*
27	18/1	A PETERBOROUGH	6,288	14/20	31	D 0-0	0-0	Ref: M Halsey	Dungey	Billy	Williams	Curran	Heathcote	James	Logan	Saunders	Littlejohn	Evans	Barlow	Illman
									Griemink	*Willis*	*Clark*	*Edwards*	*Heald*	*Bodley*	*Houghton*	*Payne*	*Carruthers*	*Charley*	*Donowa^*	*Morrison*
28	25/1	A GILLINGHAM	5,465	17/18	31	L 1-4	0-3	Evans 70 [Akinbiyi 61] / Curran 5(og), Green 9, Ratcliffe 26 — Ref: R Furmandiz	Dungey	Billy	Williams	Curran*	Heathcote	James	Saunders^	Logan	Littlejohn	Evans	Barlow	Mauge/Illman
									Stannard	*Smith*	*Butters*	*Pennock*	*Green*	*Bryant*	*Hessenthaler*	*Ratcliffe*	*Akinbiyi*	*Butler**	*O'Connor*	*Chapman*
29	1/2	H WYCOMBE	5,024	19/22	32	D 0-0	0-0	Ref: P Taylor	Grobbelaar	Billy	Williams	Saunders	Heathcote	James	Corazzin	Logan*	Littlejohn*	Evans	Barlow	Mauge/Illman
									Cheesewri't	*Cousins*	*Bell*	*Kavanagh*	*Evans*	*Forsyth*	*Carroll*	*De Souza*	*Read*	*McGavin*	*Simpson*	
30	8/2	A LUTON	6,439	19/2	33	D 2-2	0-0	Littlejohn 59, Evans 68 / Thorpe 57, 61 — Ref: T Lunt	Grobbelaar	Billy	Williams	Saunders*	Heathcote	James	Corazzin	Logan	Littlejohn	Evans	Barlow	Mauge
									Feuer	*James*	*Thomas*	*Evers**	*Davis*	*Johnson*	*Guentchev*	*Alexander*	*Oldfield*	*Thorpe*	*Marshall**	*Fotiadis/Linton*
31	15/2	H BURY	5,486	19/6	36	W 2-0	0-0	Logan 63, Corazzin 66 — Ref: M Bailey	Blackwell	Billy	Williams	Mauge	Heathcote	James	Corazzin	Logan	Littlejohn	Evans	Barlow	Saunders
									Kiely	*West*	*O'Kane*	*Daws*	*Lucketti*	*Jackson**	*Butler*	*Carter*	*Johnson*	*Matthews*	*Armstrong*	
32	22/2	A CHESTERFIELD	5,833	17/9	39	W 2-1	0-0	Evans 63, Saunders 72 / Howard 85 — Ref: R Poulain	Grobbelaar	Billy	Williams	Mauge!	Curran	James!	Corazzin	Logan!	Illman*	Evans	Saunders	Wotton
									Mercer	*Hewitt*	*Perkins*	*Curtis*	*Williams*	*Carr!*	*Beaumont**	*Davies!*	*Lormor*	*Howard*	*Gaughan^*	*Lund/Patterson*
33	25/2	A BRISTOL ROV	6,005	19/–	39	L 0-2	0-2	Cureton 22, 33 — Ref: A Butler	Grobbelaar	Billy	Williams	Mauge	Curran	James	Saunders	Logan	Littlejohn	Evans*	Barlow	Illman
									Collett	*Pritchard*	*Martin*	*Skinner*	*White*	*Tilson*	*Holloway*	*Miller**	*Cureton*	*Lockwood*	*Beadle^*	*Hayfield/Alsop*
34	1/3	H BLACKPOOL	5,585	19/13	39	L 0-1	0-1	Ellis 45 — Ref: F Stretton	Grobbelaar	Billy	Williams	Mauge	Heathcote	James	Saunders^	Logan*	Littlejohn	Illman	Barlow	Wotton/Patterson
									Banks	*Bryan*	*Barlow*	*Butler*	*Linighan*	*Clarkson*	*Philpott**	*Mellon*	*Quinn*	*Ellis*	*Preece*	*Darton*

Match notes:

24. Warnock's decision to start with Illman in attack soon pays off as the striker takes advantage of a mistake by Paul Blades. Evans shoots into an unguarded net with Cherry protesting that he had been impeded. Darren Garner's cross sets up Ian Breckin but the Millers' woes continue.

25. The Bees consolidate their top of the table position although they are flattered by the scoreline. Heathcote goes off for treatment to a broken nose and during his absence Nicky Forster scores. Illman's well-flighted shot catches Dearden out. Asaba's goal goes in after two deflections.

26. Saunders inadvertently plays a part in Argyle's victory when he asks to be taken off after feeling the pace of the game. His replacement, Logan, scores an injury-time header. By the end, a thick fog descends over Home Park and Dungey admits he could not see who scored the vital goal.

27. Grobbelaar, having spent the week in Winchester Crown Court for his match-fixing trial, is left on the bench. Attempts at any kind of passing game are almost impossible on what Barry Fry admits is the worst surface in the country. Greg Heald and Williams both hit the woodwork.

28. The referee considers a postponement because of fog. The Gills are glad he doesn't. Curran's attempted clearance of Mark O'Connor's cross flies past Dungey. Poor defending leaves the youngster exposed. Ade Akinbiyi scores on his home debut after his £250k move from Norwich.

29. Warnock sets a 50-point survival target. Both managers spend time with the referee at half-time to discuss Logan's booking for a foul on Paul Read. Warnock feels it unjustified while John Gregory thinks he should have been sent off. James makes a spectacular clearance off the line.

30. Mick Jones takes charge after Warnock is sacked in midweek via a mobile phone message. Despite a turbulent week at Home Park, the players give a wholehearted performance. Sean Evers fouls Evans who misses the resultant penalty (37) as Ian Feuer uses his 6ft 7in frame to save.

31. Blackwell keeps up his record of never having played in a losing Argyle side in a league match at Home Park. Logan nods a header past Dean Kiely. Corazzin celebrates his goal with his customary cartwheel. The victory does Jones' chances of keeping the manager's job no harm.

32. The match hits the national headlines for all the wrong reasons. Mauge is sent off (35) for a two-footed tackle. A mid-air elbow on Grobbelaar concusses the keeper and sparks a 17-man brawl which results in James, Logan, Kevin Davies and Darren Carr all being dismissed (88).

33. Argyle pay their first ever visit to the Memorial Ground. Southampton manager Graeme Souness attends to watch Evans but the striker lasts only 14 minutes. Grobbelaar is in no man's land as Jamie Cureton scores with an overhead kick and later lashes in an 18-yard blockbuster.

34. Evans signs for Southampton for an Argyle record of £500k. Without him the Pilgrims' attack lacks potency. Tony Ellis scores after sustained Blackpool pressure. Patterson makes a welcome return. McCauley states that he is ready to offer Jones the manager's job on a permanent basis.

Plymouth Argyle — Season match-by-match record (matches 35–46)

Note: each match lists the Argyle line-up first, then the opponents' line-up, followed by the match report. Figures read: League Position | Result | (figure) | Points.

No	Date	Venue	Opponent	Res	Score	Pos	Pts	Att	Scorers	Ref
—	8/3					24	42	4,717		J Brandwood
36	15/3	A	SHREWSBURY	W	3-2	15	45	3,414	Billy 52, 60, Illman 87 / Anthrobus 53, Stevens 72	S Mathieson
37	22/3	H	WREXHAM	L	0-1	17	45	5,468	Humes 40	M Halsey
38	29/3	A	YORK	D	1-1	18	46	3,917	Corazzin 54 / Bushell 77	U Rennie
39	31/3	H	WATFORD	D	0-0	18	47	6,836		M Fletcher
40	5/4	A	PRESTON	D	1-1	18	48	8,503	Saunders 36 / Reeves 18	T Bates
41	8/4	H	STOCKPORT	D	0-0	18	49	5,089		D Orr
42	12/4	A	MILLWALL	D	0-0	18	50	5,702		R Styles
43	15/4	A	NOTTS CO	L	1-2	19	50	2,423	Collins 71 / Heathcote 66(og), Jones 86	E Lomas
44	19/4	H	WALSALL	W	2-0	18	53	5,535	Saunders 75, Barlow 81	S Bennett
45	26/4	A	BRISTOL CITY	L	1-3	18	53	15,368	Williams 18 / Barnard 35, 61p, Nugent 75	J Kirkby
46	3/5	H	BOURNEMOUTH	D	0-0	19	54	6,507		G Singh

Home 6,495 Away 5,479 Average 6,495

8/3
Opponents: Pilkington, Bowman, Dillon*, Dobbin, Breckin, Richardson, Hayward^, Bowyer, Landon, Hurst~, Roscoe/Druce/Bain
Corazzin jets back from Mexico to score the all important spot-kick after Paul Dillon's clumsy challenge on Saunders. New £40k signing Simon Collins plays in an unfamiliar forward role. Patterson plays his first full game of the season after becoming a father the day before.

36 — A SHREWSBURY
Argyle: Grobbelaar, Billy, Williams, Saunders, Heathcote, Patterson, Illman, Rowbotham, Littlejohn, Collins, Barlow*, Perkins
Shrewsbury: Gall, Whiston, Dempsey, Taylor, Spink, Walton, Brown, Stevens, Anthrobus, Scott*, Currie, Seabury
Defences are on top during the first half. Darren Currie plays a part in both Shrewsbury goals. Billy scores from the edge of the area and then seizes on a mistake by Peter Whiston to double his season's tally. Illman scores from 18 yards. Student Steve Perkins gets a surprise run out.

37 — H WREXHAM
Argyle: Grobbelaar, Billy, Williams, Saunders, Heathcote, Patterson, Corazzin, Rowbotham, Littlejohn, Collins, Illman^, Perkins
Wrexham: Marriott, McGregor, Williams, Phillips, Humes, Carey, Russell, Bennett, Skinner*, Watkin, Brammer, Chalk
Another poor performance puts the Pilgrims back in trouble. The defeat prompts Jones to suggest that his side have a complex about playing at home. The finger of blame points at Grobbelaar as he starts to come for a corner and then changes his mind, allowing Tony Humes to head in.

38 — A YORK
Argyle: Grobbelaar, Billy, Williams, Patterson, Heathcote, Saunders, Corazzin, Rowbotham, Littlejohn, Collins, Barlow*, Mauge
York: Warrington, Himsworth, McMillan, Bushell, Sharples, Barras, Stephenson, Tinkler, Bull^, Tolson, Hall/Rowe!
Corazzin persuades Jones to select him despite a hip injury and repays his manager's faith by giving Argyle the lead. Steve Bushell's powerful shot equalises. Collins is poised to blast into an empty net but the ball bobbles and he slices wide. Rodney Rowe is sent (84) for swearing.

39 — H WATFORD
Argyle: Grobbelaar, Billy, Williams*, Saunders, Heathcote, Patterson, Corazzin, Rowbotham, Littlejohn, Collins, Barlow, Mauge
Watford: Miller, Gibbs, Armstrong, Palmer*, Millen, Page, Penrice, Mooney^, Phillips, Johnson, Ramage, Bazeley/Slater
Jones must be tempted to call on former goal-ace Tommy Tynan who watches the match from the terraces. Neither side look capable of scoring and there is little to entertain the shirt-sleeved crowd. There is concern over Williams, who is carried off, but the injury does not prove serious.

40 — A PRESTON
Argyle: Blackwell, Billy, Williams, Saunders, Heathcote, Patterson, Illman, Rowbotham, Littlejohn, Collins, Barlow, Mauge
Preston: O'Hanlon, Cartwright, Kidd, Jackson, Wilcox, Gregan, Kilbane, Ashcroft, Reeves, Nogan^, Bryson, Davey
Argyle's travel plans are disrupted when they are severely delayed by a bomb scare on the motorway during their journey up north on Friday. Preston boss Gary Peters is disappointed with the result after his side fail to capitalise on David Reeves' goal. Saunders' volley is a beauty.

41 — H STOCKPORT
Argyle: Grobbelaar, Billy, Williams, Saunders, Heathcote, Patterson, Corazzin, Rowbotham, Littlejohn, Collins*, Barlow, Mauge/Littlejohn
Stockport: Jones, Connelly, Todd, Dinning, Flynn, Gannon, Cavaco*, Cowans, Charlery, Armstrong^, Cooper, Durkan/Mutch
The goal-starved Home Park faithful witness Argyle firing yet more blanks. County go close after 15 minutes when Alun Armstrong heads against the bar and Barlow turns the ball against a post as he tries to clear the rebound. Jim Gannon scrambles Heathcote's header off the line.

42 — A MILLWALL
Argyle: Grobbelaar, James, Williams, Saunders, Heathcote, Patterson, Corazzin*, Rowbotham, Littlejohn, Barlow^, Mauge, Collins
Millwall: Carter, Bircham, Newman, Harle, McLeary, Witter, Hartley, Doyle, Crawford*, Sadlier^, Berry, Savage/Webber
Lions manager John Docherty is forced to re-shuffle his side after Richard Sadlier is injured and Steve Crawford is taken ill at half-time. Corazzin gets the ball in the net (51) but the effort is ruled out for a foul. Jones is pleased with an away point which virtually guarantees safety.

43 — A NOTTS CO
Argyle: Grobbelaar, James*, Williams, Saunders, Heathcote, Patterson, Corazzin^, Rowbotham, Littlejohn, Barlow, Mauge, Billy/Illman
Notts Co: Ward, Hendon, Baraclough, Redmile, Strodder, Walker, Finnan, Cunnington*, Derry, White^, Martindale, Robinson/Jones
Shaun Cunnington's shot strikes Heathcote on the way past Grobbelaar. Collins scores his first for the club with a brave header which sees him needing treatment whilst lying in the back of the net. Already relegated County seal their first home win under new manager Sam Allardyce.

44 — H WALSALL
Argyle: Grobbelaar, Billy, Williams*, Saunders, Heathcote, Patterson, Mauge, Rowbotham, Collins, Corazzin^, Barlow, Curran/Illman
Walsall: Walker, Ntamark, Evans, Viveash, Butler, Mountfield, Watson^, Keister, Lightbourne, Wilson^, Hodge, Bradley/Beckford
After a frustrating first period, Argyle grab the victory which guarantees survival. Saunders' header, which goes in off a post, is Argyle's first home goal from open play for nine hours. Barlow finds a new lucky omen as he borrows Clayton's shin pads and scores his first goal for a year.

45 — A BRISTOL CITY
Argyle: Dungey, Billy, Williams, Saunders^, Heathcote, Perkins*, Rowbotham, Logan, Littlejohn^, Collins, Mauge, Curran/Illman/Clayton
Bristol City: Welch, Owers, Barnard, Shail, Paterson, Edwards, Hewlett, Carey, Nugent, Goater^, Kuhl^, Tinnion/Agostino
A rare goal from Williams puts Argyle ahead. Dungey does not have the happiest of games. Darren Barnard's cross from the left floats over him and he then concedes a penalty by diving at the feet of Shaun Goater. Nugent scores with a simple tap-in. Perkins has a steady full debut.

46 — H BOURNEMOUTH
Argyle: Dungey, Billy, Williams^, Mauge, Heathcote, Patterson, Rowbotham, Logan*, Littlejohn, Collins*, Barlow, Illman/Wotton/Perkins
Bournemouth: Glass, Young, Vincent, Beardsmore^, Cox, Bailey, Holland, Robinson, Town^, Howe, Rawlinson, Murray/O'Neill
A drab affair is distinctly end of season. The surprise is that so many people turn up to watch it. Collins manages to hoof the ball over from inches out, but his blushes are spared by an offside flag. The 'McCauley Out' brigade stage a mini-demonstration on the pitch after the match.

NATIONWIDE DIVISION 2 (CUP-TIES)　　Manager: Neil Warnock > Mick Jones　　SEASON 1996-97

Coca-Cola Cup

		Att		F-A	H-T	Scorers, Times, and Referees	1	2	3	4	5	6	7	8	9	10	11	subs used
1:1 A	BRENTFORD 20/8	3,034 2:	L	0-1	0-0	Taylor 63 Ref: A Wiley	Grobbelaar	Billy	Williams	Mauge	Heathcote	Curran	Leadbitter	Logan	Littlejohn	Evans	Corazzin	
							Dearden	Hurdle	Anderson	Ashby	Bates	McGhee	Asaba*	Smith	Forster	Bent	Taylor	Harvey
1:2 H	BRENTFORD 3/9	5,180 2:	D	0-0	0-0	Ref: C Wilkes (Argyle lost 0-1 on aggregate)	Grobbelaar	Billy	Williams	Saunders*	Heathcote^	James	Leadbitter	Logan	Littlejohn	Evans	Barlow	Corazzin/Curran
							Dearden	Hurdle	Anderson	Bates	McGhee	Asaba	Smith	Abrahams*	Bent	Taylor		Harvey^/Hutchings

1:1 — A powerful header from Robert Taylor from Marcus Bent's cross is enough to give the Bees a slender first-leg lead. Heroics from Grobbelaar keeps the score down. Mauge retaliates after being fouled by Carl Asaba, which sparks a flare-up with several players from each side involved.

1:2 — The build-up is dominated by rumours of Warnock's threatened resignation over differences with the chairman and a planned supporters' demonstration against Mr McCauley which comes to nothing. Argyle fail to progress beyond the first round for the fourth successive season.

FA Cup

		Att		F-A	H-T	Scorers, Times, and Referees	1	2	3	4	5	6	7	8	9	10	11	subs used
1 H	FULHAM 16/11	7,104 3:1	W	5-0	1-0	Mauge 38, Evans 54p 78, Littlejohn 80, [Corazzin 88] Ref: R Harris	Grobbelaar	Billy	Williams	Mauge	Heathcote*	James	Leadbitter^	Curran	Illman"	Evans	Barlow	Saunders/Corazzin/Littlejohn
							Lange	Watson	Herrera	Cusack	Cullip	Blake	Carpenter	Cockerill*	Conroy	Morgan	Scott	Brooker
2 H	EXETER 6/12	12,911 3:5	W	4-1	2-1	Evans 30, Mauge 32, Billy 80, L'john 90; Sharpe 45 Ref: S Dunn	Grobbelaar	Billy	Williams	Mauge	Heathcote	James	Wotton	Leadbitter	Littlejohn	Evans	Barlow	Barlow Chamberl'n^ Braithwaite/McConnell
							Bayes	Richardson	Sharpe	Myers	Blake	Hare	Rowbath'm*	Dailly	Flack	Bailey	Chamberl'n^	
3 H	PETERBOROUGH 4/1	7,299 19	L	0-1	0-0	Charlery 58 Ref: C Wilkes	Grobbelaar	Billy	Williams	Mauge	Heathcote	James	Wotton*	Leadbitter^	Illman	Evans	Barlow^	Saunders/Corazzin/Littlejohn
							Griemink	Willis	Clark	Edwards	Heald	Bodley	Payne	Houghton	Carruthers* Charlery	Morrison^		Griffiths/Basham

1 — Mauge, fined two weeks' wages after off-the-field misdemeanours takes the plaudits after Argyle destroy the third division leaders. Micky Adams' side's heads drop after Evans slots in a penalty when Glenn Cockerill fouls Mauge. Littlejohn and Corazzin both score from 20 yards.

2 — Another live Sky TV match. Mauge is selected after being released on bail. The expected challenge from Peter Fox's in-form City never materialises and even John Sharpe's 25-yard effort fails to inspire them. Billy's left-foot drive from outside the area thrills a good size crowd.

3 — Warnock is unhappy that the match goes ahead. Argyle spend £800 on pimple-soled training shoes to cope with the icy surface. Ken Charlery scores as Grobbelaar thinks the ball has gone out of play. Scott Houghton bravely throws his shirt at manager Barry Fry after being substituted.

Home / Away Table

	Team	P	W	D	L	F	A	W	D	L	F	A	Pts
				Home					**Away**				
1	Bury	46	18	5	0	39	14	6	7	10	23	31	84
2	Stockport	46	15	5	3	31	14	8	7	8	28	27	82
3	Luton	46	13	7	3	38	14	8	8	7	33	31	78
4	Brentford	46	8	11	4	26	22	12	3	8	30	21	74
5	Bristol City	46	14	4	5	43	18	6	6	10	26	33	73
6	Crewe *	46	15	4	4	38	15	7	3	13	18	32	73
7	Blackpool	46	13	7	3	41	21	5	8	10	19	26	69
8	Wrexham	46	11	9	3	37	28	6	9	8	17	22	69
9	Burnley	46	14	3	6	48	27	5	8	10	23	28	68
10	Chesterfield	46	10	9	4	25	18	8	5	10	17	21	68
11	Gillingham	46	13	3	7	37	25	6	7	10	23	34	67
12	Walsall	46	12	8	3	35	21	7	2	14	19	32	67
13	Watford	46	10	8	5	24	14	6	11	6	21	24	67
14	Millwall	46	12	4	7	27	22	4	10	9	23	33	61
15	Preston	46	14	5	4	33	19	4	2	17	16	36	61
16	Bournemouth	46	8	9	6	24	20	7	6	10	19	25	60
17	Bristol Rov	46	13	4	6	34	22	2	7	14	13	28	56
18	Wycombe	46	13	4	6	31	14	2	6	15	20	42	55
19	PLYMOUTH	46	7	11	5	19	18	5	7	11	28	40	54
20	York	46	8	6	9	27	31	5	7	11	20	37	52
21	Peterborough	46	7	7	9	38	34	4	7	12	17	39	47
22	Shrewsbury	46	8	6	9	27	32	3	7	13	22	42	46
23	Rotherham	46	4	7	12	17	29	3	7	13	22	41	35
24	Notts Co	46	4	9	10	20	25	3	5	15	13	34	35
		1104	264	155	133	759	510	133	155	264	510	759	1501

* promoted after play-offs

Appearances & Goals

Player	Lge	Sub	LC	Sub	FAC	Sub	Lge	LC	FAC	Tot
				Appearances					**Goals**	
Barlow, Martin	38		1		3		1			1
Billy, Chris	44	1	2		3		3		1	4
Blackwell, Kevin	4									
Clayton, Gary		1								
Collins, Simon			1							
Corazzin, Carlo	22	8	1	1		2	5		1	6
Curran, Chris	20	2	1		1					
Dungey, James	6									
Evans, Michael	33		2		3		12	3		15
Grobbelaar, Bruce	36		2		3					
Heathcote, Mick	41	1	2		3		1			1
Illman, Neil	12	13			2		4			4
James, Tony	34		1		3		1			1
Leadbitter, Chris	17	2	2		3					
Littlejohn, Adrian	33	4	2		1	2	6		2	8
Logan, Richard	19	9	2		2		4			4
Mauge, Ronnie	29	6	1		3		3		2	5
Patterson, Mark	11	1								
Perkins, Steve	1	3								
Phillips, Lee		2								
Rowbotham, Jason	12	3								
Saunders, Mark	22	3	1	2			3			3
Simpson, Michael	10	2								
Williams, Paul	46		2		3		2			2
Wotton, Paul	5	4			2		1			1
25 players used	506	68	22	2	33	6	47		9	56

Odds & ends

Double wins: (2) Rotherham, Walsall.
Double defeats: (2) Brentford, Bristol Rov.

Won from behind: (0).
Lost from in front: (1) Bristol City.

High spots: Surprise signing of Bruce Grobbelaar.
Received record fee of £500,000 from Southampton for Michael Evans.
Lee Phillips becomes youngest ever player to play league football for the club.

Low spots: Mark Patterson breaks leg in pre-season friendly v Chelsea.
Dismissal via telephone of manager Neil Warnock.
Infamous 'Battle of Saltergate' when five players in total sent off.
Poor home record, scoring only 19 goals at Home Park.
Losing to Peterborough at home in FA Cup.

Player of the Year: Chris Billy.
Ever presents: (1) Paul Williams.
Hat-tricks: (0).
Leading scorer: Michael Evans (15).

NATIONWIDE DIVISION 2

Manager: Mick Jones   SEASON 1997-98

Fixtures

No	Date		Att	Pos	Pt	F-A	H-T	Scorers, Times, and Referees
1	9/8	A BRISTOL ROV	7,386		D 1	1-1	0-1	Heathcote 58 / Hayles 41. Ref: M Fletcher
2	16/8	H GRIMSBY	6,002	14	D 2	2-2	2-0	Logan 28, Littlejohn 42 / Donovan 66p, Nogan 73. Ref: M Bailey
3	23/8	A WIGAN	3,761	17	D 3	1-1	0-1	Logan 84 / Lowe 25. Ref: D Laws
4	30/8	H CHESTERFIELD	5,284	16	D 4	1-1	1-0	Jean 31 / Lormor 85p. Ref: K Leach
5	2/9	H WATFORD	5,141		L 4	0-1	0-0	Noel-Williams 71. Ref: A D'Urso
6	9/9	A FULHAM	8,961		L 4	0-2	0-0	Moody 57, 77. Ref: S Baines
7	13/9	H BRENTFORD	4,394	23	D 5	0-0	0-0	Ref: J Brandwood
8	20/9	A CARLISLE	5,667	22	D 6	2-2	1-2	Littlejohn 6, Wilson 74 / Jansen 2, 45. Ref: P Richards
9	27/9	H WALSALL	6,207	21	W 9	2-1	1-1	Barlow 34, 70 / Boli 31. Ref: M Halsey
10	4/10	A YORK	2,894	22	L 9	0-1	0-1	Rowe 8. Ref: R Pearson
11	11/10	A LUTON	4,931	22	L 9	0-3	0-1	Thorpe 36, 58, Davies 82. Ref: D Crick

Line-ups

1 — A Bristol Rovers

	1	2	3	4	5	6	7	8	9	10	11	subs used
Argyle	Sheffield	Collins	Williams	Rowbotham	Heathcote	Wotton	Billy*	Logan	Littlejohn	Corazzin!	Anthony	Jean
Bristol Rov	Collett	Perry	Power*	Parmenter^	Gayle	Tillson	Holloway	Penrice	Alsop*	Cureton	Hayles	Foster/Ramasut/Beadle

Rovers' £200k summer signing, Barry Hayles, puts them ahead when Sheffield failed to hold under pressure from Julian Alsop. Despite the sweltering heat, Corazzin loses his cool when he retaliates with an elbow after being clattered from behind by Steve Foster and is sent off (52).

2 — H Grimsby

	1	2	3	4	5	6	7	8	9	10	11	subs used
Argyle	Sheffield	Billy	Williams	Mauge^	Heathcote	Wotton	Rowbotham	Logan^	Littlejohn	Corazzin	Anthony	Jean
Grimsby	Davison	McDermott	Gallimore*	Handyside	Lever	Southall	Donovan	Gilbert	Liv'stone	Nogan	Groves	Clayton, Jobling/Lester

Logan's header looks goal-bound but hits Littlejohn. The rebound falls kindly however and Logan makes no mistake. Littlejohn shoots through Aidan Davison's legs for his first goal at Home Park for 16 months. Logan trips Jack Lester for a penalty. Lee Nogan completes the comeback.

3 — A Wigan

	1	2	3	4	5	6	7	8	9	10	11	subs used
Argyle	Sheffield	Billy	Williams	Mauge	Heathcote	Wotton	Rowbotham	Logan	Littlejohn	Jean	Anthony*	Wilson
Wigan	Butler	Green	Johnson	Greenall	McGibbon	Sharp	Lee	Lowe	O'Connell	Rogers	Kilford*	Broughton

Logan's decision to send his wife and new-born baby to his parents for a week to allow him to catch up on some sleep pays off as he continues his early-season scoring run. Argyle fall behind to a freak goal. David Lowe tries to find David Lee with a cross but the ball slices off his shin.

4 — H Chesterfield

	1	2	3	4	5	6	7	8	9	10	11	subs used
Argyle	Sheffield	Billy	Williams	Mauge	Heathcote	Wotton	Anthony	Logan	Littlejohn	Jean*	Wilson	Illman
Chesterfield	Mercer	Hewitt	Jules^	Curtis	Williams	Carr^	Morris	Holland	Lormor	Ebdon*	Perkins	Breckin/Beaumont/Jackson

Contract rebels Patterson and Saunders are still not considered for selection. Jean is warned by the ref after over-exuberant goal celebrations in front of the away supporters but then hugs Mr I Leach! Lormor's penalty comes after Billy is adjudged to have pushed Andy Morris in the back.

5 — H Watford

	1	2	3	4	5	6	7	8	9	10	11	subs used
Argyle	Sheffield	Billy	Williams	Mauge	Heathcote	Wotton	Anthony*	Logan	Littlejohn	Jean^	Wilson	Barlow/Illman
Watford	Chamberlain	Melvang	Kennedy	Page	Palmer	Mooney	Noel-Williams	Hyde	Lee	Johnson	Rosenthal	

McCauley announces that he is ready to sell the club. A minute's silence in memory of the Princess of Wales is impeccably observed. The tribute sets the tone for a low-key affair which is settled by Gifton Noel-Williams' goal after a Peter Kennedy free-kick is parried by Sheffield.

6 — A Fulham

	1	2	3	4	5	6	7	8	9	10	11	subs used
Argyle	Sheffield	Billy	Williams	Mauge	Heathcote	Wotton	Barlow	Logan	Littlejohn	Jean^	Wilson	Collins/Wilson
Fulham	Watton	Lawrence	Herrera	Cullip	Smith*	Blake	Newhouse*	Hayward	Moody	Morgan	Brooker^	Carpenter/Scott/Cockerill

Two decisions by referee Baines turns the match. Littlejohn is scythed down by Mark Blake as he bears down on goal but Blake escapes with a yellow card. Even Paul Moody is surprised when his first goal is allowed after Sheffield was impeded. Moody scores again with a curling shot.

7 — H Brentford

	1	2	3	4	5	6	7	8	9	10	11	subs used
Argyle	Sheffield	Billy	Williams	Mauge	Heathcote	Wotton	Barlow	Logan	Littlejohn	Jean	Wilson	Illman
Brentford	Dearden	Hurdle	Anderson	Hutchings	Bates	Oatway	Denys^	Canham	Bent	Rapley	Taylor	Bryan

The chairman takes umbrage with the local evening paper and bans them from Home Park so their reporter watches the match from a 50-foot crane erected outside the ground. Marcus Bent hits a post with the last kick after an up-and-under causes chaos between Sheffield and Wotton.

8 — A Carlisle

	1	2	3	4	5	6	7	8	9	10	11	subs used
Argyle	Sheffield	Billy	Williams	Mauge	Heathcote	Wotton	Barlow	Logan	Littlejohn	Corazzin^	Wilson	Saunders
Carlisle	Caig	Holloway	Archdeacon	Prokas	Varty	Pounew'chy	Barr^	Couzens*	McAlindon	Jansen	Aspinall	Harrison/Stevens

Saunders signs a new month-to-month contract. Teenage wonderkid Matt Jansen soon makes his mark by shooting past Sheffield. Littlejohn quickly replies by firing in a loose ball. Jansen scores again. Wilson produces a stunning volley into the roof of the net from a tight angle.

9 — H Walsall

	1	2	3	4	5	6	7	8	9	10	11	subs used
Argyle	Sheffield	Billy	Williams	Mauge	Heathcote	Wotton	Barlow	Saunders	Littlejohn	Corazzin	Wilson	
Walsall	Walker	Evans	Rogers*	Viveash	Mountfield	Peron	Boli	Skinner	Watson	Hodge	Keates^	Platt/Porter

Argyle finally win thanks to Barlow. In-form Roger Boli opens the scoring. Barlow skips past two defenders before firing in a 20-yard left-foot shot. He then scores again after a defensive error. Saddlers manager Jan Sorensen accuses the Argyle management of intimidating the referee.

10 — A York

	1	2	3	4	5	6	7	8	9	10	11	subs used
Argyle	Sheffield	Billy	Williams	Mauge	Heathcote	Wotton	Barlow	Saunders	Littlejohn	Corazzin^	Wilson	Jean
York	Samways	Murty	Hall	Bushell	Reed	Barras	Stephenson	Tinkler	Tolson	Rowe	Pouton^	Bull/Himsworth

In a turgid affair, Argyle fail to muster one shot to test Mark Samways. Neil Tolson flicks on Wayne Hall's long throw and Rodney Rowe hooks the ball in from six yards. The players become as frustrated as the fans and the referee dishes out six yellow cards in the second half.

11 — A Luton

	1	2	3	4	5	6	7	8	9	10	11	subs used
Argyle	Sheffield	Collins	Williams	Mauge	Heathcote	Wotton	Barlow	Saunders	Littlejohn	Corazzin*	Wilson*	Billy, Jean
Luton	Davis	Alexander	Small	Waddock	James	White	Spring!	McLaren	Oldfield	Thorpe^	Doherty^	Davies/Evers

Tony Thorpe confirms his liking for playing against Argyle with his seventh goal in three matches against the Pilgrims. Matthew Spring is sent off (71) on his full debut for a crunching tackle on Barlow. Jones is then sent from the dug-out for trying to get the youngster reprieved!

12 **H** 18/10 **SOUTHEND** 23 L 19 / 9

Sheffield	Collins	Williams	Mauge	Heathcote	Wotton	Barlow	Saunders	Littlejohn	Corazzin	Billy
Royce	Hails	Jones	Coulbault	Lewis	Harris	Allen	Gridelet	Rammell	N'Diaye	Clarke

Littlejohn 30, Corazzin 31 — HT 2-2 · FT 2-3
Wotton 4(og), Clarke 20, N'Diaye 75
Att 3,430 — Ref: C Wilkes

The Lyndhurst and Mayflower stands are closed by the County Council on safety grounds. Nathan Jones' shot is saved by Sheffield but the ball rebounds off Wotton and goes in. Adrian Clarke's volley is deflected. Argyle fight back but Frenchman Sada N'Diaye scores on his debut.

---

13 **H** 21/10 **BURNLEY** 23 D 24 / 10

Beresford · Brass · Vin'combe* · Harrison · Howey · Moore · Waddle · Ford · Creaney · Eyres · Weller

Jean 40, Heathcote 47 — HT 1-1 · FT 2-2
Eyres 8p, Creaney 58
Att 3,006 — Ref: P Rejer

Gerry Creaney appears to fall over his own feet but a penalty is given which David Eyres converts. Jean's low shot and Heathcote's header puts Plymouth in front. The Clarets new player-manager, Chris Waddle, begins to conjure up some of his old magic and Creaney equalises.

---

14 **A** 25/10 **GILLINGHAM** 23 L 3 / 10

Stannard · Statham · Galloway · Smith · Ashby · Green · Hess'thaler · Ratcliffe · Butler^ · Akinbiyi · Bailey^
subs: Onoura/Fortune-West, Illman/Wilson 1/Beswethr'k

Jean 4 — HT 1-1 · FT 1-2
Akinbiyi 32, Fortune-West 87
Att 6,679 — Ref: A Butler

Argyle's dream start soon goes wrong. Heathcote is stretchered off (31) after landing awkwardly. Ade Akinbiyi immediately scores. Wilson does not help the cause when he is sent off (75) for kicking the ball away having earlier been booked. Leo Fortune-West scores from 30 yards.

---

15 **A** 1/11 **PRESTON** 23 W 16 / 13

Moilanen · Parkinson* · Kidd · Murdock · Moyes · Darby · Macken^ · Ashcroft · Nogan" · Rankine · Eyres
subs: Cartwright/Gregan/Holt

Corazzin 65 — HT 0-0 · FT 1-0
Att 8,405 — Ref: A Hall

Jones's patched up side gain an elusive away win. Sheffield is concussed after coming off worse in a three-man collision but resumes after treatment with Billy ready to don the gloves. Corazzin's firm downward header past Finnish international Teumo Moilanen seals the victory.

---

16 **H** 4/11 **WYCOMBE** 20 W 14 / 16

Taylor · Cousins · Kavanagh · Ryan · Mohan · Forsyth* · Carroll · Scott · Stallard · McGavin · Simpson^
subs: McCarthy/Read, Illman

Corazzin 17p, 18, Littlejohn 54, Mauge 57 — HT 2-1 · FT 4-2
Collins 5(og), Scott 52
Att 2,993 — Ref: R Styles

Collins' attempted clearance is headed past Sheffield. Saunders is sent sprawling by Taylor in the box. Wycombe players surround the ref at the final whistle to protest about Littlejohn's goal which looked offside. A furious Jason Cousins is dragged away from Mr Styles by a steward.

---

17 **H** 8/11 **BOURNEMOUTH** 18 W 13 / 19

Glass · Young · Vincent · Howe · Cox · O'Neill* · Beardsmore · Robinson* · Warren · Fletcher · Rawlinson^
subs: Rolling/Brissett/Dean

Jean 10, Littlejohn 15, 85 — HT 2-0 · FT 3-0
Att 5,067 — Ref: P Taylor

O'Hagan is given a second chance by Jones after being released last season and leads the attack having been playing Sunday League division three football. New loan signing Lee Hodges soon wins the crowd over with some clever play. Littlejohn is back to form with two fine strikes.

---

18 **A** 18/11 **BRISTOL CITY** L 19

Welch · Locke · Bell · Hewlett · Carey · Taylor · Goodridge* · Doherty · Torpey · Goater · Tinnion^
subs: Saunders/Wilson, Langan/Brennan

Corazzin 83 — HT 0-2 · FT 1-2
Bell 33, 34
Att 10,867 — Ref: A Wiley

Argyle are immediately under the cosh as City rattle up 16 attempts on goal in the first half. Mickey Bell scores with an exquisite free-kick from 20 yards and then finds the net again with an almost identical strike. An error by Plymouth-born Shaun Taylor gifts Corazzin a late goal.

---

19 **A** 22/11 **WREXHAM** 17 D 10 / 20

Marriott · Jones · Hardy · Phillips · Humes · Skinner* · Ridler · Owen^ · Connolly · Roberts · Ward
subs: O'Hagan, Chalk/Russell

Billy 58 — HT 0-0 · FT 1-1
Ward 71
Att 3,641 — Ref: G Frankland

Littlejohn is tackled from behind by Wayne Phillips. As play continues, a linesman spots the Argyle forward spitting at his adversary and he receives a red card (27). Andy Marriott fails to hold Barlow's free-kick and Billy puts the ten men ahead. Peter Ward's shot is deflected in.

---

20 **H** 29/11 **OLDHAM** 18 L 5 / 20

Kelly · Rickers · Serrant · Boxall · Graham · Redmond · Duxbury · Hodgson · Ritchie · Reid
subs: Saunders/O'Hagan

Mauge 9(og), Rickers 90 — HT 0-1 · FT 0-2
Att 5,452 — Ref: B Knight

Pilgrim fans are urged to sign a 'Save Argyle' petition. Neil Warnock gets a warm reception on his return to Home Park and sees his side win away for the first time under his leadership. Mauge's headed clearance is misdirected past Sheffield. Paul Rickers seals it in stoppage time.

---

21 **A** 2/12 **BLACKPOOL** 20 D 9 / 21

Banks · Bryan · Dixon · Butler · Strong · Bent* · Collins · Barlow · Clarkson · Malkin^ · Philpott
subs: Brabin/Omerod, O'Hagan

HT 0-0 · FT 0-0
Att 3,281 — Ref: C Joy

The fixture planning again unkindly sends Argyle on a midweek trek to Blackpool. Hodges comes close to breaking his scoring duck but Steve Banks pushes his 20-yard shot onto an upright. Pool rarely threaten as Collins and Rowbotham both return from injury to bolster the defence.

---

22 **H** 13/12 **MILLWALL** 20 W 6 / 24

Spink · Brown · Bircham" · Veart · Fitzgerald · Black* · Witter · Hardy · Savage · Shaw · Bowry · Logan
subs: Wotton/Jean/Beswetherick, Allen/Hockton/Neill

Collins 23, Billy 43, Corazzin 78p — HT 2-0 · FT 3-0
Att 4,460 — Ref: P Danson

Visiting manager Billy Bonds pays tribute to Argyle's commitment as they defeat the highly rated Lions. Collins scores with a bullet-like header. Billy scores with a lovely shot on the turn and Corazzin picks himself up to score from the spot after being fouled by Bobby Bowry.

---

23 **A** 20/12 **NORTHAMPTON** 20 L 5 / 24

Woodman · Clarkson · Frain · Hill · Bishop* · Brightwell · Peer · Heggs^ · Freestone · Dozzell · Hunter^ · Jean
subs: Gibb/Seal/Hunt

Corazzin 45 — HT 1-0 · FT 1-2
Freestone 66, 71
Att 5,546 — Ref: D Pugh

The Cobblers give a debut to ex-Spurs star Jason Dozzell. Corazzin finishes Logan's long throw. The ref crucially refuses to allow Logan back on after treatment until a John Frain corner is taken which Chris Freestone heads in. The same combination then strike again five minutes later.

NATIONWIDE DIVISION 2 — Manager: Mick Jones — SEASON 1997-98

Each match is shown with the Plymouth Argyle line-up (roman) on the upper row and the opponents' line-up (*italic*) on the lower row.

No	Date	Att	Pos	Pt	Res	F-A	H-T	Scorers, Times, and Referees	1	2	3	4	5	6	7	8	9	10	11	subs used
24	H FULHAM 26/12	9,469	20	24	L	1-4	1-1	Barlow 5 / Ref: M Fletcher	Sheffield	Rowbotham	Williams	Hodges	Saunders"	Collins	Barlow	Logan	O'Hagan^	Corazzin	Billy*	Littlejohn/Jean/Mauge
			10					Moody 18, 80, Hayward 63, Trollope 75	*Taylor*	*Lawrence*	*Herrera*	*Trollope*	*Coleman*	*Neilson*	*Smith*	*Bracewell*	*Moody*	*Peschisolido*	*Hayward*	
25	A WATFORD 28/12	11,594	21	25	D	1-1	0-0	Saunders 86 / Ref: S Bennett	Sheffield	Collins	Williams	Mauge	Heathcote	Saunders	Barlow	Logan	Littlejohn	Corazzin	Billy	Jean
			1					Mooney 90	*Chamberlain*	*Gibbs*	*Kennedy*	*Page*	*Millen*	*Mooney*	*Noel-Williams Hyde*	*Lee*	*Johnson*	*Robinson^*	*Lowndes*	
26	H BRISTOL ROV 10/1	6,850	23	25	L	1-2	0-2	Corazzin 50 / Ref: G Singh	Sheffield	Collins	Williams*	Mauge	Heathcote	Saunders	Barlow	Jean^	Littlejohn	Corazzin	Rowbotham	O'Hagan/Phillips
			3					Cureton 23, Hayles 27	*Collett*	*Pritchard*	*Lockwood*	*Penrice*	*White*	*Foster*	*Holloway"*	*Ramasut^*	*Beadle*	*Cureton"*	*Hayles*	*Tillson/Bennett/Zabek*
27	A CHESTERFIELD 17/1	3,879	23	25	L	1-2	1-1	Corazzin 33p / Ref: K Lynch	Sheffield	Collins	Williams	Mauge	Heathcote	Saunders	Barlow	Wotton*	O'Hagan^	Corazzin	Rowbotham	Logan/Jean
			8					Wilkinson 12, 47	*Mercer*	*Hewitt*	*Beaumont*	*Curtis*	*Williams*	*Breckin*	*Creaney***	*Holland*	*Reeves*	*Ebdon*	*Willis*	*Wilkinson/Willis*
28	H WIGAN 24/1	4,345	21	28	W	3-2	0-2	Saunders 52, Barlow 77, Collins 86 / Ref: P Taylor	Sheffield	Collins	Williams	Mauge	Heathcote	Ro'botham*	Barlow	Saunders*	Littlejohn^	Corazzin	Billy	Logan/Jean
			18					Kilford 37, Lee 41	*Butler*	*Green*	*Morgan*	*Greenall*	*Kilford*	*Martinez*	*Lee*	*Rogers***	*Jones*	*Branch***	*Sharp*	*Warne/Smeets*
29	A BRENTFORD 31/1	4,783	23	28	L	1-3	1-0	Corazzin 22 / Ref: M Bailey	Sheffield	Collins	Williams	Mauge^	Heathcote	Ro'botham*	Barlow	Saunders*	Littlejohn*	Corazzin	Billy	Logan/Jean/Phillips
			22					Bates 62, Scott 66, Hogg 88	*Pollitt*	*Hutchings*	*Watson^*	*Oatway*	*Bates*	*Hogg*	*Rapley"*	*Cockerill*	*Scott*	*Canham***	*Taylor*	*McGhee/Dennis/Clark*
30	H CARLISLE 7/2	4,540	21	31	W	2-1	1-0	Heathcote 45, Corazzin 68 / Ref: A Wiley	Sheffield	Collins	Williams	Mauge	Heathcote	Rowbotham	Barlow	Saunders	Jean^	Corazzin*	Billy	Littlejohn/Phillips
			23					Stevens 51p	*Caig*	*Hopper*	*Sandwith^*	*Barr*	*Varty***	*Wallwork*	*Anthony*	*Pounew'chy Stevens*	*Wright*	*Prokas*	*McAlindon/Gray*
31	H YORK 14/2	4,382	21	32	D	0-0	0-0	Ref: M Dean	Sheffield	Collins	Williams	Logan^	Heathcote	Rowbotham	Barlow	Saunders	Jean^	Corazzin	Billy	Mauge
			12						*Samways*	*Murty*	*Hall***	*Bushell*	*Jones*	*Barras*	*Pouton^*	*Tinkler*	*Bull*	*Greening***	*Stephenson*	*Rowe/Cresswell/Jordan*
32	A WALSALL 21/2	4,612	19	35	W	1-0	1-0	Heathcote 15 / Ref: F Stretton	Sheffield	Collins	Williams	Logan*	Heathcote	Rowbotham	Barlow	Phillips*	Littlejohn	Corazzin	Billy	Mauge/Jean
			16						*Walker*	*Evans*	*Marsh*	*Viveash*	*Roper*	*Peron*	*Boli*	*Blake***	*Keates*	*Ricketts*	*Hodge*	*Platt*
33	A SOUTHEND 24/2	4,363	21	35	L	0-3	0-1	Ref: J Brandwood	Sheffield	Collins	Williams	Saunders	Heathcote	Ro'botham*	Barlow	Phillips*	Jean	Corazzin	Billy	Logan/Wotton
								Aldridge 40, Maher 62, Jobson 73	*Royce*	*Hails*	*Dublin*	*Coulbault^*	*Jobson*	*Coleman*	*Maher*	*Jones*	*Boere^*	*Aldridge*	*Clarke^*	*Rammell/Thomson/Gridelet*
34	H LUTON 28/2	4,846	21	35	L	0-2	0-0	Ref: A D'Urso	Sheffield	Collins	Williams	Saunders	Heathcote	Ro'botham*	Barlow	Conlon	Littlejohn	Corazzin	Billy	Wotton
			19					Fotiadis 80, Evers 88	*Davis K*	*Alexander*	*Thomas*	*Waddock*	*Davis S*	*Patterson*	*Evers*	*McLaren*	*Oldfield*	*Gray*	*Marshall***	*Fotiadis^/Doherty*

Match notes

24. Kevin Keegan's expensively assembled side have hardly set the division alight so far but easily outclass Argyle. Barlow's harmless looking free-kick somehow eludes everyone. The Pilgrims have no answer to Paul Moody who scores twice himself and sets up Steve Hayward's goal.

25. Despite early pressure, Argyle come close to upsetting the leaders. Jason Lee is the main culprit for the Hornets as he misses a number of good chances. Saunders' header sends hundreds of Watford fans pouring out of Vicarage Road and they miss Tommy Mooney's crucial equaliser.

26. Argyle slide deeper into trouble although Rovers boss Ian Holloway is relieved to gain maximum points. Assistant manager Kevin Blackwell is ordered back to the dugout after protesting about Jamie Cureton's opener. Barry Hayles taps in. Corazzin's low shot reduces the deficit.

27. Steve Wilkinson, with just two goals since his £150k move from Preston, silences his critics by bundling in the Spireites' first goal. Corazzin blast his penalty into the roof of the net after Barlow was bundled over by Tom Curtis. Wilkinson nets the winner after some good close control.

28. Ian Kilford puts the Latics ahead when Sheffield parried his shot but then he and Heathcote leave the ball to each other and Kilford accepts a second chance. Barlow's poor pass leads to David Lee's goal. Saunders shot beats two defenders on the line. Collins heads in from inches out.

29. Littlejohn's pace sets up Corazzin's goal. Three set-pieces from Glenn Cockerill then complete the Bees comeback. His corner is headed in by Jamie Bates. Andy Scott's diving header finishes off a free-kick and former Man Utd defender Graeme Hogg heads in from a similar situation.

30. Chairman McCauley ends his self-imposed exile from Home Park. Heathcote takes time out from his defensive duties to put Argyle ahead in this 'six-pointer'. Collins' mistimed tackle on Richard Prokas leads to Ian Stevens' twelfth goal in eleven matches. Corazzin scores on the turn.

31. City's determination not to repeat their previous away performance, a 2-7 defeat at Burnley, makes for a poor game. Logan miskicks with the goal at his mercy. Rodney Rowe, relegated to sub after a court appearance for assault, misses a hat-trick of chances in the final 20 minutes.

32. Barlow's inswinging corner to the far post somehow finds Heathcote who blasts in. The Saddler's top scorer, 22-goal Roger Boli, is booked for diving with the home side screaming for a penalty. Walsall gradually lose their discipline and manager Ian Sorensen is sent from the dug-out.

33. Despite the best efforts of man of the match Barlow, Argyle slump to a demoralising defeat. Martin Aldridge, signed on loan on Monday, makes a scoring debut. Adrian Maher scores a memorable first league goal after a flowing move. Richard Jobson soars high to head in a third.

34. With the game heading for a scoreless draw, Rowbotham's header back to Sheffield is woefully weak and Andrew Fotiadis nips in to score. Saunders is denied a penalty when he is tripped from behind by Steve Davis as he prepares to shoot. Sean Evers then scores immediately after.

Fixture log — Plymouth Argyle (matches 36–46), continued

No	Venue	Opponent	Date	Pos	Res	Pts	FT	HT	Att		Scorers / Opp scorers	Referee
	A	(Bournemouth)	3/3			36			3,545	9	Fletcher 17, 89, Vincent 80	Ref: A Butler
36	H	PRESTON	7/3	20	W	39	2-0	1-0	4,201	17	Wotton 36, Conlon 65	Ref: D Orr
37	A	WYCOMBE	14/3	22	L	39	1-5	1-1	5,508	10	Corazzin 44 / Ryan 23, Scott 47, Stallard 52, 75, [Carroll 83]	Ref: A Wiley
38	H	BRISTOL CITY	21/3	19	W	42	2-0	0-0	7,622	2	Saunders 50, Conlon 77	Ref: M Fletcher
39	A	GRIMSBY	24/3		L	42	0-1	0-0	4,661		Groves 78	Ref: P Richards
40	H	WREXHAM	28/3	19	W	45	2-0	1-0	4,749	4	Corazzin 31, Saunders 79	Ref: R Harris
41	A	OLDHAM	4/4	21	L	45	0-2	0-1	4,244	12	Littlejohn 43, 54	Ref: M Pike
42	H	BLACKPOOL	11/4	20	W	48	3-1	0-1	5,655	10	Butler 57(og), Logan 78, Corazzin 90p; Heathcote 28(og)	Ref: B Knight
43	A	MILLWALL	13/4	20	D	49	1-1	1-1	5,496	18	Corazzin 25; Hockton 4	Ref: S Baines
44	H	NORTHAMPTON	18/4	20	L	49	1-3	1-1	6,389	6	Saunders 45; Freestone 8, 47, 90	Ref: K Leach
45	H	GILLINGHAM	25/4	21	L	49	0-1	0-0	7,941	6	Smith 90	Ref: J Brandwood
46	A	BURNLEY	2/5	22	L	49	1-2	1-2	18,811	20	Saunders 25; Cooke 12, 41	Ref: P Taylor

Home Average 5,323 — Away 6,228

3/3 — Opposition line-up: Glass, Young, Vincent^, Rolling, Cox, Bailey, O'Neill^, Robinson, Teather", Fletcher, Brissett; subs Town/Dean/Howe.
A pulsating game is played on a rain-soaked pitch. Steve Fletcher puts the Cherries ahead. Saunders' glancing header levels. Jimmy Glass miscues a punch to Logan who makes no mistake. Vincent blasts home from 30 yards. Corazzin and Fletcher exchange goals in stoppage time.

36 PRESTON — Argyle: Sheffield, Collins, Rowbotham, Saunders, Heathcote, Wotton, Barlow, Logan!, Conlon, Corazzin, Billy. Preston: Moilanen, Parkinson, Kidd*, Murdock, Jackson, Appleton, Davey, Ashcroft, Sissoko^, Eyres; subs Cartwright/Mullin.
Despite torrential overnight rain, Jones orders the pitch to be watered. The injured Williams misses his first league match for 127 games. A Wotton rocket flies in from 20 yards. Logan is dismissed (72) for a second booking. Conlon scores his first league goal with a diving header.

37 WYCOMBE — Argyle: Sheffield, Collins, Rowbotham, Saunders, Heathcote, Wotton, Barlow, Logan!, Conlon^, Corazzin, Billy; subs Littlejohn/Jean. Wycombe: Taylor, Kavanagh^, Forsyth, Ryan, Cousins, Mohan, Carroll, Scott^, Stallard, Brown; subs Simpson/Read/Beeton.
A distraught Logan is sent off for the second successive week, this time for a professional foul on Mark Stallard (33). Despite the scoreline, Argyle produce one of their best away performances of the season. Keith Scott scores the goal of the match with a stunning 20-yard drive.

38 BRISTOL CITY — Argyle: Sheffield, Collins, Williams*, Saunders, Heathcote, Wotton, Barlow, Starbuck, Conlon, Corazzin^, Billy. Bristol City: Welch, Locke, Bell, Murray, Taylor, Carey, Edwards*, Hewlett, Goater, Cramb, Timion^; subs Doherty/Barclay.
Littlejohn moves to Oldham. Argyle produce the upset of the day to silence the 3,000 travelling supporters. The Pilgrims' fierce determination is rewarded when Billy's pin-point pass finds Saunders who shoots past Keith Welch. Billy's shot finds Conlon who diverts it in on the turn.

39 GRIMSBY — Argyle: Sheffield, Collins, Rowbotham, Saunders, Heathcote, Wotton, Barlow, Starbuck, Conlon, Corazzin, Billy*. Grimsby: Davison, McDermott, Gallimore^, Handyside, Lever, Burnett, Donovan, Smith, Nogan^, Lester, Groves; subs Black/Livingstone.
The Mariners' mean defence which has seen them keep 28 clean sheets in all matches this season holds out again. With 18-goal midfielder Kevin Donovan having a quiet evening, Argyle look destined for a valuable away point until Donovan crosses to find Paul Groves' head.

40 WREXHAM — Argyle: Sheffield, Woods, Rowbotham, Saunders, Heathcote, Wotton, Barlow, Starbuck^, Conlon, Corazzin, Billy. Wrexham: Marriott, McGregor, Hardy, Brammer, Humes, Carey, Connolly, Wilson, Spink^, Ward*, Roberts; subs Phillips/Currie, Skinner/Kelly.
Another battling display is interrupted only by referee Harris's desire to test the efficiency of his whistle on regular occasions. Argyle are boosted by Corazzin's surprise return from injury and he puts them ahead with a header from six yards. Saunders' volley clinches a vital win.

41 OLDHAM — Argyle: Sheffield, Woods, Williams, Saunders, Heathcote, Wotton", Barlow, Starbuck*, Conlon*, Corazzin, Collins. Oldham: Kelly, McNiven, Serrant, Garnett, Boxall, Rickers, Duxbury, Hodgson^, Littlejohn^, Reid; subs Jean/Phillips/Currie, Allott/Holt.
Perhaps it was inevitable. Adrian Littlejohn receives a hostile reception from the travelling Green Army but then reminds them of bygone days with both goals. With Sheffield suffering bruised ribs, Littlejohn shoots into the roof of the net and then scores a stunning individual effort.

42 BLACKPOOL — Argyle: Sheffield, Collins, R'botham!, Saunders, Heathcote, Wotton, Barlow, Logan, Currie^, Corazzin*, Billy*. Blackpool: Barnes, Bryan, Hills, Butler, Hughes*, Linighan, Brabin, Clarkson, Conroy, Bent, Preece; subs Lydiate^/Philpott.
Heathcote heads Junior Bent's shot into his own net. Rowbotham is booked for an altercation with Tony Butler and then sent off for a foul on Bent (41). Saunders' header hits the bar and falls to Butler who blasts past his own keeper. Marvin Bryan trips Saunders to concede the penalty.

43 MILLWALL — Argyle: Sheffield, Wotton, Rowbotham, Saunders, Heathcote, Woods, Barlow, Currie*, Conlon*, Corazzin, Billy^. Millwall: Crossley, Brown, Ryan, Bowry, Law, Witter, Allen^, Newman*, Grant, Shaw, Hockton^; subs Savage/Lavin/Harris.
Danny Hockton's early goal fails to inspire Billy Bonds' Lions who need the three points to guarantee their safety. Corazzin's 16th goal of the season ignites Argyle who look the more likely to score another. Millwall's fans round on their side who look bereft of ideas after the break.

44 NORTHAMPTON — Argyle: Sheffield, Wotton^, Rowbotham, Saunders", Heathcote, Logan, Barlow, Currie*, Conlon*, Corazzin, Billy. Northampton: Woodman, Clarkson, Frain, Sampson, Warburton, Hunt, Peer, Bishop, Seal^, Freestone, Hill; subs Jean/Mauge/Starbuck, Gibb.
Freestone is again given freedom to pick his spot. Argyle hit the woodwork three times but the hat-trick is completed after a long run by Peer. Jones' work in training on defending corners goes unheeded as Freestone is left unmarked to head in John Frain's flag-kick. Saunders levels but...

45 GILLINGHAM — Argyle: Sheffield, Collins, Williams^, Saunders, Heathcote, Woods, Barlow, Currie, Conlon*, Corazzin, Billy. Gillingham: Bartram, Patterson, Green^, Smith, Ashby*, Bryant, Hess'thaler, Pennock, Corbett^, Akinbiyi, Galloway; subs Butler/Statham/Pinnock.
Argyle suffer a sickening blow when one time Pilgrim trialist Paul Smith mis-hits a shot past the unsighted Sheffield in the final minute to end a scrappy affair. The Gills maintain their play-off hopes but even three points from the final game may not be enough to save Argyle now.

46 BURNLEY — Argyle: Sheffield, Wotton, Williams^, Saunders, Heathcote, Woods, Barlow, Starbuck^, Conlon, Corazzin, Billy. Burnley: Woods, Brass, Winstanley, Harrison, Moore, Little, Weller, Ford, Cooke, Payton, Matthew; subs Collins/Jean/Mauge.
With Brentford losing, a draw would have kept Argyle up but the combination of Damian Matthew and Andy Cooke confirms their relegation. Wotton leaves the field in tears. Crowd trouble both on the pitch and outside the ground are the final nails in a forgettable day for Argyle fans.

NATIONWIDE DIVISION 2 (CUP-TIES)

Manager: Mick Jones

Coca-Cola Cup

		Att	F-A	H-T	Scorers, Times, and Referees	1	2	3	4	5	6	7	8	9	10	11	subs used
1:1 A OXFORD 12/8	L	5,083 1:	0-2	0-1	Purse 24, Logan 78(og) Ref: P Danson	Sheffield *Whitehead*	Collins* *Remy*	Williams *Ford M*	Mauge *Robinson*	Heathcote *Purse*	Wotton *Gilchrist*	Rowbotham *Ford R*	Logan *Smith*	Littlejohn *Banger**	Corazin *Jemson*	Anthony *Beauchamp*	Wilson *Aldridge*
1:2 H OXFORD 26/8	17 L	3,037 1:13	3-5	2-0	Wilson 12, Logan 29, Smith 46(og) Beau' 47,88, Jem' 48, Pur' 64, Mur' 74 Ref: M Pierce (Argyle lost 3-7 on aggregate)	Sheffield *Jackson*	Billy *Remy*	Williams *Marsh**	Wilson *Robinson*	Heathcote *Purse*	Wotton *Wilsterman*	Ro'botham* *Ford R*	Logan^ *Smith*	Littlejohn *Aldridge^*	Jean *Jemson*	Anthony *Beauchamp*	Illman/**Ashton** *Angel/Murphy*

Formula One star Jean Alesi is amongst the crowd. Nicky Banger is lively early on. Collins is taken to hospital (37) with a suspected broken leg after an accidental collision with Sheffield. Darren Purse fires in from eight yards. Logan turns Joey Beauchamp's shot into his own net.

Argyle race into a two-goal lead to level the tie. Oxford hold their nerve despite a third when Logan's long throw caused confusion and David Smith headed past Jackson. Beauchamp's 25-yard effort inspires the comeback.Despite Sheffield's heroics, Argyle are well beaten by the end.

FA Cup

		Att	F-A	H-T	Scorers, Times, and Referees	1	2	3	4	5	6	7	8	9	10	11	subs used
1 H CAMBRIDGE 15/11	18 D	4,793 3:18	0-0	0-0	Ref: R Harris	Sheffield *Barrett*	Wilson* *Ashbee*	Williams *Wilson*	Mauge *Chenery*	Saunders *Foster*	Wotton *Campbell*	Barlow *Wanless*	Jean *Preece*	Littlejohn *Kyd**	Corazin *Butler*	Billy *Beall*	Illman *Taylor*
1R A CAMBRIDGE 25/11	17 L	3,139 3:18	2-3 aet	2-0	Mauge 21, Jean 45 Beall 74, Benjamin 77, Wilson 95p Ref: R Harris	Sheffield *Barrett*	Logan *Chenery*	Williams *Wilson*	Mauge* *Ashbee*	Saunders^ *Foster*	Wotton *Campbell*	Barlow *Wanless*	Jean *Preece**	Littlejohn *Taylor*	Corazin *Kyd^*	Billy *Beall*	Wilson/Rowbotham *Benjamin/Butler*

United belie their league form to put Argyle on the rack for much of the game. Jamie Campbell cracks a 25-yard drive against the post and Barlow clears Colin Foster's header off the line. A mist descends on Home Park for the latter stages with Argyle hanging on grimly for a draw.

Mauge puts an off the field charge of assault behind him to put Argyle ahead. It looks all over when Jean volleys in. Roy McFarland's side get a boost when Sheffield's clearance hits Trevor Benjamin in the chest and goes in. Paul Wilson scores from the spot after Campbell was tripped.

League Table

	P	W	D	L	F	A	W	D	L	F	A	Pts
1 Watford	46	13	7	3	36	22	11	9	3	31	19	88
2 Bristol City	46	16	5	2	41	17	9	5	9	28	22	85
3 Grimsby*	46	11	7	5	30	14	8	8	7	25	23	72
4 Northampton	46	14	5	4	33	17	4	12	7	19	20	71
5 Bristol Rov	46	13	2	8	43	33	7	8	8	27	31	70
6 Fulham	46	12	7	4	31	14	8	3	12	29	29	70
7 Wrexham	46	10	10	3	31	23	8	6	9	24	28	70
8 Gillingham	46	13	3	7	30	18	6	6	11	22	29	70
9 Bournemouth	46	11	8	4	28	15	7	4	12	29	37	66
10 Chesterfield	46	13	7	3	31	19	3	10	10	15	25	65
11 Wigan	46	12	5	6	41	31	5	6	12	23	35	62
12 Blackpool	46	13	6	4	35	24	4	5	14	24	43	62
13 Oldham	46	13	7	3	43	23	2	9	12	19	31	61
14 Wycombe	46	10	10	3	32	20	4	8	11	19	33	60
15 Preston	46	10	6	7	29	26	5	8	10	27	30	59
16 York	46	9	7	7	26	21	5	10	8	26	37	59
17 Luton	46	7	7	9	35	38	7	8	8	25	26	57
18 Millwall	46	7	8	8	23	23	7	5	11	20	31	55
19 Walsall	46	10	8	5	26	16	4	4	15	17	36	54
20 Burnley	46	10	9	4	34	23	3	4	16	21	42	52
21 Brentford	46	9	7	7	33	29	2	10	11	17	42	50
22 PLYMOUTH	46	10	5	8	36	30	2	8	13	19	40	49
23 Carlisle	46	8	5	10	27	28	4	3	16	30	45	44
24 Southend	46	8	7	8	29	30	3	3	17	18	49	43
	1104	262	162	128	783	554	128	162	262	554	783	1494

* promoted
after play-offs

Appearances and Goals

	Appearances						Goals			
	Lge	Sub	LC	Sub	FAC	Sub	Lge	LC	FAC	Tot
Anthony, Graham	5		2							
Ashton, Jon					1					
Barlow, Martin	41	1					4			4
Beswetherick, Jon		2				2				
Billy, Chris	41		1			2	2			2
Clayton, Gary		1								
Collins, Simon	30	2	1				2			2
Conlon, Barry	13						2			2
Corazzin, Carlo	38		1		2		16			16
Currie, Darren	5	2								
Heathcote, Mick	36				2		4			4
Hodges, Lee	9									
Illman, Neil	1	5		1		1				
Jean, Earl	16	20	1			2	4		1	5
Littlejohn, Adrian	27	4	2			2	6			6
Logan, Richard	23	4	2			1	4	1		5
Mauge, Ronnie	23	8	1				1		1	2
O'Hagan, Danny	5	4								
Phillips, Lee	3	7								
Rowbotham, Jason	23	2	2			1				
Saunders, Mark	34	3					7			7
Sheffield, Jon	46		2		2					
Starbuck, Phil	6	1								
Williams, Paul	39		2		2					
Wilson, Padi	7	4	1	1	1	1	1			1
Woods, Stephen	4	1								
Wotton, Paul	31	3			2		1	1		2
(own-goals)										1
27 players used	506	74	22	3	22	3	55	3	2	60

Season Notes

Double wins: (2) Preston, Walsall.

Double defeats: (6) Fulham, Gillingham, Luton, Northampton, Oldham, Southend.

Won from behind: (4) Blackpool, Walsall, Wigan, Wycombe .

Lost from in front: (4) Brentford, Fulham, Gillingham, Northampton.

High spots: Fine draw at eventual champions, Watford, and denied a win only by a last-minute equaliser. Consecutive home wins against highly placed Bristol City and Wrexham. Entertaining eight-goal thriller against Oxford in Coca-Cola Cup.

Low spots: Suffering relegation after a final-day defeat at Burnley. Close-season sacking of Mick Jones, whilst he was on holiday. Departure of several players at end of season on 'Bosman' transfers. FA Cup exit at hands of 3rd Division Cambridge.

Player of the Year: Martin Barlow & Carlo Corazzin.

Ever presents: (1) Jon Sheffield.

Hat-tricks: (0).

Leading scorer: Carlo Corazzin (16).

NATIONWIDE DIVISION 3 — SEASON 1998-99

Manager: Kevin Hodges

No	Date	Att	Pos	Pt	F-A	H-T	Scorers, Times, and Referees	1	2	3	4	5	6	7	8	9	10	11	subs used
1	H ROCHDALE 8/8	5,547	—	W	2:1	0:1	Mauge 52, Jean 78 / Lancashire 19p / Ref: L Cable	Sheffield / Edwards	Collins / Sparrow*	Gibbs / Stokes	McCall / Hill	Heathcote / Bayliss	Wotton / Johnson	Barlow / Farrell	Mauge / Lancashire^	Jean* / Leonard	Power^ / Peake*	Hargreaves / Stuart	Gritton/McCarthy, Gray/Bailey/Jones
2	A MANSFIELD 15/8	2,451	17/16	L 3	0:2	0:2	Peacock 8, Gibbs 23(og) / Ref: D Laws	Sheffield / Bowling	Collins^ / Williams	Gibbs / Harper	McCall / Peters^	Heathcote / Ford	Wotton / Hackett	Barlow* / Schofield	McCarthy / Clarke	Jean / Peacock*	Mauge / Christie	Hargreaves / Tallon	Power/Flash, Larmor/Ryder
3	H BARNET 22/8	5,080	7/17	W 6	2:0	1:0	Heathcote 5, McCarthy 73 / Ref: A Hall	Sheffield / Harrison	Flash / Stockley	Gibbs / Bastham	Mauge / Goodhind	Heathcote / Ford	Wotton / Doolan	Barlow / Simpson	McCarthy^ / Devine	Jean* / Currie	Power / McGleish	Hargreaves / Onwere	Power/Besweth'ck
4	A SCUNTHORPE 29/8	2,868	4/8	W 9	2:0	1:0	Heathcote 8, Jean 55 / Ref: M Cowburn	Sheffield / Clarke	Flash / Fickling	Gibbs / McCauley	Mauge / Harsley	Heathcote / Wilcox	Wotton / Hope	Barlow / Walker^	McCarthy / Forrester*	Jean^ / Eyre"	Collins / Gayle	Hargreaves / C-Garcia	Power, Logan/Bull/Stamp
5	H HALIFAX 31/8	6,544	3/4	W 12	1:0	1:0	Gibbs 42 / Ref: R Styles	Sheffield / Martin	Flash / Thackeray	Gibbs / Bradshaw	Mauge* / Sertori	Heathcote / Lucas	Wotton / Stoneman	Barlow / Butler	McCarthy / Hulme	Jean^ / Hanson	Collins / Harsfield	Hargreaves / Brown	McCall/Power
6	A CARDIFF 5/9	3,939	5/15	L 12	0:1	0:0	Wotton 88(og) / Ref: S Mathieson	Sheffield / Hallworth	Flash^ / Delaney	Gibbs / Eckhardt	Mauge / Mitchell	Heathcote / Young	Wotton / Carpenter*	Barlow / Bonner^	McCarthy / Brazier	Jean* / Thomas"	Collins / Nugent	Hargreaves / O'Sullivan	Power/Ashton, Fowler/Middleton/Williams
7	A ROTHERHAM 8/9	3,442	—	W 15	2:0	1:0	Gibbs 32p, McCarthy 51 / Ref: G Laws	Sheffield / Pollitt	Ashton / Scott"	Gibbs / Beech	Mauge / Warner"	Heathcote / Knill	Wotton / Dillon	Barlow / Garner*	McCarthy* / Thompson	Jean* / Martindale	Collins / Roscoe	Hargreaves / Wills	Power/Wills, Hudson/Rich'son/Sedgwick
8	H DARLINGTON 12/9	5,709	5/1	L 15	1:2	1:1	Mauge 19 / Gabbiadini 35, Devos 69 / Ref: C Wilkes	Sheffield / Preece	Edmondson / Reed	Gibbs / Hope	Mauge* / Liddle	Heathcote / Devos	Wotton^ / Brumwell"	Barlow / Shutt"	McCarthy / Oliver	Jean / Roberts	Collins / Gabbiadini*	Hargr'ves^ / Atkinson	Power/Wills, Tutill/Naylor/Ellison
9	A PETERBOROUGH 19/9	5,870	4/9	W 18	2:0	1:0	Heathcote 44, Barlow 54 / Ref: R Pearson	Sheffield / Griemink	Edmondson / Hooper	Gibbs / McMenamin	Mauge* / Gill	Heathcote / Bodley	Wotton^ / Edwards	Barlow / Davies	McCarthy / Payne"	Jean^ / De Souza"	Power* / Carruthers	Hargreaves / Houghton^	Jean, Farrell/Etherington/Rowe
10	H SCARBOROUGH 26/9	5,216	4/13	D 19	0:0	0:0	Ref: D Crick	Sheffield / Elliott	Edmondson / Kay !	Gibbs / Atkinson	Mauge* / Radigan"	Heathcote / Lydiate	Wotton / Mirankov	Barlow / Bullimore^	McCarthy / Jackson	Power* / McN'ghton	Collins / Brodie	Hargreaves / Robinson"	McCall/Jean, Tate/Carr/Russell
11	A TORQUAY 3/10	5,719	6/18	D 20	1:1	0:0	Gibbs 81p / Partridge 57 / Ref: B Knight	Sheffield / Gregg	Edmondson^ / Gurney	Gibbs / Herrera	Mauge / Tully	Heathcote / Robinson	Wotton / Monk	Barlow / McGorry	McCarthy / Leadbitter	Power* / Donaldson	Collins / Partridge	McCall / Waddle	Jean/Marshall

1 — Rochdale: A blatant foul in the area on Hargreaves is missed by Mr Cable who then awards Dale a spot-kick for a foul by Wotton on Graham Lancashire. Mauge and Jean fire past the otherwise impenetrable Neil Edwards. Gibbs finds a pair of glasses on the pitch and hands them to the referee!

2 — Mansfield: The old failings away from home are still there as Argyle produce an off-colour performance. Wotton allows Lee Peacock too much space to turn and fire home off the bar. Gibbs toe-pokes past Sheffield under pressure from Tony Ford and is later stretchered off – only to return later.

3 — Barnet: A forgettable first period is brought to life only by Heathcote's glancing header from Gibbs' free-kick. Sean Devine, sporting bleached hair and green boots, has Barnet's only shot on target. McCarthy slides home a second to leave Bees' boss bewildered as to his side's lacklustre play.

4 — Scunthorpe: Heathcote's header strikes a post but the rebound returns to him and he makes no mistake. Collins is surrounded by incensed opponents after a high tackle on Calvo-Garcia but is only booked. Jean rounds Tim Clarke to add a second and is later rewarded with a kiss from the chairman.

5 — Halifax: Kieran O'Regan's unbeaten Shaymen have made a promising start since being promoted from the Conference but are brought back to earth by a dominant Argyle. Mauge fails to make contact with Gibbs' free-kick but the ball continues its journey and eventually creeps inside the post.

6 — Cardiff: A lunchtime kick-off seems to catch Cardiff cold as Hargreaves goes close in the first minute. Jeff Eckhardt misses a golden opportunity when he blasts over from eight yards. Burly John Williams shrugs off Ashton. Wotton slides in to clear the cross but slices past a startled Sheffield.

7 — Rotherham: Argyle move level with the leaders as the midfield dominate. A cross from Hargreaves is handled by Kevin Dillon. Gibbs makes no mistake against Mike Pollitt who has already saved two spot-kicks this season. Jean fends off two challenges and sets McCarthy up from six yards.

8 — Darlington: Mauge's volley has too much power for David Preece who gets a hand to the shot but cannot prevent it going in. The Argyle defence have difficulty in handling the much-travelled Marco Gabbiadini who levels with a well-taken goal. He also has a hand in Jason Devos's winner.

9 — Peterborough: Barry Fry's side is decimated by a flu bug. Heathcote's powerful header gives Argyle a well-deserved lead. The second goal is a comedy of errors. Bart Griemink is penalised for handling outside the area. He then misses Barlow's free-kick, the ball strikes his body and trickles in.

10 — Scarborough: Neil Radigan's booking after just 41 seconds sets the tone for a rugged affair. Gibbs and John Kay have a running battle. And it is no surprise when the Boro skipper is sent off (72). Gibbs waves goodbye. Injury reduces Mick Wadsworth's side to nine men for the last fourteen minutes.

11 — Torquay: Ex-England star Chris Waddle makes his Gulls debut. Torquay sub Andy McFarlane is sent off (39) after he runs onto the pitch to join in a melee. Wotton commits himself to leave Scott Partridge free. Gibbs nets against his former side after McCarthy was tripped by Matthew Gregg.

12 | A | 17/10 | SHREWSBURY — Att 2,778 · Pos 23 · L · Pts 20 · 0-1 (0-1)
Sheffield Collins Beswth'k* McCall Heathcote Wotton Barlow Mauge Power Taylor Marshall Jean^
Edwards Seabury Wilding Hanmer Winstanley Gayle Berkley Kerigan^ Steele Evans Jobling Brown · Ford
Seabury 64(og)
Berkley 23, Seabury 55
Ref: M Pike

The Shrews call on a hypnotherapist to boost their confidence. Berkley scores from ten yards with Wotton claiming a foul. The one-booted Heathcote crucially slips as he tackles Seabury, and Sheffield allows his feeble shot to creep in. Jean's wayward effort deflects off Seabury.

13 | A | 20/10 | BRIGHTON — Att 1,793 · W · Pts 23 · 3-1 (1-0)
Sheffield Collins Beswth'ck Taylor Heathcote Wotton Barlow Jean Mauge Power Marshall McCall
Walton Armstrong Sturgess* Johnson Allan Thomas! Hart^ Bennett Moralee Culverhouse · Mayo/Barker/Ansah*
Collins 26, Barlow 53, 90p
Barker 84
Ref: R Styles

Jamie Moralee misses a fourth-minute chance when his shot is saved by Sheffield's legs. Collins heads Argyle in front. Barlow stuns his team-mates by scoring with his head. Barker shoots through a crowd of players. Rod Thomas handles Barlow's shot on the line and is dismissed.

14 | H | 31/10 | HULL — Att 4,285 · Pos 9 · D · Pts 24 · 0-0 (0-0)
Sheffield Crittden* Beswth'k^ Taylor Heathcote Wotton Barlow Jean Mauge McCall Power/Hargreaves
Wilson Joyce Mann Hocking Whitworth McGinty^ French D'Auria! Brown · Greaves/Hawes*
Ref: P Taylor

In atrocious conditions, Argyle fail to break down Mark Hateley's bottom-of-the-table side. David D'Auria is sent off (38) for two fouls in quick succession on McCall. This only strengthens the visitors' resolve and fans and players alike become more frustrated as the game goes on.

15 | H | 3/11 | BRENTFORD — Att 4,650 · W · Pts 27 · 3-0 (1-0)
Sheffield Collins Hargreaves Taylor Heathcote Wotton Barlow Jean^ Mauge Marshall^ Power /Crittenden|Bastow
Pearcey Boxall Anderson^ Hreidarsson Powell Bates! Falan Aspinall Owusu Rowlands Scott* · Rapley/Quinn/Hebel*
Barlow 28, Taylor 76, Bastow 85
Ref: J Brandwood

Barlow opens the scoring against the title favourites with a low 20-yard drive. Yet again, a visiting player is dismissed as Jamie Bates collects a second booking (51). YTS lad Bastow becomes the youngest ever player to score for Plymouth when his 20-yard shot takes a cruel deflection.

16 | A | 7/11 | HARTLEPOOL — Att 2,121 · Pos 7 · L · Pts 27 · 0-2 (0-2)
Sheffield Hollund Knowles Hargreaves Heathcote Wotton Barlow Power* Mauge Marshall Bastow
Lee Ingram Clark Di Lella Brightwell Miller Howard" Midgley Steph'son^ · Irvine/Rush/Hutt*
Wotton 3(og), Midgley 9
Ref: M Cowburn

Wotton misjudges a high hopeful ball in the swirling wind and it falls to Craig Midgley. Wotton slides in, attempting to recover the situation, but only succeeds in rolling the ball towards the net where the advancing Sheffield had been. Barlow's back-pass goes straight to Midgley.

17 | H | 10/11 | SWANSEA — Att 4,517 · L · Pts 27 · 1-2 (0-1)
Sheffield Collins Beswth'k^ Taylor Heathcote Wotton Barlow Mauge Phillips Marshall McCall^/Bastow
Freestone Jones Howard Cusack Smith Bound Price^ Newhouse Watkin Appleby Alsop/Jenkins*
Marshall 78
Watkin 17, Alsop 81
Ref: M Fletcher

The Swans, without a win in six and a goal in three, make the early running. Jason Price hits the post. Watkin's header from twelve yards flies into the corner. Swansea make a mess of clearing a corner and Marshall pounces. Julian Alsop scores the winner after earlier hitting the bar.

18 | A | 21/11 | SOUTHEND — Att 3,814 · Pos 10 · L · Pts 27 · 0-1 (0-0)
Sheffield Collins Beswth'ck Branston Heathcote Wotton Barlow Mauge Power Marshall^ Hargreaves
Margetson Beard" Jones Morley Newman Coleman Maher Livett Burns Rapley Houghton /Fitzpatrick/Gooding*
Newman 88
Ref: S Baines

The new fluorescent yellow ball is introduced for the winter. Argyle fail to muster one single shot on target. McCarthy is clean through but the referee, a former professional player, calls play back for a foul on Barlow. The only goal comes from Rob Newman's low shot from 20 yards.

19 | H | 28/11 | LEYTON ORIENT — Att 4,240 · Pos 12 · L · Pts 27 · 2-4 (1-1)
Sheffield Collins Beswth'ck Branston Heathcote Ashton* Barlow McCall! Joseph M Marshall McCarthy /Gritton/Bastow/Phillips
MacKenzie Wals'aerts Lockwood Hicks* Clark Ling Joseph M Griffiths Richards Beall · Ampadu/Maskell/Watts*
Joseph 9(og), Collins 74 (Griffiths 85p)
Watts 40, Ling 72, Richards 80
Ref: C Foy

After Matt Joseph's own-goal, Orient change their formation to good effect. Steve Watts punishes some hesitant defending. Argyle appeal for handball as Ling scores. McCarthy is sent off for a second yellow (82) after a lunge at Beall. Richards is tripped by Beswetherick in the box.

20 | A | 12/12 | CAMBRIDGE — Att 3,933 · Pos 13 · L · Pts 27 · 0-1 (0-1)
Sheffield Ashton Beswth'ck Branston Heathcote Wotton Barlow Mauge! Joseph Phillips Marshall^/Bastow/Sweeney
Marshall Chenery Mustoe Duncan Joseph Campbell Wanless Taylor Butler Benjamin Russell
Taylor 44
Ref: F Stretton

Argyle's slide down the table continues. John Taylor sets a new United scoring record with his 82nd goal for the club. Mauge is booked for kicking the ball away and sent off on the stroke of half-time when he clatters in to Alex Russell. Taylor's header hits the crossbar (69).

21 | H | 19/12 | CARLISLE — Att 4,236 · Pos 13 · W · Pts 30 · 2-0 (1-0)
Sheffield Ashton Beswth'ck Bastow Heathcote Branston Barlow Hargreaves McCarthy Phillips^ Marshall /Sweeney/Forinton
Caig Barr Seale Paterson Brightwell Varty Couzens Clark Stevens* Anthony Mendes · Finney/Whit'head/McGregor*
Bastow 22, McCarthy 83
Ref: B Jordan

Bastow's attempted cross flies over Tony Caig. The start of the second half is delayed by 30 minutes when an electrical fault causes floodlight failure. McCarthy scores the 150th league goal of his career when Caig sends an attempted clearance to him and his shot creeps over the line.

22 | A | 26/12 | BARNET — Att 2,519 · Pos 13 · D · Pts 31 · 1-1 (1-0)
Sheffield Ashton Beswth'ck Bastow Heathcote Branston Barlow Sweeney McCarthy Phillips Jean*/Forinton/Marshall
Harrison Stockley Currie Basham Ford Arber Searle Doolan Charlery McGleish Wilson · King*
Forinton 21
Currie 58
Ref: K Hill

New loan-signing Forinton puts the Greens ahead after Lee Harrison can only parry Bastow's 25-yard drive. With a strong wind and driving rain at their backs, Barnet level through Darren Currie's shot which deflects off Ashton. Heathcote's looping header comes off the crossbar.

23 | H | 28/12 | EXETER — Att 11,936 · Pos 12 · W · Pts 34 · 1-0 (0-0)
Sheffield Ashton Beswth'ck Bastow* Heathcote Wotton Barlow Branston McCarthy Phillips^ Jean^/Forinton/Hargreaves/Sweeney
Bayes Fry Power Holloway Gittens Gale Quailey Rees Flack Curran Gardner · Rowbotham/Breslan*
Forinton 73
Ref: P Danson

City seek their first away win since October 1997. Tempers flare when Wotton fells Chris Holloway. Beswetherick then accidentally kicks the ball against the prostrate Grecian. City's management team of Peter Fox and Noel Blake become embroiled in an argument with supporters.

NATIONWIDE DIVISION 3 — Manager: Kevin Hodges — SEASON 1998-99

Column key: No · Date · Att · Pos (Argyle league position / opponent position in italics) · Pt · F-A · H-T · players 1–11 (Argyle XI on top line, opponents in italics below) · subs used (Argyle / opponents) · Scorers, Times, and Referees.

---

24. A ROCHDALE — 9/1
Att 1,922 · Pos 13 (opp 17) · D · F-A 1-1 · H-T 1-0 · Pt 35

Argyle: Sheffield, Ashton, Besweth'ck, Mauge, Heathcote, Branston*, Barlow, Hargreaves, Phillips*, Sweeney, Forinton — subs: McCall/Marshall
Rochdale: Priestley, Sparrow, Barlow^, Hill, Farrell^, Johnson", Carden, Painter, Morris, Bryson^, Holt — subs: Stuart/Jones/Williams

Scorers: Branston 14, *Holt 62*. Ref: J Kirkby

Birthday boy Branston opens the scoring but later leaves the field with concussion after an off the ball elbow by Andy Morris which was not spotted by the officials. Mark Stuart comes on to make his mark by firing a 20-yard shot against a post with Michael Holt netting the rebound.

---

25. H MANSFIELD — 16/1
Att 4,399 · Pos 10 (opp 5) · W · F-A 3-0 · H-T 2-0 · Pt 38

Argyle: Sheffield, Ashton, Besweth'ck, Bastow, Heathcote, Collins, Barlow, Hargreaves, Marshall, McCall*, Forinton — subs: Sweeney
Mansfield: Bowling, Ford, Harper, Peters, Kerr^, Hackett, Schofield, Walker^, Lormor, Peacock", Tallon — subs: Williams/Christie/Ryder

Scorers: Marshall 13, 43, Hargreaves 46. Ref: P Dowd

Thirty-nine year old Tony Ford receives an award before the match as he breaks Terry Paine's outfield league appearance record of 824 games. Marshall looks back to his best with some opportunist finishing. Hargreaves opens his Pilgrims' scoring account with a rebound off his shin.

---

26. A HALIFAX — 23/1
Att 2,762 · Pos 10 (opp 6) · L · F-A 0-2 · H-T 0-0 · Pt 38

Argyle: Sheffield, Ashton, Besweth'ck, Wotton^, Branston, Collins, Barlow, Hargreaves, Marshall*, McCall*, Forinton — subs: Jean/Bastow/Sweeney
Halifax: Carter, Thackeray, Lucas, Sertori, Stansfield, Stoneman, O'Regan*, Hulme, Williams, Power, Butler — subs: Brown

Scorers: *Williams 62, 74*. Ref: M Jones

Offside decisions, or the lack of them, play a large part in the outcome. Peter Butler's quick free-kick from the wrong place finds the blatantly offside Andy Thackeray who sets up Marc Williams. A linesman's flag rules out Marshall's effort (69). Lee Power's pass creates the second.

---

27. A EXETER — 30/1
Att 6,746 · Pos 11 (opp 13) · D · F-A 1-1 · H-T 1-1 · Pt 39

Argyle: Sheffield, Ashton, Gibbs, Mauge, Heathcote, Collins, Barlow, Hargreaves, Marshall, Halloway, Forinton
Exeter: Bayes, Fry, Power, Clark, Richardson, Gittens, Qualley*, Rees, Flack, Gardner* — subs: Breslan/Waugh

Scorers: Forinton 27, *Fry 9*. Ref: K Leach

Gibbs returns after a four-month lay-off but his lack of fitness soon shows when he is outpaced by Chris Fry who lobs over the advancing Sheffield. A poor clearance from Steve Flack sees the ball eventually break to Forinton who smashes a shot past Ashley Bayes from 20 yards.

---

28. H CARDIFF — 6/2
Att 6,062 · Pos 11 (opp 1) · D · F-A 1-1 · H-T 1-0 · Pt 40

Argyle: Sheffield, Ashton, Gibbs, Sweeney, Heathcote, Collins, Barlow, Hargreaves, Marshall*, Bastow, Forinton — subs: Jean/Crowe
Cardiff: Hallworth, Young, Legg, Mitchell, Eckhardt, Carpenter, Fowler, O'Sullivan, Williams^, Nugent, Midleton^ — subs: Hill/Bowen

Scorers: Marshall 19, *Legg 63*. Ref: M Warren

Frank Burrows' side look anything but league leaders in the first half as Argyle dominate and take a deserved lead when Marshall is more alert than Scott Young. Welsh international Andy Legg celebrates his full City debut with a well-struck volley. Forinton goes close from 20 yards.

---

29. H ROTHERHAM — 13/2
Att 4,336 · Pos 11 (opp 6) · W · F-A 1-0 · H-T 0-0 · Pt 43

Argyle: Sheffield, Ashton, Gibbs, Sweeney^, Heathcote, Collins, Barlow, Hargreaves, Marshall*, Bastow, Forinton — subs: Jean/Crowe
Rotherham: Pollitt, Warner, Dillon*, Garner, Knill, Strodder, Ingledow^, Hurst, White^, Warne, Beech — subs: Roscoe/Sedgwick/Tracey

Scorers: Marshall 59. Ref: D Crick

Hodges names an unchanged side for the first time since September. Forinton again impresses and makes Marshall's winner. Ronnie Moore is furious with his team's display and orders them onto the team-bus right after the match. He refuses to attend the post-match press conference.

---

30. A DARLINGTON — 20/2
Att 2,643 · Pos 10 (opp 14) · W · F-A 2-1 · H-T 1-0 · Pt 46

Argyle: Sheffield, Ashton, Gibbs, Sweeney, Heathcote, Collins, Barlow, Hargreaves, Marshall*, Bastow, Jean — subs: Phillips
Darlington: Preece, Reed, Barnard, Liddle, Tutill, Bennett^, Gaughan^, Oliver, Duffield^, Gabbiadini, Atkinson — subs: Dorner/Brunmell/Ellison

Scorers: Jean 32, Marshall 72, *Dorner 75*. Ref: K Lynch

On a dreadful pitch, a rejuvenated Jean grabs his opportunity with a fine all-round display. He scores the opener with a first-time shot after a surging run from Hargreaves. Marshall's tap-in prompts optimistic chants of 'The Greens are going up' from the travelling Argyle contingent.

---

31. H CHESTER — 23/2
Att 4,208 · Pos 5 (opp 16) · W · F-A 2-0 · H-T 2-0 · Pt 49

Argyle: Sheffield, Ashton, Gibbs, Sweeney, Heathcote, Collins, Barlow, Hargr'ves*, Marshall*, Bastow, Jean — subs: Beswether'ck/Phillips
Chester: Cutler, Davidson, Smith, Richardson, Crosby, Alsford, Flitcroft, Priest^, Murphy, Beckett*, Aiston^ — subs: Cross/Woods/Shelton

Scorers: Sweeney 13, Marshall 42. Ref: M Fletcher

Cash-strapped City's stay in the West Country is partly paid for by the players themselves. Kevin Ratcliffe's side, having not conceded a goal for three matches, start the brighter but Sweeney's deflected shot turns the tide. Marshall continues his fine scoring run but misses a hatful.

---

32. H PETERBOROUGH — 27/2
Att 5,959 · Pos 7 (opp 8) · L · F-A 0-2 · H-T 0-2 · Pt 49

Argyle: Sheffield, Ashton, Gibbs, Marker^, Heathcote, Collins, Barlow, Hargreaves*, Marshall, Bastow, Jean* — subs: Phillips/Sweeney/Crowe
Peterborough: Griemink, Linton, Drury, Davies, Rennie, Edwards, Farrell, Castle, Andrews, Broughton, Scott — subs: Eth'ington

Scorers: *Andrews 3, Broughton 31*. Ref: P Rejer

Former Argyle hero Nicky Marker returns in a surprise loan deal. Heathcote almost puts through his own net (2). A minute later, Wayne Andrews is left unmarked in the six-yard box to score. Gibbs has an argument with the crowd. Collins' clearance hits Broughton and goes in.

---

33. H TORQUAY — 9/3
Att 7,856 · Pos 7 · D · F-A 0-0 · H-T 0-0 · Pt 50

Argyle: Sheffield, Wotton, Gibbs*, Mauge, Heathcote, Collins, Marker, Hargreaves, Marshall, Bastow, Jean* — subs: Phillips
Torquay: Southall, Tully, Nichols*, Robinson, Thomas, Leadbitter, Aggrey, Hapgood^, Bedeau, Harries, Platts" — subs: Herrera/McGorry/Forrester

Ref: M Pierce

Forty-year old Neville Southall turns back the clock to give a goalkeeping master-class. His save from Gibbs' 30-yard free-kick has everyone in the ground applauding. Wes Saunders fields seven players under 21 but they put up a spirited show without ever threatening Sheffield's goal.

---

34. H HARTLEPOOL — 13/3
Att 4,441 · Pos 8 (opp 23) · D · F-A 0-0 · H-T 0-0 · Pt 51

Argyle: Sheffield, Wotton, Gibbs^, Marker, Heathcote, Collins, Barlow, Hargreaves, Marshall, Bastow, Jean* — subs: Phillips/Crowe
Hartlepool: Holland, Knowles, McKinnon, Barron!, Strodder, Ingram^, Miller, Beardsley, Baker, Jones*, Clark — subs: Lee/Hughes

Ref: P Taylor

Veteran England star Peter Beardsley is outshone by the precocious Bastow. Chris Turner's side come for and get a point. Jean storms out of the ground after his half-time substitution. The already booked Michael Barron gets a red card in injury-time for a reckless tackle on Marshall.

Season fixtures — match reports (Argyle)

35. Sat 20/3 (A) HULL — L 0-1 (HT 0-0)
- Scorer (Hull): Brabin 51
- Att: 6,294 · Pts: 51 · Ref: M Messias
- Argyle: Sheffield, Wotton, Gibbs, Marker*, Heathcote, Collins, Barlow, Hargreaves, Marshall^, Bastow, Crowe. Subs: Mauge, Ashton
- Hull: Oakes, Greaves, Swales, Edwards, Whittle, Whitney, Joyce, Brabin^, Brown^, Alcide, Williams. Subs: McGinty, Faulconbridge
- *Marker completes his loan spell without having celebrated an Argyle goal. The 'Pilgrims' attack is so ineffective that Heathcote is eventually moved forward. Gary Brabin glances in a header from player-manager Warren Joyce. A jet-lagged Mauge returns from training with Trinidad.*

36. Sat 27/3 (A) CHESTER — L 2-3 (HT 1-0)
- Scorers: Marshall 37, Hargreaves 72; Beckett 46, 67, Murphy 75
- Att: 1,982 · Pts: 51 · Ref: T Jones
- Argyle: Sheffield^, Wotton, Gibbs, Mauge, Heathcote, Collins, Barlow, Hargreaves, Marshall*, Bastow, Guinan*. Subs: Jean, Ashton
- Chester: Brown, Davidson, Cross, Richardson, Crosby, Woods, Fitcroft, Priest*, Murphy, Beckett, Smeets. Subs: Alsford, Fisher
- *John Murphy's elbow concusses Sheffield (25) and Ashton is forced to take over in goal. Mauge's precision pass is converted by Marshall. Ashton watches helplessly as Luke Beckett's 20-yard curling shot finds the top corner. With a draw on the cards, Murphy fires in a loose ball.*

37. Tue 30/3 (H) SCUNTHORPE — W 5-0 (HT 2-0)
- Scorers: Guinan 25, 30, 71, Marshall 58, Sale 75
- Att: 3,589 · Pts: 54 · Ref: M Halsey
- Argyle: Dungey, Ashton, Gibbs*, Mauge, Heathcote, Collins, Barlow, Bastow, Marshall, Sale, Guinan^. Subs: Crowe, Barrett
- Scunthorpe: Evans, Witter, Dawson, Logan, Harsley, Hope, Walker*, Forrester, Eyre, Gayle^, C-Garcia^. Subs: Marshall, Stamp, Bull
- *Jean leaves the club. In miserable conditions, Argyle run riot with their new front-line all contributing. The on-loan Sale and Guinan cause all sorts of problems for the normally watertight Iron defence. Guinan's third is memorable as he controls superbly to shoot low past Tom Evans.*

38. Sat 3/4 (H) SHREWSBURY — W 2-0 (HT 1-0)
- Scorers: Marshall 40, Barlow 61
- Att: 5,749 · Pts: 57 · Ref: L Cable
- Argyle: Dungey, Ashton, Beswetherick, Mauge^, Heathcote, Collins, Barlow, Bastow, Marshall*, Phillips, Guinan^. Subs: Wotton, Crowe
- Shrewsbury: Edwards, Seabury, Hanmer, Wilding, Gayle, Tretton, Berkley, Kerrigan, Steele, Preece, Jobling*. Subs: Brown
- *Dungey performs heroics to keep the Shrews at bay. Paul Edwards flaps at Ashton's cross and Marshall heads in. Opposing manager Jake King claims later that it was pure luck and the ball hit Marshall in the face. Barlow nets a once in a lifetime goal with a volley from a narrow angle.*

39. Mon 5/4 (A) BRENTFORD — L 1-3 (HT 0-2)
- Scorers: Marshall 80; Evans 42, Mahon 45, Folan 89
- Att: 6,979 · Pts: 57 · Ref: R Olivier
- Argyle: Sheffield, Ashton, Gibbs, Mauge^, Heathcote, Collins, Barlow, Bastow, Marshall, Sale^, Guinan. Subs: Wotton, Beswetherick
- Brentford: Woodman, Quinn, Anderson, Hreidarsson, Powell, Oatway*, Scott^, Partridge, Owusu, Mahon^, Evans. Subs: Boxall, Bryan, Folan
- *Sheffield plays wearing a protective mask to guard his fractured cheekbone. Twenty-goal Lloyd Owusu turns provider to set up the big-spending Bees' first two goals. Marshall toe-pokes under the onrushing Andy Woodman but Tony Folan puts the result beyond doubt late on.*

40. Sat 10/4 (H) BRIGHTON — L 1-2 (HT 1-1)
- Scorers: Guinan 42; Hart 6, Moralee 75
- Att: 4,911 · Pts: 57 · Ref: D Pugh
- Argyle: Sheffield, Ashton, Gibbs, Mauge*, Heathcote, Collins, Barlow, Bastow, Marshall, Sale^, Guinan. Subs: Wotton, Crowe
- Brighton: Ormerod, Bennett, Mayo, Minton, Hobson, McPherson, Storer*, Arnott, Hart, Moralee, Smith. Subs: McArthur
- *Brighton are without a manager after the sacking of Jeff Wood on Thursday. Argyle are simply awful. Sheffield blasts a clearance directly at Gary Hart and the ball flies in. Guinan's equaliser fails to ignite any passion. Jamie Moralee's header puts a dent in the Greens play-off hopes.*

41. Tue 13/4 (A) LEYTON ORIENT — L 3-4 (HT 2-2)
- Scorers: Guinan 36, Marshall 45, Mauge 52; Watts 7, Mor? 9, Ingle 46, Richards 73
- Att: 4,095 · Pts: 57 · Ref: B Coddington
- Argyle: Sheffield, Ashton, Gibbs, Mauge, Heathcote, Collins, Barlow, Bastow, Marshall*, Sale^, Guinan.
- Leyton Orient: Barrett, Walsch'rts*, Lockwood, Smith, Morrison, Clark, Ling, Joseph M, Watts^, Richards, Beall. Subs: Inglethorpe, Simba
- *Several bewildering decisions by the referee incur the wrath of the Argyle players. Sale's header is inexplicably ruled out (48) and Barlow is tripped in the area but play is waved on. Plymouth fight back after early setbacks but a defensive lapse sees Tony Richards head the winner.*

42. Sat 17/4 (H) SOUTHEND — L 0-3 (HT 0-2)
- Scorers: Conlon 12, 90, Houghton 42
- Att: 3,949 · Pts: 57 · Ref: T Bates
- Argyle: Dungey, Ashton, Gibbs^, Mauge, Heathcote, Collins, Barlow, Bastow, Marshall*, Sale, Guinan. Subs: Crowe
- Southend: Capleton, Beard, Houghton, Morley, Booty, Coleman, Hodges, Unger, McGavin, Conlon, Livett. Subs: Sweeney
- *There is little sign that the play-offs are still possible as Argyle put up a gutless performance. Hodges reads the riot act and orders the players in for training at 8am the next morning. Ex-Argyle loanee Barry Conlon scores twice and just misses a hat-trick as Southend cruise to victory.*

43. Sat 24/4 (A) SWANSEA — W 3-2 (HT 0-2)
- Scorers: Guinan 72, 85, Wotton 77p; O'Leary 23, Jones 44
- Att: 5,660 · Pts: 60 · Ref: J Brandwood
- Argyle: Dungey, Wotton, Beswetherick, Mauge, Heathcote, Collins, Barlow, Bastow, Marshall*, Sale, Guinan.
- Swansea: Freestone, Jones, Coates, O'Leary, Smith, Bound, Appleby^, Thomas, Alsop, Bird*, Lacey". Subs: Watkin, Roberts, Casey
- *Argyle regain some of their pride. The 'Guinan must stay' campaign gathers pace as the on loan striker inspires an unlikely comeback. Big Julian Alsop causes problems and has a hand in both Swans' goals. Wotton equalises from the spot after Guinan was tripped by Jason Smith.*

44. Sat 1/5 (H) CAMBRIDGE — D 2-2 (HT 1-1)
- Scorers: Eustace 8(og), Crowe 61; Benjamin 38, 70
- Att: 5,006 · Pts: 61 · Ref: P Richards
- Argyle: Dungey, Wotton, Beswetherick, Mauge, Heathcote, Collins, Barlow, Hargr'ves*, Marshall*, Crowe, Guinan. Subs: Phillips
- Cambridge: Marshall, Chenery, Ashbee, Duncan, Eustace, Campbell, Wanless, Butler, Walker*, Benjamin, Russell. Subs: Kyd
- *A faulty fire alarm delays the start by 30 minutes. A minute's silence is observed for Sir Alf Ramsey. Eustace tries to recover Shaun Marshall's error but slices the ball in. Crowe scores from a yard. Trevor Benjamin adds to his growing reputation. Mauge does a farewell lap of honour.*

45. Wed 5/5 (A) SCARBOROUGH — L 1-2 (HT 1-0)
- Scorers: Brodie 3; Tate 74, 76
- Att: 2,398 · Pts: 61 · Ref: S Mathieson
- Argyle: Dungey, Wotton, Beswetherick, Mauge, Heathcote, Collins, Barlow, Phillips*, Marshall*, Sale, Brodie. Subs: Ashton, McGovern
- Scarborough: Parks, Russell*, Atkinson, Worrall, Rennison, McN'ghton, Hoyland, Jones, Tate^, ... Subs: Porter, Saville
- *Boro stare relegation in the face but find little resistance from Argyle who mathematically can still make the play-offs. Steve Brodie's header calms the nerves. Two Chris Tate goals in quick succession send the small crowd into raptures. Guinan gets a late chance but scuffs his shot.*

46. Sat 8/5 (A) CARLISLE — L 1-2 (HT 0-0)
- Scorers: Phillips 49; Brightwell 62, Glass 90
- Att: 7,599 · Pts: 61 · Ref: F Stretton
- Argyle: Dungey, Ashton, Beswetherick, Mauge, Heathcote, Collins, Barlow, Phillips*, Marshall, Crowe, Guinan. Subs: Wotton, Bastow, McGovern
- Carlisle: Glass, Bowman, Searle*, Whitehead, Brightwell, Anthony, Prokas, Hopper^, Tracey", Stevens, Dobie. Subs: Clark, Bass, Bagshaw
- *United, needing a win to stay in the league, fall behind to Phillips' first league goal. Gibbs breaks his leg. Brightwell crashes home from 30 yards. With seconds remaining, a corner is parried by Dungey to the feet of on-loan keeper Jimmy Glass who famously drills the ball home.*

Home Average 5,323 · Away 3,927

NATIONWIDE DIVISION 3 (CUP-TIES) Manager: Kevin Hodges SEASON 1998-99

Worthington Cup

Match	Att	Res	F-A	H-T	Scorers, Times, and Referees	1	2	3	4	5	6	7	8	9	10	11	subs used
1:1 H PORTSMOUTH 11/8	4,380 1:	L	1-3	1-3	McCarthy 20; Ref: R Furmandiz	Sheffield	Collins	Gibbs	Mauge	Heathcote	Wotton	Barlow	McCarthy	Jean	Power*	Hargreaves	McCall
(Portsmouth)					*McLoughlin 38p, Vlachos 40, Aloisi 45*	*Flahavan**	*Pethick*	*Simpson*	*McLoughlin**	*Whitbread*	*Awford*	*Vlachos^*	*Kyzeridis*	*Aloisi*	*Durnin''*	*Thomson*	*Knight/Soley/Claridge*
1:2 A PORTSMOUTH 18/8	5,479 1:17	L	2-3	1-2	Jean 3, McCarthy 66; Ref: P Rejer	Sheffield	Flash	Gibbs	McCall*	Heathcote	Wotton	Barlow	McCarthy	Jean^	Mauge	Hargreaves	Ashton/Power
(Portsmouth)					*Hillier 11, McLoughlin 25p, Aloisi 53* (Argyle lost 3-6 on aggregate)	*Knight*	*Thomson*	*Simpson*	*McL'ghlin**	*Whitbread*	*Awford*	*Hillier*	*Claridge*	*Aloisi*	*Durnin^*	*Kyzeridis''*	*Igoe/Robinson/Soley*

1:1 — Argyle's dismal record in the competition is set to continue as Alan Ball's Pompey prove too good. A thumping strike from McCarthy bodes well but McLoughlin's penalty after a Mauge trip on Aloisi gives the visitors heart. Two more goals see them cruise through the second half.

1:2 — Argyle put up an encouraging display. Jean's early strike is cancelled out by David Hillier's shot. Another McLoughlin penalty after Steve Claridge is tripped by Heathcote kills the tie. Aloisi's extravagant dummy leads to Pompey's third. McCarthy nets spectacularly from 20 yards.

FA Cup

Match	Att	Res	F-A	H-T	Scorers, Times, and Referees	1	2	3	4	5	6	7	8	9	10	11	subs used
1 H KIDDERMINSTER 13/11	4,284 VC:11	9 D	0-0	0-0	Ref: A Butler	Sheffield	Collins	Besweth'ck	McCall	Heathcote	Wotton	Barlow	Mauge!	McCarthy	Marshall*	Hargreaves	Phillips
(Kidderminster)						*Brock*	*Hinton*	*Hines*	*Weir**	*Smith*	*Yates*	*Webb*	*Taylor*	*Hadley*	*Arnold*	*Willetts*	*Wolsey*
1R A KIDDERMINSTER 1/12	4,471 VC:9	12 D	0-0	0-0	Ref: A Butler (Argyle won 5-4 on penalties)	Sheffield	Ashton	Besweth'ck	Bastow	Heathcote	Wotton	Barlow	McCall*	McCarthy	Jean*	Hargr'ves^	Adams/Phillips
(Kidderminster)						*Brock*	*Hinton*	*Hines*	*Webb*	*Smith*	*Yates*	*Curr'ington**	*Hadley*	*May*	*Arnold*	*Taylor*	*Willetts/Deakin*
2 A WYCOMBE 5/12	3,493 2:23	12 D	1-1	0-1	McCarthy 76 (og); Ref: P Robinson	Dungey	Ashton	Beswth'ck	Bastow	Heathcote	Wotton	Barlow	Sweeney	McCarthy	Jean	Phillips	Marshall
(Wycombe)					*Baird 31*	*Taylor*	*Lawrence*	*Vinnicombe*	*McCarthy*	*Cousins*	*Mohan*	*Simpson*	*Carroll*	*Baird*	*Scott*	*Emblen**	*Bulman*
2R H WYCOMBE 15/12	4,304 2:23	13 W	3-2	2-0	Wotton 27p, Heathcote 39, Sweeney 83; Ref: P Robinson	Sheffield	Ashton	Hargreaves	Bastow	Heathcote	Wotton	Barlow	Mauge	McCarthy	Jean*	Phillips^	Sweeney/Marshall
(Wycombe)					*Read 71, Carroll 90p*	*Taylor*	*Lawrence*	*Vin'icombe**	*McCarthy*	*Cousins*	*Mohan*	*Simpson^*	*Brown*	*Baird*	*Scott*	*Carroll*	*Beeton/Emblen/Read*
3 H DERBY 2/1	16,730 P:11	12 L	0-3	0-2	Ref: E Wolstenholme	Sheffield	Ashton	Beswth'k*	Mauge	Heathcote	Wotton	Barlow	Hargreaves	McCarthy	Jean	Phillips^	McCall/Marshall
(Derby)					*Burton 15, 82, Eranio 21p*	*Poom*	*Kozluk*	*Laursen*	*Elliott*	*Carbonari*	*Prior*	*Eranio**	*Burton*	*Sturridge*	*Bohinen^*	*Carsley*	*Harper/Hunt*

1 — The crowd are less than impressed with referee Butler after his sending off of Mauge (38). Ian Arnold hardly endears himself either, after he drops like a stone after a two-footed tackle by the Argyle midfielder and then makes a miraculous recovery. Craig Hinton hits the post late on.

1R — Injury-hit Argyle survive to progress against the non-league part-timers. McCall and Hargreaves both go off injured before half-time. Steve Taylor's miss when he blasts over the bar in the penalty shoot-out proves crucial. At 4-4, McCarthy calmly sends Stuart Brock the wrong way.

2 — Argyle's injury crisis is highlighted as Hodges names himself as a sub along with two apprentices. Dungey is recalled for the first time in nearly two years. Andrew Baird is left unmarked to head home Dave Carroll's cross. Paul McCarthy toe-pokes a cross past his own keeper.

2R — Keeper Martin Taylor does not have the happiest of nights. He shoves McCarthy for a penalty which gives Argyle their first goal for 433 minutes. He then spills the ball for Argyle's second and miscues a clearance to Sweeney who, from 30 yards out, finds the bottom corner.

3 — Without eight regulars, Jim Smith's stars simply prove too good. Dean Sturridge's pace causes all the problems and he is brought down by Wotton for a penalty. The defender concedes a second spot-kick for handball but Eranio hits the post (52). Poom's wonder save denies Jean.

League table

		Home						Away					Pts
	P	W	D	L	F	A	W	D	L	F	A		
1 Brentford	46	16	5	2	45	18	10	2	11	34	38		85
2 Cambridge	46	13	6	4	41	21	10	6	7	37	27		81
3 Cardiff	46	13	7	3	35	17	10	7	7	25	22		80
4 Scunthorpe *	46	14	3	6	42	28	8	5	10	27	30		74
5 Rotherham	46	11	8	4	41	26	9	5	9	38	35		73
6 Leyton Orient	46	12	6	5	40	30	7	9	7	28	29		72
7 Swansea	46	11	9	3	33	19	8	5	10	23	29		71
8 Mansfield	46	15	2	6	38	18	4	8	11	22	40		67
9 Peterborough	46	11	4	8	41	29	7	8	8	31	27		66
10 Halifax	46	10	8	5	33	25	7	7	9	25	31		66
11 Darlington	46	10	6	7	41	24	8	5	10	28	34		65
12 Exeter	46	13	5	5	32	18	4	7	12	15	32		63
13 PLYMOUTH	46	11	6	6	32	19	6	4	13	26	35		61
14 Chester	46	6	12	5	28	30	7	6	10	29	36		57
15 Shrewsbury	46	10	6	6	36	29	3	8	12	16	34		56
16 Barnet	46	10	5	8	30	31	6	8	9	24	31		55
17 Brighton	46	8	3	12	25	35	8	4	11	24	31		55
18 Southend	46	8	6	9	24	21	6	6	11	28	37		54
19 Rochdale	46	8	9	6	22	21	4	7	12	20	34		54
20 Torquay	46	9	9	5	29	20	3	8	12	18	38		53
21 Hull	46	8	5	10	25	28	6	6	11	19	34		53
22 Hartlepool	46	8	7	8	33	27	5	5	13	19	38		51
23 Carlisle	46	8	8	7	25	21	3	8	12	18	32		49
24 Scarborough	46	8	3	12	30	39	6	3	14	20	38		48
	1104	253	147	152	801	594	152	147	253	594	801		1509

* promoted after play-offs

Odds & ends

Double wins: (2) Rotherham, Scunthorpe.

Double defeats: (2) Leyton Orient, Southend.

Won from behind: (2) Rochdale, Swansea.

Lost from in front: (4) Carlisle, Chester, Darlington, Leyton Orient.

High spots: Sensational impact of 17-year-old Darren Bastow.

Late-season form of loan signing Steve Guinan.

Impressive 3-0 win over title favourites Brentford.

Low spots: End of season slump with play-offs in sight.

Little impact from majority of loan signings.

Sickening injury to Paul Gibbs in final game.

Enforced retirement of Richard Flash through injury.

End of season departure of popular Ronnie Mauge.

Player of the Year: Mick Heathcote.

Ever presents: (0).

Hat-tricks (1) Steve Guinan.

Leading scorer: Dwight Marshall (12).

Appearances and Goals

	Appearances						Goals			
	Lge	Sub	LC	Sub	FAC	Sub	Lge	LC	FAC	Tot
Adams, Steve	22	4								
Ashton, Jon	45		2		1		5			5
Barlow, Martin										
Barrett, Adam	21	1								
Bastow, Darren	18	8			3		2			2
Beswetherick, Jon	7	4			4					
Branston, Guy	40		1				1			1
Collins, Simon	1	1					2			2
Crittenden, Nick	3	8								
Crowe, Glen	7				1		1			1
Dungey, James	4									
Edmondson, Darren	4	1								
Flash, Richard	4	1	1							
Ford, Liam		1								
Forinton, Howard	8	1					3			3
Gibbs, Paul	27		2		2		3			3
Gritton, Martin		2								
Guinan, Steve	11	2					7			7
Hargreaves, Chris	30	2	2		4		2			2
Heathcote, Mick	43		2		5		3			3
Jean, Earl	21	8	2		4		3		1	4
Marker, Nicky	4									
Marshall, Dwight	25	3	1		1	2	12			12
Mauge, Ronnie	31	1	2		3	1	3			3
McCall, Steve	14	3	1	1	2	1				
McCarthy, Sean	14	2	1		5		3	2		5
McGovern, Brendan		2								
Phillips, Lee	8	7			3	2	1			1
Power, Lee	7	9	1	1			1			1
Sale, Mark	8									
Sheffield, Jon	39		2		4					
Sweeney, Terry	6	7			1	1	1		1	2
Taylor, Craig	6						1			1
Wills, Kevin		2								
Wotton, Paul	32	4	2		5		1	1	1	3
(own-goals)							3	1		4
35 players used	506	81	22	3	55	7	58	3	4	65

NATIONWIDE DIVISION 3

Manager: Kevin Hodges

SEASON 1999-2000

No	Date	Att	Pos	Pt	F-A	H-T	Scorers, Times, and Referees	1	2	3	4	5	6	7	8	9	10	11	subs used
1 A **SOUTHEND**	7/8	4,981	15 / 7	L / 0	1-2	1-0	Barrett 21 / Houghton 79, Tolson 81 / Ref: R Beeby	Veysey	Rowbotham	Beswetch'ck	Leadbitter	Heathcote I	Barrett	Bastow	O'Sullivan	McGregor	Hargreaves	Stoneb'ge*	Belgrave
								Capleton	Booty	Morley	Roget	Connelly	Coleman	Beard		Abiodun*	Tolson^	Houghton	Maher/Fitzpatrick
2 H **SHREWSBURY**	14/8	4,919	18 / 19	D / 1	0-0	0-0	Ref: A Wiley	Sheffield	Rowbotham	Beswetch'ck	Leadbitter	Heathcote	Barrett	Bastow*	O'Sullivan	McGregor	Hargreaves	Stonebridge	Belgrave
								Edwards	Seabury	Hanmer	Whelan	Winstanley	Wilding	Brown	Preece	Steele*	Jobling	Cullen	Jagielka
3 A **HALIFAX**	21/8	2,431	12 / 16	W / 4	1-0	0-0	Stonebridge 60 / Ref: T Jones	Sheffield	Ashton	Beswetch'ck	Leadbitter*	Taylor	Barrett	Bastow*	O'Sullivan	McGregor^	Hargreaves	Stonebridge	Bastow/Belgrave
								Adamson*	Murphy*	Jules	Mitchell*	Stoneman	Sertori	Paterson	Gaughan	Tate	Painter	Butler P*	Russell/Power/Newton
4 H **PETERBOROUGH**	28/8	4,189	10 / 5	W / 7	2-1	2-0	Stonebridge 22, O'Sullivan 35 / Farrell 90 / Ref: P Dowd	Sheffield	Row'tham*	Beswetch'ck	Leadbitter*	Taylor	Barrett	Gritton*	O'Sullivan	McGregor^	Hargreaves	Stonebridge	Bastow/Belgrave
								Tyler	Hooper	Drury	Castle	Chapple*	Edwards	Farrell	Davies*	Shields^	Broughton	Etherington	Martin/Wicks/Koogi
5 A **CARLISLE**	30/8	2,863	13 / 12	L / 7	2-4	0-2	Stonebridge 59, 74 / Tracey 41, 25, Black 44, Baker 47 / Ref: W Burns	Veysey	Ashton	Beswetch'ck	Leadbitter*	Taylor	Barrett	Bastow*	O'Sullivan	McGregor	Hargreaves	Stonebridge	Bastow/McCarthy
								Weaver	Pitts	Clark	Barr	Brightwell	Prokas*	Soley	Hopper	Baker	Tracey	Black	Thorpe
6 H **BRIGHTON**	5/9	5,444	14 / 7	D / 8	3-3	2-2	Gritton 5, 38, Stonebridge 71 / Freeman 17, Oatway 44, 66 / Ref: K Leach	Sheffield	Ashton	Beswetch'ck	McCall	Heathcote*	Barrett	O'Sullivan	Gritton	Gritton	Hargreaves	Stonebridge	Barrett/Bastow/Belgrave
								Walton	Wilder*	Campbell	McPherson	Crosby	Watson	Freeman*	Rogers	Hart	Oatway	Thomas*	Cameron/N'House/Johnson
7 H **ROTHERHAM**	11/9	4,075	14 / 11	D / 9	1-1	1-0	Heathcote 15 / Berry 49 / Ref: S Tomlin	Sheffield	Ashton*	Beswetch'ck	Leadbitter	Heathcote*	Taylor	O'Sullivan	Gritton*	O'Sullivan	Hargreaves	Stonebridge	Barrett/McCall/McCarthy
								Pollitt	Varty	Beech	Dillon	Wilsterman	Garner	Berry*	Watson	F-West	Scott	Turner^	Sedgwick/Warne
8 A **HARTLEPOOL**	18/9	2,242	17 / 19	L / 9	0-3	0-2	Freestone 4, Lee 13, Henderson 88 / Ref: M Pike	Sheffield	Barrett	Beswetch'ck	Leadbitter	Heathcote*	Taylor	O'Sullivan	Gritton	Gritton	Hargreaves	Stonebridge	Ashton/McCarthy
								Holland	Knowles	Perkins	Barron^	Lee	Vindheim	Clark	Miller	Jones	Freestone*	Steph'son^	Hen son/Westw'd/F'patrick
9 A **DARLINGTON**	25/9	5,045	20 / 3	L / 9	0-2	0-1	Nogan 23, Campbell 78 / Ref: T Parkes	Sheffield	Ashton	Beswetch'ck	Leadbitter	Taylor	Barrett	O'Sullivan	Gray	McGregor^	Hargreaves	Stonebridge	Belgrave
								Samways	Liddle	Hec'bottom Oliver*		Aspin	Brumwell	Gray	Russell	Nogan	Gabbiadini^	Atkinson	Duffield/Campbell
10 H **LEYTON ORIENT**	2/10	3,782	13 / 22	W / 12	5-0	2-0	Leadbitter 3, 48, McCarthy 17, 53, [Hargreaves 66] / Ref: R Styles	Sheffield	McCall*	Beswetch'ck	Leadbitter	Taylor	Barrett	McCarthy	O'Sullivan	McGregor	Hargreaves	Stonebr'ge*	Bastow/Gritton
								Bayes	Joseph	Morrison*	Clark	Smith	Low*	Downer	Gray	Ampadu	Inglethorpe^	Simba	Richards/Watts/Hockton
11 H **MANSFIELD**	9/10	3,809	12 / 16	W / 15	2-1	2-0	Gritton 7, O'Sullivan 34 / Peacock 64 / Ref: L Cable	Sheffield	McCall	Beswetch'ck	Leadbitter	Taylor	Barrett	McCarthy	O'Sullivan	Gritton	Hargreaves	McCarthy	Heathcote McCarthy
								Muggleton	Asher	Williams	Kerr*	Richardson	Linighan	Roscoe	Peacock	Peacock	Lormor	Clarke	Boulding

Match reports

1 — SOUTHEND: Barrett scores on his full league debut. Heathcote is sent off for the first time in his long career (41) when he loses his cool and head-butts Leo Roget. Scott Houghton scores from 20 yards. One time Argyle target Neil Tolson gets the winner after Veysey spills Martyn Booty's cross.

2 — SHREWSBURY: Hodges is offered a one-year extension to his contract. Shrews' boss Jake King is delighted with his side's defensive display and Paul Edwards pulls off a stunning save from Stonebridge's diving header. Two fans are ejected from the ground for shouting abuse at Chairman McCauley.

3 — HALIFAX: Despite spending heavily over the summer, Halifax pose little threat. Taylor plays superbly after his £30k transfer from Swindon. McGregor misses an early chance when he completely miskicks in front of goal. Stonebridge scores a breakaway goal after a fine run by Hargreaves.

4 — PETERBOROUGH: Barry Fry's side arrive with a 100% league record but leave with Fry labelling the performance a disgrace. Future Spurs star, Simon Davies, goes off (30) after feeling ill following some injections. Gritton and Stonebridge combine well up front. David Farrell scores from 30 yards.

5 — CARLISLE: Stonebridge scores twice on his 18th birthday. Several fine saves from Veysey are interspersed with three howlers from which United take full advantage. The part-time keeper can do little about Paul Baker's goal after the veteran is left to side-foot in Richard Tracey's superb cross.

6 — BRIGHTON: Gritton again impresses in a highly entertaining match, although Hodges is concerned as the defence continues to leak goals. Opposite number Micky Adams is also unhappy as his team's goals-against record doubles. Stonebridge celebrates his selection for the England Under-18 squad.

7 — ROTHERHAM: Millers' boss Ronnie Moore returns to Home Park having 'spied' on the Pilgrims in their previous match. Heathcote is allowed space to head in O'Sullivan's corner. A lapse in concentration from Ashton proves costly as he allows Trevor Berry to nip in behind him to lob Sheffield.

8 — HARTLEPOOL: Former Argyle boss Peter Shilton watches the match with son Sam amongst the home side's substitutes. Chris Freestone scores his customary goal against the Pilgrims after Sheffield misjudges a cross to set Pool on their way to an easy win to ease the pressure on boss Chris Turner.

9 — DARLINGTON: Argyle's slide down the table continues after another fruitless trip to the North East. With the experienced Marco Gabbiadini proving a threat, David Hodgson's side take the lead when Lee Nogan stoops low to head in. Sheffield is stranded as Paul Campbell's shot deflects off Barrett.

10 — LEYTON ORIENT: Leadbitter commences a fine display by unusually scoring with his head. Orient, one of the pre-season favourites for promotion, look totally inept as this heavy defeat increases the pressure on manager Tommy Taylor, recent recipient of a vote of confidence by chairman Barry Hearn.

11 — MANSFIELD: A suspiciously offside Gritton latches onto Beswetherick's pass. O'Sullivan rounds off a flowing move. Hargreaves is crudely brought down by Neil Richardson in the box (44) but Muggleton saves his spot-kick with the crowd anticipating another five-goal rout. Lee Peacock replies.

Match-by-match results and line-ups. For each match the top line lists the Argyle XI; the line in italics below lists the opposition.

12 A ROCHDALE 16/10 — D 0-0 (HT 0-0) · 15 4 16 · Att 3,105
Sheffield, McCall*, Beswethck, Leadbitter, Taylor, Barrett, McCarthy, O'Sullivan, McGregor, Hargreaves, Stonebridge, Rowbotham
Edwards, Evans, Searle, Peake, Green, Hill, Fitzcroft, Carden, Platt, Holt^, Atkinson, Jones/Dowe*
With McCall rolling back the years and rolling out the passes, Argyle settle for a point as Dale fans endure their third scoreless draw at home on the trot. In the last minute, Platt misses a chance to give Rochdale their first win over Argyle for 28 years, but Sheffield saved with his legs.
Ref: P Joslin

13 A HULL 19/10 — W 1-0 (HT 0-0) · 19 · Att 4,727
Sheffield, McCall*, Beswethck, Leadbitter, Taylor, Barrett, McCarthy, O'Sullivan, McGregor, Hargreaves, Stonebridge, Rowbotham
Wilson, Harper, Williams, Edwards, Whittle, Greaves, D'Auria, Brabin, Brown, Wood, Eyre
McGregor scores his long awaited first goal with a cross which drifts over the head of Steve Wilson. David Brown hits a post from 20 yards to briefly threaten Hull's record of failing to score for more than seven hours. Jamie Wood's injury-time appeal for a penalty falls on deaf ears.
McGregor 49
Ref: G Laws

14 H DARLINGTON 23/10 — D 0-0 (HT 0-0) · 13 5 20 · Att 4,362
Sheffield, McCall*, Beswethck, Leadbitter, Taylor, Barrett, McCarthy^, O'Sullivan, McGregor, Hargreaves, Stonebr'ge, Rowbotham/Gritton/Phillips
Collett, Liddle, Hec'bottom Campbell, Tutill, Brunwell, Russell, Oliver, Nogan^, Heaney, Atkinson, Himsworth/Naylor*
Darlo's star striker Marco Gabbiadini is out through injury thanks to a broken nose incurred in a clash with Sheffield in the recent encounter between the two sides. Endeavour outshines skill as another dull affair ensures Argyle fans aren't being overfed on a diet of high excitement.
Ref: M Warren

15 H EXETER 2/11 — W 1-0 (HT 1-0) · 23 · Att 9,412
Sheffield, McCall*, Beswethck, Leadbitter, Taylor, Barrett, McCarthy, O'Sullivan, McGregor, Hargreaves, Stonebridge
Naylor, Richardson Gale^, Buckle, Curran, Gittens, Robinson, Smith, Flack, Nyamah, Bradley^, Power/Speakman/Waugh*
Kick-off is delayed by 15 minutes to allow in the biggest Third Division crowd of the season so far. Of McCarthy's 200-plus goals this must be the easiest as he taps in from three feet after Stonebridge's shot comes off a post. Exeter recover well and Pete Smith's shot crashes off the bar.
McCarthy 22
Ref: P Taylor

16 A CHESTER 6/11 — W 1-0 (HT 1-0) · 8 23 26 · Att 2,027
Sheffield, McCall, Beswethck, Leadbitter, Taylor, Barrett, McCarthy*, O'Sullivan, McGregor, Hargreaves, Stonebr'ge, Heathcote/Belgrave
Brown, Moss, Doughty, Milosavl'vic Spooner, Shelton, Finney, Richardson Wright^, Beckett, Fisher, Cross/Nash*
The Pilgrims' improved away form continues at struggling Chester. McCall scores only the 17th league goal of his long career with a half-volley from 20 yards. Sheffield denies City twice with fine saves. Heathcote makes a welcome re-appearance and plays the last 14 minutes up front.
McCall 14
Ref: D Gallagher

17 H BARNET 14/11 — W 4-1 (HT 2-0) · 6 2 29 · Att 6,343
Sheffield, McCall, Beswethck, Leadbitter, Heathcote, Barrett, McCarthy*, O'Sullivan, McGregor, Hargreaves, Stonebr'ge, Belgrave
Harrison, Stockley, Davidson, Basham, Heald, Arber, Currie, Doolan, Charley, McGleish^, Brown, Searle/King*
Long-time league leaders Barnet are stunned by Argyle's performance. McGregor scores a nonchalant hat-trick completed by a superb long-range shot. Beswetherick's surging run down the left sets up Stonebridge. Bees boss John Still is too upset to talk to the media after the match.
McGregor 19, 69, 79, Stonebridge 35, Charley 73
Ref: P Rejer

18 A CHELTENHAM 23/11 — L 0-2 (HT 0-1) · 29 · Att 5,140
Sheffield, McCall*, Beswethck, Leadbitter, Heathcote, Barrett, McCarthy*, O'Sullivan, Belgrave^, Hargreaves, Stonebr'ge, Bastow/McCarthy/Phillips
Book, Duff, Victory, Banks, Freeman, McAuley, Howells, Milton, Grayson, Brissett^, Yates, Brough/Bloomer*
Two thousand Argyle followers descend on Whaddon Road causing a 15-minute delay to the kick-off. Without McGregor, suffering a stomach bug, Argyle's attack lacks bite. Neil Grayson's second goal, a spectacular 25-yard volley is the one moment of skill in an error-riddled game.
Grayson 5, 70
Ref: M Reed

19 A YORK 27/11 — D 0-0 (HT 0-0) · 7 18 30 · Att 2,745
Sheffield, O'Sullivan, Beswethck, Leadbitter, Heathcote, Barrett, McCarthy, Bastow, McGregor, Hargreaves, Stonebr'ge, Phillips
Mimms, Dawson, Hall, Jones, Sertori, Fairclough Fox, Bullock, Alcide, Williams, Ormerod, Hocking*
Malcolm Allison watches the match. With little to excite either set of supporters, the York fans spend most of the match calling for the sacking of manager Neil Thompson and the resignation of the chairman. Hargreaves has the best chance but his weaker right foot fails to test Mimms.
Ref: E Wolstenholme

20 H SOUTHEND 4/12 — W 3-1 (HT 2-0) · 7 13 33 · Att 4,679
Sheffield*, O'Sullivan, Beswethck, Leadbitter, Heathcote, Barrett, McCarthy, Bastow, McGregor^, Hargreaves, Stonebr'ge, Veysey/Gritton/McCarthy
Capleton, Booty^, Beard, Morley, Roget, Coleman, Connelly, Tinkler, Carruthers Tolson, Houghton, Roach/Kerrigan*
Bastow rediscovers his form and scores with a shot off the underside of the bar. Stonebridge shoots low past Mel Capleton. Sheffield goes off with a groin strain. Veysey's first touch is to pick the ball out of the net from Gordon Connelly's header. Houghton hits the post from 25 yards.
Bastow 23, Stonebr' 33, Hargreaves 68, Connelly 58
Ref: P Danson

21 A NORTHAMPTON 17/12 — D 1-1 (HT 1-0) · 8 4 34 · Att 5,039
Veysey, O'Sullivan, Beswethck, Leadbitter, Heathcote, Barrett, Bastow, McCarthy, McGregor, Hargreaves, Stonebridge
Welch, Hendon, Frain, Sampson, Howey, Parrish, Savage, Hunter, Clare, Corazzin, Spedding
McGregor scores the opening goal of an entertaining encounter with a powerful header from Beswetherick's pinpoint cross. Welch's broken rib is tested as he is forced to save at full stretch from long range efforts by Hargreaves and Stonebridge. Corazzin blasts home from five yards.
McGregor 37, Corazzin 64
Ref: P Robinson

22 H TORQUAY 26/12 — D 2-2 (HT 1-0) · 9 7 35 · Att 14,893
Veysey, O'Sullivan, Beswethck, Leadbitter, Heathcote, Barrett, Bastow, McCarthy*, McGregor, Hargreaves, Stonebridge Gritton
Southall, Holmes, Herrera, Aggrey, Russell, Thomas, Platts, Hill, Bedeau, Williams, O'Brien, Healy*
Argyle dominate the first half and take a deserved lead when Williams slices a clearance straight to McCarthy. The introduction of Brian Healy turns the tide and Williams pounces on hesitation between Barrett and Veysey. Southall's clearance falls to McGregor but Hill saves a point.
McCarthy 18, McGregor 69, Williams 52, Hill 75
Ref: C Wilkes

23 A SWANSEA 28/12 — L 0-1 (HT 0-1) · 11 3 35 · Att 9,075
Veysey, O'Sullivan, Beswethck, Leadbitter^, Heathcote, Barrett, Bastow^, McCarthy, McGregor, Hargreaves, Gritton/McCall/Wotton
Freestone, Jones, Howard, Cusack, Smith, Bound, Keegan^, Lacey^, Alsop, Boyd, Coates, Thomas/Watkin/Price
John Hollins' flu-stricken side take the points despite being decidedly second best. McCarthy grazes the crossbar with a half-volley, Jamaican international Walter Boyd scores the only goal. Argyle are furious as a penalty claim is ignored when Cusack almost rips McCarthy's shirt off.
Boyd 66
Ref: T Jones

No	Date		Att	Pos	Pt	F-A	H-T	Scorers, Times, and Referees	1	2	3	4	5	6	7	8	9	10	11	subs used
24	H	MACCLESFIELD		8	W	3-2	2-1	Stonebridge 35, 48, Taylor 38	Sheffield	McCall^	Besweth'ck	Leadbitter	Heathcote	Taylor	McCarthy	O'Sullivan	McGregor*	Hargreaves	Stonebridge	Phillips/Wotton
	3/1		6,128	*6*	38			*Askey 13, Wood 53*	*Martin*	*Abbey*	*Rioch*	*Moore*	*Tinson*	*Wood*	*Askey*	*Sedgemore*	*Barker*	*Davies*	*Durkan**	*Whittaker*
								Ref: S Dunn	Bastow is axed for ongoing disciplinary problems off the pitch and 'may not play for some time'. Leadbitter is outstanding after passing a mid-day fitness test. Both sides waste late chances, with Hargreaves firing wildly over from six yards and Askey missing a last-minute header.											
25	A	SHREWSBURY		12	D	0-0	0-0		Sheffield	McCall	Besweth'ck	Leadbitter	Heathcote	Taylor	McCarthy !	O'Sullivan	McGregor	Hargreaves	Stonebridge	
	15/1		*2,458*	*22*	39				*Edwards*	*Seabury*	*Winstanley*	*Tretton*	*Wilding*	*Whelan*	*Brown*	*Murray**	*Steele^*	*Aiston*	*Jobling*	*Berkley/Jagielka*
								Ref: M Riley	The Pilgrims battle for a point after the dismissal of McCarthy (45) for a high tackle on Spencer Whelan who is left with stud marks in his groin. The Shrews' best player, Lee Steele, clips the outside of the post but, other than that, neither side look remotely capable of scoring a goal.											
26	H	HALIFAX		12	D	1-1	0-0	McGregor 64	Sheffield	O'Sullivan	Barrett	Leadbitter	Heathcote	Taylor	Phillips	Wotton	McGregor	Hargreaves	Stonebr'ge*	Gritton
	22/1		4,841	*8*	40			*Painter 54*	*Butler L*	*Wilder*	*Jules*	*Mitchell*	*Stoneman*	*Potter*	*Paterson*	*Painter*	*Reilly^*	*Cullen*	*Butler P**	*Gaughan/Murphy*
								Ref: M Halsey	McCall is injured in the pre-match warm-up and Phillips is drafted in. Hesitation from Sheffield allows Robbie Painter to head in. McGregor beats the onrushing Lee Butler to O'Sullivan's pass but Mark Lillis's side are the more pleased with a point as Argyle's play-off hopes fade.											
27	A	PETERBOROUGH		13	L	0-2	0-0		Sheffield	**Middleton**	Besweth'ck	Leadbitter	Heathcote	Taylor	Barrett	Wotton	McGregor	Phillips^	Stonebr'ge*	Belgrave/**Morrison-Hill**
	29/1		*5,694*	*7*	40			*Castle 82, Clarke 88*	*Tyler*	*Hooper*	*Drury*	*Scott*	*Wicks*	*Edwards*	*Farrell^*	*Lee*	*Clarke*	*Forinton**	*Hanlon"*	*Martin/Green/Castle*
								Ref: A Bates	Any attempts to play good football are thwarted by a pitch which was cut up badly by the end of the warm-up. Former Argyle hero Steve Castle, now Boro's reserve-team coach comes on to break the deadlock. With Heathcote pushed into attack, Andy Clarke scores a late second.											
28	H	CARLISLE		10	W	2-0	1-0	Middleton 6, Gritton 85	Sheffield	O'Sullivan	Besweth'ck	Middleton	Heathcote	Taylor	Barrett	Wotton	McGregor^	Hargreaves"	Belgrave*	Gritton/Phillips/Wills
	5/2		4,009	*23*	43				*Weaver*	*Pitts*	*Clark^*	*Reid*	*Teale*	*Prokas**	*Barr*	*Soley*	*Dobie*	*Harries"*	*Anthony*	*Tracey/Searle/Baker*
								Ref: K Hill	Reading make a £150k bid for Beswetherick. On-loan Middleton celebrates his home debut by heading into the roof of the net. Steve Soley hits the bar. Substitute Gritton evades Billy Barr to shoot low past Luke Weaver to at last provide a modicum of excitement for the remaining fans.											
29	A	BRIGHTON		12	D	1-1	1-0	Gritton 1	Sheffield	O'Sullivan	Besweth'ck	Middleton	Heathcote	Taylor	Barrett	Gritton^	McGregor*	Hargreaves	Wotton	Belgrave/Phillips
	12/2		*5,654*	*18*	44			*Zamora 49*	*Walton*	*Watson*	*Mayo*	*Aspinall"*	*Crosby*	*Cullip*	*Freeman**	*Rogers*	*Hart*	*Oatway*	*Zamora^*	*Thomas/Ramsay/Wilkinson*
								Ref: P Taylor	Albion are in the midst of a minor crisis. Without a win in seven games, manager Micky Adams is jeered by the home fans for criticising crowd favourite Dave Cameron. Gritton adds to their woes with a first-minute goal. Debutant Bobby Zamora's header slips under Sheffield.											
30	H	YORK		11	W	2-0	2-0	Middleton 16, McCarthy 39	Sheffield	O'Sullivan	Besweth'k*	Middleton	Heathcote	Taylor	McCarthy"	Gritton^	McGregor	Hargreaves	Wotton	Barrett/Belgrave/Phillips
	19/2		4,343	*21*	47				*Mimms**	*Hocking*	*Thompson^*	*Bower*	*Sertori*	*Jones*	*Dawson"*	*Jordan*	*Hulme*	*Williams J*	*Williams M*	*HowarthTurley/Skinner*
								Ref: M Warren	Heathcote reopens a head wound during the warm-up but plays. Middleton shows his eye for goal by firing home from 18 yards. McCarthy notches the 200th goal of his career with a great strike. New City boss Terry Dolan admits he has a job on his hands to lift his side up the table.											
31	A	LINCOLN			L	0-3	0-1		Sheffield	O'Sullivan	Besweth'ck	Middleton	Heathcote	Taylor	McCarthy*	Gritton"	McGregor^	Hargreaves	Wotton	Barrett/Belgrave/Phillips
	22/2		*2,561*		47			*Thorpe 28, 46, Gordon 61*	*Marriott*	*Smith*	*Mayo*	*Barnett*	*Welsh*	*Brown*	*Fleming*	*Miller*	*Gordon**	*Thorpe*	*Gain*	*Battersby*
								Ref: M Cowburn	Argyle's dismal away form continues. Lee Thorpe runs through a statuesque defence to score. McCarthy fires wide with only Marriott to beat. Thorpe and Gordon are given the freedom of Lincoln to add to the tally. Rumours of a post-match dressing room fracas are denied by Hodges.											
32	H	HARTLEPOOL		11	D	1-1	1-0	McGregor 39	Sheffield	O'Sullivan	Besweth'ck	Middleton	Heathcote	Taylor	McCarthy	Gritton*	McGregor	Hargreaves	Wotton	Phillips
	26/2		3,917	*8*	48			*Shilton 59*	*Hollund*	*Knowles*	*Shilton*	*Barron*	*Strodder*	*Lee*	*Westwood*	*Miller*	*Jones^*	*Fitzpatrick**	*Stephenson*	*Clark/McAvoy*
								Ref: R Beeby	Heavy pre-match rain puts the game in doubt. McGregor revels in the slippery conditions and proves a constant threat to Pool's overworked defence. He rounds Martin Hollund to put Argyle in front but Sam Shilton prods in the equaliser. McGregor and Gritton hit the woodwork.											
33	A	ROTHERHAM		10	D	1-1	1-0	Hargreaves 23	Sheffield	O'Sullivan	Besweth'ck	Leadbitter	Heathcote	Taylor	McCarthy*	Barrett	McGregor^	Hargreaves	Wotton	Gritton/Barlow
	4/3		*4,496*	*1*	49			*Warne 76*	*Pollitt*	*Hurst*	*Scott*	*Berry**	*Wilsterman*	*Warner*	*Sedgwick*	*Watson*	*F-West*	*Warne*	*Turner*	*Thompson*
								Ref: D Pugh	Leo Fortune-West is presented with six pounds of best steak before the match for scoring a recent hat-trick. Hargreaves stuns the free-scoring league leaders when he heads home. Argyle withstand the aerial bombardment until Steve Thompson's shot rebounds off the post to Warne.											
34	H	CHESTER		8	D	0-0	0-0		Sheffield	O'Sullivan	Besweth'ck	Barrett	Heathcote	Taylor	Barlow^	McCarthy"	McGregor	Hargreaves	Wotton*	Stonebridge/Gritton/Phillips
	7/3		4,140	*23*	50				*Brown*	*Moss^*	*Robinson*	*Hobson*	*Hicks*	*Woods*	*Porter*	*Hemmings"*	*Finney**	*Beckett*	*Fisher*	*Doughty/Richardson/Berry*
								Ref: C Wilkes	Barlow's comeback from injury lasts just 23 minutes as he limps off again. McCarthy last only a few minutes longer. Lowly Chester are in the midst of a mini-revival. Manager Ian Atkins fumes as City are denied a penalty when O'Sullivan appears to handle Beckett's shot on the line.											

Match results (35–46)

No	Venue / Date	Opponent	Att	Pos	P	Res	Pts	Score
35	A 11/3	EXETER	4,287	20	10	D	51	0-1
36	H 14/3	LINCOLN	4,111	11	10	D	52	1-1
37	H 18/3	CHELTENHAM	4,392	11	8	W	55	1-0
38	A 21/3	BARNET	2,328	6	10	L	55	0-0
39	A 25/3	TORQUAY	4,113	11	9	W	58	4-0
40	H 1/4	NORTHAMPTON	5,448	4	9	W	61	2-1
41	A 8/4	MACCLESFIELD	2,231	13	9	L	61	1-4
42	H 15/4	SWANSEA	5,881	2	9	W	64	1-0
43	H 22/4	ROCHDALE	6,205	9	10	D	65	1-1
44	A 24/4	LEYTON ORIENT	4,113	19	9	L	65	0-3
45	H 29/4	HULL	4,233	14	11	L	65	0-1
46	A 6/5	MANSFIELD	2,031	17	12	D	66	1-2

Home 5,372 Average 5,372 Away 3,886

---

35 — A EXETER 11/3 — 0-1
Argyle: Sheffield, O'Sullivan, Beswetherick, Barrett*, Wotton, Taylor, Heathcote, Paterson, McGregor, Hargreaves, Stonebridge, Gritton
Exeter: Matthews, McConnell*, Power, Buckle, Dewhurst^, Curran, Gale, Rees, Alexander, Rowbotham, Bennett; subs Flack/Blake
Taylor 60 | Bennett 34 | Ref: R Styles

Argyle are totally out of sorts during the first half and are booed off at half-time. Sheffield pulls off a string of saves but has little chance with Frankie Bennett's close-range shot. Former City YTS player Taylor scores with an easy header after Heathcote flicked on McGregor's corner.

36 — H LINCOLN 14/3 — 1-1
Argyle: Sheffield, O'Sullivan, Beswetherick, Paterson, Wotton, Taylor, Heathcote, Barrett, McGregor, Hargreaves, Stonebridge; subs Phillips/Gibbs
Lincoln: Marriott, Smith*, Mayo, Barnett, Brown, Welsh, Gordon, Thorpe, Fleming; subs Peacock/Finnigan
Barrett 29 | Gordon 19 | Ref: D Crick

More home points are dropped as Lincoln threaten to overrun Argyle for the second time in three weeks. Gavin Gordon hits the bar and then puts City ahead, slotting low past Sheffield. Barrett's shot deflects into the roof of the net. Gibbs makes a welcome appearance after injury.

37 — H CHELTENHAM 18/3 — 1-0
Argyle: Sheffield, O'Sullivan, Beswetherick, Paterson, Wotton, Taylor, Heathcote, Gritton, McGregor, Hargreaves, Stonebridge; subs Griffin/McAuley
Cheltenham: Book, Duff, Victory, Banks, Freeman, Howells, Milton, Devaney, Yates*
Gritton 43 | Ref: P Alcock

Gritton again shows his goalscoring instinct as his close-range strike is all that separates two well-matched sides. Town manager Steve Cotterill suggests there is an element of offside about the goal. Mark Freeman wastes a late chance when he dithers over a shot in front of an open goal.

38 — A BARNET 21/3 — 0-0
Argyle: Sheffield, O'Sullivan, Beswetherick, Paterson*, Wotton, Taylor, Heathcote, McGregor, Hargreaves, Stonebridge; subs Rowbotham/Belgrave/Gibbs
Barnet: Naisbitt, Stockley, Goodhind*, Basham, Currie, Arber, Phillips^, Searle, King, McGleish, Toms, Wilson
McGleish 65 | Ref: P Robinson

Early leaders Barnet are on the slide but turn their recent poor form around. After a first-half stalemate, Argyle cannot take advantage of playing down the nine-foot Underhill slope. Scott McGleish hooks in the only goal as the Greens' defence fail to clear Frazer Toms' long throw.

39 — A TORQUAY 25/3 — 4-0
Argyle: Sheffield, O'Sullivan, Beswetherick, Ether'ton^, Wotton, Taylor, Heathcote, Rowbotham, McGregor, Hargreaves, Stonebridge; subs Gritton/McCarthy
Torquay: Jones, Holmes, Herrera, Thomas, Russell, Watson, Brandon, Guinan*, Healy, Bedeau*, Hill, Williams, Griffiths
Taylor 24, McGregor 31, 71, 78 | Ref: M Dean

A hail-storm greets the start of the match. McGregor is at his imperious best. His hat-trick is completed when he nonchanantly nutmegs the hapless Stuart Jones. After a rare away win perhaps it is perhaps understandable that three Argyle players are selected for a random drug test.

40 — H NORTHAMPTON 1/4 — 2-1
Argyle: Sheffield, O'Sullivan, Beswetherick, Ether'ton*, Wotton, Taylor, Heathcote, Rowbotham, McGregor, Hargreaves, Stonebridge; subs Gritton/McCarthy
Northampton: Welch, Hendon, Frain, Sampson, Green, Hope^, Savage*, Hunt*, Forrester, Corazzin, Spedding; subs Parrish/Howard/Hodge
McGregor 23, Rowbotham 71 | Corazzin 11 | Ref: P Danson

Carlo Corazzin celebrates in front of the Devonport End after scoring on his return to Home Park. Argyle soon level when McGregor scores his 15th of the season. Ian Sampson's header falls to Rowbotham who, from 35 yards, sidefoots a volley over the despairing Keith Welch.

41 — A MACCLESFIELD 8/4 — 1-4
Argyle: Sheffield, O'Sullivan, Beswetherick, Ether'ton^, Wotton, Taylor, Heathcote, Ro'botham!, McGregor, Hargreaves, Stonebridge; subs McCarthy^/Gritton/Gibbs
Macclesfield: Martin, Rioch, Collins, Tinson, Wood, Askey, Sedgemore, Whitehead, Davies, Durkan", Hitchen
McCarthy 66 | Askey 2, Durkan 15, Whitehead 30, 89 Martin | Ref: J Kirby

Argyle's warm-up jinx continues when Heathcote pulls a stomach muscle and is ruled out. Hodges accuses his side of 'schoolboy defending' as they conceded two early goals. Rowbotham adds to the plight when he receives a red card after appearing to stamp on John Askey (70).

42 — H SWANSEA 15/4 — 1-0
Argyle: Sheffield, O'Sullivan, Beswetherick, Gibbs*, Wotton, Taylor, Heathcote, McCarthy^, McGregor, Hargreaves, Stonebridge, Guinan; subs Leadbitter/Gritton/Phillips
Swansea: Freestone, Jones, Howard, Cusack^, Smith, Bound, Appleby, Thomas, Alsop, Watkin", Coates*; subs Price/O'Leary/Boyd
Barrett 6 | Ref: J Brandwood

Apart from Man Utd, Argyle remain the only unbeaten side at home in the league. Barrett's early header from McGregor's corner proves enough as Swansea leave everyone wondering how they have climbed to second place. Hargreaves is replaced (42), suffering a broken nose.

43 — H ROCHDALE 22/4 — 1-1
Argyle: Sheffield, O'Sullivan, Beswetherick, Gibbs*, Wotton, Taylor, Heathcote, McCarthy, McGregor, Hargreaves, Stonebridge; sub Leadbitter
Rochdale: Edwards, Ford, McAuley, Evans, Monington, Hill, Flitcroft^, Peake, Platt*, Ellis, Jones!; subs Lan'shire/Bettney/McClare
McGregor 64 | Ellis 90 | Ref: M Fletcher

McGregor's goal looks enough. Dale boss Steve Parkin is sent from the bench for foul and abusive language (70). It all goes wrong for Argyle in the last five minutes. McGregor head butts McAuley. Jones gets involved and both are dismissed (85). Tony Ellis then levels in injury-time.

44 — A LEYTON ORIENT 24/4 — 0-3
Argyle: Sheffield, O'Sullivan, Beswetherick, Gibbs, Wotton, Taylor!, McCarthy*, Guinan^, McGregor, Hargreaves, Stonebridge; subs Leadbitter/Gritton/Ether'ton
Leyton Orient: Barrett, Joseph, Lockwood, Walsch'rts*, Smith, McGhee, Beall, Ampadu, Christie, Griffiths", Brkovic; subs Watts/McLean
McGhee 26, Brkovic 78, Christie 81 | Ref: P Joslin

Argyle travel to the capital on the morning of the match to save costs. This lack of preparation is evident as they produce a toothless display. The Pilgrims do not manage a shot on target until the 89th minute. Taylor is dismissed (63) for handling to prevent Iyseden Christie going clear.

45 — H HULL 29/4 — 0-1
Argyle: Sheffield, O'Sullivan, Beswetherick, Leadbitter, Wotton, Taylor, Ether'ton", Guinan^, McGregor, Hargreaves, Stonebridge; subs Gritton/Brimacombe
Hull: Wilson, Swales, Greaves, Edwards, Whitney, Goodison^, Morgan, Brabin, Whitmore, Wood, Brown; subs Scho'f'ld/Br'shaw/Whitw'th
Wood 21 | Ref: S Tomlin

Argyle lose their unbeaten home record with a feeble performance. With nothing to play for, Hull show far more commitment as most of the home side seem to have their mind on summer holidays. Jamie Wood scores the only goal which gave Sheffield no chance.

46 — A MANSFIELD 6/5 — 1-2
Argyle: Sheffield, O'Sullivan, Beswetherick, Adams, Wotton, Taylor, McCall, Guinan, Stonebr'ge*, Hargreaves, Paterson^; subs Gritton/Ashton/Phillips/Wills
Mansfield: Mimms, Asher, Andrews, Sisson, Richardson, Williams", Bacon^, Clarke, Boulding*, Blake, Greenacre; subs Roscoe/Disley/Williamson
Guinan 9, 72 | Andrews 5, Bacon 24 | Ref: S Mathieson

The Stags, without a goal since mid-March, soon find the back of the net through John Andrews. Guinan replies with a header via the crossbar. A static defence allows Danny Bacon to score but Guinan restores some recent lost pride with another goal. Wotton's late free-kick goes close.

NATIONWIDE DIVISION 3 (CUP-TIES) Manager: Kevin Hodges SEASON 1999-2000

Worthington Cup

1:1 A WALSALL 10/8 — Att 15 L, 3,502, 2:18 — F-A 1-4, H-T 1-1
Scorers, Times, and Referees: Stonebridge 43, Bukran 35, Robins 74, Eyjolfsson 84, 88 Walker — Ref: P Walton

Team	1	2	3	4	5	6	7	8	9	10	11	subs used
Argyle	Veysey	Rowbotham	McCall	Leadbitter	Heathcote	Barrett	Bastow	O'Sullivan	McGregor	Hargreaves	Stonebridge	
Walsall	Walker	Marsh	Pointon	Viveash	Barras	Bukran	Wrack	Robins	Rammell*	Keates^	Daley*	Eyjolfsson/Lar'sson/Mavrak

Argyle sport their new all-blue away strip. The Pilgrims look the more threatening and home keeper James Walker wins the man of the match award. Hargreaves shot hits Stonebridge's back and flies in. Icelandic sub Siggi Eyjolfsson gives the Saddlers a flattering first-leg advantage.

1:2 H WALSALL 24/8 — Att 12 L, 1,834, 2:19 — F-A 1-4, H-T 1-3
Scorers, Times, and Referees: Gritton 45 [Eyjolfsson 87] Keates 4, Barras 22, Bukran 44, — Ref: S Dunn — (Argyle lost 2-8 on aggregate)

Team	1	2	3	4	5	6	7	8	9	10	11	subs used
Argyle	Sheffield	Emberson	Ashton	Beswetherick	Barrett	McCall	Bastow	Gritton*	McGregor	Hargreaves	Stonebridge^	McCarthy/Belgrave
Walsall		Marsh	Pointon*	Viveash	Barras!	Bukran	Wrack^	Robins*	Eyjolfsson	Keates	Brissett	Roper/Mavrak/Ricketts

Argyle crash out after failing to match their first-leg performance on a rain-sodden pitch. Two early goals kill the tie. Gritton's clever chip over debutant Carl Emberson provides the one bright moment for the home fans. Tony Barras is dismissed (88) for a professional foul on Belgrave.

FA Cup

1 A BRENTFORD 29/10 — Att 13 D, 4,287, 2:7 — F-A 2-2, H-T 1-0
Scorers, Times, and Referees: Stonebridge 43, McGregor 83, Owusu 56, Marshall 63 — Ref: A Bates

Team	1	2	3	4	5	6	7	8	9	10	11	subs used
Argyle	Sheffield	Rowbotham	Beswetherick	Leadbitter	Heathcote	Taylor	Barrett	O'Sullivan*	McGregor	Hargreaves	Stonebridge	Belgrave
Brentford	Woodman	Boxall	Jenkins*	Quinn	Powell	Marshall	Evans	Mahon	Owusu	Partridge	Scott	Rowlands

Eleven Pilgrims run their socks off to grab an unexpected draw. Stonebridge's header finds the top corner. Argyle's defence is penetrated for the first time in over six hours by Lloyd Owusu's 20-yard shot. Scott Marshall put the home side ahead but McGregor forces the replay.

1R H BRENTFORD 9/11 — Att 8 W, 5,409, 2:7 — F-A 2-1 aet, H-T 0-0
Scorers, Times, and Referees: McGregor 67, 112, Quinn 82 — Ref: A Bates

Team	1	2	3	4	5	6	7	8	9	10	11	subs used
Argyle	Veysey	Ashton*	Beswetherick^	Leadbitter^	Heathcote	Taylor	Barrett	O'Sullivan	McGregor	Hargreaves	Stonebridge	Bastow/McCall
Brentford	Woodman	Boxall	Rowlands*	Quinn	Powell	Marshall	Agyemang^	Mahon	Owusu	Warner*	Scott	Folan/Partridge/Bryan

McGregor is at his best as he torments the Bees. He blasts a volley straight at Andy Woodman but makes amends with a stunning goal, having dummied two players. Robert Quinn sends the game into extra-time. McGregor prevents a penalty shoot-out with a low shot into the corner.

2 H BRIGHTON 19/11 — Att 6 D, 7,414, 11 — F-A 0-0, H-T 0-0
Ref: R Harris

Team	1	2	3	4	5	6	7	8	9	10	11	subs used
Argyle	Sheffield	McCall*	Beswetherick	Leadbitter	Heathcote	Taylor	Barrett^	O'Sullivan	McGregor	Hargreaves	Stonebridge	Bastow/Belgrave
Brighton	Walton	Watson	Campbell	McPherson	Cullip!	Carr*	Freeman!	Rogers	Cameron^	Oatway	Aspinall*	Hobson/Thomas/Mayo

No repeat of the earlier six-goal league thriller as the match degenerates into an ill-tempered affair. Darren Freeman is sent off (61) for spitting at Beswetherick. Danny Cullip follows him (75) for deliberate handball. Manager Micky Adams' post-match press conference lasts 15 seconds.

2R A BRIGHTON 30/11 — Att 7 W, 5,710, 12 — F-A 2-1, H-T 1-0
Scorers, Times, and Referees: Bastow 9, Hargreaves 65, Cullip 63 — Ref: R Harris

Team	1	2	3	4	5	6	7	8	9	10	11	subs used
Argyle	Sheffield	O'Sullivan	Beswetherick^	Leadbitter	Heathcote	Taylor	Barrett	Bastow	McGregor	Hargreaves	Stonebridge	Phillips
Brighton	Walton	Watson	Johnson	Hobson	Crosby	Cullip	Freeman^	Rogers	Cameron^	Oatway	Thomas	Mayo/Ramsay

Bastow's deflected free-kick gives the Greens the perfect start. Argyle's three-man central defence stand firm against a barrage of long throws from Ross Johnson. Danny Cullip equalises but Hargreaves restores the lead with a 25-yard corner into the top corner from McGregor's pass.

3 A READING 10/12 — Att 7 D, 8,536, 2:21 — F-A 1-1, H-T 0-1
Scorers, Times, and Referees: Hargreaves 82, McIntyre 37 — Ref: A Wiley

Team	1	2	3	4	5	6	7	8	9	10	11	subs used
Argyle	Sheffield	O'Sullivan	Beswetherick	Wotton	Heathcote	Taylor	Barrett	McCarthy*	McGregor	Hargreaves	Stonebridge	Gritton
Reading	Howie	Gurney*	Polston	Bernal	Primus	Parkinson	Caskey	Murty	Williams^	McIntyre	Evers^	Sari/Scott/Grant

Argyle pay a first ever visit to the Madejski Stadium and almost pull off a shock win. Murty's cross evades two colleagues but Jim McIntyre makes no mistake. Hargreaves scores with a screamer at the end populated by almost 3,000 Argyle fans. Stonebridge almost gets a late winner.

3R H READING 21/12 — Att 8 W, 8,965, 2:21 — F-A 1-0, H-T 0-0
Scorers, Times, and Referees: Heathcote 88 — Ref: A Wiley

Team	1	2	3	4	5	6	7	8	9	10	11	subs used
Argyle	Veysey	O'Sullivan	Beswetherick	Leadbitter	Heathcote	Taylor	Barrett	McCarthy*	McGregor	Hargreaves	Stonebridge	Gritton
Reading	Howie	Gurney	Polston	Parkinson	Primus	Casper	Murty	Caskey	Williams	Scott	Smith !	Brayson

Argyle find themselves on the rack until the dismissal of Neil Smith (39) who is booked for a foul on O'Sullivan and sent off two minutes later for an off-the-ball shove on Leadbitter. With extra-time looming, Heathcote sticks out a leg to stab the ball home after a goalmouth scramble.

4 H PRESTON 8/1 — Att 8 L, 10,824, 2:2 — F-A 0-3, H-T 0-1
Scorers, Times, and Referees: [Beswetherick 77(og)] O'Sullivan 39(og), Alexander 60p. — Ref: P Durkin

Team	1	2	3	4	5	6	7	8	9	10	11	subs used
Argyle	Sheffield	McCall*	Beswetherick	Leadbitter	Heathcote	Taylor	McCarthy^	O'Sullivan*	McGregor	Hargreaves	Stonebridge	Barrett/Gritton
Preston	Moilanen	Alexander	Edwards	Murdock	Jackson	Gregan	Appleton	Rankine	Nogan*	Macken^	Eyres	Gunnlaugsson/Beresford

David Moyes' in-form side are unbeaten since October and have too much class. O'Sullivan's attempted headed clearance evades Sheffield. The keeper then fouls David Eyres and Alexander scores his seventh penalty of the season. Eyres' corner skims off Beswetherick's head and in.

Division Three

	Team	P	Home W	D	L	F	A	Away W	D	L	F	A	Pts
1	Swansea	46	15	6	2	32	11	9	7	7	19	19	85
2	Rotherham	46	13	5	5	43	17	11	7	5	29	19	84
3	Northampton	46	16	2	5	36	18	9	5	9	27	27	82
4	Darlington	46	13	9	1	43	15	8	7	8	23	21	79
5	Peterboro *	46	14	4	5	39	30	8	8	7	24	24	78
6	Barnet	46	12	6	5	36	24	9	6	8	23	29	75
7	Hartlepool	46	16	1	6	32	17	5	8	10	28	32	72
8	Cheltenham	46	13	4	6	28	17	7	6	10	22	25	70
9	Torquay	46	12	6	5	35	20	7	6	10	27	32	69
10	Rochdale	46	8	7	8	21	25	10	7	6	36	29	68
11	Brighton	46	10	7	6	38	25	9	7	7	26	21	67
12	PLYMOUTH	46	12	10	1	38	18	4	8	11	17	33	66
13	Macclesfield	46	9	7	7	36	30	9	4	10	30	31	65
14	Hull	46	7	8	8	26	23	8	6	9	17	20	59
15	Lincoln	46	11	6	6	38	23	4	8	11	29	46	59
16	Southend	46	11	5	7	37	31	4	6	13	16	30	56
17	Mansfield	46	9	6	8	33	26	7	2	14	17	39	56
18	Halifax	46	7	5	11	22	24	8	4	11	22	34	54
19	Leyton Orient	46	7	7	9	22	22	6	6	11	25	30	52
20	York	46	7	10	6	21	21	5	6	12	18	32	52
21	Exeter	46	8	6	9	27	30	3	5	15	19	42	44
22	Shrewsbury	46	6	12	5	20	27	4	7	12	20	40	40
23	Carlisle	46	6	8	9	23	27	3	4	16	19	48	39
24	Chester	46	5	5	13	20	36	5	4	14	24	43	39
		1104	246	146	160	746	557	160	146	246	557	746	1510

* promoted
after play-offs

Odds & ends

Double wins: (0).
Double defeats: (0).

Won from behind: (2) Macclesfield, Northampton.
Lost from in front: (1) Southend.

High spots: Fine home record.
Good FA Cup run to the fourth round.
Superb 4-0 win at local rivals Torquay, thanks to brilliant hat-trick by Paul McGregor.
Exhilarating 4-1 home win over leaders Barnet.
Selection of Ian Stonebridge for England Under-18 side.

Low spots: Inept late-season performances with play-offs still possible.
Loss of promising youngster Darren Bastow due to off the field problems.
Ongoing crowd protests against Chairman Dan McCauley.

Player of the Year: Paul McGregor.
Ever presents: (0).
Hat-tricks: (2) Paul McGregor (2).
Leading scorer: Paul McGregor (16).

Appearances and Goals

Player	Lge	Sub	LC	Sub	FAC	Sub	Goals Lge	LC	FAC	Tot
Adams, Steve	1									
Ashton, Jon	5	3	1		1					
Barlow, Martin	1	1								
Barrett, Adam	38	4	2		6	1	3			3
Bastow, Darren	7	6	2		3	2	1		1	2
Belgrave, Barrington	2	13			1	7				
Beswetherick, Jon	44	1	1		7					
Etherington, Craig	4	1								
Gibbs, Paul	3	4								
Gritton, Martin	14	16	1			3	6	1		7
Guinan, Steve	8						2			2
Hargreaves, Chris	44		2		7		3	2		5
Heathcote, Mick	27	2	1		7		1		1	2
Leadbitter, Chris	28	3	1		6		2			2
McCall, Steve	14	2	2		2	1	1			1
McCarthy, Sean	21	8	1		3		6			6
McGregor, Paul	44	2			7		13		3	16
Middleton, Craig	6						2			2
Morrison-Hill, Jamie		1								
O'Sullivan, Wayne	45		2		7		2			2
Paterson, Scott	5									
Phillips, Lee	3	14	1			1				
Rowbotham, Jason	7	4	1		1		1			1
Sheffield, Jon	41	1	1		5					
Stonebridge, Ian	27	4	2		7	5	9	1	1	11
Taylor, Craig	41		2		5	2	3			3
Veysey, Ken	5	1	1		1					
Wills, Kevin		2								
Wotton, Paul	21	2	1							
29 players used	506	92	22	2	77	10	55	2	8	65

NATIONWIDE DIVISION 3 — Manager: Hodges > Paul Sturrock — SEASON 2000-01

No	Date	Team	Att	Pos	Pt	F-A	H-T	Scorers, Times, and Referees	1	2	3	4	5	6	7	8	9	10	11	subs used
1	H 12/8	LEYTON ORIENT	5,649	18	0	0-1	0-1	Griffiths 27 — Ref: P Armstrong	Sheffield	O'Sullivan	Lockwood	Barrett	Wotton	McCarthy	Fleming	Barlow	Stonebridg'"	Guinan	Peake^	Phillips L/Phillips M
		(Leyton Orient)							*Bayes*	*Dorrian**	*McBhee!*	*Smith*	*Harris*	*Walschaerts^/Martin^*			*Griffiths"*	*Garcia*	*Brkovic"*	*Downer/Watts/Brissett*
2	A 19/8	HULL	5,431	19	1	1-1	0-1	Gritton 90, Whitmore 16 — Ref: A Bates	Sheffield	O'Sullivan	Besweth'ck	Barrett	Wotton	Fleming	McCarthy*	Barlow	Guinan^	Phillips L*	Phillips M	Stonebridge/Gritton/Taylor
		(Hull)							*Bracey*	*Edwards*	*Harper^*	*Goodison*	*Whittle*	*Greaves*	*Swales*	*Whitmore*	*Wood"*	*Eyre^*	*Philpott*	*Brown/Harris/Brightwell*
3	H 26/8	MANSFIELD	4,069	11	4	2-0	0-0	Hicks 52(og), McGregor 71 — Ref: W Jordan	Sheffield	O'Sullivan	Besweth'ck	Barrett	Taylor	Fleming	Barlow	McCarthy^	McGregor	Phillips L*	Peake^	Guinan/Nancekivell
		(Mansfield)							*Bowling*	*Asher*	*Andrews*	*Williams^*	*Hicks*	*Robinson*	*Corden"*	*Clarke!*	*Bradley*	*Blake*	*Greenacre*	*Sisson/Bacon*
4	A 29/8	DARLINGTON	4,415	15	4	0-1	0-1	Kaak 4 — Ref: J Robinson	Sheffield	O'Sullivan	Beswe'k*	Barrett	Taylor	Fleming	Phillips M	Barlow	McGregor^	Guinan	Phillips L*	Peake/Gritton/Nancekivell
		(Darlington)							*Collett*	*Elliott!*	*Heck'gbot'm Liddle*		*Aspin"*	*Reed*	*Gray*	*Himsworth*	*Nogan^*	*Naylor*	*Kaak^*	*Hjorth/Angel/Williamson*
5	H 2/9	MACCLESFIELD	3,888	18	4	0-1	0-0	Barker 84 — Ref: M North	Sheffield	O'Sullivan	Beswet'ck	Barrett	Taylor	Fleming	Phillips M	Barlow	McCarthy	Guinan*	Peake^	Gritton/Nancekivell
		(Macclesfield)							*Bullock*	*Hitchen*	*Ingram"*	*Collins*	*Tinson*	*Wood*	*Askey*	*Sedgemore*	*Barker"*	*Twynham**	*Durkan*	*Munroe/Whitehead/Abbey*
6	A 9/9	SOUTHEND	3,417	21	5	2-2	2-1	McCarthy 13, McGregor 38, Fitzpatrick 9, Houghton 73 — Ref: D Crick	Sheffield	O'Sullivan	Beswet'ck	Barrett	Taylor	Fleming	Phillips M*	Barlow	McCarthy*	McGregor*	Peake^	Wotton/Stonebridge/Guinan
		(Southend)							*Woodman*	*Booty"*	*Searle*	*Whelan*	*Raget*	*Morley"*	*Lee^*	*Mahar*	*Carruthers*	*Fitzpatrick*	*Connelly*	*Tinkler/Houghton/Cross*
7	A 12/9	SHREWSBURY	2,361	22	5	1-4	0-2	Peake 67, Peake 9(og), Jemson 44, 65, [Brown 53] — Ref: B Curson	Sheffield	O'Sullivan	Beswet'ck	Barrett!	Taylor*	Fleming	Phillips M	Barlow	McCarthy	McGregor	Peake	Wotton/Guinan
		(Shrewsbury)							*Dunbavin*	*Jenkins*	*Drysdale*	*Peer*	*Davidson*	*Hughes*	*Brown"*	*Murray*	*Freestone*	*Jemson**	*Aiston^*	*Wilding/Jagielka/Lowe*
8	H 16/9	CARLISLE	3,378	18	8	2-0	2-0	McCarthy 9, Peake 17 — Ref: S Dunn	Sheffield	O'Sullivan	Beswet'k*	Barrett	Mardon	Fleming	Phillips M	Barlow	McCarthy	McGregor	Peake	Wotton
		(Carlisle)							*Weaver*	*Birch*	*Hemmings"*	*Whitehead*	*Winstanley*	*Darby**	*Soley*	*Stevens*	*Hayes*	*Dobie*	*Carss*	*Squires^/Pitts/Lee*
9	A 23/9	CHELTENHAM	3,665	19	8	2-5	0-4	McCarthy 46, Mardon 55 [Howells 36], Griffin 8, Devaney 24, 41, 79p — Ref: P Joslin	Sheffield	O'Sullivan"	Beswet'k*	Barrett	Mardon	Leadbitter	Fleming"	Barlow	McCarthy	McGregor	Peake	Guinan/Wotton/Gritton
		(Cheltenham)							*Book*	*Duff"*	*Walker*	*Banks*	*Freeman*	*Griffin*	*Howells"*	*Devaney*	*Alsop*	*McAuley**	*Yates*	*Brough/White/Bloomer*
10	H 30/9	BARNET	3,423	20	8	2-3	1-0	McCarthy 45, Guinan 79, Richards 49, 59, Arber 71 — Ref: M Cooper	Sheffield	Fleming	Leadbitter	O'Sullivan	Mardon	Taylor	Phillips M	Barlow"	McCarthy	McGregor*	Peake*	St'bridge/Guinan/Nancekivell
		(Barnet)							*Naisbitt*	*Stockley*	*Goodhind*	*Bell*	*Heald*		*Currie*	*Doolan*	*Richards*	*McBleish**	*Toms^*	*Strevens/Niven*
11	A 7/10	CHESTERFIELD	4,285	21	8	1-2	0-1	McGregor 47, Parrish 38, Reeves 61p — Ref: C Webster	Sheffield	O'Sullivan"	Beswet'ck	Leadbitter	Heathcote	Taylor	Phillips M	Barlow"	McCarthy	McGregor^	Wotton	Peake/Guinan/Wills
		(Chesterfield)							*Pollitt*	*Williams"*	*Edwards*	*Tuthill*	*Blatherwick Breckin*		*Ebdon*	*Parrish*	*Reeves*	*Payne*	*Willis*	*Ingledow/Howard*

Match commentaries:

1. Without five regulars through injury or suspension. Argyle start the season in lethargic fashion. Young debutant Chris Dorrian is outstanding for the O's and he has a hand in the only goal. David McGhee is sent off (88) for tripping Lee Phillips, having been booked earlier in the game.

2. Hull's 'Reggae Boyz' Goodison and Whitmore return from Jamaican World Cup duty only a few hours before the match but are outstanding. Whitmore puts Brian Little's side ahead and Whitmore almost chips Sheffield from 25 yards. Gritton rescues a point with a shot in injury-time.

3. The Stags are forced to wear Argyle's change blue kit after their white shirts clash. Taylor's wayward header is deflected past his own keeper by Stuart Hicks. McCarthy's header sets up McGregor to volley number two. Darrell Clarke is sent off (79) for a late challenge on McGregor.

4. Dutch striker Anton Kaak scores his first goal for Darlo when he deflects Stuart Elliott's 25-yard shot. Elliott and Fleming are booked after a first-half fracas and Elliott is dismissed (46) for failing to retreat 10 yards at a free-kick. Guinan hesitates over a last-minute opportunity.

5. Last season's invincibility at home seems a distant memory as Peter Davenport's Silkmen sink Argyle. Without the injured McGregor, the Pilgrims never look like scoring despite having most of the play. Richie Barker's emphatic strike gives the Pilgrims a lesson in finishing.

6. The Shrimpers take an early lead when no one cuts out David Lee's cross and Trevor Fitzpatrick can't fail to miss. Andy Woodman blasts a clearance at McCarthy and the ball flies in off his back. McGregor heads over Woodman. Transfer-listed Scott Houghton levels from 25 yards.

7. Argyle overcome the fuel crisis but by the end are taunted by chants of "You should have saved the petrol!". Peake gets the final touch to Chris Freestone's shot. Taylor is stretchered off with ankle damage (13). Already booked, Barrett is red-carded when he clatters into Freestone (88).

8. Mardon arrives on loan from West Brom and plays his first match for 17 months. A fine strike from McCarthy and a clever lob from 20 yards by Peake give the under-pressure Hodges a crucial win in his 100th league match in charge. Phillips continues his impressive start to the season.

9. Anthony Griffin's 30-yard volley sparks first-half humiliation for Argyle who have still yet to win at Whaddon Road. McCarthy and Mardon briefly threaten a revival. Barrett is penalised for handling whilst lying on the ground. Martin Devaney completes his hat-trick from the spot.

10. Another home defeat seals Hodges' fate as he is dismissed in midweek. Only McCarthy and Phillips emerge with any credit as the midfield and defence seem non-existent. John Still's men take full advantage in the second half. Boos and jeers ring around Home Park at the final whistle.

11. Kevin Summerfield takes temporary charge for a daunting visit to the runaway leaders. The return of Heathcote after a seven-month absence seems to inspire Argyle. David Reeves' penalty, after Sheffield brings down Roger Willis gives Nicky Law's side the expected three points.

12 — H BLACKPOOL — 14/10

Pos	Pld			Result	HT
19	27	11	W	2-0	0-0

Att: 3,651
Wotton 58p, McGregor 86
Ref: M Warren

Argyle: Sheffield, O'Sullivan, Beswetherick, Leadbitter, Heathcote, Taylor, Barlow, Guinan, Stonebridge, McGregor*, Wotton — Phillips L
Blackpool: Barnes, Coid, Jaszczun, Bushell, Jones, Reid, Collins, Simpson, Ormerod*, Murphy, Maley" — Nowland*/Clarkson/Wellens

A workmanlike performance sees Argyle climb above fellow strugglers Blackpool. Wotton scores Argyle's first penalty for almost 18 months after McGregor was fouled by Brian Reid. Barnes is embarrassed as a clearance bounces over his head and McGregor is left with an empty net.

13 — H SCUNTHORPE — 17/10

Pos	Pld			Result	HT
18	10	14	W	1-0	1-0

Att: 3,437
McGregor 45
Ref: P Walton

Argyle: Sheffield, O'Sullivan, Beswetherick, Leadbitter, Heathcote^, Taylor, Barlow, Phillips M, McCarthy, McGregor*, Wotton — Guinan/Adams
Scunthorpe: Evans, Woodward*, Dawson, Stanton, Wilcox", Larusson, Hodges, Graves", Ipoua, Stamp, Calvo-Garcia — Jackson/Thom/Morrison

Summerfield's managerial aspirations are boosted by another three points as Argyle's climb from the bottom continues. A well-organised defence is finally broken down when McGregor flashes a header past Tom Evans from Phillips' cross. Heathcote goes off injured at half-time.

14 — A HARTLEPOOL — 21/10

Pos	Pld			Result	HT
19	17	15	D	1-1	0-1

Att: 2,581
Nancekivell 69, Henderson 22
Ref: E Wolstenholme

Argyle: Sheffield, O'Sullivan, Beswetherick, Leadbitter*, Adams, Taylor, Phillips M, Barlow, McCarthy, McGregor, Wotton — Nancekivell
Hartlepool: Williams, Knowles, Shilton, Strodder, Westwood, Baker, Fitzpatrick, Miller, Sperrevik, Henderson, Stephenson

Argyle fall behind for the seventh successive away match when Kevin Henderson scores after a counter attack. Nancekivell scores his first ever league goal after the bustling McCarthy upset the home defence. McGregor heads against the bar and McCarthy wastes a late chance.

15 — A BRIGHTON — 24/10

Pos	Pld			Result	HT
20	2	15	L	0-2	0-1

Att: 6,724
Carpenter 37, Zamora 85
Ref: R Harris

Argyle: Sheffield, O'Sullivan^, Beswetherick, Leadbitter, Adams, Taylor, Phillips M*, Barlow, McCarthy^, McGregor, Wotton — Guinan/Nancekivell
Brighton: Kuipers, Watson, Mayo, Culip, Wicks, Carpenter*, Zamora, Rogers", Hart^, Datway, Jones — Steele/Brooker/Melton

Hodges, in for the injured Sheffield, punches a corner to Richard Carpenter who lashes a 25-yard shot back past the debutant. McCarthy is yellow carded in the first half and then sent off following a clash with Carpenter (80). The Brighton man goes unpunished despite lashing out.

16 — A TORQUAY — 4/11

Pos	Pld			Result	HT
20	22	16	D	1-1	1-0

Att: 3,936
McCarthy 5, Williams 63
Ref: P Danson

Argyle: Hodges, Wotton, Beswetherick, Leadbitter, Adams, Taylor, Phillips M*, Barlow, McCarthy^, McGregor, Phillips L^ — Guinan/Peake/Wills
Torquay: Northmore, Tully, Holmes, Aggrey, Watson, Rowbotham, Ashington*, Ford, Mendy", Williams, Hill — O'Brien/Sissoko

New manager Paul Sturrock watches from the directors' box as Summerfield again takes charge. McCarthy taps in but then goes off (26) with a suspected broken arm after an accidental clash with Watson. Williams equalises and Mick O'Brien fails to latch on to Hodges' mis-kick.

17 — A EXETER — 2/12

Pos	Pld			Result	HT
20	21	19	W	2-0	0-0

Att: 5,145
McCarthy 47, 75
Ref: P Durkin

Argyle: Sheffield, Worrell, Beswetherick, Wotton, Taylor, Friio, Phillips M^, O'Sullivan, McCarthy*, McGregor*, Fleming — Stonebridge/McGlinchey
Exeter: V Heusden*, Campbell, Buckle, Curran, Hutchings, Roscoe, Rapley, Zabek^, Read", Roberts — Fraser/Tierney/Francis

With Sturrock's warning, 'change your ideas or change clubs' still ringing in their ears after the cup defeat by Chester, Argyle show some form again. McCarthy heads the opener and is then the unlikely winner in a chase for the ball with Jamie Campbell. City hit the woodwork twice.

18 — H YORK — 16/12

Pos	Pld			Result	HT
18	19	22	W	1-0	1-0

Att: 3,830
Taylor 3
Ref: M Jones

Argyle: Sheffield, Worrell, Beswetherick, Friio, Wotton, Taylor, Phillips M*, O'Sullivan*, McCarthy^, McGregor, Fleming — Gritton^/StBridge/Heathcote
York: Fettis, Edmondson, Potter, Sertori, Bower, Iwelumo, Agnew, Hulme*, Mathie^, Alcide^, McNiven — Jordan/Patterson

City boss Terry Dolan leaves in disbelief after seeing his side fail to score despite 18 attempts on goal. Taylor's 30-yard free-kick hits a divot and bounces over Fettis's arm. With Argyle struggling, O'Sullivan kicks out at Kevin Hulme under the nose of the referee and is sent off (67).

19 — A HALIFAX — 23/12

Pos	Pld			Result	HT
18	20	22	L	0-2	0-1

Att: 1,670
Stoneman 6, Kerrigan 65
Ref: J Winter

Argyle: Sheffield, Heathcote, Beswetherick, Friio, Wotton, Taylor, Phillips M*, O'Sullivan*, McCarthy, McGregor, Fleming — McGlinchey^/Fleming/Adams/Stonebridge
Halifax: Butler, Wilder, Murphy, Mitchell, Stoneman, Parnaby, Wainwright*, Middleton, Jones, Kerrigan, Thompson — Reilly

Another long trip north fails to bring any reward. Paul Stoneman thumps in the first. With the defence appealing for offside, Steve Kerrigan latches onto Chris Wilder's through ball. French triallist Friio is impressive. Wotton's stinging drive is parried by Lee Butler as fog descends.

20 — H CARDIFF — 26/12

Pos	Pld			Result	HT
17	4	25	W	2-1	0-1

Att: 8,543
McCarthy 74, 86, Fortune-West 15
Ref: D Crick

Argyle: Sheffield, Worrell, Beswetherick, Friio, Wotton, Taylor, Phillips M, O'Sullivan, McCarthy, McGregor, Wills* — Fleming
Cardiff: Walton, Low, Gabbidon, Evans, Eckhardt, Young, Earnshaw", Boland*, Brayson^, Fortune-West, Legg — McCulloch/Weston/Gordon

Alan Cork's City lose their ten-match unbeaten record on a heavily-sanded pitch. Leo Fortune-West beats Sheffield to a cross. McGregor's shot appears to be going wide but McCarthy diverts it past Walton. The striker's soft header then finds its way through a crowd of players.

21 — A MANSFIELD — 6/1

Pos	Pld			Result	HT
16	15	26	D	0-0	0-0

Att: 2,321
Ref: M Pike

Argyle: Sheffield, Worrell, Beswetherick, Leadbitter, Wotton, Taylor, Phillips M*, Fleming!, McCarthy, McGregor, Fleming — Pemberton/Hassall/Williams
Mansfield: Mimms, Pemberton^, Williams, Hassall, Hicks, Robinson, Corden*, Hjorth^, Barrett, Boulding, Greenacre — Bacon/Disley

Argyle adopt a safety first policy to grab an away point but the plan nearly comes unstuck when Mark Blake heads over from six yards with the goal at his mercy. Fleming is booked (71) and then sent off (89) for kicking the ball away. Adam Barrett wins the man of the match award.

22 — H DARLINGTON — 13/1

Pos	Pld			Result	HT
16	18	27	D	1-1	1-0

Att: 4,278
Taylor 39, Williams 68
Ref: D Gallagher

Argyle: Sheffield, Worrell, Beswetherick, Leadbitter, Wotton, Taylor, Phillips M^, Fleming, McCarthy, McGregor, Fleming — McGlinchey/Gritton/Stonebridge/Wills
Darlington: Collett, Elliott, Heck'gbot'm, Liddle, Kitty, Gray, Hodgson^, Brumwell, Hjorth, McMahon, Williams — Reed/Naylor/Marsh

Taylor again shows his prowess from free-kicks as he powers a low shot past Andy Collett. John Williams equalises after a frantic goalmouth scramble. The ref plays advantage instead of awarding a penalty when McGregor is pulled back by Craig Liddle but McCarthy skies his shot.

23 — H LINCOLN — 16/1

Pos	Pld			Result	HT
14	16	30	W	1-0	0-0

Att: 4,139
Stonebridge 90
Ref: K Hill

Argyle: Sheffield, Worrell, Beswetherick, Friio, Wotton, Taylor, Phillips M, O'Sullivan, McCarthy^, McGregor, Stonebridge — StBridge/Gritton/McGlinchey
Lincoln: Day, Smith, Mayo, Barnett!, Holmes, Finnigan, Walker, Schofield, Peacock, Thorpe, Garratt^ — Perkins

The attendance is boosted by a 'Kid for a Quid' scheme. Lincoln frustrate Argyle for long periods. Jason Barnett is sent off (81) for a second foul on Phillips. Stonebridge scores in the second minute of injury-time. Imps' boss, Phil Stant and his assistant, George Foster, lose their jobs.

NATIONWIDE DIVISION 3 — Manager: Hodges > Paul Sturrock — SEASON 2000-01

No	Date		Att	Pos	Opp Pos	Pt	Res	F-A	H-T	Scorers, Times, and Referees
24	20/1	A CARDIFF	9,157	15	3	30	L	1-4	0-1	Stonebridge 51 [McCulloch 90] / Earnshaw 38, 88, Fortune-West 69. Ref: M Cooper
25	27/1	H HALIFAX	4,176	14	20	33	W	1-0	1-0	O'Sullivan 33. Ref: A Bates
26	30/1	H KIDDERMINSTER	5,332	10	12	36	W	4-0	1-0	Taylor 38, St'nbr'ge 62, 80, Wotton 90p. Ref: R Beeby
27	3/2	A MACCLESFIELD	1,881	11	14	36	L	1-3	0-0	Stonebridge 50 [Priest 70, 90, Whitehead 73]. Ref: R Furmandiz
28	17/2	A CARLISLE	3,592	16	23	37	D	1-1	0-0	Frio 53 [Stevens 84]. Ref: A Kaye
29	20/2	H SHREWSBURY	5,007	13	19	40	W	3-1	0-0	Frio 56, Stonebridge 73, 78 [Rodgers 87]. Ref: L Cable
30	24/2	H CHELTENHAM	5,209	13	10	41	D	0-0	0-0	Ref: P Taylor
31	3/3	A BARNET	2,879	13	16	42	D	1-1	1-0	Wotton 13 [Currie 61]. Ref: C Roy
32	6/3	A BLACKPOOL	4,570	14	5	42	L	0-1	0-0	[Walker 90]. Ref: M Clattenburg
33	10/3	H CHESTERFIELD	5,399	13	1	45	W	3-0	1-0	Frio 20, Phillips 61, McCarthy 80. Ref: M Cowburn
34	13/3	H HULL	5,482	12	7	46	D	1-1	1-0	McGregor 3 [Wotton 84(og)]. Ref: R Styles

Line-ups (Argyle top line / opponents in italics)

#	1	2	3	4	5	6	7	8	9	10	11	subs used
24	Sheffield / *Walton*	Worrell / *Gabbidon^*	Besweth'ck / *Brazier*	Frio / *Harper !*	Wotton / *Young**	Taylor / *Weston*	O'Sullivan* / *Low*	Wilkie* / *Boland"*	McCarthy ! / *Bowen*	Stonebridge^ / *Fortune-West Legg*	McGilchrey! / *Phillips M*	/ *Brayson/Earnshaw/McCulloch*
25	Sheffield / *Butler*	Worrell / *Clarke C*	Besweth'ck / *Murphy*	Frio / *Mitchell*	Wotton / *Clarke M*	Taylor / *Hawe*	Phillips M* / *Herbert*	O'Sullivan / *Middleton*	Stonebridge / *Jones**	McGilchrey / *Reilly**	Barlow / *Thompson Fitzpatrick*	
26	Sheffield / *Brock*	Worrell / *Clarkson*	Besweth'ck / *Stamps**	Frio / *Smith*	Wotton / *Hinton*	Taylor / *Shail*	Phillips M / *Bennett*	O'Sullivan / *Durnin*	Stonebridge'' / *Broughton*	McGregor* / *Doyle*	McGilchrey^ / *MacKenzie Home*	McCarthy/Barlow/Guinan
27	Sheffield / *Bullock*	Worrell / *Adams*	Besweth'ck* / *Hitchens**	Frio / *Ingram*	Wotton / *Tinson*	Taylor / *Rioch*	Phillips M* / *Keen*	O'Sullivan / *Priest*	Stonebridge / *Askey**	McGregor / *Durkan*	Wilkie / *Tracey**	Guinan/Barlow / *Collins/Glover/Whitehead*
28	Sheffield / *Glennon*	Worrell / *Birch*	Besweth'ck / *Madison*	Frio / *Whitehead*	Wotton / *Carr**	Taylor / *Morley*	Fleming / *Soley*	O'Sullivan / *Stevens*	Stonebridge* / *Dabie*	McGregor* / *Prakas^*	Barlow / *Galloway*	Guinan/Adams / *Hemmings/Halliday/Connelly*
29	Sheffield / *Dunbavin*	Worrell / *Davidson*	Besweth'ck / *Hanmer*	Frio / *Collins*	Wotton / *McCann Redmile !*	Taylor / *Howarth*	Phillips M* / *Peer**	O'Sullivan^ / *Tolley*	Stonebridge'' / *Jemson*	McGregor / *Rodgers*	Barlow / *Aston**	Guinan/Betts/Meaker / *Seabury/Murray/Lowe*
30	Sheffield / *Book*	Worrell / *Goodridge**	Besweth'ck / *Walker*	Frio / *Banks*	Wotton / *Howells*	Taylor / *Alsop*	Phillips M* / *Wilding**	O'Sullivan^ / *Iwelumo**	Stonebridge / *McAuley**	McGregor* / *Yates*	McGilchrey^ / *Meaker*	Larrieu/Meaker / *White/Devaney/Bloomer*
31	Larrieu / *Harrison*	Worrell* / *Gledhill*	Besweth'ck / *Goodhind*	Frio / *Niven*	Wotton / *Heald*	Taylor / *Arber*	Phillips M* / *Currie*	Javary / *Gower*	Stonebridge* / *Strevens*	McGregor* / *Cattee**	McGilchrey* / *Brown*	McGlinchey/Phillips M/Adams / *Richards*
32	Larrieu / *Barnes*	Adams / *Collins*	Besweth'ck / *Jaszczun*	Frio / *Bushell*	Wotton / *Shittu*	Taylor / *Reid*	McCarthy / *Milligan**	O'Sullivan / *Simpson*	Stonebridge / *Ormerod*	McGregor / *Murphy*	McGilchrey / *Coid*	Walker
33	Larrieu / *Pollitt*	Elliott / *Breckin*	Besweth'ck / *Edwards*	Frio / *Payne*	Wotton / *Blatherwick Parrish*	Taylor / *Parrish*	Phillips M* / *Ebdon*	O'Sullivan^ / *Williams*	McCarthy / *Reeves*	McGregor* / *Beckett*	Betts* / *Richardson^*	Stonebridge/Meaker/Evers / *Howard*
34	Larrieu / *Bracey*	Elliott / *Edwards*	Besweth'ck / *Whitney*	Frio / *Swailes**	Wotton / *Whittle*	Taylor / *Brabin*	Phillips M* / *Mann*	O'Sullivan^ / *Whitmore^*	McCarthy / *Brown*	McGregor^ / *Francis*	Betts* / *Philpott*	Stonebridge/Meaker/Evers / *Eyre/Rowe*

Match reports

24 — Cardiff: McCarthy is sent off (8) for elbowing Scott Young. Earnshaw scores within a minute of coming on. James Harper gets a red card after kicking out at McGinchey (59) who follows him down the tunnel for the foul. Despite the scoreline Argyle impress and Lee Wilkie has a fine debut.

25 — Halifax: Paul Bracewell's side show plenty of spirit but lack a cutting edge without suspended top scorer, Steve Kerrigan. O'Sullivan heads his first goal of the season from Phillips' cross and is denied another by a fine double save from Lee Butler. Stonebridge hits the post with a low shot.

26 — Kidderminster: Harriers' boss Jan Molby praises Argyle as the best side he has seen this season. Taylor blasts home a free-kick from 35 yards after it has been advanced 10 yards for dissent. Phillips torments the defence. Wotton's penalty after Mark Shail's foul on Guinan completes a convincing win.

27 — Macclesfield: Off-colour Argyle take an unlikely lead when Stonebridge evades Rae Ingram to fire past Tony Bullock. The Silkmen, under caretaker boss Gil Prescott, eventually make their dominance pay off to leave the Pilgrims still looking for their first away win outside Devon for 15 months.

28 — Carlisle: On a stamina-sapping pitch, Frio arrives late in the box to head his first Argyle goal on his 28th birthday. An elusive away win looks on the cards until Ian Atkins brings on three attackers. Tony Hemmings outpaces Ian Stevens to stab home from close range.

29 — Shrewsbury: After an evenly matched first half, Frio scores again with another header. The sending off of burly defender Matt Redmile (69) suddenly gives Stonebridge more freedom and he quickly makes the game safe. Luke Rodgers curls a lovely shot past Sheffield with the outside of his boot.

30 — Cheltenham: Cheltenham's skipper, Chris Banks, plays only a week after a cartilage operation. Sheffield's dodgy back fails to last the 90 minutes to give Larrieu his debut, although the Frenchman is not seriously tested.

31 — Barnet: Argyle field three Frenchmen. Frio rolls a free-kick to Wotton who blasts past Lee Harrison. Worrell pays a high price for a last-ditch tackle on Danny Brown as he breaks an ankle. Former Argyle loanee Darren Currie leaves Larrieu helpless with a 30-yard volley into the top corner.

32 — Blackpool: Tangerines' boss Steve McMahon blasts Argyle's defensive tactics. Substitute Richard Walker turns from villain to hero as he firstly blasts a shot high over the bar from six yards but then scores with an acrobatic header in injury-time. Adams handles the tricky Paul Simpson well.

33 — Chesterfield: Argyle raise their game against the leaders who are making headlines off the pitch as well after being investigated for financial irregularities. Elliott, sent off against Argyle earlier in the season, has a good debut. Frio gets another header. McCarthy rounds it off after a keeper's error.

34 — Hull: Errors dominate. Whittle and Whitney leave the ball to each other and McGregor pounces to end his goal famine. Wotton and Elliott tangle in the six-yard box and the ball goes in with no Hull player near the action. The normally influential Whitmore plays despite a recent car crash.

Season Match Record (matches 35–46)

No	V	Opponent	Date	Result	Score	Att	Opp Pos	Pos	Pts
35	A	SCUNTHORPE	17/3	L	1-4	3,844	9	12	46
36	H	HARTLEPOOL	24/3	L	0-2	4226	4	13	46
37	A	YORK	31/3	W	2-1	3,083	18	13	49
38	H	EXETER	7/4	W	1-0	8,671	17	13	52
39	A	LEYTON ORIENT	10/4	D	1-1	4,520	5	12	53
40	H	BRIGHTON	14/4	L	0-2	7,490	2	12	53
41	A	KIDDERMINSTER	16/4	L	0-3	3,321	14	13	53
42	H	TORQUAY	21/4	W	3-1	5,711	24	12	56
43	H	SOUTHEND	24/4	D	3-3	3,619	11	12	57
44	A	LINCOLN	28/4	L	1-2	4,277	20	12	57
45	A	ROCHDALE	1/5	L	1-2	4,027	7	12	57
46	H	ROCHDALE	5/5	D	0-0	5,125	8	12	58

Home Average 4,945 — Away 3,960

---

35 — SCUNTHORPE (A) 17/3, L 1-4
Stonebridge 90 [Quailey 62, 90, Calvo-Garcia 7, Dawson 31] — Ref: H Webb
- XI: Larrieu, Elliott, Besweth'ck, Frio, Wotton, Taylor, Evers, O'Sullivan, McCarthy, Meaker
- Opp: Evans, Harsley, Dawson, Cotterill, Jackson^, Larusson^, Quailey, Sheldon*, Graves, Torpey
- Subs: McGlinchey, St'bridge/Phillips M/McGregr — Calvo-Garcia, Hodges/Wilcox/Rapley

Alex Calvo-Garcia deflects Bjarni Larusson's shot. Alex Dawson heads in from almost on the goal-line. Despite good work by Meaker, Brian Laws' men extend their lead through Brian Quailey's drive. Stonebridge replies in stoppage time but Quailey still finds time to get a second.

36 — HARTLEPOOL (H) 24/3, L 0-2
[Miller 28, Lormor 43] — Ref: M North
- XI: Larrieu, Elliott, Besweth'ck, Frio, Wotton, Taylor, Meaker^, O'Sullivan, Stonebridge^, Evans, Javary
- Opp: Williams, Knowles^, Robinson, Barron, Westwood, Sharp, Clark, Miller, Henderson*, Stephenson
- Subs: McCarthy/Phillips M/Evers — Midgley/Aspin

Evans fails to make any impact on his return following a £30k transfer from Bristol Rovers. Taylor treads on the ball and the highly rated Tommy Miller makes no mistake. Taylor is at fault again for the second when he fails to cut out a cross and veteran Tony Lormor can't miss.

37 — YORK (A) 31/3, W 2-1
Evans 45, 51 [Bower 34] — Ref: M Brandwood
- XI: Larrieu, Elliott, Besweth'ck, Adams, Wotton, Taylor, Phillips M, Javary^, Stonebridge, Evans^
- Opp: Fettis, Jones, Potter, Hocking", Bower, Cooper, Richardson^, Brass, Nugan, Alcide*
- Subs: McGlinchey, O'Sullivan/McGregor — McNiven/Mathie/Basham

McGregor announces that he is to leave at the end of the season. Evans is in inspired form and cancels out Mark Bower's opener on the stroke of half-time. The striker scores a second by beating Fettis to give Argyle their first league win outside Devon in 30 matches.

38 — EXETER (H) 7/4, W 1-0
Friio 20 — Ref: G Cain
- XI: Larrieu, Elliott, Besweth'ck, Frio", Wotton, Taylor, Phillips M, O'Sullivan, Stonebridge, Evans^, McGregor^
- Opp: V Heusdan, Epesse-Titi, Power, Roscoe*, Campbell, Buckle, Zabek, Ampadu^, Flack, Birch
- Subs: McGlinchey, McCarthy/St'bridge/Adams — Burrows/Spencer

Argyle gain another hard-working if unspectacular derby victory. On loan Gary Birch lobs Larrieu but the ball hits the bar and rebounds into the grateful keeper's arms. Friio ghosts in for another headed goal but is stretchered off on the stroke of half time with a badly bruised ankle.

39 — LEYTON ORIENT (A) 10/4, D 1-1
Meaker 27 [Watts 51] — Ref: A Hall
- XI: Larrieu, Elliott, Besweth'ck, Adams, Wotton, Taylor, Meaker^, O'Sullivan, Evans^, Guinan
- Opp: Barrett, Joseph, Harris, Downer, Smith, Opinel", Walsch'rts^, Martin, Watts, Griffiths"
- Subs: McGlinchey^, McCarthy/Phillips M/Evers — Brkovic/McElholm/Opara

Former Argyle triallist Sacha Opinel tests Larrieu with a long-range effort early on. Meaker's shot seems to surprise Scott Barrett who lets the ball in at the near post. Andy Harris's cross leads to Steve Watts' equaliser. Argyle's penalty appeal, when Taylor was bundled over, is ignored.

40 — BRIGHTON (H) 14/4, L 0-2
[Brooker 3, Zamora 16] — Ref: F Stretton
- XI: Larrieu, Elliott, Besweth'ck, Adams*, Wotton, Taylor, Phillips M, O'Sullivan, McCarthy", Evans
- Opp: Kuipers, Mayo, Culip, Watson, Crosby, Carpenter", Zamora", Brooker, Hart^, Oatway
- Subs: McGlinchey^, Stonebridge/Meaker/Evers — Rogers/Jones/Stant

More than 1,300 Seagulls fans make the journey to see their heroes clinch promotion. Any tension in Micky Adams' side is soon relieved by Paul Brooker's early goal with Larrieu claiming he was fouled. The £2 million-rated Bobby Zamora nets his 27th of the season to kill the game.

41 — KIDDERMINSTER (A) 16/4, L 0-3
[Hadley 5, MacKenzie 21, Skovbjerg 43] — Ref: P Armstrong
- XI: Sheffield, Elliott, Bance*, Frio, Wotton, Taylor, Phillips M, Javary^, McCarthy", Evans, Evers
- Opp: Clarke, Medou-Otye, Stamps, Doyle, Hinton", Smith, Bennett, Skovbjerg^, Hadley, Ducros*
- Subs: Beswerth'k/O'Sullivan/Guinan — MacKenzie — Durnin/Corbett/Davies

Friio signs a two-year contract but must be questioning the wisdom of his decision after a much-changed line up crashes to a humiliating defeat. The defence is virtually non-existent as Harriers almost score at will in the first half. Things improve slightly after early substitutions.

42 — TORQUAY (H) 21/4, W 3-1
Stonebridge 52, 60, Wills 54 [Kell 21p] — Ref: S Bennett
- XI: Larrieu, Adams, Besweth'ck, Frio, Wotton, Taylor, Phillips M, O'Sullivan, Stonebridge", Evans, Wills
- Opp: Northmore, Holmes, Green, Aggrey, Russell, Rees*, Kell, Bedeau, Sissoko^, Hill
- Subs: Gritton — O'Brien/Law

Richard Kell scores from the spot after Larrieu is spotted pulling Aggrey's shirt. Khalid Chalqi is dismissed (40) when, having been already booked, he becomes involved in argy-bargy with Frio. Wills' first league goal and two from Stonebridge send Colin Lee's side to the bottom.

43 — SOUTHEND (H) 24/4, D 3-3
Friio 2, Evans 23, Wotton 86p [Webb 45, Maher 77p, Newman 90] — Ref: M Dean
- XI: Larrieu, Adams, Besweth'ck, Frio, Wotton, Taylor^, Phillips M, O'Sullivan^, McCarthy", Evans, Wills
- Opp: Flahavan, McSweeney, Searle, Broad*, Johnson, Whelan, Webb, Maher, Rawle, Bramble
- Subs: Stonebridge/Elliott — Thurgood — Newman

Friio scores after just 73 seconds but disaster strikes when Taylor breaks an ankle (19). Evans increases the lead. Southend boss David Webb sees his son Daniel score his first league goal. Beswetherick and Rob Newman both handle for penalties. Newman heads a late, late equaliser.

44 — LINCOLN (A) 28/4, L 1-2
Stonebridge 25 [Thorpe 24, Dudgeon 84] — Ref: T Parkes
- XI: Larrieu, Elliott, Besweth'ck, Frio, Wotton, Adams, Phillips M, O'Sullivan^, Stonebridge", Evans, Guinan
- Opp: Marriott, Barnett, Bimson, Finnigan, Dudgeon, Holmes, Sedgemore*, Battersby, Thorpe", Gain
- Subs: McCarthy — Smith/Walker/Miller

Alan Buckley's Imps gain a much-needed win as they cling on to league status. McCarthy impresses as a stand-in defender. Lee Thorpe's opener is quickly cancelled out by Stonebridge's slight touch. James Dudgeon gets the winner when Larrieu is out of position from a corner.

45 — ROCHDALE (A) 1/5, L 1-2
Evans 34 [Elliott 54(og), Connor 58] — Ref: P Joslin
- XI: Larrieu, Besweth'ck, Frio", Adams, Wotton, McCarthy, Phillips M, Guinan^, McCarthy, Evans, Meaker^
- Opp: Edwards, Evans, Jones, Monington, Bayliss, Hill, Ford, Flitcroft!, Platt, Connor^, Hadland"
- Subs: Stonebridge/McGlinch'y/Wills — Ware/Lancashire

Argyle finally play at Spotland after two abortive trips earlier on the season. Evans fires Argyle ahead. Lack of communication leads to Elliott heading past Larrieu. Paul Connor smashes an unstoppable shot into the top corner. Dave Flitcroft is red-carded (77) for a late tackle on Friio.

46 — ROCHDALE (H) 5/5, D 0-0
Ref: P Dowd
- XI: McCormick, Adams, Besweth'ck, Frio", Wotton, McCarthy, Phillips M, Gritton^, Stonebridge, Wills
- Opp: Edwards, Evans, Oliver, Monington, Bayliss, Hill, Ford^, Flitcroft*, Platt, Connor, Jones
- Subs: McGlinchey, Connolly/Trudgian — Ware/Hadland"/Lancashire

Sturrock gives youth a chance and the youngsters perform well enough to deny Steve Parkin's side the win they need to clinch a play-off place. Wills in particular has a fine match and goes closest to scoring when Neil Edwards parries his goal-bound shot. Dale finish strongly to no avail.

NATIONWIDE DIVISION 3 (CUP-TIES) Manager: Hodges > Paul Sturrock SEASON 2000-01

Worthington Cup

		Att	F-A	H-T	Scorers, Times, and Referees	1	2	3	4	5	6	7	8	9	10	11	subs used
1:1 H	BRISTOL ROV 23/8	3,498 3:19 2:15	1-2 L	0-2	McGregor 72 / Bignot 32, Cameron 41 / Ref: T Parkes	Sheffield *Culkin*	O'Sullivan *Bignot*	Besweth'ck *Wilson*	Barrett *Thomson**	Wotton* *Foster*	Taylor *Pethick*	Fleming *Astafjevs*	Barlow *Hogg*	Guinan^ *Ellington^*	Gritton" *Cameron*	Phillips M *Bryant*	McGregor/McCarthy/PhillipsL *Walters/Ellis*
1:2 A	BRISTOL ROV 5/9	5,228 3:18 2:14	1-1 D	0-0	McCarthy 47 / Ellington 48 / Ref: M Brandwood (Argyle lose 2-3 on aggregate)	Sheffield *Culkin*	O'Sullivan *Bignot*	Besweth'ck *Wilson*	Barrett *Thomson*	Taylor *Foster*	Fleming *Challis**	Phillips M *Astafjevs*	Barlow *Hogg*	McCarthy *Ellington*	Guinan* *Ellis^*	Peake^ *Bryant*	Gritton/Mancekivell *Foran/Walters*

Rovers dominate the first half and Marcus Bignot scores with a fine volley. New £100k signing Martin Cameron leaves Sheffield punching thin air as he heads in a cross. A triple substitution by Hodges livens things up and McGregor dummies Nick Culkin to score into an empty net.

A much improved display is not enough to prevent Argyle's customary first-round exit from the competition. Rovers, fresh from a 6-2 win at Brentford, fall behind to McCarthy's goal. Culkin's long clearance causes confusion in the defence and Ellington runs clear to round Sheffield.

FA Cup

		Att	F-A	H-T	Scorers, Times, and Referees	1	2	3	4	5	6	7	8	9	10	11	subs used
1 A	CHESTER 18/11	2,393 3:20 NC6	1-1 D	0-0	Peake 87 / Wright 78 / Ref: P Prosser	Hodges *Brown*	Adams* *Fisher**	Besweth'ck *Doughty*	Leadbitter ! *Lancaster*	Wotton *Ruffer*	Taylor *Beesley P !*	Fleming *Carden*	Barlow *Blackburn*	Guinan^ *Beesley M"*	McGregor *Whitehall*	Phillips M" *Porter*	Wills/Stonebridge/Peake *Ruscoe*/Gaunt/Wright*
1R H	CHESTER 28/11	3,264 3:20 NC6	1-2 L aet	0-1	McGregor 73 / Whitehall 42, Ruscoe 107 / Ref: P Prosser	Hodges *Brown*	Fleming *Fisher**	Besweth'ck *Doughty*	Leadbitter *Lancaster*	Wotton *Ruffer*	Taylor *Beesley P*	Phillips M *Carden*	Barlow* *Blackburn^*	McGregor *Beesley M*	Guinan* *Whitehall^*	Peake" *Porter*	Gritton/Wills/Stonebridge *Ruscoe/Woods/Wright*

Leadbitter is harshly sent off (36) after a minor skirmish with Andy Porter. Hodges fails to hold Steve Whitehall's free-kick and Darren Wright pounces. Paul Beesley is dismissed for a second yellow (83). Peake spares Argyle's blushes with a superb curling free-kick from 30 yards.

Argyle crash to only their second ever defeat by a non-league side in the Cup. Hodges is again at fault for the first as he spills a shot from Mark Beesley. McGregor takes the game into extra time. Scott Ruscoe capitalises on more hesitancy to give Graham Barrow's side an unlikely win.

Football League Division Three — Final Table

	Team	P	W	D	L	F	A	W	D	L	F	A	Pts
			Home					Away					
1	Brighton	46	19	2	2	52	14	9	6	8	21	21	92
2	Cardiff	46	16	7	0	56	20	7	6	10	39	38	82
3	Chesterfield^	46	16	5	2	46	14	9	9	5	33	28	80
4	Hartlepool	46	12	8	3	40	23	9	6	8	31	31	77
5	Leyton Orient	46	13	7	3	31	18	7	8	8	28	33	75
6	Hull	46	12	7	4	27	18	7	10	6	20	21	74
7	Blackpool*	46	14	4	5	50	26	8	2	13	24	32	72
8	Rochdale	46	11	8	4	36	25	7	9	7	23	23	71
9	Cheltenham	46	12	5	6	37	27	6	9	8	22	25	68
10	Scunthorpe	46	13	7	3	42	16	5	4	14	20	36	65
11	Southend	46	10	8	5	29	23	5	10	8	26	30	63
12	PLYMOUTH	46	13	5	5	33	17	2	8	13	21	44	58
13	Mansfield	46	12	7	4	40	26	3	6	14	24	46	58
14	Macclesfield	46	10	5	8	23	21	4	9	10	23	41	56
15	Shrewsbury	46	12	5	6	30	26	3	5	15	19	39	55
16	Kidderminster	46	10	6	7	29	27	3	8	12	18	34	53
17	York	46	9	6	8	23	26	4	7	12	19	37	52
18	Lincoln	46	9	9	5	36	28	3	6	14	22	38	51
19	Exeter	46	8	9	6	22	20	4	5	14	18	38	50
20	Darlington	46	10	6	7	28	23	2	7	14	16	33	49
21	Torquay	46	8	9	6	30	29	4	4	15	22	48	49
22	Carlisle	46	8	8	7	26	32	3	7	13	16	39	48
23	Halifax	46	7	6	10	33	32	5	5	13	21	36	47
24	Barnet	46	9	8	6	44	29	3	1	19	23	52	45
		1104	273	157	122	843	554	122	157	273	554	843	1490

* promoted after play-offs

^ deducted 9 points

Odds & ends

Double wins: (2) York, Exeter.
Double defeat: (2) Macclesfield, Brighton.

Won from behind: (3) Cardiff, Torquay, York.
Lost from in front: (3) Barnet, Macclesfield, Rochdale.

High spots: Impact of French signing David Friio.
Convincing home win over leaders Chesterfield.
Double win over local rivals Exeter.

Low spots: Two points from last 4 games with play-offs still possible.
Departure to Australia of Player of the Year, Wayne O'Sullivan.
Career-ending injuries to John Hodges and Chris Leadbitter.
Serious injuries to David Worrell and Craig Taylor.
Defeat at home to non-league Chester in FA Cup.
Poor disciplinary record with five sending offs.
Six matches postponed through bad weather.

Appearances & Goals

Player	Lge	Sub	LC	Sub	FAC	Sub	Lge	LC	FAC	Tot
	Appearances						Goals			
Adams, Steve	12	5								
Bance, Danny	1									
Barlow, Martin	17	3	2		2					
Barrett, Adam	9		2				2			
Beswetherick, Jon	44	1	2		2					
Betts, Robert	3	1								
Connolly, Paul		1								
Elliott, Stuart	11	1								
Evans, Michael	10						4			4
Evers, Sean	2	5								
Fleming, Terry	15	2	2		2					
Friio, David	26						5			5
Guinan, Steve	7	15	2		2		5			5
Gritton, Martin	1	9	1	1		1	1			1
Heathcote, Mick	4	1					1			1
Hodges, John	2					2				
Javary, Jean-Philippe	4									
Larrieu, Romain	14	1								
Leadbitter, Chris	9				2					
Mardon, Paul	3						1			1
McCarthy, Sean	31	6	1	1	1		10	1		11
McCormick, Luke	1				1	1				
McGlinchey, Brian	17	3								
McGregor, Paul	31	2	1		2		6	1	1	8
Meaker, Michael	5	6					1			1
Nancekivell, Kevin		6				1	1			1
O'Sullivan, Wayne	38	2	2				1			1
Peake, Jason	7	3	1	1	1	1	2		1	3
Phillips, Lee	4	2			1					
Phillips, Martin	36	6	2		2	2	1			1
Sheffield, Jon	29		2							
Stonebridge, Ian	17	14			1	2	11			11
Taylor, Craig	38	1	2		2		3			3
Trudgian, Ryan		1								
Wilkie, Lee	2									
Wills, Kevin	4	6				2	1			1
Worrell, David	14									
Wotton, Paul	38	4	1		2		4			4
(own-goals)							1			1
38 players used	506	107	22	6	22	6	54	2	2	58

Player of the Year: Wayne O'Sullivan.
Ever presents: (0).
Hat tricks: (0).
Leading scorers: Ian Stonebridge and Sean McCarthy (11).

NATIONWIDE DIVISION 3   Manager: Paul Sturrock   SEASON 2001-02

No	Date	Att	Pos	Pt	F-A	H-T	Scorers, Times, and Referees	subs used
1	H 11/8 SHREWSBURY	5,087		L 0	0-1	0-0	Jemson 73. Ref: C Penton	Crowe/Gritton/Evers; Walker/Tretton/Freestone
2	A 18/8 HULL	10,755	19	D 4 / 1	0-0	0-0	Ref: G Cain	Broad/Stonebridge; Matthews/Rowe
3	H 25/8 ROCHDALE	4,198	22	L 1 / 1	1-2	1-1	Coleman 12 (og), Jones 13, Connor 78. Ref: R Harris	Besweth'ck/Banger/Broad; Connor/Townson/Ware
4	A 27/8 RUSHDEN & D	4,415	18	W 14 / 4	3-2	1-2	Evans 45, Coughlan 50, McGlinchey 71, Darby 29, 41. Ref: G Hegley	McGlinchey Gritton; Setchell/Singere
5	A 8/9 TORQUAY	4,217	14	W 21 / 7	1-0	0-0	Friio 58. Ref: M Brandwood	McGlinchey/Banger; Herrera/Nicholls/Williams
6	H 11/9 SWANSEA	3,850	8	W 13 / 10	3-1	2-0	Wotton 24p, Banger 45, Phillips 61, Stibbe 79. Ref: P Prosser	McGlinchey Hodges; Williams/Todd/Cusack
7	A 15/9 KIDDERMINSTER	2,801	9	D 16 / 11	0-0	0-0	Ref: S Baines	Banger/McGlinchey/St'bridge; Ducros/Broughton/Stamps
8	A 18/9 EXETER	5,756	8	W 24 / 14	3-2	1-2	Phillips 5, Evans 65, Stonebridge 90, Curran 7, Roberts 17. Ref: D Gallagher	McGlinchey Hodges/Stonebridge; Burrows/Diallo
9	H 22/9 MACCLESFIELD	4,227	5	W 15 / 17	2-0	1-0	Hodges 45, Friio 65. Ref: J Ross	Stonebridge Hodges; O'Neill/Byrne/Askey
10	A 25/9 YORK	2,282	7	D 15 / 18	0-0	0-0	Ref: G Cowburn	Bent; Salvati
11	H 29/9 LUTON	5,782	4	W 3 / 21	2-1	2-1	Phillips 21, Friio 45, Crowe 14. Ref: A Hall	Hodges/Wills; Forbes/Douglas/Mansell

Squad numbers in use (Argyle in bold, opponents in italic):

1 — H SHREWSBURY
Argyle: Larrieu, Adams, Beswetherick, Friio, Wotton, McGlinchey, Evans*, Stonebridge* Phillips, Coughlan, Wills
Shrewsbury: *Cartwright, Riach, Jagielka, Heathcote, Atkins, Rodgers", Jemson", Wilding^, Redmile, Murray!*
Karl Murray's sending off for two yellow cards only serves to inspire the Shrews. Heathcote makes his debut only days after signing from Argyle. Jagielka casually rolls the ball towards an open net but Beswetherick clears off the line. The wily Jemson scores after a quick break.

2 — A HULL
Argyle: Larrieu, Adams, Beswetherick, Friio, Wotton, McGlinchey, Evans*, Phillips, Coughlan, Wills, Stonebridge
Hull: *Glennon, Edwards, Mohan, Goodison, Johnson, Beresford, Dudfield^, Alexander, Whitmore*, Greaves, Whittle*
Brian Little's expensively assembled squad are favourites for promotion but Argyle defend stoutly to gain an unexpected point and frustrate the large home following. The normally influential Jamaican international Theodore Whitmore is kept quiet and the Tigers run out of ideas.

3 — H ROCHDALE
Argyle: Larrieu, Worrell", McGlinchey Adams, Wotton, Coughlan, Phillips, Evers*, Stonebridge^ Hodges, Evans, Wills
Rochdale: *Edwards, Evans, McAuley Ford*, Coleman, Bayliss, Oliver, Jones, Platt* Durkan", Filcroft*
Dale gain their first win at Home Park since 1969. Simon Coleman diverts Stonebridge's header past his own keeper but the visitors level within a minute as Gary Jones lashes home. Broad's pass is intercepted by Kevin Townson and Paul Connor sends Steve Parkin's side top.

4 — A RUSHDEN & D
Argyle: Larrieu, Adams, Beswetherick Broad, Wotton, Coughlan, Phillips, Evans*, Hodges, Wills, Gritton
Rushden: *Turley, Mustafa, Butterworth Underwood, Peters, Brady, Jackson^, Radwell, Darby, Carey, Gray*, Setchell/Singere*
The league's new boys look to be cruising as Duane Darby gives them a clear lead. Evans' goal just before the break gives Argyle hope and they reappear looking a different side. Coughlan gets his first goal for the club and a rare McGlinchey strike clinches a welcome three points.

5 — A TORQUAY
Argyle: Larrieu, Worrell, Beswetherick Friio, Wotton, Coughlan, Phillips, Adams, Stonebridge* Hodges, Evans, Wills
Torquay: *Dearden, Tully, McNeil Rees, Woods*, Woozley, Brandon, Russell, Graham, Roach", Hill^*
After a first-half stalemate, the match turns when ex-Argyle loanee Stephen Woods goes off injured. The Gulls suddenly look uncertain and Friio eventually capitalises. Torquay press hard towards the end and Hill and Graham have chances, but the Pilgrims' defence looks solid.

6 — H SWANSEA
Argyle: Larrieu, Freestone, Beswetherick Friio, Wotton, Coughlan, Phillips, Adams, Banger*, Evans, Wills
Swansea: *Freestone, Jenkins, Roberts" O'Leary, Bound, Howard, Tyson", Phillips, Stibbe, Mazzina^, Coates*
With Phillips in devastating form on the wing, Argyle prove too strong for the Welsh side. O'Leary trips Evans and Wotton blasts in the spot-kick. The lively Banger scores his first for the club and Phillips taps in. Swans manager John Hollins leaves his position the following day.

7 — A KIDDERMINSTER
Argyle: Larrieu, Worrell, Beswetherick Friio, Wotton, Coughlan, Phillips, Adams, Wills*, Evans, Banger^
Kidderminster: *Brock, Smith, Shilton* Bird*, Clarkson, Shail, Williams, Bennett, Blake, Joy, Larkin^*
The defensive combination of Wotton and Coughlan stand firm as the rest of the side put up a hard-working but indifferent performance. Jan Molby's Harriers dominate but become more frustrated as the game goes on. Substitute Banger misses two reasonable chances near the end.

8 — A EXETER
Argyle: Larrieu, Worrell, Beswetherick'k* Friio, Wotton, Coughlan, Phillips, Adams, Banger^, Evans, Hodges*
Exeter: *Gregg, McConnell, Power Curran, Watson, Campbell, Barlow, Breslan, McCarthy*, Roberts", Flack*
City quickly recover from Phillips' early goal. Ex-Pilgrim Chris Curran heads in and the dangerous Christian Roberts robs Beswetherick who is replaced at half-time. Evans restores the status quo. Phillips sets up Stonebridge in injury-time to ensure a noisy convoy back down the A38.

9 — H MACCLESFIELD
Argyle: Larrieu, Worrell, McGlinchey Friio, Wotton, Coughlan, Phillips*, Adams, Banger^, Evans*, Hodges
Macclesfield: *Wilson, Hitchin*, Abbey Keen, Tinson, Ridler, Tracey, Priest, Munroe^, Lightbourne* Glover*
Canadian international Jason Bent comes on to rapturous applause after protracted work-permit problems. Hodges becomes the ninth Argyle player to score this season when he lobs Steve Wilson. Phillips drive is only partially blocked and Friio snaffles the chance from two yards.

10 — A YORK
Argyle: Larrieu, Worrell, McGlinchey Friio, Wotton, Coughlan, Phillips, Adams, Wills*, Evans, Hodges
York: *Fettis, Edmondson, Hocking Potter, Basham, Fox*, Cooper, Bullock, Nogan, Brass, Proctor*
A hard fought draw, but the result could have been so different had Evans struck his last-minute shot with conviction. Twice Wills tests Northern Ireland international Alan Fettis with long-range efforts. The meagre crowd is another blow to the financially challenged home side.

11 — H LUTON
Argyle: Larrieu, Worrell, McGlinchey Friio, Wotton, Coughlan, Phillips*, Adams, Bent!, Evans!, Stonebridge
Luton: *Ovendale, Boyce, Taylor Holmes*, Perrett, Coyne, Spring", Nicholls, Howard, Valois^, Crowe*
Hatters boss Joe Kinnear's pre-match derogatory comments create a rivalry that is not forgotten. Dean Crowe, briefly a Pilgrim, puts Luton ahead. Argyle fight back superbly despite Evans' red card (37) for an alleged elbow on Chris Coyne. Friio bravely dives in at the near post.

Fixtures and match reports (Plymouth Argyle).

Column heading players (top row):
McCaldon · Guyett · Bolland · Hatswell · Stockley · Savage · Whitehead · Tait* · Moody · Ricketts · Omoyinmi · Thomas

---

6/10
6,071 · 13 · 22
Moody 74
Ref: P Alcock

Opponents: McCaldon, Guyett, Bolland, Hatswell, Stockley, Savage, Whitehead, Tait*, Moody, Ricketts, Omoyinmi, Thomas. Subs: Midgley/Middleton/Wood; Besweth'k/Broad/Stonebridg; Bradley/Harris.

Sturrock is September's Manager of the Month. Argyle visit the Kassam stadium for the first time. Larrieu fouls Manny Omoyinmi and Paul Moody scores from the spot. Ex-Oxford star Banger silences the taunts within two minutes of coming on as he slides a shot in at the near post.

---

13 H HALIFAX 13/10
5,085 · 21 · 25 · W · 3-0
Coughlan 15, Phillips 23, Hodges 25
Ref: M Warren

Argyle: Larrieu, Worrell, McGlinchey, Friio, Wotton, Coughlan, Phillips^, Adams, Evans^, Wills, Hodges. Subs: Stonebridge, Banger^.
Halifax: Butler, Swales, Jules*, Stoneman, Mitchell, Clarke, Harsley, Redfearn^, Jones, Kerrigan*, Smith. Subs: Midgley/Middleton/Wood.

Halifax boss Alan Little is given plenty of food for thought as he takes charge of the side for the first time. Argyle sew the game up within the first 25 minutes but then ease off. Phillips continues his uncharacteristic scoring run and Hodges is injured when he bravely stoops to head in.

---

14 A MANSFIELD 20/10
4,621 · 2 · 28 · W · 3-0
Evans 54, Friio 89, Stonebridge 90
Ref: G Frankland

Argyle: Larrieu, Worrell, McGlinchey, Friio, Wotton, Coughlan, Phillips^, Adams, Evans, Wills, Hodges. Subs: Stonebridge, Banger.
Mansfield: Pilkington, Hassell^, Pemberton, Lawrence, Reddington, Robinson, Disley, Corden, Greenacre, Williamson, White^. Subs: Bradley/Harris.

With the dangerous Chris Greenacre kept quiet, Argyle hand a first home defeat to the highly-fancied Stags. Stuart Reddington's error leads to Evans' opener. Williamson hits the post (85) before late goals from Friio and Stonebridge give the scoreline a slightly flattering appearance.

---

15 H LINCOLN 23/10
6,572 · 14 · 31 · W · 2-0
Friio 28, Coughlan 74
Ref: M Fletcher

Argyle: Larrieu, Worrell, McGlinchey, Friio, Wotton, Coughlan, Phillips, Adams, Evans, Wills, Hodges. Subs: Stonebridge, Banger.
Lincoln: Marriott, Barnett*, Bimson, Bailey, Holmes, Brown, Sedgemore^, Black, Cameron, Walker, Gain^. Subs: Battersby/Betts/Buckley.

Argyle's twelfth unbeaten match sees them hit them hit top spot. Alan Buckley's side play some attractive football but lack punch up front. A trademark header from Friio opens the scoring. Coughlan then scores from close range to already overtake his previous best scoring record.

---

16 A BRISTOL ROV 28/10
6,889 · 15 · 34 · W · 2-1
Phillips 3, Hodges 57
Cameron 84
Ref: M Halsey

Argyle: Larrieu, Worrell, McGlinchey, Friio^, Wotton, Coughlan, Phillips^, Adams, Evans^, Wills, Hodges. Subs: Stonebridge/Bent/Besweth'k.
Bristol Rovers: Howie, Wilson, Plummer, Foran, Thomson, Gilroy^, Walters", Gall, Ross, Challis^, Cameron. Subs: Cameron/Jones/Bryant.

Live coverage on ITV determines the switch to a Sunday 2.15 kick-off time. Phillips cannot fail to score as Rovers dither in clearing Wotton's corner. Hodges well-taken volley all but seals the point. Sub Martin Cameron's goal brings some consolation for the home side's late pressure.

---

17 H HARTLEPOOL 3/11
5,723 · 24 · 37 · W · 1-0
Friio 41
Ref: W Jordan

Argyle: Larrieu, Worrell, McGlinchey, Friio, Wotton, Coughlan, Phillips^, Bent, Evans, Wills, Hodges. Subs: Banger, Adams.
Hartlepool: Williams, Bass, Sharp^, Robinson, Westwood, Tinkler, Stephenson^, Barron, Humphreys^, Watson, Clarke. Subs: Simms/Lornor/Smith.

A second successive Manager of the Month award for Sturrock but the jinx that the prize normally brings still fails to strike. Top scorer Friio typically ghosts in to finish Worrell's low cross. Chris Turner's side play attractive football and look anything but a bottom of the table side.

---

18 A CHELTENHAM 9/11
5,035 · 11 · 38 · D · 0-0
Ref: B Curson

Argyle: Larrieu, Worrell, McGlinchey, Friio, Wotton, Coughlan, Phillips^, Bent*, Evans, Wills, Hodges. Subs: Stonebridge/Banger/Wills.
Cheltenham: Book, Howarth, Victory, Duff, Banks, McAuley^, Howells, Yates!, Alsop, Milton, Naylor^. Subs: Williams/Devaney.

The referee's inexplicable decision to play an additional ten minutes at the end of the first half sparks fury and an eventual scuffle between the players and management of both sides. Town skipper Mark Yates is dismissed (53) for a second yellow card when he raises studs at Larrieu.

---

19 A SOUTHEND 20/11
3,716 · 14 · 41 · W · 1-0
Adams 43
Ref: P Taylor

Argyle: Larrieu, Worrell, McGlinchey, Friio, Wotton, Coughlan, Phillips, Bent, Evans, Wills, Adams. Subs: Bent, Adams.
Southend: Flahavan, McSweeney, Searle, Cort, Whelan^, Johnson*, Maher, Rawle, Thurgood, Clark, Bramble. Subs: D'Sane/Webb.

Steve Adams heads his first ever league goal to end a 45-year wait for an Argyle victory at Roots Hall and preserve their unbeaten away record. Despite suffering concussion at Whitby, Evans, playing as the lone striker, runs his socks off. Wills crashes a 30-yard effort against the bar.

---

20 H CARLISLE 24/11
5,870 · 24 · 44 · W · 3-0
Evans 16, Bent 45, Phillips 87
Ref: R Harris

Argyle: Larrieu, Worrell, McGlinchey, Friio", Wotton, Coughlan, Phillips, Bent, Evans, Wills, Hodges. Subs: Besweth'ck/Keith/Adams.
Carlisle: Keen, Birch^, Murphy*, Whitehead, Andrews, Winstanley, McGill, Soley!, Hopper", Hadland, Halliday. Subs: Allan/Morley/Jack.

To add to the bottom club's plight, they lose top scorer Ritchie Foran after he trips over in the club shop. The game starts in a niggly manner. Soley is sent off for a second yellow (33) and Birch is replaced before he suffers similarly. The result is never in doubt after Evans' early goal.

---

21 A LEYTON ORIENT 1/12
6,342 · 13 · 45 · D · 0-0
Ref: S Dunn

Argyle: Larrieu, Worrell, Besweth'ck, Adams, Wotton, Coughlan, Phillips*, Bent*, Evans, Wills, Hodges. Subs: McGlinchey, Bent/Adams.
Leyton Orient: Barrett, Joseph, Jones*, McGhee, Smith, Leigertwood, Harris, Martin, Watts^, Ibehre, Houghton". Subs: Evers; Lockwood/Gray/Hatcher.

Both goalkeepers excel with Larrieu pulling of a world-class save from Jabo Ibehre and Scott Barrett turning Hodges' glancing header around the post. Argyle are forced to re-shuffle their line up due to injuries and Friio's suspension. O's manager Paul Brush is pleased with a point.

---

22 H DARLINGTON 15/12
5,041 · 12 · 48 · W · 1-0
Friio 81
Ref: M Cooper

Argyle: Larrieu, Worrell, McGlinchey, Friio, Wotton, Coughlan, Phillips", Bent, Evans, Wills, Stonebridg^, Hodges. Subs: Besweth'k/Keith/Adams.
Darlington: Collett, Betts, Heck'gbot'm, Wainwright, Caldwell!, Brumwell, Brightwell, Atkinson, Mellanby", Clark, Challing'th^. Subs: Maddison/Campbell.

Argyle produce a below par performance but set a new club record of 19 unbeaten matches. Substitute Sturrock makes an immediate impact by sending a slide-rule pass through to Friio who flicks it over Andy Collett. Gary Caldwell is dismissed (85) for a second bookable offence.

---

23 A SCUNTHORPE 22/12
3,602 · 6 · 48 · L · 1-2
Coughlan 51
Hodges 6, 24
Ref: G Laws

Argyle: Larrieu, Worrell, McGlinchey, Friio, Wotton, Coughlan, Phillips, Bent, Evans, Wills/Sturrock, Stonebridg^, Hodges. Subs: Keith/Sturrock.
Scunthorpe: Evans, Bradshaw*, Dawson, Stanton, Jackson, McCombe, Hodges, Calvo-Garcia, Carruthers, Torpey, Sparrow. Subs: Brough; Adams.

With the thermometer reading minus four, Sturrock refuses to blame the icy conditions as Argyle's unbeaten run ends. Former Pilgrims loan man, Lee Hodges, pounces on two bad errors. Larrieu misses Coughlan's sliced clearance for the first. Worrell then heads straight to Hodges.

NATIONWIDE DIVISION 3   SEASON 2001-02

Manager: Paul Sturrock

No	Date	Venue / Opponent	Att	Pos	Opp.pos	Pt	Res	F-A	H-T	Scorers, Times, and Referees
24	26/12	H TORQUAY	13,677	1	21	49	D	2-2	0-0	Coughlan 49, Stonebridge 51, McGlinchey 85(og), Logan 90p — Ref: P Rejer
25	29/12	H RUSHDEN & D	9,503	1	11	52	W	1-0	0-0	Keith 81 — Ref: L Cable
26	12/1	H HULL	9,134	1	6	55	W	1-0	1-0	Stonebridge 20 — Ref: C Wilkes
27	19/1	A SHREWSBURY	4,796	1	4	55	L	1-3	1-1	Evans 5; Rodgers 44, Aiston 50, Lowe 84 — Ref: D Pugh
28	22/1	H SCUNTHORPE	5,804	1	9	58	W	2-1	1-1	Wotton 44p, Keith 54; Carruthers 13 — Ref: M Fletcher
29	26/1	H OXFORD	8,239	1	14	61	W	4-2	3-2	Cough' 21, Hodges 24, S'bridge 45, 46; Morley 34, Powell 41 — Ref: B Curson
30	2/2	A LUTON	9,585	1	2	61	L	0-2	0-0	Nicholls 80p, Howard 87 — Ref: P Joslin
31	5/2	A SWANSEA	4,060	1	19	64	W	1-0	1-0	Sturrock 39 — Ref: S Tomlin
32	9/2	H MANSFIELD	14,716	1	4	67	W	1-0	0-0	Friio 85 — Ref: D Crick
33	16/2	A HALIFAX	2,330	1	24	70	W	2-0	2-0	Hodges 41, Wotton 42p — Ref: T Parkes
34	23/2	H KIDDERMINSTER	8,758	1	11	73	W	2-1	0-1	Coughlan 67, Wotton 81p; Broughton 33 — Ref: R Beeby

Squad numbers in use / subs used

24 — v TORQUAY
Argyle: Larrieu, Worrell, McGlinchey, Friio, Wotton, Coughlan, Phillips^, Adams, Keith^, Stonebridg^*, Hodges
*Torquay: Dearden, Tully, Hanson, Fowler, Hankin, Woods, Goodrige, Russell A, Logan, Graham^, Hill^*
subs used: Heaney/Wills — *Preece/Heaney/Wills*
"Both ends of the redeveloped ground are opened. Lowly United are inspired by the atmosphere. After conceding two quick goals, The Gulls hit back as the unfortunate McGlinchey turns into his own net and then fouls Eifion Williams to allow Richard Logan to convert the spot kick."

25 — v RUSHDEN & D
Argyle: Larrieu, Worrell, McGlinchey, Friio, Wotton, Coughlan, Phillips^, Adams, Keith, Stonebridg^*, Hodges
Rushden: Turley, Sambrook, Setchell, McElhatt'n^, Peters, Underwood, Hall, Butterworth, Partridge, Lowe, Gray^*
subs used: Sturrock/Evers — *Darby/Bell/Mustafa*
"Super-sub Sturrock does it again when his cross is turned in by Keith. Phillips hits the post early on but Diamonds keeper Billy Turley pulls off a string of fine saves which looks enough to clinch a point. Diamonds boss Brian Talbot complains that the ball-boys and girls were biased."

26 — v HULL
Argyle: Larrieu, Worrell, McGlinchey, Friio, Wotton, Coughlan, Phillips^, Adams, Keith^, Stonebridg^, Hodges
Hull: Muss'white, Petty, Goodison, Whittle, Holt, Wicks, Whitmore, Greaves*, Dudfield, Alexander, Johnsson''*
subs used: Evans/Bent — *Sneekes/Beresford/Williams*
"Title favourites Hull are without a win in five games. They have problems defending corners and it is no surprise when Stonebridge heads in from close range after Coughlan does well to retrieve the ball. Friio miskicks with the goal at his mercy. Larrieu saves well from Dudfield."

27 — v SHREWSBURY
Argyle: Larrieu, Worrell, McGlinchey, Friio, Wotton, Coughlan, Phillips^, Adams, Evans^, Stonebridge, Hodges
*Shrewsbury: Dunbavin, Moss, Rioch!, Tolley, Redmile, Lowe, Atkins, Fallon^, Rodgers^, Aiston^*
subs used: Keith/Stonebridge/Heaney — *Thompson/Wilding/Jagielka*
"Evans returns after compassionate leave following his wife's car accident. Greg Rioch is red-carded (16) after a second harmless foul. As in the first game of the season, ten-man Shrews then find inspiration. Lowe's 40-yard pass sets up Rodgers. Aiston shoots home from 25 yards."

28 — v SCUNTHORPE
Argyle: Adamson, Worrell, McGl'chey*, Friio, Wotton, Coughlan, Phillips, Adams, Keith^, Stonebridge, Hodges
Scunthorpe: Evans, Stanton, Dawson, Graves, Jackson, Thom, Sparrow, Carruthers*, Torpey, C·Garcia^, Beagrie*
subs used: Beswetherick/Evans — *Quailey/Hodges/McCombe*
"Manager Sturrock stays at home with flu. Larrieu is similarly afflicted and listens to the radio commentary in the dressing room. On loan Adamson makes his debut at short notice. Evans pulls down Hodges for a penalty. Worrell's dash sets up Keith. McGlinchey breaks his foot."

29 — v OXFORD
Argyle: Larrieu, Worrell, Besweth'ck, Friio, Wotton, Coughlan, Phillips, Adams, Keith^, Stonebridge, Hodges
Oxford: Woodman, Ricketts, Powell, Morley, Crosby, Bound, Whitehead, Gray*, Quinn, Savage, Scott*
subs used: Evans — *Moody/Omoyinmi*
"The new Lyndhurst Stand is opened. Coughlan and Hodges score with headers. Oxford fight back. Morley heads home unchallenged and the ball comes off Worrell's back, inviting Powell to score. Two goals in the space of a minute each side of half-time round off the entertainment."

30 — v LUTON
Argyle: Larrieu, Worrell, Besweth'ck, Friio, Wotton, Coughlan, Phillips*, Adams, Keith*, Stonebrid'g''', Hodges
Luton: Emberson, Taylor, Boyce, Nicholls, Perrett, Spring, Bayliss, Forbes, Crowe, Howard, Valois*
subs used: Evers/Evans/Heaney — *Brkovic*
"Joe Kinnear's Hatters dominate the first half of this top of the table clash. Steve Howard hits the bar and Valois has a shot disallowed. Ignoring claims of a dive, the ref adjudges that Worrell fouled Matthew Taylor. Howard converts Valois' corner and hits the crossbar for a second time."

31 — v SWANSEA
Argyle: Larrieu, Worrell, Besweth'ck, Friio, Wotton, Coughlan, Heaney^, Adams, Evans, Sturrock^, Hodges
Swansea: Freestone, Todd, Evans, Cusack, Mumford, Brodie, Sharp, Howard, Sidibe, Watkin^, Coates^*
subs used: Stonebridge/Broad — *Jenkins/Williams/Lacey*
"Colin Addison's side suffer their fifth successive defeat to add to their off the field financial problems. The manager's son scores his first goal with a left-foot shot after Todd and Mumford get in each other's way. Argyle's defence stands firm in the face of a Swans aerial bombardment."

32 — v MANSFIELD
Argyle: Larrieu, Worrell, Besweth'ck, Friio, Wotton, Coughlan, Phillips*, Adams, Evans^, Stonebrid'g^, Hodges
Mansfield: Pilkington, Hassell, Tankard, Williamson, Reddington, Barrett, Lawrence, Pemberton, Greenacre, Kelly, Corden
subs used: Keith/Sturrock/Heaney — *Corden*
"Former Manchester United keeper, Kevin Pilkington, denies Friio with two brilliant saves but the Frenchman has the final word. Beswetherick forces a corner after a surging run from halfway. Wotton's cross is met with a thundering header. Coughlan also goes close with two headers."

33 — v HALIFAX
Argyle: Larrieu, Worrell, Besweth'ck, Friio, Wotton, Coughlan, Wills*, Adams, Sturrock^, Stonebridge, Hodges
Halifax: Richardson, Woodward, Clarke M, Harsley, Clarke C, Mitchell, Bushell, Fitzpatrick^, Kerigan, Richards, Houghton*
subs used: Broad/Phillips — *Wright^/Jones/Middleton*
"Two days before the match, the entire Halifax side is up for sale. Two goals in the space of 60 seconds turn the Shaymen deeper into relegation trouble. Hodges has a simple tap in and then Wills is brought down by Paul Harsley. Wotton slams home the penalty with his usual aplomb."

34 — v KIDDERMINSTER
Argyle: Larrieu, Worrell, Besweth'ck, Friio, Wotton, Coughlan, Phillips*, Adams, Evans, Stonebrid'g^, Hodges
Kidderminster: Brock, Clarkson, Stamps, Bird, Sall, Hinton, Davies, Bennett, Broughton, Foster, Smith*
subs used: Sturrock/Heaney/Keith — *Larkin*
"The kick off is delayed by one and a half hours after a power failure. Broughton's free header is well taken. Coughlan heads the equaliser and seconds after being booked, Stamps handballs in the area. Harriers boss Jan Molby confronts the referee on the pitch as he blows for full-time."

No		Date		Att	Pos	Pts	Score
		26/2		16,369	13	76	

Fraser, McConnell, Power, Cronin", Curran, Tomlinson*, Ampadu, Flack^, Roberts, Breslan/McCarthy !/Buckle
Ref: G Cain

After conceding two soft goals, Fraser is grounded by a male streaker. Keith's superb 25-yard effort prompts a 'Mexican Wave'. A fan defies several burly stewards to do a lap of honour with a corner flag. McCarthy elbows Coughlan and is sent off within ten minutes of coming on.

36 A MACCLESFIELD 2/3 2,557 15 77 1 D 1-1
Coughlan 70
Priest 90
Ref: P Dowd
Larrieu, Worrell, Besweth'ck Friio, Wilson, Smith, Adams, Whitaker, Tinson, Wotton, Wills*, Adams, Sturrock^ Hodges, Broad/Keith
MacAuley, Priest, Byrne*, Lightb'rne^, Glover, Lambert, Hitchen/Askey

Sturrock wins his third 'Manager of the Month' award. The Silkmen, their season effectively over, take the offensive in the first half. Coughlan heads in a free-kick and threatens to become Argyle's leading scorer. Hesitancy from a throw-in allows Priest to steal a point in injury-time.

37 H YORK 5/3 10,801 21 80 1 W 1-0
Potter 45(og)
Ref: P Prosser
Larrieu, Worrell !, Besweth'ck Friio, Fettis, Hocking, Potter, Parkin, Basham, Hobson*, Coughlan, Keith^, Adams, Stonebridge Hodges, Taylor/Sturrock
Mathie, Nogan, Brass, Richardson, Wise

Pilgrims dominate the first half and force eleven corners. The breakthrough comes when Potter needlessly heads past his own keeper from Wotton's free-kick. Worrell is dismissed (53) for dissent following an earlier booking. City put the Greens under pressure but rarely threaten.

38 H LEYTON ORIENT 16/3 9,438 20 83 1 W 3-0 (Stonebridge 7, Coughlan 78, Evans 81)
Ref: M Fletcher
Larrieu, Worrell, Besweth'ck Friio", Bayes, Harris, Lockwood, Newton, Smith, Partridge, Coughlan, Keith*, Adams, Stonebridge Hodges, Evans/Bent/Sturrock
Canham*, Watts^, Christie, Martin, Hutchings, Barnard/McLean, Phillips^

The scoreline flatters Argyle who produce their worst home performance of the season. Stonebridge looks offside for the first but Orient fight back to belie their lowly position. The Pilgrims come to life after the introduction of Evans. Larrieu makes two crucial saves from Steve Watts.

39 A LINCOLN 23/3 4,019 21 86 1 W 1-0
Stonebridge 71
Ref: T Parkes
Larrieu, Worrell, Besweth'ck Friio, Marriott, Bimson*, Hamilton", Brown, Morgan, Wotton, Phillips^, Evans, Wills*, Hodges, Stonebridge/Sturrock
Black^, Walker, Thorpe, Cameron, Buckley, Gain/Smith/Battersby

Argyle gain their tenth 1-0 win of the season and Larrieu achieves his 23rd clean sheet. Sturrock is again unhappy with his side's showing but their fortunes are transformed with the introduction of Stonebridge, who scores. The Greens need only one more point to confirm promotion.

40 A ROCHDALE 26/3 4,457 6 89 1 W 3-1 (Keith 65, Coughlan 81, Hodges 83)
Simpson 54
Ref: M Pike
Larrieu, Worrell, Besweth'ck Friio, Gilks, Jobson, Griffiths, Doughty, McLaughlin Oliver, Coughlan, Adams", Sturrock^ Hodges, Keith/Stonebridge/Heaney
Fitcroft^, Platt, Townson*, Simpson, Jones/Durkan, Evans Adams^

Sturrock finally mentions the 'p' word as Argyle gain three points to clinch promotion. New Dale signing Paul Simpson scores a wonder goal from way out on the left. A triple substitution does the trick with Keith setting things off. The travelling Green Army celebrate on the pitch.

41 H BRISTOL ROV 30/3 15,732 23 92 1 W 1-0
Keith 1
Ref: P Danson
Larrieu, Worrell, Besweth'ck Friio, Howie, Wilson, Challis, Toner, Foran, Wotton, Phillips^, Keith*, Evans/Bent/Sturrock, Hodges
Carlisle !, Shore, Thomas, Quinn, McKeever * Astafjevs, Adams

The promotion party starts early. From Argyle's first attack, Adams' shot hits the bar and Keith follows up to score after just 27 seconds. The over-fussy referee books seven players and sends off Carlisle on his Rovers debut. The Argyle players do a lap of honour after the final whistle.

42 A HARTLEPOOL 1/4 3,725 9 92 1 L 0-1
Clarke 86
Ref: M Jones
Larrieu, Worrell, Besweth'ck Friio, Williams A, Barron, Lee, Robinson, Westwood, Wotton, Adams*, Evans", Sturrock/Stonebridge/Keith, Hodges
Coppinger*, Clarke, Watson^, Williams E, Humphreys Smith, Boyd/Henderson, Adams^

Three vital points are dropped in the race for the title. Both sides are evenly matched but the strain of the promotion battle looks to have taken its toll on Argyle who look jaded. Darrell Clarke's late goal gives Chris Turner's side a boost as they still harbour hopes of a play-off place.

43 H SOUTHEND 6/4 10,021 12 93 2 D 0-0
Ref: R Olivier
Larrieu, Worrell, Besweth'ck Friio, Flahavan, Broad, Kerrigan, Beard, Cort, Coughlan, Phillips^, Bent*, Evans Stonebrid^ Hodges, Sturrock/Keith/Adams
Thurgood, Maher, Searle, Belgrave* Whelan, McSweeney Wallace

The Pilgrims lose top spot for the first time since October. Another 1-0 win looks on the cards after the ref awards a penalty for handball. U's players persuade him to consult a linesman who confirms the decision. He then consults the other official and deems that it was Evans' hand.

44 A CARLISLE 13/4 3,080 17 96 1 W 2-0 (Keith 20, Wotton 53)
Ref: M Cowburn
Larrieu, Worrell, Besweth'ck Bent, Keen, Birch, Rogers, Allan^, Andrews, Wotton, Keith, Adams, Stonebridge Hodges, Halliday/Bell/McDonagh
Winstanley Hopper", Jack, Foran, Stevens^ McGill, Evans

Argyle parade their new tangerine away shirts but keep the normal green shorts as the new ones are too big. Managerless Carlisle prove no match as Keith scores with a magnificent volley. Wotton scores with a 35-yard free-kick to leave the Pilgrims needing two points for the title.

45 A DARLINGTON 15/4 4,089 16 99 1 W 4-1 (Evans 10, Keith 17, 29, Bent 59)
Clark 34p
Ref: F Stretton
Larrieu, Worrell, Besweth'ck Bent, Porter, Brumwell*, Hec'bottom Convery^, Liddle, McGurk, Wotton, Coughlan, Keith, Adams, Evans^ Hodges*, Sturrock/Phillips/McGl'chey
Ford, Atkinson, Clark, Hodgson^, Wainwright Campbell/Rundle/Sheeran

The Pilgrims remain in the north and clinch the championship in magnificent style. Evans scores from close range. Keith strikes superbly with a shot on the run and then heads home to spark early celebrations. Larrieu sends Ford tumbling. Ian Clark's spot-kick does not dampen spirits.

46 H CHELTENHAM 20/4 18,517 4 102 1 W 2-0 (Bent 4, Coughlan 24)
Ref: S Tomlin
Larrieu, Worrell, Besweth'ck Friio, Book, Griffin, Victory, Milton, Brough*, Wotton, Coughlan, Bent, Adams, Stonebrid^ Hodges, Evans/Sturrock
Duff, Finnigan, Williams^, Alsop", Naylor, Howarth/Tyson/Grayson, Keith^, Yates

It's party time at Home Park as the Championship trophy is presented. Bent drives home the first and Player of the Year Coughlan takes advantage of Book's mishandling of a clearance. Cheltenham fail to gain the point needed to gain automatic promotion and face the play-offs.

Home 8,788
Away 4,748
Average

NATIONWIDE DIVISION 3 (CUP-TIES) Manager: Paul Sturrock SEASON 2001-02

Worthington Cup

		Att		F-A	H-T	Scorers, Times, and Referees
1	A WATFORD 21/8	9,230 1:14	19 L	0-1	0-0	Gayle 81 Ref: P Armstrong

SQUAD NUMBERS IN USE

										subs used
Larrieu	Adams	McGlinchey	Friio*	Wotton	Coughlan	Wills"	Evers	Hodges	Phillips	Broad/Gritton/Stonebridge
Baardsen	Blondeau	Robinson^	Wooter*	Vega	Ward	Hughes	Foley*	Gayle	Noel-Will'ms Vernazza	Nielson/Panayi/Helguson

Argyle are far from disgraced against Gianluca Vialli's cosmopolitan side. Marcus Gayle's late goal separates the sides when extra-time looks likely. The match summarises the sides' forthcoming seasons with Argyle exceeding expectations and highly-fancied Watford under-achieving.

FA Cup

		Att		F-A	H-T	Scorers, Times, and Referees
1	A WHITBY 17/11	2,202 UL20	1 D	1-1	0-1	Phillips 72 Gildea 42 Ref: N Barry

										subs used
Larrieu	Worrell	Besweth'ck	Friio	Wotton	Coughlan	Phillips"	Adams*	Evans^	Stonebridge Hodges	Wills/Keith/Bent
Naisbett	Rennison	Gildea*	Goodchild	Logan	Williams I	Williams G	Burt^	Robinson	Ure"	Veart/Key/Ingram

Argyle break new ground by flying to the match. Match of the Day cameras are present hoping to record an upset. Gildea gives the non-league side a deserved lead. Danny Naisbett performs miracles in the Whitby goal and Jamie Burt shows why several clubs are interested in him.

		Att		F-A	H-T	Scorers, Times, and Referees
1R	H WHITBY 27/11	5,914 UL20	1 W	3-2	3-0	Bent 16, Stonebridge 40, Phillips 45 Burt 69, Robinson 72 Ref: P Durkin

										subs used
Larrieu	Worrell	McGlinchey	Friio	Wotton	Coughlan	Phillips	Bent*	Evans !	Stonebridge Hodges^	Adams/Besweth'ck
Naisbett	Rennison	Gildea*	Goodchild	Logan	Williams	Key	Burt	Robinson	Ure"	Allen/Anderson

A thrashing looks on the cards despite the first-half sending off of Evans for retaliation (37) on Goodchild. Whitby enjoy their moment of glory and respond with two fine goals to give little hint of their indifferent league form. Appreciative home fans applaud them off at the final whistle.

		Att		F-A	H-T	Scorers, Times, and Referees
2	H BRISTOL ROV 8/12	6,141 3:21	1 D	1-1	1-0	Wotton 28 Walters 60 Ref: R Beeby

										subs used
Larrieu	Worrell	McGlinchey	Friio	Wotton	Coughlan	Phillips"	Bent	Evans"	Stonebridge Hodges^	Adams/Besweth'k/Sturrock
Howie	Wilson	Trought	Faran	Thomson	Plummer*	Hogg	Mauge	Cameron	Ellington" Astafjevs^	Challis I/Walters/Gall

Given the respective sides' league form, Argyle are expected to progress easily. Former favourite Ronnie Mauge has a 90-minute battle with Friio. The introduction of 37-year old Mark Walters turns the match. Trevor Challis is sent off in stoppage time for a second yellow card.

		Att		F-A	H-T	Scorers, Times, and Referees
2R	A BRISTOL ROV 18/12	5,763 3:21	1 L	2-3	0-0	Friio 76, 86 Ommel 56, Hogg 71, Ellington 87 Ref: R Beeby

										subs used
Larrieu	Worrell	McGlinchey	Friio	Wotton	Coughlan	Phillips	Wills*	Stonebridg'^	Adams Hodges^	Keith/Sturrock/Evers
Howie	Wilson	Trought	Faran	Thomson	Challis	Hillier"	Cameron^	Ellington	Astafjevs	Walters"/Ommel/Smith

A typical cup-tie sees Rovers take a two-goal lead after some sloppy play by Argyle. Friio scores twice from close range. Astafjevs' defence-splitting pass sets up Ellington. Keith's injury-time header hits the post. Cash strapped Rovers are rewarded with a lucrative tie at Derby.

Home / Away League Table

		P	Home					Away					Pts
			W	D	L	F	A	W	D	L	F	A	
1	PLYMOUTH	46	19	2	2	41	11	12	7	4	30	17	102
2	Luton	46	15	5	3	50	18	15	2	6	46	30	97
3	Mansfield	46	17	3	3	49	24	7	4	12	23	36	79
4	Cheltenham*	46	11	11	1	40	20	10	4	9	26	29	78
5	Rochdale	46	13	8	2	45	22	8	7	8	24	30	78
6	Rushden & D	46	14	5	4	40	20	8	8	9	29	33	73
7	Hartlepool	46	12	6	5	53	23	8	5	10	21	25	71
8	Scunthorpe	46	14	5	4	43	22	5	9	9	31	34	71
9	Shrewsbury	46	13	4	6	36	19	7	6	10	28	34	70
10	Kidderminster	46	13	6	4	35	17	6	3	14	21	30	66
11	Hull	46	12	6	5	38	18	4	7	12	19	33	61
12	Southend	46	12	5	6	36	22	3	8	12	15	32	58
13	Macclesfield	46	7	7	9	23	25	6	4	14	18	27	58
14	York	46	11	5	7	26	20	5	4	14	28	47	57
15	Darlington	46	11	6	6	37	25	4	5	14	23	46	56
16	Exeter	46	7	9	7	25	32	7	4	12	23	41	55
17	Carlisle	46	11	5	7	31	21	1	11	11	18	35	52
18	Leyton Orient	46	10	7	6	37	25	3	6	14	18	46	52
19	Torquay	46	8	6	9	27	31	4	9	10	19	32	51
20	Swansea	46	7	8	8	26	26	6	4	13	27	51	51
21	Oxford	46	8	7	8	34	28	3	7	13	19	34	47
22	Lincoln	46	8	4	11	25	27	2	12	9	19	35	46
23	Bristol Rov	46	8	7	8	28	28	3	5	15	12	32	45
24	Halifax	46	5	9	9	24	28	3	3	17	15	56	36
		1104	266	146	140	845	552	140	146	266	552	845	1510

* promoted after play-offs

Appearances / Goals

	Appearances						Goals			
	Lge	Sub	LC	Sub	FAC	Sub	Lge	LC	FAC	Tot
Adams, Steve	40	6	1		2	2	2			2
Adamson, Chris	1									
Banger, Nicky	3	7					2			2
Bent, Jason	16	5			2	1	3			4
Beswetherick, Jon	27	5			1	2	3		1	4
Broad, Joe	1	6		1						
Coughlan, Graham	46				4		11			11
Crowe, Dean		1								
Evans, Michael	30	8	1		3		7			7
Evers, Sean	3	4	1							
Friio, David	41	1			4		8		2	10
Gritton, Martin		2		1						
Heaney, Neil	1	2								
Hodges, Lee	42	3	1		4		6			6
Keith, Marino	13	10			2	2	9			9
Larrieu, Romain	45				4					
McGlinchey, Brian	26	3	1		3		1			1
Phillips, Martin	37	2	1		4		6		2	8
Stonebridge, Ian	29	13	1	1	4		8		1	9
Sturrock, Blair	4	15			2	2	1			1
Taylor, Craig		1								
Wills, Kevin	13	5	1		1	1				
Worrell, David	42				4					
Wotton, Paul	46		1		4		5		1	6
(own-goals)									2	2
24 players used	506	103	11	3	44	11	71		7	78

Odds & ends

Double wins: (9) Bristol Rov, Carlisle, Darlington, Exeter, Halifax, Lincoln, Mansfield, Rushden & D, Swansea.
Double defeats: (1) Shrewsbury.

Won from behind: (6) Exeter, Kidderminster, Luton, Rochdale (a), Rushden & D, Scunthorpe.
Lost from in front: (2) Rochdale (h), Shrewsbury.

High spots: Winning Division Three title with second highest points tally ever in league history.
Development of new stadium.
Twenty-seven clean sheets.
Four players chosen for PFA Select side (Coughlan, Friio, Larrieu and Wotton).
Excellent disciplinary record.
Stability at boardroom level.
Twelve players made at least 26 appearances.

Low spots: Disappointing FA Cup defeat at lowly Bristol Rovers.
Loss of first two home matches.

Player of the Year: Graham Coughlan.
Ever presents: Graham Coughlan, Paul Wotton.
Hat-tricks: (0).
Leading scorer: Graham Coughlan (11).

NATIONWIDE DIVISION 2

SEASON 2002-03

Manager: Paul Sturrock

No	Date	Att	Pos	Pt	F-A	H-T	Scorers, Times, and Referees	SQUAD	NUMBERS	IN	USE								subs used
1	A MANSFIELD 10/8	5,309		L 0	3-4	1-1	Evans 24, Friio 86, Lowndes 90 / White 32, 67, Disley 51, Larkin 55 — Ref: G Frankland	Larrieu	Worrell	McGlinchey	Friio	Coughlan^	Wotton	Bent"	Adams	Evans	Stonebr'ge*	Hodges	**Lowndes/Broad/Phillips**
								Pilkington	Jarvis	Moore	Corden	Reddington	McKenzie	Williamson	Sellars*	Disley	Larkin^	White^	Lawrence/Christie/Bacon

After an even first half, the Stags score two quick goals after the break to take the wind out of Argyle's sails. Some unimpressive defending does not help the cause, typified by White's second when he runs from halfway and beats Coughlan and Wotton before prodding past Larrieu.

No	Date	Att	Pos	Pt	F-A	H-T	Scorers, Times, and Referees												subs used
2	H HUDDERSFIELD 13/8	8,953	15 23	W 3	2-1	0-0	Friio 58, Wotton 90 / Thorrington 89 — Ref: B Curson	Larrieu	Worrell	McGlinchy l	Friio	Malcolm	Wotton	Phillips^	Adams	Evans^	Lowndes	Hodges	Sturrock/Bent
								Bevan	Jenkins"	Sharp	Mattis^	Youds	Moses	Thorrington	Irons	Booth	McDonald*	Holland	Stead/Worthington/Heary

Argyle ride their luck, and Wotton's trademark free-kick secures a late win. McGlinchey is sent off (78) for kicking the ball away, having already been booked. Mick Wadsworth's team play attractive football and are unfortunate not gain a reward. Malcolm impresses on his debut.

No	Date	Att	Pos	Pt	F-A	H-T	Scorers, Times, and Referees												subs used
3	H LUTON 17/8	10,973	12 22	W 6	2-1	0-0	McGlinchey 57, Wotton 82 / Howard 67 — Ref: T Parkes	Larrieu	Worrell	McGlinchey	Friio	Malcolm	Wotton	Bent"	Adams	Evans^	Phillips"	Hodges	Hodges/Sturrock/Keith
								Emberson	Boyce	Davis	Nicholls*	Coyne !	Perrett	Brkovic	Spring"	Howard	Thorpe^	Robinson	Bayliss/Crowe/Neilson

Despite customary pre-match gamesmanship from Joe Kinnear, Luton again leave Home Park empty handed, with the dismissal of Coyne (8) for a professional foul not helping their cause. Hatters' coach, Mick Harford is also sent off. A rare McGlinchey goal from 30 yards is the pick.

No	Date	Att	Pos	Pt	F-A	H-T	Scorers, Times, and Referees												subs used
4	A CHELTENHAM 24/8	4,713	6 22	W 9	2-1	0-1	Coughlan 61, Wotton 74 / Spencer 33 — Ref: K Hill	Larrieu	Worrell	McGlinch'y* Friio		Coughlan	Wotton	Bent"	Adams	Evans	Stonebr'ge^	Hodges	**Beresford^** Sturrock/Phillips/Keith
								Book	Howarth	Victory	Yates	Duff	Walker	Williams^	Finnigan*	Spencer"	Naylor	Brayson	McAuley/Milton/Devaney

Yet another Wotton free-kick via the underside of the crossbar is blasted in to save the day again. Beresford's pace causes the Cheltenham defence problems. McGlinchey is stretched off after a harmless looking challenge. Spencer shrugs of two tackles to score. Coughlan nods in.

No	Date	Att	Pos	Pt	F-A	H-T	Scorers, Times, and Referees												subs used
5	H BRISTOL CITY 26/8	11,922	4 11	W 12	2-0	0-0	Wotton 65p, Coughlan 81 — Ref: W Jordan	Larrieu	Worrell	Hodges	Friio"	Coughlan	Wotton	Bent"	Adams	Evans	Lowndes^	Phillips	Sturrock/Beresford/Beadle
								Phillips	Woodman^	Fortune	Doherty*	Coles	Hill	Murray"	Brown	Peacock	Roberts	Bell	Burnell/Matthews/Beadle

Argyle lose Bent (5) with a hamstring injury. Wotton's goalscoring run continues when he nets from a penalty after a blatant shove in the back on Friio. Phillips' cross is met by Coughlan's head for number two to complete the promising start despite a lack of goals from the forward line.

No	Date	Att	Pos	Pt	F-A	H-T	Scorers, Times, and Referees												subs used
6	A QP RANGERS 31/8	14,001	3 11	D 13	2-2	1-0	Friio 33, Hodges 59 / Thomas 69, Pacquette 90 — Ref: L Cable	Larrieu	Worrell	Aljofree	Friio	Coughlan	Wotton	Beresford*	Adams	Evans*	Sturrock^	Hodges	Broad/Phillips/Keith
								Royce	Forbes	Williams	Rose	Shittu	Palmer	Doudou*	Bircham	Furlong^	Gallen	Thomas"	Pacquette/Thomson/Cor'lly

Friio's angled drive is against the run of play. Royce flaps at a corner and Hodges volleys in the loose ball. Larrieu is much the busier keeper and is finally beaten by Thomas's 15-yard shot. Richard Pacquette volleys in during injury time to deny the Greens a undeserved victory.

No	Date	Att	Pos	Pt	F-A	H-T	Scorers, Times, and Referees												subs used
7	A BARNSLEY 14/9	9,134	2 15	D 14	1-1	1-1	Sturrock 38 / Dyer 10 — Ref: M Fletcher	Larrieu	Worrell	Aljofree	Friio	Coughlan	Wotton	Phillips*	Adams	Evans^	Sturrock"	Hodges	**Lopes/Stonebridge/Broad**
								Marriott	Mulligan	Gibbs	Jones	Flynn	Curtis	Betsy	Ward	Dyer^	Sheron^	Rankin"	Fallon/Lumsdan/Holt

A mistake from the otherwise under-employed Larrieu gives Barnsley the lead. Le keeper hesitates allowing Bruce Dyer to scramble the ball home. Sturrock heads into an unguarded net. Mike Sheron blazes the best chance of the game over the bar in an otherwise uneventful match.

No	Date	Att	Pos	Pt	F-A	H-T	Scorers, Times, and Referees												subs used
8	A PETERBOROUGH 17/9	4,208	7 22	L 14	**0-2**	0-0	Clarke 58, Green 84 — Ref: M Warren	Larrieu	Worrell	Aljofree	Friio	Coughlan	Wotton	Beresford*	Adams	Lowndes	Sturrock"	Hodges^	Lopes/Stonebridge/Phillips
								Tyler	Joseph	Gill	Bullard	Edwards	Burton	Newton	Farrell"	Lee	Green	Danielsson*	Clarke/MacDonald

Wasteful Posh finishing lets Argyle off the hook after a first-half pummelling. After a 'quiet' half-time word from Barry Fry, the home side up the ante with Wotton's half-clearance thrashed home by Andy Clarke. A fine move involving the energetic Jimmy Bullard sets up the second.

No	Date	Att	Pos	Pt	F-A	H-T	Scorers, Times, and Referees												subs used
9	H CHESTERFIELD 21/9	8,547	10 11	L 14	0-1	0-0	Ebdon 69 — Ref: S Tomlin	Larrieu	Worrell	Aljofree	Friio	Coughlan	Wotton	Phillips	Adams*	Evans*	Hodges*	Hodges	Sturrock/Lopes/Beresford
								Muggleton	Howson	Davies	Ebdon	Payne*	Dawson	Booty	Rushbury	Reeves	Allott	Burt	Blatherwick

The Spireites rally after losing skipper Steve Payne (32) who is stretchered off. In the main, both sides resort to long range efforts and one finally pays off when Marcus Ebdon rifles in a fine 35-yard effort, consigning the Pilgrims to their first home defeat in almost 13 months.

No	Date	Att	Pos	Pt	F-A	H-T	Scorers, Times, and Referees												subs used
10	H CARDIFF 24/9	11,606	12 4	D 15	2-2	1-1	Wotton 8, Coughlan 90 / Earnshaw 2, 67 — Ref: C Wilkes	Larrieu	Worrell	Aljofree	Friio	Coughlan	Wotton	Phillips*	Adams*	Evans	Stonebr'ge*	Hodges	Lopes/Sturrock/Lowndes
								Alexander	Weston	Croft	Kavanagh	Prior	Gabbidon	Boland	Whalley	Thorne	Earnshaw^	Legg^	Barker/Campbell

Argyle have barely touched the ball before Earnshaw scores. Yet another Wotton free-kick equalises. Ignoring autumnal temperatures, a male streaker interrupts play (12). Earnshaw's header looks enough for victory but Coughlan pops up to level in the fourth minute of stoppage time.

No	Date	Att	Pos	Pt	F-A	H-T	Scorers, Times, and Referees												subs used
11	A WYCOMBE 28/9	6,708	10 20	L 15	1-2	0-1	Friio 60 / Currie 28p, 68 — Ref: P Danson	Larrieu	Aljofree	Friio	Coughlan	Wotton	Phillips"	Adams	Evans*	Stonebr'ge*	Hodges		Keith/Sturrock/Beresford
								Taylor	Senda	Vinnicombe	Bulman	Thomason	McCarthy	Currie	Simpson	Faul'bridge*	Rammell^	Roberts^	Johnson/Devine/Harris

A double from former Argyle loanee, Darren Currie, brings an awful September to an end. Aljofree is adjudged to have tripped Roberts for a penalty. Friio's 30-yard strike is of 'Wottonesque proportions. Currie catches Larrieu out by shooting inside the near post instead of crossing.

Plymouth Argyle — match-by-match record (matches 12–23)

12 — H NORTHAMPTON — 5/10 — Pos 11, D — HT 0-0, FT 0-0 — Att 8,530 — [12] Pts 16
Argyle: Larrieu, Worrell, Aljofree, Lopes*, Coughlan, Wotton, Phillips, Adams, Evans^, Stonebr'ge*, Hodges; subs Beresford^/Keith/Sturrock
Northampton: Abbey, Gill, Carruthers, Trollope, Sampson, Burgess, Rickers, Harsley, Gabbiadini, One*, Hargreaves; sub Asamoah
Ref: A Bates
With Phillips on fire, Argyle produce some free-flowing football with little to show for their efforts. Larrieu's finger-tip save from Ian Sampson's header is one of the best seen at Home Park for many years. The Cobblers stage a second-half fightback and are happy with a point.

13 — H WIGAN — 12/10 — Pos 10, L — HT 1-1, FT 1-3 — Att 8,746 — [3] Pts 16
Scorers: Stonebridge 18; Dinning 25, 58, Ellington 90
Argyle: Larrieu, Worrell, McGlinchey, Friio, Coughlan, Wotton^, Phillips*, Adams, Evans^, Stonebridge, Hodges*; subs Lopes*/Keith/Sturrock
Wigan: Filan, Eaden, Dinning, Jackson, De Vos, Teale*, Jarrett*, Roberts, Ellington, McCulloch, Mitchell*; sub Flynn
Ref: P Armstrong
The early spoils go to Argyle, with Stonebridge shooting home after good control. Wigan gradually take controll and the Greens' defence is unsettled by the pace of Ellington. Tony Dinning shows good composure to score twice and Ellington breaks free to side-foot past Larrieu.

14 — A CREWE — 19/10 — Pos 13, W — HT 1-0, FT 1-0 — Att 6,733 — [4] Pts 19
Scorers: Norris 45
Argyle: Larrieu, Aljofree, Friio, Coughlan, Wotton, Norris, Adams, Sturrock, Stonebridge, Hodges*; sub Evans
Crewe: Ince, Sodje, Wright, Lunt, Walton, Foster, Rix, Brammer, Hulse, Jack*, Jones; sub Ashton
Ref: F Stretton
A win at last! In-form Crewe are hot favourites but a superb debut goal from David Norris seals an unlikely victory. The new boy evades two tackles and fires a high shot past Ince from the edge of the box. All-out defence foils Dario Gradi's highly rated attack to relieve the tension.

15 — H BLACKPOOL — 26/10 — Pos 11, L — HT 0-2, FT 1-3 — Att 8,717 — [7] Pts 19
Scorers: Keith 60; Taylor 16, 40, Murphy 87
Argyle: Larrieu, Worrell, Aljofree*, Friio, Coughlan, Wotton*, Norris, Adams, Sturrock*, Stonebridge, Hodges; subs Evans/Phillips/Keith
Blackpool: Barnes, Grayson, Jaszczun, Wellens, Clarke C, Clarke P, Dalglish*, Southern, Murphy, Taylor, Hills*; subs Bullock/Coid
Ref: A Penn
Despite an unchanged line up, Argyle produce an abysmal first-half display. With Paul Dalglish causing regular panic, the dangerous Seasiders front duo take full advantage. Keith scores with his first touch. Finicky refereeing with eight yellow cards does little to cheer up the home fans.

16 — A BRENTFORD — 29/10 — Pos 12, D — HT 0-0, FT 0-0 — Att 6,431 — [8] Pts 20
Argyle: McCormick, Worrell, McGlinchey, Friio, Coughlan, Wotton^, Norris, Adams, Evans, Keith, Hodges; sub Hodges
Brentford: Smith, Dobson, Evans, Hutchinson*, Marshall, Sonner, O'Connor, Fullarton^, McCammon, Vine, Hunt; subs Williams/Frampton
Ref: M Thorpe
No doubt watching Chancellor of the Exchequer Gordon Brown is approving of the parsimonious nature of both defences. Larrieu is missing with a finger injury but McCormick performs adequately. The Bees' main strategy is to lump high balls to McCammon but without success.

17 — A TRANMERE — 2/11 — Pos 14, L — HT 1-0, FT 1-2 — Att 7,083 — [15] Pts 20
Scorers: Adams 6; Roberts 87, Hodges 90 (og)
Argyle: McCormick, Worrell, McGlinchey, Friio, Coughlan, Wotton, Norris, Adams, Evans^, Keith^, Hodges; subs Sturrock/Stonebridge
Tranmere: Achterberg, Connelly, Nicholson*, Mellon, Allen, Edwards, Taylor^, Jones, Haworth, Proudlock, Harrison*; subs Price/Hume/Roberts
Ref: S Dunn
Adams scores with a low volley. Argyle dominate in wet and windy conditions but the game turns late on. McCormick fumbles a Roberts cross into his own net. Worrell is clearly fouled but play is allowed to continue and a shot ricochets between Wotton and Hodges before going in.

18 — H OLDHAM — 9/11 — Pos 15, D — HT 2-0, FT 2-2 — Att 8,216 — [2] Pts 21
Scorers: Stonebridge 4, Friio 7; Eyres 74p, Andrews 76
Argyle: Milosevic^, Worrell, Hodges, Friio, Coughlan, Wotton, Norris*, Adams, Evans, Stonebridge, Lopes*; subs McGlinch'y/McCorm'k/Keith
Oldham: Pogliacomi, Hall, Armstrong, Murray^, Hill, Beharall, Low, Eyre*, Corazzin, Andrews, Eyres; subs Sheridan/Killen
Ref: P Crossley
Oldham's unbeaten away record looks in danger early on. Milosevic is clattered by Killen (70). Protecting their injured keeper, a mass of Argyle defenders bring down Andrews for a penalty. A second goes in past the limping debutant before his only Argyle appearance ends (79).

19 — H STOCKPORT — 23/11 — Pos 16, W — HT 3-1, FT 4-1 — Att 7,746 — [15] Pts 24
Scorers: Goodwin 6 (og), 60 (og), Keith 13, [Adams 42]; Wotton 11 (og)
Argyle: Larrieu, Worrell, Hodges, Friio, Coughlan, Wotton, Norris*, Adams, Evans^, Stonebr'ge*, Keith; subs Lowndes/Beresford
Stockport: Jones, Goodwin, Tonkin, Fradin, Challinor!, Hardiker, McLachlan^, Gibb, Beckett, Burgess*, Daly*; subs Ross/Lescott/Briggs
Ref: M Warren
National own-goal day comes to Home Park. An exciting start with three early goals and the dismissal of visiting skipper, Dave Challinor (24) for deliberate handball which prevents Evans getting clean through. Jim Goodwin completes a miserable day by getting a second – for Argyle!

20 — A COLCHESTER — 30/11 — Pos 13, D — HT 0-0, FT 0-0 — Att 3,714 — [19] Pts 25
Argyle: Larrieu, Worrell, Hodges, Wotton, Coughlan, Wotton, Norris, Adams, Evans, Stonebridge, Keith; sub Stonebridge
Colchester: Brown, Stockley*, Warren, Pinault, White, Baldwin, Keith, Bowry, Morgan, Rapley, Stockwell*; subs McGleish/Keeble
Ref: C Boyeson
Larrieu does not have to make a save for the whole game but a combination of luck, gritty defending, and poor finishing see the points shared. Evans comes closest to scoring when he bullets a header against a post and into keeper Brown's hands. A frustrating day for the Argyle fans.

21 — H SWINDON — 14/12 — Pos 13, D — HT 0-0, FT 1-1 — Att 8,111 — [18] Pts 26
Scorers: Hodges 90p; Gurney 77
Argyle: Larrieu, Worrell, Hodges, Wotton*, Coughlan, Wotton*, Norris, Adams, Evans, Keith*, Hodges; subs Sturrock/Lowndes/Beresf'rd
Swindon: Griemink, Gurney, Duke, Hewlett, Heywood, Reeves, Miglioranzi, Robinson^, Parkin, Sabin, Invincibile; sub Bampton
Ref: R Olivier
Driving rain, a fierce wind and a soaking pitch makes for a dire match. Andy Gurney curls the ball over the wall from a free-kick for a superb opener. A linesman spots a handball in injury time and, with Wotton already off, Hodges successfully takes over penalty-kick responsibilities.

22 — A PORT VALE — 21/12 — Pos 12, W — HT 2-1, FT 2-1 — Att 4,892 — [14] Pts 29
Scorers: Evans 2, Keith 40; Brooker 26
Argyle: Larrieu, Worrell, Hodges, Wotton, Coughlan, Wotton, Norris, Adams, Evans*, Keith, Hodges; sub Stonebridge
Port Vale: Goodlad, Rowland, Charnock, Boyd, Collins, Burns, Cummins, Durnin^, Brooker, Paynter, Sturrock; subs Armstrong*/McPhee/McClare
Ref: P Prosser
Mark Goodlad's first touch is to drop a Hodges free-kick at the feet of Evans to jab in. Barras's misguided header is chested down by Brooker who volleys the equaliser. Keith bundles home from a yard. The home team almost level in the last minute when a mis-hit cross shaves the bar.

23 — A BRISTOL CITY — 26/12 — Pos 12, D — HT 0-0, FT 0-0 — Att 18,085 — [3] Pts 30
Argyle: Larrieu, Worrell, Hodges, Wotton, Coughlan, Wotton, Norris, Adams, Evans*, Keith*, Hodges; subs McGlin/Stonebr'ge/Sturr'ck
Bristol City: Phillips, Coles, Bell, Doherty^, Butler, Hill, Burnell, Murray, Peacock, Roberts*, Bent; subs Rosenior/Tinnion/Beadle
Ref: A Hall
A large festive crowd is entertained by several chances for each side. Both teams hit the woodwork. Argyle are forced to reshuffle after losing Barras to injury (37). Hodges heads off the line (40) and Hill hits the post (45). Adams man-marks the creative Scott Murray out of the game.

NATIONWIDE DIVISION 2

Manager: Paul Sturrock

SEASON 2002-03

No	Date		Att	Pos	Res		Pt	F-A	H-T	Scorers, Times, and Referees
24	H NOTTS CO	28/12	11,901	12	W	16	33	1-0	0-0	Aljofree 61 — Ref: J Ross
25	H CHELTENHAM	1/1	10,927	12	W	23	36	3-1	2-1	Phillips 22, Stonebridge 35, Norris 53; Worrell 13 (og) — Ref: M Cooper
26	H QP RANGERS	18/1	10,249	10	L	7	36	0-1	0-0	Paquette 51 — Ref: P Walton
27	A NOTTS CO	25/1	6,329	12	W	19	39	2-0	1-0	Norris 38, 50 — Ref: A D'Urso
28	H MANSFIELD	1/2	8,030	10	W	21	42	3-1	1-1	Lawrence 2 (og), Phillips 68, Evans 84; Lawrence 11 — Ref: S Tomlin
29	A HUDDERSFIELD	4/2	7,294	10	L	23	42	0-1	0-0	Smith 82p — Ref: E Ilderton
30	A OLDHAM	8/2	6,657	10	W	4	45	1-0	1-0	Evans 39 — Ref: H Webb
31	H TRANMERE	15/2	8,590	8	L	10	45	0-1	0-0	Haworth 57 — Ref: D Crick
32	A CARDIFF	21/2	14,006	10	D	3	46	1-1	0-1	Wotton 86; Earnshaw 42 — Ref: M Warren
33	A LUTON	25/2	7,589	10	L	8	46	0-1	0-0	Thorpe 50 — Ref: T Bates
34	H BARNSLEY	1/3	8,228	10	D	15	47	1-1	1-0	Coughlan 14; Dyer 66 — Ref: P Rejer

---

24 — NOTTS CO (H), 28/12
Squad: Larrieu, Wotton, Hodges*, Bernard, Aljofree, Norris, Coughlan, Adams, Evans, Stonebridge, Lopes^
Opponents: Mildenhall, Ramsden, Nicholson*, Richardson, Liburd", Ireland, Caskey, Hackworth^, Baraclough, Whitley
Subs used: McGlinchey/Phillips — Harrad/Cas/Stone
A welcome win to end the year. Referee Ross makes a number of mind-boggling decisions, annoying both crowd and players alike. Aljofree's headed winner comes after a series of corners. The game ends in confusion with Mr Ross blowing for a replacement ball and not full-time.

25 — CHELTENHAM (H), 1/1
Squad: Larrieu, Worrell, Bent, Coughlan, Aljofree, Norris, Wotton, Adams, Evans*, Stonebr'ge*, Phillips^
Opponents: Book, Howarth, Yates, Duff M, Victory, Brough, Devaney, Forsyth, Alsop, Spencer^, McAuley^
Subs used: Sturrock/Friio/Keith — Duff S/Brayson
Worrell heads into his own net from Coughlan's sliced clearance. Despite the rain-soaked pitch, Argyle produce some of their best play for some time. Phillips excels in the greasy conditions. Cheltenham gradually lose goals and their discipline, with five players being booked.

26 — QP RANGERS (H), 18/1
Squad: Larrieu, Worrell, Hodges*, Coughlan, Aljofree*, Norris, Wotton, Adams, Evans*, Stonebridge, Phillips^
Opponents: Culkin, Forbes, Padula^, Carlisle, Shittu, Bircham, Palmer, Gallen, Angell, Paquette^, Cook !
Subs used: McGlinchey/Sturrock/Keith — Murphy/Oli
A disappointing result to an entertaining game, Bircham's long ball finding the unmarked Pacquette for the only goal. The match erupts at the death. Cook is sent off (90) for shoving Worrell off the ball. A fracas erupts in the tunnel at the end with players, staff and stewards involved.

27 — NOTTS CO (A), 25/1
Squad: Larrieu, Worrell, Hodges, Friio, Coughlan, Wotton, Norris, Adams, Evans*, Stonebridge, Bent
Opponents: Mildenhall, Fenton, Nicholson*, Ramsden, Richardson, Allsopp, Caskey, Stallard, Heffernan, Baraclough, Liburd
Subs used: Keith
Argyle secure their first win at Meadow Lane since 1959. County start the brighter. Heffernan hits the post but Stonebridge hits the post. Norris is the first to react and nets the rebound. The livewire midfielder then gets a second after chasing a weak back-header from Baraclough.

28 — MANSFIELD (H), 1/2
Squad: Larrieu, Worrell, Friio, Coughlan, Adams, Norris*, Wotton, Bent, Evans, Stonebr'ge*, Beresford*
Opponents: Pilkington, Hassell, Disley*, Day, Gadsby, Lawrence, Richardson, Curtis, White^, Mendes^, Disley
Subs used: Phillips/Keith/McGlinchey — Wil'mson/Beardsley/Mitchell
Liam Lawrence has an eventful start to the game, heading past his own keeper and then meeting a cross to equalise. Evans charges down a Kevin Pilkington clearance and the ball falls to Phillips to side foot in. Evans then scores with a superb overhead kick as Argyle are in control.

29 — HUDDERSFIELD (A), 4/2
Squad: Larrieu, Worrell, Friio, Coughlan, Wotton, Norris*, Adams, Evans*, Stonebr'ge*, Bent, Smith^
Opponents: Senior, Moses, Sharp, Irons*, Brown, Holland, Booth, Mattis, Stead^, Smith^
Subs used: Keith/Phillips/McGlinchey — Thorrington/Baldry/Heary
Argyle have the majority of possession but fail to carve out any clear-cut chances to test debutant keeper Phil Senior. Despite continuing to dominate, the Greens lose out on the points following a controversial penalty. Thorrington drives a cross which Aljofree is adjudged to handle.

30 — OLDHAM (A), 8/2
Squad: Larrieu, Worrell, Friio, Coughlan, Aljofree, Norris, Wotton, Adams, Evans*, Keith^, Bent
Opponents: Miskelly, Haining, Armstrong, Murray, Beharall, Hall, Duxbury*, Sheridan, Andrews, Burgess^, Carss
Subs used: Stonebr'e/McGlin'y/Bernard — Killen/Eyres
The in-form Evans strikes after beating two men and driving a shot into the far corner. Argyle are forced into rearguard action for the last 20 minutes. A tackle by Haining on Wotton provokes a touchline argument between Latics boss Iain Dowie and Pilgrims physio Paul Maxwell.

31 — TRANMERE (H), 15/2
Squad: Larrieu, Worrell, Friio, Coughlan, Aljofree, Norris, Wotton, Adams, Evans*, Bent^, Keith
Opponents: Achterberg, Allen, Roberts, Connelly, Sharps, Loran, Taylor, Jones, Haworth, Hume, Nicholson
Subs used: Keith/Phillips/McGlinchey
Aljofree 'scores' from a free-kick (30) but referee Crick orders a re-take for encroachment! The dangerous Haworth gets the only goal, heading past an out-of-position Larrieu who otherwise performs superbly. There is a seven-minute delay for treatment to a nasty Coughlan head injury.

32 — CARDIFF (A), 21/2
Squad: Larrieu, Worrell, McGlinch'y*, Friio, Aljofree*, Norris, Wotton, Bent, Evans*, Stonebr'ge*, Hodges^
Opponents: Alexander, Weston, Croft, Boland, Young, Bowen*, Barker, Kavanagh, Thorne, Earnshaw, Legg^
Subs used: Lowndes/Keith/Adams — Bonner/Prior
Stonebridge provides the miss of the season by blasting over from two yards. City capitalise on Earnshaw's pace as he runs clear to score and is then booked for over-elaborate celebrations. Wotton uncharacteristically floats a free-kick into the area but no one floats as it goes in.

33 — LUTON (A), 25/2
Squad: Larrieu, Worrell^, McGlinch'y*, Friio, Aljofree, Norris, Wotton, Bent, Evans, Stonebridge, Hodges
Opponents: Hirschfeld, Hillier, Davis, Nicholls, Coyne, Willmott, Crowe, Spring*, Howard, Thorpe, Hughes
Subs used: Keith/Lowndes — Brkovic
On-loan Canadian international Lars Hirschfeld saves the Hatters on several occasions. In an entertaining game, Thorpe prods home the only goal after a long throw from Hillier. Argyle end the game with four forwards but to no avail, as inconsistency continues to blight the season.

34 — BARNSLEY (H), 1/3
Squad: Larrieu, Worrell, McGlinchey, Bernard^, Aljofree, Norris, Wotton, Bent, Evans, Stonebridge, Keith^
Opponents: Marriott, Morgan, Donovan^, Ward, Austin, Williams, Kay, Jones, Dyer, Sheron, Neil
Subs used: Stonebr'ge*/Phillips/Friio/Lowndes — Betsy
A Wotton corner is missed by Andy Marriott and Coughlan smashes the ball into the roof of the net. A great strike from Bruce Dyer levels. The same player almost gets a second but his shot is saved by the outstretched leg of Larrieu. Both sides have penalty appeals turned down.

Match-by-match record (matches 35–46)

35 · H · 4/3 · PETERBOROUGH
Keith 9, Burton 25 (og), Gill 42 (og), McKenzie 7 [Wot'n 45, Friio 62, Bent 72]
Ref: C Penton — Att 6,931 · 10 · W · 16 · 50 · **6-1** · 4-1
Argyle: Larrieu, Worrell, Hodges, Friio*, Wotton, Coughlan, Wotton, Bent, Adams, Evans*, Keith^, Phillips · Subs: Stonebridge/Norris/Lowndes
Peterborough: Harrison, Rea, Gill, Scott, Arber, Burton^, Newton^, Jelleyman, Clarke*, Fotiadis, Phillips, Danielsson · Subs: Lee/Farrell/McKenzie
Sturrock rings the changes to good effect as his side run riot and again benefit from own-goals. Mr Penton conjures nine minutes of first-half injury time. Barry Fry makes changes at half-time which restores some parity. To think the Posh had not let in an away goal since Boxing Day!

36 · A · 8/3 · CHESTERFIELD
Keith 15, 74 | Payne 10, Reeves 17, 49
Ref: F Stretton — Att 3,668 · 10 · L · 17 · 50 · **2-3** · 1-2
Argyle: Larrieu, Worrell, Hodges, Friio*, Wotton, Coughlan, Bent*, Adams, Evans^, Keith, Phillips
Chesterfield: Williams, Payne, Close, Edwards, Blatherwick, Howson^, Allott, Rushbury, Reeves, Phillips, Brandon · Subs: Hurst/O'Hare
Without a win in ten games, the Spireites defy recent form. A soaked pitch and swirling wind contribute to several mistakes in a full-blooded encounter. The homesters lose Folan after he falls over an advertising board. Another defeat and a Frio hamstring injury makes for a bad day.

37 · A · 15/3 · BLACKPOOL
Keith 29 | Taylor 40
Ref: C Wilkes — Att 8,772 · 10 · D · 9 · 51 · **1-1** · 1-1
Argyle: Larrieu, Worrell, Hodges, Friio, Wotton, Coughlan, Bernard, Bent, Adams, Evans, Keith^, Phillips
Blackpool: Barnes, Grayson, Richardson, Southern, Flynn, Bullock, Thornley, Murphy, Taylor, Coid^ · Subs: Hills/Dalglish
Two evenly matched sides. Argyle lead through Keith's 25-yard strike. Scott Taylor, looking offside, levels when Larrieu gets a hand to his low shot but the ball trickles over the line. Veteran Colin Hendry is resolute in defence. Taylor almost snatches it, hitting the crossbar (90).

38 · H · 18/3 · CREWE
Stonebridge 47 | Jack 4, Ashton 13, 68
Ref: L Cable — Att 7,777 · 10 · L · 2 · 51 · **1-3** · 0-2
Argyle: Larrieu, Worrell*, Hodges, Bernard*, Wotton, Coughlan, Bent, Adams, Evans, Keith, Phillips · Subs: Norris/Smith/Evans
Crewe: Ince, McCready, Tierney*, Lunt, Walker, Walton, Brammer, Sorvel, Ashton", Jack, Oakes^ · Subs: Sodje/Bell/Edwards
The Argyle defence again looks susceptible to pace as Rodney Jack races clear to score. A great volley from Dean Ashton soon increases the lead. Stonebridge hooks in a shot but the impressive Ashton scores again. A male streaker is quickly apprehended by a plethora of stewards.

39 · H · 22/3 · BRENTFORD
Keith 12, 47, Smith 28
Ref: M Fletcher — Att 6,835 · 10 · W · 14 · 54 · **3-0** · 2-0
Argyle: Larrieu, Worrell, Hodges, Friio, Wotton, Coughlan, Bernard, Bent, Adams, Norris, Evans, Keith^, Smith · Subs: Wotton/Evans/Beresford
Brentford: Smith, Dobson, Sonner, Rowlands, Frampton, Sonko, Vine, O'Connor, McCam'on*, Ant'e-Curier Hunt · Subs: Williams
A route-one goal to open. Larrieu's long kick is flicked on by Smith and Keith fires home. Smith opens his Argyle account by shooting low through an inadequate defensive wall. Keith volleys in his second but misses a sitter for a hat-trick. Coughlan is added to the injury list.

40 · A · 29/3 · WIGAN
Keith 35
Ref: M Cooper — Att 7,203 · 10 · W · 1 · 57 · **1-0** · 1-0
Argyle: Larrieu, Worrell, Hodges, Friio, Wotton, Coughlan, Aljofree, Bent, Norris, Evans, Keith · Subs: Bernard
Wigan: Filan, Eaden, Baines, Bullard, De Vos, Jackson, Liddell, Jarrett, Roberts*, Ellington, McCulloch^ · Subs: Teale/Brackin
Champions-elect Wigan look out of sorts as the Greens notch up a shock win. Keith continues his hot streak by scoring via a post. Wary of the potency of the Latics attack, Coughlan and Aljofree perform superbly. Paul Jewell's men throw the kitchen sink at Argyle in the latter stages.

41 · H · 5/4 · COLCHESTER
Ref: P Taylor — Att 7,122 · 9 · D · 11 · 58 · **0-0** · 0-0
Argyle: Larrieu, Worrell, Hodges, Friio", Wotton, Coughlan, Aljofree, Bent, Malcolm, Evans, Keith · Subs: Stonebr'ge*/Smith^
Colchester: McKinney, Stockley, Edwards, Canham*, Fitzgerald, White, Izzet, Duguid, May, McGleish*, Jackson^ · Subs: Pinault/Stockwell/Morgan
Paul Sturrock is away scouting. The game is delayed after referee Taylor appears wearing a green shirt! Stonebridge is tripped (24) but Wotton fails to produce his customary power from the spot and McKinney saves with his legs. Another clean sheet but frustrating only one point.

42 · A · 12/4 · STOCKPORT
Keith 72 | Wilbraham 40, Challinor 86p
Ref: M Ryan — Att 5,494 · 9 · L · 19 · 58 · **1-2** · 0-1
Argyle: Larrieu, Worrell, Hodges*, Friio", Wotton, Coughlan, Bernard, Bent !, Norris, Evans, Keith · Subs: Evans/McAnespie/Norris
Stockport: Tidman, Goodwin, Tonkin, Clark, Challinor, Greer, Hartiker, Lescott, Wilbraham, Daly, McLachlan · Subs: Beresford
Sturrock is absent again. Argyle fail to gain a third win over a County side missing top scorer, Luke Beckett. With a draw seeming likely, Bent saves a goalbound header with his hands and is sent off. Challinor's resultant penalty gives the home side a boost in their relegation battle.

43 · H · 19/4 · PORT VALE
Coughlan 65, Norris 67, Wotton 77
Ref: M Warren — Att 7,775 · 9 · W · 16 · 61 · **3-0** · 3-0
Argyle: Larrieu, Worrell, Hodges*, Bernard, Wotton, Coughlan, Collins, Malcolm, Norris, Evans^, Keith · Subs: Lowndes/Keith
Port Vale: Delaney, Carragher, Clarke, Cummins, Walsh*, Brisco, Durnin^, Littlejohn, McPhee, Charnock, Paynter · Subs: Armstrong
A cold and swirling wind contributes to an uneventful and uninteresting first period. The entertainment is cranked up in the second half as Argyle dominate. Headers from Coughlan and, more rarely, Norris, kill the game but Wotton's 30-yard volley is easily the pick of the bunch.

44 · A · 23/4 · SWINDON
Invincibile 38, Parkin 68
Ref: M Williamson — Att 5,057 · 8 · L · 12 · 61 · **0-2** · 0-2
Argyle: Larrieu, Worrell*, Hodges*, Friio, Coughlan, Aljofree, Wotton, Norris, Bernard, Keith, Lowndes · Subs: Wotton/McAnespie/Yetton
Swindon: Farr, Lewis, Herring^, Hewlett, Heywood, Reeves, Migliaranzi*, Robinson, Parkin, Invincibile^, Duke · Subs: Bampton/Taylor/Young
The Greens get an early warning when Swindon hit the bar (4). The defence is punished for dilatory defending when Danny Invincibile pounces. Frio loses possession in a crucial area and the ball is played to Sam Parkin to score the winner. A definite end of season performance.

45 · A · 26/4 · NORTHAMPTON
Norris 19, Stonebridge 55, Stamp 66, Morison 72
Ref: E Evans — Att 5,063 · 9 · D · 24 · 62 · **2-2** · 2-2
Argyle: Larrieu, Connolly, Hodges, Friio*, Taylor, Wotton, Bernard, Broad, Stonebridge, Keith, McAnespie* · Subs: Bernard/Beresford
Northampton: Harper, Marsh, Hope, Trollope, Carruthers, Sampson, Harsley, Hargreaves, Stamp, Dudfield^, Asamoah* · Subs: Morison/Gabbiadini
The doomed Cobblers stage a spirited fightback. Sturrock again shuffles his pack, which includes a welcome return for Craig Taylor. The revised line up still looks comfortable as they notch up a two-goal lead. The failure to hold on to the three points sums up Argyle's season.

46 · H · 3/5 · WYCOMBE
Lowndes 75
Ref: G Cain — Att 10,129 · 9 · W · 17 · 65 · **1-0** · 1-0
Argyle: Larrieu, Connolly, McGlinchey, Friio, Wotton, Coughlan, Wotton, Norris, Broad, Keith^, St'bridge* · Capaldi*/Bulman · Beresford/Lowndes/Evans
Wycombe: Talia, Ryan, Vinnicombe, Senda, Johnson, Roberts, Simpson*, Harris", Cook^, Bulman · Subs: Oliver/Dixon/Holligan
Child free-entry boosts the crowd for a nothing-to-play-for match. Tony Capaldi shudders the post on an impressive debut. Lowndes converts Norris's cross from six yards. The news that fierce rivals Exeter have been relegated to the Conference induces the biggest cheer of the day.

Home average 8,981 · Away average 7,310

NATIONWIDE DIVISION 2 (CUP-TIES)   Manager: Paul Sturrock   SEASON 2002-03

Carling Cup

		Att		F-A	L	H-T	Scorers, Times, and Referees
1	A CRYSTAL PALACE	2		1-2	L	1-1	Sturrock 39
10/9		6,385 1:10	t		aet		Powell 22, Johnson 113
							Ref: C Penton

SQUAD NUMBERS IN USE: Larrieu, Worrell, Aljofree, Coughlan, Wotton, Phillips, Lopes, Lowndes", Sturrock", Hodges
*Kolinko, Fleming, Granville, Thomson^, Powell, Johnson, Mullins, Freedman", Adebola, Routledge**

subs used: Evans/Friio/Stonebridge · *Butterfield/Black/Frampton*

Argyle finally run out of legs in an evenly matched game. Sturrock tries a new 'diamond' formation. Powell heads home a free kick. Sturrock junior misses an open goal but makes amends by converting Lopes' cross. Granville goes past a tired Worrell to set up Andy Johnson's winner.

FA Cup

		Att		F-A	W/L/D	H-T	Scorers, Times, and Referees
1	A BURY	16	W	3-0		2-0	Evans 19, Nelson 32 (og), Wotton 86
16/11		2,987 3:10					Ref: H Webb

SQUAD NUMBERS IN USE: Larrieu, Worrell, Hodges, Friio, Wotton, Lopes*, Adams, Evans, Stonebridge, Keith^
Gamer, Unsworth, Swailes, O'Shaughn'y Nelson, Barrass, Stuart, Billy, Lawson^, Newby, Woodthorpe*

subs used: McGlinchey/Sturrock · *Preece/Nugent*

Argyle's extra class tells from the off. The Shakers are soon shaken by Evans' opener. With a nervous keeper, Bury never look comfortable against a three-man attack. Nelson heads a Wotton free-kick into his own net. A 35-yard free-kick from Wotton ends proceedings in style.

		Att		F-A	W/L/D	H-T	Scorers, Times, and Referees
2	A STOCKPORT	13	W	3-0		2-0	Stonebridge 9, Friio 14, Wotton 72p
7/12		3,571 15					Ref: A Butler

SQUAD NUMBERS IN USE: Larrieu, Worrell, Hodges, Friio*, Wotton, Coughlan, Adams, Evans, Stonebridge, Keith
Jones, Lescott, Tonkin, Palmer, Goodwin, McLachlan Fradin, Beckett, Gibb, Ross*

subs used: McGlinchey · *Burgess*

The Greens all but seal a third round place within the first quarter of an hour. The opener comes after a mistake by County player-manager Carlton Palmer. Jones weakly pats the ball to Friio for number two. Wotton nets from the spot after Keith is bundled over by skipper Lescott.

		Att		F-A	W/L/D	H-T	Scorers, Times, and Referees
3	H DAGENHAM & R	10	D	2-2		1-1	Stonebridge 44, Wotton 61
4/1		11,885 C:5					Terry 13, McDougald 67
							Ref: T Parkes

SQUAD NUMBERS IN USE: Larrieu, Worrell, Aljofree, Bent, Coughlan, Wotton, Norris, Adams, Evans, Stonebr'ge^ Phillips*
Roberts, Vickers, Heffer, McGrath, Matthews, Smith, Shipp, Janney, McDougald^West, Terry

subs used: Friio/Keith · *Hill*/Rooney*

Manager Garry Hill is proud of his team after they have the better of much of the game. With Coughlan having a rare off day, Argyle are grateful for a replay. Junior McDougald maintains his record of scoring in every round. The visitors do a lap of honour at the final whistle!

		Att		F-A	W/L/D	H-T	Scorers, Times, and Referees
3R	A DAGENHAM & R	10	L	0-2		0-1	Shipp 20, McDougald 85
14/1		4,530 C:5					Ref: T Parkes

SQUAD NUMBERS IN USE: Larrieu, Worrell, Hodges, Friio, Wotton, Norris, Adams^, Evans*, Keith, Stonebr'ge" West*
Roberts, Vickers, Heffer, McGrath, Matthews, Smith, Shipp, Janney, McDougald West, Terry*

subs used: Phillips/Bent/Sturrock · *Rooney*

The Daggers reach the fourth round of the Cup for the first time in their history as Sky TV gets its wish for giant-killing. Shipp's shot deflects off Hodges for the opener. McDougald scores again with a header. A fan runs on to the pitch but merely to have a conversation with Larrieu.

League Table

Pos	Team	P	W	D	L	F	A	W	D	L	F	A	Pts
			Home					Away					
1	Wigan	46	14	7	2	37	16	15	6	2	31	9	100
2	Crewe	46	11	5	7	29	19	14	6	3	47	21	86
3	Bristol C	46	15	5	3	43	15	9	7	6	36	33	83
4	QP Rangers	46	14	4	5	38	19	10	7	6	31	26	83
5	Oldham	46	11	6	6	39	18	11	10	2	29	20	82
6	Cardiff*	46	12	6	5	33	20	11	6	6	35	23	81
7	Tranmere	46	14	5	4	38	23	9	6	8	28	34	80
8	PLYMOUTH	46	11	6	6	39	24	6	9	8	24	28	65
9	Luton	46	8	7	8	32	28	9	8	6	35	34	65
10	Swindon	46	10	5	8	34	27	6	7	10	25	36	60
11	P'borough	46	8	7	8	25	20	8	9	8	26	34	58
12	Colchester	46	8	7	8	24	24	8	9	8	28	32	58
13	Blackpool	46	10	8	5	35	25	7	5	13	21	39	58
14	Stockport	46	8	8	8	39	38	7	2	14	26	32	55
15	Notts Co	46	10	7	6	37	32	3	9	11	25	38	55
16	Brentford	46	8	8	7	28	21	6	4	13	19	35	54
17	Port Vale	46	9	5	9	34	31	5	6	12	20	39	53
18	Wycombe	46	8	9	6	39	38	5	6	12	20	28	52
19	Barnsley	46	7	8	8	27	31	6	5	12	24	33	52
20	Chesterfield	46	11	4	8	29	28	3	4	16	14	45	50
21	Cheltenham	46	6	9	8	26	31	4	9	10	27	37	48
22	Huddersfield	46	7	9	7	27	24	4	3	16	12	37	45
23	Mansfield	46	9	2	12	38	45	3	6	14	28	52	44
24	Northampton	46	7	4	12	23	31	3	5	15	17	48	39
		1104	236	150	166	793	628	166	150	236	628	793	1506

* promoted after play-offs

Notes

Double wins: (3) Cheltenham, Notts Co, Port Vale.

Double defeats: (4) Chesterfield, Stockport, Tranmere, Wigan.

Won from behind: (3) Cheltenham (h & a), Peterborough (h).

Lost from in front: (2) Tranmere (a), Wigan (h), Mansfield (a).

High spots: Largely unchanged squad.
Respectable finishing position for first season in higher league.
Useful signings in Norris and Aljofree.

Low spots: Failure to capitalize on good start to season.
Inconsistency. After August never won more than two games in a row.
Disappointing defeat to non-league opposition in FA Cup.

Player of the Year: Paul Wotton.

Ever presents: (0)

Hat-tricks: (0).

Leading scorer: Marino Keith, Paul Wotton (11).

Appearances & Goals

Name	Lge	Sub	LC	Sub	FAC	Sub	Lge	LC	FAC	Tot
Adams, Steve	36	1	1		4		2			2
Aljofree, Hasney	19		1		1		1			1
Barras, Tony	4									
Bent, Jason	23	2	1	1			1			1
Beresford, David	6	10			1	1				
Bernard, Paul	7	3								
Broad, Joe	1	4								
Capaldi, Tony	1									
Connolly, Paul	2									
Coughlan, Graham	42		1		4		5			5
Evans, Michael	35	7	1	1	4		4		1	5
Friio, David	33	3	1	1	3		6		1	7
Hodges, Lee	38	1	1		3		2			2
Keith, Marino	20	17	1		3	1	11			11
Larrieu, Romain	43		1		4					
Lopes, Osvaldo	4	5	1							
Lowndes, Nathan	6	10	1	1	1					
Malcolm, Stuart	3									
McAnespie, Kieran	2	2								
McCormick, Luke	2	1								
McGlinchey, Brian	11	8				2	1			1
Milosevic, Danny	1									
Norris, David	29	4	1		3		6			6
Phillips, Martin	14	10	1		1	1	2			2
Smith, Grant	4	1					1			1
Stonebridge, Ian	30	7	1			4	5		2	7
Sturrock, Blair	5	15	1			2	1	1		2
Taylor, Craig	1									
Worrell, David	43		1		4					
Wotton, Paul	41	2	1		4		8		3	11
Yetton, Stewart							5		1	6
(own-goals)							2			2
31 players used	506	114	11	3	44	8	63	1	8	72

NATIONWIDE DIVISION 2

Manager: Sturrock > Summerfield > Williamson — SEASON 2003-04

No	H/A	Opponent	Date	Att	Pos	Pt	F-A	H-T	Scorers, Times, and Referees
1	H	GRIMSBY	9/8	9,590	–	D(1)	2-2	1-1	Keith 32, Coughlan 51 / Boulding 28, Anderson 64 / Ref: L Cable
2	A	RUSHDEN & D	16/8	4,045	21	L(1)	1-2	0-0	Capaldi 77 / Lowe 54, Jack 56 / Ref: B Knight
3	H	STOCKPORT	23/8	7,954	21	W(4)	3-1	3-1	Keith 21, Hodges 22, Bent 28 / Beckett 43 / Ref: E Ilderton
4	A	CHESTERFIELD	25/8	4,089	18	D(5)	1-1	0-0	Friio 66 / Brandon 50 / Ref: M Clattenburg
5	H	BRIGHTON	30/8	9,289	3	D(6)	3-3	1-2	Coughlan 19, St'bridge 81, Friio 89 / Connolly 14 (og), Butters 36, Knight 73 / Ref: M Fletcher
6	A	BRENTFORD	6/9	5,688	23	W(9)	3-1	1-1	Stonebridge 9, Evans 58, 84 / May 27 / Ref: S Tomlin
7	H	LUTON	13/9	9,894	8	W(12)	2-1	0-0	Evans 83, Friio 90 / McSheffrey 58 / Ref: T Bates
8	A	PETERBOROUGH	16/9	4,183	14	D(13)	2-2	1-1	Wotton 9p, Capaldi 84 / Arber 33p, Clarke 81 / Ref: R Pearson
9	A	WREXHAM	20/9	3,947	14	D(14)	2-2	1-2	Norris 30, Capaldi 49 / Lawrence 28, Jones 41p / Ref: M Ryan
10	H	BARNSLEY	27/9	8,695	5	W(17)	2-0	1-0	Coughlan 38, Evans 75 / Ref: R Beeby
11	H	BRISTOL CITY	30/9	13,923	11	L(17)	0-1	0-1	Peacock 27 / Ref: P Armstrong

SQUAD NUMBERS IN USE — subs used

Match 1 — GRIMSBY
Argyle: Larrieu, Worrell, Hodges, Friio, Wotton, Coughlan, Norris^, Bent, Keith*, St'bridge*, Capaldi
Opposition: Davison, Cas, Barnard, Campbell, Crane, Ford, Crowe, Hamilton^, T'Heuvel*, Boulding*, Anderson
Subs used: Evans/Adams/Lowndes — *Mansaram/Groves/Rowan*
Report: Baking temperatures in the mid-90s greet the new season. The Mariners score with their first chance of the game. Close-range headers from Keith and Coughlan put Argyle in front but Iain Anderson collects a corner and drills a 25-yard shot past Larrieu to give the visitors a point.

Match 2 — RUSHDEN & D
Argyle: Larrieu, Worrell*, Hodges*, Friio, Wotton, Coughlan, Norris, Bent, Evans, Keith^, Capaldi
Opposition: Turley, Bignot, Underwood, Mills, Edwards, Hunter, Hall, Bell, Lowe, Jack^, Darby
Subs used: St'bridge/Lowndes/Adams — *Burgess/Darby*
Report: Jamaican international Onandi Lowe heads the newly promoted side in front and Rodney Jack seizes on a mis-hit Hodges back pass. Capaldi employs his rarely used right foot to curl a beauty into the top corner. Home manager Brian Talbot is sent to the stands, upset at a Friio tackle.

Match 3 — STOCKPORT
Argyle: Larrieu, Worrell, Hodges, Friio, Wotton, Coughlan, Norris*, Bent, Keith*, St'bridge*, Capaldi
Opposition: Colgan, Goodwin, Hardiker, McLachlan^, Clare, Jones*, Gibb, Lescott, Beckett, Wibraham^, Ellison
Subs used: Adams/Evans/Lowndes — *Challinor/Daly/Collins*
Report: Hardly a classic but a much-needed first win of the season for Argyle. Keith needs two attempts to convert a near-post cross and two more goals in quick succession knocks the stuffing out of County. The second half is instantly forgettable with over-fussy refereeing dominating.

Match 4 — CHESTERFIELD
Argyle: Larrieu, Worrell, Hodges, Friio, Wotton, Coughlan, Adams, Bent, Keith^, St'bridge*, Capaldi*
Opposition: Muggleton, Uhlenbeek, O'Hare, Evatt, Payne, Dawson, Allott^, Hurst, Brandon, Searle, Reeves
Subs used: Evans/Norris/Lowndes — *Folan/Reeves*
Report: The normally watertight Argyle defence is again at fault as everyone stands to watch Chris Brandon roll the ball past Larrieu. Friio sends a looping header out of the reach of Carl Muggleton to notch his first goal since March and deny the Spireites their first win of the season.

Match 5 — BRIGHTON
Argyle: Larrieu, Connolly*, Hodges, Friio, Wotton, Coughlan, Norris, Bent, St'bridge, Evans, Capaldi^
Opposition: Roberts, Hinshwood, Mayo, Oatway, Cullip, Butters, Hart, Carpenter, Henderson, Knight, Harding
Subs used: Evans/Adams/B'esford — *Knight/Harding*
Report: Connolly's bizarre 40-yard lob over Larrieu sets the tone for an entertaining afternoon. Argyle look doomed after Leon Knight's header but Stonebridge heads in on his 22nd birthday and in the last minute the ball breaks to Friio who merely has to roll the ball into an empty net.

Match 6 — BRENTFORD
Argyle: Larrieu, Worrell*, Hodges, Friio, Wotton, Coughlan, Norris, Adams, Evans, St'bridge^, Hodges^
Opposition: Julian, Dobson, Fieldwick, Smith^, Roget, Sonko, Rougier, Hutchinson, May, Peters*, Hunt
Subs used: Connolly/Sturrock/Aljofree — *Tabb/Evans*
Report: Injuries force Sturrock into a number of changes. Stonebridge scores from close range. Ben May equalises but Evans proves to be the hero of the day. He finds the bottom corner from 18 yards and then bravely heads in a long clearance from Larrieu with keeper Julian rushing out.

Match 7 — LUTON
Argyle: McCormick, Worrell, Hodges, Friio, Wotton, Coughlan, Norris, Adams, Evans, St'bridge*, Hodges*
Opposition: Beckwith, Boyce, Davis, Hughes, Bayliss^, Coyne, Foley, Brkovic, Showunmi*, McSheffrey, Spring
Subs used: Keith/Bent/Sturrock — *Crowe/Hillier*
Report: More crucial late goals bring victory over old rivals. McCormick is drafted in to replace long-term injury victim, Larrieu, but is given little chance with on-loan Gary McSheffrey's header. Evans equalises and then Friio ghosts in to head home a Wotton free-kick in injury time.

Match 8 — PETERBOROUGH
Argyle: McCormick, Worrell, Hodges, Friio*, Wotton, Coughlan, Norris, Bent, Evans*, St'bridge^, Capaldi
Opposition: Tyler, Gill, Legg, Thomson, Rea, Arber, Newton, Shields, Clarke, McKenzie, Farrell
Subs used: Adams/Keith/Sturrock — *Capaldi/Farrell*
Report: Argyle take an early lead through Wotton's penalty after Capaldi is fouled by Gill. Friio is injured early on and then Arber scores from the spot after a push by Worrell on Shields. Clarke looks to have given Posh their first home win of the season but Capaldi bundles in a Keith cross.

Match 9 — WREXHAM
Argyle: McCormick, Worrell, Hodges, Adams, Wotton, Coughlan, Norris, Bent, Evans*, Keith^, Capaldi
Opposition: Dibble, Pejic, Edwards C, Ferguson, Carey, Lawrence, Whitely*, Llewellyn, One^, Jones, Edwards P^
Subs used: Evans/Sturrock — *Sam/Holmes/Thomas*
Report: 6ft 7in Trinidad international Denis Lawrence heads home from a corner, but Norris's deflected 25 yarder soon levels. Lee Jones scores from the spot after the referee spots a Hodges handball. A rare Capaldi header equalises and the Pilgrims battle through for another away point.

Match 10 — BARNSLEY
Argyle: McCormick, Worrell, Gilbert*, Adams, Wotton, Coughlan, Norris, Bent, Keith^, Capaldi*, Hodges^
Opposition: Ilic, Crooks, Gallimore, Lumsdon, Handyside^, Ireland, Garre, O'Cal'han*, Betsy, Fallon, Austin
Subs used: Sturrock/Hodges — *Kay/Carson*
Report: A first clean sheet of the season against a Barnsley side who were looking for a draw from the off. Coughlan loops a header over Sasa Ilic. Rory Fallon hits the crossbar but the recalled Evans scores with a stooping header to make Argyle the top scorers outside the Premiership.

Match 11 — BRISTOL CITY
Argyle: McCormick, Worrell, Gilbert*, Adams, Wotton, Coughlan, Norris, Bent, Evans, Keith^, Capaldi^
Opposition: Phillips, Woodman, Bell*, Burnell, Butler, Hill, Wilkshire, Tinnion, Miller, Peacock, Brown
Subs used: Stu'ck/St'bridge/Hodges — *Fortune/Lita*
Report: Evans and Stonebridge have shots cleared off the line, Capaldi hits the post, and strong penalty appeals for a handball by Craig Woodman are waved away. Lee Peacock evades Gilbert to fire home and silence the large crowd on a frustrating evening for the home side's supporters.

Match	Date	H/A	Opponent	Res	Score	Pos	Att
	4/10		(WYCOMBE)			22 18	5,708
13	11/10	H	TRANMERE	W	6-0	9 19 21	7,610
14	18/10	A	PORT VALE	W	5-1	5 3 24	5,786
15	22/10	A	SHEFFIELD WED	W	3-1	2 4 27	20,090
16	25/10	H	BLACKPOOL	W	1-0	1 18 30	12,372
17	1/11	H	OLDHAM	D	2-2	1 15 31	11,205
18	15/11	A	Q P RANGERS	L	0-3	1 3 31	17,049
19	22/11	H	HARTLEPOOL	W	2-0	3 6 34	9,000
20	29/11	A	COLCHESTER	W	2-0	2 5 37	4,332
21	13/12	H	SWINDON	W	3-2	2 13 40	9,374
22	20/12	H	NOTTS CO	W	3-0	2 22 43	9,923
23	26/12	A	BOURNEMOUTH	W	2-0	1 9 46	8,901

4/10 — (Wycombe)
Argyle: McCormick, Worrell, Short, Wotton, Coughlan, Norris, Currie, Evans, Bent, Keith, Capaldi; subs Hodges/St'bridge
Wycombe: Talia, Senda, Vinnicombe, Bulman, Branston, Thomson, Currie, Ryan*, Brown*, Holligan^, Simpson; subs Harris/Bell/Cook
Ref: M Thorpe
Wycombe had conceded 14 goals in their previous four home games but chances are few and far between in a dour encounter. Bent's 25-yard effort is the best chance but is saved well by Talia's full-length dive. Coughlan defies an injury scare to give a man-of-the-match performance.

13 H TRANMERE 11/10 — W 6-0
Scorers: Friio 6, Wotton 38, Gilbert 45, Keith 49, Evans 56, Norris 79 [Wotton 79]
Argyle: McCormick, Worrell, Gilbert, Friio^, Wotton, Coughlan, Norris, Adams, Evans^, Keith*, Capaldi; subs Hodges/St'rrock/Lowndes
Tranmere: Achterberg, Allen, Roberts, Harrison*, Connelly, Gray, Taylor^, Loran, Dagnall*, Haworth, Mellon; subs Dadi/Jones/Navarro
Ref: A Marriner
Friio returns from injury and scores within six minutes. A trademark free-kick from Wotton and a first league goal for Gilbert kill the game by half-time. Rovers are managerless and clueless as Argyle continue the rout in the second half with everyone trying to get on the score sheet.

14 A PORT VALE 18/10 — W 5-1
Scorers: Keith 35, Friio 38, 73, Adams 45, McPhee 51 [Wotton 47]
Argyle: McCormick, Worrell, Gilbert, Friio^, Wotton, Coughlan, Norris, Adams^, Evans, Keith*, Capaldi; subs Capaldi/Bent/Aljofree
Port Vale: Delaney, Brightwell^, Lipa, Pilkington, Collins, Birchall*, Cummins, Littlejohn, Paynter, McPhee; subs Armstrong/Burns/B-Wilk'n
Ref: L Probert
Third-placed Vale are demolished by Keith and Friio headers and long-range efforts from Adams. Friio again and, of course, Wotton. Many Argyle fans are stranded on the M6 and miss most of the action. Bent is allegedly racially abused by Lipa on Vale's anti-racism action day!

15 A SHEFFIELD WED 22/10 — W 3-1
Scorers: Friio 22, 64, Wotton 61p, Reddy 84
Argyle: McCormick, Worrell, Gilbert, Friio^, Wotton, Coughlan, Norris, Evans, Bent, Keith, Capaldi; subs St'bridge/Bent/Capaldi
Sheffield Wed: Lucas, Bromby, Geary, Reddy, Lee, D Smith, McLaren, Mustoe, Proudlock^, Holt, B-Murphy^; subs P Smith/Owusu
Ref: G Laws
Argyle's and Friio's form continue to blossom. The Frenchman heads Argyle into the lead. Wotton despatches a penalty with customary aplomb after a foul on Norris by Paul Smith, and another Friio header clinches an emphatic win to take the Greens to the top of the table.

16 H BLACKPOOL 25/10 — W 1-0
Scorers: Keith 43
Argyle: McCormick, Worrell, Gilbert, Friio, Wotton, Coughlan, Norris*, Adams, Evans, Keith^, Capaldi; subs St'bridge/Bent/Lowndes/Capaldi
Blackpool: Barnes, Grayson, Evans, Southern*, Davis, Clarke, Danns, Murphy, Douglas!, Coid^, Wellens; subs Taylor/Bullock
Ref: S Tanner
No doubt scared to death by Argyle's recent form, Blackpool shut up shop. They leave their top scorer on the bench and do not muster a single corner or shot on target for the whole game. Keith's close range effort is enough. Douglas, on a yellow, is sent off for a wild lunge at Friio (55).

17 H OLDHAM 1/11 — D 2-2
Scorers: Wotton 17, Evans 51, Beharall 11, 64
Argyle: McCormick, Worrell, Gilbert, Friio!, Wotton, Coughlan, Norris*, Adams, Bent, Keith*, Capaldi; subs St'bridge^/Capaldi/Lowndes/Sturrock
Oldham: Pogliacomi, Clegg^, Holden, Murray!, Beharall, Haining*, Eyre, Sheridan J!, Vernon^, Zola, Cooksey; subs Hall/O'Hall'an/Sheridan D
Ref: M Warren
A feisty encounter. After an early Latics goal Wotton's intended cross from a free-kick sails in. Friio and Sheridan are dismissed for some argy bargy which continues in the tunnel. Evans' header is cancelled out when McCormick drops the ball at Beharall's feet. Murray is also sent off.

18 A Q P RANGERS 15/11 — L 0-3
Scorers: Gallen 33, 75, Thorpe 72
Argyle: McCormick, Worrell, Gilbert, Adams, Wotton, Coughlan, Norris, Evans^, Bent*, Keith, Capaldi; subs Keith/Lowndes
QPR: Day, Edgahill*, Padula, Rowlands, Forbes, Carlisle, Bean, Bircham, Thorpe, Gallen, Shittu
Ref: T Parkes
A real off-day, and a let down for the 3,000+ travelling support. Missing the suspended Friio, Argyle are never in the game. A future Pilgrim, Kevin Gallen, scores with a deflected free-kick. Adams scuffs a clearance straight to Tony Thorpe and Gallen is left unmarked for the third.

19 H HARTLEPOOL 22/11 — W 2-0
Scorers: Keith 45, Lowndes 48
Argyle: McCormick, Connolly, Gilbert, Adams*, Wotton, Coughlan, Norris, Hodges, Lowndes*, Keith^, Capaldi; subs Wotton/Sturrock/St'bridge
Hartlepool: Provett, Westwood, Robson, Tinkler, Nelson, Craddock, Strachan*, Clarke", Williams, Humphreys; subs Gab'dini/Rob'son/Sw'ney
Ref: I Williamson
On the day England triumph in the Rugby World Cup, manager Sturrock shakes things up and makes five changes after the inept Loftus Road display. A comfortable victory ensues with Lowndes dispossessing Darrell Clarke before curling a shot into the top corner from 20 yards.

20 A COLCHESTER 29/11 — W 2-0
Scorers: Capaldi 4, Keith 11
Argyle: McCormick, Worrell, Gilbert, Adams, Wotton, Coughlan, Norris, Hodges, Lowndes*, Evans^, Capaldi; subs St'bridge/Hodges
Colchester: Brown, Stockley, Myers, Duguid, Fitzgerald*, Chilvers, Izzet, Pinault, Andrews, Fagan, Vine
Ref: K Wright
Wotton captains Argyle to their first Layer Road victory for 45 years on his 300th appearance. Two goalkeeping errors by Simon Brown hand Argyle victory on a plate. He allows Capaldi's free-kick to trickle under his body and then punches weakly to Wotton who sets up Keith.

21 H SWINDON 13/12 — W 3-2
Scorers: Capaldi 13, Norris 76, Keith 90 [Fallon 80, Parkin 90]
Argyle: McCormick, Connolly, Gilbert, Coughlan, Wotton, Aljofree, Norris, Hodges, Lowndes*, Keith", Capaldi; subs Keith/Capaldi
Swindon: Evans, Robinson, Ifil, Duke", Heywood, Gurney, Igoe^, Parkin, Hewlett*, Mooney, Miglioranzi; subs Nicholas/Fallon/Howard
Ref: B Curson
A thrilling finish. Two up with fifteen minutes left, Argyle were stunned by scrambled efforts from Fallon and Parkin. In the third minute of stoppage time, Steve Robinson is dismissed for a second yellow and, from the free-kick, Evans flicks on to Keith to slot home from 20 yards.

22 H NOTTS CO 20/12 — W 3-0
Scorers: Lowndes 28, Evans 79, 82
Argyle: McCormick, Connolly, Gilbert, Wotton, Coughlan, Aljofree, Norris, Hodges, Lowndes*, Keith^, Capaldi^; subs Sturrock/Friio/Evans
Notts Co: Mildenhall, Jenkins, Nicholson, Bolland, Fenton*, Richardson, Baldry, Caskey^, Stallard, Heffernan, Baraclough; subs Barras/Murray
Ref: R Olivier
An undeserved half-time lead thanks mainly to two great saves by McCormick. His opposite number, Steve Mildenhall, drops a Connolly cross and Evans seizes the opportunity. Three minutes later, the substitute finds the net again with a 20-yard angled drive which goes in off a post.

23 A BOURNEMOUTH 26/12 — W 2-0
Scorers: Wotton 22, Norris 40
Argyle: McCormick, Connolly, Gilbert, Friio, Wotton, Aljofree, Norris, Wotton, Hodges^, Keith*, Capaldi; subs Evans/Sturrock/Adams
Bournemouth: Moss, Buxton, Cummings, Maher, Purches, Broadhurst, Browning, Fletcher C*, Feeney, Hayter, Elliott; subs Hodges^/Hayter/Fletcher S
Ref: R Beeby
A wet and windy day at the seaside. Wotton scores the 5,000th Argyle league goal and few can have been better. Keeper Neil Moss clears the ball to the skipper who thumps it back in from 40 yards. Norris's left footer thumps into the air and spins back over the line.

NATIONWIDE DIVISION 2

Manager: Sturrock > Summerfield > Williamson   SEASON 2003-04

Match summary (figures as printed: Att · Pos · italic no. · Pt):

No	Venue	Opponent	Date	Att	Pos	—	Pt	Res	F-A	H-T
24	H	BRENTFORD	28/12	17,882	1	19	49	W	2-0	0-0
25	H	CHESTERFIELD	3/1	13,109	1	22	52	W	7-0	6-0
26	A	GRIMSBY	10/1	5,007	1	17	53	D	0-0	0-0
27	H	RUSHDEN & D	17/1	13,021	1	11	56	W	3-0	0-0
28	A	STOCKPORT	24/1	6,608	1	21	59	W	2-0	1-0
29	A	BRIGHTON	31/1	6,379	1	6	59	L	1-2	0-2
30	H	BOURNEMOUTH	7/2	13,371	1	12	60	D	0-0	0-0
31	A	TRANMERE	17/2	7,948	2	15	60	L	0-3	0-2
32	H	PORT VALE	21/2	11,330	2	5	63	W	2-1	0-0
33	A	BLACKPOOL	28/2	7,263	1	15	66	W	1-0	0-0
34	H	SHEFFIELD WED	2/3	17,218	1	12	69	W	2-0	1-0

---

24 — H BRENTFORD — 28/12
Scorers: Capaldi 47, Lowndes 53 **Ref:** P Prosser
Argyle: McCormick, Connolly, Gilbert, Friio, Coughlan, Aljofree, Phillips*, Hodges, Evans, Lowndes^, Capaldi
Brentford: Smith, Dobson, Somner, Kitamirike, Sonko, Roget!, O'Connor, Evans*, May, Wright, Hunt
Subs used: St'bridge/Sturrock · Hughes

Norris and Wotton are suspended and Keith injured. Two bone-crunching tackles sees Roget sent off (42). Shortly after half-time, Paul Smith spills Capaldi's 20-yard effort over the line. Smith then parries Evans' header for Lowndes to pick up the pieces and Argyle retain top spot.

25 — H CHESTERFIELD — 3/1
Scorers: Hodges 4, Capaldi 11, Lowndes 12, 17, [Friio 16, 36, 89] **Ref:** K Hill
Argyle: McCormick, Connolly, Gilbert, Friio, Coughlan, Aljofree, Phillips*, Hodges, Evans*, Lowndes, Capaldi^
Chesterfield: Muggleton, Uhlenbeek, O'Hare, Niven^, Blatherwick, Evatt, Allott, Hudson, Hurst, Brandon, Innes*
Subs used: Norris/St'bridge/Keith · Robinson/Davies

Argyle are rampant and go five up in 17 minutes. Every time the ball goes into the Spireites area it ends up in the net. Roy McFarland rallies his troops at half-time and gives some respectability to the second half. A first hat-trick for Friio and the biggest win at Home Park since 1936.

26 — A GRIMSBY — 10/1
Ref: E Evans
Argyle: McCormick, Connolly, Gilbert, Friio, Coughlan, Aljofree, Phillips*, Hodges, Evans*, Lowndes, Capaldi
Grimsby: Davison, McDermott, Barnard*, Groves, Ford, Edwards, Anderson^, Pouton, Boulding, Mansaram", Jevons
Subs used: Norris/Wotton/Keith · Young/Cas/Onoura

Lots of huff and puff and plenty of endeavour but little else. Both keepers are largely untroubled as defences dominate. Grimsby come closest to breaking the deadlock when Phil Jevons hits the post with a header. Coughlan is dominant as the Greens rack up yet another clean sheet.

27 — H RUSHDEN & D — 17/1
Scorers: Coughlan 47, St'bridge 58, Wotton 90 **Ref:** C Penton
Argyle: McCormick, Connolly, Gilbert, Friio, Coughlan, Aljofree, Norris, Hodges^, Evans, Lowndes^, St'bridge
Rushden & D: Ashdown, Sambrook, Bignot!, Hanlon*, Hunter*, Quinn, Hall, Burgess, Lowe, Kitson^, Jack
Subs used: Keith/Wotton · Dempster/Bell/Talbot

Norris 'scores' but the referee has already blown for a penalty for a foul on Hodges. Aljofree misses from the spot (13). Diamonds fail to force McCormick into a single save. Bignot is sent off (59) for a reckless challenge on Hodges. Wotton's 35-yard free-kick is the pick of the goals.

28 — A STOCKPORT — 24/1
Scorers: Friio 29, Coughlan 62 **Ref:** P Robinson
Argyle: McCormick, Connolly, Gilbert, Friio, Coughlan, Aljofree, Norris, Hodges, Evans*, Lowndes, St'bridge*
Stockport: Spencer, Hardiker, Jackman, McLachlan, Clare^, Griffin, Robertson*, Welsh, Lambert, Gibb
Subs used: Wotton/Keith/Adams · Wilbraham/Barlow/Mo'son

Argyle go five points clear at the top with another comfortable win. Under pressure from Evans, James Spencer drops the ball for Friio to notch his 13th of the season. Wotton comes on and immediately takes a free-kick which Aljofree flicks on for Coughlan to head in from close range.

29 — A BRIGHTON — 31/1
Scorers: Lowndes 88; Benjamin 12, Knight 34 **Ref:** P Joslin
Argyle: McCormick, Connolly, Gilbert, Friio, Coughlan, Aljofree", Norris*, Wotton, Evans, Lowndes, Hodges*
Brighton: Roberts, Virgo, Mayo, Oatway, Cullip, Butters, Watson, Carpenter, Benjamin, Knight*, Piercy^
Subs used: Adams/Keith/Sturrock · Hart/McPhee

In front of Sky TV cameras, Argyle produce their worst performance of the season so far. Trevor Benjamin's goal is the first conceded by McCormick in 642 minutes. Sturrock makes two changes at half-time. Roberts pulls off a brilliant save but the ball falls to Lowndes to score.

30 — H BOURNEMOUTH — 7/2
Ref: B Knight
Argyle: McCormick, Connolly, Gilbert, Friio, Coughlan, Aljofree, Norris, Hodges^, Evans^, Lowndes^, Capaldi*
Bournemouth: Moss, Buxton, Cummings, Browning, Fletcher C, Broadhurst, Hayter, Purches, Feeney^, Fletcher* S, Jorgensen*
Subs used: Keith/Wotton/Phillips · Elliott/Maher/O'Connor

Argyle hit the woodwork on four occasions in the second half. Referee Knight turns down four penalty appeals before finally pointing to the spot for a foul on Keith by Marcus Browning, but Moss saves Wotton's spot-kick (84) and then saves brilliantly from Norris in the last minute.

31 — A TRANMERE — 17/2
Scorers: Dadi 19, 52, Hume 22 **Ref:** M Cowburn
Argyle: McCormick, Connolly, Gilbert, Friio, Coughlan, Aljofree, Norris*, Hodges*, Adams, Lowndes, St'bridge*
Tranmere: Achterberg, Connelly, Jones, Linwood, Roberts, Allen, Mellon, Harrison, Dadi, Hume", Beresford*
Subs used: Phillips/Wotton/Sturrock · Hay/Nicholson

Manager Sturrock is absent through illness. A minute's silence for Steve Cooper who played for both sides and died aged 39. Rare defensive errors hand FA Cup quarter-finalists Rovers all three goals, although Hume's looks blatantly offside. Argyle lose top spot on a night to forget.

32 — H PORT VALE — 21/2
Scorers: Phillips 80, Stonebridge 90; McPhee 54 **Ref:** L Cable
Argyle: McCormick, Connolly, Gilbert, Friio, Coughlan, Aljofree^, Norris^, Hodges^, Adams, Lowndes^, Capaldi*
Port Vale: Brain, Rowland, Brown, Cummins*, Pilkington, Burns, Paynter, B-Wilkinson, Brooker, McPhee, Littlejohn
Subs used: Phillips/St'bridge/St'rrock · Brisco

Another unlikely victory. Steve McPhee shoots the visitors into the lead. Phillips scores his first goal for more than a year as his shot hits the crossbar and spins out but is ruled to be over the line. The winger then chases a lost cause to set up winner in the fifth minute of injury time.

33 — A BLACKPOOL — 28/2
Scorers: Stonebridge 54 **Ref:** S Mathieson
Argyle: McCormick, Connolly, Gilbert, Friio, Coughlan, Aljofree, Norris, Hodges*, Adams, Lowndes^, Capaldi^
Blackpool: Barnes, Grayson, Evans, Southern, Flynn, Bullock*, Elliott, Wellens, Murphy, Sheron, Coid
Subs used: St'bridge/Hodges/St'rrock · Blinkhorn

Stonebridge, an early replacement for Lowndes (24) who suffers double vision, justifies his 'super-sub' status by again notching the winner. The home team force three superb saves from McCormick early in the second half and threaten to take control but Argyle regain top spot.

34 — H SHEFFIELD WED — 2/3
Scorers: Evans 8, Coughlan 77 **Ref:** A Penn
Argyle: McCormick, Connolly, Gilbert, Adams, Coughlan, Aljofree, Norris, Keith, Evans^, Lowndes, St'bridge^
Sheffield Wed: Tidman, Lee", Geary, Quinn, Smith, Bromby, Chambers, B-Murphy, N-Nsungu, Shaw, Wood
Subs used: Hodges/Sturrock · Beswetherick

Evans passes a late fitness test and sends the large crowd into raptures as he is credited with an early scrambled goal from Stonebridge's corner, although Keith also claims it. Argyle's 70th league goal of the season comes from Coughlan's bullet header from Hodges' corner.

#			Pos				Score	HT												

35 A NOTTS CO 6/3 — 8,057 — 1 19 D 70 — 0-0 (0-0)
McCormick · Connolly · Gilbert · Friio · Coughlan · Aljofree · Norris · Adams · Evans^ · Keith^ · St'bridge* · Hodges/St'rrock/Lowndes
Garden · Pipe · Richardson · Baldry · Fenton" · Barras · Bolland · Caskey · Heffernan* · Curie" · Oakes · Scoffham/Scully/B'Clough
Ref: N Miller
Over 2,000 Argyle fans travel to Meadow Lane to support Kevin Summerfield, in charge after the shock departure of Paul Sturrock. County have won their last three home games. McCormick saves Paul Heffernan's weakly given penalty (68) after handball is given against Gilbert.

36 H SWINDON 13/3 — 16,080 — 1 4 W 73 — 2-1 (1-0) — Keith 11, R Evans 83 (og) / Mooney 90
McCormick · Connolly · Gilbert · Friio · Wotton · Coughlan · Norris^ · Adams · Evans" · Keith* · Capaldi · Lowndes/Bent/Sturrock
Evans R · O'Hanlon · Nicholas^ · Gurney! · Heywood · Reeves* · Igoe · Hewlett · Parkin · Mooney · Howard · Duke/Fallon
Ref: P Walton
A bizarre second Argyle goal is the main talking point. Swindon's keeper Rhys Evans mistakenly picks up a back-pass. Namesake Mickey grabs the ball and plays the indirect free-kick off the keeper into the net. Andy Gurney is dismissed (75) for a professional foul on Lowndes.

37 H PETERBOROUGH 16/3 — 13,110 — 1 20 W 76 — 2-0 (0-0) — Lowndes 55, Wotton 79p
McCormick · Connolly · Gilbert · Friio · Wotton · Coughlan · Norris · Adams · Evans^ · Keith* · Capaldi · Lowndes/Hodges
Tyler · Burton · Legg · Jenkins^ · Branston · Arber · Newton · Farrell* · Platt^ · Willock · Williams · Clarke/Gill/Logan
Ref: J Ross
Promotion looks ever more likely as Argyle open up a seven-point gap over rivals QPR. Lowndes, a half-time sub, slots home after good work between Connolly and Norris unlocks the Posh defence. Mark Arber manhandles Friio to the ground and Wotton blast home from the spot.

38 A LUTON 20/3 — 8,499 — 1 6 D 77 — 1-1 (0-1) — Adams 90 / Coyne 42
McCormick · Connolly · Gilbert · Friio · Wotton · Coughlan · Norris · Adams · Evans^ · Lowndes" · Capaldi^ · Phillips/Sturrock/Keith
Hyldgaard · Keane · Neilson · Nicholls · Boyce · Coyne* · Hughes · Robinson · Howard · Showunmi^ · Holmes · Davies/Crowe
Ref: G Salisbury
In a gale-force wind, Coyne's header gives Luton the lead. Keeper Hyldgaard is penalised for holding onto the ball too long. Lowndes tries to take the free-kick quickly and is elbowed by Kevin Nicholls who is red carded (47). Adams converts a Wotton corner in the 95th minute.

39 H WREXHAM 27/3 — 12,275 — 1 10 D 78 — 0-0 (0-0)
McCormick · Connolly · Gilbert · Friio · Wotton · Coughlan · Norris · Adams^ · Lowndes* · St'bridge" · Phillips/Hodges/Keith
Ingham · Roberts · Edwards C · Ferguson! · Morgan! · Lawrence · Barrett · Thomas* · Armstrong^ · Llewellyn · Edwards P · Spender/Sam
Ref: P Taylor
Over 70 former Argyle players attend the match. Wrexham's well-organised defence consistently frustrates Argyle's attack. Craig Morgan is sent off (57) for a second yellow card and skipper Darren Ferguson follows him down the tunnel in the last minute for the same reason.

40 A BARNSLEY 3/4 — 9,226 — 1 11 L 78 — 0-1 (0-0) — Birch 81
McCormick · Connolly · Gilbert · Friio* · Wotton · Coughlan · Norris · Adams · Keith^ · St'bridge · Hodges · Evans/Sturrock
Beresford · Austin · Murphy · Burns* · Kay · Ireland · Neil · Birch^ · Betsy · Hayward · Nardiello/Lumsdon
Ref: M Clattenburg
Lowly Barnsley are without a win in eleven games and have not scored in their last four at home, but defy the odds to overcome the leaders. Unusually, the Greens adopt safety-first tactics and seem content with a draw. On-loan Gary Birch heads in a corner on his Barnsley debut.

41 H WYCOMBE 10/4 — 14,806 — 1 24 W 81 — 2-1 (1-1) — Coughlan 39, Evans 80 / Tyson 5
McCormick · Connolly · Gilbert · Friio* · Wotton · Coughlan · Norris · Adams · Evans · Keith" · Capaldi^ · Adams/Lowndes/Sturrock
Williams" · Simpemba · Vinnicombe · Senda · Nethercott · Johnson · Bloomfield* · Simpson · Tyson · Fau'bridge^ · Currie · Bulman/Brown/Philo
Ref: D Crick
Tony Adams' Wycombe are doomed but take an early lead when the speedy Nathan Tyson outpaces the defence. After a number of chances the equaliser comes from a Coughlan header. Evans seals victory with a clever back-heel. The win takes Argyle nine points clear of third place.

42 A BRISTOL CITY 13/4 — 19,045 — 1 3 L 81 — 0-1 (0-0) — Peacock 85
McCormick · Connolly · Gilbert · Adams" · Wotton · Coughlan · Norris · Bent* · Evans · Hodges · Capaldi^ · Aljofree/Lowndes/Keith
Phillips · Carey · Hill · Murray^ · Coles · Butler · Wilkshire^ · Doherty · Peacock · Roberts" · Bell · Rougier/Tinnion/Miller
Ref: R Pearson
Promotion is put on hold after City complete the double over Argyle. Chances are few and far between in a tense affair played in front of a capacity crowd. Lee Peacock shrugs off Wotton to shoot past McCormick and keep the home team's automatic promotion hopes alive.

43 A OLDHAM 17/4 — 6,924 — 1 19 L 81 — 1-4 (0-3) — Wotton 50 / Johnson 35, Owen 43, Eyres 45, [Murray 67]
McCormick · Connolly · Gilbert" · Friio · Wotton! · Coughlan · Norris · Hodges^ · Evans · Keith · Capaldi^ · Phillips/Aljofree/Adams
Pogliacomi · Holden · Griffin · Murray · Haining · Owen · Bonner · Sheridan D · Johnson · Eyre* · Eyres^ · Vernon/Cooksey
Ref: M Cowburn
Promotion jitters set in. Three goals in ten minutes kill off Argyle. After Keith is fouled, Wotton's spot-kick is saved but he nets the rebound. He is then sent off for a second yellow (53) after taking a free-kick too quickly, one of a number of baffling decisions from Mr Cowburn.

44 H Q P RANGERS 24/4 — 19,888 — 1 2 W 84 — 2-0 (0-0) — Evans 81, Friio 86
McCormick · Connolly · Gilbert · Friio · Wotton · Aljofree · Norris · Coughlan · Evans · Keith* · Capaldi · Lowndes
Camp · Edghill · Padula · Ainsworth^ · Carlisle · Rose · Johnson" · Bircham* · Furlong · Gallen · Rowlands · Palmer/McLeod/Cureton
Ref: P Durkin
New boss Williamson clinches the title in his first game in charge after Bristol City's goalless draw. With a draw looking inevitable, Evans bullets a Norris corner past Lee Camp. Friio then chips over the advancing keeper to spark wild celebrations for the second time in three years.

45 A HARTLEPOOL 1/5 — 7,437 — 1 5 W 87 — 3-1 (2-1) — Hodges 12, Lowndes 43, Tinkler 48(og) / Boyd 11
McCormick · Connolly · Gilbert · Worrall · Coughlan · Aljofree · Norris · Hodges · Evans · Lowndes^ · Capaldi* · St'bridge/Sturrock/Yetton
Provett · Craddock · Robertson · Sweeney · Tinkler · Westwood* · Danns · Sweeney" · Boyd · Porter · Humphreys · Nelson/Clarke
Ref: A Leake
Despite clinching the title there is no let up as the Greens produce another professional performance for the 900 fans who have made the long trip. A Hodges scissors kick from the edge of the box sets up another party-like atmosphere. The impressive Boyd apart, Pool have no answers.

46 H COLCHESTER 8/5 — 19,888 — 1 11 W 90 — 2-0 (1-0) — Friio 18, Norris 47
McCormick · Connolly · Gilbert · Friio! · Coughlan · Aljofree · Norris · Hodges · Evans* · Capaldi^ · Lowndes/Adams/Wotton
Brown · Halford · Stockley · Keith · White · Brown · Izzet · Bowry" · Andrews · McGleish · Pinault/Williams
Ref: A Hall
Even the dismissal of Friio (62) for deliberate handball fails to dampen the party atmosphere. McGleish misses the resultant penalty. Despite the U's best efforts, Argyle win at a canter but the match plays second fiddle to the presentation of the Championship trophy — yet again!

Home 12,670
Away 8,068
Average 12,670

NATIONWIDE DIVISION 2 (CUP-TIES)

Manager: Sturrock > Summerfield > Williamson SEASON 2003-04

Carling Cup

		Att		F-A	H-T	Scorers, Times, and Referees	SQUAD	NUMBERS	IN	USE								subs used
1	A	COLCHESTER	12	L	1:2	1:2	Evans 23	Larrieu	Worrell	Gilbert"	Adams*	Coughlan	Aljofree^	Norris	Bent	Evans	Keith	Capaldi	Friio/Wotton/Stonebridge
		2,367	18				Fagan 22, Pinault 40	*Brown*	*Stockley*	*Myers*	*Pinault*	*White*	*Fitzgerald*	*Keith*	*Izzet*	*Fagan*	*McGleish*	*Duguid*	
							Ref: J Ross												

'Embarrassing' is Sturrock's succinct description of Argyle's defending. A mix-up between Coughlan and Larrieu allows on-loan Craig Fagan to score. Evans levels with a header from Worrell's cross but a 20-yard effort from Thomas Pinault ensures Argyle's traditional first round exit.

FA Cup

		Att		F-A	H-T	Scorers, Times, and Referees	SQUAD	NUMBERS	IN	USE								subs used
1	A	NORTHAMPTON	1	L	2:3	1:1	Friio 33, Stonebridge 63	McCormick	Worrell^	Gilbert"	Friio	Wotton	Coughlan	Norris	Bent	Evans	Keith*	St'bridge	Hodges/Phillips/Lowndes
		4,385	3:16				Walker 37, Hargr'ves 60, Asamoah 83	*Harper*	*Lyttle*	*Carruthers*	*Trollope*	*Sampso*	*Willmott*	*Low^*	*Hargreaves*	*Walker*	*Smith*	*Reeves**	*Dutfield/Asamoah*
							Ref: L Cable												

The underdogs capitalise on Argyle's failure to convert chances. Friio scores from 18 yards. Walker slots home from close range. Ex-Green Chris Hargreaves has the final touch in a goalmouth scramble. With a replay looking inevitable, Asamoah outpaces Worrell for the winner.

League Table

	Team	P	W	D	L	F	A	W	D	L	F	A	Pts
			Home					Away					
1	PLYMOUTH	46	17	5	1	52	13	9	7	7	33	28	90
2	QP Rangers	46	16	7	0	47	12	6	10	7	33	33	83
3	Bristol City	46	15	6	2	34	12	8	7	8	24	25	82
4	Brighton *	46	17	4	2	39	11	5	7	11	25	32	77
5	Swindon	46	12	7	4	41	23	8	6	9	35	35	73
6	Hartlepool	46	10	8	5	39	24	10	5	8	37	37	73
7	Port Vale	46	15	6	2	45	28	6	4	13	28	35	73
8	Tranmere	46	13	7	3	36	18	4	9	10	23	38	67
9	Bournemouth	46	11	8	4	35	25	6	7	10	21	26	66
10	Luton	46	14	6	3	44	27	3	9	11	25	39	66
11	Colchester	46	11	8	4	33	23	6	5	12	19	33	64
12	Barnsley	46	7	12	4	25	19	8	5	10	29	39	62
13	Wrexham	46	9	6	8	27	21	8	3	12	23	39	60
14	Blackpool	46	9	5	9	31	28	7	6	10	27	37	59
15	Oldham	46	9	8	6	37	25	3	13	7	29	35	57
16	Sheffield W	46	7	9	7	25	26	6	5	12	23	38	53
17	Brentford	46	9	5	9	34	38	6	6	12	18	31	53
18	Peterborough	46	5	8	10	36	33	7	8	8	22	25	52
19	Stockport	46	6	8	9	31	36	5	11	7	31	34	52
20	Chesterfield	46	9	7	7	34	31	5	5	11	15	40	51
21	Grimsby	46	10	5	8	36	26	3	6	14	19	55	50
22	Rushden	46	9	5	9	37	34	4	4	15	23	40	48
23	Notts Co	46	6	9	8	32	27	4	3	16	18	51	42
24	Wycombe	46	5	7	11	31	39	1	12	10	19	36	37
		1104	251	166	135	861	599	135	166	251	599	861	1490

* Promoted after play-offs

Odds & ends

Double wins: (8) Blackpool, Brentford, Colchester, Hartlepool, Port Vale, Sheffield Wed, Stockport, Swindon.

Double defeats: (1) Bristol C.

Won from behind: (4) Hartlepool (a), Luton (a), P Vale (h), Wycombe (h).

Lost from in front: (0).

High spots: Winning Division Two title.

Highest home victory (7-0) since 1936.

Coughlan and Friio selected in PFA divisional team.

Coughlan voted Division 2 Player of the Season.

Sturrock voted Division 2 Manager of the Season.

Low spots: Loss of Paul Sturrock to Southampton.

Disappointing defeats in both cup competitions.

Release of Jason Bent and Martin Phillips.

Player of the Year: Mickey Evans.

Ever presents: Graham Coughlan.

Hat-tricks: (1) David Friio.

Leading scorer: David Friio (15)

Appearances and Goals

Player	Lge	Sub	LC	Sub	FAC	Sub	Goals Lge	Goals LCFAC	Tot
Adams, Steve	25	11	1				2		2
Aljofree, Hasney	20	4	1						
Bent, Jason	13	5	1		1		1		1
Beresford, David		1							
Capaldi, Tony	29	4	1				7		7
Connolly, Paul	28	2							
Coughlan, Graham	46		1		1		7		7
Evans, Michael	35	9	1		1		11	1	12
Friio, David	35	1			1		14	1	15
Gilbert, Peter	40		1				1		1
Hodges, Lee	28	9		1			3		3
Keith, Marino	28	12	1		1		9		9
Larrieu, Romain	6		1						
Lowndes, Nathan	18	15		1			8		8
McCormick, Luke	40				1				
Norris, David	42	3	1		1		5		5
Phillips, Martin	3	6				1	1		1
Stonebridge, Ian	21	9		1	1		5	1	6
Sturrock, Blair		23							
Worrell, David	18		1		1				
Wotton, Paul	31	7	1		1		9		9
Yetton, Stewart		1							
(own-goals)							2		2
22 players used	506	122	11	3	11	3	85	1 2	88

COCA-COLA CHAMPIONSHIP

Manager: Bobby Williamson — SEASON 2004-05

SQUAD NUMBERS IN USE

No	Date	H/A	Opponent	Att	Pos	Pt	F-A	H-T	Scorers, Times, and Referees
1	7/8	H	MILLWALL	16,063		1	0-0 (D)	0-0	Ref: I Williamson
2	10/8	A	BRIGHTON	6,387	12	4	2-0 (W)	2-0	Cullip 11 (og), Wotton 45p — Ref: A Hall
3	13/8	A	CARDIFF	12,697	2	7	1-0 (W)	1-0	Bullock 24 (og) — Ref: P Taylor
4	21/8	H	SUNDERLAND	16,874	1	10	2-1 (W)	2-0	Wotton 1, Crawford 40 / Stewart 71 — Ref: P Crossley
5	28/8	A	WATFORD	13,104	2	10	1-3 (L)	1-1	Evans 18 / Ardley 33, Webber 46, 58 — Ref: E Evans
6	30/8	H	NOTT'M FOREST	17,538	4	13	3-2 (W)	2-1	Norris 26, Coughlan 40, Wotton 90p / Jess 44, 80 — Ref: R Olivier
7	11/9	A	QP RANGERS	15,425	4	13	2-3 (L)	1-1	Friio 7, Keith 90 / Furlong 29, 72, Gallen 89 — Ref: A Marriner
8	14/9	H	LEEDS	20,555	4	13	0-1 (L)	0-1	Keith 43 (og) — Ref: S Dunn
9	18/9	H	WOLVERHAMPTON	18,635	7	13	1-2 (L)	0-0	Friio 62 / Cort 77p, Sturridge 85 — Ref: R Beeby
10	25/9	A	IPSWICH	23,270	9	13	2-3 (L)	2-1	Adams 12, Crawford 13 / De Vos 24, Kuqi 82, 85 — Ref: G Salisbury
11	28/9	A	PRESTON	11,445	13	14	1-1 (D)	1-0	Doumbe 19 / Cresswell 66 — Ref: P Danson

---

1 — MILLWALL (H)
Argyle: McCormick, Worrell, Gilbert, Adams, Coughlan, Wotton, Lasley, Hodges, Evans^, Crawford*, Capaldi. Subs used: Milne/Keith
Millwall: Stack, Dunne^, Lawrence, Morris, Lawrence, Ward, Hill*, Elliott, Dichio, Moore. Subs used: Simpson/Wise/Cogan
The Lions show little evidence of the style that took them to the FA Cup final last season. Long-range shots are the order of the day. Millwall boss Dennis Wise brings himself in on an effort to inspire his side. The visitors almost snatch it near the end but Capaldi clears off the line.

2 — BRIGHTON (A)
Argyle: McCormick, Worrell, Gilbert, Adams, Coughlan, Wotton, Lasley, Hodges^, Keith, Crawford*, Capaldi. Subs used: Milne/Lowndes
Brighton: Kuipers, Virgo, Harding I, Nicolas, Butters, Cullip, Mayo, Reid*, Molango", Jarrett^. Subs used: Jones/Robinson/Hart
A stylish and encouraging performance from Argyle. Cullip heads against a post and the ball is deemed over the line before Kuipers scoops it back. The already booked Harding brings down Keith for the penalty and is dismissed (44), a decision that upsets home boss Mark McGhee.

3 — CARDIFF (A)
Argyle: McCormick, Worrell, Gilbert, Adams, Coughlan, Wotton, Lasley, Hodges^, Evans", Crawford*, Capaldi. Subs used: Keith/Friio/Lowndes
Cardiff: Margetson, Weston", Vidmar, Kavanagh, Page, Gabbidon, Bullock*, Langley^, Lee, Earnshaw. Subs used: Parry/Campbell/Collins
The Greens go top after more help from their opponents. Bullock diverts Crawford's header into his own net. Lenny Lawrence's men apply second-half pressure. The home crowd are baying for referee Taylor's blood when he refuses a penalty as Earnshaw is felled by Coughlan.

4 — SUNDERLAND (H)
Argyle: McCormick, Worrell, Gilbert, Adams*, Coughlan, Wotton, Lasley^, Hodges, Evans^, Crawford, Capaldi. Subs used: Friio/Makell/Keith
Sunderland: Myhre, Wright*, Arca, Robinson, Breen, Caldwell, Lawrence^, Whitehead, Kyle, Stewart, Oster". Subs used: Lynch/Thornton/Elliott
A great start as Wotton fires in a free-kick from near the left touchline taking Myrhe by surprise. The visitors are ruffled and lose composure. Crawford expertly finishes Evans' nod on. A first goal of the season is conceded as slack marking allows Marcus Stewart to head in a corner.

5 — WATFORD (A)
Argyle: McCormick, Worrell, Gilbert, Friio, Coughlan, Wotton, Norris, Hodges^, Evans^, Crawford, Capaldi*. Subs used: Keith/Makell/Lasley
Watford: Lee, Chambers, Mayo, Mahon, Cox, Dyche, Devlin, Gumarsson", Helguson, Webber*, Ardley. Subs used: Dyer/Young
The Greens dominate the first half, hitting the woodwork twice to almost add to Evans thumping volley. Neil Ardley's header provides an undeserved equaliser. Danny Webber's pace then causes problems as he puts Watford in front and then capitalises on a rare Coughlan error.

6 — NOTT'M FOREST (H)
Argyle: McCormick, Worrell, Gilbert, Friio, Coughlan, Wotton, Norris, Makell*, Evans, Crawford", Capaldi^. Subs used: Lasley/Hodges/Milne
Forest: Roche, Impey, Johnson A*, Reid, Morgan, Doig, Jess, King, Johnson D, Commons. Subs used: Robertson
Forest have manager Joe Kinnear absent and an injury crisis. Third choice keeper Barry Roche appears nervous and reacts slowly to Norris's shot. Coughlan heads in bravely. Jess's superb volley rallies the Reds. Doig trips Lasley in injury time and Wotton doesn't miss from the spot.

7 — QP RANGERS (A)
Argyle: McCormick, Worrell, Gilbert, Friio, Coughlan, Wotton, Norris, Makell*, Evans^, Crawford, Capaldi*. Subs used: Lasley/Hodges/Keith
QPR: Day, Bignot, Padula, Bean, Santos, Rose, Rowlands*, Bircham, Furlong, Gallen, Cook". Subs used: Cureton/McLeod
Friio's early goal adds to the pressure already on Rangers manager Ian Holloway. Veteran Paul Furlong's double helps his cause, the second coming after intercepting Wotton's weak back-header. Despite a blatant foul on Worrell, Gallen's third puts the game beyond Argyle's reach.

8 — LEEDS (H)
Argyle: Larrieu, Connolly, Gilbert^, Friio, Coughlan, Wotton, Norris", Makell, Evans^, Keith^, Capaldi. Subs used: Crawford/Milne/Hodges
Leeds: Sullivan, Kelly, Crainey, Wright, Butler, Carlisle, Richardson, Walton*, Deane", Joachim", Pugh. Subs used: Spring/Ricketts/McMaster
Capaldi departs early (24) with injury. After several near misses, Kevin Blackwell's men get their reward when Keith helps Butler's looping header past the recalled Larrieu. The Yorkshiremen have one of the meanest defences in the division and Argyle struggle to create anything.

9 — WOLVERHAMPTON (H)
Argyle: Larrieu, Connolly, Gilbert^, Friio, Coughlan, Wotton, Norris^, Makell, Evans^, Keith^, Adams. Subs used: Crawford/Milne/Hodges
Wolves: Jones, Clyde, Naylor, Ince, Craddock, Lescott, Newton, Olofinjana, Cort, Miller*, Seol*. Subs used: Sturridge/Cooper I/Andrews
Wolves look for their second win of the season. Mr Beeby seems impervious to their over-physical attitude. Gilbert brings down Cooper for a penalty. Cooper's knee high lunge on Gilbert sees high red for the Wolf (78) and a stretcher ride for Gilbert. Sturridge gets an undeserved winner.

10 — IPSWICH (A)
Argyle: Larrieu, Connolly, Gilbert^, Friio, Coughlan, Wotton, Lasley, Makell, Crawford, Keith^, Adams. Subs used: Capaldi/Milne
Ipswich: Davis, Wilnis I, Diallo, Wright, De Vos, Naylor, Dinning", Magilton", Bent, Counago*, Miller*. Subs used: Kuqi/Richards/Westlake
An eventful game. Argyle blow a two-goal lead despite playing against ten men for much of the game after the dismissal of Wilnis (27) for scything down Lasley. The Greens also lose Gilbert and Capaldi to injury within the first 17 minutes. Shefki Kuqi's late double breaks hearts.

11 — PRESTON (A)
Argyle: Larrieu, Connolly, Worrell, Friio, Coughlan, Wotton, Lasley, Makell*, Evans^, Crawford, Doumbe. Subs used: Hodges/Keith/Milne
Preston: Lonergan, Curtis, Davison", Alexander, Mawene, Davis, O'Neil^, Etuhu, Ndumbu-N..^, Cresswell, Lewis. Subs used: Jackson/McKenna/Daley
Injuries and the dropping of Wotton means Williamson making a number of changes. Argyle again fail to hold onto a lead. Doumbe's stooping header makes for a memorable full debut. The Pilgrims produce some neat passing play but Richard Creswell's header sees the points shared.

Argyle match-by-match results and line-ups

12 H GILLINGHAM 2/10 — 13,665 — 14 20 17 — W 2-1 (0-0)
Frio 89, 90 — Henderson 47 — Ref: B Curson
Larrieu · Connolly · Worrell · Frio · Coughlan · Doumbe · Lasley* · Makel · Crawford" · Adams · Hodges^ — Milne/Lowndes/Evans
Banks · Nosworthy · Hills* · Hes'nthaler"Hope · Johnson · Nowland · Smith · Byfield · Henderson^ · Crofts — Cox/Stidbe/Spiller
Williamson's decision to employ a lone striker at home has a bearing on a turgid first half. John Hills is stretchered off with a suspected broken ankle. Darius Henderson outmuscles Coughlan to slide the ball past Larrieu. Two late, late headers from Friio secure an unlikely three points.

13 H WIGAN 16/10 — 14,443 — 9 1 17 — L 1-2
Crawford 79 — Roberts 55, 68 — Ref: C Penton
Larrieu · Connolly · Worrell^ · Frio · Coughlan · Doumbe · Norris* · Makel · Crawford · Adams · Lowndes* — Evans/Dickson/Lasley
Filan · Eaden* · Baines · Bullard · Thorne · Breckin · Graham · Mahon · Roberts · Ellington · McCulloch — Wright
Wigan maintain their unbeaten record. Roberts misses an open goal from a yard. The pace of Wigan's expensive front two causes problems. Roberts' second has an element of luck as Ellington's shot is going miles wide but is diverted in. A flying header from Crawford gives hope.

14 A ROTHERHAM 19/10 — 5,088 — 13 24 20 — W 1-0
Doumbe 65 — Ref: M Ryan
Larrieu · Worrell · Gilbert · Adams^ · Coughlan · Doumbe · Norris · Makel · Evans · Crawford · Dickson* — Lasley/Wotton
Pollitt · Stockdale · Hurst · Garner^ · Swailes · McIntosh" · Sedgwick · Barker · Warne · Burchill · Mullin* — Vernazza/Proctor/Gilchrist
Without a win in 13 games, Rotherham show why they occupy bottom spot. Bobby Williamson gets a great reception from the club where he was a prolific goalscorer. Doumbe's close-range header from Coughlan's nod down proves enough. Warne aside, the Millers offer little threat.

15 H SHEFFIELD UTD 23/10 — 18,893 — 8 9 20 — L 1-2
Frio 87 — Bromby 78, Gray 85 — Ref: E Ilderton
Larrieu · Worrell · Gilbert · Frio · Coughlan · Doumbe · Norris^ · Makel · Crawford" · Hodges · Dickson* — Lasley/Evans/Yetton
Kenny · Bromby · Harley · Thirlwell · Morgan · Jagielka · Liddell · Tonge · Gray · Shaw · Cadamarti" — Lester
Blades' boss Neil Warnock gets one over his old club. Argyle struggle to cope with the height of the home team. Harley's deep cross eludes everyone except Bromby who sneaks in a header. Andy Gray is allowed too much room and gets a second. Friio's goal sparks a late frenzy.

16 H WEST HAM 30/10 — 20,220 — 12 4 21 — D 1-1 (0-1)
Wotton 76 — Lomas 43 — Ref: A Penn
Larrieu · Worrell · Gilbert · Frio · Coughlan · Doumbe · Norris · Makel · Evans · Crawford^ · Hodges* — Wotton/Milne
Bywater · Mullins · Brevett · Lomas · Davenport · Repka · Reo-Coker · Fletcher · Harewood · Zamora* — Etherington/Hutchison
Argyle have not beaten the Hammers at Home Park since 1954. Harewood's stunning volley is ruled out for offside. Skipper Steve Lomas heads his team in front. Enter Wotton and with his first touch blasts a 35-yard free-kick past Bywater. Alan Pardew's men hang on at the end.

17 H READING 2/11 — 14,336 — 12 3 22 — D 2-2 (2-0)
Sidwell 18 (og), Crawford 41 — Coughlan 51 (og), Kitson 90 — Ref: A Wiley
Larrieu · Worrell · Gilbert · Frio* · Coughlan · Doumbe · Norris · Wotton · Evans* · Crawford · Lasley — Adams/Milne
Hahnemann · Murty · Shorey · Sidwell · Sonko · Ingimarsson · Little · Harper · Kitson · Owusu · Convey* — Morgan
Williamson blasts his side's chalk and cheese performance against Steve Coppell's highly rated team. The home fans are in dreamland by half-time but when Coughlan turns Nicky Shorey's free-kick into his own net panic sets in. Kitson nicks an injury-time equaliser from a corner.

18 A WIGAN 6/11 — 10,294 — 12 1 25 — W 2-0 (1-0)
Wotton 40, Crawford 69 — Ref: P Prosser
Larrieu · Worrell^ · Gilbert* · Frio^ · Coughlan · Doumbe · Norris · Wotton · Evans* · Makel · Lasley — Crawford/Adams/Hodges
Filan · Wright · Baines · Bullard · Jackson · Breckin · Teale" · Mahon · Roberts · Graham · McCulloch^ · McMillan"/Eaden/Flynn
Paul Jewell's men become the last side in England to be defeated this season. Argyle are under the cosh early on. Breckin shoves Makel and from 25 yards yet another Wotton free-kick flies in. This shifts the momentum to the Greens and sub Crawford puts the game beyond doubt.

19 A COVENTRY 13/11 — 15,314 — 11 19 25 — L 1-2 (0-2)
Evans 48 — Hughes 9, Barrett 15 — Ref: M Jones
Larrieu · Worrell" · Gilbert · Frio · Coughlan · Doumbe · Norris · Wotton · Evans · Lasley* · Makel^ — Crawford/Capaldi/Milne
Steele · Carey · Giddings · Hughes · Williams · Shaw · Morrell · Doyle · McSheffrey Johnson^ · Barrett* — Adebola/Suffo
Argyle's first visit to Highfield Road for 38 years does not start as planned. Peter Reid's much-changed side goes ahead when a half-cleared corner allows Hughes to score from 10 yards. Barrett's free-kick eludes everyone. Evans' hopefully sticks out a leg and lobs over Luke Steele.

20 H STOKE 20/11 — 15,264 — 12 9 26 — D 0-0
Ref: P Taylor
Larrieu · Worrell · Gilbert · Frio* · Coughlan · Doumbe · Norris · Wotton · Evans · Crawford · Capaldi — Makel
Simonsen · Thomas · Clarke · Russel · Duberry · Hill · Brammer · Asaba* · N'l-Williams Akinbiyi · Greenacre — Henry
Referee Taylor is the central figure. This is his fourth consecutive match in charge at Home Park that has ended goalless. A number of baffling decisions infuriate players and fans alike. As fog descends towards the end, Doumbe's goal is chalked off by something only apparent to Mr T.

21 A LEICESTER 27/11 — 23,799 — 13 15 26 — L 1-2
Capaldi 9 — Scowcroft 49, Dublin 52 — Ref: P Armstrong
Larrieu · Worrell · Gilbert · Frio^ · Coughlan · Doumbe · Norris^ · Wotton · Evans · Crawford · Capaldi" — Adams/Makel/Keith
Taylor · Makin · Stewart · Nalis · Dublin · Dabizas · Gillespie^ · Gemmill · Scowcroft · Connolly · Morris* — Williams/Blake
Craig Levein has three internationals out injured and is forced to play Dion Dublin as a centre-back. Capaldi scores with an angled drive from Argyle's first attack. With Keith Gillespie causing problems, the Foxes respond with a superb headers from Jamie Scowcroft and Dublin.

22 H BURNLEY 4/12 — 13,308 — 15 8 29 — W 1-0
Wotton 90p — Ref: L Probert
Larrieu · Worrell · Gilbert · Frio · Coughlan · Doumbe · Wotton · Adams* · Evans^ · Crawford · Capaldi — Makel
Jensen · Duff · Camara · Grant · Cahill · Sinclair · Roche* · O'Connor · Moore · Blake · Branch — McGreal
Doumbe is out, sporting 24 stitches in a head wound. Wotton's last-minute penalty after a handball by Gary Cahill prevents a travesty of justice. Argyle win the shot count 15-0. Clarets boss Steve Cotterill admits his side were outplayed. Wales boss John Toshack eyes up Gilbert.

23 A CREWE 11/12 — 6,823 — 12 15 29 — L 0-3 (0-1)
Lunt 42, Ashton 57, Doumbe 80 (og) — Ref: K Wright
Larrieu · Worrell · Gilbert · Frio · Coughlan · Doumbe · Norris" · Wotton · Evans" · Crawford · Capaldi" — Makel/Crawford/Keith
Ince · Otsemobor · Moses · Lunt · Foster · Jones B* · Cochrane · Sorvel · Ashton^ · Jones S" · Vaughan — Walker/Varney/Rivers
Crewe again prove Argyle's nemesis. Lunt curls a free-kick around a six-man wall. The division's leading scorer, Dean Ashton, is watched by a host of Premiership managers and scores with a left-foot drive. Ashton, Doumbe and Larrieu collide and are left to watch the ball trickle in.

COCA-COLA CHAMPIONSHIP

Manager: Bobby Williamson

No	H/A	Opponent	Date	Att	Pos	Opp Pos	Pt	Result	F-A	H-T
24	H	DERBY	18/12	15,335	15	10	29	L	0-2	0-1
25	H	QP RANGERS	26/12	19,535	17	9	32	W	2-1	1-0
26	A	LEEDS	28/12	34,496	15	16	32	L	1-2	0-0
27	A	WOLVERHAMPTON	1/1	27,564	16	17	33	D	1-1	0-1
28	H	IPSWICH	3/1	17,923	16	1	33	L	1-2	0-0
29	A	GILLINGHAM	15/1	8,451	17	22	33	L	0-1	0-0
30	H	PRESTON	22/1	13,663	19	8	33	L	0-2	0-2
31	A	READING	5/2	19,783	20	4	34	D	0-0	0-0
32	H	ROTHERHAM	12/2	14,798	20	24	35	D	1-1	0-1
33	A	WEST HAM	19/2	25,490	20	7	35	L	0-5	0-3
34	H	SHEFFIELD UTD	22/2	13,953	21	8	38	W	3-0	1-0

---

24 — H DERBY (18/12) — Scorers: Coughlan 9 (og); Peschisolido 62. Ref: T Kettle
Argyle: Larrieu, Worrell*, Gilbert^, Friio, Coughlan, Doumbe, Norris, Wotton, Evans, Crawford, Capaldi. Subs: Gudjonsson/Keith
Derby: Camp, Kenna, Jackson, Blsgaard, Huddlestone, Santos!, Kaku, Taylor, Rasiak, Peschis'o*, Smith*. Subs: Rich/Tudgay

George Burley's men take an early lead when Paul Peschisolido's cross is deflected past Larrieu by Coughlan. The Canadian international seals his man of the match performance with a well-taken goal, rounding Larrieu to slide the ball into the net. Evans heads over from four yards.

25 — H QP RANGERS (26/12) — Scorers: Wotton 13, Evans 49; Furlong 53. Ref: T Leake
Argyle: Larrieu, Connolly, Gilbert, Friio, Coughlan!, Doumbe, Gudjonsson, Wotton, Evans*, Keith, Capaldi. Subs: Crawford
QPR: Day, Bignot, Padula^, Miller*, Shittu, Santos!, Rowlands, Bircham, Furlong, Gallen, Cook". Subs: Best/Edghill/Ainsworth

Little sign of seasonal goodwill here. The Greens take an early lead but then Coughlan is dismissed (17) for kicking out at Furlong. Santos is also sent off (40) for a heavy challenge on Friio two minutes after receiving his first yellow. Ian Holloway describes his team as 'flitty-farty'.

26 — A LEEDS (28/12) — Scorers: Crawford 90; Gilbert 46 (og), Healy 90. Ref: G Salisbury
Argyle: Larrieu, Connolly, Gilbert, Adams^, Coughlan, Doumbe, Norris, Wotton, Gudjonsson, Keith*, Hodges. Subs: Friio/Evans/Crawford
Leeds: Sullivan, Kelly, Richardson^, Butler, Lennon, Kilgallon, Gregan, Deane*, Healy, Pugh, Joachim. Subs: Wright, Carlisle

David Healy's cross is going nowhere until Gilbert's left foot diverts it into his own net. The Leeds defence finds itself under increasing pressure and Crawford's goal looks enough to earn a point but Healy produces some quality by executing a perfect 30-yard lob over Larrieu.

27 — A WOLVERHAMPTON (1/1) — Scorers: Friio 58; Seol 24. Ref: C Webster
Argyle: Larrieu, Connolly, Gilbert, Friio, Wotton, Doumbe, Norris, Gudjonsson, Evans^, Keith*, Hodges. Subs: Taylor/Capaldi
Wolves: Oakes, Newton, Andrews, Naylor, Craddock, Lescott, Cameron^, Seol, Cort, Miller, Clarke. Subs: Kennedy/Clarke

Seol is given too much time to shoot home from 25 yards. Argyle start the second half playing into a gale and the game is temporarily halted to replace some advertising hoardings that are blown down. Friio's equaliser prompts some backs to the wall defending for the last half an hour.

28 — H IPSWICH (3/1) — Scorers: Evans 87; Currie 67p, 85. Ref: D Gallagher
Argyle: Larrieu, Connolly, Gilbert, Adams^, Wotton, Doumbe, Norris*, Friio, Evans, Taylor, Hodges. Subs: Gudjonsson/Keith
Ipswich: Davis, Wilnis, Karbassi^, De Vos, Naylor, Westlake, Horlock, Kuqi, Bent, Currie, Miller. Subs: Richards/Magilton

Brief ex-Argyle player Darren Currie again shows his liking for playing against his old team. He nets from the spot after Larrieu brings down Darren Bent. Joe Royle's team consolidate top spot with another Currie goal from Jim Magilton's cross despite the late scare of Evans goal.

29 — A GILLINGHAM (15/1) — Scorers: Crofts 61. Ref: J Singh
Argyle: Larrieu, Connolly!, Gilbert, Friio, Coughlan, Doumbe, Norris, Wotton, Evans, Rose?, Hodges. Subs: Capaldi
Gillingham: Banks, Southall, Rose, Hessenth'r*, Cox, Hope, Smith, Patton, Byfield, Crofts, Henderson^. Subs: Bodkin/Hils

Argyle are sucked into a relegation battle with this defeat against Stan Ternent's struggling Gills. On a bad surface, both teams struggle to pass the ball. An unmarked Andrew Crofts heads the only goal. Connolly is sent off in the last minute for a wild and late hack at Darren Byfield.

30 — H PRESTON (22/1) — Scorers: Sedgwick 29, Agyemang 34. Ref: P Joslin
Argyle: Larrieu, Worrell^, Gilbert^, Lasley, Coughlan, Doumbe, Gudjonsson, Wotton, Evans, Taylor, Hodges^. Subs: Friio/Norris
Preston: Lonergan, Alexander, Hill, O'Neill^, Mawene, Lucketti, Sedgwick*, McKenna, Cresswell, Agyemang^, Lewis. Subs: Kozluk/Nugent/Etuhu

Williamson rings the changes and sees his side produce a dominant performance but no points. Sedgwick produces a stunning goal, chipping Larrieu from the edge of the box. Worrell then short-changes his keeper with a back-pass, leaving Patrick Agyemang the easy task of scoring.

31 — A READING (5/2) — Ref: R Olivier
Argyle: McCormick, Worrell, Gilbert, Lasley, Coughlan, Doumbe, Gudjonsson, Wotton, Blackst'ck*, Taylor*, Evans^. Subs: Evans/Friio/Capaldi
Reading: Hahnemann, Murty, Shorey, Sidwell^, Ingimarsson, Little, Harper, Ferdinand^, Forster*, Hughes. Subs: Brooker/Keown/Owusu

Given recent form, over 4,000 of the Green Army travel to the Madjeski with trepidation. Most of Reading's danger comes from attacking full-backs, Murty and Shorey and England veteran Les Ferdinand. Nicky Forster hits the bar late on but Argyle hang on for a creditable draw.

32 — H ROTHERHAM (12/2) — Scorers: Wotton 51p; Monkhouse 26. Ref: M Fletcher
Argyle: McCormick, Worrell, Gilbert*, Lasley^, Coughlan, Doumbe, Gudjonsson, Wotton, Blackstock, Chadwick, Evans*. Subs: Evans/Capaldi
Rotherham: Pollitt, Barker, Hurst, Mullin, Swailes, Gilchrist, Cam'ron*, Garner, Butler, McLaren, Monkhouse. Subs: Monkhouse/Hoskins

Again Argyle dominate the opening exchanges but go behind from Andy Monkhouse's 25-yarder. Alan Knills' team resort to time-wasting tactics almost immediately. A linesman spots Blackstock being pulled back by Chris Swailes for the penalty but more precious points are lost.

33 — A WEST HAM (19/2) — Scorers: Harewood 10p, McCormick 23 (og), Mackay 40, Sheringham 77, 86p. Ref: K Friend
Argyle: McCormick, Worrell, Aljofree, Adams, Coughlan, Doumbe, Gudjonsson!, Lasley, Blackstock, Chadwick, Evans^. Subs: Chadwick/Norris
West Ham: Bywater, Repka, Powell, Mullins^, Ferdinand, Mackay, Rebrov^, Fletcher, Harewood, Sheringham, Noble^. Subs: Reo-Coker/Lomas/Zamora

Oh dear! Five goals conceded including two penalties, an own-goal and Doumbe sent off (82). Aljofree is swathed in bandages after clashing heads with Buzsaky. Argyle are forced to borrow black socks. And it snowed! Alan Pardew is able to treat the second half as a training session.

34 — H SHEFFIELD UTD (22/2) — Scorers: Coughlan 3, Wotton 47, Blackstock 88. Ref: S Tanner
Argyle: McCormick, Connolly, Gilbert, Wotton, Coughlan, Doumbe, Norris, Blackstock, Evans*, Chadwick, Capaldi. Subs: Chadwick/Capaldi
Sheffield Utd: Kenny", Geary, Harley, Bramby, Montgomery/Cullip, Liddell, Jagielka, Shaw*, Tonge", Gray, Quinn. Subs: Thirlwell/Forte/Quinn

Coughlan's turn and shot is worthy of a striker. Paddy Kenny injures a hip and goes off (28). Blades captain Phil Jagielka is forced to go in goal. He does well but is powerless to stop Wotton's long-range strike. Blackstock's diving header buries the ghost of the previous match.

35 — CREWE (H) 26/2

Attendance 14,918 · 19 · 15 · 41 · 1-0 · W · 3-0
Wotton 25, Blackstock 68, Taylor 90
Ref: A Kaye

Argyle: McCormick, Connolly, Gilbert, Adams, Coughlan, Norris, Wotton, Evans*, Chadwick^, Buzsaky", Blackst'k/Taylor/Gudjons'on

Crewe: *Ince, McCready, Tonkin, Lunt, Foster!, Sorvel, Bell, Varney, Jones*, Buzsaky", Rivers/Moses*

Relegation fears are eased against Dario Gradi's side, who have completely lost form since the recent sale of Dean Ashton. A rare left-footer from Wotton opens proceedings. Stephen Foster is sent off (44) for a foul on Chadwick. Taylor gets his first for Argyle from point-blank range.

36 — DERBY (A) 5/3

Attendance 27,581 · 19 · 4 · 41 · 0-1 · L · 0-1
Idiakez 24
Ref: C Oliver

Argyle: McCormick, Connolly, Gilbert, Adams*, Coughlan, Norris, Wotton, Blackstock, Chadwick, Capaldi", Buzsaky/Evans

Derby: *Camp, Kenna, Makin, Bisgaard*, Huddlestone, Konjic, Bolder, Rasiak, Tudgay*, Smith, Peschisolido/Taylor*

An absorbing contest with a winning goal equal in quality as classy Spaniard, Inigo Idiakez curls a free-kick into the top corner from 30 yards. Uncharacteristically Wotton misses a penalty (67) firing high, wide and not so handsome after Coughlan had been flattened by Gregorz Rasiak.

37 — BRIGHTON (H) 12/3

Attendance 15,606 · 19 · 16 · 44 · 4-1 · W · 5-1
Chadw'k 8, Wotton 13p, 21, Norris 36, Oatway 11 [Taylor 88]

Argyle: McCormick, Connolly, Gilbert, Wotton, Coughlan, Norris, Gudjonsson, Blackstock*, Chadwick^, Capaldi", Evans/Taylor/Lasley

Brighton: *Shaaban, Mayo, Harding, Oatway, Butters, Reid, Nicolas, Hinshelwood, Carpenter!, Knight

The Seagulls are taken apart in the first half as Argyle thrash their fellow strugglers and improve their goal-difference to boot. The diminutive Oatway heads in to level Chadwick's goal. Hinshelwood handles for the penalty. Carpenter is sent off (68) for an altercation with Chadwick.

38 — SUNDERLAND (A) 15/3

Attendance 25,258 · 16 · 2 · 44 · 1-5 · L · 0-3
Taylor 88 [Caldwell 75, Thornton 90] Whitehead 31, Arca 40, Stewart 45p,
Ref: M Cowburn

Argyle: McCormick, Connolly, Gilbert, Wotton, Coughlan, Norris, Gudjonsson*, Blackstock*, Chadwick, Capaldi, Evans/Taylor

Sunderland: *Myhre, Wright, McCartney, Whitley*, Breen, Caldwell, Whitehead^, Stewart", Elliot, Arca, Lawrence/Thornton/Brown*

All the previous games' good work is undone although, remarkably, the Black Cats have just five shots on target and they all go in! Poor defending accounts for the first two. Marcus Stewart appears to slip but the linesman indicates a penalty after Mr Cowburn had waved play on.

39 — MILLWALL (A) 20/3

Attendance 11,465 · 16 · 10 · 44 · 0-3 · L · 0-1
Sweeney 15, Hayles 56, Dichio 63
Ref: P Melin

Argyle: McCormick, Connolly, Gilbert, Wotton, Coughlan, Norris*, Gudjonsson*, Evans*, Taylor, Buzsaky, Blackstock/Blackst'k

Millwall: *Marshall, Robinson, Craig, Morris*, Ward, Lawrence, Simpson^, Sweeney, Dichio^, Hayles, Livermore, Elliott/Quigley/May*

On a foggy afternoon, relegation nerves are apparent again. Peter Sweeney appears offside before lashing the ball home. Aljofree's mistake allows Barry Hayles an easy second and the Argyle defence go AWOL to allow Danny Dichio the freedom of East London and head the third.

40 — CARDIFF (H) 2/4

Attendance 18,045 · 18 · 20 · 45 · 1-1 · D · 1-1
Aljofree 60 Langley 22
Ref: R Beeby

Argyle: McCormick, Connolly, Dodd, Wotton, Coughlan, Norris, Buzsaky*, Evans, Chadwick^, Capaldi, Blackstock/Taylor

Cardiff: *Alexander, Weston*, Barker, Ardley, Gabbidon, Collins, Ledley, Langley, Thorne^, McAnuff, Vidmar/Boulding/Lee*

Both sides look anxious in their pursuit of much-needed points. McCormick flaps at a Neal Ardley corner and the ball falls to Richard Langley to shoot home despite the best efforts of Wotton on the line. City fail to clear a corner and Aljofree gets a vital goal from Evans' knock down.

41 — WATFORD (H) 5/4

Attendance 15,333 · 18 · 17 · 48 · 1-0 · W · 1-0
Buzsaky 10
Ref: C Penton

Argyle: McCormick, Connolly, Dodd, Wotton, Coughlan, Norris, Buzsaky, Aljofree, Chadwick^, Capaldi", Taylor/Lasley

Watford: *Lee, Doyley, Chambers, Mahon, DeMerit, Cox*, Eagles, Gunnars'on", Dyer", Helguson, Blizzard, Young/McNamee/Bouazza*

Adie Boothroyd promises his team will come to attack and they do. Buzsaky's beautiful left-foot strike fails to knock the Hornets out of their stride. Referee Penton limps off injured. The fourth official takes the place of a linesman but forgets his flag. Stout defence ensures a vital win.

42 — NOTT'M FOREST (A) 9/4

Attendance 28,887 · 16 · 23 · 51 · 3-0 · W · 2-0
Blackstock 3, 59, Norris 24
Ref: A Hall

Argyle: McCormick, Worrell, Dodd, Wotton, Coughlan, Aljofree, Buzsaky, Evans*, Blackstock, Taylor*, Chadwick/Capaldi/Lasley

Forest: *Gerrard, Louis-Jean, Doig, Gardner, Morgan, James*, Perch, Dobie*, Taylor, Commons, Evans/Harris/Thompson*

Forest have the injured David Friio missing. A shambolic performance sees manager Gary Megson jeered throughout. Argyle stroll to victory, aided by some Sunday League defending. By the end, most of the Forest fans have left, leaving the 3,000 travelling Green Army to celebrate.

43 — STOKE (A) 16/4

Attendance 13,017 · 15 · 12 · 51 · 0-2 · L · 0-2
Jones 26, Russell 41
Ref: C Boyeson

Argyle: McCormick, Worrell, Dodd, Wotton, Coughlan, Aljofree, Buzsaky, Evans*, Blackstock, Taylor*, Capaldi/Chadwick/Lasley

Stoke: *Simonsen, Buxton, Hill, Russell, Taggart, Greenacre*, Brammer, Jones*, N'l Williams, Clarke^, Henry/Neal/Paterson*

Argyle have never won at Stoke but must be wondering how they did not break the voodoo after dominating for much of the game. The giant Kenwyne Jones jumps higher than anyone else to head the opener. Darel Russell's 20-yard shot takes a nasty deflection and loops into the net.

44 — COVENTRY (H) 23/4

Attendance 18,443 · 15 · 18 · 52 · 1-1 · D · 1-1
Capaldi 90 John 45
Ref: L Probert

Argyle: McCormick, Worrell*, Gilbert, Wotton, Coughlan, Aljofree*, Buzsaky, Evans, Blackstock, Chadwick*, Capaldi/Doumbe/Taylor

Coventry: *Steele, Whing, Duffy, Hughes, Page, Staunto, McSheffrey, Doyle, John*, Adebola^, Dyer^, Goater/Jorgensen/Benjamin*

Wotton hesitates on the edge of his own penalty and is dispossessed. The ball falls to Stern John to score. Capaldi, who can do nothing right since coming on, equalises in the sixth minute of injury time, leaving Sky Blues boss Micky Adams in deep discussions with the officials.

45 — BURNLEY (A) 30/4

Attendance 12,893 · 15 · 14 · 52 · 0-2 · L · 0-2
Valois 87p, O'Connor 90
Ref: T Bates

Argyle: McCormick, Worrell, Gilbert, Wotton, Doumbe, Aljofree, Buzsaky, Evans*, Taylor^, Chadwick, Capaldi

Burnley: *Jensen, Sinclair, Camara, Hyde, McGreal, Cahill*, Bowditch*, O'Connor, Akinbiyi, Grant^, Branch, Oster/Valois/Duff*

Argyle are safe after other results go in their favour. The Clarets have little to play for and seem happy to settle for a stalemate, but Worrell's foul on Adi Akinbiyi and the resultant theatricals see referee Bates award a penalty. James O'Connor scores an injury-time wonder goal.

46 — LEICESTER (H) 8/5

Attendance 19,199 · 18 · 15 · 53 · 0-0 · D · 0-0
Ref: P Armstrong

Argyle: McCormick, Worrell*, Gilbert, Wotton, Doumbe, Aljofree*, Norris, Buzsaky, Gudjonsson, Taylor^, Chadwick, Milne/**Summerfield**

Leicester: *Hirschfeld, Maybury, Sheehan, Hughes, McCarthy*, Kenton^, Gudjonsson, Stewart, De Vries, Moore, Connolly, Heath/Stearman*

A definite end of season, nothing to play for encounter. The biggest cheer is reserved for Worrell as he is taken off to take the applause of the fans after being released. Patrick McCarthy seems determined to get himself dismissed and is hauled off by manager Craig Levein (35).

Home — Average 16,420
Away — 17,279
Average 16,420

CHAMPIONSHIP (CUP-TIES)

Manager: Bobby Williamson

SEASON 2004-05

Carling Cup

Carling Cup		Att	F-A	H-T	Scorers, Times, and Referees
1 A YEOVIL	2 L	6,217 2:5	2-3	2:1	Crawford 30, Wotton 42p
24|8		aet			*Johnson 28, 69, 102*
					Ref: C Penton

SQUAD NUMBERS IN USE

McCormick	Worrell	Gilbert	Adams	Coughlan"	Wotton	Lasley	Hodges*	Crawford^	Keith	Capaldi
Weale	*Lockwood**	*Rose*	*Way*	*Skiverton*	*Fontaine*	*Gall*	*Johnson*	*Jevons*	*Tarachulski"Caceres^*	

subs used: Friio/Milne/Doumbe *Terry/O'Brien/Weatherston*

A bizarre goal-swap provides the most memorable part of the game. After a Coughlan injury, Lee Johnson overhits a 'pass' to McCormick and the ball goes in. In response, Yeovil allow Crawford to walk the ball in from the restart to equalise. Johnson has the last laugh with a hat-trick.

FA Cup

FA Cup		Att	F-A	H-T	Scorers, Times, and Referees
3 H EVERTON	17 L	20,112 P:5	1-3	1-2	Gudjonsson 34
8|1					*Osman 16, McFadden 18, Chadwick 84Wright*
					Ref: M Messias

SQUAD NUMBERS IN USE

Larrieu	Connolly	Gilbert	Friio	Coughlan	Doumbe	Gudjonsson	Wotton	Evans	Hodges*	Capaldi
Wright	*Pistone*	*Naysmith*	*Carsley*	*Yobo*	*Stubbs*	*Osman*	*Kilbane*	*Beattie**	*Bent^*	*McFadden"*

subs used: Keith *Cahill/Gravesen/Chadwick*

Argyle concede two soft goals early on. In front of live Match of the Day coverage, the Toffees produce a workmanlike and professional performance. Gudjonsson gets his first Argyle goal but future Green Nick Chadwick breaks clear from halfway to put the result beyond doubt.

	P	Home					Away					Pts
		W	D	L	F	A	W	D	L	F	A	
1 Sunderland	46	16	4	3	45	21	13	3	7	31	20	94
2 Wigan	46	13	5	5	42	15	12	7	4	37	20	87
3 Ipswich	46	17	3	3	53	26	7	10	6	32	30	85
4 Derby	46	10	7	6	38	30	12	3	8	33	30	76
5 Preston	46	14	7	2	44	22	7	5	11	23	36	75
6 West Ham*	46	12	5	6	36	24	9	5	9	30	32	73
7 Reading	46	13	7	3	33	15	6	6	11	18	29	70
8 Sheffield U	46	9	7	7	28	23	9	6	8	29	33	67
9 Wolves	46	9	11	3	40	26	6	10	7	32	33	66
10 Millwall	46	12	5	6	33	22	6	7	10	18	23	66
11 QP Rangers	46	10	7	6	32	26	7	4	12	22	32	62
12 Stoke	46	11	2	10	22	18	6	8	9	14	20	61
13 Burnley	46	10	7	6	26	19	5	8	10	12	20	60
14 Leeds	46	7	10	6	28	26	7	8	8	21	26	60
15 Leicester	46	8	8	7	24	20	4	13	6	25	26	57
16 Cardiff	46	10	4	9	31	19	3	11	9	24	32	54
17 PLYMOUTH	46	9	8	6	31	23	5	3	15	21	41	53
18 Watford	46	5	10	8	25	25	7	6	10	27	34	52
19 Coventry	46	8	7	8	32	28	5	6	12	29	45	52
20 Brighton	46	7	7	9	24	29	5	5	12	16	36	51
21 Crewe	46	6	8	9	37	38	6	6	11	29	48	50
22 Gillingham	46	10	6	7	22	23	2	8	13	23	43	50
23 Nott'm For	46	7	10	6	26	28	2	7	14	16	38	44
24 Rotherham	46	2	7	14	17	34	3	7	13	18	35	29
	1104	235	162	155	762	580	155	162	235	580	762	1494

* promoted
after play-offs

Odds & ends

Double wins: (2) Brighton, Nott'm For.
Double defeats: (3) Derby, Ipswich, Leeds

Won from behind: (1) Gillingham (h).
Lost from in front: (5) Ipswich (a), Leicester (a), QP Rangers (a), Watford (a), Wolves (h).

High spots: End of season form of Akos Buzsaky.
Successful in avoiding relegation.
Attendances at a good level.

Low spots: Losing more games than any other team in the division.
Lack of impact from many of close-season signings.
Loss of crowd favourite, David Friio, to Nott'm For.
Style of play not always popular with home fans.

Player of the Year: Paul Wotton.
Ever presents: (0).
Hat-tricks: (0).
Leading scorer: Paul Wotton (13).

Player	Appearances						Goals			
	Lge	Sub	LC	Sub	FAC	Sub	Lge	LC	FAC	Tot
Adams, Steve	17	3	1				1			1
Aljofree, Hasney	12						1			1
Blackstock, Dexter	10	4					4			4
Buzsaky, Akos	14	1					4			4
Capaldi, Tony	24	11	1		1		2			2
Chadwick, Nick	11	4					1			1
Connolly, Paul	19									
Coughlan, Graham	43		1		1		2			2
Crawford, Steve	19	7	1		1		6	1		7
Dickson, Ryan	2	1								
Dodd, Jason	4									
Doumbe, Mathias	24	2	1		1	1	2			2
Evans, Mickey	33	9	1		1		4			4
Friio, David	23	5	1		1		6			6
Gilbert, Peter	38				1					
Gudjonsson, Bjarni	12	3			1				1	1
Hodges, Lee	11	8	1		1					
Keith, Marino	6	11	1		1		1			1
Larrieu, Romain	23									
Lasley, Keith	14				1					
Lowndes, Nathan	1	3								
Makel, Lee	13	6								
McCormick, Luke	23		1							
Milne, Steven	12					1				
Norris, David	33	2					3			3
Summerfield, Luke	1									
Taylor, Scott	9	7					3			3
Worrell, David	30		1							
Wotton, Paul	38	2	1		1		12	1		13
Yetton, Stewart	1									
(own-goals)							3			3
30 players used	506	103	11	3	11	1	52	2	1	55

COCA-COLA CHAMPIONSHIP

Manager: Bobby Williamson > Tony Pulis   SEASON 2005-06

No		Opponent	Date	Att	Pos	Pt		F-A	H-T	Scorers, Times, and Referees
1	A	READING	6/8	16,836		3	W	2-1	1-0	Evans 21, Chadwick 90 / Lita 54 / Ref: P Taylor
2	H	WATFORD	9/8	13,813	2	4	D	3-3	3-1	Evans 3, Capaldi 12, Wotton 43 / King 35, Young 52, 61 / Ref: L Probert
3	H	DERBY	13/8	14,279	3	4	L	0-2	0-2	Rasiak 20, Bisgaard 38 / Ref: P Dowd
4	A	CRYSTAL PALACE	20/8	18,781	13	4	L	0-1	0-0	Ward 64 / Ref: P Walton
5	H	HULL	27/8	12,329	17	4	L	0-1	0-0	Elliott 57 / Ref: A D'Urso
6	A	BRIGHTON	29/8	6,238	20	4	L	0-2	0-1	Robinson 11, Carpenter 46 / Ref: D Gallagher
7	A	NORWICH	10/9	23,981	21	4	L	0-2	0-2	Doumbe 19 (og), Ashton 37 / Ref: B Knight
8	H	CREWE	13/9	10,460	22	5	D	1-1	1-1	Taylor 12 / Johnson 8 / Ref: S Tanner
9	H	BURNLEY	17/9	11,829	23	8	W	1-0	0-0	Evans 46 / Ref: K Stroud
10	A	SOUTHAMPTON	24/9	26,331	20	9	D	0-0	0-0	Ref: A Leake
11	A	SHEFFIELD UTD	27/9	20,111	21	9	L	0-2	0-2	Shipperley 11, Quinn 31 / Ref: D Laws

SQUAD NUMBERS IN USE / subs used

1. READING (A)
Argyle: Larrieu, Barness, **Brevett**, Wotton, Doumbe, Aljofree, Norris, Buzsaky^, Evans*, Gudj'sson, Capaldi — subs: Chadwick/Djordjic
Reading: Hahnemann, Murty, Shorey, Sidwell, Sonko, Ingimarsson, Little^, Harper, Lita, Doyle, Convey^ — subs: Kitson/Hunt
Both sides seem to be champing at the bit as the action starts at a furious pace. Evans is first to meet Brevett's cross. Argyle's defence is caught napping by a quick free-kick and Lita heads in. Chadwick pokes in a deflected cross in front of the 4,000 travelling fans.

2. WATFORD (H)
Argyle: Larrieu, Barness, Brevett, Wotton, Doumbe, Aljofree, Norris, Buzsaky, Evans*, Chadwick^, Capaldi — subs: Taylor/Djordjic
Watford: Foster, Chambers, Doyley*, Bangura^, DeMerit, Carlisle, McNamee^, Blizzard, King, Henderson, Young — subs: Stewart/Mahon/Devlin
A new upbeat 'Semper Fidelis' seems to have the desired effect as Evans' head and Capaldi's left foot give Argyle an early advantage. Gavin Mahon comes on for the second half and takes command. Future England man Ashley Young adds a few quid to his ever increasing value.

3. DERBY (H)
Argyle: Larrieu, Barness, Brevett*, Wotton, Doumbe, Aljofree, Norris, Buzsaky, Evans, Djordjic*, Smith* — subs: Connolly/Norris
Derby: Camp, Edworthy, Bisgaard, Jackson, Johnson, Davies, Bolder, Idiakez, Rasiak, Smith*, Tudgay — subs: Tudgay
Lanky Pole Rasiak is the main source of Derby's attacking threat and his header loops over Larrieu and goes in via both posts. The same player then lays on the second for Morten Bisgaard to score with his chest. Djordjic misses a sitter of a header but the Rams always look comfortable.

4. CRYSTAL PALACE (A)
Argyle: Larrieu, Barness, Brevett, Wotton, Doumbe, Aljofree, Norris, Buzsaky, Evans, Mendes*, Djordjic^ — subs: Gudjonsson/Capaldi/Taylor
Palace: Kiraly, Boyce, Borrowdale, Watson", Hall, Ward, Soares^, Leigh'wood, Andrews^, Johnson, McAnuff — subs: Freedm'n/Butterf'd/Riihilahti
Argyle produce a disciplined performance but the lack of height in defence is again exposed when Darren Ward heads the ball back into the danger area. Wotton rushes his clearance which goes back to Ward to score easily. Iain Dowie makes late substitutions to run down the clock.

5. HULL (H)
Argyle: Larrieu, Barness, Brevett*, Wotton, Doumbe, Aljofree, Norris, Gudjson^, West, Taylor, Djordjic — subs: Zebroski/Buzsaky/Connolly
Hull: Myhill, Joseph!, Dawson, Ashbee, Coles, Delaney, Woodhouse, Price", Elliott, Barmby^, Fagan" — subs: Welsh/France/McPhee
Peter Taylor's men lose Marc Joseph (29) when he receives a straight red for straight arming Djordjic. Hull seem intent on a point. Myhill is booked for time wasting (55). Stuart Elliott's sublime chip over new dad, Larrieu from 30 yards is the catalyst for some terrace mutterings.

6. BRIGHTON (A)
Argyle: Larrieu, Barness, Brevett*, Wotton, Doumbe, Aljofree, Norris, Buzsaky, West, Mendes*, Djordjic^ — subs: Taylor/Zebroski/Carole
Brighton: Henderson, Hart, Reid, Buters, Hammond, Reid, McShane, Carpenter, Robinson*, Knight, Carole — subs: Kazim-Richards/Cox
The Seagulls have pace a plenty. Brevett appears to have time to clear Jake Robinson's weak shot but it dribbles over the line. Richard Carpenter scores a blinder. Doumbe skies a shot when it is easier to score. The result and manner of the performance seals Williamson's fate.

7. NORWICH (A)
Argyle: Larrieu, Barness, Aljofree^, Wotton, Doumbe, Aljofree, Norris, Wotton, West, Chadwick^, Djordjic^ — subs: Derbysh'e/Capaldi/Buzsaky
Norwich: Green, Colin, Drury, Safri, Fleming, Shackell, Marney^, Hughes, Ashton, McVeigh", Brennan — subs: Lisbie/Henderson
Nigel Worthington's side have an injury crisis. Jocky Scott's first game in charge as caretaker. He opts for a five man defence but the plan soon backfires when Doumbe helps Paul McVeigh's cross past Larrieu. Even Dean Ashton believes he is offside as the side foots home the second.

8. CREWE (H)
Argyle: Larrieu, Barness*, Brevett*, Wotton, Doumbe, Aljofree, Norris, Derbyshire^, West, Chadwick", Taylor — subs: Chadwick/Barness/Evans
Crewe: Ashton, Tonkin, Lunt, Foster, Lowe, Moss, Jones, Rivers^, Johnson*, Varney, Vaughan — subs: Higdon/Roberts
More gloom as poor defending allows Eddie Johnson to get the last touch of a goalmouth scramble. The goal drought finally ends when Taylor converts the lively Derbyshire's cross. Despite heavy pressure the Greens are unable to force a winner against Dario Gradi's fellow strugglers.

9. BURNLEY (H)
Argyle: Larrieu, Doumbe, Brevett^, Wotton, West, Aljofree, Norris, Derbyshire^, Evans, Taylor, Djordjic" — subs: Chadwick/Barness/Evans
Burnley: Coyne, Duff, Harley, Hyde, Lowe, McGreal, O'Connor, Nel-WilliamsAkinbiyi, Elliott*, Spicer, Branch — subs: Branch
Both sides are anxious to lift themselves from their current positions and are on edge. Evans' left-foot grubber just evades Danny Coyne and gives Argyle a first home win of the season. The game turns physical, resulting in seven yellows and upsetting Clarets boss, Steve Cotterill.

10. SOUTHAMPTON (A)
Argyle: Larrieu, Doumbe, Capaldi, Wotton, West, Aljofree, Norris, Gudjons'on^, Evans, Chadwick", Djordjic* — subs: Taylor/Buzsaky/Derbyshire
Southampton: Niemi, Hajto, Higginbot'm, Wise, Lundekvam, Powell, Oakley^, Quashie, Jones", Fuller, Kosowski — subs: Jones/Walcott/Crainie
A meritorious result for Tony Pulis, only 24 hours after his appointment as Argyle manager. Harry Redknapp fields an entirely different line up from the side that lost to Mansfield in midweek. Both sides have chances. Redknapp goes for broke and introduces the speedy Theo Walcott.

11. SHEFFIELD UTD (A)
Argyle: Larrieu, Barness, Brevett*, Wotton, Doumbe, Aljofree, Norris, Gudjons'on^, Evans, Chadwick", Capaldi — subs: Djordjic/Buzsaky/Taylor
Sheffield Utd: Kenny, Kozluk, Unsworth, Montgomery, Morgan, Bromby, Hill", Jagielka, Shipperley*, Kabba", Quinn — subs: Pericard/Gillespie/Webber
Neil Warnock's leaders have too much class. Larrieu pulls off a point blank save but veteran Neil Shipperley nets the rebound. A Wotton drive hits the post. There is no way back as Alan Quinn's free-kick somehow find it way through to make it ten wins from eleven for the Blades.

12 H STOKE — 1/10 — 12,604 — 23 7 12 — **W 2:1** — (0-0)

Russell 50 (og), Buzsaky 77 / *Chadwick 47* — Ref: M Russell

Lineups: Larrieu | Barness Burton | Brevett Simonsen | Wotton Russell | Doumbe Duberry | Aljofree Hoefkens | Gudjons'on^ *Chadwick"* | Norris Junior | Evans Sidibe^ | Chadwick* Gallagher | Capaldi Kolar* | Taylor/Buzsaky Sigurdsson/Dyer/Henry

Pulis gets one over his former employers now managed by Johan Boskamp. There is crowd unrest when Luke Chadwick rounds Larrieu to finish easily. Capaldi sweeps past Marlon Broomes and his cross hits Darel Russell and bobbles over. Buzsaky's bullet seals a welcome win.

---

13 H SHEFFIELD WED — 15/10 — 16,534 — 20 22 13 — **D 1-1** — (0-1)

Wotton 79p / *Buzsaky 24 (og)* — Ref: I Williamson

Lineups: Larrieu | Connolly Lucas | Brevett* Simek | Wotton Rocastle | Doumbe Coughlan | Aljofree Lee | Norris Eagles | Buzsaky* Whelan^ | Evans Peacock | Chadwick^ Graham^ | Capaldi Brunt^ | Djordjic/Taylor/Gudjonsson O'Brien/Bullen/Wood

A warm welcome back for Owls boss Paul Sturrock and captain Graham Coughlan. Buzsaky miscues an attempted headed clearance into an unguarded net. The Hungarian hits the post at the right end from 35 yards. Simek brings down Norris and Wotton does the usual from the spot.

---

14 A QP RANGERS — 18/10 — 11,741 — 19 10 14 — **D 1-1** — (1-0)

Buzsaky 39 / *Gallen 69p* — Ref: M Messias

Lineups: Larrieu | Connolly Bignot | Capaldi Dyer | Wotton Doherty* | Doumbe Shittu | Aljofree Evatt | Norris Bircham | Buzsaky* Gallen | Evans Furlong | Taylor* Nygaard | Djordjic Cook* | Chadwick/Gudjons/Brevett Ainsworth/Sturridge/Santos

The Rangers defence stand off Buzsaky and allow him to rip a 30-yard drive past Simon Royce. Argyle then defend admirably in numbers. Wotton clears a Nygaard header off the line. Larrieu's goal is finally breached by a Kevin Gallen penalty after Tylor is adjudged to handle.

---

15 A LUTON — 22/10 — 8,714 — 19 3 15 — **D 1-1** — (0-0)

Djordjic 90 / *Feeney 64* — Ref: B Curson

Lineups: Larrieu | Connolly Beresford | Capaldi Davis | Wotton Nichols | Doumbe Coyne | Aljofree Heikkinen | Norris Brkovic^ | Buzsaky^ Holmes | Evans Howard | Chadwick^ Morgan" | Capaldi Foley/Showunmi

Mike Newell's side are buoyant, being the surprise team of the division so far and having stuck four past Norwich in midweek. Carlos Edwards' superb cross finds Warren Feeney who heads powerfully past Larrieu. A rare header from Djordjic in injury-time seals another draw.

---

16 H MILLWALL — 30/10 — 11,764 — 19 24 16 — **D 0-0** — (0-0)

Ref: C Penton

Lineups: Larrieu | Barness* Marshall | Brevett Ifil | Wotton Lawrence | Doumbe Williams^ | Aljofree Robinson | Norris Wright | Buzsaky Dunne" | Evans* Hayles | Chadwick^ Asaba" | Capaldi Livermore | Djordic/Derbyshire/Chadw'k May/Craig/Elliott

A strange choice for live Sky TV coverage and most of the nation will be having a Sunday afternoon doze. A dull and uninspiring match has little excitement. Colin Lee's side show minimal enterprise and are happy with an away point, but Pulis rues more points going begging.

---

17 A IPSWICH — 5/11 — 23,083 — 21 13 16 — **L 1-3** — (0-2)

Buzsaky 51 / *McEveley 23, Juan 31, Richards 56p* — Ref: M Atkinson

Lineups: Larrieu | Connolly Price | Barness McEveley | Wotton Horlock | Doumbe De Vos | Aljofree Naylor | Norris Currie | Buzsaky Juan | Evans Parkin | Chadwick Forster* | Capaldi Richards^ | Bowditch/Westlake

Poor defending from set pieces prove costly. Jay McEveley fires a half-cleared corner through a sea of legs and Jimmy Juan is left unmarked from another corner-kick. Buzsaky curls a sublime free-kick in. Larrieu brings down Nicky Forster and Matt Richards does the spot.

---

18 H QP RANGERS — 19/11 — 13,213 — 23 11 19 — **W 3-1** — (2-0)

Wotton 7p, Doumbe 37, Chadwick 51 / *Baidoo 61* — Ref: S Tanner

Lineups: Larrieu | Connolly Bignot | Barness* Dyer | Wotton Doherty^ | Doumbe Shittu | Aljofree Evatt | Norris Ainsworth | Buzsaky* Langley^ | Evans* Gallen | Chadwick^ Santos^ | Capaldi Cook | Lastley/Taylor/Derbyshire Rowlands/Bean/Baidoo

The two-week international break seems to have worked wonders. Royce brings down Norris for an early penalty. Doumbe hooks in a corner. Chadwick glances in the third. Baidoo scores with his first touch. Not a dirty game but referee Tanner still manages to administer 12 yellows.

---

19 A SHEFFIELD WED — 22/11 — 20,244 — 17 18 20 — **D 0-0** — (0-0)

Ref: C Webster

Lineups: Larrieu | Connolly" Weaver | Barness Simek | Wotton Heckingbot' O'Brien | Doumbe Wood | Aljofree Diallo | Norris Eagles" | Buzsaky* Whelan | Evans Lee" | Chadwick* Capaldi | Capaldi Brunt | Lasley/Djordjic/Ward Graham/Corr/Partridge

Argyle's early morning flight to Yorkshire is delayed by fog. Wednesday are without the injured Coughlan. Paul Sturrock's side manage just two shots on target. Chadwick and Richard Wood have a severe clash of heads and both play out the game with heads swathed in bandages.

---

20 H READING — 26/11 — 14,020 — 18 1 20 — **L 0-2** — (0-1)

Little 20, Doyle 57 — Ref: K Wright

Lineups: Larrieu | Barness Hahnemann | Aljofree* Murty | Wotton Sharey | Jarrett Sidwell | Aljofree Ingimarsson | Doumbe Little* | Norris Harper | Evans^ Lita | Chadwick Doyle" | Capaldi Convey^ | Djordjic/Derbyshire Oster/Hunt/Cox

Steve Coppell's side are unbeaten since the opening-day defeat to Argyle and always look comfortable. Glen Little manages to chip Larrieu from 30 yards. A swift counter-attack leads to Kevin Doyle scoring from about 18 inches and he is then booked for over elaborate celebrations.

---

21 A COVENTRY — 3/12 — 18,796 — 19 21 20 — **L 1-3** — (1-2)

Norris 25 / *Morrell 36, Hutchison 45, McSheff' 49 Fulop* — Ref: N Miller

Lineups: Larrieu | Barness^ Whing | Aljofree* Hall" | Wotton Doyle | Jarrett Page | Doumbe Heath" | Norris McSheffrey Jorgensen Adebola | Buzsaky* Morrell | Evans Scawcroft^ | Chadwick Connolly | Capaldi Impey/Hutchison/Shaw | Derbyshire/Connolly

Norris converts Barness's whipped cross. Remarkably, Micky Adams is forced to bring on three subs (28) all because of injuries. His new line up does well. Jorgensen beats three players to set up Morrell. Don Hutchison scores on the turn and Gary McSheffrey fires in from 20 yards.

---

22 A WATFORD — 10/12 — 12,884 — 20 4 21 — **D 1-1** — (0-0)

Chadwick 48 / *King 90* — Ref: S Mathieson

Lineups: Larrieu | Connolly Foster | Barness Doyley | Wotton Mahon | Ward Carlisle | Aljofree Mackay | Norris Devlin | Jarrett Spring^ | Evans King | Chadwick* DeMerit | Capaldi McNamee | Derbyshire/Aljofree Chambers/Bangura

The Hornets have an injury crisis and are forced to play central defender Jay de Merit up front. The pitch, also used for rugby, cuts up badly. Chadwick scores from close range. Marlon King misses a sitter which is struck so badly it goes for a throw, in but he later makes up for it.

---

23 H CRYSTAL PALACE — 17/12 — 14,582 — 20 9 24 — **W 2-0** — (1-0)

Chadwick 1, Capaldi 90 — Ref: R Beeby

Lineups: Larrieu Speroni | Connolly Leigertwood Boyce | Barness Watson | Wotton Hall | Ward Popovic" | Doumbe Soares* | Norris Freedman | Jarrett Johnson | Evans* Morrison^ | Chadwick Hughes | Capaldi Reich/McAnuff/Macken

Chadwick scores in 12 seconds, the fastest goal in Argyle history, and Capaldi gets the second 94 minutes later. Including the kick off, it takes just five touches of the ball to take the lead, culminating in Chadwick's lob over Speroni. Iain Dowie's side recover well until Capaldi's killer.

COCA-COLA CHAMPIONSHIP

Manager: Bobby Williamson > Tony Pulis — SEASON 2005-06

No	Date	Att	Pos	Opp Pos	Pt	Res	F-A	H-T	Scorers, Times, and Referees
24	A CARDIFF 26/12	16,403	20	7	27	W	2-0	0-0	Wotton 71p, Norris 80. Ref: L Probert
25	A WOLVERHAMPTON 31/12	22,790	19	8	28	D	1-1	1-1	Ward 22; Cameron 31. Ref: P Armstrong
26	H LEEDS 2/1	17,726	19	3	28	L	0-3	0-0	Cresswell 53, Blake 60, Hulse 86p. Ref: P Taylor
27	H NORWICH 14/1	13,906	19	11	29	D	1-1	1-0	Charlton 24 (og), Huckerby 48. Ref: A Penn
28	A CREWE 21/1	5,984	20	24	32	W	2-1	2-0	Wotton 3p, 45; Rodgers 68. Ref: D Drysdale
29	H LEICESTER 24/1	12,591	19	22	35	W	1-0	0-0	Wotton 47. Ref: A Woolmer
30	H SOUTHAMPTON 31/1	15,936	16	17	38	W	2-1	1-0	Chadwick 45, Wotton 84p; Surman 70. Ref: A Hall
31	A BURNLEY 4/2	11,292	14	10	38	L	0-1	0-1	Ricketts 24. Ref: T Kettle
32	H SHEFFIELD UTD 11/2	15,017	15	2	39	D	0-0	0-0	Ref: C Penton
33	A STOKE 14/2	10,242	15	16	40	D	0-0	0-0	Ref: M Riley
34	H COVENTRY 18/2	12,958	15	14	43	W	3-1	2-0	Pericard 13, 41, 74; Wise 84. Ref: P Armstrong

Squad numbers in use

No	Plymouth XI	Opponent XI	Plymouth subs	Opp subs
24	Larrieu, Barness, Aljofree, Wotton, Ward, Doumbe, Norris, Jarrett, Evans*, Chadwick, Capaldi	Alexander, Weston, Barker^, Purse!, Loovens, Cooper*, Ledley, Ricketts, Jerome*, Koumas	Lasley	Parry/Cox/Lee
25	Larrieu, Barness, Connolly^, Wotton, Ward, Doumbe, Norris, Jarrett, Evans*, Chadwick^, Capaldi	Postma, Ross^, Lescott, Huddlestone, Gyepes, Craddock, Cameron, Anderton", Clarke", Kennedy, Miller	Lasley/Derbyshire	Ganea/Seol/Ince
26	Larrieu, Connolly^, Barness, Aljofree, Ward, Doumbe, Norris, Jarrett, Evans, Taylor*, Capaldi	Sullivan, Kelly, Crainey, Derry, Butler, Kilgallon, Miller, Douglas, Cresswell, Blake*, Hulse	Djordjic/Lasley/Derbyshire	Lewis/Hulse
27	Larrieu, Connolly, Barness, Wotton, Ward, Doumbe, Norris, Jarrett*, Evans, Chadwick*, Capaldi	Green, Colin, Drury, Charlton, Doherty, Fleming, Jarrett^, Etuhu, Ashton*, Huckerby, Henderson	Taylor	Hughes/Thorne
28	Larrieu, Connolly, Barness, Wotton, Ward, Doumbe, Norris, Nalis, Evans, Chadwick^, Capaldi	Turnbull, Otsemobor, Moss*, Lunt, Walker, Moses*, Roberts, Jones B, Jones S, Vaughan, Taylor	Hodges	Foster/Rodgers
29	Larrieu, Connolly, Barness, Wotton, Ward, Doumbe, Norris, Nalis, Evans, Chadwick*, Capaldi	Douglas, Maybury^, Johansson, Stearman, Kisnorbo, McCarthy, Wesolowski, Hughes, De Vries*, Fryatt", Gudjonsson		Smith/Hume/Hammond
30	Larrieu, Connolly, Barness, Aljofree, Ward, Doumbe, Norris, Nalis, Evans, Chadwick, Buzsaky*	Blackowski, Baird, Brennan*, Oakley, Lundekvam, Higginbot'm, Dyer, Potter, Blackstock, Pahars^, Surman	Djordjic	Kenton/Jones
31	Larrieu, Connolly, Barness*, Aljofree, Ward, Doumbe, Norris, Nalis, Evans*, Chadwick, Buzsaky*	Jensen, Duff, Harley, Hyde, Sinclair, McGreal, O'Connor J, O'Connor G, N'el-Williams, Ricketts, Elliott	Buzsaky/Zebroski	Branch/Elliott
32	Larrieu, Connolly, Barness, Aljofree, Ward, Doumbe, Norris, Nalis, Evans*, Chadwick, Capaldi	Kenny, Bromby, Armstrong, Fitcroft*, Morgan, Short, Ifill, Jagielka, Akinbiyi, Kabba^, Quinn^	Pericard	Gillespie/Ship'ley/Montgom'y
33	Larrieu, Connolly, Barness, Wotton, Ward, Doumbe, Norris, Nalis, Pericard, Chadwick*, Capaldi	Simonsen, Hoefkens, Broomes, Brammer, Duberry, Hill, Chadwick, Skoko, Sidibe^, Bangoura, Kopteel^	Evans	Sigurdsson/Sweeney
34	Larrieu, Connolly, Barness, Wotton, Ward, Doumbe, Norris*, Nalis*, Evans*, Pericard, Capaldi	Fulop, Whing, Impey, Doyle^, Williams, Heath, McSheffrey, Hutchison, John, Adebola^, Wise	Chadwick/Djordjic/Buzsaky	Scowcroft"/Wise/Jorgensen/Morrell

Match reports

24 CARDIFF — Argyle produce successive wins for the first time this season. The Greens are the better side throughout and the only surprise is the wait for the first goal. Darren Purse brings down Chadwick for a penalty and receives red being judged to be the last man. Norris makes it a merry Xmas.

25 WOLVERHAMPTON — Argyle are under the cosh until Ward heads in Postma's poor punch from a corner. Former England man, Darren Anderton hits the bar from 30 yards. Colin Cameron's shot deflects off Wotton and past the overworked Larrieu. Gradually the Pilgrims gain control and have late chances.

26 LEEDS — USA international winger Eddie Lewis gives Connolly a torrid time and sets up Leeds' first two goals. Doumbe brings down Liam Miller for a penalty to compound the misery to give Kevin Blackwell's promotion chasers a fourth consecutive win as well as ending Pulis's mini-revival.

27 NORWICH — Jason Jarrett makes a quick return, this time in opposition colours. Simon Charlton slices a clearance past his own keeper from Capaldi's badly struck corner. Darren Huckerby goes past Barness twice to tuck a shot in from a narrow angle. Pulis has already set a safety target of 53 points.

28 CREWE — Norris tumbles after a challenge by Vaughan and Wotton gives Argyle a dream start. The skipper then gets his second from a trademark 25-yard free-kick. Both defences look shaky and the Greens fail to clear a long free-kick, allowing Luke Rodgers to give hope to the bottom side.

29 LEICESTER — A rearranged game following the half-time abandonment of the original fixture in November. The Foxes have won just once in eleven games and this defeat seals the fate of manager, Craig Levein. Despite the wall being about five yards away, Wotton smashes in yet another free-kick.

30 SOUTHAMPTON — Kick off is delayed 15 minutes by a power cut. The Saints' physio pulls a muscle when running to treat an injured player! Chadwick's grass-cutter separates the sides at the break. Surman is allowed a free header to level. Referee Hall awards a penalty for reasons known only to him.

31 BURNLEY — Burnley's manager celebrates signing a new four and a half year contract with victory, courtesy of Michael Ricketts' debut goal after evading Ward's rash challenge. Argyle are restricted to long-range efforts. The home side resort to some of the physical stuff in the closing stages.

32 SHEFFIELD UTD — Neil Warnock's men lose more ground to runaway leaders Reading. The match centres on a constant midfield battle with chances few and far between. Akinbiyi misses the best chance when Larrieu's clearance hits Doumbe on the back. Vincent Pericard looks lively when he comes on.

33 STOKE — A mixed welcome back for Pulis. Stoke lose Sidibe early on when he is stretched off following an innocuous clash with Doumbe. Chadwick (the Argyle variety) misses two sitters within a minute. Larrieu pulls off the save of the match when he tips over Sam Bangoura's header.

34 COVENTRY — An emotional final appearance for Elliott Ward but the Home Park faithful have a new hero as Pericard nets the first Argyle hat-trick since January 2004. The third is embarrassingly easy. Williams and Fulop collide leaving an empty net. Wise scores three minutes after coming on.

35 A DERBY 25/2 — 0-1 L · 14 · 25,170 · 20 · 43

Larrieu · Connolly! · Barness · Nalis · Wotton · Aljofree · Norris · Hodges* · Pericard · Chadwick^ · Capaldi · Buzsaky/Evans
Camp · Edworthy · Wright · Bolder · Moore · Nyatanga · Barnes · Idiakez · Peschisolo'o*Lishie^ · Smith · Holmes/Ainsworth

The Derby fans hold a red-card demonstration against their board. Argyle are still dozing when Adam Bolder heads in Tommy Smith's cross. Connolly gets a red card of his own (73) for a second yellow, having upended the elusive Smith once too often, although the Greens still press.

Bolder 2 — Ref: K Wright

---

36 H BRIGHTON 4/3 — 1-0 W · 15 · 13,650 · 23 · 46

Larrieu · Barness · Hodges · Wotton · Doumbe · Aljofree · Norris · Nalis · Pericard · Chadwick* · Capaldi · Evans
Henderson · El-Abd · Lynch · Hammond · Butters · Hinshelwood/Carole · Carpenter · Kazim-Rich's Batting^ · Frutos* · Mayo/McPhee

Albion have not won for five games and have just lost to bottom side Crewe, but they start the brighter. A defensive mix up conjures the ball to Nalis who cleverly lobs the ball over everyone and in. The game peters out with Brighton seemingly reconciled with thoughts of the drop.

Nalis 37 — Ref: P Joslin

---

37 H PRESTON 7/3 — 0-0 D · 13 · 10,874 · 6 · 47

Larrieu · Connolly^ · Hodges^ · Wotton · Doumbe* · Aljofree · Norris · Nalis · Pericard · Evans* · Capaldi · Buzsaky/Barness/Chadwick
Nash · Mears · Alexander · McKenna · Davis · O'Neill · Sedgwick · Jarrett · Dichio · Nugent^ · Whaley · Agyemang/Ormerod/Neal

Jarrett makes another return in different colours again. The scoreline belies the quality of the match. Doumbe goes off in pain from a cracked rib. Billy Davies has three first-choice defenders suspended. Both sides have a number of good chances but indifferent finishing rules the day.

Ref: I Williamson

---

38 A HULL 11/3 — 0-1 L · 13 · 20,137 · 20 · 47

Larrieu · Barness* · Nalis · Wotton · Doumbe · Aljofree · Norris · Hodges^ · Pericard · Evans^ · Capaldi · Djordjic/Buzsaky/Chadwick
Myhill · Wiseman · Rogers · Andrews · Cort · Delaney · Green · Welsh* · Parkin · Elliott · Noble/Fagan

Yet again Argyle get no reward for a dominant day's work. On a difficult pitch bedecked with fluorescent green rugby league markings, an error by Nalis leads to the goal. The Frenchman falls and presents the ball to Keith Andrews who sets up Craig Fagan to drive low past Larrieu.

Fagan 55 — Ref: H Webb

---

39 H CARDIFF 18/3 — 0-1 L · 13 · 13,494 · 8 · 47

Larrieu · Connolly* · Hodges* · Wotton · Doumbe · Aljofree · Norris · Nalis · Evans · Capaldi · Pericard · Djordjic/Buzsaky
Alexander · Ardley · Barker · Scimeca · Purse · Loovens · Cooper · Ledley · Thompson · Jerome* · Koumas · Ndumbu-Nsungu

A presentation is made to Wotton before the game to mark his 400th appearance in a green shirt. It is not a result to remember though as Steve Thompson's header leaves Pulis looking over his shoulder at the relegation battle. Welsh international Jason Koumas masterminds the win.

Thompson 34 — Ref: R Olivier

---

40 A PRESTON 25/3 — 0-0 D · 14 · 13,925 · 6 · 48

Larrieu · Connolly* · Hodges · Wotton · Doumbe · Aljofree · Norris · Nalis · Clarke^ · Capaldi · Pericard^ · Barness/Chadwick/Evans
Nash · Alexander · Hill^ · O'Neill · Mawene · Davis · Sedgwick · McKenna · Ormerod · Stewart^ · Neal^ · Agyemang/Whaley/Mears

The referee misses a stonewall penalty (5) when Mawene clearly handles. Unlike the previous three weeks earlier, both sides are cagey. Chris Sedgwick carries North End's main threat. Seven minutes of stoppage time are added but the draw dents the Preston's promotion dreams.

Ref: N Miller

---

41 H WOLVERHAMPTON 1/4 — 2-0 W · 14 · 15,871 · 7 · 51

Larrieu · Connolly · Hodges · Wotton · Doumbe · Aljofree · Norris · Nalis · Clarke^ · Capaldi* · Pericard^ · Evans/Buzsaky/Pulis
Postma · Ross* · Jones* · Ince · Lescott · Mawene · Davies · Kennedy · Cort · Miller^ · Aliadiere · Edwards/Ricketts/Frank'ski

Glenn Hoddle makes five changes to his line up as Wolves suffer from play-off jitters. Aljofree collects a Capaldi corner and cracks in the opener. Paul Ince and Evans have a set to before the former England man turns a corner into his own net thus ensuring Argyle's survival.

Aljofree 9, Ince 80 (og) — Ref: P Melin

---

42 A LEEDS 8/4 — 0-0 D · 14 · 20,650 · 4 · 52

Larrieu · Connolly" · Hodges" · Wotton · Doumbe · Aljofree · Norris · Nalis · Clarke^ · Capaldi · Pericard^ · Evans/Buzsaky/Pulis
Sullivan · Kelly" · Crainey · Derry · Butler · Gregan · Richardson · Douglas" · Healy^ · Hulse · Blake · Beckford/Lewis/Miller

Kevin Blackwell's side are also jittery, having not won in five games. Connolly is relieved that Eddie Lewis is nursing a virus. A heavily watered pitch encourages fast flowing football. Larrieu makes his first save (90) but penalty claims are ignored.

Ref: M Thorpe

---

43 A MILLWALL 15/4 — 1-1 D · 14 · 9,183 · 23 · 53

Larrieu · Connolly · Hodges · Wotton · Doumbe · Aljofree · Norris · Nalis · Clarke^ · Capaldi* · Pericard^ · Buzsaky/Evans/Pulis
Doyle · Lawrence · Craig · Elliott · Whitbread · Phillips · Dunne^ · Williams · May · Asaba* · Livermore · Powel/Cogan

Rookie manager David Tuttle has his side ravaged by injuries. Pericard's header ignites crowd trouble with three fans charging at the directors box. With their need greater than Argyle's, Marvin Williams' header spurs the Lions into action and the Greens resort to desperate defending.

Pericard 9, Williams 30 — Ref: P Walton

---

44 H LUTON 17/4 — 1-2 L · 13 · 13,486 · 9 · 53

McCormick · Connolly · Hodges* · Wotton · Doumbe · Aljofree · Norris · Nalis · Clarke^ · Capaldi · Pericard · Buzsaky/Evans
Beresford · Edwards · Keane · Holmes · Barnett · Heikkinen" · Bell^ · Showunmi · Howard · Feeney^ · Morgan · Vine/Brkovic/Andrew

Both sides are in holiday mode and generate little excitement for an equally uninterested crowd. Pericard's header looks well over the line but Beresford persuades the referee otherwise. Buzsaky's piledriver lights a spark. Vine scores with a scissor-kick and Andrews grab a late winner.

Buzsaky 70 · Vine 79, Andrew 88 — Ref: A Hall

---

45 A LEICESTER 22/4 — 0-1 L · 15 · 22,796 · 17 · 53

Larrieu · Connolly" · Hodges^ · Wotton · Doumbe · Aljofree · Norris · Nalis · Clarke^ · Capaldi · Pericard · Chadwick/Buzsaky/Pulis
Henderson · Stearman · Maybury · Williams · McCarthy · Johansson Gudjonsson · Hughes · Fryatt^ · Welsh^ · Tiatto/O'Grady

Another definite end of season affair. Argyle wear their new predominantly black away kit for the first time. Matty Fryatt eludes Aljofree to nod home the only goal and give Rob Kelly a home win in his first game as official manager of the Foxes. Mexican waves are in abundance.

Fryatt 55 — Ref: P Joslin

---

46 H IPSWICH 30/4 — 1-1 D · 17 · 15,921 · 12 · 56

Larrieu · Connolly · Nalis · Wotton · Doumbe · Aljofree · Norris · Buzsaky* · Clarke^ · Capaldi · Pericard · Pulis/Reid/Chadwick
Supple · Casement · McEveley · Garvan^ · De Vos · Naylor · Peters · Brek-Sk'd^Westlake^ · Evans* · Currie · Parkin/Magilton/Trotter

The match is almost secondary to the farewell appearance of Mickey Evans. With the game threatening to peter out, the main man launches himself, missile-like, at Capaldi's free-kick to bullet in the winner. The final whistle elicits emotional scenes. Not a dry eye in the house.

Capaldi 28, Evans 58 · Forster 11 — Ref: B Curson

Home Average 13,776
Away 16,796

CHAMPIONSHIP (CUP-TIES)

Manager: Bobby Williamson > Tony Pulis   SEASON 2005-06

Carling Cup

Carling Cup			Att	F-A	H-T	Scorers, Times, and Referees
1 H PETERBOROUGH	17	W		2:1	2:1	Wotton 35p, Taylor 38
23|8			5,974 2:9			Plummer 21
						Ref: P Melin

SQUAD NUMBERS IN USE

											subs used
McCormick	Connolly	Barness	Wotton	Doumbe	Mendes	Norris	Buzsaky^	Evans*	Taylor	Djordjic	Zebroski/Lastley
Tyler	St Ledger	Burton	Day"	Arber	Plummer	Newton	Carden	Quinn*	Farrell^	Gain	Benjamin/Logan/Sample

Given Argyle's record in the competition, it is no surprise when they fall behind to Mark Wright's team. Chris Plummer scores after Arber's header rebounds from the bar. Farrell fouls Norris to allow Wotton to equalise. Taylor puts his side into the unknown realms of round two.

			Att	F-A	H-T	Scorers, Times, and Referees
2 A BARNET	20	L		1:2	1:1	Buzsaky 19
20|9			1,941 2:15			King 12, Grazioli 46
						Ref: R Olivier

											subs used
McCormick	Barness	Capaldi	Lasley^	Doumbe	West	Gudjonsson	Buzsaky	Chadwick	Taylor*	Derbyshire	Djordjic/Summerfield
Tynan	Hendon	Batt	Bailey	Charles	King	Lee	Sinclair	Grazioli^	Strevens	Soares*	Bowditch/Roache

Barnet are without a win in five games. Argyle begin playing down the famous Underhill slope and in red socks! Simon King thunders home a 20-yard volley. Buzsaky's curled free-kick is of equal quality. Twenty seconds after the restart, Guiliano Grazioli lobs McCormick expertly.

FA Cup

FA Cup			Att	F-A	H-T	Scorers, Times, and Referees
3 A WOLVERHAMPTON	19	L		0:1	0:1	Clarke 26
7|1			11,041 7			Ref: M Thorpe

											subs used
Larrieu	Connolly	Barness	Wotton	Doumbe	Aljofree	Norris	Buzsaky^	Evans	Hodges*	Capaldi	Djordjic/Taylor
Postma	Ross	Kennedy	Ince	Gyepes	Lescott	Cameron^	Davies	Clarke	Miller	Seol*	Cort/Rosa

A quick return to snowy Molineux a week after the league encounter. There is no romance of the Cup though. Argyle welcome back Hodges after a year's injury absence. Leon Clarke looks suspiciously offside as he latches on to Seol's long ball for the only goal. Hardly a classic.

League Table

	P	W	D	L	F	A	W	D	L	F	A	Pts
			Home						**Away**			
1 Reading	46	19	3	1	58	14	12	10	1	41	18	106
2 Sheffield U	46	15	5	3	43	22	11	7	5	33	24	90
3 Watford*	46	11	7	5	39	24	8	4	11	38	29	81
4 Preston	46	11	10	2	31	12	9	10	4	28	18	80
5 Leeds	46	13	7	3	35	18	8	8	7	22	20	78
6 Crys Palace	46	13	6	4	39	20	8	6	9	28	28	75
7 Wolves	46	9	10	4	24	18	7	9	7	26	24	67
8 Coventry	46	12	7	4	39	22	4	8	11	23	43	63
9 Norwich	46	12	4	7	34	25	6	4	13	22	40	62
10 Luton	46	11	6	6	45	31	6	4	13	21	36	61
11 Cardiff	46	10	7	6	32	24	6	5	12	26	35	60
12 Southampton	46	7	9	7	26	17	4	9	10	23	33	58
13 Stoke	46	7	5	11	24	32	10	2	11	30	31	58
14 PLYMOUTH	46	10	7	6	26	22	3	10	10	13	24	56
15 Ipswich	46	8	8	7	28	32	6	6	11	25	34	56
16 Leicester	46	8	9	6	30	25	5	6	12	21	34	54
17 Burnley	46	11	6	6	34	22	3	6	14	12	32	54
18 Hull	46	8	8	7	24	21	4	8	11	25	34	52
19 Sheffield W	46	7	8	8	22	24	6	5	12	17	28	52
20 Derby	46	8	10	5	33	27	2	10	11	19	40	50
21 QP Rangers	46	7	7	9	24	26	5	7	11	26	39	50
22 Crewe	46	7	7	9	38	40	2	8	13	19	46	42
23 Millwall	46	4	8	11	13	27	4	8	11	22	35	40
24 Brighton	46	4	8	11	21	34	3	9	11	18	37	38
	1104	234	173	145	762	579	145	173	234	579	762	1483

* promoted
after play-offs

Appearances and Goals

	Appearances						Goals			
	Lge	Sub	LC	Sub	FAC	Sub	Lge	LC	FAC	Tot
Aljofree, Hasney	36	1			1		1			1
Barness, Anthony	33	3	2		1					
Brevett, Rufus	12	1								
Buzsaky, Akos	16	18	2		1		4	1		5
Capaldi, Tony	38	3	1		1		3			3
Chadwick, Nick	26	11	1				5			5
Clarke, Leon	5									
Connolly, Paul	27	4	1		1					
Derbyshire, Matt	2	10								
Djordjic, Bojan	9	13	1			1	1			1
Doumbe, Mathias	43		2		1		1			1
Evans, Mickey	36	9	1		1		4			4
Gudjonsson, Bjarni	6	4								
Hodges, Lee	12	1			1					
Jarrett, Jason	7									
Larrieu, Romain	45									
Lasley, Keith	5		1		1					
McCormick, Luke	1		1							
Mendes, Nuno	2		2							
Nalis, Lilian	20		1							
Norris, David	44	1	1		1		2			2
Pericard, Vincent	14	1	1			1	4			4
Pulis, Anthony		5								
Reid, Reuben		1								
Summerfield, Luke						1				
Taylor, Scott	8	10	2			1	1		1	2
Ward, Elliott	15	1					1			1
West, Taribo	4									
Wotton, Paul	45		1		1		8	1		9
Zebroski, Chris		4			1		3			3
(own-goals)							3			3
30 players used	506	106	22	4	11	2	39	3	3	42

Odds & ends

Double wins: (0)
Double defeats: (1) Derby.

Won from behind: (2) Ipswich (h), Stoke (h).
Lost from in front: (2) Coventry (a), Luton (h).

High spots: Highest finish since 1986-87.
Good defensive record.
Successful battle against relegation.
Emotional farewell to Mickey Evans.

Low spots: Poor scoring record.
Unpopular early season style of play.
Tampering with traditional 'Semper Fidelis'.
Another loss to lower league opposition in Carling Cup.
Average attendance dropped by 2,644 from previous season.

Player of the Year: David Norris.
Ever presents: (0).
Hat-tricks: (1) Vincent Pericard.
Leading scorer: Paul Wotton (9).

COCA-COLA CHAMPIONSHIP

Manager: Ian Holloway

SEASON 2006-07

No	Date	Opponent	Att	Pos	Pt	F-A	H-T	Scorers, Times, and Referees
1	5/8	H WOLVERHAMPTON	15,964	—	1	D 1-1	1-0	Hayles 36 / O'Connor 47 — Ref: I Williamson
2	8/8	A COLCHESTER	4,627	8, 17	4	W 1-0	1-0	Summerfield 29 — Ref: R Booth
3	12/8	A SUNDERLAND	24,377	6, 19	7	W 3-2	2-1	Norris 8, Hayles 39, Chadwick 82 / Murphy 1, Elliott 68 — Ref: R Olivier
4	19/8	H SHEFFIELD WED	14,507	2, 19	7	L 1-2	1-0	Wotton 43p / McAllister 52, O'Brien 83 — Ref: P Melin
5	26/8	A STOKE	11,626	9, 13	8	D 1-1	0-1	Hayles 78 / Sidibe 39 — Ref: E Ilderton
6	9/9	H QP RANGERS	12,138	8, 19	9	D 1-1	1-1	Ebanks-Blake 31 / Blackstock 17 — Ref: A Marriner
7	12/9	H CARDIFF	11,665	9, 1	10	D 3-3	0-2	McNaughton 69 (og), Hay' 74, Purse 88 (og) / Thompson 8, Chopra 29, 49 — Ref: S Tanner
8	16/9	A SOUTHAMPTON	22,514	10, 9	10	L 0-1	0-0	Rasiak 51 — Ref: R Lee
9	23/9	H NORWICH	11,813	15, 10	13	W 3-1	1-0	Doherty 14 (og), Seip 47, Norris 74 / Earnshaw 90 — Ref: J Singh
10	30/9	A COVENTRY	19,545	9, 11	16	W 1-0	0-0	Samba 82 — Ref: M Halsey
11	15/10	H DERBY	13,622	7, 9	19	W 3-1	1-1	Wotton 45p, 63p, Seip 79 / Lupoli 45 — Ref: P Taylor

SQUAD NUMBERS IN USE / subs used

1 — H Wolverhampton
Argyle: McCormick, Connolly, Capaldi, Nalis^, Doumbe, Aljofree, Norris, Wotton, Chadwick^, Hayles, Hodges
Wolves: Murray, Clyde, Naylor, Henry, Breen*, Craddock, Ricketts^, O'Connor, Bathroyd*, Cort, Clapham
subs used: Ebanks-Blake/Djordjic — Edwards/Davies/Gobern

More perspiration than inspiration as both sides start the season tentatively. Hayles gets a debut goal when he stretches sufficiently to reach a Capaldi cross. O'Connor's shot loops off Doumbe's leg to leave McCormick helpless. Wolves' giant keeper Matt Murray is in superb form.

2 — A Colchester
Argyle: McCormick, Connolly, Capaldi, Summerfield'd^, Doumbe, Aljofree, Norris, Wotton, Chadwick^, Hayles, Hodges
Colchester: Davison, Elokobi, Halford, Watson, Brown, Baldwin*, Izzet^, Jackson, Cureton, Garcia, Duguid
subs used: E-Blake/**Sawyer**/Djordjic — Richards/Iwelumo

Argyle survive a first-half onslaught and go in at the interval with an undeserved lead. Brown's clearance is collected by Summerfield on the edge of the box and he lashes in a low right-foot shot. More U's pressure follows in the second period but resolute defending gains a good win.

3 — A Sunderland
Argyle: McCormick, Connolly, Capaldi, Clarke*, Doumbe, Aljofree, Norris, Wotton, E-Blake^, Hayles, Hodges
Sunderland: Alnwick, Delap, Miller*, Cunningham, Collins, Whitehead, Leadbitter, Murphy, Elliott, Lawrence^
subs used: Buzsaky/Chadwick — Wright/Stead/Brown

Despite going a goal down in 30 seconds, Argyle spoil the heralded return of Niall Quinn. Norris's half-volley loops over Ben Alnwick. Hayles intercepts a Cunningham back-pass. Elliott's header silences the home support booing. Chadwick catches Collins napping to get the winner.

4 — H Sheffield Wed
Argyle: McCormick, Connolly, Capaldi^, Summerfield'd^, Doumbe, Aljofree, Norris, Wotton, Chadwick^, Hayles, Hodges
Sheffield Wed: Jones, Simek, Spur, Lunt^, Coughlan", Bougherra, Whelan, O'Brien, Small", Brunt
subs used: Buzsaky/Djordjic/E-Blake — Boden/McArdle

A warm welcome back for Graham Coughlan. Brad Jones impedes Hayles in a chase for the ball and Wotton smashes home the penalty. Sean McAllister fires home his first ever league goal to equalise, and then Burton O'Brien chests down Lunt's pass to prod the ball past McCormick.

5 — A Stoke
Argyle: McCormick, Connolly, Hodges, Nalis, Doumbe, Aljofree, Norris, Wotton, Chadwick^, Hayles, Capaldi^
Stoke: Simonsen, Hoefkens, Higginbotham, Russell, Duberry, Hill, Chadwick", Brammer, Sidibe, Pericard^, Sweeney
subs used: E-Blake/Reid — Whitley/Harper

Argyle's fans give Tony Pulis a rough ride. Unfortunately for him, so do the home supporters. Sidibe's opener is rough justice for Argyle, who dominate the opening exchanges, only to find Steve Simonsen in inspired form. Hayles seizes on a loose ball from Connolly's long throw.

6 — H QP Rangers
Argyle: McCormick, Connolly, Hodges, Nalis, Doumbe, Aljofree, Norris, Wotton, E-Blake^, Hayles, Buzsaky^
QPR: Jones P, Rose, Milanese, Ward, Stewart, Rehman, Oliseh, Bircham*, Nygaard", Blackstock^, Cook
subs used: Chadwick/Reid — Lomas/Jones R/Gallen

Yet again, the Greens fail to seal the win despite dominating much of the game. From Rangers' first serious attack, former Argyle loanee Dexter Blackstock gets a faint touch to give them the lead. Ebanks-Blake shows great composure to curl a shot past the experienced Paul Jones.

7 — H Cardiff
Argyle: McCormick, Barness*, Summerfield, Doumbe, Nalis, Aljofree, Norris, Wotton^, Capaldi, Hodges, Hayles
Cardiff: Alexander, Gilbert, McNaughton, Scimeca, Purse, Johnson, Parry^, McPhail, Thompson^, Chopra, Ledley
subs used: Buzsaky/Nalis/Chadwick — Flood/Campbell

Dreadful defending hands the leaders three goals and seemingly three points. Argyle's defence have no answer to the in-form Michael Chopra. City's back line then goes into suicide mode. Panic struck with every Argyle attack, two own-goals contribute to the comeback of the season.

8 — A Southampton
Argyle: McCormick, Hodges^, Capaldi, Nalis, Doumbe, Aljofree*, Norris, Buzsaky*, Reid*, Hayles, Chadwick
Southampton: Davis, Makin, Dyer*, Baird, Pele, Viafara, Idiakez, Safri^, Jones^, Earnshaw, Wright
subs used: **Seip**/Wotton/Chadwick — Belmadi/Wright-Phillips

Argyle's tactics are spoiled by the loss of both Aljofree and Hodges with injury before half-time resulting in 13 minutes of stoppage time! With neither side finding any rhythm to their play, Gregor Rasiak notches the only goal as he gets the final touch to a game of ping-pong in the area.

9 — H Norwich
Argyle: McCormick, Connolly, Capaldi, Nalis, Doumbe, Seip, Norris, Wotton, Buzsaky^, Hayles^, Hodges^
Norwich: Gallacher, Colin, Doherty, Fleming, Croft^, Safri^, Cameron, Birchall*, Earnshaw, Etuhu, McVeigh
subs used: Chadwick/Sawyer/Reid — Dublin/Jarvis/Thorne

Finally a home win! Yet another own-goal sets Argyle on their way as Capaldi's inswinging corner goes in off Gary Doherty's buttock. Seip heads on his home debut. Man of the match Norris puts the game beyond doubt. Robert Earnshaw's consolation comes in the 94th minute.

10 — A Coventry
Argyle: McCormick, Connolly, Capaldi, Nalis, Doumbe, Seip, Norris, Wotton, Reid*, Chadwick^, Buzsaky^
Coventry: Marshall, Whing, Hall, Page, Ward, Birchall", Cameron, Kyle, John, Tabb^
subs used: **Samba**/Aljofree/Summer'ld — Adebola/Hutchison

The Greens dominate despite being without their two first-choice strikers, both injured. Argyle's defence are rock solid against the formidable Sky Blues front line. Aljofree's left-wing cross finds the head of fellow substitute Samba whose downward header yields a memorable debut.

11 — H Derby
Argyle: McCormick, Connolly, Capaldi, Nalis, Doumbe!, Seip, Norris, Wotton, E-Blake^, Hayles, Buzsaky^
Derby: Grant, Edworthy, Camara, Johnson, Bisgaard", Moore!, Oakley", Safri, Lupoli, Howard, Stead
subs used: Aljofree/"Summer"/Samba — Leacock/Smith/Johnson

Plenty of entertainment for the Sky TV audience. Camara trips Ebanks-Blake for a penalty. Johnson's wild shot is diverted in by the talented Lupoli. Strange decision-making culminates in a red card for Doumbe (49) for a harmless tackle. A second penalty when Johnson fouls Hayles.

Plymouth Argyle — Match-by-Match (matches 12–23)

No	Venue	Opp	Date	Att	Pos	Res		Pts	FT	HT
12	A	BARNSLEY	17/10	9,479	5	D	20	20	2:2	2:1
13	H	BURNLEY	21/10	12,817	6	D	21		0-0	0-0
14	A	CRYSTAL PALACE	28/10	17,084	7	W	12	24	1-0	1-0
15	H	IPSWICH	31/10	12,210	5	D	18	25	1-1	1-1
16	H	BIRMINGHAM	4/11	17,008	6	L	4	25	0-1	0-0
17	A	LEICESTER	11/11	21,703	7	D	15	26	2-2	1-1
18	A	SOUTHEND	18/11	9,469	7	D	23	27	1-1	1-0
19	H	LEEDS	25/11	17,088	9	L	24	27	1-2	1-1
20	H	LUTON	28/11	9,965	12	W	20	30	1-0	0-0
21	A	BIRMINGHAM	2/12	22,952	9	L	3	30	0-3	0-3
22	H	HULL	9/12	12,101	11	W	22	33	1-0	0-0
23	A	PRESTON	16/12	13,171	9	L	4	33	0-3	0-2

---

12 · A · BARNSLEY · 17/10
Ebanks-Blake 29, Hayles 34 — Kay 2, Richards 50. Ref: C Oliver

Argyle: McCormick · Connolly · Capaldi · Nalis* · Seip · Norris · Aljofree · Wotton · Hayles · E-Blake · Buzsaky^ — *subs* Summerfield/Djordjic/Samba
Barnsley: Colgan · Williams · Austin^ · Togwell · Kay · Devaney · Hassell · Howard · Hayes^ · Richards* · McIndoe — *subs* Reid/Wright/Nardiello

The match is played in misty conditions but both sides produce stunning football with goals to match. Anthony Kay belts one in from all of 40 yards. Hayles turns back time and also scores a superb goal, chesting the ball down and lashing in. No one complains about sharing the points.

13 · H · BURNLEY · 21/10
Ref: P Miller

Argyle: McCormick · Connolly · Capaldi · Nalis · Seip · Norris · Aljofree · Wotton · Hayles · E-Blake · Buzsaky — *subs* Samba
Burnley: Jensen · Sinclair · Harley · Hyde · Duff · O'Connor · Foster · Jones · Gray · N'I-Williams* · Elliot* — *subs* Lafferty/Mahon

The Clarets consider themselves lucky to keep their unbeaten away record intact after being under the cosh for much of the game. With Hayles a constant thorn in their side there looks only one winner. Steve Cotterill's men show resolute defence with McCormick virtually a spectator.

14 · A · CRYSTAL PALACE · 28/10
Chadwick 39. Ref: M Russell

Argyle: McCormick · Connolly · Capaldi · Nalis · Seip · Norris · Aljofree · Wotton · Chadwick* · E-Blake^ · Buzsaky* — *subs* Summer'ld/Samba/Sawyer
Crystal Palace: Kiraly · Lawrence · Borrowdale · Fletcher^ · Ward* · Reich* · Soares · Morrison · Freedman · Kennedy — *subs* Kuqi/Butterfield/Green

An Ebanks-Blake shot rebounds off a post and, as Darren Ward dithers, Chadwick pounces. The goal adds to the despair of Palace boss Peter Taylor under increasing pressure.

15 · H · IPSWICH · 31/10
Wotton 22 — Legwinski 1. Ref: K Friend

Argyle: McCormick · Connolly · Capaldi · Nalis · Seip · Norris · Aljofree · Wotton · Chadwick^ · E-Blake* · Buzsaky — *subs* Hayles/Samba
Ipswich: Supple · Wilnis · Harding^ · Walton · De Vos · Peters* · Legwinski · Lee · Clarke* · Richards — *subs* Roberts/Noble/Naylor

Jim Magilton's side are fresh from a 5-0 drubbing of Luton 48 hours earlier and continue in the same vein as Sylvain Legwinski heads home the first corner of the game. A rare header from Wotton levels things. Already booked, Fabian Wilnis is sent off (78) for tugging back Hayles.

16 · H · BIRMINGHAM · 4/11
Jaidi 75. Ref: G Hegley

Argyle: McCormick · Connolly · Capaldi · Nalis* · Seip · Norris · Aljofree · Wotton · Hayles · Chadwick* · Buzsaky* — *subs* E-Blake/Djordjic/Summer'ld
Birmingham: Taylor · Kelly · Sadler · Muamba · Taylor · Danns* · Clemence* · Bendtner · Jerome* · Welsh* · McSheffrey — *subs* Larsson/Gray/Nafti

The rich steal from the poor. Steve Bruce has spent £20m assembling his side and are favourites for an immediate return to the Premiership but Argyle dominate much of the game. Tunisian international Rahdi Jaidi provides the sucker punch, having been left unmarked from a corner.

17 · A · LEICESTER · 11/11
Nalis 31, Hayles 90 — Hume 29, Porter 75. Ref: M Thorpe

Argyle: McCormick · Connolly · Capaldi · Nalis · Seip · Norris · Aljofree · Wotton · Hayles · Chadwick^ · Buzsaky* — *subs* E-Blake/Djordjic
Leicester: Logan · Maybury · Johansson · Hughes · McCarthy · Sylla · Stearman · Fryatt · Hume · Welsh* · Porter

Despite the protests Ian Hume is deemed onside as he rounds McCormick for the opener. Nalis quickly replies against his former club. A slip by Seip proves disastrous, allowing Levi Porter to round the keeper Hume-style. Hayles head pops up in injury time to grab a deserved point.

18 · A · SOUTHEND · 18/11
Djordjic 5 — Gower 59. Ref: R Styles

Argyle: McCormick · Connolly · Capaldi · Nalis* · Seip · Norris · Aljofree · Wotton · Hayles · E-Blake^ · Djordjic^ — *subs* Summer'd/Buzs'ky/Chadw'k
Southend: Flahavan · Francis · Hammell · Maher · Prior* · Cam'-Ryce* · Sodje · Clarke^ · Harold · Eastwood · Gower — *subs* McCormack/Hooper/Barrett

Steve Tilson's side beat Man Utd to reach the Carling Cup last eight, but league form has so far eluded them. Djordjic soon makes the most of his first start for 13 months by firing low past Darryl Flahavan. Defensive hesitation allows Mark Gower time to pick his spot inside the post.

19 · H · LEEDS · 25/11
Djordjic 40 — Blake 3, Lewis 61. Ref: D Whitestone

Argyle: McCormick · Connolly · Capaldi^ · Nalis^ · Seip · Norris · Aljofree · Wotton · Hayles · E-Blake · Djordjic* — *subs* Chadw'k/Summer'd/Buzs'ky
Leeds: Stack · Foxe · Crainey · Derry · Heath · Kilgallon · Douglas · Westlake · Moore^ · Blake* · Lewis — *subs* Kandol/Carole

Argyle's habit of conceding early goals continues as Robbie Blake finds space and the net. The in-form Djordjic celebrates coming off the transfer list with a header, but firstly Eddie Lewis clears off the line, and then runs on to Ian Moore's pinpoint through ball to get the winner.

20 · H · LUTON · 28/11
Djordjic 61. Ref: T Kettle

Argyle: McCormick · Connolly* · Capaldi · Nalis · Seip · Norris · Aljofree · Wotton · Hayles · E-Blake* · Buzsaky* — *subs* Capaldi/E-Blake/Nalis
Luton: Kialy · Foley* · Emanuel · Robinson · Perrett · Edwards · Heikkinen · Vine · Feeney* · Brkovic — *subs* Bell/Morgan

Not pretty but another three points. Mike Newell's team are in freefall and have gone from play-off contenders to relegation battlers in a few weeks. Djordjic's goal, prodding in Connolly's cross, subjects the Hatters to an eighth consecutive defeat to equal the worst run in their history.

21 · A · BIRMINGHAM · 2/12
Bendtner 21, Upson 30, McSheffrey 41. Ref: R Beeby

Argyle: McCormick · Connolly · Capaldi · Nalis* · Seip · Norris · Aljofree · Summerfield Wotton^ · Summerfield · Buzsaky^ · Djordjic^ — *subs* Aljofree/Samba/Nalis
Birmingham: Taylor · Kelly · Sadler · Kelly · Jaidi · Larsson · Clemence^ · Bendtner* · Jerome · Bendtner* · Danns — *subs* McSheffrey/Campbell/Danns

After a promising Argyle start, on-loan Arsenal striker Nicklas Bendtner's goal turns the match. Capaldi clears off the line but the ball hits McCormick and falls to Upson to score. The Blues' third takes a huge deflection and The Pilgrims leave St Andrews a well-beaten side.

22 · H · HULL · 9/12
Ebanks-Blake 71. Ref: L Probert

Argyle: McCormick · Connolly · Capaldi · Nalis · Seip · Norris · Summerfield · Wotton* · Hayles · E-Blake^ · Buzsaky* — *subs* Djordjic^/Samba/Nalis
Hull: Myhill · Ricketts* · Dawson · Ashbee · Coles · Delaney · Welsh · Barmby · Fagan · Elliott* · Livermore* — *subs* Campbell/McPhee

Holloway is down to the bare 16 through injuries and suspensions and the situation is not helped when Wotton is stretchered off (37) with a serious knee injury after landing awkwardly. Ebanks-Blake's turn and shot provides the one moment of quality in a very lacklustre affair.

23 · A · PRESTON · 16/12
Pugh 12, Ormerod 41, Alexander 56p. Ref: K Friend

Argyle: McCormick · Doumbe · Capaldi · Nalis · Seip^ · Norris · Summerfield · Hayles · Hayles · E-Blake · Capaldi — *subs* Buzsaky/Samba
Preston: Nash · Alexander · Hill* · Whaley · St Ledger · Sedgwick^ · McKenna · Ormerod · Chilvers · Nugent · Pugh — *subs* Miller/Neal/Dichio

Play-off hopes take another knock as Paul Simpson's side notch up a comprehensive victory courtesy of some ragged defending. Pugh and Ormerod are both given the freedom of Preston to score. McKenna weaves his way into the area and is brought down by Hayles for the third.

COCA-COLA CHAMPIONSHIP

Manager: Ian Holloway

SEASON 2006-07

No	Date	Att	Pos	Pt	F-A	H-T	Scorers, Times, and Referees
24 H WEST BROM	23/12	15,172	12	34	D 2-2	2-2	Hayles 23, Nalis 40 — Phillips 45, 45 — Ref: I Williamson
25 A CARDIFF	26/12	17,299	12	35	D 2-2	1-0	Norris 33, 59 — Thompson 47, 52 — Ref: P Walton
26 A DERBY	30/12	25,775	13	35	L 0-1	0-0	Bisgaard 81 — Ref: C Webster
27 H SOUTHAMPTON	1/1	15,377	13	36	D 1-1	0-1	Hayles 66 — Rasiak 5 — Ref: K Wright
28 A NORWICH	13/1	23,513	13	39	W 3-1	0-1	Hayles 59, Buzsaky 63, 75 — Safri 45 — Ref: M Jones
29 H COVENTRY	22/1	9,841	12	42	W 3-2	2-1	Gallen 18, Buzsaky 32, Hayles 48 — Birchall 23, Mifsud 70 — Ref: S Tanner
30 A WEST BROM	31/1	19,894	11	42	L 1-2	0-1	Fallon 70 — Kamara 42p, 49 — Ref: M Thorpe
31 A WOLVERHAMPTON	3/2	19,082	11	43	D 2-2	2-1	Sinclair 28, Timar 37 — Ward 35, Olofinjana 70 — Ref: S Bennett
32 H SUNDERLAND	10/2	15,247	11	43	L 0-2	0-0	Stokes 69, Connolly 71 — Ref: K Stroud
33 H COLCHESTER	20/2	12,895	11	46	W 3-0	1-0	Norris 12, Eb'ks-Blake 59p, Gosling 67 — Ref: R Olivier
34 A QP RANGERS	24/2	13,757	11	47	D 1-1	1-0	Nalis 32 — Cook 59 — Ref: R Beeby

Squad Numbers in Use / Match Reports

24 — West Brom (H): Argyle: Larrieu, Seip, Capaldi, Nalis, Doumbe, Aljofree, Norris, Buzsaky, Hayles, E-Blake, Samba. Opponents: Hoult, Albrechtsen*, Robinson, Greening, Kamara, Davies, McShane, Carter, Hartson^, Phillips, Phillips. subs used: Djordjic^/Koumas^ — Clement I/Gera/Ellington.
Hayles coolly slides the ball under Hoult and Nalis nets a regulation header to give Argyle the advantage. In four minutes of first-half injury time Kevin Phillips scores twice, the second from 40 yards after a poor Larrieu clearance. Clement is sent off at the death for a second yellow.

25 — Cardiff (A): Argyle: Larrieu, Connolly*, Aljofree, Nalis, Seip, Aljofree, Norris, Buzsaky, Hayles, E-Blake, Capaldi. Opponents: Alexander, McNaughton/Wright*, Scineca, Purse, Johnson, Parry^, McPhail, Thompson, Chopra, Ledley. subs used: Ledley — Flood/Blake.
Yet again, Argyle gain only a point after having the better of much of the 90 minutes. Hayles tees up Norris perfectly but Dave Jones' men strike back with a quickfire double strike from big Scot Steve Thompson. The Hayles/Norris is in action again to deservedly even things up.

26 — Derby (A): Argyle: Larrieu, Connolly*, Aljofree, Nalis, Doumbe, Aljofree, Norris, Buzsaky, Hayles, E-Blake, Capaldi. Opponents: Bywater, Edworthy, Camara, Bisgaard, Moore, Leacock, Malcolm, Oakley, Howard, Stead^, Jones*. subs used: Samba/Summerf'd/Dickson — Barnes/Lupoli/Johnson.
In monsoon-like conditions, Argyle succumb to their third single-goal defeat in as many years at Pride Park. Holloway is forced to reshuffle his pack after Ebanks-Blake goes off injured (12). Giles Barnes outpaces Connolly and pulls the ball back for Morten Bisgaard to slide home.

27 — Southampton (H): Argyle: Larrieu, Seip, Capaldi, Nalis, Doumbe, Sawyer, Norris, Gosling, Hayles!, Samba^, Buzsaky. Opponents: Davis, Ostlund, Bale, Wright, Lundekvam, Baird, Pele, Prutton*, Rasiak, Wr-Phillips^, Skacel*. subs used: Summerfield/Reid/Dickson — Makin/Licka/McGoldrick.
Holloway is apoplectic at the performance of referee Wright. Rasiak is yards offside but then scores after Larrieu's scuffed kick hits him. Hayles is quickest to react to Buzsaky's saved shot but the veteran forward is sent off (84) for handball whilst charging down a Davis kick.

28 — Norwich (A): Argyle: McCormick, Gosling*, Nalis, Sawyer, Aljofree, Norris, Buzsaky, Hayles^, Gallen, Halmosi. Opponents: Gallacher, Colin^, Safri, Drury, Shackell, Croft, Etuhu, Dublin, McVeagh^, Huckerby. subs used: Hodges/Summerfield/Reid — Brown/Robinson.
Holloway is deprived of eight of his squad through injury or suspension. The new loan signings settle in well and contribute to another uncomfortable day for under-fire Canaries boss Peter Grant.

29 — Coventry (H): Argyle: McCormick, Connolly, Nalis, Sawyer, Aljofree, Norris, Buzsaky, Hayles^, Gallen, Halmosi*. Opponents: Steele, McNamee, Whing, Doyle, Page, Hall, Birchall*, Hughes, Adebola, John, Tabb^. subs used: Sinclair/E-Blake/Fallon — Thornton/Mifsud.
For once Argyle turn on the style for the TV cameras. City have caretaker Adrian Heath in charge for the first time. A power failure delays kick off by 15 minutes. Hayles scores a pearler from 25 yards. It looks comfortable until Mifsud's volley sees fingernails again being chewed.

30 — West Brom (A): Argyle: McCormick, Connolly, Capaldi, Nalis, Aljofree, Norris, Buzsaky, Hayles^, Gallen*, Halmosi*. Opponents: Kiely, McShane, Greening, Davies, Clement, Chaplow, Koren, Kamara*, Phillips*, Gera/MacDonald/Carter. subs used: Sinclair/Fallon/E-Blake — Koumas^.
It is stalemate until Buzsaky handles and Diomansy Kamara fires in from the spot. The Senegalese international then seizes on a long ball for his second. Fallon scores with a fine volley but the referee turns down two worthy penalty appeals which infuriates Holloway and his troops.

31 — Wolverhampton (A): Argyle: McCormick, Connolly, Sawyer, Nalis, Timar, Gosling, Summerfield, Fallon*, Fallon^. Opponents: Murray, Little*, Clapham, Potter, Edwards, Collins, Kightly, Henry, Keogh, Ward^, Jones*. subs used: E-Blake/Buzsaky/Gallen — McIndoe/Olofinj'a/Bothroyd.
Another dubious decision robs Argyle of a win. Sinclair's pace plays a part in his first goal. Stephen Ward equalises before Timar heads a debut goal with the linesman indicating that the ball had crossed the line. Referee Bennett awards a foul against Fallon and Olofinjana heads in.

32 — Sunderland (H): Argyle: McCormick, Connolly, Capaldi, Nalis, Timar, Gosling, Summerfield, Norris, E-Blake*, Halmosi*. Opponents: Fulop, Simpson", Collins, Whitehead, Nosworthy, Evans, Edwards, Yorke, John", Connolly, Hysen*. subs used: Sinclair/Summerfield/Gallen — Stokes/Leadbitter/Miller.
Manager Roy Keane has transformed the fortunes of the Black Cats since taking over and they show their quality. In a lively encounter both sides create several chances. £2m teenager Anthony Stokes blasts a shot past McCormick and then David Connolly coolly rounds the keeper.

33 — Colchester (H): Argyle: McCormick, Connolly, Sawyer, Nalis, Timar, Seip, Norris, Gosling*, E-Blake*, Sinclair. Opponents: Gerken, White*, Barker, Watson, Brown, Mills, Duguid, Jackson, Iwelumo*, Cureton, Garcia^. subs used: Halmosi/Fallon/Summerfield — Ephraim/McLeod/Guy.
The lure of tickets for the forthcoming FA Cup quarter-final swells the crowd. Despite a stodgy pitch Argyle produce some slick football. With U's potent pairing of Iwelumo and Cureton non existent, the Greens cruise to victory. Wayne Brown hauls down Ebanks-Blake for the penalty.

34 — QP Rangers (A): Argyle: McCormick, Connolly, Sawyer, Nalis!, Timar, Seip, Norris, Gosling*, E-Blake^, Sinclair. Opponents: Camp, Mancienne, Timoska, Lomas, Cullip, Stewart, Ainsworth, Balder, Blackstock, Rowlands^, Cook. subs used: Halmosi/Hodges — Furlong.
Holloway gets a resounding welcome back to his former club. Nalis heads Argyle in front. A blatant foul on McCormick is ignored and Cook snaps up the loose ball. Nalis is booked for protesting and then sees red (80) for kicking the ball away.

35 H STOKE 3/3 — 1-0
12,539 (12 / 0 / 48)

McCormick Connolly Sawyer Hodges Timar Seip Sinclair Summerb'd E-Blake Gallen Halmosi — Gosling/Fallon
Simonsen Hoefkens* Zakuani Russell Griffin Higginbot'm Lawrence" Diao Sidibe Hendrie^ Eustace — Dickinson/Martin/Paterson
Ebanks-Blake 44p / Russell 55 — Ref: M Russell

Holloway returns to the fold after a week's absence with flu. Potters boss Tony Pulis gets a rough ride from the crowd on his return. Carl Hoefkens brings down Halmosi for an indisputable penalty which Ebanks-Blake blasts in. A Lee Martin run sets up Darel Russell to equalise.

---

36 A SHEFFIELD WED 6/3 — 0-1 (D)
19,449 (12 / 13 / 49)

McCormick Connolly Capaldi Nalis^ Doumbe Aljofree Halmosi Gosling Fallon Gallen Sinclair — Sinclair/Hodges
Turner Simek Spurr Watson Bullen Wood Johnson* Whelan MacLean Burton Brunt — Small/Graham
Gosling 56 / MacLean 21 — Ref: R Lewis

With the FA Cup quarter-final looming, Holloway rests a few players. In an end to end game, Steve MacLean controversially opens the scoring by prodding into an empty net with McCormick lying injured. Gosling, fresh from a week's training with Chelsea, hooks in a left-foot shot.

---

37 H BARNSLEY 14/3 — 2-2 (L 2-4)
10,265 (12 / 19 / 49)

McCormick Connolly Nalis Timar Seip Sinclair^ Buzsaky^ Hayles E-Blake* Halmosi Djordjic — Hayles/Fallon/Djordjic
Colgan Austin Heckingbot' Togwell Reid Nyatanga Rajczi McCann Devaney Howard Ferenczi
Nalis 15, Ebanks-Blake 41 / Nyatanga 20, Dev'y 31,61, Ferenczi 90 — Ref: L Probert

A thrilling match enlivened by some superb long-range goals, none better than Martin Devaney's second from 35 yards which McCormick barely sees. Simon Davey's team play with a carefree attitude that belies their lowly position. The defeat all but ends Argyle's promotion bid.

---

38 H CRYSTAL PALACE 17/3 — 0-0 (W 1-0)
11,239 (13 / 10 / 52)

McCormick Connolly Sawyer Nalis Doumbe Seip Halmosi Sinclair — Fallon/Hodges
Kiraly Butterfield Borrowdale Fletcher Cort Hudson Soares^ Watson Morrison" Scowcroft Hughes* — Freedman/Grabban/Kuqi
Sinclair 48 — Ref: R Booth

Palace's run of four wins and a draw in five games is ended by a moment of brilliance from Sinclair. The youngster collects a McCormick throw in his own half and starts off on a mazy run which sees him go past three defenders before curling a right-foot shot past Gabor Kiraly.

---

39 A IPSWICH 31/3 — 0-3 (L 0-3)
21,078 (13 / 16 / 52)

McCormick Connolly Sawyer Nalis Seip Doumbe ! Sinclair* Buzsaky^ Hayles E-Blake" — Djordjic/Gallen/Fallon
Price Wilnis^ Wright Garvan De Vos Bruce Roberts^ Williams Lee Walters Richards* — Haynes/Miller/Clarke
Garvan 9, Lee 15, Haynes 90 — Ref: J Moss

On the say-so of a linesman, Doumbe suffers the quickest red card in Argyle history (2) when Walters goes down after a challenge. Two quick goals then effectively end the game. Jim Magilton's side are rarely troubled, and Danny Haynes' injury time third rubs salt into the wounds.

---

40 A BURNLEY 3/4 — 0-4 (L 0-4)
9,793 (13 / 19 / 52)

McCormick Connolly Capaldi Nalis Timar Seip Hodges" Hayles Fallon^ Sinclair — Buzsaky/E-Blake/Djordjic
Jensen Duff Harley Dj'a-Djemba Thomas Caldwell Elliott" O'Connor J^ Gray" McVeigh Jones — O'Con'r G/McCann/Akinbiyi
Duff 13, McIv' 20, Jones 38, Elliott 61 — Ref: A Hall

The Clarets end their 19-game winless streak in style courtesy of some poor defending. At 0-2 down, a clearly unhappy Holloway shuffles his formation but it makes matters worse Ebanks-Blake misses a late penalty after Wayne Thomas brings down Djordjic.

---

41 A LEEDS 7/4 — 1-2 (L 1-2)
30,034 (13 / 24 / 52)

McCormick Connolly Sawyer Nalis Timar Seip Djordjic* Norris Hayles E-Blake^ Halmosi — Sinclair/Fallon
Ankergren Richardson* Gray" Kishishev Heath Michalik Douglas Blake" Cresswell Healy Lewis — Thompson/Moore/Marques
Healy 36, Healy 45, Michalik 87 — Ref: S Mathieson

Argyle's 'week from hell' concludes with another defeat. Five changes from the Burnley debacle at least brings an improved performance. Halmosi drifts past a limpng Richardson to score, but a close-range goal from Healy and a header from Michalik all but ends Argyle's season.

---

42 H LEICESTER 9/4 — 3-0 (W 3-0)
10,900 (15 / 18 / 55)

McCormick Connolly Sawyer Nalis Seip Djordjic* Norris Buzsaky^ Hayles* E-Blake^ Halmosi — Sinclair/Fallon/Gosling
Henderson Maybury Johansson Wesolowski Kisnorbo Kenton Newton^ Jarrett Fryatt Hume Porter* — Horsfield/Hughes
Halmosi 15, Eb'ks-Blake 46, Hayles 62 — Ref: I Williamson

A classy finish from Halmosi ignites a comfortable win over Rob Kelly's strugglers. Ebanks-Blake scores within 14 seconds of the restart. Hayles scores with a diving header. The supporters give an emotional farewell to Scott Sinclair who is making his final Home Park appearance.

---

43 A LUTON 14/4 — 2-1 (W 2-1)
7,601 (13 / 23 / 58)

McCormick Connolly Sawyer Nalis Seip Doumbe Norris Buzsaky^ Hayles* E-Blake^ Halmosi — Gallen/Sinclair
Brill Keane Emmanuel" Foley Coyne Barnett Spring* Robinson Andrew Talbot" Bell — O'Leary/Idrizaj/Langley
Norris 4, Halmosi 39 / O'Leary 52 — Ref: G Salisbury

Ex-Pilgrim Kevin Blackwell's side teeter on the brink of relegation. A rare header from Norris saps the visitors' confidence even more. Halmosi adds to their misery, although a half-time rollicking sees an improved second-half performance. Stephen O'Leary grabs a consolation.

---

44 H SOUTHEND 21/4 — 2-1 (W 2-1)
11,097 (13 / 22 / 61)

McCormick Connolly Sawyer Nalis Seip Doumbe Norris Buzsaky^ Hayles^ E-Blake^ Halmosi* — Gosling/Galen/Timar
Flahavan Francis Hammell Maher Clarke Barrett Camp'l-Ryce Gower* Bradbury Eastwood* McCormack — Foran/Harrold
Ebanks-Blake 6, Hayles 90 / Clarke 25 — Ref: P Armstrong

Shrimpers keeper Darryl Flahavan is in impressive form but cannot prevent Ebanks-Blake from finishing Halmosi's cross after Peter Clarke loses the ball in a dangerous area. The Southend defender makes amends by heading in an equaliser, but Hayles sneaks in a last-gasp winner.

---

45 H PRESTON 28/4 — 2-0 (W 2-0)
13,813 (12 / 4 / 64)

McCormick Connolly Sawyer Nalis Seip Doumbe Norris Buzsaky^ Hayles E-Blake Halmosi — Gallen
Henderson Alexander Hill Soley St Ledger Chilvers Sedgwick* Davidson Ormerod" Nugent^ Pugh — Whaley/Ricketts/Agyemang
Ebanks-Blake 77p, Hayles 85 — Ref: D Gallagher

Preston withstand constant pressure as a relaxed Argyle produce their best football of the season. A long ball induces panic and Alexander handles allowing Ebanks-Blake to score from the spot. Hayles ghosts in for a second leaving the Green Army singing Holloway's name.

---

46 A HULL 6/5 — 2-1 (W 2-1)
20,661 (12 / 21 / 67)

Larrieu Connolly Sawyer Nalis Seip Doumbe Norris Buzsaky^ Hayles^ E-Blake Halmosi* — Gallen/Fallon
Myhill Doyle Dawson Ashbee Turner Delaney Marney" Parlour^ Windass Forster McPhee^ — Pelter/Elliott/Featherstone
Halmosi 45, Ebanks-Blake 59 / Elliott 61 — Ref: S Tanner

A fifth successive win. Argyle again show their spirit to come back from Ebanks-Blake's penalty miss (33) after Norris had been brought down. Another Halmosi goal adds to the clamour to make his signing permanent as the 700 travelling fans enjoy their Bank Holiday outing.

Average Home 13,011 — Away 17,571

CHAMPIONSHIP (CUP-TIES)

Manager: Ian Holloway

SEASON 2006-07

Carling Cup

	H/A	Opponent	Date	Att		Res	F-A	H-T	Scorers, Times, and Referees
1	H	WALSALL	22/8	6,407	9	L	0-1	0-0	Dann 85 — Ref: C Penton

SQUAD NUMBERS IN USE — Argyle: McCormick, Connolly, Barness, Doumbe, Aljofree, Norris, Wotton, Chadwick*, E-Blake, Capaldi^
Opposition: Ince, Westwood, Fox, Gerrard, Keates, Raper, Fanguiera*, Pead, Sam*, Constable^, Taylor
subs used: Reid/Buzsaky — Wright/Demontagnac/Dann

The Saddlers continue their unbeaten start to the season with a shock win. Despite having large chunks of possession, Argyle fail to really test Clayton Ince. Substitute Scott Dann scores within a minute of coming on, which at least spares the sparse crowd of an extra half an hour.

FA Cup

	H/A	Opponent	Date	Att		Res	F-A	H-T	Scorers, Times, and Referees
3	A	PETERBOROUGH	6/1	6,255	13	D	1-1	0-0	Aljofree 73p / McLean 78 — Ref: C Boyeson

SQUAD NUMBERS IN USE — Argyle: McCormick, Connolly!, Aljofree, Nalis, Seip, Norris, Buzsaky", Samba", Reid^, Capaldi
Opposition: Tyler, Newton, Futcher*, Butcher, Arber, Morgan, Low, Strachan", Crow, McLean, Day^
subs used: Summer'ld/Hodges/Dickson — Branston/Yeo/Benjamin

Injuries force Holloway to field an inexperienced strike-force. Connolly is sent off (64) after a needless foul on Simon Yeo. Aljofree's twice-taken penalty is cue for a number of missiles to be thrown and Posh boss Keith Alexander to be sent to the stands. McLean earns a replay.

	H/A	Opponent	Date	Att		Res	F-A	H-T	Scorers, Times, and Referees
3R	H	PETERBOROUGH	16/1	9,973	12	W	2-1	2-1	Hayles 18, Norris 27 / McLean 13 — Ref: I Williamson

SQUAD NUMBERS IN USE — Argyle: McCormick, Connolly, Aljofree, Nalis, Seip, Norris, Buzsaky^, Hayles, Reid*, Capaldi
Opposition: Tyler, Newton, Huke^, Butcher, Arber, Low", Strachan*, Crow, McLean, Day
subs used: E-Blake/Summerfield — Gain/Yeo/Benjamin

Aljofree and McCormick leave the ball to each other and McLean nips in to score. On a greasy surface Argyle quickly hit back with Hayles finishing an intricate passing move. Norris beats three players and sends a skimmer past Tyler. Round 4 looms for the first time in seven years.

	H/A	Opponent	Date	Att		Res	F-A	H-T	Scorers, Times, and Referees
4	A	BARNET	27/1	5,204	11	W	2-0	0-0	Aljofree 67p, Sinclair 84 — Ref: P Walton

SQUAD NUMBERS IN USE — Argyle: McCormick, Connolly, Capaldi, Nalis, Seip, Aljofree, Norris, Buzsaky^, Hayles, Halmosi*, Sinclair/Summerfield
Opposition: Flitney, Devera^, Nicolau, Hes'enthaler King, Yakubu, Cogan*, Bailey, Puncheon, Birchall, Graham, Hatch/Allen

Manager Paul Fairclough describes the match as one of the biggest in Barnet's history. Aljofree's precise penalty follows a foul on Noris by Joe Devera. Sinclair then scores one of the goals of the season, collecting the ball on the edge of his own area and weaving his way to goal.

	H/A	Opponent	Date	Att		Res	F-A	H-T	Scorers, Times, and Referees
5	H	DERBY	17/2	18,026	1	W	2-0	1-0	Gallen 13p, Sinclair 84 — Ref: M Dean

SQUAD NUMBERS IN USE — Argyle: McCormick, Connolly, Sawyer, Nalis, Timar, Seip, Gosling*, Norris, E-Blake, Gallen, Sinclair
Opposition: Bywater, Mears, Camara, Bisgaard, Moore !, Leacock, Johnson, Jones*, Pearson, Howard, Smith^
subs used: Halmosi — Macken/Barnes

Gallen is at the centre of the action. The loanee scores from the spot after being fouled by Leacock. He then misses a second spot-kick after Moore impedes Timar. The giant Derby defender is sent off (65) for two fouls in quick succession. Sinclair's header seals a quarter-final slot.

	H/A	Opponent	Date	Att		Res	F-A	H-T	Scorers, Times, and Referees
QF	H	WATFORD	11/3	20,652	12	L	0-1	0-1	Bouazza 21 — Ref: C Foy

SQUAD NUMBERS IN USE — Argyle: McCormick, Connolly, Sawyer^, Nalis, Timar, Seip, Gosling*, Norris, E-Blake, Gallen, Sinclair*
Opposition: Foster, Mariappa, Powell, Mahon, Shitt, DeMerit, Smith, Francis, Priskin", Kabba^, Bouazza
subs used: Hayles/Halmosi/Capaldi — Chambers/Henderson

Watford have to thank keeper Ben Foster for keeping them in the competition. The Man Utd loanee almost single-handedly saves Adie Boothroyd's Premiership strugglers. Hameur Bouzza's left-foot screamer denies Argyle a semi-final place which the performance so deserved.

Football League Championship — Final Table

	Team	P	W	D	L	F	A	W	D	L	F	A	Pts
			Home					**Away**					
1	Sunderland	46	15	4	4	38	18	12	8	3	38	29	88
2	Birmingham	46	15	5	3	37	18	11	3	9	30	24	86
3	Derby*	46	13	6	4	33	19	12	3	8	29	27	84
4	West Brom	46	14	4	5	51	24	8	6	9	30	31	76
5	Wolves	46	12	5	6	33	28	10	5	8	26	28	76
6	Southampton	46	13	6	4	36	20	8	6	9	41	33	75
7	Preston	46	15	4	4	38	17	7	7	9	26	36	74
8	Stoke	46	12	8	3	35	16	7	8	8	27	25	73
9	Sheffield W	46	10	6	7	38	36	10	5	8	32	30	71
10	Colchester	46	15	4	4	46	19	5	13	5	24	37	69
11	PLYMOUTH	46	10	8	5	36	26	7	8	8	27	36	67
12	Crystal Pal	46	12	3	8	33	22	6	8	9	26	29	65
13	Cardiff	46	11	7	5	33	18	6	11	6	24	35	64
14	Ipswich	46	13	2	8	40	29	5	6	12	24	30	62
15	Burnley	46	10	6	7	35	23	5	6	12	17	26	57
16	Norwich	46	10	5	8	29	25	6	4	13	27	46	57
17	Coventry	46	11	4	8	30	25	5	4	14	17	37	56
18	QP Rangers	46	9	6	8	31	29	5	5	13	23	39	53
19	Leicester	46	6	8	9	26	31	7	6	10	23	33	53
20	Barnsley	46	9	4	10	27	29	6	1	16	26	56	50
21	Hull	46	8	3	12	33	32	5	7	11	18	35	49
22	Southend	46	6	6	11	29	38	4	6	13	18	42	42
23	Luton	46	7	5	11	33	40	5	5	15	20	41	40
24	Leeds**	46	10	4	9	27	30	3	3	17	19	42	36
		1104	266	123	163	827	612	163	123	266	612	827	1523

* promoted after play-offs
** 10 points deducted

Odds & ends

Double wins: (6) Colchester, Coventry, Crystal P, Hull, Luton, Norwich.
Double defeats: (2) Birmingham, Leeds.

Won from behind: (2) Norwich (a), Sunderland (a).
Lost from in front: (3) Barnsley (h), Leeds (a), Sheffield W (h).

High spots: Reaching FA Cup quarter-finals.
Statistically the best finish since 1953.
Impact of several loan players.
Attractive style of football.
Five successive wins at end of season.

Low spots: Too many home points dropped to mount play off challenge.
Poor disciplinary record.
Failure to win FA Cup quarter-final after dominating game.

Player of the Year: Lilian Nalis.
Ever presents: (0).
Hat-tricks: (0).
Leading scorer: Barry Hayles (14).

Appearances and Goals

Player	Lge	Sub	LC	Sub	FAC	Sub	Lge	LCFAC	Tot
	Appearances						**Goals**		
Aljofree, Hasney	22	3	1		3			2	2
Barness, Anthony	1		1						
Buzsaky, Akos	27	9	1		3		3		3
Capaldi, Tony	30	1	1	1	3	1	3		3
Chadwick, Nick	9	7	1				2		2
Connolly, Paul	38		1		5				
Dickson, Ryan		2				1			
Djordjic, Bojan	8	9					3		3
Doumbe, Mathias	29		1						
Ebanks-Blake, Sylvan	30	11	1		2	1	10		10
Fallon, Rory	5	10					1		1
Gallen, Kevin	6	7			3		1	1	2
Gosling, Dan	8	4			3	1	2		2
Halmosi, Peter	14	2			1	2	4		4
Hayles, Barry	37	2	1		2	1	13	1	14
Hodges, Lee	11	4				1			
Larrieu, Romain	6								
McCormick, Luke	40		1		5				
Nalis, Lilian	39	3	1		5		4		4
Norris, David	41		1		5		6	1	7
Reid, Reuben	1	5			2				
Samba, Cherno	1	12		1	1	1	1		1
Sawyer, Gary	19	3			5				
Seip, Marcel	36	1			5		2		2
Sinclair, Scott	8	7			2	1	2	2	4
Summerfield, Luke	11	12				3	1		1
Timar, Krisztian	8	1			2		1		1
Wotton, Paul	21	1	1				4		4
(own-goals)							3		3
28 players used	506	116	11	2	55	11	63	7	70

COCA-COLA CHAMPIONSHIP

Manager: Ian Holloway > Paul Sturrock — SEASON 2007-08

No		Date	Att	Pos	Pt	F-A	H-T	Scorers, Times, and Referees
1	A HULL	11/8	16,633	W 3	3:2	2-1		Norris 15, Fallon 45, E-Blake 82, Windass 3, Marney 40p, Ref: G Laws
2	H IPSWICH	18/8	13,260	4 · 3	D 4	1-1	0-1	E-Blake 85, Lee 2, Ref: K Friend
3	A BARNSLEY	25/8	9,240	6 · 21	L 4	2-3	0-2	Hayles 63, Chadwick 68, Ferenczi 12, Werling 45, Howard 60, Ref: B Knight
4	H LEICESTER	1/9	11,850	11 · 9	D 5	0-0	0-0	Ref: P Taylor
5	H CARDIFF	15/9	11,591	15 · 11	D 6	2-2	1-0	E-Blake 30, 58, Rae 71, Thompson 89, Ref: R Beeby
6	A QP RANGERS	18/9	10,850	18 · 23	W 9	2-0	0-0	Halmosi 50, Norris 62, Ref: A Marriner
7	A STOKE	22/9	12,533	8 · 10	L 9	2-3	0-1	Seip 52, Fallon 59, Seip 10(og), Lawrence 66, Fuller 73, Ref: N Miller
8	H WOLVERHAMPTON	29/9	13,638	13 · 11	D 10	1-1	0-1	Chadwick 61, Elliott 41, Ref: P Joslin
9	H CRYSTAL PALACE	2/10	10,451	13 · 16	W 13	1-0	0-0	Halmosi 50, Ref: R Shoebridge
10	A BLACKPOOL	6/10	8,784	9 · 13	D 14	0-0	0-0	Ref: J Moss
11	H COVENTRY	20/10	11,576	9 · 8	W 17	1-0	1-0	Martin 16, Ref: K Hill

SQUAD NUMBERS IN USE (lineups and substitutes)

1. HULL — Larrieu, Connolly, Sawyer, Nalis, Doumbe, Seip, Norris, Buzsaky, Hayles*, Fallon*, Halmosi^ / Hodges, E-Blake, Chadwick
Myhill, Ricketts, Dawson, Coles, Delaney, Hughes, Ashbee, Marney, Windass", Barmby", Garcia / Liv'more, McPhee, Bridges*
Welcome to the new season! After three minutes Argyle go a goal down when Barmby hits a post and veteran Dean Windass reacts quickest. The Greens interval lead is cancelled out when Halmosi concedes a penalty for a harmless challenge. Ebanks-Blake's low shot proves crucial.

2. IPSWICH — Larrieu, Connolly, Sawyer, Nalis, Doumbe, Seip, Norris, Buzsaky, Hayles*, Fallon^, Halmosi / Hodges, Abdou, Chadwick
Alexander, Wright, Harding, Bruce, de Vos, Garvan, O'Cal'ghan, Miller, Lee^, Counago^, Walters / Wilnis I, Roberts, Haynes*
Manager Holloway is taken to hospital before kick off. Lee's superb header does nothing to lift the gloom. Ipswich try to run down the clock but Ebanks-Blake nicks a late equaliser. Wilnis is only on for ten minutes before being sent off for the second successive season at Home Park.

3. BARNSLEY — Larrieu, Connolly, Sawyer, Nalis, Doumbe^, Seip, Norris, Buzsaky", Hayles, Fallon*, Halmosi / E-Blake, Abdou, Chadwick
Muller, Nyatanga, Kozluk, Foster, Souza, Howard, Johnson, De Silva, Ferenczi, Odejayi, Werling^ / Christensen, Ricketts*
Argyle wear their yellow away shirts for the first time. The Tykes take the lead against the run of play. Howard's header kills the game. Argyle launch a brave fightback through a melee of players. Injured referee Knight is replaced at half-time.

4. LEICESTER — McCormick, Connolly, Sawyer*, Nalis*, Timar, Seip, Norris, Buzsaky, Hayles*, E-Blake, Halmosi / Hodges, Abdou, Fallon
Fulop, N'Gotty, Mattock^, McAuley, Kisnorbo, Hume, Wesolowski, De Vries, Clemence, Campbell", Sheehan / Cort, Porter, Kishishev*
Argyle's first goalless draw in 42 matches. City have three co-managers in charge following the sacking of Martin Allen. The home side rule the first half but cannot break down a spirited defence. Leicester also have chances but the game will not be one to talk about in the future.

5. CARDIFF — McCormick, Connolly, Sawyer, Abdou, Timar, Seip, Norris, Gosling^, Hayles, E-Blake^, Halmosi / Buzsaky, Chadwick
Turnbull, Gunter^, Capaldi, Johnson, McN'ghton, Whit'ham, Sinclair, Rae, Hass baint^, McPhail, Parry / Fowler, Thompson, Ledley*
A less than generous 'welcome' back for Tony Capaldi. Despite the plethora of internationals in the Cardiff side, Argyle take their chances. The introduction of ex-England star Robbie Fowler galvanises the visitors and they stage a fight-back. Chadwick is deprived in the last minute.

6. QP RANGERS — McCormick, Connolly, Sawyer, Nalis, Timar, Seip, Norris, Buzsaky, Hayles*, Fallon*, Halmosi / Hodges
Camp, Rehman, Barker, Cullip, Stewart, Rowlands, Nardiello", Moore^, Blackstock, Leig'twood, Bignot/Ephraim/Sahar*
An encouraging display to leave Rangers boss John Gregory under more pressure. Halmosi leaves Rehman for dead and then uses his under-employed right foot to slot home. Rowlands hits the bar. A Halmosi nod down is converged on by three Pilgrims with Norris wining the race.

7. STOKE — McCormick, Connolly, Sawyer*, Nalis, Timar, Seip, Norris, Buzsaky, Hayles*, Fallon^, Halmosi* / Hayles, Hodges
Simonsen, Zakuani, Wright, Shawcross, Hill, Delap, Lawrence, Matteo, Sidibe", Cresswell^ / Wilkinson/Sweeney/Parkin*
A well rehearsed free-kick leads to confusion and a Seip own-goal but he then levels with a header at the right end. Argyle's second sees the home crowd turn on manager Tony Pulis. McCormick completely misses a long throw leaving Lawrence to mop up and Fuller gets the winner.

8. WOLVERHAMPTON — McCormick, Connolly, Sawyer, Nalis, Timar, Seip, Norris, Buzsaky", Hayles, Halmosi* / Chadwick, Fallon, Gosling
Hennessy, Foley, Gray, Breen, Craddock, Henry, Kightly, Olofinjana, Ward", Elliott^ / Potter, Bothroyd
The visitors win the first-half corner count 14-0, which tells its own story. Lucky to be only one down, Argyle show more resilience in the second half and sub Chadwick nets an equaliser to nick an undeserved point against easily the best team seen at Home Park so far this season.

9. CRYSTAL PALACE — McCormick, Connolly, Hodges, Nalis, Timar, Seip, Norris, Gosling", Hayles*, Chadwick*, Halmosi / E-Blake, Buzsaky, Doumbe
Sperani, Butterfield", Craig, Hudson, Cort, Fletcher, Lawrence, Soares^, Dickov, Idrizaj" / Morrison/Watson/Green
A comfortable victory over a lacklustre Palace. Pernickety refereeing hardly helps add to the entertainment factor. Halmosi's superb volley is enough but no one would have argued if the margin had been greater. The result contributes to the sacking of Palace boss Peter Taylor.

10. BLACKPOOL — McCormick, Connolly, Hodges, Nalis, Timar, Seip, Norris, Buzsaky", Hayles, Chadwick*, Halmosi / Hayles, Fallon, Martin
Rachubka, Barker, Crainey, Jackson Mi, Jacks'n Ma, Southern^, T'lorF'cher, Fox, Hoolahan, Parker, Morrell^ / Vernon/Jorgensen/Welsh*
Entertaining, but not one for the purists. Argyle find it difficult to cope with the Tangerines 'up and at 'em' style of play. With the highly rated Wes Hoolahan pulling the strings in midfield, the home side look the more likely winners. The Jackson two cope well with any Argyle attacks.

11. COVENTRY — McCormick, Connolly, Hodges, Nalis, Timar, Seip, Martin, Norris, Hayles, E-Blake, Halmosi* / Sawyer
Marshall, Osbourne, Bor'wdale, Ward, Turner, Gray, Hughes M, Doyle, Mifsud, Hughes S, Simpson^ / Adebola, Kyle*
The fleet-footed Martin gets ahead of defenders to steer Ebanks-Blake's cross in and immediately endear himself to the home support. A shaky City defence leaves Marshall exposed on several occasions. Iain Dowie throws on more height but to no effect as Argyle's climb continues.

12 A CHARLTON 23/10
Att 22,123 · Pos 6 · 3 · Pts 20 · **W 2-1** (HT 2-1)
Argyle: McCormick; Connolly, Hodges", Nails, Timar, Seip, Martin, Hayes*, E-Blake*, Norris, Halmosi. Subs: Sawyer/Suzsaky/Chadwick
Charlton: Weaver; M'taouakil, Mills, Bougherra, Fortune^, Reid, Varney, Zheng, Todorov*, Iwelumo, Semedo". Subs: McLeod/Sodje/Thomas
Scorers: E-Blake 6, Hayes 38 / McCormick 12 (og) — Ref: R Styles

A first visit to the Valley for 25 years brings a memorable and unlikely victory. McCormick pushes Mills' shot onto a post but the rebound strikes the prone keeper and goes in. Argyle's two goals are both close-range efforts. Referee Rob Styles books ten players in a niggly affair.

13 A PRESTON 27/10
Att 11,055 · Pos 4 · 21 · Pts 20 · **L 0-2** (HT 0-1)
Argyle: McCormick; Connolly, Hodges", Nails, Timar, Seip, Martin", Hayes, E-Blake*, Norris, Halmosi. Subs: Easter*/Fallon/Gosling
Preston: Lonegan; Jones*, Hill, St Ledger, Mawene, Nichalls, Sedgwick, McKenna, Hawley^, Ormerod", Carter. Subs: Whaley/Mellor/Agyemang
Scorers: Ormerod 11, Carter 67 — Ref: M Pike

Oh dear! After the euphoria of Charlton, Argyle produce a dismal performance to underline Holloway's pre-match proclamation that Deepdale is his bogey ground. The wily Ormerod's prod and a volley from Carter give the previously struggling Lancastrians a comfortable three points.

14 H SHEFFIELD WED 3/11
Att 12,145 · Pos 7 · 21 · Pts 20 · **L 1-2** (HT 1-2)
Argyle: McCormick; Connolly", Hodges, Nails, Timar, Seip, Martin, Hayes^, E-Blake^, Norris, Halmosi. Subs: Easter/Fallon/Gosling
Sheffield Wed: Grant; Simek, Spurr, Hinds, Johnson M, Folly, Johnson J^, Watson, Tudgay, Sodje", O'Brien. Subs: Burton/Esajas
Scorers: E-Blake 47p / Sodje 50, O'Brien 55 — Ref: A D'Urso

Argyle's cohesive first-half display does little to suggest they will lose their unbeaten home record. Simek's clumsy challenge on Halmosi sees Ebanks-Blake score from the spot. Sodje scores from a narrow angle and then O'Brien provides an exquisite finish from Sodje's through ball.

15 A COLCHESTER 6/11
Att 4,833 · Pos 8 · 16 · Pts 21 · **D 1-1** (HT 0-0)
Argyle: Larrieu; Connolly, Hodges", Nails, Timar, Seip, Martin, Abdou*, E-Blake", Norris, Martin". Subs: Halmosi/Fallon/Easter
Colchester: Gerken; Duguid, Granville, Connolly, Baldwin, Watson, Izet", Yeates, Platt, Lisbie, Jackson. Subs: —
Scorers: Norris 88 / Lisbie 56 — Ref: G Hegley

An interval stalemate belies the fact that both sides have chances. Mark Yeates' volley is superbly saved by the recalled Larrieu but the ball falls at the feet of Kevin Lisbie who cannot miss. The U's goal then takes a continuous pounding and Norris's late leveller is well deserved.

16 H NORWICH 10/11
Att 11,222 · Pos 10 · 24 · Pts 24 · **W 3-0** (HT 1-0)
Argyle: Larrieu; Connolly, Hodges", Nails*, Timar, Seip, Martin, Hayes^, E-Blake^, Norris, Halmosi^. Subs: Easter/Abdou/Gosling
Norwich: Marshall; Otsemobor, Lappin, Taylor*, Shackell, Russell, Croft", Martin^, Cureton, Spillane, Murray. Subs: Brellier/Brown/Strihavka
Scorers: Martin 26, Connolly 47, Norris 49 — Ref: D Drysdale

New Canaries manager Glenn Roeder is left shaking his head at the task he has taken on. Argyle cruise to victory over an inept City. An early injury to Martin Taylor did little to help. Connolly's goal is his first in 149 appearances and the first from an Argyle right-back this century!

17 A SHEFFIELD UTD 24/11
Att 23,811 · Pos 7 · 12 · Pts 27 · **W 1-0** (HT 1-0)
Argyle: Larrieu; Connolly, Hodges, Nails, Doumbe, Seip, Martin, Hayes, E-Blake^, Norris, Halmosi*. Subs: Sawyer/Easter
Sheffield Utd: Bennett; Bardsley, Naysmith, Cahill, Kilgallon, Montgom'ry, Gillespie*, Armstrong, Beattie, Webber, Carney". Subs: Tonge/Sharp
Scorers: Halmosi 24 — Ref: M Russell

Argyle put the loss of manager Holloway behind them to produce a spirited performance. With Tim Breacker and Des Bulpin in charge, the Greens deserve more than the one goal by Halmosi who dinks the ball over Ian Bennett to increase the pressure on Blades boss Bryan Robson.

18 H WEST BROM 28/11
Att 14,348 · Pos 4 · 2 · Pts 27 · **L 1-2** (HT 0-2)
Argyle: Larrieu; Connolly, Hodges", Nails, Doumbe, Seip, Gosling*, Hayes^, E-Blake, Norris, Halmosi^. Subs: Abdou/Easter/Fallon
West Brom: Kiely; Hoefkens, Robinson, Barnett, Cesar, Gera, Teixeira^, Greening, Bednar, Koren, Brunt. Subs: Beattie/MacDonald
Scorers: Easter 84 / Bednar 9, 43 — Ref: S Bennett

No fairytale return for Paul Sturrock as Tony Mowbray'sBaggies prove to be a class apart. They are without their two first-choice strikers but on-loan Roman Bednar makes the most of his opportunity with both goals. Easter's late strike signals some late pressure but to no avail.

19 H SCUNTHORPE 1/12
Att 10,520 · Pos 7 · 17 · Pts 30 · **W 3-0** (HT 0-0)
Argyle: Larrieu; Connolly, Hodges", Nails, Timar, Seip, Martin", Hayes^, E-Blake*, Norris, Halmosi. Subs: Abdou/Fallon/Easter
Scunthorpe: Lillis; Logan, Williams, Crosby, Butler, Cork, Sparrow, Forte", Paterson, Baraclough^, Hurst. Subs: Ameobi/Hayes/Hurst
Scorers: E-Blake 51, Timar 64, Abdou 77 — Ref: F Graham

Struggling Iron have two suspended and lose Taylor through injury (9). The half-time introduction of Paul Hayes spurs Scunny but Ebanks-Blake's tap in eases the tension. Timar defies his size and gravity to scissor-kick the second. Abdou's left foot puts matters beyond doubt.

20 A NORWICH 4/12
Att 25,434 · Pos 6 · 24 · Pts 30 · **L 1-2** (HT 0-1)
Argyle: Larrieu; Connolly, Hodges", Nails, Timar, Seip, Martin", Hayes, Abdou*, Norris, Halmosi*. Subs: Gosling/Easter
Norwich: Marshall; Otsemobor, Camara, Taylor", Doherty, Russell, Fotingham, Evans, Huckerby, —, Cureton". Subs: Croft/Dublin/Shackell
Scorers: Timar 89 / Evans 2, Huckerby 87 — Ref: P Taylor

The Canaries have been transformed in the 23 days since the teams last met. Despite Ched Evans' early goal, Argyle start the brighter. Ebanks-Blake heads over from three inches. Some strange refereeing decisions culminate in Huckerby's penalty, despite Connolly's superb tackle.

21 H BRISTOL CITY 8/12
Att 16,530 · Pos 7 · 4 · Pts 31 · **D 1-1** (HT 1-0)
Argyle: Larrieu; Connolly, Hodges", Nails, Timar, Seip, Gosling*, Hayes^, E-Blake", Norris, Halmosi. Subs: Chadwick/Fallon
Bristol City: Basso; Orr, Fontaine, Carey, McCombe, Sproule", Johnson, Showunmi^, Noble", —, McIndoe. Subs: Trundle/Byfield/Skuse
Scorers: E-Blake 23p / Timar 71 (og) — Ref: P Dowd

Heavy rain forces a pre-match pitch inspection. Argyle open the scoring after Carey fouls Ebanks-Blake. The half-time introduction of £1m signing Lee Trundle sees City apply the pressure with Larrieu kept busy. He is eventually beaten when Timar's attempted hoof loops over him.

22 A WATFORD 15/12
Att 18,532 · Pos 8 · 1 · Pts 34 · **W 1-0** (HT 0-0)
Argyle: Larrieu; Gosling, Sawyer, Abdou, Timar, Seip, Norris, Hayes*, Hodges^, Easter, Halmosi. Subs: —
Watford: Lee; Doyley, Stewart, Jackson, DeMerit, O'Toole", Smith, King, Williamson, Priskin*, Ainsworth*. Subs: Francis/Ellington/Mariappa
Scorers: Norris 89 — Ref: D Deadman

Suspensions force Sturrock into changes but it matters little. Adie Boothroyd's Hornets quickly run out of ideas and revert to a long-ball game. Gosling, having his best game in a green shirt, sets Hayes away and he crosses for Norris at the far post to thump home a deserved late winner.

23 A CRYSTAL PALACE 22/12
Att 15,097 · Pos 7 · 15 · Pts 34 · **L 0-2** (HT 0-1)
Argyle: Larrieu; Gosling, Sawyer, Abdou, Timar, Seip, Norris, Hayes*, Hodges^, Easter, Halmosi. Subs: E-Blake/Summerfield
Crystal Palace: Speroni; Lawrence, Butterfield, Hill, Hudson, Derry, Soares, Morrison", Watson, Scowcroft, Songo'o. Subs: Scannell/Martin/Freedman
Scorers: Easter 49 / Hill 8, Scowcroft 44 — Ref: M Jones

New Palace boss Neil Warnock has lifted his side by the bootstraps. Hill opens the scoring with a header whilst Seip is off getting treatment. Scowcroft gets a faint touch to Watson's free-kick to increase the lead. Easter soon responds with a stooping header. Argyle have late chances.

COCA-COLA CHAMPIONSHIP — Manager: Ian Holloway > Paul Sturrock — SEASON 2007-08

No	Date		Att	Pos	Pt	F-A	H-T	Scorers, Times, and Referees
24	H	QP RANGERS 26/12	16,502	8 21	W 37	2-1	0-1	E-Blake 50p, 90 / Ainsworth 20 / Ref: S Bratt
25	H	STOKE 29/12	13,692	6 4	D 38	2-2	1-1	E-Blake 44, Timar 67 / Cresswell 8, Shawcross 57 / Ref: S Tanner
26	A	CARDIFF 1/1	14,965	6 12	L 38	0-1	0-1	Ledley 30 / Ref: A Wiley
27	A	BURNLEY 12/1	14,162	7 12	L 38	0-1	0-0	Blake 66 / Ref: A Taylor
28	H	SOUTHAMPTON 19/1	14,676	9 13	D 39	1-1	0-1	Fallon 51 / Wright-Phillips 13 / Ref: U Rennie
29	A	IPSWICH 29/1	20,095	11 8	D 40	0-0	0-0	Ref: T Bates
30	H	HULL 2/2	11,011	12 11	L 40	0-1	0-1	Windass 45 / Ref: P Armstrong
31	A	LEICESTER 9/2	21,264	12 20	W 43	1-0	1-0	Halmosi 34 / Ref: I Williamson
32	H	BARNSLEY 12/2	11,346	10 14	W 46	3-0	1-0	MacLean 6, Mackie 76, 85 / Ref: A Woolmer
33	A	SOUTHAMPTON 19/2	17,806	8 17	W 49	2-0	2-0	Halmosi 31, Paterson 33 / Ref: G Ward
34	H	BURNLEY 23/2	13,557	7 8	W 52	3-1	2-1	Nalis 12, Halmosi 35, 77 / O'Connor 19 / Ref: J Singh

SQUAD NUMBERS IN USE (starters / *opponents' subs & squad* / subs used)

24 QP Rangers: Larrieu, Connolly, Hodges, Nalis, Timar, Seip, Norris, Abdou*, Hayles^, E-Blake, Halmosi
Camp, Malcolm, Barter, Walton, Rehman, Rowlands, Leig'twood !/Buzsaky^, Vine, Bolder, Ainsworth*
subs used: Martin/Easter, Nygaard/Blackstock
Buzsaky is given a warm welcome back. Connolly's slip allows Rowlands to cross for Ainsworth to tap in. Walton's handball in the area gifts the equaliser. In a feisty few late minutes Ebanks-Blake slams in Halmosi's corner. Leigertwood is sent off after the final whistle for dissent.

25 Stoke: Larrieu, Connolly, Hodges, Nalis, Timar, Seip, Norris, Abdou*, E-Blake, Easter, Halmosi
Hoult !, Wilkinson, Pugh, Cort, Shawcross, Delap, Lawrence, Eustace, Sidibe^, Cresswell, Abdou*
subs used: Zakuani/Parkin^/Simonsen
Uncertain defending gifts Cresswell the opener. A Shawcross handball gives Argyle a penalty which is saved by Hoult but the rebound is netted. Shawcross claims a Hodges own-goal. Timar thumps in a header. Hoult is sent off (82) on his Potters debut for hacking down Blake.

26 Cardiff: Larrieu, Connolly, Hodges, Abdou*, Timar*, Seip, Martin*, Norris, E-Blake, Halmosi
Schmeichel, McN'ghton, Capaldi, Loovens, Whit'ham, Ledley, Rae, Hass'Baink*/McPhail, Parry*
subs used: Doumbe/Nalis/Jutkiewicz, MacLean/Thompson
The Pilgrims give a below par display. Ex-Green Tony Capaldi silences the regular booing which greets every touch by forcing Larrieu into a save which he parries to give Ledley an easy tap in. Much huffing and puffing from Argyle follows but it produces little in the way of chances.

27 Burnley: McCormick, Connolly, Hodges, Nalis*, Seip, Abdou", Sawyer, Timar, Norris, E-Blake, Halmosi
Jensen, Alexander, Unsworth, Caldwell, Varga, Elliott, O'Connor, Gudj'sson^, Gray, Jones, Harley*
subs used: Folly/Fallon/Smith, Blake/Spicer
Substitute Robbie Blake's superb volley is enough to defeat an Argyle side bereft of a number of familiar faces through transfers, injury and suspension. Sturrock's numerous tactical changes failed to ignite any fire and the Clarets are rarely troubled in gaining a comfortable win.

28 Southampton: McCormick, Sawyer, Nalis, Timar, Seip, Norris, Sum'field*, Fallon, MacLean, Easter, Halmosi
Davis, Ostlund^, Vignal, Davies, Powell, Surman, Hammill, Wright, Rasiak*, Euell, Idiakez/Thomas/John*
subs used: Folly
Saints take an early lead when Bradley Wright-Phillips collects a simple through ball. The goal shakes Argyle into action and the visitors are forced into some desperate defending. Fallon makes the most of a rare starting opportunity to hook the ball in from danger man Halmosi.

29 Ipswich: McCormick, Connolly, Nalis, Timar, Clark, Folly*, Doumbe, Seip, Fallon*, Halmosi^
Alexander, Wright, Harding, Bruce, Haynes, Miller, Garvan, De Vos, Walters, Quinn^*
subs used: Summerfield/Easter/Hodges, Lee/Roberts
It is 'backs to the wall' stuff for much of the game as a combination of brave defending and good goalkeeping give Argyle a point in the face of an onslaught. The Greens almost snatched it when a penalty is awarded against Harding but Neil Alexander saves MacLean's penalty (61).

30 Hull: McCormick, Connolly, Nalis, Timar, Doumbe, Clark*, Sum'field*, Fallon*, MacLean, Easter, Halmosi
Myhill, Ricketts, Pedersen, Brown, Ashbee, Garcia^, Walton, Windass, Campbell^, Hughes*
subs used: Easter/Abdou/Jutkiewicz, Folan/Barmby/France
A funereal atmosphere at Home Park. The players also give a dispirited and disjointed performance. Hull aren't much better but get the winner off the shin of evergreen Dean Windass. Watching England U-21 manager Stuart Pearce will not have been impressed. A day to forget quickly.

31 Leicester: McCormick, Sawyer, Nalis, Timar, Doumbe, Clark*, Abdou, Halmosi*, MacLean^, Easter, Paterson
Alnwick, Chambers, Clapham^, McAuley, Clemence, Hume, Oakley, Howard, Hayes, Bori**
subs used: Hodges/Fallon, Campbell/Laczko/Fryatt
Sweet revenge over Holloway's new team in front of live Sky TV coverage. After a tentative start, Argyle take command. Halmosi's low drive gives them a well-deserved lead. Late on, McCormick pulls off several superb saves and Hodges is fortunate to escape a handball in the area.

32 Barnsley: McCormick, Connolly, Nalis, Timar, Doumbe, Halmosi*, Abdou*, MacLean^, Easter*, Paterson
Warner, Foster, Kozluk, Nyatanga !, Souza, Howard, De Silva, Devaney, Macken, Nardiello^, Leon^*
subs used: Mackie/Wotton, Hassell/C-Ryce/Ferenczi
A sensational start with Lewin Nyatanga sent off (4) for a professional foul. Maclean gets his first Argyle goal direct from the resultant free-kick. Mackie comes on and scores within 11 seconds to set a new Argyle record and then gets a second. Wotton makes a welcome comeback.

33 Southampton: McCormick, Sawyer, Nalis, Timar, Anderson, Paterson*, Abdou, MacLean, Easter*, Halmosi
Davis, Thomas, Vignal, Powell, Wright, Sag'nowski, Euell^, John, W-Phillips^, Surman*
subs used: Teale/Mackie, Vafara/Hammill/Idiakez
Not a good first day for new Saints boss Nigel Pearson. Halmosi smashes a through ball from Nalis into the roof of the net and then Paterson gets his first goal for the club with a 25-yard drive. Little goes right for the home side who are loudly booed throughout by their fans.

34 Burnley: McCormick, Connolly, Nalis, Timar, Anderson, Teale*, Abdou, MacLean*, Easter*, Halmosi
Jensen, Alexander, Harley^, Varga, McCann", Elliott, Gjonsson, Lafferty, Blake, O'Connor*
subs used: Wotton/Mackie/Fallon, Carlisle/Unsworth/Randall
A fourth win on the trot lifts the Pilgrims back into the play-off zone. Nalis's shot slips under Jensen's considerable frame. O'Connor's header levels. In-form Halmosi's two goals clinch another well-deserved victory although Owen Coyle's side have chances but find Timar impassable.

35. A — WEST BROM — 1/3 · Att 2,503 · Pos 5 · L · Pts 52 · 0-3 (HT 0-1)
Gera 45, Miller 60, Bednar 67. Ref: U Remnie
Argyle: McCormick, Connolly, Sawyer, Nalis, Timar^, Anderson, Teale^, Abdou, MacLean, Easter, Halmosi. Subs: Mackie/Seip/Clark
West Brom: Kiely, Hoefkens, Robinson, Barnett, Albrechtsen, Greening, Texeira*, Koren, Miller^, Bednar*, Brunt. Subs: Gera/Moore/Kim
Some uncharacteristically poor defending costs Argyle dear. Zoltan Gera, an early sub (18), seizes on Abdou's uncertainty. Ishmael Miller's hopeful prod loops over McCormick. Roman Bednar slots home from close range to emphatically bring the Pilgrims' fine recent run to an end.

36. H — COLCHESTER — 4/3 · Att 11,562 · Pos 7 · W · Pts 55 · 4-1 (HT 1-0)
Ifil 11 (og), Easter 57, MacLean 60, [Sawyer 68] Lishie 64. Ref: M Russell
Argyle: McCormick, Connolly, Sawyer, Nalis, Timar", Anderson, Teale^, Abdou, MacLean, Easter, Halmosi. Subs: Fallon/Clark/Seip
Colchester: Gerken, Ifil, Balogh, Coyne, Virgo, Hammond, Izzet, Jackson, Lisbie, Vernon^, McLeod K*. Subs: Platt/McLeod I*/Elito
The game runs true to form with bottom of the table U's outclassed. Teale proves a real thorn in their side. Ifil heads into his own net after pressure from Halmosi. Vernon wastes a great chance and after that it is all one way. Sawyer rounds off the evening with his first Argyle goal.

37. H — SHEFFIELD UTD — 8/3 · Att 13,669 · Pos 6 · L · Pts 55 · 0-1 (HT 0-0)
Beattie 63. Ref: A Hall
Argyle: McCormick, Connolly, Sawyer, Nalis", Timar, Anderson, Teale*, Abdou, MacLean, Easter*, Halmosi. Subs: Mackie/Clark/Fallon
Sheffield Utd: Kenny, Geary, Naysmith, Morgan, Kilgallon, Speed, Cotterill, Tonge, Beattie*, Sharp", Carney*. Subs: Gillespie/Hulse/Ehiogu
A below par performance, resolute defending and some superb saves from Paddy Kenny deny Argyle and give the former Pilgrim, Kevin Blackwell, his first win as Blades' new boss. Former England striker James Beattie has the simple task of nodding in David Cotterill's cross.

38. A — SCUNTHORPE — 11/3 · Att 4,920 · Pos 7 · L · Pts 55 · 0-1 (HT 0-0)
Morris 55. Ref: S Attwell
Argyle: McCormick, IConnolly, Hodges, Seip, Timar, Anderson, Clark^, Abdou, MacLean, Mackie^, Halmosi. Subs: Teale/Fallon/Wotton
Scunthorpe: Murphy, Iniekpen, Baraclough, Crosby*, Butler, Goodwin, Cork, McCann, Harsfield^, Paterson", Morris. Subs: Hobbs/May/Weston
Argyle have some kit stolen before flying north, forcing Sturrock into a shopping trip to buy several pairs of boots. A wet and windy evening sees Lee Morris score via a deflection and the crossbar. McCormick is dismissed (71) for handling outside the penalty area. Hodges deputies.

39. A — BRISTOL CITY — 15/3 · Att 19,011 · Pos 7 · W · Pts 58 · 2-1 (HT 1-0)
Fallon 45, 60, Trundle 74p. Ref: T Bates
Argyle: Douglas, Connolly, Sawyer, Wotton, Seip, Anderson, Teale^, Clark, Fallon, Easter^, Halmosi^. Subs: Nalis/Abdou/Mackie
Bristol City: Basso, Orr, McAllister, Carey, Fontaine^, Elliott, Wilson^, Carle, Adebola, Byfield", McIndoe. Subs: Sproule/Vaska/Trundle
Argyle borrow Rab Douglas for one game to replace the suspended McCormick and injured Larrieu. A double from Fallon is enough to give Argyle victory over the league leaders. Easter is adjudged to have handled when charging down a free-kick leading to Lee Trundle's penalty.

40. H — WATFORD — 22/3 · Att 17,511 · Pos 6 · D · Pts 59 · 1-1 (HT 1-1)
Easter 34, Williamson 37. Ref: P Joslin
Argyle: McCormick, Connolly, Sawyer, Wotton, Seip, Anderson, Teale^, Clark*, Fallon*, Easter*, Halmosi !. Subs: Paterson/Nalis/Timar
Watford: Lee, DeMerit, Sadler, Bromby, Shittu, O'Toole, Smith, Williamson, John*, Henderson, McAnuff. Sub: Ellington
Very average football from both teams but plenty of talking points. Easter's goal is cancelled out by Williamson's exquisite free-kick. Halmosi is shown a red card whilst being stretchered off. Water is squirted at the stricken Halmosi, prompting a minor brawl involving players and fans.

41. A — COVENTRY — 29/3 · Att 18,775 · Pos 6 · L · Pts 59 · 1-3 (HT 0-2)
MacLean 82, Doyle 36, 42 Tabb 66. Ref: R Beeby
Argyle: McCormick, Connolly, Sawyer*, Wotton, Seip, Anderson^, Teale, Clark^, MacLean, Easter, Halmosi^. Subs: Mackie/Timar/Abdou
Coventry: Schmeichel, Osbourne, Fox, Dann, Ward, Hughes, Tabb, Doyle, Mifsud^, Simpson, Gray*. Subs: Thornton/Hines
Expectations are high among the 2,000 travelling fans but sadly Argyle's performance does not match. The Greens take early control. MacLean hits a post but then horrible defending changes the course of the game. MacLean's late goal is little consolation as play-off hopes take a dive.

42. H — CHARLTON — 5/4 · Att 14,715 · Pos 8 · L · Pts 59 · 1-2 (HT 0-0)
Easter 60, Lita 65, 76. Ref: I Williamson
Argyle: McCormick, Connolly, Sawyer^, Wotton", Timar", Anderson, Teale*, Abdou, Fallon, Easter, Paterson. Subs: MacLean/Mackie/Nalis
Charlton: Weaver !, Halford, Thatcher, Sodje*, McCarthy, Semedo, Zhi, Holland, Iwelumo^, Lita, Cook*. Subs: Elliot/Bouherra/Varney
A dramatic start with Addicks keeper Nicky Weaver sent off (3) for handling outside the area. A difficult wind and bumpy pitch does not lend to good football. Easter prods home from short range. McCormick misses a cross for the leveller and then allows the ball to squirm to Lita.

43. A — SHEFFIELD WED — 14/4 · Att 20,635 · Pos 12 · D · Pts 60 · 1-1 (HT 1-0)
Halmosi 2, Spurr 81. Ref: K Friend
Argyle: McCormick, Connolly, Sawyer, Nalis, Timar, Anderson, Paterson", Abdou, MacLean^, Easter, Halmosi^. Subs: Clark/Mackie/Fallon
Sheffield Wed: Grant, Gilbert, Spurr, Wood, Beevers, O'Brien, Johnson*, Bolder, Sahar", Burton, Song'o. Subs: Small/Slusarski
Both teams are desperate for a victory for differing reasons. The fit again Halmosi's free-kick is wickedly deflected past Lee Grant. With both defences looking shaky at times chances go begging. Tommy Spurr's 35-yard strike is unstoppable. The Greens play off hopes are all but dead.

44. H — PRESTON — 19/4 · Att 10,727 · Pos 10 · D · Pts 61 · 2-2 (HT 1-0)
Mackie 78, Wotton 75p, Mellor 78, Chaplow 90. Ref: A Penn
Argyle: McCormick, Connolly, Paterson, Wotton, Timar, Anderson, Mackie", Abdou, Fallon, MacLean^, Halmosi^. Subs: Easter/Nalis/Teale
Preston: Lonergan, Jones, Davidson, McKenna, Mawene, St Ledger*, Sedgwick*, Chaplow, Mellor, Hawley, Neal*. Subs: Trotman/Whaley/Carter
Play-off dreams die. The win looks sealed after a long-range deflected strike from the lively Mackie and a penalty from Wotton after Timar is hauled to the ground by Mawene. Preston immediately strike back via the dangerous Mellor and more indifferent defending allows the leveller.

45. A — BLACKPOOL — 26/4 · Att 12,911 · Pos 10 · W · Pts 64 · 3-0 (HT 2-0)
Easter 4, Fallon 25, 55. Ref: K Wright
Argyle: McCormick, Clark, Sum'field, Nalis, Timar, Anderson, Mackie, Abdou*, Fallon, Easter, Halmosi^. Subs: MacLean/Smith/Hodges
Blackpool: Rachubka, Barker, Southern, Jackson*, Evatt, Green", Jorgensen, McPhee, Dickov", Hoolahan. Subs: Burgess/Morrell/Coid
A comprehensive victory over a Blackpool side who are all at sea. Easter's early goal makes the Seasiders' heads drop. Fallon helps himself to a double. The final whistle sees emotional scenes as departing favourites Nalis, Connolly, Hodges and Wotton are brought on to say goodbye.

46. A — WOLVERHAMPTON — 4/5 · Att 26,293 · Pos 10 · L · Pts 64 · 0-1 (HT 0-0)
Olofinjana 87. Ref: M Pike
Argyle: McCormick, Doumbe, Sawyer, Sum'field, Timar", Anderson, Abdou, Clark, Fallon, Easter*, Mackie. Subs: MacLean/Teale/Folly
Wolverhampton: Hennessey, Foley", Elokobi, Gibson, Craddock, Breen, Kightly", Olofinjana, E-Blake, Keogh^, Jarvis. Subs: Eastwood/Gray/Elliott
Wolves are desperate for a win to get them into the play-offs. The match see-saws but poor Wolves finishing costs them. Timar is stretchered off (75) with a serious looking head wound. The ginormous Olofinjana gets a late goal but other results go against Mick McCarthy's men.

Home 13,000 · Away 16,494 · Average
Average 26,293

CHAMPIONSHIP (CUP-TIES)

Manager: Ian Holloway > Paul Sturrock

SEASON 2007-08

Carling Cup

			Att		W	F-A	H-T	Scorers, Times, and Referees
1	H	WYCOMBE 14/8	5,474	4	W	2-1	2-0	Bullock (og) 41, Hodges 45 / Oakes 76 / Ref: C Penton
2	H	DONCASTER 28/8	5,133	11	W	2-0	1-0	E-Blake 15, Summerfield 90 / Ref: L Probert
3	A	WEST HAM 26/9	25,774	13	L	0-1	0-0	Ashton 90 / Ref: P Dowd

SQUAD NUMBERS IN USE / subs used

1. WYCOMBE (2:21)
| McCormick | Connolly | Sawyer | Timar | Seip | Laird | Reid" | Sum'field | E-Blake" | Chadwick^ | Hodges | subs: Dickson/Fallon/Barnes |
| *Shearer* | *Williams** | *Johnson* | *Woodman* | *McCracken* | *Martin* | *Bullock* | *Bloomfield* | *Torres* | *Sutton* | *Oakes* | *McGleish* |

Youngsters Reid and Laird take the opportunity to impress against lower league opposition. An unfortunate own-goal and a rare Hodges header more or less kills the game by half-time leading to an uninspiring second half. Oakes' deflected goal fails to prevent rare progress to round two.

2. DONCASTER (1:20)
| McCormick | Connolly | Hodges | Timar | Seip | Abdou | Norris | Buzsaky^ | E-Blake | Chadwick* | Halmosi" | subs: Reid/Summerfield/Djordjic |
| *Sullivan* | *O'Connor* | *Roberts^* | *Lockwood* | *Mills* | *Guy"* | *Woods* | *Wellens* | *Hayter* | *Heffernan** | *McDaid* | *Greer/Wilson/McCammon* |

Only Ebanks-Blake manages to find the net from the numerous chances Argyle create in the first half. Rovers provide little opposition, their lack of fight frustrating the 200 travelling fans. A late Summerfield free-kick sees Argyle progress to round three for the first time in 15 years.

3. WEST HAM (P:7)
| McCormick | Connolly | Sawyer" | Timar | Seip | Nalis | Norris | Buzsaky | E-Blake* | Hayles | Halmosi | subs: Fallon/Chadwick |
| *Wright* | *Neill* | *McCartney* | *Collins* | *Gabbidon* | *Mullins* | *Ljungberg^* | *Parker"* | *Ashton* | *Cole** | *Boa Morte* | *Reid/Bowyer/Noble* |

Hammers' boss Alan Curbishley sends out a strong line up but the Pilgrims match every facet of the Premiership side's game plan. Encouraged by a 2,000 strong fan base, Argyle impress but hearts are broken at the death by England international Dean Ashton's last-minute winner.

FA Cup

			Att		W	F-A	H-T	Scorers, Times, and Referees
3	H	HULL 5/1	12,419	7	W	3-2	2-0	Abdou 23, Halmosi 26, E-Blake 58 / Windass 52, 60 / Ref: P Taylor
4		PORTSMOUTH 26/1	19,612	11	L	1-2	1-2	Clark 5 / Diarra 32, Kranjcar 42 / Ref: A Marriner

3. HULL (9)
| McCormick | Connolly | Hodges* | Doumbe | Seip | Nalis | Abdou | Sum'field" | E-Blake" | Easter | Halmosi | subs: Sawyer/Jutkiewicz/JC'wick |
| *Myhill* | *Doyle"* | *Delaney* | *Turner* | *Collins* | *France* | *Marney* | *Livermore^* | *Folan* | *Barmby* | *Elliott** | *Windass/Garcia/Atkinson* |

A five-goal thriller this wasn't. Argyle dominate a first half against an uninterested Hull, who leave out most of their first choice defence. The half-time introduction of veteran Dean Windass, who scores with a Beckhamesque free-kick, livens up proceedings but the Greens survive.

4. PORTSMOUTH (P:8)
| McCormick | Connolly | Sawyer | Timar | Doumbe | Nalis | Norris | Clark^ | Fallon | Easter* | Halmosi | subs: Jutkiewicz/Folly |
| *James* | *Johnson* | *Hre'sson* | *Pamarot* | *Distin* | *Diarra* | *Lauren* | *Mendes* | *Nugent** | *Kranjcar* | *Mwaruwari* | *Mwaruwari Mvuemba* |

England keeper David James wins man of the match which says it all. He makes several fine saves to deny Argyle a victory. Debutant Clark's shot is deflected in via the crossbar. Diarra fires in through a crowded box. Croatian international Nico Kranjcar scores from five yards out.

Final League Table

	Team	P	Home W	D	L	F	A	Away W	D	L	F	A	Pts
1	West Brom	46	12	8	3	51	27	11	4	8	37	28	81
2	Stoke	46	12	7	4	36	27	9	9	5	33	28	79
3	Hull *	46	13	7	3	43	20	8	5	10	22	27	75
4	Bristol C	46	13	7	3	33	23	7	7	9	21	30	74
5	Crystal Pal	46	9	9	5	31	29	9	8	6	27	13	71
6	Watford	46	8	7	8	26	29	10	9	4	36	27	70
7	Wolves	46	11	6	6	31	25	7	10	6	22	23	70
8	Ipswich	46	15	7	1	44	14	3	8	12	21	42	69
9	Sheffield U	46	10	8	5	32	24	7	7	9	24	27	66
10	PLYMOUTH	46	9	9	5	37	22	8	4	11	23	28	64
11	Charlton	46	9	7	7	38	29	8	6	9	25	34	64
12	Cardiff	46	12	4	7	31	31	4	12	7	28	24	64
13	Burnley	46	7	9	7	31	31	9	5	9	29	36	62
14	QP Rangers	46	10	6	7	32	27	4	10	9	28	39	58
15	Preston	46	11	5	7	29	20	4	6	13	21	36	56
16	Sheffield W	46	9	5	9	29	25	7	2	14	25	30	55
17	Norwich	46	10	6	7	30	22	5	4	14	19	37	55
18	Barnsley	46	11	7	5	35	26	3	6	14	17	39	55
19	Blackpool	46	9	5	9	35	27	3	13	7	24	37	54
20	Southampton	46	9	8	6	26	27	4	7	12	30	45	54
21	Coventry	46	8	8	7	25	26	6	3	14	27	38	53
22	Leicester	46	7	7	9	23	19	5	7	11	19	26	52
23	Scunthorpe	46	7	8	8	31	33	4	5	14	15	36	46
24	Colchester	46	4	8	11	31	41	3	9	11	31	45	38
		1104	234	171	147	790	604	147	171	234	604	790	1485

* promoted after play-offs

Appearances and Goals

Player	Lge	Sub	LC	Sub	FAC	Sub	Goals Lge	LC	FAC	Tot
Abdou, Nadjim	22	9	1				1	1		2
Anderson, Russell	14									
Barnes, Ashley						1				
Buzsaky, Akos	8	3	2				2			2
Chadwick, Nick	3	6	2	1	1			1		1
Clark, Chris	8	4			1				1	1
Connolly, Paul	42		3		1		1			1
Dickson, Ryan				1	1					
Djordjic, Bojan	1				1					
Douglas, Rab	1									
Doumbe, Mathias	10	2			2					
Easter, Jermaine	20	12		2	2		6			6
Ebanks-Blake, Sylvan	19	6	3		1		11	1	1	13
Fallon, Rory	13	16	2	1	1		7			7
Folly, Yoan	1	3								
Gosling, Dan	5	5				1				
Halmosi, Peter	41	2	2		2		8	1		9
Hayles, Barry	21	2	1		1		2			2
Hodges, Lee	20	7	2		2	1			1	1
Jutkiewicz, Lukas	1	2				2				
Laird, Scott		2								
Larrieu, Romain	15									
MacLean, Steven	14	3	3				3			3
McCormick, Luke	30		3		2					
Mackie, Jamie	4	9					3			3
Martin, Lee	10	2					2			2
Nalis, Lilian	35	5	1		2		1			1
Norris, David	27		2		1		5			5
Paterson, Jim	7	1			1		1			1
Reid, Reuben		1				1				
Sawyer, Gary	28	3	2		1	1	1			1
Seip, Marcel	32	2	3				1			1
Smith, Dan		2								
Summerfield, Luke	5	2	1	1	1	1				
Teale, Gary	8	4								
Timar, Krisztian	36	2	2		3		3			3
Wotton, Paul	5	3	3		1		1			1
(own-goals)							1		1	2
37 players used	506	117	33	8	22	5	60	4	4	68

Odds & ends

Double wins: (1) QP Rangers.

Double defeats: (1) West Brom.

Won from behind: (2) Hull (A), QP Rangers (H).

Lost from in front: (3) Charlton (H), Sheffield W (H), Stoke (A).

High spots: Return of Paul Sturrock.
Development of the Hungarian duo, Halmosi and Timar.
Encouraging performances against Premiership opposition in both Cups.

Low spots: Acrimonious departure of manager, Ian Holloway.
Sale of a number of players during January transfer window.
Release of several popular players, such as Wotton, Nalis and Hodges.

Player of the Year: Krisztian Timar.

Ever presents: (0).

Hat-tricks: (0).

Leading scorer: Sylvan Ebanks-Blake (13).

LIST OF SUBSCRIBERS

Paul 'Grizzly' Adams
Nigel Aston
Steve Billing
Graham Brooker
David Brown
Bill Dunn
Stephen Edmonds
Paul Fray
Keith Frood
Bill Hansford
Terry Harvey
Dennis Horswell
Michael Hoskin

VOTES FOR THE MOST POPULAR ARGYLE PLAYER 1974-2008

Garry Nelson
Peter Halmosi
Tommy Tynan
Micky Evans
Micky Evans
Micky Evans
Paul Mariner
Graham Coughlan
Tommy Tynan
Steve McCall
Tommy Tynan
David Friio
David Norris

Steve Lavis
Andrew Chapman
Robert Martin
Tim Matthews
Colin Parsons
David J Perry
Colin John Udy Ridge
Chris Ridley
Paul Daymond
Ian Scott
Malcolm Townrow
Gary Wake

Tommy Tynan
Tommy Tynan
Paul Mariner
Tommy Tynan
Kevin Hodges
David Friio
Paul Mariner
Paul Mariner
Keith Lasley
Graham Coughlan
Paul Mariner
Graham Coughlan